ARNHEM
LAND

Torres Strait

C. York

Gulf of Carpentaria

oper River

McArthur River

ATHERTON
TABLELAND

Cooktown

Cairns

GREAT BARRIER REEF

Normanton

Townsville

Bowen

Burdekin River

Flinders River

Cloncurry

Mackay

Percy I.

Fitzroy River

L RANGE

Alice Springs

QUEENSLAND

Rockhampton

GREAT DIVIDING RANGE

Gladstone

K

Dawson River

RAVE RANGE

Fraser I.

RANGE

Charleville

Maryborough

OUTH

Lake Eyre

Moreton Bay

TRALIA

BRISBANE

Lake Frome

Stanthorpe

FLINDERS
RANGE

Castlereagh River

GAWLER
RANGE

Darling River

Macquarie River

NEW
SOUTH
WALES

Port Augusta

Spencer Gulf

Lachlan River

MALLEE

ADELAIDE

Murrumbidgee River

SYDNEY

Kangaroo I.

Shoalhaven River

CANBERRA ACT

GRAMPIANS
RANGE

Murray River

Mt. Kosciusko

Portland

VICTORIA

MELBOURNE

Port Phillip

King I.

Bass Strait

Flinders I.

Launceston

TAS.

HOBART

A FIELD GUIDE TO

The Birds of Australia

A FIELD GUIDE TO THE
Birds of Australia

by
Graham Pizzey

Illustrated by
ROY DOYLE

PRINCETON UNIVERSITY PRESS
PRINCETON, NEW JERSEY

Copyright © 1980 by G. Pizzey and R. Doyle
Published by Princeton University Press, Princeton, New Jersey
Produced by Mandarin Offset/Printed and bound in Hong Kong

Library of Congress Cataloging in Publication Data
Pizzey, Graham, 1930-
Birds of Australia.

1. Birds—Australia—Identification.   I. Title.
QL693.P59   598.2994   80-20342
ISBN 0-691-08277-4
ISBN 0-691-08483-1

Contents

I

CONTENTS

CONTENTS

Foreword
by Dr D. L. Serventy

In the last century – and even, later, in this century – naturalists depended largely on collecting and the free use of the gun to identify birds in the field. Descriptions in bird books of that period were prepared on the basis that the naturalist had the dead bird before him, and not from the viewpoint of a field observer as we now know him.

Perhaps the pioneer of English language books on aids to identification, without having to examine a bird in the hand, was 'Birds of the Ocean' (1928) by W. B. Alexander, written after a prominent career as a zoologist in Australia. Later the American ornithologist Roger Tory Peterson established the method for land birds, and a series of books for various countries, developing his technique, has proliferated.

The House of Collins has played a notable role in these publishing ventures and has not been afraid of including within its fold even competing types of identification books. The field is a rapidly evolving one and new ideas and improving techniques are constantly coming forward.

However, with the exception of limited but tremendously useful ventures by the Melbourne Bird Observers' Club and the Gould League, Australia has been tardy in producing field identification books for birds on modern lines. New Zealand produced its field guide in 1966, but it was not until 1970 that a good collective work on bird identification in Australia appeared, illustrated by a well-known bird artist. Unfortunately it dealt only with a part of the Australian bird fauna. (A second, final volume has since been published).

The present book, by Graham Pizzey, illustrated by Roy Doyle, is the first complete one-volume field guide on Australian birds. Of Mr Pizzey little need be said to introduce him to Australian readers. He is well-known by his previous publications, in book form and in newspaper articles, and T.V. films. I have had the pleasure of being his companion in the bush (including the far outback), in museums and in the study. Throughout I have been impressed with his possession, quite remarkably, of the qualities essential in an author of a book like this one.

When I first met Roy Doyle, painting the plates for the Guide in the Australian Museum, Sydney, I was quite astonished. Few aspects of the development of Australian ornithology in recent years are more impressive than the meteoric progress of the art of bird illustration, both in painting and in photography. A group pioneered by Littlejohns and Lawrence produced the school of Keith Hindwood, Michael Sharland and their peers, and we hold them in high regard.

Then, in the recent past, appeared an almost bewildering array of glittering stars in both bird and wildlife photography. Almost each year produces new talent in these fields – and undoubtedly it will go on. There is no sign that we are reaching a plateau or witnessing any slackening off of artistic skills and genius. I had barely heard of Roy Doyle until I met him in November 1972, and when I saw his beautiful plates I recognized instantly that he was the ideal illustrator for a field guide.

The virtue of a field guide is that it contains all the information necessary, in pictures and text, to *identify* a bird. But no more. Authors should resist the temptation to include extra data.

Extraneous facts, however interesting and useful, only help in burying the essential information a reader is immediately seeking, as well as increasing the bulk of the book. After all a field guide is primarily something one takes into the bush; handbooks and reference books one studies at home. The present book conforms well to these standards. The text is sufficiently ample, but not overloaded, and is lucidly and attractively presented. For the neophyte bird observer and even for those of some experience, it is also an excellent introduction to ornithology.

Acknowledgements

Personal observations can provide only a small part of a book like this. In its preparation I have consulted much of the Australian ornithological literature, from Gould's 'Handbook' (London, 1865), through to sumptuous works like Cooper and Forshaw's 'The Birds of Paradise and Bowerbirds' (Collins, Australia, 1977).

My debt to those many books, papers, articles, special publications and notes and their many authors living and dead is considerable and freely acknowledged.

The references are much too numerous to list, but I would like in particular to draw the lay reader's attention to the several Australian journals which publish information about our birds. Seldom seen by the general reader, they place on record an extraordinary, ongoing body of observations and research data contributed by many amateur and professional ornithologists.

I include here a list of the major journals and urge anyone who wants to know our birds better to subscribe at least to his own State publication, and join the society that publishes it.

Australian Wildlife Research (formerly *CSIRO Wildlife Research*).
The Emu. Journal of the Royal Australasian Ornithologists Union.
Australian Birds. Journal of the NSW Field Ornithologists Club.
The Australian Bird Watcher. Published quarterly by the Bird Observers Club, Victoria.
The Bird Observer. Published monthly by the Bird Observers Club, Victoria.
Canberra Bird Notes. The Canberra Ornithologists Group.
Corella. Journal of the Australian Bird Study Association, (formerly the *Australian Bird Bander*).
The South Australian Ornithologist. Journal of the South Australian Ornithological Association.
The Sunbird. Journal of the Queensland Ornithological Society.
Tasmanian Bird Report. The Bird Observers Association of Tasmania.
The Western Australian Naturalist. The Western Australian Naturalists Club.

There are also the journals of the various other State and regional field naturalists clubs. These deal mostly with general natural history but birds are well represented.

The preparation of the book was assisted by several private donors through the special projects provision of the Australian Conservation Foundation. In recognition, a percentage of the author's annual royalties will be paid to the Foundation. I would like to express my sincere appreciation for that quite vital support.

Turning to individuals, I would like to pay tribute to the creator of the plates, Roy Doyle. When approached to take on the task he was not a specialist wildlife artist but became a superlatively good one. Over a period of years, as well as the challenge of representing birds accurately and pleasingly, he had to put up with the author's many requests for changes here and adjustments there. His patience was monumental. I would like most particularly to thank him, and Lesley, for their commitment and kindness.

With the text I had the enormous benefit of being able to turn to Stephen Marchant, editor of The Emu. His disciplined eye and incisive, condensing pen have been through the entire text at least three times. Unnerving at first, in time this pithy, consistent assessment became a valued restraint and regulator. Happy the author who can find such an editor and friend. I and the book owe him much.

But it will be obvious that errors of fact, significant omissions and surviving inconsistencies are mine alone.

A number of other friends or acquaintances provided me with personal observations

7

gleaned over the years, or read and commented upon all or part of the text. For these kindnesses I would like to express sincere gratitude to: Claude Austin; Sandford Beggs; Dr Graham Brown; Mike Carter; Bill Cooper; Sid Cowling; Frank Crome; Dr Doug Dorward; Allan Dear; Joe Forshaw; Tommy Garnett; Billie Gill; Murray Gunn; Dr David Hollands; Dr Leighton Llewellyn; Tom Lowe; the late Vic Lowe; Max McGarvie; Bill Middleton; Pauline Reilly; Philip Robinson; Dr D. L. Serventy; Ken Simpson; Fred Smith; Dr Gerry van Tets; Don White and not least Dr Norman Wettenhall, whose interest and support have been constant.

Roy Wheeler collated distribution data in the early days of the project and was always cheerfully helpful in other ways.

I would also mention specially John de S. Disney and Allan R. McEvey, Curators of Birds respectively at the Australian Museum, Sydney and the National Museum, Melbourne, who went to much trouble to seek answers to questions on plumage, distribution, systematics and other matters, and who provided representative skins for Roy Doyle's illustrative needs and made room for us in their crowded establishments.

Without that practical assistance the book could not have been produced. The community too little appreciates what treasures its Museums possess, or their enormous educational role.

Patricia Duncan achieved wonders of accuracy and promptness in turning an often scrambled draft into a readable manuscript.

To all I express my deep thanks.

Finally, as those who know her will understand very well, I owe my greatest debt to my wife, Sue. We have worked together on this project for over 10 years. She has been librarian, mentor, typist of drafts and superlative retriever of references, and has had to put up with its author withal. This book is at least as much hers as mine.

Introduction

According to latest revisions of the official Checklist, about 720 full species of birds have been recorded in Australia, 23 of these having been directly or indirectly introduced by man. Of the remainder, 571 species breed or are known to have bred on the Australian continent, in Tasmania or on coastal islands.

In that list of native breeding species, 329 are *endemic*: so far as is known, they breed nowhere else on earth (although some migrate to other parts of the Australian region and beyond).

The endemics include Australia's best known bird-families, whose origins are obscured by time and a paucity of fossil information. Almost certainly the early ancestors of some, like the Emus, *Dromaiidae*, were present on the land-mass that became Australia before it separated from the great southern continent Gondwanaland and commenced to drift north to its present position against the Asian shield.

Whether the early ancestors of songbird families like the Australian Warblers, *Maluridae*, or the Australian Magpies, Butcherbirds and Currawongs, *Cracticidae*, also gained their establishment in this way or colonized the continent in successive waves from Asia as long believed, is at present unknown. Such a colonization would have had to be rapid in geological terms, perhaps 20 million years at most. The subject is of fundamental interest to ornithologists.

Whatever their history may have been, many of our endemic birds have been Australian for so long that they are quite unlike any others. Coupled with the influence of birds from the Oriental region and long-distance migrants from far-northern Asia and from the sub-Antarctic, they give Australian bird-life a very distinctive stamp.

How to use this Guide

This Field Guide should enable you to identify any bird you are likely to see in Australia. It provides recognition-data on all the species that were recorded in this country up to December 1975. It illustrates all except rare vagrants and a few others.

There are 56 colour-plates and 32 black-and-white. They contain nearly 1400 separate figures, illustrating almost all the plumages our birds wear. Some birds, like the ducks and waders, are shown in flight as well as swimming or standing, because that is the way they are usually seen.

For quick reference, each bird has its own number, beside its name on the plates, in the text and on the distribution maps (page 411). Leaf through the plates. When you find a bird that looks right, note its *field marks* by using the pointers on the plates. These provide a quick method of identification, and this Guide makes full use of them. From here, locate the text-entry by number and check the sections on *Field marks*, and details of habits, *Similar species*, *Voice*, *Habitat*, *Breeding* and *Range*. Use the last, or check the appropriate map, to confirm whether the bird you saw lives in the place you saw it or not. If it belongs somewhere else, or if it is rare, the odds are you've got the wrong bird. In such a case, check *Similar species* again, or go back to the plates.

If you know the name of the bird, use the index in the normal way, locating the appropriate plate, text-entry or map by number.

9

Recognizing Birds

Getting to know birds is not difficult if you start simply and work up. All you need is a sure acquaintance with a few species to help you become familiar with basic methods of identification. From there continue to build, preferably by recording what you see in a notebook or by tape-recorder. It sounds tedious, but it helps greatly to be systematic, to keep notes (they add enormously to your competence and later enjoyment) and even to use a drill like the following, built on the word 'Recognize', with alternative spelling to suit the occasion.

R elative size – is it about the size of a thornbill, magpie, lark or heron, or some familiar bird in between?
E ssential features – what kind of bill, neck, legs, feet, wings, tail has it? Are they long, short, curved, rounded, slender or webbed?
C olour – of plumage, bill, eye and legs.
O utstanding marks – eyebrow, eye-ring, eye-mark, breastband, wing-stripe, wing-linings, tail-band. (See Field Marks, below.)
G roup it if you can – is it a wader, waterfowl, parrot or songbird?
N otes – what calls or song did you hear?
I mpression – what strikes you most – style of flight, feeding or running: was it in a flock or alone; slow or swift-flying?
S ituation – in the garden, in a swamp, at sea, in mallee, rainforest or by a roadside.
E liminate unlikely possibilities by checking text and maps for range, habitat, status, voice, even nest and eggs. *It is often as helpful to know what a bird might not be as to know what it might be.*

RARITIES

As your powers of recognition grow, *resist the temptation to see rarities*. The pleasure of watching birds lies much more in the appreciation of the bird for itself in its environment than in a feverish search for rarities or in building up the biggest list – although if your observations are careful and accurate this can quicken your senses and drive you to greater efforts. Nearly every experienced birdwatcher has known the sudden satisfaction of seeing the image of a rare bird become clear in his binoculars. But for every one of these there will be literally thousands of sightings of common birds in their proper range and habitat. Know these accurately; when a rarity eventually does appear, the record will have the assurance of good judgement and you will perhaps appreciate more clearly the reasons for it turning up where it has.

FIELD MARKS

Field marks are a quick visual shorthand to identification; they are markings, colours or other features by which birds themselves identify members of their own species, sex and, often, age-groups. Systematic eavesdropping by human observers on the birds' own means of identification was pioneered in the United States in the 1930s by Dr. Roger Tory Peterson, one of the world's best-known ornithologists and bird-artists, whose Guides to the birds of North America and of Britain and Europe have helped millions to know their birds better. Roger Peterson has graciously allowed his system to be used in this Guide. It

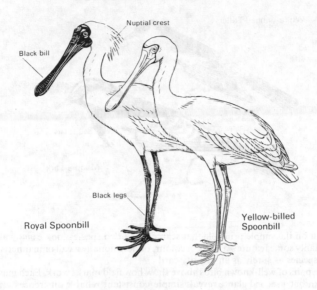

Nuptial crest

Black bill

Black legs

Royal Spoonbill

Yellow-billed Spoonbill

Heavier bill, tipped scarlet top and bottom

White tips to primaries

Black tail-band

Southern Black-backed Gull

Pacific Gull

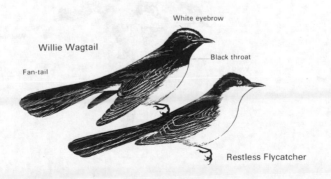

White eyebrow

Willie Wagtail

Black throat

Fan-tail

Restless Flycatcher

White-winged Triller ♂

White
neck-patch

White eyebrow

White rump
and base
of tail

Black breast

Magpie-Lark ♂

is built on the simple principle that scarcely any two species look exactly alike. There is invariably some feature – a mark, a colour, or occasionally a call or mannerism that labels each species as surely as an identity card.

The pairs of well-known birds above show how field marks work. Each may seem rather similar, but a second glance reveals simple consistent reliable differences, emphasized by the pointers. In flight, other field marks are often revealed, as indicated in the two following illustrations.

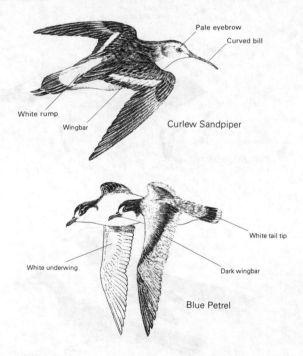

Pale eyebrow

Curved bill

White rump

Wingbar

Curlew Sandpiper

White tail tip

White underwing

Dark wingbar

Blue Petrel

THE PARTS OF BIRDS

Reference to the names of parts of birds and their plumage has been kept to a minimum in this Guide. However, certain features, including some common field marks, are referred to so frequently that it is necessary to identify them. The following figures show the most important ones. Note that in the text the feature identified here as a 'moustache streak' is mostly referred to as a 'whisker-mark'.

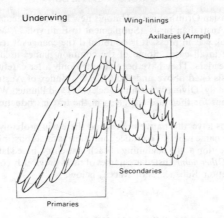

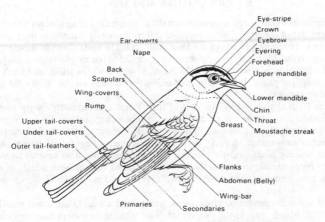

CLASSIFICATION

The classification of birds (avian taxonomy) is in some ways like the peace of God – it passeth all understanding. No secret can be made of the fact that until quite recently avian taxonomy in Aust. was in some disorder, as the formerly Revised 1926 Checklist of the Royal Australasian Ornithologists Union became progressively out of date.

Recent revision of the Australian Checklist in two parts brings the classification of our birds once more into line with present thought and knowledge. This Guide substantially follows those revisions. The first part of the new RAOU Checklist is H. T. Condon's 1975

'Checklist of the Birds of Australia, 1, Non-passerines'. The second part, still being finalized when this guide went to press, was published in 1975 by the RAOU as the 'Interim List of Australian Songbirds: Passerines' by R. Schodde. Where referred to in the text of this Guide, that list is cited as 'Schodde, 1975'.

COMMON NAMES

The Royal Australasian Ornithologists Union's new list of vernaculars, 'Recommended English names for Australian birds' (Supplement to Emu vol. 77, May 1978) was published after this book was in press. It is doubtful if the changes it recommends will win popular acceptance in all cases. Some of the common names used in this Guide will probably surprise readers. They have been adopted only after careful thought and consideration of the lists cited above and the CSIRO's 'Index of Australian Bird Names' (1969). Two names only, Diving Whistling Duck (111) and Plumed Whistling Duck (112) are my own. Reasons for their use are given in the text introduction to the subfamily *Dendrocygninae*.

Many of our birds have alternative names and there will probably never be complete agreement on which name is best. To reduce confusion as far as possible, I have provided a short *Other names* section at the beginning of each text-entry, based largely on the CSIRO Index. Some of the *Other names* listed are names of races previously considered to be good species – see the section 'Subspecies or Races', below.

EXPRESSIONS USED

Immature (Imm.) plumage as recognized here is the plumage the young bird wears for most of its first year out of the nest. This sometimes differs markedly from juvenile plumage, which is taken to be the first plumage the bird assumes in the nest, after the downy stage. *Eclipse plumage*, usually somewhat similar to female plumage, assumed by the males of a few groups after breeding. In Aust., several ducks, a triller and most fairy wrens enter an eclipse phase. It normally lasts only a few months, or less: hence the name, indicative of its brevity.

Migrants: are birds that breed in one part of their range and regularly fly (or swim or walk) to another part of the range during the nonbreeding season. Some migratory movements are short, others very long, but they are characterized by a regular, reciprocal annual pattern of movement. In Aust. there are about seven categories of migrants.

1. Migrant wading birds (mostly plovers and sandpipers but also several terns and skuas) that breed mainly in far-northern Asia and spend the northern winter in Aust.

2. Migrant land-birds (a cuckoo and two swifts) that breed in Asia and follow a similar pattern.

3. Migrant seabirds (penguins, albatrosses, petrels and a skua) that breed mostly on sub-Antarctic islands and in the NZ region, and migrate to waters over or near the Australian continental shelf in winter. A gannet, a dotterel, a tern and a cuckoo also breed in NZ and winter in Aust. (the cuckoo probably accidentally).

4. Seabirds that breed in Aust. and cross the equator to spend the southern winter in the n. Indian or n. Pacific Ocean. The outstanding example is the Short-tailed Shearwater.

5. Land-birds – a pigeon, several cuckoos, a nightjar, several kingfishers, a bee-eater, a roller, two pittas and some songbirds – that breed in Aust. and winter in northern parts of the Australasian region on Indonesian islands, in NG and the Solomons.

6. Birds that breed in southern Aust. and migrate north in winter to inland or northern Aust.

The last two categories are by no means absolute. In some species, like the Dollarbird, the whole population appears to leave Australia. In others, like the Rainbow Bee-eater, many cross Torres Strait or the Timor Sea but many also remain in northern Aust. In other species still, like Horsfield's Bronze-cuckoo, a number may spend the winter no further north than the Murray Valley, while part of the population reaches Indonesia.

7. Birds with local migratory movements. Examples are the Blue-winged Parrot that breeds in Tas. and coastal southeastern Aust. and winters in inland southeastern Aust. and the Pied Currawong, that breeds mostly in mountain forests of southeastern and eastern Aust. and disperses to coastal and sub-inland lowlands in winter.

The comparative lack of geographical barriers, fairly gradual climatic gradients and a uniformity of vegetation over large zones in Aust., coupled with irregular rainfall, results in a great deal of nomadism by migrant species, and others.

Vagrants: birds recorded in Aust. less than twenty times, so far as can be ascertained. Clearly this is a most arbitrary grouping. Vagrants in Aust. are mostly migrants at or beyond the periphery of their normal winter range. They are mostly penguins, albatrosses or petrels from the far-south or migrants from the northern hemisphere to Indonesia or NG, e.g. Garganey and Yellow Wagtail. Others, like the Manx Shearwater, may be so far from their normal range as to be apparently lost.

Introduced birds: birds like the House Sparrow and Common Starling introduced to Aust. mostly during the heyday of acclimatization societies in the 1860s and 1870s. Most of these introductions have been damaging economically and to native species, which they compete with and supplant, specially in urban areas.

BIRD-SOUNDS

One realizes the difficulty and sometimes the stupidity of trying to cramp bird-calls into human phrases. But somehow in a field guide an indication of *voice* must be given: it plays too large a part in recognition to be ignored. Many experienced observers find that they get a better idea of what birds are about by ear than by seeing them, particularly in closed habitats and in the dawn chorus. Some authors try to overcome the problem by the use of sonograms, but these are often just as difficult for the layman to follow as fanciful descriptions. However, there are some well-known calls, like the 'sweet pretty creature' of the Willie Wagtail, that have become common property over the years and appear often in the literature. These give us something to build on. In seeking out and selecting other characterizations of sounds, I have often followed descriptions from the literature by writers who seem, to my ear, to have caught the essence of bird-calls. In this connexion Dr. Glen Storr of Perth has a remarkable knack. Otherwise I have tried to capture a likeness of many calls not by direct recording but by dictating onto tape my own immediate impressions as I hear them. This has been a conscientious effort, but the method has obvious limitations. With care, there is value to be had from it and it can be used by anyone, with or without a tape-recorder.

When you hear a new bird-call well enough to put down a description of it, work at that characterization until you feel it hits the mark. You will find that by this means your ability to recognize birds by their calls will become firmly based. Some of the excellent records of Australian bird-calls now available are of great help in the regard. *Note*. Because it is considered to be of limited value in field-recognition in these cases, no 'Voice' section has been provided in the text-entries for the following families: Penguins; Albatrosses; Fulmars, Petrels, Prions and Shearwaters; Gannets and Boobies, and Frigatebirds.

HABITAT

I have avoided technical terms like sclerophyll forest: they are not in general use and tend to reduce, not enhance, clarity. But I have still tried to provide as full an indication of habitat as my own and published records have allowed, for habitat (coupled with range) often gives a lead to an identification. For example, when travelling in the Murray Valley, the large yellow parrot you see among river red gums will almost certainly be the Yellow Rosella. In parts of north-western Queensland you can expect Cloncurry Ringnecks in similar habitat. Grasswrens will mostly be found only near spinifex, as will two inland emu-wrens and the Spinifexbird. Other species (riflebirds, pittas, log-runners, several flycatchers and others) will usually be found only in rainforest, even where this occurs in isolated pockets. And you must usually go into or near mangroves to see the Mangrove Kingfisher, Mangrove Warbler and Mangrove Robin, White-breasted Whistler and Yellow White-eye. In a finer sense, sittellas and treecreepers use the trunks and limbs of trees, but lorikeets, pardalotes and most honeyeaters forage in blossoms and foliage. Fairy warblers often hover to take insects outside the foliage, but fantails hunt them in the air-space between trees. Though it is quite usual to see Nankeen Kestrels soaring round city buildings, and Little Falcons over city parks, it would be decidedly unusual to see a Grey or a Black Falcon in such situations. These distinctions cannot be learned overnight but they reflect the general reliability of habitat as a guide. *Note.* Because it is considered to be of limited value in field-recognition in these cases, no 'Habitat' section has been provided in the text-entries for the following families: Penguins: Albatrosses: Fulmars, Petrels, Prions and Shearwaters.

RANGE AND STATUS

The descriptions of *Range and Status* given here are the result of personal observation in many parts of Australia, collation and condensation of many published records, and generous assistance by many friends, particularly Stephen Marchant, Pauline Reilly and Roy Wheeler, MBE. I am aware that the information given, for which I alone am wholly responsible, makes many assumptions and statements which perhaps should not be made on so sweeping a scale. In the light of patchiness, or absence of information in many cases, the alternatives were to be conservative and simply give ranges by sections of States ('eastern NSW', 'southwestern Vic.') or to take the next step and link up apparent range-boundaries on the basis of the farthest-n., s., e. or w. records from published data or personal observations. Then a subjective judgement had to be made as to the significance of certain extra-limital or seasonal records. The result is a personal, generalized interpretation of an immense quantity of data, expressed somewhat uncritically and open to distortion by such variables as unusual seasonal factors. No doubt the section contains many errors of fact and interpretation. But it will perhaps give others a set of positive statements they can contradict, confirm or amend. In the process we may all learn more.

THE PLATES

The plates, by Roy Doyle, are mostly painted from skins selected to represent a typical example of the species or race concerned. Because some species have different male, female, breeding, nonbreeding (or eclipse) or immature plumages, they have required several figures to show their various fieldmarks. Others, particularly the hawks, ducks and waders, swifts and swallows are also shown in flight because that is the way they are often seen. Such flight-plates, and others of birds that are mostly grey, black or white, are mostly reproduced in monotone for economy and because recognition in flight is often based on pattern and style rather than colour.

The notations 'breeding', 'nonbreeding', and 'eclipse' refer to those plumages. The symbols ♂ and ♀ denote 'male' and 'female' respectively. There is a scale bar at the bottom of each plate, but *scales between plates vary greatly. Note.* Where no plate number is given after the scientific name in the text entry, the species is not illustrated.

SPECIES

The species is the natural unit of classification. By definition, members of a species breed only with members of the same species. Brown and Striated Thornbills may often be seen together and have opportunity to interbreed but they do not do so. Their co-existence as entities is taken as proof that no substantial interbreeding takes place. They are said to behave toward one another as good species. The factors that help keep them separate include colours and patterns in plumage, calls, behaviour, choice of habitat and other more subtle qualities. *All these can be used in identification by human observers.*

SUBSPECIES OR RACES

Some regard subspecies and races as somewhat different concepts. I will not try to draw a distinction. As applied here, the word 'race' is used not in the accepted, incorrect, sense of 'the human race', but in the way used to describe the races of man – African, Asian, European, Polynesian and so on.

What are races: how do they happen? When part of the population of a species is isolated or nearly isolated from the rest (usually by large climatic or geomorphological events) and if that situation continues for long, there is a tendency for the forces of mutation and adaptation to cause members of that population gradually to differ from the original stock, particularly if the habitat differs from that of the rest of the population. There are many degrees and variations of such differentiation, which man, as an interpreter of natural events, must codify in order to understand.

In one case, the process of change may be slight and involve, say, only a general paling in the plumage, under the influence of a hotter, drier environment. In such a case the population involved might be considered by taxonomists to be sufficiently different to be recognized as a *race* of the original stock. However a population that in isolation had not only developed a markedly different plumage, but also different calls and displays and adapted perhaps to a different range of habitats, might well be accorded the status of a full species, particularly if it could be shown to have come into secondary contact with its supposed parent stock *and the two had failed to interbreed.*

It would then be said to have reached a full stage of reproductive isolation: it would have become a good species.

In Aust., with its paucity of land-barriers, uniformity of vegetation and history of climatic fluctuations, there are many stages of this process of species-formation at work. The example of the Australian Magpie (720) illustrates how they are dealt with in this Guide. Our magpie has a very wide distribution. In general its black-and-white plumage is similar throughout, *except* for the shading of the back – black in the n. and e., white (or grey-white) in southeastern Aust. and Tas., and (female only) mottled black-and-white in southern WA. When the various populations of magpies were first being described, these differences were sufficient for the several forms to be regarded as separate species. Thus for over a century, at least three Australian magpies were recognized – the Black-backed (*Gymnorhina tibicen*), White-backed (*Gymnorhina hypoleuca*) and Western (*Gymnorhina dorsalis*). But as Australian ornithology became more sophisticated (and in this case, perhaps, as changes to habitats brought about by settlement accelerated) the anomalous fact that the three magpies interbred freely where their ranges overlapped could no longer be comfortably ignored. Subtler methods of expressing the situation were called for. By definition the three forms could not be 'species'; the two outlying members of the complex would be better regarded as *races* of the original stock, in this case of *Gymnorhina tibicen*. Today we know that many such former 'species' in fact are often very plastic, merge fairly imperceptibly together over a large geographical range and thus must be regarded as belonging to the one species. In some cases the change is so gradual that no steps can be observed and no races named. Such gradients are called 'clines'; the Fieldwren is an example. In others, the steps are more marked. The Queensland coastal race *laevigaster* of the well-known White-browed Scrubwren has distinctive cream-coloured underparts but can nevertheless be shown to be a continuous northward extension of that species. The inland populations of the Broad-tailed Thornbill are grey above instead of brown, with sandy-coloured rumps and white underparts; but progressive change from the more strongly coloured typical forms can be demonstrated.

Such situations are now expressed or interpreted by taxonomists by the use of a system of three scientific names, or trinomials. Thus as the supposed original magpie population was named by science *Gymnorhina tibicen*, its races, the so-called White-backed and Western Magpies, became respectively *Gymnorhina tibicen hypoleuca* and *Gymnorhina tibicen dorsalis*. For consistency when such trinomials are used, it is conventional when referring formally to the nominate race to repeat its *specific* name. Thus the nominate race of the Australian Magpie, expressed trinomially, is *Gymnorhina tibicen tibicen*. It may also be referred to simply as the 'nominate race'; similarly the subsidiary races may be referred to as 'the race *hypoleuca*', 'race *hypoleuca*', or simply, '*hypoleuca*', '*dorsalis*' etc. Such usage will be found in this Guide.

COMMON NAMES FOR RACES

Professional ornithologists use binomials and trinomials as a matter of course. Most laymen continue to use common names. This works well when only *species* are involved, but becomes very confusing when applied to races of species. In the example chosen, it will be obvious that the original common name 'Black-backed Magpie' for the nominate race will not do for the other two races, because neither have black backs. A more fitting species-name has had to be proposed, namely Australian Magpie.

Clearly, too, confusion will be caused about the status of birds if species and their races are each given different common names, which on the face of it seem to imply that they are of equal status.

Yet many people already know a number of races of common birds by common names. Examples are wide use of the name 'Spur-winged Plover' for a common bird now regarded as a race of the Masked Plover and 'Twenty-eight Parrot' for a bird now regarded as a race of the Port Lincoln Parrot.

There is no simple solution to this problem. When I first tried to organize this book I used common names for many races, but ultimately found, as others have, that the practice led to confusion. I have therefore used *common names* only for full *species*.

However because it is obvious that common names like 'Spur-winged Plover' will continue to be used for some well-known races, I have kept the link open by providing such common names in the appropriate text entry *wherever that race is referred to for the first time*, but have signalled caution by inserting the name concerned in inverted commas. All *subsequent* references to the race are by its scientific trinomial only. I hope users find this a practical compromise. For completeness, and to signal as plainly as possible wherever one former 'species' has been submerged in another, the most acceptable common name (or names in some cases) for each well-known race is also included in the appropriate *Other names* section. For an example, turn to the *Other names* section of Masked Plover (199).

NON-PASSERINES AND PASSERINES

It will be seen that the Species List on pp. 1–3 is divided into Non-passerines and Passerines. The great order, *Passeriformes*, named after the sparrows, genus *Passer*, accounts for rather more than half the species of birds known today. Passerines usually have 10 primary feathers on each wing and 12 tail-feathers. They are distinguished from all other birds by the muscular arrangement of the syrinx, which in the bird approximates the human larynx or voice-box, and by the arrangement of the foot. All Passerines have four toes, always arranged with three toes forward and one back, suitable for gripping even the finest perches. Many Non-passerines have very different feet, e.g. see family introductions for cormorants, parrots, swifts. Passerines represent the last great flowering of birds as a class, over the last 20 million years or thereabouts, when for a time there were more species extant than there are today. They have radiated to fill almost every terrestrial habitat; their songs, displays and social structure are often highly developed or complex, as in the bowerbirds. Their nest-building abilities far exceed those of non-passerine birds and their nests include the most complex structures made by any animal. So fundamental are the differences between Passerines and other birds that it is customary for ornithologists to think in terms of *Passerines* and *Non-passerines* and these expressions are to be met within this Guide, both in the species-list and in the text.

Emus   Family *Dromaiidae*

Huge flightless birds, second largest after ostriches; legs long, powerful with 3 toes. Plumage coarse, loose and drooping; feathers soft, without barbs, with aftershaft branching from main quill, as in ostriches and cassowaries. Female averages slightly larger, heavier than males.

Food: Nearly omnivorous; insects, specially grasshoppers, caterpillars, native fruits, berries, seeds, cultivated grain, grasses, herbage, blossoms.

Range: Australian mainland; distinct forms in Tas., King and Kangaroo Is. are now extinct.

Number of species: World 1; Aust. 1 (formerly 2).

1   EMU   *Dromaius novaehollandiae*

Field marks: 1.5–1.85 m. Australia's familiar largest bird; *from very pale grey-brown to almost black; skin of head and neck blue*; eye yellow, grey-brown or reddish; legs dark-grey. In breeding season female's neck plumage darker; blue skin on head and neck deepens. Juv: to 2–3 months, greyish to buff with bold black or brown stripes, crown spotted. Imm: dark-feathered head and neck; matures at 18–24 months. Singly to flocks of dozens, occasionally hundreds. Shy but curious; runs with bouncy swaying motion, in short bursts up to 50 kph; swims well.

Similar species: Ostrich (3).

Voice: Male: deep growling grunts; female: thudding drummings. Young birds, whistling peeps.

Habitat: Plains, scrublands, open woodlands, coastal heaths, alpine pastures, semi-deserts: margins of lakes; pastoral and cereal country with suitable cover.

Breeding: Eggs laid on ground, on scanty collection of leaves, grass, bark or sticks; 5–11: large, dark-green, granulated. Male alone broods, and escorts family for up to 18 months. Behaviour of female varies: remains in nest-vicinity during brooding, and accompanies male and young; disperses, or mates with another male.

Range and Status: Now confined to mainland Aust. Absent from driest deserts, heavily forested areas, and mostly from closely settled parts; common and still abundant in some pastoral areas and in some cereal-growing areas, State forests and national parks. Spring migration from desert toward coast in cw. WA. Generally highly mobile within a large home range.

Cassowaries   Family *Casuariidae*

Very large heavy flightless birds, probably related to emus, with a tall horny helmet, used like a prow to ward off obstacles as birds moves through rainforest undergrowth. Plumage black, coarse and drooping; flight-feathers reduced to coarse spines. Skin of head and neck bare and colourful, with brightly coloured neck-wattles. Legs stout and powerful, innermost of three toes with long sharp claw, used in defence. Female larger.

Food: Jungle fruits, palm seeds, vegetation; occasionally dead birds, dead small mammals.
Range: Australasian region.
Number of species: World 3; Aust. 1.

2 AUSTRALIAN CASSOWARY *Casuarius casuarius*

Field marks: 1.2–1.5 m. Our second largest bird: *black, with a horny helmet*: bare skin of head pale-blue, neck darker-blue and purple with crimson wattles; female larger, wattles and skin of neck brighter. Juv: striped; imm: brown then black; without helmet at first: wattle pinkish or yellowish. Singly, pairs, family parties; shy, most likely to be seen at edge of jungle or in clearings, especially dawn and dusk. Follows tracks to fruiting trees: swims well.
Voice: Guttural coughing; shrill whistles, often at night.
Habitat: Dense rainforest, especially near streams, edges and clearings in rainforest.
Breeding: Nest: collection of leaves added to rainforest litter, often at base of tree or in grass at edge of forest. Eggs: 3–5; very large, pale-green, granulated. Male incubates.
Range and Status: Ceram (? introduced), Aru Is, NG lowlands: coastal ne. Q, from Pascoe R. (C. York) s. to near Townsville. Common where habitat remains undisturbed, but generally uncommon; sedentary.

Ostriches   Family *Struthionidae*

Largest living birds, adult males standing up to 2.4 m; head, neck and legs bare. Legs very powerful, feet with only 2 toes – the only birds with less than 3. Gregarious, nomadic and polygamous.

Food: Omnivorous.

Range: Africa; formerly from Syria s. of Euphrates to s. Africa: now extinct in Syria, Arabia and n. Africa, except s. of Atlas Mts. and c. Ethiopia.

Number of species: World 1; formerly with 5 distinctive races. Aust. 1 introduced.

3   OSTRICH   *Struthio camelus*

Field marks: 2.1–2.4 m. An enormous bird: *male black with prominent white 'ostrich plumes' on wings and tail; female pale-brown, wings dirty white.* Juv: fawn, head and neck striped black. Imm: grey-brown, mottled. Size, bare greyish to pinkish head and neck and 'ballet-dancer's thighs' should make it unmistakable. Usually in small parties, very wary. Runs with rudimentary wings held out, at speeds up to 55 kph.

Similar species: Emu (1).

Voice: Male, hollow booming like roar of lion.

Habitat: In Aust., pastoral lands, open mulga, mallee sandhills.

Breeding: Polygamous; 3 (or more) females lay up to 20 (or more) eggs in hollow in sand. Both sexes brood. Eggs: very large, creamish, nearly round.

Range and Status: Southern Ostrich *S. c. australis*: Africa s. of Zambesi; introduced for plume-farming in 1880s to parts of SA, including Younghusband Pen.; near Port Augusta, Lake Alexandrina and Mundoo I., near mouth of Murray R. After collapse of trade following World War 1, remained feral in Narrung–Coorong and Port Augusta areas, probably gone from former by 1950s; some remain n. of Port Augusta; small numbers recently (1970) reported Redcliffe Stn., nw. of Morgan.

Grebes   Family *Podicipedidae*

Compared with ducks, grebes look sharp-billed, slender-necked and tail-less. They differ from coots and moorhens in their more delicate lines and brown, grey or white plumage. The feet are lobed rather than webbed. Larger species feed mostly underwater, but smaller species also feed much on surface. They often dive to escape danger rather than flying, quickly expelling air from plumage by muscular action. They skitter when chasing or taking flight, showing prominent white wingbar. The flight is apparently feeble, with shallow fluttering wingbeats and trailing feet, but they travel widely, usually at night. Legs set well back, they walk with difficulty, and normally are very seldom ashore. The nest is of weeds, grasses, stems and mud, floating, anchored to vegetation, or on some underwater support. It is usually sodden, and oxidization of nest-material may help maintain temperature of incubation. When leaving eggs, the brooding bird quickly throws nest-material over them. Young grebes are striped at first and ride among plumage on the back of their swimming parent, hanging on when it dives. Sexes similar.

Food: Fish; frogs and tadpoles; water-insects and larvae; crustaceans.

Range: Nearly worldwide.

Number of species: World 19; Aust. 3.

4   GREAT CRESTED GREBE   *Podiceps cristatus*   **Pl.1**

Other names: Diver, Gaunt, Loon, Crested or Tippet Grebe.

Field marks: 480–610 mm. Our only waterbird with *pointed black eartufts*: the fine sharp

23

bill, slender silvery white neck and chestnut and black frill framing the white face make it distinctive; upperparts grey-brown; frill and ear-tufts are somewhat reduced in winter. Juv: striped black-and-white head and neck. Imm: grey above, white face, neck and below, without frills or tufts. In pairs, open companies, and winter flocks on larger lakes, sheltered bays. Swims strongly, diving often and moving swiftly underwater. Flight low, seemingly feeble, neck low-hung; rapidly beating shallow-flickering wings showing much white. Elaborate mating displays: sexes face up, shake heads, dive.

Voice: A barking 'kar-arr', shrill 'er-wick' and various trumpeting moaning and whirring noises (English data).

Habitat: Lakes, flooded lagoons and swamps, reservoirs; bays, inlets.

Breeding: Nest: mass of water-weeds and mud, mostly submerged, anchored or resting on submerged stump on bank, or on small island. Eggs: 3–5; glossy, green-white, soon become limy and stained.

Range and Status: Eurasia, Africa, Aust., Tas. and NZ (but not Indonesia, Borneo, NG); e., se., and sw. Aust. and Tas.; generally uncommon and spotty, but locally and/or temporarily common: irregular through inland when conditions suitable.

5 HOARY-HEADED GREBE *Podiceps poliocephalus* Pl.1

Other names: Diver, Hoary-headed Dabchick, Tom Pudding.

Field marks: 290–305 mm. A small grebe with brushed back grey 'hair' and a pale eye; more distantly, *black chin, creamy white foreneck and breast, and narrow dark nape* are useful pointers. Winter adult has blackish crown, whitish cheeks but retains cream-white breast and dark nape-streak. Juv: striped; imm: like winter adult. More gregarious than Little Grebe; in dry seasons and winter, in dozens to hundreds on large swamps, lakes, sheltered bays, inlets. Flight – see family introduction; when disturbed often tends to fly rather than dive.

Similar species: Little Grebe (6).

Voice: Usually silent, but described as rolling guttural or soft churring; much less strident than Little Grebe.

Habitat: Larger waters; lakes, reservoirs, open waters of large swamps; sheltered coastal bays and inlets, especially in winter; rarely farm dams or tanks.

Breeding: Nest: like Little Grebe, but smaller; and often on bottom or underwater support, with others of same species or Whiskered Terns (262). Eggs: 2–4; greenish, oval, limy; soon stained brown.

Range and Status: Throughout Aust. and Tas.; fairly common, and sometimes locally very abundant in se., sw. Aust and Tas.; less usual in n. Aust. and far inland. Nomadic.

6 LITTLE GREBE *Podiceps ruficollis* Pl.1

Other names: Australian or Black-throated Dabchick, Black-throated or White-bellied Diver, Red-necked Grebe.

Field marks: 230–255 mm. Diminutive; *head and neck black, oval yellow spot between bill and yellow eye*; chestnut stripe down neck; grey-brown above, flanks pale-chestnut, stern whitish. Winter plumage duller; juv: striped; imm: grey-brown above, grey-white below, lower sides of face and throat dull-white, cheek-spot creamy-white. In pairs, family parties or small companies in autumn and winter. Dives often, but also feeds much on surface and in shallows. Flight – see family introduction.

Similar species: Hoary-headed Grebe (5).

Voice: Clear angry chitter; alarm-call, a sharp 'tik!'

Habitat: Still fresh waters generally; prefers smaller waters, usually with sub-aquatic growth; in winter, flocks occasionally with Hoary-headeds on larger open waters; more rarely in sheltered bays.

Breeding: Nest: floating mass of water-weeds, usually damp throughout. Eggs: 3–6; bluish white, limy, soon stained brown.

Range and Status: Throughout Aust., generally common; irregular inland; uncommon Tas. Sedentary or nomadic. Also Indonesia, s. NG, New Hebrides, New Caledonia, with closely related forms in NZ, Eurasia.

Penguins Family *Spheniscidae*

Penguins are recognized by three main features: modification of wings into flippers, upright stance on land, and strongly countershaded plumage. Specific recognition marks are mostly on the head: one group, the Crested Penguins *Eudyptes*, have golden crests. A few species, including our only resident, Little Penguin (16), have no distinctive head pattern. Immatures generally have obscure markings and are often difficult to identify. Penguins are the most maritime of birds, and their plumage is dense and entire. Bills are robust, legs short and rear-set, feet webbed and claws strong; balance when walking or hopping is assisted by the flippers. Propelled by the stiff, flattened flippers, penguins can make sustained dives, but generally fish near the surface: many, but not the Little Penguin, breathe while porpoising, bursting from the surface in low leaps. Most species feed and migrate in packs, maintaining contact with harsh braying or yapping calls. Most disperse from breeding colonies during winter, and two sub-Antarctic species regularly visit our waters. Gales may be responsible for the appearance of others as vagrants. Frequently in moult, some can be very difficult to identify; they should be if possible photographed for a record. Beachwashed remains should be sealed in a plastic bag, and forwarded, frozen if possible, promptly to the Curator of Birds at the appropriate State museum.

Food: Fish, squid and crustaceans.

Range: Only the Emperor and Adelie Penguins breed only on the Antarctic continent. Most species are widespread in the sub-Antarctic and s. hemisphere n. to approximately 30°S, breeding mostly on sub-Antarctic islands and coasts; the NZ region has most resident species. Only the Galapagos Penguin is equatorial, but in an area influenced by cold currents.

Number of species: World 17: Aust. 1 resident, 7 visitors or rare vagrants.

7 KING PENGUIN *Aptenodytes patagonicus*

Field marks: 915 mm. Second largest penguin, and much the largest species recorded in Aust.: head glossy black, upperparts silver-grey, breast white. *Note the orange-yellow teardrop-mark on the side of the nape, and the long straight black bill* with orange-rose fillet at base of lower mandible. Imm: shorter black bill streaked cyclamen-pink at base of lower mandible: crown tipped grey, cream patches on nape. On land looks stout and upright, bill raised aloofly: swims powerfully, 'porpoising' on surface.

Range and Status: Breeds mostly sub-Antarctic islands in far s. Atlantic and Indian Oceans: Macquarie and Heard Is. are the nearest Australian breeding stations. Records: Tas. (8); Vic.: Portland and Port Fairy, one (unconfirmed) Apollo Bay. Vagrant.

8 GENTOO PENGUIN *Pygoscelis papua*

Other names: Johnnie, Rockhopper.

Field marks: 710–760 mm. Head and throat slaty-black, otherwise bluish-black above, white below. *White band from eye to eye over crown*, scattered white spots nearby: in moult, whole head may be whitish. *Bill yellow to orange, ridge black: feet yellow or orange.* Imm: less white on head, bill paler-yellow, shorter.

Range and Status: Breeds Antarctic continent and many sub-Antarctic islands, including Macquarie I. One beachwashed, Eaglehawk Neck, Tas.: Mar. 1925. Vagrant.

9 CHINSTRAP PENGUIN *Pygoscelis antarctica*

Other names: Bearded or Ringed Penguin.
Field marks: 685–760 mm. A largish penguin, blue-black above, white below white face crossed by thin black band from behind eye across throat, *forming conspicuous chinstrap.* Bill black, feet flesh-coloured to orange-yellow. Imm: smaller, dark feathers scattered on white face.
Range and Status: Breeds Antarctic Pen. and s. sub-Antarctic islands, including Heard I. Disperses in winter mainly round S. America and in s. Atlantic. Records Macquarie I. 1953 and 1956: and s. Tas. Nov. 1968 and subsequently. Vagrant.

10 ADELIE PENGUIN *Pygoscelis adeliae*

Field marks: 610–785 mm. A sturdy penguin: bill short robust: brick-red, tipped black head and throat black: no crest but *conspicuous white eye-ring.* Otherwise blue-black above, white below, feet flesh-pink. Imm: throat white, no white eye-ring.
Range and Status: Breeds round coasts of Antarctica and islands. Ranges n. to S. Georgia, Heard and Macquarie Is. Records Portland, Vic., July 1933: City Beach, Perth, Mar. 1937: of somewhat doubtful origin – the birds may have been released by north-bound whalers. Vagrant.

CRESTED PENGUINS Genus *Eudyptes*

Four species of these golden-crested penguins have been recorded in Aust. At sea they can usually be safely identified only as crested penguins. Because most records are of beach-washed birds, the following key is provided. Note that adults in Australian waters may be imm. and/or in moult, when some features may be obscure.

1. *Golden crests meet on forehead.* Cheeks and throat white or grey (rarely blackish), forehead black, often tinged yellow   .. .. *Royal Penguin*

   Cheeks and throat dark; no yellow on forehead .. .. .. *Macaroni Penguin*

2. *Crest-line over each eye does not meet on forehead.* Sides of upper part of bill when viewed from above have parallel edges. Yellow or golden crest starts at gape of bill .. .. *Erect-crested Penguin*

   Sides of upper part of bill when viewed from above have bowed edges converging behind nostrils.
   (a) Crest-line over each eye does not reach bill; yellow crest large, straggling and drooping .. .. *Rockhopper*
   (b) Crest-line over each eye reaches bill; yellow crest smaller, neater *Fiordland Penguin*

11 ROCKHOPPER PENGUIN *Eudyptes chrysocome* Pl.1

Other names: Crested, Drooping-crested, Jackass, Tufted or Victoria Penguin.
Field marks: 455–585 mm. Smallest crested penguin. *Head, face and throat slaty black,* otherwise dark blue-grey above, white below. Crest: slender black feathers on crown increase in length from centre, edged by lemon-yellow plumes starting a space back from bill as eyebrow and projecting back in *long thin tufts; when dry, some stand wispily erect, others droop: when wet, slicked down.* Bill robust, dull-orange to red-brown with flesh-pink membrane round base: eye reddish, feet pink or whitish above, black below. Female: smaller, bill less robust, no fleshy membrane round bill. Imm: short feathers on crown, lacks yellow plumes or has them as thin pale-yellow stripe only above eye: throat dirty white: bill dull-brown. Most likely to be seen singly, but small parties occur, perhaps frequently, off s. coast.

Similar species: Fiordland (12): Erect-crested (14), Royal (15) and Little (16) Penguins.
Voice: Described as loud braying yell or loud hoarse trumpeting.
Habitat: Oceans, oceanic islands, to shores of s. continents.
Range and Status: Breeds in colonies on many islands in or near sub-Antarctic. Regular winter visitor to s. WA coast, records from Esperance to Perth: moderately common winter visitor to SA, Tas., Vic. The race most often recorded is *mosleyi*.

12 FIORDLAND CRESTED PENGUIN *Eudyptes pachyrhynchus*

Other names: Crested, New Zealand Crested, or Thick-billed Penguin.
Field marks: 510–710 mm. Like Rockhopper (11) in size but bill heavier, with no fleshy membrane round base. Crest broader than Rockhopper's, less wispy and without elongated black crown-feathers: not across forehead: begins as broad yellow eyebrow at base of bill, extends back and tends to droop down side of neck. *White streaks on cheeks are diagnostic*; caused by feathers parting to reveal whitish bases. Bill and eye red-brown, feet like Rockhopper. Imm: bill dark grey-brown, crest very short, throat whitish, distinguished from imm. Rockhopper by white streaks on cheeks.
Range and Status: Breeds w. coasts South Island, NZ: Stewart, Codfish, Solander and other NZ islands. Uncommon but possibly regular visitor to water of se. Aust., mostly imms. Records: Tas., Vic., NSW, s. WA.

13 SNARES CRESTED PENGUIN *Eudyptes robustus*

Field marks: Very similar to Fiordland Crested (12), but bill even more robust, with membrane of pink skin round base.
Range and Status: Breeds on Snares I., NZ region, ranges n. to NZ and w. to Macquarie I. Rare straggler to Aust.: near Hobart, Tas., Aug. 1951 and C. Banks, SA, Jan. 1914. Vagrant.

14 ERECT-CRESTED PENGUIN   *Eudyptes atratus*

Other name: Big-crested Penguin.
Field marks: 685–735 mm. Head, cheeks and throat velvet-black, back slightly bluish: white below. Distinctive golden crest *starts above gape, widens and sweeps up to rear of crown in brushlike effect, especially when dry.* Bill red-brown, with prominent band of white or pale-pink skin along edge lower mandible. Eye red-brown, feet pale-flesh, soles black. Imm: throat whitish, crest whiter and much smaller.
Similar species: Rockhopper (11).
Range and Status: Breeds Antipodes, Campbell, Bounty Is; disperses to NZ and Chatham I.; regular visitor to Macquarie I. Three Australian records: Julia Percy I. 1891, Carrum, Feb. 1954, Vic.; Esperance, WA, Mar. 1972. Vagrant.

15 ROYAL PENGUIN   *Eudyptes chrysolophus schlegeli*

Other name: Crested Penguin.
A race of Macaroni Penguin *E. c. chrysolophus*, of far s. Atlantic and Indian Oceans, nearest station being Heard I. The nominate race usually has *black cheeks and throat*: it has not yet been recorded in Aust.
Field marks: 660–760 mm. A distinctive large crested penguin, blue-black to blue-grey above; white below; *cheeks and throat usually white (sometimes grey or black).* Crest: loose golden-orange plumes up to 75 mm long start across forehad and extend back along sides of crown, some hanging untidily over eyes. *Bill long and massive*, flesh-pink to pale red-brown, edged with pink skin at gape, adjacent feathers sometimes tipped yellow. Eye red; feet as Rockhopper (11). Bill of female smaller. Imm: bill smaller, dull red-brown, cheeks and throat often smutty; yellow eyebrow-stripe, but crest often less-developed: distinguishable in field from imm. Rockhopper and Fiordland Crested (12) Penguins only by much greater size.
Similar species: Rockhopper (11).
Range and Status: Breeds only Macquarie I., where population may exceed 2 million. Australian records: three se. Tas., one Encounter Bay, SA: all summer or autumn. Vagrant.

16 LITTLE PENGUIN   *Eudyptula minor*   Pl.1

Other names: Fairy, Little Blue or Southern Blue Penguin.
Field marks: 380–430 mm. Smallest penguin, very simply marked: black to blue-grey above, *including cheeks*; silvery white below; flippers blue-black above, *with narrow white trailing edge*, white below. Bill black; feet flesh-white or pinkish with black soles. Imm: upper parts bluer. Adults near moult (following breeding) become dull brownish black with rusty traces, and noticeably fat; new plumage much bluer. Singly or parties up to dozens; swims low in water, often with only head and short upward-pointed tail visible. 'Flies' underwater with great speed and dexterity. Usually first noticed by calls: on land, comes and goes from burrow during darkness.
Similar species: White-flippered Penguin, *E. albosignata*: paler above: upper surface of flipper has broad white borders, which in male may be connected by white patch. Breeds South Island, NZ: not recorded Aust. Rockhopper (11), imm.
Voice: Sharp puppy-like yap; during mating or threat-display utters loud high-pitched ass-like braying, inhaling and exhaling; also deep growls, mews.
Habitat: Oceans, bays occasionally fishes round jetties, piers. Roosts through year in old burrows and places like those noted for nest, below.
Breeding: Nest: sparse, of sticks, grass, seaweed, thistle-stems: usually in burrow 0.6–1.5 m long in sand. Rookeries of dozens to hundreds on islands, but isolated pairs nest under vegetation, in cavities in rocks, seaside sheds or houses. Eggs: 2: white, become stained dirty greenish or brownish.
Range and Status: Our only resident penguin: islands and coastal waters of s. Aust. from

n. of Fremantle, WA, to se. Q. Breeds from Carnac I. near Fremantle to Port Stephens, NSW. Generally common, but probably most abundant Bass Strait islands and Tas. Best-known breeding colony is at Summerlands Beach, Philip I., Vic., where the evening return of c. 1000 birds to a protected area of dunes is viewed by over 400,000 annual visitors. Also NZ and Chatham I. The Australian race is *novaehollandiae*.

Albatrosses   Family *Diomedeidae*

Celebrated oceanic birds with extremely long slender wings and generally short tails. They are much larger than gannets and gulls and the only other sea-birds with which they should be confused are the two Giant-petrels (26–7). Adult albatrosses can usually be told apart by underwing pattern, presence and extent of white on back and wings, colour and pattern of bill and shading of head. Imms. usually have darker bills and dusky shading on head and/or breast and can be hard to separate; one (17) is mostly brown at first but has other unmistakable marks. Albatrosses probably evolved (and live mostly) in the far s. oceans. In those regions of near-constant winds, their effortless sailing flight enables them economically to cover great distances in search of food (see below) and to make extensive dispersals or migrations; they seldom resort to land except at breeding stations. There is a substantial northward winter movement of sub-Antarctic species to mostly s. offshore waters of Aust. and other s. continents. Sexes similar In the following entries reference to Voice and Habitat is omitted.

Food: Cuttlefish, fish and other marine organisms, some caught at night: carrion and offal at sea.

Range: Oceans of s. hemisphere and n. Pacific; vagrant n. Atlantic, but greatest development in far-s. hemisphere. Most species breed on sub-Antarctic islands.

Number of species: World 14; Aust. 9; 1 resident, 8 regular visitors or vagrants.

17 WANDERING ALBATROSS *Diomedea exulans* Pl.2, 3

Other names: Cape Sheep, Man-of-War Bird, Snowy or White-winged Albatross.

Field marks: 762 mm–1.35 m; span 2.7–3.5 m. Largest, longest-winged ocean bird, adult distinguished, except from Royal (18), *by white (or pale) back and dorsal surface of wings near body and white underwings*. From afar can look like a flying white cross. Seen close, note large pale-flesh bill. Imm.: very different from adult – *uniform dark-brown with contrasting clown-like white face and white underwings*. Head, back and underparts become white in untidy, mottled stages and dorsal surface of wing becomes patchy black-and-white, often with a white patch on 'inboard' part of wing; fully mature (9–11 year) males are *white with black flight-feathers*. Female: smaller, crown usually a little smutty, touch of pink on neck and breast. Singly, or loose groups disputing floating food, often with other albatrosses. On surface looks very large and white. In flight, size and especially effortless sailing distinguishing it from all but Royal and White-capped (23) Albatrosses.

Similar species: Royal (18), White-capped (23) and (for imm.) Sooty (24–5) Albatrosses and Giant petrels (26–7); Australian Gannet (73), Pacific Gull (260).

Range and Status: Breeds sub-Antarctic islands, nearest being Macquarie I. Regular visitor waters n. to Fremantle, WA, and Whitsunday I., Q; common Fremantle to Sydney. Records every month, mostly winter and spring; regular migration between c. NSW coast and S. Georgia demonstrated by banding.

18 ROYAL ALBATROSS *Diomedea epomophora*

Field marks: 760 mm–1.47 m; span 2.75–3.05 m. At all ages like adult Wandering Albatross (17), but no separate imm. plumage. In flight *outer section of wing tends to be more backswept*. Nominate race often has *large white patch on black upper surface of wing*: progressively whiter with age, old adults being white, with black flight-feathers. Smaller race *sanfordi*: *upper surface of wings almost wholly black, outwards from edge of white* *back*; tail white or with few black flecks. In both races and all ages underwing like Wandering. Note also the following, useful only at close range: head and body pure-white, usually without smutty patch on crown; black cutting edge to upper mandible, swollen forward-directed nostril tubes, black eyelids.

Range and Status: Nominate race, 'Southern Royal Albatross', breeds only Campbell I. and in the Auckland Is, NZ region. Race *sanfordi* 'Northern Royal Albatross', breeds only Otago Pen., NZ, and Chatham Is. Records: (all nominate race) mostly c. NSW coast, from Coff's Harbour s. to Bellambi; possible sight records, Vic.; specimen near Lancelin, WA, Mar. 1966. Vagrant.

MOLLYMAWKS OR MOLLYHAWKS

Seafarers reserve the proud name 'albatross' for the Wandering (17), the Royal (18) and the two Sooty (24–5) Albatrosses, calling other southern members of the family 'mollymawks', 'mollyhawks' or simply 'mollies'. Although this guide uses 'albatross' throughout, there is a certain homogeneity about 5 or 6 of the smaller species that can help you know them better. But remember that Pacific (260) and Southern Black-backed (261) Gulls are incorrectly also called mollyhawks, particularly in their brown immature plumages. Mollymawks are generally more compact than the great albatrosses and fly somewhat more tightly. Field recognition is based chiefly on underwing pattern and shading of bill and head.

19 BLACK-BROWED ALBATROSS *Diomedea melanophris*   Pl.2

Other name: Black-browed Mollymawk.

Field marks: 840–940 mm; span 2.1–2.4 m. Compact and somewhat thick-necked: wings, back and tail black; *underwing white in centre with broad black margins, into which the white merges*; *bill yellow, tipped pink*; the small black brow over the dark eye gives a beetle-browed look. NZ race *impavida* has a pale eye, heavier black brow, broader black leading edge to underwing. Imm: bill blackish; crown and nape suffused grey, *smudgy collar round foreneck, underwing nearly black*. Sub-adult: bill yellowish with dark tip, narrow white streak up underwing. Follows ships, approaches fishing-boats. Flight always seems more tight and controlled, less casual, than White-capped (23).

Similar species: White-capped Albatross (23); Grey-headed (21), imm: differs from imm. Black-browed by grey head and neck cut off cleanly from white breast: underwing more white.

Range and Status: Perhaps the most abundant albatross and the commonest species to visit Aust.; circumpolar breeding on many sub-Antarctic islands, including Macquarie I. Common migrant May–Oct. to s. waters from C. Naturaliste, WA, to Sydney: records n. to Geraldton and to Tropic in Q. Race *impavida* breeds Campbell and Antipodes Is., NZ region; ranges n. to *c.* 16°S; several sight-records NSW, Vic.

20 BULLER'S ALBATROSS *Diomedea bulleri*

Other name: Buller's Mollymawk.

Field marks: 810–865 mm; span 1.8–2.13 m. Like a heavier Grey-headed Albatross (21): head paler grey, more *distinct dark area round eyes, forehead and crown white, giving capped appearance*. Bill longer and blackish, ridge and underside of bill yellow, stripe on top broader but paler than Grey-headed, and widening at base of upper mandible. Dorsal surface paler than Grey-headed; *underwing has greater central area of white*: pattern somewhat like Yellow-nosed (22): uniformly wide black margin on leading edge much thicker than on trailing edge. Imm: bill blackish; neck and back brownish-grey: distinguish from imms. of Grey-headed and Black-browed (19) by underwing pattern.

Range and Status: Breeds Solander, Snares and Chatham Is., NZ region. Specimens and sight-records NSW coast; Sydney, Thirroul and Garie, Apr.–May and Aug. Vagrant.

21 GREY-HEADED ALBATROSS *Diomedea chrysostoma* Pl.2

Other names: Flat-billed or Gould's Albatross, Flat-billed or Grey-headed Mollymawk.
Field marks: 710–840 mm; span 2.13 m. Rather lightly built: *blue-grey head and neck sharply cut off from white breast*. Some have nearly white heads, confusable with sub-adult Black-browed (19). Bill black tipped pink, with *golden stripe along top and bottom*, dark eyemark; white crescent behind eye. Wings blackish above, back and tail greyish black: *underwing somewhat like Black-browed, but more sharply outlined; black on leading edge wider than on trailing edge.* Imm: browner, bill looks all-black: (in sub-adult, ridge, and stripe along on bottom, become yellow, tip remains black); head lead-grey, cut off from white breast; *white of underwing heavily clouded dark-grey.*
Similar species: Buller's (20) and imm. Black-browed (19) Albatrosses.
Range and Status: Breeds many sub-Antarctic Is., including Campbell and Macquarie Is., NZ region. Southerly distribution, but migrant to s. Australian waters n. to Shark Bay, WA, and s. Q, mostly May–Nov. Fairly common WA and SA, uncommon Bass Strait, uncommon to rare e. coast: common Tasman Sea off e. Tas.

22 YELLOW-NOSED ALBATROSS *Diomedea chlororhynchos* Pl.2

Other names: Carter's Albatross, Yellow-nosed Mollymawk.
Field marks: 710–815 mm; span 1.8–2 m. Smallest albatross; *long slender glossy black bill has bright yellow line along upper ridge to orange tip.* Head and neck slender, usually white; cheeks and nape sometimes washed pearl-grey. Wings blackish brown above, back greyish brown; *underwing white, with clean-cut black margins, wider on leading than trailing edge*; pattern roughly midway between Black-browed (19) and White-capped (23). Imm: *bill wholly black*; bill-ridge yellow in sub-adult, tip remains black.
Similar species: Buller's Albatross (20).
Range and Status: Breeds more northerly sub-Antarctic islands: winter migrant (May–Oct.) to s. Australian waters n. to Pt. Cloates, WA, and to near Tropic in Q. Commonest WA, where flocks of adults occur; uncommon Gt. Australian Bight, common near St Vincent Gulf, SA: rare Bass Strait, common e. coast.

23 WHITE-CAPPED ALBATROSS *Diomedea cauta* Pl.2, 3

Other names: Shy Albatross, Shy or White-capped Mollymawk.
Field marks: 1 m; span 1.9–2.4 m. Largest mollymawk, the only albatross with Australian breeding stations. It flies in the casual, droop-winged manner of Wandering (17) and has a similar underwing pattern. It is the only albatross that combines a *wholly-dark (brownish grey) dorsal surface, from wingtip to wingtip, with white underwing.* When close, note thin black eyebrow and delicate grey wash over face; whiteness of crown and nape give it a capped look. Bill: pale greyish straw, with yellowish tip; bill of imm.: lead-grey, tipped darker; darker-grey wash on cheeks and on sides of neck, in partial collar. Race *salvini*, 'Grey-backed Shy Albatross': darker-grey wash on cheeks and sides of neck, paler back: bill smaller, darker. Race *eremita*, 'Chatham I. Shy Albatross': smaller, with conspicuous bright-yellow bill; wings and back darker, sooty grey wash on cheeks and neck. Singly and open companies; Gould called it 'shy' but not so; follows ships, approaches fishing boats for scraps. Often circles feeding dolphins, watching for headless carcasses of cuttlefish they apparently discard.
Similar species: Wandering (17) and Black-browed (19) Albatrosses.
Breeding: Nest: very large cup of earth and droppings, vegetation and bones, in colony on exposed part of island. Eggs: 1; very large, white flecked red-brown at large end.
Range and Status: Nominate race breeds Albatross Rock, Bass Strait; the Mewstone and Pedra Branca, s. Tas.; Auckland and Disappointment Is., NZ region. Common all months on coasts of Vic., Tas., s. NSW; uncommon to rare SA, WA n. to Fremantle, and (occasional) e. to ne. Q. Dispersal mostly local but vagrant to US Pacific coast and S. Indian Ocean. Race *salvini* breeds Snares and Bounty Is., NZ, dispersing to S. America

and S. Africa. Sight-records from NSW to s. WA but some may be of imms. of nominate race. Race *eremita* breeds Chatham I.; no Australian records.

SOOTY ALBATROSSES

Two brown albatrosses of graceful form and buoyant wheeling flight. At sea they can be fairly easily identified as sooty albatrosses, but the species are virtually impossible to separate. Their ranges are complementary, with overlap s. of Aust.; Light-mantled Sooty (25) is the most southerly breeding albatross and has circumpolar distribution, rarely coming so far n. as s. Aust. The Sooty (24) replaces it in temperate S. Atlantic and S. Indian Oceans, with eastward extension to s. Australian waters, but apparently not to NZ. (This n.-s. distribution parallels that of many other 'pairs' of southern seabirds, e.g. Southern (26) and Northern (27) Giant-petrels, n. and s. races of Rockhopper Penguin (11).

24 SOOTY ALBATROSS *Phoebetria fusca*   Pl.3

Field marks: 840–865 mm; span *c*. 2 m. *A sooty brown albatross with very slender wings and pointed or wedge-shaped tail*; slightly darker on head. Bill slender and straight; black with a *bright-yellow stripe on lower mandible*; partial white ring behind eye. Shafts of primaries and central tail-feathers white. Imm: lacks white shafts and has *conspicuous whitish or buffish nape*, bill-stripe less pronounced: yellow, grey, bluish or violet. Follows ships on southern sea-routes, may fly in among, or alight on, rigging. Note that Light-mantled Sooty (25) has more marked two-tone appearance and a shorter bill with blue bill-stripe. But unless in hand, specific identification is virtually impossible because of overlap of shadings of both adults and imms., and because imm. Sooty may have a blue bill-stripe like adult Light-mantled.

Similar species: Wandering Albatross (17), imm.; Giant-petrels (26–7): pale heavy bills; bodies bulkier, without Sooty's elegant taper, usually fly lower and more heavily, with stiff flaps and glides.

Range and Status: Breeds sub-Antarctic islands in S. Atlantic and S. Indian Oceans, dispersing between 55°S and 30°S, with eastward extension to Australian offshore waters. Uncommon but probably regular winter migrant n. at least to Fremantle and Sydney; often on southern shipping routes. Few beachwashed records.

25 LIGHT-MANTLED SOOTY ALBATROSS *Phoebetria palpebrata* Pl.3

Other names: Grey-mantled or Light-mantled Albatross.

Field marks: 785–890 mm; span 2–2.3 m. Like Sooty Albatross (24) *but back and underparts pearly grey in 'Siamese-cat' contrast to dark smoky brown head, wings and tail*; eye-mark and white shafts like Sooty. Bill shorter, heavier than Sooty, with blue or violet stripe. Imm: like adult, but without white shafts; stripe in bill brown to blue, eyering duller. Some sight-records on Australian sea-routes probably refer to imm. Sooties; see entry.

Range and Status: Breeds sub-Antarctic islands, including Auckland, Campbell, Antipodes and Macquarie Is., in NZ region. Ranges s. into region of pack-ice and n. approximately to 35°S. Rare winter visitor offshore; few beachwashed records, some doubtful; SA, Tas., Vic., NSW, s. Q. Vagrant.

Fulmars, Petrels, Prions, Shearwaters   Family *Procellariidae*

Often simply called 'petrels'; large to very small ocean birds distinguished by tube-like nostrils. Most species have long slender wings and follow a weaving flight-path with intermittent wingbeats, covering great distances economically. Some petrels breed in small, isolated populations, based on a few islands or a single island; others are widespread; some are among earth's most abundant birds. Most petrels are gregarious at sea and some form vast feeding companies; they take food from the water in flight, while swimming on the surface or when 'flying' underwater on half-open wings; but only the Giant-petrels (26-7) regularly feed ashore. Petrels usually visit land only to breed, typically in colonies on remote islands, capes or coastal mountains, where take-off is assisted by winds and land-predators are few. After gales or during shortages of food, wrecks of birds occur on coasts or inland. After breeding, most species make extensive dispersals or migrations from which they return with remarkable precision. A distinctive musky odour which pervades the breeding grounds may guide their homecoming at night. Nests are in burrows, rock-crevices, less commonly under grass, bushes or in open. Little material is used; the single egg is very large compared with the size of bird. Although usually quiet at sea, on breeding grounds most petrels are noisy, with weird cackling cooing wailing or screeching voices. (Comparative Voice and Habitat data are omitted.)

Food: Fish, molluscs, crustaceans and plankton generally. Some species follow ships for offal or congregate at whaling stations or waste-disposal points. A few are predatory on young or eggs of other seabirds.

Range: World's oceans and bays.

Number of species: World 47; Aust. 34 with more likely to be recorded as regular visitors, vagrants or even as residents.

26 SOUTHERN GIANT-PETREL *Macronectes giganteus* Pl.3

Other names: Giant Fulmar, Glutton, Mollyhawk, Mother Carey's or Sea Goose, Nelly, Stinker, Stinkpot, Vulture of the Seas.

Field marks: 810–990 mm; span 1.8–2.05 m. Largest petrel; like a small brown albatross, but much less graceful. Flight inelegant, with heavy flapping and wheeling on stiff narrow wings; looks rather hump-backed, legs extend slightly. In high winds, wheels and weaves strongly. *Note the massive straw-white bill, surmounted by a single nostril tube*; it is *tipped green*. Mature adult, seldom seen in Aust.: grey-brown, with head neck and breast faded to dirty mottled whitish; eye pale grey. Imm: common visitor (see below): *uniform sheer blackish brown, eye dark-brown, bill more conspicuous in contrast*. A white phase, with sparse black spots, is rare locally. Solitary, but numbers gather at food; disputes over flotsam with albatrosses; occasionally near shore scavenging offal or, more rarely, ashore at stranded seals, whales. Follows ships, approaches fishing boats for scraps.

Similar species: Northern Giant-petrel (27); Sooty Albatrosses (24–5); Wandering Albatross (17), imm.

Range and Status: Breeds in colonies on coasts of Antarctica and sub-Antarctic islands between *c.* 50–60°S, including Macquarie I., dispersing widely over s. oceans. Imm. and sub-adults are common winter and spring migrants to s. Australian coasts, n. to Pt. Cloates, WA, and n. of Tropic in Q; most common Fremantle–Sydney. Few records of birds in mature plumage.

27 NORTHERN GIANT-PETREL *Macronectes halli*

Other names: Hall's (Giant) Petrel.

Field marks: Very like Southern Giant-petrel (26) but with subtle head pattern and difference in bill-colour that is diagnostic *in a good view*: *dark crown gives somewhat capped appearance*; *slight dark mask through eye usually separated from crown by indistinct pale eyebrow*. Bill horn coloured, *tipped reddish pink or orange*; eye pale-grey. Imm: uniform sooty brown, eye dark-brown; next to indistinguishable from imm. Southern, but older imms. have the slightly capped look of adults, bills tipped pink or orange. Flight and behaviour like Southern Giant-petrel; apparently does not have a white phase.

Range and Status: Breeds sub-Antarctic islands, including Chatham, Antipodes, Campbell, Auckland and Macquarie Is., NZ region; also Stewart I. Ranges generally n. of Antarctic convergence; downwind dispersal probably less extensive than Southern Giant-petrel. Adults and imms. winter in s. Australian waters certainly from Fremantle to Sydney, possibly outnumbering Southern. Described as a species in 1966, on the basis of breeding and other behaviour. Its presence and likely predominance in Australian waters only recently appreciated.

28 ANTARCTIC FULMAR *Fulmarus glacialoides* Pl.5

Other names: Antarctic, Silver-grey, Slender-billed or Southern Fulmar.
Field marks: 544–510 mm; span 1–1.14 m. A graceful thick-set white petrel; with small dark spot before eye; wings, back and tail pearl-grey, primaries blackish-grey near tips, with white inner webs, *contrast marked in flight*; underwings white. *Bill pale-flesh or yellowish, nostril and tip blackish*; feet brown or grey with flesh-pink webs. Southern relative of well-known Northern Fulmar, flies with quick shallow beats of stiff wings, wheeling glides; follows ships.
Similar species: White-headed Petrel (32); dark bill, dark pattern upperwing.
Range and Status: Breeds coasts of Antarctica and islands mainly s. of Antarctic Convergence. Rare visitor (usually winter) s. Australian waters; records WA, SA, Vic., Tas., NSW. Vagrant.

29 ANTARCTIC PETREL *Thalassoica antarctica*

Other name: Fulmar.
Field marks: 430 mm. Distinctive: ashy brown above, underparts and underwing white, throat and sides of neck washed pale-brown. Wings ashy brown with *broad white wingbar at rest*. In flight this combines with *white dark-tipped tail to form conspicuous pattern*. Bill deep, robust, with strongly hooked nail at tip.
Similar species: Cape Petrel (30).
Range and Status: Breeds Antarctica and adjacent islands, disperses n. in winter in sub-Antarctic to about 50°S. Rare straggler to s. Australian seas; recent records Vic. Vagrant.

30 CAPE PETREL *Daption capense* Pl.5

Other names: Black-and-white, Pied, Pintado or Spotted Petrel; Cape Fulmar or Pigeon.
Field marks: 355–405 mm. Sturdy and unmistakeable: *head dark grey-brown; back, wings and rump strongly chequered black and white*; white below, throat mottled grey-brown. In flight, *two large white wing-patches*; tail white with dark grey-brown terminal band. Flight fast, low, direct, with quick beats of stiff wings. Dives readily, in flight and from surface; floats high when swimming. Follows ships and in some localities regularly gathers near shore at offal.
Similar species: Antarctic Petrel (29).
Range and Status: Breeds coast of Antarctica and many Antarctic and sub-Antarctic islands, including NZ region; suspected Macquarie I. Disperses through s. oceans to beyond Tropics of Capricorn. Fairly common winter and spring (Apr.–Nov.) migrant to offshore waters of s. Aust. n. to about Exmouth Gulf, WA and Percy I., Q.

GADFLY-PETRELS Genus *Pterodroma*

Numerous small to medium petrels of tropical to sub-Antarctic distribution, called gadfly-petrels because of their high-speed swooping and soaring in great arcs, with occasional quick shallow wingbeats. *The bill is black, fairly short and usually narrow with a prominent hooked nail and a short nostril tube*; it separates them from shearwaters, which have longer thinner bills. Plumage brown, blue-grey, black and white or largely white or grey; many have pale or freckled foreheads and a dark eyemark. Field identification is based on wing-pattern, especially of the underwing, and shade of head and neck; colour of feet important but mostly of value only in the hand. Slight and often overlapping differences of form and markings and different colour-phases make classification and identification difficult in some. Most breed on remote oceanic islands, two species are known certainly to breed in Aust.; Gould's Petrel (40) on Cabbage Tree I., NSW, and Great-winged Petrel (31) on islands off s. coast WA. But Trinidade Island Petrel (35) has once (Feb. 1959) been recorded Raine I. off ne. Q in Coral Sea, and Black-winged Petrel (41) may breed on Heron I., Q. Six others are visitors or vagrants.

31 GREAT-WINGED PETREL *Pterodroma macroptera* Pl.4

Other names: Great-winged, Grey-faced or Long-winged Fulmar or Petrel; Muttonbird.
Field marks: 380–430 mm; span 910 mm–1 m. A large dark-brown petrel with *pale patch round the short deep black bill*, and long slightly angled-back narrow wings; underwing brownish, feet black. NZ race *gouldi* 'Grey-faced Petrel' has *more distinct pale patch* on face. Usually in flocks; flies spectacularly with high-towering arcs, sweeping descents; some liken it to a huge swift; others claim length of wings not conspicuous. Pays little attention to ships. Noisy round breeding islands; aerial chases day or night. At Australian stations breeding adults present most of year, but especially active and noisy Feb.–Aug.; probably wide feeding dispersal.
Similar species: Shearwaters (54–61) have longer, more slender, hooked bills. Kerguelen Petrel (37); Black (51), Westland Black (52); White-chinned (53) Petrels.
Breeding: Nest:sparse to substantial collection of material including casuarina needles or grass; usually at end of burrow *c.* 1 m long or under rock, creeper, tree-roots or scrub. Egg: 1; white, smooth, without gloss. In Aust. most eggs laid in late May, nestlings leave mid-Nov.
Range and Status: Breeds sub-Antarctic islands and NZ; in Aust. breeds only in s. WA on some islands in Recherche Archipelago and others from C. Arid (and possibly C. Pasley) w. to Eclipse I. near Albany. Non-migratory, ranges over s. oceans from 50 to 30°S; fairly common on s. Australian sea-routes, especially winter; s. coast WA n. to Abrolhos, mostly spring, vagrant SA. Flocks of unknown origin off Vic. in winter. The NZ-breeding, grey-faced race *gouldi* is possibly present through year off e. Aust. from Tas. to se. Q; uncommon.

32 WHITE-HEADED PETREL *Pterodroma lessoni* Pl.5

Other name: White-headed Fulmar.
Field marks: 405–455 mm; span *c.* 1 m. A distinctive large white petrel, slightly larger than Cape Petrel (30); *at rest and in flight, note dark wings and black eyepatch*; pearl-grey wash on crown deepens to mid-grey on back; wings darker grey, with a darker broken W pattern above; underwing grey. Note sturdy black bill with strongly hooked nail. Legs and feet flesh-white. Flight powerful, fast and wheeling in great sweeps, stiff pointed dark wings bowed; ignores ships.
Similar species: Antarctic Fulmar (28).
Range and Status: Breeds Kerguelen I., s. Indian Ocean; Auckland, Antipodes and Macquarie Is., NZ region; uncommon, mostly winter visitor s. Aust., occasionally n. to Dampier Archipelago, WA, and Richmond R., n. NSW.

33 PROVIDENCE PETREL *Pterodroma solandri*

Other names: Bill Hill Muttonbird, Bird-of-Providence, Brown-headed or Solander's Petrel.
Field marks: 405 mm. A greyish petrel, mottled white on face and forehead, with dark mark before eye. *Base of primaries white, visible in flight as a whitish patch on grey underwing.* Flight slow and easy.
Similar species: Kermadec Petrel (34).
Range and Status: Breeds only Lord Howe I., in winter. Formerly bred Norfolk I. where exterminated in the 1790s as a result of European settlement. Range extends to Tasman Sea, but uncommon e. Aust., all records NSW. Summer migrant to Japanese waters. Vagrant.

34 KERMADEC PETREL   *Pterodroma neglecta*

Field marks: 395 mm. A species of three colour-phases, all of which may interbreed. Dark phase: largely brown. Intermediate phase: body whitish, mottled darker about face. Pale phase: largely white head and body, *brown tail*. All three have wings brown above, grey below, with *white patch toward blackish wingtip*. Bill short, black; feet whitish flesh to bluish, tips of webs black; eye blackish.
Similar species: Great-winged (31), White-headed (32) and Providence (33) Petrels.
Range and Status: Breeds Kermadec and Lord Howe Is.; other races on many islands e. into S. Pacific. Disperses through warmer Pacific waters. Rare e. Aust.; specimens off Sydney, at Tuggerah and Kingscliff, NSW. Vagrant.

35 TRINIDADE ISLAND PETREL   *Pterodroma arminjoniana*

Other names: Herald or Trinidad Petrel.
Field marks: 355–380 mm. Very dark-grey above, with darker shade before and behind eye, sides of forehead white. White below, smudged grey across chest in indistinct band. Dark-grey underwing has white leading edge near body and thin median white stripe broadening into white patch towards tip, *forming diagnostic dark W on underwing*. Also a wholly dark grey-brown phase and intermediates between the two. Bill black, deep and narrow, with strongly hooked nail at tip; feet pale-flesh with outer half of webs and toes black.
Range and Status: Breeds Pacific islands near Tropic of Capricorn w. to Chesterfield Reefs in Coral Sea, also a few islands in Indian and S. Atlantic Oceans. Rare: one live bird ashore Raine I., ne. Q, Feb 1959. Vagrant.

36 TAHITI PETREL   *Pterodroma rostrata*

Field marks: 355 mm. Dark glossy brown above and on under-surfaces of wings and tail; upperbreast and flanks paler-brown; *belly and under tail-coverts* white.
Range and Status: Breeds New Caledonia, Society and Marquesas Is. Sedentary; possibly wanders to waters of ne. Q. Vagrant.

37 KERGUELEN PETREL   *Pterodroma brevirostris*   Pl.4

Other name: Short-billed Petrel.
Field marks: 330–355 mm; span 780–840 mm. *Uniform greyish colouring and short bill make confusion unlikely*; some have pale underwings. Fine mottling on forehead from pale feather-margins. Bill black, stubby and compressed laterally, strongly hooked nail at tip, legs and feet blackish. Usually solitary; flies high, somewhat swiftlike.
Similar species: Great-winged Petrel (31): larger, browner; face usually greyer.
Range and Status: Breeds few sub-Antarctic islands in S. Atlantic and S. Indian Oceans; ranges through s. oceans from 70 to about 30°S. Mainly winter visitor to s. Aust.; common sw. Aust. n. to Fremantle; rare se. Aust., SA, Vic., NSW records.

38 SOFT-PLUMAGED PETREL   *Pterodroma mollis*   Pl.5

Other name: Soft-plumaged Fulmar.
Field marks: 330–355 mm; span 760–865 mm. The combination of *grey underwing and grey partial band across white underparts* is diagnostic. Forehead whitish, mottled darker, and with *broad blackish eye-mark*, otherwise dark blue-grey above, wings dark brownish slate, tail grey, darker at tip, outer feathers grey-white freckled. (Rare wholly grey form breeds Marion I., S. Atlantic; not recorded Aust.) Bill black; legs flesh-white, webs tipped blackish. Common, flies fast in small parties near surface. Usually ignores ships.
Range and Status: Breeds sub-Antarctic islands in S. Atlantic and S. Indian Oceans, sub-tropical islands in N. Atlantic and possibly Antipodes I., NZ region. In s. hemisphere mainly in temperate waters between 30 and 50°S. Commonly in flocks in seas s. of Aust. Fairly common s. WA, many beachwashed records; rare se. Aust.: Vic. records.

39 MOTTLED PETREL *Pterodroma inexpectata*

Other names: Rainbird, Scaled Petrel.

Field marks: 305–355 mm. Distinctive; crown blackish, generally dark-grey above with black leading edge to wings; face, throat and upperbreast white, breast with brown mottlings *sometimes forming partial band, dark-grey patch on lower breast and belly*. In flight, white inner webs of primaries conspicuous on uppersurface of wing; leading portion of white underwing crossed by *thick sloping bar*. Bill black, short and hooked; feet yellow, ends of webs black. Flight fast, towering, with quick shallow wingbeats, glides.

Range and Status: Breeds NZ coastal and sub-Antarctic islands: Chatham, Snares and Bounty Is. Winter migration to n. Pacific and Arctic Sea; summer dispersal to Antarctic zone of pack-ice. Rare se. Australian waters; a few records c. NSW coast to Phillip I., Vic. and w. and nw. Tas.; once SA; mostly summer. Vagrant.

40 GOULD'S PETREL *Pterodroma leucoptera*   Pl.5

Other names: White-winged Fulmar or Petrel.

Field marks: 305 mm; span 710 mm. A contrastingly marked small petrel: forehead and underparts white; crown and patch round eye, nape and patch spreading onto sides of breast, slaty black; mantle, back, rump and tail blue-grey, latter darkening at tip. Bill black, short, narrow and with strongly-hooked nail; legs and feet grey, tipped black. In flight, note white underparts and underwing, *dark patch on sides of foreneck and dark M-mark across upperwings and rump, above a pale band formed by wing-coverts*. Usually singly; flies with quick wingbeats and glides, banks; weaves in higher winds.

Similar species: Black-winged (41) and Cook's (42) Petrels.

Breeding: Nests on ground under rocks, fallen palm fronds. Egg: 1, chalk-white.

Range and Status: Nominate race breeds only Cabbage Tree I., off Pt. Stephens, NSW. Ranges e. into Pacific; occasionally recorded on NSW coast in summer; vagrant Portland, Vic. and se. Q. Rare; movements little known. Other races breed New Caledonia, New Hebrides and Fiji group.

41 BLACK-WINGED PETREL *Pterodroma nigripennis*

Field marks: 305 mm. Blackish above, *with pale-grey back, rump and wing-coverts*; forehead and underparts white; dark mark below eye; blue-grey of mantle forms partial collar on foreneck; underwing white with broad black margins, *margin on leading edge sloping inwards and pointing to body*. Bill black, short; feet flesh-pink (occasionally blue) with outer portion black.

Similar species: Gould's (40) and Cook's (42) Petrels.

Breeding: Nest: in burrow *c.* 1 m long. Egg: 1, white.

Range and Status: Breeds Three Kings I., NZ; Kermadec and Austral Is., probably Norfolk I., possibly Lord Howe I. Very rare in Aust. At Heron I., Q, pair found in burrow without egg Jan. 1962, others recorded since, may breed; beachwashed NSW Feb. 1964, Mar. 1974. Vagrant.

42 COOK'S PETREL *Pterodroma cookii*

Other name: Blue-footed Petrel.

Field marks: 255–305 mm. Forehead white, with darker scalation merging into crown; black eyemark; pale-grey above, *tail grey edged white*; underparts white. Wing-coverts and flight-feathers brown-black, forming conspicuous shallow W in flight, extending across rump; underwing white with black margins. Bill black, *longish, comparatively slender*; legs and feet blue, ends of webs black.

Similar species: Gould's (40), Black-winged (41) and Blue (43) Petrels.

Range and Status: Breeds on NZ islands; other races in e. Pacific. Very rare Aust.; summer records c. NSW coast. Vagrant.

43 BLUE PETREL *Halobaena caerulea*   Pl.5

Field marks: 265–315 mm; span 585–700 mm. *The only petrel with a square white tail-tip*; in flight looks like a dark-headed long-winged prion with fainter dark W across wings. Face and forehead white, with faint dark mottling becoming solid black on crown and nape, and extending in patch, or series of radiating dark marks, under eye. Bill black, blue-grey stripe along ridge; it is narrow hooked and deep; feet blue-grey, webs whitish to pink. Imm: browner, forehead greyer. In flocks, to hundreds, often with prions. Flight stronger and more direct; unlike prions, follows ships.

Similar species: May be closer to Gould's Petrel (40) and other gadfly-petrels than present taxonomy suggests. See prions, (44–9).

Range and Status: Breeds sub-Antarctic islands in S. Atlantic and S. Indian Ocean: breeding suspected Macquarie I. Disperses widely over s. oceans, s. to edge of pack-ice, n. to 30–40°S. Uncommon winter and spring visitor s. Australian seas; present Tasman Sea May–Oct. Records WA, SA, Tas., Vic., and NSW.

PRIONS OR WHALEBIRDS Genus *Pachyptila*

Prions are specialized feeders on plankton, taking it on surface in a characteristic unusual manner, moving forward with head underwater, swimming or half-flying (hydroplaning). They dive often and well, 'flying' underwater on half-open wings. Their style of flight is distinctive; see Fairy Prion (49) our only resident species. *Their bills, narrow or grotesquely wide, are equipped with fine combs or lamellae, with which they retain plankton while expelling sea-water.* Form and size of the bill differs greatly between species, apparently as a result of isolation of breeding stocks on remote islands. So similar are most prions in other respects that four species can be safely identified in the field only as prions. The two exceptions are Fairy Prion and Broad-billed Prion (44); only these are illustrated. Only the Fairy Prion is known to breed in Aust.

44 BROAD-BILLED PRION *Pachyptila vittata*   Pl.5

Other names: Blue or Broad-billed Dove-petrel, Icebird, Long-billed Prion, Whalebird.

Field marks: 280–320 mm. Largest prion; with *grotesquely large, almost froglike, broad dark bill*; in hand 'comb' visible when bill closed, giving snarling look. From above, sides of bill strongly bowed. Blue-grey above to sides of neck, shaded darker on crown, with pale mark between bill and eye, pale eyebrow and blackish mark extending below and behind eye; white below. At rest, note blackish wing bar; in flight this becomes shallow W across wings and rump, leading edge of primaries being blackish from tips to bend of wing. *Tail blue-grey with broad black tip.*

Range and Status: Breeds NZ coastal islands, Chatham and Snares Is. and islands in S. Indian and S. Atlantic Oceans. Rare winter visitor s. Australian waters: beachwashed records WA, SA, Tas., Vic., NSW.

45 MEDIUM-BILLED PRION *Pachyptila salvini*

Other name: Marion Island Prion.

Field marks: 255–305 mm. Like Broad-billed Prion (44), but smaller. Comb visible when bill closed, giving snarling look; viewed from above, sides of bill not so prominently bowed as in Broad-billed. Difficult to separate from imm. Broad-billed but wing-length, usually under 200 mm.

Range and Status: Breeds Crozets and Marion Is., S. Indian Ocean. Disperses eastward through sub-Antarctic zone of surface water; common in winter off s. WA, SA, Vic., and Tas.; many beachwashed records. Uncommon NSW.

46 ANTARCTIC PRION *Pachyptila desolata*

Other names: Banks' or Blue Dove-petrel, **Banks'** Petrel or Prion, Dove-like Petrel, Dove Prion, Snowbird, Whalebird.
Field marks: 255–305 mm. Like Broad-billed Prion (44) except for bill, *which does not display combs when closed and, viewed from above, has straight, not bowed, sides.*
Range and Status: Breeds Antarctica and sub-Antarctic islands, including Auckland and Macquarie Is., NZ region. Ranges n. between 66 and 35°S., occasionally across equator. One of the most abundant sub-Antarctic seabirds. Common winter visitor offshore waters from s. WA to s. Q.

47 SLENDER-BILLED PRION *Pachyptila belcheri*

Other name: Thin-billed Prion.
Field marks: 255 mm. Like Broad-billed Prion (44), but bill slender, combs not exposed; when closed, viewed from above, *sides straight.*
Range and Status: Breeds Kerguelen and Bouvet Is., S. Indian Ocean; Falkland Is., S. Atlantic. Ranges s. to pack-ice, and n. in winter to *c.* 30°S. Uncommon winter and spring visitor s. Aust., most records s. WA; others SA, Vic., Tas., to n. NSW.

48 FULMAR PRION *Pachyptila crassirostris*

Field marks: 240–280 mm. Very like Fairy Prion (49); probably indistinguishable at sea. More sturdily built, usually paler. Bill deeper, more swollen when viewed from above; lower mandible more robust; curved nail at tip larger and more curved; space between this nail and nostril tubes *less* than in Fairy.
Range and Status: Breeds sub-Antarctic islands, NZ region; Heard I., S. Indian Ocean. Doubtful records Portland, Vic., Nov. 1954; 65 km e. Moruya Heads, NSW, Aug. 1970. Vagrant.

49 FAIRY PRION *Pachyptila turtur*   **Pl.5**

Other names: Blue or Dove-petrel, Fairy Dove-petrel, Short-billed Prion, Whalebird.
Field marks: 230–280 mm. Smallest prion, bill comparatively narrow and short with strong dertrum or hook separated only narrowly from nasal tubes. Plumage differs from all others except Fulmar Prion (48) by *wide blackish terminal band up to half length of tail and less dark shading on crown.* In flight, bounces over surface picking up plankton; tilts, flits from wave to wave; or swims underwater with half-closed wings, bobs up to swallow food on surface. In strong winds, weaves at high speed on fixed wings in typical petrel-manner, showing alternating blue and white surfaces.
Breeding: Breeds in colonies. Nest: small chamber, sometimes lined with plant material, in slender burrow 600 mm or more long, often under vegetation; also in rock crevices. Egg: 1; white, not glossy.
Range and Status: Breeds islands off Tas. and Vic. (mostly in Bass Strait) w. to Lady Julia Percy I. and Lawrence Rocks, Portland. Also NZ coastal and sub-Antarctic islands; suspected Macquarie I., Indian and S. Atlantic Oceans. Common offshore from sw. Vic. to c. NSW, Tas.; uncommon s. WA, SA, n. NSW and se. Q.

50 GREY PETREL *Procellaria cinerea*

Other names: Black-tailed Shearwater, Brown Petrel, Bully, Cape Dave, Great Grey Petrel, Night Hawk, Pediunker.
Field marks: 455–510 mm; span 1.1–1.9 m. A robust petrel, ashy grey above washed or mottled brownish, darker on head, wings and tail: *tone of head shades into whitish under-parts below eye-level; underwing and under tail-coverts grey.* Bill grey-green or greenish yellow with black nostril and ridge; feet flesh-coloured or bluish-brown, webs yellow, tipped black. Flies high, somewhat albatross-like; feet protrude a little, *giving slightly*

forked-tail look. Dives often, at times from several metres; 'flies' underwater with half-open wings; on emerging 'shakes itself like a dog'.

Range and Status: Breeds sub-Antarctic islands, including Campbell and Antipodes Is., NZ region; possibly Macquarie I. Disperses from 55 to *c*. 25°S. Records: s. WA, Vic., King I., Tas. Vagrant.

51 BLACK PETREL *Procellaria parkinsoni*

Other names: (Black) Fulmar, Parkinson's Petrel.

Field marks: 430–455 mm. *Wholly sooty black*: bill *bluish-white*, black along ridge of upper mandible and on tip: legs and feet black.

Similar species: Westland Black (52), White-chinned (53) and Great-winged (31) Petrels: Fleshy-footed Shearwater (54).

Range and Status: Breeds (in summer) on NZ offshore islands and isolated mountainous parts of w. coast of both North and South Is. One Aust. record Sydney, May 1875. Vagrant.

52 WESTLAND BLACK PETREL *Procellaria westlandica*

Other names: Westland Petrel.

Field marks: 510 mm. Indistinguishable at sea from slightly smaller, closely related Black Petrel. Bill whitish to yellowish horn with dark ridge: legs and feet black.

Similar species: Great-winged (31), Black (51) and White-chinned (53) Petrels: Fleshy-footed Shearwater (54).

Range and Status: Breeds in winter in mountains near Barrytown on w. coast, South I., NZ. Records Corrimal Beach, NSW, Jan. 1956: Cronulla, NSW, Dec. 1958. Vagrant.

53 WHITE-CHINNED PETREL *Procellaria aequinoctialis*   Pl.4

Other names: Cape Hen, Spectacled Petrel, Shoemaker.

Field marks: 485–585 mm: span 1.28–1.47 m. A large blackish brown petrel *with robust pale bill and irregular (occasionally wholly absent) white patch on chin*: underwing brown. Bill longish and rather deep: whitish, bluish, yellowish or greenish horn, with dark nostril and blackish ridge, nail strongly hooked: feet black. One of the commonest petrels of southern oceans, flight languid on broad wings, near surface: aggressive, dives well, follows ships. (A rarer race, *conspicillatus*, 'Spectacled Petrel', has band of white over crown and broad white whisker-mark: chin white. No Australian records).

Similar species: Without experience, Black (51) and Westland Black (52) Petrels probably not safely distinguished from a wholly dark White-chinned. See also Great-winged Petrel (31), Fleshy-footed Shearwater (54).

Range and Status: Breeds sub-Antarctic islands in NZ region and in S. Indian and S. Atlantic Oceans. Common on s. and se. shipping routes in winter. Records Portland, Vic., Mar. 1959, Port Kembla June 1963 and Newcastle Bight, NSW, Dec. 1968: Coolangatta, se. Q, Jan. 1974.

SHEARWATERS Genus *Puffinus*

Brown or blackish petrels: some have white underparts and underwings but most are without distinctive patterns. Wings are long and slender, tails generally short, in one, longer and wedge-shaped. Bills are mostly fairly long and slender, usually dark: legs and feet usually dark, but pale bill or feet is a useful field mark in two species. Larger species have a rather slow graceful banking gliding flight with infrequent wingbeats. Medium-sized species tend to slice fast on fixed wings in long undulating streams or, in calm weather, course low over the sea with alternate fast wingbeats and glides. Smaller species fly low and direct with quick fluttering or flapping wingbeats and short glides. Where food is abundant, they feed on surface in dark rafts, churning spray and diving to swim underwater, propelled by half-closed wings.

54 FLESHY-FOOTED SHEARWATER *Puffinus carneipes* Pl.4

Other names: Flesh-footed Petrel or Shearwater, Big or Lord Howe Island Muttonbird.
Field marks: 405–460 mm; span 990 mm–1.06 m. A large, very dark-brown shearwater: *bill robust, pale flesh or whitish green, tipped dark-grey*; *legs and feet pale-pink*; underwing brown; tail short, squarish or fan-shaped. Flight rather slow, with stiff-winged flapping and gliding near surface. Feeds in open companies but forms rafts at dusk off breeding islands and when food is concentrated; dives from surface readily, gathers round fishing boats.
Similar species: Wedge-tailed (55), Sooty (57) and Short-tailed (58) Shearwaters. Great-winged Petrel (31): short dark bill, grey face, dark feet. White-chinned Petrel (53), dark form: pale bill, dark feet.
Breeding: Nest: scraps of dry vegetation in burrow *c.* 1–2 m long, from near sea-level to high on hills. Egg: 1, large white.
Range and Status: Breeds S. America, NZ, Lord Howe I., and in s. WA on islands in Recherche Archipelago and w. to C. Leeuwin and off C. Hamelin. Common during warmer months in coastal sw. Aust. from Bunbury to coastal SA and e. Aust. from s. NSW to se Q, summer and autumn. Rare Bass Strait, e. Vic. and Tas. A winter trans-equatorial migrant. Pacific birds to n. Pacific, WA breeding birds probably to n. Indian Ocean; absent locally Apr.–Sept.

55 WEDGE-TAILED SHEARWATER *Puffinus pacificus* Pl.4

Other names: Little Muttonbird, Mourning Bird, Wedge-tailed Muttonbird or Petrel.
Field marks: 380–460 mm; span 965 mm–1.04 m. The common muttonbird of coastal e. and w. Aust., distinguished by *buoyant gentle flight on broad wings, 'wrists' well forward, wedge-shaped tail that looks pointed in flight and protrudes beyond wingtips at rest*. Bill dark grey, *feet flesh-coloured*. Note that 20–30% of birds from Shark Bay, WA, are white-breasted, as are occasional birds in e. Aust. Crooning wailing notes heard at night on many Gt. Barrier Reef islands are made by this species.
Similar species: Fleshy-footed Shearwater (54). Sooty Shearwater (57): short tail, pale wing linings, dark legs. Short-tailed Shearwater (58): short tail, dark legs; wings slender, flight more impetuous. For comparison of white-breasted phase: Grey-backed Shearwater (56).
Breeding: In crowded colonies. Nest: sparse, of grass, feathers: in long 1–2 m burrow in sand under roots, in crevice under rock, under creepers, bushes or in palm logs. Egg: 1, large, white.
Range and Status: Breeds tropical and subtropical Indian and Pacific Oceans. In Aust., islands off w. and e. coasts: in WA from Carnac and Rottnest Is., n. to Montebello Group and Forestier I.; in e. Aust. from Montagu I., NSW, n. to Raine I., Q, and many islands in Coral Sea. Common w. coast of WA and from s. of Sydney to C. York, Gt. Barrier Reef and Coral Sea. Rare across n. Aust.; rare vagrant s. Australian waters. Possibly migratory: absent from NSW from May to Aug.

56 GREY-BACKED SHEARWATER *Puffinus bulleri*

Other names: Ashy-backed Petrel, Buller's or New Zealand Shearwater.
Field marks: 405–455 mm. A large longish-necked wedge-tailed shearwater with distinctive pattern. *Dark cap, dark-brown head, wings, tail contrast with pale-grey lower back and rump*; white below, including underwing. Bill dull slate-blue; legs and feet fleshy-white, tipped black. Flight drifting, leisurely, somewhat albatross-like; dark-brown wing-coverts and back form an M.
Similar species: Wedge-tailed Shearwater (55), white-breasted phase: upperparts uniform brown.
Range and Status: Breeds in summer on islands off North I., NZ. Summer records (mostly at sea or beachwashed) NSW coast, Montagu I. n. to Cabbage Tree I., Port

Stephens. Recorded ashore both islands, but breeding not reported: summer sight-records, N. Stradbroke I., se. Q. Increasing numbers of sightings suggest it to be a regular summer visitor.

57 SOOTY SHEARWATER *Puffinus griseus* Pl.4

Other names: Ghostbird, King or New Zealand Muttonbird: Sombre Petrel or Shear-water.

Field marks: 460–535 mm: span 990 mm 1.06 m. A large dark-brown shearwater *with white wing-linings*; bill dark, longish; feet dark. Compared with Short-tailed (58) looks slimmer, *with longer bill, flight seemingly slower.* The main diagnostic feature is the white underwing, but because some Sooties lack this and some Short-taileds have silvery wing-linings, it is not a very satisfactory distinction. Try to base identification on a sampling of birds in the flock, rather than one or two.

Similar species: Fleshy-footed (54) and Wedge-tailed (55) Shearwaters: White-chinned Petrel (53).

Breeding: Nest: of grass and other vegetable material: in burrow 1–3 m long, usually beneath tussocks. In Aust., typically on high land. Egg: 1: large, white.

Range and Status: A predominantly NZ species, breeding on many NZ islands, including sub-Antarctic; also off Chile and Falkland Is. In Aust., small numbers breed Broughton, Little Broughton, Cabbage Tree, Boondelbah, Lion, Bird, Bowen, Tollgates and Montagu Is., NSW, and Courts, Tasman, Matsuyker, Breaksea Is., Tas. (also Flat and Green Is. in Port Davey). Uncommon to common off se. Aust. and Tas. in spring, summer and autumn; rare vagrant SA. Winter trans-equatorial migration to Japanese and Californian waters.

58 SHORT-TAILED SHEARWATER *Puffinus tenuirostris* Pl.4

Other names: Bonaparte's Shearwater, Sealbird, Short-tailed Petrel, Slender-billed Petrel or Shearwater, Tasmanian Muttonbird.

Field marks: 390–430 mm: span 860–960 mm. The most abundant Australian shear-water and possibly Australian bird. Dark smoky brown, *underwings slightly paler and glossed.* Some have a whitish underwing or are pale elsewhere in plumage, especially throat. *Bill slender; tail short, rounded.* Usually in flocks, some immense: they pass off-shore in undulating streams, become churning masses over food or rest on the surface in dark rafts. In light winds, flocks search randomly, with alternating easy wingbeats and glides: in high winds, flight fast and weaving on fixed wings, with bursts of quick wing-beats. Mostly well offshore, but occasionally inshore: many are wrecked on coasts or even inland, after storms or failure of plankton.

Similar species: Fleshy-footed (54), Wedge-tailed (55) and Sooty (57) Shearwaters.

Breeding: Nest: sparse grass, leaves and other vegetable material; in burrow, 5–2 m long, usually under tussocks, typically in island colony – some immense. Eggs: 1, large, white, laid between Nov. 19 and Dec. 1: incubation period 52–55 days. Chick remains in nest *c.* 94 days, the last feed *c.* 14 days before departure, which occurs from third week in Apr. to first week in May. Imms. do not return to breeding island before 2, and usually 4, years.

Range and Status: Breeds on islands from Nuyt's Archipelago, SA, round Tas. and through Bass Strait to Broughton I., NSW. After breeding, almost wholly absent from Aust. May–Sept.; imms. (and perhaps adults) migrate to n. Pacific via n. of NZ and Japan. Return is via w. coast of America. Breeding adults regularly arrive at home islands last week Sept. After 're-courtship', burrow renovation and copulation, breeding islands are vacated until egg-laying begins 19–21 Nov. During this and incubation and nestling period, disperses widely. Common to very abundant in summer off se. Aust. from c. coastal NSW, s. round Tas. and w. to offshore SA. Uncommon n. NSW and se. Q: rare s. WA.

59 MANX SHEARWATER *Puffinus puffinus*

Other name: Common Shearwater (North Atlantic).
Field marks: 355–380 mm. A medium-sized white-breasted shearwater with longish bill: brownish-black above, contrasting sharply with white underparts: boundary lying *just below eye, foreneck white*; sides of upperbreast smudged brown. Bill noticeably long, slender and hooked at tip; grey at base, with darker tip; feet pinkish flesh. Closely related to Fluttering Shearwater (60), but larger, bill bigger, flight more characteristic of larger shearwaters: stiff-winged gliding broken by few rapid shallow wingbeats.
Range and Status: Breeds Iceland, British Isles, islands off Europe, Caribbean and Arabian Seas, migrates to S. Atlantic. One Australian record: bird banded Skokholm, Wales, Sept. 1960, recovered dead Venus Bay, SA, Nov. 1961. Vagrant.

60 FLUTTERING SHEARWATER *Puffinus gavia*   Pl.5

Other names: Brown-backed Petrel, Forster's or Hutton's Shearwater.
Field marks: 330–370 mm. Much the commonest white-breasted shearwater in se. Australian waters: dark brown above, but from afar can look black, *underwing white*, axillaries (armpit) smudged brownish. Distinguished from Little Shearwater (61) by size, longer bill and smudgy border between dark above and pale below *being well below eye*, *and extending lower on sides of foreneck*; in some, almost a partial dark collar. Legs and feet blackish, with pale-flesh or whitish inner-surface. Can at times be seen from shore in large numbers, in rafts, or flying near surface, rapid wingbeats broken by quick glides: feet protrude slightly. In strong winds, 'weaves' in typical stiff-winged shearwater-manner. Spends much time on water, dives. The large race *huttoni*, 'Hutton's Shearwater' (380 mm) can be separated under good conditions by its *dusky brownish underwing*: it occurs in flocks of *gavia*.
Similar species: Little Shearwater (61): Manx Shearwater (59).
Range and Status: Breeds many NZ offshore islands and Chatham I., dispersing to coastal waters (occasionally bays and harbours) of s. and se. Aust. from se. Q to Fremantle, WA. Common and at times very abundant; present through year. Race *huttoni* breeds Seaward Kaikoura Ra. on e. coast South I. NZ above 1200 m. winter visitor coastal waters Vic. and SA (Kangaroo I.); vagrant sw. Aust.; uncommon visitor NSW: sight records Moreton Bay, N. Stradbroke I. and near Beaver Cay, Q, May–Aug.

61 LITTLE SHEARWATER *Puffinus assimilis*   Pl.5

Other names: Allied, Dusky or Gould's Shearwater or Petrel.
Field marks: 255–305 mm. Smallest Australian black-and-white shearwater: flies low, fast and straight with rapid flapping action and banking glides. Smaller and finer-billed than Fluttering Shearwater (60): *blue-black above, junction between black and white is above eye-level, resulting in dark eye standing out*; underwing white; legs and feet cobalt blue with pinkish webs. Singly or (specially in sw. Aust.) in flocks. Spends much time on water, dives.
Similar species: Fluttering Shearwater (60): Common Diving Petrel (70).
Breeding: Nest: in burrow, under rocks. Egg: 1, large, white.
Range and Status: In Aust. breeds only in WA, on islands from Recherche Archipelago to Abrolhos group. Nearest e. breeding grounds: Lord Howe and Norfolk Is.: also NZ, sub-Antarctic islands and elsewhere. Moderately common in sw. Aust.: uncommon and usually absent in winter from coastal waters of e. Aust.: records Vic., NSW, se. Q. Sedentary.

62 AUDUBON'S SHEARWATER *Puffinus lherminieri*

Field marks: 300 mm. A small shearwater, like Little (61) but upperparts brownish-black, under tail-coverts black or partly black, partly white, *legs flesh-coloured or yellowish white*.
Range and Status: Tropical Pacific, Indian and w. Atlantic Oceans. Nearest breeding

grounds are in the New Hebrides. One bird alleged collected by Sir J. Banks, June 1770, off Halifax Bay, n. Q. (?) Vagrant.

Storm-Petrels Family *Oceanitidae*

Known to sailors as Mother Carey's chickens, distinctive tiny blackish or greyish petrels sized from a pipit to a Magpie Lark. Some have white rumps or underparts. They have slight curved bills, surmounted by a typically longish nostril-tube, usually slanted upward. Northern storm-petrels, subfamily *Hydrobatinae*, differ from southern storm-petrels, subfamily *Oceanitinae*, in longer more pointed wings, shortish legs and rounded or forked tails. They swoop and skim in almost tern-like flight. Two, Leach's (68) and Matsudaira's (69) Storm-petrels, are vagrants to Australian seas. The southern storm-petrels have rather rounded wings, very long legs and butterfly-like fluttering as they skip and bounce over the waves, often running with wings spread or trailing legs as sea-anchors. They also feed while swimming, floating high on water, and swim underwater with half-open wings. Races of several southern storm-petrels are very variable. Only one, White-faced Storm-petrel (65), breeds in Aust.; migrating to tropics in winter; it is unlike any other storm-petrel and more likely to be mistaken for a prion. The next-commonest species locally is Wilson's Storm-petrel (63), perhaps the most abundant bird on earth. It breeds in sub-Antarctic, migrating n. in autumn past coasts of s. continents to tropical seas. Other species that occur locally are migratory or dispersive, their movements often little known. Some will probably be found to be regular visitors.

Food: Mostly animal plankton.

Range: Oceans of the world.

Number of species: World 21; Aust. 7: 1 breeding, 1 regular migrant, others uncommon visitors or vagrants.

63 WILSON'S STORM-PETREL *Oceanites oceanicus* Pl.5

Other names: Flat-clawed or Yellow-webbed Storm-petrel, Mother Carey's Chicken.

Field marks: 150–190 mm, span 355–405 mm. Sooty brown, with only upper tail-coverts white, overflowing onto flanks; flight feathers and tail blacker, brown or grey edges to wing-coverts form *pale loop across wing in flight*; tail blackish, slightly *forked or squarish when open*; *underwings brown.* Bill black, slender and short, with rather inconspicuous nostril-tube, legs and feet black with bright-yellow webs, tipped black. Uses long legs and feet in feeding flight, pats surface, dances, wings raised, head down. Rarely alights, but swims buoyantly, high in water. In direct flight, feet protrude slightly beyond tail.

Range and Status: Breeds Antarctica and many sub-Antarctic islands. Migrates n. in Apr.–June to winter on continental shelves of tropics and n. hemisphere. Appears on n. passage on coasts Tas., se. and sw. Aust. late autumn; common in winter coastal waters of n. Aust. from ne. Q to Kimberleys, WA; returns Sept. onwards.

64 GREY-BACKED STORM-PETREL *Oceanites nereis*

Other name: Mother Carey's Chicken.

Field marks: 165–190 mm. A small greyish storm-petrel with head to upperbreast sooty grey-brown; *underparts and underwing white. Back and rump ashy grey, each feather slightly margined white, giving lightly scaled look. Tail grey, square, with broad blackish terminal band.* Bill small, nostril-tubes not conspicuous. Flight buoyant, with rapid erratic darting and hovering.

Similar species: White-faced Storm-petrel (65): white forehead and face; dark eyemark.

Range and Status: Breeds islands in NZ region; Kerguelen and other islands in S. Indian Ocean and S. Atlantic. Ranges n. in winter, irregularly to waters of se. Aust. Specimens taken at sea en route Hobart–Sydney May 1839, June 1847: recent winter records, Tas.: two records c. coast NSW, June 1969, Oct. 1972. Vagrant.

65 WHITE-FACED STORM-PETREL *Pelagodroma marina* **Pl.5**

Other names: Frigate Petrel, Mother Carey's Chicken, White-breasted Storm-Petrel.
Field marks: 180–205 mm; span 380–430 mm. *The only storm-petrel with white forehead, face and underparts and broad dark mark through eye.* Bill slender, with prominent nostril tube; legs long and black, feet have yellow or buff webs. Singly or in open flocks; in flight, *black flight feathers and square dark tail contrast with grey shoulders and back*; underwing white; trails long legs, flutters, dips while moving into wind, picking food from surface; direct flight swift, strong and wheeling, *feet protrude a little*. Occasionally feeds while swimming or rests in flocks on calm water, floating high and buoyantly, wingtips up-slanted.
Similar species: No other storm-petrel is likely to be confused, but pattern and colour not unlike prions (44–9). Latter have distinct dark band across grey wing; flip and glide with wings more horizontal, often run on water, but do not trail legs. Bills mostly heavier, blue-grey.
Breeding: Nest: scanty lining of grass in very slim burrow like rat-hole, *c.* 1 m long; usually in colony. Egg: 1, white, finely flecked red-brown.
Range and Status: Breeds late spring and summer on many coastal islands in s. Aust. from Abrolhos Group, WA, at least to Broughton I., NSW; Bass Strait and Tas. islands: Mud and Fort Is., Port Phillip Bay, Vic.; NZ and NZ sub-Antarctic islands. White-rumped race *albiclunis* breeds Kermadec I., and in Atlantic. Migrations little understood: part of Australian population winters n. Indian Ocean from Arabian Sea to Java. Present offshore s. Aust. in summer; apparently absent in winter.

66 BLACK-BELLIED STORM-PETREL *Fregetta tropica*

Other names: Gould's Storm Petrel, Mother Carey's Chicken.
Field marks: 190–215 mm. Like closely related White-bellied Storm-petrel (67): differs in *irregular band of dark-brown down centre of white abdomen*, difficult to see in flight.
Range and Status: Breeds circumpolar sub-Antarctic islands, including NZ region, ranging n. to about 30°S in winter. Sight-records Tasman Sea between Aust. and NZ, also s. of Tas. and off Fremantle, WA; taken off coast NSW, May 1875; (old) specimens from Q and Port Essington, NT; specimens from N. Stradbroke I., Q, July 1973. Vagrant.

67 WHITE-BELLIED STORM-PETREL *Fregetta grallaria*

Other names: Broad-nailed or Vieillot's Storm-petrel.
Field marks: 175–215 mm. Variable: typical form sooty black above and on throat, mantle paler; *rump white, joining white underparts. Underwings white, margined brown: tail black, square.* Small and compact; nostril-tube conspicuous, flight erratic.
Range and Status: Breeds Lord Howe and Kermadec Is. and in S. Atlantic. Probably disperses n. into tropics. Reported in Coral and Tasman Seas and S. Indian Ocean. Vagrant.

68 LEACH'S STORM-PETREL *Oceanodroma leucorhoa*

Other name: Leach's Fork-tailed Petrel.
Field marks: 190–230 mm. A northern storm-petrel; like Wilson's Storm-petrel (63) but paler, slimmer, *tail longer and more forked.* Less white on upper tail-coverts and this area either divided by indistinct greyish central area or indented from above by extension of blackish upper tail-coverts. Little white on edge under tail-coverts. Wings longer, with slight pale-brown bar; legs shorter. Flight more erratic, darting, butterfly-like.
Range and Status: Breeds Greenland, Atlantic and Pacific coasts of n. America, Alaska, n. Asia, Japan. Migrates s. into tropical waters. One Australian record: nominate (Atlantic) race beachwashed w. Vic., July 1965. Once NZ, Aug. 1922. Vagrant.

69 MATSUDAIRA'S STORM-PETREL *Oceanodroma matsudairae*

Other name: Sooty Storm-petrel.

Field marks: 230–255 mm. A large dark-brown fork-tailed northern storm-petrel with *buffish wingbar but no white in plumage except on shafts of primaries*. Wings broad, flight strong, but slow, less erratic than smaller species.

Range and Status: Known to breed only Volcano and Bonin Is. in Pacific s. of Japan. Migrates s. after breeding, passing through Indonesian Archipelago to ne. Indian Ocean. Three specimens from waters off nw. Aust.: near Lacepede Is., WA: Seringapatam Reef, July 1965; near Montebello I., WA, Sept. 1968. Vagrant.

Diving-Petrels Family *Pelecanoididae*

Stocky small petrels of s. hemisphere remarkably like auks of n. hemisphere in structure and habits. They take much of their food when 'flying' underwater. In the hand, useful diagnostic features are nasal apertures opening upward and a small food pouch under the lower mandible, folded like a concertina.

Food: Plankton, crustaceans, small fish.

Breeding: In rock crevices and burrows on oceanic islands.

Range: Southern oceans.

Number of species: World 5; Aust 2: 1 resident, 1 vagrant.

70 COMMON DIVING-PETREL *Pelecanoides urinatrix*   Pl.5

Field marks: 200–255 mm: span 400 mm. A tubby little petrel, wings and legs set well back: glossy brownish black above, dusky white below: *short bill dark-grey*. Singly or in flocks: bursts out of water ahead of boat, *flies direct and low on fluttering narrow wings before plunging underwater*. On surface swims low: 'flies' underwater, using wings as flippers. Comes and goes from breeding islands under cover of dark: ashore, proceeds in a rat-like scurry. In hand, note small concertina-like pouch of black skin under bill, and cobalt-blue feet.

Habitat: Ocean waters, larger bays: oceanic islands.

Breeding: Nest: in burrow *c.* 0.5 m long in soil or in rock crevice, in loose colony on oceanic island. Egg: 1, dull-white.

Range and Status: Breeds many sub-Antarctic islands, including NZ region. In Aust., McHugh and Dannevig Is. in the Glennie Group and Cliffy I. (all off Wilson's Promontory, Vic.) and Lady Julia Percy I. in w. Vic.: also Kent Group, Councillor I., Black Pyramid and Maatsuyker I., Tas. Fairly common resident Bass Strait, rare elsewhere. Records: SA to se. Q.

71 SOUTH GEORGIAN DIVING-PETREL *Pelecanoides georgicus*

Field marks: 180–210 mm. Similar to Common Diving Petrel (70) but slightly smaller: distinguished in hand by bill proportionately wider at base, nostrils *rounded*, rather than elongated as in *urinatrix*. Breeds Auckland I., NZ region: also Heard, Kerguelen and Marion Is. in s. Indian Ocean. One Australian record: Bellambi Beach, NSW, Dec. 1958. Vagrant.

Pelicans Family *Pelecanidae*

Very large unmistakeable fishing birds, with enormous bills and bill-pouches used in securing food. By providing a large area of bare skin, the pouch also helps disperse body-heat, enabling pelicans to roost and nest in often hot, exposed situations. Nesting colonies are usually remote, some are very large. Pelicans waddle on land because their legs are set far apart and to rear for efficient paddling. The feet are large and like those of other pelicaniform birds are totipalmate i.e. all four toes are linked by webs. Pelicans fly and soar superbly; some dive on prey, others swim after it. Sexes similar.

Food: Mostly fish and small crustaceans.
Range: Temperate and tropical parts of all continents.
Number of species: World 7: Aust. 1.

72 AUSTRALIAN PELICAN *Pelecanus conspicillatus* Pl.9, 10

Other name· Spectacled Pelican.
Field marks: 1.5–1.9 m: span 2.4–2.6 m. An impressive black-and-white bird with *huge bill and bill-pouch.* Imm: black parts browner. Swimming groups encircle fish, plunging heads in unison; single birds swim stealthily up to fish with head low, neck cocked. Looks rotund on wing, head drawn back, bill resting on breast: *note white panel on black upperwing, white V on rump.* Flies in spectacular lines or Vs with intervals of wingbeats and glides: flocks slow-wheel to great heights on flat slender wings: over calm water skims surface in long sailing glides. Perches on piles, logs: sometimes dead trees: becomes tame where fed.
Similar species: Black-necked Stork (104): in flight, extended legs, black neck, black bar on white wing. White-breasted Sea-eagle (146): in flight, wings markedly upswept.
Voice: Away from nest rather silent: mostly gruff croaks.
Habitat: Large shallow waters generally: coastal and inland: occasionally on open sea. Also islands, mudflats, sandspits, jetties, piles.
Breeding: Nest: starts as a scrape, progressively lined with sticks, grass, seaweed during use: in small to very large isolated colonies, usually on bare islands, coastal or inland: but occasionally in vegetation over water. Eggs: 2–3: limy, dull-white.
Range and Status: Throughout Aust. and Tas. Common in suitable habitat: nomadic, movements influenced by seasonal factors. Also NG: New Hebrides, Solomon Is., Indonesia: vagrant NZ.

Gannets and Boobies Family *Sulidae*

Gannets (genus *Morus*) are large mainly white seabirds with partly or wholly black flight-feathers and tail. They inhabit mostly temperate coastal waters and form a single world superspecies. Boobies (genus *Sula*) inhabit tropical and subtropical waters: they have more extensive coloured facial skin and throat pouch: some have brightly coloured feet. Both have a streamlined silhouette, with long pointed wings and body, tapering to cone-shaped bill and pointed tail. Colour of bill, skin of face and feet is often diagnostic: feet are totipalmate – all four toes webbed. When fishing, gannets make spectacular dives from up to 50 m, submerging to about 9 m: boobies usually dive from lower levels. Sexes similar: except that in boobies colour of facial-skin and voice differ sexually.

Range: Gannets: coasts of s. Aust., NZ, s. Africa and both sides of N. Atlantic. Boobies: mostly tropical seas.
Number of species: World 9: Aust. 4.

73 AUSTRALIAN GANNET *Morus serrator* Pl.6

Other names: Australasian Gannet, Diver.
Field marks: 810–915 mm: span 1.6–1.7 m. The spectacular high-diving white seabird of s. Australian coasts. Note its *racy tapering outline, buff-washed head and black flight feathers;* central tail-feathers black: feet dark grey with yellow or green lines. Fishing gannets fly on somewhat crank-shaped wings 15–30 m above sea, bills downpointed: sighting prey, they drop with wings half-shut, plunging spectacularly. Companies wheel over shoaling fish offshore, plunging in salvos. Travelling gannets fly in lines, with alternat-

ing wingbeats and glides. They rest on calm water in white rafts and on flat surfaces of pile lights or high steep slopes of islands, but otherwise are seldom ashore. Imm: very different; grey-brown with *plentiful white spots, giving a 'salt-and-pepper' effect; head and body patchy white and brown.* Adult plumage assumed over 2 years, first with less yellow on head, at one stage with blackish brown wings, back and tail. The pattern then is albatross- or gull-like, but the whole jizz is different.

Similar species: See albatrosses (17–25); gulls (259–261); Caspian Tern (266); Red- footed Booby (74), white phase: white tail, red feet. Masked Booby (75): white head, black face and tail.

Breeding: Nest: pedestal of compacted earth, guano, seaweed and other vegetation. Egg: 1, blue-white, limy; becoming stained brown with incubation.

Range and Status: Coastal waters of s. Aust. and NZ. In Aust. breeds Pedra Branca, Eddystone Rock, s. Tas.; Black Pyramid and Cat I., Bass Strait; Lawrence Rocks, Vic. Common, widespread on s. coasts during summer, ranging n. in winter to Pt. Cloates, WA, and Mackay, Q. Local population augmented by migrant adults and imms. of NZ population. Migratory and dispersive.

74 RED-FOOTED BOOBY *Sula sula*   Pl.6

Other names: Red-footed or Red-legged Gannet.

Field marks: 660–790 mm; span *c.* 1.4 m. *Smallest booby: adult always has bluish bill, lolly-pink at base; feet flesh-pink to cherry-red.* In flight looks slender with longish tail. Plumage variable, with light and dark colour-phases and intermediates. *White phase:* white with black flight-feathers, white tail, golden wash on head. *Intermediate phase:* head and body dull-white to light buff, back and wings chocolate-brown or grey. *Dark phase:* head and body ashy-grey or ash-brown, wings and back grey. Imms. of all phases are wholly mottled brown; bill black, often tinted dull-blue, legs and feet dark-grey, becoming red. Differs from other boobies by nesting and roosting in trees; may forage over sea at night as well as by day.

Similar species: Brown Booby (76), imm: paler underwing and abdomen. Masked Booby (75); Australian Gannet (73).

Breeding: Nest: bulky, rather untidy platform, of sticks, grass: in low bush or tree, occasionally on ground. Egg: 1: limy, green-white.

Range and Status: Tropical Atlantic, Pacific and Indian Oceans: in Aust. breeds Raine I., n. Q, various cays in sw. Coral Sea s. to Capricorn Group; also Ashmore Reefs, nw. WA. Local and uncommon.

75 MASKED BOOBY *Sula dactylatra*   Pl.6

Other names: Blue-faced or White Booby, Masked Gannet.

Field marks: 735–865 mm. A robust white booby *with dark-brown flight-feathers and tail; facial skin and base of bill blue-black,* rest of bill bright-yellow in male, dull green- yellow in female; eye yellow, feet blue-grey or blue-green. Imm: brown above *crossed by mottled white bars;* wing-linings and underparts white. Bill dull-brown, blue-black at base and on facial skin; legs and feet dark. Flies and dives strongly, usually well offshore.

Similar species: Imms. of other boobies show less contrast of dark head with white underparts; no black-and-white scaly pattern above. See also Australian Gannet (73); Red-footed Booby (74), white phase.

Breeding: Nest: scrape in sand, occasionally with pebbles or grass-roots. Eggs: 2, occasionally 3; limy, blue-white. Usually only one nestling raised.

Range and Status: Tropical Atlantic, Pacific and Indian Oceans. Locally, breeds Bedout and Adelie Is., nw. Aust.; Pandora Cay and Raine I. ne. Q; Swain and Wreck Reefs, ce. Q; also many stations in sw. Coral Sea; Norfolk and Lord Howe Is. Disperses s. to Dampier Archipelago, WA, and North Reef, Q; vagrant NSW and SA. Fairly common in oceanic waters of main range; uncommon coastally.

76 BROWN BOOBY *Sula leucogaster* **Pl.6**
Other name: Brown Gannet.
Field marks: 710–760 mm: span *c.* 1.37 m. A small dark-brown booby with *sharply cut-off white belly and underwings.* Bill creamy or grey: male has blue facial skin and base of bill; female yellow facial skin, blue spot before eye; legs and feet green-yellow. Imm: same pattern but less contrast: bill blue-horn; legs and feet bright-yellow. Singly or in small flocks; often dives from low levels, takes fish from waves in flight. Roosts on coral cays, buoys, beacons, trees, ships' rigging. In s. Q and n. NSW look for it with flocks of gannets.
Similar species: Australian Gannet (73); imm. has more patchy look; larger. Red-footed Booby (74), imm: very similar, but with different pattern of grey and brown. Masked Booby (75), imm: barred above.
Breeding: Nest: scrape in sand or low collection of sponges, seaweeds; on edges of cliffs and in small clearings on islands, on ground. Eggs: 2, rarely 3: chalky, green-white.
Range and Status: Tropical Atlantic, Pacific and Indian Oceans. In nw. WA, breeds from Ashmore Reef s. to Bedout I.: in Q, from Raine I., off ne. C. York Pen., s. to Bunker Group. Common s. to Moreton Bay, Q, and Dampier Archipelago, WA: stragglers to NSW: vagrant Vic.

Darters   Family *Anhingidae*

Distinctive fishing birds, related to cormorants but with smaller head, stiletto-like bill and snakelike neck. The neck has a distinct kink, associated with a trigger process in the vertebrae that allows a sudden thrust of the slightly opened bill to impale fish and other aquatic animals while swimming underwater. On surface, darters swim with body submerged and only the slender head and neck visible, hence 'snakebird': easily-saturated plumage necessitates frequent drying of wings. As in other Pelecaniformes, all four toes are webbed, providing a large propulsive surface. The short legs are rear-placed for efficient swimming: when walking, the wings are spread for balance. Sexes dissimilar.
Food: Mostly fish.
Range: Tropical and subtropical regions throughout world.
Number of species: World 2: Aust. 1.

77 DARTER *Anhinga melanogaster* **Pl.8**
Other names: Diver, Needle-beak Shag, Snake-bird.
Field marks: 865–940 mm. Differs from cormorants (78–82) in *stiletto-like bill: snakelike kinked neck, patterns in dark plumage and larger black tail.* Male: variable but usually very dark with *white streak down side of chestnut-marked neck.* In breeding plumage, long plumes, buff with black borders, adorn back. Female and imm: head and hindneck pale grey, *foreneck white with black whisker*, breast white. Both sexes: bill and facial skin yellowish, feet pink or grey. Singly or pairs: occasionally open companies, less gregarious than cormorants. Dries wings on dead branches, fallen logs in water, on shore or navigation piles. Wary: on approach, snake-like neck writhes about. Flight distinctive – *wing-beats rapid, shallow, every few strokes interspersed with glides*: often soars high, large tail fanned.
Similar species: Black Cormorant (81).
Voice: A brassy clanging: alarm-note, a mechanical-sounding clicking.
Habitat: Larger shallow waters, fresh and salt: rivers, lakes, swamps, lagoons, reservoirs: tidal inlets, estuaries, but not open sea.
Breeding: Nest: fairly bulky platform of sticks: in dead or live trees over water, usually in small colony. Eggs: 3–5: green-white, limy.
Range and Status: Throughout mainland Aust., but patchy and often absent from apparently suitable habitats. Not recorded Tas.: once vagrant, 1874, NZ. Also Africa through s. Asia to NG.

Cormorants Family *Phalacrocoracidae*

Familiar black or black-and-white fishing birds, with bills hooked at tip, necks long and flexible, tails rather long, feet totipalmate, as in other Pelecaniformes. On the surface they swim low, body submerged, bill uptilted; underwater they propel themselves with simultaneous strokes of the feet, wings closed. The plumage is sparse and easily becomes wet; because of this cormorants must dry their wings conspicuously on piles, piers, rocks, buoys or branches. They seldom venture far to sea from coasts or islands. Some species hunt co-operatively in flocks; all roost and breed communally. Most cormorants fly with the body slightly uptilted towards the head (but see Black-faced Cormorant (78).) The flight is direct, often low over water. When travelling far in company, they often form long lines or V-skeins. Two Australian cormorants are mostly black, the other three black-and-white; two are small. Identification is based mostly on these distinctions and on colouring of bare facial skin and throat-pouch. Note that in Australia the names 'cormorant' and 'shag' are used indiscriminately but should not be. The shags are a group of sea-cormorants with distinguishing characteristics – they fly low and direct, with the head and neck on the same level as the body, or lower. One local species Black-faced Cormorant flies like a shag, roosts and nests on rock surfaces, never in trees. One authority (G. F. van Tets) has proposed that it be included in the genus of southern shags, *Leucocarbo*, with the common name Black-faced Shag.

Food: Cormorants eat what they can catch most easily: small fish, eels, frogs, crustaceans, aquatic insects and larvae and occasionally ducklings and small mammals. Contrary to belief they do not consume several times their weight in fish every day. Larger species (weighing *c*. 3 kg) are reported to take a total of 500–1000 g daily and this is approximately the weight of the largest fish they can swallow.

Range: Nearly cosmopolitan; in Aust., most inland waters but seldom more than a few kilometres to sea from coasts or coastal islands.

Number of species: World 29; Aust. 5.

78 BLACK-FACED CORMORANT *Phalacrocorax fuscescens* Pl.8

Other names: Black-faced or Black-and-White Shag; White-breasted Cormorant.
Field marks: 610–685 mm; span 1.05 m. A white-breasted cormorant: *black of crown reaches eye*; bill dark-grey, *throat-pouch and facial skin black*, extending in a point back below eye; black flank-mark. In breeding plumage, dense short white streaks on nape, rump and thighs. Imm: browner, face buff, foreneck smutty. Fishes singly or in small to large companies; roosts on offshore rocky islands, buoys, isolated jetties and breakwaters. On wing, has a distinctly *pot-bellied look, small head carried level with body*: flight straight and swift with rapid shallow wingbeats, and usually close to water.
Similar species: Pied Cormorant (79), imm: paler bill, yellowish facial skin: Little Pied Cormorant (80), imm: stubbier bill usually shows some yellow.
Voice: Usually silent: guttural croaking at roosts and in breeding colonies.
Habitat: Coastal offshore waters: islands, larger bays and inlets; on mainland coasts ashore mostly only on isolated rock-stacks, remote rocky headlands.
Breeding: Nest: rather rough scanty structure; of dry seaweed, driftwood, grass, pigface; usually in small colony on steep rocky island or offshore rock stack. (Huge colonies in SA, many substantial nests.) Eggs: 2; pale-green, limy.
Range and Status: Confined to coasts of s. Aust. from far s. NSW to Hopetoun, WA. Common Bass Strait, coasts of Tas., and Vic., w. from Wilsons Promontory through SA. Possibly absent Gt. Australian Bight. Resident Recherche Archipelago, WA, and from Israelite Bay to Hopetoun. Uncommon e. Vic.; vagrant Montagu I., NSW. Sedentary.

79 PIED CORMORANT *Phalacrocorax varius* **Pl.8**

Other names: Black-and-White Shag, Diver, Yellow-faced Cormorant.
Field marks: 660–810 mm: span 1.5 m. Largest white-breasted cormorant: *note long slender flesh-white to horn-coloured bill and patch of orange-yellow facial skin between eye and bill; throat-pouch yellowish.* At distance, looks much whiter than Little Pied (79), with slab-sided look to white neck; black flank-mark visible when perched. Imm: black areas browner: more onto sides of face and neck, often forming smutty band across upperbreast: bill dark-horn, face dull-yellow. Singly, small parties, at times companies of thousands. Shy and remote: flies in V-formations, roosts in company on piles, dead trees over water, undisturbed sandspits, mangroves. Flight strong and direct, wingbeats slower than Little Pied.
Similar species: Black-faced Cormorant (78). Little Pied Cormorant (80): much smaller, bill stubbier, yellower: adult has no black flank-mark. Little Pied Cormorant, imm, from imm. Pied by size, and stubbier, often partly yellow bill.
Voice: Guttural cacklings, croakings, mechanical sounds and loud screams, seldom heard except at colony.
Habitat: Shallower coastal waters, generally with sloping shorelines: estuaries, bays, larger lakes and rivers. Almost entirely marine in WA, in coastal mangroves and offshore islands, but in n. and e. Aust. mostly in colonies on coastal lakes, swamps, estuaries and larger rivers and on large inland waters.
Breeding: Nest: flat bulky mass of seaweed, sticks: in colonies on ground on islands, in mangroves or in dead or live trees in water; sometimes on beacons. Eggs: 2–5; dirty green-white.
Range and Status: Mainland Aust., vagrant King I., Bass Strait. Common and abundant in coastal WA and offshore islands from Cape Naturaliste to Kimberleys. Rare s. coast WA: common SA e. of Bight, breeds coastally and inland: moderately common Vic., NSW and Q, where strongholds are coastal lakes, estuaries and larger waters of Murray-Darling basin. Sedentary and nomadic. Also NZ.

80 LITTLE PIED CORMORANT *Phalacrocorax melanoleucos* **Pl.8**

Other names: Little Black-and-White Cormorant, Frilled, Little Black-and-White or Little Shag.
Field marks: 580–635 mm; span 840–915 mm. Smallest Australian cormorant: *note stubby mostly yellow bill, well-feathered head with no obvious throat-pouch.* In breeding plumage, white plumes on side of head become fuller, black crown-feather often raised in spiky crest. Imm: bill grey-brown, becoming yellow on sides; black areas of plumage browner, extending smuttily on face and neck: looks slimmer-headed than adult, and *unlike adult has a black flank-mark.* Singly or in random companies; roosts and nests communally: usually fishes alone. When flying in company, structure of flock usually random without V or line-formation. Often has rusty stains in plumage from impurities in water.
Similar species: Pied Cormorant (79).
Voice: Seldom heard except at roosts or colonies: repeated querulous croaking or cooing.
Habitat: Coasts, islands, reefs, inlets, estuaries and inland waters of all kinds, even very small; house dams, roadside ditches, garden fishponds, occasionally.
Breeding: Nest: small shallow structure of sticks (and often green sprays of eucalypt leaves); usually in colonies of few to hundreds, in trees, bushes, from 1.20 m above water: occasionally on ground or ledges on islands. Eggs: 2–5; limy, blue-white.
Range and Status: Common throughout Aust. and Tas. in suitable habitat: vagrant Lord Howe I.; sedentary or nomadic. Also Malaysia, Indonesia to NG, Solomons, New Caledonia, NZ region: vagrant sub-Antarctic islands.

81   BLACK CORMORANT   *Phalacrocorax carbo*   **Pl.8**

Other names: Big Black Cormorant, Black Shag.
Field marks: 710–915 mm; span 1.06–1.50 m. Largest cormorant; wholly blackish, with dark-horn bill, *ochre-yellow throat-pouch and facial skin*. Breeding plumage more glossy: patterned by dark feather-margins; develops *white chin and white flank-mark*, fine white flecks on head and neck. Imm: dull brown, with dull-yellow throat pouch and facial skin; centre of foreneck and breast dirty white. Singly, to very large flocks. Flight strong and direct; in undulating line or V-formations, with measured wingbeats and glides in unison. Formations drive fish, leapfrogging those in front, wheeling, skidding in and diving in rising frenzy. Very wary; rests on dead trees, usually over water, remote ends of piers, sandspits, buoys; roosts in public gardens with lakes.
Similar species: Little Black Cormorant (82): smaller; face-skin black, wingbeats quicker.
Voice: Querulous croaking, rising in cadence; rarely heard away from roosts or colonies.
Habitat: Coastal waters, bays, estuaries; larger rivers and lakes, farm dams.
Breeding: Nest: bulky platform of sticks, weed; in colony, usually in treetops over water, often with other cormorants, herons or spoonbills; occasionally on ground or cliff. Eggs 3–4; greenish white, limy.
Range and Status: Aust. and Tas., widespread; irregular throughout inland; rare n. Aust. Sedentary and nomadic. Also ne. America to Greenland, Europe, Africa, Asia, Indonesia, NG, NZ.

82   LITTLE BLACK CORMORANT   *Phalacrocorax sulcirostris*   **Pl.8**

Other names: Little Black Shag, Shag.
Field marks: 580–635 mm. *A small slender black cormorant with dark bill and dark facial skin.* Breeding plumage more bronzed, head and neck sparsely flecked white. Perhaps more typically than other cormorants, forms compact flocks, especially in autumn and winter. Very active when feeding; locating fish from the air, the birds wheel and settle progressively, driving together in rising frenzy, leapfrogging those in front. Dries wings in companies, typically on fallen trees over water, sandspits. *In flight, wingbeats quicker than Black Cormorant* (81); moves in fast-flying strings or Vs.
Similar species: Black Cormorant (81). Glossy Ibis (105): flying flocks can be confused.
Voice: Usually silent, but guttural calls at nest.
Habitat: Coastal waters, bays; inlets, mangroves; rivers, swamps, lakes, reservoirs, ornamental lakes.
Breeding: Nest: rough platform of sticks, leaves, bark, aquatic herbage; in colony, in trees over water, often with other cormorants, herons or spoonbills. Eggs: 4; greenish white, limy.
Range and Status: Aust. and Tas.: mostly coastal and on large lakes and river systems, but through inland when conditions suitable. Common; sedentary and nomadic. Also Borneo, Indonesia, NG, New Caledonia, NZ.

Frigatebirds   Family *Fregatidae*

Dark plumage, enormously long crank-shaped wings and scissor-forked tails distinguish frigatebirds. They have long slender hooked bills and very small feet, with obsolete webs. These are adaptations for economical flight; after swifts, they are the most aerial of birds, spending hours in buoyant effortless soaring; they may even sleep on wing. Lacking water-proofed plumage, they seldom alight on water, but snatch food from the surface of the sea or land. Perhaps most characteristically they harry seabirds, especially boobies, until they disgorge, recovering the booty as it falls. They usually nest near seabird colonies, where a supply of food is constant. Mostly coastal or insular, frigatebirds seldom range far to sea. In breeding plumage, males develop a crimson throat-sac, inflatable into a large conspicuous balloon, displayed in flight, on the ground, when perched and at nest. When collapsed, it shrinks to a small red mark under the chin. Sexes dissimilar, females larger.

Food: Fish, squid, crustaceans, young birds, young turtles, flotsam.

Range: Tropical seas; storm-blown individuals may wander far from normal range, particularly when following coastlines.

Number of species: World 5; Aust. 3, including one vagrant.

83 GREATER FRIGATEBIRD *Fregata minor** Pl.7

Other names: Man-o'-war Bird or Hawk, Sea Hawk.

Field marks:: 865 mm–1.01 m; span *c.* 2.13 m. For general appearance see family introduction. Male: *wholly blackish*, in flight, brownish upper wing-coverts form bar across wing. Throat-pouch usually contracted to small red patch. Eye-ring blue or black. Female: larger; *throat greyish, breast white, abdomen black*; eye-ring red; no scarlet throat-pouch. Imm: blackish-brown above with pale-brown wing-coverts, head and breast whitish washed rusty.

Similar species: Lesser Frigatebird (84); Christmas Island Frigatebird (85).

Habitat: Tropical and subtropical coastlines and islands.

Breeding: Nest: platform of sticks in top of shrub or tree. Eggs: 2; white, large, smooth and glossy.

Range and Status: Tropical Atlantic, Pacific and Indian Oceans. Breeds islands in Coral Sea, including outer Gt. Barrier Reef. Nearest breeding stations in Indian Ocean are Christmas and Cocos–Keeling Is. Probably regular but uncommon visitor to n. coasts, s. to Pt. Cloates, WA, and s. Q; more usual on islands of Gt. Barrier Reef; vagrant NSW, Vic., s. WA.

*Note contradiction between common name 'Greater Frigatebird' and specific scientific name *minor*. When first described in 1789, the species was named Lesser Pelican, *Pelecanus minor*. Under rules governing scientific names the genus *Pelecanus* can be discarded, but *minor* must stand, though smaller frigatebirds, e.g. Lesser, were later described.

84 LESSER FRIGATEBIRD *Fregata ariel* Pl.7

Other names: Man-o'-war or Sea Hawk.

Field marks: 710–815 mm; span 1.75–1.90 m. A superb soarer and relentless pursuer of other seabirds; see family introduction. Male: glossy black above, with brownish wing-bar; *black below with distinctive white 'armpits'*. Throat-sac usually as small reddish area under bill. Bill grey; eye-ring black; feet blackish or reddish brown. Female: larger, *breast white*, sometimes washed yellow or buff; *black of throat extends as wedge onto breast*; bill greyish flesh coloured, eye-ring red, feet red or pinkish; no scarlet throat-sac. Imm: head and neck deep-ginger; breast blackish, abdomen whitish, extending a little onto wings.

Similar species: Greater Frigatebird (83).

Habitat: Tropical and subtropical coastal waters and islands.

Breeding: Nest: small, flat, of sticks, grass, in trees, shrubs or on ground. Eggs: 2; white, limy.

Range and Status: Tropical Atlantic, w. Pacific and Indian Oceans. In Aust. breeds Raine I. and Gillett Cay, Q, and many cays in Coral Sea; Rocky I., NT; Ashmore Reef, Adele I., Sunday and Swan Is. (King Sound), Lacepede I., Bedout I., WA. Fairly common on n. coasts s. to *c.* Tropic of Capricorn; common on many islands on Gt. Barrier Reef; summer and autumn visitor to coastal se. Q, and n. NSW; rare further s., vagrant Vic.

85 CHRISTMAS ISLAND FRIGATEBIRD *Fregata andrewsi*

Other name: Andrews' Frigatebird.

Field marks: 940–965 mm. Male: like Greater Frigatebird (83) but *abdomen white*.

Female: like female Greater Frigatebird, but lower breast and abdomen (not throat) *white*. Imm: like imm. Greater Frigatebird. Associates in flight with Greater and Lesser (84) Frigatebirds.
Habitat: Coasts and oceanic islands.
Range and Status: Breeds Christmas I., Indian Ocean. Ranges through tropical Indian Ocean to coasts of India, se. Asia to Java, Borneo, Philippines. Sight-records, confirmed by photographs, Darwin, Jan. 21–27, 1974, at several locations. Vagrant.

Tropicbirds or Bosunbirds   Family *Phaethontidae*

Beautiful white (occasionally washed pink or gold) seabirds of tropics. Although related to gannets, cormorants and pelicans, they most resemble large-bodied terns, with strong slightly down-curved bills and elongated ribbon-like central tail-plumes, which differ in colour, length and stiffness between species; bill colour also differs. The short legs are set far back, causing them to shuffle on belly on land; feet small, the four toes connected by a web; as in other Pelecaniformes. Flight distinctive: direct and pigeon-like; with steady wingbeats, usually high above sea. They make high, gannet-like plunges after food and hover spectacularly when displaying near nest. They circle ships curiously, calling harshly.
Food: Fish, squid, etc.
Range: Pantropical seas, ranging far into temperate waters.
Number of species: World 3: Aust. 1 resident, 1 regular visitor.

86   RED-TAILED TROPICBIRD   *Phaethon rubricauda*   Pl.27
Other names: (Red-tailed) Bosunbird or Bos'nbird.
Field marks: 860 mm, including tail *c*. 400 mm. Largest tropicbird; mostly silky white, sometimes with a pink flush. The robust pointed bill is red, orange or rarely, yellow. The two rather stiff central tail plumes are *bright red*. Difficult to see from afar, their 'absence' gives the bird a *stubby silhouette*. The black feet are used as rudders in braking, turning. Imm: black bill, black-mottled upperparts, no red tail plume. Singly, in pairs or flocks far out to sea; flies high, fluttering wingbeats broken by glides. Dives like gannets or boobies, submerging completely. Over breeding grounds, hovers in display, tail depressed.
Similar species: White-tailed Tropicbird (87).
Voice: Harsh clanging rattle.
Habitat: Oceans, oceanic islands and coasts.
Breeding: Nest: scrape in cavity in cliff or under bush on shore. Eggs: 1; stone-coloured, heavily spotted red-brown.
Range and Status: Tropical Indian and Pacific Oceans. Off e. Aust., breeds Raine I., Herald Cays and Coringa Islets on Gt. Barrier Reef. Also Lord Howe and Norfolk Is. In WA, formerly bred Abrolhos Group and Rottnest I.; in recent years a small colony of *c*. 20 pairs has bred on Sugarloaf Rock, near C. Naturaliste, and nesting has been attempted on mainland beaches. Possibly regular visitor coastal waters n. of Perth and Sydney; vagrant s. NSW, Vic., Tas., SA.

87   WHITE-TAILED TROPICBIRD   *Phaethon lepturus*   Pl.27
Other names: Golden or White-tailed Bosunbird or Bos'nbird.
Field marks: 635–815 mm, including tail *c*. 400 mm. Smaller, more graceful on wing than Red-tailed Tropicbird (86): silky white, *with longer more flexible white tail-streamers, longer black comma-shaped eyebrow, and much black on wing* (parts of scapulars, secondaries and outer webs of outer primaries). Imm: mottled and barred black above, at first lacks tail streamers; bill pale-cream. Two forms in Aust. (1) nominate (Pacific) race: as above, bill yellow. (2) Christmas I. (Indian Ocean) race *fulvus*, known locally as 'Golden

Bosunbird': bill orange-pink or yellow, most have beautiful golden or apricot wash to plumage. Flight strong, direct, with rapid wingbeats, seldom glides. Hovers over fish before plunging gannet-like.

Similar species: Red-tailed Tropicbird (86).

Voice: Rattling calls in flight; harsh scream near nest.

Range and Status: Nominate race: breeds in tropical Pacific w. to Walpole I., also tropical Atlantic. Regular in Coral Sea; occasional visitor to coasts of ne. Aust.; summer and autumn straggler to s. of Sydney, NSW, mostly imms. and probably as result of cyclones. Race *fulvus*: breeds Christmas and Cocos–Keeling Is., Indian Ocean: sight-records, nw. coast, WA: specimen 400 km off Lacepede Is., July 1965.

Herons, Egrets, Night-Herons, Bitterns   Family *Ardeidae*

Mostly large, simply coloured wading birds with long necks and legs and straight sharp bills; egrets are usually white and acquire more elongated breeding plumes, when the colour of bill and facial skin also usually alters. Herons (and egrets) wade after their prey, seizing it in a lightning thrust imparted by a sudden straightening of the crooked neck; some also hunt in grassland or in pastures among grazing animals. Night-herons roost by day in company, becoming active at dusk. Bitterns, shy and part-nocturnal, cling mostly to dense cover near water: when alarmed, they point their bills skyward and freeze, relying on their streaked underparts for concealment. The flight of herons and other members of the family immediately places them: *the wings typically beat leisurely, the neck is usually folded and the long legs trail.* The voices of herons, egrets and night-herons are harsh and croaking; those of the larger bitterns typically booming. Sexes usually similar.

Food: Fish, amphibians, crustaceans, insects, small reptiles, and small mammals.

Range: World-wide.

Number of species: World 59; Aust. 14.

88   GREY HERON   *Ardea cinerea*

Field marks: 1.0 m. A large pale heron with white head and neck, dark streaks down foreneck; grey wings, back and underparts. In adults, the best field mark is the *heavy black eyebrow extending back as a drooping crest.* Bill and legs part-yellow, yellow facial-skin. Imm: greyer, without dark head-markings. In flight, black flight-feathers contrast with the otherwise grey wings. Usually solitary, motionless by water with neck extended or sunk on shoulders.

Similar species: White-necked Heron (90): black bill and legs; no head-pattern or crest; grey areas much darker, seeming blackish. In flight, two prominent white marks on leading edges of each wing.

Range and Status: Alleged early occurrences in Aust. (and once NZ). It has a wide range from Europe, Africa and Asia to Indonesia and Borneo where it is a winter visitor. Any reaching Aust. are thus most likely to occur during our summer.

89   GREAT-BILLED HERON   *Ardea sumatrana*   Pl.15

Other names: Alligator-bird; Dusky-grey or Giant Heron.

Field marks: 1–1.5 m. A very large dark grey-brown heron with *a heavy, mostly dark bill, yellow facial skin and a short crest*; eye silvery-brown, legs grey. Imm: more rufous; no crest or plumes. Usually solitary, occasionally pairs or family parties. Shy and difficult to approach, rests in trees, feeds at low tide along mangrove-lined waterways and mudbanks. Flight heavy, wings uniformly dark.

Voice: A harsh croak; deep resonant guttural roar repeated three or four times, 'like an angry bull;' often at night.

Habitat: Tidal mudflats and estuaries, mangrove-lined creeks; occasionally inland on larger rivers (e.g. Katherine Gorge, NT) and swamps or even small scrubby creeks.
Breeding: Nest: large untidy flattish structure of coarse sticks; on horizontal fork of mangrove in secluded situation, low to 2.5 m high; occasionally in taller riverside tree to 12 m. Eggs: 2; dull grey or pale blue-green; only one offspring may be reared.
Range and Status: Coastal n. Aust. and some offshore islands: from about Derby, WA, to Broad Sound, n. of Rockhampton, Q. Uncommon; sedentary. Also Burma to se. Asia, Indonesia and NG.

90 WHITE-NECKED HERON *Ardea pacifica* Pl.15
Other names: Pacific Heron, White-necked Crane.
Field marks: 760 mm–1.06 m. Our only heron with *black bill and legs, white head and neck, and slate-grey to blackish body, wings and tail*; dark spots down centre of foreneck, some streaks below. In breeding plumage, maroon plumes on back and wings. Imm: more buffy white. Singly or loose open companies, usually feeds in shallow water. Flight stately, slow-beating; neck folded; looks large and long-winged in air, *easily identified by size and white patches on leading edge of wings*.
Similar species: White-faced Heron (91); mostly pale-grey with white face; legs yellow. Pied Heron (92), imm: much smaller, dull-yellow bill and legs.
Voice: A guttural rattling croak.
Habitat: Shallow fresh waters generally, wet paddocks; rarely salt or brackish waters.
Breeding: Nest: rough shallow structure of sticks: in living tree, 6–18 m over water. Singly or in small colonies. Eggs: 3–4, blue-green.
Range and Status: Common throughout Aust. in suitable habitat; uncommon Tas. Also NG; vagrant NZ.

91 WHITE-FACED HERON *Ardea novaehollandiae* Pl.15
Other names: Blue Crane, White-fronted Heron.
Field marks: 660–685 mm. The heron familiar to most Australians, often incorrectly called 'the blue crane': *the only pale-grey heron with white face and yellow legs*. Imm: paler, less white on neck; legs greenish yellow. Singly, pairs and autumn and winter flocks. Flight stately, with deliberate beats; *note contrast of pale-grey plumage with darker grey flight-feathers*. Neck usually folded but does fly short distances with it extended. Wary: wades, pauses motionless, stirs one foot below surface; perches on fences, dead trees, telephone posts.
Similar species: White-necked Heron (90). Eastern Reef Heron (97), (grey phase): no white face, uniform grey plumage, legs greyish. Mangrove Heron (98).
Voice: A harsh gravelly croaking, in alarm or aggressively.
Habitat: Almost wherever there is shallow water: from offshore islands and mudflats to lakes, swamps, farm dams, public gardens, garden ponds, grasslands, golf-courses, orchards.
Breeding: Nest: small, untidy, shallow; of sticks in leafy branch 5–12 m high, over water, or some distance away. Eggs: 3–5; pale-blue.
Range and Status: Throughout Aust. and Tas. in suitable habitat. Common; sedentary and nomadic. Also e. Indonesia, NG. Established NZ *c.* 1940, vagrant Lord Howe, Kermadec, Chatham, Campbell and Macquarie Is.

92 PIED HERON *Ardea picata* Pl.15
Other names: Pied or White-headed Egret.
Field marks: 430–485 mm. A striking small slate-grey heron *with straw-yellow bill and legs, blackish crown and crest, white cheeks, throat and neck*. Imm: *no crest; head, neck and underparts white*, often with smutty markings; reddish brown to dark blue-grey above.

Birds in this plumage often outnumber adults. Singly or in flocks, sometimes large; associates with other herons and egrets. Flies with rather rapid wingbeats, neck folded; companies may fly together in random formation.
Similar species: White-necked Heron (90): much larger; bill and legs black.
Voice: A loud 'awk', usually in flight.
Habitat: Margins of swamps, lakes and fresh-water lagoons, tidal rivers, mudflats, mangroves; sewage ponds, stockyards, rubbish dumps.
Breeding: Nest: small shallow platform of sticks; up to 5 m high, usually over water in live tree. Eggs: 3–4; deep blue-green.
Range and Status: Coastal n. Aust.: from e. Kimberleys to coastal ne. Q, s. to Townsville; vagrant c. Aust. and Murray Valley (Gunbower). Also Borneo; Celebes to NG. Possible interchange, if not migration, between populations in Aust. and e. Indonesia.

93 CATTLE EGRET *Ardeola ibis* Pl.15, 16

Other name: Buff-backed Heron.
Field marks: 480–525 mm. Smallest egret: can look leggy and quick when feeding, walking with marked back-and-forward movement of head; but at rest often seems chunky, hunched and deep-jowled. Breeding plumage unmistakable; *orange-buff longish plumes on head, breast and lower back*; bill orange-yellow with red base; face and legs red. Non-breeding: white, sometimes with *yellow-buff wash on head and neck*; bill yellow, legs black, orange or yellow. Gregarious: parties to large, loose flocks feed among grazing cattle, horses, buffaloes, snapping up insects they disturb; also feeds in swamps. Flight rather swift; wingbeats quicker than other egrets; legs do not protrude far.
Similar species: Little Egret (95). Plumed Egret (96): often in pastures but seldom in such compact groups; movements more sedate. In flight, legs protrude further; wingbeats slower.
Voice: Guttural croak like other egrets, but softer.
Habitat: Floodplains, swamp margins, pastures, low fodder crops.
Breeding: Nest: small untidy platform of sticks in treetop-colony over water, often with other egrets. Eggs: 3–6; white, tinged blue.
Range and Status: A remarkable 'new' bird for Aust. First reported in NT in early 1900s. In 1933 eighteen birds from Calcutta were released in w. Kimberleys, to combat cattle tick but did not establish. The species began worldwide expansion from Africa to S. America (British Guiana 1930) and s. USA (Florida 1941–2). In 1948 was observed in hundreds near Oenpelli in e. Arnhem Land, NT; it reached Vic. in 1949 and NZ 1963–4. In e. hemisphere from s. Asia to s. China and Japan, Indonesia and most of coastal Aust. Breeds or has bred Kimberleys, WA, Adelaide R., NT; se. Q, ne. NSW; and possibly R. Murray swamps, Vic. Now common and widespread. Regular winter visitor to coastal se. Aust. and Tas., arriving Apr.–May, departing early Nov., after assuming breeding plumage. Vagrant NG, NZ.

94 LARGE EGRET *Egretta alba* Pl.15, 16

Other names: White or Great White Egret; White Crane.
Field marks: 760–915 mm. Much the tallest egret, about size of White-necked Heron (90). It has a gaunt lanky leaning-forward look; *when stretched out, head and neck are nearly one and a half times as long as body.* For most of year, bill pale to rich-yellow; note flat crown, yellow gape pointing back under eye; legs blackish. Breeding plumage: bill black, facial skin green; splendid wing-plumes cascade over back but no plumes on breast. Some develop plumes and breed while retaining yellow bill and black-billed birds without plumes are seen. Solitary, small parties, but in parts, e.g. floodplains of n. Aust. in wet season, very large companies. Usually forages in water, often wading deep; freezes motionless for long intervals before making lightning thrust. Occasionally takes fish from surface in flight. Sustained flight stately with deliberate wingbeats, trailing legs extend far beyond tail.
Similar species: Plumed Egret (96).

Voice: A guttural rattling croak.
Habitat: Shallows of rivers, mudflats, swamps, lagoons; sewage farms, irrigation areas, larger dams.
Breeding: Nest: scanty platform of sticks, in treetop colony over water. Eggs: 3–5: blue-green.
Range and Status: Cosmopolitan except for high latitudes and many oceanic islands. Throughout Aust., Tas. and NZ. Common to uncommon; sedentary or nomadic.

95 LITTLE EGRET *Egretta garzetta*   Pl.15, 16

Other names: Lesser or Spotless Egret.
Field marks: 560 mm. A fine-drawn small egret, about the size of White-faced Heron (91). In all plumages the fine bill is *black, with yellowish base to lower mandible, contrasting with bright-yellow facial skin*. Legs and feet black, with yellow soles in Australian race, a difficult field mark. In breeding plumage, note the ribbon-like head-plumes, luxuriant plumes on back and breast. Imm: yellow-green facial skin, grey-green legs. Away from breeding colonies, usually seen singly, but occasionally with other egrets, spoonbills or ibises; *often nervously active, dashing about in shallow water, raising and fluttering wings.*
Similar species: Large Egret (94), breeding plumage. Cattle (93) and Plumed (96) Egrets and Eastern Reef-Heron (97), white phase: bills never black.
Voice: A croaking 'kark'; a bubbling 'wulla-wulla-wulla' when breeding (European data).
Habitat: Tidal estuaries, salt-marshes, mangrove flats, swamps, lake fringes, water meadows; sewage farms.
Breeding: Nest: scanty, of sticks, in treetop colony, over water. Eggs: 3–5, pale blue-green.
Range and Status: Common n. and ne. Aust.; uncommon but regular se. Aust. to Bass Strait, inland NSW, inland Q, and WA s. of Kimberleys; in Tas., regular but uncommon winter visitor. Sedentary or nomadic. Almost annual vagrant to NZ. Also s. Europe, Africa, s. Asia to NG.

96 PLUMED EGRET *Egretta intermedia*   Pl.15, 16

Field marks: 635 mm. Like a small nonbreeding Large Egret (94) but when stretched out, *head and neck just equal body-length.* Head rounder, orange-yellow bill proportionately shorter and deeper. Looks more graceful than Large and flies with slightly quicker wingbeats, blackish legs protruding less far. Nonbreeding birds often have a *wisp of fine plumes on breast* and sometimes a reddish bill. Breeding plumage: very distinctive: bill deep-pink to orange-red, facial skin blue-green; breast-plumes long and wispy; *wing-plumes fall thickly like bridal veil, extending well beyond tail.* Birds in this plumage seldom seen far from breeding colonies. Usually singly but in n. Aust. often in open companies. Perhaps more than others except Cattle Egret (93), feeds in pastures among cattle.
Similar species: Cattle Egret (93) nonbreeding: more compact, yellow facial skin more obvious; wingbeats quicker. Little Egret (95).
Voice: A rattling croak.
Habitat: Like Large Egret, but more often in pastures; breeding in mangroves reported.
Breeding: Nest: small untidy platform of sticks, in fork of tree, in treetop colony over water. Eggs: 3–5, pale green.
Range and Status: Coastal n. and e. Aust., inland when conditions suitable. Common in n., less common s. of Newcastle, NSW, some breed on Murray R., but rare Vic. and SA (occasional breeding near Naracoorte); vagrant Tas. Sedentary or nomadic. Also from Africa through s. Asia to Indonesia–NG.

97 EASTERN REEF HERON *Egretta sacra* **Pl.15**

Other names: Blue, Sacred or White Heron; White or Blue Reef Heron; Reef Egret.
Field marks: 610–660 mm. A workmanlike beach and reef-dwelling heron, *bill longer and heavier, legs shorter,* than comparable herons or egrets. Two colour phases: (1) *uniform dark-grey,* with slight white streak down centre of throat; bill grey, facial skin yellow-green, *legs grey with dull-yellow wash.* (2) pure white, bill yellowish, often with grey or horn-coloured upper mandible, *legs dull yellow-grey.* Both have somewhat longer breeding plumes on back and breast. Roosts and nests in loose colonies; when foraging, crouches, wings sometimes open; stirs with foot, chases quarry or jabs at it while flying. Flight direct, wingbeats rather rapid, feet protrude only slightly.
Similar species: (Grey phase). White-faced Heron (91): in flight, two tones of grey, wingbeats slower. Mangrove Heron (98): dumpier, crested; more patterned, legs yellow or orange. (White phase). See egrets (93–6).
Voice: A hoarse croak.
Habitat: Exposed reefs, rocky shores; beaches, mudflats, islands; roosts and nests in woodland, scrub, pandanus adjacent to beaches.
Breeding: Nest: untidy structure of sticks, in trees, on ground under scrub or on ledges of rocks or caves; in colony. Eggs: 2–5, pale-green to blue-white.
Range and Status: Coasts and islands of n. Aust. where common, becoming less common southwards; uncommon from ce. NSW s. to far-e. Vic.; otherwise vagrant coastal Vic. and Tas.; rare SA and s. coast WA; moderately common w. coast WA. In n. Aust white and grey phases about equally common; in s. Aust. grey-phase predominates. Sedentary or part-nomadic. Also coasts from India to e. Polynesia, NZ.

98 MANGROVE HERON *Butorides striatus* **Pl.16**

Other names: Green-backed Bittern or Heron, Johnny Mangrove, Little Green Heron, Mangrove Bittern, Mangrove Jack, Little Green or Red Mangrove Heron.
Field marks: 430–510 mm. A dumpy little heron with a large head and slight drooped crest; *pink brown to greyish below* with a row of whitish and blackish marks down centre of foreneck. Bill black, eye yellow, legs and feet dull-yellow, *orange in breeding plumage.* Imm: streaked brown and buff-white below. There is a distinctive rufous race, *rogersi,* 'Red Mangrove Heron'. Small, furtive; usually seen on exposed mud near cover, stalks fish or crabs in stealthy crouch; occasionally plunges after prey from perch. When disturbed in trees, freezes bittern-like with bill held skywards. *Flies low with quick beats of rounded wings, neck folded, tail stubby;* raises crest on alighting; occasionally tame round boat areas.
Similar species: Nankeen Night-heron (99): from race *rogersi* in size, paler underparts and habitat; note range. Little Bittern (100); Black Bittern (102).
Voice: A scratchy sneeze-like 'kew!' or 'tch-aah'; also explosive 'hoo!', or startled scratchy 'kew, kew, chit, chit, kew' like screech of Swamphen (188).
Habitat: Usually mangroves, waterways and mudflats, tidal estuaries; occasionally exposed reefs.
Breeding: Nest: flimsy platform of sticks in horizontal fork of mangrove or similar leafy cover 3–9 m above water. Eggs: 2–4; blue, green, limy or mud-stained.
Range and Status: In Aust., discontinuous distribution: typical forms from far e. Vic. n. round coast to de Grey R. in WA; race *rogersi,* from Onslow s. to Carnarvon, WA. Common in main range, uncommon s. of Sydney; sedentary. Also S. America, Africa, India, Japan, se. Asia to NG and Pacific islands.

99 NANKEEN NIGHT-HERON *Nycticorax caledonicus* **Pl.16**

Other name: Nankeen Crane, Rufous Night-heron.
Field marks: 560–635 mm. A compact, rather stooped heron with a largish head. Crown and nape black, *dark-cinnamon above, creamy-white below washed buff.* In breeding

plumage, two slender white plumes fall from crown. Imm: different enough to be mistaken for a bittern: pale grey-brown, streaked whitish on head, neck and breast; *large pale spots on wings*; *cinnamon wash on wings, tail*. Roosts by day communally in leafy (occasionally dead) trees, usually near water, moves out at dusk in slow-flapping flocks, somewhat like flying-foxes, to feeding grounds where it becomes noisy and active. Occasionally flies and fishes by day.

Similar species: Australian Bittern (103) for comparison with imm.

Voice: Loud, somewhat peevish, 'kyok!', usually at night and on departure from roost.

Habitat: See comment on roosts above: within foraging range of these, shallow margins of rivers, swamps, dams, mangrove-lined estuaries; floods.

Breeding: Nest:shallow loose structure of sticks; in a tree usually in water, often high. Occasionally singly but more typically in colonies, some large, often with egrets, cormorants. Eggs: 2–5; light blue-green.

Range and Status: Throughout mainland Aust. in suitable habitat; recent breeding King I., Bass Strait. Common; sedentary or nomadic. Also Philippines to NG, Solomons, New Caledonia and other sw. Pacific islands; vagrant NZ.

100 LITTLE BITTERN *Ixobrychus minutus*   Pl.16

Other names: Leech or Minute Bittern.

Field marks: 255–355 mm. A tiny handsome bittern. Male: blue-black above, with rich-chestnut sides of head and neck; *large buff to chestnut patch on shoulder*. Female: duller, crown and back rich-brown, paler below, streaked brown. Imm: browner, more streaked. Singly or pairs; secretive, partly nocturnal; crouches with somewhat humpty-dumpty look; climbs in reeds and rushes. When disturbed, raises bill skywards. Flushes awkwardly with legs trailing, but settles into neck-folded heron-flight, *revealing conspicuous pale shoulders*.

Similar species: Mangrove Heron (98), race *rogersi*: larger, no pale shoulder-patches, habitat different.

Voice: Male in spring, 'hoch', monotonously repeated; when flushed, deep 'koh!'.

Habitat: Reed and cumbungi-choked sections of swamps, rivers, lakes; large tussocks in swampy areas.

Breeding: Nest: small shallow, loosely constructed platform in rushes or cumbungi, near water, occasionally in tree over water. Eggs: 5, white, glossy, pigeon-like.

Range and Status: Widespread e., se. and possibly n. Aust.; usually rare and spasmodic; possibly migrant; vagrant NG and NZ. Cosmopolitan.

101 YELLOW BITTERN *Ixobrychus sinensis*

Other names: Chinese Little Bittern, Little Yellow Bittern.

Field marks: 305–365 mm. A very small bittern: *yellow-brown with dark-slate crown extending in short crest*; chestnut-brown hind-neck, several black marks on bend of wing; primaries and tail black; underparts pale sandy. Bill yellow-horn, black along ridge, facial skin yellow, legs yellow. Female: duller, breast streaked brown. Imm: like female, heavier streaks below. *In flight, fawnish wings with black primaries and tail give piebald look.* Said to be solitary in habits (Japan).

Similar species: Little Bittern (100).

Voice: A deep croak (Japan).

Habitat: Reedbeds, overgrown ricefields, grassy swamps, riverside scrubs.

Breeding: Nest: very small, a hollow pad of reeds, twigs: in reeds or grass usually from 1 m over water. Eggs: 3–5; pale blue-green.

Range and Status: From n. China and Japan to India, Borneo and NG. One Australian record, Kalgoorlie, WA, 1968; unconfirmed record, Queensland. Vagrant.

102 BLACK BITTERN *Dupetor flavicollis* **Pl.16**

Other names: Yellow-necked Bittern or Mangrove Bittern.

Field marks: 540–660 mm. A slender very dark bittern with long neck and slim dagger-like dark bill. Male: sooty black above, throat whitish; *breast oddly streaked, sides of neck golden yellow.* Female: browner above, less prominently marked below. Imm: duller, feathers above edged buff; breast brown, streaked bright-yellow. Singly or pairs; secretive, keeps to leafy cover by day but may fish in shadows or tree-surrounded shallow waters. When disturbed, runs or flies to cover, creeps along branches; may point bill skyward and freeze. In flight looks black, note part-folded neck, short tail.

Similar species: Mangrove Heron (98), imm; Australian Bittern (103).

Voice: A low pronounced 'w-h-o-o-o-o', repeated at intervals.

Habitat: Leafy riverside, creekside or swampside trees, mangroves; occasionally in willows; on margins of rivers, swamps, tidal creeks, mudflats.

Breeding: Nest: flattish untidy platform of sticks on sheltered horizontal branch over water. Eggs: 3–5, whitish or very pale blue-green, rounded.

Range and Status: Coastal w., n. and e. Aust. from s. of Perth, WA, to Nadgee R., s. NSW. Probably common generally; rare s. of Sydney. Also India and se. Asia to NG and Bismarck Archipelago.

103 AUSTRALIAN BITTERN *Botaurus poiciloptilus* **Pl.16**

Other names: Boomer, Brown Bittern, Bullbird, Bunyip.

Field marks: 660–760 mm. An unusual large heron-like bird, plumage above like old leaves: *brown and buff with intricate blackish markings; dark streak through face; eyebrow and throat pale*; underparts streaked brown and buff. Bill brown, greenish below: facial skin green, eye yellow; legs green, rather short. Imm: paler. Often first seen when flushed: goes up with heavy wingbeats; note broad slow-flapping wings, folded neck, short tail, green legs protruding only slightly. Partly nocturnal but will forage by day, on feeding platform, by water in or near cover; movements very deliberate. When disturbed achieves remarkable camouflage effect as it slims feathers, points bill skywards.

Similar species: Nankeen Night-heron (99), imm. Black Bittern (102).

Voice: Unusual: note of distant foghorn with no start or finish – a deep 'woomph', repeated up to 30 times, heard from afar; thought to have inspired aboriginal 'bunyip' legends; hoarse 'cra-ak' when startled.

Habitat: Reedbeds, rushes, cumbungi, in swamps, lagoons, sluggish rivers; tussocky wet paddocks, drains.

Breeding: Nest: platform of trampled weeds, rushes, cumbungi; usually near water-level in heavy cover. Eggs: 4–6; green-brown.

Range and Status: Se. Aust., approximately s. of a line from Fraser I., se. Q, to Ceduna, SA; also Tas., Kangaroo I., SA, and sw. Aust., mostly coastal from Esperance to Moora. Uncommon but locally abundant. Also NZ.

Storks Family *Ciconiidae*

Tall, striking birds with heavy straight bills; they are bigger and more heavily built than cranes and herons and often have bold patterns in their plumage. They fly with necks and legs extended, with slow wingbeats, and forage in swamps, tidal areas, grasslands, open woodlands, agricultural lands. Sexes nearly similar.

Food: Fish, reptiles, rodents, frogs, crustaceans, insects.

Range: Almost cosmopolitan in temperate and tropical regions.

Number of species: World 17; Aust. 1.

104 BLACK-NECKED STORK *Xenorhynchus asiaticus* Pl.10, 44

Other names: Jabiru, Policemanbird.

Field marks: 1.29–1.37 m; span *c.* 2 m. An impressive very tall black and white bird with pipestem red legs: *note heavy black bill, glossy green-black head and neck*. Eye: in male black; in female yellow. Singly or pairs, sometimes accompanied by browner young; occasionally larger parties. Strides through water sweeping bill, runs after fish. Flies straight with slow wingbeats, looking rather skeletal; soars high: note the black panel on white wings.

Voice: Dull booms; also clappers its bill.

Habitat: Swamps, mangroves and mudflats; dry floodplains, irrigated lands, bore drains, sub-artesian pools; occasionally forages into open grassy woodland.

Breeding: Nest: large flat pile of sticks, grass, rushes, in live or dead tree, usually near water. Eggs: 2–4, whitish.

Range and Status: Widespread and fairly common in n. Aust., from Fitzroy R., WA, (sparse s. to Port Hedland) to Innisfail, Q; sparse in coastal e. Aust. s. to Hawkesbury R., NSW, rare and local s. coast NSW; vagrant Vic. Sedentary. Also India, se. Asia, Indonesia, NG.

Ibises and Spoonbills   Family *Plataleidae*

Their bills are their badge: long and sickle-shaped in ibises, straight and flattened with a spatulate tip in spoonbills. Our three ibises have simple bold patterns; they are typically in flocks, sometimes very large. Common and conspicuous in some areas, e.g. the Murray Valley and other irrigation areas, their flights in long wavering lines or V's are memorable. Flocks often wheel to great heights. Almost superstitiously regarded as destroyers of locusts and other insects, ibises are of undoubted great economic importance – but their reputation may be exaggerated. Highly nomadic or migratory, they breed regularly in areas of assured water regime and food, but irregularly elsewhere, depending on season. Many of their colonies are very large; two or three species often nest together.

Our two spoonbills are white; they can be separated immediately by bill and leg colours. In breeding plumage one has a crest, the other, longer breast-plumes and slight, lacy wing-plumes; both have small distinctive marks on heads. Spoonbills feed in shallow water, briskly sweeping and fossicking with the slightly open sensitive tips of their bills as they wade, locating small aquatic animals by touch. They are usually seen singly or in small parties but do form flocks to hundreds; in sustained flight, these fly in V's. Spoonbills nest singly or in small colonies, often with ibis.

Food: Crustaceans, molluscs, tadpoles, frogs, small fish, leeches, spiders; insects and larvae, especially grasshoppers, crickets.

Range: Worldwide in tropical and temperate regions.

Number of species: World: 30. Aust.: 3 ibises, 2 spoonbills.

105 GLOSSY IBIS *Plegadis falcinellus* Pl.43

Other name: Black Curlew.

Field marks: 480–610 mm. A *small dark ibis*, somewhat like a dark curlew. In good light, rich purplish brown, glossed bronze or green; Imm: browner; pale streaks on head and neck; bill shorter, straighter. Feeds in wetlands generally, sometimes with other ibises; perches in trees near water. Flies in long swift lines or compact flocks that often dash about erratically with sudden glides. These can be mistaken from afar for flocks of Little Black Cormorant (82); but note drooping extended neck and legs.

Voice: A long harsh crowlike croak; grunts.

Habitat: Wetlands generally: swamps, wet pastures; mangroves, mudflats; occasionally dry grasslands, floodplains.

Breeding: Nest: shallow platform of leafy sticks; in colony over water in shrubs, trees, cumbungi, lignum or mangroves; nests become trampled into continuous platforms. Eggs: 3–6; dull, slightly rough, deep green-blue.

Range and Status: N. and e. Aust., generally uncommon, patchy and spasmodic, specially in se. and sw.; vagrant Tas., NZ. Highly nomadic. Also warmer parts of n. and s. America, Africa, s. Europe, se. Asia, and s. NG (where possibly nonbreeding visitor from Aust.).

106 WHITE IBIS *Threskiornis molucca* Pl.43

Other names: Black-necked Ibis, Sticklebill, Sicklebird.

Field marks: 685–760 mm. White, with bare mostly black head and a black ibis-bill, black tips to flight-feathers and a *bunch of black lacelike wing-plumes over the yellowish tail.* Imm: feathered black on head and neck, no wing-plumes; bill shorter, straighter. Singly to flocks of hundreds or more; typically in pastures and swamps but also in unexpected places like woodlands, poultry-yards, garbage-tips, when the white plumage is often very soiled. Flies in lines or V's with quick wingbeats and glides. Often associates with Straw-necked Ibis (107).

Voice: Harsh barks, shouts.

Habitat: Apart from those mentioned, irrigated lands, dams, floodplains, tidal mudflats: grassed areas generally: house lawns, orchards; also rubbish dumps.

Breeding: Nest: substantial compact shallow cup of sticks, reeds, bushes; in colony over water in dense trees (often at base near water, and built tall as water rises) or in trampled swamp-growth: rushes, cumbungi, lignum; in mangroves and on ground on islands. Neighbouring nests become trampled into continuous platform. Eggs: 2–4; white, becoming dirty.

Range and Status: Aust. generally. Common and locally very abundant in coastal n., e. and se., especially Murray–Darling Basin; rare inland and in WA s. of Kimberleys. Highly nomadic, migratory or dispersive; more numerous and extending range with development of pasturelands and irrigation; vagrant Tas., NZ. Also Moluccas, NG.

107 STRAW-NECKED IBIS *Threskiornis spinicollis* Pl.43

Other names: Dryweather Bird, Farmer's Friend, Letterbird.

Field marks: 585–760 mm. A handsome ibis with *white neck, underparts and tail, straw-like tuft of breast-plumes and glossy black wings and back.* Imm: no straw-plumes, but grey, black or white feathering up neck to crown; bill shorter, straighter. In flight, the mostly black wings contrast with the white underparts, rump and tail; flocks often wheel to great heights.

Voice: Hoarse coughs, grunts.

Habitat: Somewhat drier than White Ibis (106), although they often feed together. Swamps, irrigation areas, pastures but also dry grasslands sometimes far from water: seldom tidal areas.

Breeding: Nest: shallow cup of sticks, reeds and rushes over water in colony in paperbarks, cumbungi, lignum, rushes; on ground on islands. Nests become trampled into single platform. Eggs: 4–5; white, becoming dirty.

Range and Status: Aust. generally, common in better watered coastal and inland areas, uncommon to absent arid inland; highly nomadic or migratory; vagrant Tas., NZ. Also Indonesia, NG.

108 ROYAL SPOONBILL *Platalea regia* Pl.43

Other name: Black-billed Spoonbill.

Field marks: 740–810 mm. A usually spotless white bird with *black spoonlike bill and black legs.* Breeding plumage: handsome tuft of white head-plumes, breast washed buff. Imm: bill shorter, tips of flight feathers black (as in some adults). Flies with steady

wingbeats; silhouette rather flat with extended neck inclined upwards, legs extended. Singly, or small to occasionally large flocks in suitable habitat.
Similar species: Yellow-billed Spoonbill (109).
Voice: Usually silent; near nest, soft purring grunts.
Habitat: Large shallow waters, inland and coastal; mudflats, mangroves, small islands. Does frequent farm dams but less often on such small waters than Yellow-billed.
Breeding: Nest: shallow platform of sticks, usually in a colony over water in tall trees or dense paperbarks, lignum, cumbungi. Eggs: 2–4; dull-white, spotted yellow-brown or red-brown.
Range and Status: Throughout Aust. in coastal and better-watered inland areas; occasional non-breeding visitor to King I. and Tas. Locally common; sedentary or nomadic. Vagrant to NZ before 1950, now breeding resident. Also Java to NG.

109 YELLOW-BILLED SPOONBILL   *Platalea flavipes*   Pl.43
Other name: Yellow-legged Spoonbill.
Field marks: 760–915 mm. White plumage often soiled; *spoonlike bill dull-yellow to flesh-white; legs similar.* Breeding plumage: longer breast-plumes, slight dark lacelike plumes from inner wings; black line on grey facial skin; no crest. Singly, pairs or parties. Far more than Royal (108), seeks out small isolated waters (see Habitat); rests on banks of dams or in dead trees, head on shoulders or bill laid down back. Flies with alternate shallow wing-beats and glides, neck inclined upwards, legs extended.
Voice: A feeble reedy grunt.
Habitat: Shallow waters: farm dams, roadside pools, isolated inland claypans, and tanks. Seldom on tidal areas but occasionally saltpans and saline swamps.
Breeding: Nest: platform of sticks in tree, usually in colonies over water, among cumbungi, rushes or lignum. Eggs: 2–3; dull-white.
Range and Status: Mainland Aust. in suitable habitat, even far inland; vagrant King I., Tas. and Kangaroo I., SA. Common to uncommon; nomadic.

Swans, Ducks and Geese   Family *Anatidae*

The driest continent, Aust. has fewer species of waterfowl than any comparable landmass. However, 10 of the world's 13 recognized subfamilies are represented and some species reach considerable numbers after good seasons. A characteristic of our waterfowl is their mobility, an adaptation to Australia's sparse, often irregular rainfall. Some species will breed at any time in response to suitable conditions. Some are activated by rising and spreading shallow waters, others by falling floodwaters; a few require permanent deep waters. Unlike many other Australian birds, males of some, e.g. Chestnut Teal (122) and Southern Shoveller (123) assume eclipse plumage after breeding. Reference to food will be found in the introductions for each subfamily.
Range: Almost worldwide, except oceanic regions and Antarctica.
Number of species: World: 148: Aust. 23, including 2 introduced and a vagrant recorded once.

PIED GEESE   Subfamily *Anseranatinae*

The Pied Goose (110) has no close living relatives; its unusual features include long legs and partly webbed strongly clawed feet; a long bill, narrow and strongly hooked at the tip, and in male specially, a long convoluted windpipe. It does not become flightless during moult, but replaces its flight-feathers progressively. It was once widespread in se. Aust., breeding in the Murray Valley and elsewhere. Drainage of swamps, grazing, shooting and poisoning reduced it to the status of a rare visitor s. of the Tropic. Its strongholds are now the coastal floodplains of tropical n. Aust.
Food: Bulbs of spike-rush, sedges, grasses, seeds, including wild rice.

110 PIED GOOSE *Anseranas semipalmata* **Pl.9, 10**

Other names: Black-and-white, Magpie or Semipalmated Goose.

Field marks: 865–775 mm; span 1.5 m. *Long yellow legs and knobbed head* distinguish this lanky black-and-white goose. Imm: smuttier, crown rounded. Parties to huge flocks: digs round swamp-margins, wades, swims with stern uptilted, upends; perches in heads of scrub by swamps. Whenever approached they raise thickets of black necks and a fluty clamour. Flight laboured, on broad wings with *pronounced black fingertips*, note white underparts and underwings, *large black tail*.

Similar species: In flight Black Swan (113): white wingtips; Straw-necked Ibis (107): white tail.

Voice: Falsetto honking, louder and higher-pitched in male.

Habitat: Large swamps and dams, specially with dense growth of rushes or sedges; wet grasslands, wet and dry floodplains.

Breeding: Nest: a deep cup; on mound of floating or trampled-down vegetation, in colony in swamp. Eggs: 1–9, average about 7: oval, cream-white or off-white, often stained.

Range and Status: Mostly coastal n. Aust. from Fitzroy R., WA, to Rockhampton, Q: uncommon s. Q. Locally very abundant in dry season concentrations, but generally much reduced. Sedentary or nomadic. Wandering singles or parties NSW, Vic., s. WA, SA; sometimes far inland. Also NG.

WHISTLING DUCKS Subfamily *Dendrocygninae*

Long-legged long-necked ducks, some with decorative flank-plumes. Although formerly known as tree-ducks, they seldom perch but do incessantly whistle. Aust. has two species, best identified in flight by somewhat drooping necks and long legs. They are easily separated by plumage and habits. The common names proposed here are an attempt to emphasize an outstanding feature of each.

Food: Grasses, legumes, herbs, water-lilies, spike-rush, sedges and other vegetation: seeds and cultivated grain.

111 DIVING WHISTLING DUCK *Dendrocygna arcuata* **Pl.11, 12, 14**

Other names: Red Whistler, Wandering or Water Whistling Duck, Water Whistle-duck, Whistling Tree-duck.

Field marks: 550–610 mm. Distinguished by dark rich plumage, black bill and legs and lower posture than Plumed (112) both swimming and standing. *Black crown with plain yellow-buff face and neck; shoulders chestnut.* Imm: duller, centre of abdomen paler, dividing dark underparts. In dense flocks of dozens to thousands; camps on bare margins of swamps and rivers sometimes with Plumed, but feeds in water, companies moving ahead, diving repeatedly. Flies in whistling mobs: note *chestnut underparts, blackish underwing, trailing black legs*.

Similar species: Plumed Whistling Duck (112); White-eyed Duck (127).

Voice: High-pitched single or twittering whistles, less clear-cut than Plumed.

Habitat: Deeper parts of lagoons and swamps, usually with vegetation: flooded grasslands.

Breeding: Nest: scrape in ground, usually lined with grass; in grassland, under bush or in vegetation by swamp. Eggs: 6–15; cream, smooth.

Range and Status: Coastal n. Aust., from Fitzroy R., WA, to Fitzroy R., Q: common and locally abundant, stronghold being NT floodplains. When conditions suitable, fairly widespread se. Q; irregular inland and into se. Aust. and s. WA. Also Borneo to NG and New Britain.

112 PLUMED WHISTLING DUCK *Dendrocygna eytoni* Pl.11, 12, 14

Other names: Grass Whistle-duck or Whistling Duck, Plumed Tree Duck, Grey or Red-legged Whistler.

Field marks: 415–615 mm. An erect pale-brown duck *with patchy pink bill, long pink legs and upswept cream flank-plumes*; throat and underparts pale; sides of chest reddish, finely barred darker. Imm: paler. Parties or dense flocks to thousands; camps by water during day, often dabbles but does not dive; swims with head high, flank plumes upswept. When flushed or moving out, flies with much whistling, wingbeats slow; silhouette humped, legs trailing, settles with lowered head and landing gear; in flight note *brown underwing, pale underparts, trailing pink legs*.

Similar species: Diving Whistling Duck (111).

Voice: Spirited whizzing whistles, lively twitterings; by night and day; noisy when flushed.

Habitat: By day, margins of swamps, waterholes, tanks, flooded depressions often without nearby cover; mangrove creeks, estuarine pools; at night grasslands, swamp-fringes, stubble-fields.

Breeding: Nest: scrape, low scantily lined with grass, plant-stems, in grassland or scrub, at times far from water. Eggs: 8–14; white, smooth, pointed.

Range and Status: N. and e. Aust.: from Fitzroy R., WA, to Riverina district, NSW. Stronghold inland ne. Aust. from Barkly Tableland, NT, to c. coastal Q, where common and abundant, outnumbering Diving Whistling Duck, but ratio reversed in nw. Aust. In recent years in larger numbers, breeding in se. Q, e. NSW, n. Vic. and se. SA. Under suitable conditions disperses far inland. Vagrant NG and NZ.

SWANS Subfamily *Cygninae*

Largest waterfowl, with long necks for reaching underwater vegetation; they also graze on tidal lands and in pastures. They swim with necks arched or erect and often carry feathers or wings raised in aggressive display. They fly strongly, in lines or V's, with undulating long necks, whistling wings and memorable baying, bugling or trumpeting calls. Several are migrants; our only native species, Black Swan (113), is highly nomadic. It has reached NZ naturally and has been introduced there. After breeding, swans moult and become temporarily flightless. Swans are familiar residents on ornamental lakes, becoming tame and breeding freely.

Food: Chiefly aquatic vegetation.

Range: Eurasia, the Americas, Aust.

113 BLACK SWAN *Cygnus atratus* Pl.9, 10

Field marks: 1.1–1.4 m; span 1.6–2 m. The only mostly black swan; *the white flight feathers* often show when at rest and are conspicuous in flight. Bill red, with pale bar and tip; legs and feet black. Male slightly larger, bill longer and straighter. Imm: dull grey-brown with pale edges to feathers, flight-feathers dingy-white, tipped black. Singly, or loose companies to hundreds or thousands.

Voice: Far-carrying musical bugle with a break, uttered on water or in flight; softer crooning notes.

Habitat: Large open waters: fresh, brackish and salt; flooded pastures, green crops, tidal mudflats; prefers permanent swamps and lakes with emergent and subaquatic vegetation; ornamental lakes. Occasionally on open sea.

Breeding: Nest: large heap; of reeds, grasses, weed, 1–1.5 m in diameter; in shallow water, on islands, occasionally in colonies. Eggs: 4–7; greenish white.

Range and Status: Aust. generally: common and often extremely abundant in better watered parts of se. Aust., Tas. and sw. Aust.; breeds in e. and w. Aust., s. of Atherton Tableland and North West Cape respectively. Uncommon to rare far inland and coastal n. Aust. Nomadic, movements often erratic. Introduced NZ.

114 MUTE SWAN *Cygnus olor* **Pl.9, 10**

Other name: White Swan.
Field marks: 1.3–1.6 m; span 2.4 m. A very large, wholly white, swan, wings often carried raised in heraldic manner; bill orange with black base and knob; in male, knob becomes larger in spring; legs and feet dark-grey. Imm: brownish-grey with knobless grey-pink bill. Flight strong, direct, with distinct singing of wings.
Voice: Hisses; also rarely-heard trumpet.
Habitat: Ornamental lakes, rivers; possibly sheltered sea-coasts as in Europe.
Breeding: Nest: large heap; of vegetation; on islands or among vegetation in shallows.
Eggs: 3–7 or more; green-white larger than Black Swan's.
Range and Status: Introduced from Europe to various parts of se. and sw. Aust. and Tas.; most seem to have failed. A small breeding colony persists on Avon R. at Northam, WA, and at L. Leake, Tas.

FRECKLED DUCK Subfamily *Stictonettinae*

Possibly close to original primitive waterfowl, which later differentiated into swans, geese and ducks. It has some swanlike attributes: flute-like call, lack of speculum, lack of complex displays.
Food: Algae, floating water-weeds, aquatic grasses, seeds, insects, small crustaceans.

115 FRECKLED DUCK *Stictonetta naevosa* **Pl.11, 12, 14**

Other names: Canvasback, Diamantina, Monkey, Oatmeal or Speckled Duck.
Field marks: 480–590 mm. At distance on water, a very dark duck with no obvious markings; floats high, neck short, *head large and peaked at rear. Bill has a markedly scooped-out look:* in breeding male, dark-grey *with conspicuous bright-red base*, which fades after breeding (remains red in some). Plumage blackish brown, finely freckled pale-buff to whitish; underparts paler. Female: paler, duller; bill grey. Imm: lighter brown, freckled buff. Small parties to flocks of hundreds; often far from shore by day, but where undisturbed, camps ashore and becomes quiet; sits on stumps, fence-posts, in water; associates inconspicuously with other ducks; feeds by filtering, upending, wading. Looks very dark in flight, *but distinctly paler below, with pale wing-linings*; silhouette rather hunched, neck somewhat depressed; head larger, neck shorter, wings sharper and smaller, than Black Duck (119).
Similar species: Black Duck (119), Blue-billed Duck (131), female, eclipse male and imm: bill blunter, less shapely; head rounder. Musk Duck (132).
Voice: Contact-call: soft piping; alarm-call: soft flute-like pipe, 'whee-yu', like Black Swan (113). Male: short raucous roar, 'between a sniff and a snort'; female: loud discordant quack.
Habitat: Heavily vegetated swamps; large open lakes and their shores; floodwaters.
Breeding: Nest: well-constructed bowl; of stems and sticks; in lignum or in overhanging tea-tree branch or flood-debris; close to water; sometimes uses old nest of Coot (189).
Eggs: 5–14; creamy, glossy, oval.
Range and Status: Its stronghold is the Murray–Darling Basin, and particularly the well-vegetated swamps in the NSW Riverina. It breeds here, also in permanent coastal swamps of sw. Vic., se. SA, and in coastal sw. WA. In these regions some are always present in places. It breeds in lakes of sw. Q when conditions suitable. It has been recorded sporadically in other parts of Aust., including s. Kimberleys, WA; top end and s. NT, e. Q and ne. NSW; vagrant Tas. Probably less familiar to observers than any other predominantly s. Australian waterfowl, but many shooters know it. Sedentary, irregularly dispersive.

CAPE BARREN GEESE Subfamily *Cereopsinae*

A subfamily of one species, that in the wild breeds only on islands off s. Aust. It has no close living relatives but appears to have affinities with the shelducks, subfamily *Tadorninae*, and the geese, subfamily *Anserinae*. There are thought to be *c.* 6000–8000 wild Cape Barren Geese alive today, making the species one of the world's rare waterfowl. However it may never have been numerous and particularly in recent years its status seems to have become more secure. Several of its breeding islands in Bass Strait have been proclaimed reserves.

Food: Grasses, legumes, herbs, succulents.

116 CAPE BARREN GOOSE *Cereopsis novaehollandiae*   Pl.9, 10

Other name: Pig Goose.

Field marks: 750–900 mm. An unmistakable large pale grey goose *with a square black tail, over which the grey wing-feathers tend to droop.* Note the robust short black bill, nearly covered by greenish yellow cere; white crown, large dusky spots on wings, and strong dusky-red legs; feet black. Imm: paler. Breeding pairs (on islands), family groups to flocks of 100+. Grazes mostly in open areas, including slopes of islands among rocks and tussocks. Wary and hard to approach; flight powerful, in lines or random mobs, often with a harsh clamour; wingbeats surprisingly *shallow and quick, note pale patch toward dark wingtips, black tail and under tail-coverts.* Swims seldom, stern uptilted.

Voice: Male: very loud harsh 'ark, ark-ark, ark-ark'; female: deep pig-like grunts; imm: reedy whistles.

Habitat: Offshore islands, mostly granitic and vegetated with pastures, tussocks and light scrub; in summering areas favours extensive areas of short green herbage, typically now improved pastures with clovers, margins of dams and margins of fresh or brackish swamps and lakes; often camps on banks of dams.

Breeding: Nest: shallow cup; of grass, twigs, lined with down; on ground beside bush, tussock or rock. Eggs: 3–6; dull-white.

Range and Status: Confined to coastal s. Aust.: breeds (in winter) smaller islands of Furneaux Group and other islands in Bass Strait, its stronghold; in SA: Sir Joseph Banks Group, Neptune I. and other islands in Spencer Gulf; Investigator Group and Nuyts Archipelago; in WA: Recherche Archipelago and other islands w. to near Albany. After post-breeding moult, during which it temporarily becomes flightless, flocks disperse in spring and summer to larger islands and nearby mainland areas: Flinders I.; n. Tas.; Yanakie Pen. and Western District, Vic., occasionally n. to Kerang, Mildura and exceptionally to s. Riverina and areas of Clare, Ivanhoe and Mossgiel in sw. NSW; in SA, area of L. Alexandrina and (occasional) Adelaide Plains; in WA, areas of Esperance, Hopetoun, Albany, Busselton. Introduced Kangaroo I., SA, and elsewhere. Still common in its restricted range; locally migratory or dispersive.

SHELDUCKS Subfamily *Tadorninae*

Large handsome ducks, sometimes mistaken for geese; markings bold, often with much white in plumage. The name shelduck is believed to be derived from the old English word 'sheld' meaning 'pied'. Widely distributed in Europe, Africa, Asia, Australasian region and NZ. Two species in Aust., one endemic. Sexes similar or dissimilar.

117 CHESTNUT-BREASTED SHELDUCK *Tadorna tadornoides*
Pl.11, 12, 13

Other names: Chestnut Sheldrake, Grunter, Mountain Duck.

Field marks: 550–735 mm. Conspicuous dark large duck, richly-coloured, with fine head and bill. Male: *white neck-ring, buff breast*; conspicuous white shoulder-patch; outer secondaries deep-chestnut, large green speculum. In eclipse, breast biscuit-coloured.

Female: smaller, *breast chestnut*; *white eye-ring and white round base of bill*; (males occasionally have white round bill, *never* round eye). Both sexes: bill and legs black. Imm: duller, speckled white on front of head, other white areas grey. In pairs, family parties or flocks in which pairs persist. Grazes in short grass far from cover, dabbles or upends in shallow water; flocks rest far out on water. Flight strong, wingbeats rather slow; note *white panel along leading edge and white black-tipped underwing.* Unlike other Australian ducks in Vs or long wavering lines. Migrates in summer to moult in companies on large freshwater lakes (Lake George, NSW, Coorong, SA), becoming temporarily flightless.

Voice: Male: strange deep zizzing grunt. Female: higher-pitched resounding 'ong gank, ong gank' or strident 'ow ow ow ow'.

Habitat: Large shallow waters: fresh, brackish, tidal, sandspits, islands; short grasslands, pastures, stubble-fields, young crops, irrigation areas, open woodlands; occasionally on sea.

Breeding: Nest: densely lined with down; usually in hollow tree, often far from water; at times on ground under grass or other vegetation; very occasionally in rabbit burrow, shallow cave. Eggs: 10–14; oval, cream, lustrous.

Range and Status: Stronghold is se. Aust., mainly w. Vic. and se. SA, w. to Spencer Gulf. Uncommon in e. Vic. and through Murray-Murrumbidgee region n. to area of Ivanhoe-Menindee, sw. NSW; common ACT and s. tablelands, NSW, uncommon coastal NSW. Vagrant n. NSW and s. Q, rare vagrant nw. Q (Mt. Isa); small numbers in good seasons w. SA and s. Nullarbor Plain; widespread sw. WA from Esperance to Shark Bay; irregular to near Derby, inland to Ophthalmia Ra., WA. Common e. Tas. and central highlands: augmented by regular summer migration and during droughts on mainland.

118 WHITE-HEADED SHELDUCK *Tadorna radjah*   Pl.11, 12, 13

Other names: Burdekin Duck, Rajah Shelduck.

Field marks: 485–560 mm. A conspicuous white duck *with flesh-coloured bill and legs, dark upperparts and chestnut breast-band.* Plumage sometimes rust-stained. Imm: duller, flecked grey and brown. Pairs, parties, occasional flocks. Perches in paperbarks over water; occasionally rests conspicuously on sandbars, mudflats; feeds in swamps dabbling in shallows; up-ends; busy, active, quarrelsome. Flight slow; *from below, white wings look as if 'dipped in ink';* note breastband and dark tail.

Voice: Harsh rattling notes; whistles.

Habitat: In wet season, most shallow waters: salt and brackish swamps, coastal creeks, shallow river-margins. In dry season, concentrates on permanent lagoons, paperbark swamps, man-made wetlands; mangroves, tidal mudflats, estuaries.

Breeding: Nest: in hollow tree usually in or near water. Eggs: 6–12; cream, smooth.

Range and Status: Coastal n. Aust. and islands: from Fitzroy R., WA, to Bowen, Q. Nowhere very common but reported fairly abundant on subcoastal rivers of NT e. of Darwin, with possible lesser stronghold on w. coast C. York Pen. Rare e. coast, occasionally s. to Broad Sound; vagrant se. Q and ne. NSW, rare vagrant ne. SA. Also NG, Moluccas.

DABBLING DUCKS   Subfamily *Anatinae*

Typical ducks that feed by dabbling or up-ending: some have specialized filtering techniques. The eight species in Aust. include the endemic Pink-eared Duck (126). Mallards are represented by the native Black Duck (119) and the introduced Mallard (120); shovellers by the native Southern Shoveller (123) and Northern Shoveller (124) once vagrant; teal by the Grey (121) and Chestnut (122) Teal, and by Garganey (125) which may prove to be a regular migrant from n. Sexes similar or dissimilar, speculum (flash or patch of iridescent green or purple on wing) usually present.

Food: Plankton, algae, aquatic plants, sedges, rushes, grasses, seeds, grain, insects, small crustaceans, molluscs.

119 BLACK DUCK *Anas superciliosa* **Pl.11, 12, 14**

Other names: Brown, Grey or Wild Duck.

Field marks: 480–600 mm. The familiar Australian 'wild duck': tame in public gardens. Dark wood-brown, with pale feather-margins; speculum dark green to purple, edged black. Head pattern unmistakable: *crown blackish, face and throat whitish to yellow-buff with two black stripes.* Bill dark-grey, legs dull-yellow or grey-brown. Singly, in pairs to flocks of dozens, now seldom more. Very wary; dabbles and up-ends in shallows, occasionally forages ashore in wet pastures. Perches on logs, dead trees over water. Flight strong and direct with characteristic wing-whistle; recognized from afar by white underwing contrasting with dark plumage.

Similar species: Mallard (120) female. Grey (121) and female Chestnut (122) Teal: much smaller, without facial pattern. In flight, narrow white wedge at 'armpit' and on upperwing.

Voice: Male: quick 'raab, raabraab'; when flushed, hoarse whispered 'fraank fraank'; loud 'peep' when courting. Female: hearty descending 'quark, quark, quark!'.

Habitat: Waters of all kinds: from farm dams to tidal mudflats, but prefers those with plentiful aquatic and waterside vegetation; public gardens.

Breeding: Nest: well built or sparse; on ground, in grass, swamp vegetation or old nest of other waterbird; when in stump or hollow tree, of down only. Eggs: 8–10: white or greenish cream.

Range and Status: Throughout Aust.; common to very common in Murray–Darling Basin; from Cairns to Sydney, Tas. and coastal sw. Aust. Usually in smaller concentrations elsewhere; through inland where conditions suitable. Nomadic; banding recoveries both ways across Tasman Sea. Perhaps our most abundant waterfowl; pairs find their way to any small patch of suitable water. Also Java, Sumatra to s. NG, Melanesia, Polynesia, NZ and sub-Antarctic islands in NZ region.

120 MALLARD *Anas platyrhynchos* **Pl.11, 12, 14**

Field marks: 150–610 mm. Introduced. Male: familiar as 'typical duck' in many illustrations: head glossy green, with white neck-ring, purplish breast, pale-grey wings; purple-blue speculum margined by black-and-white bars; tail white with upcurled black central feathers. Bill yellow, feet orange. Female: at first sight like pale Black Duck (119); pale-brown, streaked and mottled darker; crown dark; note *faint light eyebrow, speculum as in male, whitish tail*; bill dull-orange marked blackish, feet dull-orange. Male in eclipse resembles dark female. Flight rapid, *note white underwing and whitish tail* (both sexes). Habits like Black Duck with which it cross-breeds; hybrids usually resemble Black Duck with yellow to orange feet, *and distinctive Mallard speculum*; some hybrid males have patchy green head and curled duck-tail; some female hybrids like female Mallard with facial markings of Black Duck.

Voice: Male: quiet 'yeeb' or low 'kwck': female: boisterous 'quack, quack-quack', repeated.

Habitat: Likely to frequent any fresh water favoured by Black Duck, but usually ornamental lakes, ponds and dams.

Breeding: Nest: of grass, reeds lined with down: usually near water, under vegetation: or of down, on ground or in hollow tree. Eggs: 8–15: creamy, greenish or blue-white.

Range and Status: Eurasia, N. Africa, N. America. Introduced to Aust. first in 1860s. Now widespread se. Aust. and Tas., uncommon in wild but frequently on town lakes, farm dams. Hybridizes with Black Duck. Introduced NZ, feral and widespread: banded NZ birds have been recovered in Aust.

121 GREY TEAL *Anas gibberifrons* **Pl.11, 12, 14**

Other names: Slender or Wood Teal.

Field marks: 360–460 mm. Perhaps the most widespread Australian waterfowl: small,

almost nondescript; mottled grey-brown, easily confused with female Chestnut (122) but for *distinctly whitish throat, easily seen at distance*. Bill and feet grey, eye red. *In flight, note narrow white wing-stripe, grey-brown underwing, with narrow white wedge on 'armpit'*. Gregarious: small parties to flocks of thousands; less often in solitary pairs like Black Duck (119); in se. Aust. flocks often include Chestnut Teal. Dabbles, upends; perches in dead timber over water.
Similar species: Black Duck (119).
Voice: Male: excited clear 'pip!'; female: wild laughing chuckle; often at night.
Habitat: Almost any water, from coastal inlets and mudflats to isolated tanks in mallee-scrub or semi-desert; newly flooded depressions and billabongs.
Breeding: Nest: of down in hollow tree, among reeds, on ground under rocks, logs: in rabbit burrow (rarely). Eggs: 6–9; cream.
Range and Status: Throughout Aust.; stronghold is Murray–Darling Basin; widespread but erratic further inland. Highly-nomadic and mobile according to water conditions. Such movements extending beyond Aust.; irruptive to and/or resident Macquarie I., NZ, New Caledonia, NG, Kai and Aru Is.; Lesser Sunda Is.; Java; Andaman and Christmas Is.

122 CHESTNUT TEAL *Anas castanea*   Pl.11, 12, 14

Other names: Black, Chestnut-breasted, Green-headed, Mountain or Red Teal.
Field marks: 380–455 mm. Male: elegant small duck *with bottle-green head, rich-chestnut body, white flank-mark*, black stern. Bill dark blue-grey, legs grey-green. Eclipse plumage much duller. Female and imm: like Grey Teal (121), but darker and more ochre with heavier mottlings; *throat more buff*. In flight, both sexes *show narrow white wing-stripe and narrow white wedge on 'armpit'*, particularly obvious in male, which can look black in distance or in poor light. Often with Grey Teal, but in s. coastal areas often in parties or flocks alone.
Similar species: Chestnut-breasted Shelduck (117): much larger, white panel on wing. Black Duck (119).
Voice: Male: excited clear 'pip!', indistinguishable from male Grey Teal. Female: rapid chuckle, higher-pitched and of fewer syllables than female Grey.
Habitat: Brackish and fresh coastal swamps; saltmarshes, tidal mudflats, inlets, islands: lesser numbers on subcoastal swamps and lakes.
Breeding: Nest: lined with down; in long grass or rushes, in rock-crevice or tree hollow: takes readily to artificial nest-boxes. Eggs: 7–10; lustrous, cream.
Range and Status: Se. and sw. Aust., mostly coastal. Stronghold Tas. and islands of Bass Strait, where common to abundant; widespread but less common coastally from Sydney to Adelaide and Kangaroo I., and from Esperance to Cape Leeuwin. WA. Scarce and local, except in good years, inland in Murray Basin, on Eyre Pen., and WA n. to North West Cape; uncommon coastal n. NSW, and se. Q; straggler coastally to ne. Q (Atherton Tableland) and s. NT. Apparently increasing in s., perhaps because of widespread use of artificial nest-boxes.

123 SOUTHERN SHOVELLER *Anas rhynchotis*   Pl.11, 12, 14

Other names: Australian or Blue-winged Shoveller, Spoonbill Duck, Stinker, Widgeon, Shovelbill.
Field marks: 460–530 mm. On water, note low dark silhouette and *massive, spoonlike dark bill*, its slope rakishly repeated by neck, wingtips and tail. Male, breeding plumage: glossy grey-blue head marked by *vertical white crescent, eye yellow: shoulder and wing pale blue-grey, edged white*; chestnut below, with white flank-mark: *legs and feet orange*. Female much more sombre: finely-mottled dark-brown above: pale chestnut below: *slight pale eye-ring*; wing as male but duller: *feet green-grey to brownish*. Male eclipse: like female, but feet orange or yellow-brown. Imm: like pale female. Wary: usually well out

from shore in pairs or small parties, often among other waterfowl. Flight swift, outline racy, swept wings set well back, flies with characteristic whirr. Massive spoon-tipped bill, white underwing, blue-grey shoulder and conspicuous orange feet of male make it hard to mistake.

Similar species: Pink-eared Duck (126).

Voice: Male: soft chuckling 'took, took': muted 'clonk' and guttural grunt: female: soft husky quack: when flying, a soft chatter.

Habitat: Most waters, but prefers extensive undisturbed swamps: occasionally on shallow coastal inlets, sewage farms: exploits floodwaters.

Breeding: Nest: of grasses, lined with down: on ground in grass or other low growth, near water: occasionally in hollow tree or stump in water. Eggs: 8–11: creamy or greenish white.

Range and Status: From Cairns, ne. Q, to Eyre Pen., SA: Tas.: in WA, coastally from Esperance to North West Cape. Strongholds are Murray–Darling Basin and coastal areas of Vic. and se. SA, Tas. and sw. corner of WA. Irregular nomad to w. Q, c. Aust., NT and n. WA. Also NZ.

124   NORTHERN SHOVELLER   *Anas clypeata*

Field marks: 460–550 mm. Like Southern Shoveller (123) but male has *white breast and sides of back*. Female and male in eclipse, indistinguishable from Southern in equivalent plumages.

Range and Status: Throughout n. hemisphere: migrates s. to Africa, c. America, se. Asia, Borneo and Philippines. While in Aust. (1838–40) John Gould examined skin of an old male shot Yarrundi, NSW, (?) 1839.

125   GARGANEY   *Anas querquedula*   Pl.11, 12, 14

Other name: Summer Teal.

Field marks: 380–410 mm. About the size of Grey Teal (121), but distinctly marked: head somewhat shoveller-like. Male: long *curving pale eyebrow, dark above with long drooping black-and-white scapulars*, dark green-blue speculum margined white: rufous-brown breast. Eclipse male like female, retains blue-grey shoulders. Female: dark-brown above and on upperbreast, *almost pure-white below*; *dark line from bill through eye*. In flight, male: dark head and breast, white patch on belly, blue-grey shoulders: female: head and breast sharply cut off from white patch on belly.

Range and Status: Britain to e. Siberia. Migrates s. through Africa and se. Asia to s. NG. Until the 1960s known in Aust. only from three old Vic. records. Since then, records at Darwin NT, Yanchep, WA and in Q suggest it may be an uncommon annual visitor.

126   PINK-EARED DUCK   *Malacorhynchus membranaceus*   Pl.11, 12, 14

Other names: Pink-eyed Duck, Whistling Teal, Wigeon, Zebra Duck or Teal.

Field marks: 380–450 mm. A comical little duck with *barred flanks* and *huge square-tipped grey bill*. At distance on water looks pale-brown with dark-brown upperparts, *white forehead and face with dark-brown patch over eye* (and tiny pink 'ear-spot'). In flight, note high-held head, huge down-held bill, *pale trailing edge of wings, double crescent formed by white rump and tail tips*. Small to very large flocks, characteristic of shallow inland waters generally; often circles these closely, refusing to leave. Engages in ritual feeding in locked rotating pairs; or swims with bill submerged or dabbles in shallows, filtering food: also fossicks with head underwater; infrequently upends. Perches on low branches, logs: associates with other duck.

Similar species: Southern Shoveller (123).

Voice: Nearly continuous un-ducklike chirrup; in flight and on water.

Habitat: Inland fresh and saline waters e.g. lignum swamps, flooded claypans: irregular, specially in dry periods, to coastal inlets, mangroves, sewage farms, commercial saltfields.

Breeding: Nest: rounded mound of down in which eggs buried; in hollow tree or branch, stump, log, fence-post, old nest of waterfowl; invariably over water. Eggs: 5–8; smooth, pointed; white or creamy.
Range and Status: Mainland Aust.: essentially a species of shallow, often temporary waters, of inland. Movements and breeding much influenced by irregular flooding. Stronghold is Murray–Darling basin, sw. Vic. and se. SA; infrequent coastal e. Aust., ne. Q, top end NT and nw. Aust. Occasional Tas.

POCHARDS Subfamily *Aythyinae*

A worldwide subfamily of diving ducks that embraces the species-group of white-eyed ducks. These range from Europe to n. Africa, Madagascar, Asia, Aust., NZ and some Pacific islands. They fly swiftly and dive well, obtaining food on or under water. With feet set well back for efficient underwater swimming, they walk poorly and seldom venture far onshore. They favour deeper fresh waters, at times gathering in large rafts. The sole Australian species, White-eyed Duck (127), is typical of these small compact rich red-brown ducks. Sexes dissimilar; no speculum.
Food: Water-plants, grasses, seeds; insects, crustaceans, freshwater mussels; occasionally fish.

127 WHITE-EYED DUCK *Aythya australis* Pl.11, 12, 13

Other names: Copperhead, Hardhead, Punkari, White-wing.
Field marks: 420–580 mm. Male: a compact rich-mahogany duck *with white eye, and stern,* blackish bill crossed by blue-white band near tip. Female: paler-brown, *with dark eye; bill blue-grey*; some have whitish throat. Imm: uniform dark yellow-brown; dark eye. On water, body seems to slope rearwards; dives much; remains submerged 20–30 seconds, surfaces swimming rapidly some distance off. On larger waters occasionally in rafts of thousands. In flight both sexes show *flashing broad translucent white wing-band above, wholly white underwings and white belly.* Flight swift, shallow flickering action of slender rear-set wings.
Similar species: Blue-billed Duck (131), male.
Voice: Seldom heard; male: soft wheezy whistle; female: soft harsh croak.
Habitat: Deeper permanent swamps or lakes with emergent vegetation; also large open waters, brackish coastal swamps, ornamental lakes, sewage farms.
Breeding: Nest: neat, well-woven cup of lignum stems, cumbungi, reeds, sedges, often with canopy; close to water in reeds, cumbungi, lignum, waterside bush, shrub, bole of swamp tree. Eggs: 9–12; creamy-white.
Range and Status: In Aust. stronghold is Murray–Darling Basin, se. SA and sw. WA. At times common in other parts of c. NSW and s. Q; throughout Vic., but few breed; visits Tas., but no breeding. Irruptive or vagrant elsewhere. Extends to Java, Celebes, NG, Solomon Is., New Hebrides, New Caledonia and (formerly) NZ.

PERCHING DUCKS Subfamily *Cairininae*

A worldwide but rather disparate subfamily that includes the gorgeous Mandarin Duck of China, the American Wood-Duck, the more sombre Australian Wood-Duck (128) and the handsome small pygmy geese of Africa, Asia and Aust. Tiny to very large waterfowl with broad wings; plumage often boldly marked. Some perch on logs or trees; most usually nest in hollow trees. Sexes dissimilar.
Food: Green herbage, aquatic vegetation and seeds, insects, small invertebrates.

128 AUSTRALIAN WOOD DUCK *Chenonetta jubata* Pl.11, 12, 13

Other names: Blue Duck, Maned Duck or Goose.
Field marks: 440–500 mm. Short black bill and longish neck and legs give it the look of a

fine small goose. Male: *head and neck chocolate-brown with short black mane*; *body and wings pale-grey*, undertail black. Female: paler; *head and neck pale gingery-brown, dark eye-line bordered paler above and below*; breast mottled brown and white, pale belly and under tail-coverts. Imm: like female, duller. Typically camps in pairs to large flocks on banks of dams or tanks, moving out to feed at dusk. Near water, perches on dead logs, branches; occasionally feeds in water by dabbling. Freezes when alarmed; when with young, may flatten itself on ground or water, to look like dead wood. In flight, note male's dark head and belly, *broad grey, dark-tipped wings, broad white panel on rear edge of wing near body*; female: less contrasting pattern in flight. Wingbeats slow, but flight deceptively swift; follows courses of creeks through timber.

Voice: Female: long-drawn nasal questioning 'gnow?' rising at end; male: call shorter, higher, more rising.

Habitat: Earth dams, tanks, water among timber; swamps, lakes, reservoirs, sewage farms, ricefields; occasionally on sea, in inlets, bays.

Breeding: Nest: of down; in hollow usually of live tree; over, or far from, water. Eggs: 9–11; cream-white.

Range and Status: Aust. generally: in se. and sw. Aust. s. of the Tropic the typical waterfowl of better-watered, lightly timbered pastoral country with plentiful dams and tanks, but less common in adjacent coastal parts. Abundant on timbered watercourses and swamps of the Murray–Darling system, and in some irrigated areas. Scarce further inland and in tropical n. Aust.; visits Tas., occasionally breeding.

129 WHITE PYGMY GOOSE *Nettapus coromandelianus* Pl.11, 12, 13

Other names: Cotton Teal, White-quilled Pygmy-goose.

Field marks: 340–380 mm. Male: white and somewhat toylike; *note short black bill, black breastband, glossy blackish green above*. Female and imm: duller; *dark eyeline separated from crown by conspicuous white eyebrow*; neck shaded grey; fine dark-brown barring forms zone round upperbreast. Pairs or small parties among water-lilies; rests on logs; seldom ashore. Usually flies low; male showing flashing *white patch across primaries near wingtip*. Female: *thin white bar only on trailing edge*, rest of wing and rump dark.

Similar species: Green Pygmy Goose (130), female: greenish cap reaches eye, only slight pale eyebrow. In flight, both sexes: dark wings with white panel on rear edge; white less extensive than male White Pygmy Goose, but more extensive than female. White-headed Shelduck (118).

Voice: Male: staccato coo, uttered in flight; described as 'car car carwark' uttered several times in succession; female: soft quack.

Habitat: Deeper freshwater swamps, lagoons, dams, with water-lilies and other semi-emergent aquatic vegetation.

Breeding: Nest: high, in hollow tree or near water. Eggs: 8–15: oval, pearly-white.

Range and Status: Coastal e. Aust. from Cape York, ne. Q, to about Rockhampton–Springsure, where locally common; vagrant s. to ne. NSW. (Formerly resident s. to Clarence R., NSW). Also India, Sri Lanka, se. Asia to NG.

130 GREEN PYGMY GOOSE *Nettapus pulchellus* Pl.11, 12, 13

Other names: Goose-teal, Green Dwarf Goose.

Field marks: 300–360 mm. Small and exquisite. Male: *glossy green-black head, neck and upperparts, large white cheek-patch*, grey-white below. Bill black, tipped pink. Female and imm: *duller, faint white eyebrow*. Cheeks, neck and underparts grey-white. Pairs or small flocks among water-lilies and other aquatic vegetation. Seldom ashore: rests on logs, branches. In flight both sexes have large *white panel on rear edge of wing*, near body: otherwise wing dark above and below; note males' dark head and neck and slightly pale rump.

Similar species: White Pygmy Goose (129).

Voice: Sharp shrill 'pee-whit'; descending 'pee-yew'; high-pitched 'whit!', also high-pitched musical trill.

Habitat: Lagoons, lakes, dams with water-lilies and other semi-emergent aquatic vegetation; in wet season to shallower swamps of spike-rush and wild rice.

Breeding: Nest: usually in hollow tree in or near water, up to 10 m high. Eggs: 8–12; white or creamy white, lustrous.

Range and Status: Coastal n. Aust.; from Broome, WA, to Rockhampton, Q. Locally common; more common w. of Darwin to Kimberleys. Occasional s. to Moora, WA; Mt. Isa, Q; Lismore, NSW. Also Celebes, Moluccas to NG.

STIFFTAILS Subfamily *Oxyurinae*

A worldwide subfamily of nine species of unusual diving ducks with stiff pointed tail-feathers, prominent in their unusual displays. The tail is usually submerged when swimming but often raised and spread fanlike when at rest on surface. In male display it is pressed forward over the back – see Musk Duck (132). Sexes dissimilar.

Food: Aquatic vegetation, insects, crustaceans, molluscs.

131 BLUE-BILLED DUCK *Oxyura australis*   Pl.13

Other names: Diving, Little Musk, Spiny-tailed or Stiff-tailed Duck, Spinetail.

Field marks: 370–440 mm. Male: a small rich-chestnut duck *with prominent scooped bright pale-blue bill*, black head, dark eye. Tail black, feathers stiff and pointed, carried submerged *or raised and spread fanlike*. Male eclipse (Mar.–July): dark-brown, finely barred paler; bill dark-grey. Female: blackish brown above, feathers finely and brokenly barred buffish, giving a lightly freckled look; mixed and mottled whiter below. *Note the scooped dark-grey bill, pale throat and slight pale line back from below eye.* Imm: duller, paler. Somewhat secretive, often solitary, occasionally in large rafts far from shore on large waters. Swims low, with silhouette of largish head and bill and sloping stern; moves fast through water, diving often. Distinctive male display with spread tail, puffed feathers. Seldom seen flying; usually travels at night; flight rapid, tail-heavy, usually low; wing-beat quick and somewhat jerky, not unlike White-eyed Duck (127) with pale underparts but underwing brown.

Similar species: Musk Duck (132), female: larger, lower silhouette; stubbier triangular bill, forehead lower, less rounded. White-eyed Duck (127), male: blackish bill, tipped paler, eye and stern white; female: dark eye, generally paler red-brown, with pale stern. In flight, white wing-panel. Chestnut Teal (122) male.

Voice: Seldom heard; male in display: rapid low-pitched rattling note; female: weak quack.

Habitat: Permanent freshwater swamps, dams, lakes, larger rivers; usually with cover of dense vegetation; in winter, larger open waters generally.

Breeding: Nest: shallow cup: of rushes, reeds, sticks, cumbungi or lignum, with little down lining, often with canopy of surrounding growth pulled over it; in cumbungi, pencil-rush, lignum, tea-tree over water or on ground on islands; occasionally in old nest of other waterfowl. Eggs: 5–8; light-green, rough; become nest-stained, dirtier green.

Range and Status: Se. and s. Aust.: breeds Murray–Darling system, L. Eyre basin and se. Q, s. and w. Vic. and s. SA (not Kangaroo I.); also e. Tas., and sw. WA. Probably more common than supposed but inconspicuous by habits and nature of habitat.

132 MUSK DUCK *Biziura lobata*   Pl.13

Other names: Diver, Diving or Must Duck, Mould Goose, Steamer.

Field marks: 470–720 mm. A decidedly strange duck. Male: very large and dark with *curious large leathery flap under bill*. Bill dark-grey, almost triangular in silhouette. Female: much smaller, no obvious bill-flap. Both sexes: dark-grey or blackish-brown, feathers finely crossed with lines of lighter-brown, flight-feathers and stiff pointed tail-feathers blackish; belly whitish. Imm: like female; tip of lower mandible yellowish. Singly, or in large autumn and winter companies on open water. *Swims mostly submerged, like cormorant or platypus.* Dives constantly when feeding, brings larger items, e.g. yabbies, crabs, to surface to dismember. Often dozes on surface with tail spread fanlike. Seldom ashore, when it must shuffle on breast; rests on flattened swamp-vegetation. Occasionally associates with Blue-billed Duck (131). Male in display proceeds with repeated backward kicks, throwing splashes; fans tail forwards over back, bill raised, bill-flap expanded in prominent disc; slowly rotates in water, throwing jets with a 'k-plonk' that can be heard from afar, *and uttering simultaneously a grunt and a single shrill whistle*; often heard at night. Flies heavily, with rapid, shallow wingbeats, usually when breeze permits take off and usually at night; seldom observed on wing.

Similar species: Blue-billed Duck (131): eclipse male and female.

Voice: See above: a familiar sound, especially at night, on many permanent swamps or lakes in se. and sw. Aust.

Habitat: Lakes, reservoirs, permanent swamps with heavy vegetation; coastal swamps, brackish and fresh; shallow bays, inlets, occasionally open sea.

Breeding: Nest: rough cup: of plant-stems; in beaten-down clump of cumbungi, rushes, in grass on small island, low-hanging branch of tea-tree, often with canopy of surrounding growth drawn over it; at times sparse bed of down in hole in tree, at water level. Eggs: 1–3; greenish white, limy; becoming stained brown.

Range and Status: Se. and sw. Aust.: from Rockhampton–Fraser I., Q, through Murray–Darling Basin (further inland when conditions suitable) to s. Eyre Pen. and Kangaroo I., SA; Tas. and Bass Strait islands; in sw. WA, from Esperance to Moora; occasional n. to North West Cape. Common; sedentary and dispersive.

Ospreys, Kites, Hawks, Eagles, Harriers, Falcons

Diurnal birds of prey with strong hooked bill and usually strong feet with grasping talons. Most take live prey; some are scavengers. Some have light and dark phases; immature plumage usually different from adult. The order Falconiformes is divided into five families and several well-differentiated subfamilies, treated separately below. Sexes usually alike; females generally larger than males.

Ospreys   Family *Pandionidae*

The fish-hawk, a single worldwide species; its wings are long, legs and feet robust, the fourth toe reversible and skin of the pads rough, for effective grasp of slimy prey. Because toxic pesticides are now widespread in rivers and seas, the Osprey (133) has suffered a drastic decline in some parts of its range.

Range: Nearly cosmopolitan: breeds all continents except Antarctica, migrates to S. America.

Number of species: World 1; Aust. 1.

133 OSPREY *Pandion haliaetus*   Pl.18, 23

Other names: Fish Hawk, White-headed Osprey.

Field marks: 550–660 mm, span 1.5 m. Best identified by hunting habits: systematically quarters water at heights from 15–50 m; hovers, plunges, entering feet first with spectacular splash. On wing, looks white below, *the wing notably long and arched*, with a black mark at the wrist. Brown above, head and underparts white, *with a heavy dark line through eye and down neck*, streaked brown in broken zone across chest; legs long, feathered; eye yellow. Imm: heavier streaking across breast, underwings mottled buff. Singly, pairs or family parties; perches dead trees, piles, masts.

Similar species: White-breasted Sea-eagle (146).

Voice: Complaining high-pitched 'fee' or 'fee-ee, fee-ee'.

Habitat: Coastal waters, inlets, estuaries, offshore islands: occasionally far up larger rivers.

Breeding: Nest: large, of sticks: high in tree, usually dead: or on islands a massive tall pile of sticks, seaweed, pieces of rope, cork-floats on ground. Eggs: 2–3: dull-white, capped with reddish blotches.

Range and Status: In Aust formerly all coasts, now very rare e. SA, Vic., Tas., Bass Strait and coastal NSW s. of about Grafton. Ascends larger rivers: thus occasional sightings inland, e.g. on Murray R. near Tocumwal, NSW. Common Gt. Barrier Reef and coasts of n. and w. Aust.: (?) mostly sedentary. Cosmopolitan.

HOVERING KITES Subfamily *Elaninae*

Beautiful, somewhat falcon-like, small grey-and-white hawks of graceful flight. They hover like kestrels, but with different wing-action and often with legs dangling. On sighting prey they drop, still hovering, then parachute down with wings held high and feet out-thrust. The two Australian species are separated by underwing markings, style of flight and habits. Both hunt rodents and breed readily when these are abundant.

Food: Rodents, small reptiles, small ground-dwelling birds or their young.

Range: Europe, Africa, Asia, N. and S. America, Aust.

Number of species: World 4: Aust. 2.

134 AUSTRALIAN BLACK-SHOULDERED KITE *Elanus notatus*
Pl.20, 21

Field marks: 330–380 mm: span 900 mm. A beautiful white hawk with pale-grey wings and black shoulders: eye red, feet yellow. Imm: mottled buff or brown above: wings and flight feathers black: patchy deep-buff zone round upper breast. Singly, in pairs or family groups. Difficult to distinguish from Letter-winged Kite (135) except in flight: when note *only a small black patch on underwing near 'wrist'*. Flight direct and gull-like, with very quick wingbeats broken by intervals of gliding on upswept wings. Perches in heads of trees, telephone poles and wires, fences, stumps.

Similar species: Letter-winged Kite (135): Grey (White) Goshawk (144): Grey Falcon (154).

Voice: Clear 'chee' with sob in it, often repeatedly in flight: a harsh 'skairr!'.

Habitat: Open forests, grasslands with groups of trees: farms, market gardens, sewage farms, vacant land with rank growth: attracted to outskirts of towns by mice.

Breeding: Nest: smallish, compact, deep: of sticks: usually 7–12 m high in eucalypt, occasionally pine. Eggs: 3–5: oval, dull-white, heavily blotched chocolate-brown.

Range and Status: Throughout mainland Aust., specially better-watered parts, but sparse and occasional in far-n. Vagrant King I., Bass Strait and Tas. Common to uncommon. Sedentary and nomadic. Closely-related forms in NG and elsewhere.

135 LETTER-WINGED KITE *Elanus scriptus*
Pl.20, 21

Field marks: 350–380 mm, span 900 mm. Very like Australian Black-shouldered (134) but crown greyer, head and eyes larger, giving it a somewhat owl-like, capped look: *feet whitish. In flight, reveals variable black bar along underwing, forming a broken 'V' or 'W'*: unlike Australian Black-shouldered, secondaries translucent. Imm: like imm. (134) but more chestnut: underwing-bar variable: faint or absent in some. Flight much looser, more swooping and tern-like than adult Australian Black-shouldered, wings not held up when gliding. (But note that imm. Australian Black-shouldered also has a loose wing-beat). Forms loose flocks, sometimes numbering 50–100: typically roosts in companies in leafy trees or on dead branches by day, hunts by night.

Voice: Described as a harsh, rasping jar. Alarm-call: high, clear whistle. (D. G. W. Hollands).

Habitat: Grasslands with trees, frequently along watercourses.

Breeding: Typically in open colonies, some 20 + pairs; sometimes singly. Usually in trees along watercourses, frequently in coolibahs (*E. microtheca*). Nest: like Australian Black-shouldered but reported to be bulkier; some examined were lined with wool over dead gum leaves; frequently also lined with fur of prey discarded in pellets. Occasionally uses old nest of another hawk, or a crow. Eggs: 2–5; white to buff, spotted, blotched, or smeared reddish or brownish, most heavily at large end.

Range and Status: Its economy seems intimately connected with that of the Long-haired Rat *Rattus villosissimus*. In drought, the rat exists in refuge areas on the Barkly Tableland, NT; n. inland Q and L. Eyre Basin, SA. Irregularly, following the development of suitable conditions, its numbers increase rapidly and at times it irrupts and radiates in immense plagues towards w. and cn. NT, c. and sw. Q and sc. SA. The optimal habitat for the rat and the kite has been described as the open plains of the Barkly Tableland and the Georgina–Diamantina drainage (e. NT-far-w. Q, extending s. to L. Eyre Basin in ne. SA). When rats are abundant, colonies of kites have been observed breeding in that region and adjacent to it. Under good conditions there are probably several clutches, as in Austrlian Black-shouldered Kite. Probably as a result of increases in its own numbers, linked with subsequent rapid decline in rat populations, the kite also periodically irrupts. Single birds, pairs or flocks, as rare nomads, occasionally reach sub-coastal or open coastal parts of all mainland states, where they may associate with Australian Black-shouldered Kites. Breeding is sometimes attempted during these extra-limital occurrences. Locally common to very sparse and rare. Irruptive and nomadic.

CUCKOO FALCONS   Subfamily *Leptodontinae*

A group distinguished by crests, broad wings, usually conspicuously patterned plumage and rather feeble talons.

Food: Mostly large insects, small reptiles and amphibians.

Range: Africa and Asia to NG; n. and e. Aust.

Number of species: World 6; Aust. 1.

136   CRESTED HAWK   *Aviceda subcristata*   Pl.19, 22

Other name: Pacific Baza.

Field marks: 405–455 mm; span 750 mm. Our only hawk *with a distinct slim black crest* set off by a large yellow eye in the grey head; breast buff-white *with bold dark bars*. Female: throat whitish, upperbreast grey. Imm: dark-brown above, mottled paler; upperbreast rich-buff, undertail barred. Pairs or family parties; surprisingly tame and inoffensive. Soars high in flat circles; indulges in spectacular tumbling flights, calling. Typically hunts by plunging into foliage of trees mostly after large insects, small reptiles. In flight, from below note the *barred breast, broad rounded wings with buff linings and pale, conspicuously barred flight feathers; tail with black terminal band.*

Voice: Repeated weak piping, not unlike Wedge-tailed Eagle (147); in flight, mellow double whistle, 'wee-choo, wee-choo'.

Habitat: Treetops in rainforest, open forest, woodlands.

Breeding: Nest: small, almost pigeon-like; of sticks; on horizontal, often leafy, branch up to 30 m high. Eggs: 3–4; top-shaped; blue-white or green-white, smeared, blotched or spotted light-brown.

Range and Status: Coastal nw., ne. and e. Aust. from Kimberleys to top end NT and from C. York coastally s. to about Newcastle, NSW. Rare much s. of Grafton. Also Moluccas, NG and Solomon Is.

SOARING KITES Subfamily *Milvinae*

Broad-winged, mostly weak-footed, soaring birds of prey, both scavengers and predators. One species typically, and two others frequently, gather in companies where food is plentiful. The least-typical member is Black-breasted Kite (139), a powerful predator as well as scavenger, most often seen soaring eagle-like at great heights.

Food: Carrion, small mammals, birds, eggs, reptiles, insects.
Range: Europe, Africa and Asia extending to Aust. and Tas.
Number of species. World 6; Aust. 5

137 FORK-TAILED KITE *Milvus migrans*   Pl.19, 24

Other names: Black Kite, Kimberley Hawk, Kite-Hawk.
Field marks: 480–550 mm; span 1.2 m. Usually flying: a leisurely dark hawk with long slightly drooped wings with spread fingertips and *long forked tail, which it twists and tilts in its particularly effortless floating flight.* Tail often looks triangular, giving the impression of a 'square-tailed' kite; but see (138). Plumage dark muddy brown with fine dark streaks, dark mark round eyes, paler on throat; cere and legs yellow, latter short, feet weak. Imm: streaked fawn on head and breast, spotted fawn on wings, back and underwings; tail tipped fawn. Sub-adult: pale head, darker round eyes; wings dark with fawn band *forming a pale shoulder-patch in flight.* Singly, but *usually in loose flocks*; hundreds climb sky in slow-wheeling companies. A dead beast or smoke attracts them from afar; companies often perch on stockyards, round rubbish-dumps, slaughter-houses.
Similar species: Square-tailed Kite (138): more solitary; pale, streaked head, redder plumage; at rest wings protrude beyond tail; in flight, more upswept wings with pale half-moons, unforked barred tail. Whistling Kite (141): paler brown with contrasting black flight-feathers, unforked tail; in flight distinctive underwing pattern; note call.
Voice: Feeble plaintive trills and whinnies.
Habitat: Open country: timbered watercourses through same; beaches; towns, airfields, rubbish dumps, slaughter-yards, cattle camps, homestead environs.
Breeding: Nest: flattish, of sticks, often lined with cattle dung; typically with others in trees along watercourses; old nest of hawk or crow sometimes used. Eggs: 2–3; spotted and blotched red-brown.
Range and Status: In Aust., widespread and often very abundant in n. and inland, particularly round settlement and stock-concentrations where greater availability of food has probably considerably improved its status. Vagrant coastal sw., s. and se. Aust.; sight records Tas. Common; nomadic or migratory. Also s. Europe, Africa, Asia to NG and Bismarck Archipelago.

138 SQUARE-TAILED KITE *Lophoictinia isura*   Pl.19, 24

Field marks: 510–560 mm; span 1.2 m. Usually seen sailing harrier-like over treetops or soaring. Note the *long broad upswept wings with buff linings, prominent barred fingertips and cream half-moon at base of primaries.* The tail is long and broad with angular corners and shadowy grey and black bars below. At rest the wingtips extend past tail; note the pale, dark-streaked head, slight crest, rufous dark-streaked body, blackish back, fawn mark on shoulder. Eye pale, legs and feet flesh-coloured, feeble, with prominent buff 'trousers'. Imm: paler, dappled chestnut-brown above.
Similar species: Fork-tailed Kite (137). Black-breasted Kite (139), (pale phase): more robust, underwing pattern simpler; buffish tail much shorter. Red Goshawk (145): more robust; barred pale underwing and undertail, but no pale half-moon; quicker wingbeats and glides.
Voice: Described by D. G. W. Hollands as 'a hoarse contralto yelp', uttered near nest. Voice of male deeper than female.
Habitat: Open forests and woodlands; timbered watercourses; rocky hills and gorges.

Breeding: Nest: large, loose; of sticks; in tree, sometimes low. Eggs: 2–3; dull-white, blotched lavender and red-brown.

Range and Status: Distribution imperfectly known: scattered records from all mainland States suggest a nomadic situation with a preference for open forests, lightly-wooded foothills and timbered watercourses. Generally absent from treeless inland and from heavier forests and cleared pastoral or agricultural lands. It is possibly seen most often in WA including s. inland areas and Kimberleys, in Arnhem Land and on Divide in e. interior Q. Generally rare.

139 BLACK-BREASTED KITE *Hamirostra melanosternon* Pl.18, 23

Other name: Black-breasted Buzzard.

Field marks: 530–610 mm; span 1.5 m. Usually seen soaring high with large wings markedly upswept and somewhat backswept: note *black head and breast, round white 'window' in black wingtips, and short rounded buff tail.* At rest long wings extend to tail-tip; note contrast of black head, breast and back with rufous nape and rich-buff under tail-coverts and trousers. Bill long, robust, blue-grey with black tip; legs short, yellow. Pale phase: *pale buff with fine dark streaks* or mottlings; back black or mottled black, facial skin and legs yellow. In flight, black wingtips with indistinct white window; rest of under-wing and short rounded tail pale-buff. Imms. of both phases: like rusty-washed pale phase, facial skin and legs blue-grey. More powerful and predatory than others of sub-family.

Similar species: Square-tailed Kite (138). White-breasted Sea-eagle (146), imm.

Voice: Described by D. G. W. Hollands as 'a short, hoarse yelp', uttered singly, but repeated many times. Also 'a repeated harsh, scraping sound'.

Habitat: Plains, open scrublands, open woodlands.

Breeding: Nest: very large; of sticks; in tall tree. Eggs: 2; whitish, blotched mauve and dark-brown.

Range and Status: N. Aust. and inland parts of all mainland States except Vic., where now rare vagrant. Generally rare, commoner in nw. Q and top end NT, occurs Melville I. Uncommon; sedentary or nomadic.

140 BRAHMINY KITE *Haliastur indus* Pl.19, 24

Other names: Red-backed Kite or Sea-eagle.

Field marks: 430–510 mm; span 1.2 m. A distinctive slow soaring hawk mostly of coastal areas: *deep chestnut with whitish head, neck and breast*, black wingtips: bill pale bone. In flight, note broad rounded, somewhat drooped wings with upswept black tips, rounded pale-tipped tail. Imm: browner and mottled, head and breast streaked buff; eye dark; in flight, *pale patch at base of dark flight-feathers, not present in adult*; pale underparts and undersurface of tail. Singly, pairs or loose companies. Tame, inoffensive scavenger; seeks carrion along tide-lines, occasionally seizes fish from water, reptile or insect from ground or foliage, eats small items on wing.

Similar species: Whistling Kite (141): from imm. Brahminy in rangier build, pale brown with black flight feathers and distinctive underwing pattern. Fork-tailed Kite (137); White-breasted Sea-eagle (146).

Voice: Stuttered 'peeah-h-h'; feeble peevish trills, mews and squeals.

Habitat: Coastlines, specially with sandflats, mudflats, mangroves; islands, tidal sections of larger rivers; beaches, harbours, coastal towns.

Breeding: Nest: of sticks, seaweed, in top of tree, often mangrove. Eggs: 2–3; dull-white, bluish white or pale-green, with hairlike blackish lines and small rusty spots.

Range and Status: Coastal nw., n. and ne. Aust. and islands: from about Carnarvon, WA, to ce. NSW (Hunter R.). Common, but uncommon s. of about C. Byron, NSW. Sedentary. Also from India–Sri Lanka to se. Asia, Philippines, Indonesia, NG and Solomon Is.

141 WHISTLING KITE *Haliastur sphenurus*   Pl.19, 24

Other names: Carrion Hawk, Whistling Eagle, Whistling Eagle-hawk.
Field marks: 510–585 mm; span 1.2 m. Common and widespread, made familiar by call and effortless buoyant soaring on rather drooping wings with prominent fingertips, shoulders well forward; tail long and blunt. Plumage pale-fawn to light-brown with *plentiful pale streaks* on head, back and breast and pale spots on upperparts. At distance note *contrast of pale body with black flight-feathers.* Imm: more spotted and streaked. In flight, underwing pattern distinctive: *pale forepart of wing joins a cream band that crosses wing near tip,* leaving a large dark rectangle along trailing edge. Singly, pairs or occasionally migrating or nomadic groups or flocks; often perches on dead branch of riverside or open-forest tree or circles leisurely over treetops, whistling. Groups gather to roost or feed at carrion. Also takes live prey; harries feeding birds such as ibis, forcing them to disgorge.
Similar species: Fork-tailed (137), Square-tailed (138) and Brahminy (140) Kites. Little Eagle (148): more thick-set and powerful, with sturdy feathered legs, triangular underwing pattern; soars with much flatter wings, head more prominent.
Voice: Shrill memorable whistling call, the first note leisurely, long and descending, followed by quick upward burst of 4–6 short shrill staccatto notes; order occasionally reversed.
Habitat: Open forests and foothills; lakes, swamps, timbered watercourses, tidal inlets, estuaries, mudflats.
Breeding: Nest: bulky, of sticks; usually high in eucalypt; may be added to over many seasons until massive. Eggs: 2–3; blue-white, occasionally splotched reddish-brown.
Range and Status: Throughout Aust. and coastal islands in suitable habitat; vagrant King I., Bass Strait, and Tas. Uncommon to very common; sedentary, nomadic. Also NG, New Caledonia.

GOSHAWKS AND SPARROWHAWKS Subfamily *Accipitrinae*

The bird-hawks: powerful, agile, yellow-eyed hawks with rounded wings and long tails. Direct flight is typically of several quick beats, interspersed with glides on flat or somewhat bowed wings. Specially when mating, they often soar high, tails fanned; some perform remarkable aerobatics or circle in pairs, one or other with deep slow chesty wingbeats. A typical hunting method is to wait quietly in shelter, dashing out in fast level flight to seize prey in air or on ground. Females larger and more powerful than males.
Food: Rabbits now form an important part of diet of larger Australian species; otherwise mostly birds, small mammals, reptiles.
Range: Nearly cosmopolitan.
Number of species: World 44; Aust. 4.

142 AUSTRALIAN GOSHAWK *Accipiter fasciatus*   Pl.19, 22

Other mames: Brown Goshawk, Chicken Hawk; Pacific Goshawk.
Field marks: ♂ 405, ♀ 550 mm; span up to 1 m. A wary widespread powerful but at times deceptively sluggish hawk, female much larger than male. Adult grey-brown to powdery slate-grey above: *finely barred pale-rufous and white below, trousers more buff.* Cere, eye and legs yellow; *strong ridge over eye gives beetle-browed look.* Imm: very different: dark-brown above: off-white below *with heavy brown splashes on upperbreast, bold rufous V's or bars on underparts and undertail*; eye pale-yellow, legs dull bone-colour. Race *didimus* of n. Aust.: smaller and paler. Singly or pairs: flies with quick wingbeats and glides, rounded wings slightly arched down; note long blunt tail. Often circles on slightly upswept rounded wings, tail fanned; or glides silently over trees to surprise prey, but attacks with great speed. Specially when young and inexperienced, often raids poultry and domestic pigeons, many being shot. Widespread use of 'Brown Goshawk' probably arises from familiarity with birds in that plumage.

Similar species: Collared Sparrowhawk (143). Brown Falcon (155): tapering 'gull' wings, looser, deeper wingbeats: circles with wings more upswept; cackling calls. Note head markings.

Voice: Male: high-pitched rapid-fire 'kikikiki!': female: slower mellow whistled 'yuik yuik yuik', mostly near nest.

Habitat: Wherever there are trees, but typically more open forests and woodlands, partly-cleared farmlands, shelter-belts, roadside timber, city parks, gardens.

Breeding: Nest: flattish: of sticks, lined with eucalypt leaves: usually 6–20 m in tree. Eggs: 2–3: plain-bluish white, sometimes faintly blotched red-brown.

Range and Status: Throughout Aust. and Tas. and many coastal islands. Widespread and common in suitable habitat, including towns: probably part-migratory, with winter movement to n. Aust. Also from Christmas I. (Indian Ocean) through Lesser Sunda Is. to NG, New Hebrides, New Caledonia, Fiji and neighbouring Pacific islands.

143   COLLARED SPARROWHAWK   *Accipiter cirrhocephalus*   Pl.19, 22

Other name: Chicken Hawk.

Field marks: 300–400 mm: span up to 760 mm. Very like a small fine Australian Goshawk (142) but lacks Goshawk's beetle-brow. Sexes differ markedly in size: male often very small (300 mm): female approximates male Goshawk. At rest, *note the very slightly forked tail*, more distinct pale rufous collar on hindneck: feet less powerful with very long middle toe. Imm: like imm. Goshawk without the beetle-brow. Adult plumage varies: northern and inland birds often very pale. With practice, can be distinguished from Goshawk in flight by more square-cut tail, lighter more airy style of flight on somewhat more shapely wings. Glides with wings flat and wingtips upswept. Often soars until nearly invisible: throws itself about in dives, loops and twists: can fly straight or dive at astonishing speed. Remember that Nankeen Kestrel (156) is erroneously called 'sparrowhawk'.

Similar species: Little Falcon (153): darker, rakish pointed wings.

Voice: Shrill rapid 'kikiki', faster and thinner than Goshawk or Kestrel: can resemble alarm-call of a honeyeater: also slow mellow piping 'yuik, yuik, yuik': near nest, thin squeals.

Habitat: Temperate rainforests, coastal woodlands, to inland mulga and mallee scrubs. Perhaps most characteristic habitat is timbered gorges in inland and n. Aust. where pools attract birds.

Breeding: Nest: shallow platform of small sticks, lined with eucalypt leaves: in tree at heights from 10–30 m: occasionally uses old nest of crow or other bird. Eggs: 2–4: white or green-white, faintly blotched brown and buff.

Range and Status: Throughout Aust. and Tas., less common than Australian Goshawk but nonetheless widespread and perhaps more common than is thought. Also NG, Aru Is.

144   GREY (WHITE) GOSHAWK   *Accipiter novaehollandiae*   Pl.19, 22

Other name: White Hawk.

Field marks: 405–510 mm: span 1.05 m. More powerful and thickset than Australian Goshawk (142). Two distinct colour phases: (1) grey above, paler grey below *very faintly but regularly barred darker*, *eyes dark-red*: (2) pure-white, *eyes yellow or dark-red*. In both, cere and legs yellow, feet and talons powerful. Singly or in pairs; soars over forest or woodland showing typical round-winged silhouette and quick shallow wingbeats of goshawks, tail distinctly shorter than Australian Goshawk, giving different silhouette. The similarity of White Goshawk to Sulphur-crested Cockatoo (318) perched and in gliding flight is oft-remarked.

Similar species: Grey Falcon (154): tapering wings darker at tips: mottled upperparts: dark mark down through dark eye: note flight. Australian Black-shouldered (134) and Letter-winged (135) Kites: black shoulders, black mark on underwing: they hover and parachute.

Voice: Slow deep mellow piping 'yuik, yuik, yuik, yuik': also more rapid higher-pitched chatter.

Habitat: Temperate, subtropical and tropical rainforests, woodlands, timber along watercourses; occasionally hunts far over adjacent open country.

Breeding: Nest: large, shallow: of sticks: usually very high in live tree. Eggs: 2–3: blue-white.

Note: phases sometimes interbreed; individual young may be of either phase.

Range and Status: N. and c. Aust. and coastal islands: from Kimberley, WA, to Tas. and w. Vic.; occasional w. to about Adelaide and Kangaroo I., SA. Fairly common in suitable habitat, specially coastal rainforest: otherwise rare and spasmodic. In e. coastal rainforests, grey phase appears dominant: in Tas. and Kimberleys, white phase only. Sedentary or nomadic. Other races from Timor and Moluccas to NG, Solomon Is. etc.

145 RED GOSHAWK *Erythrotriorchis radiatus*   Pl.19, 22

Other names: Red or Rufous-bellied Buzzard.

Field marks: 500–610 mm: span 1.2 m. A large powerful goshawk: *head and breast rust red, boldly streaked black,* cheeks grey, throat pale: *trousers bright rufous, unstreaked.* Upperparts grey-brown and black, richly marked chestnut: tail grey-brown crossed by shadowy bars. Cere and skin round eye bright-yellow, legs and feet yellow, massive. Flies with quick wingbeats and glides: wing-linings rusty, undersurface of flight-feathers whitish, slightly mottled, with black tips; tail greyish below with irregular dark bands: wings more tapered, tail shorter than Australian Goshawk (142). Male much smaller and slighter than female, with finer streakings. Bold and swift and known to kill birds like ducks and cockatoos.

Similar species: Square-tailed Kite (138): roughly similar flight-pattern from below, but style very different. Spotted Harrier (149): underwing and undertail-pattern roughly similar, but lankier, note sailing flight. Little Eagle (148) (adult) and Whistling Kite (141): no rusty red underparts; note underwing patterns.

Voice: Said to be typical goshawk-chatter, deeper and slower than Australian Goshawk.

Habitat: Tree-lined watercourses, surrounding open country, lightly wooded foothills.

Breeding: Nest: like Australian Goshawk but larger, usually in a tree 10–20 m or higher: occasionally in an old nest of crow. Eggs: 2–3: blue-white, sometimes smeared blackish, brown or lavender.

Range and Status: Coastal and subcoastal n. and ne. Aust. and islands: from Fitzroy R., Kimberleys, WA, formerly s. to Sydney but now to n. NSW. Rare, except perhaps Kimberleys and coastal NT.

EAGLES AND SEA-EAGLES Subfamily *Buteoninae* (in part)

Large to very large birds of prey of powerful soaring flight. Bills strong, often nearly as long as head. Most have long robust feathered legs but sea-eagles have somewhat shorter unfeathered legs and long trousers. Sexes usually alike; males usually smaller than females.

Food: Mammals, birds, reptiles, fish, carrion; in s. and inland Aust. rabbits have become an important staple, replacing vanishing small native mammals.

Range: Nearly cosmopolitan.

Number of species: World 34; Aust. 3.

146 WHITE-BREASTED SEA-EAGLE *Haliaeetus leucogaster*   Pl.18, 23

Other names: Sea-eagle, White-bellied Fish-hawk or Sea-eagle.

Field marks: 710–890 mm: span 2 m. A large white eagle with grey-brown wings. In flight broad upswept wings and short tail give it the look of a huge butterfly; white wing-linings and grey flight-feathers divide the wing into white and grey triangles; wedge-shaped white tail grey at base. Imm: very dark-brown, streaked and spotted fawn: *tail buff-white; face and throat buff,* underparts and flight-feathers blackish: in flight, imm. looks dark and patchy, *with conspicuous white half-moon at base of primaries.* In second year, more white, patchily washed and mottled with buff. Singly, in pairs or family parties; rests on prominent trees over rivers, lake-shores, soars in slow majestic circles. Hovers low and drops into water to take fish, waterfowl etc., technique differing markedly from spectacular high dive of Osprey (133).

Similar species: Wedge-tailed Eagle (147) (adult and imm.) from imm. Sea-eagle: much rangier silhouette, tail longer and always dark. Black-breasted Kite (139), pale phase: because of pale window in wing could be confused with imm. Sea-eagle, but fawn-coloured tail short and rounded.

Voice: Strident far-carrying metallic clanking; often by two birds together, perched or in flight.

Habitat: Coasts, islands, estuaries and inlets: large rivers, inland lakes, large swamps, reservoirs; still occasionally over settled areas, where timber and waterways give refuge, e.g. Sydney Harbour. At times far from water.

Breeding: Nest: huge, of sticks; in tall dead or live tree, usually over water; or on ground, on offshore islands or remote coastal cliffs. Eggs: 2; white, sometimes smeared yellowish.

Range and Status: Throughout coastal Aust. and Tas., and on larger rivers, lakes and storages, sometimes far inland. Common to uncommon or rare in settled areas. Sedentary or nomadic. Also from India–Sri Lanka, throughout s. and se. Asia to Philippines, Greater Sunda Is., NG and (part) Solomon Is.

147 WEDGE-TAILED EAGLE *Aquila audax*   Pl.18, 23

Other name: Eaglehawk.

Field marks: 890 mm–1.06 m; span *c.* 2.5 m, but up to 3 m and more alleged. A huge dark eagle with pale bill, long feathered legs and *long diamond-shaped tail*; male smaller than female. Old adults glossy jet-black with tawny feathering on nape and in band across wing. Imms. and sub-adults up to *c.* 5 years are brown, darker on wings and tail, hind-neck and wing-coverts straw-coloured to golden-brown, bill more blue-grey at first. Singly, pairs or in hunting parties; groups at carrion. Typically rests on dead trees, inland telephone poles or on ground. Flies with easy powerful wingbeats and glides or soars often to great heights in majestic circles, wings upswept; note characteristic tail and patchy white down at junctions of feather-tracts on underwing. Conspicuous display by males over breeding territory: dives with wings half-closed, shoots up to topple forward again.

Similar species: Black-breasted Kite (139) (both phases): prominent white window in wing, short round fawn tail. White-breasted Sea-eagle (146), imm: shorter pale tail; pale halfmoon at base of flight-feathers.

Voice: Rather feeble 'pseet-you, pseet-you', seldom heard except in mating display and near nest.

Habitat: Wide – from mountain forests to nearly treeless plains; occasionally appears over cities.

Breeding: Nest: huge; of sturdy sticks, lined with fresh eucalypt leaves when in use; often added to over many seasons; in fork or on limb of tree, often high, but in inland may be near ground; on some islands on ground; old nests are used as feeding platforms. Eggs: 1–3; whitish, blotched buffish, spotted or streaked red-brown and lavender.

Range and Status: Aust. and Tas.: common where conditions suitable. In most of s. Aust., economy now linked with the introduced rabbit. Sparse to locally common; sedentary, nomadic in drought. Also s. NG.

148 LITTLE EAGLE *Hieraaetus morphnoides*   Pl.18, 24

Other name: Australian Little Eagle.

Field marks: 455–510 mm; span 1.2 m. A powerful 'pocket-eagle' with long feathered legs, square-cut tail, partial crest on nape. Dark phase: deep-sandy with long black marks on crown, crest and sides of face; dark grey-brown above with distinct fawn band across wing. Pale phase: head and sides of neck rich-buff, dark-brown above with fawn band across wing; whitish below and on trousers, washed buff (sometimes in zone across breast) and lightly streaked black. Imm: dark phase: darker than adult. Imm: pale phase; very different; patterned like adult but washed pale-chestnut on head, back and upper-breast. Can usually be recognized by flight once learned: sometimes flies with a few quick goshawk-like wingbeats and glides; *soars in rather tight circles on flat wings, with slightly upturned fingertips, tail fanned, head and neck extend well forward of wings.* Note the distinctive underwing pattern; dark phase: wing-linings coloured like breast, *leaving paler triangular area on trailing edge*; pale phase: *broad pale bar diagonally across underwing, leaving dark triangle on trailing edge.* When courting, performs high spectacular display-flights, short dives, pulling up to accompaniment of excited whistle. More than other raptor, seems to attract attacking crows, magpies, woodswallows etc.

Similar species: Whistling Kite (141) often confused, but flight more languid and floating with wings more drooped, more prominent fingertips, longer thinner tail, squarer wing-pattern. At rest, smaller head and no crest; feebler unfeathered legs. Red Goshawk (145): from imm. pale phase by yellow unfeathered legs with rich-rusty trousers; flight feathers and tail pale and barred, without the Little Eagle pattern.

Voice: Quick, double or triple-syllabled whistle, second and third syllables lower-pitched, briefer; also brief piping 'pip-it, pip-it, pip-it' in display flight.

Habitat: Plains, foothills, open woodlands and scrublands, usually near water, timber along watercourses and lakes.

Breeding: Nest: of sticks; somewhat larger than crow's, but very compact, about 0.6 m across and 0.3 m deep; often very high in leafy tree; occasionally uses old nest of other species. Eggs: 1–2; white or bluish-white, blotched and smeared red-brown.

Range and Status: Throughout mainland Aust. Uncommon generally, but very wide-spread and likely to be encountered anywhere in indicated habitat. Also NG.

HARRIERS Subfamily *Circinae*

Large slim hawks with long wings, legs and tails, small heads and owl-like facial discs of feathers that probably assist hearing when hunting. They are best-known for their low, sailing flight on upswept wings over open country; they sometimes hover heavily. Our most familiar species, commonly known as the Swamp Harrier (150), is now regarded as conspecific with the widespread Marsh Harrier, *C. aeruginosus*. Like other typical harriers, it nests on ground, our other species, the Spotted Harrier (149) nests in trees – the only harrier so to do.

Food: Small mammals, ground-dwelling birds, birds' eggs and nestlings, reptiles, amphibians, in some mainland districts and commonly in Tas., fresh corpses of rabbits and other animals killed on roads.

Range: All continents except Antarctica, and many oceanic islands.

Number of species: World 9; Aust. 2.

149 SPOTTED HARRIER *Circus assimilis* Pl.18, 21

Other names: Allied Harrier, Smoke Hawk, Spotted Swamp Hawk.

Field marks: 508–610 mm; span 1.2 m. A strikingly beautiful hawk: smoky blue-grey above with fine white spots on wings; *tail grey with narrow black bands; face and under-parts rich chestnut,* latter finely spotted white; legs long and yellow. At a distance fine markings not obvious; best distinguished from Swamp Harrier (150) on wing by more slowly beating broad wings, prominent 'fingertips' and greater contrast of dark wing-linings with whitish, *more prominently and narrowly barred underside of flight feathers and tail; the trough-shaped pointed tail.* Imm: very different; dark-brown above, head buff or pale rufous with dark streaks; dark mask edged buff; buff mark in centre of nape, large buff or rufous spots or streaks on shoulder, at a distance looking like a pale patch or broad pale band in flight. Underparts pale-buff to rufous, streaked dark-brown. Unlike adult, rump often mottled whitish; this can cause confusion with adult Swamp Harrier, but in flight note pale-buff wing-linings and pale, slightly barred undersides of flight-feathers, buff and dark-grey bands on tail. Singly or pairs; sails *very low* on broad upswept wings over grassland or through open timber in search of prey on ground, often lowers legs in flight. Hovers with wings beating deeply, long legs trailing; soars high.

Voice: Usually silent, but said to utter short shrill squeal.

Habitat: Plains and other open country, open bluebush/saltbush; more often hunts through grassy open woodlands and scrubs than Swamp Harrier.

Breeding: Nest: unique among harriers; large, of sticks lined with green eucalypt leaves in tree – usually the high leafy branch of a eucalypt. Eggs: 2–4; white and blue-white, smeared and blotched rusty.

Range and Status: Aust. generally; vagrant Tas. Common in inland and n. Aust.; uncommon in coastal e., s. and sw. Aust. Nomadic or migratory. Also Lesser Sunda Is. and Celebes.

150 SWAMP HARRIER   *Circus aeruginosus*   **Pl.18, 21**

Other names: Marsh Harrier, Swamp Hawk.

Field marks: 510–610 mm; span 1.2 m. A well-known large long-winged brownish hawk *with a white rump*; breast whitish buff with deeper streaks. Sits upright, tall and small-headed, on fence-posts, ground or swamp vegetation; *sails low over crops, paddocks or swamps on upswept wings*, rocking slightly; hovers heavily. When courting soars high, cuts agile loops and circles with wings in a stiff V, uttering a short cry; do not then confuse with Brown Falcon (155). In flight, underwing and undertail-pattern not as bold as Spotted Harrier (149); primaries dark at tips and paler toward base; flight-feathers and tail have *broad shadowy bars*. Older males often have wings and tail suffused with grey; breast and underwing sometimes nearly white. Eye yellow, legs long yellowish unfeathered with long buffish trousers. Imm: *uniform dark-brown, often with rufous tone*; whitish streaks on centre of nape; *white mark on rump small or absent*.

Similar species: Spotted Harrier (149), specially imm.

Voice: Thin short high 'kyeow', usually during courtship flights, often at great heights; feeble squeals.

Habitat: Open country, including swamps and any waters, patrols shores and shallow water areas, and adjacent swampy cover; saltmarshes, grasslands, crops; occasionally open-timbered grasslands.

Breeding: Nest: low heap of grasses, sticks, rushes or weeds; invariably on or near ground; in dense grass, crops, swamp vegetation, samphire. Eggs: 3–6; white and rounded.

Range and Status: Aust. and Tas., common to very common in coastal and better-watered parts, very scarce in arid country. There is an autumn migratory movement n. from Tas. and s. coastal districts where it is usually scarce or absent in winter. Also Europe, Africa and Asia to Greater Sunda Is., NG, Norfolk and Lord Howe Is., Oceania and NZ.

Falcons   Family *Falconidae*

Swift powerful birds of prey with long pointed wings and longish tails. Typical falcons soar high in a deceptively leisurely manner and stoop on prey with wings nearly closed, often at breathtaking speed. Typical falcons in Aust. are represented by Black Falcon (151), Peregrine Falcon (152), Little Falcon (153), (the local counterpart of the hobbies of Eurasia, which extend to NG) and the Grey Falcon (154). Less dashing, more generalized and hawklike is the widespread Brown Falcon (155), long-known as the 'brown hawk'. The kestrels, a world group of distinctive small hovering falcons, are represented by Nankeen Kestrel (156). Sexes usually alike, but females usually larger.

Food: Birds, small mammals, reptiles, insects.

Range: Cosmopolitan, except Antarctica.

Number of species: World 38; Aust. 6.

151 BLACK FALCON *Falco subniger* **Pl.20, 25**

Field marks: 480–560 mm; span 930 mm. A robust falcon; looks uniformly sooty, but seen well, note inconspicuous dark moustache-mark and pale throat – absent in some but in others, continuing to upperbreast (also sparse white spots on underwings and under tail-coverts). Bill blue-grey with dark tip, cere and eyering blue-grey: legs and feet dull straw-coloured; eye dark. Imm: noticeably patterned by paler feather-margins; cere, eyering and legs lead-grey to neutral. Singly or pairs, perches on dead trees, fence-posts; posture somewhat crouching and heavy-shouldered. In flight often looks slow and leisurely, but capable of great speed: *distinctive broad wings are slightly drooped when soaring; long tail narrow in flight, fanned when soaring, underwings more uniform dark-brown* than dark-phase Brown Falcon (155). Soars over driven stock, shooters, harvesting machines, waiting for small birds to flush. Hunts birds along timbered inland watercourses, over isolated tanks and waterholes.

Similar species: Brown Falcon, (155) dark phase: usually shows traces of pale cheek and double moustache; legs longer but feebler, sits more upright. In flight undersides of flight-feathers contrast more with dark wing-linings; 'rowing' wingbeats looser, deeper, soars with gull-wings upswept. Fork-tailed Kite (137).

Voice: Rapid chatter, 'kakakaka', softer than Peregrine Falcon (152); gull-like screeches in display-flight.

Habitat: Plains, grasslands, timbered watercourses; over crops and cultivated land.

Breeding: No nest made; uses old nest of hawk or crow. Eggs: 2–4; reddish white, minutely spotted, blotched and freckled rich red-brown.

Range and Status: Open habitats of mainland Aust., mostly inland and sub-inland. *Rare, or absent* from C. York Pen., Q; top end NT; coastal se. Q, coastal NSW, e. Vic., and from coastal WA; but occurs in Kimberleys. Uncommon; nomadic or irruptive.

152 PEREGRINE FALCON *Falco peregrinus* **Pl.20, 25**

Other names: Black-cheeked Falcon, Duck or Pigeon Hawk.

Field marks: 355–500 mm; span 900 mm. A famous large dynamic falcon: slate-blue above, mottled darker: white or creamy buff below, *unmarked upperbreast forming conspicuous pale bib*; lower breast and trousers finely barred black, they seem grey from a distance. Australian races have wholly black crown and cheeks. Bill blue-grey, tipped black; cere, eyering and legs yellow. Imm: dark-brown above including cheeks: finely margined pale-buff or rufous; buff to deep-buff below, breast *streaked or spotted blackish*; flanks and trousers with irregular V bars; cere, eyering and legs bluish. Singly, pairs, or family parties: perches in high exposed positions like dead limbs of tall trees, cliffs, broadcasting pylons. Flight magnificent and often memorable: soars with wings flat, elegantly tapered, tail fanned, white bib prominent: wingbeats quick and shallow, broken by glides. In pursuit of prey, chases with hard lashing strokes or plummets at remarkable speed on half-closed or fully-closed wings, broad shoulders giving it the look of a feathered bomb. Sometimes hawks slowly for flying insects.

Similar species: Little Falcon (153): smaller and darker with white or buff forehead, throat and partial rear collar: finely streaked below: flight more dashing on pointed wings. Brown Falcon (155): from imm. Peregrine by double cheek-mark, breast blotched or wholly brown or white with fine dark streaks: note flight. Grey Falcon (154): more uniform pale-grey, wingtips blackish: soars with wings more upswept.

Voice: Rapid hoarse complaining staccato 'chak-chak-chak-chak'. When uttered at intruder near nest, rises to angry pitch as bird dives. Near nest, high thin 'keer-keer-keer'. Male: voice higher-pitched.

Habitat: Coastal or inland cliffs and gorges, timbered watercourses, generally near rivers and swamps, plains, open woodlands: occasionally on spires or ledges of buildings.

Breeding: No nest built. Eggs: 2–3: pale-buff heavily and uniformly marked reddish-chestnut: laid on bare ledge, rock-crevice or in large tree-hollow, often deserted nest of another bird of prey or corvid.

Range and Status: Throughout Aust. and Tas.: generally uncommon, probably declining in settled regions: still well established in remote areas. Sedentary, nomadic or part-migratory. Almost cosmopolitan, but not NZ.

153 LITTLE FALCON   *Falco longipennis*   Pl.20, 25

Other names: Australian Hobby, Black-faced or Duck Hawk, Little Duck-Hawk, White-fronted Falcon.

Field marks: 350 mm: span 825 mm. Smallest Australian falcon: dark and long-winged, flight dashing and at times almost swift-like. Slate-blue to blackish above, darker on head: note diagnostic head pattern: *white or buff forehead, throat and partial rear collar*: black cheek-mark down from crown. Rufous underparts and trousers streaked blackish, flanks occasionally marked with blue-grey V-bars. Bill blue-grey tipped blackish: cere, eyering and legs yellow. Imm: feathers of upperparts margined rusty: more dusty rufous below: cere, skin eyering and legs bluish. Usually seen in swift slicing flight over treetops, but occasionally soars: female may then be momentarily confused with Peregrine (152) but no white bib. Determined hunter, flying small birds down with lashing wingbeats: occasionally kills much larger birds, e.g. ducks, herons: hawks for flying insects, eating them in flight.

Similar species: Peregrine (152): large white or pale-buff 'bib': broader wings, squarer tail: tends to fly higher, soar more: imm. Peregrine is also buffish and streaked below, but lacks partial rear collar. Spine-tailed Swift (394): can be mistaken for small dark male but note white throat and under tail-coverts.

Voice: Shrill rapid-fire peevish 'kee-kee-kee-kee-kee', more twittering, less mellow, than Nankeen Kestrel (156).

Habitat: Typically open country with large trees and timbered watercourses, but also timbered ranges to nearly treeless plains (e.g. Nullarbor). Often seen over cities, especially parks and gardens: well-vegetated suburbs.

Breeding: Nest: of sticks, large for size of bird: usually in top of tall living tree: disused nest of other species may be used. Eggs: 2–4: heavily marbled red-brown, sometimes as cap at large end.

Range and Status: Aust. and Tas.: generally uncommon: vagrant (? winter migrant) s. NG. Also New Britain, Moluccas, Lesser Sunda Is.

154 GREY FALCON   *Falco hypoleucos*   Pl.20, 25

Other names: Blue or Smoke Hawk.

Field marks: 330–430 mm: span up to 900 mm. A *pale smoke-grey falcon* of the inland and nw.: crown dark-grey, dark streak down through eye: *cere, eyering and legs conspicuously orange-yellow*, eye dark-brown. Imm: darker, heavily mottled brownish grey above, cheek-mark darker, underparts more heavily streaked: cere, eyering and legs bluish. Female larger than male: in flight has heavy-shouldered, bomb-like silhouette. When soaring, note tapered wings, *underwing pale-grey with darkish tips, wings slightly upswept toward tips*. Flies with slightly flickering shallow beats, more leisurely than Peregrine (152) but drops on prey at great speed.

Similar species: Grey Goshawk (144): finely-barred underparts: no moustache-mark: soars on rounded wings or flies with quick wingbeats and glides. Australian Black-shouldered (134) and Letter-winged (135) Kites.

Voice: Somewhat hoarse Peregrine-like 'chak-chak-chak-chak' or loud 'cluck-cluck-cluck-cluck'.

Habitat: Open habitats: semi-deserts, grassy inland plains, timbered watercourses, pastoral lands.

Breeding: Usually uses old nest of another species. Eggs: 2–4: pink-buff, heavily marbled red-brown.

Range and Status: Inland and drier coastal parts of all mainland States. Rare: sedentary or nomadic.

155 BROWN FALCON   *Falco berigora*   **Pl.20, 25**

Other names: Brown, Cackling, Striped Brown, White-breasted or Chicken Hawk.
Field marks: 405–510 mm: span 900 mm. Less robust in build and actions than a typical falcon: perhaps most readily identified by flight and behaviour. Plumage very variable but two features are constant: (1) *double moustache-mark enclosing paler cheek-patch*: (2) buff to pale red-brown 'notching' of flight and tail-feathers. Dark phase: some are nearly uniform sooty-brown, others show faint facial markings and feather-notchings as above: in flight, always with *somewhat glossy pale undersides of flight-feathers contrasting with dark wing-linings*. Typical phases: brown above, whitish below with irregular brown to yellow-buff patches, brown trousers. Pale phases: pale reddish brown above, whitish below with fine dark streaks, trousers pale or rusty. Cere, eyering and legs lead-grey or putty-coloured, legs longish, rather slender. Singly, pairs or loose companies. Rather tame except at nest: perches upright on dead trees, telephone poles, fences: makes sloping descent to seize prey on ground: pursues insects on foot. Sometimes flies with falcon-like despatch on backswept wings *but usually with loose deep 'rowing' beats of angled gull-wings: soars high on markedly upswept wings, tail fanned. Performs noisy display-flights, tumbling and diving with wings in stiff V, body swinging from side to side:* hovers clumsily.
Similar species: Black Falcon (151): much more rugged and robust with powerful feet; in flight, less contrast in underwing. Peregrine Falcon (152), imm: dark-brown cheeks and upperparts, more rufous below with regular streaks: trousers barred: far more vigorous and dashing. Fork-tailed Kite (137). Australian Goshawk (142), imm: bold pattern of brown splashes and bars on whitish breast, long tail. Note flight.
Voice: Probably noisiest Australian raptor; screeches, demented hoarse cacklings, at times like laying hen.
Habitat: General: from clearings in mountain forests to open woodlands and treeless plains: farmlands, roadsides, coastal dunes.
Breeding: Uses nest of crow or other hawk: occasionally builds a stick-nest, or lays in tree-hollow, when no material used. Eggs: 2–4: buff-white, heavily mottled red-brown.
Range and Status: Aust. and Tas.: common to very common: sedentary or nomadic. Also NG.

156 NANKEEN KESTREL   *Falco cenchroides*   **Pl.20, 21, 25**

Other names: Hoverer, Mosquito Hawk, Sparrowhawk, Windhover.
Field marks: 300–355 mm: span *c*. 750 mm. A distinctive small falcon often noticed hovering over paddocks and roadsides: *pale rufous above, with contrasting black flight-feathers*, whitish below, black mark down through eye, fine black streaks on breast. Cere, eyering and legs yellow. Slight sexual differences – male: crown and tail pale-grey: in female these are light rufous-brown, tail finely barred. Imm: like female, more mottled above. Singly, pairs or family parties: perches on dead trees, telephone posts and wires: its most conspicuous behaviour is to *hover motionless before dropping on prey*: overhead looks whitish, wingtips black, tail with subterminal black band, conspicuous in male. Soars round city buildings and spires, where it often breeds: family parties play in air currents.
Similar species: Australian Black-shouldered (134) and Letter-winged (135) Kites. Brown Falcon (155), pale phase: much larger, with double cheek-mark, plumage usually more mottled and streaked. Often has rusty 'trousers', no dark tail-band.
Voice: Shrill excited rapid-fire 'keekeekeekeekee': near nest and when playing: thin squealing 'keer keer keer'.
Habitat: Plains, open foothills, coastal dunes and cliffs: farmlands, market-gardens, city buildings, railyards.
Breeding: Eggs laid on decayed debris in hollow of tree, on bare earth of cavity in cliff or cave: occasionally in old nest of other hawk, crow, chough, or in cavity or ledge in building. Eggs: 3–5: pale-buff, closely mottled reddish-brown.
Range and Status: Suitable habitat throughout Aust. and Tas.: common in s., uncommon

in coastal n. Sedentary, nomadic or part-migratory. Vagrant NZ, Norfolk I. Also Lord Howe I., NG, Moluccas, Java, some possibly as winter migrants from Aust.

Mound Builders   Family *Megapodiidae*

Specialized fowls that differ from other birds in manner of incubation. Their large clutches are laid in incubating mounds of decomposing vegetation mixed with earth or sand, or in sand heated by sun or thermal activity. Some have complex routines for maintaining the internal temperatures of these mounds; in particular Malleefowl (158) uses remarkable techniques to create suitable incubation conditions despite an unfavourable climate. Most megapodes have powerful legs and feet; hence their name, which means 'great-footed'. Living mainly on ground in dense tropical or subtropical forests or dry scrubs, they have dark plumage or disruptive patterns. Some have bare coloured heads, necks and wattles, especially in males these enlarge and intensify in colour when breeding. All fly well, if heavily; they usually roost in trees; some noisy.

Food: Insects, soil invertebrates, generally; herbs, seeds, fallen fruits, small vertebrates; some feed at rubbish tips, glean in stubblefields.

Range: Australian and Polynesian region including islands of se. Asia, w. to Nicobar Is. in Indian Ocean.

Number of species: World 12; Aust. 3.

157 SCRUBFOWL *Megapodius reinwardt*   Pl.17

Other names: Jungle-fowl, Scrub hen; Orange-footed Scrubfowl.

Field marks: 455 mm. A large dark small-headed fowl *with short crest, bare yellow skin round eye and powerful orange legs and feet.* Usually in pairs; active, noisy, especially at dawn, dusk and during night: when disturbed, runs quickly or flaps heavily to low branch, sits motionless with outstretched neck.

Similar species: Brush-Turkey (159).

Voice: Raucous loud double crow; also cluckings, like protesting domestic fowl.

Habitat: Rainforests and scrubs; occasionally mangroves.

Breeding: Nest: enormous mound of earth and vegetation or of sand, some up to 12 m in diam. and 5 m high but usually much smaller; particularly when new. Eggs: yellowish-white to pale-pink, becoming stained pale-brown or dark red-brown. Laid singly in deep excavations in mound; at times in decaying leaves in fissures in sun-heated rocks or in sand. Number uncertain.

Range and Status: Coastal n. Aust. and many coastal islands: from Kimberleys, WA, to e. Arnhem Land and Groote Eylandt, NT; in Q, from Weipa to C. York and islands in Torres Strait, s. on e. coast to near Byfield, Q. Common; sedentary. Also Nicobar Is. (Indian Ocean); Java and Lesser Sunda Is.; Borneo, Philippines, Moluccas, NG to Solomon Is. and New Hebrides.

158 MALLEEFOWL *Leipoa ocellata*   Pl.17

Other names: Gnow, Lowan, Malleehen, Native Pheasant, Pheasant.

Field marks: 550–610 mm. A large quiet-moving fowl, *barred grey, black, buff, white and pale-chestnut above; head and neck grey with prominent black mark down centre of breast;* slim inconspicuous black crest, seldom evident unless crown-feathers raised. Bill black; legs and feet dark-grey, powerful. Singly or pairs; parties of a dozen or more sometimes feed together in wheat stubble near scrub. Wary, watchful; freezes when approached or moves away cautiously; when startled, bursts up over trees with heavy flapping. Dust-bathes, basks; during heat of day lies in shade of bushes; roosts in trees.

Voice: Male: deep three-noted booming with bellowing inflection, may carry far. Female: harsh far-carrying high-pitched crow. Also soft crooning notes, low grunts.

Habitat: Mallee and other scrubs, open scrubby eucalypt woodlands; exceptionally iron-bark forest, dry coastal heaths. Optimum habitats include sandy soils.

Breeding: Incubation mound: 2–5 m diameter and up to 1 m high; formed by filling excavation in sand or soil with dry leaves, twigs, bark. Left open to winter rains, damp material then covered with sand. Male daily works mound until temperature from decomposition stabilizes at about 33°C. Female lays 16–33 eggs singly at intervals of up to a week, while male regulates temperature, later in season uses sun-warmed sand. Eggs: very pale-pink at first, deepening to pale-brown. Chick hatches underground after approximately 7 weeks, digs way to surface. Precocious, wholly independent, able to flutter within a day.

Range and Status: Inland and w. Aust. s. of Tropic, *excluding Q*: in NSW n. to about Cobar, e. to Goonoo Forest, (*c.* 27 km e. of Dubbo) and Ingalba NR, near Temora; mallee areas of nw. Vic., e. to about Inglewood (recent report from Bendigo 'whipstick' mallee), s. to Little Desert; in SA, mallee areas of se., Murray mallee, Yorke and Eyre Pens., n. patchily to NT; in s. NT, n. to about Central Mt. Wedge; in s. WA, fairly wide-spread except heavy forests, cleared and settled areas, n. to about Rawlinson Ra.–C. Farquhar, near Tropic. Introduced Kangaroo I., probably extinct. Moderately common in most suitable habitat, otherwise scarce. Distribution and status much affected by clearing land and by food-competition from rabbits, sheep. Sedentary.

159 BRUSH-TURKEY *Alectura lathami*   Pl.17

Other names: Scrub or Wild Turkey; Yellow-wattled Brush-turkey.

Field marks: 585–700 mm. A large black fowl with prominent tail flattened sideways. Note *bare red skin of head and neck, bright-yellow wattle on lower neck*, more prominent in breeding male. (Race *purpureicollis* has bluish white wattle). Singly, pairs or parties: wary: when alarmed runs into undergrowth; pressed, flies heavily up into trees, gaining height with flapping leaps from limb to limb. Roosts high in trees during heat of day and at night, descending with heavy flappings.

Similar species: Scrubfowl (157).

Voice: Deep, fairly loud 'kyok!', with nasal quality. Also loud cluckings, deep subdued grunts.

Habitat: Mainly coastal tropical, subtropical and temperate rainforests and scrubs to sub-inland brigalow scrubs in Q.

Breeding: Mound averages approximately 4 m across by 1–2 m high, but very variable: of leaves and other plant material mixed with earth, kept friable by constant turning over. Material typically raked downhill to mound, baring ground. Male does most construction, regulates temperature at about 35°C. Eggs: white, fragile; average clutch 12–16; laid singly, at intervals of days. Incubation period about 7 weeks. Young dig way to surface unaided; precocious, independent.

Range and Status: Coastal e. Aust. and islands: from C. York to about Broken Bay, NSW, and nearer Sydney. In Q, ranges inland to about nw. of Charters Towers–Blackall–Augathella; in NSW mostly on and coastward of Divide, but reported from Pilliga scrub, Boggabri district. Near Sydney, recent records from near Glen Davis and Kurrajong, and from Macquarie Pass, Illawarra district, where formerly resident, but generally believed extinct. Introduced Dunk I., Q, and Kangaroo I., SA; feral birds (and mound) reported near Steiglitz, Vic. The distinctive small race *purpureicollis* occupies n. part of range on n. C. York Pen. s. to about Mitchell R. on w. coast and to near Cooktown in e. Common to uncommon and patchy; sedentary.

True Quails, Pheasants and Fowls Family *Phasianidae*
Button quails (Bustard-quails) Family *Turnicidae*
Plains wanderers Family *Pedionomidae*

Although only two of these families are closely related, they are treated together because of similarity in appearance and habits. Except for the introduced Domestic Fowl (164), Ring-necked Pheasant (165) and Californian Quail (166), members of the *Phasianidae* in Aust. are typical quails: small, plump, ground-living birds, almost tailless with short bills and legs, four toes and typically short wings for sudden swift flight; they are usually nomadic and partly nocturnal. Most have protectively patterned plumage and are shy; when disturbed, they squat, run or burst up with a whirr of wings. They maintain contact with brisk calls. Most exhibit sexual dimorphism; in two, females are larger and more boldly marked than males, but in King Quail (162) the reverse applies. Although superficially similar to true quails, Button-quails *Turnicidae* are probably related to rails, resembling true quails through convergence. Plump rather sturdy billed birds of richly streaked brown, buff, grey, rufous and black plumage, they lack a hind toe and differ from true quails in other ways. The large colourful females initiate courtship, typically using deep 'ooming' notes; the males brood the eggs and attend the young. Some are partly nocturnal. The family *Pedionomidae* has only one member, Plains-wanderer (173), of inland se. Aust. A rare bird of some mystery both in taxonomy and status, it combines characters of both the above families in having the hind toe of a true quail, but the brighter female plumage, polyandrous habits and voice of a button-quail.

Food: (all families) Insects; seeds of native plants and introduced cereals, legumes and weeds; other vegetation.

Number of species: *Phasianidae*: World 178; Aust. 7 (4 introduced). *Turnicidae*: World 15; Aust. 7. *Pedionomidae*: World 1; Aust. 1.

160 STUBBLE QUAIL *Coturnix pectoralis* Pl.30

Other names: Grey or Pectoral Quail.

Field marks: 175–195 mm; female larger. Perhaps our best-known quail. Male: pale-brown above, finely marbled darker and with overlying pattern of fine cream bars and *long pointed cream streaks*: three cream streaks on head start at bill – one along centre of crown, others back over each eye; *note clearly defined rich-buff throat*; *thick black streaks form blackish patch on white breast*. Female: throat pale; underparts fawn, *heavily mottled darker, buff wash in zone round upperbreast*. Bill blue-horn, legs yellow to pale olive-buff. Imm: like female but broad band of sparser irregular blackish brown spots across breast. Singly, pairs or open companies: usually first noticed by call or when flushed unexpectedly. Flies straight, far and fast with rapid whirr of wings, twisting slightly; drops tail-first into grass. Runs quickly in spurts.

Similar species: Little Button-quail (171): much smaller, bill heavier, eye pale; in flight, sandy or cinnamon rump with white sides. Brown Quail (161): uniformly darker, no distinct eyebrow, underparts finely V-barred blackish.

Voice: Brisk clear 'pippy-wheat!'; deep purring, may become 'almost a bellowing'.

Habitat: Typical habitat now appears to be cereal crops, stubble, lucerne and other crops, pastures; rank grasslands often with thistles; saltbush, bluebush, spinifex associations.

Breeding: Eggs: 5–11; dirty yellow to buffish or brownish finely and uniformly smudged and blotched dark-olive to red-brown; laid in scrape in ground, progressively lined with grass as incubation proceeds.

Range and Status: Aust. and Tas.; erratic but generally common in e., se. and coastal WA; sparse c. Aust., Kimberleys, NT and e. coastal Q; possibly absent C. York Pen.; rare Tas. Nomadic and/or migratory.

161 BROWN QUAIL *Coturnix australis* **Pl.30**

Other names: Swamp, Partridge or Silver Quail, Swamp Partridge, Tasmanian Swamp Quail or Quail.

Field marks: 175–205 mm. Largest native quail; usually looks plump and fairly dark, but colour variable; greyish or suffused warm-buff above, yellow-buff below. Very finely and uniformly streaked silver above, but when seen well the best field mark is the *fine dense pattern of wavy black barring* on the buff-grey underparts. There is a narrow stripe down centre of crown and a faint eyebrow. Bill blue-grey, tip black, legs yellowish. Female: larger than male and more heavily marked. Singly, pairs or coveys up to a dozen. occasionally (e.g. King and other Bass Strait islands) 100 +; moves very fast in spurts, bounces and bounds. Flushes noisily with a quick call, individual birds often explode in different directions; flight fast and strong.

Similar species: Stubble Quail (160): much bolder pale streaks above, paler below, without fine and close barring. King Quail (162), female: much smaller; somewhat similar breast pattern, but pale throat more distinctly separated.

Voice: A fairly loud whistled 'f-weep', 'tu-weeeee' or 'bee-quick, bee-quick': rising at end: uttered at frequent intervals. When flushed, sharp chirp or quick, rather fluty chatter. Calls heard often early morning, late afternoon and at night.

Habitat: Rank vegetation on low wet swampy ground, heavy pasture in damp paddocks, clover, lucerne, rice stubbles; grassy woodlands; in coastal areas, swampy heaths of sword grass and melaleuca and banksia-thickets.

Breeding: Eggs 7–11; dull bluish white to yellow-white, uniformly freckled olive or light-brown; laid in slight hollow under tuft of grass, lined with few grass stems and leaves. Tas. eggs distinctive, generally yellowish olive.

Range and Status: Better-watered parts of n. and e. Aust., Tas., sw. WA and coastal islands. Two forms are present in se. Aust. and Tas.; Condon, 1975 Checkl. Birds Aust., 1. treats the larger of these as a separate species, *C. ypsilophora*, Swamp Quail. Common, if frequently very local, in suitable habitat. Sedentary; perhaps nomadic in sub-inland when conditions suitable. Also NG, Lesser Sunda Is. Introduced Fiji and NZ.

162 KING QUAIL *Coturnix chinensis* **Pl.30**

Other names: Chestnut-bellied, Dwarf, Least or Little Swamp Quail.

Field marks: 115–135 mm. Male tiny: *bold black-and-white pattern on throat*, blue-grey breast, rich-chestnut underparts. Female: like miniature Brown Quail (161) but darker above, with heavier cream streaking; *whitish-buff throat cleanly separated from patterned breast*. Crown blacker, buff eyebrow broader; black line back from bill under eye and down neck. Bill grey-horn, eye brown; legs yellow-orange. Shy and hard to see; disturbed, runs or flies feebly a short distance, tail down, before dropping into dense cover.

Similar species: Little Button-quail (171): more cinnamon than female King, white below, bill much heavier, eye pale. Stubble Quail (160), female.

Voice: An elfin penetrating crow in two or three high-pitched descending notes: uttered day or night.

Habitat: Swampy heaths, dense wet native grasslands, weed-grown pastures, lucerne, crops; in coastal NT, dry sedge-plains, rice stubble.

Breeding: Eggs: 4–9; very small, pale-green, olive-yellow to pale-brown, uniformly and finely peppered reddish to blackish brown, more thickly at larger end; laid in slight hollow sheltered by tussock, at first scantily lined with grass, but improved as incubation proceeds, and hooded.

Range and Status: Coastal n., e. and se. Aust. and some coastal islands w. to Yorke Pen., SA. Confined to (often isolated) areas of suitable habitat; rare NSW, Vic. SA (?) sedentary. Also India–Sri Lanka to se. China, se Asia, Philippines, Indonesia, NG, Bismarck Archipelago. Introduced elsewhere.

163 PEAFOWL   *Pavo cristatus*

Other name: Peacock (may be used for either sex).
Field marks: 2–2.4 m including train. Male well known and unmistakable: train consists of *abnormally long glossy dark blue-green upper tail-coverts with many golden blue 'eyes'*; raised fanlike and concave in display, supported by the short rufous tail-feathers. Female: ('peahen') grey and patterned above, whitish below, without spectacular train. Singly, pairs or parties; polygamous. Feeds on ground, but flies heavily aloft to roost; noisy. A non-albino white form has been developed.
Voice: A loud discordant descending wail, bugle or crow.
Habitat: Coastal scrubs, house and public gardens, sanctuaries, grounds or surroundings of country homesteads.
Breeding: scrape in ground, usually under cover. Eggs: 3–5; brownish-buff.
Range and Status: Native to India and Sri Lanka: long-domesticated, introduced many parts of world, including Aust., Tas. and some islands. Isolated semi-feral populations, usually near settlement.

164 DOMESTIC FOWL   *Gallus gallus*

Note: The many domestic varieties are well-known. They are probably all descended from the Red Junglefowl *Gallus gallus*. Birds released on two Gt. Barrier Reef islands are reported to resemble the original ancestor, described as follows:
Field marks: 430–750 mm (including tail of male). Male: *red comb, facial skin and lappets*; chestnut to orange-red neck-hackles; *white or red ear-patch*; upperparts dark-red, and glossy blue-green; primaries and underparts black; *prominent 'cock's tail' glossy green*. Female: *facial skin red, neck streaked dark-brown and buff*; otherwise mottled dark-brown, breast more chestnut; tail brown, less-developed. Legs grey or brown.
Voice: High-pitched crow, cacklings.
Habitat: Thick scrub and woodland on islands.
Breeding: Nest: 'Usually on ground among fallen tree trunks, or up in a cavity in the base of a large *Pisonia*'. Eggs: 10–13; white.
Range and Status: Junglefowl: s. and se. Asia, Philippines, Sumatra and Java; introduced elsewhere. Domestic strains: worldwide. Feral birds resembling the ancestral type are present on North West and Heron Is., Capricorn Group, Q, as a result of release of domesticated strains in late 19th or early 20th century. In recent years the Heron I. population was reported to have declined, but to have increased since 1969.

165 RING-NECKED PHEASANT   *Phasianus colchichus*   Pl.17

Other names: Chinese Ringneck, Mongolian or Versicolour Pheasant.
Field marks: ♂ 760–890, ♀ 530–660 mm. A traditional game-bird in n. hemisphere. Male: colourful; *head glossy dark-green with horns, scarlet wattle and, in some, white neck-ring*; body-plumage of rich burnished reds; wings rounded, tail long pointed crossed with fine black bars. Female: *pale-brown with buff and blackish mottlings*; no wattle or horns, tail shorter. Wary, runs, flushes with noisy flapping.
Similar species: Superb Lyrebird (413), sometimes called Native Pheasant, unbarred grey-brown plumage; see Habitat and Range. Pheasant Coucal (375): note range.
Voice: Male: stident crow, 'korrk-kok!', often followed by flutter of wings; utters somewhat similar harsh note on being flushed.
Habitat: Scrubby eucalypt forest and woodlands, coastal scrubs, swamp paperbark thickets, rank grasslands, crops.
Breeding: Nest: scrape in ground, usually under grass, bracken, ferns. Eggs: 7–15; uniform olive-brown.
Range and Status: Introduced from British Isles, where itself much earlier introduced from Eurasia. Continuing local introduction from captive stock. Feral populations

Rottnest I., WA; King I. (and more recently, Flinders I.) Bass Strait and in other parts of Tas.; s. tablelands NSW; possibly ACT; Mt. Lofty Ras, SA.

166 CALIFORNIAN QUAIL *Lophortyx californicus*
Other name: Bob-white Quail (King I.).
Field marks: 240–260 mm. Large and distinctive, the only quail in Aust. *with small nodding black head-plume*, set off by brown crown, white forehead and eyebrow, large black throat-patch with white border. Grey-brown above, upperbreast blue-grey, flanks grey streaked white; underparts whitish, cream and chestnut in centre, all with strong scaly pattern formed by black feather-margins. Female duller, browner; no black-and-white facial pattern, shorter crest. In coveys, shy; runs with nodding topknot: flight explosive.
Voice: Three syllabled 'qua-quergo', rather lost and plaintive.
Habitat: Rank grassland in scrubs, stunted woodlands; dense tea-tree thickets.
Breeding: Nest: hollow in ground lined with grass. Eggs: 10–16; buff with dark spots.
Range and Status: Native to w. n. America; introduced to parts NSW, Vic., Tas., from 1863; also to NZ, where now widespread. In Aust., most introductions failed but remains fairly common King I., Bass Strait, where first-established from NZ about 1920. Sight-record Wonthaggi, Vic., about May 1965. Sedentary.

167 RED-BACKED BUTTON-QUAIL *Turnix maculosa* **Pl.30**
Other names: Black-backed, Black-spotted, Orange-breasted or Red-collared Quail.
Field marks: ♂ 120, ♀ 150 mm. Varies geographically; female larger, more boldly-coloured and marked than male. Constant features are: (1) *slender yellow to horn-coloured bill* (2) pale eye (3) female's *rufous to rich-chestnut sides of neck and hindneck*. Race *pseutes* of coastal nw. Aust., female: deep-rufous sides of head and flanks. Race *melanota* of e. Q – e. NSW, female: less richly coloured (yellow-buff sides of head and breast) but with black spots on upperparts and sides. Male (both races): paler, without rich colourings. Best identified by bill, and by accompanying females. Pairs, coveys; reported to be not easily flushed, but when it is, flies fast and far to cover. Following points have been described from a field observation in NSW. Female: unmistakable rufous patch on upper back; contrasting blackish markings on back and rump; indication of small (black) spots on sides of upperbreast; belly whitish. Male: slightly smaller, generally paler, no rufuous patch. Tame round habitation on some Gt. Barrier Reef islands.
Similar species: No other button-quail has such conspicuous rufous patch on hindneck, nor a fine yellowish bill. Note range and habitat.
Voice: Monotonous 'oom-oom-oom'; also described as subdued booming.

Habitat: Low marshy ground, damp coastal scrubs; grasslands, wetlands; pastures, cereal crops, lucerne.

Breeding: Eggs: 2–4; very glossy; pale slate-grey, almost entirely hidden by brown spots and larger blotches of dark-grey. Laid in hollow scantily lined with grass, protected by tuft of grass or low shrub.

Range and Status: Disjunct distribution in nw. and e. Aust., including islands in NT and Gt. Barrier Reef. Race *pseutes*: mostly coastal from e. Kimberleys, WA, to Arnhem Land and Groote Eylandt, NT. Race *melanota*: from C. York, Q, inland to Atherton Tableland to se. NSW; vagrant c. Vic. Recent NSW records: eggs from Southgate, near Grafton, sight-records from near Ballina to Diamond Head, near Taree; also near Braidwood (s. tablelands) and Finley, Riverina district, where breeding recorded. Common n. Aust. and some Gt. Barrier Reef islands; rare se. Aust. It has been suggested that heavy summer and autumn rains in e. Aust. cause a large increase in numbers. Sedentary and nomadic. Many other races from Philippines, Celebes, Lesser Sunda Is., NG, Solomon Is.

168   PAINTED BUTTON-QUAIL   *Turnix varia*   Pl.30

Other names: Butterfly, Dotterel, Scrub, Speckled or Varied Quail.

Field marks: ♂ 165, ♀ 190 mm. A quail of rich shades and patterns. *Note fine black-and-white spotting on forehead and side of face, pale-chestnut sides to neck*; breast cream-grey with large creamish spots at sides. Male: smaller, duller than female, less chestnut on neck. Bill blue-horn, eye red, legs deep yellow. Singly or small coveys; dust-bathes, scratches in debris. Runs quickly in spurts, head high; when startled flies very fast, weaving through trees on longish rather pointed wings; usually goes far before dropping and running.

Similar species: Chestnut-backed Button-quail (169).

Voice: Female: bronzewing-like 'oom, oom, oom', standing tiptoe with chest inflated. Often at night.

Habitat: Scrublands, woodlands or forests where ground is littered with fallen limbs, leaves, rocks, low shrubs; coastal tea-tree and banksia-scrubs; mallee; rank grasslands, heaths.

Breeding: Nest: slight depression lined with grass and leaves, often with partial canopy; in shelter of tussock, log, base of tree or rock. Eggs: 4; whitish, finely freckled with blue and brown over entire surface and some sparser reddish brown spots.

Range and Status: Coastal and sub-coastal e. se. and sw. Aust. and coastal islands with suitable habitat: from about Cairns, Q, to Tas., w. to Eyre Pen. and Kangaroo I., SA, n. to s. Flinders Ras; in sw. WA, from Dempsters Inlet, near Fitzgerald R., n. to Shark Bay and several of the Abrolhos Is. Widespread but nowhere common; nomadic, movements erratic.

169   CHESTNUT-BACKED BUTTON-QUAIL   *Turnix castanota*   Pl.30

Other names: Buff-backed, Buff-breasted or Olive's Quail.

Field marks: 170–220 mm. Very like Painted Button-quail (168), but more *cinnamon or sandy above with much heavier, dull-blue bill*. Birds from n. and nw. Aust. most like Painted but wings with more conspicuously broken white spots and streaks. Female larger, brighter. Females of e. race *olivei* are *large and plain – bill very robust*; pale-chestnut to *sandy cinnamon above with few darker white-edged feathers on mantle and wings; upper-breast plain grey-buff*. Both sexes – eye and legs yellow. In coveys, when disturbed, disperses running, head carried high like Painted; takes wing only when pressed and then for short distance; note pale-cinnamon or pale-chestnut rump.

Similar species: Painted Button-quail (168): note range.

Voice: Low 'oom'.

Habitat: Light woodlands, dry scrublands; stony hillsides, sandstone ridges. Race *olivei*: coastal heaths.

Breeding: Nest: shallow depression in shelter of tussock. Eggs: 4: whitish, finely freckled dark-brown with faint larger spots of purple-brown.

Range and Status: Coastal n. Aust. in broken distribution. Nominate race: from Kimberleys, WA, to top end NT, s. to Larrimah and e. to Macarthur R.; also Melville I. and Groote Eylandt. Race *olivei*: Coen–Cooktown ne. Q. This form is treated by Condon, 1975. Checkl. Birds Aust., 1. as a separate species, Buff-breasted Button-quail, *T. olivei*.

170 BLACK-BREASTED BUTTON-QUAIL *Turnix melanogaster* Pl.30

Other names: Black-breasted Turnix, Black-fronted Quail.

Field marks: ♂ 165, ♀ 190 mm. Female: unlike any other Australian quail: *eye white, head and breast black with massed prominent white spots*; grey-brown above, marbled black and chestnut, and with white black-edged streaks; in sum, a spangled appearance. Bill stout, longish, legs reddish. Male: smaller, no solid black on head and breast, *but heavily mottled black on upperbreast; note white spangling above*. Imm: dark-brown above, marbled rufous and heavily marked with black; greyish below, tipped pale-cream and crossed with black Vs, giving patterned appearance. Pairs or coveys: when feeding makes 'soup-plate' depressions in debris of forest-floor with wings and feet. Stands motionless, difficult to see. Flies reluctantly, preferring to run.

Voice: Female: deep 'oo-oom, oo-oom, oo-oom'.

Habitat: Leaf-strewn floors of drier tropical and subtropical rainforests, vine scrubs and adjacent thickets, including *Lantana*; occasionally in pastures.

Breeding: Eggs: 2–4: grey-white, finely freckled blue-grey over entire surface with bolder splotches of blackish brown and underlying blotches of blue-grey: laid in slight depression in ground in leaf-mould of forest-floor.

Range and Status: Coastal e. Q, from about Broad Sound, inland to n. of Rockhampton, Cooyar, ne. of Dalby–Cunningham's Gap, s. to ne. NSW: rare vagrant s. NSW, Vic. Rare, probably sedentary.

171 LITTLE BUTTON-QUAIL *Turnix velox* Pl.30

Other names: Butterfly, Dotterel or Swift-flying Quail.

Field marks: 125–140 mm. A small quail *with heavy blue-grey bill and pale eye*. Female: pale-brown, tawny or rich-cinnamon above, suffused with grey (each feather with black 'ladder-markings' and edged white in two parallel streaks); *whitish fawn below* washed buff on sides of neck or across breast; legs flesh-white to yellowish. Male: smaller, with pattern of darker feather-margins on sides of neck and breast. Singly, pairs or loose flocks; runs like mouse, squats; flushes with quick call, flies low and fast, appears to turn in air and drop into cover, *exposing sandy or cinnamon white-edged rump and whitish underparts*. Often active at night; associates with Stubble Quail (160).

Similar species: King Quail (162), female; Red-backed (167) and Red-chested (172) Button-quail.

Voice: Low, indeterminate 'oom oom' often at night. When flushed, squeaking note or quick 'chek chek'.

Habitat: Grasslands, plains, creekflats, open woodlands; in n. Aust., burned areas newly green after rains; also saltbush, spinifex, light mulga and other scrubs; crops, pastures, stubble.

Breeding: Nest: scanty; of grass; in hollow in shelter of tuft. Eggs: 3–4; buffish white, thickly spotted and blotched with slate-grey and chestnut with some spots of purple-brown.

Range and Status: Mainland Aust. *except* Kimberleys, top end NT, C. York Pen. Rare e. coastal areas. Highly nomadic, abundant in good years, in others apparently absent from large parts of range. Fairly regular spring–summer visitor in s. Aust. Uncommon to locally common. Nomadic or part-migratory.

172 RED-CHESTED BUTTON-QUAIL *Turnix pyrrhothorax* Pl.30

Other names: Chestnut-breasted, Red-breasted or Yellow Quail; Red-chested Turnix.
Field marks: 130–160 mm. Common name somewhat misleading; a small heavy-billed white-eyed quail that can be confused with Little Button-quail (171). Female: larger and brighter than male; *throat and upperbreast rich yellow-buff*; forehead and sides of face finely freckled white, line of white spots down centre of crown. Male: *more plentiful dark scaly markings on sides of neck and breast*. Pairs or small coveys; often difficult to flush; flies swiftly only a short distance before dropping to cover. In flight, look for heavy bill and yellow-buff chest; rump and tail brown, edged orange by feathers of flanks, unlike white flanks of Little.
Similar species: Little Button-quail (171): more cinnamon above, whiter below. Red-backed Button-quail (167): thin yellow bill, rufous patch on hindneck (female), black spots on wing and flanks.
Voice: Sharp chatter when flushed; low ooms.
Habitat: Light to medium-timbered country with good cover of long grasses; also bluebush, saltbush, light mulga and mallee-scrubs, native pines. In e. inland NSW reported mostly in pastures of native grasses and in lucerne and wheat stubble with good cover of grasses and weeds.
Breeding: Eggs: 4; buff-white, spotted slate-grey, chestnut and dark-brown, markings less dense than Little Button-quail; laid in slight depression scantily lined with grass, usually protected by tuft, or in crop or wheat stubble.
Range and Status: N., e. and se. Aust.: from top end NT (occasional) and Barkly Tableland; sub-inland and subcoastal Q, n. to the lower Norman R., e. to upper Burdekin R.–Darling Downs; w. to upper Diamantina R.–Quilpie; in e. NSW in recent years reported numerous locations (with some breeding) mostly just inland of Divide but some coastal and s. tablelands; s. to Finley and far-w. to near Ivanhoe; in Vic., vagrant s. to near Melbourne (Melton, Keilor); L. Corangamite, Minyip; in SA, sparse records w. to Langhorne's Creek, Mt. Lofty Ras, Adelaide Plains. Generally sparse, locally common; highly nomadic.

173 PLAINS-WANDERER *Pedionomus torquatus* Pl.30

Other names: Collared Plains-wanderer, Plain wanderer or Turkey-Quail.
Field marks: ♂ 150, ♀ 175 mm. Lankier than a quail and more upright, head oddly angular. Female: distinctive, much larger than male; note longish straw-yellow bill and legs, whitish eye, rufous cheeks and *prominent white-spotted black collar above rich yellow-buff or rufous breastband*. Male: smaller and paler brown; no collar and breastband; throat grey-white, breast fawn, with unusual pattern of fine black rosettes or crescents on side of neck and upperbreast, sparser below. Juv: like male; darker on crown, upperparts more heavily scalloped; breast and flanks with dark *spots* rather than crescents. Moults directly into adult plumage. Usually solitary; runs like rat through grass, stands tip-toe for better view or crouches motionless. Seldom flies unless pressed; flight weaker and less direct than Stubble Quail (160), with a rather feeble dipping or fluttering motion, legs trailing; may perch.
Voice: Repeated ooming, not unlike a button-quail.
Habitat: Native grasslands, particularly when seeding; well-grassed, ungrazed paddocks, regenerating cereal stubble and (probably) cereal crops.
Breeding: Nest: scanty, of dry grasses; in depression, in shelter of low shrub, tuft of grass. Eggs: 3–4; somewhat pointed, stone-white, freckled, blotched and smudged with umber, brown and slate-grey.
Range and Status: Inland e. Aust.: in NSW, e. to about ACT–Bathurst, n. to about Orange–Condobolin, s. to Holbrook–Deniliquin and w. (? occasionally) to about Hay–Ivanhoe, vagrant to coast and cw. (Narrabri); (? formerly) to Darling Downs–lower Dawson R., se. Q; in Vic., occasional ne., widespread in c. and w., e. to Echuca-Tongala,

s. to Melbourne (where many early records in area of Sunbury–Keilor–Laverton–
Werribee–Rockbank), sw. to Camperdown, w. to Hamilton–Horsham, nw. to Birchip–
Nyah West districts; in SA, most records in se., in a band w. through Pinnaroo-Waikerie
to plains on St. Vincent Gulf n. of Adelaide, (? occasional) Yorke Pen. and s. Eyre Pen.,
(?) vagrant n. to L. Frome, and cw. and nw. (Bon Bon, Ingomar, Everard Park Stations).
Now very rare in closely-settled former strongholds e.g. near Melbourne but still fairly
well-established if sparse in some pastoral/cereal districts. Recent capture of live birds or
breeding records Tongala, Kerang, Swan Hill districts, Vic.; Narrandera district, NSW.
Generally rare; probably nomadic.

Crakes, Rails, Bush-hen, Native-hens, Swamphens, Moorhens, Coots Family *Rallidae*

Ground or swamp-dwelling birds with small heads, longish necks and legs and slender
toes (lobed in coots) for swimming, running, or walking on floating vegetation. Crakes
and rails in particular have narrow bodies for slipping through thick vegetation, hence
'thin as a rail'. Most have short tails flicked when walking or swimming. Wings are rather
rounded, flight apparently feeble (some cannot fly); but some typically make long migrations or shorter nomadic flights, mostly at night. Habitats vary; several rails and Bush-
hen (184) live in rainforest scrubs, others in mangroves, others only on floating swamp
vegetation. Native-hens favour open margins of rivers and swamps, pastures; swamphens
and moorhens vegetated swamps and grassy surroundings; Coot (189) is mainly aquatic,
diving for much of its food, often forming large flocks far from shore on open waters.
Most have strident shrieking clacking or purring voices. Sexes similar.

Food: Aquatic vegetation, seeds, grain, corn, insects, frogs, crustaceans, molluscs, small
reptiles, larger species occasionally predatory on young birds, mammals; a few take
scraps in parks, lakes in towns.

Range: Worldwide in non-polar regions.

Number of species: World 126; Aust. 16, including 2 accidental.

174 BANDED RAIL *Rallus philippensis*   Pl.31

Other names: Banded or Buff-banded Landrail, Corncrake, Buff-banded, Painted or
Pectoral Rail.

Field marks: 280–330 mm. A large elegant rail: note *grey eyebrow and rich-chestnut
crown, nape and stripe from bill through eye*; drab-olive above, finely flecked white; grey
breast crossed by buff band; underparts black, finely barried white. Imm: duller, no white
spots on back. Singly or in pairs; shy; mostly keeps to cover. Walks somewhat hunched,
tail raised and flicked incessantly; runs fast. Difficult to flush by day but active at dusk and
after dark. In flight note rounded wings, extended neck, trailing legs.

Similar species: Lewin's Rail (175): no eyebrow or breastband.

Voice: Sharp squeak like scratching a slate; sharp 'click click' notes; coos; thudding
grunts. A sharp 'crek' or squeak when flushed. A call 'coo-aw-ooo-aw-ooo-aw', 'somewhat like a braying donkey' has been described.

Habitat: Vegetation by swamps, streams; tussocks in wet paddocks and woodlands;
crops, rank pastures; samphire in brackish swamps or saltmarsh; homestead gardens,
arrives overnight in streets, tennis-courts, cattle-yards. On islands, drier sparser habitats.

Breeding: Nest: slight or substantial shallow cup of grass and leaves in tussock, sedge or
other vegetation. Eggs: 5–8 or more; roundish; off-white, pinkish, creamy or buff,
sparsely spotted and blotched red or chestnut-brown more heavily at large end, underlying spots and blotches of lilac-grey.

Range and Status: General in better watered parts of peripheral Aust. and Tas. and on
many islands. Erratic, nomadic inland and drier coastal areas after rain. Common to

uncommon and irregular. Widely distributed from Cocos-Keeling Is. (Indian Ocean), Lesser Sundas, Celebes and Moluccas through Australasia and Oceania.

175 LEWIN'S RAIL *Rallus pectoralis* Pl.31

Other names: Lewin Water Rail; Pectoral, Slate-breasted or Water Rail.

Field marks: 215–230 mm. A dark rail with a *long, dark-tipped, pink bill and rich-gingery tone to head and nape*; throat pale-grey, *breast slate-grey, washed olive*. Imm: dark grey with faint white barrings; no chestnut tones above, breast fawn-grey. Very shy, slips through reeds or grass on margins of swamps and creeks. Usually only flies if startled or when travelling at night; flight rather clumsy, legs trailing.

Similar species: Banded Rail (174).

Voice: Loud 'jik-jik-jik', answered by other individuals; may last thirty seconds, accelerating and becoming louder, then declining; pig-like grunts and a short sharp alarm-note.

Habitat: Rushes, reeds and rank grass in swamps and creeks, samphire cover in salt-marshes; heavily grassed paddocks.

Breeding: Nest: compact cup of fine grass and rushes, often with canopy of interlaced stems; with or without trampled ramp; near water to metre or more above it; usually in swamp or tussock, sedge or rush-clump. Eggs: 4–6; pale stone-colour to warm-bone, lightly spotted pinkish brown and more heavily with lavender-grey spots.

Range and Status: In Aust. from se. Q to Eyre Pen. and Kangaroo I., SA, inland to w. slopes of Divide; Tas. and far sw. WA. Occasional on e. coast to about Cairns. Uncommon to rare; nomadic. Also Flores and NG.

176 CHESTNUT RAIL *Eulabeornis castaneoventris* Pl.31

Other name: Chestnut-breasted Rail.

Field marks: 490–520 mm, male larger. A very unusual rail with *long greenish bill*; grey head, olive-brown upperparts, pale throat and *dusky chestnut underparts*; legs and feet powerful, pale-yellow. Very shy; usually heard rather than seen. Runs rather than flies; walks like a large Banded Rail (174), tail carried high and flicked.

Voice: Unusual alternating notes rapidly repeated many times. The first resemble alarm-screech of Sulphur-crested Cockatoo (318), second, loud drumming of Emu (1); may call in response to loud note such as gun-shot.

Habitat: Mangrove thickets.

Breeding: Nest: flattish; of sticks built on low slanting mangrove, 1–2 m from ground. Eggs: 4; large, rather long, pale, pinky white, dotted with reddish chestnut, some darker spots appearing as though beneath surface of shell.

Range and Status: Coastal n. Aust. and islands: from n. Kimberleys to w. coast, C. York Pen. Possibly common but rarely recorded. Also Aru Is.

177 MALAYAN BANDED CRAKE *Rallina fasciata*

Other names: Malaysian Banded Crake, Red-legged Crake.

Field marks: 190–230 mm. Distinctive: forepart of body and upperbreast soft chestnut brown, rest of plumage brown above, *lowerbreast and under tail-coverts boldly banded with black and white; legs red*.

Similar species: Red-necked Rail (178).

Habitat: Vegetation in and near swamps and watercourses.

Range and Status: From Assam and Burma through Malaysia, migrating to Borneo and Indonesia, with possible stragglers to Kimberleys, WA. Vagrant.

178 RED-NECKED RAIL *Rallina tricolor* Pl.31

Field marks: 280 mm. Unmistakable: *head, neck and breast fiery chestnut*, rest of body very dark olive-grey; underwings barred white. Bill robust, green, eyes red, legs olive. Imm:

dull dark-brown tinged olive, light-rufous on back of neck. Pairs or small parties; shy and hard to observe as it moves about rainforest floor, flicking tail. Noisy, especially at night.
Voice: Strange pig-like grunts; 'gurk, gurk, gurk' repeated many times, descending. Also a monotonous, incessant 'clock, clock, clock'; a quick 'cluck' when startled.
Habitat: Dense tropical and subtropical rainforests and scrubs, especially along watercourses.
Breeding: Eggs laid on leaves and grass among debris or between tree-roots; 3–6; cream-white, spotted and blotched rust-brown, with underlying spots of lilac-grey over entire surface, more thickly at larger end.
Range and Status: Ne. coastal Q from C. York to about Townsville, inland to Atherton Tableland. Probably locally common. Also Moluccas to NG and islands, Bismarck Archipelago.

179 CORNCRAKE *Crex crex*
Other name: Landrail.
Field marks: 255–265 mm. A sturdy brownish rail with grey cheeks, *bright chestnut shoulders, buff breast*, tawny white-barred flanks and whitish underparts. Broad white band along inner margins of wings; tail very short. Bill horn-coloured, legs and feet dull-green. In flight, chestnut shoulders conspicuous, legs dangle at first. Solitary, skulking; active at dawn and dusk, runs swiftly; sneaks with great speed through undergrowth.
Voice: Male: persistent rasping 'rerrp-rerrp', like passing thumbnail along teeth of a comb; usually at night.
Habitat: Paddocks, crops; lush vegetation generally.
Range and Status: Europe, n. Mediterranean, Middle East to w. Siberia, migrating to Africa. Australian records: Randwick, NSW, June 1893; and on ship off Jurien Bay, WA, Dec. 1944; once NZ. Vagrant.

180 MARSH CRAKE *Porzana pusilla*   Pl.31
Other names: Baillon's or Little Crake, Little Water Crake.
Field marks: 150 mm. Smaller than Spotted Crake (181); note contrast of *tawny sides of neck with pale-grey face, throat and breast*; tawny olive above, streaked and marbled black and white; flanks and under tail-coverts barred black and white. Bill dark-brown, green at base, legs green or olive-brown; eye red. Small, shy and secretive, flicks angled short tail, slips over floating vegetation; swims or flies across open water to next cover; sometimes runs on branches of waterside trees. Flight laboured with rapid wingbeats; legs dangle.
Similar species: Spotted Crake (181).
Voice: A harsh 'krek-krek'; a whirring 'chirr' and a soft whining complaint-note.
Habitat: Vegetation growing and floating in freshwater swamps; tussocks, waterside vegetation.
Breeding: Nest: shallow cup of rushes, water-ribbons, grass and leaves, often with canopy of growing material drawn over it by sitting bird; may have trampled approach-ramp. Usually in tussock, dense water-ribbons or low bush, over or beside water. Eggs: 4–8; oval, brownish olive, faintly mottled darker.
Range and Status: Australian distribution poorly known: extends through better-watered se. and sw. Aust. n. to beyond Tropic; also Tas. and coastal ne. and nw. Aust. (Cairns area, Q, and Kimberleys, WA); irregular on suitable waters inland. Records from top end NT (S. Alligator R. and near Darwin) suggest it may be a dry-season visitor from s. Nomadic or migratory. Also throughout Old World, where usually known as Baillon's Crake, to NG. Aust. and NZ.

181 SPOTTED CRAKE *Porzana fluminea* **Pl.31**

Other name: Australian Crake.

Field marks: 170–205 mm. Note the olive-green bill (red at base of upper mandible) and legs of similar colour. Upperparts drab-olive, finely streaked and spotted white, *throat and breast dark-grey; darker round eye*: flanks barred black and white: *under tail-coverts dark with white edges*, prominent as bird flicks tail. Imm: browner above, paler-grey below, spotted white, mottled darker. Bill brown, legs dull-green. Singly, pairs or open companies; wades, swims or walks on floating weeds; ventures from cover to feed in shallow water and near cover on margins of swamps or saltmarshes.

Similar species: Marsh Crake (180).

Voice: Sharp staccato call somewhat like Fairy Tern (275). Sacred Kingfisher (402); also prolonged wheezing note somewhat like Golden-headed Cisticola (509): whirring chatterings.

Habitat: Freshwater swamps with water-ribbons and other floating vegetation; dense beds of bullrushes, clumps of spiny rush or tussocks on fresh or brackish swamps; samphire and other scrubby cover round saltmarshes and saltfields.

Breeding: Nest: shallow cup or platform, often with ramp of trampled material; of grass, rush-stems, water-ribbons; in clump of rushes, water-ribbons or tussocks, growing in or near water. Eggs: 4–5; pale-olive or olive-brown, spotted dark reddish brown and black, more plentifully at large end.

Range and Status: E. and sw. Aust.: from about Innisfail, Q, to Eyre Pen., SA, also Tas., sw. WA. Fairly common in e.; (?) rare or erratic nomad inland and nw. Aust.–Alice Springs, NT; Derby, WA.

182 SPOTLESS CRAKE *Porzana tabuensis* **Pl.31**

Other names: Leaden or Tabuan Crake, Little Swamphen or Waterhen, Spotless Water Crake.

Field marks: 200 mm. Most adults have no conspicuous white markings; but some may have pale throats. In general, *dark slate-grey, wings and back dark olive-brown*; under tail-coverts may be slightly barred or spotted white. Bill black, eye and legs red. Imm: throat dull-white; some white feathering on underparts. Usually singly; nomadic and widespread, not always shy; feeds along swamp margins, flicks tail constantly; when startled, dashes for cover or flies heavily with trailing legs; swims.

Voice: Notes very varied: shrill grebe-like chatter; others like distant motor-cycle or motor-boat, rattle of sewing-machine at high speed, popping sound of air bubbling from submerged bottle; also single soft explosive note.

Habitat: Freshwater swamps surrounded by blackberries, rushes, sedges or with heavy surface-vegetation; well-vegetated salt-swamps and saltmarsh; mangroves. On offshore islands, dry scrubs and beaches.

Breeding: Nest: shallow cup of dry grass and plants, often with flimsy canopy, usually on ground under rushes or other heavy vegetation, sometimes up to 1 m in clump of rush or tussock in water, usually near swamp edge. Eggs: 4–6; light-cream to pale-brown or pale-grey, usually mottled chestnut and lavender-grey. Resting platforms are also built.

Range and Status: Coastal e. and s. Aust. and many islands: from highlands in ne. Q (Atherton Tableland) and coastally s. from about Rockhampton to e. Tas.; s. SA and sw. WA n. at least to Abrolhos Is.–Hutt Lagoon (n. of Geraldton); occasional inland, e.g. mid-Murray Valley, and s. Riverina. Uncommon to rare; nomadic or migratory. Also widespread on islands from Philippines to Moluccas, NG, New Britain, New Caledonia, Fiji, Oceania; NZ and sub-Antarctic islands in that region.

183 WHITE-BROWED CRAKE *Poliolimnas cinereus* **Pl.31**

Field marks: 180 mm. A distinctive crake with blackish cap and *two white lines on face*, one above eye, one below, separated by black mark from bill to eye; brownish above, white below. Bill yellowish, base of upper mandible red, legs olive-green. Singly; feeds in shallows, climbs over mangrove roots; walks on floating vegetation; not particularly shy; may ignore observer.

Voice: Unusual loud chattering 'cutchee cutchee'; sometimes by several birds in chorus.

Habitat: Edges of lakes, mangroves and other waterside vegetation, either growing in or hanging low over water.

Breeding: Nest of rushes and similar coarse herbage, lined with grass; among swampy vegetation. Eggs: 4–6; oval, green-white to yellow-brown, with fleecy dots, spots and blotches, varying from yellow-brown to dull-chestnut.

Range and Status: Coastal n. Aust. from Kimberleys, WA, to about Townsville, Q; range includes suitable habitat in highlands e.g. lakes on Atherton Tableland. Probably common. Also se. Asia, Philippines, Sunda Is., Celebes, NG, Bismarck Archipelago, Solomon Is., New Hebrides, New Caledonia, Fiji, Samoa.

184 BUSH-HEN *Gallinula olivacea* Pl.31

Other names: Rufous-tailed Crake, Rufous-vented or Brown Rail.

Field marks: 255 mm. Secretive plain-coloured rail; plain olive-brown above, greyish below, with pale throat and *distinctly buff* belly and under tail-coverts. Bill heavy, pointed; when breeding green, with orange frontal shield; male's brighter; after breeding, shield dull grey-brown, remainder dull-green; legs dull-yellow. Singly, pairs or family parties; partly nocturnal.

Voice: Noisy (♀ only) when breeding: 'Eight to ten loud, harsh, shrieking notes each of one second duration, followed by five or six muted notes in quick succession'; the call is made by both male and female and is also given as a duet. Contact-calls: low single piping note and clicking notes. (J. H. Clarke).

Habitat: Rainforest fringes, floor of swamp-forests bordering marshes and lagoons, low scrub in flooded areas, creekside vegetation, tall grass, *Lantana* thickets, gardens with heavy vegetation.

Breeding: Nest: platform or cup of grasses; in tall grass or other heavy growth, drawn together overhead to form sides and roof. Eggs: 4–7; dull-white, buff-white or pale pinkish cinnamon freckled with light-chestnut, light-grey or dark-brown, mostly at large end; some with shadowy lilac or chestnut markings beneath surface.

Range and Status: Coastal n. and e. Aust.: from Gulf coast, Q, to Brisbane; inland to Camp Mountain, nnw. of Toowoomba; (? occasional) to Ballina, ne. NSW; doubtful NT. Scarce and local; (?) sedentary or migratory. Also Philippines, Moluccas, NG, to Bismarck Archipelago and Solomon Is.

185 TASMANIAN NATIVE-HEN *Gallinula mortierii* Pl.31

Other names: Narkie, Native-hen, Water-hen.

Field marks: 430 mm. A very large conspicuous nearly flightless rail: *olive-bronze above*; grey below, deepening to blackish on belly and under tail-coverts; whitish patch on mid-flank. *Bill heavy, yellow-green, legs grey.* Singly or in small parties; active, demonstrative, aggressive, tail jerks up and down. When disturbed runs very swiftly across roads, paddocks. Swims readily to escape. Noisy.

Similar species: Black-tailed Native-hen (186).

Voice: A loud rasping hacksaw-like cacophony, often from many birds; grunts.

Habitat: Open paddocks, edges of lakes, streams, swamps, with some refuge vegetation and tussocky areas; may become a pest in nearby young crops.

Breeding: Nest: platform of tussocks pulled up by the roots and trampled down, or shallow saucer of grass, roots, leaves and twigs, in undergrowth, long grass or tussocks; occasionally floating and anchored in reeds. Eggs: 6–9; stone-coloured, blotched and finely spotted chestnut, with paler underlying markings.

Range and Status: Tas. only; introduced Maria I. Common, sedentary.

186 BLACK-TAILED NATIVE-HEN *Gallinula ventralis* **Pl.31**

Other names: Black-tailed Water-hen, Gallinule, Swamphen, Waterhen.

Field marks: 320–360 mm. A dark fleet-footed native hen: *erect narrow black tail* gives it the look of a small bantam-cock. Dark olive-green above, slate-grey below, deepening to black on belly and under tail-coverts, prominent white spots on flanks, edge of outer primary white. Bill green, base of lower mandible orange, legs deep pink. Singles, parties to large massed companies; gregarious and nomadic; not uncommonly appears overnight in new districts, sometimes where seldom seen before; parties feed and run on dry margins of swamps, cross paddocks; swims readily; when pressed, flies strongly with rapid shallow wingbeats, legs trailing. Occasionally feeds with domestic fowls round homesteads.

Similar species: Dusky Moorhen (187): yellow-tipped scarlet bill and shield, tail shows white margins. A few have white streaks on flanks. Tasmanian Native-hen (185).

Voice: Usually silent, but utters a rapid harsh metallic 'yapyapyapyap', somewhat like Dollarbird (407).

Habitat: Margins of swamps, lakes and rivers, flooded claypans, watercourses in lignum and open woodland; irrigated pastures, crops, country gardens.

Breeding: Nest: flattish structure of grass; on ground among bushes or in lignum: often near others. Eggs: 5–7; pale-green, finely spotted with brown dots and few large bold blotches of chestnut-brown and underlying spots of lavender-grey.

Range and Status: Throughout Aust. *except* Gippsland, Vic., top end NT and C. York Pen.; unusual e. and se. coasts; vagrant Tas., NZ. Rare to locally very abundant: highly nomadic and irruptive, moving inland to breed after good rains.

187 DUSKY MOORHEN *Gallinula tenebrosa* **Pl.31**

Other names: Black Gallinule or Moorhen.

Field marks: 380 mm. Familiar waterhen of town lakes: *slim bill bright red at base and on forehead-shield, tipped yellow*; dark olive-brown above, slate-black below: under-edges of tail white. Some birds have a few white streaks or a continuous streak along flank. (Common Moorhen *G. chloropus* of Eurasia to Indonesia, has white flank streak: the two forms may be conspecific). Legs greenish red above 'knee', dull yellow below; toes long and slender. Imm: browner, with blackish green bill and legs. Pairs, loose colonies; often on short grass near water; runs to cover or water, head down, or flies with legs trailing. Flicks tail, swims with head jerking; skitters.

Similar species: Swamphen (188): deep-blue, heavier scarlet bill, undertail wholly white. Coot (189): bill and forehead shield white, no white in plumage. Black-tailed Native-hen (186): bantam's tail.

Voice: Noisy, strident resonant 'kerk!'; harsher repeated shrieks.

Habitat: Well-vegetated swamps, town lakes, rivers with wide grassy margins and stands of rushes or reeds, dense trees along banks or in water. Often in introduced willows.

Breeding: Nest: bulky saucer of sticks, stems, bark, grass: in rushes, reeds or other vegetation in or near water or on bole, roots or low branch of waterside tree in swamp, river or flood. Flatter, usually more exposed resting platforms are also built. Eggs: 7–10: buff or sandy, blotched and spotted purplish brown.

Range and Status: E., se. and sw. Aust.: uncommon coastal areas of nw. and e. Q: common better-watered parts of NSW, Vic., se. SA and Kangaroo I.: sw. WA. Resident King I. occasional Flinders I., Bass Strait: not recorded Tas. proper. Common: sedentary or nomadic. Also Borneo, Celebes, Moluccas, Lesser Sunda Is. to NG.

188 SWAMPHEN *Porphyrio porphyrio* **Pl.31**

Other names: Bald Coot or Waterhen, Blue Bald Coot: Blue-breasted, Purple, Eastern or Western Swamphen; Pukeko, Macquarie Waterhen, Purple Gallinule or Waterhen: Red-bill.

Field marks: 455 mm. Large and conspicuous; note *deep triangular scarlet bill and shield,* *deep-blue head and body* set off by black upperparts and prominent white under tail-coverts; legs long, reddish. The race *bellus*, 'Western Swamphen', is paler-blue. Singly to open companies; in swamps and nearby paddocks, climbs and roosts in vegetation over water. Flicks tail when walking or swimming *exposing snowy under tail-coverts*. When disturbed runs or flies heavily, legs trailing; swims with tail high.

Similar species: Dusky Moorhen (187). Tasmanian Native-hen (185): green above, bill and legs not red; undertail black.

Voice: Loud hacksaw-like screeches.

Habitat: Margins of swamps, lakes, shallow rivers with ample cover of rushes, reeds, cumbungi or scrub; often on town lakes.

Breeding: Nest: shallow platform of rushes and grass; open canopy of stems may be drawn over; often on trampled-down reeds or cumbungi; makes feeding and resting platforms. Eggs: 3–5; sandy buff, blotched and spotted chestnut with underlying spots of grey.

Range and Status: The most widespread local race, *melanotus*: e. Aust. and Tas., and coastal islands; far inland in suitable habitat, across n. Aust. to Kimberleys, WA, and coastally s. to about Onslow; vagrant NG. The race *bellus* occupies the range in sw. WA. Common in s. Aust., less common in n.; sedentary or nomadic. The species is widespread from s. Europe to Africa, s. and se. Asia, Philippines, Indonesia, NG, New Hebrides, New Caledonia, Fiji, Tonga, Samoa etc., NZ and sub-Antarctic islands in the NZ region.

189 COOT *Fulica atra*   **Pl.31**

Field marks: 380 mm. The only wholly slate-grey waterhen, darker on head; *bill and shield white to blue-white*; legs blue-grey, toes with flattened lobes. Imm: grey-brown, whitish below; bill greyish. Flocks feed ashore, in shallows or far out on surface of large waters in open flocks or rafts, diving for plant food. Skitters; sustained flight surprisingly swift with rapid shallow wingbeats. Highly nomadic; travels long distances, mostly at night.

Similar species: Dusky Moorhen (187) and Swamphen (188): reddish bills, white under-tail.

Voice: Noisy; variety of harsh notes, typically a sharp 'kyik!' or 'kyok!': repeated raucous screeches.

Habitat: Large fresh or brackish waters: inland floodwaters, permanent swamps, town lakes, reservoirs, sewage farms, brackish coastal swamps; occasionally on sheltered coastal inlets or on sheltered waters round offshore islands.

Breeding: In pairs or large companies. Nest: of sticks, swamp-vegetation, grass; in lignum, on shallow water or on low islands, stumps, logs. Eggs: 6–7: stone-coloured, finely and evenly dotted black.

Range and Status: Throughout Aust. and Tas. in suitable habitat: common, often very abundant; nomadic. Also widespread in Old World, to NG and (recently) NZ.

Cranes   Family *Gruidae*

Long-legged long-necked birds of stately carriage, usually with secondaries falling over rump in graceful bustle. Some (including those in Aust.) have bare heads – presumably an adaptation for plunging head into mud when feeding. Cranes lack the nuptial plumes of herons and fly with neck and legs extended, wingbeats shallow, often with distinctive upward flick. They are perhaps best known for their spectacular dancing displays, in which pairs or groups leap, bow and highstep. They typically form large migratory and nomadic companies; in Aust. these are best seen on remaining wetlands in north during dry season, when hundreds or even several thousands may be present on suitable swamps or floodplains. Voice, powerful brassy far-carrying trumpet, produced by large convoluted trachea or windpipe. Sexes similar.

Food: Seeds, roots, other vegetation; reptiles, small mammals and birds; insects and larvae; rarely fish.
Range: Worldwide except for S. America, NZ and Pacific islands.
Number of species: World 14; Aust. 2.

190   BROLGA   *Grus rubicundus*   Pl.44

Other name: Native Companion, Australian Crane.
Field marks: 1–1.25 m tall; span *c.* 2 m. Long-thought to be Australia's only crane: silvery grey with bustle of long secondary wing-feathers; skin of head pale-grey on forehead and crown, pale-red round rear of head, *blackish 'haired' dewlap under chin*; *eye yellow, legs dark-grey*. Imm: skin of face and crown flesh-pink. Pairs, parties or companies up to hundreds in n. Aust.; wades in shallow swamps, flooded areas; plunges head under water to dig for roots, corms. Like other cranes, renowned for group-dancing displays: leaps, bows, flaps; throws head back, arches wings when calling. Flight distinctive: neck and legs extended, wingbeats deliberate often with peculiar upward flick. Note: White-faced Heron (91) is incorrectly called 'Blue Crane'.
Similar species: Sarus Crane (191).
Voice: Far-carrying whooping trumpet, ending in staccato cacophony; uttered in flight or when standing; also hoarse croaks.
Habitat: Shallow swamps and margins; floodplains, grasslands; paddocks and ploughed fields, irrigated pastures, stubbles, crops; streets of some towns in n. and inland Aust.
Breeding: Nest: usually of grasses, plant-stems; on small islands in swamps or (standing) in water; occasionally eggs laid on bare ground. Eggs: 2; white, variably spotted and blotched brown and lavender.
Range and Status: Widespread in n., e., se. and inland Aust., extending coastally s. to about Onslow, WA, and to far-se. SA. Generally uncommon and local except in n. Aust. and suitable habitats inland, where locally abundant; nomadic. Drainage of swamps, other loss of habitat and illegal shooting have greatly reduced it in se. Aust., a former stronghold, where it is now locally extinct or casual in most closely settle districts. Once vagrant NZ. Also s. NG.

191   SARUS CRANE   *Grus antigone*   Pl.44

Note. In October 1966 a surprising addition was made to the Australian list when small parties of Sarus Cranes were discovered among Brolgas near Burketown and Normanton in nw. Q. In 1967 over 50, including imms. were seen near Normanton and in August a party was located on Atherton Tableland, on e. side of C. York Pen. Since then, gatherings of 200 +, including imms., have been recorded in the Atherton district and smaller numbers in coastal NT and in Ord River area, WA. Now accepted as a breeding resident of coastal n. Aust., overlooked previously among Brolgas.
Field marks: 1.2–1.5 m tall; span *c.* 2.4 m. Like a large somewhat darker Brolga (190), distinguished by *scarlet skin from throat and rear of head down upperneck*; no black dewlap; plumage of upperneck may be whitish and occasionally some white feathers in 'bustle', legs of adult *dull-pink or red, occasionally grey, eye deep-red*. Imm: light rufous wash over head and upperneck. In other details, including dancing displays, voice, flight and habitat, generally like Brolga.
Breeding: Nest: mass of reed and rush stems and straw, in flooded fields or marsh. Eggs: 2; pale greenish or pinkish white, sometimes spotted and blotched with brown or purple.
Range and Status: Coastal n. Aust.: (1) Ord R., WA, to top end NT, (2) Gulf coast and lower C. York Pen., from about Burketown to Atherton Tableland–Ingham. Locally fairly common. Also from w. India to se. Asia and Luzon (Philippines).

Bustards Family *Otididae*

Bustards are very large birds of plains, light scrubs, grassy open woodlands and, in some countries, cultivated lands. Typically they walk slowly with a stately air, head and bill tip raised aloofly. The long rather heavy legs have oddly small feet, without a hind toe. Bustards squat or run when disturbed and fly strongly if heavily with powerful measured wingbeats, neck and legs extended. They are gregarious and partly nocturnal; the males have spectacular displays, usually performed on a small bare display-ground or lek. Males are usually much larger and somewhat more boldly-patterned than females and those of the largest species are probably the heaviest of all flying birds. Most species, including Australian Bustard (192), have declined in the face of human expansion and shooting.
Food: Seeds, herbage, fruits, small rodents, reptiles, nestling birds.
Range: Africa, Eurasia, NG, mainland Australia.
Number of species: World 21; Aust. 1.

192 AUSTRALIAN BUSTARD *Ardeotis australis*   **Pl. 44**
Other names: Plains or Wild Turkey.
Field marks: 760 mm–1.5 m; span 1.6–2.1 m. A lordly upstanding ground-dwelling bird of open country. Male: much larger than female; crown black, neck and underparts white, with black breastband; brown above, *bend of wing patterned black and white*. Varies much; large males stand over 1 m tall and weigh up to *c.* 15 kg or more. Female: narrow brown crown; neck and breast greyer, thinner breastband. Singly, in pairs, small groups or occasionally open flocks of dozens (formerly hundreds). Moves in stately walk with head aloofly high, bill raised. Taxis to take off; flight powerful, large body, deliberately-beating broad wings and trailing legs distinctive; seems to sag at rear. Partly nocturnal, often rests through day, moves out to feed at evening. Male has distinctive display on a small display-ground or lek, cleared by constant use; conspicuously white in sunlight, he extends white-plumaged breast-sac to ground, fans tail forward over back; when a female approaches, he steps from side to side so that the now pendulous white breast swings and twists; balloons throat and roars like distant lion.
Voice: Except in display, rather silent; croaks while feeding; when startled, hoarse barking croak.
Habitat: Grasslands; light scrublands and woodlands, pastoral country; crops.
Breeding: Eggs: 1–2; buff to green-buff; laid on open bare ground or by bush, tussock.
Range and Status: Formerly widespread in suitable habitat in all mainland States. Still common away from settlement in parts of c. and n. Aust. and WA, but rare to extinct in settled districts of s. Aust.; mostly a casual visitor to far-se. Q, w. NSW, Vic., se. SA. Also s. NG.

Jacanas or Lotusbirds Family *Jacanidae*

Unusual small swampbirds with spurs on the wings, long legs and exceedingly long thin toes and hind claw, enabling them to walk on lily-pads and other floating vegetation, their usual habitat. They fly with the legs and toes trailing and seldom if ever venture on land or into heavy cover. When in danger, they ultimately seek protection by submerging with only bill protruding. Sexes similar, female usually larger. The name jacana is of Brazilian origin; in Aust., lotusbird is usual.
Food: Aquatic invertebrates, vegetable matter.
Range: Tropical regions of world.
Number of species: World 7; Aust. 1.

193 LOTUSBIRD *Irediparra gallinacea*   **Pl.31**

Other names: Jacana, Comb-crested Jacana or Parra, Lily-trotter, Skipper, Water Pheasant.

Field marks: 230 mm. Walks on floating plants on long dull-green legs and *ridiculously long toes and claws*; bill reddish, tipped black; pink comb on forehead, face and foreneck white, bordered buff, back of neck black, extending round breast in broad black band; otherwise brown above, white below. Imm: comb very small; crown ginger-brown; no buff on foreneck or dark breastband. Singly, pairs or open companies: invariably offshore on floating swamp-vegetation; active and often excitedly noisy; walks with exaggerated back-and-forward head-movement; bobs head, flicks short tail. Flies swiftly with quick shallow wingbeats, long legs and feet trailing.

Similar species: Crakes and rails (174–183).

Voice: Thin squeaky chitter or piping, usually in flight.

Habitat: Offshore vegetation on surface of lagoons, swamps and dams.

Breeding: Nest: low heap of wet floating vegetation. Eggs: 4; highly polished yellow-brown or red-brown, covered with maze of black lines.

Range and Status: Coastal n. and e. Aust., from Kimberleys, WA, to near Sydney, NSW, (Long-neck Lagoon, Pitt Town Swamp, Bakers Lagoon). Restricted to suitable well-vegetated permanent waters. Common in n.; local, scattered, rather rare in s.; sedentary. Also Borneo, Philippines, Celebes, Lesser Sunda Is., NG.

Stone-curlews   Family *Burhinidae*

Large aberrant waders known also as stone-plovers or thicknees. They have long legs with thick 'knees', but no hind-toes; the feet are part webbed. With the large yellow eyes typical of many nocturnal birds, they are active, mobile and noisy at night, but do feed by day. They typically rest with the lower leg (tarsus) flat along the ground. Their voices are usually weird mournful whistles or pipings; the wail of the curlew is celebrated in Australian literature; it gave rise to the Bush Stone-curlew's (194) aboriginal name 'willaroo'.

Food: Small rodents, amphibians, reptiles, crustaceans, molluscs, insects, and other invertebrates.

Range: Most temperate and tropical parts of world except N. America, NZ and Pacific islands.

Number of species: World 9; Aust. 2.

194 BUSH STONE-CURLEW *Burhinus magnirostris*   **Pl.44**

Other names: Bush Curlew, Southern Stone-curlew, Stone or Southern Stone Plover, Weeloo, Willaroo.

Field marks: 550–580 mm. A strange large long-legged wader-like bird that can be decidedly hard to see. Grey-brown above, buff-white below, *strongly streaked darker*. There is a dark mark along wing over a broader pale zone. Note rather robust blackish bill, whitish forehead and broad white eyebrow over blackish mark through eye and down neck. Eye large, yellow, heavy-lidded and often half-closed by day; legs greyish. Singly or pairs; shy and acutely watchful; moves slowly and deliberately, often with head horizontal. When approached, freezes stick-like, prostrates itself, walks deliberately away with head erect or runs furtively with head lowered. If pressed, taxis with long bowed wings out-spread and flies with *quick stiff wingbeats, revealing white wingpatch*. Active at night, often in noisy groups; occasionally flushed in headlights on country roads, when white wing-patches look almost luminous. Occasionally tame, e.g. on country golf-courses, and in n. Aust., in plantations, round beach-settlements and on islands.

Similar species: Beach Stone-curlew (195): bill heavier, unstreaked plumage plainer but facial and wing-patterns bolder, legs thicker.
Voice: The famous 'wail of the curlew' (do not confuse with more bubbling call of unrelated Eastern Curlew (219)). A far-carrying eerie mournful whistle of successive parts; starts low and slowly; is repeated, rises, quickens, breaks, descends and may end in staccato chorus of 'wee-wiff, wee-wiff, wee-wee' often by several birds. Usually at night.
Habitat: Open woodland with fallen branches, leaf-litter, sparse grass; timber along dry watercourses, sandy scrub near beaches; mangrove-fringes; country golf-courses and, in n. Aust., orchards, plantations.
Breeding: Eggs: 2; laid on bare ground; stone-coloured, thickly blotched dark-brown and grey, variable.
Range and Status: Aust. generally, and coastal islands, including Kangaroo I., SA; vagrant Tas. Rare in cleared or settled parts of former range in s. Aust. but persists in areas where sufficient habitat remains. In parts of coastal tropical n. Aust. remains abundant even near large towns. Sedentary. Also s. NG.

195 BEACH STONE-CURLEW *Burhinus neglectus* Pl.44
Other names: Beach or Reef Thick-knee.
Field marks: 560 mm. Hard to confuse with any other wader in its beach or reef habitat. Large and of stately bustard-like carriage. Note heavy black-tipped yellow bill; *prominent black-and-white pattern on head, bar on shoulder*, heavy yellow-green legs. Singly or pairs; shy, keeps ahead of observer or flies some distance along beach. Wingbeats slow, rather stiff; legs trail; note *surprisingly white downcurved wings with broad dark bar*.
Similar species: Bush Stone-curlew (194).
Voice: Like Bush Stone-curlew, but higher-pitched, harsher. Alarm-call: feeble 'klee-klink'.
Habitat: Open undisturbed beaches, exposed reefs, tidal mudflats and sandflats, mangroves.
Breeding: Eggs: 1–2; laid on sand, usually just above high-tide mark; creamy-white, streaked and blotched olive-brown.
Range and status: Coastal n. and e. Aust. and many coastal islands from Pt. Cloates, WA, to Tweed Heads, NSW; vagrant s. to near Coff's Harbour and Norah Head. Nowhere common, rare s. of Cairns; more usual on islands. Reclamation of mangroves and other tidal areas adjacent to river-mouths has reduced it in e. Aust. Uncommon; sedentary. Also Andaman Is., Sumatra, Borneo, Philippines to NG and New Caledonia.

Painted Snipe   Family *Rostratulidae*

Unusual wading birds in which the female is slightly larger and more colourful than male; she initiates courtship, he alone incubates. Not closely related to true snipe, Scolopacidae, and in general somewhat rail-like; the large eyes suggest partly nocturnal habits. Seasonal conditions apparently influence movements and breeding; after good rains, appears in small parties in districts where perhaps unrecorded for years, remaining temporarily to breed.
Food: Worms, molluscs, insects, some vegetable matter.
Range: Parts of S. America and from s. Africa through s. and se. Asia to Aust. and Tas.
Number of species: World 2; Aust. 1.

196 PAINTED SNIPE *Rostratula benghalensis* Pl.33, 38
Field marks: 240 mm. Unusual in appearance and habits. Female: larger and more boldly marked; *dark smoky brown hood cut off sharply on breast by creamy white 'horse collar'*. Note long white ring round eye, cream line along middle of crown, and chestnut

hindneck; otherwise patterned bronzy greenish grey above, with few rich-cream streaks, white below. Male: smaller, and greyer markings less contrasty: *large cream spots on wings*. Imm: like male, throat white. Bill shorter than Japanese Snipe (231), drooped at tip, yellow-brown in female; grey, tipped reddish in male; legs grey-green. In pairs or small parties occasionally of one sex only. Feeds deliberately, skulking, rail-like; jerks rear of body up and down while head remains steady. When disturbed freezes or flies low on rounded wings, legs trailing, revealing *black mark across grey-patterned flight-feathers*. At times flies higher, swifter, but never with dash of Japanese Snipe.

Similar species: Japanese Snipe (231).

Voice: When startled into flight, loud repeated 'kek!'. In display female utters a musical 'booo', like blowing over neck of bottle.

Habitat: Fringes of swamps, dams, sewage farms; marshy areas, generally with cover of grasses, lignum, low scrub, open timber.

Breeding: Nest: well-made saucer of twigs, reeds, grasses; often on a small hummock above water-level, usually in cover; may have light canopy of stems, grasses. Eggs: 4; rounded, tapered, creamy buff, scrawled and blotched with black, brown, underlying grey marks.

Range and Status: Aust. generally, mostly in better-watered parts; apparently more common in e. than w., but very irregular; vagrant Tas. Generally rare; nomadic. Also Africa; widespread in Asia; se. Asia to Indonesia.

Oystercatchers   Family *Haematopodidae*

Sturdy wading birds, black, or black and white; their straight stout laterally flattened red bills are used to pry shellfish off rocks, open bivalves, dismember crustaceans. Sexes similar.

Food: Crustaceans, molluscs, other marine invertebrates.

Range: Widespread on world coasts.

Number of species: World 6; Aust. 2.

197 PIED OYSTERCATCHER   *Haematopus longirostris*   Pl.32, 37

Other names: Black-and-white or White-breasted Oystercatcher, Eugerie-bird, Redbill, Seapie, Wongbird.

Field marks: 480–510 mm. A large sturdy conspicuous wader, black with sharply cut-off white rump and belly, stout straight scarlet bill, red legs. In flight, note *broad white wing-bar, white rump and belly*. Female: slightly larger. Imm: tip of bill dusky, legs paler. Singly, pairs or autumn and winter flocks. Wary, usually well out from cover; indulges in noisy aerial chases. Known to fishermen on n. NSW and Q coasts by habit of opening bivalves wedged in wet sand. Occasionally interbreeds with Sooty Oystercatcher (198).

Voice: Brisk ringing 'peepapeep, peepapeep' or 'kleep, kleep' usually in flight; musical tittering and piping in courtship.

Habitat: Undisturbed sandy beaches and spits, tidal mudflats and estuaries, islands, occasionally in paddocks near coast. Seldom rocky shores.

Breeding: Nest: shallow scrape in sand on open beach or among low growth behind beach. Eggs: 2–3; stone-grey, spotted black-brown with grey underlining marks.

Range and Status: Suitable coasts and islands of Aust. and Tas.; common in s. Aust., less so in n. Common; sedentary. Also widespread on coasts of Old World to Aru Is., NG and NZ.

198 SOOTY OYSTERCATCHER   *Haematopus fuliginosus*   Pl.32, 37

Other names: Redbill, Black Redbill, Black Oystercatcher.

Field marks: 480–510 mm. A large sturdy sooty black wader with scarlet bill and dull-pinkish legs. Imm: wing-coverts bordered buff. Bill and eyering orange-brown, legs grey; (n. race *ophthalmicus* wider bare fleshy eyering, longer bill). Habits like Pied Oystercatcher (197), but more solitary, usually singly or in pairs. These occasionally associate with flocks of Pieds and sometimes interbreed. In general it favours more rocky habitats.

Voice: Like Pied Oystercatcher.

Habitat: Undisturbed tidal rocks on ocean shores, islands; occasionally sandspits and mudflats.

Breeding: Nest: depression in sand or among rocks, seaweed, pigface, shells. Eggs: 2–3; stone-coloured, spotted and blotched purple-brown; larger, darker than Pied Oyster-catcher's.

Range and Status: Suitable coasts and coastal islands of Aust. and Tas. Generally less common than Pied.

Waders   Suborder *Charadrii*

A large and varied group whose typically long legs are suited to wading in shallow water and walking or running on open ground. Many have long bills and some have webbed feet or lobed toes for swimming; almost all nest on ground. Most species found in Aust. are migrants, breeding mostly in n. hemisphere, migrating to s. hemisphere during Aug.–Oct., leaving again in Mar.–Apr.; some overwinter. These international migrants in particular have developed long wings and powerful flight-muscles. The suborder is divided into several distinctive families, treated separately below.

Plovers and Dotterels   Family *Charadriidae*

In Aust. and NZ the smaller plovers are called 'dotterels'. Elsewhere, the name 'dotterel' is applied only to *the* Dotterel, *Eudromias morinellus*, of n. Eurasia. Well-shaped wading birds with rounded heads, large eyes, short necks and usually short bills. They tend to have bolder but simpler plumage-patterns than sandpipers, family Scolopacidae, and feed with characteristic movements: they walk or run a few steps, pause upright, then tilt forward to jab at food before moving on. Their flight is often swift and graceful and they typically form flocks of their own species or with others. Both resident and migratory species occur in Aust. The migrants breed mostly in the n. hemisphere and come here in summer. The exception is Double-banded Dotterel (206) that breeds in NZ and winters here. All the migrant species have distinctive breeding and non-breeding plumages. While in Aust. they mostly wear rather plain non-breeding plumage but newly arrived or about-to-depart individuals often show traces of, and sometimes complete, breeding plumage. An occasional adult Double-banded Dotterel that remains through summer will exhibit striking full breeding plumage. Note that the well-known endemic Masked (199) and Banded (200) Plovers are included in the widespread genus *Vanellus*, known in the Old World as lapwings because of their pulsing wingbeats in flight. They alone of the family in Aust. have coloured facial wattles. Sexes similar.

Food: Insects, small crustaceans, aquatic and marine invertebrates generally.

Range: Worldwide.

Number of species: World 63; Aust. 8 resident, 8 migrant.

199 MASKED PLOVER *Vanellus miles* Pl.36, 42

Other names: Alarmbird, (Australian) Spurwinged Plover, Spurwing or Wattled Plover; Masked or Spurwinged Lapwing.

Field marks: 350–380 mm. The species is widespread and well-known by appearance and penetrating calls. Nominate race: bill, *large facial wattle* and small spur at shoulder, *yellow*.

Crown black, tapering on nape, neck and underparts white; wings and back pale grey-brown. Race *novaehollandiae,* 'Spurwinged Plover': facial wattle smaller; crown and *back of neck black, extending to side of upperbreast in black 'lapels',* somewhat darker grey-brown above, white below. In flight (both races), note white underwings with black flight-feathers, white rump and tail with broad black sub-terminal band. Flies with quick beats of rounded wings. Noisy; groups stand tittering and erect in display; vocal flocks in autumn. Aggressive when nesting; dives at intruders. Intermediates from interbreeding of races are like *novaehollandiae,* but less black on nape and sides of neck; wattles bigger.

Similar species: Banded Plover (200): black breastband, strong white wingbar.

Voice: Strident grating staccato 'kekekekekek' or single piercing 'kek!'; often at night. In display, running trills.

Habitat: Swamp-margins, paddocks with dams, beaches; airfields, orchards, gardens; vacant suburban lots; has bred in grounds and even on flat roofs of suburban factories.

Breeding: Nest: scrape or shallow cup of twigs, grasses, pebbles or dry cow-dung; on ground or small hummock in water. Eggs: 3–4; yellow-olive to dark-olive, spotted, blotched, brown-black.

Range and Status: The species ranges from about Dampier, nw. WA, through Kimber-leys, n. NT, nearly throughout Q, NSW, Vic., Tas., islands of Bass Strait, e. and s. SA and Kangaroo I. It occurs on many coastal islands. Nominate race occupies the range in n. Aust. s. to about Cairns, Q; the race *novaehollandiae,* se. Aust. and n. on the e. coast to about Mackay, Q. Their breeding ranges overlap in a broad zone between those limits and extending inland. Intermediates, mostly resembling *novaehollandiae* with reduced black, occur in the overlap zone and more widely in interior. Nominate race occasional s. to Menindee, sw. NSW, Mildura, Vic.; Coopers Creek, Coward Springs and near Adelaide, SA. Race *novaehollandiae* occasional n. to about Mt. Isa and Birdsville, Q. Both occur fairly frequent at Alice Springs, NT; both are vagrant to far-s. WA. Nominate race vagrant (? or migrant) to s. NG and islands; race *novaehollandiae* has colonized NZ from Aust. Common; sedentary, nomadic or part-migratory. Also Moluccas; Christmas I., Indian Ocean.

200 BANDED PLOVER *Vanellus tricolor*   Pl.36, 42

Other names: Banded Lapwing; Black-breasted, Brown, Flock or Plain Plover.

Field marks: 250–280 mm. Distinguished from Masked Plover (199) by black sides of neck continuing down *to form prominent breast-band.* Bill and facial skin yellow; small red wattle, *white bar behind eye.* In flight, white bar across base of black flight-feathers *gives zigzag appearance;* underwing white, tipped black. Wary; usually in small parties, occasionally large winter flocks far from cover; takes flight with quick clipped wingbeats, wild cries.

Similar species: Red-kneed (203) and Black-fronted (212) Dotterels.

Voice: Wild plaintive cries; quick metallic 'er-chill-char, er-chill-char'; strident 'kew-kew, kew-kew'; often at night.

Habitat: Open bare paddocks, plains, airfields, stony ground, and other areas of very short grass; bare margins of dry swamps; usually far from cover; occasionally beaches; seldom wades.

Breeding: Nest: scrape in ground; sparsely lined grasses, rootlets, pieces of dung. Eggs: 3–4; rounded at large end, tapering; ground-colour varies from deep olive-green to stone coloured, spotted and blotched brown or blackish brown, underlying grey marks.

Range and Status: Aust., except far-n.: in Q, n. to Cairns–Atherton Tableland–Mt. Isa; in NT, n. to Alice Springs; in WA, n. to Ashburton R.; also Tas. Fairly common if patchy in suitable habitat in s., scarcer in n.; nomadic.

201 GREY PLOVER *Pluvialis squatarola* Pl.35, 40, 41

Other names: Black-bellied Plover, Grey Sandpiper, Maycock.

Field marks: 280–305 mm. A large plover of 'hunched dejected appearance'; note large head and dark eye, shortish black bill, graceful carriage and method of feeding. *Nonbreeding plumage:* pale grey above, mottled darker; whitish below. *Breeding plumage:* underparts wholly black from face to legs but *under tail-coverts white*; head and side of neck white; deep grey back strongly chequered white. Birds gaining or losing this plumage look patchy. In flight (all plumages) *whitish rump, barred tail, white wingbar and black 'armpits' (axillaries) contrasting with white underwing*; flight swift and graceful, pointed wings longer than Eastern Golden Plover (202). Shy; singly or small parties aloof from other waders; usually far out on exposed mudflats, sandspits. In a few places, e.g. Mud I., Vic., flocks of hundreds.

Similar species: Eastern Golden Plover (202): smaller and buffer; indistinct wingbar in flight, no black 'armpit'. In breeding plumage, underparts *and* under tail-coverts black. Knot (236); Great Knot (237).

Voice: Sweet plaintive drawn-out 'tlee-o-weee'; usually in flight.

Habitat: Mudflats, saltmarsh, tidal reefs and estuaries; rarely inland.

Range and Status: Breeds n. Russia, Siberia, Arctic n. America; winters widely in tropical and temperate regions including NG, Aust. and NZ. Regular migrant to coastal Aust. and islands Aug.–Apr. Not uncommon some areas, but rather local.

202 EASTERN GOLDEN PLOVER *Pluvialis dominica* Pl.35, 40, 41

Other names: American, Lesser or Pacific Golden Plover.

Field marks: 230–280 mm. Smaller, more elegant and upright than Grey Plover (201), distinguished in nonbreeding plumage by *pale-buff forehead, face and upperbreast*. Has similar dark ear-coverts, but brownish, not greyish, above often with buffish spanglings. In breeding plumage: *beautifully spangled golden-buff above; entire undersurface from face to under tail-coverts black*, margined white from forehead over eye and down side of neck. Newly-arrived and soon-to-depart birds often *patchy below*. Singly, small parties or occasionally large open companies, usually far from cover. Flight swift and graceful; in flight differs from Grey Plover by *brownish rump and tail; only faint wingbar; white streaks (shafts) on primaries, grey underwing without black armpits*.

Similar species: Grey Plover (201); Oriental Plover (210): plainer, without spangling; legs longer; note habitat.

Voice: 'Too-weet'; a musical whistling 'tlooi'; rough scratchy 'kree kree kree'.

Habitat: Estuaries, mudflats, saltmarshes; mangroves; on rocky reefs and stranded seaweed on ocean shores; margins of shallow open inland swamps; sewage farms, short grassy paddocks, sports-grounds, airfields, ploughed lands.

Range and Status: Breeds ne. Siberia and w. Alaska; regular common widespread migrant to NG, Aust. and islands and NZ., Aug.–Apr. Mostly coastal, occasional inland in suitable habitat.

203 RED-KNEED DOTTEREL *Erythrogonys cinctus* Pl.36, 42

Other name: Sandpiper.

Field marks: 175–190 mm. Distinctive: *black hood and breastband separated by gleaming white bib*; otherwise bronze-brown above, with prominent white streak along bend of wing; chestnut flanks. Bill deep-pink, tipped black; eye black, longish legs deep-pink to 'knee', blue grey below. Imm: brown where adult black; white below; breastband absent, smudgy or as brown band, with age. In flight, wings show *conspicuous broad white trailing edge; white rump and tail, with narrow dark centre*. Usually on still shallow waters; actions somewhat jerky, bobs head, runs, wades; occasionally swims.

Similar species: Hooded Dotterel (204); Black-fronted Dotterel (212); Banded Plover (200).

Voice: Musical trilling; on taking flight, rather liquid 'chet chet'.

Habitat: Shallow parts of fresh and brackish swamps, floodwaters, claypans, sewage farms.

Breeding: Nest: may be of twigs; in a depression, often under bush or in open among pebbles or on damp ground among swamp-vegetation. Eggs: 4; stone-coloured, with wavy streaks and blotches of dark-brown and black.

Range and Status: Inland parts all mainland-States. Coastward movement in dry season, often remains to breed in shallow coastal swamps. Moderately common but patchy; rare s. WA; vagrant Tas. (summer). Also s. NG.

204 HOODED DOTTEREL *Charadrius rubricollis*   Pl.36, 42

Field marks: 190–215 mm. A tubby dotterel of ocean beaches in se. Aust. and beaches and inland salt lakes in s. WA. *Head and throat black with broad white rear collar*; black on shoulders sometimes extends to sides of breast; otherwise silvery grey-brown above, white below. Bill red, tipped black, eyering red; the short legs are flesh-coloured. Imm: plainer, no hood; grey above with smudgy grey 'lapels'. In pairs or family parties; potters slowly round jetsam and along edges of spent waves. When approached runs, turns its back and squats motionless, or flies briskly over waves to settle further along beach, revealing *broad white wingbar crossing black flight feathers; white tail with black hourglass pattern*.

Similar species: Habitat simplifies identification, but see Red-kneed (203) and Black-fronted (212) Dotterels and Common Ringed Plover (205). Sanderling (246): from imm. by absence of rear collar, longer bill and legs, quicker movements; dark mark on wing.

Voice: Short piping; also deep-toned barking 'kew kew'; in flight, guttural flock-calls.

Habitat: Ocean beaches and adjacent dune-wilderness, occasionally bays; rock-shelves and reefs at low tide; tidal flats. In s. WA (only), extends to inland salt-lakes.

Breeding: Nest: scrape in sand, pebbles, shells with some seaweed; often near debris. Eggs: 2–3; pale stone-coloured, blotched blackish brown, lavender.

Range and Status: Suitable habitat on s. coasts, from about Shoalhaven Heads, s. coast NSW, to Spencer Gulf and Kangaroo I., SA; islands in Bass Strait and Tas. (perhaps its stronghold). In s. WA, from about Israelite Bay to n. of Geraldton and inland on salt lakes to Balladonia and L. Deborah, nw. of Bullfinch. Fairly common; probably mostly sedentary and local.

205 COMMON RINGED PLOVER *Charadrius hiaticula*

Field marks: 178–190 mm. A small sand-plover with black breastband, black band *above the white forehead*, and a heavy black mark back through eye to nape. The white throat extends in a white rear collar; no black on shoulders, otherwise brown above with black flight feathers, white below. *Bill orange with black tip, eyering and legs orange* but legs can look dark when muddy. Imm: somewhat like female or imm. Red-capped Dotterel (211); dusky-brown breastband, often incomplete; no black forehead-band. Birds seen in Aust. may be in imm. plumage or moult, with incomplete dull brown markings. Active; feeds over exposed sand or mudflats, rarely wades. In flight, note prominent white wingbar and white edges and tips to tail; wingbeats regular; flocks twist and turn in flight.

Similar species: Red-capped Dotterel (211) from imm. Common Ringed: smaller, black legs, no white tip to tail. Black-fronted Dotterel (212). Little Ringed Plover *C. dubius*: breeds from n. Africa to NG; not yet recorded in Aust. Second white line behind black forehead-band, dull pink legs. In flight, no wingbar.

Voice: Reported to utter a clear 'dzerwit' and a wavering 'too-o-ee' in flight.

Habitat: Sandy or muddy shores.

Range and Status: Several races breed through n. Europe to Arctic Asia and Arctic Canada, etc., some migrating s. to Africa and s. Asia. Occasional (?) from Malaysia to NG. Recent sight-records: Long Bay, and Kooragang I., mouth of Hunter R., NSW. Feb., Oct.–Dec. 1967; supposed old record Port Stephens, NSW. Vagrant.

206 DOUBLE-BANDED DOTTEREL *Charadrius bicinctus* **Pl.35, 40, 41**
Other name: Banded Dotterel.
Field marks: 175–190 mm. Nonbreeding plumage like Mongolian Sand-plover (207) *but more suffused with buff*; dark ear-patch merges into yellow-buff on side of head. Whitish below, with brownish breast-band or suggestion of same. Bill black, rather slim, legs dull yellow-grey or light grey-green. Breeding plumage, often seen on arrival and before departure, unmistakable: forehead and underparts white, *black band across lower throat, broad chestnut breast-band*. Moulting birds show two shadowy bands. Imm: speckled sandy above; off-white below with single shadowy breast-band. Singly, with other small waders or in large open flocks; often far from water. In flight, note thin white wingbar, white shafts to primaries, pale sides to rump and tail.
Similar species: Mongolian Sand-plover (207); Red-capped Dotterel (211): female and imm.
Voice: Incisive staccato high-pitched 'pit pit' or 'chip chip'.
Habitat: Mudflats, saltmarsh, beaches; shallow brackish and freshwater swamps; clay-pans, bare margins of lakes and large dams; bare paddocks, ploughed fields, airfields; sometimes far from water.
Range and Status: The only wader to breed in NZ and (part of population) to migrate to Aust. Breeds North and South Islands, coastal islands and Chatham and Auckland Is. Usually begins to arrive in se. Aust. in Feb.; most depart by Aug., but records every month. Disperses coastally n. to Cairns and w. to Eyre Pen., SA; inland to suitable habitats in Vic., s. SA, s. NSW and Tas.; stragglers to s. coastal WA. Common and locally abundant in s., less common in n.

207 MONGOLIAN SAND-PLOVER *Charadrius mongolus* **Pl.35, 40, 41**
Other names: Lesser Sandplover; Mongolian Plover, Dotterel or Sand-dotterel.
Field marks: 190–205 mm. Like small Large Sand-plover (208) with which it often associates. In e. Aust. it usually gathers in much larger flocks. It can be distinguished by *quicker movements, darker upperparts, slighter black bill, darker-grey legs*. Flight-pattern less bold – narrower white wingbar and less white on sides rump and tail. Nonbreeding: grey-brown above with white forehead; dark mark from bill through eye broadens onto ear-coverts; partial band extends to sides of breast. Breeding plumage: forehead, throat and underparts white; face black, rusty sides of neck and broad breast-band, some nearly brick-red; breastband edged black above. Moulting birds often show pinkish flush on breast. Singly, parties to flocks of many hundreds in places, e.g. Kooragang I., mouth of Hunter R., NSW.
Similar species: Double-banded Dotterel (206); Large Sand-plover (208).
Voice: A short 'drrit', or 'drit, drit, derreet'; a soft 'tikit'; trills.
Habitat: Mudflats, wide sandy beaches, estuaries; tidal areas in mangroves; airfields.
Range and Status: Breeds Himalayas, China and s. and ne. Siberia; winters coasts of India, Africa, se. Asia; vagrant to NG and NZ. Widespread migrant to Australian coasts Sept.–Mar., sometimes remaining as late as May; more abundant than Large Sand-plover in e. Aust., vice versa in w. Common on n. and e. coasts to s. NSW, uncommon Vic.; rare Tas. and SA. In WA, more plentiful in nw. than s. Occasional inland.

208 LARGE SAND-PLOVER *Charadrius leschenaultii* **Pl.35, 40, 41**
Other names: Great or Large Sand-dotterel, Large-billed Dotterel.
Field marks: 200–230 mm. In nonbreeding plumage, a large plain wader: *fawn to pale grey-brown above*, white below, with *sturdy black bill, longish for a sand-plover, nearly equalling length of head*. Note white forehead and face with dark mark through eye to ear-coverts; sometimes washed buff across breast and with beginnings of band at sides. Legs medium-long, *pale-bluish or greenish grey, sometimes yellow-buff*. Breeding plumage: forehead black with white spot between bill and eye; ear-patch black, margins of crown,

nape and neck rose-pink to rufous; narrow to broad rose-pink or pale orange-red breast-band. Female: much paler band. Solitary, or with other waders, especially Mongolian Sand-plover (207); occasionally small flocks. Favours remote undisturbed areas but often less shy and jumpy than other waders: on approach lowers head, slinks away or flies a short distance. Flight strong but not very rapid; note prominent white wingbar, white underwing; dark rump with whitish sides; tail pale, darker towards end, finely tipped white.

Similar species: Mongolian Sand-plover (207). Oriental Plover (210), nonbreeding: more slender, bill slighter, legs longer, face and underparts grey-buff. In flight underwing grey, no obvious wingbar, rump and tail grey-brown.

Voice: Quiet clear mellow 'tweep tweep'; melodious trill.

Habitat: Undisturbed wide sandy beaches and sandspits; mangroves, saltmarsh; mudflats, exposed reefs; occasionally away from water in dune-wastes.

Range and Status: Breeds Turkey, s. USSR and Mongolia; winters Arabian Pen., Africa, se. Asia to NG, Solomon Is., Aust. and NZ (occasional). Regular migrant Aug.–May to coasts and islands of Aust. in suitable undisturbed habitats. Common in WA and apparently so in n. Aust.; less common on e. and s. coasts; scarce Tas.

209 CASPIAN PLOVER *Charadrius asiaticus*

Recorded in Aust. once, an old skin (SAM) from near Pine Creek, NT; Sept. 1896. Smaller than Oriental Plover (210), with *white 'armpits' and wing linings*. Breeds: s. Russia, s. Siberia, sw. China; winters e. and s. Africa.

210 ORIENTAL PLOVER *Charadrius veredus*   Pl.35, 40, 41

Other names: Asiatic or Eastern Dotterel, Caspian Plover.

Field marks: 220–255 mm. Like a small Eastern Golden Plover (202) with longer wings and legs, *but plainer sandy or grey-brown above, with no spanglings*. Nonbreeding: pale-buff forehead extends back as pale eyebrow; brownish mark back through eye over ear-coverts to nape; *buff rear collar*; whitish below, with faint zone across upperbreast, sometimes as very pale-rufous breast-band. Bill black, slender; *legs long, pinkish or greenish grey, pale-brown or yellowish*. Breeding plumage: male: *broad rufous breast-band, edged black below*; female: *breastband much paler*. Small parties or singly s. Aust.; in flocks n. and inland, often with Australian Pratincole (254). Wary, erect, runs, bobs head; stands on rocks, stumps. Flight strong, graceful or erratic with swift turns; *underwing grey, tail brown, narrowly tipped white*.

Similar species: Eastern Golden Plover (202), Large Sand-plover (208): bill heavier, longer; underwing white. Australian Pratincole (254): chestnut belly, white rump, short black tail. Oriental Pratincole (253): white rump, forked tail. Both pratincoles have shorter curved bills; see imms.

Voice: In flight, loud deliberate 'chip-chip-chip'; melodious trills; short piping 'klink'.

Habitat: Open plains or bare rolling country, often far from water; ploughed lands, muddy or sandy wastes near inland swamps or tidal mudflats; coastal saltmarshes and grassy airfields.

Range and Status: Breeds n. China; winters Sunda Is., Moluccas, NG, Aust., and NZ. Regular migrant to Aust. Sept.–Mar., records all States, but regular only across coastal and inland n. Aust., where common and often very abundant.

211 RED-CAPPED DOTTEREL *Charadrius ruficapillus*   Pl.35, 40, 41

Other names: Red-capped or Red-necked Plover; Sandlark, Sandpiper.

Field marks: 140–165 mm. A plump lively little wader with short black bill. Often runs ahead along shore on twinkling black legs; bobs head. Male: pale-brown above, pure white below; *forehead white, crown and nape fox-red*. Slight black marks as follows: a line separating white forehead from red crown; a wedge back from bill through eye; a slight 'lapel' on sides of white upperbreast. Female: duller; markings less intense; brown mark through eye. Imm: like female; mottled above, forehead greyish. Singly, pairs or post-breeding flocks of hundreds, both coastal and inland. Associates with other small waders; flocks plunge and wheel like sandpipers, now brown, now white. In flight, note white underparts, blackish flight feathers, thin white wingbar, blackish centre of rump and tail edged white.

Similar species: Common Ringed Plover (205); Double-banded Dotterel (206). Red-necked Stint (242): smaller head, longer tapering bill, mottled greyer above; feeding actions differ.

Voice: Brisk 'tik', uttered singly or repeatedly, accelerating into a rapid hard trill; thin churrings; peeps.

Habitat: Sandy and shelly shores, bare areas adjacent and those in saltmarsh; dune wilderness; mudflats and reefs; open shores and bare ground round salt, brackish and (occasionally) fresh waters, coastal and inland.

Breeding: Nest: scrape in sand, shingle or bare earth, sometimes lined with shells, stones or vegetation. Eggs: 2, occasionally 3; pale-sandy to greenish stone; blotched and mottled grey, lavender, dark-brown and black.

Range and Status: Aust. and Tas. and coastal islands: typically coastal, but on suitable (mostly saline) waters far-inland. Common; sedentary or nomadic. Vagrant NZ.

212 BLACK-FRONTED DOTTEREL *Charadrius melanops*   Pl.36, 42

Other names: Guttersnipe, Sandpiper.

Field marks: 160–180 mm. A widespread native dotterel of disruptive pattern. Note *black band across forehead, back through centre of crown and through eyes below white eyebrow; bold black Y on white breast*. Mottled brown above with chestnut scapular region and pale mark along wing. Bill red to orange, tipped black; eyering red; legs flesh-pink to yellowish. Imm: no breastband or black on forehead; wingbar paler-chestnut, more white on wing. Singly, pairs or loose companies; typically along edges of shallow fresh water; carriage horizontal; lively, bobs head, tips, runs; occasionally swims. When courting, aerial chases with excited churring; often active and vocal at night. Flight easy and undulating or jerky and dipping, wings seemingly too large. Note white wingbar, chestnut wingpatch and rump; black on central tail-feathers broadens at end, tip and outer tail-feathers white.

Similar species: Red-kneed Dotterel (203): plain black hood, white bib; in flight, wide white trailing edge. Hooded Dotterel (204): head wholly black with white rear collar; breast wholly white; note habitat. Common Ringed Plover (205).

Voice: Single or repeated liquid explosive 'dip!'; tinkling rattles and churrings, often in flight.

Habitat: Shallow margins of rivers, lakes, on pebbles, gravel or mud; swamps; edges of dams, including those isolated in bush; occasionally saltmarsh areas of brackish lakes, tidal streams; rarely sandy seashores.

Breeding: Nest: scrape in sand, shingle, bare ground among leaf-litter; may be partly lined with small sticks etc.; sometimes far from water. Eggs: 3, occasionally only 2; yellowish stone-coloured, closely scribbled or marbled black-brown and lavender.

Range and Status: Suitable habitat throughout Aust. and Tas. Common except Tas.; colonized NZ *c*. 1954 now widespread.

213 AUSTRALIAN DOTTEREL *Peltohyas australis*   Pl.36, 40, 41

Other names: Desert Plover, Inland Dotterel.

Field marks: 190–230 mm. An unusual wader: sandy-buff above, strongly streaked brown; *forehead and throat white or buff-white, with black bar across crown and down through the large dark eye*. Another line down side of neck to form *prominent black Y on buff breast*; belly rich-chestnut, under tail-coverts conspicuously white; tail short. Imm: buffer, without bold black markings; somewhat like small Eastern Golden Plover (202).

Parties to flocks of dozens; posture upright; runs, freezes, bobs head. Flight low and swift; note long wings and contrast of buff underwing, *dark belly and white under tail-coverts*; rump and tail brownish. Active day or night; flocks occasionally seen in headlights on outback roads.

Similar species: Australian Pratincole (254): white rump. Oriental Pratincole (253): white rump and forked tail. Both have easier ternlike flight; neither has such distinctive facial or breast-pattern.

Voice: Described as a brisk 'quoick'; also 'kr-root'.

Habitat: Bare, stony or sparsely-vegetated plains and uplands; gibber; stock-routes, outback roads and tracks; occasionally on ploughed land; seldom near water.

Breeding: Nest: scrape in bare ground often ringed with ridge of sandy soil, pebbles, stems or pieces of dung. Eggs: 2–3; cream to buff-brown or light olive, heavily streaked and blotched dark-brown, specially on large end; underlying violet marks. On leaving nest, bird covers eggs; young often shelter in burrows.

Range and Status: Arid parts of all mainland States mostly s. of Tropic; to w. coast between about Onslow–Geraldton, WA, and s. coast between about Esperance, WA, and Murray R., SA, ne. to Pinnaroo; in nw. Vic., s. to about Wyperfeld NP and e. to about Mystic Park; in NSW, e. to about Deniliquin-Griffith-Collarenebri (vagrant e. to Bathurst and to Long Reef Golf Course, Sydney); in Q, e. to about Cunnamulla-Longreach, n. to about Julia Creek–Mt. Isa; s. NT n. to Attack Creek, n. of Tennant Creek. Uncommon; nomadic, apparently with regular seasonal movements.

Stilts and Avocets   Family *Recurvirostridae*

Slender waders with very long slender legs, feet partly or fully webbed. Bills straight (stilts) or upturned (avocets). When feeding, they probe, or sweep bill sideways. Plumage mostly white with solid areas of black, rich-browns. Voices distinctive; clear tootings, yaps. Sexes similar.

Food: Mainly animal: crustaceans, molluscs, aquatic insects; some seeds.

Range: Almost worldwide in temperate and tropical regions.

Number of species: World 7; Aust. 3.

214 PIED STILT   *Himantopus himantopus*   Pl.32, 37

Other names: Black-winged or White-headed Stilt; Longshanks, Stiltbird.

Field marks: 355–380 mm. Bold pattern and *extremely long pink legs make it unmistakable*. Head and body white, nape and wings black; bill black, long and needle-like. Imm: crown and nape greyish. Pairs, small parties, companies of many hundreds where conditions suitable, but seldom in compact flocks like Banded Stilt (215); wades in shallows, seldom swims. In flight, wings black above and below, trailing pink legs nearly double length of body. Noisy and demonstrative near nest.

Similar species: Banded Stilt (215), imm: wholly white head, neck and body, black-and-white wings. Red-necked Avocet (216).

Voice: Falsetto yaps or repeated 'boo', mostly when nesting; imm. has thin whistle.

Habitat: Fresh or brackish swamps, shallow river or lake-margins; dams, sewage farms, commercial saltfields; estuaries, mudflats.

Breeding: Nest: of water-plants, weeds, often built up; usually in open colonies, on low hummocks in water, among dead bushes, at times floating; or in depression on dry ground with little lining. Eggs: 4; dark-olive, blotched and spotted dark-brown.

Range and Status: Throughout Aust. in suitable habitat; vagrant Tas. Fairly common; nomadic. Almost worldwide, including NG and NZ.

215 BANDED STILT *Cladorhynchus leucocephalus* **Pl.32, 37**
Other names: Bishop or Rottnest Snipe.
Field marks: 360–450 mm. Adult *white with chestnut breastband*, black mark on centre of belly, black and white wings (moulting birds may be without breastband). Bill black, long and needle-like, legs long, flesh-pink to orange-yellow, feet partly webbed. Imm: wholly white head, neck, breast and back; no breast-band. Typically in compact flocks, often in thousands; occasionally small parties. Wades, swims buoyantly like a black-and-white gull; often with Red-necked Avocets (216). Lone individuals, usually imms. occasionally seen with other waders e.g. godwits. Flight strong, *typically in close-packed flocks that twist, dive and turn.* Note breast-markings, *white panel on trailing edge of blackish wing.*
Similar species: Pied Stilt (214); Red-necked Avocet (216).
Voice: Wheezy puppy-like bark.
Habitat: Salt-lakes, tidal mudflats, saltmarsh, commercial saltfields; occasionally shallow freshwater lakes.
Breeding: In colonies (some huge) on low islands in large inland salt lakes. Eggs: 3–4; laid on scrape in sand; variable, pure-white to deep-fawn; scrawled, blotched black, dark-brown.
Range and Status: Shallow salt lakes, shallow marine inlets and commercial saltfields from Rottnest I., off Fremantle, WA, e. to near Melbourne, Vic. In WA, coastally n. to about Pt. Cloates, far-inland when suitable conditions occur; in SA, n. to L. Eyre – L. Callabonna, s. to Kangaroo I. and the Coorong, commonly occurs commercial saltfields on Eyre and Yorke Pens. and near Adelaide; in w. Vic., salt lakes n. to about Little Desert, occasional n. to Swan Hill–Mystic Park, Vic. and Balranald–Wentworth, NSW; e. to commercial saltfields near Geelong and w. of Melbourne; vagrant (? mostly imms. with other waders) to e. coast NSW (Illawarra district and lower Hunter R.), e. Q and Tas. When water-conditions are suitable and brine shrimps correspondingly abundant, frequently gathers in dense flocks; tends to move coastwards in summer; movements erratic. Breeding seldom recorded: has occurred irregularly in area of L. Grace and elsewhere in s. WA; L. Callabonna and elsewhere in n. SA. Optimum conditions of water-level and food are apparently necessary. Rare and sparse to locally common and abundant; highly nomadic.

216 RED-NECKED AVOCET *Recurvirostra novaehollandiae* **Pl.32, 37**
Other names: Cobbler, Cobbler's Awl, Painted Lady, Scooper, Trumpeter, Yelper.
Field marks: 400–460 mm. *Long upturned fine black bill, rusty head,* white body and black-and-white wings make it very distinctive. Long legs pale blue-grey, feet fully webbed. Parties, occasionally flocks. Wades, swinging bill from side to side; swims, tips up duck-like. In flight, note flickering effect of black-tipped wings with angled black bar on upper surface; legs trail well beyond tail. In flight away, two black bars down back are diagnostic. Often associates with Pied (214) and Banded (215) Stilts.
Voice: Musical fluty 'toot', mostly when nesting.
Habitat: Estuaries, tidal mudflats; fresh, brackish and salt swamps; shallow inland waters, claypans; commercial saltfields.
Breeding: Nest: scrape with scant lining of sticks, rootlets; often near small bush, or on small hummock in shallow water, when built-up of weeds, mud. Eggs: 4; dark-olive to creamy stone, blotched, spotted black, stained grey.
Range and Status: Through much of Aust. but patchy; widespread and fairly common in suitable habitat inland se. and coastal s. and sw. Aust.; sparse or absent e. Vic., uncommon coastal e. Aust., sparse or absent in C. York Pen. and top end NT; vagrant Tas. Nomadic; moves toward coast in summer (s. Aust.) and dry season (n. Aust.). Vagrant NZ.

Sandpipers, Stints, Curlews, Snipe   Family *Scolopacidae*

A large family of swift-flying wading birds, varying greatly in size. In general they are smaller-headed than plovers, with longer necks; unlike plovers, their bills are usually long, slender and straight or downcurved, rarely upcurved. Recognition depends mostly on size, shape of bill and patterns on wings, rump and tail in flight. The family is divided into a few characteristic, easily remembered groups. *Sandpipers* are small to medium graceful waders, generally with straight medium-long tapering bills. *Stints* (known as 'peeps' by American birdwatchers) are tiny sparrow-sized sandpipers, the smallest migrant waders. *Curlews* (including whimbrels) are the largest members, characterized by moderately to very long downcurved bills and brown mottled plumage which shows little change from summer to winter. *Godwits* have long straight or very slightly upturned bills, which they ram to the hilt in mud when feeding. *Snipe* for their size have even longer straighter bills than godwits, but have short legs and prefer grassy muddy ground, not shores. Most scolopacids are gregarious, feeding and flying in swift groups or flocks that instantly wheel and twist (sandpipers and stints) or string out in wavering lines or echelons (curlews and godwits). Sexes usually similar but may differ in size; in a few, e.g. godwits, females are larger. All species recorded in Aust. are regular international migrants that breed mostly in n. Asia and winter in s. hemisphere. Most arrive Aug.–Sept. and depart in Mar.–May. Some, like Eastern Curlew (219), commonly stay through our winter. The greatest number of species and the largest concentrations occur coastally, but there is a substantial movement across the continent, involving most members of the family. While in Aust. most wear rather dull and often confusingly similar nonbreeding plumage, but newly arrived and about-to-depart birds are often seen in partial or full breeding plumage; this is usually richer and more colourful than nonbreeding plumage and usually includes strong rusty, buff or even pinkish tones, usually without the bold simple patterns of plovers.

Food: Insects, crustaceans, molluscs, worms and other animal life; some vegetable matter.

Range: Almost cosmopolitan.

Number of species: World *c.* 80; Aust. 35 recorded to date; but more will be added with advancing numbers and skill of observers.

217 RUDDY TURNSTONE   *Arenaria interpres*   Pl.36, 42

Other names: Beachbird, Calico-bird, Eastern Turnstone, Sea-dotterel.

Field marks: 210–255 mm. A distinctive rather tubby wader; short black bill seems *slightly upturned*; *short legs conspicuously orange*. Nonbreeding: smutty grey-brown above: *throat white, upperbreast smutty to blackish, cut off by white underparts*; head and breast often show signs of harlequin breeding plumage. (See flight-pattern below.) Breeding plumage unmistakable: *black-and-white harlequin-pattern* on head, black patch on white underparts; wings and back red-brown mottled black. Imm: like non-breeding adult but more dusky. Solitary or a few with other waders, but very abundant in some localities e.g. Gt. Barrier Reef islands: winter flocks of 20–200 +. Potters slowly when feeding, 'bulldozing' shells and heaps of seaweed with bill. Looks sturdy on wing; indulges in brisk noisy aerial chases, showing *conspicuous white wing-panel*; *white lower back and tail crossed by two black bars*.

Voice: Clear rattling 'kitititit'; deep husky rattle 'quitta . . . . quitta . . . quit-it-it'; ringing 'kee-oo'.

Habitat: Tidal reefs and pools, weed-covered rocks washed by surf, pebbly seaweed-strewn shores; mudflats; occasional inland shallow waters, sewage farms, commerical saltfields or bare open ground near coast.

Range and Status: A cosmopolitan shorebird that breeds along coasts of far-n. hemisphere and winters widely in s. hemisphere. Regular migrant Sept.–Apr. mostly to coastal

Aust. and Tas.; but some inland. Some overwinter and may remain in breeding plumage. Common in suitable habitat.

218 EUROPEAN CURLEW *Numenius arquata*
Other name: Common Curlew.
Field marks: 538–580 mm. Very like Eastern Curlew (219) but slightly smaller, with slightly shorter bill (*c.* 140 mm against *c.* 180 mm), and with *white rump extending up back*, conspicuous in flight. Habits, voice and habitat generally as Eastern Curlew, with which it probably associates.
Similar species: Whimbrel (220).
Range and status: Breeds w. Europe and Russia to sw. Siberia, winters s. Europe, Africa; occasional e. to Malaysia, Borneo, where summer and winter records. In Aust., sight records Darwin, NT, Mar.–Apr., 1948 and Point Peron, s. WA, Nov. 1969. Vagrant.

219 EASTERN CURLEW *Numenius madagascariensis*　　　　Pl.32, 37
Other names: Sea or Australian Curlew.
Field marks: 530–610 mm. Our largest migrant wader, easily distinguished by size, call, *very long (180), down-curved bill*, nearly half length of body, *and brown rump*. Plumage: pale-buff to greyish fawn, liberally streaked and barred dark-brown, indistinct pale eyebrow and eyering; legs grey. Flight strong, wings tapering, bill very prominent; note blackish patch on leading edge of outer part of wing and very pale-grey mottled area on trailing edge. Wary; solitary to large dispersed feeding companies. When removing to new feeding areas or roosts, flocks to several hundred fly in drawn-out lines or V-formations, often low over water, calling hauntingly. Parties occasionally roost in tall trees on islands or in mangroves. Active and vocal at night.
Similar species: European Curlew (218); Whimbrel (220) and (in that entry) American Whimbrel.
Voice: Wild haunting sometimes grating 'curlee, curlee' or 'crooeee, crooeee' mostly in flight; also bubbling trill, rising then sinking; day or night.
Habitat: Mainly coastal; sandspits, mudflats, waterways in saltmarsh, mangroves; occasionally fresh or brackish lakes, bare grasslands near water.
Range and Status: Breeds ne. Asia, migrates to e. China, Korea, Japan, Taiwan, Philippines, Indonesia, NG, Solomon Is., Aust. and NZ. Common migrant Sept.–May to suitable tidal areas on coasts and islands of n., e. and se. Aust. and Tas., less common SA and s. WA; sparse inland. At some places, e.g. Kooragang I., lower Hunter R., NSW, and Westernport Bay, Vic., flocks of hundreds. Smaller numbers regularly overwinter.

220 WHIMBREL *Numenius phaeopus*　　　　Pl.32, 37
Other names: Jack or Little Curlew, Mayfowl, Shipmate.
Field marks: 380–430 mm. Like a small Eastern Curlew (219), but bill proportionately shorter and less curved; crown has two dark-brown stripes separated by median stripe of buff-grey and bordered by greyish eyebrows. In flight, note *white rump, extending in pointed blaze up lower back, quicker wingbeats and distinctive call: a rapid shrill tittering 'ti-ti-ti-ti-ti'*. Usually in small compact flocks or singly, with other waders. In places, e.g. near settlements on Gt: Barrier Reef islands, becomes tame; elsewhere wild, wary and difficult to approach without putting it to noisy flight. Occasionally roosts in trees on islands and in mangroves. Birds even in same flock can differ in size – beware of seeing 'Little Whimbrels' on size alone.
Similar species: European Curlew (218) has a white rump, but its other curlew features effectively identify it. American Whimbrel or Hudsonian Curlew *N. hudsonicus*, (not recorded in Aust., but vagrant NZ) similar to (220) except for *warm-brown rump*. As some whimbrels can appear wholly dark above unless seen well, caution is advised. Little Whimbrel (221).

Habitat: Estuaries; channels among mangroves, tidal flats, coral cays, flat exposed reefs; flooded paddocks; occasional on sewage farms, bare grasslands, sportsgrounds, lawns.

Range and Status: Widespread northern hemisphere wader with breeding populations in n. America, n. Europe and ne. Siberia. Birds of the latter race, *variegatus*, winter in se. Asia to NG, Aust. and NZ. Regular migrant from Sept.–Mar. to coastal Aust.; common in n. and e. and (particularly) on islands of Gt. Barrier Reef; uncommon and local in se. and sw. Aust.; occasional Flinders I., Bass Strait and n. Tas. Some regularly overwinter, mostly in n. Aust.

221 LITTLE WHIMBREL   *Numenius minutus*   Pl.32, 37

Other names: Little or Pygmy Curlew.

Field marks: 310–360 mm. A slender, tiny curlew, about the size of a long legged Eastern Golden Plover (202). *Bill shortish and only slightly downcurved*; plumage dark-brown above, feathers edged buff, giving strong pattern. *Crown somewhat peaked at rear* – rufous-brown, divided by pale median stripe; *area round eye, eyebrow and throat whitish or pale-buff*, dark mark runs through eye to rear; breast buff, mottled brown. Legs longish, light blue-grey or greyish fawn. In large flocks in n. Aust. but mostly small parties, pairs or singles s. of Tropic. Walks rapidly; wary, when approached squats, freezes or flushes with quick calls; tame near settlement. Flight buoyant: *note brown rump, whitish shafts on outer primaries*, blackish flight-feathers; wings thrown up on landing.

Similar species: See American Whimbrel, under Whimbrel (220).

Voice: Less shrill than Whimbrel; hoarse 'tit-tit-tit-tit'; a 'tchew-tchew-tchew' call has been described as being harsher and of lower pitch than Greenshank (227).

Habitat: Open areas of short grass; floodplains, margins of drying swamps; tidal mud-flats; also airfields, playing fields, wet paddocks, crops, commercial saltfields.

Range and Status: Breeds c. and e. Siberia, migrates to Japan, Philippines, Borneo, Celebes, Moluccas, NG and islands, and to Aust. Sept.–Apr. Records all States, including some far inland; regular and common nw. Aust. from Pt. Cloates, WA, to top end NT and Gulf Coast, of NT and to about Tropic in coastal Q. Mostly rare s. of Tropic; vagrant Tas. It has been described as the most abundant wader in nw. Aust.; flocks of many thousands gather on floodplains and grasslands of NT and nw. Q particularly on arrival and before departure.

222 UPLAND SANDPIPER   *Bartramia longicauda*

Other names: Bartram's Sandpiper; Upland Plover.

Field marks: 280–320 mm. An unusual, upstanding thin-necked small-headed wader that looks like a sandpiper and behaves like a plover. Pale-brown, mottled darker, paler round eye, on throat and underparts. *Bill short, dark, yellowish at base*; *legs long, dull-yellow*. Flight rather stiff; note *longish wedge-tail*, dark wingtips, white barred underwing; rump and tail dark in centre, pale on sides. Holds wings up on alighting.

Similar species: Sharp-tailed (238) and Pectoral (239) Sandpipers; Ruff (249).

Voice: Mellow whistled 'kip-ip-ip-ip'.

Habitat: In America, grassy paddocks, plains.

Range and Status: Breeds N. America; migrates to s. America; vagrant Europe, Russia; once Aust.; Sydney 1848. Vagrant. Sight record NZ, Feb. 1967.

223 WOOD SANDPIPER   *Tringa glareola*   Pl.33, 38

Field marks: 200–230 mm. A usually shy wader most often found in localized shallow freshwater situations, often among dead timber and other cover. Note longish straight black bill, long white eyebrow and whitish eyering, longish yellow-green legs. Nonbreeding: grey-brown above *with white freckling*; whitish below, washed grey across breast.

Breeding plumage: richer, darker, more white-mottled. Singly, pairs or parties, occasionally in flocks. Nervous; bobs head, flicks tail, perches dead branches, fence-posts. Flushes with clear calls, flight fast and twisting with clipped wingbeats; when startled typically zigzags high. Note white rump, barred at sides; light-grey underwing, yellow legs extend beyond tail.

Similar species: Green Sandpiper *T. ochropus* (not recorded in Aust.) should be kept in mind: darker, slightly larger; in flight, white rump, tail and belly contrast with dark upperparts; but *wing-linings blackish*. Flight call, ringing, 'tluitt, weet-weet'. Marsh Sandpiper (229): whiter, unspotted; more stilt-like legs, needle-like bill.

Voice: Shrill excited 'chitt-chitt-chitt', less strident than Greenshank (???); liquid 'tlui',

Habitat: In addition to above, mangroves, margins of tidal mudflats, saltmarshes, sewage farms.

Range and Status: Breeds far-n. Eurasia from Norway to ne. Siberia and s. to about 50°N.; winters Africa, s. and se. Asia, Japan, Philippines, Sunda Is., NG and Australian region. Regular migrant to Aust. Sept.–Apr. Moderately common n. Aust., uncommon but fairly regular coastal and subcoastal s. Aust.; sparse through inland on suitable habitat; vagrant Tas.

224 GREY-TAILED TATTLER *Tringa brevipes* Pl.33, 38

Other names: Grey-rumped Sandpiper, Asiatic Tattler.

Field marks: 255 mm. An elegant, softly shaded wader. Nonbreeding: plain-grey above; white eyebrows nearly meet across forehead; whitish below, washed grey across breast; occasionally with faint barrings on flanks. Bill straight, grey, occasionally yellowish near base; *nasal groove extends approximately half total length*: legs dull orange-yellow or yellow-green. Breeding plumage: throat, breast and flanks finely barred dark-grey, *but belly and under tail-coverts unmarked*. Singly or with other waders, parties or small flocks. Not shy, but of nervous appearance; bobs head, wags rear of body up and down. Perches on snags, rocks; typically flies low across water with clipped wingbeats, calling; on alighting, raises wings vertically, *showing grey 'armpits' and white wing-linings*.

Similar species: Wandering Tattler (225). Knots (236–7): sturdier, more mottled above; both have more-or-less pale rump. Wood Sandpiper (223): freckled white above, white rump and tail barred darker.

Voice: Drawn-out liquid 'tlooeep' or 'weet-eet'; more scratchy 'peep, peepeepeep' or strident 'klee-klee, klee-klee, tooee, tooee'. None really staccato.

Habitat: Estuaries, wave-washed rocks and reefs; waterways in mangroves; tidal mudflats, beaches.

Range and Status: Breeds c. and e. Siberia (see next species); winters se. China, Taiwan, Japan, se. Asia, Philippines, Sunda Is. to NG, Solomon Is. and islands in n. Indian Ocean and w. Pacific. Fairly common regular migrant Sept.–Apr. to coasts and coastal islands of n. Aust. from about Shark Bay, WA, to about Sydney, NSW; uncommon on s. coasts, regular but uncommon Tas. Some overwinter, mostly in n.

225 WANDERING TATTLER *Tringa incana* Pl.33, 38

Field marks: 265–285 mm. In nonbreeding plumage distinguished from Grey-tailed Tattler (224) only by darker upperparts; *nasal groove extending three quarters length of bill*; *different call*: a rippling trill of 6–10 accelerating notes of decreasing volume. Breeding plumage: *entire underparts, including under tail-coverts, heavily barred dark-grey*; traces of barring may persist in nonbreeding plumage.

Habitat: Like Grey-tailed Tattler, but in Aust. most typically reefs, islands and beaches, occasional other tidal areas.

Range and Status: Breeds ne. Siberia, Alaska and n. Canada; winters c. and s. America and widely on islands in w. Pacific s. to NZ. Rare but probably regular migrant Sept.–Mar. to Gt. Barrier Reef islands and (much less commonly) to coasts of e. Aust. s. to c. NSW (Botany Bay). Also Lord Howe I.

226 COMMON SANDPIPER *Tringa hypoleucos* Pl.33, 38

Other name: Summer Snipe.

Field marks: 195–215 mm. A dainty slender sandpiper, characterized by constant nervous teetering while perched or walking. *Bronze-brown above*, white below; washed brown at sides of breast; eyebrow and eyering whitish, slight dark mark from bill through eye; *white of breast forms slight white 'hook' round bend of wing*. Bill fine, brown with base of lower mandible buff; legs grey-green, tinged yellow. Solitary, or occasional small parties; feeds on margins of shallow water; perches rocks, branches, boats, jetties, piles. Flight very distinctive: clipped shallow wingbeats, with pause after each downstroke or every few strokes to glide on strongly down-arched wings; note broad white wingbar and white sides of brown rump and tail.

Similar species: Wood Sandpiper (223): darker and greyer, spotted white above, white rump; no wingbar.

Voice: Plaintive, piping 'twee-wee-wee' somewhat like Varied Sittella (571) or Welcome Swallow (420).

Habitat: Pebbly or muddy edges of rivers and streams, coastal to far inland; dams, lakes, sewage farms; margins of tidal rivers; waterways in mangroves or saltmarsh; mudflats; rocky or sandy beaches; riverside lawns; drains, street gutters.

Range and Status: Breeds w. and n. Europe to far-n. Asia and n. Japan; winters s. Europe, Africa, India, s. and se. Asia to Sunda Is., NG, Aust. and NZ. Regular migrant to Aust. both coastal and inland, July–May; more common in n. and e. Aust. and on w. coast than in se. and Tas., where rather rare. Some overwinter.

227 GREENSHANK *Tringa nebularia* Pl.33, 38

Other name: Common Greenshank.

Field marks: 305–340 mm. A distinctive largish wader of lively nervous character and strident calls. *Note longish slightly upturned lead-grey bill* and grey-green legs. Nonbreeding: general appearance very pale with greyish crown; nape and wings slightly streaked darker. Breeding plumage: browner-grey above with some black feathers on wings and back. Often solitary but small parties to flocks of dozens or even hundreds are seen, specially in n. Aust. Nervously active; often dashes about while feeding; very wary, bobs head, flushes with ringing alarm-calls. Flight fast with clipped wingbeats; *white back and rump contrast with dark wings*; *no wingbar*.

Similar species: Marsh Sandpiper (229): smaller, whiter, note black needle-like bill; the proportionately longer legs protrude in flight.

Voice: Strident 'tew-tew', or 'tew-tew-tew' with somewhat sobbing intonation: often heard at night.

Habitat: Mudflats, estuaries, saltmarshes, margins of inland swamps and lakes, sewage farms.

Range and Status: Breeds from Scotland to s. and ne. Siberia; winters Africa, s. China, Japan to s. and se. Asia and Sunda Is., Moluccas, NG, Aust. and NZ. Regular widespread migrant to Aust. and Tas. Sept.–Apr. Coastal districts, coastal islands and in lesser numbers in suitable habitat through inland. Common to uncommon; some overwinter.

228 REDSHANK *Tringa totanus*

Other name: Common Redshank.

Field marks: 280 mm. Like a small brownish Greenshank (227), *but bill orange-red at base, tipped black*; *legs orange-red*. Grey-brown above, mottled darker; paler below and streaked; *tail barred black and white*. Imm: buffer, with yellowish legs. In Aust. has been met singly, with other waders and in a flock. Nervous, bobs head; perches on low objects; noisy. Flight fast and direct, with quick, clipped wingbeats, showing conspicuous unusual combination of *white rump and broad white trailing edge of wings*.

Similar species: Greenshank (227). Godwits (234–5): bills longer, pink at base; no red on legs.

Voice: Usual call: musical down-slurred 'tleu-hu-hu'. Alarm-call strident, high-pitched repeated yelping 'teuk' or 'chip'. When flushed, a volley of high-pitched notes. (European data).

Habitat: Records from near Darwin, NT, refer to a tidal sandbar at the mouth of a tidal creek and a beach, with mudflats beyond mangroves; a (? tidal) pool at the edge of rocks and a freshwater lagoon near Daly R., NT.

Range and Status: Breeds across n. Eurasia mainly below 60°N; winters Africa, Asia Minor, s. Asia, se. Asia to Philippines, Borneo and Indonesian region, including Timor. Australian sight-records: on coast within 20 km ne. of Darwin, NT, (single bird and flock of 17 during July 1970); single birds Elizabeth Downs Station, Daly R., c. 140 km ssw. of Darwin, Nov. 1973, and Lee Point, near Darwin, Jan. 1975. Vagrant on present records but may prove regular uncommon migrant to coastal n. Aust.

229 MARSH SANDPIPER *Tringa stagnatilis*   Pl.33, 38

Other name: Little Greenshank.

Field marks: 200–230 mm. Like a small fine Greenshank (227); nonbreeding plumage fairly similar, but more *needle-like bill black, legs proportionately longer and more stiltlike, yellow-green to green-grey*. Breeding plumage: feathers above have black centres and buff edges giving spotted look. Singly, parties, occasionally in flocks. Active, wades to full length of legs; sometimes swims, head high, busily picking food off surface. Flight very fast, wingbeats clipped, contrasting pattern of dark wings, white rump extending up back in long wedge, and white tail; *legs protrude noticeably farther than Greenshank.*

Similar species: Wood Sandpiper (223).

Voice: Soft 'teeoo'; on being flushed, sharp 'yip-tchik' or 'chiff, chiff'; twittering trills.

Habitat: Freshwater swamps, bore-drains, salt or brackish lakes; sewage farms, commercial saltfields, mangrove swamps, occasional tidal mudflats, estuaries.

Range and Status: Breeds from Austria to n. Mongolia; winters Africa, Asia Minor, India, se. Asia to Moluccas, Sunda Is., Aust., vagrant NZ. Regular migrant to Aust. Aug.–May; records all States, coastal and inland. Fairly common n. Aust.; regular but scarce to rare s. Aust. and Tas. but of recent years recorded more frequently, and in larger numbers. (Flocks of 60–200 + Kooragang I., Hunter R., NSW, Oct. 1972, and c. 80 Langhorne's Ck., SA).

230 TEREK SANDPIPER *Tringa terek*   Pl.33, 39

Field marks: 215–250 mm. An unusual wader, about the size of Curlew Sandpiper (244); easily distinguished by *long slightly upcurved black bill (occasionally yellow at base) and conspicuous orange-red or orange-yellow legs.* Nonbreeding: pale-grey to grey-brown above, white below, streaked faintly on breast; shoulder darker, part-visible white bar on wing (secondaries), two black lines down back. Breeding plumage: browner. Usually singly or small parties, but recorded in high-tide concentrations of hundreds on e. coast. Can look rather squat and hunched but when alert stands upright, revealing a longish neck; active; jerks tail, bobs head; shape of bill seems suited to its habit of dashing about after small crabs etc. in a crouched posture, with head lowered, also probes mud rapidly with bill. Flight strong and direct, often high; note *broad white trailing edge of wings near body contrasting with dark primaries.*

Voice: Described as a pleasant muscial trill, 'teerrr-da-weet, teerr-da-weet-a-weet' repeated; a rapid high-pitched 'tee-tee-tee'; also fluty 'du-du-du-du-du'!

Habitat: Tidal mudflats, estuaries; shores and reefs of offshore islands; coastal swamps; commercial saltfields.

Range and Status: Breeds s. Finland, Russia to ne. Siberia; winters Africa, Persian Gulf, India, se. Asia, Indonesia to NG, Aust. and NZ. Regular migrant to coastal Aust.

Sept.–May; fairly common from n. WA to Hunter R., NSW; elsewhere rare or scarce, vagrant Tas. Some overwinter.

231 JAPANESE SNIPE *Gallinago hardwickii*   **Pl.33, 38**

Other names: Australian, Common, Jack or Latham's Snipe; Bleater, Longbill.
Field marks: 240–260 mm. Its most striking feature is the *very long (75 mm) straight bill*, and large dark eye, set high in head. Plumage 'camouflaged' and somewhat like dead leaves; *crown dark-brown, split by buff line, upperparts divided by bold brown stripes and cream streaks*; flanks barred, belly whitish; legs short. Singly, loose parties or occasionally large open companies. Shy; feeds busily, ramming bill vertically into mud with rapid sewing-machine action. Usually flushed unexpectedly, bursting up in fast twisting or zigzagging flight, alarm-call flushing others nearby. *Note the very long bill, conspicuous white belly and underwing.* May dash wildly into sky and check and quickly drop to cover. In hand, 18 or fewer tail feathers; Swinhoe's Snipe has 20 or more.
Similar species: Swinhoe's Snipe (232); Painted Snipe (196). Godwits and other long-billed sandpipers are often incorrectly called snipe.
Voice: When flushed, quick explosive 'zhak!', like a quick tearing of cloth or sandpaper.
Habitat: Typically soft wet ground or shallow water with good cover of tussocks or other growth such as wet parts of paddocks, seepage below dams, irrigation areas; also scrub and open woodland, from sea-level to 2000 m. It seeks out such places even though they may be small local pockets in otherwise unsuitable habitat. It frequently occurs on alpine bogs and occasionally on bare muddy margins of rivers, reservoirs, lakes and swamps, in 'samphire' *Arthrocnemum* on tidal saltmarsh and mangrove fringes.
Range and Status: Breeds Japan (Hokkaido and Honshu); Kuril Is., USSR. Regular migrant to n., e. and se. Aust. and some coastal islands Aug.–Apr. Its stronghold here seems to be from Darling Downs, se Q, through e. and s. NSW, Vic., Tas. and se. SA; it occurs on Kangaroo I., SA, w. (? occasional) to Eyre Pen. and Ooldea. Mostly coastal and sub-coastal, but substantial inland movement through Murray–Murrumbidgee irrigation areas; records w. to Mt. Isa-Augathella, Q; Ivanhoe-Hay, NSW; Mannahill–Orrorroo, SA. Some overwinter. Common locally, but generally uncommon. Also NG; occasional L. Howe I. and NZ.

232 SWINHOE'S SNIPE *Gallinago megala*

Other names: Chinese, Marsh or Pintailed Snipe.
Field marks: 260–290 mm. Like Japanese Snipe (231) and probably not safely distinguishable in field; *slightly larger and paler, with broad white tips to tail feathers.* Note limited Australian range. In hand, note more than 18 tail-feathers; length of wing (measured from body along underwing to tip) under 150 mm. (Japanese Snipe: 18 tail-feathers, or fewer; wing over 152 mm).
Voice: A sharp rasping alarm-note is reported.
Habitat: Wet grassy ground, edges of reedy swamps.
Range and Status: Breeds c. Siberia and Mongolia; winters widely from s. Asia to NG. Probably a regular migrant to top end NT and elsewhere in coastal n. Aust. during our summer. Note: the identity and status of snipe observed in coastal n. Aust. is open to question as other Asian species occur on migration in Indonesian region and may reach n. Aust.

233 ASIATIC DOWITCHER *Limnodromus semipalmatus*

Field marks: 250–350 mm. Nonbreeding: like a small grey Bar-tailed Godwit (235), with shorter blackish legs and *longer blunt black bill. Note dark line through eye and thin off-white eyering. Darker brown* above than a godwit, streaked paler, flanks pale with brown scaly markings; under tail-coverts white, barred brown. Breeding plumage: head, neck underparts rufous, back rufous with large spots. Note characteristic feeding behaviour:

walks jerkily, plunging bill into the mud with a sewing machine action, near or in water, sometimes submerging head.
Similar species: Bar-tailed Godwit (235).
Voice: Not recorded in Aust.
Habitat: Tidal mudflats and sandflats, shingle or gravel-banks on shoreline.
Range and Status: Breeds Siberia, Mongolia, ne. China; winters s. Asia, w. to Aden, Malaysia, Indonesia. Australian records: Darwin NT, Oct 1971, Little R., Vic., Jan. 1973 and Queenscliff, Vic., Jan. 1974; Moreton Bay, Q, Jan. 1976. Vagrant.

234 BLACK-TAILED GODWIT *Limosa limosa*   Pl.32, 37

Field marks: 355–430 mm. Like Bar-tailed Godwit (235) but bill straighter. Nonbreeding: *greyer, less streaked and mottled but bold wing and tail markings in flight.* Breeding plumage: head, neck and breast rich rusty; eyebrow cream; upperparts richly patterned black and rusty; flanks barred black and white; wing and tail markings as above. Imm: buffish neck and breast. Singly, small flocks, but in places e.g. near Darwin, Brisbane and Kooragang I., Hunter R., NSW, in companies of hundreds; often with Bar-taileds; compare bills and look for Black-tailed's white underwing when stretching wings. Movements unhurried, deeply probes mud. Flight swift, often low over water, occasionally erratic; *note bold white wingbar and underwing, black flight feathers; white rump and black tail; legs extend farther than Bar-tailed.*
Similar species: Bar-tailed Godwit (235). American or Hudsonian Black-tailed Godwit *L. haemistica* (vagrant to NZ): black armpits (axillaries) and dusky underwings, white wingbar less conspicuous.
Voice: Staccato, slightly harsh, 'witta-wit' or 'reeta reeta reeta'; when feeding, single 'kuk'.
Habitat: Tidal mudflats, sandspits, swamps, shallow river-margins; reservoirs, sewage farms; inland on larger shallow fresh or brackish waters.
Range and Status: A widespread n. hemisphere species breeding from Iceland and w. Europe to n. Asia. The race that occurs in Aust., *melanuroides*, breeds from Mongolia to n. Siberia; winters s. and se. Asia, Philippines, Indonesian region, Bismarck Archipelago; occasional NG and NZ. Regular migrant to Aust. Sept.–May; common from n. WA to c. NSW coast; coastal islands in n. and e. and on Gt. Barrier Reef; widespread but scarce in s. Aust.; vagrant Tas. Inland records in nw. and sw. Q, w. NSW and nw. Vic. indicate a regular inland passage; some overwinter.

235 BAR-TAILED GODWIT *Limosa lapponica*   Pl.32, 37

Other name: Eastern Bar-tailed Godwit.
Field marks: 380–455 mm. A large, pale-brown, streaked wader with *a conspicuously long, slightly upturned bill;* female larger and longer-billed. Nonbreeding: pale grey-brown above, streaked and mottled darker brown; fawn eyebrow runs back and up from behind eye; pale below, fine dark streaks on neck and upperbreast. When bird stretches, *note finely barred underwing.* Breeding plumage, male: head and body orange-rufous or brick-red, upperparts richly patterned black and buff. Female: head and body deep-buff. All plumages: *bill pink at base, blackish toward tip; rump and tail whitish, barred darker.* Singly, parties or, in suitable roosts, flocks of many hundreds. Not shy; rams bill deep into soft ground when feeding, often wades deep. Sometimes roosts in vegetation e.g. mangroves. Flight swift, direct, often in staggered lines or chevrons low to water, *revealing whitish rump and tail, barred darker.* Note that European race, *lapponica,* suspected in Aust., has unbarred white rump and whitish underwings.
Similar species: Black-tailed Godwit (234). Greenshank (227): much paler; heavier lead-grey bill. Note call.
Voice: Staccato, muted but rather scratchy 'ketta-ket'; soft 'kit-kit-kit-kit'.
Habitat: Tidal mudflats, estuaries, sewage farms; occasionally on shallow river-

margins, brackish or salty inland lakes, flooded pastures, airfields, usually in places where soft sand or mud permits probing.
Range and Status: The race *baueri* of this widespread n.-hemisphere wader breeds in n. Siberia e. from about lat. 110°, and in nw. Alaska; winters China, Taiwan, Japan, Philippines, Indonesia, NG, Aust. and NZ and islands in NZ region. Common widespread migrant to Aust. and Tas. Sept.–Apr. Commonest on coasts and coastal islands, except sw. WA where uncommon; many inland records and probably regular inland passage; often overwinters (usually in non-breeding plumage).

236 KNOT *Calidris canutus*   Pl.34, 38

Other names: Common, Grey-crowned, Lesser or Red Knot; Knot-Snipe.
Field marks: 255 mm. A rather squat horizontal wader: note robust tapering black bill and rather short dull-green legs. Nonbreeding: white eyebrow, shadowy dark mark from bill through eye; grey above with *inconspicuous scaly pattern from fine pale margins of wing-feathers*; pale below, with slight flecking. Breeding plumage: head and body rust-red; crown and upperparts richly speckled black and silver, pale rump and wingbar; female duller. Moulting birds often show rusty traces. Small numbers with other waders, or *close flocks* (packs), sometimes large in suitable high-tide roosts. Feeds with rapid down-thrusts of bill, head often submerged. In flight, note *robust bill, pale wingbar, dark-flecked pale rump and darker tail*.
Similar species: Great Knot (237). Sanderling (246): smaller, runs more. Nonbreeding: whiter; blackish shoulder. In flight, whiter wingbar, dark centre to white rump.
Voice: Throaty 'knut-knut', screeched 'nyut', whistling 'twit-twit', higher-pitched 'too-it–wit'; subdued musical chatter while feeding or in flight.
Habitat: Tidal mudflats and sandflats, beaches, saltmarshes; occasionally wet or flooded pastures or ploughed lands.
Range and Status: Breeds throughout Arctic; winters on s. continents and islands, to NZ and NZ sub-Antarctic islands. Regular, mostly coastal, migrant to Aust. and Tas. Aug.–Apr.; moderately common in n., mostly scarce on s. coasts; sparse (? but regular) sub-inland. Some overwinter, some assuming full breeding plumage.

237 GREAT KNOT *Calidris tenuirostris*   Pl.34, 38

Other names: Japanese, Slender-billed or Stripe-crowned Knot; Great Sandpiper.
Field marks: 280–300 mm. *A thickset low-slung wader*, larger and heavier than Knot (236); near Grey Plover (201) in size, with longish heavy-based black bill and dark-streaked crown; legs sturdy, green-grey. Nonbreeding: grey above, heavily mottled and streaked dull white and blackish; *white below, usually with dark spots on breast and flanks*. Breeding plumage: head and neck strongly striped black and brown; upperparts chestnut, brown, buff and grey, *large black spots on chest* sometimes forming a black band. With other waders, specially godwits or in small to large *compact* flocks. Feeds slowly, deeply probling mud or sand. Flight strong and direct; *faint white wingbar, whitish rump with few dark mottlings; tail grey-brown*.
Similar species: Knot (236).
Voice: Usually silent, but said to utter double whistle; other calls similar to Knot's.
Habitat: Tidal mudflats, sandy ocean shores; occasionally inland fresh and salt-lakes.
Range and Status: Breeds ne. Siberia, winters Persian Gulf, s. and se. Asia, Philippines, Indonesia, NG; regular migrant to Aust., coastal islands and Tas. Sept.–Mar.; inland occurrences nw. Q, nw. Vic. Common and abundant top end NT, apparently becoming so in coastal e. Q, where large numbers have been observed Plantation Creek estuary, n. of Burdekin R. Scarce to rare other States but occasionally locally abundant. Many more records in recent years of a bird that before about 1950 was seldom observed (? or recognized) in Aust. Some overwinter, specially in n. Aust.

238 SHARP-TAILED SANDPIPER *Calidris acuminata* **Pl.34, 39**

Other names: Asiatic or Siberian Pectoral Sandpiper, Sharp-tailed Stint, Snipe.
Field marks: 180–230 mm. The somewhat pointed tail is *not* a useful field mark. Non-breeding: note the *rufous crown* with fine dark streaks; fawn eyebrow, most obvious behind eye, and the well-marked feathers of upperparts, specially the *long pointed dark, pale-edged scapulars* (feathers down sides of back); neck and breast fawnish with *sparse streaks and spots*; underparts whitish. Breeding plumage: buffer, breast and flanks more heavily marked with darker spots, 'boomerangs' on flanks. Bill straight, pale grey-brown, darker at tip, legs usually dull olive-yellow, yellow-grey or grey-olive. Imm: more ochre; crown rufous. In flight no obvious wingbar; rump and tail dark-brown in centre, white on sides. Small to large parties; feeding habits, like form and plumage, are generalized; associates freely with other waders. There is much variation in size, some males very large.
Similar species: Pectoral Sandpiper (239); Long-toed Stint (243); Curlew Sandpiper (244), non-breeding; Ruff (249).
Voice: On taking flight, dry 'trit-trit'; musical twitter.
Habitat: Varied: tidal mudflats, mangrove swamps, saltmarshes; shallow fresh, brackish, salt inland swamps and lakes; flooded and irrigated paddocks; sewage farms, commercial saltfields.
Range and Status: Breeds Arctic Siberia; winters India to NG and sw. Pacific islands, Aust., NZ and NZ sub-Antarctic islands, including Macquarie I.; vagrant Europe, n. America. *One of the commonest most widespread wader migrants* to coastal and inland Aust. and Tas.. Aug.–Apr.; mostly passage migrant n. Aust.; seldom overwinters.

239 PECTORAL SANDPIPER *Calidris melanotos* **Pl.34, 39**

Other name: American Pectoral Sandpiper.
Field marks: 180–240 mm. The n. American close relative of Sharp-tail (238). It is 'different': a plainer, browner, subtly longer-billed, longer-necked bird. Main field mark is the *heavily brown-streaked neck-and-breast, sharply cut off from the whitish underparts*; the crown is brownish like neck, not tawny. Bill slightly downcurved, olive-yellow at base, tipped dusky; legs pale to deep-yellow, generally but not always brighter than Sharp-tail. Some males very large. Rare in Aust., usually solitary or with Sharp-tails and easily over-looked; occasionally in small pure flocks. Rather shy, with characteristic mannerisms: when approached, may crane upright 'on toes', or freeze flat on ground; when flushed, zigzags like a snipe, uttering distinctive flight-call. *From below, dark wing-linings are said to form a band with sharply cut-off dark upperbreast.*
Similar species: Ruff (249); non-breeding.
Voice: Harsher and distinctly different from Sharp-tail: a deep reedy rather musical chirp or chirrup, like Budgerigar (337); also dry 'trrt-trrt'.
Habitat: Rather than mudflats, *favours shallow fresh water*, often with low grass or other green herbage, on swamp-margins, flooded pastures, sewage farms; occasional tidal areas, saltmarsh.
Range and Status: Breeds American Arctic and ne. Siberia; winters s. South America, many fewer to Japan, Korea, Hawaiian Is., Samoa, NG and NZ; vagrant Europe, Africa. Regular, scarce to rare migrant to Aust. and Tas., Aug.–Apr.; scattered records all States, mostly coastal; inland in Murray–Darling Basin and w. Vic.

240 BAIRD'S SANDPIPER *Calidris bairdii*

Field marks: 175–190 mm. Nonbreeding: larger and buffer than Red-necked Stint (242), *back with dark scaly pattern*; forehead, eyebrow, throat and belly whitish; *upperbreast buff-brown*; bill and legs black. Breeding plumage: deeper buff. Likely to be met singly; rather quiet; when feeding, picks rather than probes; carries itself horizontally, *dark wingtips protruding beyond tail*. In flight, general buffishness contrasts with black flight-feathers; note faint white wingbar, conspicuous white sides to dark rump.

Similar species: Sharp-tailed (238) and Pectoral (239) Sandpipers, Buff-breasted Sandpiper (247).
Voice: Flight-call, shrill 'kreep', not unlike Sanderling (246).
Habitat: Tidal mudflats, damp grassy areas.
Range and Status: Breeds e. Siberia, Arctic n. America, Greenland; winters round Pacific and to S. America. Vagrant s. Asia and Africa. Australian records: Derwent Estuary, Tas., Oct. 1966; Mystic Park, Vic., Nov. 1974. Vagrant.

241 WESTERN SANDPIPER *Calidris mauri*

Field marks: 140–170 mm. Rather like a large Red-necked Stint (242), *with longer heavier black bill, drooped downwards at tip*; legs black. Nonbreeding: grey-brown above, *white eyebrow and rusty marks on crown and scapulars*. Breeding plumage: rusty crown, back and scapulars contrast with white face and underparts, some blackish or rusty mottling at sides of breast; dark line from bill through eye isolates long white eyebrow running from forehead back past eye. Singly or with other small waders; active; runs, wades, submerges head when feeding. In flight, dark centre and white edges to rump and tail.
Similar species: Red-necked Stint (242); Dunlin (245); Broad-billed Sandpiper (248).
Voice: Variously reported to be a high-pitched 'cheep', a thin 'jeet' not drawn out, a thin 'chree-rp'.
Habitat: Tidal shores and mudflats, salt and freshwater marshes.
Range and Status: Breeds ne. Siberia and on coasts of n. and w. Alaska; winters mostly S. America, Australian records: Sandford, Tas., Sept. 1969 and Ticehurst Swamp near Ivanhoe, NSW, May 1974. Vagrant.

242 RED-NECKED STINT *Calidris ruficollis*   Pl.34, 39

Other names: Land-snipe, Little Dunlin or Stint; Red-necked Sandpiper, Rufous-necked Stint.
Field marks: 150 mm. A tiny common wader, in parties or dense small to large flocks that plunge and wheel, settling instantly to run about and feed with sewing-machine action. Nonbreeding: grey-brown above, streaked and mottled darker, slight dark mark from bill through eye; *forehead, eyebrow, cheeks and underparts white*; grey-brown of back extends to side of neck, often with zone of fine streaks across upperbreast; bill black, straight, tapering; legs black. Breeding plumage: head, neck and upperbreast *washed deep salmon-pink*; upperparts mottled black, brown and chestnut. In flight, *white wingbar, white margin to rump and tail*.
Similar species: Long-toed Stint (243): browner with brown breastband; legs greenish-yellow. Sharp-tailed (238); Curlew (244) and Broad-billed (248) Sandpipers.
Voice: When feeding, constant twitterings: when flushed, weak 'chit, chit' or quick high-pitched trill.
Habitat: Tidal mudflats, saltmarsh, sandspits; sandy or shell-grit beaches; shallow margins of salt, brackish or freshwater lakes often far inland; sewage farms, commercial saltfields.
Range and Status: Breeds n. and ne. Siberia, n. Alaska; winters China, Japan, Taiwan, Andaman and Nicobar Is., Philippines, Indonesia, NG; Aust. and NZ; vagrant NZ sub-Antarctic islands. Very common widespread regular migrant to coastal and (less-commonly) inland Aust. and Tas., Aug.–May. Often overwinters, usually in nonbreeding plumage.

243 LONG-TOED STINT *Calidris subminuta*   Pl.34

Other name: Middendorf's Stint.
Field marks: 145–165 mm. Tiny; like a rounder-headed Red-necked Stint (242) *with greenish-yellow legs and a more distinct breastband*. Nonbreeding: mouse-brown above,

slightly mottled darker, faint white eyebrow; whitish below *with broad grey or brown zone across breast*. Breeding plumage: crown chestnut; rest of head, neck and upperbreast dull cinnamon-brown; *a broad dark stripe from bill through eye, with whitish streak above and below*; back and wings mottled black and chestnut; underparts whitish. Look for it among flocks of (238, 242). Feeds slowly and mouse-like or actively, making quick little runs; stands tiptoe and cranes neck to view intruder or freezes flat. In flight (described in one account as snipelike, zigzagging and towering) no obvious wingbar; darker rump edged white, tail dark, without conspicuous white margins.

Similar species: Sharp-tailed (238) and Pectoral (239) Sandpipers.

Voice: Loud for size, usually in flight; described as resembling short bursts from bicycle-bell, a trilled 'chrreee-chrreee', 'chring' or 'trring-trring'; also 'chee', singly or rapidly repeated.

Habitat: Shores of coastal and inland freshwater or brackish lakes and swamps; streams with muddy fringes; floating masses of weed along tidelines.

Range and Status: Breeds across Siberia, from Ural Mts. to far-n. Pacific, and islands; winters s. and se. Asia, w. to India and e. to Sunda Is., Celebes and e. NG. Regular but scarce migrant to Aust. Sept.–Apr.; recorded nearly annually in Vic. (mostly near w. of Melbourne, also Kerang district). Other records: se. SA; ne., nw. and sw. Q; nw. and inland s. WA; top end NT.

244   CURLEW SANDPIPER   *Calidris ferruginea*   Pl.34, 39

Other names: Curlew-stint, Pygmy Curlew.

Field marks: 200–215 mm. In nonbreeding plumage a medium-small grey-brown wader, whitish below and with distinctive *slim longish downcurved black bill* and longish black legs. Apart from bill, the field marks are *white eyebrow and rump, coupled with white wingbar in flight*. Breeding plumage: except for pale patch round base of bill, *rusty to deep-rosy chestnut*, upperparts richly marked darker; in flight, white wingbar, white rump sparsely barred darker. Moulting birds often scattered through flocks show irregular chestnut scaly pattern. Small parties (often with Sharp-tails (238) and Red-necked Stints (242)), to very large compact flocks. Wades to depth of legs, plunging head underwater; active, groups chase in flight; at times flocks of thousands wheel and turn.

Similar species: Dunlin (245); Broad-billed Sandpiper (248).

Voice: Distinctive liquid 'chirrup'; during chases musical twittering 'tirri-tirri-tirri'.

Habitat: Tidal mudflats, reefs, estuaries; saltmarsh, commercial saltfields; shallow fresh, brackish or salt inland waters; sewage farms.

Range and Status: Breeds ne. Siberia; winters Africa, s. and se. Asia to Indonesia, NG and NZ. Widespread common regular and at times very abundant migrant to Aust. Sept.–Apr.; mostly coastal but inland records all States. Perhaps mostly passage migrant in n. Aust. Some overwinter.

245   DUNLIN   *Calidris alpina*

Other name: Red-backed Sandpiper.

Field marks: 170–220 mm. Somewhat like a squat, short-legged Curlew Sandpiper (244) with heavier black bill, *decurved only at tip*. Nonbreeding: grey-brown above streaked darker; pale eyebrow; breast grey, *finely but often uniformly streaked darker, cut off fairly sharply from whitish underparts*. Breeding plumage: chestnut above, mottled and streaked black, face and underparts whitish with *large black patch on lower breast*. Imm: smudgy mark on sides of lower breast. In flight, all plumages, note white wingbar and *black centre to white rump*. Singly or in small parties or with Curlew Sandpipers (244), Sharp-tails (238) and Red-necked Stints (242). Feeds actively, posture hunched.

Similar species: Curlew Sandpiper (244); white rump. Broad-billed Sandpiper (248), non-breeding: difficult to distinguish except for cream stripes on head and back.

Voice: Flight note described as rather weak 'treep' or 'teerp' (England); soft 'pur-r-r-r' (Japan); nasal, rasping 'cheezp' (USA).

Habitat: Tidal beaches and mudflats, commercial saltfields.

Range and Status: Breeds widely in far n. hemisphere, migrating to more southerly parts of n. hemisphere. Few s. hemisphere records but published sight-records from Cairns, Q; w. shores Port Phillip Bay, Vic.; and near Hobart, Tas. – several birds in each area. Dunlins reaching Aust. are possibly of the large race *sakhalina*, breeding far-ne. Siberia. Vagrant.

246 SANDERLING *Calidris alba*   Pl.34, 39

Field marks: 175–205 mm. In nonbreeding plumage the *whitest* sandpiper, crown and upperparts pale-grey with fine black streaks on crown and black centres to feathers of upperparts; *note the rather straight bill and black legs*; *dark bend of wing*; black primaries. Breeding plumage: dark-brown above, mottled rusty or gold, rusty and dark-brown mottlings over throat and upperbreast, cut off sharply from white underparts; moulting birds often patchy. Solitary or with other waders; occasionally in small to large flocks in certain localities, plump and active, potters round beach-debris, chases retreating waves, jabbing bill repeatedly into sand; flies to avoid waves, settles again. In flight, shows the *largest white wingbar of any sandpiper*, near trailing edge of wing, contrasting with dark wing-coverts and flight-feathers.

Similar species: Hooded Dotterel (204), imm.

Voice: Liquid 'twik-twik'; soft querulous 'ket ket ket'.

Habitat: Low beaches of firm sand 'where the waves ebb and flow', often near reefs; occasionally inlets, tidal mudflats.

Range and Status: Breeds throughout Arctic; winters on coasts of s. continents; occasional NZ. Regular migrant coastal Aust., Tas. and coastal islands, Sept.–May. Generally scarce and very patchy, but regular on certain favoured beaches. Some over-winter, and may assume breeding plumage.

247 BUFF-BREASTED SANDPIPER *Tryngites subruficollis*

Field marks: 185–220 mm. About size of Sharp-tailed Sandpiper (238) but more plover-like; bill short, head rounded. *Uniform sandy buff from head to under tail-coverts*, sparse dark spots on breast near bend of wing. Bill black; pale eyering; *legs yellow to orange-yellow*. In flight, *white underwing contrasts buff body*; short rounded brown tail has pale tips. On settling, wings may be held aloft; carriage upright, walks with head jerking.

Similar species: Sharp-tailed (238) and Baird's (240) Sandpipers.

Voice: Subdued sharp 'chek-chek' or 'pik', like stones chipped together; soft 'twut-twut' and low trilled 'pr-r-reet'.

Habitat: Open areas of short grass or succulents; dry ground, margins of freshwater or brackish swamps; occasionally tidal flats.

Range and Status: Arctic n. America and Wrangel I., ne. Siberia; winters S. America; vagrant Europe, Asia, Aust. Sight-records – Vic.: Altona, Mar.–May 1962 and Jan. 1966; Carrum Swamp, Dec. 1965; L. Tutchewope, (2 records) Jan.–Mar. 1966; Swan Hill, Mar. 1976; NSW: Botany Bay, Apr. 1965. Vagrant.

248 BROAD-BILLED SANDPIPER *Limicola falcinellus*   Pl.34, 39

Field marks: 165–190 mm. Intermediate in size between Red-necked Stint (242) and Curlew Sandpiper (244); with *longish black bill stout at base, broadening and turning down near tip*; legs dark olive-grey or greeny-brown. Nonbreeding: grey above, often heavily mottled with blackish centres to feathers; some with rich-tawny margins. *Note dark centre-line on crown, margined on either side by whitish stripe starting at bill*, each stripe splitting into two just past eye. White below, finely streaked darker in zone across fore-head and breast. Breeding plumage: blackish above, feathers edged cream, warm-buff and tawny; similar mottling across breast; *snipe-like creamy double streaks on crown and along back.* Solitary; with other waders or occasional flocks. Runs rapidly; feeds deliberately, with jabbing action, at times with head underwater. Looks very dark in flight: note prominent bill, streaked plumage, *black patch on wing-coverts*; white wingbar, white-edged dark rump and pointed tail.

Similar species: Curlew Sandpiper (244); Dunlin (245) nonbreeding.

Voice: Short trill, 'trii-trii-trit', short high nasal 'treet'; also in flight, 'chetter-chetter'.

Habitat: Tidal flats, exposed reefs, saltmarsh; occasionally freshwater swamps, sewage ponds.

Range and Status: Breeds across n. Eurasia; winters coasts of s. and se. Asia, Sunda Is., Moluccas to NG, Aust., vagrant NZ. Migrant mostly to coastal Aust. and islands Sept.–Apr. Generally scarce to rare, but locally abundant in places e.g. Cairns waterfront, Q; Kooragang I., Hunter R., NSW; a few inland records in se. Aust.: Fletcher's Lake, NSW, Jan. 1963; Mystic Park, Vic., Jan.–Feb. 1966: ACT, Feb. 1969.

249 RUFF (REEVE) *Philomachus pugnax* Pl.34, 38

Field marks: ♂ 300 mm; ♀ 230–275 mm. Note that male is termed Ruff, the much smaller female, Reeve. In nonbreeding plumage somewhat like a very large erect Sharp-tail (238) *with slender neck and small head* without the rufous cap. Bill straight, shortish or faintly downcurved; black or yellow-green at base with black tip; legs long, yellow, orange-yellow, orange-red, green, brown or grey. Head and neck light grey-brown, slightly streaked darker; buff edges of dark-brown feathers of upperparts *give it a scaly look.* Throat and belly whitish, breast uniform mouse-grey to warm-brown or with shadowy scalloping or untidy rufous or black spotting. Breeding plumage (unlikely in Aust.), Ruff: *enormous neck-ruff and ear tufts* variable in pattern and colour: black-and-white, white, finely barred dark-grey, rufous or buff, or mixtures of these. Reeve: more or less heavily mottled blackish above and on upperbreast; throat and belly whitish. Imm: foreneck and sides of breast pinkish-buff. Usually singly in Aust., often with Sharp-tails; feeds deliberately, erect posture becoming somewhat hunched and round-shouldered. Flight strong with regular wingbeats and glides; thin white wingbar and *distinctive large oval white patch on each side of dark rump; toes extend beyond tail-tip.* (In hand, note that feet are partly webbed).

Similar species: Pectoral (239) and Buff-breasted (247) Sandpipers.

Voice: Usually quiet; when flushed, a low 'tu-whit'.

Habitat: Shallows of fresh, brackish and salt lakes; tidal mudflats; commercial saltfields; sewage farms.

Range and Status: Breeds n. Eurasia from France to ne. Siberia; winters Europe, Africa and s. and se. Asia, to Philippines, Borneo and Aust. Rare but probably regular summer migrant mostly to coastal s. Aust. Records, mostly Sept.–Apr.; WA: King R. (s. WA); Hamelin Pool, near Shark Bay. SA: Port Gawler; Kadina (Yorke Pen.); Langhorne's Creek, ICI saltfields, Adelaide Plains (frequently). Tas.: Barilla Bay, near Hobart. Vic.: L. Tutchewope; L. Murdeduke; Carrum Swamp; Altona; Werribee; Little River. NSW: Kooragang I., Hunter R.; Windsor. NT: Darwin.

Phalaropes   Family *Phalaropodidae*

A family of three species of aberrant sandpiper-like waders, sometimes called sea-snipe. They have longish necks, small heads and sharp straight bills; their wings are carried rather low; their toes are not webbed, but lobed like those of coots and grebes. Their plumage is thick and they float high like small gulls. All breed in n. hemisphere and two species winter pelagically in oceanic zones, far from land, feeding on plankton. Even when feeding in shallow waters, they usually swim, typically spinning like tops, dabbing bills into water. Females are larger and in breeding season more colourful than males.

Food: Small crustaceans, molluscs, insects, spiders, vegetable matter.

Range: Circumpolar in n. hemisphere; migrate to continents and oceans of s. hemisphere.

Number of species: World 3; Aust. 3, vagrant.

250 RED-NECKED PHALAROPE *Phalaropus lobatus*

Other name: Northern Phalarope.

Field marks: 165–205 mm. In nonbreeding plumage, a dainty black-and-white wader in size between a Red-necked Stint (242) and Sharp-tailed Sandpiper (238). Note the longish slender neck and shortish legs; the body looks rather flat and broad. Head white with prominent black, curving 'phalarope-mark' *through eye to ear-coverts*; *wings back and tail dark-grey* with several white stripes and bars. Bill black, needle-like, *about same length as head*; legs grey-green. In flight, note dark-grey wings with *prominent pale stripes*, rump dark-grey with white sides, tail grey. Breeding plumage: unmistakable; dark-grey above, including crown and face, throat white; sides of neck and upperbreast reddish rufous; wings and back with snipe-like golden-buff stripes. Male smaller and paler than female. In Aust. has usually been seen singly with other waders; typically swims when feeding and frequently spins, occasionally feeds ashore, jabbing mud; note short legs.

Similar species: Wilson's (251) and Red (252) Phalaropes.

Voice: In flight, described as 'chek', singly or repeated, or 'chick-chick-cher'.

Habitat: Ocean; bays; shallows in saltmarsh and coastal fresh, brackish and salt lakes; commercial saltfields; sewage farms.

Range and Status: Breeds virtually circumpolar in Arctic regions; winters at sea in parts of Atlantic, Pacific and Indian Oceans and e. Asia. Common (*in n. winter*) in seas n. of NG w. from New Britain–New Ireland and, to w. of NG, off Ceram, Ambon, Buru and Celebes. Unknown in Aust. before Dec. 1962 when a presumed male in breeding plumage identified by F. T. H. Smith and H. E. A. Jarman at Werribee Sewage Farm, Vic. Subsequent sight-records of birds in nonbreeding plumage: Werribee, Altona, and Seaholme, Vic., and near Whyalla, SA, (all Nov.–Feb.), and near Darwin, NT, Jan. and Mar. Specimens, (nonbreeding): Langhorne's Creek, near L. Alexandrina, SA, Nov. 1966 and Darwin (East Point), NT, Jan. 1974. Several NZ records. Vagrant.

251 WILSON'S PHALAROPE *Phalaropus tricolor*

Field marks: 215–255 mm, male smaller. Nonbreeding: about the size and colour of a large nonbreeding Curlew Sandpiper (244), with longer neck, smaller head and black needle-like bill *somewhat longer than head*; legs dull-yellow or dark greenish. Forehead, face and underparts white with grey 'phalarope-mark', from bill through eye curving down side of neck; upperparts plain-grey. In flight, note plain darkish wings, *white rump* and grey tail. Breeding, male: grey-brown above, *white spot on nape*; throat white, foreneck warm-buff. Female: black 'phalarope-mark' *extends down neck, merges into chestnut stripe that forks across wing and back*. Flight swift, erratic. More than other phalaropes feeds ashore or on floating weed; reported to run actively about with lurching gait, picking insects with quick sideways movements of head, legs bent, head close to ground, tail raised in manner of a feeding Terek Sandpiper (230). Occasionally flattens itself on water, darting bill at insects.

Similar species: Red-necked (250) and Red (252) Phalaropes.

Voice: A low nasal 'wurk' or 'chek chek chek'.

Habitat: Shallow lakes, swamps, pools, mudflats, saltmarsh; perhaps small dams.

Range and Status: Breeds interior n. America; winters s. S. America; vagrant Europe. Sight-records Vic.: L. Murdeduke, Feb. 1966; Golf-links Swamp, Altona, Nov. 1967–Jan. 1968 and Nov. 1968. (All records F. T. H. Smith, with others.) Vagrant.

252 RED PHALAROPE *Phalaropus fulicarius*

Other name: Grey Phalarope.

Field marks: 190–225 mm. *Bill shorter and sturdier than Red-necked Phalarope (250)*, *black at tip, often yellowish at base* in adults (black in imms.); legs yellowish. Nonbreeding: paler than Red-necked, with more obvious white forehead; plainer, less streaked above, with distinct 'phalarope-mark'. Has been described as resembling a Sanderling (246) with phalarope mark. In flight, wings greyer, large white wingbar, white side of rump; generally less-contrasting pattern than flying Red-necked Phalarope. Breeding, female: forehead and crown blackish, face white, *whole underparts deep-rusty red*; male: duller and paler.

Voice: Described as a shrill 'whit' or 'prip', like Sanderling (246).

Habitat: Oceans; bays; lakes, swamps.

Range and Status: Breeds circumpolar in Arctic regions; winters at sea mostly in s. hemisphere 'mainly w. of Africa and w. of S. America' (Checkl. Birds NZ, 1970). Rare vagrant to e. coast, NZ, where three females in breeding plumage have been collected in the past 100 years. One Australian sight-record: near Woorinen, Swan Hill district, Vic., Feb. 1976. (F. T. H. Smith). Vagrant.

Pratincoles and Coursers   Family *Glareolidae*

Pratincoles are graceful long-winged aberrant waders of plains and dry wastes. They fly easily like terns or swallows and take insects on wing and on ground, hence alternate name swallow-plover. Bills are short and somewhat curved, with a wide gape. True pratincoles genus *Glareola* are a compact group of 3 species distributed in Europe, Africa and Asia; one, Oriental Pratincole (253) migrates to Aust. They have short legs and longish, deeply forked tails. Another group of 3 species are separated by some in the genus *Galachrysia*. The Australian Pratincole (254) is now usually separated in the monotypic genus *Stiltia*. It is regarded by some as a courser and like members of that group has long legs, long wings and a short tail. It stands more upright than true pratincoles, slopes more to rear and wags rear of body up and down. Unlike either pratincoles or coursers, it lacks pectinations (comb-like processes) on the claw of the middle toe. Like coursers but unlike practincoles, it has no hind toe.

Food: Mostly insects.

Range: Temperate and tropical Europe, Africa, Asia, Aust.; vagrant NZ.

Number of species: World 17; Aust. 2.

253 ORIENTAL PRATINCOLE *Glareola maldivarum*   **Pl.35, 40, 41**

Other names: Grasshopper-Bird, (Little) Storm-bird, Swallow-plover, Swarmer.

Field marks: 230 mm. A small graceful, almost tern-like wader, *forked tail longer than wings*. Apart from the tail, distinguished from Australian Pratincole (254) by shorter legs, lower posture, generally darker colour. Nonbreeding: dusky olive above, rump and tail white, inside margin of fork black; underparts buffish to white. Breeding plumage: *throat creamy buff with black border*. Bill black, short, curved, gape red; legs short, black. Imm: broad breastband of dark streaks. In large to very large cohesive noisy migratory flocks in n. Aust.; mostly singly or in small flocks to s. Aust., associating with Australian Pratincoles and Oriental Plovers (210); and reportedly, in flight, with swifts. On ground runs well, despite short legs; bobs head. Flight very graceful and swallow-like; conspicuously hawks flying insects; note contrast of rich-chestnut underwing, *white trailing edge, abdomen and mostly white forked tail*.

Similar species: Australian Pratincole (254). Note: Black-winged Pratincole *G. nordmanni* of s. Europe and Russia is similar except for black underwing. Unlikely to occur in Aust. but check underwing colour of any Oriental Pratincole.

Voice: Noisy in flight, hard ternlike 'chik chik' or 'kyik', also soft plover-like 'toowheet, toowheet'.

Habitat: Open plains; bare ground on swamp-margins and claypans; mudflats, airfields.

Range and Status: Breeds c. and s. Asia; winters s. to Philippines, Greater Sunda Is. and Aust.; vagrant NG and NZ. Regular migrant mainland Aust. Oct.–May; common and often very abundant in n., rare in s. In WA, numerous, if sporadic, in summer in coastal nw., s. to about Port Hedland. Recent, mostly summer, sight-records of singles and flocks from near Brisbane, Q, (Lockyer Valley); near Sydney, NSW, (Bakers Lagoon, 56 km nw.); Mystic Park and near Melbourne, Vic., (Werribee Sewage Farm); near L. Alexandrina, SA, Dec. 1973, and on Eyre Highway, w. of Nullarbor Stn., SA, May 1974.

254 AUSTRALIAN PRATINCOLE *Stiltia isabella* **Pl.35, 40, 41**

Other names: Australian Courser, Roadrunner, Swallow-plover.

Field marks: 220–240 mm. An upstanding short-tailed wader, ploverlike on ground, ternlike on wing. Sandy rufous above; *long black wingtips extend much beyond tail*; breast washed sandy, lower breast dark-chestnut, abdomen and under tail-coverts white. Bill shortish and curved: red, tipped black; legs long, deep-red. Imm: brown above, feathers margined pale-buff, buff-brown zone with blackish mottlings crosses upperbreast. Bill and legs black. Open flocks; pairs or singly; on ground runs gracefully, bobs head, see-saws rear of body; occasionally wades. At dusk, flocks hawk high for flying insects. In flight, note black underwing, chestnut lower breast, white belly and under tail-coverts and *white base and sides to short black tail*.

Similar species: Oriental Pratincole (253).

Voice: Shrill thin, rather ternlike 'quirree-peet'.

Habitat: Open plains, gibber, claypans; bare dry margins of swamps and stock-tanks, dry floodplains.

Breeding: Eggs: 2–3; laid on bare ground, pale-stone to creamy white, with irregular spots and blotches of grey, brown and black. Young reported to take refuge in burrows, fallen hollow fence-posts.

Range and Status: N. and inland Aust.: coastally s. to about Roebourne–Onslow, WA, and to coastal plains near Townsville, Q. In se. Aust., e. to about Darling Downs, Q; vagrant to near Brisbane (and to Heron I.); in nc. NSW, e. to L. Narran–Macquarie Marshes, in Riverina, e. and s. to about Narrandera–Deniliquin; in Vic., occasional to plains of nw. (Echuca–Kerang–Swan Hill), vagrant Millewa, ne. Vic. and L. Murdeduke, s. Vic.; in SA, many records in recent years s. to L. Alexandrina–Adelaide Plains, (breeding); in s. WA, (?) vagrant to near Naretha (w. Nullarbor) and Pelican Point, Perth. Nomadic, part-migratory: breeds sporadically throughout its range, but probably the main breeding takes place in far-inland and n. sub-coastal areas. Mostly dry season visitor to n. coasts; summer visitor to se. s. and sw. Aust., the extent of the movement depending on seasonal conditions. Migrant to Borneo, Java and NG; (?) resident in s. NG.

Skuas Family *Stercorariidae*

Robust seabirds related to gulls, but with hooked bills, swifter more direct flight and elongated central tail-feathers. They are characterized by relentless pursuit of other seabirds, forcing them to disgorge food, which is seized as it falls. They are also predators and scavengers, following ships for scraps. Two groups are recognized: Great Skua (255) has breeding populations in n. Atlantic and far-s. hemisphere, mostly on sub-Antarctic islands and in Antarctica. Some treat the n. and s. populations as separate species. The most widespread s. race, *lonnbergi*, 'Great Southern Skua', is the usual form on our coasts. Large and blunt in silhouette, it is a powerful predator. Some treat the smaller, paler far-s. form *maccormicki* as a full species. Members of the second group, the Arctic (256), Pomarine (257) and Long-tailed (258) Skuas, breed in far-n. hemisphere and winter in oceans and on coasts of s. hemisphere; two are regular summer migrants to Australian waters. Smaller than the Great Skua, they can be distinguished by their swept pointed wings, swift effortless, almost falcon-like flight, and by the shape of their elongated central tail-feathers. These are prominently developed in breeding adults, but smaller, broken or absent in nonbreeding adults and immatures. The Arctic and Pomarine Skuas have distinctive light and dark phases, with variable intermediates. Imms. have different, mottled plumage.

Food: Whole prey disgorged by other seabirds; flotsam, scraps, refuse from whaling and fishing operations and other carrion; fish, squids, small mammals, young and eggs of other seabirds. Small species take insects on wing.

Number of species: World 4; Aust. 4 (1 as rare vagrant).

255 GREAT SKUA *Stercorarius skua*   Pl.26

Other names: Antarctic Skua; Bonxie; Dark, Southern (or Dark S. or Great S.) Skua; Port Egmont Hen, Robber Gull, Sea Hawk.

Field marks: 610–660 mm; span 1.5 m. Like a stout dark-brown gull with *white patch at base of primaries*, conspicuous in flight; tail short, central pair of tail-feathers scarcely protrude, but separate to form a slight notch. Bill black, gull-like but hooked; feet black, webbed. Flight powerful and hawklike with regular easy wingbeats; when attacking, accelerates wingbeats, hurtles at gannets, gulls, terns or petrels and despite size and bulk follows with close twists until victim disgorges. Follows ships, perching on masts; approaches fishing boats for offal; enters harbours, ashore in places, e.g. Hobart, Tas.; Albany, WA, but usually offshore; scavenges on dead seals, whales, etc., and offal near disposal points.

Similar species: Pacific Gull (260), imm: less bulky; no white wing-patches, plumage more mottled, often with pale rump; bill heavier, often pale and dark-tipped; note flight, habits, habitat.

Voice: Gull-like.

Habitat: Oceans; bays, harbours; sometimes ashore at wharves, beaches.

Range and Status: The race *lonnbergi* breeds Antarctic, sub-Antarctic and NZ region, including w. coast South Island; winters n. to *c.* 33°S. in Pacific, crossing equator in Indian Ocean. Regular uncommon winter visitor to Australian coasts and bays occasional n. to Sandy C., Q, and Geraldton, WA; more common s. WA. Small pale race *maccormicki*, 'South Polar Skua' breeds Antarctica; distinguished by yellowish streaks on nape, winters n. Pacific; vagrant NG. One Australian record: SA, May 1958.

256 ARCTIC SKUA *Stercorarius parasiticus*   Pl.26

Other names: Arctic Gull, Boatswain-bird, Parasitic Jaeger; Parasitic or Richardson's Skua; Parasite or Robber Gull; Sea Pirate, Teaser.

Field marks: 455–510 mm; span 1–1.15 m. A graceful dark seabird: flies high above sea with easy buoyancy and long glides; harries gulls and terns on tapering, sharply angled wings. Note the *two pointed central tail-feathers* that may extend *c.* 100 mm, usually less. First-year birds lack them; imms. and moulting adults often have them short or broken. Adult: light and dark phases, with intermediates. Light phase: grey-brown above, with *black cap and straw-yellow cheeks and neck*; *white below*. In flight, white shafts to primaries on uppersurfaces of wing and a whitish patch along base of primaries on underwing. Dark phase: *uniform dark brown*; in flight, *conspicuous white shafts to primaries*; inconspicuous pale patch below. Imm., all phases: dark-brown above, streaked, barred or mottled buff or white; paler below, with irregular brown barrings. Usually patchy, some show partial pale rear-collar. In flight, *white bases to primaries form an untidy pale patch* on wing; tail squarer than adult, points inconspicuous. Imms. usually outnumber adults in our waters; often in moult, with gaps in wings. Singly or small parties, usually well offshore; apart from parasitism, scavenges scraps and often escorts ships, hanging overhead among gulls; rests on floating planks or boxes; when swimming floats high, wing-tips and tail uptilted.

Similar species: Pomarine (257) and Long-tailed (258) Skuas.

Voice: Mostly silent at sea. Described as a nasal squealing 'eee-air'; alarm-call 'ya-wow', repeated.

Habitat: Coastal offshore waters, larger bays, occasionally coastal inlets, lakes, usually in storms.

Range and Status: Breeds circumpolar regions n. of Arctic Circle and n. Europe, winters oceans and coasts s. hemisphere. Fairly common Oct.–Apr. e. Aust. s. of about Fraser I., Q, to se. Aust., Tas. and SA; uncommon sw. Aust. n. to about Cockburn Sound; some overwinter. Also seas off NG, Bismarck Archipelago, Solomon Is., New Caledonia and NZ.

257　POMARINE SKUA　*Stercorarius pomarinus*　　　　　　Pl.26

Other names: Pomarine Jaeger; Pomatorhine or Twist-tailed Skua.

Field marks: 480–540 mm. Larger and heavier than Arctic Skua (256) with a longer deeper bill; flight less buoyant. Note the *two blunt twisted central tail-feathers*, which project up to 100 mm, giving the tail a heavy look. Some adults and many imms. lack them or have them much-reduced. Plumage: light and dark phases and intermediates as Arctic. Imm: as Arctic; often patchy and with gaps in wings; *white bases to primaries generally more conspicuous, above and below.* When without tail-plumes, adults and imms. best-distinguished by greater size and heavier appearance.

Similar species: Arctic Skua (256).

Voice: Described as a harsh quick 'which-youu'.

Habitat: Offshore waters; enters bays and harbours less often than Arctic.

Range and Status: Breeds from Arctic n. America to Arctic n. Russia – n. Siberia; winters tropical seas and continental waters in s. hemisphere. Fairly common off e. Australian coasts Sept.–Apr., less common to rare (usually well-outnumbered by Arctic) in Bass Strait, Tas. and from Port Phillip Bay to SA waters; regular but scarce off s. WA. Also seas off NG, Bismarck Archipelago, New Hebrides; rare but probably regular NZ.

258　LONG-TAILED SKUA　*Stercorarius longicauda*

Other name: Long-tailed Jaeger.

Field marks: 510–560 mm, including tail 125–250 mm. Like a small slender pale-phased Arctic Skua (256) except for *whiter underparts and very long central tail-feathers, projecting up to 250 mm*; black forehead and crown cut off more sharply from the pale throat and neck, giving it a more capped appearance; shafts of primaries less conspicuously white. Imm: like imm. Arctic, but plainer; *legs blue-grey.* Flight tern-like with light deep wing-beats; wings narrower than Arctic; it lacks the Arctic's heavy-shouldered look; is said to have Arctic's habit of resting on floating driftwood. Usually well offshore.

Similar species: Arctic Skua (256).

Voice: Seldom vocal except at breeding-grounds.

Habitat: In Aust., coastal offshore waters, larger bays.

Range and Status: Breeds round Arctic in scattered colonies; winters at sea in s. hemisphere, perhaps regular but rare in sw. Pacific. Rare summer–autumn visitor to se. Aust.; sight records: Stradbroke I., Q, Apr. 1973; Sydney Harbour *c.* 1930 and off Sydney Heads, Mar. 1973 (other sight-records off Sydney); Port Phillip Bay, Vic., Apr. 1965; near Robe, SA, Apr. 1971. 3 beachwashed Byron Bay, NSW, Jan. 1974. Vagrant NZ.

Gulls, Terns and Noddies   Family *Laridae*

Gulls are sturdier, broader-winged and longer-legged than terns; bills usually more robust and deeper, tails usually squared or rounded. Most have white bodies with grey or black wings and backs; their young are mottled or largely brown and may be taken for different species. Gulls tend to be coastal rather than oceanic in distribution and in Aust. one gull (and some terns) occurs and may breed far inland. Terns in general have sharp fine bills and are more slender with longer narrower wings and typically deeply forked tails; they are more inclined to be migratory and oceanic. They fly gracefully and typically take living food by plunging below, or skimming, the surface; only a few species feed over land. Terns of the largest and most typical group have black caps, greyish wings, white under-parts; most have a characteristic nonbreeding plumage, in which they typically become whiter on the head; imms. are usually like nonbreeding adults. A few species are black or grey-brown above. *Noddies* are a small group of five mostly tropical oceanic terns; the three typical species are sooty, with white or pale-grey caps. The remaining two species belong to different genera and are frequently called terns or ternlets; one is pale-grey, the other spotless white. Most terns (and some gulls) lay their eggs in a scrape in sand; gulls typically build cup-shaped nests on the ground or in low bushes. Noddies typically nest in bushes or trees. Most species form breeding colonies, some immense.

Food: Varied: small aquatic and marine animals, including fish; other animal food, some vegetable food; carrion and refuse.

Range: Nearly worldwide, tending to favour coasts and inland waters. Some terns make long migrations; Arctic Tern (268) makes the longest-known regular annual migration, from breeding grounds in the far-n. hemisphere to the Antarctic zone of pack-ice. At least four terns breed in n. hemisphere and winter Aust. One is a regular migrant from NZ.

Number of species: Gulls: World 43; Aust. 3. Terns: World 35; Aust. 17. Noddies: World 6; Aust. 5.

259 SILVER GULL   *Larus novaehollandiae*   Pl.26

Other names: Hartlaub's, Jameson's, Kitty, Mackerel, Red-billed or Red-legged Gull, Seagull or Sea Pigeon.

Field marks: 380–430 mm. Our familiar seagull: white with pale silver-grey upperparts, wings *tipped black, with white windows*; eye white; *bill, eyering and legs scarlet*. Juv: mottled buff and brown above; bill and legs black. Imm: grey wings marked with several lines of brown spots; dark tips to tail-feathers. Eye brown, bill and legs black at first, then dull yellow-brown. Gregarious; large local populations where food is plentiful: e.g. during upsurges of plankton and at fishing centres, rubbish-tips; newly-ploughed fields. Follows ships near coast and in harbours. In rough weather shelters on town-lakes, playing fields, airfields. Has adapted well to urban areas.

Similar species: See terns (262–277).

Voice: Noisy; usual call, short harsh guttural 'karr' or 'keow'; long call – a harsh grating 'karrr-karrr-karrr', often in chorus. Imms: peevish squeals and trills.

Habitat: Coasts and islands; seldom far to sea; inland on almost any large water.

Breeding: Usually in colonies, some large. Nest: scanty or well-made saucer of seaweed, rootlets, plant-stems; on ground, in low vegetation on islets, rocks, salt-piles, jetties; occasionally fish-boxes, old boats, etc. Eggs: 1–3; pale-brown or even bluish to dark olive-green, thickly blotched, spotted or striped dark-brown and black.

Range and Status: Aust., Tas. and many coastal islands. Common to extremely abundant in s. coastal regions; widespread, but much less common in n. and usually only locally abundant e.g. in vicinity of breeding colonies of other seabirds; occurs throughout inland in suitable habitat. Breeds coastal islands, rocks and reefs; islands in commercial saltfields, and in inland lakes, storages, floodwaters. Sedentary or dispersive. Also New Caledonia, NZ and some NZ sub-Antarctic islands; s. Africa. Vagrant Norfolk I.

260 PACIFIC GULL *Larus pacificus* **Pl.26**

Other names: Jack or Larger Gull; Mollyhawk, Nelly.

Field marks: 580–660 mm; span 1.3–1.5 m. Striking large white gull with black wings and back *and very deep, heavy bill, yellow with broad scarlet tip* – the most robust bill of any gull. At rest, bill and bright-yellow legs are the best field-marks. In flight, look for the *black band across the white tail* – but moulting adults in late summer may have stumpy all-white tails. Imm: differs so much from adult as often to be taken for a different species, *Mollymawks* (see *Mollymawks*, p. 30). Stages between brown first-year plumage and adult plumage in fourth year are confusing but can be recognized as follows:

(1) Fairly uniform dark-brown; glossy black bill and dark eye; legs dark grey-brown.

(2) More mottled (pale edges to feathers) lighter-brown, with paler rump, darker tail. Bill horn-coloured with dark tip; eye pale-brown, legs dark grey-brown.

(3) As above, whiter on forehead, tail nearly black, rump whitish. Bill cream to pale-yellow with dark tip; eye white; legs yellowish.

(4) Like smutty adult *with black tail*, bill yellow with dark tip, legs yellow.

Singly, pairs or loose gatherings, often with Silver Gulls (259). Aggressive, occasionally with noisy displays, especially on breeding islands. When foraging, typically flies steadily along tidelines at about 15 m; in high winds sails majestically; soars up vertically to drop molluscs on rocks; often plunges in shallow water; follows fishing boats, ships.

Similar species: Southern Black-backed Gull (261); Great Skua (255).

Voice: A shouted 'ow! ow!' or more muffled 'auk auk auk'; similar gruff note repeated staccato, almost in a chuckle; whining stutters when disputing food.

Habitat: Coasts and bays, rarely far to sea except round offshore islands. Occasionally on farmland, swamps, rubbish tips near coast; occasionally inland, along rivers.

Breeding: Single pairs, loose colonies on offshore islands. Nest: cup of sticks, stalks, grasses, lined with finer materials; in elevated position. Eggs: 2–3; olive-brown, blotched brown and grey.

Range and Status: Coasts and islands of s. Aust.: from about Hunter R., NSW to Tas. and w. to Eyre Pen., SA, and in s. WA, from Recherche Archipelago to Shark Bay, occasional n. to Pt. Cloates. Vagrant inland, and coastally n. in e. Aust. to se. Q: sight-records Noosa R., Aug. 1971; Bramble Bay, Jan. 1972. There are three main breeding zones: Bass Strait islands (its stronghold); islands in Gulf areas of SA; islands off s. WA. Common; adults sedentary; imms dispersive along coasts.

261 SOUTHERN BLACK-BACKED GULL *Larus dominicanus* **Pl.26**

Other names: Kelp Gull, Dominican Gull.

Field marks: 535–590 mm; span 1.25–1.40 m. Like Pacific Gull (260) but more slender; calls totally different. The main distinguishing marks at rest are (a) *slimmer pale-greenish yellow bill with scarlet spot on lower mandible only*; (2) conspicuous white tips to primaries as well as secondaries; (3) greenish-grey, sometimes yellow legs. In flight, note *pure white tail, white window at wingtips* and broader white trailing edge. Imm: *at first finely speckled brown on white, neck streaked*; bill black, eye dark-brown, legs grey-brown. Several stages before gaining adult plumage in fourth year: head and body become paler, wings darker; bill passes to yellow-brown with dark subterminal ring, to yellow with orange and then red spot; legs to blue-grey, grey-green, dull-yellow or yellow; eye to brown, yellow-brown and finally white. At all stages the more slender bill is a useful mark. Singly or pairs, occasionally flocks.

Voice: *Yelping or laughing* 'yo-yo-yo-yo-yo-yo-yo' with sobbing intonation, like 'seabird calls' often heard in films and on radio. No other local gull has a call remotely like it; also squeals; chucklings.

Habitat: Coastal, offshore or on beaches, sandspits, reefs, jetties, offshore islands.

Breeding: Nest and eggs like Pacific Gull, but eggs slightly smaller.

Range and Status: In Aust. first recognized at Newcastle, NSW, Jan. 1939 but probably overlooked earlier (unrecognized imm. specimen from near Perth, WA, 1923). First bred Moon I., NSW, 1958; subsequent breeding there and other islands in NSW, Vic., Tas. Generally scarce, locally common, becoming established in parts of se. and sw. Aust.; probably most successfully in se. Tas., (Orford–Derwent R. estuary–Bruny I.) where now common resident. Sight-records n. to Cairns and Green I., ne. Q, and to Jurien Bay, WA. Sedentary and dispersive. Also S. Africa, s. S. America, NZ and many sub-Antarctic islands. Closely resembles Lesser Black-backed Gull L. *fuscus* of n. hemisphere. Photographs of a pair of gulls at Gove Pen., ne. Arnhem Land, NT, Oct. 1974 (Aust. Bird Watcher 6:162) may refer to that species.

262 WHISKERED TERN *Chlidonias hybrida* **Pl.27, 29**

Other name: Marsh Tern.

Field marks: 255–270 mm. Largest of the three cosmopolitan marsh terns, see also (263–4); only the Whiskered breeds in Aust. Breeding plumage: black cap extends well down nape *but is cut off at eye-level by white cheeks*, hence 'Whiskered'. These are shaded below by deepening silver-grey underparts; *whole abdomen blackish*. Bill dark-red, legs red. Nonbreeding: bill and legs black, head and underparts white; crown streaked blackish, joining black area that spreads back from eye and merges into grey on nape *leaving no white collar*. Imm: heavily mottled brownish above at first, then like nonbreeding adult, with slight dark mark along wing and noticeably pale rump. Parties to flocks; like other marsh terns, these work into wind over swamps, dipping to surface or plunging with upheld wings, breaking surface but seldom submerging. Associates with the more slightly-built White-winged Black Tern (263) and easily confused. Although the last is in non-breeding plumage when Whiskered is in breeding dress, there are often confusing stages of moult in mixed companies. In general Whiskered is larger, heavier and without a white collar; its wings are more pointed and tipped dark-grey; underwing whiter; tail deeper-forked and greyer. Its flight is more direct, somewhat slower and more laboured, with deeper wingbeats.

Similar species: White-winged Black Tern (263). Common Tern group (267–9) have much deeper-forked, whiter tails.

Voice: A sharp 'kitt' or 'kittitt'; feeding or roosting flocks often chatter excitedly.

Habitat: Freshwater swamps, lakes, flooded inland claypans and depressions; brackish and salt lakes, commercial saltfields, irrigated pastures, sewage farms.

Breeding: Usually loosely colonial. Nest: small pile of vegetation, on islands or floating. Eggs: usually 3; glossy, pale-green to pale-brown to dark-stone, spotted, blotched grey and black, denser toward large end.

Range and Status: Widespread mainland Aust. in suitable habitat; nomadic in n. and inland, mostly breeding migrant in s. between Sept.–Mar.; some overwintering. Locally common, to uncommon and irregular. Vagrant Tas. Also s. Europe, Africa, s. and se. Asia, n. to China and Manchuria, e. to Philippines, Indonesia, NG and NZ.

263 WHITE-WINGED BLACK TERN *Chlidonias leucoptera* **Pl.27, 29**

Other names: Black or White-tailed Tern, White-winged Sea-swallow.

Field marks: 230 mm. Breeding plumage unmistakable, not often seen in Aust.: *black, with white shoulders, rump and tail*; in flight, wing-linings black, remainder of underwing white. Bill black, some tinged red at base, legs red. Nonbreeding: wings above, rump and tail grey; black or smutty band from eyes round rear of crown and *nearly separate patch down over ear-coverts, separated from grey back by white collar*; *rump, underparts and underwing white*. Bill black, legs pinkish black. Imm: similar but shoulders *buffish and blackish*; white rump more definite. Moulting birds are patchily black on sides of face, underparts and underwings, 'like a Dalmatian dog'. Some show the black wing-linings of breeding plumage. Parties to flocks, sometimes large, or with other terns, specially Whiskered (262). Flight more fluttery and buoyant than Whiskered, wings not finely pointed; tail short, barely forked – see Whiskered.

Similar species: Most likely to be confused with nonbreeding Whiskered (262) and Black (264) Terns. The Common Tern group (267–9) and Little (274) and Fairy (275) Terns all have more deeply forked tails, more pointed wings.

Voice: Flocks noisy while feeding. Calls described as buzzing, less shrill than Whiskered: 'keeek-keeek-keeek' with accent at beginning and end of each 'keeek'; rapid 'kik-kik-kik' or single sharp 'kik', a harsher 'kek-kek-kek' or thin rising 'krrreeeek'.

Habitat: In Aust., usually coastal lakes and swamps, fresh, brackish and salt; commercial saltfields, sewage farms; estuaries, coastal waters.

Range and Status: Breeds e. Europe to e. Siberia and Mongolia, s. to Middle East, e. Africa; winters Africa, s. and se. Asia, Philippines, Borneo and Indonesia to Aust., fewer to NG and NZ. Regular migrant Sept.–May in fluctuating numbers to n., e. and se. Aust. Fairly regular in flocks 50 + coastally and in estuaries, coastal and subcoastal swamps s. to about estuary of Hunter R., NSW; larger companies observed offshore. Regular in smaller numbers to se. Tas., coastal Vic., mostly w. of Westernport, and s. SA, from L. Alexandrina to Port Gawler–Yorke Pen. Rare and irregular inland: Richmond, Thargomindah, Q; L. Bathurst and L. Cowal, Booligal and Finley, NSW; Mystic Park, Vic. By late Apr.–May many acquire full breeding plumage; some overwinter. Irruptions into sw. WA have followed tropical cyclones in nw.; vagrant Lord Howe I. from similar causes.

264 BLACK TERN *Chlidonias nigra*

Field marks: 240–255 mm. Breeding plumage: *black with slate-grey wings, back and tail, whitish wing-linings, white under tail-coverts.* Bill black, rather long and slender, legs red-brown. Nonbreeding: like White-winged Black Tern (263); but *uppersurface (wings, back, rump and tail) uniformly grey*; forehead, sides of face and undersurface white; rear of crown, nape and ear-coverts blackish, somewhat more extensive than non-breeding (262–3); *dark shading of back extends in a finger onto sides of breast.* In flight, also note *whitish wing-linings,* never patchy black (moulting birds show patchy black on sides of neck and on breast only). Imm: browner above than adults, may have brownish patches on sides of breast and along leading edge of underwing; bill may be yellowish at base, legs slightly yellower than adult. Flight and feeding habits like other marsh terns with which it associates, wingbeats described as 'fuller and more dynamic' than White-winged Black.

Similar species: Whiskered (262) and White-winged Black (263) Terns, nonbreeding. See also Common Tern group, (267–9).

Voice: Rather quiet; utters rather squeaky, high-pitched 'kik', 'ki-ki-ki' or 'keek keek'.

Habitat: Coastal seas and inlets; freshwater swamps, lakes, rivers; brackish or salt coastal lakes.

Range and Status: Breeds w. Europe to Asia Minor, Russia and Siberia; N. America from Alaska to California; winters Africa, s. Asia and S. America. Australian sight-records: Tuggerah Lakes, NSW, Sept. 1958; Newcastle, NSW, Jan., Mar. 1968; L. Joondalup, s. WA, Dec. 1973. Vagrant.

265 GULL-BILLED TERN *Gelochelidon nilotica* Pl.27, 29

Other name: Long-legged Tern.

Field marks: 355–430 mm. A largish unusual tern with *rather deep, black bill.* Very pale-grey above; white below; at rest wings extend well beyond short tail; legs black, rather long. Breeding plumage: black cap well pulled down over eyes. Nonbreeding: head white, black mark through eye over ear-coverts, with shadowy extension on nape. Imm: more shadowy eyemark. Singly or small flocks, sometimes accompanied by dependent young. In flight looks almost white; wings broad with dark tips; tail white, forked but short. Skims and hawks gracefully over land for insects; gathering where such food abundant, occasionally follows the plough – probably our only tern so to do. Hawks and skims over water but seldom plunges.

Voice: Mostly quiet except when nesting. Reported are a throaty rasping 'ka-huk, ka-huk' or 'za-za-za', an insect-like buzz and a stuttered 'kerr' and 'tirruck-tirruck', some-what like Little Corella (316).

Habitat: Grasslands, plains, ploughed lands, airfields; inland swamps and tanks; floods, wet paddocks; fresh and brackish lakes; beaches, tidal mudflats.

Breeding: Usually colonially on sandspits or islands in lakes. Nest: variable – a scrape in sand or soil to a well-made cup of dry twigs and feathers, on or near ground in low vegeta-tion; once on old nests of Black Swans. Eggs: 2–3; buff-white, pale-grey, pale-brown or grey-green, irregularly blotched purplish red or brown and lilac.

Range and Status: Cosmopolitan. Breeds, often irregularly, some parts of all continents. Endemic Australian race *macrotarsa* occurs sparsely throughout continent and some coastal islands. Status not well understood. Probably mostly winter visitor to coastal n. Aust. and NG; erratic throughout inland, breeding opportunistically, often in hundreds where conditions suitable. Small numbers all months coastal e. Aust. s. to about Hunter R., NSW. Summer visitor (mostly Sept.–Mar.) to coastal and inland se. Aust., breeding opportunistically; small numbers overwinter. Similar, less regular, in smaller numbers in s. WA. Vagrant Tas., Lord Howe I., and NZ. Part-migratory, highly nomadic.

266 CASPIAN TERN *Hydroprogne caspia*   **Pl.27, 29**

Field marks: 480–550 mm; span 1.1–1.3 m. Largest tern, unmistakable by *size and powerful scarlet bill.* Breeding plumage: crown black; pale-grey above, short tail and underparts white; legs black. Nonbreeding: white forehead and crown streaked black, deepening to black round eye and nape. Imm: orange-red bill with blackish tip, white forehead, shadowy black marking on crown and round eye. In flight, note long slender wings *blackish at tip below, and short slightly forked tail.* Patrols with easy wingbeats, plunges spectacularly; occasionally hovers. Noisy and aggressive over nest.

Voice: Deep harsh 'kraa-uh' or sharper 'kah', mostly at intruders near nest or when attacking predators.

Habitat: Large waters generally: fresh, brackish or salt lakes; larger rivers, reservoirs; estuaries, tidal mudflats, beaches, shallow coastal waters.

Breeding: Usually singly or with a few other pairs on sandspits, islands; occasionally (as overseas) in large colonies. Nest: scrape on ground or sand, occasionally with few pieces of seaweed, grass, sticks. Eggs: 1–2; creamy grey to pale-brown, lightly spotted and blotched blackish, dark-brown.

Range and Status: Nearly cosmopolitan. Throughout Aust. and Tas. in suitable habitat, including coastal islands; widespread but nowhere numerous except when breeding, when companies up to 200 + reported. Movements little understood, may be mostly a summer breeding visitor to coastal s. Aust. and mostly a dry season visitor with some breeding, to coastal and subcoastal n. Aust.; sporadic inland. Nomadic or part migratory.

267 COMMON TERN *Sterna hirundo*   **Pl.27, 29**

Other name: Asiatic Common Tern.

Field marks: 305–380 mm. With Arctic (268) and Roseate (269) Terns, forms a distinctive group whose nonbreeding and imm. stages can easily be confused. Usually seen in non-breeding plumage: forehead white, hinder part of head, from round eyes, black; upper-parts pale-grey with smutty bar on shoulder; white below. At rest, rear of body and the long wingtips are characteristically upswept; tail streamers long *but do not protrude beyond wingtips.* Bill and legs usually blackish. Birds recently arrived or soon to depart often have *underparts washed pearly grey.* In flight, note dark-grey webs to primaries, black edge to tail-streamers. Imm: similar but with some blackish mottling above. Breeding plumage: black cap pulled well down over eyes; *underparts washed pearl-grey;* in flight shows a *translucent patch on inner primaries; bill black* in the usual local race *longipennis,* Eastern Common Tern; feet black or dark-red. *Flight light and buoyant, body rising and sinking at each wingbeat;* hovers, dips and plunges, quickly flutters up again. Rather noisy and excitable; associates with other terns. In some localities e.g. Sorrento, Vic., parties typically frequent a particular local jetty or other resting-place through the summer, returning each year; distribution can thus be surprisingly local and patchy.

Similar species: Arctic (268), Roseate (269) Terns. White-fronted Tern (270): larger, whiter, no black on tail-streamers. Imm: has stronger pattern, much more black on shoulder.

Voice: Brisk rapid 'kik-kik-kik', 'keer, keer, keer' or high-pitched grating 'keeee-yaah'.

Habitat: Offshore waters; beaches, reefs, bays, tidal mudflats; lower reaches of large rivers with sandbars; commercial saltfields; sewage farms; occasionally freshwater and brackish swamps near coast.

Range and Status: Common Tern is the English vernacular for this widespread migrant that breeds in n. Europe to ne. Asia and n. America and winters coastally in s. hemisphere. Regular migrant to Aust. Sept.–Apr.; generally uncommon, but locally abundant, e.g. c. 1500 Newcastle Bight, NSW, Feb. 1972. Most records coastal e. Aust. The usual race in Aust. is probably 'Eastern Common Tern', *longipennis*, breeding in Asia from Lake Baikal to Kamchatka and Commander Is.: bill and legs black in all plumages. Some overwinter. Nominate race, breeding through much of n. hemisphere except ne. Asia, recorded twice: Fremantle, WA, Jan. 1956 and Gunbower, Vic., Oct. 1968; possible sight records elsewhere. Breeding plumage: bill scarlet or orange-red, usually tipped black; legs red. Other races may occur.

268 ARCTIC TERN *Sterna paradisaea* Pl.27, 29

Field marks: 380 mm. Very like Common Tern (267), but 'different': bill about a third shorter, forehead higher; *legs very short*; *at rest, specially in breeding plumage, the outer tail-feathers extend well beyond the wingtips*. In flight, *all* the flight-feathers are translucent when seen overhead; dark tips of primaries form grey margin on trailing edge. Nonbreeding: very like Common; generally whiter, with less black on head and less-definite shoulder-mark; primaries not so definitely black; rump whiter. Legs (and bill) often quite black, with no trace of red. Imm: shoulder-mark fainter than imm. Common. Breeding plumage: (seldom seen here): bill wholly blood-red, legs red, black cap pulled well down over eyes; throat and sides of face white, deepening to *deep pearl-grey breast*. Tail white, outer web of streamers black. Behaves like Common; flight very light and graceful.

Similar species: Common (267) and Roseate (269) Terns. Also Antarctic Tern, *S. vittata*; see FG Birds NZ (Collins 1966).

Voice: 'Kee-yahr' with rising inflection, sharper than Common Tern; high whistled 'kee-kee'.

Habitat: Coastal: beaches, tidal mudflats, saltmarsh.

Range and Status: Breeds n. Eurasia and far-n. America; winters in region of Antarctic pack-ice, travelling s. through Atlantic and e. Pacific. Casual visitor to s. Aust. (Fremantle, WA,–Hunter R., NSW) mostly Sept.–May. Five Arctic Terns banded respectively nw. USSR, Sweden, Finland and UK (two) had been recovered in Aust. to Mar. 1974; Fremantle, WA, (two); Eaglehawk Neck, Tas.; Bega and Bateman's Bay, NSW, respectively May, June, Dec. (two) and Sept. Other records from s. WA, SA, King I., Bass Strait; Tas., Vic. and NSW; a number have been of dead or dying birds, perhaps reflecting the influence of westerly gales in their movements to our coasts. Records also NZ, Macquarie I.

269 ROSEATE TERN *Sterna dougallii* Pl.27, 29

Other name: Graceful Tern.

Field marks: 340–405 mm. The only resident member of a confusing group (267–9); note range. Breeding plumage: unmistakable; very white, silver-grey above, washed very *pale-pink below*; black cap reaches bill; rump white; at rest, the *long, wholly white tail-streamers extend c. 100 mm beyond wing-tips. Bill black with scarlet base, legs red*. Nonbreeding:

forehead white, crown heavily dark-mottled, blacker on rear and nape; bill black, legs orange-brown. Some retain rosy tinge on breast. Imm: black spot before eye, forehead freckled dark-brown and white, crown black streaked paler; slight dark shoulder-mark and often dark mottling on mantle; outer pair of tail-feathers white. Bill black, legs orange-red. In flight, both adult and imm. have narrow white trailing edge to wing. Flight extremely graceful, wingbeats shallow. Forages, breeds, roosts in flocks; associates with Black-naped Tern (271).

Similar species: Common (267) and Arctic (268) Terns, nonbreeding. White-fronted Tern (270): very like nonbreeding Roseate, even has slight roseate tinge but more robust, forehead much whiter; usually winter only; note range.

Voice: Distinctive: guttural rasping 'aach, aack'; soft 'chu-ick'; angry, chattering 'kekekekek'.

Habitat: Offshore waters, islands, coral reefs, sand cays.

Breeding: Nest: flattened area on low bush, cavity in low rocky surface or scrape in sand. Eggs: 1–2, occasionally 3; creamy grey to stone-coloured, spotted and blotched with dark browns and greys.

Range and Status: Coastal seas and islands of ne., n. and w. Aust.: in WA, breeds Bedout I., Fraser I. off Pt. Cloates, the Abrolhos Group and small islands s. to Green Islets, 160 km n. of Fremantle; stronghold being the Abrolhos, where colonies of up to 2500 + nests have been reported; occasional coastally s. in winter to Fremantle, Rottnest I., Cockburn Sound, WA, and n. to coastal Kimberleys. In Q, breeds E. Strait I. in Torres Strait, Cairncross and Bushy Is. off ne. C. York Pen.; Franklin I.; Wilson and One Tree Is. (Capricorn Group) and Lady Musgrave I. (Bunker Group), on s. Gt. Barrier Reef off Rockhampton. Breeding-sites alter; occupied only when nesting. Generally uncommon; locally abundant; sedentary, dispersive. The Australian race is *gracilis*. Other races breed in n. America, Britain, n. Europe, n. Africa, n. Indian Ocean to s. China, se. Asia and in isolated colonies from Malaysia to NG, Solomon Is. and New Caledonia.

270 WHITE-FRONTED TERN *Sterna striata*   Pl.27, 29

Other names: Black-billed or Southern Tern.

Field marks: 380–420 mm. Breeds in NZ, part of population, mostly imms., wintering in coastal se. Aust. Nonbreeding: a whitish, rather robust tern, somewhat smaller than Crested Tern (276); pale-grey above, white below, with deeply forked, white tail. Note *conspicuously white forehead* with black rear-cap extending forward through eye. Bill black, *long slender and slightly downcurved*; legs red-brown. Imm: perhaps the most boldly patterned, imm. tern locally. Like adult, with blackish brown barring or mottling on mantle, strong brownish-mottled or black shoulder-mark; webs of primaries dark, all but central tail-feathers with wide dark-grey margin: legs blackish. Breeding plumage: black cap separated from black bill by *conspicuous white saddle and from grey back by white collar*; some have rosy wash over throat and breast; silvery grey above; white, deeply forked tail; at rest long streamers extend c. 20 mm beyond wing-tips. Bill black, *legs bright-red to red-brown*. Feeds in flocks, often with Crested Terns, often far to sea; flight more buoyant, wingbeats quicker; hovers, dives; follows fishing boats.

Similar species: Common (267); Arctic (268) and Roseate (269) Terns.

Voice: A high-pitched, rasping 'kee-eet' or 'siet'.

Habitat: In Aust., offshore coastal waters, bays, reefs, rocky islands.

Range and Status: Probably most abundant NZ tern; breeds North and South Is., and on Stewart, Chatham and Auckland Is.; part of population (mostly first and second-year birds, but some adults) winters off coastal se. Aust., Mar.–Oct. Mostly NSW, Vic., Bass Strait and e. and n. Tas., occasional n. to Rockhampton, Q, and w. to Fleurieu Pen.–Adelaide, SA; accidental inland, Wyperfeld NP, Vic. Up to 400 recorded Moon I., NSW; in some winters, very large companies at sea off s. NSW.

271 BLACK-NAPED TERN *Sterna sumatrana* Pl.28

Field marks: 305–355 mm. An elegant, mostly white, small tern with black bill and legs and a *widening black line back from just before eye to form black nape.* In some (winter adult or imms.) black on nape indistinct. Crown and underparts may be suffused pale-rose; tail white, long and forked. Imm: nape brown, flight-feathers grey. In flight, looks very white, wingbeats short and choppy with diving swoops to pick food from surface. Often with Roseate (269) and other terns and noddies.

Similar species: Little Tern (274) nonbreeding and imm: greyer above, less black on nape; often has dark shoulder-mark; flight-feathers dark. Roseate Tern (269), nonbreeding and imm: greyer, crown mottled black.

Voice: Described as short sharp high 'tsii-chee-chi-chip'; alarm-call 'chit-chit-chit-rer'.

Habitat: Tropical and subtropical oceanic waters; on Gt. Barrier Reef, forages over lagoons and outer edges of reefs. Ashore mostly on islands, but to mainland coasts in places.

Breeding: Colonies on islands and cays. Eggs laid in rock crevices and depressions on coral or shingle beaches or in shelter of roots and other vegetation. Eggs: 2, occasionally 3; white to creamy white, spotted and blotched purplish black, mauve-grey and blackish brown with underlying markings of lavender.

Range and Status: Tropical Indian and w. Pacific Oceans, from Madagascar to China, Japan and e. to Samoa. In Aust., breeds on coastal islands and cays from Bunker and Capricorn Groups, Q, n. to Torres Strait and w. at least to Sir Edward Pellew Group in Gulf of Carpentaria, e. NT. Occasional in winter s. to Bribie and Stradbroke Is., se. Q; w. to Groote Eylandt and n. Arnhem Land, NT; to shores of mainland in places. Common, sedentary and dispersive.

272 SOOTY TERN *Sterna fuscata* Pl.28

Other names: Egg-bird, Whale-bird, Wideawake.

Field marks: 400–465 mm. A very distinctly marked tern; black above, white below, forehead white, *but no long white eyebrow*; outer edge of tail-streamers white; bill and legs black. Imm: very different; *the only wholly sooty grey tern with a forked tail; prominent pale crescents on mantle and spots on wings* form a broad pale panel in flight. Flocks skim and dip when foraging, seldom plunging or settling on water; they often soar high. They resort to land only to breed and after breeding, disperse far to sea; some believe they sleep on wing.

Similar species: Bridled Tern (273): greyer, smaller white forehead, longer white eyebrow. Compared with Sooty imm., no noddy has such an obviously forked tail or pale spots.

Voice: High-pitched nasal 'ker-wack-wack', hence sailors' name of 'Wideawake'; incessantly at colonies; other harsh notes.

Habitat: Tropical and subtropical seas; on islands only to breed.

Breeding: Noisy, often immense, colonies on oceanic islands and cays in tropical and subtropical seas. Nest: scrape in sand in open or under low shrub. Egg: 1 (when more, probably laid by more than one female); white, pinkish or cream, finely spotted and broadly blotched dark-brown or deep-chestnut with shadowy grey markings.

Range and Status: In Aust., breeds Lord Howe and Norfolk Is., many stations in Coral Sea; Michaelmas, Upolu and Oyster Cays, ne. Q; Sir Edward Pellew Group, NT; Ashmore Reefs and Bedout I., nw. Aust., and Abrolhos Group, WA. Rare on mainland coasts, usually in summer after storms and cyclones; coastal records from Townsville to s. of Sydney, many being imms; some inland; vagrant Vic., SA, where in Dec. 1972 one present in breeding colony of Crested Terns (276), Brothers I., sw. Eyre Pen.; in WA occasional s. to Bunbury, Oct.–Apr. Common; migratory or dispersive. Also Moluccas; NG, Solomon Is., New Caledonia, and throughout tropical and subtropical Indian, Pacific and Atlantic Oceans.

273 BRIDLED TERN *Sterna anaethetus* Pl.28

Other names: Brown-winged, Dog, Panayan, or Smaller Sooty Tern.

Field marks: 360–420 mm. Like a small slender Sooty Tern (272) but with narrower white forehead, *longer fine white eyebrow*; black cap contrasts with grey-brown upperparts, *the two separated by a variable pale collar*; duller-white below. Tail relatively longer, more white on streamers and inner feathers. Imm: crown grey, streaked white; blackish line from eye to nape, upperparts have a pale barred patterned look; *underparts pale*. Shyer, swifter and more graceful than Sooty; dips to surface, plunges; associates with noddies when foraging but usually well offshore. Unlike Sooty, reported to settle on water. Like Sooty, often feeds and is vocal at night.

Similar species: Sooty Tern (272).

Voice: A toy bark, like puppy or Pied Stilt (214).

Habitat: Tropical and subtropical oceans and some temperate waters; rarely to mainland shores.

Breeding: Pairs and small to very large, loose colonies on islands. Egg: 1; usually laid in crevice under ledge, among coral blocks or boulders or under bush; cream-white, irregularly spotted and blotched dark red-brown and indistinct blue-grey.

Range and Status: In Aust. breeds on islands from C. Leeuwin, WA, n. coastally to Bunker Group, Gt. Barrier Reef, Q. Recent breeding Baudin Rocks; vagrant Troubridge I., SA. Fairly common offshore in summer from C. Leeuwin n. round coast to about Rockhampton, Q; uncommon s. to Q–NSW border. Uncommon on mainland coasts generally. Range extending s. in WA, and may explain SA breeding. After summer breeding, leaves vicinity of breeding islands. A northward winter, possibly transequatorial, migration is suspected. Widespread tropical Indian Ocean and w. Pacific, from Madagascar, Red Sea, Persian Gulf to China, Japan, se. Asia to Philippines, Indonesia, NG; tropical Atlantic.

274 LITTLE TERN *Sterna albifrons* Pl.28, 29

Other names: Sea-swallow, White-shafted Ternlet.

Field marks: 200–250 mm. A tiny pale-grey and white tern whose main field mark in breeding plumage is the *black wedge from bill to eye*, an extension of the black crown; forehead white. Bill yellow, *usually with black tip*; *legs yellow*. Nonbreeding and imm: no dark mark from bill to eye or only shadowy trace; blackish shoulder-mark, dull-yellow legs. Bill black, occasionally yellow at base. Because of probable overlap of migrants from n. hemisphere and local populations, either plumage may be seen in any month. Small parties to flocks of hundreds, often with other terns. *Flies with rapid deep wingbeats, hovers on rapidly beating wings; plunges or parachutes down on stiff upheld wings before plunging.* In flight, the shortish white forked tail often seems a *single spike*.

Similar species: Fairy Tern (275).

Voice: Short high-pitched, rather feeble 'jeep' or sharp 'kweek'; while hovering, urgent 'peep-peep-peep'; excited chitterings in courtship flights.

Habitat: Coastal waters, bays, shallow inlets; salt or brackish lakes, commercial salt-fields, sewage farms near coast.

Breeding: Usually in loose colonies on sandy islands, lonely sandspits, beaches, dune-wastes. Eggs: 1–2, sometimes 3; stone-coloured, spotted and blotched dark-brown, umber and grey; laid in scrape in sand or shell-debris.

Range and Status: Coastal n., e., se. Aust. and Tas.: from about Broome, WA, to C. York, Q, s. to Tas. and w. to Yorke Pen., SA. The usual race in Aust. is *sinensis*, which breeds from s. and e. Asia to Philippines, Moluccas, NG and Aust., summer migrant NZ. It occurs here as (1) regular non-breeding migrant, mostly Sept.–Apr., in flocks of hundreds s. to about Sydney, smaller numbers to Vic. and s. SA. Mostly in non-breeding plumage but birds remaining into May–June frequently assume full breeding plumage. (2) Summer resident, breeding from ne. Q and some Gt. Barrier Reef islands to se. Vic. (L. Victoria,

Lakes Entrance), with recent expansion of breeding to e. Tas. (St Helens–Bicheno) and to se. SA (Coorong–L. Alexandrina). Common; migratory – the species as a whole is scarce in se. Aust. in winter. Almost cosmopolitan in temperate/tropical zones. Note that the race *saundersi*, breeding from Red Sea to w. India, is treated by Condon, 1975, Checkl. Birds of Aust. 1. as a full species. One Aust. record: Wollongong, NSW, 1903.

275 FAIRY TERN *Sterna nereis*   Pl.28, 29

Other names: Little Sea-swallow, Sea-swallow, White-faced Ternlet.

Field marks: 215–270 mm. Very like Little Tern (274); breeding plumage differs in *white gap* between base of bill and the black extending from crown round eye; there is less suggestion of an angular start to a white eyebrow. Bill more orange-yellow, usually without black tip, legs orange-yellow. Nonbreeding: white forehead more extensive; base and near-tip of bill blackish but *central part probably always dull-yellow*; legs dull-yellow; only faint greyish mark along shoulder; imm: bill black, legs dull orange-brown. These stages very difficult to distinguish from Little, whose behaviour and flight are similar. In general, Fairy is paler and slightly chunkier, bill somewhat deeper from top to bottom, legs shorter – at rest, 'knees' are nearly hidden in plumage. Calls sometimes help; note distribution. Small parties to large flocks; in nw., flocks of thousands have been observed. Very demonstrative, specially near nest.

Similar species: Little Tern (274). Common (267) and Arctic (268) Terns, nonbreeding and imm: best distinguished by style of flight when foraging.

Voice: Very vocal; hard loud low-pitched 'tchi-wick', excited chittering 'kirrikiki-kirrikiki', rapid high-pitched 'ket-ket-ket-ket'.

Habitat: As Little Tern.

Breeding: As Little Tern; colonies mostly small, but some to hundreds of pairs. Eggs: slightly more rounded than Little Tern, and paler ground-colour, cream-yellow to yellow-grey.

Range and Status: Aust. is its stronghold. Breeds coasts and islands from about Derby, n. WA, coastally s. and e. to Port Albert, Vic., King, Flinders (? and other) islands, Bass Strait, and n. and e. Tas. Replaces Little Tern through most of this range, but overlap recently recognized in c. coastal Vic., Tas. and se. SA; vagrant to Botany Bay, NSW. Common, dispersive, possibly part-migratory. Also North I., NZ; New Caledonia.

276 CRESTED TERN *Sterna bergii*   Pl.28, 29

Other names: Diver; Greater Crested, Ruppell's Swift, Torres Strait or Bass Strait Tern.

Field marks: 440–480 mm. Our commonest tern and second largest after the Caspian (266); named after *shaggy fringe on rear of black crown*. Bill long slender straw-yellow; legs black. Breeding plumage: black cap separated from bill by conspicuous white saddle. Nonbreeding: whole forehead whitish, top of crown mottled blackish. Imm: bill paler; less white forehead; crown mottled blackish-brown, blackish mottlings on sides and back of neck; dusky shoulder-mark and flight-feathers. Singly, flocks often with gulls and other terns on beaches, sandspits, jetties; flies gracefully on rakish narrow wings; tail deeply forked. Often in flocks over shoals on surface; plunges spectacularly.

Similar species: Lesser Crested Tern (277).

Voice: Noisy: a somewhat rasping 'carrik' or 'kirrik'; imm: peevish whistles.

Habitat: Offshore usually near coast; bays, inlets, tidal rivers; salt or brackish coastal swamps or lakes; occasionally large fresh waters, occasionally follows rivers well inland.

Breeding: Nest: scrape in sand or depression in bare rock; in colony (some very large e.g. c. 8000 pairs N. Solitary I., NSW) usually on an island. Eggs: 1, rarely 2; sandy white to pale stone-coloured, scrawled and blotched black, red-brown and umber, with shadowy markings of grey.

Range and Status: Australian coasts, coastal islands and Tas.; common throughout, very common in s.; occasionally ascends rivers. Sedentary and dispersive. Widespread from Fiji to Philippines, coasts of s. and e. Asia, Red Sea to s. Africa.

277 LESSER CRESTED TERN *Sterna bengalensis*   Pl.28, 29

Other name: Allied Tern.

Field marks: 365–415 mm. Smaller and paler than Crested (276), but distinguished by *conspicuous orange bill* and, in breeding plumage, by the black cap extending nearly to bill, legs shorter. Nonbreeding: bill remains orange, forehead all-white, streaked black on crown; frequently breeds in this plumage. Imm: blackish shoulder-mark, outer tail-feathers sooty. Flight and foraging generally like Crested, looks smaller on wing. Associates frequently with other terns.

Similar species: Crested Tern (276).

Voice: Somewhat like Crested.

Habitat: Tropical and subtropical offshore waters; islands, cays reefs, ocean beaches.

Breeding: Nest: scrape in sand; in colony on offshore island. Egg: 1; light stone-coloured, blotched and spotted dark-purple, with underlying lavender marks.

Range and Status: Coastal n. Aust. and islands, breeds from Bedout and Adele Is., WA, to Capricorn and Bunker Groups, Q; ranges s. to Shark Bay, WA, and to Fraser I., Q, occasional s. to Moreton Bay and N. Stradbroke I. Generally scarcer, breeding colonies much smaller than Crested. Also from NG to coasts of se. and s. Asia, to e. Africa, s. Mediterranean, Morocco.

NODDIES

A distinctive group of six, mostly tropical, small terns. The three typical species (278–80) are sooty brown with pale caps; two others, vagrant to mainland Aust., are blue-grey or white. Noddies fly delicately, swiftly and erratically; they skim and hover rather than plunge when feeding; some probably forage at night. They are best distinguished from dark shearwaters by their longer pointed bills, broader wings, style of flight and, when near, by their pale caps. Like other marine terns, noddies breed on islands, oceanic or well offshore, usually in large colonies; unlike other terns, some noddies nest in trees or low bushes.

278 COMMON NODDY *Anous stolidus*   Pl.28

Other names: Greater Noddy, Noddy Tern, Noddy.

Field marks: 380–405 mm. Largest noddy, doubtfully distinguished in flight *by contrast of smoky-brown plumage with dark-brown flight-feathers and the dark heavily pointed or wedge-shaped tail*, often notched at tip. *Facial marking*: well-defined black mark between eye and bill, cut off sharply by edge of white forehead; cap shades from white forehead to grey crown to brown nape. Bill black, fairly robust, legs black. Imm: cap absent or patchier than adult, slight mottlings on wing. Flight ternlike, with long glides; reported to hover near surface when feeding, with tail fanned and elevated. Rests on water; reefs, cays, offshore piles and buoys.

Similar species: See other noddies (279–80). Sooty Tern (272), imm: pale spots and barrings above; tail deeply forked.

Voice: Ripping 'karrk'; round 'kwok, kwok', also 'eyak'.

Habitat: Tropical and subtropical seas.

Breeding: Nest: untidy shallow cup of dry seaweed, grass and twigs, lined with few shells or pebbles on trampled platform in low shrub or similar structure; on ground in open or in tussocks with rim of shells and pebbles; eggs may also be laid on bare ground or among coral rocks. Egg: 1; variable; dull-white or creamy, blotched red-brown and purplish or finely spotted blackish brown.

Range and Status: In Aust. breeds Abrolhos Group, Bedout and Lacepede Is., WA;

Ashmore Reefs in Timor Sea; Bramble Cay, Torres Strait, s. to offshore cays near Cairns, Q, Lady Elliott I. in Bunker Group, islands in Coral Sea and Lord Howe I. Very large colonies on Abrolhos, Bramble Cay and Raine I., status on n. coasts uncertain; common e. Torres Strait, less common to accidental s. along Gt. Barrier Reef except near breeding colonies. After breeding, probably disperses far to sea; occasional flocks off Stradbroke I., se. Q; after storms, vagrant NSW s. to Kiama, and to C. Naturaliste, WA. Dispersive or migratory. Breeds widely in tropical Indian, Pacific and Atlantic Oceans.

279 LESSER NODDY *Anous tenuirostris*   Pl.28

Field marks: 305–340 mm. Smaller and darker than Common Noddy (278) with *proportionately longer finer bill and rounder tail*; pale-grey of head *shades evenly down sides of face, neck and hindneck without abrupt margin*: black mark round eye does not extend to bill. Imm: cap paler. Flight fairy-like, buoyant, erratic.
Similar species: Common Noddy (278); Black Noddy (280) – note range.
Voice: At colonies and probably at sea, soft rattling 'churrr'.
Habitat: Tropical and subtropical oceans; oceanic islands.
Breeding: Colonially, on limbs of trees, typically mangroves; the site relocated from time to time. Nest: platform of wet seaweed and leaves and later guano; dries and hardens with use; slight concave egg-cavity. Egg: 1; pale-stone or cream, irregularly blotched dull-chestnut, shadowy dark-brown markings.
Range and Status: A species of the Indian Ocean. In Aust., breeds only Abrolhos Group, WA, on Pelsart and Wooded Is. Sedentary, seldom observed away from Abrolhos except when winter storms drive numbers ashore from Fremantle s. to C. Naturaliste, WA.

280 BLACK NODDY *Anous minutus*   Pl.28

Other name: White-capped Noddy.
Field marks: 330–360 mm. Darkest noddy; on wing *looks uniformly blackish* with prominent white crown; bill proportionately longer and more slender than Common Noddy (278). In darkest individuals, *sides of face blackish up to level of eye, cut off sharply by white cap before and behind eye*; cap merges into powdery grey on sides and rear of neck. Flight very buoyant; note forked tail, shorter than Common; flocks forage along edge of reefs and far to sea.
Similar species: Common (278) and Lesser (279) Noddies; note range.
Voice: Nasal rattling 'chrrr' or 'krrrrr'; also tern-like 'kik-kirrik'.
Habitat: Tropical and subtropical oceans; breeds oceanic islands, cays and atolls.
Breeding: Nest: untidy mass of leaves and seaweed, bound with excreta; in aust. usually colonially in branches of leafy trees, e.g. *Pisonia*, also *Casuarina*, *Pandanus* etc. Egg: 1; pale creamy white, spotted and blotched reddish brown or purplish grey.
Range and Status: Breeds islands in tropical Pacific w. to NG, Borneo, Sumatra, Philippines, also w. Atlantic Ocean. In Aust., principally Capricorn and Bunker Groups, Gt. Barrier Reef; (probably also Quoin I. off e. Cape York); near Darnley I., Torres Strait; islands in Coral Sea and Norfolk I. Sedentary, locally very abundant in Capricorn and Bunker Groups ('tens of thousands', Heron I.); uncommon n. through coastal waters of ne. Q; occasional in Q s. of Bunker Group, vagrant Stradbroke I; rare vagrant NSW: off Terrigal, Mar. 1969; Forster, Apr. 1972; sight-record Long Reef, Feb. 1969.

281 GREY NODDY *Procelsterna albivittata*

Other name: Grey Ternlet.
Field marks: 280–305 mm; span 610 mm. A delicate small noddy: *pale blue-grey, with white cap*, wing-linings and underparts. Eye dark, appearing larger by fine blackish surrounding ring; bill and feet black, webs yellow. Loose flocks round breeding colonies,

but solitary vagrant mainland Aust. Flight graceful and fairy-like; tail tapered, tips often separated; occasionally settles on water.
Voice: Round breeding colonies, a rolling or purring 'cror-r-r-'.
Habitat: Oceanic islands and oceans.
Range and Status: Breeds through subtropical Pacific Ocean, nearest colonies to Aust. are Lord Howe and Norfolk Is. Rare vagrant e. Aust.; occasionally beachwashed NSW coast mostly near Sydney, summer and winter; sight-record N. Stradbroke I., se. Q, Apr. 1973. Vagrant NZ.

282 WHITE NODDY *Gygis alba*

Other names: Fairy, Love or White Tern.
Field marks: 285–330 mm; span 715–760 mm. A fairy-like *all-white tern*, the 'most ethereal of seabirds'; when seen against blue sky, wings and forked tail almost translucent. *Eye dark-brown, seemingly made larger by surrounding fine black eye-ring*; noticeable at distance. Bill black, deep blue at base; *legs black*. Imm: black spot before and round eye, smudged brown or grey on nape and back; shafts of flight and tail-feathers blackish. Flight airy, or swift and darting; swoops to take food from surface.
Similar species: Grey Noddy (281).
Voice: Reported to be a guttural 'heech, heech'.
Habitat: Oceanic islands and tropical and subtropical oceans.
Range and Status: Tropical and subtropical Pacific, Indian and Atlantic Oceans. Near Aust. breeds Norfolk, Kermadec and recently Lord Howe I. Vagrant coastal e. Aust. Records: NSW; once inland, Grafton June, 1951; two far off c. NSW coast; Q: Brisbane R., Apr. 1973; sight-record Stradbroke I., May 1973. Vagrant NG, NZ.

Pigeons and Doves   Family *Columbidae*

Plump, small-headed, densely-plumaged seed or fruit eating birds. Generally, larger members of the family are called pigeons, the smaller, doves. Six of the world's 24 groups are represented in Aust. For field-identification it is perhaps more effective to remember two main groupings selected on the basis of habitat. Group 1: pigeons and doves of rainforests and similar dense, humid habitats of e. and n. Aust. These include the highly colourful, boldly marked fruit pigeons and other arboreal species which feed mostly on whole fruit and berries. This group also includes the White-headed Pigeon (289), the Brown Pigeon (293), the Green-winged Pigeon (297) and the Wonga Pigeon (307). Group 2: pigeons and doves of drier, usually more open habitats; mostly modestly-coloured, ground-feeding birds, some with a brightly coloured bronze patch (speculum) on the wing. Some members of both groups are highly nomadic in response to seasonal availability of food. Some are highly gregarious; travelling, feeding (or watering) in flocks. Most pigeons and doves have a strong direct flight, and many take off with a characteristic clatter. When courting, some make clapping sounds with their wings in conspicuous aerial displays. Sexes similar or dissimilar.
Food: Seeds, shoots, fruit, berries; also insects and other invertebrates.
Range: Almost cosmopolitan; absent from the high latitudes and some oceanic islands.
Number of species: World 280; Aust. 22; 3 introduced.

283 BLACK-BANDED PIGEON *Ptilinopus cinctus* Pl.45

Other names: Banded or Black-banded Fruit Dove or Pigeon.
Field marks: 330–355 mm. Distinctive: *black breastband* separates white, yellow-washed, forepart of body from blue-grey underparts. Wings and back dark-slate, rump grey; tail black, *broadly tipped pale-grey*. Imm: pale-grey where adult white. Singly, small parties or flocks; usually shy, best-observed by locating one of its food trees, which include figs.

When feeding it may reveal itself by flapping for balance. Flight fairly swift; when it drops down the steep escarpments of its home it travels rapidly with whistling wings. Occasionally suns itself on exposed limb. Note range and habitat.

Similar pecies: Torres Strait Pigeon (287).

Habitat: Patches of rainforest scrub in deep gullies and gorges in the sandstone and conglomerate escarpments of w. Arnhem Land, NT; marginally into adjacent eucalypt woodlands.

Voice: Reported to sound like Common Bronzewing (298), but slower: a deep booming.

Breeding: Nest: undiscovered until May 1971 – a loose open flimsy structure of short sticks; 2–7 m high, mostly on horizontal forks near end of slender branches in leafy softwoods shrubs or trees growing among rocks or in patch of rainforest, near the base of sandstone escarpments. Egg: 1; pure-white, sub-elliptical; smooth but not glossy.

Range and Status: Confined to nw. Arnhem Land, NT, from Oenpelli s. to S. Alligator R. Sedentary, local and scarce.

284 PURPLE-CROWNED PIGEON *Ptilinopus superbus* Pl.45

Other names: Purpled-crowned Fruit Dove or Pigeon, Superb Fruit Dove or Pigeon.

Field marks: 220–240 mm. A gorgeous tiny pigeon, mostly rich golden green above and with many other colours; from below, both sexes can be identified by *cream-white abdomen, edged and partly barred green, and broad white or grey tips to black tail.* Male: crown rich-purple, hindneck fiery orange-chestnut; *blue-black breastband* separates pale-grey upperbreast from abdomen. Bill olive-green or blue-grey; eye yellow, legs coral-red. Female: *purple-blue patch on rear of crown*; no breastband. Imm: mostly green with yellow on wing-coverts and broad white broken areas below. Singly, pairs or parties; difficult to see in foliage. Listen for call, quick fluttering of wings for balance, falling fruit or wing-whistle in quick short flights.

Similar species: Red-crowned Pigeon (285): abdomen apricot-yellow; tail tipped yellow.

Voice: Described as a loud double coo; also a low 'oom', uttered singly or as a series but not accelerating.

Habitat: Tropical and subtropical rainforests and scrubs; wooded stream-margins, lantana thickets; occasionally large isolated trees: figs, pittosporums.

Breeding: Nest: flimsy; of few twigs; among branchlets or on fork usually up to about 8 m high. Egg: 1; creamy white.

Range and Status: E. coastal Q and coastal islands from C. York to near Rockhampton, inland to Atherton and Eungella Ras, but not certainly breeding s. of Proserpine. Common in n.; uncommon s. of Cardwell, occasional se. Q and n. coastal NSW; vagrant Sydney area, s. coastal NSW, Vic., Tas. Incidence of imms. reported has led to speculation about possible extra-limital breeding in rainforests in area n. of Maitland, NSW. Nomadic, possibly migratory; generally absent from s. parts of range May–Sept. Also Sulu Archipelago and Celebes to NG, Bismarck Archipelago.

285 RED-CROWNED PIGEON *Ptilinopus regina* Pl.45

Other names: Pink Cap, Pink-capped, Red or Rose-crowned Fruit Dove or Pigeon; Ewing's or Swainson's Fruit Pigeon.

Field marks: 200–230 mm. A gorgeous tiny pigeon, best identified by *rich yellow-pink underparts and broad yellow tail-tip.* Glossy rich-green above with deep-pink crown; on neck and breast pale-grey feathers form a pointed pattern over pale-green base. Bill green, legs greyish or green, eye orange-yellow. Female: duller. Imm: mostly green above, with yellow margins to wing and tail-feathers, yellow abdomen. Singly or pairs; shy and inconspicuous among foliage. Climbs after fruit, when observed often freezes. Listen for call, falling fruit or quick whistling flights. Sustained flight fast and direct. The nw. Australian race *ewingi.* 'Rose-crowned Pigeon' differs only slightly; crown paler, throat yellower. It seems tamer; often seen Darwin Botanic Gardens.

Similar species: Purple-crowned Pigeon (284).
Voice: A surprisingly loud explosive call; begins slowly and deliberately, accelerates until the falling notes run rapidly together, somewhat like Pheasant Coucal (375): 'hook-coo; hook-coo; hook-coo; coo coo coo-coocoocoocoo'; also a different call, 'OO, uk-COO, uk-COO'.
Habitat: Tropical and temperate rainforests, woodlands, scrubs; mangroves, wetter eucalypt forests, isolated groups of berry or fruit-bearing trees.
Breeding: Nest: frail platform of twigs; usually in low growth or vines. Egg: 1; pure-white, oval.
Range and Status: Coastal nw. and e. Aust. and coastal islands: from n. Kimberleys, WA, to Arnhem Land, NT, e. to Pellew Is. and from C. York, Q, to about Hunter R., NSW. Fairly common in suitable habitat; probably part-migratory. Vagrant s. coast NSW, Vic., Tas. Also e. Lesser Sunda islands, including Timor, from Flores to Aru Is. and (probably) s. NG.

286 WOMPOO PIGEON *Ptilinopus magnificus* **Pl.45**
Other names: Bubbly Jock, or Mary; Green, or King Pigeon; Magnificent Fruit Dove or Fruit Pigeon; Painted or Purple-breasted Pigeon or Fruit Pigeon.
Field marks: 350–560 mm. A magnificent large pigeon: pale-grey head and neck shade into rich-green upperparts, broken yellow band across wing; *breast and belly plum-purple, underparts rich-yellow.* Bill red, tipped straw-yellow; eye red, legs green. Singly to companies where fruit or berries are plentiful; feeds high in canopy or low, colours blending with foliage; revealed by unmistakable call or sound of falling fruit. Behaviour sedate but flight swift and direct, exposing *yellow wing-lining.* Note: races in ne. Q and NG are noticeably smaller than nominate race in s. Q–NSW.
Voice: Typical calls: a deep gruff bubbling or gobbling 'wollack-a-woo', 'bock-bock-oo' or quieter 'wampoo'.
Habitat: Rainforests and scrubs to nearby trees in open and along scrubby creeks.
Breeding: Nest: very flimsy; usually on horizontal branch, palm frond or in leafy twigs, 2–10 m high in thick scrub, often over a stream. Egg: 1; largish, white; often seen through nest.
Range and Status: Coastal e. Aust. and forested coastal islands: from C. York, Q, formerly s. to Illawarra district, NSW, now to about Hunter R. region, mostly on and e. of Divide. Fairly common in n., now much scarcer in s.; sedentary, with local feeding movements. Also NG and adjacent islands.

287 TORRES STRAIT PIGEON *Ducula spilorrhoa* **Pl.45**
Other names: Nutmeg, Spice or White Nutmeg Pigeon; Australian Pied Imperial Pigeon; Torres Strait Imperial Pigeon.
Field marks: 380–440 mm. Large and striking; a mostly white pigeon with *slate-grey flight-feathers and end of tail.* Head may be soiled brownish by fruit. Bill pale, eye blackish; legs and feet blue-grey. Singly or small parties; conspicuous when feeding in or flying over the dark canopy of scrub or rainforests. Males in display fly up steeply, stall and tip forward to glide down again. When breeding, provides a spectacle as *small to very large flocks* travel daily to and from breeding colonies on offshore islands and mainland feeding areas, flying swiftly, high over the sea or low.
Similar species: Black-banded Pigeon (283); White-headed Pigeon (289).
Voice: Described as a deep 'roo-ca-hoo'; low moaning 'up-oooo' deep 'ooms'; higher pitched sounds when feeding.
Habitat: Tropical rainforests, scrubs along creeks and rivers; mangroves.
Breeding: Nest: substantial structure of sticks, in usually dense colony in mangroves or rainforest canopy, mostly on offshore islands. Egg: 1; large, white.
Range and Status: Coastal n. Aust. and coastal islands: from n. Kimberleys to top end NT, s. to Katherine–Elsey–Borroloola; in ne. Q, from C. York s. to Norman R. on Gulf

154 PIGEONS AND DOVES

coast and to about Mackay and Cumberland Is. on e. coast. A migrant, arriving from n. during Aug.–Oct. to breed, usually departing Mar.–Apr.; some overwinter. Fairly common: some breeding colonies large, but in general much-reduced by clearing of rainforests and, on breeding islands, by shooting. Also NG and adjacent islands. The wintering areas of birds that breed in Aust. are not certainly known.

288 TOPKNOT PIGEON *Lopholaimus antarcticus* Pl.45
Other names: Flock Pigeon; Quook Quook.
Field marks: 400–460 mm. A large grey pigeon with a *curious backswept ginger black 'hair-do'*. Flight-feathers and long tail slaty black, tail crossed by *a narrow but distinct buff-grey band*. Bill rose-red with green nostril; eye orange-yellow, feet red. Imm: bill brown. Small parties to flocks of 50–100 traverse rainforests, flying strongly and circling somewhat like large Domestic Pigeons (290), looking *slender-winged with long, square, banded tails*. They feed in canopy, clambering, flapping and skirmishing and rest in high open trees above canopy or in nearby eucalypt forest. Note that birds in ne. Q are smaller than in s.
Voice: Seldom-heard unless near: a soft low rumbling grunt; when skirmishing, a short screech surprisingly like a distant flying fox or domestic pig.
Habitat: Rainforests, stands of palms, adjacent eucalypt forests and woodlands; fruiting trees in open paddocks.
Breeding: Nest: flat, loose but bulky; of long twigs; 3–30 m high in a leafy tree. Egg: 1: white, large, oval and slightly glossy.
Range and Status: Coastal e. Aust. and forested islands: from C. York to s. coast NSW, on and e. of Divide. Common in suitable habitat in mid-part of range from ce. NSW to Atherton Tableland; scarce n. of Cooktown; irregular s. coastal NSW to Illawarra district, but large flocks still occur; occasional s. to Barren Grounds and far-e. Vic. (Mallacoota); rare vagrant elsewhere in Vic. and in Tas. In general highly nomadic in response to availability of food in rainforests and other wooded areas.

289 WHITE-HEADED PIGEON *Columba leucomela* Pl.45
Other names: Baldy; White-headed Fruit Pigeon.
Field marks: 380–410 mm. Our only pigeon that combines *white head and breast with wholly blackish upperparts and tail*. The white is often buffish or smutty; flanks greyish; feathers of wings and back with glossy margins. Bill red, tipped paler; eye pale-orange or yellow; eyering and legs red. Female: duller and greyer. Imm: crown, nape and breast grey. Singly, pairs or small parties; rather shy. Often seen in swift direct flight between patches of scrub or through rainforest. In early morning and late afternoon moves out from cover to forage in foliage, low vegetation, on ground under trees, (? locally) on fallen grain in cornfields. At times perches conspicuously in heads of live or dead trees.
Similar species: Torres Strait Pigeon (287); Black-banded Pigeon (283) – note range.
Voice: Described as a loud 'whooo-hoo' uttered several times, or a series of gruff melancholy 'ooms'.
Habitat: Tropical and subtropical rainforests and scrubs; isolated trees or secondary growth in cleared country; occasionally street trees. Often in introduced camphor laurels.
Breeding: Nest: scanty platform of twigs; usually high in canopy. Egg: 1; cream-white.
Range and Status: Coastal ne. Aust. and forested islands: from Cooktown, Q, to Illawarra district, NSW; occasional s. to about Narooma. Inland to Bunya Mts., Q. Fairly common, nomadic.

290 DOMESTIC PIGEON *Columba livia* Pl.46
Other names: Feral, Homing or Rock Pigeon, Rock Dove.
Field marks: 330–340 mm. Typically blue-grey with glossy reddish or purplish green sheen on neck, black chequered pattern or *two black bars on wing*, dark flight-feathers and

tail-tip. General colouring may be paler or darker blue-grey to nearly black, or red-brown to sandy or nearly white or mixtures of these; patchy white, sometimes pure-white. Influence of fancy strains is seen in enlarged wattles, neck-ruffs, feathered legs, fan-tails, somersaults in flight etc. Imm: cere (raised nostrils) brownish, eye brown. Singly, pairs, flocks; feeds on ground, wheels high, showing white underwings. Males in display clap wings, sail with *wings upheld in a V*. In rural areas, usually fewer or fast-flying compact flocks of 'homing' birds.

Voice: A deep 'coroocoo' or 'rackitty-coo'; persistent 'ooms'.

Habitat: Ledges and cavities in buildings; grain-handling installations; railyards; wharfs; streets, parks, gardens. Scattered feral populations in light woodlands, occasionally coastal cliffs; bare paddocks, ploughed lands, stubblefields, sand-dunes, beaches.

Breeding: Nest: scanty; of twigs or grass; on ledge or cavity in a building, under eaves, on roof-beams or in guttering; crevice in rock-face, tree-hollow. Eggs: 2; white, oval and glossy.

Range and Status: Common in and round most towns and cities. Breeds away from settlement mostly in better-watered cereal-growing or agricultural regions of e., se. and sw. Aust. and Tas. Long a commensal of man, and domesticated. Probably introduced to Aust. from earliest days of settlement. The wild ancestor, Rock Pigeon *C. livia*, is still widespread in Europe, w. Asia and n. Africa.

291 SPOTTED TURTLE-DOVE *Streptopelia chinensis* Pl.45

Other names: Burmese Spotted, Indian Laceneck, Necklace or Spotted Dove; Chinese or Indian Turtle-dove.

Field marks: 315 mm. A large, rather long-tailed, grey-brown dove with pale-grey head and *black, white-spotted patch on back of neck*; upperparts mottled; underparts plain pinkish fawn, varying in depth. Imm: plainer; no chequered patch. Singly, pairs, open companies; feeds on ground, walking sedately. Flight direct, with wing-clatter when startled: *note blue-grey shoulders, broad white tips to black outer tail-feathers when spread*. Raises and lowers tail as it alights. Displaying males fly clattering up at steep angle, glide down slow-circling, wings and tail spread.

Similar species: Bar-shouldered Dove (296): barred coppery nape; blue-grey face and upperbreast. Laughing Dove (292): no collar but distinctive breast-marking.

Voice: Mellow, slightly rough, 'coo'; phrasing varies: 'coocoo, croo(oo)', or 'coo-coo, krroo, kook'.

Habitat: City and suburban streets, parks, gardens; grain installations, roadsides, close-settled rural areas; crops; secondary growth; lantana thickets, scrubby creeks.

Breeding: Nest: scanty platform; of twigs and rootlets; 1–15 m high in shrub or densely foliaged tree, often an exotic; ledges or beams of buildings; occasionally on ground. Eggs: 2; white, slightly glossy.

Range and Status: The species occurs naturally from India and Sri Lanka to s. China, Taiwan, se. Asia to Celebes, Moluccas and Sunda Is. Introduced se. Aust. in 1870s and later elsewhere; long known as Indian Turtle-dove but Australian populations are thought to be derived from the races *tigrina* and *chinensis*, of Burma–Malaya and s. China. Common and established cities; expanding in settled and agricultural districts of coastal e. and se. Aust., from about Cooktown, Q, to parts of Eyre Pen. and Kangaroo I., SA. Also Tas., mostly round Hobart, Launceston. On mainland, ranges inland to about Moree–Gunnedah–Albury, NSW; in c. Vic., n. to Murray R.; in SA, upstream on Murray R. at least to Loxton and n. to Port Augusta; in WA, from Perth n. to Dongara; populations Kalgoorlie, Katanning and on Rottnest and other islands. Common; sedentary.

292 LAUGHING DOVE *Streptopelia senegalensis* Pl.45

Other names: Egyptian or Senegal Dove, or Turtle-dove; Garden, Palm, Town or Village Dove.

Field marks: 255 mm. A small pinkish fawn dove with *distinctive blue-grey shoulder and wing and black-speckled deep-buff band* across lower throat; white below. Male brighter than female; imm: duller, with no specklings or blue-grey on wing. Singly, pairs to small flocks after breeding season. Rather tame; walks quietly in hunched posture. Flight direct, exposing prominent white tail-margins on take-off and alighting. Display-flight like Spotted Turtle-dove (291).

Similar species: Spotted Turtle-dove (291).

Voice: 'Coo-oo, coocoo'; described as having a bubbling laughing quality.

Habitat: City and suburban areas; country towns; parks and gardens, railyards, roadsides, farms, specially in wheatbelt.

Breeding: Nest: like Spotted Turtle-dove but smaller. Eggs: 2; white, smaller than Spotted Turtle-dove.

Range and Status: Natural range Africa to India; introduced some Mediterranean countries. Introduced Perth, WA, from 1898; extended into wheatbelt areas; e. to about Southern Cross, n. to Geraldton; occasional n. toward Shark Bay; s. to Albany; populations Kalgoorlie, Esperance; Rottnest and Garden Is. *Not elsewhere in Aust.* Common; sedentary.

293 BROWN PIGEON *Macropygia amboinensis* Pl.45

Other names: Brownie, Brown Cuckoo Dove; Large-tailed or Pheasant Pigeon, Pheasant-tailed Pigeon.

Field marks: 400 mm. A graceful *long-tailed* brown pigeon: dark-coppery brown above, buffish cinnamon below, paler on throat, broad shadowy bars on undertail. Imm: upperparts have rufous or buff feather-margins; underparts more chestnut with faint black barrings. Pairs, parties, feeding companies of dozens. Not shy; often feeds near ground by roads or tracks in rainforest or secondary growth in clearings. Flight strong and graceful with easy wingbeats, somewhat like King Parrot (329).

Voice: Mellow, high-pitched 'coo-crrork' or 'cucu-rrorrk', rising at end ('Did you walk?'), repeated deliberately several times. In display, a rolling 'c-croor'.

Habitat: Rainforests, mostly on margins, clearings, by tracks; secondary growth; thickets of wild tobacco, inkweed and similar regrowth.

Breeding: Nest: scanty structure of few twigs laid crosswise; usually fairly low, often near edge of tracks. Egg: 1; creamy white.

Range and Status: Coastal e. Aust. and islands: from Pascoe R. ne. Q, s. to Tanja, near Bega, NSW; inland to Atherton Tableland, Bunya Mts., Toowoomba, Chinchilla, Q; Gloucester and Blue Mts., NSW. Occasional (?) far-e. Vic. (Mallacoota NP). Common; sedentary or locally nomadic. Also Philippines, Indonesia, NG and Bismarck Archipelago.

294 PEACEFUL DOVE *Geopelia striata* Pl.45

Other names: Doodle-doo, Doo-doo; Four o'clock, Ground or Zebra Dove.

Field marks: 175–230 mm. A diminutive grey-brown dove with blue-grey head and neck and *a dense pattern of fine black-and-white barrings in a broad zone round neck and upper-breast*; coarser black barring on wings; cere and skin round eye blue-green. Imm: paler; fawn on wings and blue-green line back from eye. Pairs, small parties, winter flocks; feeds on ground, flushes with a 'frrr' of wings, flies in a quick undulating flip-flip style; note *chestnut wing-lining* and white tips to black outer tail-feathers. Tame in streets, gardens.

Similar species: Diamond (295) and Bar-shouldered (296) Doves.

Voice: Typical is a falsetto, musical, oft-repeated, 'doodaloo'; also falsetto 'co-co-coo'.

Habitat: Open scrublands, foothills and grassed woodlands near water; scrubby or lightly timbered watercourses; rainforest-fringes, coastal scrubs; agricultural country; roadsides, parks, gardens, fowlyards, railyards.

Breeding: Nest: scanty, of sticks; up to 7 m on horizontal branch or fork in leafy bush or tree, often exotic: citrus in orchard, pepper-tree near homestead. Eggs: 2; white, rounded.

Range and Status: Mainland Aust. and coastal islands, but *absent from* w. part of continent s. of about Murchison R., WA, and about Banka Banka, NT; extends s. through e. NT and e. SA to Adelaide and lower Murray R.; thence throughout e. Aust., *except* coastal Vic. between about Yarram and Portland; introduced Kangaroo I., SA. Generally common, but becoming rare in s. SA and s. Vic., perhaps by competition from Spotted Turtle-dove (291). Sedentary. Also Malaysia, Luzon, Indonesia, s. NG.

295 DIAMOND DOVE *Geopelia cuneata* Pl.45

Other names: Little or Red-eyed Dove or Turtle-dove.

Field marks: 190–215 mm. A dimunitive blue-grey dove, washed smoky brown above, *with red eyering and scattered fine white spots on wings.* Female: duller, slightly browner; eyering smaller. Some inland birds show uneven rufous tinge. Imm: browner, with very pale-buff markings giving barred appearance somewhat like Peaceful Dove (294). Pairs, small parties, winter flocks; feeds on ground with 'quick, toddling run'; flushes with a whistling 'frrr', flies fast and direct, showing white outer tail-feathers and *chestnut on primaries.*

Similar species: Peaceful Dove (294).

Voice: Common call: slow, level, mournful four-note coo, syllabized 'oh-my-papa'; also plaintive slow high-pitched 'coo-cooooo'.

Habitat: Near water in dry inland scrubs and woodlands; hilly country with scrubby trees; timbered watercourses.

Breeding: Nest: fragile platform of twigs, grasses and rootlets; in low shrub or scrubby tree or on stump. Eggs: 2; white, rounded.

Range and Status: Wide distribution in drier parts all mainland states, generally *absent* coastal e., se. Aust.; sw. WA s. of Murchison R. Fluctuates with the seasons; irregular movements coastwards during dry periods inland, mostly in summer. Fairly common, but patchy; highly nomadic.

296 BAR-SHOULDERED DOVE *Geopelia humeralis* Pl.45

Other names: Barred-shouldered, Mangrove or Scrub Dove; Kook-a-wuk; Pandanus or River Pigeon.

Field marks: 265–300 mm. A fairly large dove, mostly brown above with *bold dark scaly pattern on upperparts;* this extends only to sides of neck *not round breast;* blue-grey face and upperbreast contrast with *pale-copper nape and shoulders;* underparts plain pink-buff, paling to white below; cycring grey, red-brown in breeding male. Imm: duller, coppery shades on blue-grey neck, buff eyering. Feeds mostly on ground in pairs or small parties; occasionally flocks. Flight swift and direct, *head carried distinctly high;* note pale-coppery shoulders, blue-grey neck, chestnut underwing and patch on flight-feathers; white margins to tail less prominent than in Spotted Turtle-dove (291).

Similar species: Peaceful Dove (294); Spotted Turtle-dove (291).

Voice: Distinctive: very high-pitched melodious 'coolicoo'; also an emphatic 'hook, coo! hook, coo!'.

Habitat: Typically vegetation near water: tropical and subtropical scrubs, inland and coastal; scrubby vegetation and mangroves by creeks and swamps; eucalypt woodlands; crops, plantations, lantana thickets; gardens.

Breeding: Nest: scanty platform; of twigs and grasses; in shrub, low tree, mangrove or vine. Eggs: 2; white, rounded and glossy.

Range and Status: Coastal n. and e. Aust. and coastal islands: from Onslow and

Hamersley Ras., WA, through Kimberleys; top end NT; all coastal Q, inland to Rolleston–upper Barcoo–Warrego Rs.; in NSW, coastally s. to about Newcastle, local populations s. to Wyong; inland to Lightning Ridge–Cobar–L. Cargelligo–Griffith; vagrant near Nowra on s. coast and Hattah Lakes NP, Vic. Common in undisturbed habitat in main range, but being adversely affected by clearing, and, in e. Aust., perhaps by expansion in range of Spotted Turtle-dove (291). Sedentary. Also s. NG.

297   GREEN-WINGED PIGEON   *Chalcophaps indica*   Pl.45

Other names: Emerald or Green-winged Dove; Lilac-mantled, Little Green or Little Green-winged Pigeon.

Field marks: 230–255 mm. A small dark *purplish brown pigeon with glossy emerald-green wings*, lower back crossed by two pale-grey bars. Bill and legs reddish. Male: white patch at shoulder; female: smaller grey mark. Imm: dark markings on head, wings and below. Singly, pairs or parties; feeds unobtrusively on ground usually under cover, becomes tame round settlement. Flight fast and low, soon to settle and remain motionless: in good light note pale shoulder-patch, chestnut webs of flight-feathers and bars on lower back.

Voice: Described as monotonous low-toned 'coo-coo', and 'hoo-hoo-hoon', with nasal ending.

Habitat: Rainforests, tropical and subtropical scrubs; wet eucalypt forest, streamside timber; lantana thickets, coastal and island scrubs, mangroves; margins of tracks or under large fruiting trees; farms, gardens, tourist centres. More open, drier habitats in winter.

Breeding: Nest: scanty platform; of twigs in shrub, fern, on horizontal limb or fork, in vine or lantana scrub, up to 5 m. Eggs: 2; creamy-white.

Range and Status: Coastal n. and e. Aust. and forested coastal islands: from Kimberleys through coastal NT and from C. York s. generally e. of Divide to Shoalhaven R., NSW; occasional far-e. Vic.; vagrant Lower Tarwin, Vic., and near Perth, WA. Common; sedentary. Also India through se. Asia to se. NG, New Hebrides, New Caledonia; Norfolk and Lord Howe Is. (perhaps introduced).

298   COMMON BRONZEWING   *Phaps chalcoptera*   Pl.46

Other names: Bronzewing; Common or Forest Bronzewing Pigeon, Scrub Bronzewing, Squatter.

Field marks: 305–355 mm. A large plump pigeon; apart from extensive bronze on wing, the upperparts are brown with *pale margins of feathers giving a bold scaly appearance*. Male: forehead buffish, throat pale and unmarked; *conspicuous curving white line* back from bill under eye and a little down side of neck; *breast pinkish grey*. Female: duller, forehead and breast greyer. Imm: duller generally. Singly, pairs, open companies; feeds on ground, in stubble at edge of scrub, under wattles; travels considerable distances at dawn and dusk to drink at creeks, isolated tanks, etc., often in half-light. Very wary; flies with a clatter to depart swiftly or settle motionless but head-bobbing on high limb. Sustained flight very swift with continuous wingbeats and characteristic whistle of wings, *note buff wing-linings*. Occasionally tame in gardens, farmyards.

Similar species: Brush Bronzewing (299): plainer, darker brown above, with chestnut patch on throat; deeper blue-grey below. In flight, rusty flight-feathers.

Voice: Repeated 'oom-oom-oom' of fugitive but carrying quality, repeated monotonously.

Habitat: Eucalypt forests, woodlands and scrubs; mallee, native pine, vegetation of inland plains and hills; thickets of wattles and other acacias; coastal tea-tree scrubs, banksia thickets and heaths; alpine woodlands to over 2000 m in summer.

Breeding: Nest: scanty platform or fairly substantial shallow saucer; of twigs and rootlets; up to 12 m in shrub or tree, usually on horizontal branch, fork or in mistletoe; or near ground on stump, concealed by coppice growth; occasionally in old nest of babbler, chough or magpie. Eggs: 2; white, oval.

Range and Status: Nearly throughout Aust. and Tas. in suitable habitat *except* waterless regions inland. Fairly common; mostly sedentary but probably nomadic in dry conditions.

299 BRUSH BRONZEWING *Phaps elegans* Pl.46

Other names: Box-poison Pigeon, Little Bronze-Pigeon.

Field marks: 280–300 mm. Best field marks are the *rich-chestnut shoulders, sides of neck and throat-patch and the blue-grey underparts.* Wings and back *plain olive-brown* with two bronze bands on wing. Male: forehead buff, crown grey; *bold chestnut line back from eye, margined white below; chestnut throat-patch.* Female: forehead less buff or greyish; much less chestnut on upperparts, none on nape; throat-patch smaller or absent. Imm: like duller female. Singly or pairs; feeds quietly on ground under trees or shrubs; flight swift; note rich-chestnut shoulders, *rusty flight-feathers.*

Similar species: Common Bronzewing (298).

Voice: Muffled 'oom', uttered incessantly when breeding; higher pitched than Common Bronzewing.

Habitat: Generally in cover with a scrubbier thicker understorey than Common Bronzewing: coastal scrubs and heaths; understorey of eucalypt forests and woodlands; mallee scrubs; alpine woodlands in summer. Drier sparser scrubs on coastal islands.

Breeding: Nest: scanty; of twigs and rootlets; in shrub or tangle of fallen branches and leaves, near or on ground under cover. Eggs: 2; white.

Range and Status: Mostly coastal se. and sw. Aust. and islands: from se. Q (Fraser I. and Noosa Plain) s. to Bass Strait islands and Tas., w. to Kangaroo I. and Streaky Bay, Eyre Pen., SA, where it has been described as 'much more common' than Common Bronzewing in coastal parts. It occurs inland in scrubby understorey of forests on parts of Gt. Dividing Ra. and Grampians, Vic., and appears to be extending inland in mallee areas of nw. Vic. – se. SA. In s. WA, mostly w. of a line from Esperance to Dongara, and Abrolhos Group. Generally scarce, locally common; sedentary. Vagrant Lord Howe I.

300 FLOCK PIGEON *Phaps histrionica* Pl.46

Other names: Flock or Harlequin Bronzewing.

Field marks: 280–305 mm. A conspicuous long-winged pigeon usually seen in flight in parties or flocks, often high over plains. Male: sandy copper above, blue-grey below; *head black with conspicuous white forehead, ear-mark and bib.* Female: duller, browner; forehead and throat dull-white with broad smutty area on lower throat bordered by whitish bib. Imm: duller. Gregarious and highly nomadic; flocks feed on ground far from cover; single birds or parties travel across sky on long, backswept wings; courting males fly with quick shallow wingbeats, hold wings in a stiff V and glide. At dawn and especially toward dusk, large, at times spectacular, flocks fly to water, rising and falling like petrels. They settle some distance off to walk in or they drop to surface of open water, supported by spread wings as they drink before springing off.

Similar species: Squatter (302) and Patridge (303) Pigeons: no white forehead; habits differ.

Habitat: Grassy plains; saltbush, spinifex, open mulga; stock-tanks, bore-drains, pools in water courses. Occasionally feeds in crops, including lucerne.

Breeding: Nest: a scrape on ground in cover of low bush or tussock; many pairs reported to nest in proximity. Eggs: 2; creamy white.

Range and Status: It ranges through n. inland Aust. but its occurrence is often very spasmodic. It occurs most consistently on Barkly Tableland of e. NT and adjacent nw. Q. It occurs w. to the Kimberley region, WA, and e. to about Hughenden–Longreach, Q, occasional e. to near Townsville. At times it ranges s. to about the Tropic in WA, s. through the NT to L. Eyre Basin, ne. SA, and s. through w. Q into nw. NSW to about Darling R., occasional s. to about Ivanhoe. Formerly recorded in huge flocks, it declined following settlement and by the early 1900s was feared extinct. Since the 1950s it has again been frequently observed, at times in flocks of thousands. Fairly common but very patchy; highly nomadic.

301   CRESTED PIGEON   *Ocyphaps lophotes* .   Pl.46

Other names: Crested Bronzewing or Dove; Saddleback, Topknot; Whistling-winged Pigeon; Wirewings.

Field marks: 305–355 mm. Our only *greyish pigeon with a slender black crest*. Wings with fine wavy black bars; coloured bronze wing-patch edged white; tail longish, black toward end, tipped paler. Imm: duller, almost without bronze on wing. Singly, pairs, parties or open flocks; feeds on ground; runs with crest erect; perches and suns itself on dead trees, fences, overhead wires. Flight swift, with *bursts of whistling wingbeats or single wingbeats and flat-winged tilting glides, crest flat*; on alighting, tips tail. Courting males perform steep upward display-flight, descending in curving glide.

Similar species: Spinifex Pigeon (306). Do not confuse by name with Topknot Pigeon (288).

Voice: 'Whoop!' singly in alarm, or repeated.

Habitat: Open country generally, where water is present; in settled districts often on roadsides, stubble-fields and other croplands, weed-grown paddocks; sportsgrounds, farmyards, country railyards.

Breeding: Nest: frail platform; of twigs, usually in rather dense low bush or tree, up to 5 m. Eggs: 2; oval, pure white and glossy.

Range and Status: Australian mainland; formerly confined to arid and semi-arid inland and drier coastal regions and islands. Has progressively extended range n. into Gulf lowlands in Q, into e. coastal areas to s. of Sydney; occasional to near coast in w. Vic., s. SA; in s. WA, coastally to s. of Perth. The Gt. Dividing Range and associated forests have apparently inhibited its coastward spread in se. Aust. and the Darling Ra. and forests similarly in s. WA. *Absent or scarce* C. York Pen. n. of Mitchell R. and top end NT. Introduced Kangaroo I., SA. Common; sedentary.

302   SQUATTER PIGEON   *Petrophassa scripta*   Pl.46

Other names: Partridge Bronzewing or Pigeon.

Field marks: 270–320 mm. A dull-brown pigeon; pale feather-margins give it a scaly pattern; *note strong black-and-white facial pattern combined with white throat*; *whitish sides to grey breast form a distinct broad V.* Skin round eye blue-grey or blue-white (apricot-coloured in birds from ne. Q); feet dull-blue or purplish. Small parties in sparse grassy cover; when alarmed, squats or runs twisting through grass with neck craned and feathers of crown raised in small rough crest. Bursts up with a clatter or whirr, broad dark tips of outer tail-feathers prominent; flies with alternate flaps and glides, settles again on ground or horizontal branch, where it squats or stands erect and motionless. Said to be attracted to cattle camps to feed on ticks; tame near settlement.

Similar species: Partridge Pigeon (303).

Voice: Low quiet conversational double 'coos'.

Habitat: Grassy plains, well-drained river flats; open grassed woodlands and foothills, dry watercourses; environs of homesteads and cattle-camps.

Breeding: Nest: scrape on ground lined with grass. Eggs: 2; creamy white, rounded.

Range and Status: Nearly confined to Q, except settled parts of coastal se., the far-sw. and perhaps n. C. York Pen.; extends a short way into n. NSW, to about Inverell, occasional further s.; (?) vagrant Marrapinna Stn. *c.* 150 km nne. Broken Hill. Formerly common and more widespread, ranging further s. in NSW. Now much reduced, locally common in n. but generally uncommon. Sedentary or part-nomadic.

303 PARTRIDGE PIGEON *Petrophassa smithii* **Pl.46**

Other names: Bare-eyed Pigeon, Naked-eye Partridge Pigeon, (Smith's) Partridge Bronzewing.

Field marks: 250–280 mm. A squat dull-brown pigeon with a *heavy black bill, prominent red facial skin outlined in white, and white throat*; breast pinkish brown with prominent white sides forming a V; *in centre of breast a grey area with black scaly marks*. Small flocks, to dozens; squats or runs with feathers of crown raised in rough crest; when startled, birds disperse in different direction with almost a roar of wings, showing broad dark tail-tips. They quickly glide to ground on set wings and run or settle on horizontal branch and freeze.

Similar species: Squatter Pigeon (302).

Voice: Soft rolling double 'coo'.

Habitat: Grassy woodlands, open ground by streams and watercourses; roadsides, areas of newly burned grass or bush; seldom far from water.

Breeding: Nest: depression on ground; lined with grass. Eggs: 2; cream-white or greenish white.

Range and Status: Coastal nw. Aust. and Melville I.: from Kimberleys, WA, s. to Cockatoo Spring; top end NT s. to Mataranka–Mallapunyah; possibly extreme nw. Q. Locally fairly common; sedentary.

ROCK-PIGEONS

Two closely related specialized rock-dwelling pigeons of nw. Aust. Their plumage is dark-brown, finely patterned by paler feather margins. This pattern matches remarkably the dark granular rocks of their habitats. Both have black bill and legs and black facial skin from bill to round eye, margined above and below by a fine white line. In the Chestnut-quilled (305), greyish centres to feathers of head and neck give it a subtly patterned look; in White-quilled (304) these are whiter and mostly confined to throat. They are best distinguished by different coloured wingpatches, usually visible only in flight. Their ranges do not overlap.

304 WHITE-QUILLED ROCK-PIGEON *Petrophassa albipennis* **Pl.46**

Field marks: 280–300 mm. A sturdy small-headed darkish-brown pigeon that crouches. Smaller than Chestnut-quilled (305) and with white across base of outer primaries, barely visible or disappearing at rest, *but forming a conspicuous white patch in flight*. Singly, pairs, small loose flocks; runs, squats motionless, relying on protective colouring. Flies with a loud whistling whirr in very rapid 'flip-flip-glide' flight; when flushed from base of rocky escarpments, typically flies steeply uphill to cover of rocks. N.B. the small race *boothi*, occupying e. part of range in the area of lower Victoria R., NT, shows little or no white in wing.

Similar species: Chestnut-quilled Rock-pigeon (305).

Voice: Like Chestnut-quilled.

Habitat: Sandstone escarpments, ridges and gorges with horizontal niches and ledges. Typically rough and broken with large blocks and boulders, vegetated with spinifex, stunted eucalypts and other trees; may extend to open country at base of escarpments.

Breeding: Nest: fairly substantial, of sticks and leaves or of a few leaves and stalks of spinifex very loosely arranged, with little material beneath eggs; on shaded rock-ledge or horizontal crevice in cliff face. Eggs: 2; creamy white, smooth and glossy, elliptical.

Range and Status: Confined to area of lower Victoria R., NT, w. through Kimberleys, WA, s. to Argyle Downs, w. to inland of Derby. Locally common; sedentary.

305   CHESTNUT-QUILLED ROCK-PIGEON   *Petrophassa rufipennis*   **Pl.46**
Other name: Red-quilled Rock Pigeon.
Field marks: 300–320 mm. A squat, wing-drooping dark-brown pigeon, *primaries mostly chestnut*, forming a streak sometimes visible at rest and a large chestnut wing-patch in flight. Imm: duller. Singly, pairs parties to 20 + that chase along ledges, preen and doze together. Feeds along foot of rocky escarpments in early and latter part of day, flying up when disturbed to take refuge among rocks. Flies with musical loud whirr and stiff flips and glides on level wings.
Similar species: White-quilled Rock-pigeon (304).
Voice: Reported to be low coos and a loud 'coo-carook'.
Habitat: Rugged fissured sandstone escarpments, deeply dissected by gullies and gorges; no woodland as such, but with numerous trees including eucalypts, figs and other softwoods and some pockets of rainforest.
Breeding: Nest: fairly substantial for pigeon; platform of sticks fitted into irregularities in rock, hollowed and lined with thick pad of spinifex leaves and stems; on shaded ledge or crevice in rock-face. Eggs: 2; creamy white, elliptical, smooth and glossy.
Range and Status: Confined to Arnhem Land, NT, from Oenpelli s. to upper Katherine R. Locally common; sedentary.

306   SPINIFEX PIGEON   *Petrophassa plumifera*   **Pl.46**
Other names: Plumed Bronzewing, or Pigeon, Red or White-bellied Plumed Pigeon, Plumed or Ground Dove.
Field marks: 200–235 mm. A plump, erect little sandy buff to rich ruddy buff pigeon with *a very tall erect sandy crest, wavy black barrings on wings and prominent facial pattern*. Nominate (and other) races have white or buff-white underparts; the race *ferruginea*, 'Red-bellied Spinifex Pigeon', is rich ruddy buff above and below. Pairs to small flocks; runs and dodges swiftly like quail through spinifex and over rocks; flushes with sudden whirr or clatter, flying with single flips and glides, displaying *large copper patch* on rounded wings and blackish outer tail-feathers. Tame round habitation.
Similar species: Crested Pigeon (301).
Voice: Soft high-pitched 'coo' or 'cooloo-coo' also deep guttural 'coo-r-r-r'.
Habitat: Always near water: rocky hilly spinifex country; spinifex-covered sand-ridges; occasionally sandy scrub without spinifex; sandy creekbeds.
Breeding: Nest: none or little; on ground in shelter of spinifex clump or low bush. Eggs: 2; white.
Range and Status: Inland and n. Aust.; from Gascoyne R., WA, n. to Kimberleys, e. to about Winton–Longreach, Q, and n. to dry interior of lower C. York Pen.; s. inland to far-nw. NSW and n. SA; absent top end NT and Gulf coast. The race *ferruginea* occupies w. end of range from Gascoyne R., WA, n. through the Pilbara to Eighty Mile Beach, inland to about Meekatharra. Common but patchy and discontinuous; mostly sedentary.

307   WONGA PIGEON   *Leucosarcia melanoleuca*   **Pl.46**
Other name: Wonga Wonga.
Field marks: 430 mm. A stately pigeon, slaty above with *prominent white forehead; breast white, with deep blue-grey wedge down from throat in centre and similar stripe on either side; forming a bold double V-pattern*; black spots on white flanks. Singly or pairs; feeds on forest-floor or ground near cover specially morning and late afternoon; stands or crouches motionless in shadow, flies up with a clatter; usually settles motionless on branch with back to observer or sits lengthwise. Typically spends middle of day perched; often calling incessantly.
Voice: Loud far-carrying high-pitched whistling coo or 'wonk', easily imitated by blowing through cupped hands; repeated monotonously.
Habitat: Rainforests, wet eucalypt forests; timbered gullies to drier woodlands; margin-

ally in newly planted corn; thistle-beds, banana plantations; quiet gardens near bush, where it becomes tamer.

Breeding: Nest: shallow platform; of thin sticks, twigs and stems; usually on horizontal fork of forest tree up to 12 m. Eggs: 2; large, white and rounded.

Range and Status: E. coastal and highland areas up to c. 1200 m, from Shoalwater Bay n. of Rockhampton, Q, s. to about Gippsland lakes, L. Tyers, Vic.; inland to about Chinchilla, Q; Mudgee and Tumut, NSW; Fraser NP–Powelltown, Vic. Generally uncommon, locally common; sedentary.

Parrots, including Cockatoos

Parrots are mostly very colourful birds distinguished by powerful curved bills with both mandibles articulated for crushing or tearing hard objects; short legs and muscular zygodactylous feet, i.e. two toes forward and two back. Like a few other groups, they produce powder-down, friable specialized down growing in several patches that breaks into powder during preening and serves as a feather-dressing. Most species in our arid inland habitats are nomadic, moving and breeding irregularly in response to irregular rainfall. Following good rains and growth of vegetation, parrots like the Cockatiel (334) and the Budgerigar (337) may enjoy a spectacular increase. Species of more coastal range have more regular breeding seasons. Most Australian parrots nest in tree-hollows but the small group of 'anthill' parrots (352–4) burrow in termite mounds and one grass-parrot (359) nests in rock-cavities. The Ground (335) and Night (336) Parrots, alone, build nests of plant-material on or near ground in heavy low cover. Most parrots are gregarious, forming small to large flocks specially when not breeding. Some, particularly Galah (314) have become more abundant and widespread as a result of pastoral and agricultural development. Others have been severely reduced as a result of settlement and at least four are in danger of extinction or are seriously reduced by loss or fragmentation of habitat or by illicit trapping.

Range: Throughout the tropics, extending into temperate, cool temperate and even alpine zones in Asia, N. and S. America, Africa, Aust. and NZ and some oceanic and even sub-Antarctic islands.

Number of species: World 328; Aust. 55.

Cockatoos Family *Cacatuidae*

Cockatoos are perhaps best described as large, simply coloured parrots with mobile crests. The Australian region is their stronghold; beyond NG, a few species range to the Philippines. Aust. has eleven species, all fairly easily identified: five (308–312) are blackish and large to very large with massive bills; four (315–8) are mostly white and two are smaller and distinctive: dark-grey with some red (Gang Gang 313), or pink-and-grey (Galah 314). Most have loud voices. Sexes similar or dissimilar.

Food: Seeds, nuts, berries, fruits, blossoms, corms and roots, palm shoots and invertebrates, especially large wood-boring larvae of moths and beetles.

308 PALM COCKATOO *Probosciger aterrimus*   Pl.48
Other names: Cape York or Great Palm Cockatoo, Black Macaw.
Field marks: 560–640 mm. A large, uniformly dark-grey cockatoo. *Bill huge, dark-grey, facial skin orange-pink, scarlet when excited; crest very long and erectile.* Female: bill and facial patch smaller. Imm: feathers of underparts and wing-linings margined pale-yellow; bill pale at first. Singly, pairs or parties; perches conspicuously in leafless branches of emergent trees above rainforest or eucalypt woodland, calling and displaying. Flies with full slow beats of broad wings, bill tucked onto breast; glides on downcurved

wings when coming in to settle. Occasionally feeds on ground, e.g. on fallen nuts of *Pandanus*.

Similar species: Red-tailed Black Cockatoo (309) is the only other black cockatoo on C. York Pen.

Voice: Whistling 'hweet-kweet'; deep and mellow, then shrill and far-carrying, usually when perched; also harsh deep screech and wailing cry in flight.

Habitat: Tropical rainforest and adjacent open eucalypt woodlands; stands of paper-barks.

Breeding: Nest: layer of splintered twigs; in hollow tree-trunk, *c.* 9 m high. Egg: 1; white.

Range and Status: C. York Pen., Q, s. to Archer R. on w. coast and to Princess Charlotte Bay in e. Fairly common; sedentary. Also NG and Aru Is.

309 RED-TAILED BLACK COCKATOO *Calyptorhynchus magnificus* Pl.48

Other names: Banks' Black, Banksian, Great-billed or Red-tailed Cockatoo.

Field marks: 590–660 mm. The only black cockatoo in much of n. and inland Aust.; con-spicuous and often noisy. Male: *broad scarlet panels in tail* conspicuous on take-off and alighting. Bill blackish and robust; crest rounded, erectile forward over bill like helmet. Female and imm: *bill whitish*, plumage duller with fine yellow spots and barrings, *tail-panels yellow-orange*, finely barred black. Pairs, parties to flocks of 200 +; feeds much on ground, camps in tall trees, specially by rivers, in w Vic. and se. SA reported to associate with (311) and in sw. WA, with (312). Flocks travel in steady level buoyant flight with deep slow wingbeats.

Similar species: Glossy Black Cockatoo (310): smaller, duller, but easily confused; note comparatively more massive bill, softer wheezy calls; female: patchy yellow on head and neck. Yellow-tailed (311) and White-tailed (312) Black Cockatoos.

Voice: Hoarse brassy far-carrying bugle or trumpet, 'kreee'; uttered in flight or at 5–8 second intervals when perched; reminiscent of loud rusty windmill.

Habitat: Open forests and woodlands; (in w. Vic. and se. SA, stringybark woodlands); grasslands, scrublands; trees along watercourses. Note: sometimes behaves like Glossy Black by feeding in casuarinas, cracking the seed-capsules.

Breeding: Nest: on decayed debris in large tree-hollow, entrance usually high. Egg: 1, white.

Range and Status: N. and interior Aust.: from Kimberleys, WA, to top end NT, C. York Pen. and e. Q s. to about Burnett R.; s. through inland Q and nw. NSW to about the Darling R. Occasional in se. Q and e. NSW, where however some sight-records are probably misidentifications of Glossy Black Cockatoos. There are (? separate) popula-tions in: (1) w. Vic. and se. SA: Grampians n. to Little Desert, s. to Hamilton–Mt. Gambier, w. to Penola–Bangham, SA. (2) Central Aust.: Macdonnell Ras., NT, s. to NT–SA border, occasional Everard Ras. and elsewhere in n. SA. (3) s. WA: from timbered lands of far-sw. corner n. coastally and on Darling Ra. to Murchison and possibly Minilya Rs.; inland limits not clear. Uncommon to rare in s. Aust.; common in interior and n. Aust.; sedentary, nomadic or part-migratory.

310 GLOSSY BLACK COCKATOO *Calyptorhynchus lathami* Pl.48

Other names: Casuarina (Black) Cockatoo, Leach's Black Cockatoo.

Field marks: 460–510 mm. Misleadingly named – a dull-black cockatoo with a *massive bulbous bill* and red panel in tail. Male: bill dark-grey. Female: bill paler, grey-horn; *usually has irregular clear-yellow markings on head and neck*; flecked yellow on underparts and underwing (carpal joint); red in tail barred black, edged yellow on inner webs. Imm: like female but usually no yellow on neck. Pairs or parties; more approachable than Red-tailed Black Cockatoo; flight laboured. Typically feeds in casuarinas, breaking seed-capsules with its massive bill; seldom on ground. Easily, and in e. NSW and se. Q probably frequently, mistaken for Red-tailed Black; look for yellow head-markings of females.

Similar species: Red-tailed Black Cockatoo (309). Yellow-tailed Black Cockatoo (311): browner, with pale feather-margins; yellow spot on cheek, pale-yellow panel in tail; note calls.

Voice: Feeble whining wailing, described as a soft 'tarr-red, tarr-red'.

Habitat: Usually associated with casuarinas in coastal forests and woodlands, timbered watercourses. In inland NSW and Q, in hilly rocky ridge country where casuarinas occur, and in brigalow scrub.

Breeding: Nest: on decayed debris; usually in hollow of dead tree, often high. Egg: 1; white, oval.

Range and Status: E. Aust., from n. of Yeppoon, Q, coastally s. to far e. Vic. (Wingan Inlet); isolated population Kangaroo I., SA (formerly in Mt. Lofty Ras.). Inland in Q to Chinchilla (? and Carnarvon Ras.–Augathella); in NSW to Inverell–Warrumbungle NP and on hills w. to about Cobar–Hillston-Griffith, including Harvey Ras.; Mt. Hope; Lachlan and Cocoparra Ras. and hills nw. of Ardlethan. Sedentary; generally local and very uncommon. Clearing of woodlands containing casuarinas is probably responsible for decline.

311 YELLOW-TAILED BLACK COCKATOO *Calyptorhynchus funereus*
Pl.48

Other names: Black or Funereal Cockatoo; Yellow-eared Black, or Yellow-tailed Cockatoo; Wylah.

Field marks: 630–690 mm. A large, somewhat glossy brownish black cockatoo with *round yellow mark on ear-coverts and pale-yellow panels on upper surface of tail*; undertail: basal part pale-yellow, remainder black. Male: upper mandible deep-grey, lower paler; eyering deep-pink. Female: whitish bill, grey eyering, brighter-yellow spot on earcoverts; yellowish margins to breast-feathers, yellow tail-panels spotted and finely zigzagged brown. Imm: browner; more prominent pale feather-margins. Pairs, family trios, small flocks to autumn and winter flocks of hundreds. Tears bark and wood of acacias and eucalypts to attack 'white grubs'; opens seed-capsules of hakeas, banksias and introduced pines; occasionally feeds on ground. Flight very distinctive: buoyant and level with *deep slow wingbeats*, long tail prominent; weird calls.

Similar species: Red-tailed (309) and Glossy (310) Black Cockatoos.

Voice: Weird wail, 'wee-yu' or 'wy-la'; grinding noises when feeding; harsh alarm-screeches.

Habitat: Temperate rainforests, mountain and coastal eucalypt forests and woodlands, coastal heaths; plantations of introduced pines.

Breeding: Nest: on decayed debris; in tree-hollow, usually high. Eggs: 1–2; white, oval; only one offspring survives.

Range and Status: Se. Aust., mostly coastal and on ranges, to snowline: from near Rockhampton, Q, to s. SA; in Q, inland to Taroom–Chinchilla (? Carnarvon Ras.); in NSW w. to higher slopes of Divide, vagrant s. Riverina (Moulamein); all Vic. except nc. and nw.; s. SA, w. to Mt. Lofty Ras., s. Eyre Pen. and Kangaroo I. Also Fraser I., Q; larger islands of Bass Strait, and Tas. Uncommon to common; sedentary and nomadic.

312 WHITE-TAILED BLACK COCKATOO *Calyptorhynchus baudinii* **Pl.48**

Other name: Baudin's Black Cockatoo.

Field marks: 530–580 mm. Smaller and browner than (311), *yellow tones replaced by white*; sexual differences, habits, flight and voice similar. Two races are recognized: (a) nominate race has long narrow bill adapted to extract seeds from fruit-capsules of marri *Eucalyptus calophylla*, and to tear wood in search of wood-boring larvae. (b) *latirostris* has a shorter broader bill, adapted for cracking hard seed-capsules of hakeas, dryandras, banksias. Pairs, small flocks; larger flocks in non-breeding season (Jan.–June); causes damage in apple and pear orchards; may damage almonds. The species is now a regular seasonal visitor to plantations of introduced pines, to extract seeds from cones; this food has become important in its economy.

Similar species: Red-tailed Black Cockatoo (309).

Habitat: Nominate race: heavy forests, woodlands; *latirostris*: woodlands, scrublands, wheat-belt and sandplain areas. Both visit pine plantations.

Breeding: Nest: on decayed debris; in hollow of an isolated tree, usually at some height. **Eggs:** 1–2; white, oval; typically one egg fails to hatch or one offspring fails to survive. **Range and Status:** Confined to sw. WA, from Murchison R. to Esperance, inland to near Southern Cross and Norseman. Nominate race inhabits wetter zone from Gin Gin, n. of Perth, to e. of Albany; includes Darling Ras., heavy karri and most of the mixed jarrah and marri forests and woodlands of sw. corner. In nonbreeding season it forms flocks of 1000–1500+. Race *latirostris* inhabits mostly the drier zone making up the rest of range. It breeds round Perth, wheatbelt, and coastal areas n. of Perth and e. of Albany. After breeding it forms wandering flocks (of c. 50–500+); smaller flocks moving coastwards into range of nominate race. Common.

313 GANG-GANG COCKATOO *Callocephalon fimbriatum* Pl.48

Field marks: 330–355 mm. A somewhat owl-like small dark-grey cockatoo; pale margins to rather square feathers give it a patterned look. Male: *bright-red head and untidy crest*. Female: *grey head and crest*, feathers of underparts margined light-red. Imm: like female, wings and undertail barred and marbled whitish yellow; imm. males have light-red marks on head and crest. Pairs, small parties or flocks; quiet and inconspicuous in foliage, often first located by growling notes, cracking of seed-capsules or falling debris. When flushed, typically swoops low, swings up into next tree. Flight loose and tilting with deep wing-beats; note short squared tail.

Voice: Unmistakable – a strong stuttered creaky growl, with rising inflection, like rusty hinge; usually in flight.

Habitat: Forests and woodlands, from sea level to over 2000 m; timbered foothills and valleys; in autumn–winter disperses to open lowlands, timbered watercourses, coastal scrubs, farmlands, suburban gardens; often in hawthorn and other berry-bearing hedges.

Breeding: Nest: on decayed debris in tree-hollow, usually in woodland or forest. Eggs: 2–3; white, rounded.

Range and Status: Se. Aust., from about Hunter R., NSW, (sight record near Ebor, New England), s. coastally and on Divide to far-se. SA. Inland (occasional) to Mudgee–Wagga Wagga and downstream on Murray R. to about Tocumwal; e. and s. Vic., inland to about Warby Ras.–Mt. Alexander–Grampians. Vagrant King I. and Tas. Fairly common in suitable habitat; sedentary and nomadic or part-migratory.

314 GALAH *Cacatua roseicapilla* Pl.48

Other names: Goolie, Goulie, Roseate or Rose-breasted Cockatoo; Willie-willock, Willock.

Field marks: 340–380 mm. Well known: *pale-grey above, rose-pink to deep rose-red below, with low cap-like crest*. Male's eye dark-brown; female's reddish. Nominate race has whitish crown and crest, deep-red eyering; race *assimilis* has pinker larger crest, upperparts whiter, *specially rump and tail*; eyering pale-grey. Imm: (both races) breast washed grey; eyering grey. Singly, pairs to very large noisy flocks, easily identified from afar by the alternation of grey and pink as they wheel. Feeds much on ground but also in foliage: often a pest in grain, haystacks, domestic fruit or nut-trees. Waters and roosts in noisy antic companies; hangs with wings spread, flies wildly.

Voice: Unmistakable thin high-pitched splintered call, 'chill chill'; harsher screeches.

Habitat: Open country with suitable trees, typically on watercourses. Expansion of

grasslands, cereal crops and provision of waterholes and tanks has greatly expanded habitat; town parks, playing fields, even beaches.
Breeding: Nest: in hollow tree, living or dead; occasionally in cliff. Two unusual features: bark is typically stripped from round entrance; nest-hollow is lined with green eucalypt leaves and twigs. Eggs: 2–5; white, oval.
Range and Status: Formerly inland and drier coastal areas where water available; has greatly expanded range coastwards since settlement. Now very widespread in suitable habitat *except* some wetter coastal areas. Nominate race: e. and se. Aust.; vagrant King I. and other Bass Strait islands; in Tas., recent records (? escapes) mostly near Hobart and Launceston; also Legana, e. Tas. *assimilis*: n. SA, s. NT and s. WA. Common to very abundant; sedentary.

315 LONG-BILLED CORELLA *Cacatua tenuirostris* Pl.48

Other names: Dampier or Slender-billed Cockatoo.
Field marks: 355–410 mm. Slightly larger than Little Corella (316) with *much longer whitish bill*; pink before eye and across forehead more conspicuous, *mark of similar colour across throat*; *general pinkish tinge in underfeathers*. (Race *pastinator* has less pink, none across throat). Crest small and cap-like; when folded, can look crestless. Parties to flocks, occasionally in thousands; flight swift and pigeon-like; on wing looks large-headed. Associates with Galahs (314) Sulphur-crested Cockatoos (318) and Little Corella (316) where ranges overlap; digs for roots, corms; head and breast often dirt-stained.
Similar species: Little Corella (316); Pink Cockatoo (317).
Voice: Distinctive: quick wavering falsetto 'currup!' or 'wuk-wuk'; other quavering or squeaky conversational notes; also harsh screech like Sulphur-crested Cockatoo (318).
Habitat: Open forests, woodlands, timber along watercourses, adjacent grasslands; pastoral and grazing country; grain crops, stubble.
Breeding: Nest: on decayed debris; in hollow in eucalypt, usually high. Eggs: 2–3; dull-white, oval.
Range and Status: Widely separated range in se. Aust. and s. WA. Nominate race: far-se. SA (w. to Glencoe–Lucindale–Frances) to sw. Vic., n. to Dimboola–Horsham–Ararat and less abundantly e. through L. Corangamite region to about Dean's Marsh–Winchel-sea–Creswick. Also s. Riverina, NSW, from about Euston n. to Hay-Griffith (occasional n. to Lachlan R.), e. to about Finley-Barooga; along Murray R. in Vic. in parts adjacent to this range e. at least to Barmah Forest; s. on Goulburn R. to about Nagambie. Formerly reported to be scarce, now locally very abundant; (?) sedentary. The isolate s. WA race *pastinator* (regarded by some as a race of Little Corella, 316) formerly more widespread, now occurs from Geraldton–Mullewa s. to Moora–Wongan Hills; isolated colonies in Darling Ra. s. of Perth and L. Muir. Uncommon; sedentary.

316 LITTLE CORELLA *Cacatua sanguinea* Pl.48

Other names: Bare-eyed, Blood-stained or Short-billed Cockatoo.
Field marks: 355–395 mm. A small nearly crestless white cockatoo; note the *short whitish bill, pink stain between bill and eye and bare blue-grey eye-patch*. No pink bar across throat as (315) but underfeathers of head and throat rich-pink, seen when bird preens or wind ruffles feathers; plumage often dirty. Pairs and small to immense flocks, in trees by water or in white crowds on ground; noisy. *Flight swift, direct and pigeon-like, wings slender*; underwings and undertail washed yellow. Associates with other cockatoos. Except when with (315), presence soon apparent by calls.
Similar species: Long-billed Corella (315); Sulphur-crested Cockatoo (318).
Voice: Like Long-billed Corella; noisy.
Habitat: Timbered watercourses; dams and tanks, and surrounding open country; grasslands, sandhills with spinifex, gibber, saltbush, mulga and mallee-native pine associa-

tions; crops, stubble. In n. Aust., mangroves, lightly timbered offshore islands; cliffs; street trees.
Breeding: Nest: on decayed debris; in hollow of tree, sometimes cavity in cliff or termite-mound. Eggs: 3–4; white, oval.
Range and Status: Inland e. Aust., coastal n. and w. Aust. and islands off n. and nw. coasts: from Geraldton, WA, to Kimberleys; top end NT s. to Tennant Creek and in e. to SA border–L. Eyre Basin. Widespread in Q., n. to w. Cape York Pen. e. to Hughenden–Barcaldine–Charleville, occasional to ne. coast and, in s., to Chinchilla–Darling Downs. In NSW, s. to Darling R., occasional e. to Rankin Springs and on Murray e. to Euston; occasional nw. Vic., s. to Wyperfeld NP, e. to about Koondrook; vagrant s. to near Geelong (You Yangs) and to ne. Vic. (Warby Ras.–L. Mokoan). All e. SA, s. to L. Alexandrina, less common w. SA. Small populations, probably from aviary escapes, near Perth, Sydney and coastal n. NSW and se. Q. Common to very common and abundant; sedentary and nomadic. Also s. NG.

317   PINK COCKATOO   *Cacatua leadbeateri*   Pl.48

Other names: Chock-a-lock, Cockalerina, Joggle-joggle; Leadbeater's Cockatoo, Major Mitchell; Wee Juggler.
Field marks: 330–360 mm. A very beautiful *pink-washed* white cockatoo, upswept crest whitish when folded, when spread shows *bands of scarlet and yellow*. Male: eye dark-brown. Female: eye reddish; crest has broader yellow band. Pairs or flocks, rarely of more than 20–50; feeds on ground, often on pademelons, and in foliage, e.g. of saltbush or native pines. Flight distinctive: wingbeats quick, shallow and irregular, with glides on downcurved wings; note gorgeous *sunset-pink underwing and undertail*. Associates mostly with Galahs (314) and corellas (315–6).
Similar species: Sulphur-crested Cockatoo (318); corellas (315–6).
Voice: Peculiar stuttered quavering falsetto cry; in alarm, harsh screeches.
Habitat: Grasslands, gibber, saltbush and mulga, often near timbered watercourses; stands of native pine, sheoak or belar; larger mallee with suitable nest-hollows and mallee associated with riverine woodlands, e.g. black box, river red gum.
Breeding: Nest: on decayed debris that may include bark-fragments or pebbles; in tree hollow. Eggs: 2–4; white, oval.
Range and Status: Mostly arid and semi-arid interior, to w. coast in WA, from Jurien Bay to about Shark Bay; inland to s. Kimberleys; in NT n. to Hooker Ck and e. to Macdonald Downs; in Q, n. to Birdsville and e. to St. George, occasional e. to Darling Downs; in NSW, e. to Warrumbungle NP–Parkes–Griffith, occasional e. to Moulamein; in nw. Vic., s. to Wyperfeld NP, e. to about Swan Hill; vagrant near Geelong (You Yangs); in SA, s. to mallee areas adjacent to Murray R., to Eyre Pen., and w. along Bight coast into WA; *absent* sw. WA w. of Esperance–Toodyay–Jurien Bay. Widespread but usually much less abundant than other white cockatoos; sedentary or nomadic.

318   SULPHUR-CRESTED COCKATOO   *Cacatua galerita*   Pl.48

Other name: White Cockatoo.
Field marks: 455–510 mm. A pure-white cockatoo with upswept *plain yellow crest*; faint yellow mark on cheek, undertail and underwings washed yellow. Pairs, parties to flocks of hundreds that whiten ground when feeding or dead trees when perched. At rest, favours isolated trees in farmland or emergent (usually dead) trees above rainforest. Flight distinctive: wings blunt, wingbeats rather stiff, often gives *a quick flap-flap-glide*. Very noisy, specially in roosts at dusk and dawn. Associates mostly with corellas (315–6).
Similar species: Long-billed (315) and Little (316) Corellas; Pink Cockatoo (317). White Goshawk (144) can be mistaken; note yellow cere and legs.
Voice: Raucous shattering screech; perched and in flight; clear whistles, sharp squawks.
Habitat: Very varied; tropical and temperate rainforests, palm forests, swamp woodland;

eucalyptus forests and woodlands; mallee, timbered watercourses; even mangroves. Grasslands, farmlands, crops; occasionally city parks and gardens. **Breeding:** Nest: on decayed debris; in hollow of eucalypt, usually high. Eggs: 2–3; white, oval. **Range and Status:** N., e. and se. Aust., Tas. and coastal islands: mostly in zone of higher rainfall from Kimberleys, WA; top end NT s. to Victoria and Roper Rs.; n. and e. Q, inland to Mt. Isa–Barcaldine–Quilpie; NSW w. to about Darling R.; most Vic. except drier mallee areas; Tas. (midlands, w. and s.); se. SA mostly on and s. of Murray R., w. to St. Vincent Gulf and Kangaroo I. Common to very common and abundant; probably extending range; sedentary. Also NG and islands; introduced NZ.

Typical Parrots   Family *Psittacidae*

Medium-sized short-tailed parrots that typically feed on fruits in rainforest but also forage in eucalypt woodlands. Represented in Aust. by two species confined to C. York Pen., regarded as relics of NG fauna. Sexes markedly dissimilar, specially in Eclectus Parrot (319).

319 ECLECTUS PARROT   *Eclectus roratus*   Pl.49

Other names: Red-sided Parrot, Rocky River Parrot.
Field marks: 400–430 mm. Note apparent reversal in colour of sexes. Male: *bright-green with very large orange bill*; red flanks (not always visible); flight-feathers and bend of wing blue; in flight scarlet wing-lining and flanks contrast with blackish underside of flight-feathers and tail. Female: *mostly scarlet to deep wine-red, with blue-shoulders and broad blue band across breast, bill black*: in flight, note blue wing-linings, orange tip to tail. Imms. like adult with brownish bill. Pairs, parties or flocks; some liken it more to a cockatoo than a parrot. Noisy and conspicuous; forages in rainforest on fruits and blossoms, also in eucalypt woodlands. When disturbed, may circle up, screeching. Roosts in noisy companies, some large. Flight described as 'slow and direct with full, deliberate wingbeats, interspersed with brief periods of gliding'; wings not raised above body-level, giving a distinctive flight-pattern. In poor light on wing it can look very dark.
Voice: Flight-call harsh rolling screech described as 'kraach-krraak' or 'kar!, kar!, kar!'; also a wailing cry and flute-like whistle.
Habitat: Tropical rainforest, adjacent eucalypt woodlands.
Breeding: Nest: on decayed debris; in tree hollow, usually high. Eggs: 2; white, oval.
Range and Status: In Aust. restricted to e. coastal C. York Pen. from Pascoe R. s. to Massy Creek, inland to Iron and McIlwraith Ras. Locally common; sedentary. Possible sight-records L. Barrine Sept. 1953 and Herberton Ra., Aug. 1955. Also Moluccas, Lesser Sunda Is., NG, Bismarck Archipelago and Solomon Is.

320 RED-CHEEKED PARROT   *Geoffroyus geoffroyi*   Pl.49

Field marks: 200–250 mm. A compact bright-green parrot. Male: *red face and forehead, blue crown*; *wing-lining blue*, abdomen and underside of tail yellow-green. Bill, upper mandible red, lower greyish. Female: *head olive-brown, bill grey*. Imm: like female, head greener; imm. males may show traces of adult colour on head and bill. Pairs and parties; when feeding in tops of dense rainforest trees heard more readily than seen; flutters, hangs to reach fruits. In morning dispersal single birds are reported to perch conspicuously in tops of bare trees, calling. *Flight reported to be fast, direct and starling-like.*
Voice: Described as a piercing metallic 'hank', uttered in flight and perched, repeated in quick succession; guttural chatterings, high-pitched screeches like Rainbow Lorikeet (321).
Habitat: Dense tropical jungles, occasionally in adjacent eucalypt woodlands.

Breeding: Nest: on decayed debris; in tree-hollow or hole in palm, often excavated in rotten wood. Eggs: 2–3; white rounded.

Range and Status: In Aust., confined to C. York Pen., Q, between Pascoe and Rocky Rs. and inland to McIlwraith Ra. Locally common; sedentary. Also Moluccas, Lesser Sunda Is. and NG.

Lorikeets   Family *Loriidae*

Distinctive swift-flying, mostly small, green parrots, found only in the Australian region. They have brush-tipped tongues for blossom-feeding and a simplified alimentary system. It was long assumed that nectar was the staple diet but a study of the Purple-crowned Lorikeet (326) in s. WA showed that pollen is probably the main food, although nectar is important. Blossom-feeding demands a high level of daily and seasonal mobility. Lorikeets travel in small hurtling flocks and occasionally large high-flying wavering lines, attracting attention by their thin piercing shrieks. Blossom is located by sight and by calls of birds already feeding. When it is abundant, large numbers of several species often gather noisily, clambering through foliage and blossoms and making brief quick flights. They remain while blossoming lasts. Lorikeets also eat insects and their larvae and other invertebrates found in blossom and foliage. Most species exploit ripening soft fruit, part-ripened grain (maize, sorghum) and (occasionally) cultivated flowers. From time to time they cause economic damage. In many places they come to feed on specially provided sweet food. Daily feeding of thousands of Rainbow (321) and Scaly-breasted (323) Lorikeets at the Sanctuary near Currumbin in Q has become one of Australia's largest single tourist attractions. Sexes similar.

Food: Nectar, pollen, plant-shoots, fruits, berries, insects.

321   RAINBOW LORIKEET   *Trichoglossus haematodus*   Pl.47

Other names: Blue Mountain Lorikeet or Parrot, Blue-bellied Lorikeet, Blue-bonnet, Bluey, Coconut Lory, Lorikeet, Lory.

Field marks: 250–320 mm. A large dark-green lorikeet, familiar to many in e. and se. Aust. Note scarlet bill, *streaky blue head, yellow-green nape*; red-orange chest and trousers, *blue belly*. Imm: duller; bill blackish. Pairs, small to occasionally very large flocks; usually seen in flight or clambering among foliage and blossoms of eucalypts and other trees with noisy shrieks. In flight, a fast compact colourful bird with tapering swept wings and pointed tail; wingbeats shallow and very rapid, exposing *red wing-lining and narrow yellow wingbar*. May damage fruit, flowers, maize; becomes tame when provided with nectar in gardens.

Similar species: Red-collared Lorikeet (322): orange-red nape, black belly; overlaps Rainbow only in w. C. York Pen.

Voice: A musical rolling screech, slightly deeper than Musk Lorikeet (325): raucous chatterings, softer conversational shrieks.

Habitat: Rainforest, eucalypt forests and woodlands; swamp woodlands; coastal scrublands and heaths; occasionally mangroves; plantations, gardens; flowering street trees.

Breeding: Nest: on decayed debris; in tree-hollow, usually fairly high in eucalypt or paperbark. Eggs: 2–3; white, oval.

Range and Status: Mostly coastal e. and se. Aust. and coastal islands from C. York Pen. through e. Q, e. NSW; s. Vic. n. to Wimmera district in w.; s. SA w. to Mt. Lofty Ras., Yorke and s. Eyre Pens. and Kangaroo I. Recent, (? natural) occurrence near Perth, WA. Fairly common to very common and abundant; (?) vagrant Tas. Sedentary and nomadic. Also s. Moluccas, Lesser Sunda Is. to NG, Solomon Is., New Hebrides and New Caledonia.

322 RED-COLLARED LORIKEET *Trichoglossus rubritorquis* **Pl.47**

Field marks: 270–310 mm. Differs from Rainbow Lorikeet (321) in *orange-red nape, black belly*; broader yellow wingbar in flight, breast and trousers usually yellow-orange rather than orange-red.

Habits, Voice, Habitat and Breeding: Like Rainbow Lorikeet.

Range and Status: Replaces Rainbow Lorikeet in n. Aust. and coastal islands from w. of about Georgetown–Normanton, Q, across top end NT, s. to Daly Waters and w. through Kimberleys to area of Broome, WA. Some intergraduation in sw. C. York Pen. Common; sedentary and nomadic.

323 SCALY-BREASTED LORIKEET *Trichoglossus chlorolepidotus* **Pl.47**

Other names: Green-and-gold Lorikeet, Greenie.

Field marks: 220–240 mm. The only lorikeet with *unmarked green head*; neck and breast have *distinctive yellow scaly pattern*; often a touch of orange-red at sides of upperbreast. Bill and eye red. Imm: bill *brownish*, less yellow in plumage. In flight, note orange-red wing-linings. Often with Rainbow (321) and sometimes Musk (325) Lorikeets: same general habits; occasionally interbreeds in wild with either.

Similar species: Note: in flight, both Purple-crowned Lorikeet (326) and Swift Parrot (338) also show red-wing lining.

Voice: Like Rainbow Lorikeet, but higher-pitched.

Habitat: Mostly coastal eucalypt woodlands and forests; flowering street trees.

Breeding: Nest: on decayed debris; in hollow usually of eucalypt. Eggs: 2–3; white, oval.

Range and Status: Mostly coastal e. Aust. and coastal islands: from about Cooktown, Q, s. to Illawarra district, NSW; occasional colony or irruptions mostly along watercourses w. of Divide; records w. to Augathella-Charleville, Q; Pilliga scrub (Baradine), NSW. Aviary escapes elsewhere. Common to very common and abundant; sedentary or nomadic.

324 VARIED LORIKEET *Psitteuteles versicolor* **Pl.47**

Other names: Red-crowned, Red-capped or Variegated Lorikeet; Varied Lory.

Field marks: 170–200 mm. A pale-green, softly but gorgeously coloured small tropical lorikeet; the only one *with deep-rose cap, white goggles*; lime-green ear-patch, washed blue round neck and pink on breast; plentiful fine white or lime-green streaks; bill orange-red. Female: duller, with olive-green cap. Pairs, parties, small flocks; quieter than other lorikeets; flight swift, green wing-linings contrast with blackish underside of flight-feathers. Gathers in flowering eucalypt woodlands and swamp woodlands; ventures from woodlands far over grasslands to feed on blossoms in bare branches of such trees as 'kapok' *Cochlospermum* and bauhinias.

Voice: Thin rolling screech, less strident than Rainbow (321) or Red-collared (322) Lorikeets.

Habitat: Eucalypt and paperbark woodlands, flowering trees in foothills, along watercourses and in grasslands.

Breeding: Nest: on decayed debris or fragmented eucalypt leaves; in tree-hollow. Eggs: 2–3; white, oval.

Range and Status: Confined to n. Aust. and coastal islands: from Fitzroy R., WA, through Kimberleys, top end NT s. to Victoria R.–Elliott and Gulf coast; in Q, n. on C. York Pen., and s. to about Mt. Isa–Hughenden; occasional s. to sw. Q (Boulia–Windorah) and occasional s. on e. coast to Townsville–Mackay. Fairly common in main range; nomadic.

325   MUSK LORIKEET   *Glossopsitta concinna*   Pl.47

Other names: Green Keet or Leek; King Parrot, Musk Lory; Red-crowned or Red-eared Lorikeet.

Field marks: 195–230 mm. A sturdy lorikeet with *scarlet patch back from forehead through eye to ear-coverts*, bluish wash on crown and sides of face; mantle bronze-brown; yellow area on side of upperbreast. Bill blackish at base, tipped red. Female: duller, markings less bold. Imm: bill dark-brown; cheek-patch orange-red. Pairs or flocks, in which pairs often persist. Associates with Purple-crowned (326) and Little (327) Lorikeets, and with Swift Parrot (338). Flight very swift; sturdy build and short wedge-shaped tail give somewhat bomb-shaped look; *wing-lining pale green*, inner webs of tail-feathers scarlet. Raids orchards, vineyards, maize or wheat-crops.

Similar species: Little Lorikeet (327): tiny; bill black; face and chin red, none behind eye; thinner 'zit' call. Swift Parrot (338): longer, with thin reddish tail, forehead and throat red; tinkling calls.

Voice: Rolling screech, higher-pitched than Rainbow Lorikeet (321), much deeper and fuller than Purple-crowned or Little; chatters while feeding.

Habitat: Eucalypt woodlands and drier forests on foothills and fringes of plains; roadside timber, shelter-belts, timbered watercourses.

Breeding: Nest: on decayed debris; in hole in eucalypt, usually high. Eggs: usually 2; white, rounded.

Range and Status: Se. Aust. and Tas.: from about Rockhampton, Q, (occasional n. to about Bowen) to s. SA. Mostly coastal in Q; in NSW, w. to Moree–Warrumbungle NP, w. slopes of Divide and w. along Murrumbidgee and Murray Rs. to about Finley; most Vic., usually in taller woodland and open forest of foothills, edges of plains and along watercourses; se. SA w. to Mt. Lofty Ras., s. Eyre Pen. and Kangaroo I.; in Tas., mostly e. of Devonport–Huonville. Uncommon to locally very common; nomadic, mostly in autumn–winter.

326   PURPLE-CROWNED LORIKEET   *Glossopsitta porphyrocephala*   Pl.47

Other names: Blue or Porphyry-crowned Lorikeet; Zit Parrot.

Field marks: 150–170 mm. A tiny pale-green lorikeet with *pale-blue breast* and distinctive head markings: *reddish yellow forehead, patch of similar colour on ear-coverts*; *dark-purple crown*. Bill black. Imm: no purple on crown. Small parties to large strung-out flocks; often with Musk (325) and Little (327) Lorikeets. Tame and often quiet when feeding, save for quick 'zit' notes; crawls like mouse through leaves and blossoms; occasionally dashes off and returns. In flight, *crimson flanks and wing-linings*. Long regarded as the only lorikeet in s. WA, but see Rainbow Lorikeet (321).

Similar species: Little Lorikeet (327): all-green, with red face and throat; green wing-linings.

Voice: Thin quick 'zit' or 'zit-zit'; uttered as birds feed and specially in flight.

Habitat: Like Musk Lorikeet, with a stronger preference for mallee associations; often in blossoming street trees.

Breeding: Nest: on decayed debris; in spout or hole in eucalypt; several to many pairs typically nest in neighbouring hollows in a large tree, such as a river red gum. Eggs: 3–4; white, rounded.

Range and Status: S. Aust.: far-s. NSW s. of about Bega–Albury–Jerilderie–Euston, (probably further n. in mallee areas of inland NSW when blossom abundant); most Vic., *except* ne. highland areas; s. SA, n. to mallee areas bordering Murray R.–Sutherlands–Mt. Lofty Ras.; Kangaroo I., Eyre Pen., n. to Gawler Ras. and w. along Bight coast and n. of Nullarbor Plain to Gt. Victoria Desert, n. to lower Murchison R. district–Shark Bay. Vagrant ne. NSW, se. Q. Fairly common, locally very abundant; nomadic.

327 LITTLE LORIKEET *Glossopsitta pusilla* **Pl.47**

Other names: Gizzle, Green Parrakeet, Jerryang; Green or Little Keet; Red-faced Lorikeet.

Field marks: 150–165 mm. A tiny green lorikeet with *black bill and a red patch over forehead and throat*, just reaching eye; mantle bronze-brown, underparts yellowish green. Imm: duller, less red on face; bill brownish. Pairs, parties; larger companies where blossom abundant; often hard to see as it clambers mouselike in foliage and blossoms. Flight bullet-like, showing pale-green wing-linings. Often with Rainbow (321), Musk (325) and Purple-crowned (326) Lorikeets; occasionally raids soft fruit.

Similar species: Musk (325) Purple-crowned (326) Lorikeets. Fig-parrot (328): usually in rainforest; blue and red on face, sky-blue on primaries; more squeaky 'zit' calls.

Voice: Thin quick slightly rolling 'zit' or 'zit zit'; more screeching and metallic than Purple-crowned.

Habitat: Forests and woodlands; isolated large trees or stands of trees in open country; timbered watercourses, roadside trees and shelter-belts; flowering street-trees. Seldom mallee.

Breeding: Nest: on decayed debris; in hole in eucalypt, often high. Eggs: 4–5; white, rounded.

Range and Status: Coastal e. and se. Aust., some e. coastal islands and Tas.: from about Cairns, Q, to se. SA. In Q, inland to about Atherton Tableland–Carnarvon Gorge NP–Chinchilla; in NSW, w. to about Warialda–Warrumbungle NP–W. Wyalong–Deniliquin; in Vic., rather widespread in suitable habitat *except* ne. alpine and nw. mallee areas; se. SA w. to Sutherlands–Mt. Lofty Ras. and Yorke Pen.; vagrant Kangaroo I. Status in Tas. uncertain; perhaps rare vagrant. Fairly common generally; uncommon Vic. s. of Divide and in SA; nomadic.

Fig-Parrots or Lorilets Family *Opopsittidae*

Tiny fruit-eating parrots with rather large heads, broad robust bills and very short, rounded tails. Sexes dissimilar.

Food: Fruit, particularly native figs; also berries, seeds, nectar and possibly lichens or fungi.

328 DOUBLE-EYED FIG-PARROT *Psittaculirostris diophthalma* **Pl.47**

Note: The three Australian fig-parrots, formerly given species-rank, are now regarded as races of the Double-eyed Fig-parrot of NG; each occupies an isolated or nearly isolated range in tropical and temperate rainforests in coastal ne. Aust. Apart from range, they can be told apart by head-markings, specially of males.

Field marks: 130–160 mm. The species (as a whole) is the smallest Australian parrot, with very short tail and *robust pale-grey, dark-tipped bill*. The large bi-coloured bill, distinctive head-markings (see below), yellow sides of breast and deep-blue primaries readily separate all races from Little Lorikeet (327), the only similar species.

Race *marshalli* 'Cape York' or 'Marshall's Fig-parrot'. 130–135 mm. Male: red forehead and red cheeks with blue lower edge. Female: no red on head, blue forehead, blue whisker-mark encloses creamish patch on cheek.

Race *macleayana* 'Northern' or 'Red-browed Fig-parrot'. 130–140 mm. Male: small red patch on forehead separated from red cheek by *pale-blue between bill and eye*, violet-blue whisker-mark borders red cheek. Female: like male, but cheek not red.

Race *coxeni* 'Southern' or 'Blue-browed Fig-parrot'. 140–160 mm. Male: blue on forehead nearly replaces red; red cheek-patch smaller. Female: no red on forehead, red cheek-patch duller.

Pairs or flocks, quiet and difficult to observe when feeding; they creep like mice through foliage, sometimes drawing notice by calls, small sounds of falling pieces of fruit. Seen to bathe in wet foliage, like lorikeets. They forage on trunks and limbs, possibly eat fungi and lichen. Flight swift and darting, over and through canopy.

Voice: Thin feeble quick 'zeet zeet', frequently uttered in flight; a chattering twitter is also described.

Habitat: Rainforest, timber along watercourses, swamp woodlands; adjacent drier woodlands and coastal scrubs; visits gardens and plantations round Cairns, Innisfail.

Breeding: Nest: on decayed debris in tree-hollows, from low to *c*. 10 m from ground. Eggs: 2, white, rounded.

Range and Status: Race *marshalli*: area of Lockhart and Claudie Rs., ne. C. York Pen., probably ranging beyond these limits in suitable habitat. Race *macleayana*: coastal areas and highlands from Cooktown s. to Paluma Ra., near Townsville, Q. Race *coxeni*: coastal areas and highlands from Maryborough, Q, s. to Macleay R., NSW, inland to Blackall Ras. and McPherson Ras. Generally uncommon; probably sedentary or locally nomadic.

Longtailed Parrots   Family *Polytelitidae*

Medium-to-large long-tailed parrots of easy graceful flight. They occupy habitats from inland semi-deserts to coastal rainforests and are identified by usually strong plumage-patterns and characteristic calls, often uttered in flight. Sexes dissimilar.

329   KING PARROT   *Alisterus scapularis*   Pl.49

Other names: Blood Rosella, King Lory; Scarlet-and-Green or Spud Parrot.

Field marks: 410–440 mm. Male: the only Australian parrot with unmarked *bright-scarlet head and body*; wings dark-green with pale-green band; rump dark-blue, tail blue-black; bill red above, black below; eye yellow. Female: *mostly dark-green with red belly*; bill grey, eye yellow. Imm: like female, eye brown. Pairs to flocks, in which green birds predominate. Feeds in foliage and on ground usually near cover. Wary, flies quickly to cover. Flight strong, with deep wingbeats; easy but erratic, with twists and sudden changes in direction. Disperses into open country in autumn and winter and may attack fruit in orchards, unripe maize, sorghum or newly dug potatoes. Becomes tame in farmyards, other places where food is available.

Similar species: Crimson Rosella (341): blue cheek and wing-patch, latter conspicuous in flight. Imm: from female and imm. King Parrot in more olive-green upperparts and rump, blue cheek, often patchy crimson head. Red-winged Parrot (330), female and imm: note range.

Voice: Flight-call, scratchy brassy 'chack! chack!'; male, a long drawn-out ringing 'creee' or 'swee'; both sexes, harsh screeches in alarm.

Habitat: Rainforests, wetter eucalypt woodlands and clearings; coastal woodlands and scrubs; areas of secondary growth with berry-bearing shrubs; crops; potato-fields; orchards, parks and gardens.

Breeding: Nest: on decayed debris; in a hollow tree, usually eucalypt; may be well below entrance, at times near ground-level. Eggs: 3–5; white, rounded.

Range and Status: Coastal e. Aust. and highland areas from about Cooktown, to s. Vic.; also Fraser I., Q and (? vagrant) other coastal islands. In Q, inland to Atherton Tableland–Blackall–Carnarvon Gorge NP–Miles–Warwick; in NSW, inland to Bingara–Warrumbungle NP–Mudgee–Holbrook–Albury; in Vic., e. of Hume Highway, s. to Wilson's Promontory NP; (? isolate) population Otway Ras., occasional w. to near Portland. Common to uncommon; dispersive in autumn–winter.

330 RED-WINGED PARROT *Aprosmictus erythropterus* **Pl.49**

Other names: Crimson-winged Parrot, Crimson or Red-winged Lory.
Field marks: 305–330 mm. Male brilliant and conspicuous: *bright pale-green with prominent scarlet shoulder*, black mantle, deep sky-blue lower back. Female: mostly grass-green; *thin scarlet band across wing, blue rump*. Both sexes: bill scarlet or reddish. Imm: like female. Pairs to small flocks, seldom far from water, usually feeds in foliage and blossoms. Wary; when disturbed, flies noisily to distant trees. Flight distinctive: erratic with deep pumping wingbeats. Associates with Pale-headed Rosellas (345), Mallee Ringnecks (348).
Similar species: Superb Parrot (331), female: duller and more slender with longer pointed tail; rump green, no scarlet on wing. King Parrot (329), female and imm: darker-green, bill grey, belly red.
Voice: Flight-call, rapid brassy 'ching ching' or 'ching-ching-chink'; also thin screech like Rainbow (321) and Red-collared (322) Lorikeets.
Habitat: Varied: open woodlands, timbered watercourses, mulga, casuarina and native-pine scrubs; mangroves and cultivation in n. coastal areas.
Breeding: Nest: on decayed debris; in hollow tree, usually eucalypt near water; usually well below entrance, sometimes to ground-level. Eggs: 3–6; white.
Range and Status: N. and inland e. Aust.: from Broome, WA, through Kimberleys, top end NT s. to Elliott–Mallapunyah; widespread in Q 'in regions of medium rainfall', n. to C. York, inland to Mt. Isa–Hughenden–Blackall–Quilpie and on large sw. watercourses (Diamantina R.–Cooper's Creek); to e. coast mostly during dry periods inland; sparse in coastal se. but recorded Bribie I.; inland NSW, e. to about Inverell–Gunnedah–Wellington s. to Nymagee–Ivanhoe, occasional s. to near Hay and w. to near Broken Hill–Menindee; occasional ne. SA (presumably down watercourses from sw. Q) s. to Innamincka, Mutooroo (s. of Barrier Highway); vagrant s. to Renmark. Common in main range; sedentary, dispersive. Also s. NG.

331 SUPERB PARROT *Polytelis swainsonii* **Pl.49**

Other names: Barraband Parrot or Parrakeet; Green Leek.
Field marks: 360–420 mm. A graceful very slender long-tailed grass-green parrot. Male: *forehead and throat yellow cut off from breast by red crescent*; bill usually coral red; eye yellow. Female: plainer; duller-green, *lightly washed blue-grey on cheeks, underside of tail black, marked pinkish*. Both sexes, eye yellow. Imm: like female; eye brown. Pairs to flocks, some of males only or family parties. Feeds on ground in herbage and grain crops, at times with other parrots on spilt grain on roadsides; also in foliage on seeds and blossoms of acacias, eucalypts. Flight swift, slipping, graceful with swept wings and long slim tail. Note range.
Similar species: Regent Parrot (332).
Voice: Rolling grating 'currack currack' usually in flight; less harsh than Regent Parrot.
Habitat: Riverine forests and neighbouring woodlands of river oaks; yellow box and other eucalypts; also stubble, pastures, sugar-gum windbreaks, homestead gardens.
Breeding: Nest: on decayed debris; in hollow limb of eucalypt, usually near or over water. Eggs: 4–6; white, rounded.
Range and Status: Inland e. NSW; Forshaw (1969) noted two discrete populations: (1) from Hay to ACT along Murrumbidgee R., s. to n. Vic. and n. to the Lachlan R. In w., confined to riverside red gum forests and black box woodlands; in e. Riverina extending into other eucalyptus woodlands, nearby farmland and eucalyptus windbreaks in irrigation areas. (2) from Gilgandra to Coonamble along Castlereagh R., w. to Warren on Macquarie R. and near Gunnedah on Namoi R. Main habitat, flooded zone eucalyptus community. In recent years s. population recorded w. to near Balranald, n. to L. Cargelligo, Round Hill NR and to Goonumbla near Parkes; e. to Cowra–Rye Park–Yass; s. on Edward R. and to Murray R. near Barham, Mathoura, Barooga and Albury. Formerly s.

to c. Vic. but now only near Murray R.: vagrant Hattah Lakes NP, Robinvale, Mystic Park, Kerang; (?) occasional Barmah Forest, Ulupna I. and near Cobram. In recent years the n. population recorded w. to Hermidale and ne. to Narrabri. Locally common; part-nomadic. Occurs from time to time well beyond indicated range e.g. to Sydney area but confusion from aviary escapes.

332   REGENT PARROT   *Polytelis anthopeplus*   Pl.49

Other name: Black-tailed Parrot or Parrakeet; Plaide-wing Parrot, Rock Pebbler or Peplar; Smoker.

Field marks: 380–410 mm. Distinctive *old-gold or deep-yellow, specially bright on shoulders*, contrasting with blue-black flight-feathers and long slender black tail. Note narrow *soft-red band across wing.* Bill coral-red. Female and imm: duller, less red across wing, outer tail-feathers margined and tipped deep-pink; race *westralis*, greener and duller. Pairs, parties to flocks of 50 +, mostly in non-breeding season; in s. WA, at times flocks of hundreds. Feeds on ground or in foliage and blossom of eucalypts, acacias. Appears to disperse into more open habitats in winter. Flight swift, slipping and graceful on swept wings, long tapering tail prominent. In good light, contrast of old-gold and black striking and beautiful.

Similar species: Superb Parrot (331). Yellow Rosella (343): pale-yellow, blue cheek and wingpatch; blue-white margins to tail.

Voice: Harsh rolling 'carrak, carrak', often heard before birds fly into view; when perched or feeding, soft warblings.

Habitat: In e. Aust. mostly river red gum forests, black box woodlands and adjacent cleared country; larger more open mallee-native pine associations; rank weedy clearings, vineyards, cereal and legume crops, stubblefields, golf-courses. In sw. WA, wheatbelt, timbered watercourses, dry woodlands to cleared lands in coastal woodlands and forests.

Breeding: Nest: on decayed debris; at bottom of hollow in eucalypt or native pine; nest-chamber may be some distance below entrance; occasionally in hollow stump. Eggs: 4–6; white, rounded.

Range and Status: Nominate race: inland se. Aust., on or near river systems and lakes; sw. NSW e. to about Balranald, occasional e. along Murrumbidgee R. to Hay; in Vic., e. to near Swan Hill, s. to L. Hindmarsh, occasional s. to St Arnaud–Little Desert; in SA, w. along Murray R. to Morgan–Sutherlands, s. to Bordertown–Langhorne's Ck. Race *westralis*: sw. WA, w. of about Israelite Bay–Dundas–Kalgoorlie–Ajana, n. of Geraldton; occasional much further inland. Locally common; in WA, generally abundant. Sedentary, locally nomadic.

333   PRINCESS PARROT   *Polytelis alexandrae*   Pl.49

Other names: Alexandra's, Princess Alexandra's or Queen Alexandra's Parrot; Rose-throated Parrot.

Field marks: ♂ 460 mm; ♀ 340 mm. Long, slender, pastel-coloured and very beautiful. Mostly soft olive-green above, with *pale-blue crown, rose-coloured throat* and under tail-coverts; lime-green shoulders, sky-blue rump and *very long, slim pale blue-green tail.* Bill red. Female and imm: duller with shorter tail. Pairs or small flocks; feeds on ground in spinifex and in foliage and blossoms of eucalypts, mulgas. Perches lengthways on limbs. Flight easy and undulating, *long streaming tail conspicuous.*

Voice: Flight-call described as a prolonged rolling note; when feeding or resting, re-strained but constant cackling chatterings; alarm-call, sharp 'queet, queet'.

Habitat: Dry interior–eucalypt-lined watercourses; desert oaks and other casuarinas, mulga and spinifex, at times far from water.

Breeding: Nest: in hollow of eucalypt on watercourse or tree such as casuarina; several pairs may breed in proximity. Eggs: 4–6: white, glossy, rounded or elliptical.

Range and Status: Interior c. and w. Aust., exact range uncertain because rare, highly nomadic and irregular. Known to arrive and breed in places where previously unknown or long absent. In WA reported n. almost to Fitzroy R. and s. to Wiluna, occasional Menzies; e. through Gt. Victoria and Gibson Deserts; in NT n. to Sturt Plains, Newcastle Waters, and s. to e. of Alice Springs; in n. SA e. to about Oodnadatta; unconfirmed early record far sw. Q.

334 COCKATIEL *Nymphicus hollandicus*   Pl.51

Other names: Cockatoo-parrot, Crested Parrot, Quarrion, Weero.

Field marks: 300–330 mm. The only smallish Australian parrot with a crest. *Grey plumage set off by prominent white shoulders*, central tail-feathers long and slender. Male: pale-yellow forehead, face and crest; large orange-red cheek-spot; tail grey. Female: duller, head and crest greyer, cheek-spot duller, outer tail-feathers and underwing pale-yellow, finely barred grey. Imm: like female; young males yellower on head. Pairs to very large flocks; often heard before seen. Feeds mostly on ground; typically settles on dead trees, often perching along limbs. Associates with Galahs (314) and other parrots – specially in inland with Budgerigar (337), at times in great congregations at water. Flight easy, slipping and graceful; swept wings and tail conspicuous.

Voice: Melodious loud rolling chirrup, hence aboriginal name Quarrion; penetrating 'queel queel'.

Habitat: Open woodlands, scrublands, grasslands; timber along watercourses, spinifex associations, Mitchell-grass plains; pastures, grain crops; stubblefields, roadsides.

Breeding: Nest: on decayed debris; in hollow, usually of eucalypt. Eggs: 4–7; white, rounded.

Range and Status: Widespread drier parts all mainland States; usually absent far-ne. Q, coastal e. and se. Aust., se. SA and sw. WA but regular spring–summer movement in fluctuating numbers to sub-inland e. and se. Aust. In dry years often extends into coastal regions, sometimes breeding. Uncommon to locally very common and abundant; highly nomadic. Occasional records Tas.; ? aviary escapes.

Broadtailed Parrots   Family *Platycercidae*

Ranging in size from the Budgerigar (337) to the large Port Lincoln Parrot (349), the broadtails are perhaps the most characteristically Australian parrots. They inhabit temperate and subtropical forests, woodlands and grasslands, with representatives in the tropical and arid zones. Most are generalized feeders in grasses or low herbage or in foliage and blossoms; but one, the Swift Parrot (338), has a brush-tongue and feeds much like a lorikeet. The grass-parrots of the genus *Neophema* are wholly or largely terrestrial. Most broadtails nest in tree-hollows but one neophema, the Rock Parrot (359), lays its eggs in rock-cavities of coastal islands, and three distinctive members (352–4) of the genus *Psephotus* make nest-tunnels in termite-mounds. The flight of most broadtails is strong and undulating; that of the Swift Parrot is impetuous and lorikeet-like. This and several neophemas are regular migrants within Aust.; some of the inland forms, e.g. Budgerigar, are highly nomadic in response to seasonal conditions. Other members of the family are sedentary or are mobile locally in post-breeding flocks of adults and immatures.

GROUND AND NIGHT PARROTS

Distinctive terrestrial parrots, characterized by green-and-yellow plumage, with dark streaks, barrings or mottlings; the Ground Parrot (335) lives mostly in coastal heaths; the Night Parrot (336) in inland, in spinifex *Triodia* associations. It is partly or wholly nocturnal; its present status is unknown. Unlike other Australian parrots, both construct nest-platforms of plant-materials at or near ground-level in grass-tussocks or low shrubs.

335 GROUND PARROT *Pezoporus wallicus* Pl.52

Other names: Button-grass or Swamp Parrot.

Field marks: 280–320 mm. A slender long-tailed bright grass-green parrot, *finely but strongly streaked black, black feathers barred yellow*; *forehead red.* Imm: yellowish forehead, head and breast more heavily marked with black, underparts yellower. Singly, pairs or open companies; partly nocturnal. Disruptive pattern, extreme wariness and denseness of its usual habitats make it difficult to observe, but red forehead and barred appearance are diagnostic. Usually it flushes unexpectedly, going up suddenly with brief sound of wings striking herbage but without calling. The flight is very distinctive: fast, usually low, with *bursts of wingbeats broken by glides on stiff downcurved wings, and quick snipelike changes of direction.* Note yellow wingbar and long barred tail. After going 20–200 metres, it usually plunges into cover again, running swiftly on long legs. Rarely perches but does climb low plants, e.g. blackboys, for seed.

Similar species: Night Parrot (336). The green neophemas (357–60) likely to be found in or near its habitats are much smaller and plainer-green, with blue on forehead and wings; they fly higher, with zizzing or tinkling calls.

Voice: Reported to call regularly for an interval at dawn and dusk and irregularly by day or night. Calls described as thin and high-pitched, carrying well in still conditions, or beautiful and sweet: three or four measured bell-like notes 'tee...tee...stit', occasionally followed by notes ascending scale, ending with drawn-out 'tee...tee...tee...tee...–ee'; uttered by a single bird from cover or in voluntary flight and answered by others; several birds may call at once.

Habitat: Low ground-cover, usually in extensive swampy heaths; preference for drier ridges in same. Such habitats often include Rope-rush *Hypolaena* or Twine-rush *Leptocarpus*; the bird's barred plumage resembles their massed stems. In Tas., coastal and sub-alpine button-grass flats and slopes. Occasionally in grasslands, pastures.

Breeding: Nest: shallow excavation, thickly lined with bitten-off stems; well hidden near or in base of tussock or stunted bush. Eggs: 3–4; white, slightly glossy, slightly pointed.

Range and Status: Coastal areas of se. Aust., Tas. and sw. WA: from Fraser I. and ne. of Gympie., Q, in sparse scattered and now-isolated colonies in suitable habitat along coasts of NSW and Vic. to extreme se. SA. Widespread Tas., mostly s. and w.; Hunter I., Bass Strait, formerly King and Flinders Is., but not recently. In sw. WA formerly n. to Geraldton, now restricted to s. coast. Local, scarce to rare, probably endangered except perhaps in Tas. Sedentary; possibly some autumn–winter movement.

336 NIGHT PARROT *Geopsittacus occidentalis* Pl.52

Other name: Night Parakeet, Spinifex Parrot.

Field marks: 220–240 mm. An unusual rather dumpy smallish parrot with a large head and eye and short tail, shaped like a rounded wedge. Rich olive-green to dull faded olive-green, *intricately barred and mottled black, dark-brown and pale-yellow*; *no red on forehead*; yellowish below, outer tail feathers barred black and yellow, probably conspicuous when spread. Described as extremely shy and elusive; rests by day in cavity in spinifex-clump; disturbed by driven stock or vehicle, flies briefly before dropping to cover or runs and squats, keeping close to cover. Birds thus disturbed were described as bright-green, about size of Mulga Parrot (351) but heavier. They flew swiftly 20–30 m, just clearing spinifex, before dropping. No calls were heard. Early observers noted that on emerging at night it flew to water before moving on to feed on seeds of spinifex and other plants; one remarked its liking for open areas of bare ground at night. Flight to water after dusk reported to be low and direct, but flight of another possible Night Parrot in headlights was 'weak and fluttering'. A captive bird moved in short hops and runs.

Similar species: Ground Parrot (335). Note that Bourke's Parrot (356) is commonly called 'Night Parrot' from its habit of crepuscular drinking.

Voice: Reported to utter a squeak when flushed; also a harsh loud double note, a peculiar froglike croaking alarm-note and a long-drawn mournful whistle.

Habitat: Predominantly spinifex *Triodia* particularly on stony rises and breakaway country but also on sandy lowlands; also samphire *Arthrocnemum* on margins of salt lakes and watercourses; unconfirmed reports of sightings on saltbush *Atriplex* plains in sw. NSW and in saltbush, bluebush *Kochia* and bindii *Bassia* associations in SA; also in introduced Ward weed *Vella*.

Breeding: Nest reported to be a scrape in ground in centre of spinifex-clump, densely lined with terminal sections of spinifex spines, *c.* 125 mm long, in chamber about 250 mm across, reached by tunnel some 75 mm across; another suspected nest was a platform of small sticks above ground-level in similar cavity in samphire bush. Eggs: 4; white, about size of Crested Pigeon's (301).

Range and Status: Mostly confined to arid interior and possibly coastal nw. WA. Old specimens or sight-records from scattered localities all States: nw. Vic.; far-w. NSW; Eyre Pen., Gawler Ras. and ne. SA; far-sw. Q through s. NT to nw. and wc. WA. Probably highly nomadic and subject to considerable fluctuations from seasonal conditions. Seen by many observers 1870–1900 but thereafter declined markedly. Lost and present status unknown, often stated to be extinct, but still the subject of unconfirmed sightings, some no doubt authentic.

337 BUDGERIGAR *Melopsittacus undulatus*   Pl.52

Perhaps the world's best-known parrot and one of the most popular cage-birds, in blue, yellow, grey, white and other varieties. But note that the monotypic wild Budgerigar has only one plumage, mostly yellow and green. Sexes nearly similar.

Other names: Budgerygah, Betcherrygah; Canary Parrot, Flightbird, Lovebird; Scallop, Shell, Undulated or Zebra Parrot; Warbling Grass Parrot or Parakeet.

Field marks: 170–200 mm. A tiny *grass-green parrot with yellow forehead and throat*; yellowish to pale-brown above *with close dark barrings*; cere blue in male and non-breeding female, brown in breeding female. Imm: duller, forehead barred. Parties to very large flocks; busy, active and vocal. Feeds in grass, flushes chattering, flight swift, slightly undulating; note *prominent yellow wingbar, yellow black-tipped short outer tail-feathers*. Rests in foliage during heat of day; congregates morning and afternoon to drink, at times in immense flocks. Associates with Cockatiel (334), Red-rumped Parrots (350), Zebra Finches (672).

Similar species: Neophemas (356–62): plainer-green above; forehead and wing banded blue; calls more tinkling.

Voice: Musical mellow chirrup; continuous when flocks gather to water; also sharp rasping scolds; when alarmed, zizzing chatter.

Habitat: Grasslands, spinifex associations; saltbush, mallee, mulga, timber along watercourses; grasslands, crops, roadsides.

Breeding: Much influenced by rainfall and state of vegetation; many pairs may nest in proximity, some in same hollow. Nest: on decayed debris; in hollow limb, hole in tree or cavity in stump or fence-post. Eggs: 4–6, occasionally 8; white, rounded.

Range and Status: Chiefly drier regions of mainland Aust., usually absent from wetter parts of coastal e., se. sw. and ne. Aust. but regular spring–summer movement in fluctuating numbers to subcoastal se. Aust. and s. SA; limits difficult to define because of nomadism; vagrant Kangaroo I., SA. Common to very abundant; highly nomadic.

338 SWIFT PARROT *Lathamus discolor*   Pl.47

Other names: Clink, Red-faced or Red-shouldered Parrot; Swift-flying or Swift Lorikeet or Parakeet.

Field marks: 230–255 mm. A streamlined green parrot with a *dusky red spike-shaped tail*; *forehead and throat red, crown and cheeks blue*; *note red mark on secondaries and red under tail-coverts.* (Neither marking shown on plate.) Bill pale-horn, eye yellow. Imm:

duller, with pale wingstripe. Usually seen in flight; first noticed by distinctive calls, flocks weave through woodlands at great speed or travel high, with random changes in direction, often settling on a high bare branch before proceeding; in flight note *red underwings and under tail-coverts*. Single birds or parties are easily approached as they feed in blossoms and foliage of eucalypts on nectar and sugary lerp insects; they often hang head-down. Wintering flocks may feed in a district for weeks, returning to the same tree 'nightly to roost with much noisy swooping and circling. Associates with lorikeets; occasionally attacks soft fruits, cultivated berries.

Similar species: Lorikeets (321–7) have broader, mostly green tails; none has pale bill or eye, similar facial markings, red spots on wing, or red under tail-coverts; calls differ. Mulga Parrot (351), male: yellow forehead, yellow slash on wing, red thighs.

Voice: Bursts of high-pitched tinkling chattering; and a piping 'pee-pit pee-pit pee-pit'; quite unlike screeches of lorikeets.

Habitat: Foliage and blossoms of eucalypts, banksias, etc. in forests, open woodlands, plantations, parks, gardens or city streets; occasionally feeds in green grasslands.

Breeding: Nest: on decayed debris; in hollow, 6–20 m high, usually in eucalypt. Several pairs may breed in proximity. Eggs: 3–5; white, rounded.

Range and Status: Breeds Tas. and islands of Furneaux Group (unconfirmed reports of occasional breeding in s. Vic.). After breeding, most of population migrates in Feb.–Apr. to mainland, where it becomes a nomad in response to availability of blossoms and other food. It is usually plentiful in c. Vic. in winter, but extends w. to Mt. Lofty Ras. and n. to Sutherlands, SA; n. to Swan Hill district, Vic.; in NSW, inland to about Ivanhoe–Griffith–Warialda, but mostly se., often abundant in winter round Sydney and ACT; in Q, recorded inland to Chinchilla, vagrant n. to Caloundra, once to Bowen. Returns Tas. Aug.–Oct., where common, mostly s. and e. of a line from Rocky Cape to Southport.

339   RED-CAPPED PARROT   *Purpureicephalus spurius*   **Pl.49**

Other names: King Parrot, Hookbill, Pileated Parrot, Red-capped Parakeet, Western King Parrot.

Field marks: 355–375 mm. Male very gaudy: dark-green; *cap crimson, cheeks and rump bright lime-green; breast soft-purple, thighs and under tail-coverts red*. Female: duller, may have some green in crown; underparts grey-mauve. Imm: duller, crown green, sometimes with red on forehead, pale violet-grey breast, green touches on red under tail-coverts. Pairs or small parties; feeds on ground under eucalypts or grass or quietly in foliage. The curiously long, curved bill is adapted for removing seed from the deep capsules of marri *E. calophylla* and other eucalypts; also feeds on seeds of casuarinas, grevilleas, hakeas and grasses; becomes a pest in orchards. Flight undulating and 'somewhat fluttering; *note contrast of lime-green rump and dark upperparts*; female and imm: show pale wingbar.

Similar species: Port Lincoln Parrot, (349) race *semitorquatus*: dark rump in flight.

Voice: Grating rosella-like chatter 'checkacheck, checkacheck'; when alarmed, harsh clanging screeches.

Habitat: Eucalypt forests and woodlands and clearings in same; paddocks with shelter-belts and trees left standing; timbered watercourses and roadsides; orchards, parks, gardens.

Breeding: Nest: on decayed debris; in eucalypt hollow, usually very high. Eggs: 4–6; white, rounded.

Range and Status: Confined to s. WA: from Dandaragan, n. of Perth, generally w. of Gt. S. Rly, but in s. eastwards to Lake Grace and Esperance. Common, sedentary.

340   GREEN ROSELLA   *Platycercus caledonicus*   **Pl.50**

Other names: Green, Mountain or Tasman Parrot, Tasmanian Rosella, Tussock Parrot; Yellow-bellied or Yellow-breasted Parrot.

Field marks: 320–360 mm. A very dark, Tasmanian rosella: *dark-green above, with heavy* *black mottling*; *head and underparts deep-yellow*, red forehead-band and blue throat-patch; blue shoulder and edge of wing, tail edged blue-white. Female: smaller, duller, throat washed orange-red. Imm: duller, olive-grey above, dull olive-green rump and tail, olive-yellow below; pale wingstripe in flight. Pairs, parties to flocks of 20 + in autumn and winter; these may be wholly or mostly of imms. Feeds on ground and in foliage, of eucalypts, etc., also introduced hawthorns, briars; raids orchards, grain crops; associates with Eastern Rosella (344). Flight strong and direct, sometimes very high; *note rich-yellow head and underparts*.

Similar species: Eastern Rosella (344) is the only other rosella in Tas.

Voice: Curious loud 'kussik, kussik', repeated; also bell-like contact note and shrill piping alarm-notes.

Habitat: Dense mountain forests to lightly timbered farming country; timber along rivers; briar-scrub and roadside hawthorn hedges; crops, orchards, gardens.

Breeding: Nest: on decayed wood debris; in hollow trunk or branch. Eggs: 4–8; white, rounded.

Range and Status: Confined to Tas. and islands of Bass Strait: Flinders I., King I. and Kent Group. Common and widespread Tas. and Flinders I.; locally common King I. and Kent Group. Sedentary.

341 CRIMSON ROSELLA *Platycercus elegans*   Pl.50

Other names: Crimson Parrot, Mountain or Red Lowry or Parrot.

Field marks: 320–370 mm. One of our showiest and most familiar parrots: *deep crimson, with blue cheek, shoulder and tail*; *mantle heavily mottled black*. Imm: often taken for a different species; mostly deep golden-olive, crimson patch on forehead and throat, under tail-coverts crimson, *cheek-patch and bend of wing blue*; in flight note its *golden-olive upperparts*, pale wingbar. Specially in n., some imms. assume adult plumage from nest. Size decreases northwards, race *nigrescens* in ne. Q smallest, darkest. Pairs, parties, flocks to about 20 often largely of imms. Feeds in foliage and on ground at edge of clearings; dashes for cover when alarmed. Flight fast and swooping, often with deep exaggerated wingbeats, brassy cries; note contrast of crimson body and rump and *flashing two-toned blue wings*, tail margined bluish white. Often tame in parks, gardens, comes to bird-tables.

Similar species: King Parrot (329).

Voice: Contact-call, mellow ringing 'trip-klee' or slow bell-like 'klee-kleekeee'; in flight, raucous brassy clanging 'klee klee klee'.

Habitat: Rainforests; wetter forests and woodlands to above snowline; fern-gullies. In autumn and winter disperses into more open country, timbered roadsides, shelter-belts and watercourses, coastal scrubs; cultivated paddocks, gardens.

Breeding: Nest: on decayed debris; in tree hollow, often very high, at times near ground; rarely, in cavity in building. Eggs: 5–8; white, rounded.

Range and Status: Coastal e. and se. Aust.: widespread from se. Q (Blackall Ras.–Gympie) s. coastally and on Divide to e. and s. Vic. and se. SA, w. to Kangaroo I.; disperses in autumn–winter, recorded inland to Moree–Warrumbungle NP (breeds)–Finley, NSW; in Vic., n. to Bendigo–Little Desert; in se. SA, n. to Bordertown–Fleurieu Pen. The race *nigrescens* occurs in highlands of ne. Q, from Eungella Ra., near Mackay, n. to near Cooktown. Common; dispersive. Occasional records from King I., Bass Strait and n. Tas. may be vagrants or escapes. Introduced Norfolk I. and NZ.

342 ADELAIDE ROSELLA *Platycercus adelaidae*   Pl.50

Field marks: 340–360 mm. Has plumage characteristics of Crimson (341) and Yellow (343) Rosellas, of which it may be a natural hybrid. Unlike Yellow Rosella, *always has some red showing through yellow plumage*; *feathers of mantle usually margined yellow-red*. Some are mostly yellow but reddish about forehead, mantle and breast; others are red on head, breast, underparts and rump, merging into yellow on nape, sides of neck and rump. Birds in s. Flinders Ras. are usually pale, other populations variable. Imm: olive-green above, duller below, *forehead, throat, thighs and under tail-coverts dull-red*. In flight, like Yellow Rosella, but note reddish tones; imm. has pale wingstripe. Like Crimson Rosella in habits, calls, breeding; often flies with the same deep exaggerated wingbeats. **Similar species:** Yellow Rosella (343): generally paler, margins of black feathers on mantle yellow to whitish yellow without reddish tinge.

Habitat: Varied: timbered valleys in Mt. Lofty Ras., open forests and woodlands; timber along watercourses; occasionally mallee, timbered farmlands and roadsides.

Range and Status: Confined to Mt. Lofty and s. Flinders Ras., SA: from Willunga, s. of Adelaide, n. to about Quorn, e. to about Murray Bridge, Mannum, Morgan and Peter-borough. Reported to intergrade with Yellow Rosella (343) near Mannum and Morgan, along watercourses. Common; sedentary.

343 YELLOW ROSELLA *Platycercus flaveolus*   Pl.50

Other names: Murrumbidgee or Swamp Lowry or Rosella; Murray Smoker.

Field marks: 300–340 mm. Mostly pale-yellow; forehead red, *cheeks and shoulders blue*; *feathers of mantle black, with broad yellow margins* giving heavily mottled look; tail blue with whitish margins. Some of both sexes have reddish wash on throat or breast. (See Adelaide Rosella (342) with which it may interbreed in SA). Imm: upperparts and rump *dull olive-green*, yellow-green below; pale wingstripe in flight; some assume (dull) adult plumage from nest. Pairs to small flocks; habits like Crimson Rosella (341) but more sedentary, seldom far from water. Feeds on ground in open forest, grassland, and in foliage and blossoms of eucalypts and acacias; fond of peppercorns and fruit; visits orchards and gardens. In flight, note *contrast of pale-yellow plumage with blue wing-patches*. Occasionally with Superb Parrots (331) Mallee Ringnecks (348).

Similar species: Adelaide Rosella (342).

Voice: Flight-call, ringing 'rik-rik'; when perched, bell-like call of two slow notes, then two very short notes: 'ding-ding, didit'.

Habitat: River red gums on and near watercourses, woodlands of black and grey box and mallee; grassy clearings, grazing country and cropland; timber along roadsides, shelter-belts; parks, gardens.

Breeding: Nest: on decayed debris; in tree-hollow, usually high; often in river red gum overhanging or standing in water. Eggs: 4–5; white, rounded.

Range and Status: River red gum forests along Murray, Darling, Lachlan, Murrumbidgee, Goulburn and other rivers and tributaries in s. and sw. NSW, n. Vic. and se. SA: from Yass–Jugiong on upper Murrumbidgee R. system and from about Hume Reservoir on Murray R., downstream to about Mannum, SA. In NSW, extends upstream on Lachlan R. to about Booligal, and up Darling R. to Menindee. In Vic., extends s. on Ovens R. to near Wangaratta–Warby Ras., s. on Goulburn R. to about Shepparton and, in nw. Vic., to Hattah Lakes. Intergrades with Adelaide Rosella (342) on watercourses near Morgan and Mannum, SA. Common; sedentary.

344 EASTERN ROSELLA *Platycercus eximius*   Pl.50

Other names: Common, Red-headed or White-cheeked Rosella; Golden-mantle, Non-pareil or Polly Parrot; Rosehill Parakeet, Rosy.

Field marks: 290–340 mm. Extremely colourful: *head and upperbreast bright-scarlet, cheeks white*; black mottled above, with blue shoulders, mostly yellow below, under tail-coverts red. Female: slightly duller, patchy green on rear crown. Imm: nape and crown more patchy green; pale wingstripe in flight. The n. race *ceciliae* has more golden-yellow nape and mantle, pale blue-green to pale-turquoise rump, conspicuous in flight. This race interbreeds with Pale-headed Rosella (345). Pairs, parties and small flocks in autumn, winter. Often on roadsides or perched on fences; raids fruit or nuts in orchards, gardens. Feeds much on ground, retreats noisily to trees when disturbed. Flight strongly undulating with alternating bursts of wingbeats and dips; *note brilliant bright yellow-green to turquoise rump*. Associates with Crimson Rosellas (341), Pale-headed Rosellas (345) and Red-rumped Parrots (350).

Voice: Flight-call, brisk high-pitched 'pink-pink'; contact-call, slow ringing 'pee-p-peeee', usually from leafy tree: also soft chatterings. Calls higher-pitched than Crimson Rosella.

Habitat: Open forests and woodlands with adjacent grasslands: timbered watercourses; paddocks, grain-crops; roadsides, parks, gardens.

Breeding: Nest: on decayed debris; in tree-hollow, occasionally in stump or hollow fence-post. Eggs: 4–7; white, rounded.

Range and Status: Se. Aust. and Tas.: from about Gympie (and Bribie I.) Q, through e. NSW, inland to Moree–Parkes–Griffith–Euston; most Vic., to se. SA, n. to Bordertown–Salt Creek, also perhaps downstream along Murray R. from Vic.; (?introduced) population in s. Mt. Lofty Ras. Nominate race and *cecilae* intergrade in area of latitude 32°S–Hunter R., NSW. In Tas., widespread mostly from nc. coast through midlands to the se. Common; sedentary.

345 PALE-HEADED ROSELLA *Platycercus adscitus* **Pl.50**

Other names: Blue-cheeked Parakeet or Rosella; Blue, Mealy, Moreton Bay or White-headed Rosella.

Field marks: 280–320 mm. Palest-headed Australian parrot. A variable species, easily recognized in all its forms by *white or pale-yellow head* and rosella-like behaviour and calls. Nominate race: *head white or yellow-white with large white and small blue throat-patches,* feathers of mantle black, edged yellowish or bluish; shoulders blue, sides of breast yellow, underparts and rump pale blue-grey to cobalt-blue, under tail-coverts red. Race *palliceps:* *head pale-yellow, deeper on nape; feathers of mantle black, edged yellow; cheeks white, without blue throat-patch; underparts and rump pale blue-grey to pale-turquoise.* Imm: like adult but duller, some with pink on head; female and imm. show patchy traces of pink or red on head and body. Pairs to flocks; feeds on ground and in foliage, and blossoms; may raid crops, orchards. Flight strongly undulating with regular dips and shoots; note colour of *rump: greyish or yellowish* (n. and e. Q); *conspicuous pale-turquoise* (s. Q and n. NSW). Interbreeds with Eastern Rosella (344) where ranges overlap in n. NSW–s. Q.

Voice: Flight-call, 'crik crik', deeper and harder than equivalent 'pink pink' of Eastern Rosella. Also ringing rapid, high-pitched 'fee fee fee'.

Habitat: Open woodlands and scrublands, timber along watercourses, grasslands adjacent to these; clearings in woodland and forest; roadsides, farmlands, orchards, agricultural land and small crops; lantana thickets.

Breeding: Nest: on decayed debris; in tree hollow. Eggs: 3–5; white, rounded.

Range and Status: E. Aust. and some coastal islands: from C. York Pen., Q, s. to Clarence R. and Woolgoolga, NSW; in Q, inland to about Richmond–Longreach–Cunnamulla; in NSW inland to about Bourke–Walgett. Four races are recognized by Condon, 1975. Checkl. Birds Aust., 1.; but only the northernmost (nominate) and southernmost (*palliceps*) are outlined here. Nominate race occupies the range from about Cooktown, Q, w. to Gilbert R. and s. to about Atherton Tableland–Cairns in n. Q. According to Condon, the s. race *palliceps* occupies the range from near Longreach–Richmond, Q, also Fraser I., to n. NSW. Common; sedentary.

346 NORTHERN ROSELLA *Platycercus venustus* **Pl.50**

Other names: Brown's Parakeet, Parrot or Rosella; Smutty Parakeet, Parrot or Rosella.

Field marks: 280–300 mm. Distinctive: a yellowish rosella *with a black cap; fine dark margins to feathers of underparts give scaly look;* cheek-patch, shoulders and tail blue, under tail-coverts red. (In some, cheeks almost wholly white). Imm: duller; may have reddish marks on head and breast; in flight, pale wingbar. Pairs to (usually) small flocks;

feeds on ground and in foliage of shrubs and trees. Flight swift and strongly undulating.
Similar species: Hooded Parrot (353) male: conspicuous golden shoulder, blue-green underparts.
Voice: Rapid succession of high-pitched notes, 'trin-se, trinse'; chatterings when feeding.
Habitat: Open woodlands and scrublands and clearings in same; timber along watercourses; occasional mangroves; roadsides, crops, gardens.
Breeding: Nest: on decayed debris; in tree-hollow, usually of eucalypt near water. Eggs: 2–4; white, rounded.
Range and Status: N. Aust. and coastal islands: from Spring Creek, nw. WA and Kimberleys to far-nw. Q; s. in NT to Pearce Pt.–Katherine–Macarthur R. and to Nicholson R. in far-nw. Q. Generally uncommon; sedentary.

347 WESTERN ROSELLA *Platycercus icterotis* Pl.50

Other names: Stanley Parakeet or Rosella, Yellow-cheeked Parrot or Rosella.
Field marks: 250–280 mm. Smallest rosella, unlike any other parrot in sw. Aust. Male: *scarlet head and body set off by prominent yellow cheek-patch*, feathers of mantle black, margined grey-green. Female: green above, cheek-patch duller; *head and breast mostly green*, with red forehead and touches of red and yellow below. Imm: greener, no cheek-patch. The race *xanthogenys* is redder and greyer above; female paler than nominate female. Pairs, small parties; quiet and often tame; feeds in foliage of shrubs and trees and on ground, flies up to nearest tree on being disturbed. Flight gentle with few undulations; female and imm. show pale wingbar.
Voice: Soft 'chink chink'.
Habitat: Open forest and woodland with clearings; trees along watercourses, grasslands or crops with few trees; farmlands, roadsides, orchards, surroundings of homesteads, gardens.
Breeding: Nest: on decayed debris; in tree-hollow, usually in eucalypt, often at no great height. Eggs: 3–7; white, rounded.
Range and Status: Confined to sw. WA roughly s. of Dongara–Israelite Bay, e. to Southern Cross–Norseman. Nominate race confined to better-watered coastal districts; race *xanthogenys* in drier parts of range; some intergradation. Fairly common; sedentary.

RINGNECKS Genus *Barnardius*

Robust parrots, closely related to rosellas; they occur in several geographical forms, each distinguished by a yellow rear-collar but differing in other features. In the past they have been treated as four, three or two species. Condon 1975. Checkl. Birds Aust., 1. retains Mallee Ringneck (348) *B. barnardi* and Port Lincoln Parrot (349) *B. zonarius*.

348 MALLEE RINGNECK *Barnardius barnardi* Pl.49

Other names: Barnard's Parakeet, Bubba-bulla, Buln-buln; Cloncurry, Mallee or Scrub Parrot, Eastern Ringneck.
Field marks: 325–355 mm. Pale blue-green head and body and pale-turquoise shoulders contrast with *deep blue-grey mantle*; note red mark on forehead, yellow rear-collar and *irregular yellow or orange-yellow breastband*. Female: duller, back grey-green. Imm: brownish crown, mantle and mark through eye. Both adults and imms. of race *whitei* have brownish head and green back. The small race *macgillivrayi*, 'Cloncurry Ringneck', formerly regarded as full species, has no red on forehead; pale blue-green above, yellower below; in flight, looks much less contrasty. Pairs, family parties; feeds on ground or in foliage. Flight undulating, rosella-like, wingbeats deep; note flashing contrast of pale-turquoise nape, wingpatches and rump with dark mantle and wingtips.
Similar species: Port Lincoln Parrot (349): blackish head, blue cheeks, upperparts dark-green.

Voice: Flight-call, clanging 'kling-kling-kling' or 'put-kleep, put-kleep, put-kleep', less strident than Port Lincoln.

Habitat: Scrub-country: mallee, native pine, mulga, bulloak, open eucalypt woodlands, especially on edges of open country and clearings; river red gums and other timber along creekbeds and lakes; paddocks, homestead-gardens. Race *macgillivrayi* is mostly confined to river red gums and other timber along watercourses, nearby woodlands and scrubs.

Breeding: Nest: on decayed debris; in hollow of eucalypt, either living or dead. Eggs: 4–6; white, rounded.

Range and Status: E. inland Aust.: from nw. Q and perhaps adjacent e. NT to s. NSW, nw. Vic. and e. SA. Nominate race: c. Q, n. to Windorah–Winton, e. to Blackall–Carnarvon Ras.–Goondiwindi; in NSW, e. to Moree–Dubbo–Wagga; in w. Vic., e. to Kerang and s. to Little Desert–Edenhope; in SA, from about Innamincka s. to Naracoorte–Kingston, w. to Flinders Ras.–Port Augusta–Salt Creek, *except* wetter parts of Mt. Lofty Ras. The race *whitei*, whose colouration reflects interbreeding with Port Lincoln Parrot, occupies the range from Flinders Ras. s. to mallee areas w. of Murray R. The race *macgillivrayi* has an isolated range in far-nw. Q, from Boulia e. to Kynuna, n. to the drainages of the Gregory Leichhardt and Cloncurry Rs., w. to Camooweal, Q, and upper Nicholson R. in e. NT. (Some consider this form more logically treated as an isolate of Port Lincoln Parrot.) Common; sedentary.

349 PORT LINCOLN PARROT *Barnardius zonarius* Pl.49

Other names: Twenty-eight Parrot; Western Ringneck; Yellow-banded Parrot.

Field marks: 345–370 mm. Distinctive and robust; *the only green Australian parrot with a blackish head*, some have red mark on forehead; bill whitish, cheeks blue, yellow rear-collar; yellow zone across breast. Imm: duller, head brownish black; imm. female; pale wingstripe in flight. Race *semitorquatus*, 'Twenty-eight Parrot', is larger, darker; distinguished by *usually wholly green underparts*. Race *occidentalis*: paler; head grey-black, no red on forehead; upperparts bluer; yellow of underparts extends to vent. Pairs, parties to flocks; feeds on ground and rather inconspicuously in foliage and blossoms. When disturbed, usually flies strongly, uttering strident alarm-calls; head somewhat raised and with marked undulations or exaggerated deep chesty wingstrokes; *deep-green mantle and lighter-green rump contrast with blackish head and flight-feathers.* May become a pest in crops, orchards, vineyards.

Similar species: Mallee Ringneck (348).

Voice: Flight-call, strident ringing 'put-kleepit-kleepit' or rapid 'kling-kling-kling-kling-kling' like striking a silvery anvil; alarm-note described as a sharp 'vatch'. The race *semitorquatus* has distinct ringing triple note, hence 'Twenty-eight'.

Habitat: Wide: wet coastal forests and woodlands to river red gums along inland watercourses; mallee, mulga scrub, desert oak and spinifex associations; usually near water. In settled areas, roadsides, farmlands, surroundings of homesteads, orchards, parks, gardens.

Breeding: Nest: on decayed debris; in hollow, usually of eucalypt. Eggs: 4–7; white, rounded.

Range and Status: Widespread in w. half of continent: from Eyre Pen. and w. of Flinders Ras., SA, n. to Banka Banka, NT, e. to 136°E, occasional to NT–Q border; w. in NT to s. edge of Tanami Desert. In WA, from the far-nw. (? occasional s. Kimberleys) s. throughout State; the pale race *occidentalis*, from Marble Bar and de Grey R. s. to Geraldton and e. to L. Way. Race *semitorquatus* occupies wetter coastal parts of s. WA. Common; sedentary. Note: local colonies, founded by escaped birds, Melbourne and ACT; often reported feral in other States. Its size and strength apparently enable it easily to force its way out of aviaries.

350　RED-RUMPED PARROT　*Psephotus haematonotus*　　　Pl.51

Other names: Grass Parrot, Green Leek, Ground or Red-backed Parrot.

Field marks: 255–280 mm. Male: brilliant small long-tailed parrot, head and neck bright emerald-green, underparts rich yellow; *yellow mark on shoulder*; *lower back orange-red or brick-red*, prominent in flight. Female differs: head and upperparts olive grey-green, dull-white below, edge of wings blue, *rump green*. Imm: like adults, but duller. In flight both female and imm. show pale wingbar. Male of inland race *caeruleus*: paler and bluer than nominate race, whiter below; female paler, duller. Pairs to flocks, in which pairs persist. Feeds much on ground; flies up to fences and trees with pleasing calls. Rests during heat of day in foliage; feeds on eucalypt and other blossom, spilt grain on roadsides, fowlyards. Flight fairly swift and direct with slight undulations.

Similar species: Mulga Parrot (351). The green *Neophema* grass parrots (357–62) are smaller, often with yellowish 'mask' and blue forehead-band; distinctive zizzing or tinkling calls, darting low or very high flight with distinctive hesitant wingbeat.

Voice: Pretty warbling song, unusual for parrot. Flight-call, cheery 'chee chlip, chee chlip, chee chip' with slight break in it.

Habitat: Seldom far from water; open woodlands and adjacent crops, grasslands and paddocks; timber along watercourses; clearings, paddocks with living or dead eucalypts; roadside, stubble, golf-courses, playing fields, farmyards, suburban allotments.

Breeding: Nest: on decayed debris; in tree-hollow, usually of living or dead eucalypt; fence-post or hollow stump. Eggs: 4–6; white, rounded.

Range and Status: Mostly inland se. Aust.: confined to near water in more arid parts of range; from Windorah–Augathella–Chinchilla, Q, e. to Brisbane, where it is scarce; in NSW, w. to about Bourke–Darling R.; most of Vic., rare or absent e. from Port Phillip Bay to s. Gippsland and se. corner; widespread e. SA, w. to s. Mt. Lofty Ras. and Yorke Pen., n. to Burra–s. Flinders Ras.; colony reported near Kimba, Eyre Pen. Race *caeruleus*: apparently isolate in Lake Eyre Basin, ne. SA– far-nw. NSW, probably extending to sw. Q. Common; sedentary but apparently extending coastwards and into the Divide in e. Aust. from s. Q to s. NSW. Present in w. parts of Sydney area, where recent large irruptions have occurred; also Melbourne and Adelaide outer suburbs.

351　MULGA PARROT　*Psephotus varius*　　　Pl.51

Other names: Many-coloured or Varied Parrot.

Field marks: 255–305 mm. Male: a rather slender brilliant emerald-green parrot with *scarlet patch on belly and thighs, prominent in flight*; *note yellow mark on forehead and shoulder*; *red mark on centre of nape and rump*, prominent pale-green band across lower back. Female: dull brownish-green; no scarlet thighs but red mark *on nape and shoulder*, *green rump*. Imm: like duller adults; young male has little or no red on thighs but may have reddish tinge to yellow on shoulder. In flight both female and imm. show pale wingstripe. Pairs or family parties; feeds on ground near trees, on roadsides or in foliage of saltbush, mulgas and eucalypts; keeps more to cover than Red-rumped Parrot (350). Flight very swift and direct; with quick fluttering interrupted wingbeats producing an undulating effect, and distinctive calls.

Similar species: Red-rumped Parrot (350). Swift Parrot (338).

Voice: Brisk distinctive flight-call, somewhat resembling 'swit swit', repeated.

Habitat: Usually not far from water; in mallee, mulga and other inland scrubs; saltbush plains with trees, timbered inland watercourses.

Breeding: Nest: on decayed debris; in tree-hollow, often near ground in stunted woodland; also in taller trees, e.g. along watercourses. Eggs: 4–5; white, rounded.

Range and Status: Interior of s. Aust., n. to MacDonald Downs, NT, and Windorah–Charleville–Moonie, Q; thence s. through w. NSW e. to Moree–Gilgandra–Grenfell–Griffith–Moulamein; nw. Vic., e. to about Swan Hill–L. Boga, s. to Little Desert; most of SA, *except* coastal se. and higher rainfall areas of Mt. Lofty Ras.; widespread in WA n. to

Pilbara region but not sw. WA, s. of Dundas–Northam–Moora. Common only in suitable habitat; sedentary or nomadic.

352 GOLDEN-SHOULDERED PARROT *Psephotus chrysopterygius* Pl.51

Other names: Ant-bed or Ant-hill Parrot; Golden-winged Parrot.

Field marks: 250–270 mm. Male: a slender upright pale-turquoise parrot: small blackish cap separated from bill by *pale-yellow forehead*; mantle and wings pale-brown with *pale golden bar along wing*; deep salmon-red belly and thighs and under tail-coverts. Female: dull-yellowish green, bronze wash on crown and nape; lower breast, sides of body and rump pale-blue, belly and under tail-coverts grey-green *with some pale-red*. Imm: like female; young males are greener, with darker crowns. Females and imms. show pale wing-stripe in flight. Pairs or small parties; feeds chiefly on ground, flying up to trees when disturbed; flight swift and slightly undulating.

Similar species: Hooded Parrot (353).

Voice: Chirruping calls; soft pleasing whistles.

Habitat: Open eucalypt or paperbark woodlands and scrublands where termite-mounds occur; mangroves.

Breeding: Nest: in cavity excavated at end of narrow tunnel in termite-mound, often one standing in ground that becomes swampy in wet season. Eggs: 4–6; white, rounded.

Range and Status: S. and c. C. York Pen. Q; recorded n. to Watson R. on w. coast, e. to Coen, lower Morehead, Normanby, upper Palmer Rs. and to s. of Bulimba and Normanton, but now probably much reduced and mostly reported in ne. part of that range. Locally common but threatened by illegal activities of bird-trappers.

353 HOODED PARROT *Psephotus dissimilis* Pl.51

Field marks: 255–275 mm. Like Golden-shouldered Parrot (352) but male has *entire crown black to below eye and more golden yellow on shoulder*. Female: forehead and face pale-blue; neck and upperbreast yellow-green, *under tail-coverts salmon-red*. Imms: like female but duller; young males may have slightly darker heads, brighter colouring. Pairs to parties, occasionally flocks. Feeds much on ground; flight, swift and undulating; in male note contrast of dark upperparts with turquoise body and rump and golden shoulders. Habit of perching on telephone wires sometimes brings it to notice.

Similar species: Golden-shouldered Parrot (352). Northern Rosella (346).

Voice: Singular jarring cry: a sharp metallic 'chissik-chissik' or 'chillik'.

Habitat: Dry open woodlands and spinifex-associations; eucalypts on rocky open grasslands bordering watercourses. Usually where termite mounds occur.

Breeding: Nest: on impacted debris in cavity excavated in termite-mound, reached by short tunnel. Eggs: 2–5; white, rounded.

Range and Status: Semi-arid areas of top end NT, from w. edge of Arnhem Land e. to Macarthur R. Patchy and uncommon and now most frequently reported at the w. extremity of its range, from upper S. Alligator R. w. to Pine Creek and s. to about Mataranka.

354 PARADISE PARROT *Psephotus pulcherrimus* Pl.51

Other names: Ant-hill Parrot, Beautiful Parakeet or Parrot; Ground Parakeet, Scarlet-shouldered or Soldier Parrot.

Field marks: 275–300 mm. *Possibly now extinct*: an exceedingly beautiful small long-tailed parrot. Male: *forehead scarlet*, crown and nape blackish 'like a tight little cap'; *dark-brown above with scarlet shoulders*; *face and breast bright emerald-green*, shading into turquoise-blue on sides of neck and flanks to rump; underparts and under tail-coverts scarlet; tail bronze-green and blue above, margined white. Female: duller and much paler; less scarlet on shoulder, *face and breast buff-yellow with brownish orange markings*; rump turquoise-blue; underparts pale-blue, under tail-coverts with some red. Imms: like poorly coloured adults. Female and imm. show pale wingstripe in flight. Pairs to family parties; reported to feed quietly on ground, flying up into nearby tree when disturbed. Flight probably swift and undulating *with contrasting dark-brown upperparts and blue rump.* Posture when perched very upright, hence 'Soldier Parrot'.

Similar species: Some 'sightings' may be mis-identifications of Blue Bonnet (355), race *haematorrhous:* sturdier and much paler grey-brown with a blue facial patch and a gold mark below red on shoulder; calls differ.

Voice: Alarm-call reported to be short sharp but musical whistle, uttered before taking flight; probably same call described as metallic 'queek', repeated several times. Also (male): musical animated song.

Habitat: Grassy eucalypt woodlands and scrubby grasslands, particularly where termite mounds occur.

Breeding: Like Golden-shouldered Parrot (352). Nest: on impacted termite-debris; usually excavated in terrestrial termite-mound; tunnel approximately 40 mm in diameter ending in large nest-chamber; occasionally in tunnel in creekbank or in hollow stump. Eggs: 3–5; white, rounded.

Range and Status: Formerly reported s. Q and ne. NSW: n. to the Tropic, possibly further n. in region of Lynd R.; w. to Mantuan Downs–Upper Comet–Upper Dawson–Roma–Goondiwindi, e. to Rockhampton–Howard–Esk; in n. NSW, formerly Inverell district, (? vagrant) e. to Casino. Probably always uncommon and local; now very rare or extinct, probably as a result of habitat-changes and trapping. Unconfirmed reports of occurrence still circulate, but last confirmed sighting was in mid-1920s, in area of Gayndah, Q.

355 BLUE BONNET *Northiella haematogaster*   Pl.51

Other names: Bulloak Parrot, Crimson-bellied Parrot, Little Blue Bonnet, Naretha, Oak or Pine Parrot; Red-vented or Yellow-vented Parakeet.

Field marks: 270–350 mm. The only pale grey-brown parrot *with deep-blue forehead, cheeks and throat, not bonnet.* (1) Nominate race: *wing deep olive-yellow,* bend of wing blue; underparts *including under tail-coverts pale-yellow,* red patch on centre of belly and red thighs. Female: similar. Imm: duller, with smaller red belly-patch; female and imm. show pale wingstripes in flight. There is a similar but paler race, *pallescens,* see Range and Status. (2) Race *haematorrhous,* 'Red-vented Blue Bonnet': conspicuous *dark-red patch on wing* with a green mark above and bordered by blue curve of wing; lower breast pale-yellow; thighs, patch on centre of belly and *under tail-coverts, dark-red.* (3) Race *narethae,* 'Naretha or Little Blue Bonnet': smaller, two-tone blue on head, *more olive-green above, rump olive-yellow;* under tail-coverts red but *belly and thighs pale-yellow without red.* Pairs to small parties; note upright stance. Feeds much on ground, flies a distance to trees with sharp alarm-calls. Flight fast, undulating and rather erratic, with distinctive rapid shallow wingbeats; note chunky build. In flight, all blue bonnets show pale brown upperparts with *deep-blue on flight-feathers, and blue-white outer tail-feathers; lemon belly with more or less red,* according to race.

Similar species: Bourke's Parrot (356): smaller and more softly-coloured; no blue on face. Paradise Parrot (354).

Voice: Flight-call; harsh abrupt distinctive 'jak, jakajak' or jagged 'chak chak chak chak'; also piping whistle.

Habitat: Open woodlands and scrubs, native pine, belar, sheoak, bulloak; mulga and other *Acacia* sp.; sugarwood; larger, more open mallee; saltbush; grasslands sparsely broken with these; watercourses; farmlands, crops, roadsides; rail sidings, environs of homesteads. Race *narethae:* typically in desert sheoak (belar) *Casuarina cristata* with acacia species.

Breeding: Nest: on decayed debris; in hollow limb or trunk, usually of eucalypt or casuarina. Eggs: 4–7; white, rounded.

Range and Status: Interior Aust.: from s. Q to se. WA. Nominate race: greatest part of range, n. to Windorah-Charleville in sw. Q; inland NSW e. to Warialda–Wellington–Wagga–Barooga; in n. Vic., s. to Rochester–Inglewood–Dimboola; widespread in e. and n. SA from Bordertown–Salt Creek to n. of Adelaide, n. Yorke and Eyre Pens., to Simpson Desert in ne. and Malbooma and Commonwealth Hill Station in w.; recorded Musgrave Ras. in nw.; mostly absent from Flinders Ras. Race *pallescens* occupies the L. Eyre basin. Race *haematorrhous* occupies range e. of nominate race, extending ne. to Mitchell–Condamine–Goondiwindi, Q, and e. to Warialda–Orange–Grenfell in NSW. The zone of intergradation is imperfectly known, specially in cs. Q; in c. NSW, said to be Barellan–Rankin's Springs and Cobar–Hermidale. Both above races common in suitable habitat. Race *narethae*: nearly confined to the Nullarbor Plain, from e. of Kalgoorlie, WA, to Mundrabilla–Eucla; recently recorded in SA e. of Ooldea, within 200 km of nominate race (? possibly liberated trapped birds). Uncommon. The species is probably mostly sedentary.

GRASS PARROTS Genus *Neophema*

Small distinctive, ground-frequenting, mostly green parrots, of inland and s. Aust., Tas. and islands off s. coasts. Best identified as neophemas by size, calls and characteristic swift darting flight with wings briefly left open between wingbeats, giving a hesitant irregular style, reminiscent of flight of some small waders. There are three colour-groups: (1) a single aberrant brownish inland form. Bourke's Parrot (356); (2) scarlet or brick-red patches in plumage of males and blue faces of females; e.g. Turquoise Parrot (361) (only this group shows marked sexual dimorphism); (3) mostly green with blue forehead-band and blue on wings. Three members of this group, Blue-winged (357), Elegant (358) and Rock (359) Parrots are easily confused in field.

356 BOURKE'S PARROT *Neophema bourkii* Pl.52

Other names: Bourke Parrot, Bourke's Grass Parrot; Blue-vented or Pink-bellied Parrot or Parakeet; Night or Sundown Parrot.

Field marks: 185–225 mm. *A small soft-brown parrot with whitish eye-ring*; pale edgings to feathers on wings give a strong pattern; *breast washed pink, deeper on abdomen*. Male: forehead-band and bend of wing mid-blue; flanks, under tail-coverts and sides of rump pale-blue. Female: duller; no blue on forehead, less blue on wing. Imm: like female; no pink on upperbreast; adult and imm. females show pale wingstripe in flight. Pairs to flocks; feeds on ground and in foliage; when disturbed, freezes or darts quickly into branches, often of dead tree, matching colour of wood. In flight, note pale-blue underwing and sudden flash of white margins to tail. At morning and evening, in darkness or full daylight, flocks pass fast and low through scrub to water, uttering soft calls, wings whistling softly. Sometimes called 'night parrot' for this reason – but see (336).

Similar species: No other parrot should be confused, but see Blue Bonnet (355). Peaceful (294) and Diamond (295) Doves: in flight, grey plumage and white tail-edges can cause confusion.

Voice: Flight-call, mellow 'chu-wee'; also soft chirrupy twitter, less strident and carrying than that of Budgerigar (337); alarm-call, shrill metallic note.

Habitat: Mulga and other inland acacia-scrubs; less typically native pine-scrubs and open eucalypt woodlands.

Breeding: Nest: on decayed debris; in tree-hollow, usually of acacia or casuarina, at no great height. Eggs: 3–6; white, rounded.

Range and Status: Mostly s. inland Aust., to coast in mid-w. WA, from near Geraldton to near North West Cape, thence to Ashburton R., e. to s. NT, n. to Devil's Marbles; far-s. Q, n. and e. to Windorah–Adavale–Cunnamulla–Dirranbandi; inland NSW, s. to about Lightning Ridge–Nyngan, occasional s. to L. Cargelligo–Ivanhoe, vagrant e. to Peak Hill–Narrandera; in e. SA, s. to L. Frome–Barrier Highway, occasional s. to near Murray R., w. to n. of Port Augusta–Woomera–Musgrave Ras.; in s. WA, s. to Gt. Victoria

· Desert, w. to Morawa. Fairly common and locally abundant, but patchy and irregular; probably increasing. Nomadic.

357 BLUE-WINGED PARROT *Neophema chrysostoma*   Pl.52

Other names: Blue-banded or Blue-winged Grass Parrot or Parakeet; Hobart Ground Parrot.

Field marks: 200–230 mm. Male: dull olive-green, crown more golden-green in contrast with rest of upperparts, yellowish facial mask, *blue forehead-band does not extend past eye*; *whole shoulder, bend of wing and flight-feathers uniform very deep-blue*; pale-yellow below, some orange-yellow between legs. Female: duller, smaller frontal band. Imm: duller than female, no blue on forehead; blue on wing smaller and duller, pale wingstripe in flight. Pairs, parties, flocks, large open companies; feeds quietly on ground, sometimes in foliage. When approached, typically flits along, settling again on ground, fence or branch or darts upwards with snipe-like erratic twists; when migrating or travelling a distance, flies swiftly and directly at great heights, revealed by *tinkling double calls* and distinctive flight. In SA, far-sw. NSW associates with Elegant Parrot (358).

Similar species: See Elegant Parrot (358) for differences. Imms: difficult to tell apart; look for adults, note calls and range. Orange-bellied Parrot (360): deeper-green, no yellow from bill to eye, less blue on wing, distinctive calls. Rock Parrot (359): brownish green, less blue on wing; overlaps in coastal SA. Turquoise Parrot (361), female.

Voice: Flight-call, double high-pitched silvery tinkling note, 'brrrt brrrrt'; when startled into flight, a staccato burst of notes; 'chappy-chappy-brrt-chippy-chippy-brrt'; soft low twittering when feeding.

Habitat: Open grassy woodlands and forests; heathlands, coastal scrubs, dune and salt-marsh vegetation; short grasslands; clearings and regrowth in alpine areas to over 1200 m; airfields, saltfields, golf-courses; roadsides, ploughed fields; orchards (autumn–winter roosting); inland in mallee, mulga and saltbush; canegrass areas, margins of inland swamps and lakes; stock-tanks.

Breeding: Nest: on decayed debris; in hollow, from over 20 m high in snow gums in Tas. to stumps of felled trees in coastal Vic.; pairs may nest in proximity. Eggs: 4–6; white, rounded.

Range and Status: Breeds e. and n. Tas.; coastal s. Vic. and se. SA. Partial winter migrant from this region (through Bass Strait islands) to inland se. Aust., moving n. mostly in Mar.–Apr., returning Aug.–Oct. During that period it may be found almost anywhere in e. SA; Vic. (including e. montane areas); NSW w. of the Divide and coastal far-se. (Nadgee) and s. Q. Records: w. to Whyalla and Streaky Bay, n. to Flinders Ras.–L. Callabonna, SA; Tibooburra–Adelaide Gate, nw. NSW; Thargomindah–Chinchilla, Q; e. in inland NSW to Moree–Gilgandra–Barooga. Common Tas. and coastal mainland; scarce and local elsewhere; flocks of dozens to hundred gather to roost, or where suitable food-plants occur.

358 ELEGANT PARROT *Neophema elegans*   Pl.52

Other names: Elegant Grass Parrot or Parakeet.

Field marks: 220–240 mm. Easily confused with Blue-winged (357), but *more uniform golden-olive above*, pale-yellow below; more obvious yellow facial mask; *blue forehead-band continues slightly through eye. Less blue on wing and distinctly of two tones.* Small patch of orange on centre belly, sometimes faint. Female: duller, yellow facial mask more prominent than female Blue-winged. Imm: nearly without blue on forehead. Solitary, pairs or small flocks; watchful but often approachable. Flight similar to Blue-winged; *golden-olive rump and pale-yellow tail-margins more prominent.*

Similar species: Blue-winged (357) and Orange-bellied (360) Parrots. Females of Turquoise (361) and Scarlet-chested (362) Parrots.

Voice: In flight, single sharp 'tsit'; when feeding or flushed, sweet feeble twitterings.

Habitat: Open woodlands and scrublands, coastal and inland; grasslands, saltbush, mallee and mulga-scrubs; clearings with rank secondary growth; saltmarsh vegetation, commercial saltfields.

Breeding: Nest: on decayed debris; in hollow spout or hole in trunk of tree, at times at some height. Eggs: 4–5; white, rounded.

Range and Status: Disjunct distribution in se. SA and parts of adjacent States, and in sw. WA. (1) In SA, limits are roughly from lower sc. (Port MacDonnell–Bunns Bore) n. coastally to Langhorne's Ck–Fleurieu Pen. and Kangaroo I.; n. through Adelaide Plains–Mt. Lofty Ras –Flinders Ras , the far-n. limits being about Maree–L. Callabonna. Recorded w. to Quorn–Port Augusta, and near Whyalla (suspected sightings elsewhere on Eyre Pen.). It has been recorded e. to Sutherlands and patchily e. through the mallee and pastoral region between Murray R., Barrier Highway and the Olary Ridge to far-w. NSW, where recorded Menindee–Broken Hill ne. to Wilcannia–Pirie L., mostly in nomadic flocks. There are sight-records from the Vic. mallee. (2) In s. WA, mostly sub-inland from Esperance to Moora, e. to Merredin, expanding coastwards into forest belt, Perth area, and n. in pastoral country to Fortescue R. Fairly common, part-nomadic, movements unpredictable.

359 ROCK PARROT *Neophema petrophila* Pl.52

Other names: Rock Elegant Parrot, Rock Parakeet or Grass-Parakeet.

Field marks: 210–230 mm. The dullest neophema, of specialized habitat. Male: *brownish olive above*, yellower below; forehead-band dark-blue, slight pale-blue facial mask *extends slightly past eye*; bend of wing and flight-feathers *narrowly edged dark-blue*, margined pale-blue; some have orange patch on belly. Female: duller. Imm: duller with less blue; pale wingstripe in flight. Pairs to flocks of 100 + ; feeds on ground among low growth, when disturbed flits and lands again or settles on rocks, shrubs; *posture rather upright* or darts skywards and flies very fast and high. At Albany, WA (? and elsewhere) feeds on spilt grain in railyards.

Similar species: Blue-winged (357) and Orange-bellied (360) Parrots.

Voice: 'Tsit, tsit, tsit . . .' like Purple-crowned Lorikeet (326); when flushed, described as rapid streams of 'tsit, tsit' notes, slowing down once out of danger.

Habitat: Granite and limestone islands and coastal formations; dunes, low coastal scrubs, grasslands, swamps, wastelands; golf-courses.

Breeding: Nest: on ground among rocks, under raised slab of rock or under cover of vegetation, mostly on rocky offshore islands, often within reach of spray. Eggs: 4–5; white, rounded.

Range and Status: Coasts and coastal islands of s. SA and sw. Aust.: from about Robe, SA, to Shark Bay, WA. Common, mostly sedentary but some autumn–winter dispersal coastally into suitable near-coastal habitats.

360 ORANGE-BELLIED PARROT *Neophema chrysogaster* Pl.52

Other names: Orange-bellied or Orange-breasted Grass Parakeet or Parrot.

Field marks: 200–215 mm. Male: sturdier than Blue-winged Parrot (357) and readily distinguished by *brilliant deep grass-green plumage*, yellowish green below, orange-yellow patch on centre of abdomen; undertail bright-yellow. Bright-blue forehead-band stops at eye; bend of wing dark-blue, paler inwards. Female: duller, forehead paler-blue, orange patch on abdomen. Imm: dull-green, richer on back and rump; little if any blue; smaller orange patch; pale wingstripe in flight. Parties to small flocks, occasionally to 70 + ; feeds on open ground and in low ground-cover; perches tops of shrubs. Often quiet but, if not cautiously approached, dashes into sky, calling; on wing looks *dark and sturdy*.

Similar species: Blue-winged (357) and Elegant (358) Parrots also have orange on belly; both are more slender. Blue-winged: duller olive-green with large dark-blue wingpatch; male has distinct yellow facial 'mask' under the blue forehead-band; calls more tinkling.

Elegant: distinctly golden-olive with blue forehead-band through eye, note range and habitat. Rock Parrot (359): browner-green; overlap likely only coastal se. SA.

Voice: When flushed, a distinctive, rapid metallic buzzing 'zizizizizizizizi'; harder and with little of tinkling quality of other neophemas.

Habitat: Mostly coastal: in sw. Tas., areas of button-grass *Mesomelaena* on wet peat plains; (? and possibly eucalypt woodland). Elsewhere: open areas of bare ground and low succulents, low shrubs, etc., on margins of tidal inlets, saltmarsh, brackish coastal lakes and sand-dunes; beaches; paddocks, in weeds, grass and introduced capeweed; at times feeds on kelp on tidelines.

Breeding: Little known: few records from Tas.; e.g. eight pairs in hollows in living eucalypts near Macquarie Harbour, Tas., in Nov. (1918–23). Nest: in tree-hollow. Eggs: 4–6; white, rounded.

Range and Status: Fragmentary evidence suggests breeding in sw. Tas. (Port Davey), part at least of population migrating Mar.–July through n. Tas., King I. and possibly Hunter Group, Bass Strait, to coastal s. Vic. and s. SA from Westernport and Altona–Corio Bay, Mud I., L. Connewarre, inland to near Colac, Vic., w. to Robe–Coorong, SA, occasional w. to L. Alexandrina, (? formerly) Outer Harbour and saltfields n. of Adelaide; vagrant Yorke Pen. Return Tas. Sept.–Nov. Formerly bred Long Bay, Sydney; apparently extinct NSW. Very rare and local; probably declining.

361 TURQUOISE PARROT *Neophema pulchella* Pl.52

Other names: Beautiful Parrot or Grass Parrot; Chestnut-shouldered Grass Parrot or Parakeet; Chestnut-winged Parrot or Grass Parrot; Red-shouldered Grass Parrot, Parakeet or Parrot, Turquoisine Parrot.

Field marks: 190–210 mm. Male distinctive: grass-green above, *bright-blue forehead and cheeks*, broad two-tone blue band round bend of wing surrounding *reddish chestnut patch on shoulder*; *rich-yellow below*. Female: duller; whitish-yellow from bill to eye, usually no chestnut on wing. Differs from other female neophemas except Scarlet-chested (362) in *greater contrast of green with yellow below*. Some males and females have orange belly. Imm: like female, but duller; young males have deeper-blue face, faint chestnut shoulder-patch. Pairs, small flocks; typically on ground or in low grass, weeds, heaths; usually not shy, moves ahead of observer, flies to trees on being disturbed. Flight swift and direct or erratic and fluttering; note bright buttercup-yellow outer tail-feathers; females (adult and imm.) show a pale wingstripe in flight.

Similar species: All other adult neophemas *except* female Scarlet-chested (362) differ from female Turquoise in blue band across forehead. Female Scarlet-chested: next to indistinguishable in field; note range and habitat. Orange-bellied Parrot (360): deeper green, much less blue on face and on shoulder; note range.

Voice: Sharp tinkling double flight-call like Blue-winged Parrot (357) but weaker and higher-pitched; also single high-pitched note that has been likened to that of Azure Kingfisher (396); continual musical twittering when feeding or at water.

Habitat: Open woodlands, grasslands or areas of weeds, heaths or clearings bordering woodland or scrub; slopes and bottoms of (sometimes rocky) foothills, with living or dead timber; occasionally roadsides or orchards.

Breeding: Nest: on decayed debris; in dead stump or spout of eucalypt. Eggs: 4–5; white, rounded.

Range and Status: Se. Aust.; patchily distributed through areas of suitable habitat: in Q now probably n. only to Chinchilla–Gayndah, most records from granite belt in inland se., recently discovered near coast at Cooloola; in NSW, w. to Moree–Pilliga scrub–Warrumbungle NP–Parkes–Temora–Albury, further w. near Nymagee, Round Hill (Mt. Hope) and Cocoparra NP; in n. Vic., rare and local, records from near Chiltern, Wangaratta, Glenrowan and Bendigo, also e. Gippsland. Becoming more common NSW, including area w. of Sydney; scarce and local elsewhere; partly nomadic.

362 SCARLET-CHESTED PARROT *Neophema splendida* Pl.52

Other names: Scarlet-breasted Parrot, Scarlet-chested or Scarlet-throated Grass Para-keet or Grass Parrot, Splendid Parrot or Grass Parrot.

Field marks: 175–215 mm. Male brilliant and unmistakable: *head bright light-blue, deeper on chin, chest deep-scarlet*, underparts rich-yellow. Female: *more blue on face and greater contrast between green above and yellowish below* than any except female Turquoise (361), which it closely resembles. Imm: like female but duller; males darker-blue on face; in flight, females show pale wingstripe. Pairs, small parties, at times large flocks. Quiet and inconspicuous; feeds usually on ground; when disturbed flits a short distance to settle again on ground or tree. Flight erratic and fluttering or direct and very swift; rich-yellow margins of blackish outer tail-feathers show on taking-off and alighting. Unlike other parrots, seldom seen at water; apparently gains much of its moisture from dew or succu-lent plants.

Similar species: Turquoise Parrot (361) female. Other adult neophemas have blue fore-head but no blue on face, less pale-blue on wing and less marked green-yellow contrast.

Voice: Feeble twittering, lacking the carrying quality of voices of other neophemas.

Habitat: In inland WA, open eucalypt woodlands and scrubby associations dominated by belar but principal habitat appears to be mallee and mulga-scrubs, in association with more open spinifex, saltbush and other food-plants, e.g. parakeelya, *Calandrinia*.

Breeding: Nest: on decayed debris, but sometimes with some leaves; in hollow, often of mallee or mulga, often low, but up to 8 m. Eggs: 3–5; white, rounded. Several pairs may nest in proximity.

Range and Status: S. inland Aust. n. to lower Finke R. and Petermann Ras., NT, w. to Murchison R., WA, thence s. to Corrigin–Kalgoorlie–Balladonia and Nullarbor Plain; e. to n. Eyre Pen.–Flinders Ras., SA, mallee areas s. to Murray R.; (rarely) to mallee of nw. Vic. and w. NSW; vagrant sw. Q. Scarce to rare; occasionally locally abundant; reported to be common in better-vegetated s. part of Gt. Victoria Desert, from where it may periodically irrupt. Highly nomadic.

Cuckoos Family *Cuculidae*

Cuckoos look much like songbirds; the main external difference is that their feet are zygodactylous: two toes point forward, two back. In Aust. they can be divided into two broad groups and three distinctive large species – Koel (373), Channel-billed Cuckoo (374) and Pheasant Coucal (375). Reflecting their uncuckoo-like appearance, the last two are illustrated respectively with the currawongs (Plate 84) and the lyrebirds (Plate 17). *Typical cuckoos* are represented here by a group of five species (363–7) of graceful, mostly greyish, slender birds that look somewhat like small to large wattlebirds in silhouette, but whose manner and bearing are distinctive. The wingtips often droop and the longish tail hangs vertically or is carried horizontally and raised and lowered. Flight is generally swift, graceful, undulating and rather hawklike with swept wings. The species are fairly easily separated by colour or pattern of underparts, development of white spotting or 'notching' on wings and tail-feathers, colours of eyes and legs, and calls. *Bronze-cuckoos* are wide-spread in Africa and from Asia to New Zealand. The Australian species (368–72) are rather like small honeyeaters, but their wingtips often droop. Most are glossy bronze-green above and whitish below with dark barrings. Except for the pale-brownish Black-eared Cuckoo (368), they are not easy to separate in the field and the racial details of one form (372) are not clear. Cuckoos are most frequently noticed when calling insistently from the tops of dead trees or overhead wires or in noisy courtship flight. They feed in foliage or in the open, typically perching on fences or stumps, flying down to take food on or near the ground. Often the prey is a hairy caterpillar, which cuckoos, unlike many birds, eat in great quantities. Courting males prepare and present such prey to females. The best-known aspect of cuckoo-behaviour is parasitism: all species in Australia *except*

Pheasant Coucal are brood-parasites, depositing their eggs in nests of other birds, often removing an egg of the host species at the same time. Over 100 species of Australian birds are known to have their nests parasitized, but there are no Australian data about the number of eggs female cuckoos lay in a season. Certainly they lay more than one and many nests are parasitized by each breeding female. Two species only, Koel and Channel-billed Cuckoo, lay more than one egg in the same nest; broods of up to five young of the last have been reported. Soon after hatching, the nestlings of most other parasitic cuckoos instinctively expel the eggs or young of the host from the nest. Cuckoos are usually recognized by host-species and other birds, and they typically elicit alarm, scolding calls or mobbing, specially when breeding is in progress. The commotion can be a useful pointer to their presence. Male cuckoos become noisy and conspicuous when breeding and this may serve to divert the attention of intended hosts. Young cuckoos, whether in the nest or following foster-parents when fledged, can often be recognized by their insistant sibilant begging calls; birds other than their foster-parents frequently feed them. Most cuckoos in Aust. are migrants, moving n. in non-breeding season to inland or n. Aust., NG or beyond; these movements are imperfectly understood. Two, Oriental Cuckoo (363) and Shining Bronze-cuckoo (370), breed elsewhere and come here as non-breeding migrants.

Food: Insects and larvae, especially hairy caterpillars; larger species take fruits, berries and vertebrates, including small lizards, mice and the young (and eggs) of other birds.

Range: Almost cosmopolitan in tropical to temperate regions.

Number of species: World 107; Aust. 14.

363 ORIENTAL CUCKOO *Cuculus saturatus*   Pl.53

Other names: Blyth's or Himalayan Cuckoo (Asia).

Field marks: 300–330 mm. A large longish-tailed grey cuckoo with *white lower breast and abdomen boldly barred dark-brown.* No white mark on nape or at shoulder or white spots on wing, as in Pallid (364); upperparts can look steely blue-grey or shot-chestnut; tail darker, lightly spotted white above, shadowy dark barrings below; *eye whitish with a yellow eye-ring; legs bright-yellow.* Imm: chestnut-brown above, with dark-brown barrings below, from throat down. Singly, pairs to small gatherings where food abundant. Most observers comment on its hawklike bearing and powerful long-winged flight, often likened to that of Little Falcon (153) and described as low, swift, slipping or, when weaving through trees, erratic. Not easy to approach, slips swiftly out of trees and away.

Similar species: Pallid Cuckoo (364): see above; breast plain-grey, eye and legs dark. Barred Cuckoo-shrike (428): paler, with sturdier black bill, dark mark round eye and black legs; tail squarer, without spots.

Voice: Usually fairly quiet; described calls include mournful subdued trill on three notes, repeated with rising crescendo, somewhat like Fan-tailed (367); when feeding, a harsh 'gaak-gaak-gak-ak-ak-ak', somewhat like cackling of Dollarbird (407).

Habitat: Open woodlands; vegetation along watercourses; rainforest pockets; leafy trees in paddocks, along river-flats and roadsides; habitats on passage include mangroves and coral cays on Gt. Barrier Reef.

Range and Status: Breeds in Himalayas, Siberia, China, Korea, Japan; winters s. Asia to Aust., occasional NZ. Regular migrant to coastal n. and e. Aust. and islands: from e. Kimberleys, WA, to Cape York Q, s. to Brisbane–Toowoomba, occasional to area of Sydney, NSW; arrives Sept.–Oct., departs Apr.–May, some winter records. Generally uncommon; rare NSW.

364 PALLID CUCKOO *Cuculus pallidus*   Pl.53

Other names: Brainfever-bird; Grasshopper or Mosquito Hawk; Harbinger-of-spring; Rain, Scale, Semitone, Storm or Weather-bird.

Field marks: 280–330 mm. A graceful longish-tailed grey cuckoo; note *curving dark line* *through eye; white mark on nape and at shoulder; flight-feathers notched and spotted white,* tail prominently notched whitish; eye black with yellow eye-ring, legs dark-olive. Sub-adult: buff spot on nape, spotted above with buff; often looks untidy. Imm: at first striking with large head, boldly-mottled black-and-white plumage, short tail. Singly, pairs or chasing trios; often first noted by well-known call. Flight swift, hawklike, slipping and slightly undulating; note small head and pointed wings; on alighting, tail often raised and lowered.

Similar species: Oriental Cuckoo (363). Fan-tailed Cuckoo (367): smaller, breast buff to pale-rufous, wings not spotted. Cuckoo-shrikes (427–33): plainer grey, no yellow eye-ring or white spotting. In flight they look blunter, tails shorter, squarish; flight more undulating, often in groups.

Voice: Male utters the well-known 'harbinger-of-spring' call: upward scale of about eight whistled notes, the second note slightly below the first, then rising in quarter-tone or chromatic scale; uttered persistently day or night. When pursuing females, a demented 'crookyer, crookyer', becoming wilder; also staccato 'pip-pip-pip-pip'. Female: hoarse brassy whistle.

Habitat: Open forests, woodlands and scrublands; mangroves; cleared country; roadsides, railway reserves, paddocks, gardens.

Breeding: Eggs: flesh-coloured, spotted pink, laid singly, usually in open cup-nests of insectivorous birds; honeyeaters are the usual hosts, but also flycatchers, woodswallows, Magpie Larks, orioles, shrike-thrushes and cuckoo-shrikes.

Range and Status: Aust., Tas and coastal islands: regular migrant in coastal s. Aust., and Tas., usually arriving in Sept. (sometimes June–July) departing from Jan. to Apr., after breeding; some overwinter; near Perth arrives end May, leaves Dec. Breeding recorded in NT and n. Q; movements of n. birds little known. Common but numbers fluctuate notably. Winter vagrant NG, Moluccas.

365 BRUSH CUCKOO *Cuculus variolosus*   Pl.53

Other name: Square-tailed Cuckoo.

Field marks: 220–240 mm. A rather dull cuckoo with grey head and throat; *breast grey, washed buff, under tail-coverts buff.* Upperparts olive-to rufous-brown with slight greenish sheen; tail-feathers tipped white *but 'notchings' on edges scarcely apparent. Eye-ring grey,* legs grey-pink. Imm: very different: brown, mottled buff; wing and tail-feathers notched buff; paler below, intricately streaked and spotted dark-brown in fine barred pattern. Singly, pairs or displaying small parties; made apparent by persistent call, otherwise unobtrusive. Perches quietly in rainforest or woodland when feeding, flies from branch to branch and into foliage. Sustained flight swift, direct, slightly undulating.

Similar species: Fan-tailed Cuckoo (367): breast more rufous; tail longer, outer feathers notched white.

Voice: A shrill far-carrying deliberate, usually descending phrase of about 7 or 8 (sometimes 3 or 4) notes, 'fear-fear-fear-fear . . .', a characteristic call of e. rainforests in spring. Displaying males very noisy with repeated shrill rising phrases like 'where's-the-tea', 'where's-the-tea-Pete' or 'where's-the-pippy', becoming demented.

Habitat: Rainforests and woodlands, to high country in se. Aust. in summer; leafy trees along watercourses, mangroves, roadsides.

Breeding: Egg: whitish, with faint purplish brown and lavender markings. Usually in cup nest of Flame (442), Scarlet (443) or Eastern Yellow (449) Robin; Leaden Flycatcher (482), Grey Fantail (487) or a honeyeater; occasionally in domed nest of fairy warbler, fairy wren or scrubwren.

Range and Status: Coastal n. and e. Aust. and many coastal islands: from about Derby, WA, to Cape York, Q, s. coastally and on Divide to near Melbourne, Vic., occasional cw. Vic., in forests in Bendigo–Daylesford–Maryborough areas; vagrant Vic. mallee. Status in n. Aust. little known; some appear to be present all year. In se. Aust. it is a regular breeding migrant, arriving Sept.–Oct., departing Feb.–Apr. Common. Also Solomon Is., NG, Indonesia, Malaysia.

366 CHESTNUT-BREASTED CUCKOO *Cuculus castaneiventris* Pl.53

Field marks: 235 mm. Somewhat like a small Fan-tailed Cuckoo (367), but much darker: *slightly glossy slate-blue above, rich-chestnut below, tail-feathers notched white on inner webs* and these not obvious; eye brown, eye-ring and legs yellow. In flight shows pale wingbar. Imm: chestnut-brown above, buff-brown below, without barrings of imm. Fan-tailed. Fairly seldom observed in Aust.; foraging methods typical of cuckoos have been described – watches from low perch, flies to ground for insects or larvae; has been seen to hover low, tail downpointed. Another report described a bird as moving high in tallest rainforest trees.

Voice: Described as a feeble note like trill of Fan-tailed Cuckoo; a single whistling 'chir-rip', uttered infrequently; notes 'like loud honeyeater calls' noted in NG.

Habitat: Tropical rainforests and scrubs; thick scrubby vegetation along watercourses; possibly dense mangroves.

Breeding: Egg and host-species not certainly recorded in Aust.

Range and Status: Coastal e. C. York Pen., s. to Bloomfield R., (Cooktown–Mossman) inland to McIlwraith Ra. Unconfirmed sight-records near Ayr, Q, in mangroves; and 65 km n. of Charters Towers, Q. Uncommon; apparently sedentary. Also NG and Aru Is. Condon 1975. Checkl. Birds Aust., 1, regards it as a non-breeding visitor to Aust.

367 FAN-TAILED CUCKOO *Cuculus pyrrhophanus* Pl.53

Other name: Ash-coloured Cuckoo.

Field marks: 255–270 mm. A slender graceful cuckoo with a fairly long and slim, not obviously fan-like, tail. Slate-grey above and on throat, *tail-feathers prominently notched white on outer webs; breast warm-buff to pale-rufous, under tail-coverts buff.* Eye black, eye-ring yellow, legs olive-yellow. Female: breast duller, may be greyish, pale-rufous on throat. Imm: very different; buff-brown head and body, head and neck streaked dark; rufous-brown wings mottled and barred darker, *underparts finely mottled black, grey and brown in irregular fine-barred pattern.* Singly, pairs; sits quietly on stumps, wires, branches, posture upright, tail downpointed. Flight easy and undulating, note pale wingbar and marking of tail-feathers; tilts tail on alighting.

Similar species: Pallid Cuckoo (364). Brush Cuckoo (365): breast greyer and paler; no conspicuous notching on outer webs of tail-feathers. Chestnut-breasted Cuckoo (366): much deeper tones, no notching on outer webs of tail-feathers; note range.

Voice: Strong, but rather sad, slow downward trill: 'peeeeer', day or night; also a still small voice, somewhat like 'get-woorrk', with rising inflection. Female (?): excited shrill slurred high-pitched 'pree-eee', or 'too-brrreeet'.

Habitat: Somewhat denser wooded habitats than Pallid Cuckoo, from rainforest to river red gum forests, but often seen in open country, paddocks, roadsides, orchards, gardens, mangroves.

Breeding: Egg: mauve-white with reddish or brownish spots forming zone at large end. Typically in domed nest of fairy wren, thornbill or scrubwren but sometimes in open-cup nest of honeyeater, white-eye or flycatcher.

Range and Status: Widespread in e. Aust. from C. York, Q, to Tas. and s. Eyre Pen., SA; also s. WA. Common: sedentary, nomadic or part-migratory. In se. Aust., breeds wetter coastal areas and on Divide, dispersing inland in autumn to n. Vic., interior NSW, lower n. of SA, but many overwinter; apparently a seasonal passage across Bass Strait. In s. WA, occurs coastally from Israelite Bay n. to Murchison R.; reported to move inland in winter from its stronghold in coastal karri forests, returning after breeding; vagrant (? passage migrant) Groote Eylandt, NT, May 1948. Also Fiji, New Caledonia, New Hebrides, Solomon Is., NG and Aru Is.; vagrant NZ.

368 BLACK-EARED CUCKOO *Chrysococcyx osculans* **Pl.54**

Field marks: 190–205 mm. An inconspicuous but distinctive inland cuckoo; pale-brown above with slight olive-bronze sheen; *curving black mark through eye margined white*; *rump whitish*, tail dark-brown with white tips, outer feathers barred white; *breast salmon-pink to fawn-white*. Imm: eyebrow pale, ear-coverts dark-brown; brownish green above, off-white to pale-grey below. Shy and unobtrusive, feeds mostly in low shrubby vegetation but in spring courting males chase noisily with calls and tail-spreading. Flight swift and direct like other bronze-cuckoos; *note pale rump*.

Similar species: Horsfield's Bronze-cuckoo (369), imm. lacks warm tones below and has rufous on base of tail. Some adults are pale and buffish, but note barred breast. Spiny-cheeked Honeyeater (581): pale rump can cause confusion in flight, but plumage generally darker; bill partly reddish.

Voice: A quiet descending mournful 'peeeeeer', singly or repeated; when several display, livelier calls described as 'pee-o-wit-pee-o-weer' repeated.

Habitat: Drier woodlands, scrublands: mallee, mulga, sheoak, broombush, lignum and samphire on saltflats; in inland and n. Aust., thickets on watercourses.

Breeding: Egg: small for size of bird; uniform brownish chocolate; colouring can be rubbed off with wet finger. Laid mostly in domed nests on or near ground; in se. Aust., Speckled Warbler (546) is an important host, as are Fieldwren (545) and Redthroat (544) in s. inland areas and sw. WA; all lay red-brown eggs, apparently imitated by the cuckoo. Also Buff-rumped (563) and Broad-tailed (558) Thornbills; White-browed Scrubwren (540); Mallee Heathwren (543); Variegated Wren (515); occasionally White-browed Babbler (500), Rufous Songlark (510).

Range and Status: Interior of Aust. and (mostly) drier coastal regions. Probably autumn–winter visitor to n. Aust., from Kimberleys to lower C. York Pen., rare top end NT; fairly widespread WA, except forested sw. corner. Regular winter–spring breeding migrant to s. SA, s. to Eyre and Yorke Pens, L. Alexandrina–Naracoorte; mostly spring–summer migrant in subcoastal se. Aust., breeding s. in Vic. to about Edenhope–Grampians You Yangs–Melton–Kinglake–Broken R.–Chiltern and e. in NSW to about Grenfell–Gilgandra, smaller numbers to ACT, to w. of Sydney and lower Hunter R. valley, rare near coast; in Q, occasional e. to Darling Downs; Atherton Tableland–Cairns. Probably nomadic through inland, breeding irregularly in response to suitable conditions. Rare generally; common locally. Also NG, Kai and Aru Is. and s. Moluccas.

369 HORSFIELD'S BRONZE-CUCKOO *Chrysococcyx basalis* **Pl.54**

Other names: Horsfield, Narrow-billed or Rufous-tailed Bronze-cuckoo.

Field marks: 145–170 mm. Dullest bronze-cuckoo: not easily distinguished from races of (370) except by *bright-rufous at bases* of *near-outer tail-feathers*, often hard to see. Note too the dark eye, *whitish eyebrow over strong brownish mark curving from eye down neck*, pale margins to wing-feathers. Head brown, upperparts bronze or purplish brown with green gloss in good light. Some are very pale, head biscuit-coloured, prominent pale margins to wing-feathers. Breast dull-white with bold dull-brown bars not meeting in centre, throat irregularly *streaked, not barred*. Imm: grey-brown above with slight wash of green; *tail as adult*; light-grey below, at first without bars, then shadowy barring on flanks. Singly, pairs or loose winter flocks; unobtrusive except in mating displays and chases. Feeds in foliage, perches watchfully on overhead wires, fences. Flight swift and direct, slightly undulating; on pointed wings; pale wingbar.

Similar species: 'Golden Bronze-cuckoo' – see Shining Bronze-cuckoo (370), race *plagosus*: greener above without pale feather-margins; whiter below, bars bolder, extending up throat; eye pale, less distinctive eyebrow and mark on side of neck, no rufous in tail. Note call. Little Bronze-cuckoo (371): red eye, red or brown eye-ring, white side to face without dark broad mark. Black-eared Cuckoo (368).

Voice: Single long-drawn *descending* 'tseeeeuw', 'prrelll' or 'pir-r-r', repeated persistently, usually from some high point. During mating displays, calls become more animated but lack the piercing staccato character of (370).

Habitat: Open woodlands, scrublands and most open or partly open country; mallee, mulga and saltbush in inland to saltmarsh, samphire or mangroves on coast; roadsides, golf-courses, orchards, gardens. In n. and ne. Aust., rainforests and margins.

Breeding: Egg: whitish, with fine pink or red-brown speckles and spots, usually laid in domed nests in low situations; over 60 host-species recorded, commonest being fairy wrens and warblers, thronbills and Weebill (547); less-often, lays in cup nests of robins (specially Red-capped – 444) also flycatchers, chats, honeyeaters.

Range and Status: Widespread all States including Tas.; mostly in open habitats; coastal islands. Unlike (370) occurs through inland to s. NT and drier coastal areas, breeding when conditions suitable. Regular breeding migrant to s. Aust., arriving July–Sept., departing Dec.–Mar.; many overwinter, specially in warmer sub-inland. Present n. Aust. throughout year, breeding in summer, but scarce coastal areas and C. York; movements uncertain. Part of populations migrant in winter to w. NG, Aru Is., Indonesia and Christmas I., Indian Ocean.

370 SHINING BRONZE-CUCKOO *Chrysococcyx lucidus*   Pl.54

Other names: Broad-billed Cuckoo, Golden Bronze-cuckoo; Green back.

Field marks: 140–165 mm. Nominate race breeds NZ, reaching Aust. as an uncommon migrant. It differs from the Australian race *plagosus* (see below) in *white scalloping on forehead, whiter sides to face; more uniform green upperparts*; breast-bars bronze-green rather than bronze-brown. Imm: no barring on throat or centre of breast. Usually singly in Aust. and inconspicuous because not breeding – see Range and Status. The race *plagosus* 'Golden Bronze-cuckoo', the resident form in Aust.: bright metallic bronze-green above, *without pale feather-margins*; duller and more purplish on head; white below, with bold bronze-brown bars complete across breast *and extending finely to throat*; indefinite dark mark from eye down neck; *eye creamish grey to pale-brown*. Imm: grey-brown above with dull bronze-green sheen; suggestion of dark ear-mark and pale eye-brow as in adult Horsfield's (369); underparts off-white, without bars at first; then shadowy bars on flanks. Singly or pairs; inconspicuous in foliage; noticed more in breeding season when males call from high positions, overhead wires; display and chase. Flight swift, direct and slightly undulating on pointed wings.

Similar species: Horsfield's Bronze-cuckoo (369). Little Bronze-cuckoo (371): greener above, eye red or brown, sparser bars on breast.

Voice: (Race *plagosus*). Somewhat like person whistling dog; clear high-pitched deliberate 'feee, feee, feee, feee', each note rising at end; often ends in descending 'pee-eerr'. Males, displaying and chasing, utter staccato notes.

Habitat: (Race *plagosus*). Tends to less-open habitats than Horsfield's; rainforest, forest, woodlands, scrublands and adjacent open country; golf-courses, orchards, gardens.

Breeding: (Race *plagosus*). Egg: uniform olive-green or bronze-brown; colouring removable with wet finger. Over 60 recorded hosts, mostly builders of domed nests: Yellow-rumped Thornbill (565) is perhaps principal but also Brown Thornbill (557), fairy wrens, fairy warblers, Weebill (547), scrubwrens; less frequently lays in cup-nests of flycatchers, chats, white-eyes, sittellas, honeyeaters.

Range and Status: Nominate race: breeds NZ, migrates in autumn through Lord Howe (? breeds) and Norfolk Is. to Solomon Is and Bismarck Archipelago, irregular to coastal e. Aust. and islands, occasional to s. Vic., as 'wrong-way' spring migrant. Race *plagosus*: e. and sw. Aust.; in Q, from C. York Pen. w. to Mitchell R.–Georgetown–Springsure–Chinchilla; in NSW, inland to Moree–Gilgandra–Griffith; in Vic., fairly widespread *except* for the nw., where rare vagrant; in Tas., fairly widespread in summer to 1000 m, probably more usual than Horsfield's; in SA, from se. coastal areas n. to Bunns Bore, Murray mallee to Blanchetown–Sutherlands (occasional e. along Murray), w. to Mt. Lofty Ras., s. Eyre Pen. and Kangaroo I.; in WA, from Esperance through sw. corner n.

to about Carnarvon. Breeding migrant in s., arriving June–July (s. WA) and Aug.–Sept. (se. Aust.) adults usually leaving by Dec.–Jan., young departing by Mar.; some over-winter. Part-migrant or resident in Q, movements uncertain, mostly in higher parts of Divide in n.; breeds n. to Atherton Tableland. Some winter Bismarck Archipelago, NG, e. Lesser Sunda Is. Fairly common.

371 LITTLE BRONZE-CUCKOO *Chrysococcyx malayanus* Pl.54

Other name: Malay Bronze-cuckoo.
Field marks: 140–152 mm. The Australian race, *minutillus*, of a small bronze-cuckoo widespread from se. Asia. Resembles a small (370), with bronze *dark-bluish green* head contrasting *with paler bronze-green back and wings*; outer tail-feathers heavily spotted black and white, inner webs of next feathers rufous; *face white, usually with white line above eye* and a few white feathers above bill; underparts white, with fine bronze-green bands on throat and breast, broader copper-bronze bars on belly; some may have rufous wash on sides of breast. Male: eye and eye-ring red. Female: eye brown, eye-ring tan. Imm: duller with breastbars less defined; eye brownish. Habits as other bronze-cuckoos.
Similar species: Rufous (372), Horsfield's (369) and Shining (370) Bronze-cuckoos.
Voice: Similar to Rufous Bronze-cuckoo.
Habitat: Rainforest, edges of monsoon forest, open forest, woodland and swamp woodland, often near water; mangroves.
Breeding: Egg: uniform greenish olive. Hosts include White-throated (555) and Large-billed (549) Warblers and Bar-breasted Honeyeater (634).
Range and Status: Widespread from se. Asia to the Australian region, including NG. Its races and precise distribution have still to be clarified. In Aust., apparently distributed along the n. coast and coastal islands from Kimberleys, WA, e. to C. York and s. coastally to the Q–NSW border, with reported breeding near Dorrigo, ne. NSW. Near Brisbane, regarded as migrant, arriving in Sept. (sometimes July), departing Dec.–Jan. In coastal nw. Aust. and NT common, but whether migratory or sedentary is unknown.

372 RUFOUS BRONZE-CUCKOO *Chrysococcyx russatus* Pl.54

Other names: Rufous-breasted or Rufous-throated Bronze Cuckoo.
Field marks: 150 mm. No other bronze-cuckoo has so much rufous in plumage: *rufous bronze-green above with rufous margins to flight-feathers*; tail rufous-green above; outer feathers spotted black-and-white below. No white feathers above bill nor prominent white on face. Whitish below with dark shadowy barring on breast, copper-bronze bars on belly and flanks; *rufous zone across upperbreast or on sides of breast*. Male: *eye and eye-ring red*. Female: eye brown, eye-ring tan. Imm: duller with few or no bars and no rufous on breast; eye pinkish brown. Habits like other bronze-cuckoos.
Similar species: Little Bronze-cuckoo (371). Horsfield's Bronze-cuckoo (369): larger, duller, no rufous on breast.
Voice: Trill of silvery grasshopper-like notes rapidly repeated, 'a bubbling downward trill'. Also a distinctive call, 'chu-chu-chu-chu'; other calls described as canary-like.
Habitat: Open forest and woodlands, tropical scrubs, mangroves; orchards, gardens.
Breeding: Egg: buff-olive, minutely freckled with dark-brown; also described as 'a dark chocolate colour'. Usually laid in suspended domed nest; hosts include Large-billed (549) and Fairy (554) Warblers, Yellow-breasted Sunbird (651).
Range and Status: Coastal ne. Q and coastal islands: from C. York to Bowen; sight-records s. to Yeppoon, Apparently sedentary except in s. Common year-round resident Cairns–Innisfail, Atherton Tableland. Also s. NG. Note: some regard it as a race of *C. malayanus* – see (371).

373 KOEL *Eudynamys scolopacea*   Pl.53

Other names: Black or Flinders' Cuckoo; Cooee or Rainbird; Indian Koel.
Field marks: 410–460 mm. A large cuckoo with distinctive voice, plumage and habits.
Male: glossy blue-black with a *long rounded tail*; *bill blue-grey or horn-coloured*; *eye red*.
Female: cocoa-brown *with white spots and bars*; crown and face black, white stripe
through eye to side of neck, throat chestnut, bill pale olive-green, eye red. Imm: like
female, but with broad pale eyebrow; eye stone-coloured, later orange. Singly, pairs,
occasionally small displaying groups. Feeds in foliage of leafy trees on fruit, specially
native figs; occasionally raids cultivated fruits, berries. Often shy and elusive, taking cover
or flying when approached. But visible, noisy and active during mating period; males
often perch in high exposed positions with constant feverish calling, flight-chases and
display.
Similar species: Satin Bowerbird (694), male. Spangled Drongo (692).
Voice: Very vocal day and night during breeding period, specially in wet; rather silent
after breeding. Males utter repeated far-carrying 'kooeel'; also brisk rising 'quoy-quoy-
quoy-quoy', falsetto 'quodel-quodel-quodel' or slightly mad, rising 'weir-weir-weir-
weir!' Female: shrill four-note brassy piping.
Habitat: Rainforest, open forest; tall leafy trees on fringes of rainforest or woodland
along streams or in stands in farmland, parks and streets.
Breeding: Egg: salmon-pink, marbled reddish and violet-grey specially at large end; egg-
mimicry has been suggested. Hosts include Noisy (585) and Little (586) Friarbirds, Blue-
faced Honeyeater (588), White-rumped Miner (591), Olive-backed Oriole (689), Paradise
Riflebird (701), Magpie Lark (710).
Range and Status: Regular summer breeding migrant to n. and e. Aust. and coastal
islands, from Kimberleys, WA, to s. coast, NSW; inland to Larrimah, NT; Mt. Isa–
Hughenden–Chinchilla, Q; mostly coastwards of Divide in NSW; rare s. of Illawarra
district; vagrant ACT, Kosciusko region, NSW, Mallacoota, Vic., and (once) 160 km e.
of Perth, WA. Arrives Aug.–Sept., departs Apr.–May; in NSW the usual months are
Sept.–Mar. Common coastal lowlands, much less common inland and on highlands.
Winters NG, Aru Is.; other races range to India and s. China.

374 CHANNEL-BILLED CUCKOO *Scythrops novaehollandiae*   Pl.84

Other names: Flood, Rain or Stormbird; Giant or Storm Cuckoo; Fig Hawk, Hornbill,
Channel-bill, Toucan.
Field marks: 580–650 mm. An unmistakable large grey bird with a *conspicuous curved
straw-coloured bill*; note red bare skin round eye; *tail long with a terminal black band
tipped white*. Singly, pairs or small flocks; shy, generally keeps to heads of large trees,
where it feeds on native figs and other fruit; active morning and evening, also after dark.
Much harrassed by other birds; usually first noted by extraordinary call. Flight strong
and hawklike, often high, somewhat pointed wings and long tail prominent.
Voice: Awful: a raucous, deliberately-spaced shout of 'oik', 'awk' or 'wark', repeated,
rising slightly. Uttered flying or perched, often at night.
Habitat: Open forests, woodlands, swamp woodlands and scrublands, sometimes
rainforest.
Breeding: Eggs: dull-white to buff or stone-coloured, blotched reddish or purplish
brown, sometimes as if beneath the surface. Unlike other Australian cuckoos, it may lay
two or more eggs in one nest; hosts include Pied Currawong (713), Australian Magpie
(720) or Torresian Crow (725).
Range and Status: Regular breeding migrant to n. and e. Aust. and coastal islands: from
Kimberleys to area of Sydney, NSW, arriving Aug.–Sept., departing Mar.–Apr., earlier
(Dec.–Feb.) in NSW. Mostly coastal in Kimberleys and top end NT, but extends nearly
throughout Q, occasional on inland drainages to far ne. SA (Coopers Creek and Diamantina R., L. Eyre basin); in NSW, inland to Moree–Warrumbungles–Barellan–

Mudgee. Uncommon nw. Aust., common more humid parts Q and ne. NSW; vagrant s. coast NSW, ACT, far e. and c. Vic. (Bendigo) and Tas. Winters Bismarck Archipelago, NG and parts of Indonesia.

375 PHEASANT COUCAL *Centropus phasianinus*   Pl.17

Other names: Swamp Pheasant or Cuckoo, Coucal, North-west Pheasant.

Field marks: 510–660 mm. A skulking long-tailed short-legged pheasant-like bird, probably more often heard than seen. Breeding plumage: *head, body and tail blackish, wings and back chestnut.* Non-breeding: *rufous above, head and underparts yellow-buff.* The plumage is intricately streaked and patterned, shafts of feathers on head and body glossy black in breeding plumage, straw-coloured in non-breeding. Bill black, deep, strongly-curved, eye red. Female slightly larger than male; voice deeper. Imm: fawner; bill brown, paler below; eye brown. Singly or pairs; sits watchfully and rather ludicrously in heads of small leafy trees and bushes, runs heavily across roads and clearings or threads through rank grass; when flushed, flies heavily, flopping into cover. Sometimes takes eggs or nestlings and is frequently mobbed by other birds.

Similar species: Really none, but see Ring-necked Pheasant (165) and lyrebirds (412–3). Note ranges.

Voice: Frequently heard in subtropical and tropical coastal Aust. – a deep, hollow '*coop*-coop-coop-coop-coop-coop', slow at first, accelerating and descending like liquid glugging from a bottle; also harsh, though not loud, scolding notes.

Habitat: Rank growth in and round swamps, wet heathlands, margins of timber; regrowth in clearings; vegetation along watercourses; lantana thickets, pandanus clumps, mangrove-fringes, sugar-cane, overgrown roadsides, gardens; occasional in brigalow-scrub.

Breeding: Builds its own nest; saucer-shaped; of grass lined with leaves; blades and stems drawn together overhead to form canopy, which may be open at either end; usually in rank tussock, sometimes in low bush, clump of pandanus, stool of sugar-cane, citrus tree in orchard up to 2 m from ground. Eggs: 3–5, occasionally 7; dirty white, limy; may be stained brownish or scratched. The chicks have a strange long white hairlike covering at first, prolongations of horny sheaths covering the developing feathers.

Range and Status: Mostly coastal n. and e. Aust. and coastal islands: from Minilya R., WA, Kimberleys, top end NT s. to Mataranka–Macarthur R.; n. and e. Q, inland to Carnarvon Ras.–Mitchell–Warwick; coastal NSW s. to about Conjola (48 km s. of Nowra); occasional inland. Common to fairly common; mostly sedentary. Also NG.

Owls   Families *Strigidae* and *Tytonidae*

Owls are divided into two world-wide families, each poorly represented in Aust. The hawk owls *Strigidae* have large forward-directed eyes, usually bright-yellow. The barn owls *Tytonidae* have dark eyes surrounded by a large heart-shaped facial disc of partly erectile feathers, which probably assists the highly developed hearing. They hunt by ear as much as by sight and a Barn Owl (380) has been shown capable of capturing a mouse moving on dry leaves in a totally dark room. In keeping with these sensory developments, most owls have comparatively larger more mobile heads than hawks, mounted on remarkably flexible necks. Their legs are usually long and typically wholly or partly feathered; the feet are usually powerful, the outer toe reversible and usually directed sideways. Barn owls only, have pectinations on the middle claw of each foot, probably to aid grooming. The renowned silence of flight of owls is enhanced by soft plumage and by modification of the outer web of the outer flight-feathers to a short, comb-like ridge that helps silence the flow of air over the wingtips. Most Australian owls are wholly nocturnal, roosting by day in tree hollows or dense foliage, but Barking Owl (379) is sometimes vocal and active by day.

Food: Entirely animal: mammals, including possums, rabbits, rodents; also birds, reptiles, insects.
Range: Worldwide, except Antarctica.
Number of species: World: Strigidae 126; Tytonidae 10. Aust.: Strigidae 4; Tytonidae 4.

376 RUFOUS OWL *Ninox rufa*   Pl.55

Field marks: 440–510 mm. A large richly coloured owl with rather flat crown; upperparts dark rufous-brown with indistinct paler barrings; underparts *orange-buff with close dense fine light-brown horizontal bars;* tail barred below; eyes greenish yellow, feet dull-yellow. Female smaller and darker. By day perches singly or in pairs in dense foliage of tree in rainforest or swamp-woodland; habits little known.
Voice: Slow 'woo-hoo!' like Powerful Owl (377) but softer and not so far-carrying; occasional sharp single note.
Habitat: Tropical rainforest and scrub; swamp woodlands.
Breeding: Nest: on debris in hollow tree. Eggs: 2–3; white, glossy.
Range and Status: N. and ne. Aust.: broken distribution in suitable habitat: n. Kimberleys, WA; top end, NT; n. and e. Q: Gulf Coast of C. York Pen. and e. coast from Claudie R. s. to near Rockhampton, inland to Atherton Tableland–upper Burdekin R.; local, generally uncommon. Also NG, Aru Is.

377 POWERFUL OWL *Ninox strenua*   Pl.55

Other names: Eagle Owl, Great Scrub Owl.
Field marks: 600–660 mm. A very large owl with golden eyes. Dark grey-brown above, *mottled and barred whitish; white below with bold grey-brown V-barring;* legs feathered to ankle, powerful feet dull-yellow. Male larger than female. Imm: back and wings paler, more heavily barred white; face white with dark eye-patches; whitish below with sparse fine dark streaks, faint barring on flanks. Lives permanently in pairs (J. Calaby). By day roosts singly, in pairs or family groups of 3 or 4; in foliage or on branch of fairly open tree in forest or woodland, often clutching part-eaten remains of prey. Several roosting sites are used and may be occupied intermittently for many years. Easily approached by day; shy and difficult to observe by night.
Similar species: Barking Owl (379).
Voice: An impressive low slow, far-carrying 'whoo-hooo'.
Habitat: Dense mountain gullies; coastal forests and woodlands; coastal scrubs, pine plantations.
Breeding: Nest: on decayed debris; in large hollow limb or trunk 10–20 m or more high. Eggs: 1–2; dull white oval.
Range and Status: Coastal ranges and forests of e. and se. Aust. from Dawson R., Q, to sw. Vic. and nearby se. SA (Mt. Burr). Mostly within 200 km of coast; inland to Chinchilla, Q; Tenterfield, (?) Pilliga scrub–Brindabella Ra., NSW; in Vic., e. highlands and inland in w. to about Mt. Alexander–Pyrenees–Grampians. Uncommon.

378 BOOBOOK OWL *Ninox novaeseelandiae*   Pl.55

Other names: Mopoke, Morepork; Northern or Red Boobook Owl; Cuckoo, Marbled or Spotted Owl; Tasmanian Spotted Owl.
Field marks: 300–360 mm. A small brown owl that seems to wear *large pale-rimmed goggles bordering the dark patch round each eye;* irregular large pale spots on wings; underparts reddish brown *with thick brown and white streaks or heavy irregular white mottling;* legs closely feathered. Female slightly larger and darker. Considerable colour variation; race *ocellata* widespread in n., inland and w. Aust. (except sw. Aust.) mostly very pale; race *lurida* of humid coastal ne. Q: dark reddish-brown. Most mainland races have *grey-green eyes,* but eyes of the small dark Tasmanian race *leucopsis* are *yellow.* This

form may migrate across Bass Strait in winter. Imm: eyes brown. Singly, pairs, family parties; roosts by day in thick foliage; when disturbed, slips silently out, often mobbed by small birds. At dusk sits watchfully on exposed branches, fences, telephone poles; from time to time flies up to capture flying insects, as it does under street-lights at night; looks dark and deceptively large in flight.

Similar species: Barking Owl (379): larger, greyer, brilliant-yellow eyes; grey to rufous streaks on whitish breast.

Voice: Well-known: falsetto 'boo-book' or 'morepork', repeated at intervals; also a rarely heard falsetto 'yo yo yo yo'; near nest, a drawn-out rising cat-like 'brrrwow' and monotonously repeated low 'mor-mor-mor'.

Habitat: Varied: rainforests to mallee and mulga scrubs to margins of almost treeless plains; woodlands, lightly timbered farming country; pine forests, orchards, parks, gardens, streets.

Breeding: Nest: on decayed debris; in tree-hollow. Eggs: 2–3; white, rounded.

Range and Status: Widespread in a number of well-marked races in Aust., islands and Tas. Generally common; part-migratory or nomadic; scarcer inland, but sometimes in numbers in cereal-growing areas during mouse-plagues. Also e. Lesser Sunda Is., including Timor, s. NG, Norfolk and Lord Howe Is; NZ.

379 BARKING OWL *Ninox connivens*   Pl.55

Other names: Winking Owl.

Field marks: 380–430 mm. A medium-sized robust owl; *smoky brown above with large white spots on wings*; *whitish below with dark-grey to rusty streaks*; legs feathered, feet powerful. Male much larger than female. Typically roosts by day in pairs in leafy trees, sometimes in exposed position; when approached instantly alert with head snapping in direction of intruder; note piercing yellow eyes. At rest, often clutches remains of prey. At times abroad before dark.

Similar species: Powerful Owl (377): much larger, head relatively smaller, underparts with bold V-bars. Boobook Owl (378).

Voice: Unmistakable: quick dog-like 'wook-wook', repeated; soft at first, becoming explosive and far-carrying; when heard close, preceded by a growl; sometimes in duet, male's deeper. Also, occasionally, a drawn-out wavering sobbing scream, usually during the winter breeding season.

Habitat: Open forests, woodlands, dense scrubs; foothills and timber along watercourses, often those penetrating otherwise open country; swamp woodlands.

Breeding: Nest: on decayed debris; in tree-hollow, usually from few to 10 m or more high. Eggs: 2–3; dull-white, roundish.

Range and status: Mainland Aust. and some coastal islands in n.: in WA, the sw. corner and n. from Ashburton R., through Pilbara district and Kimberleys; top end NT s. to Roper and upper Macarthur Rs.; fairly widespread Q; in NSW, fairly widespread *except* far-nw.; rare e. of Divide; in Vic., mostly n. of Divide; in SA mostly e. of Cooper's Ck.– Spencer Gulf. Apparently absent or very rare in arid regions or those without large trees. Nowhere common except perhaps parts of Q and in Kimberleys, WA. Also NG and Moluccas.

380 BARN OWL *Tyto alba*   Pl.55

Other names: Delicate, Lesser Masked, Screech or White Owl.

Field marks: 300–360 mm. *The 'white owl', made distinctive by its large facial disc*; plumage of upperparts beautifully blended grey, brownish grey, buff-grey or yellow-buff with sparse black and white spots; *pure-white below* with sparse dark spots; legs slender, sparsely feathered white to above 'ankle'. Female slightly larger. Imm: heavier spotting on breast. Sometimes flushed by day from hollow tree or dense foliage, often then harried by other birds; looks very white and long-winged, with large head and short tail. At night, floats like ghost in headlight-beams; occasionally hovers or sits white and upright on roadside fence-posts.

Similar species: Pale n. form of Masked Owl (381): note fully-feathered legs, much heavier feet and talons. Grass Owl (382).

Voice: Hoarse thin wavering reedy screech: 'sk-air!' or 'skee-air!'; in flight and perched.

Habitat: Open forests and woodlands, grasslands with stands of timber; offshore rocks, islets and islands; farmlands, suburbs, cities; occasionally roosts or nests in buildings; drive-in cinema screens; in treeless areas, e.g. Nullarbor Plain and rocky offshore islands, roosts and/or nests in caves, ledges.

Breeding: Nest: on decayed debris in hollow tree-trunk; carpeted with accumulated remains of prey. Eggs: 3–4, occasionally 5 or 6; white, rounded.

Range and Status: Widespread mainland Aust. and some coastal islands; rare Tas. Local populations increase rapidly in response to upsurges of mice and native rodents, specially autumn–winter and as quickly decline. In s. Aust. during colder months many are found dead, apparently undamaged, probably starving. Nearly cosmopolitan; the Australian race is *delicatula*.

381 MASKED OWL *Tyto novaehollandiae*   Pl.55

Other names: Tasmanian Masked Owl; Cave, Chestnut-faced or Maw-faced Owl.

Field marks: 330–500 mm. The largest *Tyto*; distinguished from Barn Owl (380) by size, *usually darker upperparts and facial disc, with chestnut shading round eyes; fully feathered legs and more powerful feet.* Colour very variable: females in s. Aust. and Tas. have facial disc buffish to chestnut, outlined black; upperparts blackish brown to light chestnut-brown, with silver-white freckling; underparts pale-chestnut to rufous, spotted brown. Male: much smaller and paler, upperparts yellow-brown; underparts yellow-buff to fawn-white. In n. and nw. Aust. plumage often almost as pale as Barn Owl. Shy and secretive; roosts by day in tree-hollows, thick foliage; hunts by night in woodlands and clearings. The race *troughtoni* roosts and nests in caves and blow-holes of Nullarbor Plain. Cave-roosting also reported elsewhere.

Similar species: Barn Owl (380).

Voice: Seldom heard; loud version of Barn Owl: drawn-out rasping 'cush-cush-sh-sh' or 'quair-sh-sh-sh'.

Habitat: Forests, open woodlands, adjacent cleared country; timbered watercourses; underground caves of Nullarbor Plain.

Breeding: Nest: on decayed debris and discarded remains of prey; in hollow trunk of eucalypt 12–20 m high or on bare sand or limestone of underground caves. Eggs: 2–3; dull-white, elongated.

Range and Status: Aust., except arid interior; widespread but generally very scarce *except* in Tas., where fairly common. Present in caves on Nullarbor Plain. Also s. NG, Manus I. and some e. Indonesian islands.

382 GRASS OWL *Tyto longimembris*   Pl.55

Field marks: 330–380 mm. A seldom-seen ground-dwelling owl, usually darker than Barn Owl (380) and with *noticeably longer legs* poorly covered with short sparse feathers, lower part of 'shin' bare. Upperparts *rich yellow-buff, heavily marbled blue-black or dark-grey* with fine silvery spots; large triangular facial disc *buffish; underparts pale orange-buff to dull-white*, with sparse dark spots. Rests by day in 'form' – a trampled platform in a large tussock or other heavy growth, often with well-used approach-paths or over shallow water. When disturbed, bursts out, flies rather slowly, revealing *long legs with feet extending beyond tail* (in Barn Owl, only the toes protrude); on wing looks *dark and large-headed* and by one report, 'T-shaped'; another observer considers the dark wingtip, contrasting with rich-buff centre-patch, to be diagnostic. May sail on still wings before dropping precipituously back into cover. (Take care – Barn Owls also roost in long grass, far from timber). Like Barn Owl, occasionally caught in headlights on roadside fence-posts; posture tall and upright.

Voice: Like Barn Owl; has also been heard to utter a 'thin quavery little whistle'.

Habitat: Tall grass-tussocks in extensive swampy areas; grassy plains; swampy heaths; clumps of cane-grass or lignum on floodplains, sedges and dense stands of cumbungi on bore-drains.

Breeding: Nest: in trodden-down grass; usually in cover of substantial tussocks and approached by passages or runs. Eggs: 4–6; pure-white, smooth, oval or elongate.

Range and Status: Sparse, generally very rare but status may be obscured by patchiness of suitable habitat, difficulty of observation, and the bird's (probably) nomadic, irruptive economy, which like that of the Barn Owl is probably linked with incidence of rodents. Recorded at least once all mainland States, probably most-frequently in coastal e. Q. Recent records: In NT, Humpty Doo, Feb. 1968. In Q, Innisfail, 1966 (breeding); Coopers Creek, July 1974; Birdsville, Aug. 1974; Noosa Plains (Cooloola), Aug. 1975. In NSW, Tenterfield, Feb. 1963; near lower Clarence R., Sept. 1964–65; Harrington, Apr. 1973 (breeding). In SA, Goyders Lagoon, far-ne., Aug. 1975; Sept.–Nov. 1976; sight-records, specimens; locally common following plague of Long-haired Rats, *R. villosissimus*. Has been regarded as a n. and e. coastal species but recent inland observations (and Storr, 1973) suggest that grasslands of ne. NT–nw. Q, Channel Country in sw. Q, and L. Eyre Basin, ne. SA, may be a stronghold. Also Fiji, New Caledonia, NG to se. Asia, se. China, India. A similar, possibly conspecific, form in Africa.

383 SOOTY OWL *Tyto tenebricosa*   **Pl.55**

Other names: Black or Dusky Barn Owl.

Field marks: 350–450 mm. A robust *short-tailed, sooty grey owl with oval white facial disc outlined in black and silver; eyes black, very large*; upperparts sooty, with silvery white spots, underparts whitish, heavily mottled dark-grey, sparse bars lower; legs sparsely feathered whitish, feet very powerful. Female larger than male. Secretive; roosts by day in hollow of tall forest tree or in heavy vegetation. When disturbed, may blunder out with heavy wingbeats or remain quiet and seemingly drowsy.

Voice: Weird far-carrying descending strident or mellow whistle, like falling bomb, uttered at intervals; other very loud calls; also described are duets and part-duets in a series of down-rolling cricket-like chirruping trills.

Habitat: Dense tropical, subtropical and temperate rain-forests and fern-gullies.

Breeding: Nest: on decayed debris; in hollow trunk of eucalypt; one of few recorded nests was over 30 m high. Eggs: 1–2; white, oval.

Range and Status: Coastal e. Aust.: nominate race mostly on and e. of Divide from Dandenong Ras., e. of Melbourne, to extreme se. Q, w. to Warwick, n. to near Brisbane; (?) vagrant, Flinders I., Bass Strait. The small, heavily spotted n. race *multipunctata* is apparently isolated in ne. Q from Mt. Spec NP, near Townsville, to near Cooktown. Perhaps commoner than records suggest, but remains one of our least-known birds of prey. Also NG and Jobi I.

Frogmouths Family *Podargidae*

Often mistaken for owls, frogmouths have small, weak feet and are probably aberrant nightjars. They are named for their very broad, slightly hooked bills used to seize moving prey on ground or branches at night, in a hunting technique similar to that of kooka-burras. At night, when plumage is relaxed, they look large, with big, round red or yellow eyes. By day, there is a remarkable change – specially when approached. The plumage slims, the bill is raised skywards and the birds assume a slim stick-like immobility while following your movements with the eyes closed to slits and the head moving imperceptably. Intricately patterned plumage, tufts of coarse plumes over the bill and jagged tips to the tail make the bird look like dead wood. Frogmouths have no preen-gland but produce powder-down in two patches under the rump-feathers; this is spread through the plumage as a feather-dressing. There is still doubt about the taxonomic status of several Australian forms. The tendency to produce rufous (erythristic) plumage phases adds confusion.

Food: Chiefly insects, but also vertebrates small enough to be swallowed whole, e.g. mice, lizards.

Range: Oriental and Australasian regions.

Number of species: World 12; Aust. 3.

384   TAWNY FROGMOUTH   *Podargus strigoides*   Pl.56

Other names: Mopoke, Morepork, Freckled Frogmouth, Night Hawk, Podargus, Tawny-shouldered Frogmouth.

Field marks: 330–470 mm. A strange large night-bird with a very broad bill and *large yellow eyes*. Plumage mostly grey, *heavily and intricately mottled and marbled paler-grey or brownish tawny and with dark streaks*; *often tawny to rufous on shoulders, wings and back*; paler below, finely dark-streaked. Varies in size and colour; there is an uncommon rich-rusty phase. Very small forms in coastal n. Aust. and islands are either pale-grey or rust-red with very fine moth-like markings, and fine dark streaks. Singly, pairs or family parties of 3 or 4; usually roosts branch-like by day; sometimes stumplike on ground. Startled, flies strongly but silently on downcurved wings. Active at dusk; sits on open branches, fence-posts, flying silently to capture moving food. Often takes prey from road-surfaces, looking very large and pale in headlights; many are killed by traffic.

Similar species: Papuan Frogmouth (385), grey phase: eye red, tail longer. Marbled Frogmouth (386): generally browner and more mottled; greater contrast between dark above and pale below; eye orange-yellow; note range.

Voice: Low repeated 'oom-oom-oom-oom', slow or quite rapid and repeated up to 40 times; seems to have no clear beginning or end, difficult to locate.

Habitat: Timbered country–heavy forests to open woodlands; in inland, timber along watercourses or in hills; mallee, belar, coastal tea-tree and banksia-scrubs; roadsides, golf-courses, suburban and city parks; gardens.

Breeding: Nest: shallow flimsy platform; of small sticks sparsely lined with leaves; on horizontal fork 5–10 m high; sometimes uses old nests of other species, e.g. White-winged Chough (712) or Australian Magpie (720). When disturbed, sitting bird adopts 'broken-branch' posture. Eggs: 2; white, rounded.

Range and Status: Aust., coastal islands and Tas.; widespread and common in better watered regions, sparse in arid regions; mostly sedentary, possibly migratory in Q.

385   PAPUAN FROGMOUTH   *Podargus papuensis*   Pl.56

Other names: Large or Plumed Frogmouth.

Field marks: 450–580 mm. Largest Australian frogmouth: *eye red, tail long and pointed or mitre-shaped*. Dark form: richly mottled and marbled tawny and grey above, with underlying whitish and blackish barrings, overlaid with black streaks, *may have buffish bar along shoulder*; forehead, sides of face and throat greyish, finely streaked black; greyer below than above. Grey form: few rich-rufous or tawny shades. Probably similar in habits to Tawny Frogmouth (384).

Similar species: Tawny (384) and Marbled (386) Frogmouths.

Voice: Repeated 'oom' like Tawny Frogmouth; also weird rapid ghostly laugh, 'hoo-hoo-hoo'.

Habitat: Open eucalypt woodlands, lowland rainforest scrubs, heavy vegetation along watercourses, swamp woodlands, mangroves.

Breeding: Nest: scanty; of sticks; on horizontal fork of tree. Eggs: 1–2; white, variable.

Range and Status: In Aust., confined to ne. Q, and some islands, from C. York s. on Gulf coast to Staaten R.; s. on e. coast to Mt. Spec NP, near Townsville. Common in n., scarce, mostly coastal, s. of Cooktown. Also NG, Aru and other islands.

386 MARBLED FROGMOUTH *Podargus ocellatus* Pl.56

Other name: Plumed Frogmouth.

Field marks: 330–380 mm. Slender and long-tailed, *eye orange-yellow*. Male: *brownish* above, finely mottled grey and buff, *indistinct buff eyebrow and wingbar*; *flight-feathers barred buff and rufous*; *longish pointed tail light-brown and rufous, banded grey*; underparts whitish, finely freckled brown, streaked darker, specially in line down side of neck. Female: some are darker and more rufous; brown below, blotched buff-white; a series of squarish buff-white blotches on side of neck. *Note*: the little-known 'Plumed Frogmouth' of rainforest scrubs of coastal se. Q and ne. NSW s. to Manning R., is now regarded as a race, *plumiferus*, of this species. It has large black-and-white banded tufts of plumes over bill. Variable; some redder than others, markings on underparts more distinct, less chestnut.

Similar species: Tawny Frogmouth (384): greyer, eye yellow. Papuan Frogmouth (385): larger, more uniformly coloured; eye, red.

Voice: Reported to be a monotonous 'kooloo-kooloo-kooloo'.

Habitat: Rainforests and vine-scrubs.

Breeding: Nest: flat platform; of twigs; on branch of tree in thick scrub. Eggs: 2; white, rounded.

Range and Status: In Aust., nominate race ranges from n. C. York Pen. s. to Claudie R. on e. coast and possibly Ducie R. on w. Extralimital sight records: Morehead R., near Princess Charlotte Bay, and (?) Yungaburra. The race *plumiferus* perhaps confined to ne. NSW and nearby se. Q. Other races occur from Solomon Is. to NG and some e. Lesser Sunda Is.

Owlet-nightjars Family *Aegothelidae*

Small night-birds with characters of both nightjars and frogmouths. The tiny broad bill is surrounded by prominent bristles, the large eyes are forwardly directed and the head has almost owl-like mobility; the feet are rather feeble. Unlike frogmouths, owlet-nightjars have a preen-gland. The single Australian species lays small white frogmouth-like eggs. It nests and roosts by day in tree-hollows.

Food: Mostly insects.

Range: Australasian region only: including NG, Moluccas, New Caledonia.

Number of species: World 8; Aust. 1.

387 OWLET-NIGHTJAR *Aegotheles cristatus* Pl.56

Other names: Fairy, Little or Moth Owl, Banded Goatsucker, Crested Owlet-nightjar.

Field marks: 205–240 mm. Like a miniature owl except for the weak pink feet. Bill very short and broad; eyes large, blackish brown. Plumage moth-like; dark-grey, freckled and barred light-brown and buff. Note head-marking: *dark crescent starts above eye, goes back and returns under eye*, encircling a grey, buff or rufous ear-patch; *twin dark and buffish (or rufous) collars on hindneck*. Inland and n. forms more reddish brown. Imm: more buff or rufous. The distinctive n. race *leucogaster* has white underparts. Roosts by day in hollow limbs or spouts; occasionally suns itself in entrance. Emerges at dusk, occasionally by day, to take insects in flight, on branches or ground; flight swift silent and direct. Sits crossways on limbs; posture more upright than a true nightjar; its dark forward-directed eyes do not glow in spotlight.

Voice: A very common night-sound: high-pitched slightly weird 'chirr chirr', repeated

several times, uttered perched, in flight or from roosting hollow by day.
Habitat: Forests, woodlands and scrublands from wetter coastal areas to dry inland; favours drier, more open mature forests, taller scrublands, e.g. mallee; timber along inland watercourses.
Breeding: Nest: on lining of *Eucalyptus* leaves plucked green, in tree-hollow or spout. often near ground; sometimes in hollow stump or fence-post. Eggs: 3–4; white, rounded.
Range and Status: Widespread and fairly common in suitable habitat throughout Aust. and Tas. and on timbered coastal islands. The race *leucogaster* is found in n. Aust. from Kimberleys, WA, to C. York Pen., Q. Also w. NG.

Nightjars   Family *Caprimulgidae*

Nocturnal insectivorous birds with large eyes, short bills, huge gapes, long wings and ample tails. Their legs are very short and the feet tiny; the middle toe has a comb-like process for grooming. The plumage is beautifully patterned like dead leaves with black, grey, chestnut, buff, cream and white. Nightjars usually nest and roost by day sitting low on ground among leaf debris with the large dark eye closed to a slit. They are very difficult to see and often wait until almost underfoot before taking flight with startling suddenness, looking dark and long-winged. They often settle lengthwise along open branches. They are mostly seen hawking for insects at dusk over treetops, clearings, roads or waterways; the characteristic flight is wheeling and very graceful, with unusual stiff-stroking flicks and glides on raised wings. In headlights, their eyes, unlike those of Owlet-nightjar (387), reflect brilliantly, usually blazing pink. Their calls are unusual and most species are probably heard more than seen.
Food: Mostly flying insects.
Range: Almost worldwide, except for far-n. Eurasia and N. America, s. S. America, NZ and oceanic islands.
Number of species: World 72; Aust. 3.

388   WHITE-THROATED NIGHTJAR   *Caprimulgus mystacalis*   Pl.56

Other names: Fern or Laughing Owl, Moth or Night Hawk.
Field marks: 330–345 mm. Largest and darkest nightjar; *no white on tail and only small white mark on flight-feathers* (third or fourth primaries). White on throat forms two crescents no more conspicuous than in other species. Imm: mottled reddish brown and black. Singly or pairs; looks very dark in flight, white on wing not conspicuous; call distinctive.
Similar species: Spotted Nightjar (389): richer-rufous above, buff spots on wings; in flight white patch on wingtips; call differs. Note range. White-tailed Nightjar (390): conspicuous white patch on wingtips, white corners to tail; call differs.
Voice: A weird laugh, starting with a loud deep 'kook', accelerating and becoming higher-pitched; also described as three or four mellow repeated upscale whistles, followed by a rapid chuckle.
Habitat: Forests and woodlands with bare ground strewn with leaves, rocks and branches, mostly on ridges and slopes; woodlands with understorey of bracken or heath; wallum country on ce. coast.
Breeding: Egg: 1; dark-cream, sparsely blotched and spotted with dark-purplish brown or light-brown, irregular black spots mostly at large end and underlying lines of light-grey; laid on leaf-litter or bare ground.
Range and Status: E. Aust.: from Cairns, Q. to Otway Ras., Vic.; mostly coastal but inland to lower Dawson R.–Warwick, Q; Inverell–Mudgee–ACT and Mt. Kosciusko, NSW; Jamieson–Nagambie–Toolern Vale, Vic. Moderately common in mid-part of range; scarce Vic. and n. of Tropic; probably migratory. Condon, 1975. Checkl. Birds

Aust., 1. states: 'Migrates, in winter and spring, to e. and c. NG w. to Fly and n. to Idenburg R.' Another race in NG and Solomon Is.

389 SPOTTED NIGHTJAR *Caprimulgus guttatus* Pl.56

Field marks: 290–330 mm. Our most widespread nightjar, typical of drier country: *more buff or rufous than others*, specially on hindneck and underparts. Note *cream-buff spots and white patch on wings*; *no white on tail*. Imm: more rufous, with unusual rusty pink tone. Singly or pairs; roosts nearly invisibly on ground by day. Emerges at dusk to hawk for insects over treetops and along clearings and roads; in headlights, note the blazing pink eyes and *glistening small white patch on wingtips*.

Similar species: White-throated Nightjar (388): darker, little white on wing, none in tail. White-tailed Nightjar (390): greyer, conspicuous white corners to tail. Note ranges.

Voice: Weird 'caw-caw-caw-gobble-gobble-gobble' or 'wokka-wokka-chokka-chokka-chooka-chooka'; sometimes by day.

Habitat: Drier eucalypt woodlands mostly on ridges; mallee, mulga or pine scrubs, specially where ground strewn with leaves, rocks, branches.

Breeding: Egg: 1; light greenish cream to pale-green when fresh, spotted and dotted black and grey-brown to reddish purple, some markings as if below surface; on ground on leaf-litter.

Range and Status: Mainland Aust.; widespread in drier habitats mostly w. of Divide but reaching coast Cooktown–Townsville and possibly Hinchinbrook I., ne. Q. In s. Q, e. to lower Dawson R.; in NSW e. to Inverell–Wellington–Cowra; in Vic., s. to Benalla–L. Eppalock–Edenhope (occasional You Yangs, Portland); in SA, s. to Penola–Chauncey's Line–Kangaroo I. Throughout WA, commoner in n.; coastal islands nw. Aust. Fairly common in suitable habitat. Possibly migratory within Aust. and to Aru Is.

390 WHITE-TAILED NIGHTJAR *Caprimulgus macrurus* Pl.56

Other names: Large-tailed Nightjar; Axe, Carpenter or Hammerbird.

Field marks: 260–280 mm. The only Australian nightjar with *white on both wing and corners of tail*; *from below, lower half of tail wholly white*. Note bands of buff spots across closed wings. Rests on ground by day, often in shade of large tree, or low branch. At night sits on ground, fence-posts or open branches, from time to time sallying into air after insects, announcing its presence by repeatedly calling.

Similar species: Other nightjars, (388–9) also Owlet-nightjar (387).

Voice: An unbirdlike monotonous succession of 4–50 dull chopping notes, like an axe struck against a hollow log; mostly heard in summer, a familiar sound in n. Aust.; deep froglike croaking note when disturbed.

Habitat: Rainforest scrubs with open leafy ground beneath; tropical forests and woodlands, drier parts of mangrove areas; watercourse vegetation; tropical plantations, gardens.

Breeding: Eggs: 2; light to rich-cream or pinkish stone-coloured clouded with fleecy markings of pale-slaty lilac as if beneath surface; laid on leaf-litter on ground.

Range and Status: N. and ne. Aust. and coastal islands: top end NT, from Pt. Keats n. to Melville I. and e. to Gove Pen., Groote Eylandt and Pellew Is.; n. and e. Q, from Normanton to C. York, s. to Gin Gin and Fraser I., mostly coastal and forested coastal islands but inland to Mt. Surprise, near Georgetown. Common in n., scarce in highlands; patchy s. of Ingham. Also New Britain to NG, Indonesia to se. Asia, to sw. China, w. Pakistan.

Swifts   Family *Apodidae*

The fastest and most aerial birds, somewhat like swallows, but flight much swifter, direct and sustained, on swept bladelike wings. Plumage generally sombre, dull blackish to glossy blue-black, with diagnostic paler patches on back, rump, throat or under tail-coverts. The wings are very long, tapering and backswept, shape of tail varies from deeply forked to short and square with feather-shafts extending as short spines. The small feet have strong sharp curved claws; in some species, all four toes are directed forwards to facilitate clinging to vertical surfaces; in some, the short, spine-tipped tail acts as a prop. True swifts cannot perch and usually need a vertical drop to reach flying speed. These species roost and nest on walls of cliffs, caves, tree-trunks, in hollow trees or on buildings. Some species build tiny saucer-like nests chiefly of hardened saliva, reinforced with fine twigs or similar material and attached to the wall of a cave, interior of a hollow tree, chimney or other part of a building. Such nests typically contain a single egg; in Borneo, Malaysia and elsewhere in se. Asia they provide the raw material of bird's-nest soup. Swifts copulate on the wing and at the nest and drink in flight from surface of rivers, lakes and reservoirs. Some species probably sleep on wing. Swifts form small to large, sometimes enormous, open flocks, feeding on flying insects, rising under some conditions to thousands of metres. Depending on circumstances, flight is slow and wheeling or very fast and direct with downward raking dashes and dives at speeds estimated to exceed 150 kph, with a clearly audible swish as they pass. After arrival in Aust. on summer migration, from Asia, Spine-tailed (394) and Fork-tailed (395) Swifts become nomadic within their Australian ranges, their movements irregular and influenced by weather systems that govern the incidence of flying insects. Rapid movement of flocks across Australian States is indicated. Three smaller species, one resident, are recorded from ne. Q.

Food: Flying insects.

Range: Nearly worldwide, except for parts of the Arctic, Antarctica and some oceanic islands; vagrant NZ.

Number of species: World 71; Aust. 5 (or 6); 1 breeding resident, 2 summer migrants; 2 (or 3) vagrants.

391 WHITE-BELLIED SWIFTLET *Collocalia esculenta*   Pl.57

Other names: Edible-nest, Glossy or White-breasted Swiftlet.

Field marks: 90–115 mm. Smallest and most distinctive swiftlet: *glossy black with white belly*; tail shortish, square or slightly forked. Small parties to flocks; reported to fly more slowly and often lower than other small swifts, with frequent changes in direction.

Similar species: Grey Swiftlet (392): belly not white. Uniform Swiftlet (393).

Habitat: Over forests and forest-clearings, open country, timbered watercourses; forest trails and streams.

Range and Status: Widespread from Malay Pen. to NG, Solomon Is., New Caledonia and New Hebrides. Vagrant ne. and e. Q: C. York (before 1929); Claudie R. (Iron Ra.) Jan. 1966: Finch Hatton Gorge, (Eungella Ra., near Mackay), April 1975. Possibly regular summer visitor in small numbers.

392 GREY SWIFTLET *Collocalia spodiopygia*   Pl.57

Other names: Grey-rumped Swiftlet, Mothbird.

Field marks: 115 mm. A small swift, *dark-grey with grey-white rump, tail slightly forked*. Parties to large flocks; soars and dips like stiff-winged swallow, with erratic changes in direction, often near tree-top le£el. Rests on walls of caves, occasionally tree-trunks.

Similar species: White-bellied (391) and Uniform (393) Swiftlets.

Voice: In flight, high-pitched cheep; in caves, metallic incessant clicking, a means of echo-location.

Habitat: Over rainforest, cleared country, beaches and in gorges; breeds in secluded caves and cavities between boulders, near sea on coastal islands or in gorges and hills.
Breeding: Nest: small, basket-shaped; of dry grass, sheoak needles and twigs, cemented with saliva secreted by bird, some with few feathers as lining; in clusters on sloping walls or roofs of caves in dense colonies to hundreds of nests; some attached to one another. Egg: 1; white, elliptical, slightly glossy.
Range and Status: Coastal ne. Q and highland areas, from Claudie R., C. York Pen. s. to Eungella Ra. near Mackay; continental islands with caves, s. to Dunk, Family Group and Hinchinbrook Is. Common below 500 m but to over 1000 m in places e.g. Mt. Bartle Frere. Sedentary.

393 UNIFORM SWIFTLET *Collocalia vanikorensis*
Other name: Lowland Swiftlet.
Field marks: 125 mm. A small wholly dark swiftlet, tail slightly forked. Glossy greenish-black or bronze-brown above, greyer-brown below.
Habitat: Coastal and open lowland areas.
Range and Status: Some *Collocalia* swiftlets (of NG to se. Asia) are very hard or impossible to identify in field; therefore data here are tentative. This species ranges from Celebes and Moluccas to NG, Solomon Is. New Caledonia and New Hebrides. One specimen from Peak Pt., C. York, Q, Sept. 1913. A sight-record, Atherton Tableland Jan., 1971 of four small dark swifts, in flocks of (394) may have been this species.

394 SPINE-TAILED SWIFT *Hirundapus caudacutus* Pl.57
Other name: Needle-tailed Swift.
Field marks: 190–215 mm; span 500 mm. A large, powerful swift, one of world's fastest birds. *Dark, with white forehead, throat and under tail-coverts and short square tail*; (with inconspicuous needle-like shafts); brown on mid-back fades almost to whitish. Parties to very large widespread flocks often make their appearance during unsettled thundery weather, they head consistently in one direction or soar in rising columns, from grass-level to several thousand metres. Typical flight is of upward flutters or downward swoops comprising several (6–8) quick wingbeats followed by fast raking glides. They sometimes indulge in diving displays, dropping sharply with folded wings. In se. Aust., has occasionally been seen to settle briefly on trunks of dead trees or in foliage but roosting habits are not known.
Similar species: Fork-tailed Swift (395): flight less dashing; cigar-shaped body, long forked tail; only rump white. Little Falcon (153): at distance can be confused because of similar shape and wingbeat.
Voice: Rapid high-pitched chitter, usually when birds chase.
Habitat: Aerial, even over cities; feeding concentrations frequently over hilltops and timbered ranges.
Range and Status: Breeds Asia, from w. Siberia, Himalayas, e. to Japan: regular summer migrant to Aust.; arrives from mid-Oct., extending through e. Aust. to Tas., departing by mid-Apr. Numbers greatest in e. and se. Aust. w. to se. SA specially during Jan.–Mar.; rare in c. and w. Aust. where outnumbered by Fork-tailed; occasional NZ; vagrant Macquarie I.

395 FORK-TAILED SWIFT *Apus pacificus* Pl.57
Other names: Migrant or White-rumped Swift.
Field marks: 165–190 mm; span 430 mm. A dusky swift with *cigar-shaped body and long forked tail*; *throat paler, rump pure white in a saddle visible at sides*. Usually in flocks, sometimes immense; movements often precede or accompany thunderstorms. Associates with Spine-tailed Swift (394), swallows, martins, woodswallows. Flies more buoyantly and slowly than Spine-tailed; feeds with erratic flutters and turns. Roosting has not been

observed in Aust., but may spend nights on wing under some circumstances.
Similar species: Spine-tailed Swift (394). Grey Swiftlet (392): smaller, tail less-forked, no white throat.
Voice: High-pitched long squeak 'dzee, dzee' or 'skree-ee-ee'; twitterings and buzzing notes.
Habitat: Aerial; over open country generally, semi-deserts to coasts and islands; sometimes over cities.
Range and Status: Breeds Siberia and Himalayas e. to Japan, s. to China, Taiwan and se. Asia; regular migrant, arriving n. Aust. early Oct., extending through WA and SA where common, usually far outnumbering Spine-tailed; a few mass movements annually into e. States where otherwise uncommon to rare; flocks reach Tas. some years, usually in late summer. Most flocks leave Aust. by mid-Apr. Status in c. Aust. little known; may generally inhabit region centering on the 250 mm rainfall isohyet round the continent. Also NG; vagrant NZ, Macquarie I.

Kingfishers   Family *Alcedinidae*

Plump, short-tailed erect often colourful birds with large heads and oversized bills, very short legs and syndactylous toes, i.e. united over part of length. One Australian species (405) has very long central tail-plumes. There is considerable range of size: Little Kingfisher (397) and Laughing Kookaburra, (398), 100 and 450 mm respectively, are the extremes in Aust. Despite their name, only two Australian species, Azure (396) and Little Kingfishers, typical Kingfishers, subfamily *Alcedininae* – hunt exclusively over water. Other Australian species, being tree kingfishers, subfamily *Daceloninae*, hunt mostly over land. Often seen perched on telephone wires, fence posts, branches, they dart to ground, foliage, surface of water or mud of mangroves for food, returning to a perch. Kookaburras in particular discern movement from afar and make spectacularly long sloping glides to seize prey, which occasionally includes snakes. All our species, the two kookaburras included, sometimes plunge into shallow water after prey or when bathing. The calls of kingfishers are usually harsh, those of kookaburras being among our loudest and most famous sounds.
Food: Small mammals, small birds, nestlings and eggs; reptiles, fish.
Range: Cosmopolitan; absent from high latitudes and some remote islands.
Number of species: World 90; Aust. 10.

396 AZURE KINGFISHER *Ceyx azureus*   Pl.58
Other names: Blue, Creek, Purple, River or Water Kingfisher.
Field marks: 170–190 mm. A sparrow-sized kingfisher; rich glossy dark-blue above *with white or buff spot on side of neck*; *orange-rufous below clouded blue on sides*; *feet red*. Imm: dull-blue above; underparts paler. Singly or pairs; usually first revealed by distinctive call. Perches on roots or low branches overhanging water; bobs head, raises tail, *darts off arrowlike low over water to next perch*. Dives from such points; occasionally hovers.
Similar species: Little Kingfisher (397): white below, black feet. Forest Kingfisher (400): white wingpatch in flight; male has white collar.
Voice: Shrill squeaked 'peet peet', often in flight.
Habitat: Mostly tree-lined creeks, rivers, lakes and swamps with suitable banks for nesting; tidal creeks and well-vegetated estuaries, mangroves.
Breeding: Nest: in chamber at end of burrow up to 1 m long; in bank of creek or river or in earth adhering to roots of fallen tree. Eggs: 5–7; white, rounded, glossy.
Range and Status: N. and e. Aust., Tas., and some coastal islands: from Derby, WA, through coastal Kimberleys; top end NT s. to Victoria and Macarthur Rs.; in Q, Gulf coast s. to Riversleigh; C. York Pen. and e. Q, inland to Mt. Surprise–Thomson R. (Muttaburra–Longreach)–Carnarvon Ras.–Chinchilla. In NSW, mostly e. of Divide, but

w. to Inverell–Wagga, along Riverina streams w. to Balranald and downstream along Murray R. to about Dareton; in Vic., widespread except in nw.; sparse and local but well-established along Murray R. and tributaries downstream to about Swan Hill–Dareton; in SA, 'streams and creeks in s. parts of State', w. to Mt. Lofty Ras.; 'very rare visitor' along Murray R. near Renmark and L. Meretti–Chowilla. In Tas., streams on n. and w. coasts. Uncommon; (?) sedentary. Also NG, Tanimber and Aru Is. to n. Moluccas.

397 LITTLE KINGFISHER *Ceyx pusillus* Pl.58

Field marks: 115–130 mm. Tiny – the smallest Australian kingfisher; deep glossy purplish above *extending to side of white breast*; *white spot before eye and on side of neck, feet black*. Shy; perches low over water; plunges, returns to perch. Flight very swift and direct, low over water.

Similar species: Forest Kingfisher (400): paler-blue back, no spot on neck, but white wing-patch in flight. Azure Kingfisher (396).

Voice: High-pitched squeak.

Habitat: Creeks and other waters in tropical rainforest and scrub, up to 700 m; well-vegetated coastal creeks, small tidal mangrove-lined creeks and swamps.

Breeding: Nest: in chamber at end of small burrow in creekbank. Eggs: 4–5; white, rounded, glossy.

Range and Status: N. Aust.: (1) NT, from Anson Bay and Melville I. to e. Arnhem Land and Groote Eylandt. (2) n. Q, from Normanton on w. coast C. York Pen. to C. York, s. coastally and on some coastal islands e.g. Hinchinbrook, to e. Barrata Creek, s. of Townsville. Probably occurs along Gulf coasts. Uncommon to fairly common; (?) sedentary. Also Moluccas, NG, Solomon Is.

398 LAUGHING KOOKABURRA *Dacelo gigas* Pl.58

Other names: Alarmbird, Breakfastbird; Bushman's, Settler's or Shepherd's Clock; Brown, Great Brown, Giant or Laughing Kingfisher; Jack, Jackass, Jacko, Jacky, John, Johnny; Kooka; Laughing Jack, John, Johnass, or Johnny; Ha Ha or Woop Woop Pigeon.

Field marks: 410–470 mm. One of world's largest kingfishers. Bill long and robust, head and breast cream-white, *dark-brown crown and brown mark through eye*; pale-blue mottlings on brown wings; tail rufous, margined white and barred black; eye brown. Males often have some blue-green in centre of rump, in females much-reduced or absent. Imm: shorter dark bill, base of tail tinged blue, fine brownish margins to white feathers. Pairs or family parties consisting of a mated pair and one or two auxiliaries and/or young. Such groups 'laugh' together in noisy territorial display. Normal flight rather heavy and direct; note large white patch on wing; raises tail on alighting. In winter and spring, has conspicuous high display-flight over territory with deep, stiff wingbeats.

Similar species: Blue-winged Kookaburra (399): dark-streaked white head, whitish eye; bluer wing and rump; blue or chestnut tail.

Voice: Famed boisterous 'laugh' – a chuckle or repeated 'kook-kook-kook' developing into a rising staccato shouted 'kook-kook-kook-ka-ka-ka', then fading. Usually taken up by other members of group in chorus, inciting other groups to respond. Heard usually morning and evening. Also a raucous staccato squawk, usually when attacked.

Habitat: Open woodland, forests, clearings, farming country with trees; orchards, gardens, city parks. Farther inland, mostly confined to timbered watercourses.

Breeding: Nest: on decayed debris; in hollow trunk or limb up to 20 m high. Occasionally in hole in creekbank, termite-nest or tree, haystack, cavity in wall. Eggs: 2–4; white, roundish.

Range and Status: Originally confined to e. Aust.: from near C. York s. through e. Q, inland to Longreach–Cunnamulla–Eulo; in NSW inland to the Darling and tributaries but in cw. mostly along river-systems; throughout Vic. in suitable habitat; in se. SA n. to

Port Augusta and s. Flinders Ras., and w. to s. Eyre Pen. Introduced: sw. WA (1897 on), now widespread Geraldton–Esperance; Tas. (1905), now widespread in e. and n.; Kangaroo I., SA (1926); Flinders I., Bass Strait, c. 1940. Common to uncommon; sedentary.

399 BLUE-WINGED KOOKABURRA *Dacelo leachii*   Pl.58

Other names: Barking or Howling Jackass; Fawn-breasted or Leach's Kingfisher.

Field marks: 405–440 mm. Differs from Laughing Kookaburra (398) in *streaked white head, whitish eye; larger blue patch on shoulder, uniform pale-blue rump;* tail: *deep-blue* (male); *red-brown* (female); barred darker in both. Imm: lighter streaking on head, slight dark mottlings on white plumage. Singly or pairs; shyer than Laughing Kookaburra; in heat of day often remains quietly in foliage. In flight note pale head, blue rump, prominent white wing-patch.

Similar species: Laughing Kookaburra (398).

Voice: Appalling: starts off with guttural 'klock, klock, klock, klock' and develops into cacophony of squawks and screeches, somewhat like machine-driven hacksaw; usually by several birds in chorus.

Habitat: Tropical and subtropical woodlands, paperbark swamps, timber along watercourses.

Breeding: Nest: on debris; in hollow limb or trunk of tree; occasionally in arboreal termite-nest. Eggs: 3–4; whitish, rounded.

Range and Status: N. Aust. and coastal islands: from Wooramel R. (Hamelin Pool), WA, inland to upper Gascoyne R. (Mt. Clere), and n. through Hamersley Ras., Pilbara and Kimberleys; top end NT, s. to Victoria and Macarthur Rs.; n. and e. Q, inland to Mt. Isa–Hughenden–lower Dawson R.–Toowoomba. In Brisbane area, uncommon, reported on upper Brisbane R. and watercourses in open country to about 30 km s. of Ipswich, never near coast. Fairly common in n., uncommon in s.; (?) migratory. Also Torres Strait islands, s. NG.

400 FOREST KINGFISHER *Halcyon macleayii*   Pl.58

Other names: Blue, Bush or Macleay's Kingfisher.

Field marks: 180–230 mm. A beautiful kingfisher of strong contrasts: brilliant deep-blue above, *paler on back and rump; spot before eye and underparts pure white; male has broad white rear-collar.* Imm: duller; back greener, white areas tinged buff. In flight note large *white spot on wing;* flight swift, direct.

Similar species: Sacred (402) and Mangrove (403) Kingfishers: green or blue-green above; no wingpatch; white areas of Sacred usually washed buff. Little Kingfisher (397).

Voice: Loud high-pitched scratchy 'krree-krree-krree' and a high-pitched rattle, drier and harder than Sacred. Scolding screech and chatterings near nest.

Habitat: Open woodlands, timber and scrub along watercourses; swamps, beaches, mangroves; open lands generally on margins of woodland and forest.

Breeding: Nest: on decayed debris; in hollow branch or trunk of tree or in cavity excavated in termite-nest, 3–25 m high.

Range and Status: Coastal n. and e. Aust.: from Derby, WA, through Kimberleys and top end, NT, to C. York Pen. Q, and s. to Macleay R., NSW; occasional s. to Sydney, inland to Mt. Surprise–Chinchilla, Q, and to Moree in NSW. A migrant in s. part of range, arriving to breed Sept., departing Mar. Also NG, as resident and migrant from Aust.; New Britain and Kai Is.

401 RED-BACKED KINGFISHER *Halcyon pyrrhopygia*   Pl.58

Other name: Golden Kingfisher.

Field marks: 195–240 mm. A dry-country kingfisher, paler than others. Male: *crown whitish, streaked grey-green,* wings and tail dusty pale-blue, *back and rump orange-tan;*

whitish below. Female: duller, greyer above. Singly or pairs, often far from water or cover; perches conspicuously in exposed places, including overhead wires. Flight swift, direct.

Similar species: Sacred Kingfisher (402): colours deeper, no streaks on crown, rump bluish; note habitat.

Voice: Mournful level whistle, 'peel'; repeated monotonously from top of tree or telephone wires; rather noisy when mating, with parrot-like chatter and far-carrying 'k-prrr, k-prrr'.

Habitat: Most inland habitats, often miles from water; gibber; spinifex and other grasslands; scrubby foothills, mulga and mallee-scrubs, open woodlands, tree-lined dry watercourses.

Breeding: Nest: in cavity at end of tunnel; in bank of creek, cliff, road-cutting, sand-dump, termite-mound; occasionally in hollow branch. Eggs: 4–5; white, rounded.

Range and Status: Inland and drier parts all mainland States, with seasonal coastward movements. Breeds through inland when conditions suitable. Small numbers winter in coastal e. Aust., from ne. Q (Cairns–Townsville) to se. Q–n. NSW (Fraser I. s. to about Grafton). Regular breeding migrant to sub-inland se. Aust. arriving Sept.–Oct., departing Jan.–Feb.; in NSW, e. to about Finley (occasional ACT); in Vic., s. to about Nagambie–Bendigo–Wyperfeld NP, occasionally further s.; in SA, s. to Bunns Bore–L. Alexandrina–s. Eyre Pen.; in WA widespread, but normally absent s. of Norseman–Geraldton; in Kimberleys and NT commoner in subcoastal rather than coastal zone, where it is a scarce dry season visitor. Generally uncommon.

402 SACRED KINGFISHER *Halcyon sancta*   Pl.58

Other names: Green, Tree, or Wood Kingfisher.

Field marks: 200–230 mm. Perhaps our most familiar small kingfisher. Note *white to buff horizontal wedge before eye and a more or less dark band through eye to nape above a white to buff rear-collar.* Male: shoulders blue, rump bright-blue, tail bright deep-blue; collar and underparts white. Female: usually larger; duller and greener; tail dull dark-green; collar and underparts white. In winter plumage (both sexes) the breast becomes buff, male upperparts duller. Imm: sexes respectively like adults, with buffish margins to feathers of upperparts; underparts deep to pale-buff or nearly white, depending on age; buff stages have well-marked to slight dark margins to feathers. It usually has sufficient *buffish tinge in white plumage* and on underwing to separate it from Forest (400) and Mangrove (403) Kingfishers. Singly, pairs or loose companies during migration. Noisy in breeding season. Flight swift, direct. Note: in n. coastal areas often found in habitat of Mangrove Kingfisher and can be easily mistaken.

Similar species: Forest Kingfisher (400): glossy blue above, whiter below; in flight, prominent white wing-spot. Mangrove Kingfisher (403): see entry below.

Voice: Clear measured 'dek dek dek' or 'dik dik dik', familiar spring and summer bush sounds; at or near nest, peevish rising 'keer keer keer'; also harsh scoldings and rising musical trill.

Habitat: Open forests and woodlands, usually but not always near water; margins of rivers and lakes, seashores, mangrove-fringes, tidal inlets and mudflats, offshore islands; towns, gardens.

Breeding: Nest: on debris in tree-hollow or termite-nest on stump or in tree; occasionally in tunnel in river bank. Eggs: 3–5; white, slightly glossy, becoming dull with age.

Range and Status: Aust., coastal islands and Tas.: generally absent from arid inland except as passage migrant, but there are breeding populations in n. Aust. and on many islands. In coastal, subcoastal and riverine areas of s. Aust. and Tas., from n. of Brisbane to n. of Perth, it is a regular breeding migrant, arriving Sept.–Oct. usually departing by Mar.–Apr. Many winter in inland and a few in s., mostly in sub-inland or milder coastal areas, e.g. Carnarvon, WA; Newcastle, NSW. Many migrate n. in autumn through C.

York and nw. Aust. Common. Resident, or winter migrant from Aust., from s. Philippines, Sunda Is., including Timor, e. to NG, Bismarck Archipelago and Solomon Is. Resident New Caledonia, Loyalty, Norfolk, Lord Howe Is. and NZ.

403 MANGROVE KINGFISHER *Halcyon chloris* Pl.58

Other names: Collared or White-collared Kingfisher.

Field marks: 255–290 mm. *Like a larger whiter Sacred Kingfisher (402) with a distinctly longish bill, seemingly slightly upturned and often carried partly open*; crown blacker than Sacred, back darker bronze-green, shading to almost peacock-blue on wings and tail; individuals may be slightly buff on forehead and sides of breast but usually much less so than Sacred. Imm: duller with faint barrings on underparts. Note habitat, different call.

Similar species: Sacred (402) and Forest (400) Kingfishers.

Voice: Somewhat like Sacred but slower and louder: deliberate 'kek, kek' or 'kek, kek, kek'; in *both, second note higher*. Also loud clear 'pukee pukee pukee' and peevish rising 'keer keer', similar to Sacred.

Habitat: Mangroves, tidal creeks; adjacent beaches, mudflats and jetties.

Breeding: Nest: usually in hollow in trunk of mangrove or cavity tunnelled into tree-termite nests, up to 10 m or more high. Eggs: 3–5; rounded, whitish, becoming stained.

Range and Status: Coasts and islands of n. Aust.: from Carnarvon, WA (occasional s. to Shark Bay) to ne. NSW (Tweed R.), occasional to Ballina and possibly further s. Common; sedentary. Also coasts and islands from Red Sea and n. Indian Ocean to se. Asia and w. Pacific.

404 YELLOW-BILLED KINGFISHER *Syma torotoro* Pl.58

Other names: Lesser Yellow-billed Kingfisher; Saw-billed Kingfisher.

Field marks: 180–210 mm. Our only yellow-billed kingfisher. *Head cinnamon-rufous, black mark round eye, black crescent on hindneck*, back and wings blue-green, tail blue; whitish below. Female: *black patch on crown, broader black crescent on hindneck*. Perches low, keeps to cover; remains still when approached and often hard to see. Generally heard more often than seen.

Voice: Trilling whistle in ascending scale, frequently repeated and continually heard when nesting; at times seems ventriloquial, difficult to locate.

Habitat: Lower parts of tropical scrubs and rainforest, margins of open woodland bordering scrub.

Breeding: Nest: in chamber at end of short burrow in termite nest, 3–12 m high on tree, usually at edge of scrub or open forest; or in a tree-hollow. Eggs: 3; white, rounded.

Range and Status: In Aust., confined to ne. C. York Pen., Q, from Claudie to Chester Rs. Common; sedentary. Also NG and islands.

405 WHITE-TAILED KINGFISHER *Tanysiptera sylvia* Pl.58

Other names: Buff-breasted Paradise Kingfisher; Long-tailed, Racquet-tailed or Silver-tailed Kingfisher.

Field marks: 300–360 mm, including tail of 175–250 mm. Distinctive and beautiful, the only Australian landbird with *two elongated stiff white tail-plumes. Bill orange-red; brilliant-blue and black above; centre of back, rump and tail white, buff-yellow to yellow-chestnut below*. Imm: bill black, wings dull-blue, back blackish grey; breast dirty cream; at first lacks white tail-plumes. Singly or pairs; shy, often remains high in canopy of forest. Flight described as rapid, floating; slowly raises and lowers tail-plumes on alighting.

Similar species: Yellow-billed Kingfisher (404): yellow bill, cinnamon-rufous head, short green tail.

Voice: Described as steady ascending 'chop chop chop chop chop', or 'choga choga choga', repeated four or five but up to fourteen times; also high-pitched trill heard all day during nesting season.

Habitat: Dense lowland rainforest with open ground below, scrubby mountain gullies; usually where there are small ground-termite nests, suitable for breeding.
Breeding: Nest: in chamber in low active termite-nest, usually on ground but reportedly sometimes in tree; entrance to nest-tunnel in terrestrial nests may be only 150 mm from ground. Eggs: 1–3; white, rounded.
Range and Status: In Aust., breeds in coastal ne. Q from C. York s. to Mt. Spec., near Townsville. Regular migrant from NG, arriving Oct.–Nov., leaving Mar.–Apr.; several June–Aug. observations suggest some may overwinter. Locally common. Also e. NG and Bismarck Archipelago.

Bee-eaters   Family *Meropidae*

Distinctive colourful birds with slender curved bills and small, syndactylous feet; i.e. toes partly united. Needle-like shafts of two central tail-feathers extend 25 mm or more, slightly enlarged at tip when new. Flight swift, graceful and soaring, like swallows or woodswallows. The family is strongest in Africa, with numerous attractive members. The single Australian species is migratory and nomadic. Like other bee-eaters, it removes or renders harmless the stings of bees or wasps before swallowing or feeding to mate or young.
Food: Flying insects generally, not only bees.
Range: Europe and Africa through Asia to Australasian region.
Number of species: World 23; Aust. 1.

406   RAINBOW BEE-EATER   *Merops ornatus*   Pl.58

Other names: Rainbow Bird; Australian or Pintailed Bee-eater, Berrin-berrin, Gold-digger, Gold-miner, Golden Swallow, Kingfisher, Pintail Sandpiper, Spinetail.
Field marks: 230–280 mm, including tail-points. A gorgeous pale-green and blue bird of graceful flight. Note *fine curved black bill, blue-edged black eye-mark, pale-orange throat with black mark in centre.* Male: golden-bronze crown; shafts of two central tail-feathers *extend 25–50 mm as wires,* slightly enlarged at tip. Female: less bronze on crown, shorter tail-wires. Both often lose or break them during nesting. Imm: greener, plainer, with paler throat, no black throat-patch or tail-points. When breeding (often in loose colonies) pairs and trios sit on fences, gates, dead trees – dashing into air after insects. Flight swift, undulating, soaring, with erratic twists and turns; *note coppery flight-feathers.* Occasionally plunges into water after prey. In n. Aust. specially, conspicuous migratory or nomadic flocks drift high overhead, often with woodswallows and often first noted by calls; indulges in massed high-soaring at dusk and in mornings; may move at night.
Similar species: None – but it is nevertheless often called 'kingfisher' – see 402 for comparison.
Voice: Melodious 'pirr, pirr, pirr', usually in flight.
Habitat: Open country: in s. Aust. chiefly at suitable breeding places in areas of sandy or loamy soil: sand-ridges, riverbanks, road-cuttings, sand-pits, occasionally coastal cliffs; on migration in n. flocks roost in mangroves, rainforest canopy, woodlands.
Breeding: Nest: in chamber at end of burrow, up to 1·6 m long, tunnelled in flat or sloping ground, sandy bank or cutting. Eggs: 4–5; white, glossy, rounded.
Range and Status: Mainland Aust. except extreme coastal se. and sw. and cooler wetter forested areas. Resident coastal and subcoastal n. Aust.; regular breeding migrant in s. Aust., arriving Sept.–Oct., departing Feb.–Mar., some occasionally present to Apr.–May. In Vic. it has bred s. to Pearcedale and Anglesea. In the far-inland it seems mostly a passage migrant. Large numbers winter in coastal and subcoastal n. Aust., but many migrate n. in autumn through C. York, and through nw. Aust., wintering in Lesser Sunda Is., NG, Bismarck Archipelago and Solomon Is. Common.

Rollers   Family *Coraciidae*

Rather robust, colourful birds with large heads, wide short, somewhat hooked bills and small syndactylous feet, i.e. toes partly united. Wings are long and flight strong. During courtship, typically perform spectacular swooping, looping and rolling displays, hence family name. Most species are noisy, conspicuous and aggressive. Sexes similar.

Food: Mostly insects caught in flight, and in outer foliage of trees.

Range: Europe and Africa, through s. Asia to Australasian region; absent from NZ.

Number of species: World 16; Aust. 1.

407   DOLLARBIRD   *Eurystomus orientalis*   Pl.58

Other names: Broad-billed or Eastern Broad-billed Roller; Starbird.

Field marks: 280–305 mm. A strange-looking stocky greenish bird with *short wide red bill and large dark-brownish head*. Note also red eye-ring and legs and short black-tipped green tail; wings and back greenish blue, flight-feathers deep-blue, throat a streaked lilac blue. Imm: duller, bill blackish, then flesh-coloured. Singly, pairs or open companies; sits watchfully upright on high dead limbs over forest canopy or water; sallies after flying insects, returns to perch. Flight swooping and erratic with deep loose beats of long wings; note *prominent large white spot* at base of flight-feathers, hence 'Dollarbird'. Birds often active at dusk, dipping low, fluttering high; in gloaming may be mistaken for a thickset nightjar, fanciful as that may sound.

Voice: Loud rasping accelerating 'kak, kak, kak-kak-kak-kak-kak' or 'yap, yapapapap'.

Habitat: Forests, open woodlands and timber along watercourses; over open swamps at dusk; timbered suburbs of towns and cities.

Breeding: Nest: on decayed debris; in hollow limb or hole in tree, usually high. Eggs: 3–5; white, glossy, pointed.

Range and Status: Regular breeding migrant to n. and e. Aust. and coastal islands, arriving Sept.–Oct., departing Feb.–Apr. Ranges from Kimberleys, WA, through top end NT, s. to Victoria, Roper and Macarthur Rs.; in Q, inland to Mt. Isa–Blackall–Charleville, occasional along river systems of sw. Q and adjacent ne. SA; in NSW mostly coastal but w. to Warrumbungle NP–Hay, regular in small numbers along Murray R. w. to Barham, occasional to Mildura; more rarely to about Morgan, SA. Regular ne. Vic., rare s. of Divide; occasional Seville–Wonga Park area e. of Melbourne and sw. Vic. to Naracoorte, SA. Vagrant Tas. and NZ. Common. Winters Solomon Is., Bismarck Archipelago, NG and islands, Kai Is. and Moluccas. Range extends through Sunda Is., Philippines, Andamans to se. Asia, Japan, Korea, se. China, e. India and Nepal.

Pittas   Family *Pittidae*

Very distinctive, brightly and boldly coloured, ground-feeding birds of rainforests and tropical scrubs, somewhat like stumpy long-legged thrushes with very short tails and rounded wings with large white wingpatches seen in display and in flight. They have strong whistling voices and are heard more than seen. Seldom venturing from cover by day, they hop briskly over leaf-litter, throwing leaves aside with their bills, and noisily crack shells of land-snails on rocks; such anvils become surrounded with discarded shells. The flight is strong and usually low but they do fly up to perch; they normally roost high and often call from near treetops. Some species are migratory, apparently travelling at night. The word 'pitta' is of Telegu (Indian) origin.

Food: Molluscs, insects and other invertebrates; berries and fruit.

Range: Africa to se. Asia and tropical parts of Australasian region.

Number of species: World 26; Aust. 3 (a fourth doubtfully recorded).

408 RED-BELLIED PITTA *Pitta erythrogaster*   **Pl.59**
Other names: Blue-breasted or Macklot's Pitta.
Field marks: 175–190 mm; legs 40 mm. A typical pitta; note dull-red nape, *broad pale-blue breastband and red underparts.* Habits like Noisy Pitta (410).
Voice: A mournful whistle.
Habitat: Tropical rainforests and scrubs.
Breeding: Nest: large, domed on ground against root of tree. Eggs: 3.
Range and Status: In Aust. confined to C. York Pen., Q, s. to about Rocky R. Breeding migrant, arriving from NG Oct., departing Mar.–Apr. The range extends through NG, Celebes, Philippines.

409 BLUE-WINGED PITTA *Pitta moluccensis*
Other names: Crowned, Indian or Fairy Pitta.
Field marks: 175–190 mm. Somewhat like Noisy Pitta (410) but *with a whitish throat*; more extensive cobalt-blue on shoulders and rump, crown buffy brown with black central streak; broad black band from bill through eye to nape; no dark mark in centre of buffish underparts. In Borneo reported to fly more readily than other pittas when disturbed, flushing with quail-like whirr, often settling on low branch.
Voice: A short whistle uttered sharply three times, first note shrillest (Borneo). Loud clear double whistle (India).
Habitat: Rainforests, mangrove-forests, native gardens (Borneo).
Range and Status: Widespread in s. and se. Asia: through India from Himalayas southward, and Ceylon; n. to Indo–China, Korea and Japan, e. to Borneo and Sumatra. Migratory and nomadic. Known in Aust. only from two old specimens in WA Museum, from nw. Aust. Vagrant.

410 NOISY PITTA *Pitta versicolor*   **Pl.59**
Other names: Buff-breasted Pitta, Painted Thrush, Dragonbird, Dragoon.
Field marks: 175–210 mm; legs 40 mm. The only common Australian pitta with *a mustard-yellow breast.* Note sturdy black bill, chestnut crown, black face and throat; legs fleshy straw-coloured. Singly or pairs; hops on forest-floor; throws leaves aside with bill; stands boldly upright; flicks short tail. Advises presence by calls, sounds of rustling leaves or by sharp raps as it hammers snails on rock-anvil. Flight swift and kingfisher-like: looks blue-green with *prominent white windows in black flight-feathers.*
Similar species: Blue-winged Pitta (409): white throat.
Voice: Three-note whistle; often syllabized 'walk-to-work'; also sharp 'keow' repeated at intervals, and a single liquid mournful note. Calls by day and night, from ground or aloft; heard mostly in spring and summer; rather silent in winter.
Habitat: Rainforests, tropical and subtropical scrubs, occasional in wet eucalypt forests.
Breeding: Nest: domed; with ramp of sticks to rather large side-entrance; of twigs, leaves, bark and mosses, lined with plant-fibres and few feathers; marsupial dung may be spread inside and on ramp. On or near ground, between roots or on stump. Eggs: 3–5; rounded, delicate-white or blue-white, spotted and blotched dark purple-brown, with shadowy spots of blue-grey, usually near larger end.
Range and Status: E. coastal Aust. and mountain areas from C. York to near Port Macquarie, NSW; also NG. Fairly common. A coastwards winter movement has been suggested; part of population may migrate to NG in winter.

411 RAINBOW PITTA *Pitta iris*   **Pl.59**
Other name: Black-breasted Pitta.
Field marks: 150–180 mm from head to tail-tip; legs 40 mm. The only resident pitta in nw. Aust. and the only Australian pitta *with black head and breast.* Note bright tan streak

on sides of crown. Habits and flight in general like Noisy Pitta (410) including white window in wing.

Voice: Double or triple whistle, easy to imitate.

Habitat: Remnants of rainforest, scrubs along watercourses, bamboo-thickets, mangroves.

Breeding: Nest: large, domed, with side-entrance; of dead bamboo-leaves and other plant material loosely put together; in mangroves or clumps of bamboo 2 m high, sometimes on ground or in tussock of grass; lightly roofed over in open situations. Eggs: 4; creamy white with sepia blotches and underlying markings of dull purplish grey.

Range and Status: Kimberleys, WA, to top end NT, s. to about Victoria R., e. to Groote Eylandt. Fairly common, mainly coastal. (?) Sedentary.

Lyrebirds   Family *Menuridae*

A famous Australian family of two species of very large, specialized songbirds of temperate and subtropical rainforests. They feed entirely on the ground, excavating and turning over soil and humus with their large powerful feet and claws. Their plumage is mostly brown or chestnut and the males especially have spectacular long tails, of 16 feathers modified into three kinds. In Superb Lyrebird (413) resemblance of the two outer plumes (lyrates) to the shape of a Greek lyre gives the family its name. The tail is normally carried horizontally; the upright position in which it is often pictured is assumed only momentarily as it is raised and spread forward over the body in display. Albert's Lyrebird (412) does not have lyrates. Lyrebirds have developed perhaps the most powerful of all songbird-voices. They have their own characteristic songs but have become consummate mimics of the calls of many other birds, and include these in the song-pattern. The stream of song and mimicry produced by male lyrebirds is highly directional, being 'beamed' toward females and rival males, often while in spectacular display on an arena. Males and females annually claim (separate) territories where males display to and attract females for mating and where each mated female builds a nest and rears her single young. Song and display reach a peak during winter breeding season but sub-adult males often continue to sing and display through summer. Ordinarily lyrebirds are very shy but they have become accustomed to visitors in such places as Sherbrooke Forest Park in the Dandenong Ras. near Melbourne, where feeding and even displaying birds can be easily seen.

Food: Insects, earthworms, crustaceans and other soil-invertebrates.

Range: Temperate and subtropical coastal e. Aust.

Number of species: World 2: Aust. 2.

412   ALBERT'S LYREBIRD   *Menura alberti*   Pl.17

Other names: Northern Lyrebird, Prince Albert's Lyrebird.

Field marks: Male 890 mm including tail; female 760 mm. Smaller and *richer-chestnut* than Superb and *more richly-coloured below*; *tail black, simpler, without lyrate plumes*. Generally rich-chestnut above, throat and foreneck rufous-buff; rich buff-grey below; legs and feet grey, powerful. Tail of male of 14 rather fuzzy filamentaries, glossy black above, fine, wiry and lace-like at tips; two dark central ribbon-like plumes extend some 75 mm beyond end, cross at tip and curve outwards. Tail of female (and imm.) somewhat shorter, less lacy; two central plumes shorter, broader, straighter than male's. Singly or pairs; seldom seen; when surprised, half-runs, half-flies heavily into cover or ascends a tree in series of leaps. Males tread down display-platforms of vine-stems and other vegetation; display and sing on these and on ground, logs. In display, inverts tail over back, droops wings.

Similar species: Superb Lyrebird (413).

Voice: Male: powerful, mellow, far-carrying; typical phrase deliberate ringing 'caw-cree craw-craw-wheat' or 'caw-caw-kee-kee-wheat'; also mellow rising 'wooo' like start of howl of dingo. Local dialects differ somewhat. Also mimicry linked with refrain of own notes; females also mimic. Alarm-call, piercing 'whisk-whisk', indistinguishable from Superb.

Habitat: Dense subtropical rainforests and scrubs.

Breeding: Nest: large, globular with side-entrance; of sticks, bark, leaves, fern-fronds, thickly lined with bird's rufous flank-feathers, readily distinguished from grey feathers of Superb. In cleft in rock, between boulders, buttress of tree, on stump. Egg: 1; purplish-stone to purplish-brown, blotched irregularly with blackish brown in zone round large end and marked overall with blackish-brown streaks and spots.

Range and Status: Confined to extreme se. Q and ne. NSW. Probably extinct Blackall Ra., Q; locally common from Mt. Tambourine n. to Wilson's Peak, and Dalrymple Ck., Q, s. to McPherson Ras. and adjacent ranges in ne. NSW.

413 SUPERB LYREBIRD *Menura novaehollandiae*   Pl.17

Other names: Lyretail, Native Pheasant, Queen Victoria's Lyrebird.

Field marks: Male up to 1 m, including tail; female 860 mm. More often heard than seen: looks dark, long tailed and pheasant-like; *plain rich-brown above, tinged coppery on wings*; *grey-brown below*; legs and feet dark grey and powerful. *Tail of male long, clubbed and train-like*: of two lyrates 600 mm or longer; glossy black and rufous above, silvery below, with notched 'windows'; each plume handsomely curved and each ending in a club; 12 lacy filamentaries, black above and silvery below; two slim down-curved 'guard-plumes'. Full tail acquired irregularly over 3–9 years and moulted each year. Tail of female *simpler*: *shorter, more drooping and pointed*; of 14 simple brown plumes, central pair longest; outer pair like small lyrates often hidden; the tail typically becomes bent during incubation. Imm: like female, but throat rufous, tail more slender. Singly, pairs or small parties in summer; often glimpsed crossing roads or tracks, running along logs; flees in flying bounds. Roosts high in trees but spends much of day on ground turning over soil in search of food; scratchings often extensive. Flies heavily, usually downhill or in vol-planing descent from trees; ascends trees in flying bounds from limb to limb. In autumn, mature male sings frequently and rakes up numerous low display-mounds, about 1–2 m across, in territory; displays on these (and elsewhere) by inverting the trail forward in silvery shower, turning slowly about while pouring out a stream of song and mimicry. This display often climaxes in a dance, in which the bird, still covered by the spread tail, jerkily leaps forwards and back in time to a thudding song-phrase. Copulation takes place on or near mound. Several females may take up separate breeding territories near one male, each building a nest and rearing single chick unaided. During spring, song diminishes as males moult tails, which are renewed by Jan. During summer, in loose feeding parties of both sexes, females typically accompanied by young.

Similar species: Albert's Lyrebird (412). Note that bushmens' name 'pheasant' for Superb may cause confusion with (165) or (375).

Voice: Magnificent, mellow, far-carrying, usually heard 'in valley below'. Song: stream of mimicked calls of many other birds, interwoven with lyrebird's own refrain, which varies much in local dialect. Conspicuous note, common throughout range: a loud clear 'blick blick' or 'bilik, bilik', usually uttered during display. Males commonly sing while feeding or from logs, branches. Females sing (and mimic), usually less powerfully than males. Both sexes and large nestlings have high-pitched piercing alarm-screech, 'whisk! whisk!'.

Habitat: From sea-level to above snowline in denser temperate and subtropical rain-forests, woodlands, fern-gullies; rugged wooded sandstone country; rocky gullies. Sometimes in new forest plantations or gardens adjacent to forests; attracted to newly turned soil.

Breeding: Nest: domed, bulky; of sticks, bark, bracken, fern-fronds, moss, lined with fibrous rootlets; dense mat of bird's own grey breast and flank-feathers added during incubation. On ground, bank, rock-shelf or crevice, stump, log or in head of tree-fern or

up to 25 m high in tree fork, usually facing downhill. Egg: 1; stone-grey, deep-khaki or purple-brown, spotted, streaked and blotched with deep-grey and blackish brown.
Range and Status: From Dandenong Ras., Kinglake and Wandong districts e. and ne. of Melbourne, Vic., to highlands in extreme se. Q (n. to Wyperba district, n. of Wallangàrra). Common. Successfully introduced Tas. in Mt. Field NP and near Lune R. etc.

Scrub-birds   Family *Atrichornithidae*

A supposedly ancient Australian family of two smallish songbirds, probably related to lyrebirds and, like them, characterized by primitive arrangement of muscles of syrinx (voice-box) and absence of a furcula or wish-bone. They have sombre brown plumage with blackish and paler markings below. The feet and legs are powerful; the wings short and rounded, tail-feathers abruptly graduated. Strongly territorial, they dwell in heavy undergrowth, fly feebly and are extremely elusive. The female Noisy Scrub-bird is reported to occupy a small nesting area at the edge of the male's territory. They are almost invariably heard before (and usually without) being seen. Voices of males, in particular, have an extraordinarily sharp penetrating quality; they may mimic other species. Females are seldom heard or seen. The present distribution of the family suggests a much wider former range, sundered by climatic changes.
Food: Insects and other invertebrates.
Range: Restricted to two isolated coastal areas, one in ce. Aust., the other on s. coast of WA.
Number of species: World 2; Aust. 2.

414   RUFOUS SCRUB-BIRD   *Atrichornis rufescens*   **Pl.59**
Field marks: Male 190 mm; female 165 mm. A small stocky noisy, but almost unbelievably elusive bird of dense lower growth of mountain rainforests. Male: dark rufous-brown above, *throat whitish with black mottlings down centre and onto breast; under tail-coverts rich-buff.* Eye large, brown; legs powerful. Female: breast more yellow-buff. Imm: darker above; dull red-brown below, throat greyer. Usually only single males are located and then usually heard rather than seen. It calls loudly at intervals or mimics local birds. It moves mostly near ground, creeping mouse-like beneath fallen leaves; bounces along logs, occasionally hangs momentarily on a tree-trunk or rocks. Female quieter and even shyer; almost impossible to locate except when nesting. Both sexes often hold the longish pointed tail erect over back and slightly droop wings. When pressed, they fly feebly a few metres between cover.
Similar species: Noisy Scrub-bird (415); note range.
Voice: Remarkably powerful; despite the bird's size, its calls can frequently be heard from afar through thick scrub. Male: typical call, sharp high-pitched 'cheep, cheep, cheep' starting deliberately, falling in pitch and accelerating; there can be four to more than twelve syllables to a call, the last few being given very rapidly. Other calls, a repeated ringing note, and a harsh scolding 'churr-churr-churr'. Seemingly less vocal when nesting (Nov.–Dec.). Female usually silent but, when eggs or young approached, utters sharp 'tick'; also feeble squeaks. An accomplished mimic.
Habitat: Densest tangles of ferns, undergrowth or tussocks, surrounding of fallen logs; in temperate rainforests including stands of Antarctic Beech *Nothofagus* to over 1000 m in McPherson Ras., Q. Very local; individuals often confined to small areas.
Breeding: Nest: globular; about 150 mm across with rounded side-entrance approximately 30 mm in diameter; usually of broad dry grass, interlaced but not interwoven and incorporating dry leaves, fern; lined with wood-pulp apparently applied when wet, drying to smooth almost cardboard-like consistency. Eggs: 2; very pale-pink, sparsely spotted with red-brown, forming zone at large end.
Range and Status: From McPherson Ra., se. Q, s. on e. of Divide to Barrington Tops NP, nw. of Dungog, NSW, inland to Gibraltar Ra. NP, near Glen Innes. Generally uncommon; sedentary.

415 NOISY SCRUB-BIRD *Atrichornis clamosus* Pl.59

Other name: Western Scrub-bird.

Field marks: ♂ 220–255; ♀ 200 mm. Distinctive and celebrated; rare, local and elusive, usually heard rather than seen, though male may approach observer, calling loudly. Brown above; throat and breast dull-white, under tail-coverts rich yellow-buff. Male: *black patch on upperbreast extends in point up centre of throat, giving the white sides of throat the appearance of two white streaks*; these marks form an inverted V when bird raises bill to call. Wings stubby, tail rather long, flattish and slightly downcurved. Bill dark-horn above, paler below, strong, pointed with narrow ridge on top of upper mandible at base, giving head somewhat triangular appearance. Legs and feet powerful. Female and imm: no black patch on breast. Usually singly, though the fledged chick may remain with the female for a period. Moves like a rat on or near ground in thickest cover, at times with great speed, rarely revealing itself; tail often cocked. Flies feebly and probably only when hard-pressed; appears to use runs through undergrowth. Female usually silent; scarcely ever seen.

Similar species: Western Bristlebird (531): plain fawn-grey breast. Calls differ.

Voice: One of the most extraordinary of Australian bird-voices. Powerful, penetrating and directional; seemingly ventriloquial in quality. Typical territorial call of male: sweet descending crescendo, 'chip, chip, chip, chip-ip-ip-ip!!', at first well-spaced and deliberate, falling and accelerating into an ear-splitting almost explosive crack; other calls described include a short song, given by the male alone, or the male and female together; a three-noted call which has been characterized 'zip da dee', repeated once or twice, and three calls described respectively as the zit, squeak and chip calls, the first two probably being alarm-calls. Females are reported normally to give only single calls.

Habitat: Dense, damp vegetation in watercourses of low, heath-covered coastal prominences and adjacent low-lying swampy areas; in thickets of stunted eucalypts, principally of Bullich *E. megacarpa*; tea-tree, banksia, sheoak, rush, saw-sedge and tall grass.

Breeding: Nest: domed; of rush, grass or dead leaves, with small side-entrance; lined with hard smooth thin cardboard-like material, apparently of masticated decayed rush, plastered when wet on inner walls and bottom of nest-chamber. Usually in rushes, tangle of shrubs or clump of *Juncus*, on rough platform of same material as nest, 90–700 mm from ground. Egg: 1; described as long oval; dull, very pale-buff, with blotches of orange-brown, most prominent at large end.

Range and Status: Known at present only in one small population, confined to the area of Mt. Gardner, near Two People Bay, e. of Albany, WA; rediscovered 1961, when long thought to be extinct. There are thought to be some 40 pairs resident in the area, which has been declared a reserve. Rare; sedentary.

Larks   Family *Alaudidae*

Smallish birds typically of grasslands, light scrub and other open habitats; plumage brown, blackish or reddish brown and streaked; local soil-colouring may influence shade. They are characterized by stout bills, crown feathers that can be raised in low rounded crest, longish legs (often flexed in a crouched position), very long hind claws and white outer tail-feathers. They run rather than hop and, when disturbed, may crouch behind low cover. Most species become conspicuous during the breeding season by indulging in song-flights, in which the bird rises high or flies round on quivering wings, pouring out a stream of song, often mixed with mimicry of other species. Outside the breeding season, they may form large loose flocks. Note that neither Songlarks (510–11) nor the Magpie Lark (710) belong to this family despite their common names.

Food: Insects and other invertebrates, seeds and other vegetable matter.

Range: All continents except Antarctica, but very poorly represented in Aust. and the Americas, absent from many oceanic islands; introduced NZ.

Number of species: World 76; Aust. 2, including one introduced.

416 SINGING BUSHLARK *Mirafra javanica* Pl.67

Other names: Australian Skylark; Brown, Cinnamon, Horsfield's, Rufous-winged Bushlark; Croplark.

Field marks: 125–150 mm. Somewhat like a boldly-marked Common Skylark (417) but smaller and stockier with shorter tail, sturdy sparrow-like bill and distinctive fawn to rufous eyebrow returning round side of face to below eye. Colour variable, often in relation to soil of its habitat: *sandy, rufous, reddish grey or blackish above; with strong pattern from pale edges of wing-feathers;* fawn to pale-rufous below. Imm: wider more conspicuous pale margins to wing-feathers. Singly to open flocks; inconspicuous and often overlooked; runs nimbly, legs well bent, usually keeping close to cover; when surprised may freeze; when put to flight, flutters in almost shivery jerky tail-down manner a short distance, before dropping into cover, *rufous in wings* and white edges to tail prominent. When breeding, performs typical lark-like song-flight, hovering on quivering wings, singing gloriously, often at night. In places, may perch on telephone-lines crossing grasslands, unusual behaviour for a lark.

Similar species: Common Skylark (417): larger, tail longer, lacks bold rufous margins to wing-feathers; song more robust and sustained; direct flight stronger, showing pale trailing edge. Richard's Pipit (423): larger, longer, usually paler, with longer finer bill, legs, teeters longer tail up and down.

Voice: Sweet clear, if spasmodic, song; typically uttered while hovering 3–100 m high or descending on quivering wings; also sings in low undulating flight or when perched on stump, fence-post or ground; notes alternately shrill and trilling or rich and melodious. Accomplished mimic. When disturbed, often utters a chirrup.

Habitat: Grasslands, especially those with rank cover; open woodlands and scrublands; cereal or legume-crops; dust-bathes on dirt-roads, margins of crops.

Breeding: Nest: cup-shaped, partly or fully (if flimsily) domed; among grass tussocks, sometimes in depression. Eggs: 2–4; medium-oval, smooth, glossy; ground-colour from greyish stone to whitish, finely speckled or distinctly blotched pale-grey and lavender, sepia, dark-brown and blackish, evenly distributed or in zone at large end.

Range and Status: Most of Aust. n. of Tropic and through much of Q, NSW, Vic. and se. SA, w. to Eyre Pen.; apparently absent C. York Pen., Q and many parts of Divide in e. Aust., but recorded in alpine herbfield near Mt. Kosciusko. Probably migratory, certainly locally nomadic, but movements little understood. Generally regarded as a summer breeding migrant in s. Aust., arriving Oct.–Nov., departing Feb.–Mar., but many probably winter in coastal se. Aust., unnoticed because silent. Generally uncommon, except locally, when sometimes very abundant. Also NG to Asia.

417 COMMON SKYLARK *Alauda arvensis* Pl.67

Other name: English Skylark.

Field marks: 175–190 mm. A large lark, pale eyebrow encircles cheek; *feathers of crown often raised in low rounded crest, tail longish and slightly forked with conspicuous white sides.* Buff-white below, upperbreast boldly dark-streaked. Bill short, sturdy. Singly, in pairs to open companies; typically crouches, turns back on observer or flattens itself behind tuft of grass; flushes suddenly with a chirrup, flying strongly with marked undulation, displaying broad wings with *whitish trailing edge* and white edges to tail. Most conspicuous habit is to *hover up, singing gloriously, to great heights;* descends still singing, suddenly closes wings and plummets silently; occasionally sings from fence-posts, stumps. In coastal se. Aust., travelling single birds or parties are often heard or seen passing overhead, specially spring and autumn.

Similar species: Singing Bushlark (416). Richard's Pipit (423): slimmer; longer, slimmer bill and legs; more conspicuous pale eyebrow; tail less forked, teeters it up and down; perches more.

Voice: Sustained clear beautiful song of runs, trills and repeated throbbing phrases; also a mellow chirrup, often heard from passage birds high overhead.

Habitat: Short grasslands generally; pastures, wastelands, coastal sand-dunes.
Breeding: Nest: compact, grass-lined cup; in depression on ground, usually in shelter of tussock. Eggs: 3–5; greyish white, freckled and blotched brown.
Range and Status: Introduced to various places from Britain in 1850s and 1860s. Common in Tas., se. SA, Adelaide area, Kangaroo I. and most Vic., less common NSW Riverina, e. coastal NSW and tablelands. Nomadic or part-migratory.

Swallows and Martins Family *Hirundinidae*

Well-loved small graceful birds that spend much of their time on the wing in pursuit of flying insects. They have very short, wide bills, short necks and long pointed wings; in some, tails are deeply forked; others have shorter squarer tails. Swallows superficially resemble swifts, but their flight, though swift and slipping, is much slower and less dashing. They usually feed lower and also perch much on wires, dead branches, twigs over water or settle on ground, which most swifts cannot do. Plumage black or deep-blue and glossy above, paler below; some have distinctive pale rumps. The four species of swallows that breed in Aust. can also be recognized by nesting habits: one builds a bracket-like nest of mud, another tunnels, one nests in hollow limbs; the last makes a bottle-nest of mud-pellets; the last 3 breed in colonies. Though in Aust. the name 'martin' tends to be given to smaller species, there is no technical distinction from swallows. Note that wood-swallows (704–9) are not true swallows.
Food: Flying insects.
Range: All continents except Antarctica; absent from many oceanic islands.
Number of species: World 74; Aust. 5, including one rare but possibly regular migrant to ne. Aust.

418 WHITE-BACKED SWALLOW *Cheramoeca leucosternum* Pl.57
Other names: Black-and-white, White-breasted or White-capped Swallow.
Field marks: 125–150 mm. Distinctive: a chunky dull-black swallow of drier habitats: *crown, throat and back white*; tail deeply-forked. Imm: duller. Usually in small flocks or colonies. Flight less dashing than Welcome Swallow (420), more fluttering, irregular, like the martins. Has the unusual habit of using its own and occasionally burrows of other species, for roosting. More than a dozen have been discovered at night in one burrow and torpid birds have been taken from burrows in winter.
Similar species: Tree (421) and Fairy (422) Martins: dark backs, white rumps, shorter tails.
Voice: Dry 'jk, jk' uttered in flight; also attractive twittering song.
Habitat: Open inland areas, extending to drier coasts where there are suitable breeding habitats; usually near sandy or gravelly banks of creeks, road-cuttings, sandpits.
Breeding: The only Australian swallow that burrows in the ground. Nest: sparse lining of grass or leaves at end of tunnel 50 mm in diameter and 30–100 cm long; in creekbank, road-cutting, sandpit. Eggs: 4–6; pure-white.
Range and Status: Widespread; inland parts of all mainland States, to coasts in WA, SA and ne. NSW. Common *except* in n. half NT, n. and se. Q n. of Mt. Isa and e. of Divide, most of NSW e. of Divide, s. Vic., Tas. and extreme sw. WA. Breeding colonies may be far apart.

419 BARN SWALLOW *Hirundo rustica* Pl.57
Other names: Chimney or European Swallow.
Field marks: 160–170 mm. Like Welcome Swallow (420) but chestnut face and throat separated from *whiter underparts by distinct thin black band*. Imm: duller, with shorter, less deeply-forked tail. Habits like Welcome Swallow. Flight swift and slipping; perches

on overhead wires. Occurs in small to largish migratory flocks or as single vagrants with (420).

Voice: Reported as a high 'tswit', becoming rapid twitter when excited; alarm-call, high 'tswee'. Song: pleasant weak mixture of rapid twittering and warbling notes.

Habitat: Coastal open country generally, especially near water; also towns, on wires.

Range and Status: Breeds almost throughout the n. hemisphere, wintering in s. hemisphere. Birds presumably of n. Asian origin regularly winter s. to Philippines, Sunda Is. (including Timor) and NG. Probably a frequent summer visitor to coastal n. Aust., although records comparatively few. Sight-records (mostly Nov.–Mar.) from: Derby, WA; near Darwin and Adelaide R., NT; Mossman and Innisfail districts, ne. Q. and Fraser I. and Canungra, se. Q. Congregations of dozens to hundreds (some in successive seasons) at Derby, Adelaide R. and near Innisfail. Migratory.

420　WELCOME SWALLOW　*Hirundo neoxena*　　　　Pl.57

Other names: Australian or House Swallow.

Field marks: 150 mm. Our familiar swallow of houses and outbuildings: *forehead, face and throat dull-tan; pale-grey below*; tail deeply forked; in flight, row of lace-like white spots near ends of inner tail-feathers but no white rump. Imm: duller, tail shorter. Singly, pairs or small to large gatherings where flying insects abundant or during seasonal movments. Flight swift and slipping, often low above ground or water; may feed high, specially in humid weather. Courting males descend on stiffiy downheld quivering wings.

Similar species: Barn Swallow (419). Tree (421) and Fairy (422) Martins: stumpier, with whitish rumps; no tan on throat.

Voice: A single 'chep', usually in flight; spirited twittering song, also a rising 'seep seep seep'; in alarm, high-pitched puny 'seeet'.

Habitat: Widespread except in heavy forest and drier inland; perches, roosts and nests on and in many man-made structures, specially verandahs, garages. Under natural conditions, margins of lakes, rivers and swamps, perching on snags, exposed roots, dead branches.

Breeding: Nest: cup of mud-pellets bound with grass, densely lined with feathers, fur, hair or grass; in large cavity in tree, wall of cave, riverbank, on vertical surface or shelf under eave of building, parapet, mineshaft, even in boat, railway carriage. Eggs: 2–5; whitish, streaked and spotted red-brown and lavender.

Range and Status: S. and e. Aust., coastally n. to Port Hedland, WA; all SA; rare in far-n. and in s. NT, but occasional Alice Springs; all Tas., Vic., NSW; most Q, n. to Thursday I., w. to Mt. Isa–Birdsville; many islands off e. coast. Although many winter in s. Aust., there is a dispersal from se. Aust. to Murray–Darling basin and probably n. coastally during autumn–winter. Very common in s., less so in inland and n. Part-migratory. Self-introduced to NZ.

421　TREE MARTIN　*Cecropis nigricans*　　　　Pl.57

Other name: Tree Swallow.

Field marks: 125–140 mm. The larger and darker of our two small white-rumped swallows, the other being the Fairy Martin (422). *Note glossy-black crown and cheeks.* Both often mingle in small to large companies, usually near water. But when breeding, Tree Martin typically haunts large trees, e.g. river red gums, and sweeps and dips blithely round their heads, plunging into small hollow spouts. In flight both martins look smaller, stubbier and trimmer than Welcome Swallow (420); without deeply forked tails; flight more clipped and erratic with quicker wingbeats. At times very large companies of Tree Martins form temporary roosts in reedbeds.

Similar species: Fairy Martin (422).

Habitat: Colonies in large spreading trees in open woodland, usually near lakes, watercourses but at times far from water; occasionally in urban areas, nesting in buildings.

Voice: Dry little 'drrrt drrrt' and twitterings; animated twittering song.
Breeding: Nest: collection of grass and leaves; in hollow spout of tree;sometimes partly closed off by mud; several pairs may use single entrance to hollow, diving in at speed with breath-taking accuracy; occasionally nests in holes in cliffs or buildings, or usurps nest of Fairy Martin. Eggs: 3–5; pinkish white, finely freckled pale rusty-brown specially towards larger end.
Range and Status: Aust. and Tas.; migratory in s., arriving to breed July to Oct., departing Mar. to May. Common to very common. Also Lesser Sunda islands, Moluccas, NG, New Caledonia.

422 FAIRY MARTIN *Cecropis ariel* Pl.57

Other names: Bottle, Cliff or Land Swallow.
Field marks: 120–130 mm. A small white-rumped swallow like the Tree Martin (421), but slightly smaller, *whole crown pale rust-red, rump and underparts whiter, tail squarer.* When overhead, differences hard to see until birds bank, showing crown. Usually in companies, over water, open country generally and specially noticeable near nest-colonies. During migration often gathers with Tree Martins. It is the only Australian bird that builds a bottle-shaped mud nest. Like Tree Martin, gathers mud at puddles and often settles on bare ground, e.g. dirt roads.
Similar species: Tree Martin (421), Welcome (420) and White-backed (418) Swallows.
Voice: Slight churring 'drrt drrt' or rolling 'dzee dzee', higher pitched than Tree Martin.
Habitat: Open country generally, locally near water and suitable breeding places. Less often round large trees than Tree Martin.
Breeding: Nest: bottle-shaped; of mud-pellets; swollen nest-chamber *c.* 150 mm in diameter; neck or spout, from 50 to 300 mm long, narrows and may droop toward entrance. In colonies of few to dozens, nests often run together; on walls and ceilings of caves, overhung creekbanks, cavernous trees; now often in culverts, under bridges or eaves of buildings. Old nests are used by some pardalotes, House Sparrow (663), snakes and bats. Eggs: 4–5; whitish finely freckled reddish or yellowish brown.
Range and Status: Throughout Aust.: rare n. C. York Pen. and extreme sw. WA; accidental Tas. Common; a regular breeding migrant in se. Aust. from Aug.–Sept. to Apr., occasionally wintering. Straggler to NG.

Pipits and Wagtails Family *Motacillidae*

Pipits are ground-dwelling birds somewhat like larks; their bills and legs tend to be longer and more slender. They walk with slight swagger, teetering the longish tail up and down; they perch more. When breeding, they sing short, poorly developed songs from stumps, fence-posts or dead branches or fly high with repeated short quivering dives, calling. The single Australian species is commonly but incorrectly called a groundlark. *Wagtails* are more boldly marked or more colourful than pipits, and have much longer tails that they constantly teeter as they walk or run about. Familiar throughout Eurasia, they occur in Aust. only as rare migrants or vagrants. Identification is made difficult by the large number of races in several species, some of which have confusingly differing markings. These difficulties are compounded by the fact that while here they are usually in either nonbreeding or immature plumage, or transitional stages. Note that our familiar Willie Wagtail (489) is a fantail and not related, despite its common name.
Food: Chiefly insects and similar invertebrates; also seeds and other vegetable matter.
Range: Pipits: all continents except Antarctica and many oceanic islands. Wagtails: Eurasia and Africa, reaching Australasian region on migration.
Number of species: Pipits: World 43; Aust. 1. Wagtails: World 11; Aust. 3 rare migrants.

423 RICHARD'S PIPIT   *Anthus novaeseelandiae*   **Pl.67**

Other names: Groundlark; Australian, Indian or New Zealand Pipit.

Field marks: 165–190 mm. Familiar, slender streaked brownish bird with a *slender pale-brown bill and long pale pinkish brown legs*. Note the *long fawn eyebrow and double fine dark streak down either side of throat*; fine dark streaks on fawn breast, white edges to tail. Singly or pairs; walks and runs easily, with slight swagger, teetering tail up and down, perches on rocks, stumps, fences, dead branches. Flight somewhat fluttering, tail often spread and depressed, *white edges prominent*. Courting male performs high display-flight, swings up, swoops with wings quivering and tail elevated, swings up again, each dip accompanied by a high quavering note like 'peer'.

Similar species: Singing Bushlark (416) and Common Skylark (417). Rufous Songlark (510): dark from bill to eye; more 'netted' pattern on wings, tawny rump; no white in tail; different voice, habits.

Voice: Usual call: brisk splintered 'pith' or rasping drawn-out 'zwee'.

Habitat: Most grasslands from inland plains to cultivated pastures, alpine meadows; also open woodlands, coastal sand-dunes, roadsides.

Breeding: Nest: deep well-constructed cup of grasses; in depression usually in shelter of tussock or stone. Eggs: 3–4; grey, dull-white or buff-white, plentifully and finely freckled with deeper grey, slate-brown and umber.

Range and Status: Throughout Aust. and Tas. Very common; sedentary. Also e. Europe and Africa to Asia, Indonesia, NG and NZ.

424 YELLOW WAGTAIL   *Motacilla flava*   **Pl.79**

Field marks: 165–190 mm. Shaped somewhat like a long-tailed pipit. Plumage varies with race, sex, age and moult. Birds reaching n. Aust. belong to all age-groups and probably several races. Adults: head grey, blackish or olive, according to race, usually with a *long white, cream or yellow eyebrow; the ear-coverts are frequently grey or brown, the combination forming a simple distinctive facial pattern*. Upperparts grey to brownish, usually tinged greenish-yellow; some may have a golden-olive rump, causing confusion with Grey Wagtail (426). Wing-feathers dark-brown edged pale-brown to off-white, the pale tips of the wing-coverts sometimes forming two fine bars. Underparts clear bright-yellow to pale-yellow, buff, cream or whitish, frequently with irregular yellow markings and washed olive-grey at sides, sometimes across breast. The tail is longish, black, with white outer feathers. Females are duller. Imm: browner, underparts whitish, with a *necklace of brownish spots or streaks across breast*. In all plumages the legs are *brown to blackish*, helping separate it from Grey Wagtail. In Aust., usually singly or in small parties. Shy and active, walks with back-and-forward head-movement, bobs tail, leaps into air for insects. Flight strong and undulating; sometimes perches in trees.

Similar species: Yellow-hooded Wagtail (425): adults have more yellow on head; imms. may be difficult to tell apart; the white wingbars are broader. Grey Wagtail (426): usually bluer-grey above, with contrasting yellowish rump, tail longer; legs pinkish to pale-brown. In flight, a narrow pale wingbar. Calls differ. Imms may be hard to tell apart, but note leg-colour.

Voice: Described as a pronounced 'zweep, zweep'; also 'zip-zip-did-did-diddt'.

Habitat: Water-meadows; areas of short grass or bare ground, usually near water, swamp-margins; short grasslands with trees; airfields, ploughed land.

Range and Status: Ranges widely through Europe and Africa to Alaska, migrating to Africa, se. Asia, Indonesia, NG. Birds that reach n. Aust. probably belong to race *tschutschensis* that breeds ne. Siberia and Alaska and winters s. to Java and West Irian; other races that breed in se. Asia winter in Indonesia; some may reach Aust. In Aust., recorded near Derby, WA; Darwin, NT, Innisfail and old specimen Dawson R., Q; most records Nov.–Feb. Vagrant.

425 YELLOW-HOODED WAGTAIL *Motacilla citreola*
Other names: Citrine Wagtail, Yellow-headed Wagtail.
Field marks: 165–175 mm. Male breeding plumage distinctive: *head and underparts bright lemon-yellow*; *nape black, clearly-defined*; back, wings and rump ashy grey to black, with two whitish wingbars; tail long and blackish with broad white edges. Nonbreeding male; female: *crown and nape grey, forehead and eyebrow yellow*, underparts yellowish white. Imm: like female but whiter, said to be hard to tell from imms. of some races of Yellow Wagtail (424). In Aust. most likely to be seen singly, near water or in nearby trees. Walks, runs and perches with sprightly restless movements, jerks tail up and down. Flight jerky and undulatory, showing white band on wing, tail acting as a sort of pendulum behind; shrill call repeated on every up-curve.
Similar species: Yellow (424) and Grey (426) Wagtails.
Voice: Described as double high-pitched 'chip', with ringing inflexion, often in flight; also as a wheezy 'peep' or 'dzeep', similar to Yellow Wagtail.
Habitat: See above. The one Aust. sight-record refers to an area of swampy grassland adjacent to a mangrove-fringed shore.
Range and Status: Nominate race breeds ne. Russia; nw., cs. and c. Siberia; n. China; other races in ce. Russia; cw. Siberia; n. Afghanistan, Kashmir, Himalayas, Tibet and sw. China. Migrates s. to Pakistan, most of India, Bangladesh and Burma. One Australian record: adult male in breeding plumage seen Botany Bay, NSW, June–July 1962. Vagrant.

426 GREY WAGTAIL *Motacilla cinerea*
Field marks: 180–190 mm. Male, breeding: *throat black, rest of underparts yellow*; *upperparts blue-grey, white eyebrow not reaching bill, flight-feathers black with inner white bar*; *rump olive-yellow*; *very long black tail* prominently edged white. Nonbreeding: as above but throat white, breast buffish. Female: both plumages, tinged greenish above, rump olive-yellow, dull-white eyebrow and white throat. Both sexes: legs flesh-pink to pale-brown. Imm: eyebrow absent or indistinct; grey-brown above, rump yellow-buffish below, under tail-coverts yellow. In Aust., likely to be solitary; habits and actions like other wagtails.
Similar species: Yellow (424) and Yellow-hooded (425) Wagtails.
Voice: Described as a single note like an alarm-note of Tawny Grassbird (505), repeated quickly a number of times. Also described as 'a clear, sharp, metallic "chitik".' (se. Asia.)
Habitat: In Borneo, gravel beds of mountain torrents. In NG, mountain streams in forest or grasslands; cultivated mountain gardens. At Innisfail, Q, observed near running water on floor of disused lowland quarry.
Range and Status: Breeds w. Europe to Asia; migrates to Africa, Malay Archipelago, Borneo and NG, where it is 'the usual wagtail'. One Australian sight-record, probably imm.; near Innisfail, n. Q, Feb. 1970. Vagrant.

Cuckoo-shrikes and Trillers   Family *Campephagidae*

Neither cuckoos nor shrikes, the family takes its name from the cuckoo-like slender greyish form and flight of some typical members and from the somewhat shrike-like bill. In Asia they are widely known as greybirds. Apart from some African species and the small colourful Asian minivets, cuckoo-shrikes are mostly grey, black or white with barrings and other markings of one or other of these shades. They range in length from 125 mm to 380 mm. They forage singly, in pairs or small parties in branches and foliage of trees and at times on ground; some species hover. One aberrant Australian form, Ground Cuckoo-shrike (431) mostly of inland, has longish legs and walks and runs actively on ground when feeding. A characteristic of larger species is their habit of refolding or shuffling wings on alighting. A physical peculiarity of many is the presence of thick-matted, slightly spiny, feathers on lower back and rump. These are not normally visible but may be erected during display or in the presence of a predator when brooding. In this posture, the head and tail are depressed and the hump formed by the raised feathers of the rump becomes the highest part of the bird, making it look remarkably like a bump on the branch on which the tiny nest is placed. These plumes are easily shed. One member of family, White-winged Triller (432) is unusual among passerines in moulting twice a year; the male has a distinctive eclipse plumage. This and several other local species, including Black-faced Cuckoo-shrike (427) and Cicadabird (430) are wholly or partially migratory, moving north in winter. Cuckoo-shrikes make very small inconspicuous bowl-shaped nests of spiders' web, often decorated externally with lichen, usually high on the horizontal branch of a live tree.

Food: Insects, especially in foliage, other invertebrates, berries and fruit.

Range: From Africa and s. Asia to Australasian region and Samoa; absent from NZ.

Number of species: World 72; Aust. 8.

427 BLACK-FACED CUCKOO-SHRIKE *Coracina novaehollandiae* Pl.81

Other names: Blue or Grey Jay, Cherry Hawk, Leatherhead, Shufflewing, Summerbird.

Field marks: 305–355 mm. Widespread and familiar; blue-grey *with black face and throat, white below*. Flight-feathers blackish edged pale, tail broadly margined black, tipped white. Race *subpallidus* in coastal c. WA very pale-grey. Imm: black mark extends only from bill through eye and over ear-coverts; *crown, whitish throat and breast finely barred greyish*. Singly, pairs and family parties to small or occasionally large loose migratory companies. Flight strongly undulating, with wing-closed 'shooting': on alighting (and when courting and at other times) *has characteristic habit of repeatedly refolding wings*. Feeds mostly in foliage; hovers over trees or low over grass.

Similar species: In e. and se. Aust. note possible double confusion with Little Cuckoo-shrike (429), race *robusta*: dark-phase adult also has black face and upperbreast, can best be distinguished by duller, less uniform black of those parts with indistinct barring on breast; note size; different calls. Typical adult *robusta* can be confused with imm. Black-faced, having an approximately similar area of black through eye to ear-coverts but is plain pale-grey below; note size and call.

Voice: Unusual musical rolling purring or churring note; also a higher note, 'chereer, chereer' uttered in flight, when perched or when courting, often continually while shuffling wings; also harsh scolding 'skair'.

Habitat: Grasslands with trees, timber along watercourses, woodlands, scrublands, forests; orchards, parks, gardens.

Breeding: Nest: unusually small neat shallow cup; of fine twigs, bound with cobwebs, fitted snugly to horizontal limb or fork, 6–20 m high. Eggs: 2–3; blue-green, olive-green or olive-brown, blotched and spotted brown, reddish brown and grey, some as though below surface.

Range and Status: Throughout Aust. and Tas. Common; partly migratory and nomadic. There is a substantial movement n. from Tas. and se. Aust. in autumn after breeding, to inland and n. Aust.; many apparently cross to NG and islands. Also Lesser Sunda Islands, NG and Solomon Is.: some consider it conspecific with forms ranging to India and Himalayas.

428 BARRED CUCKOO-SHRIKE *Coracina lineata* Pl.81

Other name: Yellow-eyed Cuckoo-shrike.

Field marks: 255 mm. A distinctive small cuckoo-shrike: *note pale-yellow eye and finely barred white underparts*; bill and legs black. Pairs to small flocks; forages among foliage of trees for insects and fruit, often with other fruit-eating birds; active, frequently moving from tree to tree.

Similar species: Oriental Cuckoo (363): more slender, tail longer; darker above, more boldly barred below; note yellow eye-ring and legs.
Voice: Pleasant chatter, often uttered in flight: described as 'aw-loo-ack, aw-loo-ack, aw-lack, aw-lack' with tone of toy mouth-organ; a plaintive whistled 'whee' has also been described (NG).
Habitat: Tropical and subtropical rainforest, scrub and scrub-margins, eucalypt forests and woodlands, clearings in secondary growth, swamp woodlands, timber along water courses, plantations, gardens.
Breeding: Nest: shallow saucer of fine twigs bound with cobweb; on horizontal fork or branch, to 20 m high. Eggs: 2; white, spotted brown and purplish grey.
Range and Status: Coastal e. Aust. from C. York to Manning R., NSW. Generally uncommon, rare in NSW; nomadic. Also NG, Bismarck Archipelago, Solomon Is.

429 LITTLE CUCKOO-SHRIKE *Coracina papuensis* Pl.81
Other names: Papuan, White-bellied or White-breasted Cuckoo-shrike.
Field marks: 265–280 mm. Pale-grey above, white below; *note the black facial mark from bill, just reaching or just through eye.* The large race *robusta* has breast washed grey. This race also has a rare dark phase, in which the face, neck and upperbreast are *smutty black, breaking into irregular bars on breast.* The amount of black varies; some have all-black heads. Like other cuckoo-shrikes, the blackish flight-feathers have pale margins, giving a distinct pattern from rear; tail black, tipped white, slightly forked. Imm: head and upperparts mottled grey and brown; grey mark from bill to eye. Habits like Black-faced Cuckoo-shrike (427) but more solitary and much less common, particularly in s.; also apparently less migratory.
Similar species: Black-faced Cuckoo-shrike (427), imm: from adult Little by size, larger black facial mark, faint barring on underparts. Adults are usually present; calls differ. Adult Black-faced from dark phase *robusta* by size, purer black face, and different calls.
Voice: Typical call is a peevish 'kissik, kissik' or 'quizeek'.
Habitat: Woodlands, scrub, timber along watercourses, mangroves; plantations, gardens.
Breeding: Nest and eggs like Black-faced, but smaller.
Range and Status: Moluccas, NG and Solomons in many races; nominate race occurs w. and n. NG. In Aust. there are two races: *hypoleuca* from Kimberleys, WA, through top end NT and far nw. Q approximately to Burketown; *robusta* meets it in s. coastal areas of Gulf of Carpentaria and replaces it over much of e. half Q, NSW, Vic. and se. SA. Both are common in n. but *robusta* progressively less common southwards, being rare s. of Divide in Vic. and in se. SA. Nomadic or sedentary.

430 CICADABIRD *Coracina tenuirostris* Pl.82
Other names: Caterpillar-eater, Jardine Caterpillar-eater or Triller.
Field marks: 265 mm. A small slender cuckoo-shrike, more often heard than seen. Male: *slate-grey, blackish from bill to cheeks; centres of some flight-feathers black; tail black and slightly forked, central feathers grey;* bill and legs black. Female and imm: grey-brown above; creamy buff below; *with broken dark-brown barrings on sides of neck and breast. Note conspicuous pale eyebrow,* sides of face blackish, streaked; tail brown with pale-buff edges and tip; bill dark-brown. Singly or pairs, usually high in trees and usually first noted by call. Movements quicker than other cuckoo-shrikes; does not appear to shuffle wings. Flight swift and undulating.
Similar species: White-winged Triller (432), female, and Varied Triller (433), female.
Voice: Male: like cicada beginning to call: a strange, loud, rather harsh, staccato buzzing repeated 8–20 times or more, slowing and dropping slightly; when chasing, reported to utter a soft, explosive 'twik' or 'twok'; alarm-call, quick, slightly rolling 'chuit'.

Habitat: Heads of trees in tropical and temperate rainforests, scrubs, open woodlands, paperbark-swamps, mangroves.

Breeding: Nest: very small for bird's size; shallow bowl of small twigs and stems, bound with cobweb and camouflaged on outside with lichen; on fork or horizontal branch, 10–25 m high. Egg: 1; pale blue-grey to green-grey, heavily marked with dull-brown, grey-brown and lavender.

Range and Status: Coastal n. and e. Aust.: from Kimberleys, WA, through top end NT and from C. York to near Melbourne. Local, generally uncommon. A regular breeding migrant in s. from Oct. to Mar., with general n. movement in winter, some to NG. Also Celebes, NG and Solomon Is.

431 GROUND CUCKOO-SHRIKE *Coracina maxima* Pl.81

Other names: Ground or Long-tailed Jay.

Field marks: 330–355 mm. The only cuckoo-shrike adapted to feeding mostly on ground; *slender and long-legged.* Head and upper body pale-grey, *wings and long, slightly forked, tail black, contrasting with finely barred white underparts, lower back and rump. Eye pale.* Imm: fine broken barrings above and on throat; eye dark. Pairs or small parties; walks and runs with back-and-forward head-motion. Rather shy, flies readily: flight strong and easy; wingbeats interspersed with glides on depressed wings, *white back and rump contrasting strongly with dark wings and tail.* Perches stumps, fence posts, hawks for flying insects.

Voice: Flight-call, distinctive far-carrying 'pee-ew, pee-ew'; also 'chill-chill . . . . . kee-lick, kee-lick'.

Habitat: Open country generally, with dead trees and belts of live trees; timber along watercourses; open mallee, mulga and native pine scrubs; claypans, pastures, vineyards.

Breeding: Nest: shallow cup of stems, bark and grasses bound with cobwebs, spiders' egg-sacs and sometimes wool; on horizontal branch or fork 3–15 m high. Occasionally built on old nest of Magpie Lark (710) or White-winged Chough (712). Eggs: 2–3; glossy; olive with brown or red-brown markings toward larger end and with few irregular black spots.

Range and Status: Interior Aust., reaching coast at Gulf of Carpentaria; occasional e. and s. of Divide. Generally uncommon; probably nomadic.

432 WHITE-WINGED TRILLER *Lalage sueurii* Pl.82

Other names: Jardine or White-shouldered Caterpillar-eater or Triller.

Field marks: 155–185 mm. A small cuckoo-shrike, longish-tailed and graceful. Male: glossy black above, to eye; pure white below. *Note conspicuous white shoulders and white edges to coverts in netted pattern; pale-grey lower back and rump, white corners to black tail.* Bill and short legs black. Adult male is unusual among passerines in entering eclipse plumage Mar.–Aug. when crown and back brown like female, *wings and tail remain black, rump purer-grey, underparts whitish.* Displays and sometimes breeds while in eclipse. Female: brown above, off-white below slightly streaked brown, wing-feathers margined fawn-white *in distinctive netted pattern; note dark line through eye, slight pale eyebrow.* Imm: male more buff on head, mantle, wing-coverts and breast than eclipse male. Singly, pairs or loose companies; conspicuous on migration and specially when breeding, when males fly from tree to tree calling or display with spread wings and partly spread, cocked tail; defend territories aggressively. Normal flight strong, undulating and rapid. Feeds among foliage, sometimes hovers close to ground or forages on ground near trees; sometimes feeds among blossoms, presumably on nectar.

Similar species: Varied Triller (433), male: bold white eyebrow, no white shoulders, lightly barred breast, ochre under tail-coverts. Female differs from female White-winged in same features; no pale margins to wing-feathers. Rufous Songlark (510): tawny rump.

Voice: Male territorial song: clear sustained and variable, sounding in part like slightly descending 'chiff-chiff-chiff-joey-joey-joey' or 'deet-deet-deet-dip-dip-dip-dip-drrr' ending in a canary-like trill. Uttered flying from tree to tree, gliding down with outspread wings and tail; perched, or white brooding or low in dense cover. Female seldom calls.

Habitat: During migration: open country with trees, from inland plains to coastal farming country, suburban areas. Breeds in open woodlands and scrublands, woodland along watercourses, native pine and other scrubs.

Breeding: Nest: small shallow cup; of dry grasses, rootlets, pieces of bark and small fine twigs, bound with cobweb; usually on horizontal branch or fork, from 1–20 m high; several nests often in same tree or group of trees, or near nests of Willie Wagtail (489), Restless Flycatcher (485), Magpie Lark (710). Eggs: 2–3; green, heavily streaked and blotched brown, chiefly at large end.

Range and Status: Throughout Aust., vagrant Tas. Resident near water in n. Aust.; otherwise migrant with nomadic tendency, moving s. into s. Aust. from Aug.–Oct. to Dec.–Mar., n. again in autumn, part of population regularly crossing to NG. Breeds soon after arrival in s. but not always in same localities as previous year. Common. Also Java, Celebes, Sunda Is., NG.

433 VARIED TRILLER *Lalage leucomela* **Pl.82**

Other names: Pied or White-eyebrowed Caterpillar-eater.

Field marks: 175 mm. Male: a small cuckoo-shrike, somewhat like male White-winged Triller (432) without white shoulders, *but with prominent short white eyebrow, black line through eye, two prominent white bars on wing and biscuit-coloured wash on finely-barred underparts, to yellow-buff under tail-coverts.* Female and imm: dark-brown above, with similar pale markings; greyer and more heavily barred below. Singly or pairs; moves quietly and often high in foliage. The frequently heard distinctive call usually first reveals its presence.

Similar species: White-winged Triller (432).

Voice: Typical call, unusual harsh trill, a loud rolling 'brreeer', repeated 4 to 8 or more times, each phrase swelling and falling away. Others take up call, a common sound in n. forests.

Habitat: Chiefly coastal in tropical and subtropical rainforests and scrubs, open woodland and forest, thickets along watercourses; mangroves; plantations, gardens.

Breeding: Nest: very small shallow cup; of fine twigs, rootlets and grasses, bound with cobwebs; on horizontal branch or fork, 1–20 m high. Egg: 1; greenish, blotched with red-brown.

Range and Status: N. and e. Aust. from Kimberleys, WA, through top end NT, and from C. York s. almost to Port Stephens, NSW. Common in n., rather rare in NSW. Sedentary. Also NG and Bismarck Archipelago.

Bulbuls   Family *Pycnonotidae*

Active, often bold, inquisitive birds of moderate size and often rather inconspicuous plumage. Many are noisy, with continual musical chatterings or pleasant songs. Some are crested and many are characterised by a patch of somewhat hair-like feathers on the nape and rather long rump feathers. Their colours and patterns are plain but many have small patches of yellow or red about the head; the under tail-coverts are often similarly coloured. As a rule bulbuls have adapted well to alteration of woodland and forest habitat, many now live in cultivated lands and round cities, villages and gardens. Sexes usually similar, male slightly larger. The family is represented in Aust. by one introduced species Red-whiskered Bulbul (434). A second species, the Red-vented Bulbul *P. cafer*, was formerly reported in Melbourne and Adelaide. Apparently an aviary escape, it has not become established.

Food: Insects, fruit, nectar, etc.

Range: Africa to Asia as far east as Moluccas.

Number of species: World about 120; Aust. 1, introduced.

434 RED-WHISKERED BULBUL *Pycnonotus jocosus* Pl.62

Field marks: 230 mm. Jaunty and distinctive; now one of Sydney's characteristic birds: olive-brown above, extending onto sides of white breast. *Note forward-inclined black crest, conspicuous white cheek, bordered below by fine blackish line; red mark behind eye, pink or red under tail-coverts.* Singly and pairs in local colonies; restless, quick, prominent on wires or other high points round houses in urban areas, often calling; captures insects on wing. During winter sometimes congregates in large companies, specially where attracted to berries, soft fruits.

Similar species: Eastern Whipbird (492): much darker, breast black; no red in plumage; lower denser habitat.

Voice: Jaunty, pleasant liquid notes, hard to describe, but easily recognized when once identified; familiar sounds in Sydney parks and gardens.

Habitat: Gardens, suburban trees, public parks, wasteland, thickets; marginally in native woodland and scrubland.

Breeding: Nest: shallow untidy open cup; of fibrous bark, shreds of leaves and rootlets, lined with very fine short twigs or rootlets; up to 3 m high in thick bush or other cover. Eggs: 2–4; glossy, whitish, heavily but finely spotted and sometimes heavily blotched reddish or purplish brown.

Range and Status: Naturally in India, China, se. Asia. Introduced Mauritius and Aust. Common, widespread in Sydney area with apparently recent extension to lower Hunter Valley; also now established Coffs Harbour, NSW. In Vic., a smaller colony persists in and round the suburb of South Yarra; reported Adelaide, but apparently not established.

Flycatchers, Thrushes, Whistlers and Allies   Family *Muscicapidae*

This is a very large and diverse family divided into several sections. Brief introductions are provided for the more important sections that occur in Aust.

THRUSHES

A very large cosmopolitan group of mostly plump slender-billed songbirds that take much of their food on the ground. Note that the shrike-thrushes are not closely related. Most thrushes have melodious voices; their plumage is usually brown to reddish brown, often with distinctive spots and other markings. Thrushes in Aust. fall into two groups. Most familiar round settlement in many parts se. Aust. are the introduced Blackbird (436) and Song Thrush (437); less well-known is the native Scaly Thrush (435); it also ranges through se. Asia into Siberia. The endemic scrub-robins (438–9) are longish-tailed birds with thrush-like characters and mannerisms but more terrestial habits; they nest on the ground. Their distribution is divided; one lives in humid ne. rainforests, the other in southern arid scrubs.

Food: Insects, molluscs, other invertebrates; seeds, fruit, berries.

Range: Practically worldwide, except for Antarctica and NZ.

Number of species: World *c.* 300; Aust. 5, including 2 introduced.

435 SCALY THRUSH *Zoothera dauma* Pl.60

Other names: Ground, King, Mountain, Speckled or White's Thrush; Spotted Ground Thrush.

Field marks: 255–290 mm. A large handsome thrush: grey-brown to golden-brown above with buff mottlings; whitish below, *with bold overall scaly pattern of dark half-moons*; legs flesh-coloured. Singly or pairs; quiet and inconspicuous on ground among leaf-litter. Stands motionless, hops or runs forward, may rock back and forward a little, jabs bill vigorously into ground. When approached, freezes or flies away low through trees, *showing prominent pale wingbar.*

Similar species: Song Thrush (437): plainer above, breast spotted; no scaly pattern.

Voice: Seldom heard; typically two clear notes connected by a slurred upward slide. At times the song is developed into a sustained melody. Heard mostly in winter and spring, usually very briefly at dawn, but during day in dull weather and in denser habitats. Flight or contact-note, a thin 'seep'.

Habitat: Shady areas and damp gullies of wet woodlands, rainforests, coastal scrubs; in winter to scrubs, woodlands, secondary growth in sub-inland; sheltered gardens.

Breeding: Nest: large, bowl-shaped, rather untidy; rim thick and rounded; of fine roots, strips of bark, decorated outside with moss and lichen; usually in vertical fork, 2–10 m high. Eggs: 2–3; variable, pale-stone to green or whitish green, thickly freckled red-brown or with few fine red-brown markings round larger end.

Range and Status: Coastal e. Aust., from Atherton Tableland, Q, to Bass Strait islands and Tas., w. to se. SA, Mt. Lofty Ras. and Kangaroo I.; occasional Flinders Ras. Mostly on or coastwards of Divide. Sedentary, but some dispersal to more open country in winter, including parts of Murray Valley. Also wide overseas distribution, from Solomon Is., and NG to se. Asia, Siberia and e. Europe.

436 BLACKBIRD *Turdus merula*   Pl.60

Field marks: 255 mm. Male: a well-shaped, *uniformly black bird with yellow-orange bill and eye-ring and black legs.* Female: dark-brown above, rufous-brown below with faint paler eyebrow; *throat dull-white or buff, finely streaked darker; bill yellow-brown.* Imm: like female, but mottled rufous, bill brown; sub-adult male: uniform brownish black, bill blackish. Singly or pairs; typically moves with vigorous hops; droops, flicks wings and longish tail; pauses, head on side to 'listen', jabs bill vigorously into soil for worms. Short flights are low and undulating, but flight fast and direct when moving over open country. Strongly territorial and vocal when breeding, aggressive at bird-baths, feeding tables; often a pest in fruit trees; fond of berries. Albinos or part-albinos not unusual.

Similar species: Common Starling (687): oily gloss on plumage, often with fine white spots; sharper, paler-yellow or blackish bill, shorter tail; legs reddish. Feeds often in flocks with fast fussy movements; song wheezy. Song Thrush (437): from female and imm. Blackbird in cream-white underparts with sparse darker spots; song differs.

Voice: Serene mellow, often loud, song in measured phrases; lacks repetitions of Song Thrush. At dawn, dusk and in presence of predators, small chucking notes, a ringing 'tchink, tchink', an anxious drawn-out 'tsoi?'. A screeching chatter in alarm; flight-call, a thin 'tseee'; whisper-song in autumn includes mimicry of native birds.

Habitat: Gardens, parks, orchards; understorey of wetter woodlands and forests; thickets, timber along watercourses, denser coastal scrubs.

Breeding: Nest: substantial cup of grass, rootlets or bark, reinforced with mud or occasionally horse-manure; lined with fine grass and rootlets. Eggs: 3–5; blue-green, freckled, streaked or blotched pale red-brown or grey.

Range and Status: Naturally, in Europe and Asia. Introduced Melbourne 1862 and later there and Sydney; Adelaide 1863. Common and widespread in Tas., most of Vic. and s. SA except mallee areas, occasional Flinder Ras.; e. NSW n. and w. to Cobar and w. along Murray and watercourses of s. Riverina and in vineyards and citrus-groves to Waikerie–Moorook, SA.

437 SONG THRUSH *Turdus philomelos*   Pl.60
Other name: English Thrush.
Field marks: 230 mm. Mid-brown above; *cream-white to buff-white below with sparse dark spots*; in flight, note buff underwing. Singly or pairs; moves on ground with short runs and pauses or bouncing hops. Smashes shells of garden snails by using a rock for an anvil. Flight swift and slipping.
Similar species: Scaly Thrush (435): larger; distinctive scaly pattern overall; pale wing-bar in flight; song differs. Blackbird (436), female and imm: much darker below.
Voice: Clear spirited fragmented song, easily recognized by phrases repeated 2–4 times between pauses; for minutes to several hours. Heard most frequently at dawn and dusk June–Nov., sometimes into autumn; mimics Australian species. Alarm-call, tinny scolding chatter; flight-call, quiet 'sip'.
Habitat: Gardens, parks, wetter woodlands and forests, thickets.
Breeding: Nest: bowl-shaped and somewhat untidy on exterior; of tangled grasses, roots, fine twigs; inner part more tightly woven and smoothly plastered with mud and often horse-manure; usually in dense bush, shrub or creeper against house or bank. Eggs: 3–5; pale-blue with sparse fine black spots.
Range and Status: Introduced Melbourne in 1860s; subsequently Sydney, ACT and elsewhere; now resident only Melbourne and other parts of Vic. including Warragul, parts of Mornington Pen., Dandenong Ras., Yellingbo, Macedon, Werribee, Geelong, Lorne districts; usually rather rare and local, near habitation. Also introduced NZ. Occurs naturally in Europe, n. Africa and w. Asia.

438 NORTHERN SCRUB-ROBIN *Drymodes superciliaris*   Pl.60
Other name: Eastern Scrub-robin.
Field marks: 210 mm. Like a boldly-marked Southern Scrub-robin (439): rich-brown above with chestnut rump and central tail-feathers, face and underparts fawn-white, breast and flanks washed tawny. *Note conspicuous vertical black eyeline; black, white-tipped, wing-coverts, double white wingbar and white tips to black outer tail-feathers.* Reported to hop briskly over leaf-litter, cocks, raises and lowers tail; rather tame.
Voice: Described as a long drawn-out whistle, like a quail-thrush.
Habitat: Leaf-litter on floor of tropical rainforests and vine-scrub, specially in more open areas and margins of same.
Breeding: Nest: a depression lined with dead leaves, fine fibres, with outside, a thick wall of twigs. Eggs: 2; oval, light stone-grey, thickly covered with small umber blotches, heavier at large end.
Range and Status: Confined in Aust. to n. part C. York Pen., Q, s. to lower Archer R. and Coen. Sedentary. Also NG, Aru Is.

439 SOUTHERN SCRUB-ROBIN *Drymodes brunneopygia*   Pl.60
Other name: Pale Scrub-robin.
Field marks: 200–230 mm. A spirited ground-dweller of mallee and other dry scrubs. Dull-brown above, grey-white below, *with rufous-brown lower back and tail*, buffish flanks and under tail-coverts. Note large dark eye with *vertical blackish eyemark, fine white double wingbar and longish mobile white-tipped tail*, which it raises and lowers or flicks rudderlike. Singly or pairs; unobtrusive, feeds on ground among debris; flips leaves, occasionally flies up to snap insects. Runs swiftly if approached, scolds harshly from cover but will often inquisitively approach quiet observer.
Voice: Distinctive sweet musical 'chee-too-kwee?', or 'whip-whip, paree?' while perched on stick, low bush or high in dead tree; contact-call, long high-pitched 'seeep'; also a frequently heard, dry rattling scold.
Habitat: Mallee, broombush and other dry scrubs; lignum on claypans; heaths, coastal tea-tree thickets.

Breeding: Nest: cup-like depression on ground, in litter, lined with fine twigs, rootlets, strips of bark; rimmed with distinctive low barricade of 'dog-legged' criss-crossed heavy twigs. Usually in open or at base of tree or beside fallen branch. Egg: 1 usually; green-grey, spotted and blotched brown.

Range and Status: Drier areas of s. Aust.: sw. NSW, n. to about Mt. Hope, e. to near Griffith (Cocoparra NP); nw. Vic., s. to near Natimuk; se. SA n. in Flinders Ras., and w. to Eyre Pen.; Bight coast and in sw. WA n. to Shark Bay, but not in extreme sw. corner. Generally uncommon; sedentary.

OLD WORLD FLYCATCHERS

As presently understood, a large assemblage of mostly insectivorous small birds distributed from Europe to Africa, Asia, the Australian region, NZ and Pacific Islands. Australian representatives are mostly colourful plump small birds with finer bills than typical flycatchers. All *except* the four *Microeca* flycatchers (451–4) take their food mostly on the ground and are called 'robins', a name probably first applied in nostalgia for the robin red-breast of Europe, actually a thrush. Another vernacular altogether would be better but 'robin' is probably here to stay. The worst identification problems in the group (for observers in s. and e. Aust.) are found in red-breasted robins (440–4) in their brown female or imm. plumages. As a group, they can usually be identified by their upright posture, quick flicks of slightly-drooped wings and of tail. When in open country during autumn–winter dispersal they frequently dart to ground to seize an insect, then move ahead in short flights, alighting on ground, thistles, posts etc. In these dispersals, Flame Robin (442) is the only species usually in flocks. Identification of males is based on shade of upperparts, extent and colour of red on breast and presence of a red cap or white in tail. 'Brown birds' are more difficult: only two regularly show red to any marked degree but because a few females of most species may have reddish breasts, it is not always a reliable character. Identification is based on general shade, the shade and extent of a 'broken-arrow' wingbar and presence or absence of white in tail. The 'uncoloured robins' (445–7) and (457–8) are individualists and present no special problems. The yellow robins (448–50) have a characteristic 'jizz'. Confiding birds of usually closed habitats, they typically cling sideways low on a vertical trunk or vine, watching for food on the ground. They present no serious identification problems. One species, the White-breasted Robin (448) of sw. Aust., has entirely lost yellow pigmentation. The four *Microecas* (451–4) complete the group in Aust. Small graceful birds with flat triangular bills and soft tones of plumage, they form a distinctive company. Unlike other members of the family in form, behaviour and feeding habits, their flycatcher-like ways may have developed coincidentally in isolation. They are particularly noted for their tiny shallow nests – the smallest of any Australian birds. Note that one, the Yellow-footed Flycatcher (451) is not only a new-comer to the genus, but has a new common name. It was formerly called Little Yellow Robin. The Brown-tailed Flycatcher (453) is once-more raised to species rank. There are identification problems with both – see text.

Food: Chiefly insects and their larvae.

Range: Europe, Africa, Asia, Australasian region and parts of Oceania.

Number of species: World 200 + ; Aust. 16.

440 ROSE ROBIN *Petroica rosea*   **Pl.63**

Other name: Rose-breasted Robin.

Field marks: 100–120 mm. *Smaller, more slender and longer tailed* than other red-breasted robins, with more flycatcher-like jizz. Male: small white forehead; *uniform deep-grey above*, extending over throat; *breast bright rose red, underparts and undertail white, outer tail-feathers mainly white*. Female: greyish brown above with broken whitish bars on wing; *greyish white below sometimes washed pale-rose on breast*; *tail dark-brown, edged white*. Imm: like female. Singly or pairs, graceful and active; takes insects from tips of leaves or darts into air in tumbling pursuit; the most arboreal red robin, often high in forest canopy.

Similar species: Pink Robin (441): 'brown birds' are richer olive-brown with a rich-buff wingbar; no white on tail.

Voice: Male: pretty trilling territorial song, 'dick, dick-didit-deer-deer', with something of quality of ball-bearing bouncing on hard surface, last two notes pitched higher; also described as 'a-ree-a-ree-a-ree'; alarm-call, an agitated chirring. Both sexes: dry 'tick' like snapping twig.

Habitat: Breeds in dense gullies and other parts of wet forests, temperate and subtropical rainforest; in NSW and Vic. known to breed near sea-level (Otway Ras. and elsewhere) but in Q breeding appears to be restricted to higher altitudes. Disperses in autumn–winter to drier more open woodland, sub-inland and coastal scrublands and riverside vegetation.

Breeding: Nest: smaller than Pink Robin; deep cup; of green moss bound with spiders' web, lined with fur or plant-down; heavily decorated externally with lichens; generally on horizontal lichen-covered fork or branch, low to 18 m high. Eggs: 2–3; pale-green or blue-grey, freckled brown and purple, more heavily at large end.

Range and Status: Coastal and mountain forests of mainland se. and e. Aust., from sw. Vic. to about Rockhampton, Q, and better-vegetated coastal islands. There is an autumn–winter dispersal to woodlands in coastal and sub-inland lowlands, w. to coastal se. SA and (? occasional) to Fleurieu Pen. and Adelaide suburbs in Mt. Lofty Ras.; inland to near Dimboola, Vic. and Murray Valley (Mystic Park–Chiltern–Yackandandah); in ACT to Brindabella Ras.; in NSW w. to Parkes-Peak Hill–Warrumbungle NP–Inverell; in Q, inland to Chinchilla and n. (? exceptionally) to Eungella NP, inland of Mackay. Locally common; part-migratory or dispersive.

441 PINK ROBIN *Petroica rodinogaster* Pl.63

Other name: Pink-breasted Robin.

Field marks: 115–127 mm. Male: distinguished from other red robins by *the absence of white from wings and tail*; wholly sooty black above, usually with very small, white mark over bill; *throat and upperbreast sooty, cut off from dusky rose-pink breast and underparts.* Female: darkest female red-breasted robin; *deep olive-brown above with rich-buff double wingbar*; may have small buff-white mark over bill and slight paler edges to tail *but no white*; underparts fawn, washed grey-buff across breast, occasionally with faint pink wash. Singly or pairs; quiet, tame; feeds low in cover, often darting out to seize an insect on open ground.

Similar species: Rose Robin (440), male: rose breast extends to throat; longish tail edged white. Female: much paler; wingbars nearly white; longish tail edged white.

Voice: Song of male described as subdued simple warble. Both sexes utter sharp 'tick' like snapping a dry twig; also scolding 'chur-r-r-r-'.

Habitat: Breeds in dense gullies in temperate rainforests, dispersing to more open forests, woodlands and scrublands, including sub-inland belar and native pine; coastal tea-tree scrubs; occasionally to gardens, plantations round homesteads, shrub-cover on golf-courses; seldom to treeless areas.

Breeding: Nest: somewhat larger than Rose; rounded cup; of fine strips of bark, green moss, bound with spiders' web, lined with fern-fibre, hair or fine grass; exterior typically covered with lichen; in tree-fern, leafy shrub or tree, 1–6 m high. Eggs: 3–4; greenish white, thickly sprinkled with light-chestnut and purple-brown.

Range and Status: Its breeding stronghold is Tas., where it is fairly widespread (including coastal islands and suitable habitat on islands of Bass Strait); also breeds mountain woodlands and forests of s. and e. Vic. and (probably) adjacent se. NSW (Kosciusko NP). There is an autumn–winter dispersal to woodlands, scrubs and even gardens in coastal and sub-inland lowlands, in which 'brown birds' are far more frequently seen than coloured males. In this dispersal it has been recorded w. to coastal se. SA, inland to the Murray

Valley (Mystic Park–Corowa), the ACT–L. George and n. to near Sydney and (exceptionally) to Pittsworth–Irongate, sw. of Toowoomba in se. Q. Locally common, generally uncommon; migratory or dispersive.

442 FLAME ROBIN *Petroica phoenicea*   Pl.63

Other names: Bank or Flame-breasted Robin, Robin Redbreast.

Field marks: 125–140 mm. Male: distinguished by *bright flame-red from throat to underparts*; dark-grey above, smallish white patch above bill, bold white slash across wing, white edges to tail. Female: buffish grey-brown above, *prominent buff-white broken arrow wingbars*; *outer tail-feathers mostly white*; throat and breast brownish grey-buff, deeper across breast, underparts whitish. Note that a minority of 'brown birds' have *yellow-orange wash (or spots)* on breast. This may be a mature female character, but so far the use of plumage details as a means of telling females from imms has proved impossible. It is safe to refer only to 'brown birds'. Usually in pairs during spring–summer; open companies during autumn–winter dispersal. These feed in open country and form communal roosts in nearby woodland, orchards. It is the only red-breast regularly to form flocks. These may be 'brown birds' only, but often adult males are present and their bright breasts are conspicuous on farmlands, golf-courses, snowfields, etc.; occasional Scarlet Robins (443) join these companies.

Similar species: Scarlet Robin (443), male: black above, with black upperbreast. Female: darker above, usually has pink wash on breast. Seldom in flocks.

Voice: Male; pleasing high-pitched song, in little runs of distinctive tinkling lilting quality; louder and merrier than Scarlet Robin's, syllabized imaginatively 'you may come, if you will, to the sea'; in winter dispersal, feeding 'brown birds' utter brief 'peep'.

Habitat: Breeds in forests, woodlands and scrubs of both coastal and sub-inland foothills and ranges to about 1,800 m; disperses in autumn and winter to lower, more open country, grasslands, treeless sub-inland plains; paddocks and ploughed land, golf-courses, orchards, parks, gardens.

Breeding: Nest: bulky, somewhat rough cup; of fine bark-strips and grass bound with spiders' web; decorated with moss, lichen or hanging bark-strips; lined with fur, hair or plant-down; in cavity in tree, often charred; behind bark on tree-trunk; in overhanging bank or rock fissure among roots of upturned trees; woodpile; open shed, or old mine-shaft. Sometimes in broken tree-fork or spout to 20 m high, or in low dense bushes less than 1 m high, usually then with overhanging cover. Eggs: 3–4; greenish white, freckled; spotted with yellowish chestnut and lilac markings, sometimes in zone at large end.

Range and Status: Se. Aust. and Tas.: breeds mostly in timbered foothills and high country of the Divide, from tablelands of n. NSW to Vic., islands of Bass Strait, Tas., and possibly se. SA. In s. NSW, Vic. and Tas. there appears to be a widespread autumn–winter dispersal to lowlands, when it extends w. to Yorke Pen. and Kangaroo I., SA, inland to about Balranald-Hay, NSW, and n. to about Chinchilla, Q. Birds breeding from about Blue Mts., NSW and further n. may be more sedentary in high country. A trans-Bass Strait migration of Tas.-breeding birds has long been suspected, but not proven. Common, part-migratory, dispersive or sedentary.

443 SCARLET ROBIN *Petroica multicolor*   Pl.63

Other names: Robin Redbreast, Scarlet-breasted or White-capped Robin.

Field marks: 120–140 mm. Male distinctive: jet-black above with *white forehead*, bold white slash on wing, white edges to tail; *upperbreast black, breast scarlet*. Pale males can be mistaken for Flame Robins (442) but see below. Female: the only female red-breasted robin usually to have a pale-red wash on breast (but see group-introduction): *greyish olive-brown above; small buff or buff-white forehead, bold buff-white broken arrow on wing, buffish edges to secondaries*; tail edged white. Imm: grey-white below, washed buff, with no red. Usually in pairs in spring and summer; in winter moves into more open country, usually singly or pairs; sometimes associates with Flame Robins.

Similar species: Flame Robin (442), male: does not have black upperbreast. Misletoe-bird (652), male: glossy blue-black above without white marks.

Voice: Territorial song of male, pretty ringing repeated 'wee-cheedalee-dalee'; both sexes utter quiet single tick.

Habitat: Breeds in woodlands and forests mostly of ranges, foothills and watercourses dispersing in autumn–winter to more open habitat in valleys, grasslands, sub-inland scrubs and river red gum forests; golf-courses, parks, orchards, gardens.

Breeding: Nest: often untidy cup of strips of bark, moss or grass bound with spiders' web, decorated externally with strips of bark or lichen, lined with hair, fur or feathers; usually 1–3 m high, sometimes to 16 m in fork or on horizontal branch, behind loose bark, especially in stringybark or in sheltered cavity in tree, often one that is charred; in sw. Aust. occasionally in fork in blackboy. Eggs: 3; pale-green, pale-blue or dull-white, heavily spotted brown, purplish-brown and blue-grey in irregular zone round large end.

Range and Status: Widespread in suitable habitat in se. and sw. Aust.: from granite belt of sub-inland se. Q, (? winter visitor) n. to about Chinchilla, occasional e. to near Brisbane. In NSW, mostly on Divide, w. slopes, e. foothills and nearby open country; uncommon near Sydney; occurs inland to about Moree–Warrumbungle NP; winter visitor to the Riverina, mostly in river red gum forests of Murray R. and tributaries, w. to about Moulamein–Barham. In Vic., fairly widespread in suitable habitat, except far nw. mallee; in Tas., widespread resident, also Flinders I., Bass Strait; in SA, from se. n. to Mt. Lofty Ras. and s. Flinders Ras., w. to s. Eyre Pen., also Kangaroo I. In sw. WA, widespread in suitable habitat from Esperance to Lancelin, inland to L. Grace. Fairly common; part-migratory, dispersive or sedentary. Also Norfolk I. and from Solomon Is. to Fiji and Samoa.

444 RED-CAPPED ROBIN *Petroica goodenovii* Pl.63

Other name: Redhead.

Field marks: 115–120 mm. Male unmistakable: small, *with brilliant-scarlet cap and breast*; black above with bold white wing-slash, white edges to tail. Female: smallest, palest female red robin; *pale buff-grey above, whitish below, washed buff-grey on upperbreast*; note *largish dark eye, pale eye-ring, buff-white broken arrow on wing*; (? old) females have *distinctly reddish or pale-chestnut forehead.* Imm: male similar, but slightly washed pink on breast. Singly or pairs; tame and often curious; sits watchfully on stumps, low branches; takes much food on ground but also flying insects.

Similar species: Crimson Chat (646), male; dark mask through eye, dark-brown above, white throat; red rump. Jacky Winter (454): from female Red-capped by pale eyebrow, no broken arrow on wing; wags tail.

Voice: Male: dry but pretty insect-like trill, 'dit-dit-drr-it'; also sparrow-like scolding. Both sexes: sharp single or double 'tick', like pebbles struck together.

Habitat: Scrubs and woodlands in drier parts of continent, inland and coastal, in winter disperses into open eucalypt forests, river red gum forests and woodlands; drier coastal habitats in moonah, coastal tea-tree and banksia-scrubs; occasional in wetter coastal ranges; shelter-belts, golfcourses, orchards, gardens.

Breeding: Nest: neat beautiful well-camouflaged small rounded cup; of soft fine-shredded bark and grasses, bound with spiders' web, covered externally with lichen; on fork or horizontal branch, 1–3 m high. Eggs: 2–4, blue-green or grey-green, heavily marked with fine purple-brown spots, often heaviest round middle.

Range and Status: A species typical of inland and more arid coastal (and island) habitats throughout much of mainland *except* tropical Aust. n. of about 19°S – i.e. mostly absent from Kimberleys, top end NT; Gulf lowlands and ne. Q n. of upper Einasleigh–Burdekin Rs.; *unusual* coastwards of Divide in se. and in coastal sw. WA, but there is a surprising irregular occurrence (?) across the S. Alps in e. Vic. – to Mallacoota, Tabberaberra, Connors Plains and elsewhere in Gippsland. Common; dispersive in nonbreeding season.

445 HOODED ROBIN *Melanodryas cucullata* Pl.63

Other names: Black-and-white or Pied Robin.

Field marks: 165 mm. Male distinctive: *black hood goes down white breast in a wedge*; *prominent white bars on shoulder and wing*; tail black, tipped white *with prominent white panels*. Female: grey-brown where male black, *prominent white wingbar but no white shoulder-mark*; grey-white below, whiter on abdomen, sometimes buffish. Imm: like female but young male has shadowy markings of adult. Usually in pairs, sits quiet and watchful on dead branches or stumps, flying down to take prey on ground. *In flight, note white wingbar and prominent hour-glass tail-pattern.*

Similar species: White-winged Triller (432), male: wholly white throat and underparts. Pied Honeyeater (642), male: bill distinctly longer, curved; more white on shoulder; white wingbar less prominent in flight; pale rump.

Voice: Usually quiet but utters variety of notes. Male's song prominent in pre-dawn chorus, specially when breeding: 'YAP-yapyapyapyapyap', yaps becoming shorter; described also as clear 'whee-whew, whee-whew, whee-whew' beginning long before daylight.

Habitat: Drier woodlands and scrubs, including mallee, belar and other casuarinas, native pine and mulga; cleared paddocks with stumps and dead trees or secondary growth; drier open coastal scrubs.

Breeding: Nest: open cup of strips of bark, rootlets and grasses, bound with spiders' web; usually inconspicuous on top of stump, in cavity of broken trunk, on horizontal fork or branch, in stunted eucalypt, nearly always on or near dead wood, 1–6 m high. Eggs: 2–3; apple-green to pale olive, sometimes with faint tint of red-brown on large end or clouded with rich-brown.

Range and Status: Throughout mainland Aust., *except* C. York Pen.: distribution very patchy in coastal areas of e. Aust. from Gulf to e. and s. Vic., confined locally to drier ridges on Divide, and scrubby, sandy habitats coastally. Fairly common; probably sedentary.

446 DUSKY ROBIN *Melanodryas vittata* Pl.63

Other names: Dozey; Stump, Tasmanian or Sleepy Robin.

Field marks: 165 mm. Plainest robin; *uniform olive-brown above, bend of wing whitish, fine white bar across secondaries*, tail finely edged buff-white; fawn below, washed olive-buff on throat, sides of breast and flanks. Female: duller. Imm: streaked paler above and mottled darker below; wing-feathers edged paler. Singly or pairs; quiet and often tame; sits watchfully on stumps and posts, darts to ground for food. Does not flick wings and said to remain so still as to appear part of wood. In flight, note *irregular white patch on outer part of wing.*

Similar species: Female red-breasted robins (441–3) have larger whitish or buff wing-markings and usually a white spot over bill. They are less uniform in shading and some have pink on breast.

Voice: Brightest notes have been syllabized 'choo-wee; choo-we-er', repeated and carrying far; other shorter notes.

Habitat: Forest margins and tracks, open scrub, newly cleared areas, coastal scrubs.

Breeding: Nest: cup-shaped, somewhat more untidy than Flame (442); of grasses, strips of bark and rootlets, lined with hair or wool; in cavity of stump, bole of eucalypt, fork in bush or tree or crevice in bark on side of tree, near ground to 6 m high. Eggs: 3–4; pale apple-green to olive-green, faintly tinged brown on large end, forming faint cap or with distinct zone of brown spots or smudged brown.

Range and Status: Tas. and Bass Strait islands. Common; sedentary.

447 MANGROVE ROBIN *Eopsaltria pulverulenta* Pl.63

Other names: Ashy or White-tailed Robin.
Field marks: 145–165 mm. Distinctive: metallic blue-grey above, wings brown; whitish below, washed fawn; grey wash on sides of upperbreast; *tail blackish, outer feathers white at base, forming broad panel on either side when spread.* Imm: like adult but patchily brown and rufous above. Tame and quiet, but hard to observe because of habitat; often heard before seen. Flies silently; sits almost motionless on branches and exposed roots of mangroves; often flutters wings. Takes food among leaves, branches, exposed mud, seldom leaving cover. Note range.
Voice: Like Little Grassbird (506) – a long mournful double note sounding far away even though close; a repeated 'chig'; a single soft chirring note and a musical excited song.
Habitat: Typically mangroves: on coasts, tidal creeks and river mouths.
Breeding: Nest: small well-camouflaged compact cup; mostly of strips of bark and plant-fibre, bound with spiders' web; long strips of dry bark hang on outside; lined with dry roots and grass; usually in fork of dead or living mangrove, 1–5 m high. Eggs: 2; light-green to dark olive-green, with small spots of red-browns and lilac, latter as though below surface.
Range and Status: Coasts of n. Aust.: from Exmouth Gulf, WA, to Burdekin R., Q. Locally common; sedentary. Also NG and Aru Is.

448 WHITE-BREASTED ROBIN *Eopsaltria georgiana* Pl.64

Other names: White-bellied Robin, White-breasted Shrike-Robin.
Field marks: 150–165 mm. Distinctive member of yellow robin complex, confined to sw. WA. *Dark blue-grey above, pure-white below*; narrow white mark along bend of wing; *distinct white wingbar in flight.* Imm: mottled browner. Coastal population between Lancelin–Geraldton paler blue-grey above than main population in wetter habitats s. of Perth. Habits typical of other yellow robins.
Voice: A variety of calls are described: a liquid 'chee-op' ending in a slight whipcrack; a loud 'zhip', uttered singly, repeated; alarm-call, a harsh 'chit'; in aggression, a harsh 'zhzhurr'. Male has a quiet animated chirruping song.
Habitat: Typically in lower denser more humid cover than Western Yellow Robin (450). Thickly vegetated creekbeds and gullies, understorey of dense forest, e.g. karri forests, thickets of acacia and melaleuca typically with well-developed canopy, little undershrubbery and much litter.
Breeding: Nest: loosely constructed cup, of dry grasses and rootlets bound with spiders' web; typically without lining but decorated outside with lichen or hanging bark-strips, and inconspicuous. In low cover such as bracken or 1–2 m high in fork of paperbark or other shrub or tree, but occasionally to 6 m. Eggs: 2; variable; olive, light-brown to pale-blue, with very fine red-brown specks and streaks.
Range and Status: Confined to sw. WA and some forested coastal islands: coastal thickets from Geraldton to Moore R., and forested sw. corner from near Canning Dam in the Darling Ra. s. of Perth to Two People Bay and the Stirling Ras. Common; sedentary.

449 EASTERN YELLOW ROBIN *Eopsaltria australis* Pl.64

Other names: Bark, Creek, Eastern, Northern or Southern Yellow Robin; Yellow-breasted Robin; Yellow Bob, Yellowhammer.
Field marks: 150–170 mm. Widespread and familiar; *grey above, washed olive on lower back and rump; chin grey-white, breast clear-yellow.* Bill blackish, fairly robust; eye large and dark, legs blackish. Note that race *chrysorrhoa* has *rump and upper tail-coverts bright-yellow.* Juv.: streaked and spotted paler, with slight buffish broken arrow wingmark. Singly, pairs or family parties; quiet and confiding; when agitated becomes sprightly; flirts wings, cocks tail. Quiet colouring in gloom of habitat makes it inconspicuous *but in flight pale wingbars,* and, in *chrysorrhoa, bright-yellow rump.*

Similar species: Pale-yellow Robin (455): differs subtly; pale-grey mark over bill, olive rump, duller yellow-olive underparts, flesh-coloured legs. Golden Whistler (463): black cap and breastband.

Voice: Specially at dawn and dusk, oft-repeated quick explosive 'chop-chop!' also a high-pitched piping, continuous and monotonous or irregular; scolding note, low 'k-k-kair'; soft drawn-out squealing whistles, especially during courtship.

Habitat: Shaded cover, from lower levels of mountain rainforests to coastal swamp-woodlands and tea-tree thickets; sub-inland mallee and acacia scrubs; orchards, golf-courses, parks, gardens.

Breeding: Nest: well-camouflaged cup; of bark shreds, bound with spiders' web, lined with grass, thin twigs or leaves; decorated outside with strips of bark, lichens and moss; usually in fork 1–5 m high. Eggs: 2–3; apple-green or light blue-green, spotted blotched or minutely dotted deep brownish red and yellow-brown with indistinct lilac spots.

Range and Status: E. and se. Aust. and better-vegetated coastal islands: from about Cooktown, ne. Q, to about Millicent–Naracoorte in se. SA; in Q, inland to Atherton Tableland–Carnarvon Gorge–St. George; in NSW, inland to about Moree–Macquarie Marshes–Nymagee–Mt. Hope–Cocoparra NP; in Vic., n. to about Echuca–Inglewood–Little Desert, thence w. into se. SA. Nominate race occupies the s. part of the range coastally n. to Hunter R., NSW, thence n. inland to the upper Dawson R. in ce. Q; the yellow-rumped race *chrysorrhoa* replaces it in the mountain and coastal forests of ne. NSW and se. Q, thence n. to Cooktown. Common; probably sedentary.

450 WESTERN YELLOW ROBIN *Eopsaltria griseogularis* **Pl.64**

Field marks: 150–160 mm. Like Eastern Yellow Robin (449) but has *white throat and grey upperbreast; yellow confined to lower breast.* The colour of rump varies from yellow in coastal s. WA (nominate race) to olive-green from inland s. WA, e. to Eyre Pen., SA (race *rosinae*). Habits and actions like Eastern Yellow Robin, but range of habitat wider; feeds and nests higher in large trees of savannah-woodland.

Similar species: Golden Whistler (463): black cap and breastband.

Voice: Somewhat harsher than Eastern Yellow Robin; an explosive 'chip chip', or 'chip chair'; of lower pitch and differing tone from White-breasted Robin (448).

Habitat: Open forests, woodlands, scrublands, coastal scrubs and mallee; woodland-saltbush associations; generally avoids dense wet thickets favoured by White-breasted Robin.

Breeding: Nest: well-camouflaged cup; of bark shreds, bound with spiders' web, lined with dry leaves; decorated externally with long strips of bark, and blending well with support, usually a fork of sapling or tree, at a height of 1–6 m. Eggs: 2; oval; cream, buff or olive, blotched brownish or red-brown, often in zone round large end.

Range and Status: Sw. Aust.: from Shark Bay, WA, to Kalgoorlie and Esperance, coastally e. to Eyre Pen., SA, and n. to Gawler Ras. Common; sedentary.

451 YELLOW-FOOTED FLYCATCHER *Microeca griseoceps* **Pl.64**

Other names: Formerly known as Little Yellow Flycatcher or Robin.

Field marks: 120 mm. Bill typical of *Microeca* flycatcher: *flat and broad, dark-horn above, cream below; note also the yellow legs.* The first identifies its group; the second, its species. *Grey above, specially on head;* washed olive on wing-coverts, back and rump; flight-feathers and tail brownish; throat whitish-grey, upperbreast lightly washed buff, wing-linings and underparts washed very pale-lemon. A little-known species, until 1960 thought to be an *Eopsaltria* and known as Little Yellow Robin. Usually singly, high in canopy and difficult to see. Its behaviour has been likened to that of Yellow-breasted Boatbill (474): cocks tail, almost continually on the move, making short flights to pick insects from leaves, and on wing.

Similar species: Lemon-breasted Flycatcher (452): dark legs; head less distinctly grey.

Grey Whistler (465): much larger, bill dark and glossy, longer but narrower, hooked; *more olive green above and on tail.*
Voice: Reported to utter low subdued piping 'zzt, zzt, zzt' or a loud clear whistle, repeated 5–10 times. Latter noted to continue with scarcely a break while feeding. Song has been likened to that of Yellow-breasted Boatbill.
Habitat: Tropical rainforests, often with entangled masses of climbing plants; borders of scrub and open forest.
Breeding: Nest and eggs have not been described.
Range and Status: In Aust. confined to n. C. York Pen., Q, s. to Claudie R. Scarce. Also NG.

452 LEMON-BREASTED FLYCATCHER *Microeca flavigaster* Pl.64
Other names: Yellow-bellied or Yellow-breasted Flycatcher.
Field marks: 125–140 mm. This attractive little bird behaves much like its cousin the Jacky Winter (454). Colours subtle: *dull olive green above, with a pale throat; lemon underparts washed olive across the breast.* Bill short and broad, dark-horn above, cream below; legs dark-grey. Female: similar. Imm: browner above, mottled paler; whitish below, mottled brownish. Singly or pairs; a species of great charm, active and attractively vocal. Perches on heads of trees, telephone wires; darts into air for insects or hovers in open, about branches. Conspicuous song-flight; soars up in circles often to great heights singing, then drops back to cover. Often tame, but pugnacious to intruding birds.
Similar species: Brown-tailed Flycatcher (453). Yellow-footed Flycatcher (451): smaller; legs yellow. Eastern Yellow Robin (449). Grey Whistler (465): could be confused in ne. Q larger; bill glossy black, longer but narrower and slightly hooked.
Voice: Glorious sweet clear varied song, somewhat like Common Skylark (417), Clamorous Reedwarbler (503) or Brown Honeyeater (625); loudest and most sustained at dawn, with seldom a phrase repeated; also in songflight. Typical cadences: brisk 'quick, quick, come with me, Tito', or 'do be sweet, to Cynthia' or just 'sweet-to-Cynthia'; also a clear bouncing 'chauncey-chauncey *chew*'!
Habitat: Grassy open woodland, typically near water; fringes of dense growth along watercourses; occasionally parks, gardens.
Breeding: Nest: shallow cup, so small that sitting bird nearly conceals nest; of fine fibrous bark and grass bound with spiders' web. Egg: 1; pale-blue, finely spotted all over with purple or purplish red.
Range and Status: Coastal n. Aust.: from e. Kimberleys, WA,. (Ord R.) and Carlton Reach, far-w. NT, nearly to Broad Sound, Q; s. in Kimberleys to about Ivanhoe Station and in NT to Elsey–lower Macarthur R.; mostly coastal s. of C. York Pen. and scarce above 550 m. Locally common; (?) sedentary. Also NG.

453 BROWN-TAILED FLYCATCHER *Microeca tormenti* Pl.64
Field marks: 130 mm. Grey-brown above, tinged buff; *washed olive-green on wing-coverts and rump, tail brown, without white edges,* but inner webs of the three outer tail-feathers have a whitish spot. Underparts grey-white, chest and flanks washed buff-grey. In hand, the underwing-coverts are yellow-buff. *Bill short and broad, coloured dark-horn;* legs black. Female: similar, slightly smaller. Identified as much by range and habitat as by appearance. Reported to be shy, concealing itself in thickest mangroves, feeding on small crabs and other marine life, also large black ants.
Similar species: Lemon-breasted Flycatcher (452): yellower below; imms. are whiter below and could be confused; note range and habitat. Brown Whistler (466): different bill, glossy black but narrower, slightly hooked; typical 'whistler' calls.
Voice: Reported to utter loud notes resembling those of Yellow-faced Honeyeater (599).
Habitat: Dense coastal mangroves, outskirts of mangroves, dense thickets.
Breeding: One nest described. A very small cup, of bark and spider's web covered on the outside with small pieces of leaf. In dead mangrove, 1.5 m over water. Egg: 1; oval, smooth

and slightly glossy; pale blue-grey, spotted all over, particularly at the large end, where an irregular zone is formed, with chestnut and purple, the last appearing as though beneath the surface.

Range and Status: Thought to be confined to coastal Kimberleys, WA, from Augustus I., Napier Broome Bay, w. to King Sound near Derby and to C. Baskerville, *c.* 80 km n. of Broome. Described as very uncommon; probably sedentary. Few ornithologists have seen it alive, and from the beginning its descriptive history was marred by error. Field observers have further confused the situation by apparently mistaking the Brown Whistler for it, thus inferring an extension of range to top end NT and nw. Q. It is treated here as a full species in consistency with Schodde, 1975. An alternative treatment is to regard it as the race *tormenti* of Lemon-breasted Flycatcher.

454 JACKY WINTER *Microeca leucophaea*   Pl.64

Other names: Brown Flycatcher, Peter Peter, Postboy, Postsitter, Spinks, Stumpbird.
Field marks: 125–145 mm. A plain little bird of much charm: grey-brown above, whitish below, washed grey-buff across breast; note *slight whitish eyebrow and eyelids, blackish tail with conspicuous white edges and corners.* Bill short and rather broad. Inland and n. races much paler, some almost pure-white below. Imm: streaked and mottled, especially in zone across upperbreast. Singly or pairs; perches on dead trees, fence-posts, stumps; *restlessly wags tail from side to side.* Flies into air to take flying insects or hovers over grass; white edges of tail prominent. When courting, performs slow wavering song-flight above treetops or pours out sustained beautiful song from high perch.
Similar species: Brown-tailed Flycatcher (453): less white in tail, back greenish; note range. Female red robins (440–4) have broken creamish or whitish arrow-mark on wing; flick wings and tails; less aerial.
Voice: Musical variations of phrase 'peter-peter-peter'; clear, beautiful and surprisingly far-carrying; uttered from tree-top or in song-flight; prominent in dawn chorus.
Habitat: Open woodlands and scrublands, paddocks with dead timber or stumps; fences, timbered roadsides, orchards, parks. In arid parts of range, timber along watercourses.
Breeding: Nest: very small, shallow cup; of dry grass, etc., bound with spiders' web and camouflaged on exterior with bark and lichen; usually on horizontal branch or fork 1–20 m high and blending so well with support as to be practically invisible. Eggs: 2; pale green-blue spotted purplish brown or lilac, often in cap at large end.
Range and Status: Areas of suitable habitat nearly throughout mainland Aust. Absent from more heavily forested parts, from wetter coastal habitats, and mostly from treeless areas. Intolerant of human activity, it has become scarce in settled areas. Otherwise common, if patchy. Mostly sedentary. Some winter dispersal to open areas; suspected n. autumn migration in e. Aust. Also NG.

455 PALE-YELLOW ROBIN *Tregellasia capito*   Pl.64

Other name: Large-headed Robin.
Field marks: 130 mm. Often mistaken for Eastern Yellow Robin (449), but readily distinguished. *Breast paler greenish-yellow,* washed grey on flanks; *note whitish grey area from above bill to below eye joining to pale-grey throat.* This patch sharply edged above by dark-grey forehead, which becomes paler over crown, cheeks and nape. In the race *nana,* from n. of Townsville, the mark from bill to eye is *buff.* Back and rump *olive-green; legs yellowish flesh-colour.* Behaves much like Eastern Yellow Robin but in general a daintier bird; seldom leaves gloom of its habitat.
Similar species: Eastern Yellow Robin (449). White-faced Robin (456): whole face and throat white. Note range.
Voice: Short single or double squeak not unlike Rufous Fantail (486) or Red-browed Firetail (665); seems ventriloquial; also harder, more peevish note like honeyeater. In display or territorial defence, soft churring trill; alarm-note, loud harsh scolding 'scairr'.

Habitat: Tropical and subtropical rainforests, specially where lawyer-vine occurs; dense vegetation along watercourses.

Breeding: Nest: neat cup; of grasses and rootlets bound with spiders' web, decorated on outside with moss, bark, lichen or leaves; usually at junction of stem and leaves of lawyer-vine, 1–6 m high. Eggs: 2; green-white with yellowish, deep-brown or chestnut markings, forming irregular zone at large end.

Range and Status: Occurs patchily in suitable habitat, coastally and in highlands to *c.* 1500 m, from about Mt. Poverty, *c.* 50 km s. of Cooktown, Q, to near Port Stephens, NSW. Common in n., scarce in s. Sedentary.

456 WHITE-FACED ROBIN *Tregellasia leucops* Pl.64

Other names: White-faced Yellow Robin, White-throated Robin.

Field marks: 120–125 mm. Distinctive: à *small yellow robin with black head, sharply contrasting clownlike white forehead, face and chin*; upperparts olive-green; legs pale-yellow. Like other yellow robins in actions. Quickly becomes tame, settling close to inspect observer.

Similar species: Pale-Yellow Robin (455); note range.

Voice: Harsh grating 'chee-chee' rapidly repeated; musical five-note song in breeding season also reported.

Habitat: Tropical rainforests and vine-scrubs.

Breeding: Nest: neat cup; of bark and lawyer-vine fibre, bound with spiders' web, decorated on outside with moss and bark-strips; usually in lawyer-vine or fork of sapling, 1–10 m high. Eggs: 2; green-white, spotted red-brown, specially at large end.

Range and Status: Confined to far ne. Q, from C. York s. to Rocky R. Common; sedentary. Also NG.

457 WHITE-BROWED ROBIN *Poecilodryas superciliosa* Pl.63

Other names: Buff-sided Robin, White-browed Shrike-robin.

Field marks: 140–170 mm. Dark brown above with *long white eyebrow, white bar across base of flight-feathers, and white tailtips*; white below, upperbreast washed grey. Note that the nw. race *cerviniventris* 'Buff-sided Robin' *has buff flanks and under tail-coverts*, white tips to secondaries. Singly or pairs; quiet and sprightly; raises and lowers tail; droops wings; hops actively through lower branches and vines. Feeds on ground but also on tree-trunks, occasionally takes flying insects.

Voice: Piping whistle repeated four times very loudly, somewhat like a rosella.

Habitat: In n. Q; rainforests, vegetation along watercourses, coastal scrubs, nearby eucalypt woodlands, especially in wet season. In nw. Aust.: pockets of jungle, swamp woodlands, bamboo and pandanus thickets by watercourses and springs; mangroves.

Breeding: Nest: frail cup; of twigs lined with rootlets, with pieces of paperbark or patches of lichen loosely attached to outside; in shrub, vine or tree 1–10 m high. Eggs: 2; variable; rich apple-green to bluish, spotted with chestnut or purple, some with zone round large end.

Range and Status: N. and ne. Aust.: race *cerviniventris* from Kimberleys, WA, through NT s. to Larrimah, into Gulf coast of Q. Nominate race: C. York Pen, coastally and in some highland areas e.g. Atherton Tableland, s. to Rockhampton. Local, generally uncommon and patchy; sedentary.

458 GREY-HEADED ROBIN *Poecilodryas albispecularis* Pl.63

Other name: Ashy-fronted Robin.

Field marks: 165 mm. Attractive and robust; *head and breast grey*; *deep olive-brown above with rufous rump and base of tail*; *bold double white mark on black wing*. Note *slight dark mark round eye, separated by white mark down through eye to white throat*; underparts yellow-brown; bill robust and black, legs flesh-coloured. Singly or pairs; quiet and unobtrusive. Perches motionless, often sideways, on trunk or vine; darts to ground with strange jerking of tail; hops briskly and upright.

Similar species: White-browed Robin (457): browner above, paler below; white eyebrow and tail-tips.

Voice: Described as one of most characteristic sounds of mountain scrubs of ne. Q: loud thin whistle followed by three, slightly lower ones, monotonously repeated and heard in all months; also chattering like scrubwren; chirpings.

Habitat: Mountain rainforests above c. 240 m and margins of roads, tracks; lawns in rainforests reserves.

Breeding: Nest: flattish untidy cup; of rootlets, twigs, lawyer-vine fibre and leaves, decorated with lichen and green moss; usually in lawyer vine, at base of leaf in small palm or fork in small shrub 1–2 m high. Egg: 1 or 2; cream, brownish or pale-green, freckled and blotched dark-brown and purplish grey, specially at large end.

Range and Status: Ne. Q: coastal highlands from Bloomfield R. to Mt. Spec near Townsville. Common, sedentary. Also NG.

SHRIKE-TITS Genus *Falcunculus*

Australia's shrike-tits are now treated as isolated races of a single species, Crested Shrike-tit (459). In colouring, habits and in the development of the strong, notched bill for removing bark, opening seed-capsules or dealing with large insects, they have similarities to true tits, Paridae, of n. hemisphere. However, they are regarded (by some) as aberrant relatives of the whistlers. Sexes generally alike.

Food: Insects, their larvae, and other small invertebrates and vertebrates; also seeds.

Range: Aust. and NG.

Number of species: World 2; Aust. 1.

459 CRESTED SHRIKE-TIT *Falcunculus frontatus* Pl.62

Other names: Bark or Crested Tit; Eastern, Northern, Western, White, Yellow-bellied or Yellow-breasted Shrike-tit.

Field marks: 150–190 mm. A striking, rather robust, smallish crested bird with *strong black-and-white head-pattern and yellow breast*; upperparts olive-green; *throat black in male, olive-green in female*. Bill robust, slightly hooked, tail slightly forked. Imm: like female; young males have mixed yellow and black throats. The race *leucogaster* of s. WA *has white abdomen cut off sharply from yellow breast, yellow under tail-coverts*; wings and tail washed yellow-green. The small race *whitei* of nw. Aust. has brighter-yellow underparts than nominate race and is yellower-green above, flight-feathers and tail washed yellowish. Pairs or family parties; typically feeds high in eucalypts, first detected by strange calls or noise made tearing off bark in search of insects. The powerful bill is also used to open leaf-galls, seed-cases or to dismember hard-shelled insects like cicadas. Flight swift, swooping between trees.

Similar species: Golden Whistler (463), male; no crest or head pattern; throat white; black breast-band.

Voice: Mournful mellow drawn-out whistle, uttered singly but usually four or more times, becoming louder. Also a repeated chuckled or stuttered note, described as 'knock-at-the-door' or 'knock-at-the-door-whack'; mimics.

Habitat: Eucalypt forests and woodlands; in inland districts, timber along watercourses; occasionally in acacias, coastal tea-tree or banksia or native pine scrubs; golf-courses, orchards, parks, gardens.

Breeding: Nest: deep cup; of bark-fibre bound outside with spiders' web, often decorated with lichen, lined with fine grass; concave inner walls probably help retain eggs when nest sways in wind. Usually built round vertical twigs at top of tall eucalypt or sapling 5–25 m

high; twigs, leaves and buds above nest are usually nipped off. Eggs: 2–3; whitish or grey-white, dotted and spotted brown, slate-grey and black.
Range and Status: E., se., sw. and nw. Aust.: *nominate race* occurs in highlands of ne. Q from about Atherton to Kirrama and in se. Aust. s. from about Rockhampton–Charleville, in the w. mostly along rivers; in NSW, w. to the Darling R. and tributaries and in timber on watercourses through the Riverina; all Vic.; in SA, w. along Murray R. in small numbers and from coastal se. to Yorke Pen., Mt. Lofty Ras. to Flinders Ras. Race *leucogaster*: sw. WA s. from Geraldton–Norseman to s. coast e. of Albany. Race *whitei*: nw. Aust.; recorded only at a few localities, s. to Larrimah–Borroloola, NT, also at Napier Broome Bay, Kimberleys. Uncommon to rare; probably mostly sedentary.

WHISTLERS Genus *Pachycephala*
SHRIKE-THRUSHES Genus *Colluricincla*

Songbirds with rather large rounded heads and fairly robust bills, short in some but longish and slightly-hooked in others. The whistlers *Pachycephala* were formerly known in Aust. as thickheads. Smaller than shrike-thrushes, their sexes are usually dissimilar, females being plain greyish or at least much less boldly-marked and coloured than males. Whistlers take their food, mostly insects, while methodically scrutinizing foliage and branches, often flying to seize prey from leaves. Many of their actions, especially a characteristic see-saw posturing in courtship display, and their strong undulating flight, reflect those of shrike-thrushes. However their voices are higher-pitched and the sequences of notes longer. The memorable explosions of song by several species place them among our most outstanding vocalists. Their small notes, especially in species like Red-lored (461) and Olive (460) Whistlers, are highly characteristic pensive still small voices of a curiously indrawn quality. Not closely related to true thrushes (435–9), the shrike-thrushes *Colluricincla* are active medium-sized birds of mostly soft-browns, greys or rufous. Their sexes are nearly alike. They search for food on limbs, trunks, bark and the ground; one species is terrestrial in sandstone escarpments and gorges. They are sometimes predatory on smaller birds, eggs and young and have been known to take surprisingly large items like feathertail gliders and green tree-frogs. Although their song-patterns are shorter than those of whistlers, their voices are strong, mellow and beautiful. Whistlers and shrike-thrushes are strongly territorial when breeding. They build open cup-nests; the former usually place them in forks in smaller branches and foliage, the latter usually in larger forks near trunks, in cavities or hollows, overhung banks and in the terrestial species, in caves or fissures in rocky cliffs. Eggs are usually white to buff or olive, with brown and grey markings.
Food: Insects and other invertebrates; small mammals, birds and occasionally nestlings; small reptiles and amphibians.
Range: Mostly Australasian region and many Pacific islands; Malaysia, Indo-China.
Number of species: Whistlers. World *c.* 28; Aust. 9. Shrike-thrushes. World 4; Aust. 4.

460 OLIVE WHISTLER *Pachycephala olivacea* Pl.65
Other names: Mystery Bird, Native Thrush, Olive Thickhead, Whipbird.
Field marks: 205–215 mm. A largish, plainly coloured whistler. Male: *rich olive-brown above, contrasting with grey crown and sides of face; throat whitish with very fine broken dark barrings*; grey or grey-buff zone across upperbreast, merging into deep olive-buff underparts. Female: duller, more olive crown and nape, breastband less definite. Bill of male blackish; female has pale lower mandible. Except when breeding, usually solitary. Feeds on or near ground, perching on logs, tree-buttresses. Elusive, often maddeningly so; usually first located by calls, often travels unseen for considerable distances near ground with short flights between thickets; in taller forest country moves ahead of observer in swooping, strongly undulating flight.
Similar species: Golden Whistler (463); female.

Voice: Very sweet, pensive, ethereal; but some notes powerful. Typical territory call, 'cho cho cho cho', or 'jiff, jiff, jiff, jiff', repeated monotonously swelling. Also a long-drawn ringing 'peeee' – a calm, still small voice. In McPherson Ras., Q, birds call thoughtful 'peee-pooo', with distinct drop between syllables; may reverse call, 'pooo-peee'; other variations include 'pee-sweet' or 'pee weee'. A common call of s. birds has been syllabized 'tu-wee-e-tchow', last syllable loud and sharp, ending almost in crack; in s. coast scrubs and Bass Strait islands, a slow, ringing 'cheer, ritty', rising and with slight whipcrack effect.

Habitat: Dense, closed habitats, from alpine thickets to the undergrowth of wetter rainforests, forests and woodlands; vegetation along watercourses, dense coastal scrubs and heaths, blackberry thickets, well-vegetated gardens. More open habitats in autumn–winter. The typical habitat of the n. population is beech forest *Nothofagus* above *c.* 750 m. In Tas., the range is much wider, and includes lightly timbered lowlands.

Breeding: Nest: large compact cup; of coarse twigs, bark and leaves, neatly lined with fine grass and rootlets, somewhat like a shrike-thrush; usually 1–3 m high in dense shrub or tree, but at times in bracken or sword-grass. Eggs: 2–3; tapering at both ends; yellow-white to buff-white, with irregular dots, spots and small blotches of brown, underlying markings of lavender or grey.

Range and Status: S. and se. Aust., Bass Strait islands and Tas.: from Millicent–Beachport in se. SA, inland to Ballarat–Blackwood in cw. Vic. to ne. Vic., Brindabella Ra., ACT and Blue Mts., NSW; with (? isolated) highland populations n. to McPherson Ras. in far se. Q. Ranges from sea-level to over 1500 m. In many parts, to lower or more open habitats in autumn–winter, and is then seen unexpectedly in parks, gardens. Fairly common in s., scarce in n. Sedentary or dispersive.

461 RED-LORED WHISTLER *Pachycephala rufogularis* Pl.65

Other names: Buff-breasted or Red-throated Whistler.

Field marks: 195–215 mm. In and out of breeding season, often first located by sweet wistful voice. Male: deep olive-grey or grey-brown above, flight-feathers *margined olive or buff*, *bill to eye, and throat to under tail-coverts pale reddish buff*, brightest on head and throat; breast grey. Female: greyer below. Both sexes: eye deep-red. Imm: streaked below, eye brown. Usually singly except when breeding. Rather shy and elusive; typically seen in tops of shrubs and low trees, but feeds much on ground, usually near cover. When disturbed, often moves some distance; flight strong and undulating. Note range.

Similar species: Rufous Whistler (467), male: white throat, bold black breastband. Female: pale below, prominently streaked. Gilbert's Whistler (462), male: black mark between bill and eye. Female: more uniformly grey.

Voice: Sweet, wistful, haunting, unmistakably made by a whistler; a typical call is a slow swelling 'see-saw' – a loud clear whistle followed quickly by sound like breath in-drawn between partly closed lips. One variation is a leisurely three-note 'see-saw-sik', dipping on second syllable, rising on last.

Habitat: Low shrubby mallee with spinifex; native pine and broombush scrubs.

Breeding: Nest: substantial cup; of bark, twigs and dry leaves, lined with grasses; rim typically well rounded and often with interwoven green tendrils of vine, leaves of broom-bush, or rootlets; usually in top of clump of spinifex under overhanging mallee foliage or in low fork. Eggs: 2–3; buff-white to pinkish, spotted brown with less distinct irregular marks of brown, purple and lavender, heaviest at large end.

Range and Status: Mallee areas of e. SA, nw. Vic., and sw. NSW from about Hartley, SA, to Murray mallee n. of Waikerie, n. and e. to Round Hill NR–Cocoparra NP–in s. NSW; s. to n. of Bordertown, SA and Wyperfeld NP, Vic. Rare, apparently sedentary.

462 GILBERT'S WHISTLER *Pachycephala inornata* Pl.65

Other names: Black-lored or Red-throated Whistler or Thickhead.

Field marks: 190–205 mm. A plain greyish whistler; male: *black mask*; *throat rich* *reddish-buff*, touch of rich-buff in centre of lower breast, under tail-coverts pale-grey. Female: *very plain*, uniform grey above, sometimes with dark streaks on breast or faint buff wash on centre of breast and under tail-coverts. Both sexes have red eyes. Imm: like female, eyes brown. Shy except when breeding, when more than ordinarily vocal. At other times, usually heard before seen, feeds inconspicuously in tops of shrubs and trees or on ground; when disturbed, moves continually ahead in strong undulating flight.

Similar species: Golden Whistler (463), female: less uniformly grey, no black on ear-coverts; pale bar across wing. Red-lored Whistler (461): no black on ear-coverts; more extensive reddish buff below.

Voice: Famed for its rich and far-carrying or sweet, haunting calls: one call like man whistling dog, single or repeated 'perweee, perweee, perweee', each note rising strongly at end. Also an explosive 'jock-jock-jock-jock'; swelling, repeated in sequence of 11–18 or more; also swelling 'pew, pew-pew-pew-pew-PEW-PEW-PEW' . . . breaking into explosive wheezy 'ee-cha,ee-ch' or 'EE-chop, EE-chop'. Also soft in-drawn calls, typical of whistlers, e.g. slow descending 'wee-e-e-woo', or 'persweee?', rising at end; also low plaintive whistle like quail-thrush.

Habitat: Drier scrubs and scrubby woodlands; mallee-spinifex associations, mulga; coastal tea-tree scrubs and eucalypt woodlands including secondary coppice-growth; in riverine black box and lignum.

Breeding: Nest: bulky and well built or somewhat untidy; of twigs, leaves and grass, occasionally with wool interwoven, lined with fine grass and plant-fibre; in low fork in shrub, often among heavy growth of vine, in low mistletoe clump, on top of stump among coppice growth or on old nest of babbler or butcherbird. Eggs: 2–3; 4, 5; oval to somewhat pointed; whitish to light-buff, irregularly spotted different shades of brown and occasionally blackish with underlying markings of lilac, in zone at large end or evenly distributed.

Range and Status: S. interior of Aust.: in WA, suitable habitat mostly e. of Northam–Albany, probably ranging n. to mulga–eucalypt line, to se. of Yalgoo and in Gt. Victoria Desert e. to SA, where it occurs n. at least to Ooldea–Gawler Ras.–mallee areas of Murray R.; in Vic., s. to Edenhope–Maryborough–(vagrant You Yangs)–Nagambie and e. to Chiltern; in NSW, e. to Temora–Cowra–Orange, n. to Gilgandra. Uncommon to rare, sedentary or nomadic.

GOLDEN WHISTLER COMPLEX

The Australian golden whistlers are members of a superspecies extending from Java to Fiji, New Caledonia, Norfolk and Lord Howe Is. More than 70 races have been described; in most places where these come together, interbreeding takes place, demonstrating that they belong to a single species. The main Australian population, Golden Whistler *P. pectoralis* (463), ranges from Cooktown, Q, to Tas. and w. coastally through SA to near Carnarvon, WA. Another population inhabits mostly mangrove habitats in coastal n. Aust., from North West Cape, WA, to coastal e. Q s. to near Bowen and the Whitsunday Is. Its most striking feature is that females, instead of being grey, have partly or wholly yellow underparts. Because of these differences, and because the two populations, despite an apparent overlap of *c.* 800 km in ne. Q, appear not to interbreed, they are regarded as separate species, the northern form being known as the Mangrove Golden Whistler, *P. melanura* (464).

463 GOLDEN WHISTLER *Pachycephala pectoralis* Pl.65

Other names: Cutthroat; Golden-breasted, White-throated or Yellow-breasted Whistler or Thickhead; Ring-coachie, Thunderbird, Whipbird.

Field marks: 165–185 mm. Male: distinctive; *head black, extending round upperbreast in broad band, separating white throat from rich-yellow underparts*. Olive-green above with yellow rear-collar from breast; tail black, grey or grey with black tip. Female: grey-brown above, progressively washed deeper olive-green from se. Aust. to Q. Note pale-grey tips to greater wing-coverts, *giving subtle pale line across wing.* Grey-white below, with buff wash of varying intensity, scarcely apparent in coastal se. Aust., but warm-buff in sw. Aust.; some females, specially from coastal n. NSW and s. Q, have *lemon wash on under tail-coverts.* Bill black. Nestling: rich-rufous. Imm: like female, *but with broad rufous margins to wing-feathers.* Bill brown, straw-coloured at base. Length of bill varies from stubby (Tas.) to longish (Q). Pairs during breeding season; mostly solitary for rest of year; but often in feeding companies with other small passerines. In spring, males display and call vivaciously, with characteristic see-saw posturing. Sings and breeds in imm. plumage.

Similar species: Mangrove Golden Whistler (464). Gilbert's Whistler (462), female: more uniform grey; faint blackish ear-coverts, no pale wingbar. Grey Whistler (465): smaller, no pale wingbar.

Voice: Range of sweet notes, many robust and ending in fairly sharp crack, others with curious in-drawn quality typical of whistlers. Typical phrases: rising 'wheat-wheat-wheat-WHITTLE!' a brisk 'dee-dee-dee-ah-WHIT!'. Contact-call: a single rising 'seeep'. Like other whistlers, males often call after thunder, car backfire, shot or other sudden loud noise, hence 'Thunderbird'.

Habitat: Closed habitats; rainforests, forests, woodlands, riverside vegetation, coastal and sub-inland scrubs including mallee, brigalow and other acacias; at times mangroves (but see following species); orchards, shelter-belts, golf-courses, parks, gardens.

Breeding: Nest: open cup, neat and rounded inside, rough externally; of strips of bark bound with spiders' webs, plant-stems, rootlets, skeleton leaves, dead fern-fronds, grass, twigs; usually in upright fork of bush or low tree, 1–4 m high, sometime higher; also in blackberries, treeferns or long grass. Eggs: 2–3; oval, variable; typically cream-white to cream buff, freckled dotted or blotched with dark-brown, with underlying spots of dark-grey evenly distributed or in cap or zone round large end; also white with lavender or heavy brown or blackish markings, or salmon-pink spotted or splashed with red, brown and grey.

Range and Status: S. and e. Aust., coastal islands and Tas.; in sw. WA, s. from Carnarvon, inland to se. of Yalgoo, e. of Bonnie Rock, s. of Coolgardie–Karonie and e. coastally to Eucla; s. SA; all Vic.; NSW about e. of Darling R.; s. and e. Q e. of St. George–Roma–Emerald–Charters Towers–Lynd–Burdekin Divide, to mountain rainforests of Atherton Tablelands and tablelands near Cooktown; not in coastal lowlands n. of Johnstone R. and usually above 450 m n. of Innisfail. Present some islands off e. coast: Stradbroke to Fraser Is. Common. Mostly sedentary in coastal sw. and se. Aust., with inland winter dispersal; n. winter or altitudinal migration on e. coast.

464 MANGROVE GOLDEN WHISTLER *Pachycephala melanura* Pl.65

Other names: Black-tailed or Robust Whistler or Thickhead.

Field marks: 150–170 mm. See discussion in introduction. The species is split into several races along n. coast, from North West Cape, WA, to near Bowen, Q. Males: smaller than Golden Whistler (463), bill distinctly longer, slightly hooked; *underparts brighter orange-yellow extending round neck in much broader collar, also across rump*; tail jet-black and short. Females: differ from Golden Whistler, female, in the greater amount of yellow on underparts. This varies racially; see Pl.65. Imms: probably like female, with brownish or straw-coloured bill. Habits like Golden Whistler; sometimes feeds among tidal debris.

Similar species: Golden Whistler (463). Brown (466) and Grey (465) Whistlers: smaller than female Mangrove Golden; shadowy buff-grey breastband, no distinct yellow on underparts.

Voice: Like Golden Whistler.

Habitat: Mangroves, pockets of coastal rainforest or monsoon forest and riverside thickets, coastal scrubs and subhumid scrubs on coastal islands.

Breeding: Nest and eggs like Golden Whistler.

Range and Status: Coastal n. Aust. and coastal islands: from North West Cape, WA; in

NT, inland to Adelaide R.–Borroloola; in Q, n. to C. York and s. on e. coast to Springcliff near Bowen and possibly to n. of Mackay; said to be *absent* coastally from Cape Tribulation to Townsville; present Daydream I. and other islands of Whitsunday Group. Nominate race *melanura* occupies range from North West Cape to Napier Broome Bay, WA. Race now designated *robusta* occupies remainder of range from w. Kimberley coast, WA, to e. coastal Q. Fairly common; sedentary. Related forms from Java to NG and many Pacific islands.

465 GREY WHISTLER *Pachycephala griseiceps* Pl.65

Field marks: 140–150 mm. Crown and nape grey, otherwise olive above, flight-feathers grey with olive margins; *throat whitish, upperbreast washed greyish olive-buff, paling to lemon wash below*; legs and feet grey. Female: less lemon on abdomen. Imm: like adult but secondaries have broad buff margins. Bill glossy black; *longish, narrow, slightly hooked – an important field-mark*. Singly or in pairs; moves quietly; forages from undergrowth to considerable heights in canopy, where observation and identification are difficult; some actions recall those of flycatchers, especially habit of fluttering momentarily round foliage.
Similar species: Yellow-footed Flycatcher (451): short, broad bill, with creamy base to lower mandible, legs yellow; actions more lively, feeds more on wing.
Voice: Two short notes and loud clear whistle of five or more notes. Has been syllabized: 'one two three four five' or 'catch a fish alive'; territorial song of male, a series of loud clear musical notes. The calls lack the whipcrack quality of other whistlers.
Habitat: Rainforests and pockets of same; mangroves, paperbark-swamps, coastal scrubs.
Breeding: Nest: open cup; of coarse grass, leaves, vine tendrils and rootlets, loosely bound with spiders' web. Eggs: 2; whitish to pale-buff, spotted dull-brown and deep-lavender, mostly on large end.
Range and Status: Coastal ne. Aust.: from C. York s. to about Cardwell, inland to Atherton Tableland; also Hinchbrook and other coastal islands of ne. Q. Common to scarce; probably sedentary. Also NG and islands, and Moluccas.

466 BROWN WHISTLER *Pachycephala simplex* Pl.65

Field marks: 140–150 mm. Grey-brown above, with slight olive wash; fawn-white below with faint dark streaks on throat and distinct grey-buff wash on sides that may form band across breast. *The only other mark is the narrow white margin round bend of wing.* Bill *glossy black, longish, slightly hooked.* Solitary or in pairs, forages from undergrowth to high in canopy; flutters round foliage like a fairy warbler or a flycatcher.
Similar species: Lemon-breasted Flycatcher (452), imm. Brown-tailed Flycatcher (453): note range, specialized habitat, calls. In both, bills are shorter.and flatter.
Voice: Described as a single note repeated four times and a rich melodious song. The calls lack the whipcrack quality of other whistlers.
Habitat: Monsoon forest, dense mixed forests, swamp woodlands, mangroves, occasionally to nearby open forest.
Breeding: Nest: open cup; of grass, leaves, vine-tendrils and rootlets, loosely bound with spiders' web. Eggs: 2; whitish to pale-buff, spotted dull-brown and deep-lavender, mostly on large end.
Range and Status: Coastal NT, from Port'Keats on w. coast to Gove Pen. and Groote Eylandt, possibly to Gulf coast. Common to scarce.

467 RUFOUS WHISTLER *Pachycephala rufiventris* Pl.65

Other names: Coachwhip-bird, Echong, Joey Joey, Mock Whipbird; Rufous-breasted Whistler or Thickhead; Ring Coachman, Thunderbird.
Field marks: 165–175 mm. Male: grey above, blackish mask extends down side of neck round breast in *broad black band, separating white throat from rufous underparts.* Female:

brownish-grey above, with touch of olive; *whitish below, washed buff, and with dark streaks.* Imm: like female but more olive above and with rufous margins to flight-feathers. Some males are intensely coloured, others have ill-defined masks, breasts pale sandy; some females are almost whitish below, streaked blackish. Birds in n. Aust. are noticeably small. Usually solitary or in feeding associations with other small songbirds in non-breeding season. Habits and actions typical of family – see introduction. In breeding season highly animated, both sexes displaying characteristically, males especially vocal.

Similar species: White-breasted Whistler (468), female: more robust bill; note range and habitat.

Voice: Specially when courting, male pours out impetuous spirited song; components include a sharp 'pllik, chik' and a ringing almost explosive "ee-chong!", uttered singly several times before loud rippling bursts of melody; also associated is a clear penetrating 'joey-joey-joey', rapidly and monotonously repeated on one level 30 or more times. In autumn, both sexes utter beautiful subdued sub-song.

Habitat: Typically more open forests, woodlands, scrubs, from coasts to mallee and mulga scrubs in arid inland; less usual, but present in taller denser, more humid forests of Divide.

Breeding: Nest: thin, fragile loosely constructed cup; of few long thin twigs and dry grass, lined with finer material; usually in upright slender fork 1–5 m high, occasionally to 15 m and usually in cover. Eggs: 2–4; variable; pale olive-green to olive-brown, freckled and spotted with pale red-brown to dark-brown, with fainter shadowy margins; faint, evenly distributed, or in zone round large end.

Range and Status: Widespread in suitable habitats in mainland Aust. and many coastal islands. Resident or nomadic in WA. Part-migratory in e. Aust., and regular breeding migrant in se. Aust., between Sept. and Apr.; occasionally overwinters. Vagrant King I., Bass Strait and Kangaroo I., SA. Common. Also Moluccas, NG, New Caledonia.

468 WHITE-BREASTED WHISTLER *Pachycephala lanioides* **Pl.65**

Other names: Torres Strait or White-breasted Thickhead.

Field marks: 190–210 mm. Note robust, somewhat hooked bill. Male: grey above, white below, *crown and nape black, joining broad black band across breast*, finely bordered rich-rufous on lower side; tail black tipped grey. Female: grey-brown above, sometimes washed olive, wings and tail browner; *fawn-white below, washed grey-buff on sides of neck and breast and finely streaked dark-brown.* Imm: like female but darker above, buffer below. Usually in pairs; feeds in foliage and under mangroves on mud. Often first located by calls.

Similar species: Rufous Whistler (467), female. Grey Shrike-thrush (472); from female by buffish under tail-coverts and/or ginger eyebrow and eye-ring.

Voice: Described as a deep whistle of four to six notes, with a pause between each, or rich and mellow, poured out impetuously; also soft clear whistle slightly falling at end; harsh, sharp alarm-call.

Habitat: Mangroves; less typically, pockets of dense rainforest fringing coastal streams and springs.

Breeding: Nest: often rather scanty cup; of twigs and rootlets, lined with finer rootlets and fastened to branches with spiders' web; usually in fork of mangrove 1–3 m high. Eggs: 2; buffish, with zone of brown and lavender spots at large end.

Range and Status: Coasts and islands of nw. and n. Aust. in suitable habitat: from Carnarvon, WA, to Norman R., Q. Fairly common; sedentary.

469 RUFOUS SHRIKE-THRUSH *Colluricincla megarhyncha* **Pl.60**

Other names: Little Shrike-thrush; Red or Rufous Thrush.

Field marks: 190 mm. A rufous-coloured thrush with a *longish robust pinkish-brown bill.* Olive-brown above, grey on head and back; *rich-dusky buff below,* paler and slightly streaked on throat and upperbreast. The nw. race *parvula*, 'Little Shrike-thrush': *whitish* *from bill to eye* with slight pale eyebrow. Singly or pairs; feeds on ground or in undergrowth, on tree-trunks, in high masses of vines and in canopy; often first located by calls or rustling sounds when throwing leaves aside or stripping bark.

Voice: Sweet clear notes, lower-pitched than those of Grey Shrike-thrush (472); phrases characteristically end with such repetitions as 'wot wot' or 'shee-oh, whee-oh'; a typical call may be syllabized 'a cup of tea, wot-wot-wot'. Birds of a pair may call in unison; when alarmed, loud clear chirps or a harsh wheeze. Typical call of *parvula* has been syllabized 'eeee, butch-butch-butcher'.

Habitat: Tropical and subtropical rainforest, dense vegetation along watercourses, paperbark-swamps, coastal open forest; mangroves.

Breeding: Nest: deep cup, smaller and more compact than Grey Shrike-thrush; of fibres, dead and green leaves, and rootlets bound with supple stems and spiders' web, lined with fine plant-fibre and rootlets; in fork of small shrub or sapling, or in mass of vines; low, to 10 m high. Eggs: 2–3; pearly white to pale-pink, spotted and blotched brown, underlying markings of lilac, evenly or in zone at large end.

Range and Status: Coastal nw. and e. Aust. and coastal islands: from C. York s. to Edward R. on w. coast and on e. coast s. to Hastings R., NSW. Common in n., uncommon and local in s.; sedentary. Race *parvula*: nw. Aust. and coastal islands from n. Kimberleys, WA, to Groote Eylandt, NT, s. to Coomalie Creek and upper S. Alligator R. Uncommon; sedentary. Also Torres Strait islands, NG and many satellite islands; Celebes.

470　BOWER'S SHRIKE-THRUSH　*Colluricincla boweri*　　　Pl.60

Other names: Bower or Stripe-breasted Shrike-thrush or Thrush.

Field marks: 210 mm. An odd-looking shrike-thrush, *characterized by somewhat large head, large blackish bill and rather short tail*; grey-brown above, *underparts rich olive-buff with faint to bold dark streaks*. Singly or pairs; rather quiet, watches for prey from perch, descends to seize it before taking watch again; reported to feed on lawns near rainforest and to associate with Tooth-billed Catbird (699). Reported to replace Rufous Shrike-thrush (469) above 600 m on Big Tableland, Cooktown. Note restricted range.

Similar species: Rufous Shrike-Thrush (469): smaller, less-streaked; bill pinkish brown.

Voice: Quieter than other shrike-thrushes; call, loud 'chuck' or single clicking chirps; in anger or alarm, harsh gratings.

Habitat: Rainforests above 400 m in coastal ranges of ne. Q; feeds on lawns of parks and houses near rainforests.

Breeding: Nest: open cup; of leaves, skeleton leaves and bark, lined with rootlets; in lawyer-vine or tree-fork, 1–8 m high. Eggs: 2–3; pearly or pinky white, with small sparse blotches of red-brown, and underlying marks of grey, mainly at large end.

Range and Status: Highlands of ne. Q: from Mt. Amos near Cooktown to Mt. Spec near Townsville, inland to Herberton Ra. Common in suitable habitat; sedentary.

471　SANDSTONE SHRIKE-THRUSH　*Colluricincla woodwardi*　　　Pl.60

Other names: Brown-breasted or Woodward's Shrike-thrush or Thrush; Cliff or Rock Thrush.

Field marks: 265 mm. A distinctive rock-dwelling shrike-thrush. Head greyish, merging into *olive-brown upperparts*; pale mark between bill and eye and on throat; *underparts rich olive-buff with slight wash of grey on upperbreast*. Bill blue-grey. Singly or pairs; active and difficult to observe. Flicks wings and somewhat longish rounded tail, throws head back when calling. Makes short quick flights, hops quickly over and round rocks and up rock-faces; apparently seldom perching on trees or bushes. Often first noted by splendid calls.

Similar species: Rufous Shrike-thrush (469), race *parvula*: smaller, underparts paler; both may occur in same area, but habitats differ.

Voice: Glorious clear strong notes unmistakably of shrike-thrush origin; echoed and accentuated by surrounding rocks and cliffs; contact-call, a rather strident 'peter!'

Habitat: Sandstone and similar escarpments and gorges of nw. Aust.

Breeding: Nest: large untidy cup; of bark, porcupine grass, rootlets; in crevice of rock, on ledge. Eggs: 2–3; creamy-white, blotched brown about large end.

Range and Status: Recorded in three disjunct populations in n. Aust. (a possible further population in Pilbara region, WA): Kimberleys, WA, from Derby to se. of Kununurra; nw. Arnhem Land Plateau from King R. to S. Alligator R., NT; Macarthur R., NT, e. to Nicholson R., extreme nw. Q. Fairly common in suitable habitat; sedentary.

---

472 GREY SHRIKE-THRUSH *Colluricincla harmonica* **Pl.60**

Other names: Brown, Harmonious or Western Shrike-thrush (or Thrush); Grey or Native Thrush; Duke Wellington, Jock Whitty, Joe Wickie, Pluff, Whistling Dick.

Field marks: 220–265 mm. Familiar and widespread, occurring in several geographical forms. Nominate race in se. Aust.: *grey above, with olive-brown back and grey-to-white underparts.* Northwards, it becomes plainer grey-brown above and paler below. *Bill black* in se. Aust., but northwards becomes *browner and nearly cream* in coastal n. Aust. Race *rufiventris* 'Western Shrike-thrush': greyer above, *with buff wash over much of undersurface, specially under tail-coverts.* Both races: male; *white mark from bill to eye.* Female: underside of bill usually paler than upperside; less-distinct white mark from bill to eye; back less brown, *slight dark streaks on throat.* Sexual differences become less marked northwards and inland. Imm: rufous or ginger eyebrow and eye-ring, slight brown streaks on throat and breast; pale-rufous or buff margins to flight feathers. Habits fairly constant, except that the bird adapts well to settlement in se. Aust. and breeds round human habitation but in sw. WA it has retreated before settlement. Singly, pairs or family parties; actively searches branches, trunks and bark; hops over ground and logs – see introduction.

Similar species: Female whistlers can be confused, especially the plain-grey female Gilbert's (462). Note their details and behaviour (see group introduction). Remember, the true thrushes (435–9) are not closely related to shrike-thrushes. Mostly brown with spots or scallops, they should not be confused.

Voice: During breeding season specially, voice of male rich and beautiful. Typical phrases have been syllabized 'purr-purr-purr *quee yule*', 'yoh-ho-*ee*', 'pip-pip-pip-pip-ho-ee', 'e-all, ee-all, *queel*' or 'crook crook per *kweee*', last syllable rising strongly. In winter utters single loud ringing note, 'dite' that depending on locality and ear of observer, can also sound like 'yorrick' or 'ching'. Flying young still being fed utter distinctive clear ringing call.

Habitat: Most forests and woodlands (generally more open parts); coastal scrubs, mallee and other inland scrubs, vegetation along inland watercourses; in e. Aust. especially, homesteads, golf-courses, parks, gardens.

Breeding: Nest: large cup or bowl; of strips of bark, grass, rootlets and other material; in fork of shrub or leafy tree, hollow top of broken stump, tree-cavity, sawn-off buttress of tree surrounded by coppice-growth; palms overhanging bank, vine against wall of house, down-pipe or hanging tin, sometimes in sheds, usually 2–6 m high. Eggs: 2–4; white, finely freckled red-brown and blue-grey.

Range and Status: Widespread in Aust. and Tas. and forested coastal islands. Nominate race: se. Aust. and Tas., and coastal n. Aust., with following limits: w. to Spencer Gulf–L. Eyre in SA, n. to C. York, Q, and in coastal n. Aust. s. to Nicholson R.–Larrimah–Sturt Creek in NT and to Roebuck Bay in nw. WA. Race *rufiventris*: c. and w. Aust.; SA e. to Spencer Gulf–L. Eyre and through s. NT e. to Toko Ra. in far w. Q; n. to Brunchilly in NT and to Fortescue R. in cw. WA; thence nearly throughout s. WA. Apparently intergrades with nominate race in Flinders Ras., SA, and Georgina R. of far w. Q–NT border area. Common; sedentary. Also s. and e. NG.

473 CRESTED BELLBIRD *Oreoica gutturalis* **Pl.62**

Other names: Bell-bird, Bunbundalui, Dick (Dick-Dick)-the-devil, Pan-pan-panella.
Field marks: 205–230 mm. Best known for remarkable call; appearance unusual. Male: *forehead and throat white, bordered by area of black down from slender black crest through eye and enlarging to form a broad band round breast*, rest of head grey; upperparts light-brown with chestnut tinge on rump; whitish below, *under tail-coverts buffish*; tail not tipped white. Female: no conspicuous black or white markings nor breastband; generally browner. Eye of male reddish orange, of female yellowish. Imm: like female. Singly, pairs, family parties or small loose companies; feeds much on ground, stumps and low branches, hops briskly. When disturbed, often moves some distance in strong undulating flight to cover. When calling, perches high, usually on dead branch, turns this way and that when calling, hence perhaps 'ventriloquial' quality of call.

Similar species: Do not confuse by name with unrelated and dissimilar Bell Miner (589). Wedgebill (494): more uniform brown, no dark or white mark on face; tail rather full, with prominent white tips. Western Whipbird (493): greyer and greener; centre of throat black with whitish whisker-mark. In flight, pale tips to outer tail-feathers; note range and habits; calls differ.

Voice: Territorial call of male is one of most unusual and lovely sounds of inland and drier coastal districts; of fugitive ventriloquial quality, tone and phrasing differ between individuals and districts. Typically consists of series of notes of varied syllables that start softly and intensify: 'did-did-did, didee-dit' or 'pan-pan, panella', last syllable lower and usually rendered as a liquid plonk, resembling tolling of mellow cow-bell; from distance, last note alone heard. Other calls, thin 'seep, seep' like quail-thrush, followed by mellow 'plunk plunk' or 'plunka-plunka-plunka'; also somewhat harsh note, syllabized 'chuck-a-chuck-chuck'.

Habitat: Drier inland and sub-inland scrubs and woodlands, drier coastal areas, specially in SA and WA.

Breeding: Nest: somewhat untidy cup; of bark-strips, leaves and twigs, lined with fine grass and rootlets; usually on top of stump, or in fork of shrub or tree, 1–3 m high. Eggs: 3–4; white, blotched dark-brown and grey. Nests with eggs usually have live, immobilized caterpillars placed round rim.

Range and Status: Throughout interior and drier coastal areas of mainland: in WA apparently absent only from 1000+ mm rainfall zone of sw. corner; present on drier coastal islands and from e. of Albany along coast to Eyre Pen. SA, and absent only from se. corner SA; in Vic., confined to nw. and n., e. to about Chiltern; throughout NSW w. of Divide, occasionally to n. coast; in Q widespread, mostly in s. and w. interior, less well established elsewhere but e. to Bunya Ras., catchments of Dawson, Burdekin and Herbert Rs. and drier parts Atherton Tableland; apparently absent from C. York and Gulf coast; but in NT, n. to Borroloola–Larrimah–Timber Creek. Common interior, uncommon and local in better-watered coastal areas. Sedentary or nomadic.

MONARCH FLYCATCHERS Genus *Monarcha*

Distinctive flycatchers with rather large heads, broad ridged bills surrounded by bristles, and bold, simple plumage-patterns. Most feed in and round foliage of trees. In Aust., they fall into two sections and three atypical species. (1) Genus *Monarcha* (475–8): mainly grey or blackish above, with buff or white underparts, and black or white markings; females resemble males. Then come two distinctive members of the genus *Arses* (479–80) boldly-marked, unusual little black-and-white birds with feathers peaked to a crest on the nape and bare bluish skin round eye. They feed more on trunks and branches than other members of the group. Equally distinctive is the small, brightly-coloured Yellow-breasted Boatbill (474) with its grotesquely large, flattened and rounded bill. (2) Genus *Myiagra* (481–5): glossy black to grey upperparts and either white, buffish or rusty underparts;

females are typically buff or rusty below. Monarch flycatchers locate insects in careful scrutiny of foliage and branches, sitting still or with tail *quivered vertically or sideways*, darting into foliage or air for prey. Their voices are usually somewhat harsh and rasping but they also have clear penetrating whistles. Their nests are beautiful cups decorated with lichen or green moss; eggs are whitish or buffish, marked with brown. Sexes similar or dissimilar.

Food: Mainly insects.

Range: Africa south of the Sahara, s. Asia to Aust.; many Pacific islands.

Number of species: World *c.* 133; Aust. 11.

474 YELLOW-BREASTED BOATBILL *Machaerirhynchus flaviventer* **Pl.66**

Other names: Boat-billed or Yellow-breasted Flycatcher; Wherrybill.

Field marks: 110–125 mm. Unlike any other Australian bird: a small colourful flycatcher with a *grotesquely large broad flattened bill*. Male: black and olive-grey above *with bold yellow eyebrow*, white marks on wings, edges and tips of tail; *throat white, sides of neck and underparts bright-yellow*. Female: olive-grey above, eyebrow whitish yellow; wings, tail and throat as male; *yellow-green below, upperbreast and flanks faintly barred*. Imm: like dull female. Usually in pairs; vivacious; works through branchlets and leaves snapping up insects; sallies from feeding stations to take flying insects. Calls often.

Voice: Song of male described as a characteristic soft insect-like trilling, 'wit, zee-ee-ee, wit'; other peculiar notes and pretty warblings have been described.

Habitat: Rainforests and heavy creekside vegetation; occasionally to adjacent eucalypt woodland.

Breeding: Nest: small saucer or basket; of fine twigs or plant-stalks, bound with spiders' web; usually on slender horizontal fork at end of branch or sapling, but usually among leaves, 4–20 m high. Eggs: 2; white, with zone of reddish purple or reddish yellow spots at large end.

Range and Status: Coasts, highlands and forested coastal islands of ne. Q: from Archer R., on w. C. York Pen., to s. of Ingham. Locally common; generally uncommon; sedentary. Also NG.

475 BLACK-FACED MONARCH FLYCATCHER *Monarcha melanopsis*
Pl. 66

Field marks: 165–190 mm. A distinctive robust flycatcher: beautiful pale-grey upperparts *and upperbreast contrast with sharply cut off pale-rufous underparts*; *black forehead and throat form a patch round base of the pale blue-grey bill*; tail grey, without white tips. Imm: no black on face. Singly or pairs, rather slow-moving and sedate, but, when breeding, becomes more active and conspicuous; often first noted by call. Feeds among foliage with frequent sallies into air after insects.

Similar species: Black-winged Monarch Flycatcher (476); shoulders, wings and tail black; note range. Spectacled Monarch Flycatcher (477): rufous underparts extend to throat; tail tipped white.

Voice: Notes vary greatly, but typical call is rich, clear 'Why-you, which-you', a harsher 'which-a-where' or a descending, clear mellow 'which you' or 'why you, witch', or again 'weech you', first syllable rising, second falling. Also a repeated downward-slurred 'r,r,rerr' or 'shsh-shsh-shirr', like calls of Satin Bowerbird (694) and White-browed Babbler (500).

Habitat: In coastal n. Aust.: rainforests, eucalypt woodlands, coastal scrubs. In se. Aust.: during breeding season, usually damp gullies in temperate rainforest; disperses after breeding into more open woodland.

Breeding: Nest: deep cup; of fine strips of bark, rootlets or occasionally casuarina needles; bound with spiders' web, often decorated externally with hair-like green moss; usually in horizontal fork, often concealed by leaves 1–12 m or more high. Eggs: 2–3; white,

minutely and irregularly dotted and spotted reddish or red-brown, sparse underlying pale purplish blotches.
Range and Status: Coastal e. Aust. and islands: from C. York, Q, to Dandenong Ras., Vic., vagrant to w. of Melbourne. Rarely far inland, mostly along Divide. Resident in ne. Q; regular migrant in coastal e. Aust., moving s. during Aug.–Sept., and n. in Mar.–Apr. after breeding; part of population migrates to NG. Common in n., fairly common to scarce in s.

476   BLACK-WINGED MONARCH FLYCATCHER   *Monarcha frater*

Other name: Pearly Flycatcher.
Field marks: 150 mm. Like Black-faced Monarch Flycatcher (475), but *wings and tail mostly black, contrasting with grey upperparts.* Imm: face grey.
Similar species: Black-faced Monarch Flycatcher (475): mostly grey wings and tail; note range. Spectacled Monarch Flycatcher (477); different facial pattern; white in tail.
Voice: Probably like Black-faced.
Habitat: Rainforests and nearby woodlands.
Breeding: Probably like Black-faced.
Range and Status: In Aust., confined to C. York Pen., s. to Claudie R. on e. coast. Resident, or migrant from NG, where widespread in highlands.

477   SPECTACLED MONARCH FLYCATCHER   *Monarcha trivirgatus*
Pl.66

Other names: Black-fronted or White-bellied Flycatcher.
Field marks: 150–165 mm. A slender, active flycatcher, deep blue-grey above, throat and breast rich buff, with *black cloverleaf pattern on face and throat;* underparts white. Tail blackish, *outer feathers prominently tipped white.* Race *albiventris* of n. Q: only upper-breast buff, rest of underparts pure-white. Imm: no black on head, centre of throat greyish; outer tail-feathers tipped buff-white. Singly, pairs, small parties; tame, vivacious; flutters, hovers and dodges in foliage, works industriously over trunks and vines, longish tail carried at slight angle, slightly fanned and used much like that of fantail: white tips prominent. Often first located by chatterings.
Similar species: Black-faced (475) and Black-winged (476) Monarch Flycatchers: upper-breast grey; no white in tail.
Voice: Scratchy chattering or fussy jigging scolding, somewhat like distant party of rosellas; also clear 'zwee zwee zwee', each syllable rising end; song unpretentious, a soft short squeaky warble.
Habitat: Gloomier parts of mountain and lowland rainforests, adjacent thickly wooded gullies; typically well below canopy.
Breeding: Nest: pretty cup; of fine bark and other fibres, leaf skeletons and moss, bound with spiders' web; may be decorated externally with white or greenish spiders' cocoons; usually in fork of open shrub, low tree or hanging vine 1–6 m high; often near water. Eggs: 2; oval; pink-white to creamy white, minutely freckled rich-pink, red-brown or dull-purple, more heavily on large end.
Range and Status: Coastal ne. and e. Aust. and many coastal islands from C. York s. to Watson R. on w. coast, and to Port Stephens, NSW, in e. Resident s. to Rockhampton; total migrant in s. Q and ne. NSW, arriving Sept.–Oct. to breed, departing by May. Common in humid ne. Aust.; elsewhere locally common and only in suitable habitat. Also s. NG, Moluccas, Timor.

478   WHITE-EARED MONARCH FLYCATCHER   *Monarcha leucotis* Pl.66

Field marks: 135–145 mm. Very distinctive; has been likened to a miniature Magpie Lark (710): *black above, with bold white marks round eyes, on sides of head and wing; rump white, outer tail-feathers broadly tipped white;* white below, black of upperparts coming well down on sides of neck: breast and flanks washed grey. Female: duller. Uncommon; said to be usually in isolated pairs. Very active; feeds on flying insects disturbed as it flutters among leaves in treetops or lower; active during heat of day; calls often.

Similar species: Pied (480) and Frilled Monarch (479) Flycatchers. White-browed Robin (457).

Voice: Vivacious: calls freely and chatters incessantly near nest; calls described as repeated drawn-out 'phew-phew-phew', or 'ee-ooo, ee-ooo', much like Horsfield's Bronze-cuckoo (369); an oft-repeated musical whistle has been syllabized 'you-GET-awaaay' or 'ta-ta-taaaa'!

Habitat: Coastal rainforests and dense scrubs, swamp woodlands, mangroves; similar on coastal islands; usually in denser parts but occasionally at edge of scrub.

Breeding: Nest: deep cup or goblet; of soft mosses, spiders' cocoons and web, lined with palm-fibre; in upright fork of small shrub or tree. Eggs: 2; blunt oval; whitish, with small uneven red-brown spots.

Range and Status: Coastal e. Aust. and forested coastal islands: from C. York Pen., Q, to ne. NSW (records Murwillumbah and Iluka; once vagrant Lithgow). Breeds s. to Stradbroke I., Q. Fairly common in suitable habitat in mid-part of range, uncommon to rare in s.; mostly coastal, uncommon in highlands; nomadic autumn and winter, possibly migrant.

479 FRILLED MONARCH FLYCATCHER *Arses telescophthalmus* Pl.66

Other names: Frilled, Frill-necked or White-lored Flycatcher.

Field marks: 140–165 mm. Note range: very like Pied Monarch Flycatcher (480), but *no black breastband*; white rear-collar more extensive and conspicuous. Female: white spot before eye. Habits like Pied; when singing, reported to make short whirring flights from twig to twig.

Voice: Noisy; harsh scolding calls and a trilled song have been described (NG data).

Habitat: Rainforest, chiefly in middle spaces but into lower treetops (NG data).

Breeding: As for Pied Monarch Flycatcher.

Range and Status: Confined to n. C. York Pen., Q: s. to Chester R. on e. coast and to Archer R. on w. coast. Fairly common; sedentary. Also NG and Aru Is.

480 PIED MONARCH FLYCATCHER *Arses kaupi* Pl.66

Other name: Black-breasted Flycatcher.

Field marks: 150–160 mm. Two small blue-black and white flycatchers with erectile neck frills inhabit ne. Q. This is the s. form. Apart from range, easily distinguished by its *broad black breastband*. Note the long white scapulars (feathers covering join of wings and back). They form a conspicuous white patch on back. Note also *pale-blue eye-ring, all-white chin and throat and wholly black tail*. Female: rear white collar incomplete. Imm: white hindneck heavily flecked black, mantle grey-brown, no white scapular patch, throat greyish, breastband grey-brown. Pairs to small parties, vivacious, raises collar in slight frill; searching for insects, it creeps and hops up or down tree trunks somewhat like treecreeper, wings half-open; jerks tail downward; darts out after flying insects, tail spread like fantail.

Similar species: Frilled Monarch Flycatcher (479).

Voice: Quaint soft 'quacking' notes while feeding have been described.

Habitat: Rainforests, palm and vine-scrubs, especially near running water; adjacent eucalypt woodlands.

Breeding: Nest: miniature hanging basket; openly woven of fine twigs or tendrils, held together with spiders' web and decorated externally with lichen. Usually slung between hanging creepers or attached to hanging branch, 6–10 m high. Eggs: 2; nearly elliptical; glossy; pink-white, finely spotted or freckled red-brown, reddish chestnut and purple-grey, most heavily large end.

Range and Status: Coastal ne. Q from Cooktown to Townsville, inland to Atherton Tableland. Fairly common; sedentary.

481 BROAD-BILLED FLYCATCHER *Myiagra ruficollis*   Pl.66

Field marks: 150–165 mm. Deep glossy blue-grey above, *outer tail-feathers edged whitish;* slight pale eye-ring. Upperbreast uniform pale to rich buff, underparts whitish. Female: less glossy above, paler below. Imm: browner above, wing-feathers margined buffish. *The pale edges of the tail help* separate it from female Leaden (482) and Satin (483) Flycatchers. Bill somewhat broader, crown flatter; head looks rather large. Singly or pairs; quiet, seeks insects in and about heads of mangroves and other leafy trees. Note habitat.

Habitat: Mangroves, monsoon forest, swamp woodlands, riverside vegetation; occasional in coastal woodlands.

Voice: 'Hrinney, hrinney, hrinney . . .', clear and far-carrying; also soft churring.

Breeding: Nest: shallow cup; of strips of bark or plant-fibre, bound with spiders' web; decorated externally with lichen; usually in dead or living mangrove 1–3 m high above high-tide mark or over stream. Eggs: 2–3; round-oval, glossy; whitish, spotted and blotched dark-brown and grey in zone, leaving large end bald.

Range and Status: Mostly coastal n. Aust. and islands: from Fitzroy R., Kimberleys, WA, to Rocky R., e. C. York Pen., Q. Common. Also s. NG and Timor.

482 LEADEN FLYCATCHER *Myiagra rubecula*   Pl.66

Other names: Blue Flycatcher, Frogbird.

Field marks: 140–165 mm. Male: *glossy blue-grey above and on upperbreast;* greenish gloss on head, throat and upperbreast makes these look darker; *dark-grey to blackish from bill to eye;* white below cut off sharply from dark upperbreast. Female: *dull lead-grey above,* slightly browner on back; *throat pale orange-buff, becoming paler on breast,* dull-white below. Imm: like female, wing-feathers and tail edged buffish, mottled band across upperbreast. Singly or pairs; alert and active; sits watchfully upright; darts into foliage or air after insects; often raises feathers of crown in slight peak when calling; *rapidly quivers tail up and down or sideways.*

Similar species: Satin Flycatcher (483); male: blue-black, and without contrast between dark face and upperparts. Female: darker blue-grey above, more uniform and often richer-buff below. Calls more strident. Note range. Broad-billed Flycatcher (481): both sexes very like female Leaden, but distinctly larger than small n. race of Leaden. *Note white edges to tail.*

Voice: Deep, slightly harsh, guttural 'zhirrp', singly or repeated; also strident, far-carrying 'see-hear, see-hear, see-hear' or 'see-kew, see-kew', or 'liprick, liprick'. When breeding, vivacious little song.

Habitat: Dense forest gullies in Divide to open eucalypt forests, woodlands, coastal scrubs and especially in n. Aust., swamp woodlands, riverside vegetation and mangroves. In lowlands of e. coast, more typical of coastal scrubs and woodlands than Satin.

Breeding: Nest: neat cup; of fine bark, bound and covered with spiders' web, beautifully decorated round rim with small pieces of lichen and bark; usually on fairly slender dead branch, often in cover of foliage, in woodland or forest, 10–25 m high, at times down to 3 m. Eggs: 2–3; oval; white or blue-white, spotted in zone round middle or large end with shades of brown, purple-brown and underlying violet spots.

Range and Status: N. and e. Aust. and coastal islands, from Fitzroy R., Kimberleys, WA, across n. Aust., and e. Aust. s. to sw. Vic.; occasional Tas. and se. SA. Sedentary in n.; breeding migrant in se. Aust. Sept.–Apr. Mostly coastal but occurs well inland, specially on watercourses. In NT s. to Katherine; in Q inland to Blackall–Roma; in NSW to Moree–Barham, vagrant further w., along Murray R.; in Vic. w. to Warby Ras.–Portland; vagrant Mt. Lofty Ras., SA. Common n. coasts and islands; fairly common to uncommon elsewhere. Also NG.

483 SATIN FLYCATCHER *Myiagra cyanoleuca* Pl.66

Other names: Satin Sparrow, Shining Flycatcher.
Field marks: 150–175 mm. Male: *glossy blue-black, cut off sharply across breast by white underparts.* Female: *slightly glossy dusky blue-grey above, throat and upperbreast rich-buff,* underparts white. Imm: like female. Singly or pairs; lively, active and showy. Usually in tops of taller trees; darts from branch to branch, sallies into air after insects. Raises crown feathers to form peak; *quivers tail rapidly usually up and down, sometimes sideways.*
Similar species: Willie Wagtail (489): black fan-tail; white eyebrow and whisker. Leaden Flycatcher (482), male: more blue-grey, with contrasting darker face. Female: somewhat paler above and below. Broad-billed (481): both sexes like female Satin *but white edges to tail.* Restless Flycatcher (485): underparts white from bill down.
Voice: Generally more strident than Leaden; guttural 'zhurp!' or 'bzzurt', oft repeated. Also strident clear carrying 'wu-*chee*-wu-*chee*-wu-*chee*' or 'chellee chellee chellee' and associated clear high-pitched 'weir-to-weir-to-weir', or 'thurp, pewit pewit pewit'.
Habitat: When breeding, favours heavily vegetated gullies in forests and taller woodlands; during migration coastal forests, woodlands and scrubs, swamp woodlands, mangroves; trees in open country, gardens.
Breeding: Nest: neat cup; of strips of bark, green moss, bound and matted with spiders' web; usually at tip of dead branch 6–25 m high, often in cover of foliage. Eggs: 2–3; noticeably rounded at one end; dull-white to faint bluish or greenish white, spotted, blotched dark-brown, purple-grey, with zone of underlying dull purple-grey spots leaving large end bald.
Range and Status: E. Aust. and coastal islands: from C. York to Tas. and w. Vic.; vagrant SA and Bight coast of WA. Breeds se. Aust. and Tas., arriving Aug.–Oct., departs Feb.–Apr.; some winter in n. Q, but apparently most pass to NG. Generally scarce except in Tas., which appears to be the breeding stronghold. Vagrant NZ. Uncommon.

484 SHINING FLYCATCHER *Myiagra alecto* Pl.66

Other names: Glossy Flycatcher, Satinbird.
Field marks: 170–190 mm. Unmistakable. Male: *entirely glossy jet-black.* Female: *crown and nape glossy black, rest of upperparts rich-chestnut;* white below. Imm: like dull female. Singly, pairs or displaying small groups; vivacious, raises crown-feathers in low crest, habitually flicks tail upward. When feeding, moves very fast, pausing before making sudden dart at invertebrates on leaves or on mud. Male often seems shyer than female; if disturbed, quickly vanishes.
Voice: An 'amazingly varied repertoire' of calls and songs has been described, from pretty whistlings to peculiar croakings. One call of male is a deep 'zhip, zhip, zhipipipip'. A warning call has been described as three clear distinct whistles.
Habitat: Always seems to be associated with water. Dense mangroves, pockets of rainforest near water, riverside vegetation, including paperbarks and pandanus.
Breeding: Nest: deep, closely woven cup; of strips or rough pieces of bark, bound with spiders' web; decorated externally with bark and closely resembling supporting branch; sometimes so deep in fork as to be nearly invisible. Almost always over water and sheltered by leaves; in mangroves, on slender dead or living branch or vine, 1–6 m high. Eggs: 2–3; glossy, rounded at large end; blue-white or green-white with minute spots or blotches of various browns and underlying marks of lilac-grey at one end, or in zone round large end.
Range and Status: Coastal n. and ne. Aust. and some coastal islands from Broome, WA, (with possible gap on Gulf coast) to C. York Pen., Q, and s. to Fraser I. and Noosa R.; unconfirmed sight-records s. to Tweed Heads, NSW. Occasional some distance inland on watercourses, e.g. S. Alligator R. near El Sherana, NT. Common in NT and s. to Herbert R. in Q, scarce to rare s. of there. Also NG and adjacent islands; Bismarck Archipelago, Aru Is. and Moluccas.

485   RESTLESS FLYCATCHER   *Myiagra inquieta*   **Pl.66**

Other names: Crested Wagtail, Dishlick, Dish Washer, Razor or Scissors Grinder, Who-are-you?

Field marks: 165–210 mm. Handsome and distinctive; deep glossy blue-black above; *entire underparts silky white, often washed pale yellow-buff across breast*; bill longish and fairly robust. Imm: dull blackish above, scapulars tipped dull-white. Singly or pairs; active, restless; raises slight crest; gracefully sweeps tail from side to side. Flight swooping, graceful, with deep wingbeats. Seeks insects, food in foliage, branches; *hovers near ground while hunting, uttering distinctive call*; perches on stumps, occasionally feeds on ground. Rather vocal, often heard before seen. The n. race *nana* is small (170 mm).

Similar species: Satin Flycatcher (483), male. Willie Wagtail (489).

Voice: A rasping 'zhap', singly or repeated and run together: '*zhap*-zhapzhapzhapzhap'. While hovering, a curious sustained grinding churring; also utters a clear repeated whistle, 'chewee, chewee, chewee', each phrase rising at end like man whistling a dog.

Habitat: Open forest and woodlands, especially near water; during autumn and winter dispersal ranges to sub-inland scrubs, including mallee; also golfcourses, orchards, roadside timber, parks, gardens.

Breeding: Nest: like Willie Wagtail but thinner-walled and slightly larger; of shreds of bark and fine grass, bound and felted on outside with spiders' web; often decorated externally with lichen. Usually on horizontal branchlet, in scrub or woodland, 1–20 m high. Eggs: 3; oval, glossy; off-white, with distinct zone of dark-brown and grey spots round larger end.

Range and Status: N., e. and s. Aust. and some coastal islands: from Broome, WA, through n. half NT s. to Morphett Creek–Alexandria; in Q, inland to Mt. Isa–Fermoy–Toompine; most NSW *except* far nw.; all Vic.; s. half SA and s. WA n. to Gt. Victoria Desert–Kalgoorlie–Moora. Race *nana* occupies most of n. range from Broome to C. York Pen., Q, to Edward R. Fairly common; nomadic or part-migratory. Also s. NG.

FANTAILS   Genus *Rhipidura*

A large group of distinctive flycatchers distributed from s. Asia to NZ, reaching its greatest development in s. Asia and NG; Aust. has four species only. Their characteristic feature is the conspicuous fan-like tail, carried partly cocked, alternately spread and closed or switched this way and that, either when bird is on ground or when it clambers, flits and flutters through branches and foliage. These actions, often jerky and abrupt, serve to disturb insects. On wing, fantails are very sprightly, performing spinning looping aerial chases after insects. They are often tame and several species frequently appear about or at times inside buildings. Their voices are perky and spirited; their nests are neat cups, sometimes shaped like a wine glass without a base.

Food: Mostly insects.

Range: S. Asia, Australasian region, NZ and parts of Oceania.

Number of species: World 38; Aust. 4.

486   RUFOUS FANTAIL   *Rhipidura rufifrons*   **Pl.66**

Other names: Rufous-fronted or Wood Fantail; Rufous Flycatcher.

Field marks: 150–165 mm. In dark cover, it can look like a darting flame with its *fiery orange-rufous rump and base of tail*; rest of tail blackish, tipped paler. Note also *orange-rufous forehead and eyebrow, white breast crossed by black band or zone of blackish spots*. Imm: more rufous above, underparts washed brown. Singly, territorial pairs, migrant companies; less madly active than Grey Fantail (487); tends to keep lower in denser cover. Flight after insects quick and jerky, usually without aerobatics; feeds more in branches, sometimes running on ground and logs. Tame, occasionally enters buildings.

Voice: A single high-pitched faint or penetrating squeak, accelerating into a brisk squeaky *descending* see-saw song; higher-pitched than Grey.

Habitat: Dense, usually rather damp, undergrowth of tropical rainforests and scrubs, monsoon forest, swamp woodland, denser sub-inland and coastal scrubs; mangroves, vegetation along watercourses; parks, gardens. On migration, individuals stray to open country, farms, gardens, streets, buildings.

Breeding: Nest: larger than Grey Fantail; neat tailed cup; of fine strips of bark, moss and fine grasses, felted externally with spiders' web; usually near ground in fork in bush, but to 5 m or higher, often near or over water. Eggs: 2–3; glossy; stone-coloured, yellow-buff or yellow-white, speckled brown and lavender-grey, usually in zone at large end.

Range and Status: Mostly coastal n. and e. Aust. and coastal islands: from C. Bertholet, c. 80 km n. of Broome, WA, e. through top end NT to C. York, Q, thence coastally s. to sw. Vic.; vagrant n. Tas., se. SA. Mostly e. and s. of Divide, occasional inland–Nebo–Dalby, Q; Orange–Hay, NSW; Mystic Park, Vic. Total migrant in se., arriving in Oct. to breed, departing Mar.–Apr., with apparently regular return to breeding haunts. Part migratory (? also altitudinal) in n.; apparently some regular movement to NG. Also resident NG, Solomon Is., Celebes and Guam.

487 GREY FANTAIL *Rhipidura fuliginosa* Pl.66

Other names: Cranky Fan, Mad Fan, Snapper, White-fronted or White-shafted Fantail.
Field marks: 140–165 mm. The outer feathers of the *large dark-grey fan-tail* are white and *all but the central feathers have broad white tips and prominent white shafts*. (The race *albicauda* of c. Aust. has most white in tail). Note too the broken white eyebrow, *two fine white bars across wing* and white edges to flight-feathers; *white throat separated from fawn-to-buff breast by dark breastband*. S. birds, specially from Tas., are darkest. Imm: duller, browner; buffish head-markings, wing-coverts tipped buff, breastband ashy-brown. Singly or pairs; companies during winter dispersal. Restlessly active; wings drooped, tail spread; more so than other fantails, flutters, loops and stunts after flying insects.
Similar species: Northern Fantail (488): a 'different' more sedate bird, a larger head and bill give more flycatcher-like 'jizz'; note markings.
Voice: An oft-repeated, fairly sharp 'dek'. When breeding, this develops into tinny but sweet, animated song of fiddle-like see-saw character, usually *ascending*, often ending in several drawn-out rising notes of silvery quality; surprisingly loud, prominent in dawn chorus.
Habitat: Almost any cover with some moisture, from coastal scrubs and mangroves to rainforests, inland scrubs and vegetation lining watercourses and rocky gorges. A population is confined to mangroves n. from Shark Bay, WA. Also golf courses, orchards, parks, gardens.
Breeding: Nest: small beautiful tailed cup like baseless wine-glass; of fine grasses and strips of bark, occasional leaves and wood-fibre, bound with spiders' web, giving it smooth grey look; on slender horizontal or vertical fork of shrub or tree or dead branchlet, low to 12 m high. Eggs: 2–3 (sometimes 4 in s. Vic. and Tas.); slightly glossy; yellowish or fawnish white, spotted with light-brown, rufous and grey, especially at large end.
Range and Status: Aust, and Tas. and coastal islands: widespread except driest coverless habitats; common in wetter coastal areas. In se. and sw. Aust., substantial sub-inland dispersal after breeding; migration across Bass Strait is suspected, as are migratory movements elsewhere, but the picture is complex and confused. Also NZ, e. NG (where rare); Solomon Is., New Hebrides, New Caledonia.

488 NORTHERN FANTAIL *Rhipidura rufiventris* Pl.66

Other name: White-throated Fantail.
Field marks: 165–185 mm. More flycatcher-like than other fantails; head larger, bill longer and broader, tail shorter and less fanned, edged and tipped white, *but no white shafts*. Dark grey-brown above with faint white eyebrow; throat white, *broad streaked or spotted grey-brown breastband*; underparts creamy buff-white. Imm: browner, with

buffish margins to wing-feathers and tail-tips. Singly or pairs; actions subdued; forages in foliage, sits on exposed branches to sally after flying insects.
Similar species: Grey Fantail (487). Mangrove Robin (447): no breastband, tail not fanlike; note white panels at base.
Voice: Quiet; a short metallic 'chip'; beautiful tinkling song, prefaced with almost inaudible notes, oft-repeated.
Habitat: Margins of rainforests and vine scrubs; monsoon forests, swamp woodlands, riverside vegetation to open eucalyptus forest in wet; mangroves.
Breeding: Nest: tailed cup, larger and somewhat untidier than Grey Fantail; of shreds of bark and fine grasses, felted with spiders' web on outside; on branch of shrub or open tree, often paperbark, acacia or eucalypt, usually 1–6, occasionally to 20 m high. Eggs: 2–3; creamy-white, with zone of dull-brown spots with few indistinct underlying spots of blue-grey.
Range and Status: N. Aust. and coastal islands: from C. Bertholet, *c.* 80 km n. Broome, WA, to about Mt. Spec–Townsville, Q; sight-record Eungella NP, near Mackay; seldom far inland e.g. to Larrimah, NT. Fairly common; apparently has seasonal (? altitudinal) movements in parts of n. coast. Also Lesser Sunda Is., Moluccas, NG, Bismarck Archipelago, Solomon Is.

489 WILLIE WAGTAIL *Rhipidura leucophrys* **Pl.66**
Other names: Black-and-white Fantail or Flycatcher, Frogbird, Morningbird, Shepherd's Companion.
Field marks: 190–215 mm. One of our most widespread, well-loved birds. Black and fantailed, with white underparts sharply cut off below breast; note *white eyebrows and slim white whiskermark.* Imm: duller with rusty feather-margins, indistinct buffish eyebrow. Singly, pairs, family parties; active, perky and bold; uses low branches, fence-posts, stumps or even backs of animals as look-outs. Takes insects in twisting flight, in foliage or while running on ground or floating vegetation, disturbing them by jerky twitching of tail or (some individuals) by sudden opening of wings. Large butterflies are transferred to feet for carriage in flight. Sustained flight quick and direct with slight undulation. Frequently skirmishes with larger birds, specially other black-and-white species like Australian Magpie (720), Magpie Lark (710).
Similar species: Satin Flycatcher (483), male: glossy, no white eyebrow, quivers slim tail up and down. Restless Flycatcher (485): glossy blue-black above, no white eyebrow; throat and underparts wholly white.
Voice: Usual call spirited, sweet, often characterized as 'sweet-pretty-creature', but varies much; often heard on moonlight nights. Other common call, a scolding, rattling 'rikka-tikka-tikka-tik'.
Habitat: Most habitats except dense forests; includes mangroves, vegetation on Gt. Barrier Reef islands to nearly treeless (and often apparently waterless) parts of Nullarbor Plain, Barkly Tableland; spinifex-scrub associations in Simpson Desert; lightly timbered river valleys, open margins of streams and swamps; also golfcourses, orchards, parks and gardens.
Breeding: Nest: shallow cup; of fine grass, bark shreds and rootlets felted on outside with spiders' web until grey and smooth, lined with hair, wool, feathers, plant-down; usually on small horizontal branch. 1–15 m high; sometimes over water, or near nest of Magpie Lark (710) or White-winged Triller (432). Or on fallen branches, trees in orchards, roots from overhanging banks; clothes hoists, street-lamps, fence-wires; sheltered parts of buildings or boats. Often uses the same nest-site in successive years; after first brood, may lay again in same nest or remove it and use material elsewhere; 2–3 broods in a season are common. Eggs: 2–4; light creamy buff to yellowish white, spotted and marked with light red-brown, wood-brown, olive or grey, usually in belt near centre.
Range and Status: Mainland Aust. and many coastal islands; vagrant Kangaroo I., SA; Flinders and King Is. and possibly to n. Tas. Very common, widespread, mostly sedentary. Also Moluccas, NG, Bismarck Archipelago, Solomon Is.

Logrunners, Whipbirds, Wedgebills and Quail-thrushes
Family *Orthonychidae*

The two chowchillas or logrunners (490–1) are terrestial songbirds with robust legs and feet and a specialized tail, the rather stiff feather-shafts extending in resilient spines. When feeding, they clear leaves from soil by rapid scratching, throwing debris aside and behind, sometimes propping themselves on the spread tail and using both feet to excavate. Characteristic small cleared areas result. Logrunners move in pairs or small parties, and are very noisy, specially at dawn and dusk; Northern Logrunner (491) is an accomplished mimic. In Aust. the species are widely separate in range; curiously, only the Southern Logrunner (490) occurs in NG. Whipbirds have bold patterns of plumage in dull colours, feed mostly on or near the ground and live in scrub or undergrowth. They need vocal contact and so have strong or far-carrying voices. One species, Western Whipbird (493) has become adapted to drier habitats. It is generally rare and perhaps declining. Wedgebill (494) is plainer; it lives in scrubs in more open habitats; vocal contact is important to it and indeed the two races of wedgebill, treated by some as species, are separated mainly on voice. Quail-thrushes (495–8) are highly-distinctive birds of bold but cryptic patterns. They live on the ground in open forests of the se. and in scrubs or open country of the s. inland; there is one in NG. Usually shy and secretive, they move in pairs or small groups that freeze when disturbed or burst up with a quail-like whirr, flying low, fast and straight in spurts, displaying white-tipped dark tails, landing at flying speed and running. Their taxonomy is still debatable. Colours of upperparts have changed to match the soil of their various habitats, but their markings below, being of greater importance for recognition and display, have remained more alike. They are clearly closely related and females of inland forms look very similar in the field.

Food: Insects, their larvae and other invertebrates.

Range: Endemic to the Australasian region.

Number of species: World 11; Aust. 10.

---

490 SOUTHERN LOGRUNNER *Orthonyx temminckii* Pl.59

Other names: Scrub-quail, Spinetail, Jungle Spinetail; Spinetailed Chowchilla or Logrunner; Scrub-hen.

Field marks: 205 mm. Of distinctive appearance, habits and calls. Male: rufous above, mottled black; *black flight-feathers crossed by several pale bars*; rump rufous, tail dark-brown and full, spines not prominent; sides of face white or pale-grey; *throat white, margined by black collar.* Female: similar *but throat distinctive orange-rufous.* Imm: like female, plainer. Moves in pairs or small parties, noisily turning over leaves, bark and debris. When disturbed while feeding, hops, runs, hides under leaves or flies with quail-like whirr on short rounded wings. Parties call noisily in concert; chase and chatter with much excitement, wings drooped, tails spread.

Voice: Distinctive and varied: typical call: loud resonant 'be-kweek-kwekk-kweek-kweek', often quickly repeated; also short piercing loud note, sometimes rapidly repeated, described as 'quick!' or 'tweet'.

Habitat: Open leafy floors of rainforests and where logs, fallen limbs, debris, ferns and vines cover the ground.

Breeding: Nest: large, globular, domed, with approach-ramp, which is often muddy, of sticks, ferns, fibrous leaves, treefern fibres, mosses; dome or cowl typically of green moss; interior reinforced round base with wood-pulp and lined with soft fibrous material, such as rootlets or skeletal leaves matted together; on or near ground on bank, against stone or log, in tree buttress, ferns or vine-moss. Eggs: 2; large, white.

Range and Status: Isolated populations in coastal and mountain areas s. from Blackall and Bunya Ras., se. Q, to Illawarra district, s. coast NSW. Common in Q, uncommon to rare NSW; sedentary. Also NG.

491 NORTHERN LOGRUNNER *Orthonyx spaldingii*   Pl.59

Other names: Auctioneer-bird, Black-headed Logrunner, Northern Chowchilla; Spalding's Spinetail.

Field marks: 280 mm. Male: head black; rest of upperparts dark-brown, *throat and breast white*. Female: *throat and upperbreast rich-rufous*; white below. Shafts of tail-feathers end in short spines, not very conspicuous; legs and feet powerful. Pairs or small parties; active, hops or runs on forest-floor; scratches among debris like a fowl, breast close to ground. Rarely takes wing and then only in whirring short flights. Noisy, specially in early morning.

Voice: At dawn reported to drown most other voices; becomes quieter during middle of day. Typical call 'chow chowchilla'; other strange, raucous notes; mimics.

Habitat: Leafy debris-strewn floor of tropical rainforests, mostly highland.

Breeding: Nest: large, bulky and domed; loosely made of twigs, roots and mosses; on ground among roots of vines, on stump or elk-horn fern, to 4 m high. Egg: 1; oval, white.

Range and Status: Coastal ranges and tablelands of ne. Q: from about Cooktown to about Mt. Spec near Townsville. Common; sedentary.

492 EASTERN WHIPBIRD. *Psophodes olivaceus*   Pl.62

Other names: Coachwhip or Stockwhip-bird, Whipbird.

Field marks: 255–305 mm. Male: a noisy but secretive *blackish crested bird with a longish white-tipped fan-tail*; note *white patch on either side of throat*; upperparts dark olive-green. Female: smaller, throat mottled whitish. Race *lateralis* in ne. Q: paler above, slightly browner below, dull-white tips to tail. Imm: dull olive brown, wings and tail greener; no white on throat. Pairs appear to stay together throughout year. Often hard to see, but presence soon becomes known by well-known whipcrack call and loud rustling as it feeds in forest-litter, throwing aside leaves and bark with bill. Hops and bounces briskly like a babbler over ground and through undergrowth, hangs on sides of trunks, logs, vigorously probes rotten wood. In mating skirmishes, males move rapidly and call together, spreading crests and tails. Flight not strong, rarely sustained.

Similar species: Northern Logrunner (491): no crest, white or chestnut below.

Voice: The remarkably loud, well-known whipcrack call varies geographically. It is typically uttered as duet by (? mated) pairs. Male's long drawn-out explosive whipcrack is immediately answered by female with a quick 'choo-choo', 'weece-weece', 'awee-awee' or 'witch-a-wee' or similar. Heard close, the whipcrack is preceded by chuckle, soft creaking notes or sustained 'eee' or 'swish': Females sometimes 'answer' without male call; males sometimes utter only the 'swish'. Also scolding chatters when feeding and a remarkable range of guttural chuckles, clucks, croaks and gurgles.

Habitat: Dense closed habitats, near ground: coastal scrubs, creek and riverside vegetation; undergrowth and floor of rainforests; wetter eucalypt forests and woodlands; dense thickets of blackberries, bracken, lantana; overgrown gardens.

Breeding: Nest: well-constructed flattish cup; of long twigs, grass and bracken, lined with rootlets; in undergrowth, bracken, shrub or sapling, 1–2 m high, occasionally higher. Eggs: 2–3; blue-white to blue-green, with black and blue-grey hieroglyphic markings.

Range and Status: Nominate race: coastal e. Aust. from ranges n. and e. of Melbourne through e. and ne. Vic.; in NSW on and e. of Divide, in se. Q n. to Byfield (n. of Rockhampton), inland to Toowoomba–Bunya Ra.–Kingaroy–Biggenden–lower Dawson R.; also well vegetated coastal islands. Race *lateralis*: coastal ne. Q from Mt. Spec near Townsville n. to Mt. Amos near Cooktown, inland on Atherton Tableland; mostly above 300 m, but to coast in wetter areas. The species is common in suitable habitat. Sedentary.

493 WESTERN WHIPBIRD *Psophodes nigrogularis* **Pl.62**
Other names: Black-throated or Mallee Whipbird; Rainbird.
Field marks: 200–255 mm. Usually first noted by song or by discovery of nest. A highly elusive *greyish olive-green bird with a slight crest; black throat bordered on either side by white whisker;* outer tail-feathers *crossed by subterminal black band and prominently tipped white.* Imm: throat dull grey-brown, tinged yellow-olive. Note that isolate race *leucogaster,* 'Mallee Whipbird' of mallee/broombush associations in e. SA and nw. Vic., is paler with central underparts whitish. Singly or pairs, rarely observed; feeds in and keeps to undergrowth or bare ground below scrub. Runs swiftly; flies fast, low and direct, displaying white tips to outer tail-feathers.
Similar species: Crested Bellbird (473); Wedgebill. (494).
Voice: Peculiar, harsh and grating. Territorial call of male in sw. Aust. consists of scratchy ventriloquial phrase of *four slow notes, somewhat like repeated cyclic creaking of unoiled cartwheel*; syllabized as 'Lets scratch teacher' with emphasis on 'teach'; beginning softly, swelling in volume. Female completes this call with phrase 'pick it up'; also a 'chitter-chitter' alarm-call. Calls in Vic. described as strange, rattling, staccato repeated 8–10 times or more and uttered as if with difficulty. After calling for a time, may remain silent for hours, specially if disturbed.
Habitat: Big Desert, Vic.: undulating sandhills with dense short mallee and spinifex, teatree and broombush-scrubs; particular stages of regeneration after burning may be important to it. In dunes in inland se. SA, coastal areas of s. SA, and Kangaroo I.: heath, mallee and dry eucalypt woodlands. In Gnowangerup, Borden, Ravensthorpe districts, s. WA: mallee, banksia, and stunted heath associations.
Breeding: Nest: substantial cup; of fine twigs, strips of bark and grass, sometimes with interwoven fine green sprigs; typically below 1 m high in top of clump of spinifex under overhanging mallee-branch, also in small shrub or clump of sword-grass. Eggs: 2; delicate-blue, marked with fine black, brownish or greyish spots, last appearing as though below surface of shell, or scrawls and hieroglyphs.
Range and Status: Five widely-separated isolate populations in s. Aust.: mallee areas of nw. Vic. and se. SA in Big Desert and near Peebinga respectively; very rare. Kangaroo I.; s. Yorke Pen and s. Eyre Pen., SA; fairly common. Esperance–Stirling Ra.–Albany, WA; rare. Sedentary or locally nomadic.

494 WEDGEBILL *Psophodes cristatus* **Pl.62**
Other names: Chimesbird, Crested Wedgebill, Daylightbird, Kitty-lintol, Waggonbird, Wheelbarrow-bird.
Note: Recent field research has established that there are two forms, e. and w. whose appearance is nearly identical but whose habits and calls differ markedly. They are treated here as races of a single species.
Field marks: 195–220 mm. *A plain brownish bird with a slim upright crest; middle flight-feathers edged whitish, visible as white streak when wing closed,* tail rather prominent and rounded, blackish brown outer feathers broadly tipped white. (Nominate race has slight dark streaks on breast). Bill short, robust, wedge-shaped, dark-brown; legs and feet strong. Imm: bill horn-coloured, secondaries and wing-coverts margined buff. Pairs to parties of dozens; when approached, *cristatus* often stays perched on an exposed bush, continuing to call; *occidentalis* reported to drop quickly out of sight. Feeds much on ground; runs rather than hops, moves quickly. Flight low, swift and direct, with long flat glides like a babbler; tail usually partly spread, pale wing-streak and white outer tail-tips conspicuous. Parties of *cristatus* seem to be very gregarious, streaming off babbler-like in one direction when disturbed or calling in company.
Similar species: Crested Bellbird (473). Western Whipbird (493): olive-green above, crest black, throat margined by white streak.
Voice: Nominate race 'Chirruping Wedgebill': calls often heard as duet. One bird utters a call like 'sitzi-cheeri' or 'sit 'n-cheer', the first notes sweet but soft, so that only the loud

shrill 'cheeri' note is heard, reminiscent of rolling chirrup of Budgerigar (337). This call is often immediately answered by (?) female with an upward-rolling r-e-e-e-t CHEER! and the two are combined in an endless rondo, echoed by others elsewhere, giving an unusual effect. Race *occidentalis* 'Chiming Wedgebill': a phrase of four or five notes (sometimes three or only two notes) in a descending scale or chime, with the final note stressed; somewhat peculiar and metallic, but sweet and far-carrying with ringing quality; typical sequence like rapid 'but-did-you-get-drunk' with almost cyclic pattern, the 'but' very short and soft, the 'did' high and sweet, the rest rapidly descending with metallic plonk on the 'drunk'. Usually uttered by males, sometimes by females, *but not in a duet*. Often monotonously repeated, sometimes by moonlight.

Habitat: Nominate race: areas of low shrubs like bluebush, nitrebush and emu bush, scattered clumps of acacia; lignum-canegrass associations; *occidentalis*: thickets of acacia, tea-tree and similar often dense cover.

Breeding: (Both races). Nest: flattened, loosely constructed cup; of twigs; in low shrub, 1–3 m high. Eggs: 2–3; beautiful blue or pale-greenish blue, sparingly spotted with black especially at large end or with mauve-grey or purplish black spots or hieroglyphs.

Range and Status: Nominate race: e. inland Aust.; from Oodnadatta district, SA, s. through Flinders Ras. and n. Murray mallee; occasional in far nw. Vic.; widespread in NSW w. of Darling R.; in Q e. to Cunnamulla and n. to lower Diamantina R.; possibly in NT n. of Simpson Desert. Locally common. Race *occidentalis*: w. interior, from a line w. of L. Torrens, SA, passing through Oodnadatta district to lower Finke R. in s. NT; n. limits in WA are about Wittenoom and 20°S on n. Canning Stock Route; s. limits about Payne's Find-Leonora, thence e. through Gt. Victoria Desert. Locally common, sedentary or nomadic.

495 SPOTTED QUAIL-THRUSH *Cinclosoma punctatum* **Pl.61**

Other names: Groundbird, Ground Dove or Thrush.

Field marks: 255–280 mm. The only quail-thrush in coastal se. Aust. and Tas. Male: *face and throat black, with white eyebrow and throat-patch*; upperparts grey-brown, heavily mottled black, shoulders black spotted white; breast grey with black band; *flanks spotted black*. Female and imm: *eyebrow and throat buff-white, throat-patch yellow-ochre*, breast plain-grey with no black band; buff-white below, flanks spotted black. Pairs or family parties; usually shy and elusive.

Similar species: Scaly Thrush (435): no black face; scaly pattern; actions more deliberate.

Voice: Contact-call: fugitive, very high-pitched thin drawn-out 'seep'. Territorial song of male, uttered from bare stick or branch, described as 10–12 even, rather soft but far-carrying fluty notes, somewhat like one call of White-throated Treecreeper (572) heard distantly; in alarm, a low, harsh chatter.

Habitat: Floor of drier forests, woodlands and scrubs from sea-level to snowline. Favours areas with litter, fallen branches, rocks, tussocks small shrubs; often seems to be found on the sunny side of a dry ridge.

Breeding: Nest: loose cup of bark, grass, leaves and rootlets; in depression on ground, often sheltered by overhanging rock, leaning tree, stump, tussock or fern; dead leaves may be built up round nest. Eggs: 2–3; dull-white to cream-coloured, heavily marked dark-brown and purplish grey.

Range and Status: Coastal and highland areas of e. and se. Aust. from s. of Rockhampton, Q, to se. SA; isolate population Mt. Lofty Ras., SA; also Tas. Local, generally sparse. Sedentary.

496 CHESTNUT QUAIL-THRUSH *Cinclosoma castanotum* **Pl.61**

Other names: Chestnut-backed Quail-thrush, Chestnut Groundbird, Copperback.

Field marks: 230–255 mm. A large, dark inland quail-thrush: *olive-brown above, lower back and rump crossed by band of chestnut*. Male: *eyebrow white, throat and breast glossy* *black with white streak or patch on side of throat.* Female and imm: no black on face or breast; *eyebrow and mark on throat yellow-buff*, rest of throat and breast grey, cut off sharply by whitish lower breast; flanks olive-buff. Inland forms brighter chestnut above. Pairs or family parties; wary, usually keeps well ahead of observer. Unless startled, walks and runs rather than flies.

Similar species: Cinnamon Quail-thrush (497), males, all races: smaller, black breast divided by white or chestnut band. Nullarbor Quail-thrush (498), male: much smaller; similar breast-markings to male Chestnut, but upperparts rich-cinnamon. Cinnamon and Nullarbor Quail-thrush, females: smaller and paler than female Chestnut; upperparts more uniformly cinnamon or chestnut.

Voice: Repeated high-pitched 'seep', usually at dawn; song described as soft-toned, but far-carrying, tremulous and somewhat ventriloquial, usually uttered at dawn from song-perch to 6 m high.

Habitat: Prefers dense mallee in sandy areas, but has the widest habitat-range of all inland quail-thrushes: mallee, mulga and native pine scrubs, especially those with shrub layer; also lighter mallee-spinifex associations; desert woodlands, saltbush, stunted desert-heaths and dunes, tea-tree thickets near coast in drier areas.

Breeding: Nest: neat deep cup; of strips of bark, fine grass or sticks; in depression near mallee-trunk, against fallen branch, under low bush or in sparse tuft of grass. Eggs: usually 2, occasionally 3; roundish, white, spotted and blotched with different shades of brown.

Range and Status: S. Aust., mostly inland: sw. NSW, to about 100 km n. of Ivanhoe, irregularly e. to about Grenfell; mallee areas of nw. Vic.; much of SA *except* se. and ne. corners; extends from nw. SA into NT to n. of Tropic and across s. WA n. to about Shark Bay, but absent sw. corner. Common in suitable habitat, specially mallee; sparse patchy and uncommon in open habitats. Sedentary or nomadic.

---

497 CINNAMON QUAIL-THRUSH *Cinclosoma cinnamomeum* **Pl.61**

Other names: Chestnut-breasted, Cinnamon or Western Groundbird, Ground-thrush or Quail-thrush.

Field marks: 175–240 mm. As now recognized, a species of a great range of shade, reflecting the colour of its various arid, exposed habitats. Nominate race is the palest quail-thrush. Male: *upperparts pale-buff to pale cinnamon-rufous*; shoulder black, spotted white. Bold head and breast-pattern: *white eyebrow; black face and throat*, large white or buff mark on side of throat; *breast white to buff or cinnamon, with bold black band, often connecting with black throat*. Female: much plainer; like male above, with creamy-white eyebrow and patch on side of throat; throat and upperbreast buff-grey, cut off from white underparts. Imm: like female, young males may have shadowy breastband. Race *castaneothorax*, 'Chestnut-breasted Quail-thrush': patterned similarly, but larger and darker above, much richer below; crown and mantle olive-brown, *rest of upperparts deep rust-red.* Male: facial-pattern similar, but upperbreast rich rust-red. Female: eyebrow orange-buff; throat creamy, broad rufous-grey band across upperbreast; flanks dull cinnamon-brown to bright pale-rufous; underparts white. The two races reported to intergrade near McNeil Ra. in w. Q. Race *marginatum*, 'Western Quail-thrush': like nominate, but larger, brighter and more boldly-marked. Male: crown and nape olive-brown, *back and wings chestnut-cinnamon, richer on rump; upperbreast pale-chestnut.* Female: like female Chestnut-breasted, broad grey-buff breast-band; flanks rufous, belly whitish. Pairs and family parties; shy; runs swiftly, flies in rocketting bursts, or alighting, runs and dodges; uses low bushes for concealment, shade or as lookouts or song-perches. When not disturbed, walks deliberately and rather slowly; flicks tail.

Similar species: Chestnut (496) and Nullarbor (498) Quail-thrushes.

Voice: A very high-pitched long thin insect-like 'see see see', almost beyond hearing, interspersed with 'see whit, see whit', uttered from ground or top of low bush, dead stick or branch; alarm-call, deliberate ringing 'si si si'. Singing males appear to answer one another.

Habitat: Nominate race: sandy desert and open gibber with sparse low saltbush, blue-bush, shrub-grown gullies in same; stony tablelands. Race *castaneothorax*: mulga and mulga-box associations; stony ridges and grassy scrub-patches. Race *marginatum*: mulga, gidgee and other inland scrubs, often on stony ground.

Breeding: Nest: shallow cup; of leaves and bark; in slight depression, with thin apron of leaves and bark; usually near a low shrub. Eggs: 2–3; buffy-white, thickly spotted blackish brown and blue-grey.

Range and Status: The species occurs across arid inland Aust., from w. Q and nw. NSW to ce. WA. Nominate race: se. NT n. to about Alice Springs; sw. Q s. of Boulia and w. of Beal and Grey Ras.; NSW nw. of White Cliffs; SA, n. of Flinders Ras. and Port Augusta, extending sw. into n. Eyre Pen. Common. Race *castaneothorax*: s. central Q, s. of Blackall and w. to Windorah, McGregor and Grey Ras.; and n. c. NSW s. to about Cobar–Bourke. Uncommon. Race *marginatum*: far-sw. NT and se. WA w. to coastal areas near Shark Bay. Comes into contact with Chestnut Quail-thrush in s. and se. part of range; hybrids are reported. Common. Sedentary or nomadic.

498 NULLARBOR QUAIL-THRUSH *Cinclosoma alisteri* **Pl.61**

Other name: Black-breasted Groundbird.

Field marks: 175–190 mm. Male: *wholly rich-cinnamon above*, shoulders black, spotted white; *face and underparts like male Chestnut* (496). Female: upperparts olive-brown tinged cinnamon, less bright than male, eyebrow and large patch on sides of throat cream-white; throat and upperbreast uniform buff-grey, cut off sharply from whitish lower breast; flanks cinnamon-buff. Imm: like female, less well-marked. Pairs or family parties; very shy; habits like other quail-thrushes.

Similar species: Cinnamon Quail-thrush (497): similar above, but male has a white or buff-white band across black breast. A well-marked female Cinnamon is nearly identical to female Nullarbor, but usually without clear-cut buff-grey zone across breast, and less distinct cream-white throat-patch.

Voice: Probably like Chestnut Quail-thrush.

Habitat: Low vegetation of Nullarbor Plain: saltbush, samphire and other sparse low shrub-cover.

Breeding: Nest: neat cup; of dry grass in a depression, under a dead bush. Eggs: 2–3; creamish, lightly marked with grey and brown.

Range and Status: Confined to Nullarbor Plain about from Ooldea, SA, to Naretha, WA. Uncommon.

Babblers Family *Timaliidae*

Australian babblers are rather sturdy birds with brown, chestnut, grey and black plumage with some prominent white markings. The bill is longish, pointed and arched; wings short and rounded; the longish white-tipped tail is often carried cocked and partly spread. As their fund of common names suggests, they are gregarious, noisy and energetic. They live in groups of three to about a dozen, feeding, preening, dust-bathing and roosting together. They cooperate to build a number of large domed stick-nests of which usually only one is used for nesting, others for roosting. Probably more than one female contributes to the clutch. Certainly more than a single pair cooperate in the rearing of young. Babblers feed a good deal on the ground, moving briskly in boucing hops; they also search crevices in bark on trunks and limbs, anchored by their strong feet. They fly in follow-my-leader style from cover to cover, rapid wingbeats interspersed with short glides on level wings. They are very demonstrative and the sudden appearance of an observer nearby sends them into furious scolding activity. Groups sometimes take up residence in the vicinity of home-steads.

Food: Small crustaceans, insects, small amphibia and reptiles, fruits, seeds.
Range: Parts of Europe, Africa, Asia and the Australasian region.
Number of species: World about 250; Aust. 4.

499 GREY-CROWNED BABBLER *Pomatostomus temporalis*   Pl.61

Other names: Apostlebird, Barker, Cackler, Catbird, Chatterer, Codlin Moth Eater, Dogbird, Happy Family, Happy Jack, Hopper, Jumper, Parsonbird, Pine-bird, Quackie, Red-breasted Babbler, Yahoo.
Field marks: 290 mm. The largest babbler: *note the very large white eyebrows, bordering narrow pale-grey crown; eye pale-yellow*; upper parts dark-brown to brown-black; tail black, longish and full, prominently tipped white. White throat shades into grey breast, underparts rufous to dark-brown. (Note that populations w. of about Normanton–Winton, Q, have *pale-rufous* breast rather than grey; formerly treated as a separate species, 'Red-breasted Babbler.') Habits like other babblers, but tends to feed higher, in larger trees, than White-browed Babbler (500). In flight, the species has a chestnut wing-patch that separates it from other babblers.
Similar species: White-browed Babbler (500): smaller, duller brown; crown brown, white brows narrower; calls differ.
Voice: Typical call clear 'yahoo' or brisk 'gowahee, gowahee, gowahee', rather like braying of distant donkey; also a strident 'peeoo peeoo peeoo', heard afar, or falsetto 'put-yair, put-yair, put-yair', incessant fussy chatterings.
Habitat: Open forest, scrubby woodlands and scrublands.
Breeding: Nest: large, domed with spout-like entrance, lined with grass, bark-fibres, rootlets, feathers or wool; 3–6 m high in shrub or sapling. Many may be built; some serve as communal roosts. Eggs: 2–6; buff, light-brown, dark purple-brown or dark-grey, marked with hairlike scribbles of dark-brown or black.
Range and Status: Scattered in suitable habitat in mainland e., n. and w. Aust.: the e. population occurs in far-se. SA; through Vic., *except* for nw. mallee areas or Gippsland; NSW, *except* far-w. or the coastal se; Q., *except* w. of about Eulo–Blackall–Winton–Normanton. The so-called 'red-breasted' population occurs in nw. Q w. of about Winton–Normanton, s. to about Boulia, through NT *except* the arid sw., extending into n. SA s. to about Oodnadatta; in WA, through Kimberleys and Pilbara, coastally s. to Wooramel R., extending s. inland to upper Murchison R.–Wiluna. The species is still common in lightly settled parts of range but has disappeared from, or is becoming rare, in settled districts, apparently being unable to adapt to disturbance of habitat. Sedentary. Also s. NG

500 WHITE-BROWED BABBLER *Pomatostomus superciliosus*   Pl.61

Other names: Apostlebird, Catbird, Go-aways, Happy Family, Stickbirds, Cackler, Twelve Apostles, Jumper.
Field marks: 180–220 mm. The dullest-brown babbler, *white of throat shades into brown lower-breast*. Note that white eyebrow is relatively *smaller* than in Grey-crowned Babbler (499); *crown dark-brown, eye dark*.
Similar species: Hall's Babbler (501): much darker; white throat sharply cut off on mid-breast. Grey-crowned Babbler (499): larger white brow, grey crown, pale eye; in flight, note rufous patch on wing, blacker tail. Chestnut-crowned Babbler (502): chestnut crown, white wingbars.
Voice: Extraordinary variety of falsetto chattering miaowing notes; usual call, whistled rising 'sweet-sweet-sweet-miaow', last note drawn-out and descending, somewhat like automobile starter-motor failing to engage; alarm-call, brisk 'wit-wit' or a rapid tearing

'chiew-chiew'; when disturbed, parties throw up a high-pitched frenzied chattering caco-phony.

Habitat: Scrubby woodlands; mulga, mallee, native pine scrubs; timber and scrub along watercourses.

Breeding: Nest and eggs like Grey-crowned Babbler, but smaller.

Range and Status: S. Aust.: throughout s. WA (patchy in sw. corner) n. to about North West Cape; s. NT to 50 km n. of Alice Springs, thence e. into far-w. Q to about the Georgina and lower Diamantina Rs.; also patchily in s. Q from about St. George to Warwick, n. to about Chinchilla; widespread NSW mostly w. of the Divide but e. to near Muswellbrook, Hunter R.; occasional ACT; in Vic. generally patchy s. of the Divide, absent Gippsland, widespread n. of Divide; throughout SA *except* for arid far ne. Generally common; sedentary.

501 HALL'S BABBLER *Pomatostomus halli*   Pl.61

Other names: White-breasted or White-throated Babbler.

Field marks: 230 mm. Like a sooty-brown or sooty-black White-browed Babbler, (500) *but with only a small white bib; rest of underparts dark-brown*; eye red-brown. Habits like other babblers.

Voice: Calls more like Grey-crowned (499) than White-browed (500) Babbler: lacks the 'yahoo' of (499) and the madder staccato bursts of (500); the main calls seem to be squeaky chatterings and a frequent liquid note.

Habitat: Light mulga and other acacia scrubs to open eucalypt woodlands and nearly treeless spinifex associations.

Breeding: Nest smaller and neater than Grey-crowned Babbler; eggs not recorded.

Range and Status: A recently-described species, first collected May 1963 5 km e. Langlo Crossing near Charleville, Q. Large range in w. Q and far-nw. NSW, some outer limits being: s. to Barrier Ra. and Mootwingee, NSW; n. to the Finucane Ra., n. of the Winton–Boulia road in w. Q; between these, w. at least to the Beal Ra., w. of Windorah, and the McGregor and Grey Ras. in far-sw. Q. The approximate e. limits are 58 km w. of Long-reach and Langlo Crossing to near Cunnamulla. Common in suitable habitat. Probably sedentary.

502 CHESTNUT-CROWNED BABBLER *Pomatostomus ruficeps*   Pl.61

Other names: Chatterer, Red-capped Babbler.

Field marks: 215 mm. Somewhat like White-browed Babbler (500) but more interestingly marked. Note *rich-chestnut crown bordered by white eyebrows and double white wingbar*; white of throat and breast narrower than White-browed, *bordered by dark sides of breast like half-open waistcoat*; eye dark. In flight, white wingbars not easily seen, but present. Habits like other babblers specially White-browed but often seems shyer; reported to form playgrounds by chasing round and round under low shrub, cutting noticeable track.

Similar species: White-browed Babbler (500).

Voice: Usual flock-call, 'we-chee chee chee'; a strident but melodious territorial song from top of tall mulga or similar vantage-point, in phrasing like Song Thrush (437), but in quality more like piping of Little Eagle (148). When approached, flocks chatter fussily, uttering loud 'chack-a-chack'.

Habitat: Inland scrubs generally: mallee, mulga, belar, lignum, saltbush; appears to favour drier habitats than White-browed.

Breeding: Nest: larger and often higher than White-browed Babbler. Eggs: 3–5; like White-browed.

Range and Status: Se. inland Aust.: e. SA, w. to about Swan Reach–Quorn–Leigh Creek–Innamincka; sw. Q n. to Nappamerrie–Windorah–Mitchell–Dirranbandi; w. NSW, e. to Lightning Ridge–Nyngan–Balranald; far-nw. Vic. Scarce to locally common; sedentary.

Old World Warblers   Family *Sylviidae*

A large widespread family of songbirds. The few Australian forms are medium to small birds with streaked or unstreaked brownish plumage and rather pointed tails. They live usually in grassy or swampy habitats and several have rich voices characteristic of family. Spinifexbird (507), the sole member of the genus *Eremiornis*, occupies an unusually arid habitat; its unstreaked plumage, longish tail and voice simplify identification. The two grassbirds *Megalurus* (505–6), have in general a more coastal distribution, in heavy grass or swamp and saltmarsh vegetation. They are best identified by heavily streaked upperparts, calls and habitat. The two songlarks *Cinclorhamphus* (510–511) are not larks at all, but were so-called because of their conspicuous but not specially lark-like song-flights when breeding. The widespread reed warblers are represented by the Clamorous Reed Warbler (503), also of NG to se. Asia and Eurasia, it is readily identified by its outstanding song, plain appearance and habitat. A similar species, the Great Reed Warbler (504), has been collected in NT. The two cisticolas belong to a complex assemblage that ranges over much of Africa, s. Europe and Asia; Golden-headed Cisticola (509) is widespread and well-known in n. and e. Aust., but it was not until 1950s that Zitting Cisticola (508), a form widespread in se. Asia, was found in coastal n. and ne. Aust. Cisticolas construct singular domed nests, using spiders' web to stitch living leaves into the fabric in a way somewhat like the tailorbirds of Asia; they are sometimes incorrectly called 'tailorbirds' for that reason.

Food: Mostly insects and other small invertebrates; also seeds and other vegetable matter.

Range: Widespread in Europe, Africa and Asia, extending to Aust. and Tas.

Number of species: World 339; Aust. 9, including 1 rare vagrant.

---

503 CLAMOROUS REED WARBLER   *Acrocephalus stentoreus*   Pl.67

Other names: Australian Reed Warbler, Nightingale, Reedbird, Reedlark, Swamp Tit, Water Sparrow.

Field marks: 150–165 mm. The outstanding singer of the summer reedbeds: *plain unstreaked olive-brown above, with faint fawnish eyebrow*; fawn-white below. Clings sideways to reed-stems or feeds on floating vegetation. When singing, puffs throat, raises crown-feathers, inside of mouth yellow. In flight over water from one reed-patch to another, *note tawny rump*.

Similar species: Great Reed Warbler (504). Tawny (505) and Little (506) Grassbirds: heavily streaked above. Song of Brown Honeyeater (625) can be confused, but check range and habitat.

Voice: Rich variable liquid phrases, some metallic and guttural, others sweet, repeated in chant: 'chutch chutch chutch, dzee-dzee-dzee, quarty-quarty-quarty'. Alarm-call, sharp 't!'; also dry scolding rattle.

Habitat: Stands of reeds, cumbungi, river red gum regrowth; weeping willows, bamboos, even tall cereal crops over or beside lakes, swamps or rivers, lantana thickets: often in public gardens.

Breeding: Nest: very deep cup; of strips of reed-sheaths and other aquatic growth woven round several vertical stems. Eggs: 3–4; variable; blue-white to buff-brown, spotted and blotched blue-grey, olive-brown or blackish brown.

Range and Status: Formerly known as Australian Reed Warbler, *A. australis*, but now considered conspecific with the wide-ranging Eurasian species *stentoreus*. Widespread in Aust. and Tas.; breeding migrant to s. Aust., arriving Aug.–Oct. departing Mar.–Apr. Often winters in warmer districts of s. Aust., when silent and easily overlooked. Common. Also NG to se. and s. Asia, w. to ne. Africa.

504 GREAT REED WARBLER *Acrocephalus arundinaceus*
Field marks: 190 mm. Probably indistinguishable in field from Clamorous Reed Warbler (503) but inside of mouth *salmon*. In hand, outer (9th) primary *longer* than 6th; in Clamorous, 9th primary much shorter than 6th. (Field Guide to the Birds of South-East Asia, King et al, Collins 1975).
Range and Status: Africa, Eurasia, s. Asia migrant in n. winter to se. Asia, Philippines, Celebes and Greater and Lesser Sunda Is., including Timor. Specimen Melville I., NT, (1912). Vagrant.

505 TAWNY GRASSBIRD *Megalurus timoriensis*   **Pl.67**
Other name: Tawny Marshbird.
Field marks: 190 mm. *Larger and tawnier* than Little Grassbird (506); crown plainer and tawnier; underparts fawn, unstreaked; tail *fuller and more wedge-shaped*. Singly or pairs in loose colonies, shy, flies more above cover than Little. Breeding male has conspicuous song-flight. Has habit of climbing high stem to watch observer, uttering short sharp alarm-call. Drops to cover when approached.
Voice: Breeding male frequently flies above cover in fluttering, somewhat tail-down, manner, uttering sweet song somewhat like Rufous Songlark (510), with overtones of reeling song of Superb Blue Wren (513): alarm-call, sharp 'jk' or 'jk-jk' like stones struck together, uttered throughout year.
Habitat: Wet coastal heaths, rank grasses, 'canegrass', cumbungi swamps; also sugar-cane, corn, other crops.
Breeding: Nest: deep-cup; of fine grasses, lined with rootlets; in rank grass or thick low vegetation. Eggs: 3; pink-white, freckled purplish brown and grey.
Range and Status: From Kimberleys, WA, across top end NT to C. York Pen. and e. Aust. generally e. of Divide, (but w. to Gilgandra, NSW), to s. of Sydney. Locally common, generally uncommon. Possibly migratory in s. Also NG to Philippines.

506 LITTLE GRASSBIRD *Megalurus gramineus*   **Pl.67**
Other names: Little Marshbird; Striated Grassbird or Reedbird; Marsh Warbler.
Field marks: 140 mm. A common widespread skulking little bird, heard more than seen. Note *tawny crown, slight buff eyebrow*, rest of upperparts grey brown, *heavily streaked darker*; breast unstreaked except for zone of fine markings on throat; *longish pointed tail* is often *carried slightly cocked*. Keeps much to cover, sneaks to tops of bushes to view intruder or to call, dropping out of sight if approached: *runs* over mud or floating swamp growth. When flying to cover, reveals plain tawny-olive rump *and tail without bars or white tips*.
Similar species: Fieldwren (545): more obvious pale eye-brow and more streaked below. Cocks tail more; in flight, shows dark tail-band and pale tips. Tawny Grassbird (505): larger, more tawny crown and rump; calls differ.
Voice: Mournful whistle of three notes on one level, 'p-peee-peee'; the first note very short, the rest drawn-out, sometimes through the night; also a dry scolding rattle.
Habitat: Low dense swamp and marsh-vegetation, including mangroves and samphire on tidal marshes; cumbungi, reeds, rushes, cane-grass, lignum and other inland swamp-cover, vegetation along inland bore-drains.
Breeding: Nest: very deep, somewhat untidy, cup of grasses and stems, narrower at neck and sometimes part-domed, deeply lined with feathers; in sturdy grass or reed stems or dense low shrub. Eggs: 3–5; whitish to pink-white, speckled greyish to red-purple, zoned round large end.
Range and Status: S. and e. Aust. (n. to Atherton Tableland, Q), Tas. and Bass Strait islands. Extends very patchily through inland in suitable vegetation on isolated swamps and bore drains n. to about Mt. Isa, Q,–Barkly Tableland, NT. Locally very common in coastal and subcoastal areas; sedentary. Also w. NG.

507 SPINIFEXBIRD *Eremiornis carteri* Pl.67

Other name: Desertbird.

Field marks: 140–165 mm. Distinguished as much by its preference for spinifex as by appearance. *Unstreaked brown above, buff-white below*; crown a little more rufous, *eyebrow buff*; bill longish, dark-brown tail equals length of body and usually carried cocked. Climbs to peer at intruder from top of spinifex-clump, into which it scrambles to hide; dashes on ground between clumps with tail cocked, or flies with tail pumping up and down.

Similar species: Grasswrens (522–9): heavily streaked above, some with throat-markings, calls differ. Fieldwren (545), rusty forms: different habitat; tails have dark bands and pale tips.

Voice: Loud repeated 'cheerywheat' somewhat like Stubble Quail (160); also 'cheerit' repeated perhaps every three seconds for half a minute, then 'cheeroo', descending, similarly repeated; sharp alarm-call like pebbles struck together, as Tawny Grassbird (505).

Habitat: Tall spinifex and other dense grasses, not necessarily in thick or unbroken tracts, but often along creekbeds or on rocky ground.

Breeding: Nest: cup of fine grasses lined with rootlets, usually in spinifex. Eggs: 2; pink-white, finely freckled pale-lilac, purplish and red-brown.

Range and Status: Areas of suitable habitat in arid inland and central-w. Aust., and on Barrow, Hermite and Thevenard Is. in the Dampier and Montebello Groups, WA. The mainland distribution is said (Parker, *Emu* Vol. 74) to be in 'four separate hilly or broken areas, mostly above 300 m elevation . . .' (1) Central w. WA, from Pilbara s. to Minilya R. and e. to Rudall R. (2) Fitzroy R. drainage e. to Victoria R. drainage (Kimberleys, WA, to w. NT). (3) Southern highlands of the NT, n. to Banka Banka district. (4) Highlands of Mt. Isa–Opalton area, Q. The situation in intervening areas little known. Locally common, generally uncommon. Sedentary.

508 ZITTING CISTICOLA *Cisticola juncidis* Pl.67

Other names: Streaked Cisticola or Fantail-warbler.

Field marks: 100 mm. Like non-breeding Golden-headed Cisticola (509) and difficult to separate in field. *Somewhat more streaked above, on nape as well as crown*; rump more rufous; whiter below, without such golden-buff tones; note more prominent whitish tailtips.

Voice: Distinctive call is described as just like that of Red-backed Wren (519).

Habitat: Reported to prefer more saline situations than Golden-headed. Rank grasses and similar vegetation on coastal flats.

Breeding: Nest oval, domed; of grasses drawn together with spiders' web, plant-down, at times with leaves stitched into structure. Eggs like Golden-headed but less glossy.

Range and Status: Certainly known in Darwin area, NT; also reported Gulf coastal area of Burketown–Normanton, n. of Morehead R., e. C. York Pen., coastal areas between Townsville–Proserpine, and lower Fitzroy R. area, Q. Local and elusive. Also Indonesia to Japan and s. Asia, s. Europe and n. Africa.

509 GOLDEN-HEADED CISTICOLA *Cisticola exilis* Pl.67

Other names: Barleybird, Cornbird, Golden-capped Grass-warbler, Golden-headed Fantailed Warbler, Grassbird, Grass-warbler, Tailorbird.

Field marks: 90–115 mm. Diminutive spirited dweller of tall ground-cover in moist situations. Note two distinct seasonal plumages. Breeding male: *head plain golden-buff*; back buff, heavily streaked black; *tail short, blackish tipped buff*. Female and non-breeding male: *crown streaked blackish, unstreaked buff nape; tail noticeably longer;* whitish below, washed golden-buff at sides, rump golden-buff. Imm: underparts washed yellowish. Breeding males call incessantly from grass-tops, fences, telephone wires; flutter up in bouncing song-flights or make longer jerky flights over territory before dropping to cover. **Similar species:** Zitting Cisticola (508): difficult to separate from non-breeding Golden-headed; but note streaked nape, less golden-buff tones, more rufous rump, generally whiter underparts and tailtips. Habitat and call differ. Little Grassbird (506): no golden-buff tones.

Voice: Perched and in flight, breeding males utter incessant far-carrying insect-like 'bhzzt' followed by loud liquid 'lek' or 'pillek', call varying locally; high-pitched chatter-ings and scolds.

Habitat: Tall grasses, rushes and other rank herbage round swamps, drainage and in wet or neglected paddocks; roadsides, overgrown margins of irrigated pastures; crops, black-berries, samphire on margins of saltmarshes.

Breeding: Nest: small, domed; of fine grass, plant-down, often with several broad living green leaves stitched into fabric with spiders web or plant-fibre. Eggs: 3–4; blue, spotted, dotted, blotched red-brown.

Range and Status: Nw., n., e. and se. Aust. and coastal islands, including Gt. Barrier Reef islands: from Fortescue R., WA, to mouth of Murray R., SA; also King I., Bass Strait, where common. Possibly n. Tas., where early probable nesting record (s. Spring-field). Patchy, mostly coastal; inland in n. Aust. to Barkly Tableland, NT; area of Long-reach, Q, and in se. Aust., along Murray R. Common; sedentary or part-migratory. Also irregularly from Bismarck Archipelago and NG to Moluccas, Celebes, Lesser Sunda Is., Philippines, to se. Asia, s. China, India.

---

510 RUFOUS SONGLARK *Cinclorhamphus mathewsi* Pl.67

Other names: Rufous Singing Lark, Skylark.

Field marks: ♂ 190, ♀ 165 m. Slender and somewhat pipit-like; the best field mark is *the tawny rump*, best seen in flight. Note also the pale-fawn eyebrow and *netted pattern formed by pale margins to wing-feathers*; greyish fawn below with slight necklet of spots or streaks across lower throat. Female smaller. Singly or in loose companies, males polyga-mous. The singing and territorial behaviour of breeding males makes them conspicuous, but otherwise rather shy and easily missed; perches on stumps, fence-posts or moves shiftily through grass and foliage of shrubs and trees.

Similar species: Brown Songlark (511), female. Richard's Pipit (423): white edges to tail, which it carries horizontally but raises and lowers. White-winged Triller (432), female: no rufous rump.

Voice: Males very vocal when breeding; song has sweet, splintering, almost ventriloquial quality; often begins with clear loud trill, then develops into full refrain, 'a-witchy-weedle', repeated; uttered from conspicuous high perches in territory e.g. large dead or live tree, telephone wire or pole, and in flight between such points or while descending to ground; also a scolding rattle; alarm-call, a sharp 'tik'.

Habitat: Open grassy woodlands or scrublands.

Breeding: Nest: deep cup; of grasses in depression or in shelter of tussock. Eggs: 3–4; white, speckled reddish all over, mostly at large end.

Range and Status: Most of mainland Aust. *except* C. York Pen.; patchy and occasional near-coastal districts e. of Divide and extreme sw. corner WA. Migratory, moving s. in spring to breed, n. in autumn. Uncommon to locally and/or seasonally common.

---

511 BROWN SONGLARK *Cinclorhamphus cruralis* Pl.67

Other names: Australian Skylark, Black-breasted Songlark, Brown Singing Lark, Corn-crake, Harvestbird.

Field marks: ♂ 255, ♀ 190 mm. Male is the only Australian bird with fawn crown con-trasted with *sooty-brown face and breast*; upperparts patterned by pale feather-margins; legs long, flesh-coloured; an *upright, lanky bird*; *typically carries the longish tail cocked*; the tail-feathers are pointed. Female: much smaller and paler, *washed ochre above*, feathers of upperparts have brown centres with paler margins, giving strong pattern; dull white below with brown markings. Imm: like female; subadult (? and moulting) males may be plain fawnish, blackish round eyes, or patchy dark-brown on centre of breast and belly. Singly or in loose companies; runs through grass; sits upright on stumps, fences, telephone poles and wires over grassland, tail cocked. Songflight conspicuous: takes off singing, rising on sloping line in fluttering flight broken by glides with *wings upswept, undercarriage lowered*; descends in this attitude, drops steeply to ground. Song and display conspicuous in spring and summer; usually silent for rest of year in s. and e. Aust.

Similar species: Common Starling (687) imm: more uniform mouse-brown, throat paler; legs and tail shorter, latter not cocked. Rufous Songlark (510): like female Brown, but generally less buff or ochre on sides of face and breast; feathers of upperparts less strongly marked; rump rufous. Richard's Pipit (423): pale eyebrow, white edges to tail, which it raises and lowers but carries horizontally.

Voice: Song of male strange, metallic, guttural and far-carrying; hence school childrens' name 'skit-scot-a-wheeler'.

Habitat: In settled districts, chiefly pastures and croplands; in inland, open country of most kinds: grasslands, open scrubs and sparse low shrub-vegetation, e.g. saltbush or bluebush.

Breeding: Nest: deep cup; of grasses, in shelter of tussock or tuft of grass. Eggs: 3–4; salmon-pink, speckled pinkish red mostly on large end.

Range and Status: Throughout Aust. but sparse n. Kimberleys, WA, n. half of NT, C. York Pen.; patchy and occasional in some e. coastal areas, and sw. corner WA; occurs Kangaroo I., SA. Nomadic or migratory in s., arriving to breed from June onwards, departing by March. Locally and irregularly common.

Australian Warblers   Family *Maluridae*

An assemblage of mostly small insectivorous birds confined to the Australasian region. A puzzling aspect to the beginner is the use of the name 'wren', in various combinations, specially because it is also used for some members of the next family. The name was probably first used by early settlers for almost any small brown bird but particularly those that cocked their tails in the manner of the Common Wren of Britain and Europe. The most obvious candidates for the name in the areas of first settlement were the fairy wrens *Malurus* particularly in their brown plumage phases. The matter became and remains complicated when other small Australian birds were also described as 'wrens', with a prefix denoting the supposedly favoured habitat. Different groups within the family have their own introductions below.

Food: Mostly insects, larvae and other invertebrates; spiders, earthworms, small crustaceans, seeds and other vegetable matter.

Range: Mostly Aust. and Tas., but also NZ, New Caledonia, NG; with one fairy warbler in Borneo.

Number of species: World 26; Aust. 21.

FAIRY WRENS   Genus *Malurus*

Familiar small Australasian wrens with long cocked tails. Males are extremely colourful during breeding season (mostly spring and summer) but in autumn and winter moult into an eclipse plumage that in most species resembles brownish female plumage. But the bill remains black, and this, together with the absence of the rich brownish plumage round the eyes (as in females) and the retention of a blue tail and sometimes blue flight-feathers, distinguishes them. Immatures also resemble females but young males usually acquire a coloured tail during their first winter. The presence of many 'brown birds' in wren-parties led to the belief that males are polygamous; but family parties of the Superb Blue Wren (513) stay together through winter and young females mostly disperse as spring approaches. Young males are less dispersive and one or more frequently remain with the territorial pair and assist in the feeding of the first brood of the new season. These supernumerary males do not assume breeding plumage until several months after the dominant male. Female wrens typically build and lay again within a week of the first brood leaving the nest and the supernumerary male(s) then frequently rear the first family, leaving the pair to attend to the second brood. By six weeks of age, the young of the first brood join in the feeding of the second brood. By these auxiliary means, up to three successful broods may be produced in a season. Other fairy wrens probably have a similar social structure; in several species more than one male has been seen to feed young. There are three distinctive species: Lilac-crowned (512), Blue-and-White (518) and Red-backed Wrens. They present few identification problems. The rest are conveniently divided into two groups, the blue wrens, and the red-shouldered wrens, that also have blue in their plumage. The blue wren group consists of two species (513–4), one having several races which replace each other successively across s. Aust., in a way that simplifies recognition, males differing in colour of underparts, shade of blue of head and breast, and presence or absence of a black band over rump. Identification in the red-shouldered group (515–7) is in general based on the colour of crown, back and breast of males. One species, Variegated Wren (515), covers much of the continent, but is replaced by very similar, closely-related species on Eyre Pen., SA and in sw. WA. It has two very distinctive races, formerly regarded as good species, in nw. and ne. Aust.; their females are soft blue-grey above, simplifying identification.

512 LILAC-CROWNED WREN *Malurus coronatus*   Pl.68

Other name: Purple-crowned Wren.

Field marks: 140–150 mm. Unlike any other Australian bird. Male, nominate race: brownish above, whitish below, *crown deep-lilac with black centre*; *face black, extending round nape in broad black band*; tail rich-blue. Male eclipse: head brown, with black eyepatch. Female: brown above, whitish below, *pale from bill to eye, distinctive chestnut face and ear-coverts, blue tail*. Race *macgillivrayi*, male: darker above, with broader black band round nape. Female: differs from nominate race in *crown and nape dark blue-grey*, face chestnut, ear-coverts black. Imm: like female. Usually in small parties, often high in pandanus and paperbarks.

Voice: Typical fairy wren reeling, with elements of scrubwren about it; also described as shrill, high-pitched, 'cheepa-cheepa-cheepa'; contact-call like short 'drrt' or 'jk' note of Fairy Martin (422); also described as a chirrup.

Habitat: Usually near water: dense pandanus and paperbark thickets and groves; tall cane-grass; occasionally mangroves.

Breeding: Nest: domed and bulky, side-entrance having a platform; of strips of paperbark and blades of canegrass, in canegrass or other low cover. Eggs: 3; pink-white, marked all over, mostly at large end, with ill-defined spots and splashes of deep brownish pink.

Range and Status: Apparently broken distribution in two races. Nominate race: on rivers e. from Fitzroy R. (Kimberleys, WA) to lower Victoria R., NT. Race *macgillivrayi*: from Macarthur R. in e. NT e. to the Gregory R. and (?) Leichhardt R. in nw. Q, s. to Mallapunyah NT, Riversleigh (? and Kamilaroi) in Q. Very local; common in parts. Sedentary.

513 SUPERB BLUE WREN *Malurus cyaneus*   Pl.68

Other names: Blue Bonnet, Bluecap, Blue Wren; Cock-tail, Jenny Wren, Mormon Wren; Superb Warbler.

Field marks: 140 m. The well-loved blue wren of southeastern Australia. Male: no red shoulders; note the glossy *blue-black throat and chest*; *grey-white underparts*; tail dark-blue. Male eclipse: brown like female, but bill black, no red-brown feathers round eye;

tail deep-blue; often seen in patchy intermediate stages. Female: plain mouse-brown, *throat whitish,* underparts fawn-white; *bill red-brown, pale red-brown feathers from bill to round eye,* tail brown, washed greenish blue. Imm: at first like female, with plain-brown tail; young males usually acquire blue tail before first winter. Pairs, family parties, in which brown birds usually predominate; they move briskly through thickets and undergrowth and bounce over ground to snap up insects; pausing to sing briskly from tops of shrubs, thickets, or fences. When breeding, males and females persistently battle their own reflections in windows, hub-caps and other reflective objects.

Similar species: All other male blue wrens have either red shoulders or blue underparts.

Voice: Song: accelerating series of notes, breaking into brisk merry trill, loud for size of bird; often only partial song on one note; like tinny alarm clock. Contact-call: brisk splintered 'prip-prip'. Alarm-call: very thin high-pitched 'seee'.

Habitat: Almost wherever dense low cover is found in association with open areas or clearings: coastal heaths, saltmarsh vegetation; riverside thickets, areas of bracken; undergrowth of forests, woodlands where the cover is broken; blackberry thickets, margins of roads and tracks; road-reserves, shelter-belts. In inland parts of range, margins of mallee and bluebush but more typically in riverside vegetation and lignum, reeds, tussocks, canegrass in swamps. Also golf-courses, orchards, parks, gardens.

Breeding: Nest: domed, often with slight porch over entrance; of grass, moss, rootlets and twigs, bound with spiders' web and egg-sacs, usually in dense tussock or foliage near ground. Occasionally up to 5 m in foliage, mostly where ground-cover removed or damaged. Eggs: 3–4; pink-white, spotted red-brown, mostly at large end.

Range and Status: Se. Aust. and Tas., (including Flinders and King Is.), from Kangaroo I. and s. Eyre Pen., SA, almost to Tropic in Q. Approximate inland limits: SA, n. to Tothill Ra. in n. Mt. Lofty Ras. and Swan Reach–Jabuk–Pinnaroo in Murray mallee. A population extends from Overland Corner–Moorook on Murry R. e. to area of Mildura, Vic. Throughout Vic. except drier Mallee and Wimmera districts; occurs along Murray R. and environs except possibly Mildura–Robinvale section. Throughout e. NSW; widespread in s. Riverina, mostly in riverside or swampy areas or about homesteads and urban areas; present (? in parts only) along Murrumbidgee and Lachlan Rs., with (? isolate) occurrence reported Willandra Creek near Mossgiel; Bogan R. is given as w. limit in n. inland NSW. In Q, mostly se. interior, w. to Goondiwindi–Surat–Morven–Springsure, n. to about 24°S, and e. to Eidsvold–Kilcoy–w. Brisbane suburbs and to coast near Southport. Common; sedentary.

514 SPLENDID WREN *Malurus splendens* Pl.68

Other names: Banded Blue Wren, Banded Wren or Superb Warbler; Black-backed Wren; Splendid Fairy-wren; Turquoise Wren.

Field marks: 135 mm. Nominate race: the familiar blue wren of south-western Aust. Male: perhaps the most brilliant Australian bird, glossy violet-blue, forehead and ear-coverts lighter-blue, black band across nape and breast, *but no band across lower back;* tail shorter and broader than other fairy wrens. Male eclipse: brown like female, wing-feathers pale-blue, tail dark-blue; bill black. Female: brownish grey above, whitish below; *tail dull-blue, slightly tipped white; bill and feathers round eye pale-tan.* Imm: like female. Race *callainus,* 'Turquoise Wren', male: *paler, and with black band across lower back;* blue of upperparts paler than underparts; blue of abdomen less violet. Tail longer. Imm: like nominate; young males acquiring adult plumage develop blue wings while having whitish underparts. Race *melanotus,* 'Black-backed Wren': differs from *callainus* in glossy cobalt-blue underparts similar to upperparts *but ear-coverts much paler;* black breastband *narrower.* Both races, male eclipse and female: indistinguishable in field from nominate race (and from each other) except by range. Usually in family parties, 'brown birds' predominating; in WA, reported to feed and sing higher in shrubs and foliage of trees than other fairy wrens.

Similar species: Variegated Wren (515), male: red shoulder, whitish underparts. Female:

prominent dark-chestnut eye-feathering. Superb Blue Wren (513), male: upperbreast blue-black, underparts grey-white. Female: darker than female of race *callainus*; *tail not blue*.

Voice: Somewhat like Superb Blue Wren, but harder, more metallic; in WA, less loud and sharp than red-shouldered wrens.

Habitat: Nominate race: rather wide; undergrowth on margins and in clearings of forests and woodlands; vegetation along watercourses and swamp-margins, including swamp-woodlands; golf-courses, orchards, parks, gardens, but unlike Superb in se. Aust., shuns built-up areas. Inland in areas of larger saltbush, mulga, mallee and other scrubs, sometimes in association with spinifex. Race *callainus*: mallee, dense mulga; thickets of saltbush and bluebush; shrubby, grassy gorges in inland ranges; vegetation along dry watercourses; canegrass swamps. Race *melanotus*: mallee-spinifex associations; dense mulga, brigalow and other acacia-scrubs, belar with understorey of smaller shrubs; watercourse vegetation, including lignum and cumbungi.

Breeding: Nest: domed, somewhat untidy; of dry grasses; usually near ground in thicket, tussock, reeds but at times to 10 m in tree e.g. paperback. Race *callainus*; nest: domed, of grasses bound with spiders' web and plant-down; in mulga-shrub, saltbush, canegrass. Race *melanotus*: like *callainus*; often in a spinifex-clump. Eggs: 2–4; white, finely spotted red-brown, with heavier zone at large end.

Range and Status: The species ranges from inland e. Aust. to s. WA. Nominate race: s. WA, n. to Shark Bay, inland to upper Ashburton R.–w. Gibson Desert–Wiluna–Laverton, and e. coastally to near Eucla. Common, sedentary; often very local. Race *callainus*: s. central Aust.; from Gibson and Gt. Victoria Deserts, inland WA, (where reported to intergrade with nominate race) through sw. SA s. to about Ooldea–n. Eyre Pen.–Port Germein, thence n. mostly w. of Flinders Ras. to Simpson Desert; in s. NT, mostly in deserts circling the ranges, e. to about Finke, n. to about Central Mt. Wedge. Patchy and uncommon; part-nomadic. Race *melanotus*: inland e. Aust.; e. from about Mannum–Annadale, SA, and the e. fringes of Mt. Lofty–s. Flinders Ras.; n. limits in SA poorly documented; range extends to sw. Q w. to Thargomindah–Windorah–upper Diamantina R., n. to near Winton and e. to Tambo–Mitchell; e. in NSW to Mungindi–Bogan R.– c. NSW mallee areas–Cocoparra NP; thence s. through mallee areas of nw. Vic. e. to near Swan Hill, s. to Wyperfeld NP and Murray mallee of SA, s. to about Coonalpyn. Patchy; possibly part-nomadic.

515 VARIEGATED WREN *Malurus lamberti* Pl.69

Other names: Lambert's; Lavender-flanked, Lovely or Purple-backed Wren.

Field marks: 120–140 mm. The most widespread and longest tailed red-shouldered fairy wren: note jet black throat and upperbreast, *deep lilac-blue back* and chestnut to brick-red 'shoulders'; the sky-blue of crown is mostly *darker* than ear-coverts, but in nominate race *lamberti* of coastal NSW crown is nearly as pale as ear-coverts. Male eclipse: like female, but bill black, no chestnut round eye; tail blue. Female: pale-brown above, fawn below, tail washed blue; bill pale-tan, *deep-chestnut mark from bill round eye*. Race *amabilis*, 'Lovely Wren': this, the following race, and less-markedly, a race of Lilac-crowned Wren (512), are the only fairy wrens whose females are mostly *blue-grey* above. As the main ranges are separate in each case, it becomes a useful field mark. Male: *crown and large cheek-patch more uniform blue than nominate race; black rear-collar broader*; more conspicuous whitish tail-tips. Female: *deep grey-blue above and on ear-coverts, whitish from bill round eye*; fawn-white below. Imm: probably like female; but young males with faint chestnut shoulders and indications of respective male and female plumage in fledglings have been noted. Habits like Variegated, but habitat more restricted; feeds to 15 m high in margins of rainforest. Race *dulcis*, 'Lavender-flanked Wren', male: bill longish; black nape-band broader; *deep lilac-blue spot on flank below bend of wing, more prominent white tail-tips*. N.B. Despite the illustrations, it is not certainly known whether males of *amabilis* or *dulcis* have an eclipse phase. Female: *wholly blue-grey above, tail* *bluer*; wings brown; plain fawn-white below. Note that females of this race *have distinctive whitish feathering from bill round eye* while those of the Kimberley race *rogersi* have this area *dark-chestnut*. Pairs and parties; 'brown birds' usually predominate but coloured males are frequently seen together, and sometimes with other species of wrens. Often feeds higher in shrubs and trees than other wrens.

Similar species: In s. WA and on Eyre Pen.: Blue-breasted Wren (516); in s. WA only, Red-winged Wren (517). Females of the 'blue-wren' group lack the distinctive dark-chestnut eye-ring, have shorter tails.

Voice: Like Superb (513) and Splendid (514), but somewhat more high-pitched; lesser range of notes.

Habitat: Nominate race: wide; typical are shrub associations, undergrowth, margins of clearings in forests and woodlands; heaths, sandplain and dune-vegetation; mallee, mulga, saltbush, lignum and spinifex in arid lands; shrubby or rank grassy vegetation along watercourses; coastal blackberry thickets; golf-courses, orchards, parks, gardens. *Amabilis*: rainforest-margins; timber and scrub along watercourses; paperbarks and other swamp-vegetation; dense dune-vegetation; shrubs and rank grass on roadsides; vine and lantana-thickets, mangrove-fringes. *Dulcis* and *rogersi*: shrubs and spinifex in rugged sandstone hills and gorges; rank shrubbery and grass along watercouses; pandanus and paperbarks round freshwater springs and pools.

Breeding: Nest: domed, loosely woven; of soft grasses, strips of bark and plant-down, and occasionally spiders' web and egg-sacs; usually near ground in undergrowth or low shrub, or tall tuft of grass. Eggs: 3–4 (*amabilis*, *dulcis* and *rogersi* 2–3); white, finely speckled with reddish purple, most at large end.

Range and Status: Nominate race: widespread in mainland Aust., but *absent from* Kimberleys, WA; top end NT, n. of Larrimah; C. York Pen. and from n. and e. Q approximately n. and e. of Georgetown–upper Burdekin R.–Maryborough. Also *absent from* extreme se. corner of NSW (s. Tablelands, ACT, and coastal areas s. from Narooma); from ne. and s. Vic., from extreme se. SA and Kangaroo I.; *absent from* sw. Aust. s. and w. of Geraldton–Eucla, but with long coastal extension s. from Geraldton to City Beach, Perth; *amabilis*: ne. Q; C. York Pen. s. to Edward R. on w. coast and to Saunders Beach, 24 km nw. Townsville, in e.; *dulcis*: w. Arnhem Land, NT, from King R. w. at least to upper Alligator R. and Plum Tree Creek; *rogersi*: through Kimberleys, WA, e. at least to WA–NT border. Fairly common; probably sedentary.

516 BLUE-BREASTED WREN *Malurus pulcherrimus* Pl.69

Other names: Blue-breasted Superb Warbler, Purple-breasted Fairy Wren.

Field marks: 135–140 mm. Very like Variegated Wren (515); but in male the *throat and upperbreast are deep, slightly glossy blue-black* rather than jet-black. Hard to discern in field, it contrasts slightly with the jet-black of mark from bill through eye to nape. Crown lilac-blue, showing less contrast with blue ear-coverts than in Variegated. Female, imm. and eclipse male not safely distinguished from Variegated.

Similar species: Variegated (515) and Red-winged (517) Wrens.

Voice: Like Variegated Wren.

Habitat: Undergrowth in forests and woodlands; sandplain-scrubs and heaths; tea-tree and mallee associations; low dense dune-vegetation, acacia-thickets, saltbush. In SA, (Eyre Pen.) heath country and swampy localities.

Breeding: Nest and eggs like Variegated Wren.

Range and Status: Discontinuous distribution in sw. WA and SA. In sw. WA it occupies a band crossing from w. coast n. of Perth to Bight coast e. of Albany, between ranges of Variegated and Red-winged Wrens. The approximate n. and e. limits are from Tamala sandplain, s. of Shark Bay, to Mingenew–Bunjil–Wongan Hills–Gibb Rock–Norseman and e. to Bight coast s. of Mundrabilla; it may extend coastally e. to Eucla. The s. and w. limits in WA are from mouth of Namban R., about 170 km n. of Perth, passing inland of

Perth to wheatbelt and s. to near Katanning and to s. coast near Warriup, e. of Albany. Note that it overlaps range of Variegated Wren on w. coast between Tamala and Namban R. In SA, confined to s. Eyre Pen., n. and e. to Kimba–Whyalla. Common to locally very common in WA; uncommon SA. Sedentary.

517 RED-WINGED WREN *Malurus elegans*   Pl.69

Other names: Elegant Fairy-wren, Graceful Blue Wren, Marsh Wren.

Field marks: 145 mm. Note its specialized habitat, reflected by the alternative common name of Marsh Wren. Male: like Blue-breasted (516) but easily separated by following: (a) *feathers of back have white bases, making mantle conspicuously blue-white*; (b) *forehead sides of head and cheeks mostly pale silvery blue*; throat and upperbreast deep-blue. Female: like female Blue-breasted *but bill blackish*. Imms. and eclipse males like female. Sometimes associates with Splendid Wren (514).

Similar species: The only other red-shouldered wren regularly in contact is Blue-breasted (516). See above, and that entry. Variegated (515) approaches Red-winged on Swan coastal plain n. of Perth, where about 11 km of unsuitable sandplain is reported to separate them. Male Variegated has deeper lilac-blue head and back, and black upperbreast; female has reddish brown bill.

Voice: Song like Splendid Wren: three or four short clear notes followed by trilling warble. 'Pripping' notes sharper and louder.

Habitat: Thick scrub and swamp-vegetation along margins of freshwater swamps and permanent streams; neighbouring gardens, orchards; swamp woodlands; jarrah forest and moist gullies in Darling Ra.; coastal dune vegetation.

Breeding: Nest: larger, rounder and more sturdily constructed than Splendid Wren; of grass, bark-strips and leaves; usually in rush-clump in swampy vegetation, usually in reeds or rushes over water or near ground in base of rushes. Eggs: 2–3; white, lightly spotted and blotched red-brown, mostly at large end.

Range and Status: Suitable habitat in (mostly) coastal sw. WA, and Darling and Stirling Ras., from Moora to e. of Albany. Common, sedentary.

518 BLUE-AND-WHITE WREN *Malurus leucopterus*   Pl.69

Other names: Black-and-white, Pied, White-backed or White-winged Wren.

Field marks: 115–130 mm. Male: *the only Australian bird with bright deep-blue body and tail, pure-white wings* (primaries brown). Male eclipse: like female, but bill dark-horn. Female: *dullest and palest female fairy wren*: pale mouse-brown above, tail washed pale grey-blue; off-white below, flanks buffish, *bill sandy-brown*. Imm: bill paler, some yellowish. Nominate race, 'Black-and-White Wren': note island range. Male distinctive: *glossy black with white wings* (primaries brown); tail washed deep-blue; examples of nominate race from adjacent w. coastal areas are at times very dark or blackish; conversely some 'Black-and-White Wrens' have blue in plumage. Female, imm. and eclipse male: like nominate race, but last two often with patchy black in plumage and white on wings; bill and legs darker brown. Usually in parties, brown birds far outnumbering coloured males, which are usually shy and elusive. In flight, male's white wings against blue (or black) body are conspicuous and butterfly-like. Distinctive call is often first clue to its presence.

Similar species: Females and 'brown birds' of other fairy wrens are generally darker, specially in richer brown mark from bill to eye. Not safely separated unless males present, but note calls.

Voice: Rapid undulating musical reeling, like fishing reel rapidly wound. Contact-call, splintered 'prip prip' typical of fairy wrens, but thinner, more insect-like.

Habitat: Race *leuconotus*: tall grasses, low dense shrubs or other low tangled thickets or clumps on open, generally treeless arid and desert areas; saltbush, bluebush, roly-poly, spinifex, dead finish; lignum and canegrass in dry swamps or watercourses; samphire on margins of salt lakes and coastal inlets; commercial saltfields. Nominate race: low heath and scrub, including melaleuca, thryptomene and saltbush.

Breeding: Nest: domed, of grasses, plant-stems, bound with spiders' web and plant-down; usually in low shrub or grass near ground. Eggs: 3–4; white, finely spotted red-brown or purplish with or without zone at large end.

Range and Status: Race *leuconotus*: w. coastal and inland Aust., from Pilbara region, WA, to Tanami–Banka Banka, NT, across Barkly Tableland to Mt. Isa–Richmond–Roma–Goondiwindi, Q; all w. NSW, e. to foothills of Divide; nw. Vic., e. to Kerang area; Murray mallee, SA, to coastal areas near Adelaide; *not* Yorke or s. Eyre Pens; coastally w. from Streaky Bay, SA, to Esperance, WA, thence to near Perth, excluding sw. corner and better-watered country ne. of Perth, but extending s. to Perth coastal suburbs along coastal dunes; said to be extending range sw. The range includes deserts–recorded frequently in Simpson Desert crossings. Common to very common. Part-nomadic, specially in post-breeding season. Nominate race: confined to Dirk Hartog and Barrow Is., WA; 550 km apart. The two island populations are considered by some to have evolved independently. Very common; sedentary.

519 RED-BACKED WREN *Malurus melanocephalus* Pl.69

Field marks: 120–135 mm. Male: unlike any other Australian bird; *chocolate-brown to jet-black, with conspicuous crimson to fiery orange-red back*; tail blackish, shorter than most other wrens. Male eclipse: like female but often with traces of red back. Female: no chestnut round eye; pale-brown above, slight ochre wash to ear-coverts and flanks; fawnish white below; tail brown. *Bill and legs pale-brown to pinkish horn.* Imm: like female. Usually in parties, 'brown birds' predominating. Shy but tamer round settlement.

Similar species: Variegated Wren (515), female: dark-chestnut mark round eye; tail distinctly longer, bluish.

Voice: Reeling call louder, stronger and more irregular than Variegated Wren; other notes rather robust.

Habitat: Tropical and subtropical grasslands with or without canopy of taller vegetation; tropical woodlands including more humid eucalypt forests, swamp-woodlands; lantana and other scrubby thickets, plantations, gardens; occasional in rainforest. Further inland, typically in tall grass along watercourses and in foothills; low scrubs or spinifex.

Breeding: Nest: globular, neat and compact; of grass, bark-strips, leaves; usually in grass, less often in low shrub or thicket. Eggs: 3–4; white, very finely spotted light-red, more heavily at large end.

Range and Status: N. and e. Aust. and coastal islands: from about Broome, WA, across Kimberleys and top end NT, s. to Tanami–Tennant Creek–Barkly Highway; in Q, inland to Mt. Isa–Richmond–Carnarvon Ra.–Bunya Mts.–Warwick; n. coastal NSW, s. to area of Port Stephens, inland to Casino and about 30 km w. of Gloucester. There is circumstantial evidence that it once occurred nearer Sydney; recent sight records from near Wyong and Warriewood. Common, probably sedentary.

EMU-WRENS Genus *Stipiturus*

Emu-wrens are like small buffish dark-streaked fairy-wrens with very long thin tufty tails of only six feathers. These are curiously like stiff emu-feathers in their coarse open structure and in colour. No other Australian bird has such a tail and no known bird has fewer tail-feathers. The males have beautiful lavender-blue throats. One emu-wren (521) lives in s. coastal heathlands; the other two forms, now regarded as races of a single species (520), are spinifex-dwellers in arid lands. Their ranges are mostly well separated.

520 RUFOUS-CROWNED EMU-WREN *Stipiturus ruficeps* Pl.68

Field marks: 120–145 mm. The only emu-wren of the interior and central-west. *Note the plain unstreaked rufous crown and nape*; tail-feathers shorter and somewhat less flimsy than Southern Emu-wren (521). Race *mallee*, 'Mallee Emu-wren': somewhat darker, crown more streaked. Sexual differences like Southern Emu-wren (521). Pairs or parties; perches on tall seed-stems of spinifex, flies feebly before dropping to cover, crawls mouselike through spinifex-clumps.

Similar species: Southern Emu-wren (521) darker and more streaked, crown not rufous, tail longer. Fairy wrens (512–19) in brown plumage: 'normal' tail-feathers; upperparts unstreaked, no fine streaks on ear-coverts.

Voice: Contact-call: feeble insect-like 'prip, prip'; alarm-call: very high-pitched squeak, 'seeeeeeet'.

Habitat: Spinifex, typically on sides and gullies of rocky ridges, with sparse shrubs or trees.

Breeding: Nest: oval, with side-entrance; of fine grasses, shreds of bark, plant-down, often with spiders' web and egg-sacs, in spinifex-clump or small low shrub. Eggs: 2–3; white, speckled and blotched brown and red-brown, forming a zone at large end.

Range and Status: Nominate race: arid inland Aust., from c. Q to coastal n. WA between Pilbara region and NW Cape, n. to about 20°S in Gt. Sandy Desert, and s. to the E. Murchison district–Kathleen Valley–Naretha and n. part of Gt. Victoria Desert, (to about 100 km e. of Neale Junction), possibly into nw. SA. In sw. NT, s. to James Ra., Macdonnell Ras. and n. to Wauchope–Frewena. Unknown in Q until 1969, when discovered near Opalton; further observations indicate occurrence in area of Winton–Fermoy–Opalton. also on Buckingham Downs Stn., about 125 km n. of Boulia. Probably widespread in w. Q, perhaps continuous with population in NT. Local, sedentary; seemingly scarce, but status uncertain. Race *mallee*: confined to Murray mallee in se. SA and mallee areas of nw. Vic., e. to about Wyperfeld and Hattah NPs. Probably fairly common in suitable habitat, but because elusive, status uncertain.

521 SOUTHERN EMU-WREN *Stipiturus malachurus* Pl.68

Other names: Button-grass Wren, Sticktail.

Field marks: 185–200 mm. Tail very long (100–125 mm) and filmy, carried erect except in flight. Male: *grey-rufous above, streaked darker, face and throat lavender-blue*. Female: no blue, dark streaks above *and (finely) on grey ear-coverts; bright-buff underparts*. Imm: like female, less streaked above, tail shorter. Pairs or family parties; shy, moves nimbly through thick low cover, bounces or runs over ground, climbs to exposed positions on tussocks, low shrubs or low dead branches. Flight feeble, long tail streaming.

Similar species: Rufous-crowned Emu-wren (520): note habitat and range. Fairy-wrens (512–19) in brown plumage: 'normal' tail-feathers; upperparts unstreaked; no fine streaks on ear-coverts.

Voice: Like that of fairy-wrens, but higher-pitched and more splintered. Male, pretty trilling song; contact call: 'prip prip', high-pitched and insect-like. Alarm-call: very high-pitched 'seee'.

Habitat: Swampy heaths; rushes, sedges, scrubby thickets, occasionally lignum; also montane gullies, subalpine grasslands, heaths and woodlands. In Tas., button-grass plains with shrubs, montane moors. On Kangaroo I., reported in mallee. In sw. Aust. habitats wider: scrubby dune-vegetation, sandplain-heaths, dry eucalyptus and acacia-spinifex thickets.

Breeding: Nest: domed, loosely made of fine grass, rootlets, moss; lined with finer grass; usually in tussock or dwarf scrub near ground. Eggs: 3; white, tinged pink, minutely dotted overall with light red-brown and blotched at large end with same colour.

Range and Status: Confined to pockets of suitable habitat in coastal se. and sw. Aust. and Tas., from sea-level to over 1000 m. In WA, from Shark Bay–Dirk Hartog I., s. and e. to Israelite Bay, inland to Wongan Hills–Mt. Holland (Hyden–Norseman). In se. Aust. from s. Eyre Pen., Kangaroo I. and s. Mt. Lofty Ras., through coastal se., inland to about Naracoorte. In Vic. mostly coastal, inland to Grampians–Colac–Yellingbo and s. foothills of Divide in Gippsland, (? occasional) on High Plains. In NSW, inland to foothills

of se. highlands and probable on S. Tablelands; local in Blue Mts., inland to Kanangra
Boyd NP; n. coastally at least to lower Clarence R.; inland to Gibraltar Ra. NP. In se. Q
(?) isolate population recently found in the Cooloola area. Sedentary, uncommon;
habitats fragmented by clearing, land-development and sand-mining.

GRASSWRENS Genus *Amytornis*

Grasswrens are in many ways the most distinctive Australian wrens. Somewhat like large
fairy wrens, they are characterized by long white streaks, mostly on upperparts, markings
harmonizing with the streaked appearance of their spinifex and canegrass cover. Otherwise their colours reflect their arid, sandy or rocky homes—black through reddish brown
to cinnamon and grey. Several have white throats or underparts and a bold black whisker-
mark, an important field mark that has been used to indicate relations within the genus.
In most, females have chestnut flanks. Having been sternly dealt with by past climatic
phases, five of the eight species are isolated in very restricted refuge-areas in arid inland
or n. Aust. Two of these, Eyrean (526) and Grey (527) Grasswrens, inhabit small exclusive
canegrass habitats in sw. Q–nw. NSW, and n. SA, respectively, while Black (522), White-
throated (523) and Carpentarian (524) Grasswrens are similarly isolated in rocky escarpments in n. and nw. Aust. In these species, *Range* is the best clue to identification. The
remaining species: Thick-billed (529), Dusky (528) and Striated (525) Grasswrens have
much wider ranges (mostly s. of the Tropic). Note the following: because they were
apparently recently derived from a common ancestor, the Thick-billed (formerly known
as the Western) and Dusky Grasswrens are the most confusingly similar forms. Their
ranges now overlap in sw. NT–nw. SA, but the Thick-billed inhabits low shrubby vegetation on sandy lowlands and the Dusky is confined to rocky hills with spinifex. Being the
most widespread species, the Striated Grasswren partly overlaps ranges of several others,
mostly s. of the Tropic, but it can be fairly readily separated by its colour and prominent
black 'whisker-mark'. Grasswrens are among our most elusive least-known birds; they
move briskly in pairs or parties, hopping on ground or rock-surfaces with erect tails, run
with heads and tails lowered or, when breeding, climb to the top of grass-clumps, shrubs
or rocks to sing their pretty liquid territorial songs. When disturbed, they dash or fly to
hide in vegetation, flood debris or rock crevices and thus large areas of apparently suitable
habitat can often be traversed without sight or sound of them. Because of their extreme
shyness and the generally remote rugged nature of their homes, the Grey Grasswren was
not proved to exist until 1967; three others became 'lost' for decades and the unsuspected
(or continued) existence of others has only recently been proved in States far from their
next occurrence.

522 BLACK GRASSWREN *Amytornis housei*   Pl.70

Field marks: 230 mm. Male: our only bird that is *mostly black with prominent white
streaks*. Female: *underparts light-chestnut*. Imm: uniformly dark with faint white streaks.
Apart from appearance, *Range* is diagnostic. Usually in parties; runs and hops over rocks,
flicks tail, bobs; makes short downward glides. When alarmed, runs with head and tail
lowered, disappearing into cracks in rocks or scuttles ratlike along ledges.
Similar species: White-throated Grasswren (523).
Voice: Calls described as somewhat like fairy-wren but harsher and more continuous.
Alarm-call: loud ticking notes interspersed with grating sounds.
Habitat: Rough country of piled-up masses of sandstone, shading from red to black, with
which its colouring harmonizes. Gullies in sandstone hills, shaded and with tumbled rocks,
spinifex and trees.
Breeding: No data.
Range and Status: First discovered 1901; then 'lost' and rediscovered in 1968 in area of
Charnley R., Manning Creek and Mt. Elizabeth, Kimberleys, WA, where perhaps
common but because of remoteness of habitat, seen by few observers. Sedentary.

523 WHITE-THROATED GRASSWREN *Amytornis woodwardi* **Pl.70**

Field marks: 215 m. Note range. A large distinctive grasswren with black white-streaked upperparts, red-brown rump; black whisker-mark, *white throat separated from rusty underparts by incomplete black-and-white streaked breastband.* Female: richer-rusty underparts. Singly, territorial pairs or parties of 6–7. Not particularly shy but very nimble; runs in bursts over rock-faces of its rugged home with head and tail lowered; when disturbed, darts into crevices or under rocks slabs.

Similar species: Carpentarian Grasswren (524): smaller, less black; wings red-brown, underparts white with no breastband. Note range.

Voice: Song described as a rich attenuated series of rising and falling notes and trills. Feeding parties keep up animated chirping with snatches of song. Alarm and contact calls described as strong sharp 'trrrt' or 'tzzzt', repeated sporadically.

Habitat: Rounded sandstone escarpments and tors of w. Arnhem Land, NT, with ledges and plateaux of gravelly soil vegetated with spinifex and low shrubs.

Breeding: Nest: domed, of grass, leaves and paperbark, in top of spinifex tussock. Eggs: 2; slender, oval, rounded at both ends; slightly glossy, finely and sparingly speckled and blotched with red-brown, purple-grey and pale sepia, more heavily at large end, forming zone.

Range and Status: W. Arnhem Land, NT, from area of Oenpelli in n., sw. to El Sherana–Plumtree Creek and to upper Mary, S. Alligator and Katherine Rs.; e. limit unknown, but probably to about 134°E. Locally fairly common; sedentary.

524 CARPENTARIAN GRASSWREN *Amytornis dorotheae* **Pl.70**

Other names: Dorothy's or Red-winged Grasswren.

Field marks: 170 mm. Note isolated range. Like a smaller White-throated Grasswren (523) *but lores orange-brown; back red-brown, wing-feathers margined reddish-brown. Throat and upperbreast white with black whisker-mark but no streaked breastband;* underparts pale orange-buff, probably darker in female. Pairs, small parties; bounces quickly with short flights over rocks and steep slopes of rugged habitat, taking shelter in rock-crevices.

Similar species: White-throated Grasswren (523).

Voice: Described as like that of other small grasswrens.

Habitat: Sandstone escarpments, ledges and plateaux with large clumps of spinifex, small shrubs, and sparse eucalypts.

Breeding: Nest: bulky, domed, loosely-woven; of spinifex seed-stems and leaves, placed in a clump of spinifex near top. Eggs: 2–3; oval, rounded or elongated; smooth and glossy; pink-white, with irregular fine markings of red-brown and mauve, mostly at large end.

Range and Status: Sandstone escarpments of a small area of e. NT, near Macarthur R., between Western and Clyde Cks. An isolated form, seldom seen by ornithologists.

525 STRIATED GRASSWREN *Amytornis striatus* **Pl.70**

Other name: Rufous Grasswren.

Field marks: 150–175 mm. Widespread; the only grasswren occurring mostly s. of the Tropic that is red-brown above and has a *strong black whisker-mark*; head and back marked with prominent white streaks, underparts buff-white; note orange-buff eyebrow and white throat. Female: flanks chestnut. Nominate race: dull chestnut-brown above, underparts washed grey, sometimes with fine dark streaks. Birds in inland and WA (now grouped in a single race, *whitei*, which includes the former 'Rufous Grasswren') show much variation but are generally much brighter rufous-brown above, abdomen creamy-cinnamon to rusty. Pairs, small parties; behaves like other grasswrens.

Similar species: Thick-billed Grasswren (529): cinnamon-buff below, no whisker-mark;

bill heavier. Eyrean Grasswren (526): whiter below, no whisker-mark, bill heavier; note range and habitat. Mallee Heathwren (543): darker-brown above; no white streaks or whisker-mark; blackish tail with white tips. Fieldwren (545): rusty inland forms; smaller, no pale streaks or whisker-mark; habits differ; seldom in spinifex.

Voice: Song: a sweet rippling melody, interspersed with 'tu-tu-tu' notes. Alarm call: thin high-pitched squeak; also splintered twittering scolding, like a fairy wren or Striated Thornbill (567).

Habitat: Spinifex, often associated with mallee, acacia and other inland scrubs; coastal scrubs in w. WA.

Breeding: Nest: cup-shaped; usually of spinifex spines interwoven in spinifex clump. Eggs: 2; oval, white, irregularly spotted and streaked red-brown.

Range and Status: Inland and w. Aust.: from Vic. mallee (e. to Annuello–Kooloonong) s. to Little Desert; w. to Bunns Bore and near Murray Bridge, SA, n. through Murray mallee and Flinders Ras. to L. Eyre basin and Simpson Desert; also nw. and w. SA; (? isolate) population n. Eyre Pen.; in NT, n. to about 18°S in Tanami Desert; in WA, n. to about 20°S on Canning Stock Route; w. to Pilbara and to coast near Pt. Cloates–North West Cape; s. inland to E. Murchison district–Wiluna–Laverton–Gt. Victoria Desert. The desert race *whitei* occupies the inland and w. part of range, intergrading with nominate in n. Flinders Ras. Isolate populations recently discovered in Q, in area of Opalton–Fermoy–Santos; and in area of Cobar–Hillston–Ivanhoe, NSW, where last-reported 1883, (earlier records from elsewhere in NSW). Common locally, but patchy according to habitat; sedentary.

526 EYREAN GRASSWREN *Amytornis goyderi*   Pl.70

Field marks: 140 m. Note very restricted range. Very small, about the size of Blue-and-White Wren (518) but reported to seem larger when scurrying between clumps of cane-grass. Crown and nape grey-brown, back and upper tail-coverts *bright rufous-brown, streaked white*; *underparts off-white*, without strong whisker-mark; flanks pale-rufous. Bill short, greyish.

Similar species: Thick-billed Grasswren (529): larger, browner above, buffer below; note range and habitat. Striated Grasswren (525).

Voice: Reported to be almost inaudible: faint two-syllable whistle, 'swi-it, swi-it'.

Habitat: Dense clumps of canegrass, mostly *c.* 1 m high and 3 m apart, on sand with local small hummocks and dunelets.

Breeding: Nest: almost globular, semi-domed, with opening near top; mostly of cane-grass leaves with a few interwoven canegrass stems. Eggs not described.

Range and Status: First described 1871, then 'lost'; rediscovered 1961 at Christmas Waterhole (lat. 27°35′54″) of Macumba R. in Simpson Desert n. of L. Eyre, SA, in general area of original discovery. Local, apparently rare.

527 GREY GRASSWREN *Amytornis barbatus*   Pl.70

Field marks: 185–205 mm. *The palest, greyest grasswren: crown black, streaked white; upperparts sandy grey-buff prominently streaked with black-edged white lines.* Eyebrow, face and underparts white, with distinctive black mark through eye and black pattern on throat, *joining in centre of throat in a 'necklet'*; breast crossed by zone of fine black streaks, flanks pale-buff. Female: similar. In field, head and throat markings reported not to be distinctive; main feature being the bird's general greyness. Small parties; perches in top of canegrass and lignum-clumps; when approached, descends into clump; when flushed, flies rapidly and low to another clump with tail trailing like a fairy wren; runs and bounces between cover; perhaps tends to fly more frequently than other grasswrens.

Similar species: Striated Grasswren (525), desert forms: bright red-brown above; black whisker simpler, not meeting in centre of throat; note range and habitat. Eyrean Grasswren (526): red-brown above; unmarked white throat.

Voice: When disturbed, reported to utter a prolonged twittering from interior of dense thickets, notes being soft, double-syllabled and high-pitched.

Habitat: Canegrass and lignum of overflow channels and swamps.

Breeding: Nest: bulky, very loosely made, semi-domed with opening at side; of grass. **Eggs:** 2; rounded-oval, slightly glossy, variable; dull-white, tinged pale-pink, speckled with fine nutmeg-brown markings, with freckled cap at large end; or white, unevenly but boldly speckled and blotched with heavy irregular nutmeg to red-brown markings.

Range and Status: Discovered 1967 in overflow channels of the lower Bulloo R. (the Bulloorine) in border area of far-nw. NSW and far-sw. Q. Since reported in canegrass and swamps, Tibooburra area, NSW, and Goyder's Lagoon, ne. SA. Uncommon; sedentary.

528   DUSKY GRASSWREN   *Amytornis purnelli*   Pl.70

Other names: Thin-billed or Buff-throated Grasswren.

Field marks: 165–175 mm. *Darker, slimmer and finer-billed* than the closely-related Thick-billed Grasswren (529). Note rufous touch to forehead, absence of black whisker-mark, cinnamon-brown upperparts with long pale streaks and *rich-buff underparts*; *flanks of female pale-chestnut*. Shy; bounces over rock-faces and boulders; takes cover in crevices; normally carries the longish tail cocked but, when distrubed, dashes with tail lowered; occasionally flies, low and straight, frequently downhill.

Similar species: Thick-billed Grasswren (529): bill much heavier, paler above, underparts distinctly paler. Note habitat. Striated Grasswren (525): redder above, whiter below with black whisker-mark.

Voice: Song: a reeling trill, like blue wren but more sibilant and regular. Song of female has been syllabized 'sree-sreeee-sreé-teu-teu'. Alarm-call, harsh loud 'chip-chip!', also long very high-pitched 'seet'.

Habitat: Rocky ranges and gorges, vegetated with spinifex and shrubs.

Breeding: Nest: half-domed; loosely constructed of fine soft dry grass; within 45 cm of ground in spinifex-clump, tussock or dense low bush. Eggs: 2–4; swollen oval, fine, rather glossy; white or pinkish, spotted and blotched light to dark red-brown and lilac-grey, forming a cap at large end.

Range and Status: Rocky hills of interior: from Everard, Mann and Musgrave Ras., n. SA, w. to Rawlinson, WA, and n. through Macdonnell, Harts and other ranges of s. NT to near Powell Creek (s. of Elliott and L. Woods). In 1966 a population was discovered in rocky hills in area of Mt. Isa–Cloncurry, nw. Q; it probably occurs in other rocky ranges of w. Q. Fairly common locally but elusive; sedentary.

529   THICK-BILLED GRASSWREN   *Amytornis textilis*   Pl.70

Other name: Western Grasswren.

Field marks: 165–185 mm. A thickset *dull grasswren with a stout conical bill* but no black whisker-mark; upperparts brownish rufous, streaked paler; underparts grey-buff with pale streaks on throat and breast (nominate race) or plain pale-fawn (race *modestus*); female has chestnut flanks. Birds from the region of L. Eyre, SA, reported to be paler with deeper bills than those from WA and (formerly) from NSW. Shy and elusive, said to fly more than other grasswrens. *Note habitat.*

Similar species: Dusky Grasswren (528): thinner bill, different habitat. Striated Grasswren (525), desert forms: redder above, paler below; black whisker-mark. Eyrean Grasswren (526): redder above, mostly white below; bill comparatively *heavier*; note habitat.

Voice: Reported to be rather quiet but a clear silvery song and a very high-pitched alarm squeak.

Habitat: Typically on sandy plains and depressions in gibber, in dense low saltbush, cottonbush, bluebush and nitre-bush; also clumps of canegrass, mostly on watercourses. Noted to take refuge in heaps of old flood debris on dry sandy watercourses. In area of L. Way, WA, in stunted heath and samphire.

Breeding: Nest: varied; cup-shaped, half-domed or domed with large opening on side, rather loosely made, of dead dry grass, strips of dry bark, lined with finer grass, and a little fur or feathers; on or near ground in clump of canegrass, low shrub or flood debris. Eggs: 2–3; variable, white or pink, heavily spotted or blotched red-brown and purplish grey, or with fine red-brown specks.

Range and Status: S. inland and s. WA, range possibly disjunct: (1) s. interior, from sw. NT and Macdonnell Ras., s. to w. side of Flinders Ras., SA, (Murnpeowie–Farina–Lyndhurst–Copley), and sw. to ne. Eyre Pen. Formerly c. and w. NSW (near Mt. Arrowsmith Stn.; Mossgiel; lower Namoi R) (2) WA, e. of Tropic and roughly w. of longitude 123°E; absent from sw. corner, but reaching central w. coast, e.g. Peron Pen., and (formerly) Dirk Hartog I. Common locally, but generally sparse; its extreme elusiveness may often cause it to be overlooked.

BRISTLEBIRDS Genus *Dasyornis*

So-called because they have four or more stiff forward-curving bristles growing from near the base of the bill (a feature also present in some other songbirds), Bristlebirds are the giants of the *Maluridae*. Their behaviour is furtive and they are easily confused with scrub-birds (414–5). Their field marks are rather subtle dark or rufous markings on brownish plumage and rather large frequently cocked or fanned tails. Their calls are silvery, clear and far-carrying. Their extraordinarily divided east-west ranges, like those of scrub-birds, seem to indicate that they were formerly much more widespread but are now in a period of decline.

530 EASTERN BRISTLEBIRD *Dasyornis brachypterus* Pl.59

Other name: Brown Bristlebird.

Field marks: 200–220 mm. Rare, shy and more often heard than seen. *Dark olive-brown or reddish brown above, washed chestnut on crown and nape*; *short rounded wings and long graduated tail, half total length*; grey-brown to pale grey below, washed tawny on sides of breast, flanks and under tail-coverts. Moves with furtiveness and agility of a rat through dense undergrowth, *tail usually raised and often fanned*. Most flights short and low; sings from bushes.

Similar species: Rufous Bristlebird (532): rufous cap and ear-coverts. Rufous Scrub-bird (414), (e. only): smaller, darker, call differs. Note habitat. Pilotbird (533): rich-buff face, throat and breast; voice can be confused.

Voice: Loud and melodious, with sweet but strangely penetrating quality; ends in something of a whipcrack.

Habitat: Coastal scrubs, wet heathlands, reedbeds and thickets overgrown with rank vegetation; in McPherson Ras., Q, heathy country above 600 m.

Breeding: Nest: domed; of sticks, bark and grass; in low shrub, vine or tussock, on or near ground. Eggs: 2; buff-white, with irregular fine blotchings of red-brown to purplish brown, forming heavy zone round large end.

Range and Status: Se. Aust.: scattered, apparently isolated, populations from about Marlo in e. Vic. to the McPherson Ras. in far se. Q. The Marlo population may no longer exist. Some places where reported include: Wingan Inlet NP, Mallacoota NP, Vic.; Barren Grounds, Jervis Bay, Dorrigo Plateau, NSW; Binna Burra, Mt. Lindesay, and Cunningham's Gap, Q. Generally rare and local; sedentary.

531 WESTERN BRISTLEBIRD *Dasyornis longirostris* Pl.59

Other names: Brown or Long-billed Bristlebird.

Field marks: 170–190 mm. Probably derived from the same stock as the somewhat larger Eastern Bristlebird (530) which it resembles in habits and actions. Bill longer; *crown, nape and mantle distinctly dappled with grey*; slight dark scaly pattern on throat and breast.

Similar species: Rufous Bristlebird (532): larger; cap and ear-coverts distinctly rufous; head and upperparts not dappled. Noisy Scrub-bird (415): note different breast-markings and calls. The two species occur in the same locality.

Voice: Call of male has been syllabized as a quick 'chip-pee-tee-peetle-pet'; that of female as 'tink'. There is a fairly high-pitched alarm-call.

Habitat: Dense coastal scrubs, wet heaths.

Breeding: Nest: large, globular, with a side entrance; of wiry grass, without lining; in grass or low shrub, under cover. Eggs: 2; dull-brownish white, blotched and freckled purplish brown, mostly heavily at large end. Some blotches appear to be below surface of shell.

Range and Status: S. WA: apparently now confined to a small range e. of Albany, including the Mt. Gardner area at Two People Bay, where Noisy Scrub-bird also occurs. Rare; sedentary.

532 RUFOUS BRISTLEBIRD *Dasyornis broadbenti*   **Pl 59**

Field marks: 240–265 mm. The largest bristlebird, with widely-divided range. Note: *rich-rufous cap and 'ear-mufflers'* contrasting with olive-grey upperparts; underparts pale-grey *distinctively mottled darker*. Rather shy and elusive; more often heard than seen. When briefly glimpsed, can look like female Blackbird (436), but flies less readily; *runs swiftly; raises and spreads longish full tail*.

Similar species: Eastern (530) and Western (531) Bristlebirds: no distinctive rufous on crown and cheeks. Noisy Scrub-bird (415): in s. WA, known range is well-separated.

Voice: Male call: clear and penetrating, not unlike Pilotbird (533); three or four pairs of silvery notes with rising inflection in quick succession, ending with double whip-like crack, last three notes often echoed by female. Syllabized as rich 'chip, chip, chip, chewee' followed by softer 'chew-a'. Variations: 'chip, chip, chip, chip-choowee' or 'chit, chit, chit, chit, chewee-wit'; also a 'charming chuckling sub-song in depths of thickets'; short, sharp alarm-call.

Habitat: heavy coastal scrubs and thickets; coastal gullies with rank growth of sword-grass and blackberries; undergrowth in gullies in temperate rainforest.

Breeding: Nest: largish, rough-looking, domed; of thin twigs; usually in small tea-tree, clump of wire-grass or sword-grass usually over 0.5 to 2 m high. Eggs: 2; whitish, very heavily and uniformly freckled red and purplish.

Range and Status: Note widely divided range: coastal se. SA and w. Vic., from mouth of Murray R. (Younghusband Pen.) e. to near Torquay, Vic.; ranges some distance inland in suitable habitat e.g. to s. of Terang–Colac, Vic.; fairly common. In s. WA restricted to strip of coast from C. Naturaliste to C. Leeuwin, where now possibly extinct.

Scrubwrens, Fairy Warblers, Thornbills and Allies Family
Acanthizidae

A large and diverse family of small or smallish birds mostly endemic to Australasia. The most important groups are introduced separately.

Food: Mainly insects, their larvae, other small invertebrates; nectar.

Range: Australasian region, including NG and NZ and some NZ sub antarctic islands; Melanesia; Greater and Lesser Sunda Is., Philippines; to se. Asia (one species).

Number of species: World 59; Aust. 37.

SANDSTONE WARBLERS

Confined to se. Aust., both Pilotbird (533) and Rock Warbler (534) have simple patterns and unusual rufous or buff underparts. To some degree they replace one another geographically. However the Pilotbird is larger and its voice and nest are more like those of bristlebirds, with which it is illustrated. Their habits and habitats differ and neither presents serious problems of identification; the Rock Warbler is distinctive in a number of ways.

533 PILOTBIRD *Pycnoptilus floccosus* **Pl 59**

Other name: Guinea-a-week

Field marks: 165–175 mm. A richly coloured, plump, rather tame ground-dweller of dense temperate rainforests. *Forehead to upperbreast rich buff with slight scaly pattern*, eye red; *tail usually carried high, flicked up and down.* Feeds mostly on ground; hopping briskly; when disturbed, moves quickly almost like rat through densest undergrowth; flight not strong but at times up into trees or after insects. Unusual name apparently because it accompanies Superb Lyrebirds (413), like pilotfish with shark, snapping up soil-organisms they uncover.

Similar species: Rock Warbler (534).

Voice: Piercing and sweet; male: silvery far-carrying 'ee-see-a-week', often imitated by Superb Lyrebird, and similar notes; answered by female: 'whit-a, whit-ee' or 'qui-wit-tui-wit-tee'; also softer notes, 'tui-wit', etc.

Habitat: Floor and lower level of temperate rainforest and wet woodland; among leaf-litter, ferns, sword-grass, wire-grass, fallen logs.

Breeding: Nest: like miniature lyrebird's; untidy, globular with side-entrance; of strips of bark, dead leaves, rootlets; on or near ground among fallen branches, sword-grass, ferns. Eggs: 2; largish, short and swollen; green to dark-grey, smoky brown or rich purple-brown, with darker zone at large end.

Range and Status: Forested coastal and highland areas from just e. of Melbourne (Dandenong Ras.–Wilson's Prom., Vic.) to Blue Mts. and Sydney area, NSW, mostly on ranges and denser coastal forests. Fairly common; sedentary.

534 ROCK WARBLER *Origma solitaria* **Pl 71**

Other names: Cataract-bird, Cavebird, Hanging Dick, Rock Robin, Sandstone Robin.

Field marks: 120–140 mm. The only bird confined to NSW. Somewhat like a scrubwren; olive-brown above, washed rufous on rump; *throat grey, breast and underparts plain rich-rufous.* Imm: throat tinged tawny. Solitary pairs or family parties. Very active, restless; moves body from side to side; flicks tail sideways; hops swiftly over rocks; creeps mouse-like into crevices. Note range, and absence from some areas of apparently suitable habitat.

Similar species: Pilotbird (533).

Voice: Shrill melancholy call described as 'good-bye', uttered three or four times; shorter high-pitched variation of this, uttered intermittently, and rasping but slightly liquid note; harsh scolding.

Habitat: Rocky hillsides, gullies and caves in reddish weatherbeaten sandstone and lime-stone; usually near water.

Breeding: Nest: bulky ragged hanging mass, tapered at both ends; with side-entrance; of root and bark fibre, moss and grasses bound with spiders' web; suspended from sloping wall or roof of cave, overhanging rock, stalactite, road culvert, mineshaft; also in houses and other artificial situations. Eggs: 3; glossy, usually pure-white.

Range and Status: Confined to outcrops of Hawkesbury Sandstone and adjoining lime-stone in NSW from upper Hunter R. to Pigeon House Mt. in s. coastal NSW; n. to Scone, inland to Munghorn Gap NR, near Mudgee. Fairly common; sedentary.

SCRUBWRENS (including SCRUB TIT and FERNWREN)

Typical scrubwrens are mostly undergrowth-dwelling small birds of strong voices and sombre plumage, enlivened by bold patterns on face, throat or breast that show up clearly in the gloom of their homes, and by which they are best identified. They mostly have pale eyes, and wing-coverts marked with black and white. Unlike their wren namesake, they do not cock their tails. Note that two apparently closely related problem species have been dealt with as follows by Schodde (1975): the Scrub Tit (541) of Tas. is treated as a scrubwren. The Fernwren (535) of ne. Q is linked with the mouse-babblers of NG in the genus *Crateroscelis*, of which it is the sole Australian representative. The heathwrens, (542–3) and the Redthroat (544) are now also included in *Sericornis*. However this Guide differs from the new Checklist in retaining separate genera for the Fieldwren (545) and Speckled Warbler (546). Their affinities are not understood.

535 FERNWREN *Crateroscelis gutturalis* Pl.71

Other name: Collared Scrubwren.

Field marks: 125–140 mm. A distinctive ground-dweller with many features typical of scrubwrens. Rich olive-brown plumage makes it difficult to see in gloom of rainforest but, head on, *shows distinctive facial pattern of white eyebrow and throat, margined below by black 'bib'*; note dark eyes and longish bill. Usually in pairs; not shy. Scratches vigorously on forest-floor; hops about, bows low, elevates short tail, flicks leaves.

Similar species: Yellow-throated Scrubwren (538): similar in dim light but centre of breast yellowish.

Voice: Described as extraordinarily penetrating high-pitched whistle; also harsh scolding of five rapid staccato notes, descending the scale, followed by three more prolonged and higher 'chips'.

Habitat: Ferns and undergrowth in dense mountain rainforests.

Breeding: Nest: domed; entrance with slight overhang; firmly made of rootlets, twigs, skeleton leaves, moss and lichen; on ground under overhanging bank or small cave amid ferns and mosses; usually in dark places. Eggs: 2; oval, white, smooth, glossy, sometimes finely spotted chestnut and tan.

Range and Status: Confined to highlands from Cooktown s. to Mt. Spec, Paluma Ra., ne. Q, mostly above 400 m. Fairly common; sedentary.

536 ATHERTON SCRUBWREN *Sericornis keri* Pl.71

Other name: Bellenden Ker Scrubwren.

Field marks: 135 mm. Like Large-billed Scrubwren (537) *but dark olive-brown of upperparts extends over forehead and face* without contrast between dark crown and distinctive buff face. Darker below; central pale area of lower breast and belly *forms yellowish stripe; tail more reddish brown*. Slightly larger and longer-legged than Large-billed; inhabits lower levels of rainforest; feeds low in trees and on ground, in contrast to fluttering arboreal behaviour of Large-billed.

Voice: Not recorded; probably differs somewhat from Large-billed Scrubwren.

Habitat: Understorey of mountain rainforests.

Breeding: Nest: domed with side-entrance; of dried plant material, skeleton leaves; lined with feathers; in roadside bank among grass, ferns. Eggs: 2; like Large-billed Scrubwren.

Range and Status: Apparently confined to rainforests of Atherton Tableland, Q. above 600 m.

537 LARGE-BILLED SCRUBWREN *Sericornis magnirostris* Pl.71

Field marks: 115–130 mm. *Note longish straight bill, seemingly stuck to head at slight upward angle.* Plain buff-brown above, fawnish below; no obvious markings but *buff face paler than crown, making large dark eye noticeable*; rump and base of tail slightly rufous. Pairs, small parties; behaves more like thornbill than scrubwren; flutters high in foliage or hangs acrobatically on vines, trunks, branches; descends infrequently to feed on or near forest-floor.

Similar species: Atherton Scrubwren (536): face not buff; habits more terrestial.
Voice: While feeding, occasional sharp little chatter 'sip-sip-sip' like Striated Thornbill (567); also typical penetrating scrubwren territorial call: 's-cheer, s-cheer, s-cheer, s-cheer, s-cheer'.
Habitat: Tropical subtropical and temperate rainforests, from sea level to about 1500 m.
Breeding: Nest: domed; loosely built of bark-fibres, grass, moss; in creeper or among twigs. Eggs: 3–4; dull-white to pale purplish brown with pale streaks and fine spots, forming cap at large end. In many parts of coastal e. and ne. Aust. commonly usurps nest of Yellow-throated Scrubwren (538) and less commonly of Brown Warbler (548).
Range and Status: Coastal and highland forests of se. and e. Aust., from the Dandenong Ras. and area of Kinglake, e. and n. of Melbourne, to near Cooktown, ne. Q. In Vic. it is mostly found in highland forests of the Divide; in NSW and Q it extends from highlands to (mostly) dense coastal forests and in places further inland e.g. to near Chinchilla, Q. Also some islands off coast, e.g. Fraser I. The range in ce. Q may be discontinuous. Fairly common in n., uncommon in s.

538 YELLOW-THROATED SCRUBWREN *Sericornis citreogularis* **Pl.71**
Other names: Blacknest-bird, Devilbird.
Field marks: 120–135 mm Handsome and distinctive: large black mask bordered above by long white to yellowish eyebrow, *below by prominent yellow throat*; eye brown. Legs pink, longish. Female: facial pattern duller, mask and forehead brown, not black. Singly or pairs; hops briskly and quietly through undergrowth, often venturing into tracks through forest. 'Devilbird' supposedly refers to its unexpected presence in dim dark surroundings. Often first noted by call; scolds intruder at nest. Note voice.
Similar species: White-browed Scrubwren (540): pale eye, no yellow throat, white whisker below eye; black-and-white mark on wing-coverts. Its race *laevigaster* has more prominent cream-white breast.
Voice: Brilliant vocalist; clear sweet song usually includes interwoven mimicry. Contact-call, sharp 'tick' like stones tapped together.
Habitat: Ground and understorey of coastal and mountain rainforests, forests and woodlands and heavily vegetated gullies; often near water.
Breeding: Nest: distinctive, often conspicuous; untidy, bulky, domed; long and slender or globular; of blackish rootlets, palm-fibre, skeleton leaves, twigs, ferns, mosses and dry grasses, decorated with moss, lichen or plants, including orchids. Usually slung from leafy twig or lawyer-vine in dark place, over water. Eggs: 3; glossy, pale chocolate-pink to chocolate-brown, banded with two or three shadowy zones.
Range and Status: Note broken range: highlands between Cooktown and near Towns-ville, ne. Q, inland to Atherton–Ravenshoe; coastal se. Q and NSW, from Cooroy–Bunya Mts., Q, s. to Illawarra district, s. coast NSW. Common; sedentary.

539 TROPICAL SCRUBWREN *Sericornis beccarii* **Pl.71**
Other name: Little Scrubwren.
Field marks: 115 mm. The typical form is a clearly marked small bird somewhat like a small brownish White-browed Scrubwren (540), with *pale-orange to deep orange-scarlet* eyes; its facial pattern also differs: *eyebrow broken, blackish mask reduced mainly to 'scorched' area before eye*; rump cinnamon, no tail band. Female: duller. A much less well-marked race, *dubius*, occupies s. part of the species' Australian range on C. York Pen.: more brownish buff, with only faint markings, and somewhat resembles Large-billed Scrubwren (537). Active, usually in pairs or parties; fossicks among dead leaves and debris on ground or high among masses of fallen vines and trees.
Voice: Generally like White-browed Scrubwren.
Habitat: Rainforests, monsoon forests, river-scrubs.
Breeding: Nest: domed; of leaves, rootlets, lined with feathers; suspended in hanging

roots on banks of dry creeks, in dead leaves in bushes; or in vine clinging tree about 1 m high. Eggs: 2–3; faint reddish-brown, with light-brown fleecy markings on large end. **Range and Status:** C. York Pen., s. to Archer R., Coen and Rocky R. The typically-coloured race *minimus* occupies the n. part of the range. It is reported to merge with *dubius* in the area of Iron Ra.–Lockhart R. on e. coast, and in area of Wenlock–Watson–Archer Rs. in w. Common; sedentary. Also NG where nominate race, and others occur.

540 WHITE-BROWED SCRUBWREN *Sericornis frontalis* Pl.71

Other names: Brown, Buff-breasted, Spotted or White-fronted Scrubwren; Cartwheel-bird.

Field marks: 110–135 mm. Widespread in several races; typical male of coastal se. Aust.: *narrow blackish mask from bill to eye, margined above by white eyebrow and below by silvery white whisker*; *pale eye*; *blackish mark on shoulder, checked white*; throat whitish, slightly streaked black, centre of underparts cream-yellow. Female: facial pattern much less bold, 'mask' brown, not black. Imm: duller and browner than female. The n. coastal race *laevigaster* 'Buff-breasted Scrubwren', is more contrastingly-marked; and has a *larger black facial mask, a more obvious white throat and glowing creamy white underparts.* Race *humilis*, 'Brown Scrubwren': larger (135 mm), with a *much less-distinct facial pattern*; throat greyish with faint darker markings, *small white mark on wing*. Race *maculatus* 'Spotted Scrubwren': greyer above and whiter below, specially in more arid parts of range; *throat and upperbreast prominently marked with long blackish spots or streaks*, longer white eyebrow; tail may be tipped white. The form in wetter coastal areas of sw. Aust. has yellower underparts. Calls harsher. Singly, pairs or parties; hops briskly on ground, logs, through undergrowth, shrubbery and lower levels of trees. Wary, alert, fussy and inquisitive; often scolds intruder; becomes tame in gardens.

Similar species: Tropical (539) and Yellow-throated (538) Scrubwrens. Heathwrens: (542–3) have bright chestnut rumps, and cock their tails. Thornbills (556–67): smaller, with smaller bills, much less pronounced facial patterns.

Voice: Vocal and excitable; characteristic scolding call, a deep insistant zizzing, uttered at intruders near nest, snakes, cuckoos. Territorial song varies; typically a clear far-carrying 'tseer-tseer-tseer' or 'seat-you seat-you seat-you', oft-repeated.

Habitat: Dense dim undergrowth of forests woodlands and scrubs, from sea-level to above snowline; riverside thickets in drier country, coastal scrubs and heaths; bracken, saltmarsh, mangroves; parks, gardens with low shrubs and creepers. Race *maculatus*: range of habitat wider, from mangroves, coastal forests and scrubs to thickets of mulga, and saltbush in drier regions.

Breeding: Nest: untidy, domed; loosely woven of grasses, twigs, fine roots, leaves. Usually well-hidden in undergrowth, sword-grass, tussock or fork of shrub; round houses, sometimes in an artificial situation–a hanging tin, old coat, disused golf-bag in outhouse. Eggs: 2–3; stout, oval; grey-white to very pale-buff, blotched and spotted dull-brown to purplish brown, more heavily at large end.

Range and Status: Coastal e., s. and sw. Aust. and Tas.: from Cairns–Atherton Table-land, ne. Q, to Shark Bay and Bernier I., WA. Widespread in e. Aust., inland in suitable habitats on Gt. Dividing Ra., Carnarvon Ras., Q, and Mt. Lofty Ras., SA; present in river red gum forests of the Murray Valley w. to about Barham, NSW; present on many coastal islands, including Kangaroo I., SA. The nominate race occurs in se. Aust.; the cream-breasted race *laevigaster* occupies the coastal range in ne. NSW and Q; the large plain race *humilis* occurs in Tas. and Bass Strait islands, where intergradation seems to take place with nominate race; the race *maculatus*, and other forms with streaked breasts, occupy the range coastally w. of about Spencer Gulf, SA, (where intergradation also occurs) along the Bight coast and in sw. WA, inland to about L. Grace–Narrogin–Moora. Common; sedentary.

541 SCRUB TIT *Sericornis magnus*   Pl.71

Other names: Fern Weaver, Mountain Wren, White-breasted Scrub Tit.
Field marks: 115 mm. Like a scrubwren: note *longish curved bill*, brown eye, conspicuous white throat and upperbreast; white marks on wing; flanks chestnut-olive. Shy, inconspicuous; moves mouse-like in dense scrub; hops up tree-trunks, flies to base of another tree to ascend again, like treecreeper.
Similar species: Brown (557) and Tasmanian (559) Thornbills: no white throat. Whitebrowed Scrubwren (540) race *humilis*: bill straight, eye pale; throat and breast not conspicuously white.
Voice: Like Brown Scrubwren and Brown Thornbill; practice is said to be required to differentiate. A typical call is described as simple 'to-wee-to', with pleasant whistling.
Habitat: Dense undergrowth of temperate rainforests, fern-gullies; on King I. reported in paperbark areas, as well as fern-gullies.
Breeding: Nest: domed with slightly hooded side-entrance; of strips of bark, grasses, leaves, hair-like treefern fibre, green moss, lichen; usually among ferns, bushes or blackberries. Eggs: 3–4; white, finely freckled dull-red or reddish brown.
Range and Status: Endemic to Tas.: where widespread except drier e. coast forests; King I. sparse in suitable habitat. Fairly common; sedentary.

542 HEATHWREN *Sericornis pyrrhopygius*   Pl.71

Other names: Chestnut-tailed or rumped Groundwren, Heathwren or Hylacola; Scrub Warbler.
Field marks: 135–140 mm. Known as much by song and mimicry as by appearance. Olive-brown above, whitish below, breast streaked grey-brown; note *prominent pale eyebrow, rich-chestnut rump, pale-chestnut under tail-coverts; outer tail-feathers with dark subterminal band and pale tips; tail usually cocked.* Female: duller. Imm: buff eyebrow, buffish unstreaked below. Singly or pairs; hops briskly; disappears like india-rubber ball when disturbed. Note song.
Similar species: Mallee Heathwren (543). Fieldwren (545): greener; streaked above; no chestnut on rump. White-browed Scrubwren (540): black mask, whitish whisker, no conspicuous chestnut rump; does not cock tail.
Voice: Song: usually from low bush; begins softly, gradually swells till air rings with melody; like full-voiced canary. Mimicry imperceptibly interwoven. Female may duet with male. Contact-call, harsh 'zeet' or 'sweet'.
Habitat: Wet coastal heaths, coastal and subcoastal open woodlands and scrublands.
Breeding: Nest: globular, often untidy; slight platform below side-entrance; of grass, rootlets, strips of bark, on ground, in grass or shrub near ground. Eggs: 3; salmon-pink, freckled and blotched light chocolate-brown, more heavily at large end.
Range and Status: Coastal and subcoastal se. Aust.: from se. corner SA to a few locations in extreme se. Q (Cunningham's Gap, and n. of Wallangarra). Scattered populations in Flinders and Mt. Lofty Ras. and Fleurieu Pen., SA. In Vic. ranges inland to Grampians–Bendigo to n. of Divide in ne., but more usual in coastal parts; likewise in NSW, but inland to Temora–Warrumbungle NP. Uncommon; sedentary.

543 MALLEE HEATHWREN *Sericornis cautus*   Pl.71

Other names: Red-rumped, Shy or Western Groundwren or Heathwren or Hylacola.
Field marks: 115–140 mm. A small bird of character, very like Heathwren (542), which it replaces (? or merges with) in sub-inland se. Aust. and drier coastal parts of SA and s. WA. Note darker upperparts, *whiter underparts, with conspicuous blackish streaks, white mark on wing, more fiery-chestnut rump*; all tail-feathers except inmost pair tend to be wholly blackish, tipped white. Distinctions are fairly subtle and apparently irregular. Imm: washed fawn on throat and breast. Pairs or small parties; moves over ground like bouncing ball, *tail cocked*; flight low and quick. Shy, but at times curious and can be squeaked up.

Similar species: Grasswrens (522–9): streaked whitish above, no contrasting rump. Field-wren (545): reddish inland races: upperparts paler, some heavily streaked; no distinct chestnut rump; distinct blackish sub-terminal tail-band, and pale tips.

Voice: Song rich and sweet, with considerable range of notes and mimicry; typical contact-call syllabized 'chcc-chcc-chick-a-dee'.

Habitat: Shrub woodland, mallee and other inland scrubs; stony hillsides with low heathy scrub; open low dwarf banksia-scrub.

Breeding: Nest: domed, with side-entrance and slight platform forming doorstep; loosely woven of grass and bark-strips; in depression on ground among debris at foot of mallee sapling or in shelter of dwarf bush. Eggs: 3; oval, glossy; olive-grey with very dark indistinct spots below surface, forming zone at large end.

Range and Status: Inland se. Aust., and s. inland and coastal s. and sw. Aust.: from about Condobolin–W. Wyalong, NSW, mallee areas of nw. Vic. and se. SA, (and Kangaroo I.), to sw. WA n. to Kalgoorlie and Murchison R.; *except* w. of line from Dongara to Stirling Ras. Uncommon.

544 REDTHROAT *Sericornis brunneus* Pl.71

Other name: Red-throated Scrubwren.

Field marks: 115 mm. Soberly coloured; male: *face and underparts plain greyish, small rusty throat-mark*. Female: whitish areas between bill and eye, unmarked greyish white throat. Usually in pairs, not abundant; spends much time on ground. Shy, disappears hopping mouse-like into cover; often emerges again to inspect intruder, or flies quickly to cover, *revealing largish black white-tipped tail*. Breeding males sing conspicuously, beautifully; this and Mallee Heathwren (543) are sweetest singers of inland scrubs.

Similar species: Broad-tailed Thornbill (558), all races: streaked breasts, reddish rumps. Mallee Heathwren (543): whitish streaked darker below; rump chestnut; cocks tail. Slate-backed Thornbill (561): dark-streaked crown, distinct pale-chestnut rump.

Voice: Rich, almost canary-like song; phrasing varies, but typical phrase may be rendered 'jur-jerrig-jerriganee, a-pitta-pitta-pit'; from high points in territory, dead top of native pine, mulga or mallee; expert mimic. Song of female less rich.

Habitat: Inland scrubs, typically mulga and mallee-associations, eucalypt re-growth, tea-tree, saltbush, bluebush, spinifex.

Breeding: Nest: globular with side-entrance; of strips of bark, grass; in low shrub, spinifex or occasionally in low tree-hollow, lizard-burrow. Eggs: 3–4; purplish brown, darker at large end.

Range and Status: Inland Aust. to w. coastal WA: from near Winton, Q, s. to nw. Vic. and Murray mallee in SA w. to Lake Grace and Moora, WA, thence coastally n. to Pilbara and through s. NT (Macdonnell Ras.). Generally uncommon.

545 FIELDWREN *Calamanthus fuliginosus* Pl.71

Other names: Cock-tail, Desertwren, Fieldlark, Mock Quail, Reedlark, Rock, Rufous, Rusty or Streaked Fieldwren, Rush Warbler, Sandplain-Wren, Stinkbird.

Field marks: 125–140 mm. A lively small bird of open places that carries its tail cocked; note *bold blackish streakings above and below, prominent pale eyebrow*, often slightly orange before eye. Usually first noticed singing from top of low shrub, tussock, fence-post or wire, dives into cover when approached; often flushed by cars from roadside cover, when it shows *white-tipped dark-banded tail*. Formerly divided into four species now regarded as local colour variations of a single species that form a cline, i.e. gradually merge together. Most are streaked; the form in se. Aust., Bass Strait islands and Tas. is *greenish-grey above, yellow-white below*; sides of breast washed buff; the smaller sw. Australian form is *greyer* above, whiter below; inland forms are *rich rust-brown above, some without streaks; whitish below*. Note that eyes vary from light-brown or cream in se. Aust. to red-brown in inland races, and yellow on c. WA coast.

Similar species: Heathwren (542), and Mallee Heathwren (543). Grasswrens (522–9): *pale* streaks, longish tails without black bands; note specialized habitat. Little Grassbird (506): slimmer; darker rufous and grey-brown above; head and breast much less streaked; tail seldom cocked. Richard's Pipit (423): pale-brown, longer; lifts and lowers white-edged tail, does not cock it.

Voice: A spirited small voice in vastness of habitat; syllabized 'whirr-whirr-chick-chick-whirr-ree-ree', last note liquid; note singing positions (above).

Habitat: Open country with low cover; rank grass of swamp-fringes; alpine tussocks; wet heaths, dune-vegetation, saltmarsh. Inland: saltbush, roly-poly and similar cover typically in claypans; low sparse shrubs and other cover in gibber or rocky areas.

Breeding: Nest: domed, untidy with side-entrance; of grasses, plant-stems; on or near ground, usually hidden in or by a tussock, sedge, small shrub; occasionally on open ground; often found only by flushing bird. Eggs: 3–4; buff to light-chestnut or pale chocolate-brown, thickly freckled darker, spotted and blotched rufous and chestnut, more heavily at large end.

Range and Status: S. Aust. and Tas.: much of WA s. of Exmouth Gulf and Tropic (and coastal islands, e.g. Dirk Hartog and Dorre Is.) *except* sw. corner (Lancelin–Albany); e. throughout SA *except* perhaps extreme n. and ne. In Vic. and NSW there appears to be a broken distribution: the greenish or buffish coastal form is found through the s. half of Vic. and into se. NSW, n. to Sassafras Ra.; grey or reddish inland forms occur in nw. Vic. and w. NSW e. to about 80 km nw. of White Cliffs and possibly to s. of Broken Hill w. of the Darling. Common but patchy and local; sedentary.

546 SPECKLED WARBLER *Chthonicola sagittatus* Pl.71

Other names: Blood Tit, Chocolate-bird, Jenny Wren, Little Fieldlark or Fieldwren, Speckled Jack, Streaked Warbler.

Field marks: 115–125 mm. A creamish breasted small bird with bold black streaks. Note distinctive facial pattern: *blackish line over long whitish eyebrow and creamish area round large dark eye.* Female: chestnut streak in eyebrow. Pairs, small parties; associates with other small ground-feeding passerines, specially Buff-rumped Thornbill (563). Hops over ground, logs, lower trunks and branches. Not shy; but under observation near nest may freeze motionless for long periods.

Similar species: Heathwren (542): rump chestnut; cocks tail. Fieldwren (545), coastal form: greener; cocks tail; habitat more open.

Voice: Sweet little song, somewhat like White-tailed Warbler (552): often mimics; also deep rasping scolding.

Habitat: Open forests, woodlands and scrublands with sparse tussocks, stick debris, rocks.

Breeding: Nest: domed with hooded side-entrance; of grasses and bark-shreds or moss, often lined with fur, resembles surrounding debris; on ground among branches or near shrub or tree-trunk. Eggs: 3–4; rich-reddish chocolate, with shadowy zone at large end.

Range and Status: Se. Aust.: e. inland Q from inland of Mackay (Suttor Creek H.S.) s. to near Rockhampton, w. to Tambo–Charleville; e. NSW, w. to about Moree–Griffith, exceptionally w. to near Cobar; all Vic. *except* s. Gippsland, sw. coast and far nw.; (w. limits appear to be Otways–Grampians–Inglewood). Fairly common but local.

547 WEEBILL *Smicrornis brevirostris* Pl.72

Other names: Brown or Yellow Weebill, Short-billed Scrub Tit; Short-billed, Southern or Yellow Tree Tit.

Field marks: 80–90 mm. Diminutive: note *very short horn-coloured bill, pale creamy-buff eyebrow, whitish eye and streaked ear-coverts*; tail brownish with broad blackish band and pale tips. S. and e. races are tinged olive-green above, creamish buff below, slightly streaked darker on throat and upper breast. Inland and n. races paler and yellower above, *distinctly yellow below*, without steaks. One race, *flavescens*, formerly known as Yellow Weebill, at *c*. 80 mm, is the smallest Australian bird. Pairs, small parties or in feeding associations with other passerines. Active; flutters in and round foliage. Noisy for its size; usually heard before seen (but inland and n. birds seem quieter).

Similar species: Thornbills (556–67) have longer, sharper bills; spotted, scalloped or streaked crowns. Yellow Thornbill (566): richer yellow-buff throat, dark eye.

Voice: Robust for size of bird; a deep clear far-carrying 'weebill', 'weebit, weebee!' or 'willy-weet, willy-weetee!'; also a continual quick rather deep '*ti*did, *ti*did', like Yellow or Striated Thornbill (567).

Habitat: Foliage of trees and shrubs generally, from drier coastal forests and woodlands to sparse inland scrubs and vegetation along watercourses.

Breeding: Nest: like baby's woollen bootee with side-entrance; of plant-down, leaves, grass and spiders' web; slung among small branches or outer foliage, 1–5 m high. Eggs: 2–3; white to buff-white to grey-brown, very finely freckled brownish, mostly on large end.

Range and Status: Almost throughout mainland Aust., except dry treeless and wetter forest and agricultural areas, e.g. ne. coast from C. York to Rockhampton, Q, higher rainfall areas of Divide, s. coastal Vic. and far sw. WA. Generally common, often conspicuously so; ? nomadic.

FAIRY WARBLERS Genus *Gerygone*

A genus of small fine-billed birds of great charm; their songs distinguish them–sweet plaintive 'falling-leaf' melodies in the minor key. Unlike thornbills (556–67), they are usually seen singly or in pairs; their shape is distinctive, their patterns simple. Unlike thornbills, they do not have streaks, scallops or a differently coloured rump but are identified by general colour, eye-colour, facial and tail-patterns. Their most typical behaviour is to hover *outside* the foliage of trees and saplings, seeking leaf-insects; they take flying insects with an audible snap. They are largely replaced by thornbills in s. Aust. and often only one (if any) species is present in a given district. In much of coastal n. Aust. reverse is the case.

548 BROWN WARBLER *Gerygone mouki* Pl.72

Other names: Brown Bush Warbler, Citronbird, Northern Warbler.

Field marks: 95–110 mm. Rather like a thornbill in shape and actions; note warm olive-brown upperparts set off by *long grey-white eyebrow, plain pale-grey sides of face and breast; flanks washed buff*, abdomen creamish; eye red or red-brown. When fluttering round foliage, note tail markings: *broad blackish subterminal band, white spots near tips*. Pairs or parties; incessantly active and vocal; searches among, or flutters round foliage often to great heights; snaps flying insects. Note distinctive call.

Similar species: Mangrove Warbler (551). White-tailed Warbler (552): greyer above, whiter below; much more white in tail.

Voice: Differs markedly from typical call of other fairy warblers: brisk, cheerful and incessant 'which-is-it, which-is-it'; 'which-is-it-is-it', or 'diddle-it-did-dit', repeated; in quality like thornbill, scrubwren or insect.

Habitat: Rainforests, heavy vegetation along watercourses, occasionally mangroves.

Breeding: Nest: beautiful, domed, with hooded or spoutlike entrance and tapering tail; of rootlets, bark-fibre, bound with spiders' web, decorated with moss, lichens, usually suspended from twig or vine in dark situation. Eggs: 3; whitish, finely but heavily speckled red-brown, mostly at large end.

Range and Status: Coastal e. Aust. from e. Vic. (Mitchell R.) nearly to Cooktown, Q (Mt. Amos). The typical fairy warbler of e. coastal and mountain rainforests, ranging inland to Tweed and McPherson Ras.; Bunya Mts.; Eungella Mts.; Mt. Spec and Atherton Tableland; n. from Tully, found only above about 250 m. Uncommon to common; sedentary.

549 LARGE-BILLED WARBLER *Gerygone magnirostris* **Pl.72**
Other name: Floodbird.
Field marks: 105–115 m. Sandy-grey above, whitish below, breast washed fawn. Distinguished from other brown-plumaged fairy warblers *by absence of white eyebrow* (but small white spot above bill and fine white eyelids) and by tail-markings; *broad blackish sub-terminal band without white tips.* Note somewhat larger size, heavier bill; eye brown or red. Singly or pairs; feeds in and flutters round foliage from near ground to 25 m or more high.
Voice: A slight descending reel of 3 or 4 notes in the minor key, uttered continually; also described as long series of double notes, followed by succession of triple, slightly descending, liquid calls.
Habitat: Remnant patches of rainforest, usually near water; vegetation along streams and watercourses; paperbark-swamps, mangroves, eucalypt woodlands; plantations, gardens.
Breeding: Nest: domed, with hooded side-entrance and long ragged tail; of grasses, rootlets, leaves and plant-fibres bound with spiders' web; typically suspended from vine or bare branch over stream, waterhole or swamp; often near wasps' nest; sways in wind and often resembles flood-debris. Eggs: 2–3; whitish, lightly freckled red-brown, mostly at larger end.
Range and Status: Coastal n. Aust. and coastal islands: from Mackay, Q, to Kimberleys, WA. Common; sedentary. Also NG and islands.

550 DUSKY WARBLER *Gerygone tenebrosa* **Pl.72**
Field marks: 115 mm. The plainest brown-plumaged fairy warbler, and the only one with *pale (whitish or straw-coloured) eyes.* Note small buff-white mark on forehead; *whitish line from bill toward eye, fine white eyelids; no obvious marks on tail.* Habits like other warblers; often hard to follow in dense mangroves.
Similar species: Mangrove Warbler (551): distinct white eyebrow and white spots at tail-tips. White-tailed Warbler (552): note white base of tail, dark subterminal band, white spots at tail-tips.
Voice: Repeated descending trills somewhat like White-tailed; also hesitating little song, a slow rather thoughtful 'chew chew chew wee' or 'chif chif choowet', somewhat like whistler or silvereye.
Habitat: Dense mangroves, adjacent swampland and creekside scrub; vegetation in rocky gorges.
Breeding: Nest: domed; of bark-fibre bound with spiders' web; suspended from limb of mangrove. Eggs: 2; white, spotted red-brown mostly at large end.
Range and Status: Coastal mangroves and nearby vegetation from coastal w. Kimberleys, to Carnarvon, WA. Probably common.

551 MANGROVE WARBLER *Gerygone levigaster* **Pl.72**
Other names: Buff-breasted Warbler, Queensland Canary.
Field marks: 110 mm. Over its long coastal range distinguished from other brownish fairy warblers except Brown Warbler (548) by *distinct white line from bill over reddish eye and blackish lower half of tail with large white spot near tip of each outer tail-feather.* Bill longer and more robust than Brown Warbler; underparts whiter. Imm: no white eyebrow, yellowish eyelids, yellowish wash on throat, slight striations on upperbreast. Singly, pairs, family parties. Perhaps flutters outside foliage less than other fairy warblers, feeding more *among* leaves.
Similar species: Brown Warbler (548): *voice differs markedly;* darker olive-brown above, buffer below; bill shorter; note habits and habitat. White-tailed Warbler (552): note range.

Voice: Typical fairy warbler song: rich sweet fugitive 'falling-leaf' call in minor key; somewhat like White-throated Warbler (555).

Habitat: Mainly mangroves; adjacent coastal woodlands, gardens.

Breeding: Nest: globular, with hooded side-entrance and wispy tail; of dry grasses, bark fibre, occasionally strands of seaweed, bound with spiders' web, usually in outer branches of mangrove from just over water-level to 5 m high, over water or in open woodland near water. Eggs: 3; pinkish white, freckled red-brown, mostly at large end.

Range and Status: Coastal n. and e. Aust. from Derby, WA, to near Newcastle, NSW, (Kooragang I.). Generally common; sedentary.

552　WHITE-TAILED WARBLER　*Gerygone fusca*　　　　　Pl 72

Other names: Inland or Western Warbler; Sleepy Dick.

Field marks: 100 mm. A brownish grey warbler with inconspicuous white eyebrow, red eye, *whitish underparts and much white at base and near tips of tail*, leaving broad blackish subterminal band. Imm: more olive above, *with yellowish wash on throat and underparts*. Singly or pairs, habits like White-throated Warbler (555), of which it is the inland and w. counterpart. It is the common (and only) fairy warbler round Perth.

Similar species: Brown Warbler (548): rounder and darker, no white at base of tail; calls, habits and habitat wholly different. Dusky (550) and Mangrove (551) Warblers: note range and habitat. Jacky Winter (454): plumper, larger, bill broader; *edges* of tail white, wags from side to side.

Habitat: Varied: foliage of trees from coastal open forests and woodlands to sparse scrubs.

Voice: One of the sweetest and most oft-repeated but elfin and elusive Australian bird songs: a falling silvery thread of sound that seems to finish before the end. A frequently-heard bush-sound near Perth, WA.

Breeding: Nest: oval, with hooded side-entrance and a long wispy tail; of fine grass and bark-fibre bound with spiders' web; usually suspended among foliage up to 10 m high. Eggs: 2–3; pink-white, blotched and speckled red-brown, mostly at large end.

Range and Status: An apparently broken distribution in w., c. and e. Aust.: (1) coastal and sub-coastal WA, from e. of Albany n. to the Pilbara region. (2) Inland n. and c. Aust., s. to Everard Ras., SA, and w. to Gibson Desert, WA. (3) Inland e. Aust. from Normanton, Q, to nw. Vic. and the You Yangs, w. of Melbourne; mostly w. of Divide, but breeding e. to the coast in parts from Rockhampton to Sydney, thence s. to Kosciusko NP and ne. Vic., (Mt. Beauty–Warby Ras.). Breeding also recorded patchily Eyre Pen. and elsewhere s. SA. Apparently migratory in se. Aust. but details unknown. Common in s. WA, sparse and uncommon elsewhere. Also s. NG.

553　GREEN-BACKED WARBLER　*Gerygone chloronota*　　　　Pl.72

Field marks: 100 mm. The greenest fairy warbler: *olive-green above, duller or bluer-green on head*; *whitish below*, washed buff-grey on sides of upperbreast; tail blackish brown, outer feathers with slight subterminal blackish band; *eye red*. Singly or in pairs, rather shy; actions like other fairy warblers; hovers round foliage.

Similar species: White-throated Warbler (555): yellow breast. Lemon-breasted Fly-catcher (452): bill shorter and broader, yellower below; habits more aerial; song differs.

Voice: A slighter version of other warbler-songs.

Habitat: Dense vegetation especially near water, monsoon and heavy mixed forests, bamboo-thickets, paperbark-swamps, mangroves, and adjacent eucalypt forest; Darwin gardens.

Breeding: Nest: domed, with side-entrance; typically suspended from a mangrove. Eggs: 2–3; whitish with fine red-brown freckles.

Range and Status: Kimberleys, WA, and top end NT, including Melville I. and Groote Eylandt. Mostly coastal. Common. Also NG and Aru Is.

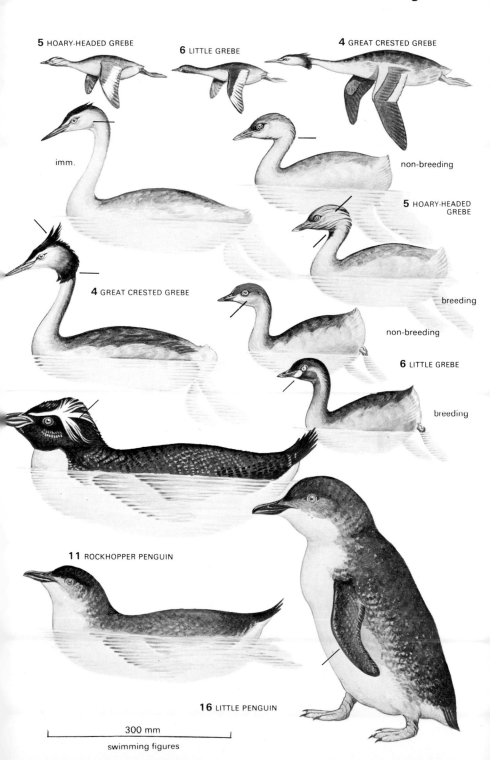

5 HOARY-HEADED GREBE

6 LITTLE GREBE

4 GREAT CRESTED GREBE

imm.

non-breeding

5 HOARY-HEADED GREBE

4 GREAT CRESTED GREBE

breeding

non-breeding

6 LITTLE GREBE

breeding

11 ROCKHOPPER PENGUIN

16 LITTLE PENGUIN

300 mm

swimming figures

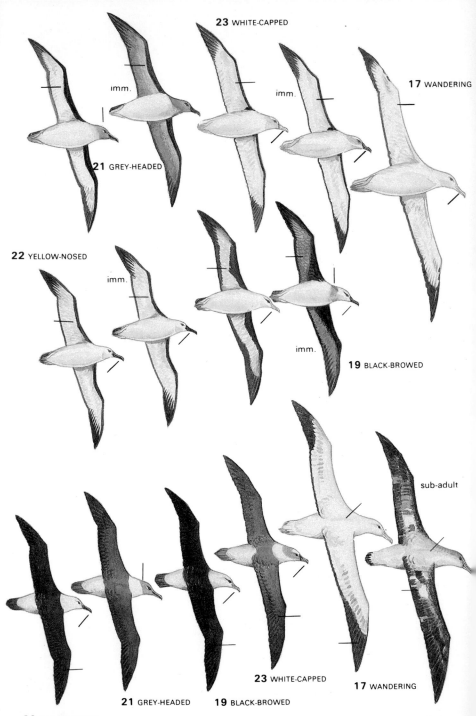

23 WHITE-CAPPED

17 WANDERING

imm.

imm.

21 GREY-HEADED

22 YELLOW-NOSED

imm.

imm.

19 BLACK-BROWED

sub-adult

23 WHITE-CAPPED

17 WANDERING

21 GREY-HEADED

19 BLACK-BROWED

22 YELLOW-NOSED

300 mm

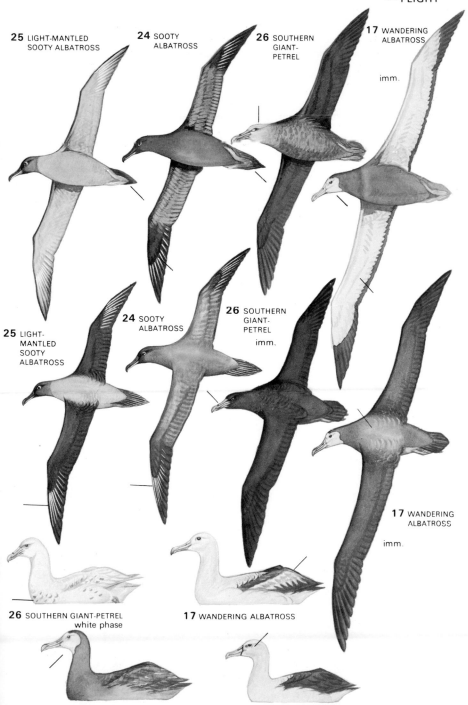

25 LIGHT-MANTLED SOOTY ALBATROSS

24 SOOTY ALBATROSS

26 SOUTHERN GIANT-PETREL

17 WANDERING ALBATROSS

imm.

25 LIGHT-MANTLED SOOTY ALBATROSS

24 SOOTY ALBATROSS

26 SOUTHERN GIANT-PETREL imm.

17 WANDERING ALBATROSS

imm.

26 SOUTHERN GIANT-PETREL white phase

17 WANDERING ALBATROSS

17 WANDERING ALBATROSS imm.

23 WHITE-CAPPED ALBATROSS

300 mm
flight figures

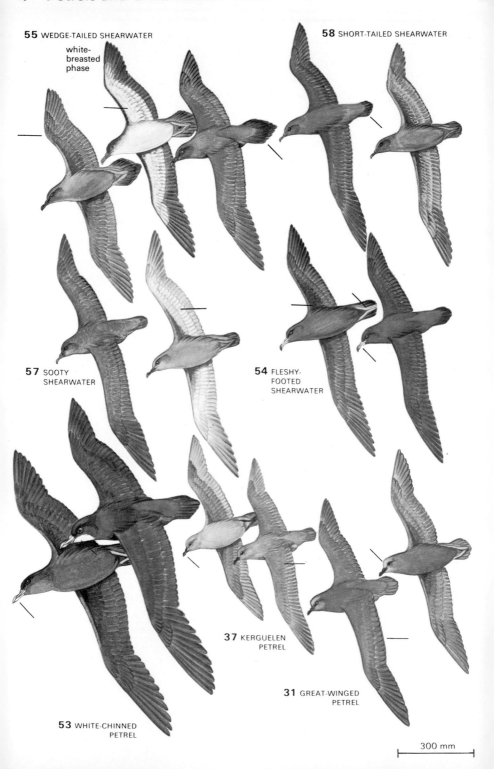

55 WEDGE-TAILED SHEARWATER

white-breasted phase

58 SHORT-TAILED SHEARWATER

57 SOOTY SHEARWATER

54 FLESHY-FOOTED SHEARWATER

37 KERGUELEN PETREL

31 GREAT-WINGED PETREL

53 WHITE-CHINNED PETREL

300 mm

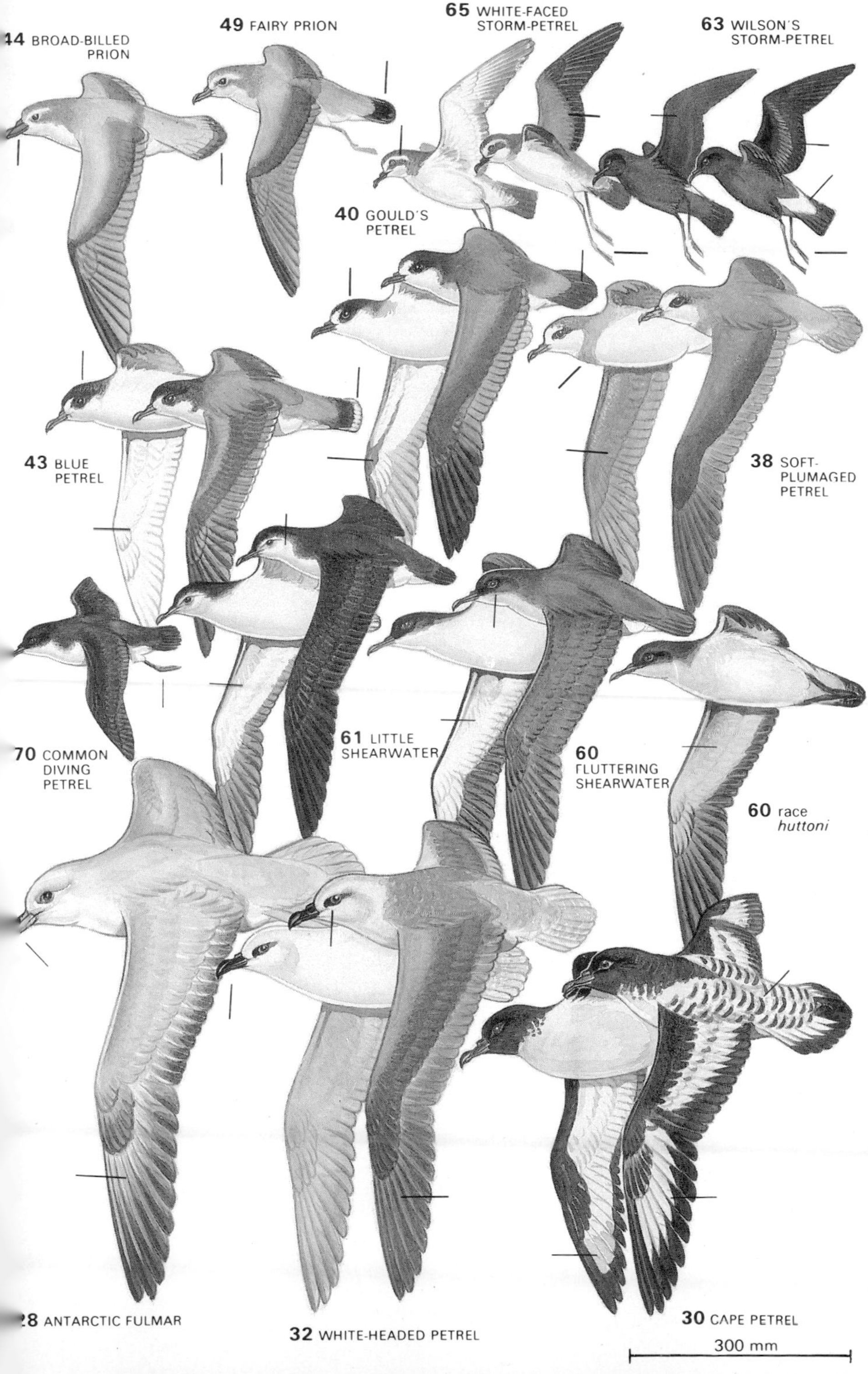

44 BROAD-BILLED PRION

49 FAIRY PRION

65 WHITE-FACED STORM-PETREL

63 WILSON'S STORM-PETREL

40 GOULD'S PETREL

43 BLUE PETREL

38 SOFT-PLUMAGED PETREL

70 COMMON DIVING PETREL

61 LITTLE SHEARWATER

60 FLUTTERING SHEARWATER

60 race huttoni

28 ANTARCTIC FULMAR

32 WHITE-HEADED PETREL

30 CAPE PETREL

300 mm

imm.

imm.

76 BROWN BOOBY

75 MASKED BOOBY

adult

imm.

sub-adult

73 AUSTRALIAN GANNET

imm.

dark phase

white phase

300 mm

74 RED-FOOTED BOOBY

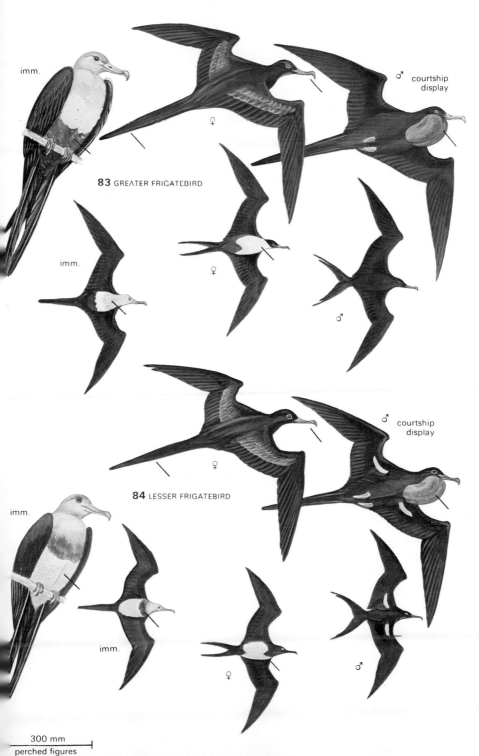

imm.

♀

♂ courtship display

83 GREATER FRIGATEBIRD

imm.

♀

♂

♀ courtship display

84 LESSER FRIGATEBIRD

imm.

imm.

♀

♂

300 mm
perched figures

77 DARTER

81 BLACK CORMORANT

82 LITTLE BLACK CORMORANT

78 BLACK-FACED CORMORANT

79 PIED CORMORANT

80 LITTLE PIED CORMORANT

82 LITTLE BLACK CORMORANT

78 BLACK-FACED CORMORANT

77 DARTER

81 BLACK CORMORANT breeding

imm.

imm.

imm.

81 BLACK CORMORANT

79 PIED CORMORANT

80 LITTLE PIED CORMORANT

breeding

77 DARTER

♂

♀

300 mm

perched figures

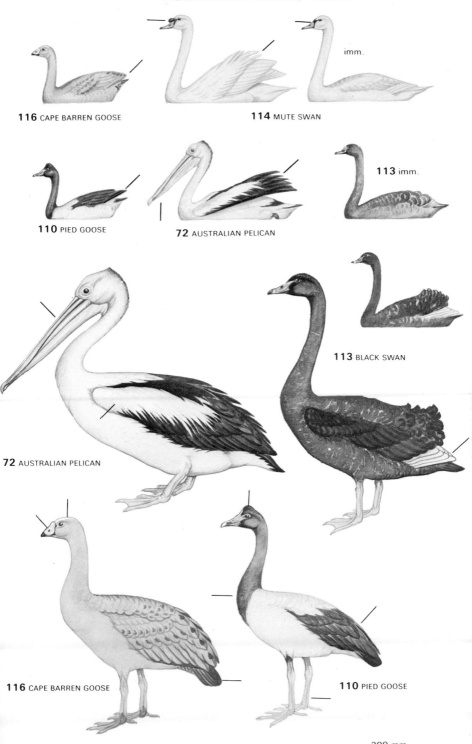

116 CAPE BARREN GOOSE

114 MUTE SWAN

imm.

110 PIED GOOSE

72 AUSTRALIAN PELICAN

113 imm.

113 BLACK SWAN

72 AUSTRALIAN PELICAN

116 CAPE BARREN GOOSE

110 PIED GOOSE

300 mm
standing figures

10 Australian Pelican, Geese, Swans and Black-necked Stork —FLIGHT

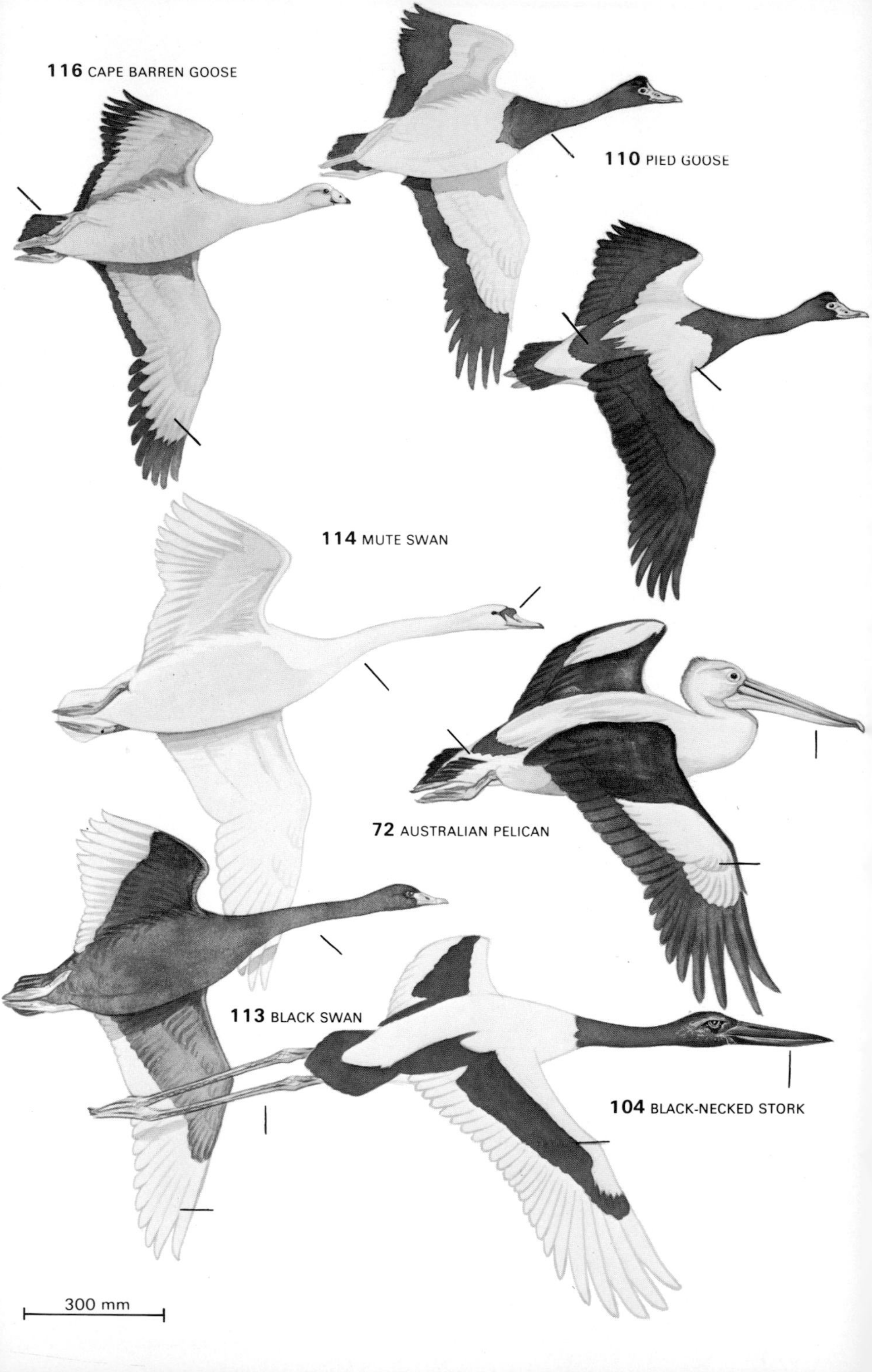
116 CAPE BARREN GOOSE
110 PIED GOOSE
114 MUTE SWAN
72 AUSTRALIAN PELICAN
113 BLACK SWAN
104 BLACK-NECKED STORK
300 mm

120 MALLARD

127 WHITE-EYED DUCK

122 CHESTNUT TEAL

115 FRECKLED DUCK

126 PINK-EARED DUCK

19 BLACK DUCK

121 GREY TEAL

123 SOUTHERN SHOVELLER

17 CHESTNUT-BREASTED SHELDUCK

128 AUSTRALIAN WOOD DUCK

112 PLUMED WHISTLING DUCK

118 WHITE-HEADED SHELDUCK

111 DIVING WHISTLING DUCK

125 GARGANEY

129 WHITE PYGMY GOOSE

130 GREEN PYGMY GOOSE

300 mm

120 MALLARD ♂ ♀

127 WHITE-EYED DUCK ♂ ♀

122 CHESTNUT TEAL ♂ ♀

115 FRECKLED DUCK

126 PINK-EARED DUCK

119 BLACK DUCK

121 GREY TEAL

117 CHESTNUT-BREASTED SHELDUCK ♂ ♀

123 SOUTHERN SHOVELLER ♂ ♀

128 AUSTRALIAN WOOD DUCK ♂ ♀

118 WHITE-HEADED SHELDUCK

112 PLUMED WHISTLING DUCK

111 DIVING WHISTLING DUCK

125 GARGANEY ♀ ♂

129 WHITE PYGMY GOOSE ♂ ♀

130 GREEN PYGMY GOOSE ♂ ♀

300 mm

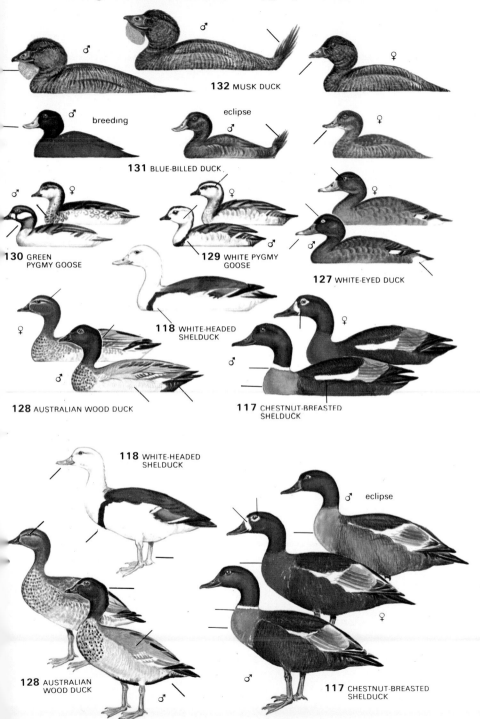

132 MUSK DUCK

breeding eclipse

131 BLUE-BILLED DUCK

130 GREEN PYGMY GOOSE

129 WHITE PYGMY GOOSE

127 WHITE-EYED DUCK

118 WHITE-HEADED SHELDUCK

128 AUSTRALIAN WOOD DUCK

117 CHESTNUT-BREASTED SHELDUCK

118 WHITE-HEADED SHELDUCK

eclipse

128 AUSTRALIAN WOOD DUCK

117 CHESTNUT-BREASTED SHELDUCK

300 mm

♂ breeding

♂ eclipse

♂ eclipse

♀

125 GARGANEY ♀

122 CHESTNUT TEAL

♂ breeding

121 GREY TEAL

123 SOUTHERN SHOVELLER

126 PINK-EARED DUCK

♂ eclipse

♀

♂ breeding

♂ non-breeding

♂ eclipse

120 MALLARD

♂ breeding

♀

♀

115 FRECKLED DUCK

♂ breeding

119 BLACK DUCK

112 PLUMED WHISTLING DUCK

111 DIVING WHISTLING DUCK

111 DIVING WHISTLING DUCK

112 PLUMED WHISTLING DUCK

300 mm
swimming figures

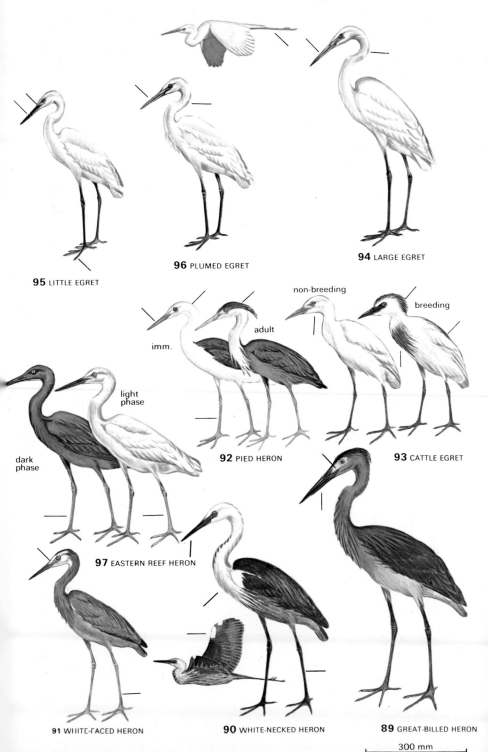

96 PLUMED EGRET

94 LARGE EGRET

95 LITTLE EGRET

imm.

adult

non-breeding

breeding

light
phase

dark
phase

92 PIED HERON

93 CATTLE EGRET

97 EASTERN REEF HERON

91 WHITE-FACED HERON

90 WHITE-NECKED HERON

89 GREAT-BILLED HERON

300 mm

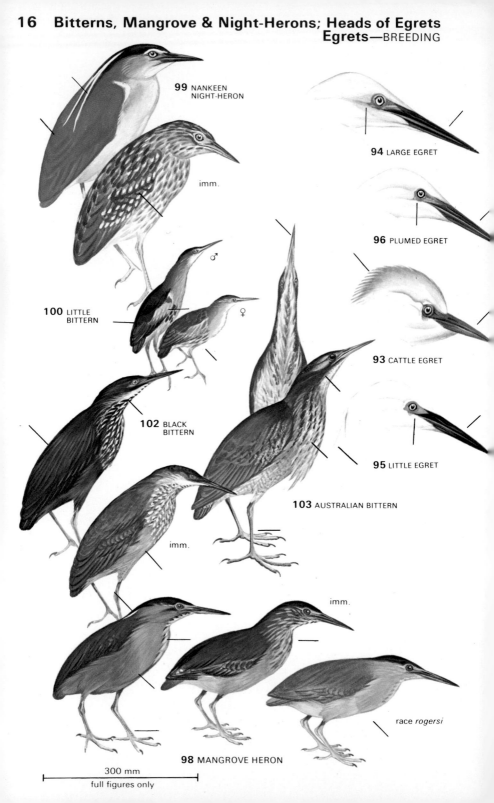

99 NANKEEN NIGHT-HERON

imm.

94 LARGE EGRET

96 PLUMED EGRET

100 LITTLE BITTERN

♂

♀

93 CATTLE EGRET

102 BLACK BITTERN

95 LITTLE EGRET

103 AUSTRALIAN BITTERN

imm.

imm.

race *rogersi*

98 MANGROVE HERON

300 mm

full figures only

159 BRUSH-TURKEY

158 MALLEEFOWL

157 SCRUBFOWL

breeding

non-breeding

375 PHEASANT COUCAL

♂ ♀

165 RING-NECKED PHEASANT

412 ALBERT'S LYREBIRD

♂ ♀

♂ ♀

413 SUPERB LYREBIRD

300 mm

147 WEDGE-TAILED EAGLE

imm.

148 LITTLE EAGLE

dark phase

imm. pale phase

pale phase

139 BLACK-BREASTED KITE

pale phase

150 SWAMP HARRIER

imm.

133 OSPREY

149 SPOTTED HARRIER

imm.

imm.

146 WHITE-BREASTED SEA-EAGLE

300 mm

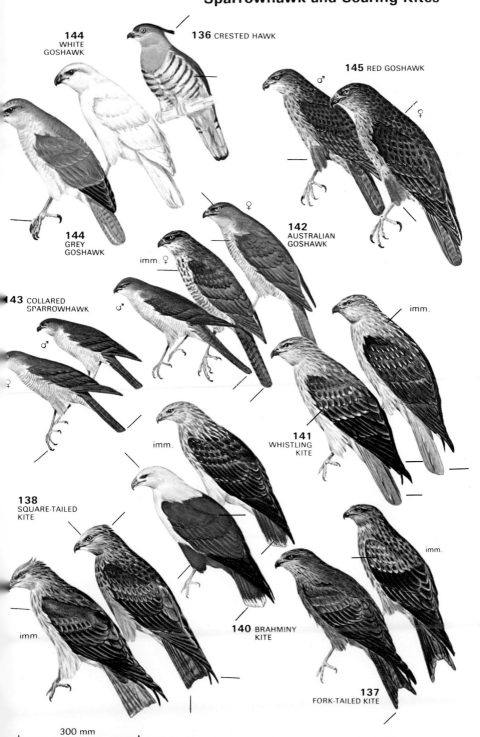

144 WHITE GOSHAWK

136 CRESTED HAWK

145 RED GOSHAWK ♂ ♀

144 GREY GOSHAWK

142 AUSTRALIAN GOSHAWK ♀

imm. ♀

143 COLLARED SPARROWHAWK ♂ ♀

♂

imm.

141 WHISTLING KITE

imm.

138 SQUARE-TAILED KITE

imm.

140 BRAHMINY KITE

imm.

137 FORK-TAILED KITE

300 mm

135 LETTER-WINGED KITE

imm.

134 AUSTRALIAN BLACK-SHOULDERED KITE

imm.

156 NANKEEN KESTREL

♀

♂

imm.

153 LITTLE FALCON

imm.

imm.

152 PEREGRINE FALCON

154 GREY FALCON

dark phase

imm.

155 BROWN FALCON

pale phase

151 BLACK FALCON

300 mm

135 LETTER-WINGED KITE

134 AUSTRALIAN BLACK-SHOULDERED KITE

134 AUSTRALIAN BLACK-SHOULDERED KITE

156 NANKEEN KESTREL

imm.

adult

150 SWAMP HARRIER

imm.

adult

adult

imm.

adult

149 SPOTTED HARRIER

imm.

300 mm

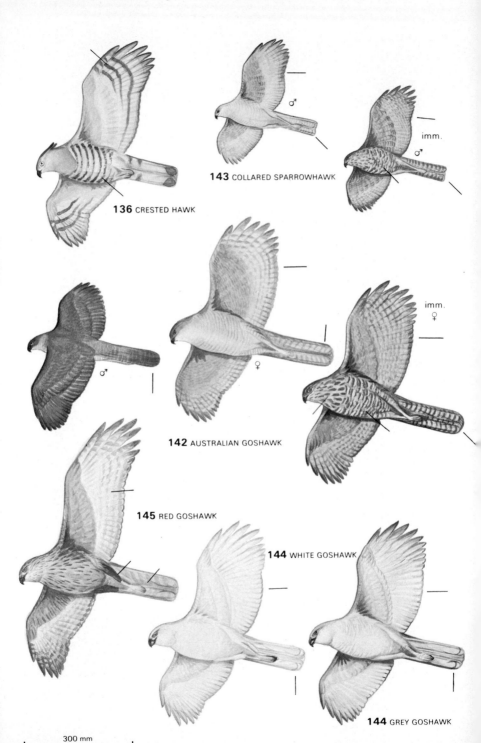

136 CRESTED HAWK

143 COLLARED SPARROWHAWK

♂

imm.

♂

142 AUSTRALIAN GOSHAWK

♂

♀

imm.

♀

145 RED GOSHAWK

144 WHITE GOSHAWK

144 GREY GOSHAWK

300 mm

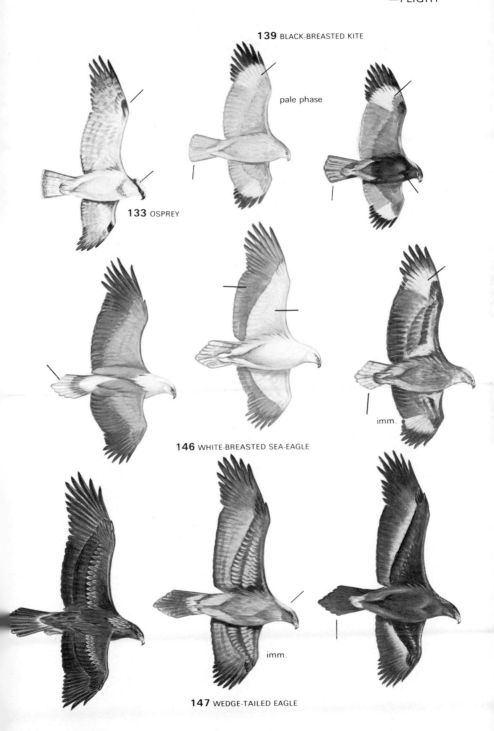

139 BLACK-BREASTED KITE

pale phase

133 OSPREY

146 WHITE-BREASTED SEA-EAGLE

imm.

imm.

147 WEDGE-TAILED EAGLE

300 mm

dark phase

pale phase

148 LITTLE EAGLE

138
SQUARE-TAILED
KITE

imm.

140 BRAHMINY KITE

141 WHISTLING KITE

imm.

137 FORK-TAILED KITE

300 mm

155 BROWN FALCON

dark phase

156 NANKEEN KESTREL

♂

♀

51 BLACK FALCON

imm.

153 LITTLE FALCON

imm.

154 GREY FALCON

imm.

imm.

152 PEREGRINE FALCON

300 mm

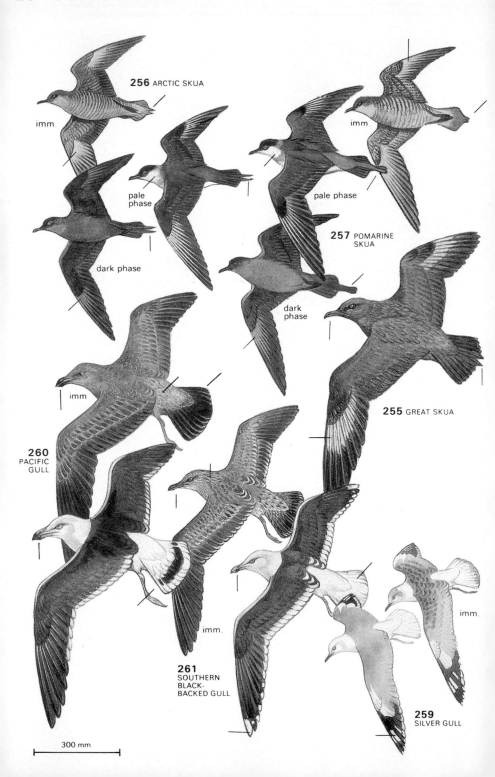

256 ARCTIC SKUA

imm.

pale phase

dark phase

imm.

pale phase

257 POMARINE SKUA

dark phase

255 GREAT SKUA

imm

260 PACIFIC GULL

imm.

261 SOUTHERN BLACK-BACKED GULL

imm.

259 SILVER GULL

300 mm

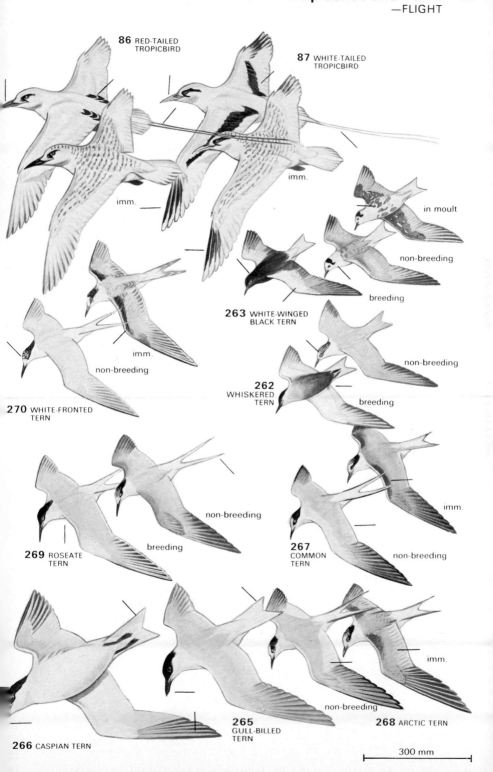

86 RED-TAILED TROPICBIRD

87 WHITE-TAILED TROPICBIRD

imm.

imm.

in moult

non-breeding

breeding

263 WHITE-WINGED BLACK TERN

imm.

non-breeding

270 WHITE-FRONTED TERN

non-breeding

262 WHISKERED TERN

breeding

non-breeding

imm.

269 ROSEATE TERN

breeding

267 COMMON TERN

non-breeding

imm.

non-breeding

268 ARCTIC TERN

266 CASPIAN TERN

265 GULL-BILLED TERN

300 mm

272 SOOTY TERN

imm.

imm.

273 BRIDLED TERN

277 LESSER CRESTED TERN

breeding

breeding   imm.

276 CRESTED TERN

breeding

275 FAIRY TERN

imm.

274

271 BLACK-NAPED TERN

imm.

breeding

274 LITTLE TERN

279 LESSER NODDY

278 COMMON NODDY

280 BLACK NODDY

300 mm

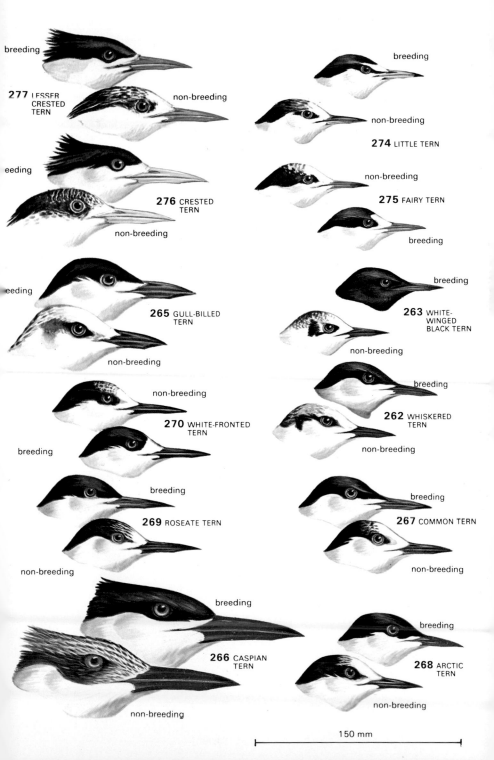

breeding

277 LESSER CRESTED TERN

non-breeding

breeding

non-breeding

274 LITTLE TERN

eeding

276 CRESTED TERN

non-breeding

non-breeding

275 FAIRY TERN

breeding

eeding

265 GULL-BILLED TERN

non-breeding

breeding

263 WHITE-WINGED BLACK TERN

non-breeding

non-breeding

270 WHITE-FRONTED TERN

breeding

breeding

262 WHISKERED TERN

non-breeding

breeding

breeding

269 ROSEATE TERN

breeding

267 COMMON TERN

non-breeding

non-breeding

breeding

breeding

266 CASPIAN TERN

268 ARCTIC TERN

non-breeding

non-breeding

150 mm

167 RED-BACKED BUTTON-QUAIL

168 PAINTED BUTTON-QUAIL

169 CHESTNUT-BACKED BUTTON-QUAIL

170 BLACK-BREASTED BUTTON-QUAIL

172 RED-CHESTED BUTTON-QUAIL

160 STUBBLE QUAIL

161 BROWN QUAIL

173 PLAINS-WANDERER

162 KING QUAIL

171 LITTLE BUTTON-QUAIL

150 mm

Crakes, Rails, Native-hens, Waterhens and Lotusbird

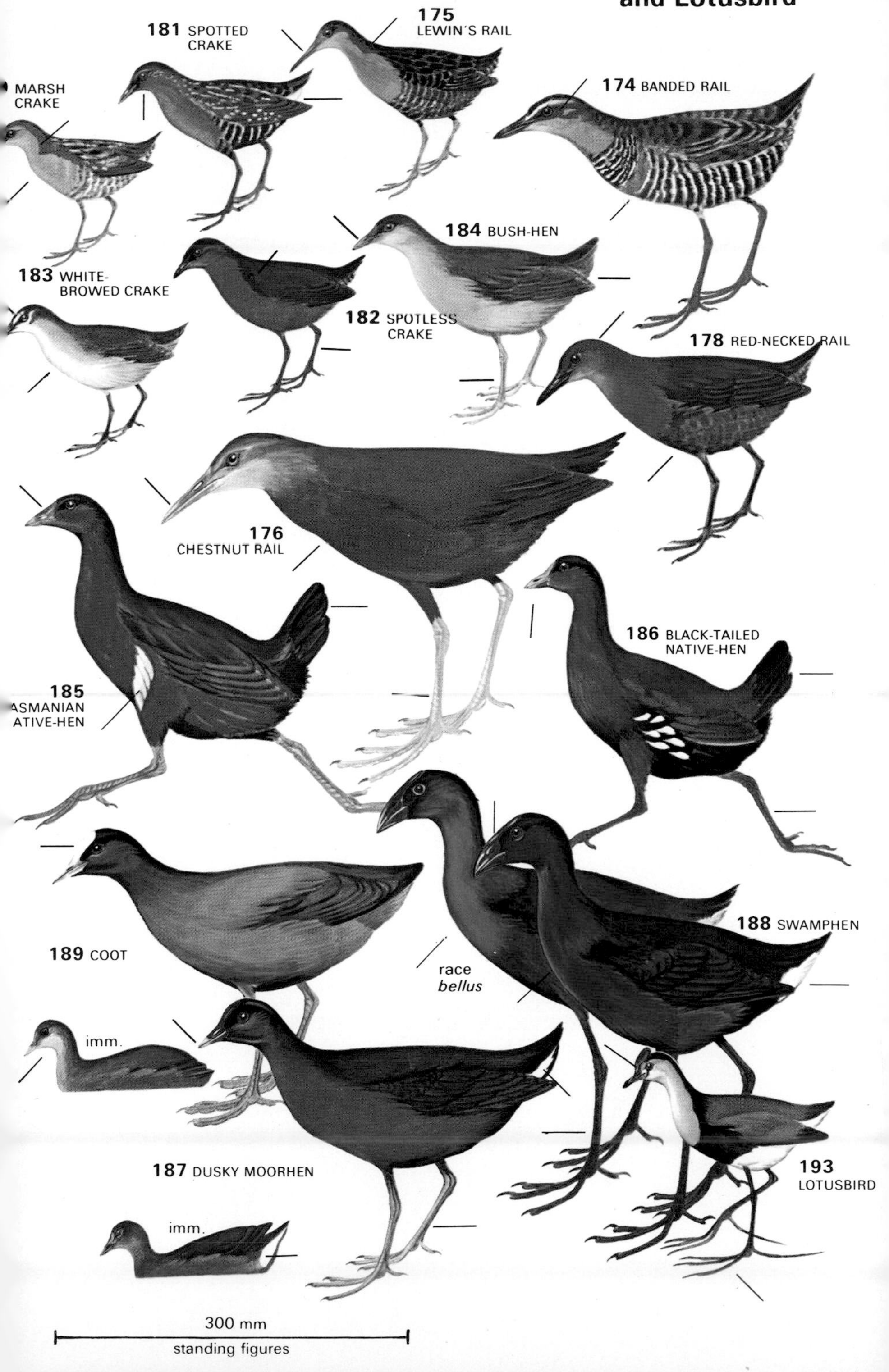
181 SPOTTED CRAKE
175 LEWIN'S RAIL
MARSH CRAKE
174 BANDED RAIL
184 BUSH-HEN
183 WHITE-BROWED CRAKE
182 SPOTLESS CRAKE
178 RED-NECKED RAIL
176 CHESTNUT RAIL
185 ASMANIAN ATIVE-HEN
186 BLACK-TAILED NATIVE-HEN
188 SWAMPHEN
189 COOT
race *bellus*
imm.
193 LOTUSBIRD
187 DUSKY MOORHEN
imm.
300 mm
standing figures

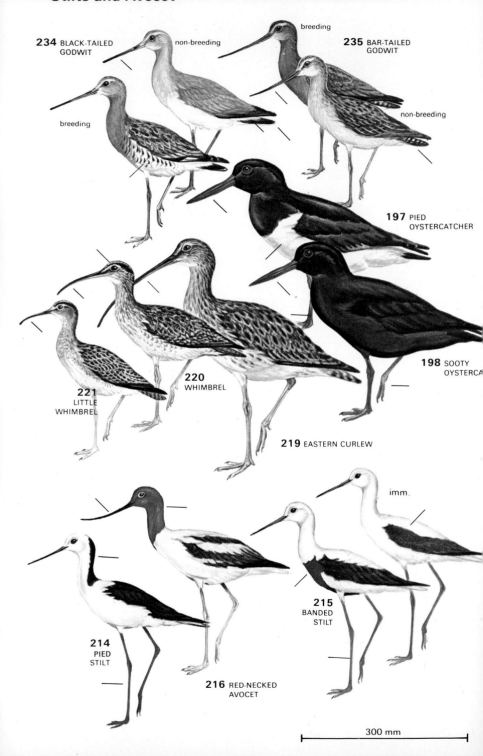

234 BLACK-TAILED GODWIT

non-breeding

breeding

breeding

235 BAR-TAILED GODWIT

non-breeding

197 PIED OYSTERCATCHER

221 LITTLE WHIMBREL

220 WHIMBREL

198 SOOTY OYSTERCA

219 EASTERN CURLEW

imm.

215 BANDED STILT

214 PIED STILT

216 RED-NECKED AVOCET

300 mm

196 PAINTED SNIPE

♀

♂

231 JAPANESE SNIPE

breeding

223 WOOD SANDPIPER

non-breeding

226 COMMON SANDPIPER

229 MARSH SANDPIPER

230 TEREK SANDPIPER

breeding

224 GREY-TAILED TATTLER

breeding

225 WANDERING TATTLER

224 GREY-TAILED TATTLER

non-breeding

breeding

non-breeding

27 GREENSHANK

non-breeding

150 mm

242 RED-NECKED STINT
breeding
non-breeding

243 LONG-TOED STINT
breeding
non-breeding

imm

adult non-breeding

248 BROAD-BILLED SANDPIPER
breeding
non-breeding

238 SHARP-TAILED SANDPIPER
non-breeding

imm.

adult non-breeding

239 PECTORAL SANDPIPER

237 GREAT KNOT
breeding
non-breeding

236 KNOT
breeding
non-breeding

244 CURLEW SANDPIPER
breeding
non-breeding

246 SANDERLING
breeding
non-breeding

non-breeding

249 REEVE ♀

249 RUFF ♂
breeding
non-breeding

150 mm

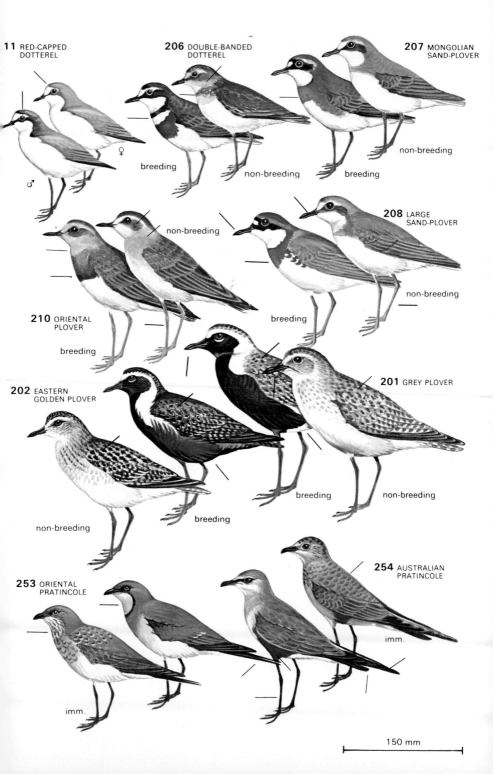

11 RED-CAPPED DOTTEREL

♀

♂

206 DOUBLE-BANDED DOTTEREL

breeding

non-breeding

207 MONGOLIAN SAND-PLOVER

non-breeding

breeding

non-breeding

208 LARGE SAND-PLOVER

breeding

non-breeding

210 ORIENTAL PLOVER

breeding

202 EASTERN GOLDEN PLOVER

non-breeding

breeding

201 GREY PLOVER

breeding

non-breeding

253 ORIENTAL PRATINCOLE

imm.

254 AUSTRALIAN PRATINCOLE

imm.

150 mm

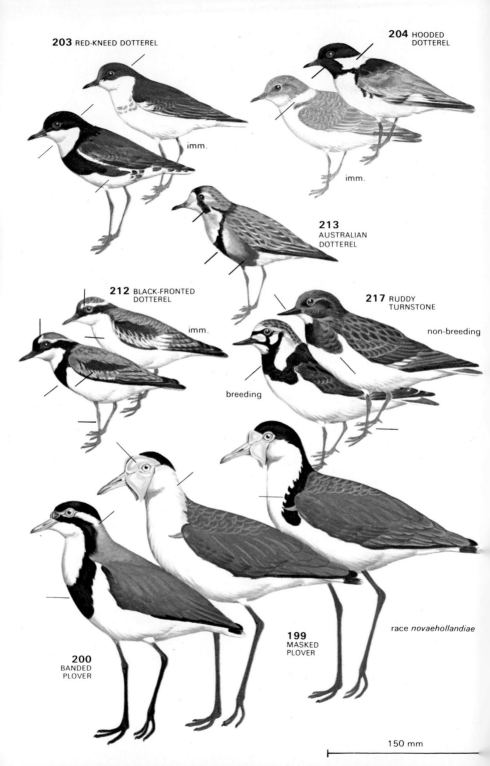

203 RED-KNEED DOTTEREL

imm.

204 HOODED DOTTEREL

imm.

213
AUSTRALIAN
DOTTEREL

212 BLACK-FRONTED
DOTTEREL

imm.

217 RUDDY
TURNSTONE

non-breeding

breeding

200
BANDED
PLOVER

199
MASKED
PLOVER

race *novaehollandiae*

150 mm

imm.

adult

imm.

imm.

214 PIED
STILT

adult

215
BANDED
STILT

216 RED
NECKED
AVOCET

adult

219
EASTERN
CURLEW

198
SOOTY
OYSTER-
CATCHER

197
PIED
OYSTER-
CATCHER

220
WHIMBREL

235
BAR-TAILED
GODWIT

221
LITTLE
WHIMBREL

breeding

non-breeding

234
BLACK-TAILED
GODWIT

non-breeding

breeding

300 mm

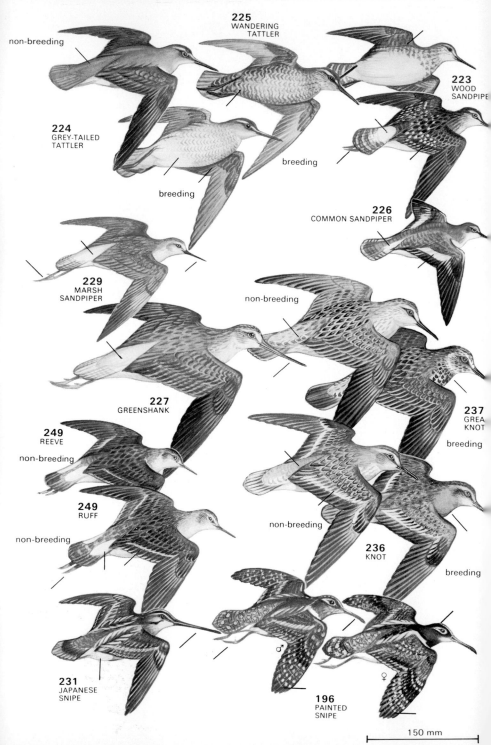

225
WANDERING TATTLER

non-breeding

223
WOOD SANDPIPE

224
GREY-TAILED TATTLER

breeding

breeding

226
COMMON SANDPIPER

229
MARSH SANDPIPER

non-breeding

227
GREENSHANK

237
GREA
KNOT

breeding

249
REEVE

non-breeding

249
RUFF

non-breeding

non-breeding

236
KNOT

breeding

231
JAPANESE SNIPE

♂

♀

196
PAINTED SNIPE

150 mm

248
BROAD-BILLED
SANDPIPER

breeding

242
RED-NECKED
STINT

n-breeding

238
SHARP-TAILED
SANDPIPER

breeding

244
CURLEW-
ANDPIPER

n-breeding

239
PECTORAL
SANDPIPER

breeding

246 SANDERLING

n-breeding

230
TEREK
SANDPIPER

150 mm

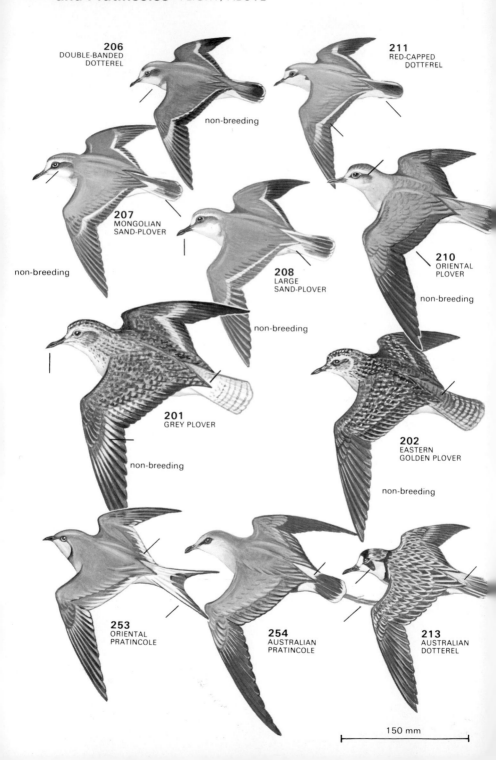

206
DOUBLE-BANDED
DOTTEREL

non-breeding

211
RED-CAPPED
DOTTEREL

207
MONGOLIAN
SAND-PLOVER

non-breeding

208
LARGE
SAND-PLOVER

non-breeding

210
ORIENTAL
PLOVER

non-breeding

201
GREY PLOVER

non-breeding

202
EASTERN
GOLDEN PLOVER

non-breeding

253
ORIENTAL
PRATINCOLE

254
AUSTRALIAN
PRATINCOLE

213
AUSTRALIAN
DOTTEREL

150 mm

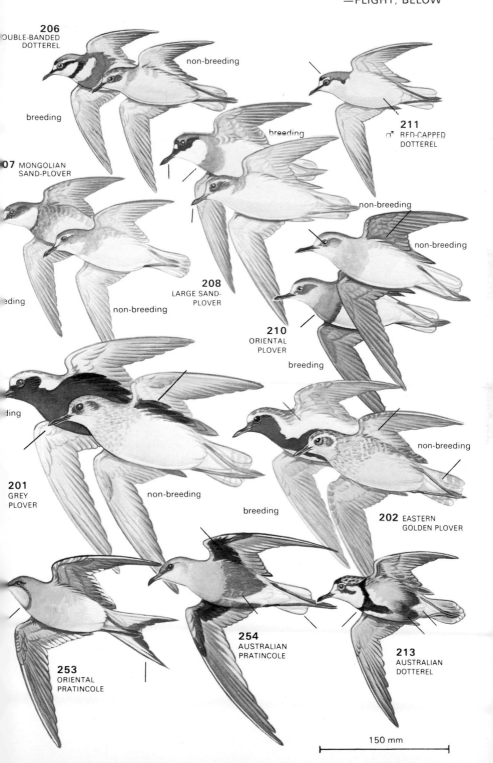

206
OUBLE-BANDED
DOTTEREL

non-breeding

breeding

211
♂ RED-CAPPED
DOTTEREL

breeding

07 MONGOLIAN
SAND-PLOVER

non-breeding

eding

non-breeding

non-breeding

208
LARGE SAND-
PLOVER

non-breeding

210
ORIENTAL
PLOVER

breeding

ding

201
GREY
PLOVER

non-breeding

non-breeding

breeding

202 EASTERN
GOLDEN PLOVER

254
AUSTRALIAN
PRATINCOLE

213
AUSTRALIAN
DOTTEREL

253
ORIENTAL
PRATINCOLE

150 mm

203
RED-KNEED
DOTTEREL

imm.

imm.

204 HOODED
DOTTEREL

212
BLACK-
FRONTED
DOTTEREL

imm.

breeding

non-breeding

217
RUDDY
TURNSTONE

race
novaehollandiae

non-breed

199
MASKED
PLOVER

200
BANDED
PLOVER

150 mm

106
WHITE
IBIS

107 STRAW-NECKED
IBIS

imm.

adult

105 GLOSSY IBIS

breeding

non-breeding

108 ROYAL
SPOONBILL

109
YELLOW-
BILLED
SPOONBILL

300 mm

standing figures

191 SARUS CRANE

190 BROLGA

192 AUSTRALIAN BUSTARD

194 BUSH STONE-CURLEW

195 BEACH STONE-CURLEW

104 BLACK-NECKED STORK

191 SARUS CRANE

190 BROLGA

300 mm
standing figures

285 RED-CROWNED PIGEON

284 PURPLE-CROWNED PIGEON

286 WOMPOO PIGEON

289 WHITE-HEADED PIGEON

287 TORRES STRAIT PIGEON

♂

♀

288 TOPKNOT PIGEON

283 BLACK-BANDED PIGEON

293 BROWN PIGEON

297 GREEN-WINGED PIGEON

295 DIAMOND DOVE

294 PEACEFUL DOVE

292 LAUGHING DOVE

296 BAR-SHOULDERED DOVE

291 SPOTTED TURTLE-DOVE

150 mm

303 PARTRIDGE PIGEON

300 FLOCK PIGEON

♂ ♀

302 SQUATTER PIGEON

306 SPINIFEX PIGEON

race *ferruginea*

299 BRUSH BRONZEWING

♂ ♀

304 WHITE-QUILLED ROCK-PIGEON

298 COMMON BRONZEWING

305 CHESTNUT QUILLED ROCK PIGEON

♂ ♀

301 CRESTED PIGEON

290 common variations

307 WONGA PIGEON

290 DOMESTIC PIGEON

150 mm

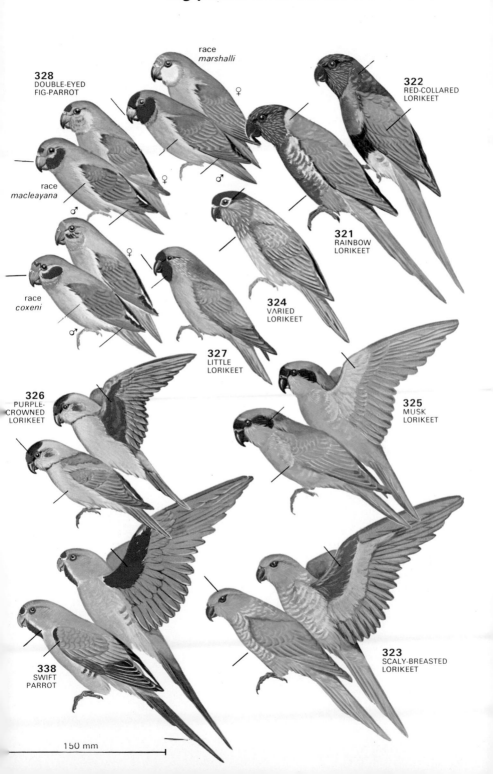

328
DOUBLE-EYED
FIG-PARROT

race
marshalli
♀

race
macleayana
♂
♀

♀
♂

race
coxeni
♂

322
RED-COLLARED
LORIKEET

321
RAINBOW
LORIKEET

324
VARIED
LORIKEET

327
LITTLE
LORIKEET

326
PURPLE-
CROWNED
LORIKEET

325
MUSK
LORIKEET

323
SCALY-BREASTED
LORIKEET

338
SWIFT
PARROT

150 mm

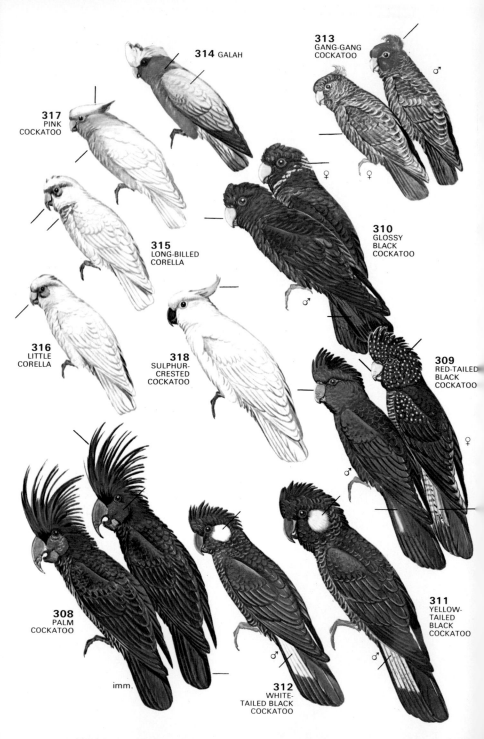

314 GALAH

313 GANG-GANG COCKATOO ♂

317 PINK COCKATOO

315 LONG-BILLED CORELLA

310 GLOSSY BLACK COCKATOO ♀ ♂

316 LITTLE CORELLA

318 SULPHUR-CRESTED COCKATOO

309 RED-TAILED BLACK COCKATOO ♂ ♀

308 PALM COCKATOO imm.

312 WHITE-TAILED BLACK COCKATOO ♂

311 YELLOW-TAILED BLACK COCKATOO ♂

300 mm

race *macgillivrayi*

race *occidentalis*

race *semitorquatus*

348
MALLEE
RINGNECK

349
PORT
LINCOLN
PARROT

331
SUPERB
PARROT

♀

♂

332
REGENT
PARROT

♀

♂

339 RED-CAPPED
PARROT

♀

♂

333
PRINCESS
PARROT

320
RED-
CHEEKED
PARROT

♀

♂

♂

♀

♀

329
KING
PARROT

♀

♂

♂

330
RED-WINGED
PARROT

319 ECLECTUS PARROT

300 mm

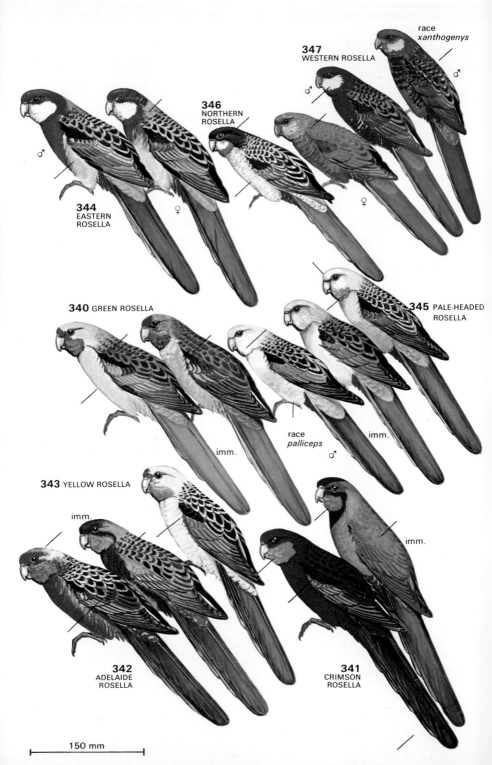

347
WESTERN ROSELLA

race
xanthogenys

♂

♂

♀

346
NORTHERN
ROSELLA

♂

344
EASTERN
ROSELLA

♀

340 GREEN ROSELLA

345 PALE-HEADED
ROSELLA

race
palliceps ♂

imm.

imm.

343 YELLOW ROSELLA

imm.

imm.

imm.

342
ADELAIDE
ROSELLA

341
CRIMSON
ROSELLA

150 mm

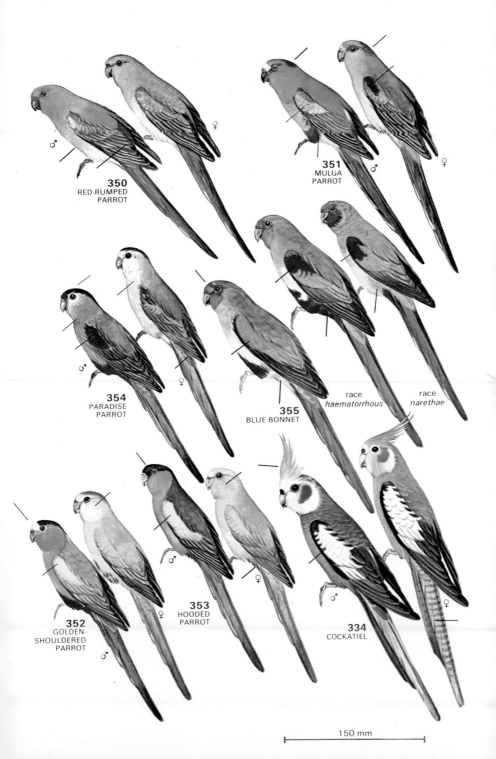

350
RED-RUMPED
PARROT

351
MULGA
PARROT

354
PARADISE
PARROT

355
BLUE BONNET

race
haematorrhous

race
narethae

352
GOLDEN-
SHOULDERED
PARROT

353
HOODED
PARROT

334
COCKATIEL

150 mm

337 BUDGERIGAR
♂

356 BOURKE'S PARROT
♀
♂

362 SCARLET-CHESTED PARROT
♂
♀

361 TURQUOISE PARROT
♂
♀

358 ELEGANT PARROT
♀
♂

360 ORANGE-BELLIED PARROT
♀
♂

357 BLUE-WINGED PARROT
♀
♂

359 ROCK PARROT
♀
♂

335 GROUND PARROT

336 NIGHT PARROT

150 mm

imm.

363 ORIENTAL CUCKOO

sub-adult

364 PALLID CUCKOO

imm.

imm.

365 BRUSH CUCKOO

♂

imm.

367 FAN-TAILED CUCKOO

imm.

♂

imm.

♀

373 KOEL

366 CHESTNUT-BREASTED CUCKOO

150 mm

TAILS: under upper

imm.

371 LITTLE
BRONZE-CUCKOO

imm.

372 RUFOUS
BRONZE-
CUCKOO

imm.

369 HORSFIELD'S
BRONZE-CUCKOO

imm.

370
race
plagosus

370 SHINING
BRONZE-CUCKOO

368 BLACK-EARED
CUCKOO

imm.

imm.

150 mm

381 MASKED OWL

♂ pale phase

♀ dark phase

380 BARN OWL

383 SOOTY OWL

376 RUFOUS OWL

382 GRASS OWL

379 BARKING OWL

378 BOOBOOK OWL

race *ocellata*

377 POWERFUL OWL

300 mm

384 TAWNY FROGMOUTH
race *phalaenoides*

386
MARBLED
FROGMOUTH

385
PAPUAN
FROGMOUTH

red phase

387 OWLET-
NIGHTJAR

imm.

389

390

388

imm.

388 WHITE-THROATED NIGHT

389
SPOTTED
NIGHTJAR

390
WHITE-
TAILED
NIGHTJAR

150 mm
perched figures only

392 GREY SWIFTLET

391 WHITE-BELLIED SWIFTLET

395 FORK-TAILED SWIFT

394 SPINE-TAILED SWIFT

419 BARN SWALLOW

422 FAIRY MARTIN

421 TREE MARTIN

420 WELCOME SWALLOW

418 WHITE-BACKED SWALLOW

419 BARN SWALLOW

422 FAIRY MARTIN

421 TREE MARTIN

418 WHITE-BACKED SWALLOW

420 WELCOME SWALLOW

150 mm

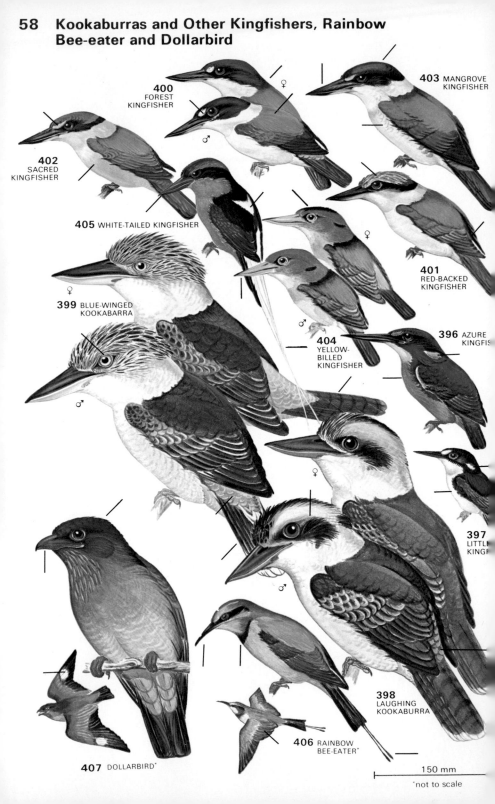

400 FOREST KINGFISHER

403 MANGROVE KINGFISHER

402 SACRED KINGFISHER

405 WHITE-TAILED KINGFISHER

401 RED-BACKED KINGFISHER

399 BLUE-WINGED KOOKABURRA

404 YELLOW-BILLED KINGFISHER

396 AZURE KINGFIS

397 LITTL KING

398 LAUGHING KOOKABURRA

407 DOLLARBIRD*

406 RAINBOW BEE-EATER*

150 mm

*not to scale

Pittas, Logrunners, Pilotbird, Scrub-birds 59
and Bristlebirds

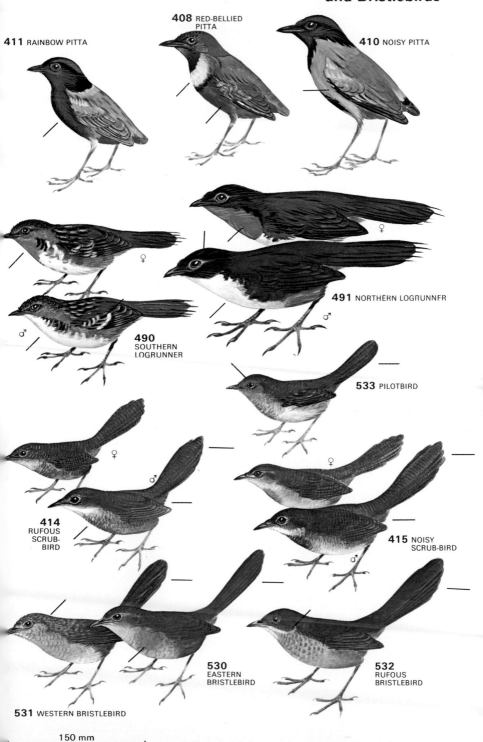

411 RAINBOW PITTA

408 RED-BELLIED PITTA

410 NOISY PITTA

490 SOUTHERN LOGRUNNER

491 NORTHERN LOGRUNNER

533 PILOTBIRD

414 RUFOUS SCRUB-BIRD

415 NOISY SCRUB-BIRD

530 EASTERN BRISTLEBIRD

531 WESTERN BRISTLEBIRD

532 RUFOUS BRISTLEBIRD

150 mm

470 BOWER'S SHRIKE-THRUSH

469 RUFOUS SHRIKE-THRUSH

race *parvula*

471 SANDSTONE SHRIKE-THRUSH

472 GREY SHRIKE-THRUSH

imm.

♂

race *brunnea*

race *rufiventris*

439 SOUTHERN SCRUB-ROBIN

438 NORTHERN SCRUB-ROBIN

436 BLACKBIRD

♀

♂

435 SCALY THRUSH

437 SONG THRUSH

150 mm

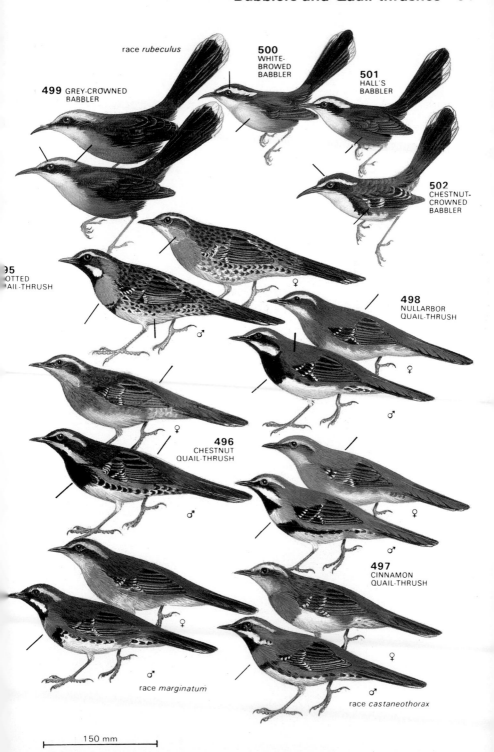

race *rubeculus*

500
WHITE-
BROWED
BABBLER

501
HALL'S
BABBLER

499 GREY-CROWNED
BABBLER

502
CHESTNUT-
CROWNED
BABBLER

95
OTTED
AIL-THRUSH

498
NULLARBOR
QUAIL-THRUSH

♀

♂

♀

♂

496
CHESTNUT
QUAIL-THRUSH

♀

♀

♂

497
CINNAMON
QUAIL-THRUSH

♀

♂

race *marginatum*

♀

♂

race *castaneothorax*

150 mm

race *leucogaster*

459
CRESTED
SHRIKE-TIT ♂

♀

♂

imm.

492
EASTERN
WHIPBIRD

434
RED-WHISKERED
BULBUL

493
WESTERN
WHIPBIRD

494
WEDGEBILL

473
CRESTED
BELLBIRD ♂

♀

150 mm

443 SCARLET ROBIN

♂

♀

444 RED-CAPPED ROBIN

♂

♀

441 PINK ROBIN

♂

♀

442 FLAME ROBIN

♂

♀

445 HOODED ROBIN

♂

♀

440 ROSE ROBIN

♂

♀

446 DUSKY ROBIN

♂

♀

447 MANGROVE ROBIN

♂

♀

race *erviniventris*

457 WHITE-BROWED ROBIN

458 GREY-HEADED ROBIN

150 mm

454
JACKY WINTER

452
LEMON-
BREASTED
FLYCATCHER

453
BROWN-TAILED
FLYCATCHER

451
YELLOW-
FOOTED
FLYCATCHER

455
PALE-YELLOW
ROBIN

456
WHITE-FACED
ROBIN

449
EASTERN
YELLOW
ROBIN

449
race
chrysorrhoa

450
WESTERN YELLOW
ROBIN

448
WHITE–
BREASTED
ROBIN

150 mm

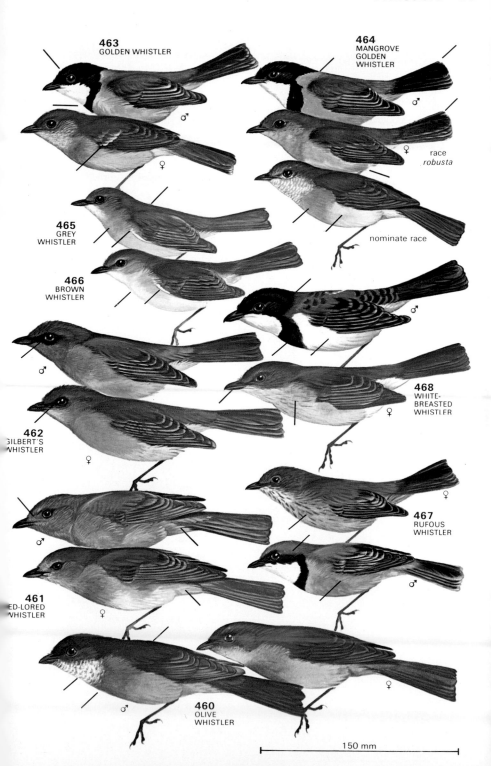

463
GOLDEN WHISTLER

♂

♀

464
MANGROVE
GOLDEN
WHISTLER

♂

♀

race
robusta

nominate race

465
GREY
WHISTLER

466
BROWN
WHISTLER

♂

468
WHITE-
BREASTED
WHISTLER

♀

♂

462
GILBERT'S
WHISTLER

♀

♀

467
RUFOUS
WHISTLER

♂

♂

461
RED-LORED
WHISTLER

♀

♂

♂

460
OLIVE
WHISTLER

150 mm

487
GREY
FANTAIL

486
RUFOUS
FANTAIL

488
NORTHERN
FANTAIL

489
WILLIE
WAGTAIL

482
LEADEN
FLYCATCHER
♂
♀

485
RESTLESS FLYCATCHER
♂

483
SATIN
FLYCATCHER
♀

481
BROAD-
BILLED
FLYCATCHER

484
SHINING
FLYCATCHER

imm.

475
BLACK-
FACED
MONARCH
FLYCATCHER

imm.
♂

♀

477
SPECTACLED
MONARCH
FLYCATCHER

474
YELLOW-
BREASTED
BOATBILL
♂
♀

480
PIED MONARCH
FLYCATCHER

479
FRILLED MONARCH
FLYCATCHER

478
WHITE-EARED
MONARCH FLYCATCHER

150 mm

509
GOLDEN-HEADED
CISTICOLA

♀

♂ eclipse

eeding

503 CLAMOROUS REED WARBLER

507
SPINIFEXBIRD

♀

♀

♂

508
ZITTING CISTICOLA

510
RUFOUS SONGLARK

♂

511
BROWN
SONGLARK

♀

506
LITTLE
GRASSBIRD

♂

light example

dark example

505
TAWNY
GRASSBIRD

417 COMMON
SKYLARK

423
CHARD'S
PIPIT

416
SINGING
BUSHLARK

150 mm

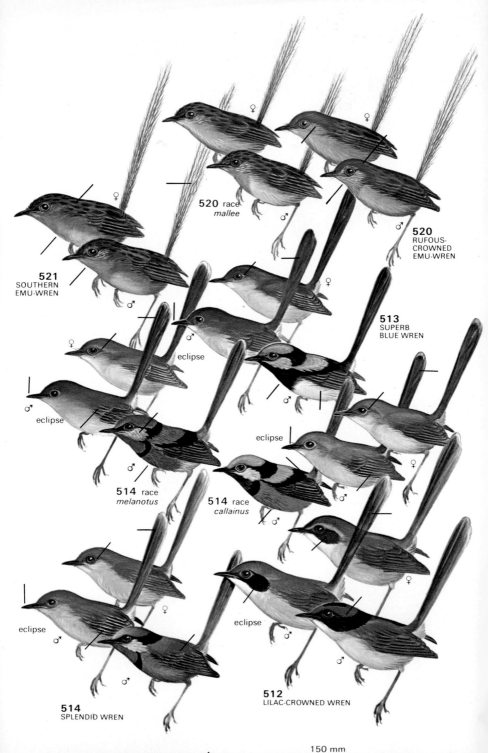

520 race *mallee*

♀

520 RUFOUS-CROWNED EMU-WREN

♂

521 SOUTHERN EMU-WREN

♂

♀

eclipse

513 SUPERB BLUE WREN

♂

eclipse

♀

♂

eclipse

514 race *melanotus*

♂

514 race *callainus*

♂

eclipse

♀

♂

♀

eclipse

512 LILAC-CROWNED WREN

♂

♂

♀

eclipse

♂

514 SPLENDID WREN

150 mm

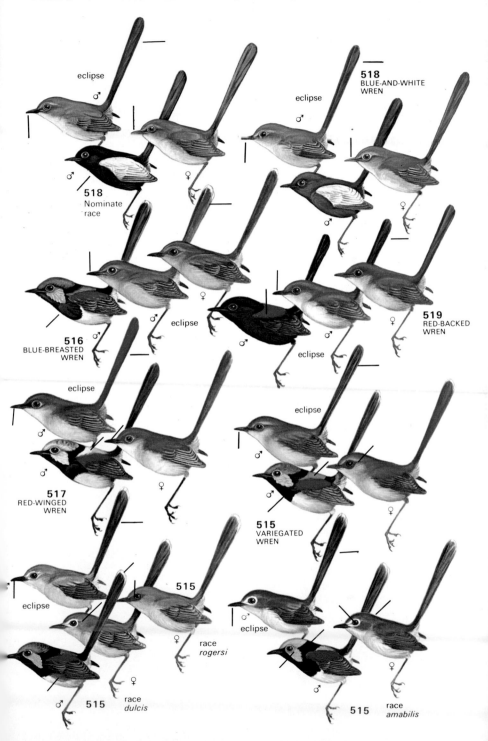

eclipse

♂

♂ **518**
Nominate
race

♀

518
BLUE-AND-WHITE
WREN

eclipse

♂

♂

♀

516
BLUE-BREASTED
WREN

♂

♀

eclipse

♂

eclipse

♀ **519**
RED-BACKED
WREN

eclipse

♂

♂

517
RED-WINGED
WREN

♀

eclipse

♂

♂

♀

515
VARIEGATED
WREN

eclipse

♂

♀

515

race
rogersi

♂ **515** race
dulcis

eclipse

♂

♀

515 race
amabilis

150 mm

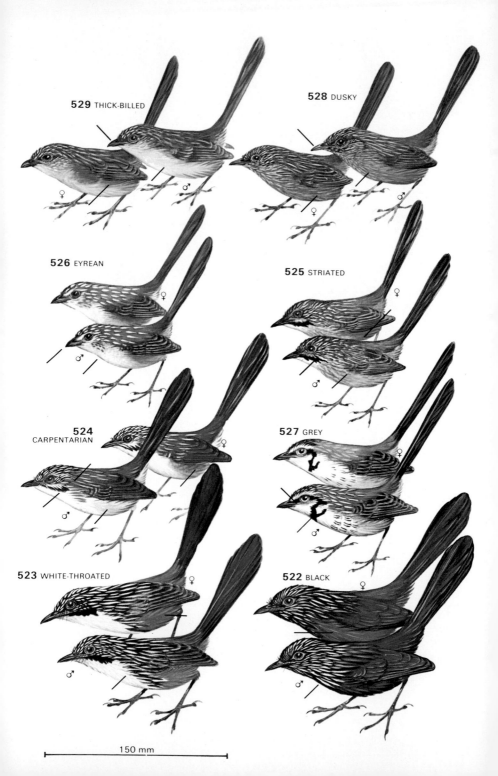

529 THICK-BILLED ♀ ♂

528 DUSKY ♀ ♂

526 EYREAN ♀ ♂

525 STRIATED ♀ ♂

524 CARPENTARIAN ♀ ♂

527 GREY ♀ ♂

523 WHITE-THROATED ♀ ♂

522 BLACK ♀ ♂

150 mm

race *humilis*

540
WHITE-BROWED
SCRUBWREN

♀

race *maculatus*

♂

♂

538
YELLOW-THROATED
SCRUBWREN

537
LARGE-
BILLED
SCRUBWREN

536
ATHERTON
SCRUBWREN

535
FERNWREN

race
dubius

541 SCRUB TIT

539
TROPICAL
SCRUBWREN

♂

545
FIELDWREN

544
REDTHROAT

♀

♂

inland form

546
SPECKLED
WARBLER

543
MALLEE
HEATHWREN

534
ROCK
WARBLER

542
HEATHWREN

150 mm

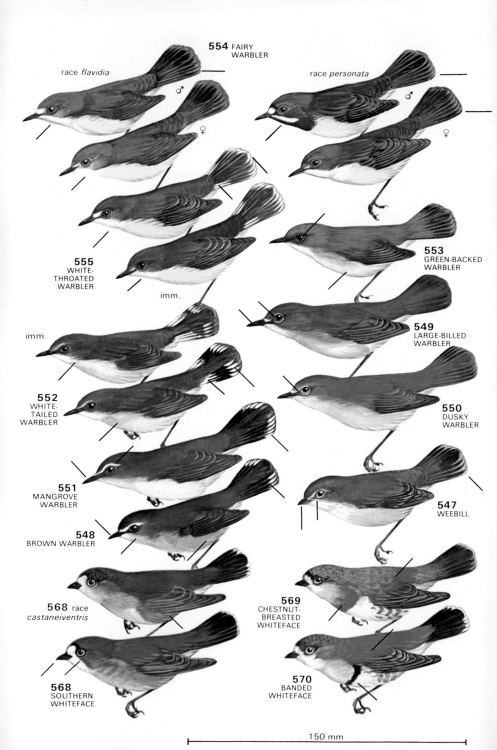

554 FAIRY WARBLER

race *flavidia*

♂

♀

race *personata*

♂

♀

555 WHITE-THROATED WARBLER

553 GREEN-BACKED WARBLER

imm.

imm.

549 LARGE-BILLED WARBLER

552 WHITE-TAILED WARBLER

550 DUSKY WARBLER

551 MANGROVE WARBLER

547 WEEBILL

548 BROWN WARBLER

568 race *castaneiventris*

569 CHESTNUT-BREASTED WHITEFACE

568 SOUTHERN WHITEFACE

570 BANDED WHITEFACE

150 mm

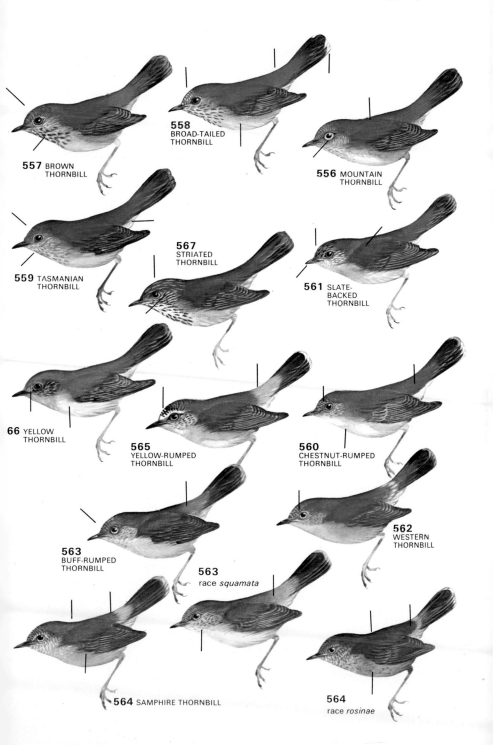

557 BROWN THORNBILL

558 BROAD-TAILED THORNBILL

556 MOUNTAIN THORNBILL

559 TASMANIAN THORNBILL

567 STRIATED THORNBILL

561 SLATE-BACKED THORNBILL

66 YELLOW THORNBILL

565 YELLOW-RUMPED THORNBILL

560 CHESTNUT-RUMPED THORNBILL

563 BUFF-RUMPED THORNBILL

563 race *squamata*

562 WESTERN THORNBILL

564 SAMPHIRE THORNBILL

564 race *rosinae*

150 mm

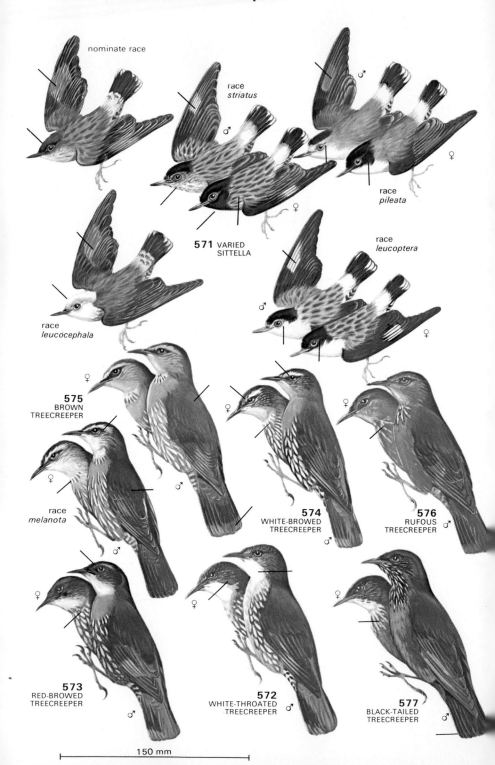

nominate race

race
striatus

race
pileata

♂

♀

race
leucocephala

571 VARIED
SITTELLA

race
leucoptera

♂

♀

♀

♂

575
BROWN
TREECREEPER

♀

574
WHITE-BROWED
TREECREEPER
♂

♀

576
RUFOUS
TREECREEPER ♂

race
melanota

♂

♀

♀

573
RED-BROWED
TREECREEPER
♂

♀

572
WHITE-THROATED
TREECREEPER ♂

♀

577
BLACK-TAILED
TREECREEPER ♂

150 mm

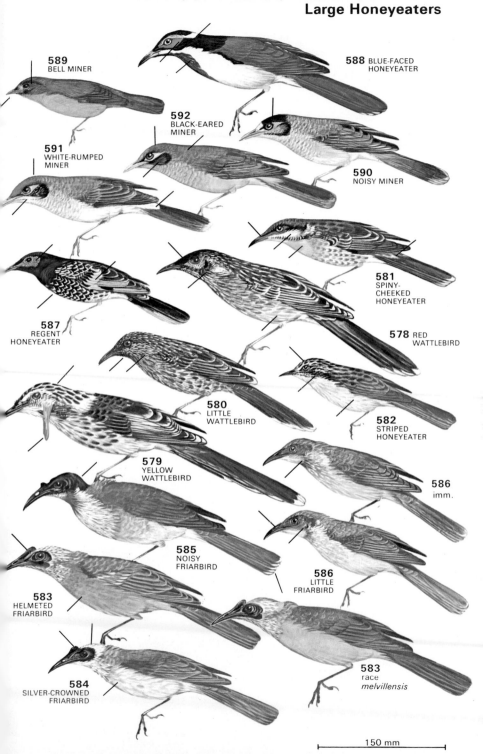

589 BELL MINER

588 BLUE-FACED HONEYEATER

592 BLACK-EARED MINER

591 WHITE-RUMPED MINER

590 NOISY MINER

581 SPINY-CHEEKED HONEYEATER

587 REGENT HONEYEATER

578 RED WATTLEBIRD

580 LITTLE WATTLEBIRD

582 STRIPED HONEYEATER

579 YELLOW WATTLEBIRD

586 imm.

585 NOISY FRIARBIRD

586 LITTLE FRIARBIRD

583 HELMETED FRIARBIRD

584 SILVER-CROWNED FRIARBIRD

583 race *melvillensis*

150 mm

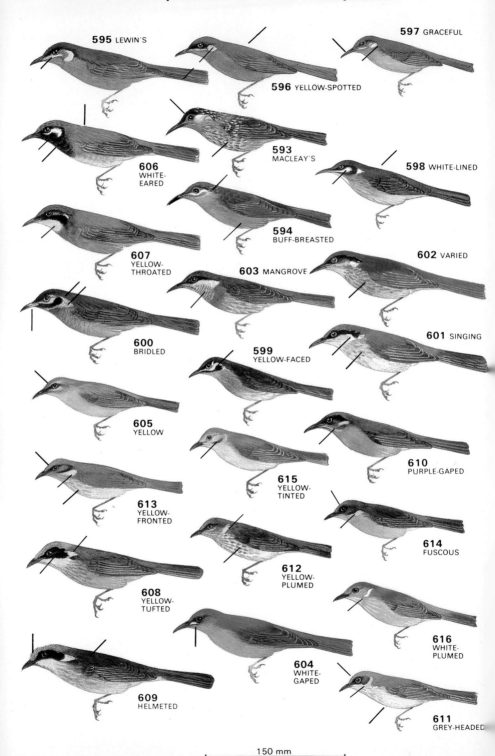

595 LEWIN'S

596 YELLOW-SPOTTED

597 GRACEFUL

606 WHITE-EARED

593 MACLEAY'S

598 WHITE-LINED

607 YELLOW-THROATED

594 BUFF-BREASTED

602 VARIED

600 BRIDLED

603 MANGROVE

599 YELLOW-FACED

601 SINGING

605 YELLOW

610 PURPLE-GAPED

613 YELLOW-FRONTED

615 YELLOW-TINTED

614 FUSCOUS

608 YELLOW-TUFTED

612 YELLOW-PLUMED

616 WHITE-PLUMED

609 HELMETED

604 WHITE-GAPED

611 GREY-HEADED

150 mm

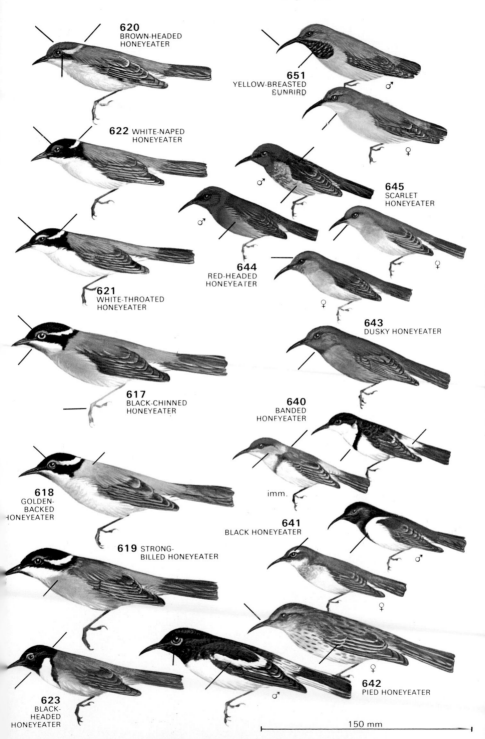

620
BROWN-HEADED
HONEYEATER

651
YELLOW-BREASTED
SUNBIRD

♂

♀

622 WHITE-NAPED
HONEYEATER

♂

645
SCARLET
HONEYEATER

♂

♀

621
WHITE-THROATED
HONEYEATER

644
RED-HEADED
HONEYEATER

♀

643
DUSKY HONEYEATER

617
BLACK-CHINNED
HONEYEATER

640
BANDED
HONEYEATER

618
GOLDEN-
BACKED
HONEYEATER

imm.

641
BLACK HONEYEATER

619 STRONG-
BILLED HONEYEATER

♂

♀

♀

642
PIED HONEYEATER

623
BLACK-
HEADED
HONEYEATER

♂

150 mm

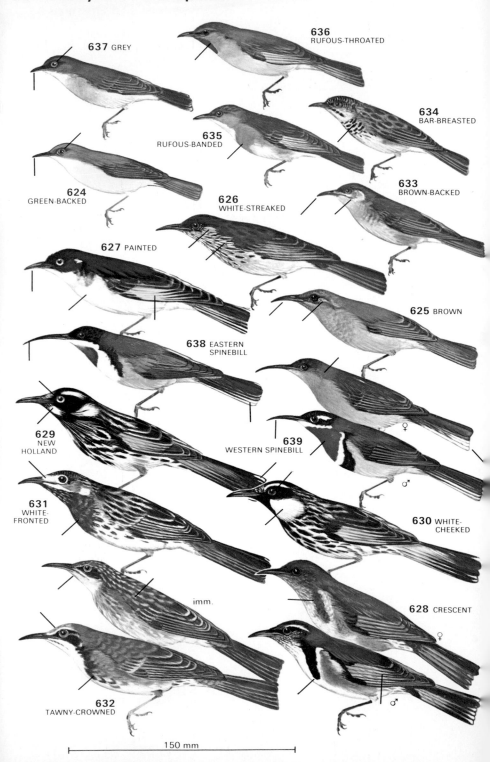

637 GREY

636 RUFOUS-THROATED

635 RUFOUS-BANDED

634 BAR-BREASTED

624 GREEN-BACKED

626 WHITE-STREAKED

633 BROWN-BACKED

627 PAINTED

625 BROWN

638 EASTERN SPINEBILL

629 NEW HOLLAND

639 WESTERN SPINEBILL

♀

♂

631 WHITE-FRONTED

630 WHITE-CHEEKED

imm.

628 CRESCENT

♀

632 TAWNY-CROWNED

♂

150 mm

646
CRIMSON
CHAT

649
WHITE-FRONTED
CHAT

648
YELLOW
CHAT

647
ORANGE
CHAT

650
DESERT
CHAT

non-breeding

non-breeding

424 YELLOW WAGTAIL

150 mm

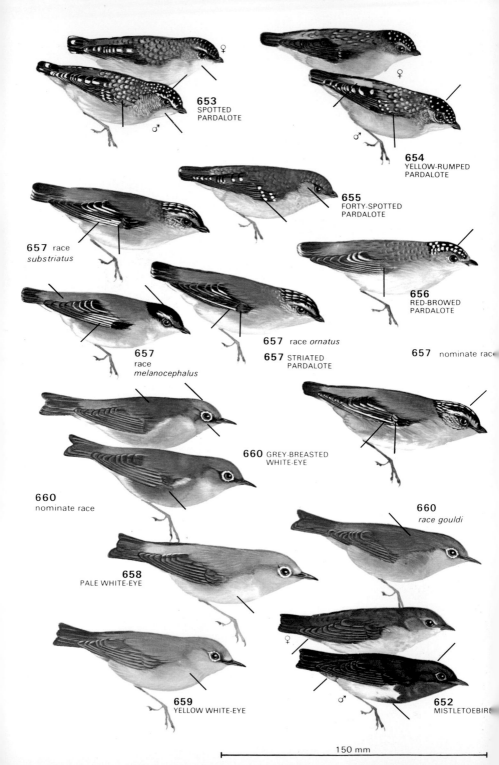

653 SPOTTED PARDALOTE ♀ ♂

654 YELLOW-RUMPED PARDALOTE ♀ ♂

655 FORTY-SPOTTED PARDALOTE

656 RED-BROWED PARDALOTE

657 race *substriatus*

657 race *melanocephalus*

657 race *ornatus*

657 STRIATED PARDALOTE

657 nominate race

660 GREY-BREASTED WHITE-EYE

660 nominate race

660 race *gouldi*

658 PALE WHITE-EYE

659 YELLOW WHITE-EYE

652 MISTLETOEBIRD ♀ ♂

150 mm

dark phase

429
race
robusta

429 LITTLE
CUCKOO-SHRIKE

imm.

imm.

428
BARRED
CUCKOO-
SHRIKE

imm.

427
BLACK-FACED
CUCKOO-SHRIKE

431 GROUND CUCKOO-SHRIKE

150 mm

708 DUSKY
WOOD SWALLOW

707
BLACK-FACED
WOODSWALLO

709 LITTLE
WOODSWALLOW

704
WHITE-
BREASTED
WOODSWALL

706
WHITE-
BROWED
WOODSWALLOW

705
MASKED
WOODSWALLO

432
WHITE-WINGED
TRILLER

♂ eclipse

430
CICADABIRD

433
VARIED TRILLER

150 mm

imm.

imm.

719
PIED
BUTCHER-
BIRD

♂

710
MAGPIE
LARK

rufous
phase

716
BLACK
BUTCHERBIRD

718
BLACK-
BACKED
BUTCHER-
BIRD

717
GREY
BUTCHERBIRD

imm.

imm.

adult

712 WHITE-WINGED
CHOUGH

720
AUSTRALIAN
MAGPIE

♂

711
APOSTLE-
BIRD

♀

♂

720
race *hypoleuca*

♀

♂

720
race *dorsalis*

300 mm

374 CHANNEL-BILLED CUCKOO

715 race *arguta*

715 GREY CURRAWONG

715 race *melanoptera*

714 BLACK CURRAWONG

713 PIED CURRAWONG

721 AUSTRALIAN RAVEN

725 TORRESIAN CROW

723 LITTLE RAVEN

724 LITTLE CROW

300 mm

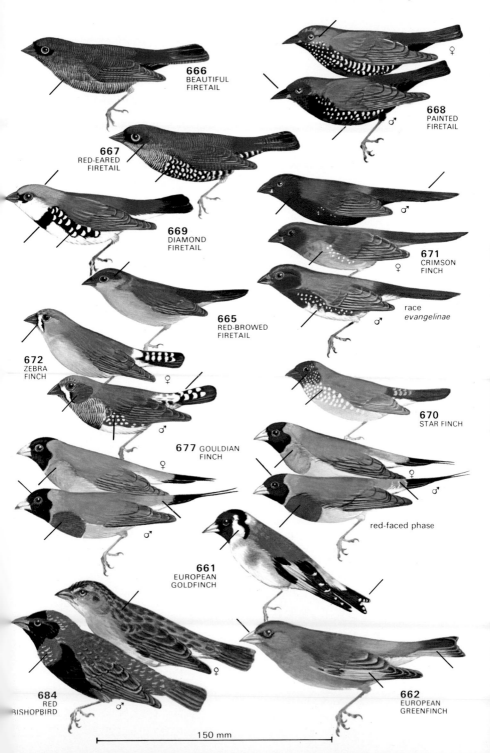

666
BEAUTIFUL
FIRETAIL

♀

668
PAINTED
FIRETAIL

♂

667
RED-EARED
FIRETAIL

669
DIAMOND
FIRETAIL

♂

♀

671
CRIMSON
FINCH

race
evangelinae

♂

665
RED-BROWED
FIRETAIL

672
ZEBRA
FINCH

♀

♂

670
STAR FINCH

677 GOULDIAN
FINCH

♀

♂

red-faced phase

661
EUROPEAN
GOLDFINCH

684
RED
BISHOPBIRD

♂

♀

662
EUROPEAN
GREENFINCH

150 mm

673 DOUBLE-BARRED FINCH

race *annulosa*

682 PICTORELLA MANNIKIN

678 BLUE-FACED FINCH

681 CHESTNUT-BREASTED MANNIKIN

680 YELLOW-RUMPED MANNIKIN

679 PLUM-HEADED FINCH

683 NUTMEG MANNIKIN

676 BLACK-THROATED FINCH

674 MASKED FINCH

race *leucotis*

race *atropygialis*

675 LONG-TAILED FINCH

♂ winter

663 HOUSE SPARROW

♂

664 TREE SPARROW

♀

150 mm

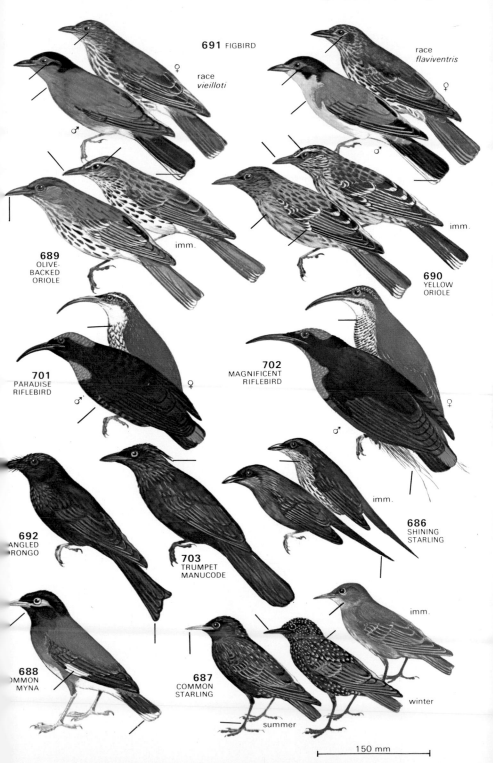

691 FIGBIRD

race *vieilloti*

race *flaviventris*

689 OLIVE-BACKED ORIOLE

imm.

690 YELLOW ORIOLE

imm.

701 PARADISE RIFLEBIRD

702 MAGNIFICENT RIFLEBIRD

692 DRONGO

703 TRUMPET MANUCODE

imm.

686 SHINING STARLING

688 COMMON MYNA

687 COMMON STARLING

summer

imm.

winter

150 mm

693 GOLDEN BOWERBIRD ♀ ♂

695 REGENT BOWERBIRD ♀ ♂

700 GREEN CATBIRD

694 SATIN BOWERBIRD ♀ ♂

race *guttata*

696 SPOTTED BOWERBIRD

699 TOOTH-BILLED CATBIRD

698 FAWN-BREASTED BOWERBIRD

697 GREAT BOWERBIRD

150 mm

554   FAIRY WARBLER   *Gerygone palpebrosa*   **Pl.72**

Other names: Black-throated Warbler; Hornet-nest Bird; Yellow Warbler.
Field marks: 100–115 mm. There are two distinctive Aust. races– *flavida* and *personata*,
'Black-throated Warbler'. Race *flavida*, male: olive-buff above, forehead whitish, centre
of throat and entire underparts pale-lemon, *with a small black mark on chin*, white whisker
on either side of throat; tail has blackish subterminal band, *with small white tips*. Female
similar, but no whitish whisker. Race *personata*: male: greenish above with *extensive dull-
blackish throat and prominent white whisker* down either side of throat from bill; breast
lemon. Female: whitish throat merges into pale-lemon breast; in both sexes, tail has faint
blackish band, *but no white*. Imm. (both races): throat washed yellow. The two forms
intergrade in the region of Cooktown–Innisfail and Atherton Tableland, where some
males have dull blackish throats. Singly or pairs, usually among outer branches and foliage
of trees; hovers like other fairy warblers.
Similar species: White-throated Warbler (555): more white on throat and in tail. Imm:
easily confused; look for adults.
Voice: Animated undulating warble: song less developed than White-throated.
Habitat: Nest: globular, with pronounced hood and wispy tail; of bark and plant-fibre
bound with spiders' web; suspended from fine branch, usually over or near water and
often near wasp nest. Eggs: 2–3; pink-white, finely freckled and spotted reddish brown.
Range and Status: Ne. Q and some coastal islands. Race *flavida* coastally from about
Rockhampton n. to near Cairns–Atherton Tableland. Race *personata*: C. York Pen., n.
from about Atherton Tableland–Hartley's Creek on e. coast and from Staaten R. on w.
coast. Fairly common; sedentary. Nominate (and other) races occur in NG and Aru Is.

555   WHITE-THROATED WARBLER   *Gerygone olivacea*   **Pl 72**

Other names: Bush or Native Canary; White-throated Bush Warbler or Flyeater.
Field marks: 100–115 mm. A *wholly white-throated warbler with clear-yellow breast*; eye
red, upperparts buff-grey, tinged olive; tail blackish, *outer feathers white near base and
tipped white*; northern forms have less white in tail; some lack it entirely. Imm: *yellowish
throat*. Singly or pairs; moves actively through and hovers outside foliage, *when white in
tail seen most clearly*. Usually first noted by charming song, especially when breeding.
Similar species: Fairy Warbler (554). Yellow Thornbill (566): from imm. in greener
upperparts, richer buff-yellow throat, streaked ear-coverts, no white in tail; calls differ.
Voice: Beautiful, oft-repeated 'falling-leaf' song in minor key, with upward recovery
toward end, then tails off; silvery thread of song.
Habitat: The foliage of trees in open forest and woodlands, specially those with some
sapling re-growth; lightly timbered hills; patches of scrub, large trees along watercourses.
Breeding: Nest: domed, rather globular, *with hooded side-entrance and wispy tail*; of
bark-fibres or grass, bound with spider web; usually hung from thin branch of tree or
sapling, low to 15 m high. Eggs: 2–3; white or pink-white, heavily spotted blotched and
freckled red to red-purple, with zone at large end.
Range and Status: N. and e. Aust.: from Kimberleys, WA, to e. and c. Vic. w. to about
Anglesea–Bendigo–Inglewood; occasional breeding w. to Millicent and Mt. Lofty Ras.,
SA. Mostly on and e. of Divide, but inland to Augathella–Richmond, Q; Narrabri–
Warrumbungles NP, NSW. Sedentary in n. Aust., regular breeding migrant in se.,
arriving Sept., departing Apr.; a few winter, when quiet and inconspicuous. Common to
uncommon and patchy.

THORNBILLS   Genus *Acanthiza*

Endlessly active, mostly 'small brown birds' with fussy insect-like voices; usually in
parties or small flocks. According to species they feed in and round high foliage, low
foliage, undergrowth, ground cover or on open ground near cover and these preferences

can aid identification. Look for five plumage features: (1) General shade–grey, brown or greenish yellow. (2) Eye–pale or dark. (3) Forehead and crown–plain, scalloped or streaked. (4) Breast–plain or streaked. (5) Rump–buff, yellow or brown to rusty. No two species of thornbills in the same part of Aust. combine the same markings. Even if you have five species in your district, sometimes all in one tree together, they *can* be separated. Remember too that *voice* is often a ready means of separating them, once learned. For example, Brown (557) and Striated (567) Thornbills can be immediately told apart by their calls.

556 MOUNTAIN THORNBILL *Acanthiza katherina* Pl.73

Field marks: 100 mm. Somewhat like a greenish, more plainly marked Brown Thornbill (557), *but with a yellowish white eye*; indistinct scalloping on forehead; slight dark streaks on whitish to yellow-buff underparts; flanks olive-buff. Pairs and small parties; generally feeds high in foliage.
Similar species: Most likely to be confused with fairy warblers (548–555) but none is streaked and none in Q has pale eyes. Habits and calls differ.
Voice: Probably like Brown Thornbill (557).
Habitat: Rainforests and adjacent wooded streams, mostly above 450 m.
Breeding: Nest: bulky, domed; externally of green moss. Eggs unknown.
Range and Status: Confined to highlands of ne. Q from s. of Cooktown to Mt. Spec near Townsville. Locally fairly common.

BROWN AND BROAD-TAILED THORNBILL COMPLEX

Ten (or more) races of brownish thornbills occupying most of the continent mostly below the Tropic. Their *markings* are similar (scalloped forehead, red to brown eyes, dark-streaked breasts) but the range and intensity of shading varies greatly. Generally, but not invariably, the forms in wetter coastal areas of s. and e. Aust. and in Tas. tend to be darker and more sombrely coloured; in drier coastal and sub-inland areas, the shades are brighter and more contrasting, but in arid far-inland habitats, generally paler and less-contrasting.

557 BROWN THORNBILL *Acanthiza pusilla* Pl.73

Other names: Browntail, Brown-rumped or Brown Tit, Scrub Thornbill, Titbat, Tit-warbler.
Field marks: 100 mm. The typical small brown garden bird of coastal se. Aust. Note *largish dark-red eye*; *fine buff and brown scalloping* on the forehead; *blackish arrowlike markings* on greyish throat and breast, appearing plain-grey at distance. The rump and base of tail are more tawny than the back; rest of tail grey-brown with blackish sub-terminal band and somewhat paler tips; flanks olive-buff. Singly, pairs, family parties or in feeding associations with other small passerines. Restless and active; feeds in foliage, branches of lower trees, shrubs, undergrowth; hangs upside down; flutters to snap insects. In flight, flirts, opens and closes tail.
Similar species: Striated Thornbill (567): pale-streaked crown and ear-coverts, greener back, yellower-white underparts; calls differ. Broad-tailed Thornbill (558). Tasmanian Thornbill (559).
Voice: Notes varied, many surprisingly deep: typical call is baritone 'pee-orr'; also many fussy squeaks and churrs. Excellent mimic, specially when under stress and during sub-song; alarm-call, a deep zizzing scolding like scrubwren.
Habitat: Foliage and undergrowth of rainforests, wetter eucalypt forests, woodlands, scrubs; creekside vegetation; bracken, rushes on swamp and river-margins; dune-vegetation on coast; saltmarsh vegetation; mangroves; parks, gardens.

Breeding: Nest: domed with hooded side-entrance, untidy; of bark-shreds and grasses almost always with a little green moss; bound with spiders' web often with egg-sacs; often near ground. Eggs: 3; whitish, blotched and freckled red-brown, mostly round large end.
Range and Status: Mostly coastal se. Aust., and Tas. (where fairly widespread); from Mt. Dryander, n. of Proserpine, Q, to Yorke Pen. and Kangaroo I., SA. The precise inland range, and whether it merges with that of Broad-tailed Thornbill (558), is unknown. Some present-known inland limits in Q are L. Elphinstone about 110 km sw. of Mackay, Cracow–Toowoomba–Wallangarra; some w. limits in NSW are Inverell–Warrumbungle NP–Wellington–Cowra–The Rock; in the Murray Valley it extends w. at least to Gunbower State Forest, thence throughout Vic. except far nw. mallee–mulga areas; to se. SA and Mt. Lofty Ras. Also King I. (? and other islands in Bass Strait) and off e. coast, including Stradbroke, Bribie and Fraser Is. Common, except in drier parts of range; sedentary.

558 BROAD-TAILED THORNBILL *Acanthiza apicalis* **Pl.73**
Other names: Inland, Red-rumped, Red-tailed, Tanami or Whitlock's Thornbill; Red-rumped or Tanami Tit.
Field marks: 95–115 mm. Paler above and whiter below than Brown Thornbill (557), *rump conspicuously more red-brown*; forehead-scalloping *whitish* rather than buff; tail-band wider, outer tail-feathers *conspicuously tipped white*. Seemingly more conspicuous in habits and even more demonstrative; *often carries tail cocked*. Races of farthest arid inland are generally palest. The following races span most recognizable plumage variations: (1) Nominate race: brownish olive above, rump dull-tawny, white tips of outer tail-feathers not conspicuous. (2) Race *albiventris*: grey-brown above, rump rich red-brown; underparts whitish, prominent black streaks on throat and upperbreast, flanks washed buff. (3) Race *whitlocki*: much paler; buff-grey above, rump pale-tawny, underparts whitish fawn. (4) The form in inland Q (e. to Opalton–Winton and possibly n. to Mt. Isa): plain pale-grey above, rump pale-chestnut; underparts white with strong black streaks on throat and upperbreast. Bill noticeably long.
Similar species: Chestnut-rumped Thornbill (560): unstreaked whitish breast; pale eye. Slate-backed Thornbill (561): blue-grey above, crown streaked black; underparts unstreaked.
Voice: Like Brown Thornbill but stronger; also mimics, specially in threat-display or under stress. Sweet spirited territorial song, somewhat like Mallee Heathwren (543); also high-pitched 'see-see' contact-call, like Chestnut-rumped Thornbill.
Habitat: Most dry scrubs and woodlands in sub-inland e. and se. Aust. generally; in sw. Aust. heavy forests, wet coastal scrubs, heaths; mangroves.
Breeding: Nest: like Brown Thornbill; in foliage of low tree or shrub, usually near ground. Eggs: 3; whitish, freckled, spotted and blotched red-brown, most heavily at large end.
Range and Status: *Nominate race*: most of WA s. of Tropic, except extreme sw. corner where replaced by darker race *leeuwinensis*. Race *whitlocki*: Nullarbor Plain, n. Eyre Pen. and Flinders Ras., SA, to s. Barkly Tablelands; a similar but paler race, *tanami*, in Tanami Desert, w. NT. Race *albiventris*: s. Eyre Pen. through Murray mallee of SA and nw. Vic., much of inland NSW e. to about Moulamein–Cocoparra NP–Pilliga Scrub–Moree; inland Q, e. to near Darling Downs–Blackall–Winton and (? race) n. to Mt. Isa. Common.

559 TASMANIAN THORNBILL *Acanthiza ewingii* **Pl.73**
Other names: Browntail, Ewing's Thornbill or Tit.
Field marks: 100 mm. Like Brown Thornbill (557), but bill shorter, forehead rich-brownish without conspicuous scallopings; breast greyer, less-distinctly streaked; *flanks and under tail-coverts whiter*; 'like white underpants'; tail slightly longer. Habits generally

like Brown Thornbill, but where they occur together, shows preference for denser, wetter habitats.

Similar species: White-browed Scrubwren (540) race *humilis*: larger, faint white eyebrow, black-and-white shoulder-mark, yellow-white breast. Scrub Tit (541): much more white–on eyebrows, edges to inner wing-feathers, throat and underparts.

Voice: Most notes like Brown Thornbill; a typical call has been characterized as 'zit zit zit whoorl'.

Habitat: Forests, woodlands and scrub.

Breeding: Nest: like Brown Thornbill but neater and more compact, sometimes covered with moss. Eggs: 3–4; pinkish white, lightly freckled red-brown.

Range and Status: Tas., coastal islands, King I. and Furneaux Group, Bass Strait. Common; sedentary.

560 CHESTNUT-RUMPED THORNBILL *Acanthiza uropygialis* Pl.73

Other names: Chestnut-tailed Thornbill or Tit.

Field marks: 100–115 mm. A plain pale thornbill *with pale-chestnut rump*; upperparts greyish mouse-brown; *underparts whitish and unstreaked*; *forehead tinged buff and finely scalloped paler*; *eye whitish*. Usually in small flocks; feeds on ground, in shrubs and low trees. Flies bouncingly, revealing chestnut rump and contrasting blackish white-tipped end of tail. Associates with other thornbills, whitefaces; often first noted by call.

Similar species: Slate-backed Thornbill (561). All races of Brown (557) and Broad-tailed (558) Thornbills have dark eyes, streaked breasts.

Voice: Contact note, penetrating 'see' or 'see-see'. Animated far-carrying territorial song based on this, from tops of mulgas, etc.; also double buzzing scold and 'tchik, tchik' flight-call.

Habitat: Widespread in inland habitats: drier woodlands, scrubs and thickets including saltbush, bluebush, lignum, grasslands in farming country, mostly among dead trees, stumps.

Breeding: Nest: domed; of grasses, fur, feathers; unusually for a thornbill, placed in a hollow stump, fence-post or tree-hollow; 1–15 m high. Eggs: 2–4; white, spotted red-brown, mostly at large end.

Range and Status: S. (mostly inland) Aust.: s. WA s. of Fortescue R. *except* sw. corner, w. of Moora–Lake Grace–Esperance; e. through s. NT, n. to about Tea Tree–Jervois Ra., nearly to Winton–Charleville–Chinchilla in Q, with a record 115 km e. of Hughenden; in NSW, e. to about Moree–Grenfell–Corowa, thence s. to Nagambie–Bendigo–Kiata, Vic., and Murray mallee–Yorke Pen.–Eyre Pen., SA. Common; sedentary.

561 SLATE-BACKED THORNBILL *Acanthiza robustirostris* Pl.73

Other names: Large-billed, Robust-billed or Thick-billed Thornbill; Robust Thornbill, Thick-billed Tit.

Field marks: 95 mm. Handsome but seldom-observed dweller of far-inland: *head and back noticeably blue-grey, crown with fine dark streaks*; (the only thornbill with these); bill shortish and robust, eye red; rump and base of tail tawny or pale-chestnut; underparts unstreaked, whitish, washed buff. Usually in pairs, feeds in foliage; associates with inland races of Broad-tailed Thornbill (558).

Similar species: Broad-tailed Thornbill (558), inland forms: more buff-grey above, with scalloped foreheads, streaked breasts. Chestnut-rumped Thornbill (560): pale eye, unstreaked whitish breast.

Voice: Somewhat similar to Broad-tailed Thornbill group, including 'see-see' contact-call; also harsh 'thrip thrip' alarm-call, high-pitched twitterings.

Habitat: Denser inland scrubs, mainly mulga; in WA also reported in swamp herbage near salt-lakes.

Breeding: Nest: domed, with hooded side-entrance, of dried grasses, bound with spiders' web; upper part rather fragile. Eggs: 3; white, with faint tinge of pink, finely speckled red-brown, in cap over large end.

Range and Status: W. inland Aust.: from far-sw. Q (26 km w. of Eromanga), w. through s. NT n. to Hermannsburg and s. to Everard–Musgrave Ras. in SA; thence to w. coastal WA near Shark Bay, n. to Peak Hill–Ophthalmia R. and s. to Yalgoo–Broad Arrow. Uncommon.

562 WESTERN THORNBILL   *Acanthiza inornata*   Pl.73

Other names: Bark or Plain-coloured Tit.

Field marks: 100 mm. The plainest thornbill: grey-brown above, tawny-olive on rump, tail buff-brown with blackish subterminal band; *creamy buff below without streaks*; *eye pale*. Pairs or parties, feeds in foliage, descending to lower bushes and ground. The w. representative of the Buff-rumped Thornbill group (562–4), its different habits probably reflect absence of intra-specific competition. Note range.

Similar species: Samphire Thornbill (564): contrasting buff rump; ranges probably do not overlap.

Voice: Quiet tinkling twitter; mimics.

Habitat: Tall forests to open woodlands and coastal scrubs.

Breeding: Nest: domed with side entrance; of grasses, plant-stems and fibres, and spiders' web; usually in centre of bushy tree against trunk, in tree-hollow, upright small branches of shrub or tree or under bark. Eggs: 3; fleshy white, freckled with irregular red-brown markings, with heavy zone toward large end.

Range and Status: Confined to sw. WA from Hill R.–Moora s. and e. to the Stirling Ras. Common; sedentary.

563 BUFF-RUMPED THORNBILL   *Acanthiza reguloides*   Pl.73

Other names: Bark or Buff-rumped Tit, Buff-tailed or Varied Thornbill.

Field marks: 110 mm. Plain greyish olive above, *contrasting with yellow-buff rump and blackish pale-tipped tail*; underparts washed yellow-buff and unstreaked; forehead and sides of face have fine deep-buff scalloping; *eye pale*. Pairs or parties; active, moves quickly over ground and bark of lower parts of trees. When disturbed, flies bouncingly ahead, *disclosing flashes of buff rump*. Note that n. birds, specially race *squamata*, 'Varied Thornbill', *are greener above, rump and underparts yellower*; without care they can easily be mistaken for Yellow-rumped Thornbills (565).

Similar species: Yellow-rumped Thornbill (565). In w. Vic. (Little Desert) and adjacent areas of SA, Samphire Thornbill (564), race *hedleyi*, may cause confusion but note smaller area of buff on rump; faint streaks on dirty white underparts; specialized habitat.

Voice: Rapidly repeated musical tinkling call on two alternating notes. 'pit-pit-pit-pitta-pitta' or 'zizizip-zizizip'; harder and more metallic than Yellow-rumped and not cyclic.

Habitat: Ground, trunks and lower limbs in untidy open forest, woodland and scrubs; often among tussocks, fallen branches, shrubs.

Breeding: Nest untidy, domed; of grasses, bark-fibre and spiders' web; on ground among debris, fallen limbs, base of tree, in tussock, under bark or among accumulated debris in tree fork. Eggs: 4; whitish, freckled or streaked red-brown and few spots of purplish lilac; usually with zone at large end.

Range and Status: E. and se. Aust.: subcoastal e. Q n. to Atherton Tableland and w. nearly to Einasleigh–Hughenden in n. and Blackall–Mitchell–Warwick in s.; e. NSW w. to lower foothills of Divide and w. in river red gum forests of Murray R., Edward R. and Billabong Creek to about Wanganella–Barham; throughout Vic. *except* for nw. mallee areas; se. SA w. to Mt. Lofty Ras. Patchy and generally uncommon. The range in ne. Q is occupied by the very yellow race *squamata*. Common; sedentary.

564 SAMPHIRE THORNBILL *Acanthiza iredalei* Pl.73

Other names: Dark, Slender or Slender-billed Thornbill.

Field marks: 80–95 mm. A sombre-plumaged thornbill divided into three isolated races, each differing in intensity of shading. All have *pale eyes and pale scalloped pattern on forehead. Rump buff, but extent varies*; tail blackish with slightly paler tips. (1) *Nominate race*: the palest; pale grey-brown above, washed olive; *breast pale buff-white, almost without dark streaks; largish buff rump*. (2) Race *rosinae*: darkest race; dark grey-olive above; *throat and breast grey-white with fine blackish streaks*, rest of underparts deep olive-buff; *buff rump scarcely evident*. (3) Race *hedleyi*: paler olive-grey above, dirty-white below, with slight dark streaks; small buff rump. Usually in small flocks, feeds on ground or in low bushes. When disturbed, moves some distance in low bouncing flight, buff rump contrasting with blackish tail.

Similar species: Buff-rumped Thornbill (563): larger, deeper yellow-buff below; larger rich-buff rump; voice distinctive; note habitat.

Voice: Contact-call: tinny rattling 'tsip tsip tsip'.

Habitat: *Nominate race*: often in saltbush and near dry salt-lakes, samphire on margins of inland salt-lakes, also on coast in mangroves, and scrubby vegetation of Nullarbor Plain. Race *rosinae*: samphire in saltmarshes; saltbush. Race *hedleyi*: dwarf banksia, casuarina-scrubs and similar heath-vegetation.

Breeding: Nest: domed, with side-entrance near top; of grasses and plant-down; usually in top of low shrub. Eggs: 3; white finely-speckled reddish brown, mostly at large end.

Range and Status: *Nominate race*: from Carnarvon–Shark Bay, WA, e. through mid-WA (s. of Wiluna and n. of Kalgoorlie) to Port Augusta–Flinders Ras., SA, possibly extending to s. NT. Race *rosinae*: confined to head and e. shores of St. Vincent Gulf, SA. Race *hedleyi*: Lake Albert, near Meningie, SA, e. to the Little Desert in w. Vic. Local and uncommon; sedentary or nomadic.

565 YELLOW-RUMPED THORNBILL *Acanthiza chrysorrhoa* Pl.73

Other names: Chigaree, Tomtit; Yellow-tailed Thornbill, Yellow-rumped or Yellow-tailed Tit.

Field marks: 100–120 mm. Largest and most distinctly marked thornbill, with *bright-yellow rump, white eyebrow, white-spotted black crown, pale eye*. Inland races and nw. Q. race, *normantoni*, are distinctly paler, being more greenish above, whitish below, washed yellow. Pairs or small flocks; feeds much on ground, hops, teeters tail. Flies bouncingly to settle again or shelter in tree or shrub, *yellow rump contrasting with black white-tipped tail*. Note pretty calls and characteristic flight-note.

Similar species: Buff-rumped Thornbill (563): plainer and buffer, without strong head-pattern; its ne. race, *squamata*, has yellowish rump and underparts, but no white eyebrow or white spots on crown.

Voice: Song: vivacious merry tinkling with cyclic pattern; flight-call repeated 'check'.

Habitat: Open woodlands, scrublands, grasslands; paddocks and roadsides with nearby stands of trees; plantations, often including introduced pines and cypresses; parks, gardens.

Breeding: Nest: unusual, somewhat untidy. Domed, with hooded, hidden side-entrance; and with an additional (often tilted and rudimentary) open cup-like 'nest' for an upper storey; of grasses, plant-fibres and rubbish, felted and bound with spiders' web, often with egg sacs attached. In shrub, low foliage of tree, including introduced pine, up to 8 m, outer sticks of nest of hawk or eagle, or old nest of babbler. Eggs: 3–4; dull-white, lightly-spotted red-brown, mostly at large end.

Range and Status: S. Aust. and Tas.; and much of Q: from Murchison and upper Gasgoyne and Ashburton Rs., WA, to s. NT, n. to Tennant Ck.; and to Mt. Isa–Croydon, Q, with (? isolate) population n. to Burketown–Normanton on Gulf. Not in e. coastal Q n. of Rockhampton. Common, sedentary.

566 YELLOW THORNBILL *Acanthiza nana* **Pl.73**

Other names: Little Thornbill or Tit; Yellow-breasted Thornbill or Tomtit; Yellow Dicky. *Note:* Although long known as 'Little Thornbill', this species is not obviously smaller than others but *is* distinctly yellower. Revival of an earlier common name, Yellow Thornbill, thus seems sensible.

Field marks: 100 mm. *The yellowest thornbill:* greenish above, *with dark eye; plain (bright or pale) yellowish below, washed ochre on chin and throat.* No white streaks on crown but dark ear-coverts streaked paler. Inland populations are much paler. Singly, pairs, parties or feeding associations with other small passerines; moves quickly through outer branches or foliage; hovers round leaves, showing dark tail, pale tips. Even more than other thornbills, always seems to be moving somewhere.

Similar species: Weebill (547). Striated Thornbill (567): crown (as well as ear-coverts) streaked whitish; underparts prominently streaked brown. Fairy Warbler (554): greyer above, with some white on throat; unstreaked; calls differ. White-throated Warbler (555) imm: throat yellowish, no streaks on cheeks.

Voice: Brisk 'chidid' or 'chidid-tis-tiz', somewhat harsher than Striated, more like Weebill; uttered constantly.

Habitat: Drier woodlands, sub-inland scrubs, riverine forests, timber in paddocks, mangroves; golf-courses, orchards, parks, gardens. Seems to have a particular affinity for acacias.

Breeding: Nest: domed and untidy, with side-entrance; of bark-shreds, grasses, tendrils, mosses and lichens, bound with spiders' web; usually suspended high in small branches or foliage. Eggs: 2–4; whitish, blotched, freckled red-brown, chocolate and lilac.

Range and Status: Widespread in e. and se. Aust.: in Q, from Mackay w. to Blackall–Cunnamulla; in NSW, w. to Ivanhoe–Cobar; widespread in Vic.; in SA, s. and w. to Goolwa–Adelaide, n. to Flinders Ras. There is an isolate population in area of Atherton Tableland, ne. Q. Common but patchy; sedentary, (?) part-nomadic.

567 STRIATED THORNBILL *Acanthiza lineata* **Pl.73**

Other names: Striated Tit, Striped Tit-warbler.

Field marks: 100 mm. Often confused with Brown Thornbill (557), but of richer shades, more distinctive pattern, and calls; eye pale-brown. *Note white streaks on warm-brown crown (the only thornbill with these); dense pale streaks on face and ear-coverts;* back greenish, rump and tail warm-brown; yellowish white below, streaked black. Imm: more fawn. Parties to small flocks; feeds in and hovers round foliage and bark of taller shrubs and large trees, often to great heights, showing *dark tailband.* Forms feeding associations with other small passerines; often associates with Yellow Thornbill (566).

Similar species: Weebill (547): short bill, creamish eyebrow; no pale streaks on crown. Brown Thornbill (557): browner above, greyer below; forehead scalloped, ear-coverts not streaked; eye dark. Yellow Thornbill (566).

Voice: Quick, insect-like 'tiziz, tiziz', many other high-pitched, insect-like notes, more splintered than Brown Thornbill.

Habitat: From temperate rainforests to drier woodlands; mangroves, parks, gardens.

Breeding: Nest: neat, rounded, with hooded side-entrance; of bark-fibres, grasses, bound with spiders' web; suspended from outer small branches in foliage, 1–20 m high. Eggs: 2–4; pinkish-white, irregularly freckled with various red-browns, usually with zone at large end.

Range and Status: Coastal and sub-inland se. Aust.: se. Q from near Maryborough inland to Bunya Mts.–Toowoomba–Warwick; in NSW, inland on w. slopes of Divide to about Coonabarabran–West Wyalong; also river red gum forests of Murray V. to about Gunbower–Barham; widespread in Vic. n. to Bendigo–Grampians, w. to coastal se. SA, Kangaroo I., and n. to Mt. Lofty Ras. Common in suitable habitat; sedentary.

WHITEFACES Genus *Aphelocephala*

Three species of mostly ground-feeding small birds of mainly inland districts. They are apparently related to thornbills. Their sturdy bills reflect a catholic diet that includes seeds as well as insects. All have whitish faces and are easily recognized.

568 SOUTHERN WHITEFACE *Aphelocephala leucopsis* Pl.72

Other names: Eastern or Western Whiteface; Squeaker, Tom tit.

Field marks: 100–125 mm. A simply marked, sturdy small bird: grey-brown above, *white mask from above bill to below eye, margined blackish above. Bill fairly sturdy, slightly curved; eye whitish to straw-yellow.* Underparts pale-grey with the colour of the flanks becoming more reddish toward the w. part of range: forms in e. Aust. have buff-grey flanks; with darker mark near legs; flanks are reddish buff in SA, c. Aust. and se. WA, and *rich pale-chestnut* in the c. WA race *castaneiventris* 'Western Whiteface'. All races have broad black tailband, tipped white. Pairs to small flocks, feeds mostly on or near ground, often with ground-feeding thornbills and in inland with other whitefaces; investigates stumps, fence-posts; continually flirts tail. When disturbed, takes cover in shrubs.

Similar species: Chestnut-breasted Whiteface (569): chestnut breastband, rusty-buff lower back and rump. Banded Whiteface (570): black breastband, rusty-buff above. Zebra Finch (672), imm: greyer, black tail with white ladder-pattern.

Voice: Continual squeaking 'tweet-tweeter' on one note; flight-call, brisk 'wit, wit-awit'.

Habitat: Open grasslands, sparse open forest and inland scrubs, usually with dead trees, stumps; where overlapping range of Banded Whiteface, reported to favour mulga thickets rather than open plains.

Breeding: Nest: large untidy, domed; of grasses, rootlets or bark; in hollow limb, stump or fence-post or in foliage of shrub or low tree; also in sheds, boxes. Eggs: 2–5; variable; whitish to buff or purplish grey, freckled or blotched brown to reddish often with zone at large end.

Range and Status: Widespread in inland s. Aust.: ranges e. to Darling Downs, Q; Armidale–Sydney area–Goulburn, NSW; Wodonga–Yea, Vic; in s. Vic. approaches coast at You Yangs, thence w. to Horsham–Edenhope; in SA s. to Joanna–Adelaide area–Eyre Pen.; all s. WA *except* sw. corner w. of Eucla–Mullewa; ranges n. to beyond Tropic in WA and NT e. to Jervois Ra.; and n. to Birdsville–MacGregor Ra.–Chinchilla Q. Locally common, but patchy; sedentary.

569 CHESTNUT-BREASTED WHITEFACE *Aphelocephala pectoralis* Pl.72

Field marks: 100 mm. The whiteface of most restricted and remote range; seldom observed. Like Banded Whiteface (570) *but with broad pale-rusty breastband.* Imm: paler breastband, with a few dark spots. Pairs or small flocks, usually hopping on ground; shy; when approached flies to take cover in low bushes. Associates with Southern Whiteface (568) and Banded Whiteface. The call, once known, should alert observer to its presence.

Similar species: Banded Whiteface (570).

Voice: Silvery tinkling trill weaker and softer than Banded Whiteface.

Habitat: Semi-desert tablelands: sparse bluebush interspersed with bare ground or gibber; fringes of mulga and similar sparse scrubs.

Breeding: Nest: (one described); globular with side-entrance near top but no entrance-spout; very loosely constructed of dead twigs; lined with a little wool and small feathers; in bluebush 30 cm from ground. Eggs: 3; described as rounded, oval, pale-pink without gloss; coloured with purplish grey markings, densest on large end.

Range and Status: Confined to ce. SA, from near Port Augusta n. to Oodnadatta, w. to about Coober Pedy and e. to about L. Frome. Status little known but appears to be local and uncommon.

570 BANDED WHITEFACE *Aphelocephala nigricincta* **Pl.72**

Other names: Black-banded Squeaker or Whiteface.
Field marks: 110–125 mm. A whiteface with *distinct black band across whitish breast*; *sandy-buff above, richer on rump*; tail blackish, tipped buff-white. Pairs or small flocks, often with other whitefaces or thornbills. Feeds mostly on ground, hops actively; takes cover in low bushes. Male has distinctive song-flight; rising high at an angle, flutters momentarily, singing, before dropping back to cover (other whitefaces may behave similarly).
Similar species: Southern Whiteface (568). Chestnut-breasted Whiteface (569). Double-barred Finch (673).
Voice: Song, musical trill or tinkle, sometimes in flight; somewhat like 'alarm-clock' note of White-plumed Honeyeater (616); alarm-call, harsh cricket-like 'bzz-bzz'.
Habitat: Open mulga and other inland scrubs, vegetation along watercourses; saltbush, bluebush and grasslands, gibber; sandhills with sparse low shrubs.
Breeding: Nest: domed; of sticks, with spoutlike entrance; in open bush (WA); *or of* grasses, bark; in hollow spout. Eggs: 3–4.
Range and Status: Inland and cw. Aust. e. to far-sw. Q (e. and n. to beyond Warri Gate–Betoota–Bedourie); n. in NT to Tarlton Downs–Barrow Creek–Tanami; n. in WA to Godfrey's Tank–Jigalong, w. and s. to middle Gascoyne R.–Cue; s. in SA to Musgrave Ras.–L. Eyre Basin. Fairly common.

Sittellas Family *Neosittidae*

Small climbing birds with longish, slightly upturned bills, large strong feet, large wings and short tails. They resemble the nuthatches of the n. hemisphere. They live in flocks of up to twenty or more and travel between trees in bouncing flight, with a scatter of high-pitched calls, revealing large wings, prominent coloured wingpatches (orange in s. Aust., white in n.) and pale rumps. They settle head-downward on high branches and typically work downwards with a jerky rocking-horse action, making short flights between branches, often opening and shivering wings. Gripping with strong feet, they probe crevices in bark and lever flakes of bark away to reach their small animal food. Sittellas in Aust. are now treated as a single species, in five or six races that occupy abutting or marginally over-lapping ranges over almost the whole Australian mainland except denser rainforests and treeless regions. In the following accounts, references to habits, voice and breeding are given for the nominate race only; other races vary little in these respects but, because habitat is probably one reason why several races maintain separate status, an indication of habitat (and range) is given for each race. The nest, placed in a deep fork, is a master-piece. A very deep cup, it fills in the gap between the forks, and is hung with flakes of bark so as to be nearly invisible.
Food: Insects, spiders and other small invertebrates.
Range: Mainland Aust. and NG.
Number of species: World 3; Aust. 1.

571 VARIED SITTELLA *Daphoenositta chrysoptera* **Pl.74**

Other names: Orange-winged, White-headed, Black-capped, White-winged, Striated Sittella; Barkpecker, Treerunner, Woodpecker.
Field marks: 115–125 mm. Nominate race: the least clearly-marked form; *head grey or blackish*, back paler grey-brown with broad dark streaks, rump whitish, tail black with white tips; *wings blackish with pale-orange patch across primaries*, conspicuous in flight; throat and underparts whitish grey, *very lightly streaked in Vic., streaking increasing through n. NSW and inland s. Q.* Bill blackish brown with pale tip, base of upper mandible

orange. Unlike other races, sexes do not differ greatly but females tend to have darker cheeks. Imm: paler, wing-coverts tipped buff; underparts whitish.

Voice: Usual call, high-pitched thin 'seewit-seewee', often in flight; flying flocks let fall continual rain of 'chip chip' notes; feeding flocks, insect-like notes; alarm-call, rapid high-pitched 'didididit'; song described as 'tzir, zit-zit, tzir-zit-zat-zat'.

Habitat: Eucalypt woodlands and forests (except heavier rainforests); also mallee, acacia and coastal tea-tree scrubs; golf-courses, shelter-belts, orchards, parks, scrubby gardens.

Breeding: Nest: extremely beautiful well-camouflaged deep cup; of flakes of bark and lichens, bound with spiders' web and moulded to resemble bulge of wood; usually in upright fork of living or dead branch in eucalypt, sheoak, paperbark or coast tea-tree, 5–20 m high. Eggs: 3; blue-white to grey-white, speckled and blotched glossy black, olive-brown; many faint grey underlying markings in zone at large end.

Range and Status: Central and e. Vic.; e. NSW and inland s. Q, merging there with *leucocephala*. Merges with *pileata* in w. Vic. and central NSW. Common; sedentary or nomadic.

Race *leucocephala* 'White-headed Sittella': like n. examples of nominate race *but head and neck wholly whitish in both sexes*. Some imms. reported to have white heads, others grey. **Habitat.** In s. part of range, usually in forests and woodlands of Divide and coastal plain e. of Range; in n. parts, where apparently no competition with nominate race, ranges into more open grassy woodlands. **Range.** From Clarence R., n. NSW, to Darling Downs–Mitchell–Blackall–Suttor Ck, Q, and to coast near Mackay. Merges with nominate race in ne. NSW and se. Q, and with *striatus* in zone n. to Townsville–Charters Towers.

Note. 'Pied Sittella' race *albata* has been 'lost' since several were collected near Bowen, Q, in late 19th. century. It appears to be an intergrade between *leucocephala* and *striatus*. Principal field mark is *unique combination of creamy white head and white wing-patches*.

Race *pileata* 'Black-capped Sittella': more boldly marked and clean cut than nominate race, from which it differs in *glossy black crown, pure-white unstreaked underparts and back plain grey-brown or with slight dark streaks*; note also basal third of bill deep-yellow, rest dark-brown. Male: black crown isolated by white forehead and white sides to face. Female: black continues over forehead and cheeks. Imm. greyish-black crown, streaked whitish in juvs. In flight, *orange wing-patch*, white rump, white tips to black tail conspicuous. **Habitat.** From coastal eucalypt forests and woodlands to inland scrubs, including mallee, mulga and native pine; in inland areas timber lining watercourses, gullies and gorges of ranges; golf-courses, orchards, parks, gardens. **Range.** WA s. of Tropic; s. NT, all SA; w. Vic. (occasional to inland e. Vic.); w. NSW and sw. Q. Merges with nominate race in c. Vic. and c. NSW and with *leucoptera* in c. Q. to c. NT and mid-nw. WA.

Race *leucoptera* 'White-winged Sittella': very like *pileata*, but *wing-patch white instead of pale-orange*. Bill golden-yellow with black tip. Imm: head greyish. *In flight, white wing-patch very conspicuous*. **Habitat.** Grassy woodlands, timber along watercourses and scrubby timber on ranges. **Range.** From Opalton–Winton–Cloncurry n. to Gulf in nw. Q, w. through top end NT to Kimberleys, s. to about Tropic in Q and NT, and to about Broome in WA. Merges with *striatus* in area of lower Flinders R.–Cloncurry, nw. Q, and with *pileata* in s. NT and mid-nw. WA.

Race *striatus* 'Striated Sittella': *darkest-headed and most streaked sittella*. Both sexes grey-white above, *streaked brownish black, whitish underparts finely streaked blackish*. Male: crown black. *Female: head, throat and sometimes upperbreast black. Wing-patch white*; bill yellow with black tip. Imm: no streaks on breast. **Habitat.** Eucalypt forests, grassy woodlands and scrublands. **Range.** Ne. Q, from Townsville n. to C. York, and w. to Normanton. Merges with *leucocephala* in area of Charters Towers–Townsville and with *leucoptera* in area of lower Flinders R.–Cloncurry.

Australian Treecreepers Family *Climacteridae*

Rather robust small birds with strong legs, large feet and claws for gripping trunks of trees and strong, slightly curved bills for probing crevices in bark. Unlike Old World treecreepers, they do not have stiff pointed tail-feathers to serve as props when ascending vertical trunks and their approach to a tree is usually the reverse of that of sittellas. Foraging singly or in pairs, they usually start with a downward planing glide from high in one tree to base of the next, then hop briskly upwards, spiralling round the trunk. They are very agile and often perform the impossible by hopping upside-down along the underside of limbs. Several species, specially those in drier open habitats, feed much on ground. They build untidy nests concealed in hollow trunks or branches. Their calls are brisk, sharp and piping. In plumage they are mainly brownish above with streaked underparts and all have a prominent buffish or whitish wingstripe. Species are recognized mostly by general shade, colour and length of eyebrow-stripe, and intensity of streaking on underparts. Females are distinguished by rust-coloured eyebrows or rusty marks on neck or upperbreast.

Food: Insects, specially ants; other small invertebrates; also seeds.
Range: Aust. and Tas.; NG.
Number of species: World 7; Aust. 6.

572 WHITE-THROATED TREECREEPER *Climacteris leucophaea* Pl.74

Other names: Little Treecreeper, Woodpecker.
Field marks: 160–175 mm. *A dark treecreeper with prominent white throat.* Olive-grey above, outer tail-feathers with broad subterminal black band; *underparts washed yellow-buff, sides of breast dark-grey with prominent black-bordered whitish streaks.* Female: small orange spot below and behind ear-coverts. Imm: distinctive; streaked pale above, *rump distinctly chestnut.* Singly, pairs or family parties. Seldom on ground; otherwise behaves like other treecreepers. When moving any distance, flight fast and swooping, displaying prominent pale-fawn wingbar. Note that the isolate n. Q race, *minor*, 'Little Treecreeper' (regarded as a full species by Schodde, 1975) is *much smaller (140 mm) and darker*; white throat much-reduced, upperbreast deep grey-buff; underparts buff, heavily streaked white with black margins.
Similar species: Red-browed Treecreeper (573): rufous eyebrow and eyering; more completely streaked below.
Voice: A loud high-pitched piping, beginning with several clear single notes or in a burst; repeated interminably, falling slightly and slowing; also a whistle sounding like someone wishing to attract attention, turning up at end; in courtship, beautiful rapid mellow trill or warble.
Habitat: Subtropical and temperate rainforests, wetter eucalypt forests and woodlands, tall humid coastal tea-tree and banksia-scrubs; riverine forests, drier woodlands to sub-inland scrubs including taller mallee, belah and brigalow.
Breeding: Nest: loose collection of shreds of bark, thickly lined with fur and feathers, often including charcoal; usually in hollow branch or trunk, 5–15 m or more high, occasionally in cavity in wall of building, mine-shaft. Eggs: 2–3; white, finely spotted red and purple-brown.
Range and Status: E. and se. Aust. and some coastal islands: from Cooktown, Q, to Mt. Lofty Ras., SA. The race *minor* occupies the n. part of the range, mostly in rainforest above 300 m from near Cooktown s. to Eungella Ra., inland of Mackay and probably further s. Nominate race: s. from Rockhampton, inland to Carnarvon Ra.–Darling Downs; through e. NSW to w. slopes of Divide, s. Riverina and sw. NSW in river red gum forests on and adjacent to Murray R. and tributaries; all Vic. except drier mallee of far nw.; se. SA w. to Mt. Lofty Ras. Common; sedentary.

573 RED-BROWED TREECREEPER *Climacteris erythrops* **Pl.74**

Field marks: 135–150 mm. A dark treecreeper somewhat like White-throated (572) *but with rich-rusty eyebrow and eyering*; throat whitish, upperbreast grey-brown, underparts like White-throated *but more uniformly patterned with black-bordered white streaks.* Female: more conspicuous rusty-red eyebrow and eyering, *upper breast streaked rusty.* Imm: grey instead of rusty markings round eye, no streaks below. Pairs or small parties; shyer and quieter than White-throated; usually higher in trees. Flight fast and undulating, displaying grey-buff wingbar.

Similar species: White-throated Treecreeper (572).

Voice: Usual call like White-throated, but softer, less piping and sustained; harsh high-pitched medley also described.

Habitat: Wetter denser temperate rainforests and wetter eucalypt forests mainly in hilly and mountainous country.

Breeding: Nest: collection of bark-shreds lined with fur, in hollow, 6–30 m high. Eggs: 2–3; delicate pink-white, finely spotted red and purple-red.

Range and Status: Se. Aust.: from se. Q (Tewantin) through forested highlands and coastal parts of NSW, e. and se. Vic. in highlands and forests on coast s. to Wilson's Prom. and w. to ranges e. and n. of Melbourne. Not common anywhere; sedentary.

574 WHITE-BROWED TREECREEPER *Climacteris affinis* **Pl.74**

Field marks: 140–145 mm. Like Brown Treecreeper (575) but smaller; note *bolder whitish eyebrow, and bolder streaks on ear-coverts; greyer upperparts, bolder and whiter stripes on underparts.* Male: small cluster of black streaks in centre of upperbreast. Female: eyebrow starts with orange-rufous spot; *breast-streaks rufous, broader and extending over whole breast.* Imm: underparts not heavily streaked. Pairs, family parties; feeds much on ground among fallen trunks, stumps; when disturbed, flies to nearest stump or tree. In taller growth behaves like other treecreepers.–see introduction. In flight, note greyish fawn wingbar, dark subterminal tailband.

Similar species: Brown Treecreeper (575). Black-tailed Treecreeper (577): sooty above, no white eyebrow.

Voice: Rather quiet; typical treecreeper-calls: a sharp thin 'peep, peep' and a scolding chatter; also 'peter-peter' like Jacky Winter (454); other calls described as tinkling.

Habitat: Semi-arid and arid inland scrubs, mulga, native pine, sheoak, desert-oak, corkwood; black box-lignum associations n. of Murray in SA, to saltbush associations. In open, sparsely vegetated country, dry gravelly ridges, stands of belar in mallee country.

Breeding: Nest: collection of grass and shreds of bark, lined with fur or hair; in hollow stump or tree usually near ground. Eggs: 2–3; pink, covered with fine deep-pink and purplish red spots.

Range and Status: S. inland Aust., extending to drier w. and Bight coasts: from upper Gasgoyne R.–Murchison R.–Mingenew, WA, s. to Southern Cross– Kalgoorlie and e. through n. Nullarbor Plain to Gawler Ras., s. Flinders Ras. and Murray mallee, SA; nw. Vic., s. to Wyperfeld NP; through far-w. NSW and sw. Q e. to Mitchell and n. to Blackall, thence w. through Channel Country to Coniston, NT. Uncommon to rare; probably sedentary.

575 BROWN TREECREEPER *Climacteris picumnus* **Pl.74**

Other name: Woodpecker.

Field marks: 165–175 mm. A rather plain treecreeper; *head grey, rest of upperparts pale-brown; note short buff eyebrow, dark mark through eye*; upperbreast plain mouse-grey, cut off by regular black-edged pale-buff streaks on underparts. Male: cluster of fine black streaks in centre of upperbreast. Female: cluster of rufous streaks. Imm: breast nearly unstreaked. Singly, pairs or family parties. Very active; in flight, pale-buff wingbar, dark subterminal tail-band. Note that the n. race *melanota*, 'Black Treecreeper' is uniform

blackish brown above, with long cream-white eyebrow; because of general darkness of tail, the blackish tail-band is not apparent in flight.
Similar species: White-browed Treecreeper (574): stronger whitish eyebrow, black-streaked ear-coverts, bolder black and white streaks below; note range. Black-tailed Treecreeper (577): note range.
Voice: Strident 'spink!' uttered once, twice or rapidly repeated, becoming slower and descending; also harsh sparrow-like rattle.
Habitat: Drier forests and woodlands; timber along watercourses and round shores of lakes (especially further inland); taller scrublands; paddocks with standing dead timber; among stumps; margins of denser wooded areas.
Breeding: Nest: collection of grass, lined with fur; usually in tree-hollow 3–10 m or higher; or in stump or fence-post near ground where base may be substantially built up with grass or horse, cow or kangaroo dung. Eggs: 2–3; pink, thickly freckled and streaked red and purple, most heavily at large end.
Range and Status: E. Aust., from e. SA to n. Q. Nominate race: from Spencer Gulf–L. Frome, SA, throughout Vic. *except* wetter forests and woodlands and s. coastal districts; (?) vagrant Flinders I., Bass Strait; all NSW *except* wetter forests and woodlands in e.; in Q, widespread w. to Channel Country and Richmond, n. on e. coast to about Townsville. Race *melanota*: C. York Pen., from drier parts of Cardwell Ra.–Conjuboy–Forsayth to s. of Normanton, n. to about Weipa on w. coast but seldom to e. coastal areas. Common in suitable habitat; sedentary.

576 RUFOUS TREECREEPER *Climacteris rufa* Pl.74

Other name: Woodpecker.
Field marks: 150–175 mm. The richest-coloured treecreeper: *buff-grey above, with rufous eyebrow; rusty below,* centre of breast finely streaked black and buff in male, buff only in female. Imm: plainer, with distinct rufous rump. Habits like Brown Treecreeper (575); colour makes it rather conspicuous as it spirals up trunks. In flight, note rufous wingbar, dark subterminal tail-band.
Voice: Single penetrating 'peep'; churring scolds.
Habitat: Wider than other treecreepers. Jarrah-karri forests in humid sw. corner of WA; timber along watercourses, golf-courses, parks, wandoo and salmon-gum woodlands further inland; marble gum and mallee-spinifex associations n. of Nullarbor; on Eyre Pen. SA in mallee-woodland associations.
Breeding: Nest: collection of soft grasses, lined with plant-down and feathers; base often built up with fur or dung; usually in hollow near ground, but up to 8 m high. Eggs: 2–3; whitish, with reddish spots and splashes.
Range and Status: Sw. Aust.: from sw. WA, e. to Eyre Pen., SA, except for unsuitable habitat on Nullarbor Plain; n. to Shark Bay, inland to Laverton–Vokes Hill–Gawler Ras. Common in suitable habitat; sedentary.

577 BLACK-TAILED TREECREEPER *Climacteris melanura* Pl.74

Other names: Allied or Chestnut-bellied Treecreeper.
Field marks: 170–200 mm. The darkest treecreeper. Sooty-brown to blackish above, earthy rufous-brown below; *no pale eyebrow but ear-coverts finely streaked black and white.* Male: centre of throat and upperbreast *streaked black and white.* Female: *throat white, streaking into rich-chestnut on upperbreast.* Primaries crossed by broad buff-white band, showing as streak when wing closed, bold wingbar in flight. Habits typical of treecreepers.
Similar species: Care needed where range approaches that of Brown Treecreeper race *melanota* (575) in region of Leichhardt and Flinders Rs., nw. Q. In flight away from observer, both look blackish with buff-white wingbar.
Voice: Clear strident 'pee, peepeepeepeepeepee, pee, pee'.

Habitat: Open eucalypt forest, grassy woodlands and open scrub in hilly and breakaway country and lowlands; in nw. Aust. large timber, river gums along watercourses.
Breeding: Nest: of grass, lined with feathers; in hollow 4–10 m high. Eggs: 2–3; pink-white, spotted all over with rich purple-red and purple, most heavily on large end.
Range and Status: Nw. and n. Aust.: from Carnarvon, WA, through Hamersleys and Kimberleys into NT s. to Banka Banka–Alexandria; in nw. Q, e. to lower Leichhardt R.–Cloncurry. An apparently isolate small pale race *wellsi* occurs in c-w. WA, roughly between the de Grey and Gascoyne Rs. Common; sedentary.

Honeyeaters Family *Meliphagidae*

One of our most characteristic, widespread and well-differentiated families, owing much to the dominance of eucalypts, acacias, banksias, grevilleas and other nectar-bearing, insect-attracting flowering plants in the Australian flora. They occupy every vegetational zone and feed mainly on insects and nectar from blossoms, and on fruits and berries, including mistletoe-berries. They probably rival insects in importance as pollinators. Perhaps their most districtive features are the generally longish curved bill and long fine flexible tongue, curved on the edges near the base and divided toward the tip, each section being edged with a fine brush-like process. When feeding, the tongue can often be seen darting from the tip of the bill. Honeyeaters range in size from the Scarlet Honeyeater (100 mm) of e. Aust. to the Yellow Wattlebird of Tas. (400 mm). Colours vary, but grey-greens, greys and browns predominate, often with streaks, or black, white or yellowish markings. Several groups have bare skin on the head, colourful in some; others have distinctive features such as knob on bill or coloured wattles. In some other species e.g. Brown (625) and Fuscous (614) Honeyeaters, the gape (skin at corners of mouth) and/or orbit (fleshy ring round eye) may be either yellow or black. The reasons for this are not fully understood. However there is evidence that black coloration of these parts is indicative of breeding condition. *When honeyeaters feed in blossoms heavy with pollen their heads and faces may be heavily dusted cream to orange–a fact to note.* Honeyeaters are active vigorous birds, darting or threading through foliage and blossoms when feeding, often flying up to snap flying insects. Their voices are clear and strong; several have attractive sustained songs, but the calls of large forms are raucous. Dependence on blossoming plants has caused much mobility in many species. About half the inland forms are nomadic in response to blossoming of plants and abundance of insects after rainfall, and even in better-watered coastal areas there is considerable movement related to blossoming. Some species are regular migrants. In particular, autumn migration of Yellow-faced (599) and White-naped (622) Honeyeaters in coastal se. Aust. can be spectacular, with seemingly-endless streams or parties of birds travelling at treetop level. Many honeyeaters have adapted well to altered habitats, and in most parts of Aust. one species or several are common in orchards, vineyards or suburban areas, feeding in native or introduced trees and shrubs. Except for larger species that build shallow nests of sticks, the typical honeyeater nest is a fragile suspended cup of great beauty, evidence of remarkable structural skill. Two species, Brown-backed (633) and Bar-breasted (634) Honeyeaters, build domed nests and Blue-faced Honeyeater (588) may use the old nest of another bird as a base for its own. Eggs are typically pinkish with darker spots; the family is heavily parasitized by cuckoos.
Food: Mainly insects, nectar, pollen, berries and fruit, including mistletoe.
Range: The Australasian region, including NZ and NG; Lesser Sunda and Bonin Islands, and Micronesia, Melanesia, Polynesia and Hawaii.
Number of species: World, about 169; Aust. 68.

578 RED WATTLEBIRD *Anthochaera carunculata* **Pl.75**

Other names: Barkingbird, Butcherbird, Gillbird, Gilly-wattler, Muttonbird, What's o'clock.

Field marks: 335–360 mm. Largest, longest-tailed honeyeater in mainland s. Aust.: grey-brown, with *bold pale streaks*; *white edges and tips to flight and tail-feathers*; *lemon on belly*. Note head-markings: *plain black crown, white mark on face below the red eye, blackish ear-mark, fleshy red neck-wattles* (that lengthen and become deeper red with age). Female: smaller, tail shorter. Imm: paler, plainer, no wattle, less yellow on abdomen. Singly, pairs, nomadic and migratory open flocks, sometimes of hundreds. Noisy and aggressive; feeds acrobatically; takes flying insects or hops on ground after insects. Flight strong, direct and undulating; when travelling, typically settles on high bare branches before continuing. Tame round gardens; attracted to vineyards, soft fruits, garden nectar-feeders; punctures garden flowers like hibiscus, foxgloves, for nectar.

Similar species: Little Wattlebird (580): fine silvery streaks, no wattles or bold head-markings. Yellow Wattlebird (579), (Tas.): larger, dark-streaked head, long pendulous yellow wattles. Grey Butcherbird (717): very dissimilar, but many seem to confuse the two.

Voice: Usual call, harsh single, double or treble cough as though clearing throat; hacking 'yak', 'yakayak' or 'yaak, yakyak'; also mellow deep ringing 'tew-tew-tew-tew'; alarm-call, single emphatic 'chock'.

Habitat: Forests, woodlands and scrubs, including mallee; vegetation along water-courses, coastal scrubs and heaths; orchards, golf-courses, parks, gardens.

Breeding: Nest: untidy saucer of sticks, leaves and grass; lined with strips of bark, fur or hair; usually 2–16 m high in fork of shrub or occasionally supported on bark against trunk. Eggs: 2–3; pale-pink to reddish buff, spotted red-brown or reddish purple, mostly at large end.

Range and Status: Se., s. and sw. Aust., from Darling Downs and Brisbane, Q, s. through e. NSW inland to about Inverell–Warrumbungle NP–Macquarie Marshes–Hillston, and throughout mallee areas of sw. NSW. Throughout Vic.; throughout s. SA and Kangaroo I., n. at least to s. Flinders Ras.–Gawler Ras., and coastally w. along Bight. In WA, it extends along the Bight coast, throughout the sw., and coastally n. to Shark Bay, the approximate inland limits being Gt. Victoria Desert–Kalgoorlie–Paynes Find–Pindar. Also offshore islands: Recherche Archipelago, Rottnest I. Common. A highly-mobile species with complex movements related to blossoming. In e. Aust. there is an altitudinal movement from mountains e. to coastal lowlands in autumn, and return in spring, and a similar movement w. to sub-inland plains. In summer, it occurs up to 2000 m in the Kosciusko alpine area, NSW, and Bogong High Plains, Vic. In e. Aust. there is apparently a regular n. coastal migration in autumn and return in spring. In s. WA, there appears to be a w. movement into coastal areas in autumn.

579 YELLOW WATTLEBIRD *Anthochaera paradoxa* **Pl.75**

Other names: Long or Tasmanian Wattlebird.

Field marks: 375–450 mm. Largest honeyeater: face and chin whitish, *prominent dark eye; note long pendulous rich-yellow to orange neck-wattles.* Upperparts grey to dusky brown, *crown and nape streaked black, back and shoulders streaked buff-white*; wings blackish brown, flight-feathers edged grey, primaries tipped white. Throat, breast and flanks grey, *streaked blackish*; centre of lower breast and abdomen rich-yellow; *tail long, graduated*, grey, edged blackish-brown, tipped white. Imm: no wattle. Singly, pairs or flocks; open companies when blossoms abundant. Active and acrobatic; flight strong, direct, slightly undulating. Fairly tame, enters gardens for food; at times becomes a pest in orchards. Associates with Little Wattlebird (580).

Similar species: Little (580) and Red (578) Wattlebirds, note range.

Voice: Harsh curious gurgling guttural notes, inelegantly likened to coughing and vomiting.

Habitat: Mountain shrubberies and subalpine forest to lowland forests, open woodlands, coastal and other scrubs, particularly those dominated by banksias; golf-courses, orchards, parks, gardens.

Breeding: Nest: large open saucer-shaped structure of twigs and strips of bark; bound with wool; lined with grass and wool; up to 13 m high in fork in foliage of shrub or tree. Eggs: 2–3; salmon-red, spotted and blotched red-brown, purplish red and blue-grey.
Range and Status: Tas. region: common e. and c. Tas., rare on n. coast w. of Tamar R., and w. coast. Extends to above snowline in subalpine regions. Resident, altitudinal migrant or nomad. Uncommon King I. Note: although no material evidence exists of it ever straying across Bass Strait, there are two possible autumn sight-records for the s. Mornington Pen., Vic.

580 LITTLE WATTLEBIRD *Anthochaera chrysoptera* Pl.75

Other names: Biddyquock, Brush Mockingbird or Wattlebird; Cookaycock, Mocker, Mock Gillbird or Wattlebird.
Field marks: 260–305 mm. A rather slim dull-brown longish tailed honeyeater, much smaller than Red Wattlebird (578) and without its red wattles, lemon belly or bold white wing-markings; *note dark shading down chin and throat, and fine silvery streaks above and below, densest and most silvery on sides of neck*; eye brown. In flight, *rufous patch on wings, white tips to secondaries, not primaries*. Race *lunulata*, sw. WA: bill longer; plumage less-streaked but more silvery sides of throat. Imm: browner, pale streaks less distinct. Singly, pairs, loose companies, specially where banksias blossoming. Streaked plumage makes it inconspicuous among banksia blossoms and old woody seed capsules. Active, noisy and aggressive; postures jerkily with bill and tail raised, rattling bill. Flight active and darting, sometimes with long glides. Much less-frequently seen in travelling flocks above treetops than Red Wattlebird. Tame in orchards, gardens; pugnacious.
Similar species: Striped Honeyeater (582): whitish head and upperparts prominently streaked black; rump paler; calls differ. Spiny-cheeked Honeyeater (581): black-tipped pink bill, pink to buff throat and breast; whitish rump. Red Wattlebird (578). Yellow Wattlebird (579), (Tas.): larger, paler, boldly streaked, long yellow wattle; calls differ.
Voice: Harsh and vivacious with many squeaky musical lilting notes; characteristic calls: strident 'cookay-cock'; rough raucous 'fetch the gun, fetch the gun' or mellow, guttural 'yekop, yekop, yekop' accompanied by rapid bill-rattling; rough 'squark', head rapidly ducked, thrown up, bill rattled; alarm-call, explosive 'kwock', often with nasal 'shnairt'.
Habitat: Banksia woodlands and scrubs; scrubby eucalypt woodlands, sandplain-heaths; in se. Q in thickets of lantana, native tobacco; often in parks, gardens.
Breeding: Nest: loosely made, untidy cup of twigs; lined with shredded bark or plant-down; usually 1–10 m high in fork of banksia, tea-tree or gum sapling. Eggs: 1–2, invariably 1 in WA and often in mid-NSW; salmon-pink to reddish salmon, spotted red-brown to purplish red, mostly at large end.
Range and Status: Coastal se. Aust. and some coastal islands, Tas. and sw. WA: from n. of Noosa Heads, se. Q inland (in winter) to near Toowoomba. Coastal NSW; breeding to c. 600 m in Blue Mts. (Woodford), inland in se. to ACT (irregular) and Kosciusko NP. In Vic., mostly s. of Divide, but in w., n. to Grampians–Little Desert–(uncommon) Wyperfeld NP; vagrant n. to Narungarra, near Swan Hill on Murray R. In SA w. coastally to Mt. Lofty Ras. (n. to Nuriootpa) and to Yorke Pen. and s. Eyre Pen.; also Kangaroo I. Coastal e. and n. Tas., sparser inland; once Strahan, w. coast. In sw. WA, from Israelite Bay n. to Geraldton, inland to Stirling Ras.–L. Grace–Northam. Common; sedentary, in se. Aust. and Tas., locally nomadic or part-migratory elsewhere.

581 SPINY-CHEEKED HONEYEATER *Acanthagenys rufogularis* Pl.75

Other name: Spring-cheeked Honeyeater.
Field marks: 225–260 mm. A graceful brownish long-tailed honeyeater; the dark-tipped bill is *deep-pink at base*; there is a strong dark mark through eye over a broad white streak along the cheek; this ends in stiff *yellowish buff brushlike feathers*; *throat and upperbreast pale-pink to deep sandy buff*; eye blue-grey. Imm: cheek-spines bright-yellow. There is

much variation in shade with locality, age and state of moult. Singly, pairs or parties; graceful and active. Raising its bill skyward, it utters distinctive calls from exposed dead branches, tops of leafy shrubs, overhead wires. Flight swift and undulating, *white rump and tail-tip contrast with brown upperparts.* Male in song-flight rises steeply 30 m calling, before dropping. Feeds much on insects and berries, including mistletoe.

Similar species: Striped Honeyeater (582); Little Wattlebird (580).

Voice: Many unusual calls, including liquid gurgling notes. Song, a distinctive rising then falling 'widit, widit-ear, peer-peer, peer-peer, peer-peer' or 'wee-ear, chonk-chonk-chonk chonk' etc. In song flight, phrases like 'give-the-boy-a-go', repeated, ending in single abrupt note as bird closes wings and drops. Alarm-call, single 'tok!' like cricket ball hitting bat; mimics.

Habitat: Varied: drier inland forests, woodlands and scrubs; saltbush, samphire on margins of salt-lakes, desert shrub-associations; vegetation along inland watercourses; coastal tea-tree scrubs, heaths; orchards and gardens near suitable habitat.

Breeding: Nest: flimsy deep slung cup of soft grass, needle-like leaves; bound with spiders' web and egg-sacs; lined with fur, soft grass, often incorporating string, cotton or wool; usually in outer hanging foliage, 2–3 m high. Eggs: 2–3; white, yellowish to creamish buff, darker at large end, spotted and blotched red-brown and brown, usually in cap at large end.

Range and Status: Interior of all mainland States; often thought of as a characteristically inland bird, but resident in many coastal areas from nw. WA to s. Vic., irregularly reaching e. coast at points n. to Townsville, usually during dry periods inland. Its approximate limits across n. Aust. are Charters Towers–Normanton, Q; Alexandria–Newcastle Waters–Tanami, NT and Fortescue R., WA. It is absent from the higher-rainfall areas of sw. WA, s. and w. of a line through Dongara–Moora–Northam–Broomehill–Bremer Bay. In SA, it is absent from forested parts of Mt. Lofty Ras.; vagrant Kangaroo I. In Vic. it is present (patchily) in drier coastal habitats e. to the e. shore of Port Phillip, occasionally e. to Westernport, and Gippsland Lakes; it is common in mallee and similar habitats of the far-w. and nw., e. to the Loddon R., and patchy in drier habitats of central Vic., e. to about the You Yangs–Melton–Tallarook. In NSW it is fairly common e. to about Finley–Temora–Peak Hill–Warrumbungle NP–Moree; frequently e. of that line, and to coast irregularly–a few records in Sydney area (Normanhurst, Mt. Kuringai, Woolooware Bay), and to Woodburn on n. coast. In Q, e. to Goondiwindi–Chinchilla–Blackwater and to coast near Bundaberg–Rockhampton and at Townsville. Locally common to very common; sedentary with local movements in wetter coastal habitats; highly nomadic in drier habitats, movement perhaps influenced by availability of berries as much as blossoms; records in humid coast or subcoastal districts (e.g. Murphy's Ck., Q) during drought.

582 STRIPED HONEYEATER *Plectorhyncha lanceolata* **Pl.75**

Other name: Lanceolated Honeyeater.

Field marks: 210–230 mm. A distinctive medium-sized brownish grey honeyeater *with whitish head, nape and mantle heavily streaked black; heavy black streak bordering whitish throat.* Bill fine and pointed. Singly, pairs or small nomadic parties in non-breeding season. Active; feeds and chases round trees and taller shrubs, when distinctive calls often draw attention; sometimes attracted to cultivated fruit. In flight, rump and wings plain-brown without markings; *tail longish, slightly forked, square at corners.*

Similar species: Spiny-cheeked Honeyeater (581): reddish bill with black tip; throat buff to pale-orange; in flight, pale rump. Little Wattlebird (580): silvery streaks on dark plumage.

Voice: Calls attractive, mellow and rolling; somewhat like Olive-backed Oriole (689), but longer, higher-pitched, random phrases. Typical calls, rolling 'cherree-cherree-chirrarip', 'cherree-cherree-chew' or 'free-wheat-peeler-peeler' rising then falling. Song, longer and more rambling; also in songflight above treetops.

Habitat: Drier scrubs and woodlands; stands of belar and other casuarinas; mulga, native pine, mallee and saltbush. In (parts of) e. coastal Aust.: sheoak, banksia and tea-tree scrubs, swamp woodlands. Also orchards, gardens.

Breeding: Nest: deep cup of fine rootlets, plant-down, emu feathers, wool etc.; bound with spiders' web; slung in drooping foliage or hanging twigs, 1–6 m high. Eggs: 2–4; flesh-pink, minutely sprinkled red-buff and blue-grey; eggs in coastal NSW more heavily coloured than inland.

Range and Status: A predominantly inland species that appears to be extending and consolidating its range in coastal e. Aust. and some coastal islands, from n. of Sydney (Gosford area) to about Cairns, ne. Q, thence n. on highlands to near Cooktown. It is rare or absent from wetter areas of Dividing Ra., and e. of the Divide is mostly associated with coastal scrubs and swamp-woodlands, extending inland along valleys e.g. of Hunter and Richmond Rs. In Q it ranges w. to Cloncurry and possibly the Channel Country. In NSW its far-inland range is uncertain but probably extends throughout; its se. limit is Deniliquin–Albury–Wagga–Cowra. In nw. Vic., it ranges e. to about the Loddon R. and s. to Wyperfeld NP. It occurs through e. SA from L. Frome s. through the Murray mallee to the Coorong and coastally w. to Yorke Pen. Fairly common but patchy, in suitable habitats. Nomadic inland, probably sedentary on coast.

FRIARBIRDS   Genus *Philemon*

Large pale-brown honeyeaters nearly the size of wattlebirds. Depending on species, the dark (black or grey) skin of their heads is partly or wholly unfeathered, hence the common name 'leatherhead'. Most friarbirds have large, curved almost bladelike bills surmounted by a knob or raised ridge. The size and shape of this knob is a useful guide to species and/or age–young friarbirds have little or no knob and the Little Friarbird (586) lacks it completely. In the knob-billed species, the plain pale-brown plumage, with close, plushlike or frilled silvery white or silvery brown feathers on parts of the crown, nape and throat, is distinctive. Also distinctive are friarbirds' extraordinary voices–varied, curiously harsh and loud, or falsetto and mellow. When friarbirds gather in blossoming trees, often with other honeyeaters and lorikeets, the din they create can be heard afar. Note that the large Helmeted, Melville Island and Sandstone Friarbirds are all treated in this Guide as races of the widespread species *P. buceroides* (583), which has an island range from Indonesia to n. Aust., NG and New Britain. In plumage and calls the Australian races are nearly identical, but differ somewhat in size. Differences in the frilled plumage of the nape, described in other guides, are probably due to feather-wear. The remaining species are easily-identified. Friarbirds are frequently hosts to larger cuckoos, notably the Koel (373).

583   HELMETED FRIARBIRD   *Philemon buceroides*   Pl.75

Other names: Melville Island, New Guinea or Sandstone Friarbird.

Field marks: 325–350 mm. This species as now recognized includes 'Melville Island' and 'Sandstone' Friarbirds, formerly regarded as good species. A large plain-brown honeyeater, paler-brown below; sexes alike, eye of male scarlet, of female dark-orange. Distinguished by (1) the strong, curved bladelike bill surmounted by a *low, rounded knob* that blends with the head-contour; (2) black facial skin; (3) *pale silvery brown* plushlike plumage of crown, frilled nape and throat. Imm: no knob on bill, facial skin grey, mantle with slight pale scaly pattern formed by pale feather-margins; wings washed olive-yellow. Singly, pairs or small flocks. Usually feeds high in foliage and blossoms. Active, noisy and aggressive, but often rather shy and difficult to approach; bolder near habitation.

Similar species: Silver-crowned Friarbird (584): much smaller; knob on bill more prominent; silvery white head-plumage contrasts more; underparts paler than above. Noisy Friarbird (585): angular knob on bill; wholly bare black head; broad pale tail-tips.

Voice: Loud, strange and extremely varied: a common call in e. Aust. is frequently syllabized as 'poor-devil', constantly repeated; many other more complex calls like Noisy Friarbird. Calls of birds in Arnhem Land escarpments are described as deeper; they include a metallic 'chillanc chillanc' a monotonous 'chank, chank, chank', and a three-note 'whack-a-where'. It is impossible to describe in words the range, variety and strangeness of the remarkable utterances of the species as a whole.

Habitat: Rainforests, monsoon forests and margins; open forests and woodlands, especially vegetation along watercourses; mangroves; other tropical scrubs, coastal scrubs and similar island vegetation including sheoaks and pandanus; blossoming and fruiting trees in gardens and towns. The habitat in the Arnhem Land escarpment is described as heavily overgrown shrubby vegetation in sandstone gorges, adjacent woodlands during blossoming.

Breeding: Nest: large cup of strips of bark, stems and rootlets; slung usually from horizontal fork amid foliage, usually at some height. Nesting noted with Shining Starling (686); Figbird (691) and Spangled Drongo (692). Eggs: 3–4; pale-pink, spotted brown, dark-red and purple.

Range and Status: The Aust. range is divided: (1) Race *yorki*; ne. Q and coastal islands: from C. York s. to Weipa on w. coast of the Pen.; s. to Mackay on e. coast. Mostly in coastal lowlands, but ranges to Divide and Tablelands; sight-record from the Hughenden basalt tableland. (2) Race *melvillensis*: Melville Island, adjacent coastal NT (? and Groote Eylandt) from about Darwin (and probably further sw.) e. to Yirrkala, inland to about Oenpelli. (3) A large form occurs on the Arnhem Land escarpment, sw. and to *c.* 100 km s. of Oenpelli. Common in coastal ne. Q, less common on Divide and in the NT. A blossom nomad, appearing when eucalypts, paperbarks and other trees are in flower. In coastal NT, seasonally nomadic; reported to be an irregular visitor to the Darwin area, commonest in Dec. and Jan. in mangroves, monsoon forest and gardens, occasionally wandering into nearby open forests; mostly absent in winter, when it apparently moves inland in response to blossoming in sub-coastal woodlands. Also Torres Strait islands, New Britain, NG and islands, Lesser Sunda Is.

584 SILVER-CROWNED FRIARBIRD *Philemon argenticeps* Pl.75

Field marks: 270–315 mm. Much the smallest 'knob-billed' friarbird, comparable in size with the Little (586). Apart from size, it is best distinguished from Helmeted group by (1) *the more prominent knob on the bill, rising and rounding off more abruptly.* (2) *The silvery white plumage of the crown, frilled nape and throat*, that contrasts more strikingly with the black facial skin and the other plumage. (3) The paler underparts. Imm: lacks knob on bill at first; throat washed yellowish; some irregular scalloping on sides of mantle, and faint yellow wash on flight-feathers and tail. Pairs, parties or feeding flocks; active; acrobatic and noisy when feeding, attracting attention from afar; often difficult to approach.

Similar species: Helmeted Friarbird (583): larger, lower, rounded knob on bill; brown head-plumage and underparts. Noisy Friarbird (585) wholly black bare head.

Voice: Many nasal, catlike calls with much variation. Diagnostic call of males in Arnhem Land has been described as a harsh reiterated 'more tobacco, uh, more tobacco, uh'; a call heard near Macarthur R., NT, resembled 'weeloo' of Yellow-tailed Black Cockatoo (311).

Habitat: Tropical open forests and woodlands, scrubs on hills, vegetation along watercourses; mangroves; trees and shrubs on margins of cultivation; gardens and towns.

Breeding: Nest: cup-shaped; of bark-fibre and grass; bound with spiders' web; suspended from fork in foliage 3–13 m high. Eggs: 2, occasionally 3; pale salmon-pink to pinkish buff, sometimes with few faint bluish spots at large end, spotted and freckled red-brown, purplish brown and purplish grey.

Range and Status: Coastal n. Aust.: from Derby, WA, e. through Kimberleys; NT s. to Larrimah–Mallapunyah; also Groote Eylandt; in Q, s. to Cloncurry–Flinders R. on Gulf coast, and from C. York Pen. s. on e. coast to Townsville and Magnetic I. Common; a blossom nomad, possibly with some regular migratory movements.

585 NOISY FRIARBIRD *Philemon corniculatus*   **Pl.75**
Other names: Four-o'clock, Knobby-nose, Leatherhead, Monk, Pimlico, Poor-Soldier.
Field marks: 315–350 mm. A strange large honeyeater mid-brown above, whitish brown below, *with bare black head and an angular knob on bill*; there is a *pronounced ruff of long creamish feathers on hind-neck* and longish silvery white pointed plumes on upperbreast. White tail tips more prominent than in other friarbirds, a good field mark in flight. Imm: no knob on bill at first, feathers extend like cowl up nape to rear of crown; pale scaly pattern on mantle; throat and upperbreast lightly washed yellow; slim dark collar under throat. Singly, pairs or parties, nomadic or migratory flocks; associates with Little Friarbird (586). Noisy and aggressive; feeds blossom, actively searches foliage for insects; attracted to grapes, soft fruit; roadside blackberries, syrup from sugar-cane after burning.
Similar species: Other knob-billed friarbirds have partly-feathered heads. No other Australian bird has bare black head and angular knob on bill.
Voice: Harsh and peculiar, with many and varied calls; some common calls have been syllabized 'tobacco, tobacco', 'keyhole, keyhole'; 'four-o'clock' or 'poor soldier'; a harsh 'yakob'; in pursuit, a loud brassy shout like screech of Swamphen (188); also a clear liquid ringing 'chog!', often followed by 'eeyit', descending; or 'ch-will' or mellow 'chew, chewip', both very like common calls of Little Friarbird (586).
Habitat: Open forests and woodlands, trees along watercourses, swamp woodland, coastal scrubs, taller sub-inland scrubs; blossoming trees in orchards, vineyards, parks, street, gardens.
Breeding: Nest: large deep, somewhat untidy, cup of wool and stringy bark with few leaves; lined with rootlets; suspended in leafy branch, 3–10 m high. Eggs: 2–4, usually only 2 in ne. Aust.; deep-pink, spotted and blotched chestnut-red and purplish grey.
Range and Status: E. Aust. and coastal islands: from C. York Pen., Q, to Vic., and w. along Murray R. into SA. Approximate inland limits in Q are Croydon–Hughenden–Blackall–Eulo; it extends down Paroo and Warrego Rs. into nw. NSW; otherwise in NSW, w. to Bourke–Nyngan–West Wyalong–Leeton–Tocumwal. In Vic., regular summer migrant to ne. high country, and e. Gippsland w. to Bairnsdale, vagrant further w. to Port Phillip; in c. Vic., regularly s. to about Mansfield–Nagambie–Bendigo, vagrant s. to outer Melbourne suburbs and to the Grampians in sw. Vic. It extends downstream in river red gum forests of Riverina and w. along the Murray R. to Overland Corner, SA, occasional further w. Common, a blossom nomad in Q, a regular summer breeding migrant in s., arriving Sept.–Oct., departing Feb.–April; some overwintering, with nomadic movements, when blossom abundant. In coastal ne. NSW and se. Q, the n. autumn movement in Apr.–May of migrating flocks is at times conspicuous, with hundreds passing in a day. Also s. NG.

586 LITTLE FRIARBIRD *Philemon citreogularis*   **Pl.75**
Other names: Little Leatherhead, Yellow-throated Friarbird.
Field marks: 250–290 mm. Smallest friarbird, comparable in size only with Silver-crowned (584). Distinguished by *absence of knob on bill*, and from other large honeyeaters by *patch of bare blue-grey skin* back from bill under eye, widening on face like 'mutton-chop' whiskers. Head rather small, bill fairly prominent; some have a partial pale collar. Flight distinctive; wing-beats shallow and rather quivering, tail rather square-cut and with slight pale tips. Female: smaller. Imm: distinctive; chin and throat and sometimes upper-breast, washed yellow; some have an obvious pale-grey collar; tail more rounded. Because of imm's 'different' look, it was described as the Yellow-throated Friarbird, hence *citreogularis*. Singly, pairs to flocks in nonbreeding season. Usually feeds high on blossoms and fruits, but occasionally low in blossoming shrubs, hawks flying insects. Raids orchards, vineyards, gleans syrup from sugar-cane after burning. Noisy, but less so than other friarbirds. Associates with Noisy (585) and other rriarbirds.
Similar species: Adults of other friarbirds: knob or ridge on bill; blacker facial skin; silvery plushlike plumage on crown and neck. Calls harsher. Little (580) and Red (578)

Wattlebirds: plumage darker and more streaked; no bare facial skin. Calls differ.

Voice: Oft-repeated liquid mellow 'gee-wit' or 'chewip'; when breeding, extended into song, viz: 'cheweep, chewip, chewip, chew-will, chew-will, chew-will'; other calls, quick falsetto phrase like 'I've-got-red-hair-air', repeated; rough chattering scoldings.

Habitat: Open forests and woodlands, particularly along watercourses; swamp-woodlands, mangroves; inland scrubs and shrub-communities, specially when flowering and in good seasons; orchards, vineyards, parks and gardens, specially near rivers.

Breeding: Nest: deep cup of grass and bark-fibres, small twigs and rootlets, lightly bound with spiders' web; lined with rootlets and hair; often flimsy and eggs visible from below; suspended from twigs, 2–10 m high among drooping foliage. Eggs: 2–3, 4; whitish pink to salmon-red or pale-purplish red, with fine to heavy spots of purplish red, purple or chestnut markings occasionally forming zone at large end.

Range and Status: N. and e. Aust. and some coastal islands: from Pt. Hedland, WA, n. through Kimberleys; top end NT s. to Elliott; n. and e. Q, inland at least to Mt. Isa–Opalton–Quilpie; NSW, except far nw.; mostly w. of Divide, generally confined to the vicinity of water in the far-w. parts of State; irregular spring–autumn breeding visitor to central coastal areas and Sydney with occasional wintering; vagrant ACT and s. coast. Regular summer migrant through well-watered parts of the NSW Riverina and the Murray Valley, regularly extending s. in Vic. in summer along Goulburn R. and other streams of the Murray R. system, (? less regularly) s. to Nariel–Licola, occasional to coastal e. Gippsland–Melbourne area–Bendigo–Little Desert NP. It intrudes into mallee areas of nw. Vic. near water e.g. Hattah Lakes NP; in SA, it extends downstream along Murray R. and associated watercourses to about Morgan, vagrant s. to Murray Bridge, n. to near Yunta and w. to Nuriootpa and possibly w. Eyre Pen. Generally common: sedentary or a blossom nomad in n.; seasonal migrant in se. Aust., arriving Sept.–Oct. to breed, moving n. in Mar.–Apr. Also s. NG.

587 REGENT HONEYEATER *Xanthomyza phrygia* **Pl.75**

Other names: Embroidered or Warty-faced Honeyeater; Flying Coachman, Turkeybird.

Field marks: 200–225 mm. Unusual: *mostly black, with bold netted or scaly pattern of cream and yellow; wing and tail-feathers with conspicuous broad golden-yellow edges;* abdomen and under tail-coverts yellowish white. Area of pinkish warty skin round eye. Bill black. Female: often much smaller. Imm: black areas greyish to dark-brown; bill yellowish. Pairs in breeding colonies, parties or nomadic flocks of dozens. Very active, often in mistletoes, constantly flying from tree to tree, at times in fluttering display-flight. In flight, yellow patches and margins on wing and broad golden edges of tail contrast strongly with dark plumage.

Similar species: Painted Honeyeater (627).

Voice: Not specially noisy, but calls very distinctive, when breeding. Common call is anvil-like ringing 'chink-chink-chink', somewhat like call of Magpie Lark (710); slow mellow 'quippa-plonk-quip', 'quip kik' or quicker 'quip, quip'; also liquid 'cloop-cloop-cloop', mewing or turkey-like; calls accompanied by bowing, or uttered in flight; subsong reported.

Habitat: Open forests and woodlands, timber along watercourses, coastal heaths and banksia scrubs, sometimes mallee; also stands of timber along roadsides, shelter-belts; occasionally trees in streets, gardens.

Breeding: Nest: cup of grasses and strips of bark, lined with hair or down; more sub-stantial than most honeyeater nests and like small nest of Grey Shrike-thrush; usually 2–10 m high, in upright fork of sapling or tree, occasionally in mistletoe. Eggs: 2–3; salmon-buff, spotted deep red-brown and purplish red, mostly in zone towards large end.

Range and Status: Se. Aust.: from near Rockhampton, Q, to Mt. Lofty Ras., SA; *except s.* Gippsland and Otway Ras., Vic. Its range is mostly coastal and subcoastal, the approxi-mate inland limits being: Chinchilla, Q; Inverell–Warrumbungle NP–Wellington–Cowra–Holbrook–Finley, NSW; Bendigo–Maryborough–Harrow, Vic.; Naracoorte–

Mt. Lofty Ras., SA, n. to Sutherlands–Clare. Its stronghold appears to be from about the Hunter R. Valley through se. NSW to c. Vic.; but even within this zone, although locally common, and resident in parts, it is generally highly nomadic and irregular, depending on blossoming, often arriving and breeding in a district after an absence of years, and just as quickly departing. In Q, it is mostly an autumn–winter visitor. In SA it is rarer, possibly part-migratory; vagrant Kangaroo I.

588 BLUE-FACED HONEYEATER *Entomyzon cyanotis* Pl.75

Other names: Banana-bird, Blue-eye, Gympie, Pandanus-bird.

Field marks: 300–320 mm. A vigorous distinctive large honeyeater; golden-olive above, whitish below, head-pattern distinctive; *crown and nape black, with white nape-band*; *patch of bright to darkish blue facial skin*; *dusky mark from chin down throat widens into a black bib.* Bill black pale-grey at base; eye white. The small n. race *albipennis* has *large patch of white on base of primary wing-feathers prominent in flight.* Imm: facial skin buffish, then olive-green; 'bib' grey. Pairs when nesting; otherwise family parties or small flocks; given to noisy displays, mobbing of owls, goannas. Inquisitive and aggressive; feeds in foliage, blossoms, probes bark; flight strong and undulating. Becomes bold round habitation, raids fruit, takes food in poultry yards, visits rubbish dumps for sweet food, gleans syrup from sugar-cane after burning.

Voice: Strong, strident and distinctive: a common call is a penetrating querulous 'woik, woik, woik', or 'queet, queet', each note rising at end; also softer 'hwit, hwit'.

Habitat: Open forests and woodlands, timber along watercourses, timber in farmlands, roadsides, taller sub-inland scrubs. In n. Aust. pandanus, swamp woodlands; also sugar-cane, banana plantations, orchards, golf-courses, parks, gardens.

Breeding: Nest: sometimes builds the typical honeyeater-nest of a suspended deep cup, often rather small, of bark-shreds, rootlets, grass, sometimes with spiders' web on outside; lined with plant-down or hair; other nests are large and untidy, sometimes like flood-debris, with bulky foundation of twigs; situated in bark debris in forks of trees, or in a narrow upright fork of two or three branches, 3–10 m high. Often uses old nest of babbler, Magpie Lark or Apostlebird as base. Eggs: 2–3; buff-pink to salmon-pink, spotted red-brown and purplish red.

Range and Status: Coastal n. and e. Aust., and inland se. Aust.: from Kimberleys through top end NT s. to Larrimah, Gulf coast of nw. Q s. to Mt. Isa. From C. York Pen. it ranges s. coastally to about the Myall Lakes, NSW; thence to Maitland–Windsor–Albury, occasional e. to Kosciusko NP; its inland limits in e. Aust. are Richmond–Blackall–Charleville in Q and Lightning Ridge–Nyngan–L. Cargelligo in NSW. It is widely distributed in open red gum forests of the Murray and Murrumbidgee Rs. and associated watercourses and lakes in the NSW Riverina and adjacent n. Vic., w. along Murray R. to about Morgan, SA. It extends marginally into ne. Vic. (formerly s. to Bright), thence s. to Murchison–Bendigo–Maryborough–Beaufort, and w. in a narrow band s. of the mallee areas to Naracoorte SA; occasional w. to lower Murray R. area (Langhorne's Ck.–Mannum). Note that the form in n. Aust. w. of Burketown is the distinctive small race *albipennis.* Common in coastal n. Aust. and Q; uncommon to patchy in se. Aust. Sedentary nomadic or locally migratory. Also s. NG.

589 BELL MINER *Manorina melanophrys* Pl.75

Other name: Bellbird.

Field marks: 190 mm. *Plain olive-green*, wings slightly darker. Note subtle facial pattern and *triangle of scarlet waxy skin behind eye. Bill orange-yellow, legs pale-orange.* Imm: skin behind eye olive-yellow, becoming orange, then red at 6–8 months. Colonies of mated pairs (often with 'helpers') and family parties; some colonies are large, numbering hundreds. Almost always first noted by well-known distinctive call; the bird itself is often surprisingly hard to detect in foliage. Active, aggressive and demonstrative; often descends to lower branches to scold intruders. Flight direct, glides with wings in V at end of flight, especially when joining group-display. Near nest, shrieking distraction-display; birds crouch, depress and fan tail, raise fluttering wings, drop to ground.

Similar species: None, but do not confuse by name with unrelated Crested Bellbird (473).

Voice: Best-known by clear high-pitched bell-like 'tink', varying in pitch. Typically uttered by many birds in colony with beautiful tinkling effect, but can be tryingly persistent. Other notes, sharp repeated 'jak jak jak'; hard complaining 'kwee-kwee-kwee-kwee' like Noisy Miner (590); also harsh scolding churring alarm-call, harsh mewing shrieks in distraction display; imms make a continual 'yik, yik'.

Habitat: Temperate rainforest, wetter eucalypt or angophora woodland, with fairly dense shrubby understorey; typically in well-watered valleys or gullies near rivers or creeks, but occasionally far from foothills in suitable woodland, or in well-timbered suburbs. Visits garden feeders.

Breeding: Nest: large, somewhat untidy, deep bulky cup of grasses, leaves and plantdown; bound with spiders' web; decorated with spiders' egg-sacs; usually supported in upright fork, 1–4 m high, seldom in canopy. Eggs: 1–3, usually 2; white to pale-pink, spotted or purplish or red-brown. Communal nesting is practised in that more than a mated pair may feed young.

Range and Status: Coastal se. Aust.: from e. suburbs of Melbourne to upper Mary R., near Gympie, Q. (Vagrant w. of Melbourne to Blackwood and Lerderberg Gorge and once to Glenelg R. near Casterton, far-w. Vic.). Mostly on or immediately coastwards of the Dividing Ra., with occasional vagrant occurrences further inland e.g. Nagambie and Chiltern, Vic. Common; mostly sedentary but subject to sudden short-range re-locations; apparent expansion in recent years.

590 NOISY MINER *Manorina melanocephala* Pl.75

Other names: Cherry-eater; Micky or Micky Miner; Snakebird; Soldierbird.

Field marks: 240–275 mm. A demonstrative largish grey honeyeater with deep-yellow bill and legs and distinctive head-pattern: forehead pale-grey, *crown and cheeks black, with triangle of rich-yellow skin behind eye.* Colonial, aggressive and inquisitive, with noisy group-displays and mobbing choruses. Feeds in foliage and/or trunks, probes bark; often feeds on ground. Male in song-flight rises steeply 30 m or more, calling. Normal flight level and direct, frequently ends in glide on upraised wings, especially when joining group-display. *In flight, rump grey like back*; *whitish tips to tail.* Tame in parks, gardens, when fed. May damage soft fruits.

Similar species: White-rumped Miner (591): paler, no black on crown, yellowish streak on face, white rump. Black-eared Miner (592): darker; no black cap, but black extends round eye in more complete mask; note range.

Voice: High-pitched penetrating complaining 'yoi-yoi-yoi-yoi' or 'pwee pwee pwee', rising at end peevishly; used in mild alarm, group-displays, mobbing chorus. Alarm-call, strident piping deliberate 'pee, pee, pee', taken up by distant birds, also urgent 'weedidit', reiterated. Also quieter liquid chucklings.

Habitat: Open forests and grassy woodlands, usually in larger trees; in drier inland districts confined to large trees along watercourses, also banksia, paperbark associations, at times in heaths, especially during winter dispersal; shelter-belts, roadside timber, large trees in farm paddocks; orchards, vineyards, golf-courses, parks, gardens.

Breeding: Nests in loose colonies. Nest: untidy large cup, of twigs and grasses; bound with spiders' web, often including wool or similar material; lined with fine grass, rootlets, hair, fur, or wool; 2–13 m high, usually in fork of leafy branch. Eggs: 2–4; buff-white to pale or deep-pink, freckled, spotted or blotched all over or principally at large end with red-brown, blue-grey or pale-lilac. Communal nesting is practised.

Range and Status: E. Aust. and Tas.: in Q, local populations n. to about Musgrave on e. C. York Pen., replaced by White-rumped Miner in drier parts of ne., e.g. near Townsville; elsewhere in e. Q, widespread in suitable habitat, inland to about Clermont–

Charleville. In NSW, widespread in suitable habitat, inland to about Bourke–Cobar–Ivanhoe–Balranald. In Vic., widespread in suitable habitat; in nw., confined to larger timber on watercourses. In SA, in suitable habitat through se., along Murray R., w. to Yorke Pen. and n. to Burra–Jamestown–Melrose; sight-records from s. Flinders Ras. In drier inland areas, it typically occurs in larger timber along watercourses, while White-rumped Miner occupies adjacent drier habitats. In some localities this leads to a mosaic distribution-pattern e.g. in c. NSW, from Nyngan s. and w. to about Mt. Hope, the Noisy Miner occurs in mixed eucalypt woodland and pine-mallee associations, while the White-rumped Miner is prevalent round Nyngan, and far to the east. Locally as in NSW s. Riverina, both may occupy the same acacia or black box habitats, but the colonies do not mingle. In Tas., confined to ce. of State, approximate w. limits being Devonport–Great Lakes–Hobart area; absent from ne. coast n. of St. Helens and e. of the Tamar R. Colonial, common in suitable habitat, but patchy; mostly sedentary, but local autumn–winter feeding movements.

591 WHITE-RUMPED MINER *Manorina flavigula* Pl.75

Other names: Yellow-throated Miner; Micky. Locally in s. WA, 'Dusky Miner'.

Field marks: 250–275 mm. Much paler than Noisy Miner (590), *rump and whole under-surface whitish.* Note head markings: *crown grey, not black*; *black mark extends from bill under eye and spreads over ear-coverts*; yellow skin behind eye, yellow of gape extends under eye; *forehead and sides of neck may be washed yellow, chin yellowish.* Imm: browner above, markings less distinct: throat yellower at first. Behaves like Noisy Miner, but appears to form larger companies, especially where it is the only miner occupying timber on watercourses. Locally travelling flocks venture much farther from woodland-cover than Noisy.

Similar species: Noisy (590) and Black-eared (592) Miners. Spiny-cheeked Honeyeater (581): can be confused in flight away, but greater contrast of pale rump and tail tips with brown upperparts; flight more undulating.

Voice: Stridently vocal; calls seemingly keener and higher-pitched than Noisy Miner.

Habitat: Drier woodlands and scrublands, grasslands with flowering shrubs; drier coastal scrubs, banksia-woodlands and heaths. In far-w. NSW and Q, the interior and w. of continent, river red gums along watercourses, habitat usually pre-empted by Noisy Miner elsewhere. Also golf-courses, orchards, gardens.

Breeding: Nest: like Noisy Miner, but often placed lower. Eggs: 3–4; salmon-pink to salmon-red, spotted and blotched all over with similar but richer shades.

Range and Status: Replaces Noisy Miner in drier parts of all mainland States, with considerable overlap in ec. NSW–Q (see Noisy Miner, Range and Status). In Q, n. to Gulf lowlands, Georgetown and lower Staaten R. on w. C. York Pen., occasional e. to Townsville; in s., colonies e. to Springsure–Darling Downs. In NSW, e. to about Inverell–Warrumbungle NP–Peak Hill; in se., to Moulamein–Jerilderie–Urana, (? isolated colonies) reported e. to Lalalty–Albury. In Vic., widespread in nw., mostly mallee, e. at least to Kerang, and to s. of Wyperfeld NP. In SA, s. through Murray mallee, Yorke Pen. and s. to about Arno–Streaky Bay on Eyre Pen. Nearly throughout NT, patchy in coastal top end and Arnhem Land; present some coastal islands of NT and nw. WA. Nearly throughout WA, including Kimberleys, but absent from forest-zone of far-sw.; extends along the Bight coast to SA. Note that the form in sw. WA is the large dark race *obscura*, 'Dusky Miner', once erroneously allied with Black-eared Miner (592). Inland, White-rumped is present in nearly all but arid treeless deserts; marginally into Simpson Desert. In places where Noisy Miner does not occur or is sparse e.g. Darling R. at Menindee, NSW, White-rumped occupies tall red gums along watercourses, habitat normally pre-empted by Noisy where they occur together. Common, patchy to locally very abundant. Sedentary, with local nomadic movements related to blossoming.

592 BLACK-EARED MINER *Manorina melanotis* **Pl.75**

Other name: Dusky Miner.

Field marks: 250 mm. Somewhat like Noisy Miner (590) but darker, uniform grey from crown to rump: *no black across crown, but black sides of face give masked appearance.* Bill, small spot behind eye and legs deep-yellow. Absence of pale tail tips helps separate it from Noisy Miner in flight. Usually in small parties, as part of colony. Unlike other miners, generally shy and fugitive; when observed, inspects intruder, calls complainingly and vanishes; associates with White-rumped Miner (591). Note range and habitat. So-called Dusky Miner of sw. WA is local race of White-rumped Miner.

Similar species: Noisy (590) and White-rumped (591) Miners.

Voice: Like Noisy Miner, with same complaining tone.

Habitat: Mallee-scrubs, also belar, buloke; shares habitat with White-rumped but not Noisy Miner.

Breeding: Nest and eggs generally like Noisy and White-rumped Miner.

Range and Status: In small, very local colonies in mallee of a small continguous region of sw. NSW, nw. Vic. and e. SA: e. to Wyperfeld and Hattah NPs, Vic., n. to near Euston, NSW, and w. into Murray mallee of SA, the approximate n. limits being Gluepot–Calperum n. of Murray R., s. and w. to Chapman's Bore–Hartley area, n. of L. Alexandrina. Sedentary, or locally nomadic. Uncommon to rare, or locally plentiful; shy and seldom observed.

593 MACLEAY'S HONEYEATER *Xanthotis macleayana* **Pl.76**

Other names: Buff-striped, Mottle-plumaged or Yellow-streaked Honeyeater.

Field marks: 200 mm. A stocky, long-billed, short-tailed strikingly marked honeyeater: *upperparts brown with angular whitish spots*; throat grey, upperbreast dark-brown; *underparts yellow, more or less striped* dark-brown. Note also the head and facial markings: *black-cap, patch of yellow-buff skin round eye; small white and large yellow patch on ear-coverts.* Singly or pairs: often untidy, likened to a scruffy Regent Honeyeater (587). Quiet, movements heavy and deliberate. Reported to climb trunks of forest trees like treecreeper; hangs upside down to feed; enters orchards and gardens to feed on oranges, mandarins; comes to bird-tables.

Voice: Often described as silent, but a cheerful call like Yellow-faced Honeyeater (599), but not so loud, and a rapid staccato call, have been described.

Habitat: Rainforests, vegetation along watercourses, swamp woodlands, adjacent eucalypt forests and woodlands; gardens.

Breeding: Nest: cup of palm-fibre, leaves and shreds of bark; bound with spiders' web; in shrub or low tree. Eggs: 2; pinkish-buff, spotted red or chestnut with lilac and dark-grey markings.

Range and Status: Ne. Q: from Cooktown coastally s. to Mt. Spec NP near Townsville, inland to high altitudes on coastal Gt. Dividing Ra., including Atherton Tableland. Fairly common, probably sedentary.

594 BUFF-BREASTED HONEYEATER *Xanthotis flaviventer* **Pl 76**

Other names: Tawny-breasted, Streaked or Streaked-naped Honeyeater.

Field marks: 185–200 mm. Unlike other Australian honeyeaters except Macleay's (593), whose bolder streaking easily separates it. *Note the heavy longish downcurved black bill and pale short streaks on nape, and distinctive buffish underparts, with touches of yellow.* The facial markings are also distinctive: grey skin round eye, white curved line from bill under eye; with a lower yellowish line this encloses greyish olive ear-coverts. Singly, pairs or parties, active and rather noisy, usually feeds in high foliage and blossoms of trees or lower at edge of scrub or vegetation on watercourses; pugnacious.

Similar species: Magnificent Riflebird (702), female: pale eyebrow, dark eyeline without yellow streak; barred underparts.

Voice: Varied; one distinctive note described as 'which-witch-is-which'; also rather loud whistled song.

Habitat: Vine scrub, edges of rainforests, eucalypt woodlands, heathlands, mangroves.

Breeding: Nest: compact cup of bark-shreds, including paperbark; lined with rootlets and strips of bark; suspended from horizontal fork in foliage of shrub of leafy tree, including mangrove, 3–16 m high. Eggs: 2; whitish pink with small red-brown and grey spots; glossy.

Range and Status: Ne. Q: C. York Pen. s. to Watson and Rocky Rs. Common to uncommon. Also NG and satellite islands.

595   LEWIN'S HONEYEATER   *Meliphaga lewinii*   **Pl.76**

Other names: Banana-bird, Brasseye, Lewin or Yellow-eared Honeyeater; Orange-bird, White-lug.

Field marks: 200–215 mm. Largest darkest and most widespread member of trio with Yellow-spotted (596) and Graceful (597) Honeyeaters; *wide whitish streak from bill to eye, and broad pale-yellow half-moon earmark*. Bill black, strong; eye grey. Birds of non-coastal n. NSW and s. Q brighter olive-green, head and throat almost blackish, well defined; earmark very yellow. Singly or pairs; bold, aggressive, feeds actively, often hanging head downwards; hovers, takes flying insects, often raids cultivated fruit, comes to houses, picnic tables for food. Flight strong, undulating, irregular, with 'flop-flop' of wings.

Similar species: Yellow-spotted (596) and Graceful (597) Honeyeaters; see details, note range.

Voice: Long tremulous machinegun-rattle, somewhat like postman's whistle; a common sound of e. coast forests; also single loud peevish note.

Habitat: Rainforests, from coast to over 600 m; other forests and woodlands, sub-inland scrubs, brigalow and belar; coastal scrubs and heaths, mangroves; vegetation on margins of cultivation, plantations, canefields, orchards; thickets of blackberries and similar tangles on edges of clearings; roadsides, gardens.

Breeding: Nest: large untidy strongly built cup of bark-fibre, grass and occasionally moss and lichen; bound with spiders' web and cocoons, often with broad leaves or scraps of paper, fabric included; lined with plant-down; slung in foliage of leafy shrub or tree 1–6 m high. Eggs: 2; 3; white, spotted deep-red, usually most heavily at large end.

Range and Status: E. Aust. and some coastal islands from Cooktown, Q, to near Melbourne, Vic.; inland in Q to Carnarvon Ras.; in NSW to Mt. Kaputar NP (near Narrabri)–Ben Bullen (near Lithgow); ACT–Mt. Kosciusko NP; in Vic. mostly on and s. of the Divide, w. to the Dandenong Ras., *c.* 40 km. e. of Melbourne, and s. to Gippsland lakes and Strzelecki Ras. Common in n., uncommon and part-migratory in s.

596   YELLOW-SPOTTED HONEYEATER   *Meliphaga notata*   **Pl.76**

Other name: Lesser Lewin Honeyeater.

Field marks: 175 mm. Member of trio with Lewin's (595) and Graceful (597) Honeyeaters; *somewhat brighter olive-green above than Lewin's*; *eye brown, not grey*; olive-grey below; forehead and cheeks blackish; fine bright-yellow stripe from bill to below eye, *and rounded* yellow earmark. Female and imm. similar. Singly or pairs, active, bold, impulsive, aggressive. Flight swift, undulating, feeds acrobatically, takes insects on wing. Inquisitive like Lewin's; easily called up, becomes tame round habitation. Note range.

Similar species: Graceful Honeyeater (597); bill longer, eye grey. Lewin's Honeyeater (595): larger, darker, gape-streak whiter, earmark more angular, eye grey; note call.

Voice: Single melodious 'chip'; alarm-call, sharp 'queak-queak-queak'; also machinegun-like rattle similar to Lewins's, but inferior in tone and volume, repeated at varying speeds; also loud ascending scolding notes.

Habitat: Rainforests. coastal scrubs, nearby eucalypt woodlands, vegetation along watercourses, mangroves; banana plantations, cultivated lands, lantana thickets at edges of clearings and roadsides; gardens. Occurs in highlands, but is most common below c. 400 m.

Breeding: Nest: delicate almost transparent cup of bark-shreds; bound with spiders' web and decorated outside with pale-green lichen; lined with plant-down; suspended 1–3 m high from twigs in low bush or shrub, mangroves. Eggs: 2; white to delicate pink-white, irregularly spotted reddish or purple mostly at large end.

Range and Status: Confined to ne. Q.: c. York Pen. s. to Watson R. on w. coast; and e. coastal areas, lower foothills of Divide, and coastal islands. s. to Townsville (where locally uncommon). Common; sedentary.

597 GRACEFUL HONEYEATER *Meliphaga gracilis* **Pl.76**

Other names: Grey-breasted, Lesser or Little Yellow-spotted Honeyeater.

Field marks: 140–165 mm. The smallest of trio with Lewin's (595) and Yellow-spotted (596) Honeyeaters; paler olive-green above, with grey cheeks and underparts, thin yellow streak from bill to below eye, with a rounded pale-yellow earmark; bill is *proportionately longer and slimmer*. Female and imm: similar. Singly or pairs; quiet, unobtrusive, feeds among foliage, blossoms, lantana thickets: takes flying insects.

Similar species: Yellow-spotted Honeyeater (596): slightly larger, earmark yellower; voice distinctive. Lewin's (595): much larger, darker; earmark brighter-yellow, more angular; voice stronger, more distinctive.

Voice: Sharp 'tuck', 'tick', or 'pick' helps separate it from (595) and (596).

Habitat: (Mostly) lowland rainforest, vine scrubs, eucalypt woodlands and coastal scrubs, denser vegetation on small streams; lantana thickets, citrus orchards, gardens.

Breeding: Nest: delicate cup of grass and moss, bound with spiders' web, heavily decorated with moss or lichen: lined with plant-down; slung from twigs and usually low, sometimes over water. Eggs: 2; rich salmon-pink, dotted and spotted red, chestnut and purple-grey, most heavily at large end.

Range and Status: Ne. Q, from C. York s. to Edward R. and on w. coast and to Hinchinbrook I. and Ingham on e. coast. Fairly common; sedentary. Also s. NG and Aru Is.

598 WHITE-LINED HONEYEATER *Meliphaga albilineata* **Pl.76**

Other name: White-striped Honeyeater.

Field marks: 190 mm. A seldom-observed tropical species, somewhat like a dark Singing Honeyeater (601). Dark grey-brown above, lighter below, with soft dark mottlings on upperbreast; dark-grey of face margined *by fine silvery white line below eye, extending to and enlarging on ear-coverts*; feathers of wings and tail edged yellow-olive. Juv. reported to lack the white stripe but to have ear-coverts extensively tipped yellowish white; underparts plainer. Singly or pairs; scolding, vigorous, flirts tail. Schodde and Mason (1975) remarked 'has the typical meliphagid habit of forming loose flocks in trees where it feeds and of behaving aggressively towards smaller competitors. On occasions it is rather solitary and retiring, spending much of its time foraging through the dense upper branches of shrubbery, where it is much more often heard than seen'. Flight quick, undulating; with 'flop flop' of wings.

Similar species: Singing Honeyeater (601): much paler, with bold black mark through eye above narrower yellow-white mark.

Voice: Described as 'a most melodious series of disconnected phrases uttered in a rich, flutelike voice' (Deignan, 1964). Schodde and Mason commented 'the first whistle is invariably given with a rising inflexion, the second, sometimes omitted, undulates and usually falls a little and the third and strongest usually rises rather wildly before falling away. In quality, the notes are not unlike those of the accelerating 'brain-fever' call of the Brush Cuckoo (365)'. Other observers have described how the calls ring through the sandstone gorges; one described the phrases as a loud clear 'tuuuheer-tuu-uu-eee', uttered occasionally.

Habitat: Scrub on the slopes and sides of sandstone escarpments and nearby hills, associated pockets of rainforest, swamp woodland and flowering eucalypt woodlands.

Breeding: Nest: deep cup of fine interwoven strands of vine-like creeper, rim re-inforced by spiders' web and fine vegetable fibre that binds nest to supporting stems, lined with fine plant-stems and fibre; 1–5 m high in outer twigs of small shrub or tree. Eggs: undescribed.

Range and Status: Known only from two regions of suitable habitat in nw. Aust. (1) w. Arnhem Land, NT, from area of King River to Wellington Ra. and Mt. Borradaile s. along the w. escarpments of the Arnehem Land Plateau 'at least as far as the e. headwaters of the Mary R.' (e. of Pine Ck); possibly extending to Katherine Gorge (*fide* Schodde and Mason). (2) n. Kimberleys. WA, in area of Mitchell R. and adjacent coastal islands. Locally common.

599 YELLOW-FACED HONEYEATER *Lichenostomus chrysops* Pl,76

Other names: Chick-up, Lovebird, Quitchup, Yellow-gaped Honeyeater.

Field marks: 160–170 mm. A plain olive-grey honeyeater obscurely streaked darker, with pale chin and *a fine curving yellow streak back from bill below eye, boldly margined black above and below, and ending in whitish tip*; slight yellowish mark behind eye; sides of breast buffish. Birds in n. Q smaller, darker, bills longer. Active like other honeyeaters in foliage and blossoms, often near ground; sometimes hovers. Singly or in pairs, but in autumn–winter migrates in flocks of dozens to hundreds and these may total tens of thousands a day at peak, attracting local attention; presence in mixed flocks revealed by oft-uttered flight-call. Familiar and tame round gardens, raids fruit.

Similar species: Bridled Honeyeater (600): darker; broader black mark on lower side of facial streak in almost mutton-chop effect. Singing Honeyeater (601): larger, paler; black mark through eye, broader yellow-white facial streak without lower black border.

Voice: A brisk cheery 'chickup' or clear descending 'calip, calip, calip' often expanded into ringing, descending song. Flight-call: short 'dip' or 'dep'; alarm-call, single scratchy peevish 'kree'.

Habitat: Varied: coastal scrubs, mangroves, woodlands and forests to treeless alpine heaths and tussocks over 1800 m; blackberry and other thickets; golf-courses, orchards, parks, gardens.

Breeding: Nest: small neat cup of grasses, bark-fibre and moss, often decorated with lichen and often thin enough to see through; slung from horizontal fork in branchlets 1–6 m high. Eggs: 2–3; pink to deep red-buff, spotted and blotched chestnut-red and purplish grey.

Range and Status: E. and se. Aust.: (?) isolate population in ne. Q s. coastally from Cooktown to Herbert R. and inland on Tablelands. Main range s. from Mackay Q to Mt. Lofty and (? isolate population) Flinders Ras., SA; inland to Suttor Ck–Carnarvon Ras.–Chinchilla–Goondiwindi in Q; all e. NSW inland to Moree–Warrumbungle NP– Wellington; far-w. record from Booligal; all Vic. *except* nw. but occasionally to Mystic Park; regular winter visitor Bendigo; se. SA w. to Fleurieu Pen.–Mt. Lofty Ras.; vagrant Murray mallee. *Not* Tas. or Furneaux Group; but present King I., Bass Strait and other islands off e. coast n. to Fraser I, Q. Common; part-migratory in s.

600 BRIDLED HONEYEATER *Lichenostomus frenatus* Pl.76

Other name: Mountain Honeyeater.

Field marks: 200 mm. A dark honeyeater: *bill black with yellow base*; *a fine whitish or yellow line (or 'bridle') extends back from gape and swings up behind eye*. A broader black 'line below this *widens noticeably behind eye. Below this again, a grey line extends back to enlarge on side of neck*. There is a grey mark behind eye, and yellow spot on ear-coverts. Upperparts dark-brown, wing-feathers and tail edged olive; grey-brown below slightly streaked. Singly, pairs or small flocks, active and pugnacious.

Similar species: Yellow-faced Honeyeater (599).

Voice: Noisy: calls clear and melodious, usually described as 'we-are', and 'wachita-wachita'. Call also described as loud and imperious, the first part reminiscent of Spangled Drongo's (692) harsh rattle, latter, part of the Willie Wagtail's 'sweet pretty creature', but in faster time; varied in length and composition.

Habitat: Highland rainforests and margins; vegetation along watercourses in hills, wetter eucalypt woodlands, to lower levels in winter; swamp woodlands; adjacent drier open eucalypt forests and woodlands.

Breeding: Nest: cup of fine twigs and stems lined with plant-fibre; suspended in leafy twigs of tree or vine in scrub or rainforest, usually at no great height. Eggs: 2; whitish, spotted red-brown, grey-brown, purplish grey.

Range and Status: Ne. Q: from Cooktown s. on highlands to Eungella Ra., near Mackay. Common; probably sedentary.

601 SINGING HONEYEATER *Lichenostomus virescens* **Pl.76**

Other names: Black-faced or Forrest's Honeyeater; Grape-eater or Grey Peter.

Field marks: 180–220 mm. The name 'Singing' is an exaggeration; only in coastal WA are calls sufficiently sustained and vivacious to be song-like. A medium-sized pale grey-brown honeyeater with *bold black mark from bill through eye to sides of neck, with thinner line of yellow below, ending in a broad silvery white mark*; pale-fawn below with slight dark streaks. Female: smaller. Often solitary; feeds quietly in low shrubs; when disturbed, flies low, undulating to next cover. Attracted to soft fruits, grapes; pugnacious to other birds.

Similar species: Yellow-faced Honeyeater (599): yellow facial-streak bordered black above and below. Varied (602) and Mangrove (603) Honeyeaters. Yellow-fronted Honeyeater (613): no black line through eye; strong yellow-and-black mark on throat.

Voice: Calls vary: scratchy peevish 'scree scree'; dry 'prrit prrit prrit', like Rainbow Bee-eater (406); alarm-call, 'crik-crikit-crikit-crikit', accelerating into running, almost machinegun-like note, somewhat like Lewin's Honeyeater (595).

Habitat: Varied: coastal dune vegetation to inland mulga and mallee; often shows a marked preference of isolated shrubs or thickets, being prepared to cross much open ground to reach them; in inland, often in vegetation near watercourses; also orchards, vineyards, gardens.

Breeding: Nest: frail rather untidy cup of faded green grass or plant-stems; bound with spiders' web; lined with hair, fur, fine grass or plant-down; slung from fine branchlets in dense shrub 1–4 m high. Eggs: 2–3; pink-white to light-yellowish buff, thickly spotted with fine indistinct red-brown marks, or nearly without spots, but deeper in tone at large end.

Range and Status: Widespread in mainland Aust. *except* for higher-rainfall areas. Mostly absent from Gippsland and the Dividing Range in Vic., and from areas e. of Divide in NSW and Q, but extends to near coast in ce. Q, and n. to Mitchell R. on w. coast C. York Pen. Present on many drier coastal islands. Fairly common, if localized in suitable habitat. Sedentary.

602 VARIED HONEYEATER *Lichenostomus versicolor* **Pl.76**

Field marks: 195 mm. Usually first noticed by conspicuous noisy ways. Olive-brown above with yellow on wings and tail; *yellowish below with distinct brown streaks*; black mark from bill through eye down sides of neck, broad yellow streak below, ending in white patch on ear-coverts. Singly, pairs or demonstrative parties; constantly on the go, moving quickly through foliage and blossoms and from tree to tree. Some regard it as conspecific with Mangrove Honeyeater (603), which replaces it s. from Townsville.

Similar species: Singing Honeyeater (601): much paler, without yellow on underparts. Mangrove Honeyeater (603): feathers of throat and upperbreast scaly brown and yellow, not streaked; calls differ. Note range.

Voice: Loud and rollicking; includes clearer, sometimes melodious, notes somewhat like Singing and Mangrove Honeyeaters; other common calls, often repetitive, described as shouted 'go-bidger-roo', 'which-way, which-way-you-go'; 'get-your-whip' or 'hear-hear'.

Habitat: Coastal scrubs, adjacent drier woodlands, mangroves; trees along waterfront, streets, gardens of coastal towns.

Breeding: Nest: flimsy cup of plant-stems, leaves, drier sea-grass, rootlets and plant-fibre; bound with spiders' web; sometimes lined with plant-down; usually in mangrove, sometimes in leafy tree such as introduced mango, up to 4 m or more high. Eggs: 2; pale-pink, deeper at large end, finely spotted red-brown.

Range and Status: Coastal ne. Q and many coastal islands, from C. York s. to Halifax Bay, near Ingham. Locally common, sedentary. Also Torres Strait islands, NG and islands.

603 MANGROVE HONEYEATER *Lichenostomus fasciogularis* Pl.76

Other names: Fasciated, Island or Scaly-throated Honeyeater.

Field marks: 190–205 mm. Dark like Varied Honeyeater (602), but with a *curious brown and yellow barred or scaly pattern on throat and upperbreast*; blackish mark from bill through eye above broad yellow streak that ends in silvery white patch on ear-coverts. Female: often distinctly smaller. Pairs or small parties; active, noisy and aggressive; feeds usually in outer foliage of mangroves; at low tide descends to feed among lower trunks, roots.

Similar species: Varied Honeyeater (602). Singing Honeyeater (601).

Voice: One of the best singers among honeyeaters. Calls strong and clear; some like Varied Honeyeater, but less varied; once learned, difference in tone easily recognized; also chatter somewhat like alarm-call of Lewin's (595).

Habitat: Mangroves, nearby blossoming eucalypt woodlands, blossoming trees in coastal towns.

Breeding: Nest: deep cup of fine dry grass or dry sea-grass; bound with spiders' web and egg-sacs; lined with fine rootlets; in fork of mangrove down to 60 cm above high water. Eggs: 2; pale salmon-pink, spotted red-brown mostly round large end.

Range and Status: Coastal e. Aust. and coastal islands, and some islands in Capricorn Group, from near Townsville, Q, s. to Stuarts Point, near Macksville, NSW. Common in n., rare in s. Sedentary.

604 WHITE-GAPED HONEYEATER *Lichenostomus unicolor* Pl.76

Other names: Erect-tailed or River Honeyeater.

Field marks: 180–215 mm. Demonstrative and very evident, despite dull plumage: plain grey-brown; faint olive wash on outer edges of primaries. The one diagnostic mark is the *white, creamish or yellow wedge-shaped mark on gape between bill and eye*. Pairs, or parties or flocks; noisy, aggressive, given to group-chases; displays with wings fluttering, tail erect, unusual for honeyeater.

Similar species: Lewin's Honeyeater (595): yellowish ear-mark.

Voice: Various loud rollicking calls, e.g. 'whit whit, awhit-whit, awhit-whit'; an explosive 'chiew' or 'chop', repeated at intervals, also described, 'a short trill followed by melodious whistles'.

Habitat: Vegetation near water; pandanus thickets; mangroves; swamp woodlands and nearby grassy woodlands; homestead environs; trees in streets and gardens.

Breeding: Nest: deep cup of fine grass, rootlets, hair, plant-fibre and some bark; bound with spiders' web; lined with soft grasses; usually in horizontal fork of leafy tree or shrub 2–16 m high. Eggs: 2; whitish pink, spotted and blotched red and purple.

Range and Status: Coastal n. Aust. and some islands: from near Broome, WA, and inland on Fitzroy R., through Kimberleys, top end NT s. to Newcastle Waters; e. along Gulf coast and coastal rivers and n. to Archer R. on w. coast C. York Pen., crossing (patchily, mostly on rivers) to e. coast of Q from Cooktown s. to Burdekin R., inland to Atherton Tableland–Georgetown. Common coastal n. Aust. and some coastal towns e.g. Darwin, Townsville; generally uncommon on e. coast. Probably sedentary.

605 YELLOW HONEYEATER *Lichenostomus flavus* Pl.76

Field marks: 175 mm. *A plump bright yellow-green honeyeater* with slight dark line through eye. Singly and pairs, rather placid and often tame. Feeds in blossoms and foliage, enters orchards and gardens to feed on soft fruits. Flight undulating, with distinctive 'flop-flop' of wings

Similar species: Yellow-tinted Honeyeater (615): smaller, paler, black-over-yellow mark on sides of neck; calls differ.

Voice: Varied: loud clear whistle or piercing 'whcc, whee' or merry 'whee-a, whee-a'; also metallic 'tut-tut-tut', short trill ending in sharp whistle. Alarm-call, peevish, scratchy 'jab!'.

Habitat: Vegetation on watercourses, eucalypt woodlands, margins of rainforests and tropical scrubs, mostly below 450 m; swamp woodlands, mangroves; orchards, plantations, gardens; urban areas.

Breeding: Nest: shallow cup of bark, grasses or palm-fibre; bound with spiders' web; suspended 1–10 m high from small branches of leafy shrub or tree often in orchard, garden. Eggs: 2; whitish to deep-pink, spotted or blotched red-brown, chestnut and purplish-grey.

Range and Status: N. Q: from Flinders R. on Gulf coast s. to Mt. Isa, n. to Cape York (Jardine R.) and s. on e. coast to Broad Sound, *c.* 100 km n. of Rockhampton. Patchy, fairly common; probably sedentary.

606 WHITE-EARED HONEYEATER *Lichenostomus leucotis* Pl.76

Other name: New Norcia Honeyeater.

Field marks: 200–205 mm. Distinctive: *black from face to upperbreast with large white ear-mark*; crown grey, upperparts deep-olive green, yellow-olive below. Female: less black on breast. Imm: duller, crown olive-green. Singly or pairs; active, bold, aggressive; feeds less on nectar than many other honeyeaters, forages in foliage, on limbs and trunks, often attracts attention by noise made while fossicking under bark, and 'flop-flop' of wings in flight, sometimes attacks fruit in orchards. Known to alight on heads or clothing of observers to remove hair or other fibre for nest-building. Near nest, performs distraction display.

Similar species: Yellow-throated Honeyeater (607); (only Tas. and on larger Bass Strait islands): throat yellow, white ear-patch smaller; underparts grey.

Voice: Various calls; jarring descending 'chung-chung-chung', mellow 'chockup, chockup', or 'beer-brick', 'beer-brick'. Inland populations have somewhat lighter calls of more syllables, e.g. mellow 'cherrywheet, cherryweet', or a quick 'chittagong', also rapid machinegun-like 'chock-chock-chock-chock-chock'; many other calls during breeding season.

Habitat: Varies geographically: in coastal e. and se. Aust. in wet forests and woodlands, vegetation along streams, coastal scrubs, to sub-inland mallee, brigalow, belar. In sw. Aust. confined to drier habitats, typically mallee, salmon-gum woodlands, and tea-tree thickets round salt-lakes.

Breeding: Nest: deep cup of bark-shreds and grass, bound with spiders' web and lined with wool, fur, hair; usually slung from branchlets 1–3 m high, or in low growth like bracken. Eggs: 2–3; whitish to pale cream, sparingly spotted and blotched red and red-brown, mostly towards large end.

Range and Status: E. and sw. Aust.: inland e. Q, from Tropic (? vagrant n. to Hughenden–Charters Towers) inland s. to Blackall–Carnarvon Ras.–Goondiwindi; patchily e. to Westwood–lower coastal ranges Gin Gin–Gympie;–Glasshouse Mts.–

Cunningham's Gap; e. NSW, *except* coastal areas n. of Clarence R.; inland to Pilliga scrub (Moree–Baradine), central mallee areas (Mt. Hope–Rankin Springs) and mallee areas of sw. NSW; throughout Vic., including nw. mallee areas, but mostly *absent* from red gum forests of Murray Valley; in SA, mallee areas of lower north–Orroroo–s. Flinders Ras.–Gawler Ras. and Kangaroo I., thence coastally w. to Gt. Victoria Desert, WA. Present in drier parts of sw. WA, n. to lower Murchison R. on w. coast; *absent* from the higher rainfall zone w. of Stirling Ras.–Wickepin–Wongan Hills. Common except in n. of range; mostly sedentary or locally nomadic, but regular altitudinal and (? winter migratory) movements in se. Aust.

607   YELLOW-THROATED HONEYEATER *Lichenostomus flavicollis*   Pl.76

Other names: Green Dick or Linnet.

Field marks: 200 mm. Distinctive; the only Tas. member of its genus: *blackish face and upperbreast offset by bright-yellow throat and small creamy-white mark behind eye*; crown and rest of underparts grey. Female: similar. Behaviour like White-eared Honeyeater (606), including habit of sometimes alighting on observer's head or coat to pluck hair for nest.

Similar species: White-eared Honeyeater (606).

Voice: Common call has been syllabized 'tonk, tonk, tonk', 'tchook, tchook' or 'chur-uk, chur-uk'; also 'pick-em-up'.

Habitat: Varied: most forests, woodlands, except rainforest; coastal scrub; golf-courses, orchards, parks, gardens.

Breeding: Nest: small cup of grass, bark-shreds and leaves; bound with spiders' web and lined with fur, treefern fibres; sometimes wool used for body and lining of nest; often within 1 m of ground in low bush or tussock, occasionally to 10 m high in foliage. Eggs: 2–3; pale-pink or fleshy buff, marked with prominent small dots of chestnut-red and a few indistinct dots of purplish grey.

Range and Status: Confined to and widely distributed in Tas., King I. and Furneaux Group. Bass Strait. Common, apparently sedentary.

608   YELLOW-TUFTED HONEYEATER *Lichenostomus melanops*   Pl.76

Other names: Black-faced or Golden-tufted Honeyeater; Yellow-whiskers, Whisky.

Field marks: 195–220 mm. A striking medium-sized honeyeater: *sides of head glossy black with bright-golden ear-tufts*; *crown and upperparts olive-green*, to olive-brown on wings and tail, sides of throat bright-yellow; centre of throat and breast yellow-grey. When stressed may raise crown feathers, but these do *not* form a fixed helmet on forehead. The race *gippslandica* is the largest and darkest form, very like Helmeted Honeyeater (609), except that it lacks such a conspicuously-raised forehead tuft, and the colours of crown, nape and mantle *merge*, without abrupt transition as in Helmeted. The palest race is *meltoni* (see below). Singly, pairs, small flocks as part of colony, or nomadic companies. Active, aggressive; feeds in blossoms and foliage high or low, and on sap exuding from treetrunks; probes bark. Parties often play and chase, chattering, wings drooped, tails raised.

Similar species: Helmeted Honeyeater (609).

Voice: Contact-call, sharp 'yip!', also scratchy 'jeow!' or sharp single 'querk', in chorus like Bell Miners (589). Notes too varied to describe, some harsh and scratchy, others softer, clear, almost whistling. Voice of *gippslandica* most like Helmeted, but short contact-call deeper and more scratchy.

Habitat: Varies: eucalypt forest and woodland, usually with good undergrowth; coastal scrubs and heaths. Inland drier woodlands, specially red ironbark and red stringybark, also mallee, native pine, brigalow and belar.

Breeding: Nest: skilfully woven substantial cup of grass and strips of bark bound with spiders' web and egg-sacs, often with paper, wool or dead leaves incorporated; lined with plant-down, fine grass and feathers; slung in slender fork in many situations: fallen

branches near ground, down old mine shafts, tussocks, shrubs or saplings, sometimes in foliage or hanging bark from tree at heights to 20 m. Eggs: 2–3; pinkish-buff, spotted and blotched red-brown and purplish grey, mainly at large end.
Range and Status: Se. Aust.: from extreme se. SA (Naracoorte) n. and e. to Tropic in brigalow belt s. of Clermont, Q, coastally to near Noosa Heads, Q. Approximate inland limits: Little Desert–Mystic Park, Vic.; Jerilderie–Wellington–Warrumbungle NP–Moree, NSW; Goondiwindi–Carnarvon Ra., Q. The darkest race *gippslandica* extends e. from Noojee, Vic., mostly on streams flowing s. from Divide, to coast near Metung, thence to se. NSW. The palest race *meltoni* extends from se. SA across inland Vic. to NSW and Q, does not appear to cross the Divide in e. Vic.; thus the dark and pale ends of the population appear to remain apart. The dark se. coastal forms appear to be sedentary; the inland forms sedentary or nomadic and irruptive, probably in response to less-dependable rainfall, and fluctuations in blossoming of eucalypts, grevilleas etc. They appear irregularly from time to time beyond the stated inland limits e.g. to mallee areas of nw. Vic. Generally patchy, locally common to rare.

609 HELMETED HONEYEATER *Lichenostomus cassidix* Pl.76
Field marks: 210 mm. One of our rarest birds, now confined to a small colony e. of Melbourne. It closely resembles the race *gippslandica* of Yellow-tufted Honeyeater (608), differing in the *fixed short crest or helmet of golden, almost plush-like feathers on forehead, projecting slightly over base of bill*; not a conspicuous field mark, but clearly visible under good conditions. When agitated, feathers of crown also raised, enhancing helmet. When wet or cold the bird is reported to ruffle feathers and thus temporarily obscure the distinctive head-contour. Unlike all races of Yellow-tufted, gold of crown and nape *cut off rather sharply from blackish-olive upperparts*; conspicuous white tail-tips. Female and imm: slightly smaller, with smaller helmet. Pairs and parties, as part of the colony. Very active and vocal; forages in foliage, hangs upside down, often descends to undergrowth or to water to bathe. Parties often perch close together with drooping trembling wings, calling, or chase with loud chattering notes.
Similar species: Yellow-tufted Honeyeater (608).
Voice: Contact-call: sharp scratchy 'jik', longer calls described as 'jor, jor, jor, jor, jircc, jiree', 'churl, churl, churl, churl'; also soft gurgling and almost flute-like notes.
Habitat: Restricted and specific: appears to require combination of manna and swamp gums with shrubby tea-trees, bracken and dense tussocks of grass and saw-sedge along watercourses.
Breeding: Nest: deep untidy cup of grass, strips of bark, ferns and leaves; loosely bound with spiders' web and egg-sacs, lined with fine bark-shreds and plant-down, fur or feathers; usually in low shrub or bracken, occasionally to 6–10 m high. Eggs: 2; pinkish-buff, deepening to reddish-buff at large end, spotted and blotched red-purple with underlying purplish grey markings, mainly at large end; or pink-buff with evenly-distributed spots.
Range and Status: Some now treat the Helmeted as a large dark end-race of (608). Others still consider it a full species, the only one endemic to Vic.; proclaimed a State Faunal Emblem 10 Mar. 1971. A small population of probably less than 200 occurs along a section of Woori–Yallock Ck. and several tributaries mostly in the Yellingbo State Wildlife Reserve, *c.* 50 km e. of Melbourne. A smaller colony on Cardinia Ck. near Gembrook may be extinct. Efforts have been made by members of the Bird Observers Club, private landowners and the Victorian Fisheries and Wildlife Division to expand and consolidate suitable habitat in the Yellingbo area. Formerly more widespread in colonies in ranges and watercourses e. of Melbourne, n. to Upper Yarra R., w. to Bass R. area and possibly Strzelecki Ras., s. Gippsland. Sedentary.

610 PURPLE-GAPED HONEYEATER *Lichenostomus cratitius* Pl.76

Other names: Lilac-wattled or Wattle-cheeked Honeyeater.

Field marks: 170–190 mm. A large, dark, yellow-plumed honeyeater: head grey, upperparts olive-green, brighter on wings, underparts pale-grey washed yellow. Note blackish mask through eye and *line of lilac skin along gape, above yellowish streak down throat*; *a second yellow mark or plume behind grey ear-coverts*. Imm. gape yellow. Singly, pairs, parties to flocks when blossoms abundant; T. R. Garnett has remarked that it *climbs* through foliage, without flitting movements. Wary; probably most easily observed when it drinks at waterholes, tanks.

Similar species: Grey-headed Honeyeater (611): paler-grey head, breast yellowish. Note range. Yellow-plumed Honeyeater (612): prominently streaked below; no yellow streak down throat. Yellow-fronted Honeyeater (613): underparts fawn.

Voice: Noisy; utters a variety of calls: clicking notes, a harsh single chirp, a loud whiplike whistle and soft parrotlike warble are reported. In flight, a sharp 'twit-twit', harsh chatterings.

Habitat: Usually mallee associations and nearby woodlands; in sw. Aust. into open grassy woodlands and scrubby timber along watercourses; occasionally blossoming street trees.

Breeding: Nest: delicate cup of strips of bark, grasses; bound with spiders'web and egg-sacs; lined with fine grass and plant-down; slung from slender leafy branchlets often below 1 m high. Eggs: 2; white, tinged pink, spotted and speckled red-brown forming zone at large end.

Range and Status: Divided distribution in semi-arid s. and sw. Aust: mallee areas of sw. NSW and nw. Vic. (s. to Little Desert with irruptions reported s. to Bendigo); Murray mallee, SA, s. to Coorong thence w. to Kangaroo I., York and Eyre Pens. In WA from Wongan Hills (occasionally w. to Northam) s. to L. Grace–Stirling Ras.; mostly in mallee areas of wheatbelt; sight-records of birds at tanks in drought from Kathleen Valley, WA, far-inland from above locations. Generally uncommon, but gathers in large local companies where blossom abundant. Apparently highly nomadic.

611 GREY-HEADED HONEYEATER *Lichenostomus keartlandi* Pl.76

Other name: Keartland's Honeyeater.

Field marks: 150–160 mm. Unmistakable: *crown clear-grey*; *underparts lemon, slightly streaked darker*; black mark back through eye broadens to patch on side of head, distinctive yellow plume or cut-throat mark, margined black above, joining yellowish underparts. Imm: yellow gape, dark oily mark round base of bill. Pairs and parties, usually colonial. Behaves like White-plumed Honeyeater (616), very active but less excitable; seems attracted to native figs in rocky parts of habitat.

Voice: Somewhat like White-plumed but less strident; one distinctive call described as 'chee-toyt, chee-toyt'; also weak, mellow 'chickowee'; peevish 'check, check, check' uttered in flight; alarm-call weak 'alarm-clock' trill.

Habitat: Seems to favour rugged lightly wooded hillsides and gorges above watercourses. Drinks at these but in many parts of range denied permanent occupation by White-plumed; where this aggressive species is locally absent e.g. Mt. Olga, NT, Gregory R., Q, the Grey-headed occupies watercourse habitat. Also woodlands and inland scrubs, including mallee and mulga.

Breeding: Nest: cup of fine strips of bark, plant-down; bound with spiders' web; suspended from small branches or supported in slender fork, usually in low shrub. Eggs: 2; whitish to pale-pink, slightly spotted with pale-brown to reddish spots or reddish blotches.

Range and Status: Widespread in suitable habitat in interior, reaching w. coast from Minilya R., WA, n. to Derby and s. (n. to Oscar Ras.) Kimberleys; in NT, ranges n. to Roper R.–Mallapunyah; in nw. Q ranges from upper Nicholson R.–Cloncurry R. se. to area of Opalton, thence sw. to Birdsville. Apparently *absent* from Simpson Desert, in s. NT it ranges s. through the Macdonnell Ras. and other ranges s. to Oodnadatta–Musgrave Ras. in n. SA, thence w. through Rawlinson Ras. and other ranges of e. central WA to Carnarvon. Distribution apparently influenced by occurrence of rocky ranges with creeks. Probably sedentary.

612 YELLOW-PLUMED HONEYEATER *Lichenostomus ornatus* **Pl.76**

Other names: Graceful or Mallee Honeyeater.

Field marks: 130–160 mm. The only one of its group with a *whitish strongly streaked breast*. Head olive-green, note dark-olive mark round eye and *bright-yellow neck-plume, without adjacent dark mark*. Singly, pairs or parties as part of overall colony; active, vivacious, behaves much like White-plumed Honeyeater (616); performs song-flight, rising steeply, 15 m or more, calling, then dropping steeply.

Similar species: Purple-gaped Honeyeater (610); grey below. Yellow-fronted Honeyeater (613): fawn below, with fainter streaks; yellow neck-plume more strongly margined black above. White-plumed Honeyeater (616): white neck-plume; underparts scarcely streaked.

Voice: Calls somewhat like White-plumed but flatter and harder: common contact-call, brisk but liquid 'joe-joe-*hik*'; also brisk 'chickwididee'; call uttered by male in song-flight resembles 'hit joe-joe, hit joe-joe, hit'; alarm-call, trill of flatter more machinegun-like quality than White-plumed.

Habitat: Mallee and taller sub-inland eucalypt woodlands and forests; nearby stands of native pine and belar; in more coastal parts of range, banksias, sheoaks, sandplain-heaths, tea-tree thickets; woodlands and forests in sw. WA. During nomadic movements, river red gums along watercourses and in good seasonal conditions, flowering semi-arid zone shrubs often far from surface water.

Breeding: Nest: delicate shallow cup of dry grasses; bound with plant-down, some spiders' web; usually suspended among foliage 1–3 m in mallee, sometimes to 12 m in taller eucalypts. Eggs: 2; whitish to pale reddish-buff, deepening to salmon toward large end, finely freckled and spotted red-brown, mainly at large end.

Range and Status: S. inland Aust.: from mallee areas of c. NSW e. to Gilgandra–Goonoo Forest–Orange–Temora, to mallee areas of nw. Vic.; widespread in s. SA, including York and Eyre Pens. (and nearby Flinders I., SA) n. to L. Frome–Ooldea; w. through (but apparently not north of) Nullarbor Plain to Gt. Victoria Desert–Coolgardie, WA, to ne. of York and n. to Tamala Sandplain (s. of Shark Bay). Common in suitable habitat; nomadic, possibly migratory; frequent movements far from 'normal' range: inland to near Kathleen Valley, WA, and to Everard Ras., SA; in Vic., s. to Portland, se. to area of Melbourne.

613 YELLOW-FRONTED HONEYEATER *Lichenostomus plumulus* **Pl.76**

Other name: Grey-fronted Honeyeater; Plumed Honeyeater.

Field marks: 130–160 mm. A well-marked honeyeater with longish square-cut tail; dark olive-fawn above, paler below with darker fawn streaks. Tone of crown and nape are quite deep and against this, *the yellow neck-plume, edged blackish above, is very conspicuous – a bright-yellow mark against darker background*, opposite in effect to neck-marking of Yellow-tinted Honeyeater (615). Note also *darkish shading from bill to round eye*. Imm: base of bill yellowish, underparts more strongly streaked. Usually solitary or in well-spaced pairs, but numbers gather in blossoming trees. Wary; when approached, usually flies some distance to next group of shrubs or trees.

Similar species: Yellow-tinted Honeyeater (615): note distinction above; usually colonial near water. Yellow-plumed Honeyeater (612): more conspicuously streaked below; usually in mallee.

Voice: One call, probably uttered in upward song-flight, has been syllabized 'it-wirt, wirt, wirt, wirt'; single sharp note, 'boink', probably alarm-call, may be likened to the 'peet' of

Little Woodswallow (709), but deeper. A canary-like song reported in sub-inland SA.
Habitat: Dry-country vegetation generally, including mallee, mulga, low shrubs, scrub along dry watercourses, sparse timber and scrub on rugged hills. In w. NSW the preferred mallee habitat is described as 'low mallee with an understorey of porcupine grass and other ground vegetation . . . also . . . low coppiced mallee shoots regenerating after a bushfire'. (Australian Birds, 10:3, p. 44).
Breeding: Nest: small cup of finely shredded bark; bound with spiders' web and eggsacs; lined with plant-down; suspended from branchlets often below 2 m. Eggs: 2, occasionally 3; pale salmon-pink, very finely spotted pale red-brown in regular zone at large end.
Range and Status: Widespread in interior: n. to Kimberleys (Napier Broome Bay), WA; in NT, n. to about Mataranka–Mallapunyah; in Q, n. to Karumba on Gulf thence e. to Barcaldine–Mitchell; mostly 'dry mallee' areas in w. NSW, e. to Nyngan–Condoblin–Binya (e. of Cocoparra NP), to similar habitats in nw. Vic. and Murray mallee of SA, n. and s. of Murray R., also n. Eyre Pen.; throughout WA s. of Kimberleys *except* coastal areas s. from about North West Cape, and the heavily forested sw. Generally patchy, confined to suitable habitat. Sedentary or nomadic.

614 FUSCOUS HONEYEATER *Lichenostomus fuscus* Pl.76

Field marks: 150–160 mm. A rather plain honeyeater *with dark shading round eye that gives it a bruised look*; *small lightly black-edged yellow plume on side of neck*. Grey-brown above, tinged olive, wings and tail washed olive; paler below. Bill black, but nonbreeding adults of either sex may be seen with yellow base of bill and eyering; these 'soft parts' become black when breeding. Imm: bill brownish, yellow at base; eyering yellow. Note: the ne. Q race *subgermana* is paler, with crown and face washed yellow-olive, and pale grey-brown underparts, usually without streaks, centre of belly off-white. It has frequently been confused with the Yellow-tinted Honeyeater (615), which some consider conspecific. (Note Voice and Habitat). Pairs, family parties as part of a colony, or nomadic flocks. Often feeds high and inconspicuously, but calls are a feature of any woodland it inhabits. Male song-flight: calls while rising steeply 30 m or more before abruptly dropping to cover. Often tame round habitation, especially where food is provided.
Similar species: Yellow-fronted Honeyeater (613): shading round eye less conspicuous, yellow plume more conspicuous. Yellow-tinted Honeyeater (615): yellower head, against which black mark combined with yellow plume stands out distinctly; calls and habitat differ. White-plumed Honeyeater (616): head plain olive-green or olive-yellow; without dark shading round eye; prominent white neck-plume.
Voice: Often characterized as 'arig-arig-a-taw-taw'; much local variation: a common call in Vic. is quick, slightly guttural, 'pitt-quoll, pitty-quoll' or 'guinea-a-week'. In song-flight, deep metallic rather twanging 'tew-tew-tew-tew', 'permewan-permewan-permewan' or 'clitchit-clee-you, clitchit-clee-you' repeated. Alarm-call, short querulous note somewhat like Yellow-tufted (608), but less rasping.
Habitat: Drier open forests and woodlands (as on Atherton Tableland, ne. Q) but in parts e.g. Grampians, Vic. in wetter forests and woodlands; (in parts) river red gums along watercourses, margins of rainforest; inland scrubs, including belar and other casuarinas, and brigalow; occasionally tall mallee, coastal banksia-scrubs and heaths; gardens, even in city suburbs.
Breeding: Nest: neat cup of fine strips of bark, grass; bound with spiders' web; lined with hair, wool or plant-down; slung in leafy outer branchlets 1–20 m high. Eggs: 2–3; yellowish to buff-pink with few faint red-brown or pale-lilac spots, evenly sprinkled or forming zone at large end.
Range and Status: E. and se. Aust.: from Cooktown and Atherton Tableland, ne. Q, to e. SA. In Q, inland to upper Walsh R.–Mt. Garnet–Charters Towers–Duaringa–Chinchilla–Wallangarra; in NSW, inland to Bingara–Pilliga scrub–Warrumbungle NP–L. Cargelligo–s. Riverina and w. in river red gum forests of Murray R. and associated water-

courses and lakes into e. SA; in Vic., in ne. (s. to about Omeo) and n.-central and central districts s. to outer Melbourne areas and w. Gippsland (Lang Lang); through w. Vic. in parts (Grampians, Maryborough) to se. SA (Bool Lagoon), n. to Sutherlands and Flinders Ras. Generally common, but rare in SA; part-migratory or nomadic in s., probably sedentary in n.

615 YELLOW-TINTED HONEYEATER *Lichenostomus flavescens* Pl.76

Other name: Pale-Yellow Honeyeater.

Field marks: 140–160 mm. A somewhat nondescript honeyeater with one safe field mark. The neck plume is a small blackish mark or smudge above a larger yellow mark. *In the field, only the blackish part is conspicuous, looking somewhat like the ear-opening of a lizard*; this easily separates it from the Yellow-fronted (613), in which the *yellow* is the more conspicuous. Fawn above, face and underparts pale-yellow, breast often faintly streaked ashy, or yellowish fawn. Imm: base of bill yellow, brownish shading on crown. Usually in resident colonies or small nomadic flocks. Brisk and active; some consider it conspecific with Fuscous Honeyeater (614).

Similar species: Fuscous Honeyeater (614): away from ne. Q, darker, with 'bruised' shading round eye. But in region w. of Atherton Tableland, s. to about Townsville, the two seem often to be confused. Note Voice and Habitat. Yellow-fronted Honeyeater (613): white neck-plume, adjacent black mark not conspicuous. Calls differ.

Voice: Usual contact-call: sharp little 'jer', 'jer-jer' or harsh descending 'tew', tew, tew' uttered almost continuously; alarm-call, rather feeble trilled 'weeweeweewee'. Song (? in song-flight) described as high clear 'porra-cheu, porra-cheu-cheu, chi-porra cheu, porra-cheu-cheu-cheu'.

Habitat: Mostly timber and vegetation along watercourses; nearby grassed woodlands, occasionally mangroves.

Breeding: Nest: cup of bark-shreds and grass; bound with spiders' web and egg-sacs or caterpillar-silk; lined with fine pieces of bark; attached to fine twigs in small shrubby tree, 2–3 m high. Eggs: 2; pink, lightly spotted red-brown mostly at large end.

Range and Status: N. Aust. and some coastal islands: from Fitzroy R., WA, through Kimberleys and across top end NT s. to Larrimah–Macarthur R., nw. Q s. to Mt. Isa and e. to Mitchell R., C. York Pen. Situation in ne. Q s. of C. York Pen. is confused: specimens from Georgetown, sight-records from Atherton Tableland (w. of Herberton), and from area of Innisfail and Hervey Ra., 43 km nw. of Townsville. It has been suggested that, in Gulf drainage, Yellow-tinted is essentially a bird of waterside thickets, whilst Fuscous in ne. Q predominantly inhabits open forests. Common, probably sedentary. Also se. NG.

616 WHITE-PLUMED HONEYEATER *Lichenostomus penicillatus* Pl.76

Other names: Australian or Native Canary, Chickowee, Greenie, Linnet, Ringeye, Ringneck.

Field marks: 155–170 mm. In e. and se. Aust. a *plain olive-grey* honeyeater with yellow-olive head and wash on wings and *longish clear-cut white neck-plume, sometimes margined blackish above*. In inland, n. Aust. and WA, plumage much yellower, head golden-yellow. Imm: rich-yellow base to bill, giving somewhat different appearance, white neck-plume less distinct. Singly, pairs or parties, often as part of a general colony. Feeds from low, to tops of tallest trees; nervously active; mobs sleeping owls, goannas, possums. Male has conspicuous song-flight, rising steeply 15–30 m or more, calling, before closing wings and dropping to cover.

Similar species: Yellow-plumed Honeyeater (612): yellow neck-plume; whitish breast strongly streaked darker.

Voice: Common call; brisk 'chickowee' or 'chickabiddy', also variety of rapid glancing chatterings, difficult to describe; alarm-call, a rapid high-pitched strident trill, like alarm-clock; carries far and alerts many birds; a characteristic bush sound. In song-flight male utters repeated 'chickowee, chickowee-chickowee' or 'chick-wert, chick-wert, chick-wert' etc., differing geographically.

Habitat: Seldom far from water and tends to be restricted to particular eucalypt habitats; in higher rainfall areas of coastal Aust. typically in open forests, woodlands or isolated stands of smooth-barked eucalypts; in inland districts mostly confined to river gums along watercourses, but in good seasons extends into nearby mallee; also shelter belts, road reserves, golf-courses, orchards, parks, gardens.

Breeding: Nest: deep and apparently fragile cup of grasses; bound with spiders' web; lined with plant-down, horsehair; slung from outer branchlets 1–25 m high. Eggs: 2–3; white, pale-buff to deep-pink, minutely spotted chestnut-red, toward large end; some with larger purple-red or deep-lilac spots as though below surface.

Range and Status: Through much of mainland Aust. *except* far-n. coastal regions: nearly throughout se. Aust., from n. Eyre Pen., SA, (vagrant Kangaroo I.) to inland ne. NSW; formerly uncommon round Sydney, now becoming consolidated. In Q, ranges e. to coast near Rockhampton, otherwise e. to Texas–Dalby–Charters Towers–the middle Herbert R. and n. to Richmond–Mt. Isa and rivers of Gulf coast; in NT n. to Alexandria–Brunette Downs; widespread in river red gums on watercourses of s. NT and adjacent interior; in mid-WA, widespread inland and coastally from Pilbara region s. to Geraldton thence inland s. to Moora–Norseman; vagrant Perth but *absent* from better-watered sw. corner WA, Bight coast and Nullarbor Plain. Common, probably mostly colonial and sedentary.

BLACK-CAPPED HONEYEATERS Genus *Melithreptus*

Seven species (*six* by Schodde, 1975) of small to medium-sized honeyeaters distributed over most parts of Aust., one extending to NG. Characteristic pattern is the black crown and nape with white band back from behind eye, joining round nape. Rest of upperparts generally olive-green, underparts whitish. Identification is based on *extent of the nape-band, colour of the small crescent of bare-skin above or round eye and presence or absence of dark mark down centre of throat.* Mostly gregarious and colonial, feeding and travelling in small to large flocks in local nomadic or extensive migratory movements. Several species are known to be communal breeders, in the sense that more than the mated pair feeds the young in the nest and after they have fledged. Although not included in the genus the large distinctive Blue-faced Honeyeater (588) is regarded by many as a giant *Melithreptus.*

617 BLACK-CHINNED HONEYEATER *Melithreptus gularis*   Pl.77

Other name: Black-throated Honeyeater.

Field marks: 165 mm. Patterned like others of its group; nape-band forms rather straight line. Note *vivid blue eye-crescent, blackish mark on chin and a little down centre of throat; underparts white, strongly washed grey-buff; legs yellowish.* Imm: duller and more fawn, head browner, underparts whitish; bill orange, tipped brown; *legs bright orange.* Pairs or parties; usually as part of a colony; active, demonstrative; feeds on limbs, trunks and in foliage, usually fairly high. Often first noted by calls and robust song. Considered by some conspecific with Golden-backed Honeyeater (618) and possibly with Strong-billed (619).

Similar species: Golden-backed Honeyeater (618): yellow-olive eye-crescent; golden-yellow above, whiter below.

Voice: Curious high-pitched grating, croaking notes, developed into song; often uttered in concert of several birds together and in flight; suggestive of some calls of Spiny-cheeked Honeyeater (581), but less guttural. Contact-call: 'chirrup', somewhat like Rainbow Bee-eater (406).

Habitat: Taller, drier eucalypt forests, woodlands, and timber along watercourses often without understorey; scrubs. On w. slopes, NSW, and in n. and c. Vic., the typical habitat is ironbark forests.

Breeding: Nest: rather fragile cup of bark-shreds, grass, other plant-fibre and occasionally wool; bound with spiders' web; slung from twigs in drooping outer foliage, usually high. Eggs: 2; pale salmon-pink with deep reddish-yellow spots at large end.

Range and Status: Replaces Golden-backed Honeyeater in e. Aust. In Q it ranges inland to w. of Charters Towers–Barcaldine–Charleville; in NSW, inland to w. of Moree–Warrumbungle NP–Mudgee; it extends into ne. and c. Vic., s. to outer Melbourne environs (Lower Plenty–You Yangs) and through w. Vic. to Naracoorte–Mannum–Mt. Lofty Ras., SA, thence n. to Port Augusta–s. Flinders Ras. It extends w. in river red gum forests of the Murray R. and associated river systems and lakes from Swan Hill downstream into SA. It approaches the e. coast mostly where drier forests occur. There are resident populations in Sydney area. Except for one sight record of a pair with fledged young in the Snowy R. Valley, far-e. Vic., there are few published records for Gippsland. Probably nomadic in drier inland parts of range.

618 GOLDEN-BACKED HONEYEATER *Melithreptus laetior* Pl.77

Other name: Yellow-backed Honeyeater.

Field marks: 150–165 mm. The brightest member of its group: *striking golden-olive above, brighter on mantle and rump*; *eye-crescent yellow-green*; chin dark, underparts white washed grey; imm: duller, head brownish; eye-crescent white; lacks distinct golden tones above. Usually in pairs, parties or flocks (more than one pair seen to feed young). A bold beautiful inquisitive and somewhat aggressive honeyeater, often first noted by call. Possibly conspecific with Black-chinned (617).

Similar species: White-throated Honeyeater (621): eye-crescent blue-white; upperparts greener, underparts all-white. Black-chinned Honeyeater (617): eye-crescent blue; upperparts much less golden; greyer below.

Voice: Like Black-chinned: conspicuous far-carrying, deep, somewhat scratchy, croaking 'chee-chee, creep-creep-creep'; other variations, uttered while perched and in flight. Single sharp contact-note.

Habitat: Open woodlands and scrublands; river red gums along watercourses; swamp woodland; mallee.

Breeding: Nest: deep cup of soft grass, bark-fibre, and plant-down; bound with spiders' web, cocoons, suspended by rim in hanging foliage, 5 m or more high. Eggs: 1–2; pale-fleshy buff, spotted and blotched and with underlying faint markings of purplish buff.

Range and Status: Wide but patchy range in n., c. and nw. Aust., and some coastal islands: from Exmouth Gulf, WA, inland through Hamersley Ras. and Pilbara region, and from Fitzroy R. through Kimberleys, nearly throughout NT in suitable habitat from Marrakai (top end) to Macdonnell Ras. and timbered watercourses elsewhere in s. NT, probably extending into ne SA; in Q, e. along Gulf coast to C. York Pen., n. to Archer R. on w. coast and to Iron Ra. on e. coast; it extends s. at least to Mt. Isa, and se. to Opalton. Sedentary to nomadic, specially in arid inland parts of range.

619 STRONG-BILLED HONEYEATER *Melithreptus validirostris* Pl.77

Other names: Barkbird, Blackcap, Black-capped Honeyeater.

Field marks: 150–170 mm. The Tas.-equivalent of the Black-chinned Honeyeater (617), and *the only honeyeater on mainland Tas. with a white nape-band*; *eye-crescent blue*; whitish *below with blackish mark down from chin*; *underparts washed grey-brown*. Imm: skin round eye pale-yellow, nape-mark yellowish white. Pairs or flocks; works over limbs, trunks or boles of trees, probing bark with robust bill; noise thus made by flocks often considerable; occasionally feeds on ground. Associates with Black-headed Honeyeater (623) outside breeding season.

Similar species: White-naped Honeyeater (622) – Deal I., Kent Group: eye-crescent red; underparts whiter. Black-headed Honeyeater (623): the only other black-capped honeyeater in Tas. proper: head and throat wholly black, except for white eye-crescent.

Voice: Short sharp note, 'cheep, cheep'.

Habitat: Timbered areas, especially those with heavy undergrowth, from heavy forests to coastal scrubs.

Breeding: Nest: deep cup of bark-shreds, grass and fur, hair and wool; slung from twigs in top of sapling or outer foliage. Eggs: 2–3; pinkish buff, spotted dark red-brown and purplish grey.

Range and Status: Confined to Tas., King I. and Furneaux Group, Bass Strait; more generally distributed in Tas. proper than Black-headed. Common; sedentary.

620 BROWN-HEADED HONEYEATER *Melithreptus brevirostris* Pl.77

Other name: Short-billed Honeyeater.

Field marks: 100–135 mm. Markings duller than others of its group: *crown brownish, face blackish-brown, skin round eye yellowish to pale-cream*; *nape-band dull-cream*; upperparts washed olive; underparts pale-fawn. Imm: brighter; washed olive-green on crown and wings, skin round eye pale-blue, nape-band duller. Usually in flocks, conspicuous by calls and bouncing flight between trees, working systematically and somewhat sittella-like over limbs, trunks and foliage high and low, hanging acrobatically and fluttering, always moving. More than two adults reported feeding nestlings. Gathers hair for nest-building from cattle, koalas, human garments.

Similar species: Imms: of White-throated (621) and White-naped (622) Honeyeaters: check for nearby adults.

Voice: Loud 'chips' while feeding and from flocks in flight, suggestive of a small blizzard of notes. Song: animated staccato 'chip-chip-chip-chip-chip' starting with separate notes, accelerating and splintering, ending again with separate 'chips'. Alarm-call, flat hard trill.

Habitat: Rainforests, forests, woodlands, swamp woodlands and scrublands, including mallee, belar, coastal tea-tree and banksia-scrubs.

Breeding: Nest: firmly woven, deep cup of bark-shreds, grass and hair; lined with fur; slung from branchlets in sapling or tree, 3–15 m high. Eggs: 2–3; whitish pink to pale-salmon, lined, dotted and spotted chestnut-red with similar markings below surface, chiefly at large end.

Range and Status: Widespread in s. Aust., *except* for arid inland. In e. Q, ranges n. to (? hinterland of) Bowen, inland to Tambo–Cunnamulla, and e. to lower Dawson R.–Chinchilla–Toowoomba–Cunningham's Gap; mostly *absent* coastal se. Q, Brisbane area, and coastal ne. NSW n. of Clarence R.; otherwise widespread e. and s. NSW, inland to Bourke–Ivanhoe; throughout Vic. in suitable habitat; s. SA n. to L. Frome–Flinders Ras.–n. L. Torrens–Ooldea; thence w. along Bight coast, and possibly n. of Nullarbor Plain, to sw. WA, inland to Menzies, probably nomadic to mulga-eucalypt line n. to Shark Bay. Present on coastal islands with eucalypt woodlands of scrublands, including Kangaroo I., SA; Stradbroke I., Q. Common; sedentary, nomadic or part-migratory.

621 WHITE-THROATED HONEYEATER *Melithreptus albogularis* Pl.77

Other name: White-chinned Honeyeater.

Field marks: 125–145 mm. Very like White-naped Honeyeater (622), but *eye-crescent whitish to pale-blue, nape-band bolder, nearly reaching eye; chin and entire underparts white*. Imm: duller; crown tawny-grey, eye-crescent dull blue-white; faint nape-mark, yellowish wash on flight-feathers; underparts tinged grey. Behaviour like White-naped, but not strongly migratory.

Similar species: Brown-headed (620) and White-naped Honeyeaters. Rufous-throated Honeyeater (636), imm: like imm. White-throated, but no nape-band; duller-white below.

Voice: Calls sharper than White-naped: a peevish 'psee'; a repeated 'T-tee, T-tee, T-tee' or 'gorgee, gorgee' somewhat like double note of Leaden Flycatcher (482); flight-call, explosive 'dip'; song, ringing 'chick, chick-chick, chick-chick, chick', usually from tree-top. Alarm-call, flat hard trill, like Brown-headed.

Habitat: Forests and woodlands generally; swamp woodlands, timber along water-courses, occasionally mangroves; parks, gardens adjacent to natural habitat.

Breeding: Nest: delicate cup of bark or other soft material; bound with spiders' web; slung from slender fork, usually in outer foliage, 5–16 m high. Eggs: 2; light-pink, blotched and freckled red-brown.

Range and Status: N. and e. Aust. and coastal islands; from Broome, WA; top end NT s. to Victoria River Downs–Renner Springs; Gulf coast of Q, s. to Mt. Isa–Gregory R.; n. to C. York, and s. through e. Q, inland to Glendower–Carnarvon Ra.–Ipswich; s. coastally to Stuart's Point, 20 km s. of Nambucca Heads, ne. NSW. Common: sedentary part migratory or nomadic. Also s. and se. NG.

622 WHITE-NAPED HONEYEATER *Melithreptus lunatus* Pl.77

Other names: Black-cap, Black-capped or Lunulated Honeyeater.

Field marks: 135 mm. A small, neat member of its group: crown and nape black, upperparts olive-green; underparts white. *The white nape-band stops well short of eye and in se. Aust. is frequently rather faint; crescent of skin over eye orange-red, chin blackish.* Imm: duller, crown brownish, eye-crescent orange; face black; no nape-band. Forms in sw. WA are larger, bill longer, chin darker. Eye-crescent *whitish* in race *whitlocki* from s. coastal area; *greenish* in *chloropsis* n. from Perth. Pairs or small companies; usually as part of colony; moves actively and often acrobatically through higher foliage; investi-gates hanging strips of bark, flocks chase through treetops with little chittering calls. In e. Aust. noisy migratory flocks, flying at and above level of treetops. Associates in these movements with other migratory species, specially Yellow-faced Honeyeater (599).

Similar species: Brown-headed Honeyeater (620) for imm. White naped. White-throated Honeyeater (621): bolder nape-band nearly reaches eye; eye-crescent whitish to pale-blue; chin and throat pure-white; note range.

Voice: Thin scratchy 'shirp, shirp, shirp'; constant cheeps; liquid mellow 'tsew-tsew-tsew', characteristic of any forest where it occurs; alarm-call, taken up by many birds when flying predator appears; tense quiet 'pew, pew, pew'.

Habitat: Forests and woodlands: in se. Aust. prefers smooth-barked eucalypts like manna gums; but also in stringybarks, ironbarks and coastal scrubs; to adjacent parks and gardens.

Breeding: Nest: delicate hanging cup of fine grass, bark-shreds, plant-down; bound with spiders' web; slung from slender horizontal fork, 5–20 m high. Eggs: 2–3; pink to buff, finely spotted red-brown and grey, especially on large end.

Range and Status: E. and sw. Aust.: (? isolate) population in highlands of ne. Q from Atherton Tableland s. to Mt. Spec, near Townsville; and from Tropic (Rockhampton) to Yorke Pen., SA, and Deal I., Bass Strait. In Q, ranges inland to Duaringa–Carnarvon Ras.–Warwick; in NSW, inland to Mt. Kaputar NP–Warrumbungle NP–Cowra–Finley–Moulamein: widespread in e. and s. Vic.; winter visitor, Kiata, Mystic Park, Swan Hill and elsewhere in nw. Vic. In se. SA, w. to Yorke Pen. and Mt. Lofty Ras., occasional (? winter visitor) n. to Morgan–Waikerie on Murray R., and Mt. Mary Plains–Clare. In sw. WA, occupies humid zone w. of a line of about Esperance to Moora. Common; in se. Aust. part of population is migratory, moving n. in Apr.–May, some at least as far as se. Q, returning in Aug.–Oct., but with many overwintering in s. At places, e.g. Mallacoota NP, Vic., Blue Mts. and Tuggerah Lakes, NSW, n.-bound autumn flocks numbering dozens to hundreds and aggregating tens of thousands in a day stream through conspicuously, sometimes for consecutive days. Generally the s. movement in spring is less conspicuous.

623   BLACK-HEADED HONEYEATER   *Melithreptus affinis*   Pl 77

Other names: Black-cap or King Island Honeyeater.

Field marks: 125–140 mm. Note range: immediately distinguished by *black head and throat set off by small whitish eye-crescent*; *no nape-band*; olive-green above, white below with *black mark on sides of breast*. Imm: head dun-brown, throat yellowish-white. Usually in flocks; active and pugnacious. Associates in flocks with Strong-billed Honeyeater (619). Raids fruit.

Voice: A common call has been described as a distinctive sharp whistle; others like White-naped Honeyeater (622).

Habitat: Forests and woodlands; coastal heaths; orchards, gardens.

Breeding: Nest: deep cup of fibrous bark, fine grass, plant-down, hair and fur; bound with spiders' web; slung from twigs in foliage often at considerable height. Eggs: 2–3; pale-pink, spotted red-brown and purple-grey.

Range and Status: Confined to Tas., King I. and Furneaux Group, Bass Strait; well-distributed in n. and e. Tas., but probably only a straggler to suitable pockets of habitat on w. coast. Recorded up to 900 m in subalpine forest. Common; sedentary.

624   GREEN-BACKED HONEYEATER   *Glycichaera fallax*   Pl.78

Other names: Puff-backed or White-eyed Honeyeater (NG).

Field marks: 110–120 mm. An active, elusive, nondescript small honeyeater, with *rather long, slightly curved grey bill*; *eye grey-white, with a narrow ring of whitish feathers*; dull olive-green above, wings browner, tail blackish brown; throat whitish or grey underparts yellowish; legs blue-grey. Usually in pairs; somewhat like a white-eye, but bill longer and more curved. Difficult to distinguish as it feeds high in rainforest; but it also feeds in foliage or branches of lower trees, hopping quickly along limbs, often hanging head-down or upside-down or hovering to pry out insects, taking insects on wing, and flitting from tree to tree. Reported to feed wholly on insects; forms feeding associations with other small passerines. Note range.

Similar species: Fairy Warbler (554), female: said to look very similar in field, needing careful examination to separate; bill shorter and straighter. Yellow-footed Flycatcher (451); Grey Whistler (465); Grey-breasted White-eye (660).

Voice: Reported to be distinctive and unlike that of other honeyeaters; three calls have been described: a thin, insect-like 'peep'; a thin twitter, sometimes with upward inflexion, in flight or on alighting; an aggressive call, rapidly-uttered 'twit' or 'twee-twee-twit-twit', uttered as single loud 'twit' when scolding, and very like a call of Graceful Honeyeater (597).

Habitat: Rainforests and tropical scrubs, adjacent eucalypt woodlands.

Breeding: Not recorded.

Range and Status: In Aust. confined to far ne. (and possibly nw.) C. York Pen. At present best-known on Claudie R. near Iron Ra.; may extend from upper Pascoe R. s. to Lockhart R. or to Rocky R. Locally fairly common. Also NG and islands to w., including Aru Is. The Australian race is *claudi*.

625   BROWN HONEYEATER   *Lichmera indistincta*   Pl.78

Other name: Least Honeyeater.

Field marks: 130–150 mm. A plain dull-brown honeyeater, *with longish curved bill and tiny yellowish and silvery white spot behind eye*; flight and tail-feathers margined yellowish. The gape (skin at corners of mouth) is usually yellowish, but becomes black in breeding males. Imm: yellow-white mark near gape, no yellow spot behind eye. Singly, pairs, parties or flocks; active and acrobatic; with strong and distinctive song.

Similar species: Dusky Honeyeater (643): smaller, darker, more uniform; no yellow spot behind eye. Red-headed (644) and Scarlet (645) Honeyeaters: females. Grey Honeyeater (637): greyish brown above, whitish below with grey wash on chest; bill shorter.

Voice: Song remarkably strong sweet and varied, reminiscent of Clamorous Reed Warbler (503) or Jacky Winter (454); a typical phrase, 'sweet-sweet-quarty-quarty'; alarm-call somewhat harsh and grating.

Habitat: Varied: from karri and jarrah forests in sw. Aust. to inland scrubs, subtropical and tropical woodlands, rainforest-margins; coastal scrubs, swamp woodlands and mangroves; in inland, occurs typically in vegetation along watercourses; also golf-courses, parks, gardens.

Breeding: Nest: deep cup of grass, bark-shreds, leaves, palm-fibre; bound with spiders' web occasionally with egg-sacs attached; suspended in foliage or branchlets 1–6 m high, occasionally in small mangroves. Eggs: 2–3; white with red-brown spots.

Range and Status: Widespread on Australian mainland and many coastal islands *except for* a section s. of a line from w. coast of Gt. Australian Bight, WA, to about Thirroul, s. of Sydney, NSW. In WA it extends from Twilight Cove (Bight coast) inland at least to Coolgardie–Barlee Ra.; throughout NT; most of Q *except* sw. corner w. of Charleville–Cunnamulla; possibly occurs n. SA; in inland NSW, recorded s. to about Bourke–Dubbo. Generally common, but in NSW uncommon inland and s. of Hunter R. Sedentary or nomadic. Also s. NG, Aru Is., Lesser Sunda Is.

626 WHITE-STREAKED HONEYEATER *Trichodere cockerelli* Pl.78

Other names: Brush-throated or Cockerell's Honeyeater.

Field marks: 155 mm. Head and sides of face dark-grey; otherwise olive-brown above with strong yellow wash on wings and outer tail-feathers. *Whitish below with strong grey streaks radiating from throat down breast*; clear-yellow line from bill to below ear-coverts and long golden-yellow tufts behind ear-coverts. Bill black, strong and curved, naked skin at gape dark blue-grey or yellow, eye red. Female and imm: eye brown, naked skin at gape pale-greenish blue. Active and restless; feeds among foliage and blossoms, takes flying insects.

Voice: Seldom silent; calls described as loud scolding, also a sweet four-note whistle like Brown Honeyeater (625).

Habitat: Vine scrub, flowering eucalypt woodlands, coastal heaths, swamp woodlands.

Breeding: Nest: frail cup of fine rootlets and grasses, partly bound with spiders' web, lined with fine grass; suspended in fork of small tree up to 1 m or more high. Eggs: 2; salmon-pink, spotted and blotched darker.

Range and Status: Confined to C. York Pen. s. to Archer R. and Coen. Fairly common; sedentary, with local feeding movements.

627 PAINTED HONEYEATER *Grantiella picta* Pl.78

Other name: Georgie.

Field marks: 160 mm. Unusual and showy: *blackish above, white below; note conspicuous yellow margins to flight-feathers, yellow panels in tail*; often has small blackish spots or streaks on sides of neck, breast and flanks. Bill fleshy pink; eye red-brown. (NB. Plate 78 is in error). Female: slightly smaller, duller brownish black above, fewer spots below, on flanks. Imm: like female, but more spotted below. Singly, pairs and colonies of mated pairs; small nomadic flocks. Unusually for a honeyeater, feeds mainly on mistletoe berries (and nectar), moving deliberately, often very high and inconspicuously, at other times made conspicuous by calls and behaviour. Males active when establishing territories, calling from treetops and pursuing one another in dipping weaving flight. In song-flight, calls while rising steeply to 30 m or more, drops swiftly.

Similar species: Regent Honeyeater (587). Banded Honeyeater (640): black breastband; white rump, no yellow. Black Honeyeater (641), male: smaller; black throat continues down centre of abdomen; no yellow. Pied Honeyeater (642), male: prominent white shoulder and wing-patch, white rump; black throat and upperbreast; no yellow.

Voice: Specially when breeding, incessant peculiar sing-song notes; at its peak, song has been described as even more strident and melodious than that of Brown Honeyeater (625). Calls usually characterized as 'georgie'; also 'pretty-pretty', 'tort-tee, tort-tee' (or reversed, first note short) or 'et tee, et tee'.

Habitat: Frequently in trees afflicted with mistletoes; also open eucalypt forest and woodland, swamp woodlands, timber along watercourses; belar and other casuarinas, mulga and other acacias; mallee: visits nearby gardens, said to feed on peppercorns.

Breeding: Nest: flimsy delicate cup of plant-fibres and rootlets; eggs may be seen through fabric; bound with spiders' web and rootlets; in leafy extremities eucalypt, casuarina or paperbark, 3–20 m high. Eggs: 2–3; oval, slightly glossy, pale salmon-red, spotted and speckled red-brown and lilac, most heavily at large end.

Range and Status: N. and e. Aust.: in n. Aust. it ranges w. to the Macarthur R., e. NT, nw. to Arnhem Land and to inland of Darwin, NT. In e. Aust. it has a very wide, mostly inland range, from n. Q (Atherton Tableland–Mt. Isa) to inland se. NSW (Sydney–ACT–Jerilderie) and inland Vic. (Corryong–Wangaratta–Lower Plenty–You Yangs–Grampians–Edenhope). Its far-w. limits are uncertain, but it has been recorded c. 130 km w. of Ouyen (Vic. mallee) and doubtfully in nearby SA, near Manya; c. 160 km n. of Tibooburra, nw. NSW and c. 20 km w. of Thargomindah, in far sw. Q. One acceptable SA record (near Curdimurka, L. Eyre South, May 1970) is in the same region. Said to be very irregular in its movements, following the fruiting of mistletoes parasitic on eucalypts, casuarinas and acacias, but in se. Aust. this movement becomes a regular summer migration, s. in Oct.–Nov., departing by early Apr., after breeding. This pattern has been noted from the Hunter R. Valley and Sydney (shale) areas to ACT, inland se. NSW and Victorian locations within the stated range. It appears to be faithful to the same breeding locations but in some years, or for years in succession, birds may fail to arrive at all. Further n., it has been recorded at Taree, NSW, in Aug., and is reported to be an uncommon breeding visitor to inland ne. NSW and Darling Downs and Bunya Mts., se. Q, in Sept.–Feb. In far-inland and n. Q it appears to be an irregular winter visitor. Locally common; generally scarce.

628 CRESCENT HONEYEATER *Phylidonyris pyrrhoptera*   Pl.78

Other names: Chinawing, Egypt; Horseshoe or Tasmanian Honeyeater.

Field marks: 150–155 mm. Male: a dark-grey honeyeater with bold yellow panel on wing and outer tail-feathers, throat and breast white, flanks grey; note *black-and-white eyebrow and white-margined black crescent or broken horseshoe on either side of breast.* Bill longish, curved. Female: browner, duller; yellow on wings and tail and crescent on breast less distinct. Imm: like adults but markings less distinct, crescent absent. Singly or pairs; companies where insects and blossoms plentiful. Often first recognized by distinctive call. Usually wary but tamer in gardens, specially where food provided.

Similar species: Tawny-crowned Honeyeater (632): browner, crown tawny, no yellow in wings or tail, less conspicuous crescent on breast. Eastern Spinebill (638): curved needle-like bill; no eyebrow; dark patch on white throat; no yellow in wings or tail; rufous underparts.

Voice: High-pitched emphatic jagged 'eejik' ('Egypt'), usually during spring and summer; like one call of White-cheeked Honeyeater (630). In winter, usually simple sharp 'jik'.

Habitat: Alpine woodlands, temperate rainforests, wetter eucalypt forests and woodlands, dense vegetation on creek sides and gullies, wetter coastal scrubs and heaths; mallee on Kangaroo I., SA; orchards, gardens near suitable habitat.

Breeding: Nest: deep cup, somewhat bulky; of strips of stringy bark; bound with some spiders' web; lined with finer strips of soft bark, dry grass, plant-down or hair, occasionally with feathers; in fork of thick low shrub, swordgrass or ferns, 1–2 m high. Eggs: 3; pale-pink to reddish buff, deep toward large end, heavily marked at large end with pinkish, reddish, chestnut-brown or purplish brown spots.

Range and Status: Se. Aust., Tas. and Bass Strait islands: mostly coastal and highland; from Kangaroo I. and Mt. Lofty Ras., through coastal se. SA; e. through s. Vic., n. to Grampians–Ballarat through e. Vic. in Gippsland and on the Divide; in NSW widespread in high country and coastal regions of se., the n. limits being the Hunter R. Valley on coast and further n. on Divide to Gloucester–Barrington Tops NP, but rare n. of Blue Mts. An altitudinal migrant with local coastal and sub-inland winter dispersal; vagrant upstream on Murray R. to Waikerie, SA; inland to Mystic Park–Yackandandah, Vic. and Burrinjuck, NSW; autumn–winter visitor to gardens in Sydney, Canberra, Melbourne, Launceston and Hobart. On mainland common but patchy; one of the noisiest birds in the high country of e. Vic. and elsewhere ranges to high altitudes, e.g. alpine region, Kosciusko NP, Brindabella Ra., ACT, and Blue Mts., NSW. In Tas. its stronghold, common to over 1500 m in summer; widespread coastally and on lowlands in winter.

629 NEW HOLLAND HONEYEATER *Phylidonyris novaehollandiae*   Pl.78

Other names: Fuchsia-bird; Long-billed, White-bearded Honeyeater; Yellow-winged Honeyeater; Yellowings.

Field marks: 175–180 mm. A boldly streaked black-and-white honeyeater *with white eyes*; back browner; bold yellow panel on wing, yellow on outer tail-feathers, tail black *tipped white*. Note head-markings: *face black with narrow white eyebrow, white 'whisker-tuft' either side of throat, larger white 'ear-tuft' on sides of neck*; sparse spiky 'beard' on centre of throat. Bill black, longish, curved. Imm: browner, eye *grey*. Pairs or parties, usually in a colony. Restless, lightning chases and group displays; mobs sleeping owls, larger honeyeaters. Often sits calling from top of shrub or low tree, drops to cover when approached, but when feeding may disregard observer.

Similar species: White-cheeked Honeyeater (630): longer white eyebrow, large white cheek-patch, dark-brown eye; no pale tail-tips.

Voice: Sharp 'jik' or quick high-pitched squeaky 'phseet'; alarm-call, uneven high-pitched piping, mixed with harsh jigging scolding, and explosive chattering; or machinegun-like tinny rattle.

Habitat: Varied, but strong affinity for banksias and grevilleas; undergrowth in taller eucalypt forests and along creeks, coastal woodlands and heathlands, swamp woodlands, drier sub-inland woodlands, semi-desert heaths and mallee-spinifex associations in good seasons; scrub along dry watercourses; shelter-belts, golf-courses, orchards, parks, gardens.

Breeding: Nest: rather large rough cup of small twigs, grasses and stems; bound with spiders' web; lined with soft white or brownish plant-down; usually in fork of low shrub, tree or bracken, gorse 1–3 m high. Eggs: 2–3; whitish buff to pink, spotted and blotched chestnut-red, red and slate-grey mainly at large end.

Range and Status: Se. and sw. Aust. and well-vegetated coastal islands; from about Gympie, se. Q to Eyre Pen. and Kangaroo I., SA, Bass Strait islands and Tas. Mostly coastal: in Q, inland on D'Aquilar Ra. and to about Stanthorpe; in NSW, inland to Gibraltar Ra. NP–Barrington Tops NP–Wellington–Burrinjuck; in Vic., mostly on and s. of Divide in e., n. occasionally to Mt. Beauty–upper Broken R.; in w. Vic. ranges further inland, breeding n. to Wyperfeld NP, vagrant to Mystic Park–Irymple and to Balranald and w. of Euston, in NSW; in se. SA n. in mallee-heath areas to near Murray R.; wetter parts of Mt. Lofty Ras., ne. to Mt. Mary Plains; also Yorke and s. Eyre Pen.; vagrant n. to Peterborough, s. Flinders Ras. (Telowie Gorge), and to near L. Frome. In sw. WA, widespread s. of a line from Twilight Cove, sw. Nullarbor Plain, to Moora. Common except coastally n. of Sydney; mostly sedentary, local autumn–winter feeding dispersal; perhaps more nomadic in sw. WA.

630 WHITE-CHEEKED HONEYEATER *Phylidonyris nigra* **Pl.78**

Other name: Moustached Honeyeater.

Field marks: 160–180 mm. Like New Holland Honeyeater (629), but darker, with *dark-brown eye and single large white cheekpatch*; tail black, without white tips. Pairs, parties, active but appears less vivacious than New Holland; but has a more conspicuous song-flight, flying steeply up calling, dropping swiftly back to cover. When calling, unlike New Holland, often perches just within top of low leafy tree or shrub.

Similar species: New Holland Honeyeater (629).

Voice: Typical notes include squeaky 'chip-chew, chippy-chew' like Crescent Honey-eater (628); also a quick 'chip' or 'hiccup'. Song: a repeated 'twee-ee-twee-ee' often uttered on wing; also rapid 'hee-hee-hee-hee-hee-hee', probably an alarm-call.

Habitat: In coastal e. Aust.: rainforest margins and wetter woodlands, vegetation along watercourses, nearby eucalypt woodlands, banksia scrubs, swamp-woodlands, wet coastal heaths, swamps with sedges and similar vegetation. In sw. WA: coastal thickets, wet heaths, drier sandplain-heaths, and stands of banksias, dryandras and casuarinas, especially where these form tall understorey in woodlands.

Breeding: Nest: somewhat rough cup of twigs, strips of bark, grass and rootlets; bound with spiders' web; lined with plant-down; in low shrub or heath, under trees or somewhat exposed, occasionally in tall grass, most under 3 m high and usually less than 1 m. Eggs: 2–3; like New Holland.

Range and Status: E. and sw. Aust.: an isolate race on subhumid highlands of ne. Q from Atherton Tablelands s. to Valley of Lagoons (upper Burdekin R.) and Paluma Ra., near Townsville. The main e. coast population ranges s. from Fraser I. and Cooloola NP (n. of Noosa) and Bribie, Moreton and Stradbroke Is. through se. Q and coastal NSW s. to Wallaga Lake, near Bermagui, and some coastal islands. Mostly coastal, but resident populations on highlands of New England NP to 1500 m, and to 1000 m in Blue Mts. (Katoomba–Wentworth Falls). Common n. of Sydney, scarce on s. coast, specially s. of Ulladulla; mostly sedentary. In sw. WA, from Israelite Bay to Murchison R.; uncommon n. of Perth, *absent* from heavy forest zone of far-sw.; inland to e. of a line through Ravens-thorpe–Katanning–Narrogin–Northam. Common; sedentary.

631 WHITE-FRONTED HONEYEATER *Phylidonyris albifrons* **Pl.78**

Field marks: A rather odd-looking streaked dark honeyeater: blackish, rather scaly head, throat and upperbreast, *white mask from forehead to eye*; small fleshy red spot behind eye, silvery streak from bill down side of neck; streaked whitish underparts cut off from black upperbreast; flight-feathers washed yellow; eye brown. Female: browner. Singly or pairs, travelling parties or large loose feeding companies. Shy and elusive, usually first noticed by peculiar calls, uttered from top of shrub.

Similar species: New Holland Honeyeater (629): more streaked, no white mask; face black, eye white.

Voice: Strange metallic fugitive calls: 'pert-pertoo-weet', first note rather harsh, second and third loud and musical; or 'quack-peter-peter-peter'; also 'peter-peet-peet' in minor key; and sweet or peevish, grating canary-like 'tweet'; alarm-call, scolding 'dick, dick'.

Habitat: Drier scrubs and heaths, mulga, mallee, flowering arid-zone shrubs generally; timber along watercourses, to taller eucalypt woodlands and coastal scrubs at extremities of range.

Breeding: Nest: cup of grass and bark-shreds; bound with spiders' web; lined with plant-down; in fork in small shrub near ground; or on ground at base of a mallee. Eggs: 2–3; pale-buff, clouded reddish and spotted with chestnut and purplish grey, most heavily at large end.

Range and Status: Interior and more arid parts of all mainland States; to w. coast from near Broome, WA, s. to near Perth (Gingin Brook), its approximate sw. limits being Northam–Katanning–Bremer Bay; e. of that point s. irregularly to Bight coast. In SA s.

irregularly in spring to any coastal area, including Flinders I. off Eyre Pen., Kangaroo I. and the Coorong; has penetrated timbered areas of Mt. Lofty Ras. In Vic. irregular spring visitor to nw. mallee areas, occasional s. to Little Desert NP, (once) e. to Inglewood, where it bred; vagrant You Yangs. In NSW, s. and e. to Moulamein–Cocoparra NP–Griffith; in ec. NSW rarely coastward of w. slopes, but vagrant Sydney coastal plain. In Q, occasional e. to Warwick and n. to Richmond–Mt. Isa. In NT, to a little n. of Tennant Ck. Generally uncommon; an irregular blossom nomad that may become locally very common remaining to breed when blossoms abundant. Large directional movements of thousands, lasting days, been observed. There is a tendency to move n. into coastal and subcoastal se. Aust. in summer, into subcoastal WA in winter, and a general coastwards movement in droughts.

632   TAWNY-CROWNED HONEYEATER   *Phylidonyris melanops*   **Pl.78**

Field marks: 140–175 mm. An elegant slender pale-brown, white-breasted honeyeater with a fine curved bill. *Crown tawny to cream, separated by white eyebrow from blackish mark that runs from bill through eye, and widens into a bold black crescent on sides of the white breast.* This partial 'horseshoe' mark is not outlined in white as in Crescent Honeyeater (628). Imm: distinctive, brownish with buff streaks above; yellow from about bill to throat, with brown streak on either side; flight feathers washed yellow. Singly, pairs; loose flocks or open companies in winter or when blossom abundant. Rather shy and elusive; when seen well, note tawny crown and breast-markings, but quick view in flight often suggests only a plain-brown bird with slightly forked tail, pale at edges, confusable with Richard's Pipit (423) as it flies away. Typically feeds in (sometimes isolated) low shrubs, on top of which it sits to observe and sing; also on high dead twigs, telephone and fence wires. When flushed, flies low to cover or far and high. Male in songflight flies steeply up tiltingly to perhaps 60 m, spreads wings and performs quivering hovering flight, singing; closes wings and drops.

Similar species: Crescent Honeyeater (628); Eastern (638) and Western (639) Spinebills.

Voice: High-pitched, fluty but metallic, ascending 'a-peer-peer-pee-pee-pee', or quicker call from top of bush or in song-flight; difficult to hear except in still conditions, when it can be beautiful and ethereal.

Habitat: Low coastal (and other) heathlands; stunted banksia scrubs; sandplain vegetation; mallee; 'grass-tree country'; shrubby re-growth on cleared lands; button-grass country (Tas.). In autumn–winter, or in occasional irruptions at any time, flowering woodlands, street trees, gardens.

Breeding: Nest: deep, rather untidy, cup of dry faded grass and strips of bark; bound with spiders' web; lined with whitish plant-down or wool; suspended but supported by upright stems of low shrub, near or occasionally on ground, in herbage. Eggs: 2, exceptionally 1–4; large for size of bird, pointed at one end, white or whitish blotched chestnut-red, either faintly or clear-cut, usually at large end.

Range and Status: Se. and sw. Aust. In se. Aust., from about Evans Head, n. NSW, to s. Eyre Pen and Kangaroo I., SA; Tas. and Bass Strait islands. In e. NSW almost exclusively coastal, *except* for Blue Mts. Plateau (where breeding reported near Wentworth Falls) and winter vagrant occurrences near Dripstone, Orange and ACT. In Vic. mostly coastal, but occurs in Grampians, Little and Big Deserts and in the mallee, where it sometimes breeds in numbers; rare autumn–winter visitor to Murray Valley (Mystic Park) and far-s. and sw. NSW (Wentworth–Barham–Finley). In Tas. mostly coastal and uncommon; not recorded far-sw. In SA mostly coastal, but occurs n. to Mt. Lofty Ras. and the Murray mallee; occasional s. Flinders Ras. In WA it may occur along Bight coast but at present recorded e. only to Toolinna–Point Culver, e. of Israelite Bay; coastally w. and n. to Murchison R. and possibly to Peron Pen.; inland to Norseman–Southern Cross–Wongan Hills. In sw. WA forms nomadic autumn–winter flocks that enter flowering forests and woodlands. In se. Aust. probably more sedentary but in autumn–winter small numbers disperse well inland; in exceptional years numbers irrupt in spring or autumn, appearing in gardens, flowering street trees and woodlands well beyond normal range and habitat. Locally common; generally uncommon.

633   BROWN-BACKED HONEYEATER   *Ramsayornis modestus*   Pl.78

Field marks: 105–120 mm. Nondescript: dull olive-brown; dirty white below, *with indistinct brownish barring on breast and streaking on flanks and abdomen; small white spot under eye with black lower margin*. Bill rather large, down-curved, pinkish brown; legs and feet reddish. Imm: breast more streaked, rump more rufous. Pairs or small flocks; mostly in colonies; lively, associates with other honeyeaters in numbers when blossom abundant.

Similar species: Bar-breasted Honeyeater (634). Rufous-banded (635) and Rufous-throated (636) Honeyeaters, imms: distinct yellow margins to flight-feathers.

Voice: Usual calls: lively chattering 'shee-shee-shee' and sharper 'chit' rapidly repeated; flight-call, 'mick-mick-mick'.

Habitat: Vegetation along streams, waterside thickets; swamp woodlands; nearby open forest when trees are blossoming; mangroves.

Breeding: Nest: *domed*, elongated, with side entrance near top nearly concealed by overhanging hood; of strips of soft paperbark; bound with spiders' web and egg-sacs; lined with fine strips of paperbark; often in paperbark, suspended from tips of twigs. 1–16 m high, often over water, and in colonies of 8–20 nests, with other colonies nearby. Sometimes two nests, old and new, adjoin. Eggs: 2; white, finely dotted purplish black specially at large end. See Bar-breasted Honeyeater, nest.

Range and Status: Coastal ne. Q and coastal islands: from C. York s. on Gulf coast to Archer R., and s. on e. coast to near Rockhampton; inland in parts e.g. to Coen, Atherton Tableland, lower Dawson R. Common on coast, more patchy in higher, drier parts of range. Migratory. Also islands of Torres Strait, NG and islands.

634   BAR-BREASTED HONEYEATER   *Ramsayornis fasciatus*   Pl.78

Other names: Fasciated or White-breasted Honeyeater.

Field marks: 140–150 mm. A smallish, unusually marked, honeyeater, possibly conspecific with Brown-backed Honeyeater (633). Brown above, crown scalloped black and white; *face and underparts white with fine black scaly pattern from upperbreast down; black line from base of bill down sides of throat.* Imm: forehead and underparts streaked darker, primaries edged yellow-buff. Usually in pairs, but often in considerable numbers with other honeyeaters when blossoms plentiful; active, but quiet and often rather inconspicuous.

Similar species: Brown-backed Honeyeater (633): crown darker; no scalloped pattern on forehead or throat. Note range.

Voice: Undistinguished: one note, soft 'mew'; also shrill rapidly repeated piping.

Habitat: Vegetation along watercourses, mangrove fringes, monsoon forest, swamp woodlands, especially when paperbarks, grevilleas are in blossom. In ne. Q also montane heathland.

Breeding: Nest: *domed*, with side entrance and resting place below opening; usually of strips of paperbark and rootlets; bound with spiders' web; lined with soft bark; strongly woven and practically rain-proof; strips of bark often hang from sides and bottom of nest; suspended from fine twigs, often in paperbark over water and often about 1 m high. Eggs: 2–3; white, finely freckled and dotted light red-brown, sometimes forming indistinct zone at large end. (This and Brown-backed are the only Australian honeyeaters that build domed nests.)

Range and Status: Coastal n. Aust.: from Derby, WA, through top end NT s. to Roper and Macarthur Rs. and e. along Gulf coast, Q, to Mitchell R., w. coast C. York Pen. Part-migratory, common to uncommon.

635 RUFOUS-BANDED HONEYEATER *Conopophila albogularis* **Pl.78**

Other names: Red-breasted or Rufous-breasted Honeyeater.
Field marks: 110–125 mm. A stocky dull-brown honeyeater, greyer on head, whiter below, *with broad reddish buff breastband*. Note bold yellow edges to flight-feathers, finer on tail-feathers. Imm: whitish throat extends to upperbreast; breastband absent or partial. Pairs and small parties; active, associates when feeding with other honeyeaters including the very similar Rufous-throated Honeyeater (636).
Similar species: Rufous-throated (636), adult: rufous patch on throat, no breastband. Imm: difficult to tell apart but imm. Rufous-throated has much the smaller area of white on throat.
Voice: Call of male: repeated rising 'zzheep' like call of a young cuckoo. When several together, brisk little rondo 'sweeta-swee, sweeta-swee', with silvery tone suggestive of Pilotbird (533).
Habitat: Vegetation along watercourses, mangroves, swamp woodlands, monsoon forest, nearby open forest, coastal scrubs; surroundings of cultivation, gardens.
Breeding: Nest: small hanging cup of strips of paperbark; bound with plant-fibres and spiders' web; lined with soft grass; suspended among foliage, often over water. Eggs: 2–3; white, spotted and dotted red-brown, sometimes forming cap at large end.
Range and Status: Coastal n. Aust. and coastal islands: top end NT s. and w. to Victoria R. Downs and Timber Ck, s. to Katherine and Roper R., and e. along Gulf coast to far-nw. Q. In Q, w. coast C. York Pen. s. to Staaten R. Fairly common. Also NG and Aru Is.

636 RUFOUS-THROATED HONEYEATER *Conopophila rufogularis* **Pl.78**

Other name: Red-throated Honeyeater.
Field marks: 130–140 mm. Like Rufous-banded (635) but instead of a breastband *has only a distinctive small rufous patch on chin and centre of throat*; primaries prominently edged yellow; grey-white below, flanks rusty. Imm: plain-whitish throat, less intense than imm. Rufous-banded. Frequently in demonstrative small parties or flocks that perform noisy, rather conspicuous, wing-fluttering displays. Very active and acrobatic when feeding; associates with other honeyeaters in blossoming trees.
Similar species: Rufous-banded Honeyeater (635).
Voice: Contact or alarm-call, sharp 'zit-zit', somewhat like Tawny Grassbird (505), but stronger; in group-displays chatters like House Sparrow (663), tone sweet or scratchy and peevish.
Habitat: Vegetation round water; swamp woodlands, mangroves, drier scrublands and grassed woodlands when conditions suitable; surroundings of cultivation; gardens, street trees in coastal towns.
Breeding: Nest: delicate deep slung cup, smaller at top than bottom; of fine strips of paperbark or fine grass; bound with spiders' web; often lined with plant-down; some mainly of white kapok or cotton-like material; in outer foliage of eucalypt, vine, mangrove or other low shrub, 1–6 m high. Eggs: 2–3, variable; usually white with evenly distributed pink and red spots.
Range and Status: Coastal n. Aust.: from w. Kimberleys, WA, (C. Bertholet *c.* 40 km n. of Broome) to Noosa R., Q. In the NT, inland to Tennant Ck.; in nw. Q, inland to *c.* 100 km s. of Mt. Isa. Absent from ne. C. York Pen., extends n. to Archer R. on w. coast and Coen in e.; present in drier w. parts of Atherton Tableland, thence s. inland to Burdekin R. near Charters Towers and in coastal lowlands s. from Ingham. Common in n., scarce and patchy on e. coast. Migratory.

637 GREY HONEYEATER *Conopophila whitei* **Pl.78**

Other name: White's Honeyeater.
Field marks: 105–115 mm. Probably our most inconspicuous and nondescript honey-eater: no distinctive markings *except for somewhat darker sides of face and faint ring of*

pale feathers round eye. Bill black, short, down-curved. Upperparts brownish grey, flight-feathers darker and slightly margined olive-yellow; tail dark-brown tipped white; underparts whitish with greyish wash on throat and breast. Imm: yellowish wash on cheeks and throat, buffish feathers round eye. Singly or pairs; behaves rather unlike a honeyeater; feeds on insects in and round foliage of shrubs and trees like a white-eye or a fairy warbler. Said to associate with thornbills. A bird collected near Granville Downs, SA, contained mistletoe berries.

Similar species: White-tailed Warbler (552): white eyebrow; white panels in tail. Grey-breasted White-eye (660): greener, with more distinct white ring round eye, straighter bill. Rufous-banded (635) and Rufous-throated (636) Honeyeaters, imms: browner above, more yellow on wings.

Voice: Rapid succession of five or six high-pitched sibilant notes, reminiscent of a White-eye or Richard's Pipit (423).

Habitat: Semi-arid mulga and other acacia-scrubs, in which the occurrence of mistletoe may be an important factor; homestead gardens in inland WA.

Breeding: Nest: frail somewhat untidy cup of horsehair; bound with spiders' web and cocoons; slung from slender twigs in outer foliage of mulga. The eggs may be seen through the fabric. Eggs: 2; swollen oval, slightly glossy; white lightly spotted with red-brown and dull-purplish grey, latter as if below surface.

Range and Status: Far-inland Aust., extending to near w. coast from Geraldton, WA, n. to upper Minilya and upper Ashburton Rs. Not recorded in NSW or Q, but may occur in mulga areas in far-w. of either State. In NT, n. to Tanami Ra. and e. to near Hermannsburg; recent (?doubtful) sight-record from near Frewena. In inland SA, s. to Musgrave and Everard Ras.; specimen from *c.* 200 km wnw. of Oodnadatta. In inland WA, s. to Thundelarra (*c.* 70 km nw. of Paynes Find), Wanjarri (*c.* 90 km ese. of Wiluna) and possibly Leonora. Rare and little known. Probably nomadic.

638 EASTERN SPINEBILL *Acanthorhynchus tenuirostris* Pl.78

Other names: Cobbler's Awl, Hummingbird, Spine-billed Honeyeater, Spiny.

Field marks: 150–165 mm. The two spinebills are best identified by their very fine long curved bills. In this species the underparts are buff-grey, wings gunmetal grey, *underparts pale-rufous.* Male: black crown extends down in a *crescent on either side of the white upper-breast*; *note the rufous and black patch in centre of white throat*; nape and mantle rufous-buff; tail black, outer feathers conspicuously white. Female: duller, crown grey, fainter crescent on breast. Imm: plainer; dull olive-grey above, plain fawn below. Singly or pairs, loose companies where blossom abundant and in winter; very active and vivacious; hovers at blossoms somewhat like hummingbird. Flight very fast and erratic, with distinctive quick 'flip flop' of wings, tail flirted, *flashing prominent white outer feathers.* Courting males perform song-flight, calling while rising waveringly but steeply 30 m or more.

Similar species: Crescent Honeyeater (628): white eyebrow, yellow patch on wing. Tawny-crowned Honeyeater (632): browner, with pale eyebrow, dark eyemark. In both, bills heavier; neither have prominent white in tail.

Voice: Clear high-pitched staccato piping, sometimes long-repeated, may be brisk and explosive or soft and wavering; calls in songflight more muted.

Habitat: Forests and woodlands, thickets along watercourses; chiefly in coastal areas or on Divide; occasional inland; coastal scrubs and heaths; well-vegetated gardens, specially on cultivated fuchsias, abutilons.

Breeding: Nest: small cup of grass, moss and hair; bound with spiders' web; lined with feathers; attached to small fork in shrub or tree, 1–5 m high, occasionally higher. Eggs: 2–3; whitish to pink-buff, spotted chestnut and brown, most heavily on large end.

Range and Status: Se. and e. Aust., coastal islands and Tas. (uncommon Flinders I., rare or absent King I.): from Kangaroo I. through se. SA n. to Mt. Lofty and s. Flinders Ras., occasional e. along Murray R. to about Renmark; throughout s. and ne. Vic., winter visitor Maryborough–Bendigo–Albury; winter vagrant Vic. mallee, Mystic Park and s. and w. NSW (Broken Hill, Leeton, Moulamein). Otherwise in NSW mostly on and e. of Divide but regular w. to Wagga–Warrumbungle NP–Moree. Coastal in se. Q n. to Maryborough, and in ranges from near Stanthorpe n. to Gayndah, inland to Carnarvon Ra. An apparently isolate population in coastal highlands of ne. Q from Eungella Ra. near Mackay n. through Atherton Tableland to Big Tableland near Cooktown. Common to uncommon; resident or partial migrant, with altitudinal and inland dispersal in autumn–winter, and local coastal movements.

639 WESTERN SPINEBILL *Acanthorhynchus superciliosus* Pl.78

Field marks: 150 mm. Note *very fine, long curved bill*. Male: crown black; a black mark through eye separates the white eybrow from the white throat; *orange-chestnut rear collar expands into broad chestnut band across lower throat and upperbreast, bordered below by a whitish and a black band*; outer tail-feathers white, conspicuous in flight. Female: duller and plainer, with rufous shading on nape, breast rufous-buff, without bands. Imm. like dull female. Like Eastern Spinebill (638) in actions and behaviour, but has adapted less successfully to urban environments.

Similar species: Tawny-crowned Honeyeater (632): plainer and browner; white throat enclosed by black crescent; bill heavier; no conspicuous white in tail.

Voice: High-pitched staccato piping.

Habitat: Undergrowth of forests and woodlands; sandplain-heaths, coastal scrubs, particularly thickets of banksias and dryandras.

Breeding: Nest: compact cup of bark-shreds and fine plant-stems; bound with spiders' web; lined with plant-down; 1–5 m high in shrub or low tree. Eggs: 1–2; blue-white or pink-white, spotted and blotched chestnut and purple-brown, usually in band or zone round large end.

Range and Status: Confined to sw. WA: from Cockleshell Gully, n. of Jurien Bay, se. to Israelite Bay; inland to Moora–Corrigin–L. Grace, and e. along the s. coast. Common, nomadic.

640 BANDED HONEYEATER *Certhionyx pectoralis* Pl.77

Field marks: 115–135 mm. A handsome small honeyeater with *black upperparts offset by conspicuous white rump*; *underparts white with black breastband*. Female: usually described and portrayed as having mottled tawny back, but this appears to be an imm. character. Imm: distinctive; *crown and back tawny, with or without blackish mottling, according to age*; *flight-feathers blackish edged tawny, gape and sides of face yellow*; underparts white, breastband may be incomplete. Pairs or small flocks; active, aggressive, rather noisy, often in considerable numbers when blossom abundant.

Similar species: No other black-and-white honeyeater has a black breastband.

Voice: Various single or double calls, including throaty 'dup' or scratchy 'jap', peevish, somewhat finch-like 'tweet'; also clear, cheerful song.

Habitat: Eucalypt woodlands, swamp woodlands, coastal tropical scrubs, mangroves, vegetation along watercourses; extends to drier open habitats when such trees as bauhinias are blossoming.

Breeding: Nest: flimsy cup of fine grass and bark; bound with spiders' web; lined with grass; suspended from slender fork, usually in foliage of tea-tree or paperbark from near ground to 6 m high. Eggs: 2; cream-buff, with band of deeper buff round large end.

Range and Status: N. and ne. Aust.: from w. Kimberleys, WA, through top end NT, Gulf coast and all C. York Pen., Q, s. to near Cooktown; approximate inland limits are Larrimah, NT, and Mt. Isa–Charters Towers, Q. Between Charters Towers and Cooktown present in drier parts of highlands, but rare coastally. Fairly common otherwise; highly nomadic, erratic movements influenced by blossoming of eucalypts, paperbarks, bauhinias, mangroves.

641 BLACK HONEYEATER *Certhionyx niger*   **Pl.77**

Field marks: 95–120 mm. Male dapper and distinctive: plain black above and upper-breast, *white below with black extending down middle of belly*; bill longish and curved, tail slightly forked. Female: different; *brownish-grey above with dull-whitish eyebrow back from above eye, whitish below*, upperbreast washed brownish. Imm: like female, but more smutty grey. Pairs or flocks, active, darts through foliage and between trees; perches on exposed dead limbs, darts after flying insects. Male song-flight: from exposed perch, flies steeply upwards 15 m or more, descends in steps on quivering, stiffly down-arched wings, calling. Note habitat; often gathers in numbers in blossoming vegetation.

Similar species: Pied Honeyeater (642); Hooded Robin (445).

Voice: Clear but elusive 'seep' or 'see-see' like a quail-thrush or Little Grassbird (506), usually from top of dead mallee or mulga; during song-flight repeatedly at each dip while descending; also sparrow-like chirp animated chatter.

Habitat: Inland scrubs, eucalypt woodlands at extremities of range; when breeding, prefers low scrub with dead, sometimes fire-blackened, branches; also in scrubby re-growth.

Breeding: Nest: frail shallow cup of grass, twigs, rootlets bound with spiders' web; usually in fork or dead shrub or in fallen branches, near ground. Eggs: 2; buffish, with zone of grey and olive-green spots and indistinct markings round large end.

Range and Status: A highly-nomadic honeyeater of the arid interior; in some years, mostly after good-breeding conditions inland, irrupts into near-coastal areas, where it may breed. Recorded coastal Kimberleys, WA, Gulf lowlands of nw. Q, and e. to Orange, Sydney and Albury areas, NSW, s. to Maryborough, Bendigo and the You Yangs, Vic., and Adelaide-Fleurieu Pen. SA. Locally common.

642 PIED HONEYEATER *Certhionyx variegatus*   **Pl.77**

Field marks: 140–175 mm. Male: striking; black above and on upperbreast, with con-trasting *white shoulder, wingbar, rump and underparts*; *tail black with white panel on either side at base*. Female: dull grey-brown above with pale eyebrow; pale margins to wing-feathers form pattern; brownish-white below the zone of fine darkish mottlings across upperbreast; in flight, rump looks pale. *Note longish curved grey bill, black at tip*; *spot of blue-grey skin below eye, larger in male than female*. Imm: like female. Singly or pairs; shy and unobtrusive. Most likely to be found where arid-zone vegetation flowers after rain. Courting males in songflight rise steeply, descending with fanned tail, uttering a sharp call. In flight, *note conspicuous tail-pattern*. Female and imm. not easily recognized: look for the typical honeyeater-like bill, and restless habit of flirting tail.

Similar species: Black Honeyeater (641), male: much smaller, no white above; black of upperbreast extends down belly. Female: best separated by size; rump not pale. White-winged Triller (432), female, and Rufous Songlark (510): shorter straighter bills; usually less nervous and active. White-winged Triller (432), male.

Voice: Usually rather silent. In song-flight male utters piercing drawn-out 'te-titee-tee-tee'.

Habitat: Dry scrublands, often sparse; associations of flowering semi-desert shrubs, to woodlands at extremities of range.

Breeding: Nest: large for size of bird; robust cup of grasses and fine twigs, bound with spiders' web; usually in fork of shrub or tree to 5 m high. Eggs: 2–3; 4; pale-fawn, with small blotches of pale-grey and groups of well-defined blackish-brown spots.

Range and Status: A highly nomadic honeyeater of the arid interior, reaching w. coast between about Geraldton and Onslow, WA; in NT, n. to Tanami–Tennant Ck.; in Q, n. and e. to Mt. Isa–Longreach–Cunnamulla; in NSW, mostly far-w., vagrant e. to Nandewar Ra. (Tamworth–Inverell); in Vic., occasional to nw. mallee areas, s. to Kiata; in SA, nomadic s. to Murray mallee and n. Eyre Pen.; in s. WA, regular s. to Kathleen Valley, nomadic s. to L. Grace. Locally common but very irregular.

643 DUSKY HONEYEATER *Myzomela obscura* **Pl.77**

Field marks: 125 mm. A uniform dark coppery grey small honeyeater with *longish curved bill and slightly darker mark on chin.* Some are as pale as Brown Honeyeater (625), but note darkish mark under chin and absence of other markings. Pairs or parties; chattering chasing pugnacious and at times inquisitive little bird that hangs or hovers to feed on blossoms and darts into air after insects; associates with Red-headed (644), Scarlet (645) and other honeyeaters.

Similar species: Red-headed (644) and Scarlet (645) Honeyeaters

Voice; An obscure squeak, excited 'see see see' notes when several birds chase; also a short mournful whistle with soft trilling chatter, 'in definite sequence'.

Habitat: Coastal woodlands and scrubs, rainforests; vegetation along watercourses, mangroves, swamp-woodlands; gardens; usually near coast and on islands, but to mountain rainforests in ne. Q.

Breeding: Nest: frail cup of rootlets and grasses, bound with spiders' web; slung from branchlets in outer foliage, from few to 5 m high. Eggs: 2; pink-white, finely spotted red-brown and dark-grey.

Range and Status: N. and ne. Aust. and many coastal islands: coastal NT from Port Keats to Port Bradshaw, s. to Katherine Gorge; in Q, from Edward R. n. round C. York and coastally s. to Brisbane, inland to about Kenilworth. Common, less so s. of Rockhampton. Also s. NG, Aru Is. and Moluccas.

644 RED-HEADED HONEYEATER *Myzomela erythrocephala* **Pl.77**

Other name: Bloodbird.

Field marks: 110–125 mm. Male: distinctive; bill longish and curved; *red head and rump cut off abruptly from dark-brown wings and back, and from dark-grey underparts.* Female and imm: *plain brownish, lightly washed red on forehead and throat.* Usually in pairs; active and darting, flicks tail like finch, darts into air after insects. Not shy, but often difficult to watch because of density of habitat.

Similar species: Scarlet Honeyeater (645), male: scarlet back, whitish underparts. Female: less red forehead. Note range.

Voice: Male, brisk, rather harsh 'chiew-chiew-chiew'; female, sibilant squeak.

Habitat: Chiefly mangroves, adjacent tropical shrubs, flowering eucalypt woodlands, vegetation along watercourses, swamp woodlands, parks and gardens.

Breeding: Nest: delicate cup of fine strips of bark, bound with spiders' web, occasionally with leaves attached to outside, lined with soft bark and rootlets; usually in fine leafy branches of mangrove up to 12 m over water. Eggs: 2; whitish, with fine reddish spots and blotches at large end.

Range and Status: Coastal nw. and n. Aust. and coastal islands: from Derby WA to Rocky R. e. C. York Pen., Q; inland to Katherine Gorge NT. Common, conspicuous round Darwin. Also NG and e. Lesser Sunda Is.

645 SCARLET HONEYEATER *Myzomela sanguinolenta* **Pl.77**

Other names: Bloodbird, Crimson Honeyeater, Hummingbird.

Field marks: 100–110 mm. Male: brilliant small bird with longish curved bill; head and throat pale-scarlet, *extending down back to rump; underparts whitish;* wings and tail blackish. Female: much plainer; crown, face and upperparts tawny brown; slight reddish wash on chin; pale-brown below. Singly, pairs and open companies; incessantly active and aggressive, darts through blossoms or in bouncing flight to next trees. Males call conspicuously from tops of trees, high bare branches.

Similar species: Red-headed Honeyeater (644), male: brown back; dark-grey underparts. Female: more extensive reddish wash on forehead and throat. Note range. Dusky Honeyeater (643): coppery brown, darkish mark on throat.

Voice: Song of male: explosive silvery tinkling, descending and tailing away; typically uttered while perched high; also short varied tinkling phrases, squeaks and twitterings.
Habitat: Rainforests; eucalypt forests and woodlands, heaths and coastal scrubs; swamp woodlands; vegetation along watercourses; flowering street-trees; parks, gardens.
Breeding: Nest: very small delicate cup of fine bark-shreds and similar material bound with spiders' web; slung from twig up to 10 m high, in foliage. Eggs: 2–3; whitish, spotted and blotched red-brown, brown-yellow and pale-mauve, mainly at large end.
Range and Status: Coastal e. Aust. and coastal islands: from e. C. York Pen. Q, to Mallacoota, Vic.; inland to Mt. Surprise–Carnarvon Gorge, Q; Inverell–Mudgee, NSW; rare vagrant coastal e. Vic. to w. of Port Phillip. Nomadic in n.; part-migratory or nomadic in NSW. Fairly common; local and scarce s. of Sydney.

Australian Chats   Family *Ephthianuridae*

A small distinctive endemic Australian family. Males are brilliantly coloured or boldly marked; females and imms. have similar but duller tonings. They live in family parties or flocks, feed on or near ground in open habitats, walk and run swaggeringly rather than hop and fly strongly and often high in a characteristic wing-flirting manner. Probably best-known is White-fronted Chat (649). Two of the inland species (646–7) are highly nomadic, irrupting and breeding after suitable rainfall. Another (650) is a desert-resident. The rare and seldom observed Yellow Chat (648) is largely confined to five coastal river-valleys in n. Aust., but has (?recently) colonized parts of w. Q by exploiting bore-waters.
Food: Mostly insects and other small invertebrates.
Range: Aust. and Tas.
Number of species: World 5; Aust. 5.

646 CRIMSON CHAT *Ephthianura tricolor*   Pl.79

Other names: Crimson-breasted Nun, Saltbush Canary, Tricoloured Chat.
Field marks: 100–120 mm. Male: note blackish 'mask'; *crimson crown and breast contrast with white throat. Brown above except for crimson rump.* Female and imm: brownish above, buffish below, *crimson wash on rump and breast.* Pairs or small to large open flocks. Feeds on and near ground; occasionally in blossoming trees; flies in strong bouncing manner typical of family, often high and far, revealing *scarlet or pink rump and black, white-tipped tail.*
Similar species: Red-capped Robin (444): black and white above, no red on rump.
Voice: High-pitched 'seee', or 'seeet'; in flight, soft 'dik-it, dik-it' or brisk 'check check'; also small harsh rattles and silvery trills.
Habitat: Open plains, with mulga and low sparse ground-cover, saltbush or bluebush; spinifex on plains and hills, margins of more open inland scrubs; mallee scrubs when in blossom.
Breeding: Nest: deep cup; of grasses, fine twigs and stems; near ground in low shrub or grass. Eggs: 3–4; white, spotted reddish purple, heaviest at large end.
Range and Status: Widespread in inland Aust., extending to w. coastal WA, Gulf coast of Q and probably irregularly along Gt Australian Bight. In e. Aust. ranges irregularly s. and e. to nw. Vic., occasional to Little Desert–Swan Hill; in NSW e. to Balranald–Forbes, rarely further; in Q, e. to St George–Blackall–Hughenden. Nomadic according to rainfall, with superimposed regular movements s. in spring, n. in autumn. When conditions favourable, huge numbers may appear in a district after absence of years or perhaps where never before known, breed freely and depart.

647 ORANGE CHAT *Ephthianura aurifrons* **Pl.79**

Other names: Orange-fronted Chat or Nun, Saltbush Canary.
Field marks: 90–115 mm. Male distinctive: yellow body *washed orange on head and breast, face and throat black, rump yellow.* Female and imm: *no black on face,* streaked sandy brown above with *yellow rump; plain yellow-fawn below. Eyes of both sexes brown-red.* Typically in parties or loose flocks. Feeds on or near ground, perches conspicuously on low shrubs. When flushed, flies high and far in bouncing manner typical of family, *revealing yellow rump and blackish pale-tipped tail.* Often with Crimson Chats (646).
Similar species: Desert Chat (650): like female Orange, but sandier, with pale eye; only sides of rump yellow. Usually in pairs only.
Voice: Flight-call, canary-like 'chee-chee-chee'.
Habitat: Sparse open grasslands, gibber, areas of low succulents; saltbush, bluebush, samphire round claypans; in SA and cw. WA where range extends to coast, on salt-lakes and saltmarsh.
Breeding: Nest: cup-shaped; of grasses and rootlets; in low shrub near ground. Eggs: 3; white, freely sprinkled with purplish red, heaviest at large end.
Range and Status: Inland and w. Aust.: to w. coast WA (Onslow–Geraldton); e. to Mt Isa–Richmond–Cunnamulla, Q, and Forbes–Hay, NSW; s. to Kerang–Wycheproof, Vic. and to Bordertown–Langhorne's Creek–Eyre Pen. and occasional to Bight coast, SA. Generally scarce, locally abundant; highly nomadic in response to seasonal conditions.

648 YELLOW CHAT *Ephthianura crocea* **Pl.79**

Other names: Yellow-breasted Chat, Bush Chat or Nun.
Field marks: 110–120 mm. Male: *eye white;* face, underparts and rump rich golden-yellow, *with black breastband,* narrow black line between bill and eye; tail blackish, tipped yellow. Female: *eye white;* no breastband, yellowish face, neck, rump and below. Pairs or small parties. Habits differ from other chats: feeds typically by swamps, rivers or drains, among swamp vegetation, or on muddy water-margins. Note widely disjunct distribution.
Similar species: Orange Chat (647), male: black face and throat; no breastband. Female: less yellow about head and neck, eyes dark.
Voice: Three distinct calls have been described: one rather like metallic 'tang' of White-fronted Chat (649); a rather strident churring noise like a cricket; and a musical 'pee-eep'.
Habitat: Swamp-vegetation, including rushes; long grass, trees bordering swamps; bore drains, and swamps associated with same.
Breeding: Nest: cup-shaped; of plant-stalks and grasses. Eggs: 3; white with minute dots and spots of blackish red, mostly at large end.
Range and Status: Distribution poorly known; isolate populations on rivers, swamps: Fitzroy R. and Wyndham area, WA; top end NT; far-nw. Q from Normanton w. to border on Gulf coast; in far-w. Q, on bore-drains and associated swamps near Coorabulka, se. of Boulia; coastal areas of e. Q near Broad Sound and Fitzroy Vale. Apparently sedentary.

649 WHITE-FRONTED CHAT *Ephthianura albifrons* **Pl.79**

Other names: Baldyhead, Banded Tintack, Bumps, Clipper, Dotterel, Jenny Wren, Moonbird, Nun, Ringlet, Ringneck, Single-bar, Tang, Tintack, White-faced Chat, White-fronted Nun.
Field marks: 110–130 mm. Male unmistakable: *forehead, face and underparts white, black hood extends down to form bold black breastband; eye whitish to orange.* Female and imm: plain grey-brown above, black breastband much thinner. Pairs, parties or large open companies on or near ground; walks and runs with back and forward head-movement. Perches prominently on tussocks, low bushes, fences. Flight strong and bouncing, with characteristic flirting of wings revealing *shortish black tail broadly tipped white.*
Similar species: Double-barred Finch (673): dark eye, two breastbands; note range.

Banded Whiteface (570): narrower breastband, no black hood, rufous back and flanks; note range.

Voice: Usual contact call metallic 'tang' and similar rapid fussy notes.

Habitat: Low ground-cover, usually in damp situations: tussocks in wet parts of paddocks, margins of swamps, low heath or tea-tree, samphire and margins of mangroves on saltmarshes and inlets, coastal dune-vegetation, low roadside shrubs and tussocks; inland saltbush-plains, samphire on margins of salt-lakes and other low open cover.

Breeding: Nest: neat deep cup; of grasses and twigs, deep in tussock or low shrub, near, rarely on ground. Eggs: 3–4; white; spotted reddish or purplish brown, forming zone at large end.

Range and Status: S. Aust.: s. of Shark Bay, WA, and St George–Darling Downs, Q; Tas. Common, mostly sedentary, but possibly nomadic or migratory in n. parts of range.

650 DESERT CHAT *Ashbyia lovensis* **Pl.79**

Other names: Gibberbird, Gibber Chat.

Field marks: 125 mm. *A mottled sandy bird with yellowish face and breast and pale eyes*; in flight, note yellow flanks, sandy rump with yellow sides, black tail. Female: duller. Note long-legged upright carriage; walks and runs with slight swagger; stands on stones. Makes short flights in tail-down fluttering manner, rather like Richard's Pipit (423); when disturbed, flies high and strongly, in typically chat-like manner. Usually in pairs, rather than flocks; difficult to locate unless accidentally flushed.

Similar species: Orange Chat (647).

Voice: Flight-call, squeaky 'dip dip', somewhat like Yellow-faced Honeyeater (599).

Habitat: Arid: open gibber, with sparse dwarf bushes, tufts of grass; wind-scalded areas in saltbush-bluebush.

Breeding: Nest: cup-shaped; of grasses and twigs; in depression in ground. Eggs: 3; white with red-brown spots at large end.

Range and Status: Arid parts of se. NT, sw. Q, w. NSW and SA, n. limits little known. In SA, ranges s. to about Lyndhurst–Quorn, occasional s. to Sutherlands. Formerly (?isolate) population sw. of Ivanhoe, NSW. Nomadic; uncommon.

Sunbirds Family *Nectariniidae*

Small brightly coloured sometimes highly-burnished nectar-and insect-eating birds of the Old World tropics and subtropics. Most are found in Africa, where they are as much a feature of blossoming trees as are honeyeaters in Australia. The bills of sunbirds are mostly long, slender and markedly down-curved, the edges of the mandibles often being serrated; they are used to probe and pierce blossoms for nectar and take insects and larvae from flowers, leaves and in flight. Many spiders are eaten. Sunbirds are volatile, and aggressive; group displays are frequent. Flight is typically urgent and darting; their calls are sharp, high-pitched and sibilant, elaborated into song by breeding males.

Food: Nectar, insects and larvae, spiders and other invertebrates.

Range: Africa south of the Sahara, southern parts of the Middle East, southern Asia and the Australian region.

Number of species: World 118; Aust. 1.

651 YELLOW-BREASTED SUNBIRD *Nectarinia jugularis* **Pl.77**

Other name: Olive-backed Sunbird (se. Asia).

Field marks: 112 mm. A gorgeous small short-tailed olive-green bird with *long curved bill*. Male: *throat and upperbreast burnished blue-black*; *underparts lemon-yellow*. Female: *whole throat and breast lemon-yellow*; *slight yellowish eyebrow*. Imm: like female. Singly or pairs in temporary groups; assertive; flits about blossoms, hovers to feed; takes quite large spiders, dismembering them while hovering before their webs. Direct flight swift and darting. Associates with smaller honeyeaters, which it resembles in form but not colour. Groups gather in animated display, uttering brisk calls. Tame about houses, where it often nests.

Voice: Thin squeaky notes uttered in flight; staccato in display.

Habitat: Margins of rainforest, vegetation along watercourses, coastal scrub, mangroves; agricultural areas, streets and gardens.

Breeding: Nest: beautiful, pendulous and tailed, 300–600 mm long; side entrance often slightly hooded; of bark, grass and leaves, bound with spiders' web and including debris found in webs; fabric loose and soft but nest-chamber quite substantial, lined with plant-down and feathers. Suspended from vine or branch, sometimes over water, 2–6 m or more high, often in or near houses or sheds, verandah rafters and other structures. Eggs: 2–3; grey-green, heavily mottled brownish.

Range and Status: Coastal n. Q and many coastal islands: from C. York s. to Staaten R. on w. coast and to Gladstone on e. coast. Common; sedentary. Also Solomon Is. and NG to Andaman and Nicobar Is., se. Asia and se. China.

Flowerpeckers Family *Dicaeidae*

A large family of colourful specialized small birds best-represented in se. Asia. The one Australian species, Mistletoebird (652), is a small bird with a stubby tail, fine bill and a tongue adapted to nectar-eating. However its staple is the fruit of mistletoes and to deal with this food it has a simple, specialized alimentary system. The stomach is a blind sac, with an entrance that opens to admit food like insects requiring muscular digestion but is bypassed by more easily-digested food like mistletoe-fruit. Eaten in quantity, the flesh-covered stones are adeptly squeezed from their tough cases and swallowed. They pass through the bird quickly (under 30 minutes in one observation) and are still tacky when excreted, numerous seeds often being linked like beads in a glutinous thread that, assisted by the bird's restless switching about, adheres to a branch, where the seeds subsequently germinate. There is thus mutual dependence, the bird's movements across the continent being influenced by fruiting of mistletoes.

Food: Fruits, especially of mistletoes; also berries, nectar, insects.

Range: Oriental and Australian regions, excluding Tas. and NZ.

Number of species: World 58; Aust. 1.

652 MISTLETOEBIRD *Dicaeum hirundinaceum* Pl.80

Other names: Australian Flowerpecker or Flower-swallow, Mistletoe Flowerpecker.

Field marks: 95–110 mm. Male: tiny; *glossy blue-black above; throat, upperbreast and under tail-coverts scarlet; grey-white below with black mark down centre.* Bill black, sharp. Female: grey above, tail black; underparts whitish, *under tail-coverts pale-red.* Bill dark grey. Imm: like female, *but bill orange to reddish.* In pairs when breeding, otherwise solitary; difficult to observe because so small in foliage, blossoms and mistletoes. Posture upright, restlessly switches this way and that. Flight swift and darting on longish pointed wings.

Similar species: Behaviour separates it from other Australian birds with red breasts.

Voice: Most notes have a glancing splintered quality. Flight-call, distinctive sharp 'dzee!' or 'tsew!'. Song of male, clear penetrating 'kinsey-kinsey-kinsey'; 'wait-a-bit, wait-a-bit, zhipp!; or 'swizit, swizit, weet-weet-swizit'; also soft warbling song that includes mimicry.

Habitat: Wide, yet specialized: vegetation of any kind that supports mistletoes.

Breeding: Nest: beautiful pear-shaped purse like baby's bootee, with slit-like side-entrance; of plant-down or wool felted together, decorated with brownish to grey material that may include excreta of insect larvae, lichen or faded wattle-blossom; hung from leafy twig, from few or 15 m or more high. Eggs: 3–4; white.

Range and Status: Throughout mainland Aust. Common, highly nomadic. Also some e. Lesser Sunda Is. and w. NG.

Pardalotes Family *Pardalotidae*

Pardalotes are small stubby birds of fine markings. The name means 'spotted' and they are also commonly known as 'diamond-birds'. They are mostly pale-brown with black, white, yellow, orange or red markings. Four species are spotted white on crown or wings; the other group, the stripe-crowned pardalotes, are different and their taxonomy is rather complex; they are now treated as races of one species, *P. striatus* (657). All pardalotes have short robust partly-notched bills used to remove invertebrates from leaves and smaller branches of eucalypts. Hard to see as they move like mice in foliage, they are usually first located by calls or by chipping sounds while feeding. Calls are persistent and distinctive, placing the caller in either the spotted or the stripe-crowned group. When travelling, they frequently alight on high dead branches and call, restlessly switching body this way and that. Similarly, courting male pardalotes display on high bare branches, standing stretched upright and calling, with chin tucked in (Spotted – 653) or spreading and quivering wings and tail (stripe-crowned group). The Spotted and several of the stripe-crowned races flock in autumn and winter, making extensive sub-inland dispersals. In flight, their short tails make them look like flying beetles; they are often pursued by honeyeaters. Sexes usually similar; females in spotted group plainer than males.

Food: Mainly insects and larvae, specially lerp and scale insects; other smaller invertebrates.

Range: Confined to Aust. and Tas.

Number of species: World 5; Aust. 5.

653 SPOTTED PARDALOTE *Pardalotus punctatus* Pl.80

Other names: Bank or Ground Diamond; Diamondbird, Diamond Sparrow, Headache-bird.

Field marks: 80–95 mm. Tiny and jewel-like. Male: crown, wings and tail black, *finely spotted white*; eyebrow white; sides of face and neck grey; throat yellow; *rump chestnut-red*; *under tail-coverts bright-yellow*. Female: duller, no yellow on throat, creamish spots on crown. Imm: like female but duller, crown greyish with indistinct pale-yellowish spots, eyebrow very faint. Singly, pairs or large loose winter flocks.

Similar species: Yellow-rumped Pardalote (654): rump brilliant-yellow; note range and habitat. Striated Pardalote (657): crown plain black or black, streaked white; outer primaries streaked rather than spotted white; no red rump or yellow under tail-coverts. Forty-spotted Pardalote (655): dull olive-green, white spots on wings only; from imm. Spotted by yellow-olive ear-coverts. Note range.

Voice: A slow, high-pitched 'sleep-may-be', in minor key, the 'sleep' clear and piping, the 'may-be' higher but descending, the call often ends with a sharp 'peep'; and this may be answered by female. Sometimes the whole call consists only of a soft 'maybe' or 'wee-wee', a lost plaintive note. Also single loud penetrating note. Persistent calls in breeding season inspire name Headache-bird.

Habitat: Coastal forests, woodlands and scrublands to drier open forests; in sub-inland areas usually in red gum and other eucalypts along watercourses; also mallee-fringes, stands of sheoak; golf-courses, orchards, parks, gardens.

Breeding: Nest: globular; of fine strips of bark, lined with soft grass; in chamber at end of burrow 600 mm long usually placed under overhanging cover near top of a creekbank, road-cutting, sandpit, earth on roots of fallen trees; unusually in garden sandheap, hanging fern-basket. Eggs: 3–4, sometimes 5; roundish, white.

Range and Status: E., s. and sw. Aust. and some coastal islands: ne. highlands s. from Atherton Tableland to Eungella Ras., inland of Mackay; thence through se. Q lowlands to Carnarvon Ra.; all coastal NSW inland to w. slopes of Divide and s. Riverina on frontages of Murray R. and tributaries; all Vic. except nw. mallee areas; coastal se. SA, and Mt. Lofty Ras.; in sw. WA, confined to areas of higher rainfall from Stirling Ras. n. to near Jurien Bay, inland to Northam–Moora. Also Tas., Flinders and King Is. Common in s., scarce in n.; there is a regular autumn dispersal from s. to n. in se. and sw. Aust. and from coastal areas to sub-inland; possible seasonal migration across Bass Strait.

654 YELLOW-RUMPED PARDALOTE *Pardalotus xanthopygus* Pl.80

Other names: Golden-rumped Diamondbird, Yellow-tailed Pardalote.
Field marks: 90–100 mm. Very like Spotted Pardalote (653) *but rump bright golden-yellow rather than chestnut*; whitish eyebrow less marked. Female: duller, no yellow on throat. Habits like Spotted, but often easier to see in its lower mallee habitat.
Similar species: Spotted Pardalote (653).
Voice: Somewhat like Spotted Pardalote; slow plaintive 'wee-wee' in minor key, second note semi-tone lower than first; when heard nearby, preceded by abrupt 'chk!'; other softer notes.
Habitat: Usually confined to mallee but at times in nearby tall eucalypt woodlands, mallee and mulga or vagrant in drier tall woodlands elsewhere.
Breeding: Nest: cup or sphere; of bark-shreads and dry grass; in chamber at end of short tunnel in sloping ground or sandhill, often near clump of spinifex. Eggs: 3–4; whitish, rounded.
Range and Status: Mostly mallee areas of s. Aust.: from w. NSW, nw. Vic. and s. SA (including Kangaroo I.) w. to Stirling Ras.–L. Grace, WA, inland to Flinders Ras.–Gawler Ras.–Ooldea–Gt. Victoria Desert–Norseman. Common in mallee habitats; apparently nomadic, sometimes occurring far from presumed regular range, e.g. to near Mudgee, NSW; Melbourne suburbs, You Yangs and Aireys Inlet, Vic. and Mt. Lofty Ras., SA.

655 FORTY-SPOTTED PARDALOTE *Pardalotus quadragintus* Pl.80

Other names: Diamondbird, Many-spotted Pardalote.
Field marks: 95 mm. Confined to Tas.; the dullest, rarest paradalote. Generally olive-green, paler and greyer below, brownish margins to feathers of upperparts give slightly patterned appearance. The only field marks *are the pale yellow-olive ear-coverts and under tail-coverts. and white spots on brownish-black wing-feathers.* Bill short and stubby even for a paradalote. Singly, pairs or parties; habits like other pardalotes; sombre colouring and habit of feeding actively in taller trees make it difficult to observe.
Similar species: Spotted Pardalote (653).
Voice: Usual call described as double note in montone, like one note of Spotted, but harsher; also simple piping note of two syllables; higher-pitched trill suspected.
Habitat: Wet and dry eucalypt forests; perhaps in sub-alpine forests.
Breeding: Nest: almost entirely of strips of stringy bark; usually in holes in trees, 1–15 m high; sometimes in ground. Eggs: 4; roundish, white.
Range and Status: Most recent records are from coastal se. Tas. from Bruny I. in s. to Coles Bay in n., including Hobart environs; inland to just w. of Granton. Vagrant King I. Scarce and local; sedentary or locally dispersive.

656 RED-BROWED PARDALOTE *Pardalotus rubricatus* Pl.80

Field marks: 120 mm. An unusual pale pardalote with rather large bill. *Crown black with large white spots, eyebrow orange then deep-buff, no dark eyeline; distinctive broad golden-buff wingstreak*; throat and underparts pale buff-white with area of pale-yellow in middle of upperbreast. Imm: duller. Singly or pairs, elusive; tends to feed high.
Voice: Unusual, easily memorized: five somewhat parrot-like whistled notes, first two

slow and rising, other three quicker and on higher level; or one slow followed by five quicker high notes.

Habitat: Drier eucalypt woodlands, scrublands and open mulga; occasionally in river red gums along watercourses, more usually the habitat of Striated Pardalote (657).

Breeding: Nest: globular or cup-shaped, and compact; of strips of bark lined with dry grass; in chamber at end of tunnel in bank. Eggs: 2–3; roundish, pure dull-white.

Range and Status: Arid interior, w. coastal and n. Aust., *except* for top end NT, n. of Victoria R.–Roper R. Ranges over much of Q s. from C. York, *except* (?) coastal areas (occasional to coast near Townsville) and se. Q, e. and s. of lower Dawson R.–Mitchell; in nw. NSW, occurs s. to Barrier Ra.; n. SA, s. to n. Flinders Ras and (probably well s. of) Everard Ras.; in WA, s. to Gt. Victoria Desert and Gasgoyne R.; n. to Kimberleys. Fairly common, scarce eastward in Q.

STRIPE-CROWNED PARDALOTE COMPLEX

Replacing one another in four regions over Aust. are four pardalotes of common ancestry. They have yellow-and-white eyebrows and a black crown, or a black crown streaked with white; white outer margins to the primaries, and a bright-red or bright-yellow spot on the wing-coverts. Because the three mainland-breeding forms hybridize, all are now treated as races of a single species, Striated Pardalote *Pardalotus striatus*, (657), which breeds in Tas. and migrates to the mainland in winter. Differences between the nominate race and the two races it overlaps in se. mainland Aust. are slight, but with great care can be discerned in the field. Look for (1) the colour of the spot on the wing-coverts (whether red or yellow); (2) the width of the white streak along the primaries (whether narrow or broad). Note that fluffy flank feathers may obscure this wingstreak and that hybrids may show intermediate features; they should simply be called 'striated or stripe-crowned pardalotes'. The situation in inland s. and sw. Aust., in n. Aust. (and in Tas.) is simpler, as only one race occurs in each region.

657 STRIATED PARDALOTE   *Pardalotus striatus*   Pl.80

Other names: Pickwick, Wittachew; Chip-chip, Chippie, Chookchook.

Field marks: 95–115 mm. A widespread species of several distinctive races. An olive-fawn pardalote with yellow of throat often dividing and extending along the flanks, which are otherwise buffish. *Crown plain black or streaked white; bold white eyebrow starting with yellow to orange mark before eye. Bright-red or yellow spot on wing-coverts ('wingspot'), wing-feathers black, white outer margins of primary feathers forming a narrow or a broad white streak along wing.* Females are slightly duller; imms often have grey-black unstreaked crowns.

Nominate race, 'Yellow-tipped Pardalote': largest and dullest of the complex, with *striped crown, small bright-yellow wingspot, narrow white wingstreak.* Singly, pairs or family parties. On mainland (mostly autumn–winter–spring) associates with other races, principally *ornatus*, less often with *substriatus*, occasionally, in n. parts of winter range, with *melanocephalus*. Interbreeding not certainly known.

Race *substriatus*, 'Striated Pardalote': somewhat more boldly marked; striped crown, orange to red wingspot; broad white wingstreak, formed by outer webs of first and third to seventh or eighth primaries. (Because of wear, first often lacks white.) Specially in winter forms travelling flocks, often with other pardalotes or other small passerines. Hybrids with *ornatus* resemble the latter; hybrids with *melanocephalus* have less-streaked crowns, more orange start to eyebrow.

Race *ornatus*, 'Eastern Striated Pardalote': very like *substriatus*, but with *orange to red wingspot and narrow white wingstreak*, formed by white edges of first and third primaries. A proportion of birds (25 % in one study) also have fourth primary edged white, giving a wingstreak nearly as broad as *substriatus*. Field identification is thus chancy without the clearest sighting. Forms winter associations like *substriatus*, frequently associating and hybridizing with latter in w. parts of range; occasionally associates with *melanocephalus* in n. part of range.

Race *melanocephalus* (and others), 'Black-headed Pardalote': *crown plain-black*, bold white eyebrow begins with orange mark, black eyeline cut off below by white sides of face, no chestnut on secondaries, wingmarks otherwise identical to *substriatus* (Pl. 80 incorrectly omits red wingspot); rump richer, tinged rufous in e. coastal Q, nearly golden buff in far-n., coastal NT and Kimberleys, WA. Behaves like other races but does not appear to form flocks in nonbreeding season. Often interbreeds with *substriatus*, hybrids have partly striped black crown, chestnut margins to secondaries.

Similar species: Spotted (653) and Yellow-rumped (654) Pardalotes: by spotted upper-parts, no wingstreak, and scarlet and/or yellow rump; yellow under tail-coverts, note range. Red-browed Pardalote (656): large white spots on crown; broad golden-buff wingstreak.

Voice: A sharp double 'chip-chip' or 'pick-pick'; a trisyllabic 'pick-it-up', 'wittachew' or 'pretty-de-Dick', with emphasis on first syllable; a stuttered 'pretty-de-Dick' or 'widididup'. Also a flat hard trill and a soft 'cheeoo' or 'pee-ew, pee-ew'.

Habitat: Mostly eucalypt forests, woodlands and scrublands, including mallee; timber along watercourses; *substriatus* and *melanocephalus* in mulga and other drier acacia-scrubs; *melanocephalus*: rainforests, mangroves. (All): roadsides, golf-courses, parks, gardens.

Breeding: Nest: globular, of bark fibre, rootlets and fine grasses; in tree-hollow or knot-hole 3–25 m high, but sometimes near ground; or in chamber at end of a tunnel up to 60 cm (2 ft) long in creekbank, road-cutting, sandpit; the entrance usually in exposed mid-section of the bank. In WA, under natural circumstances, *substriatus* typically nests only in tree-hollows. Artificial situations, like cracks in brickwork, are sometimes used by *ornatus*, *substriatus* and *melanocephalus*. Eggs: 2–5; white, round-oval.

Range and Status: The species is distributed in suitable habitat throughout Aust. and many coastal islands.

Nominate race: breeds only Tas., Bass Strait islands, and (? occasionally) coastal s. Vic. Common Tas. Oct.–Mar., migrating to mainland Mar.–Oct.; ranges through e. Vic., e. coastal and highland NSW, se. Q n. to Rockhampton. Inland limits: Chinchilla–lower Dawson R. in Q; Inverell–Wagga, NSW; w. and nw. Vic., occasional se. SA (Tintinarra–Hartley). Generally scarce on mainland. Common Tas., where it is the only stripe-crowned pardalote. Migratory.

Race *substriatus*: widespread in mainland Aust., mostly w. of Divide; n. to about Rockhampton–Diamantina R., Q; Tennant Ck.–Tanami, NT, and Fitzroy R., WA. Also some coastal islands, including Kangaroo I., SA. Common; nomadic or migratory.

Race *ornatus*: se. Aust.; e. Vic., occasional to se. SA; in NSW, occasional w. to Darling R.; in Q probably mostly winter visitor, n. to Bowen, and inland to w. of Charleville. Common, nomadic or migratory.

Race *melanocephalus*: ne. and n. Aust. and coastal islands; from Hunter R., NSW, n. coastally and on n. tablelands; in Q, widespread, w. at least to Barcaldine, and on Gulf coast s. at least to Cloncurry; in NT, s. to about Brunette Downs–Larrimah; through Kimberleys to about Broome. Commonest and most evident pardalote round Brisbane and through n. coastal area; less common inland. Sedentary or nomadic.

White-eyes   Family *Zosteropidae*

A widespread, originally tropical, family of small birds formerly known in Aust. as silvereyes. They show remarkable physical similarity despite an enormous world range. Most species are characterized by fine, slightly decurved bills, brush-tipped tongues, grey to olive-green plumage and a conspicuous ring of fine white feathers round the eye. When not breeding they associate in parties or flocks, some making long migrations. This gregarious mobility, coupled with a liking for sweet food, makes them a serious economic pest in orchards and vineyards. But they also destroy quantities of harmful insects like aphids. White-eyes have high-pitched voices and attractive songs. They sling their beautiful cup nests from twigs in bushes or scrubby trees, often in gardens, where they become tame. Sexes alike.

Food: Insects, berries, fruit, nectar.

Range: Africa, Asia, Australasian region, parts of Oceania and some sub-Antarctic islands.

Number of species: World 79; Aust. 3.

658 PALE WHITE-EYE *Zosterops citrinella* Pl.80

Other name: Pale Silvereye.

Field marks: 120 mm. Note range. Probably best recognized by *whitish underparts*; olive-green above, yellower on head and rump; *forehead, eyeline, throat and under tail-coverts clear-yellow*; note white eyering. *Bill longer and much more robust* than other Austrlian white-eyes, except race *chlorocephala* of Grey-breasted White-eye (660) on Bunker and Capricorn Groups on s. Gt. Barrier Reef. Behaviour like other white-eyes.

Similar species: Yellow White-eye (659): underparts bright-yellow; note range and habitat.

Habitat: Wooded and forested islands.

Breeding: Nest: small neat cup; of fine grass bound with spiders' web; suspended in slender fork of shrub or foliage of tree. Eggs: 2–4; pale blue-green.

Range and Status: Islands in Torres Strait and off e. coast C. York Pen. s. to Quoin, Eagle and Palfrey Is. Also islands off s. NG, e. Lesser Sunda Is. Sedentary.

659 YELLOW WHITE-EYE *Zosterops lutea* Pl.80

Other name: Yellow Silvereye.

Field marks: 95–120 mm. Distinctive: *uniform yellow-olive above*; *forehead and underparts bright-yellow*; note *white eye-ring*. Colours blend well with yellow-green leaves of mangroves. Habits like other white-eyes; but note specialized habitat.

Similar species: Grey-breasted White-eye (660), w. race *gouldi*.

Voice: Calls like other white-eyes, but with distinct dialect; usual call reportedly lower in pitch and more nasal and metallic than Grey-breasted; song perhaps loudest of any Australian white-eye.

Habitat: Mainly coastal mangroves; also low coastal thickets, monsoon thickets, vegetation along coastal rivers; trees and gardens in nw. towns.

Breeding: Nest: deep cup; of soft grasses bound with spiders' web; suspended from horizontal fork, usually of mangrove. Eggs: 3–4; paler-blue than Grey-breasted.

Range and Status: Coasts and some coastal islands of (mostly) n. Aust.: from Shark Bay, WA, to ne. C. York Pen., Q. Isolate colony at Leschenault Inlet, Bunbury, WA; also reported from mangroves at Ayr and Burdekin R., e. coastal Q (far from w. C. York Pen); extends some distance inland along rivers. Common; sedentary.

GREY-BREASTED WHITE-EYE COMPLEX

In e. Aust., Tas. and sw. Aust. lives a complex of variable races or geographical forms now recognized as belonging to one species, Grey-breasted White-eye (660), *Zosterops lateralis*. In s. WA, the bird is mostly olive-green above; in e. Aust., the back is grey, but the colours of the throat, flanks and under tail-coverts change geographically, resulting in a very different appearance – sometimes even in members of a single flock. These difficulties (for observers) are compounded by extensive movements of various colour-forms throughout se. Aust. on migration or at least during non-breeding dispersal. Despite banding-studies, such movements are generally little understood, although the regular migrations of Tas.-breeding birds are now fairly well-known.

660 GREY-BREASTED WHITE-EYE *Zosterops lateralis*   **Pl.80**

Other names: Blightbird, Grape-eater, Greenie; Green-backed, Grey-backed, Grey-breasted or Western Silvereye; Little Grinell, Ringeye, Silvey, Spectacled Blightbird, Waxeye.

Field marks: 100–125 mm. In most of s. and e. Aust. it is *the only small grey and olive-green bird with a conspicuous white eyering.* Colours of underparts vary geographically: (1) Migratory population breeding in Tas. and Bass Strait islands: *throat grey, flanks buff to chestnut, under tail-coverts whitish.* (2) Population breeding mostly n. from Sydney: *throat bright-yellow, flanks grey or slightly buffish, under tail-coverts lemon-yellow.* There are various intermediates between these extremes and because of migration and nomadism, any may be seen almost anywhere from s. Q to s. SA. The WA, race *gouldi* differs in its *more uniform olive-green upperparts,* pale yellow-olive upperbreast, grey underparts and buff-washed flanks. Apparent intergradation between *gouldi* and e. races is seen in green-backed birds from Eyre Pen. and Kangaroo I., SA. Pairs when breeding, otherwise mostly parties to flocks. These show remarkable cohesion; banded members of same party have been retrapped together several years apart. The birds move rapidly through bushland, orchards and gardens, calling constantly. When migrating, dozens to hundreds gather in trees then, with a blizzard of calls, dash into the air on next stage of journey. There is some nocturnal movement. A pest in orchards and regular visitor to bird-tables and nectar-drinkers; aggressive.

Similar species: Yellow White-eye (659): much yellower, specially below; note range. Pale White-eye (658): may be confused in coastal e. Q and islands; larger; yellow above, whiter below.

Voice: Contact call, thin peevish 'psee'; another common call, wavering 'wee-ee-ee-ee-ee', also used in alarm. Male: surprisingly loud beautiful warbling territorial song of rapid succession of high-pitched notes and trills, warbles and slurs. Also quiet or autumn sub-song that includes mimicry. Calls of *gouldi* harsher, flight-note almost a staccato 'chip chip'.

Habitat: Practically every vegetational type in coastal and sub-coastal s. Aust.

Breeding: Nest: beautiful suspended cup; of grass, thistle-down, moss and sometimes horsehair, bound with spiders' web; suspended between forks of slender twig, usually in low shrub. Eggs: 2–4; usually 3; delicate pale-blue.

Range and Status: E., s. and sw. Aust. and coastal islands: s. coastally from C. York Pen., inland to Charters Towers–Springsure–Morven, with a resident robust-billed race *chlorocephala* on Capricorn and Bunker Groups, s. Gt. Barrier Reef; nearly throughout NSW, vagrant w. of Darling R.; all Vic.; Tas.; s. SA n. to Flinders and Gawler Ras, w. occasionally on Nullarbor Plain into WA; the w. race *gouldi* occurs s. of Nullarbor Plain in SA, w. along Bight coast, and throughout sw. WA, n. to Wongan Hills–Shark Bay and coastally n. to Pt Cloates. Common and often abundant; highly nomadic and migratory. Part of the Tas.-breeding populations leaves Tas. from mid-summer through autumn, dispersing throughout se. Aust., n. to Q, where mid-winter it makes up *c.* 5 % of the total population round Brisbane. Returns to Tas. Aug.–Oct. Also NZ and Pacific islands to Fiji.

Finches   Family *Fringillidae*

In general larger and more robust than the Australian grass-finches, most true finches have short, sharp bills for seed-cracking; their voices are usually strong, with chirruping calls and songs. They build cup-shaped nests, and their eggs are bluish and often spotted. Though most native grass-finches have declined round cities in se. Aust., the two introduced members of this family and specially European Goldfinch (661), have been highly successful and are now very numerous in some districts.

Food: Mainly seeds, also insects.

Range: Worldwide natural distribution *except* for Australasian and Malagasy regions.

Number of species: World 122; Aust. 2 (introduced).

661 EUROPEAN GOLDFINCH *Carduelis carduelis*   Pl.85

Other name: Thistle-finch.

Field marks: 120–135 mm. A handsome pale-brown finch with *sharp whitish bill, deep-red face, white down side onto throat, crown and nape black*; *wings black, tipped white, and with broad bright-yellow band; rump whitish, cleft tail black*; underparts pale with buff sides. Imm: plainer, mainly grey-buff, streaked darker, with yellow bar on black wings. Pairs, small to large flocks, specially in autumn–winter. Feeds fluttering in seeding grasses, thistles, and on ground; perches on fence and telephone wires, restlessly switching about, calling. Flight dancing, bursts of wingbeats accompanied by tinkling notes; note yellow wingbar and pale rump.

Similar species: Flame (442) and Scarlet (443) Robins: in flight, off-white wingbar, brown rump; tails have white edges. European Greenfinch (662): greener, more robust, with yellow panels on either side of tail.

Voice: In spring, pretty tinkling catchy song: 'twiddle-ee-twiddle-ee-dee'; also deep scratchy long-drawn canary-like 'tweet'; in flight, tinkling notes.

Habitat: Grasslands, weedy wastelands, farmlands, orchards, roadsides, vacant suburban land, shrubby wastes near beaches; prefers to nest and roost in introduced trees.

Breeding: Nest: neat cup of fine twigs, rootlets, grass; felted inside with plant-down, fur; 1–10 m high in shrub or tree. Eggs: 4–6; delicate blue-white, finely but variably spotted or blotched pale red-brown; some almost plain, others with zone or cap of spots at large end.

Range and Status: Native from w. Europe and n. Africa to c. Asia; introduced NSW, Vic., SA in 1860s and 1870s; established round Brisbane from 1919; in s. WA, apparently by aviary escapes from 1930s. Widespread in suitable habitat s. from Brisbane area and Darling Downs, Q, through e. and s. NSW, inland to Moree–Gilgandra–L. Cargelligo and in sw. NSW to arid country n. of Balranald–Wentworth, extending to high country of ne., s. tablelands and se. alpine region. Nearly throughout Vic., commonest coastal areas and w. plains. In Tas., widespread in e., in w. mostly near settlement; recorded to *c.* 1200 m, Mt Wellington; also most Bass Strait Islands. In SA, through se. n. to about Barrier Highway, also Yorke and s. Eyre Pens, Kangaroo I. In sw. WA established round Perth and Albany. Common; locally nomadic in autumn–winter.

662 EUROPEAN GREENFINCH *Carduelis chloris*   Pl.85

Other name: Green Linnet.

Field marks: 145–160 mm. A robust dull yellow-green finch, about size of House Sparrow (663). Note *short robust pale bill, yellow streak on wing, yellower-green rump and blackish forked tail with conspicuous yellow panel on either side.* Imm: dull-brown, streaked darker; yellow parts less conspicuous than adult. Pairs, small autumn–winter flocks. Feeds on ground, often near cover, flies up with strong bouncing flight and distinctive notes, *revealing yellowish leading edge to wing, yellow wingbar and tail panels.* Male sings on prominent perch and in slow wavering, weaving song-flight.

Similar species: European Goldfinch (661), imm.

Voice: Male in spring: grasshopper-like but robust descending 'birrzz', uttered from top of tree; in song-flight, utters similar call and canary-like trills and twitterings; also canary-like but harsh rising 'tsooeet?' and hard flat trill.

Habitat: Open farmlands and grasslands, weedy wastelands, coastal and dune-scrubs, swamp-woodlands; roadsides; orchards, parks, golf-courses, gardens, urban areas; favours introduced trees for roosting and nesting.

Breeding: Nest: cup of fine twigs; bound with hair; lined with rootlets, hair, feathers; in shrub or among foliage of pine or cypress. Eggs: 4–6; whitish to pale-greenish blue, spotted, streaked red-brown, violet.

Range and Status: Native of Europe and Middle East to Caspian Sea; introduced Melbourne from 1863, Adelaide during 1870s; apparently self-introduced to Tas., from *c.* 1945, via King I. Now well established, but apparently discontinuous. In NSW, parts of Sydney area, including Botany Bay; patchily w. to Orange, also ACT–Albury. In Vic., patchy, but now widespread over much of State, except for mallee areas of nw., commonest coastally. In Tas., in n., e. and midlands, less widespread than European Goldfinch; records on w. coast s. to Henty R.–Strahan. Mostly coastal. Common King I.; local and less common Flinders I. In SA, through coastal se., n. to Adelaide and Mt Lofty Ras.

Old World Sparrows   Family *Passeridae*

The family, which consists of true sparrows, rocksparrows, and some specialized weavers, is widespread in Africa and Eurasia. The species are all small (sparrow-sized), usually dull-coloured, thick-billed (for eating seeds) and usually nest in holes or crevices, making bulky nests, often domed. Two species have been introduced into Aust.

Food: Mainly seeds and insects.

Range: The Ethiopian, Palaearctic and Oriental Regions.

Number of species: World 27; Aust. 2 (introduced).

663 HOUSE SPARROW   *Passer domesticus*   Pl.86

Other name: English Sparrow.

Field marks: 140–160 mm. Well known, but markings seldom noted well. *Male: crown grey, nape and sides of neck chestnut, cheeks grey-white.* Rest of upperparts richly marked, black centres to feathers with buff and rufous margins, prominent whitish bar on shoulder; grey below. In summer, throat and upperbreast *black*; in winter, duller and greyer, black much reduced, mottled. Female: brown above, with indistinct paler and darker streaks, *bold buff eyebrow back from eye*; *one fairly prominent and a fainter pale bar on wing*; dingy fawn-grey below. Bill short and robust, blackish in male, horn-coloured paler below in female. Imm: like female. Singly, pairs to large flocks; bold, perky and adaptable; gleans spilt grain and much other free food in city and country; pest in grain-fields, poultry-yards, raids food-tables, damages flowers but eats aphids. Flight swift and undulating. Courting males hop round females, cheeping, legs bent, tails cocked, wings drooped.

Similar species: Tree Sparrow (664): bill less robust, whole crown chestnut; black ear-mark on whitish cheek; smaller dark throat-mark; quieter.

Voice: Garrulous and persistent; most common note, loud insistent 'cheep'; also tinny grating rattle, uttered as alarm-call or in aggression; many other notes.

Habitat: Towns generally; farm buildings, farmlands, especially where dead trees and hollows suitable for nesting; grain fields; sometimes far from settlement and well inland, in mallee, mulga, saltbush, timber and scrub along watercourses.

Breeding: Nest: bulky, untidy, domed, with side entrance; of dry grass; lined with feathers; in dense shrub or tree, hollow branch, any accessible crevice or sheltered place in building; occasionally uses nest-hole of kingfisher, mud-bottle nest of Fairy Martin (422); it displaces native hole-nesters like pardalotes, whitefaces. Eggs: 4–6; grey-white, finely but closely spotted and freckled grey and pale-brown.

Range and Status: Native to Eurasia, nw Africa, India to China; widespread elsewhere by introductions. First to Aust. from about 1863. Common, well-established e. Aust. and some coastal and Gt Barrier Reef islands, from Cooktown, Q, inland to Mt Isa–Bedourie; nearly all NSW and Vic.; in Tas., widely in e., but mostly near settlements in w.; Bass Strait islands; in SA n. to Oodnadatta–William Ck–Mt Willoughby, also Kangaroo I. and smaller coastal islands; ranges w. to beyond Tarcoola, in good seasons w. to Nullarbor

Station, where it has bred; yet to cross Nullarbor Plain in sufficient numbers to become established in WA. Stowaways ashore from ships at ports in WA are destroyed if possible. Sparrows seen anywhere in WA should be immediately reported to appropriate authorities.

664 TREE SPARROW *Passer montanus* Pl.86

Other name: Mountain Sparrow.

Field marks: 130–150 mm. Less common and familiar than House Sparrow (663). Differs in *rounder, wholly chestnut crown and nape, black ear-mark on whitish cheek*, smaller blackish patch on throat; rump yellow-brown. Bill less robust. Unlike House Sparrow, sexes similar. Imm: paler, with less distinct markings. Pairs to flocks, mostly winter; often with House Sparrow. Feeds on ground or in foliage, takes flying insects.

Similar species: House Sparrow (663).

Voice: Quieter than House Sparrow; short metallic 'chik', repeated 'chit-tchup' and rapid twitter; flight-call, 'tek, tek'.

Habitat: Suburban areas generally; has not penetrated so successfully into open country as House Sparrow, but does occur round farm buildings and homesteads far from urban areas in parts.

Breeding: Nest: like House Sparrow but smaller; in hole in building or tree. Eggs: 4–6; like House Sparrow but smaller, browner and more glossy.

Range and Status: Native to Europe and Asia e. to Japan and s. to Philippines, Greater Sunda Is., Celebes and Ambon; introduced America. Introduced se. Aust. from 1863. Now established from Melbourne and towns of c. and ne. Vic. to s. NSW (Moama–Albury), where it is fairly common, to Sydney area–Newcastle–Hunter R. Valley, NSW, where it is rare. In Vic., it has been recorded w. to Dimboola, and in NSW w. to Wagga–Cowra, recently recorded Weethalle, Hay. Said to have been introduced to Tas., but not recorded recently.

Australian Grass-finches and Allies   Family *Ploceidae*

This large family, as now arranged, includes finchlike birds of great diversity of form, colour and behaviour. Most are African, but two subfamilies are represented in Aust. The Australian Grass-finches, subfamily *Estrildinae*, range from the Australian region to se. Asia and Polynesia. Most of the 18 species which occur naturally in Aust. live in the tropics, but two (668, 672) have adapted to arid inland habitats and two others (666–7) are confined mostly to cool, wet s. coastal woodlands and scrubs. The rest occupy woodlands or grasslands between these extremes. Grass-finches are highly social, gathering in small to large flocks, specially in the non-breeding season; the pair-bond is strong; some appear to mate for life. Mating displays by males include posturing with a long piece of grass gripped in the bill. Nests are typically untidy domed structures, mostly of grass, with a long entrance-spout. Some species nest in loose colonies. Most species build domed roosting nests in the non-breeding season. These are less elaborate than breeding nests, and generally lack an entrance-spout. In better-watered coastal districts breeding is fairly regular, but in more arid regions it may occur in any month, following rain. Some species have long been favourite cage birds and two in particular, Zebra (672) and Gouldian (677) Finches, are nearly as well-known outside their native land as within it. One grass-finch, Nutmeg Mannikin (683), has become established in Aust. as a result of aviary escapes. It is now widespread. The true weavers, *Ploceinae*, whose stronghold is Africa, are or have been represented in Australia by Red Bishopbird (684) and White-winged Widowbird (685). Both apparently became established as a result of aviary escapes. Particularly near cities and towns, observers should be aware of the possibility of such aviary escapes. They may be exotic members of the family not included in this book,* or native species so far outside their natural range, or so confined to one locality, as to be reasonably considered escaped birds or their progeny. Thus for example, Chestnut-breasted Mannikin

(681) is reported feral in Melbourne outer suburbs, and near Finniss in SA, w. of L. Alexandrina.

Food: Mostly seeds and insects.

Range: Africa through s. Asia to NG, Aust., Fiji and Samoa.

Number of species: World *c.* 240; Aust. 19, including 1 introduced.

* e.g. the Black-headed Mannikin, *Lonchura atricapilla*, was reported feral from a few swampy areas near Sydney shortly before this book went to press.

665 RED-BROWED FIRETAIL *Emblema temporalis* Pl.85

Other names: Redbill, Red-browed Finch, Redhead, Temporal Finch, (Sydney) Waxbill.

Field marks: 110–115 mm. *A small grey-and-olive finch with scarlet bill, prominent scarlet eyebrow and rump*; golden-olive mark on shoulder, tail black. Imm: browner with blackish bill, no scarlet eyebrow. Small race, *minor*, of ne. Q: head paler, grey, back more yellow-olive, throat and underparts whiter, undertail-coverts darker. Pairs to flocks; feeds on or near ground in grass or on lawns, seldom far from cover. Darts to nearest shrubbery in erratic bouncing flight. Has adapted well to settlement; often at bird-tables where seed provided.

Similar species: Beautiful Firetail (666): darker; underparts patterned; no red eyebrow, but black mask round eye. Diamond Firetail (669): no red eyebrow, white below with black breastband and white-spotted flanks.

Voice: Typical contact-call, high-pitched squeak, an outburst when flocks disturbed; alarm-call, dry single note, or brisk chatter.

Habitat: Undergrowth and margins of forests, woodlands, coastal scrub and heaths; well-watered grasslands with low shrubs and trees; vegetation along watercourses, margins of canefields and other cultivated lands, roadsides; blackberries and other thickets; golf-courses, orchards, parks, gardens.

Breeding: Nest: large, bottle-shaped, some untidy with or without flimsy spouts, others with well-made spout 25–150 mm long; of stiff green or dry grass; lined with soft grasses, plant-down, feathers, fur; usually 1–2 m high in dense low shrub, prickly bush, orchard citrus, introduced cypress or pine; occasionally to 10 m in leafy tree. Eggs: 4–6; white.

Range and Status: E. and se. Aust.; recently introduced to sw. WA from aviary escapes. In e. Aust. from Weipa–Pascoe R., C. York Pen., Q. coastally s. to se. SA; inland to Laura–Atherton Tableland–Carnarvon Ras.–Warwick, Q; and to Moree–Pilliga Scrub–Warrumbungle NP, NSW, rare in the Riverina and mostly near Murray R. and associated watercourses w. to about Moulamein; in Vic., commonest s. of Divide, but in suitable habitat in all districts except the nw. mallee; in SA, coastal se., n. to Mt. Lofty Ras. and Nuriootpa; also Kangaroo I. Common; mostly resident, locally nomadic in autumn–winter. In WA, became established from avaiary escapes after about 1960 in Darling Ra. e. of Perth, between Bickley and Mundaring Weir.

666 BEAUTIFUL FIRETAIL *Emblema bella* Pl.85

Other name: Firetail Finch.

Field marks: 115–120 mm. A plump dark finch with *bright-red bill and rump, small black mask round eye, and pale-blue eyering*. The plumage is dark bronze-brown above, crossed with fine dark-brown barrings; *underparts very finely barred black and white*. Male: centre of abdomen and undertail coverts black. Female: only latter black. Imm: duller, bill blackish. Pairs to small groups or flocks; quiet and unobtrusive. Feeds on ground in small clearings or at edge of scrub, seldom far from cover. Hops rapidly through grass like plump dark mouse. When approached, quickly flies into cover with burr of wings, red rump noticeable against dark plumage. Sustained flight swift and direct. In spring and summer, males call from high perches above cover. Associates with Red-browed Firetail (665).

Similar species: Red-eared Firetail (667): note range. Red-browed Firetail (665).

Voice: Calls simple: commonest has been described as a mournful piping penetrating 'weee'; two or three high notes ending with a staccato downward run; also clear drawn-out 'pee-oo, pee-oo, pee-oo'.

Habitat: Dense vegetation, usually but not invariably in damp situations. In Tas., fairly varied and include low-altitude heaths, grassy woodlands, dry and wet eucalypt forests; sub-alpine forest and tussock moors. On Flinders I. (Tas.) and Kangaroo I. (SA) stands of she-oaks near creeks, and nearby clover pastures. On mainland mostly in dense damp coastal heaths and paperbark thickets, scrubby eucalypt woodlands and forests with dense undergrowth, saw-sedge and other large tussocks, dense bracken.

Breeding: Nest: bulky, bottle-shaped with long (170 mm) entrance spout; of grass, collected when green, reinforced with stems of creepers; lined soft grass, plant-down, feathers; usually 1–6 m high in dense shrub or tree. Eggs: 5–8; pure-white, smooth, without gloss.

Range and Status: Mostly coastal se. Aust., from near Newcastle, NSW, to Mt. Lofty Ras. and Kangaroo I., SA; in NSW occurs inland in Blue Mountains (area of Blackheath)–Thirlmere Lakes NP–Braidwood–ACT (? vagrant). In Vic. patchily inland in suitable habitat e.g. Yellingbo State Faunal Reserve and near L. Eildon and Mt. Beauty. In SA, confined to se. coast, suitable habitat in Mt Lofty Ras., and Kangaroo I. In Tas., widespread *except* drier e. woodlands; also Flinders I. and other Bass Strait islands, but not King I. Generally rare, locally common; sedentary. Distribution will become even more patchy as scrublands are cleared.

667 RED-EARED FIRETAIL *Emblema oculata* Pl.85

Other name: Red-eared Finch.

Field marks: 115–120 mm. Note range. A plump dark finch with *bright-red bill, ear-coverts, and rump*; small black mask and pale-blue eyering. Upperparts olive-brown, throat and upperbreast buffish, finely barred; *rest of underparts black, spotted white*. In breeding season, ear-coverts of male deep-scarlet, of female orange-scarlet. Imm: duller, bill black, eyering dull-blue, no black mask or red on ear-coverts. Grey-brown above, rump dull-red; no white spots below but finely barred light and dark-brown. Singly, pairs, or family parties only; does not flock in non-breeding season. Shy, secretive; feeds near ground among grass, sedges and low shrubs less often on ground, when it hops. Flight low, fairly slow and without undulation; scarlet rump conspicuous.

Similar species: In its restricted range in sw. WA it could be confused only with recently introduced Red-browed Firetail (665): plainer grey and olive-green with long red eyebrow.

Voice: Described as a mournful directionless 'wee-ee', or 'oo-wee', singly or oft-repeated.

Habitat: Mostly restricted to undergrowth of heavy forests, heavy vegetation along creeks and gullies in ranges, dense coastal scrubs, wet coastal heaths, paperbark swamps.

Breeding: Nest: bulky, bottle-shaped, with long entrance spout, totalling up to 400 m in length, the largest nest made by an Australian grass-finch; firmly constructed of initially green plant-stems and tips; lined with fine grass, plant-down and feathers; hidden in foliage in small shrub, sapling or at end of leafy branch up to 16 m high. Eggs: 4–6; pure-white, somewhat translucent.

Range and Status: Confined to suitable pockets of habitat in coastal and near-coastal sw. WA: from about Mundaring Reservoir in Darling Ras. near Perth s. to Manjimup–Pemberton and coastally e. to Hamersley R. near Hopetoun; also Lucky, Mississippi and Duke of Orleans Bays, e. of Esperance. Common to uncommon; sedentary and often very local.

668 PAINTED FIRETAIL *Emblema picta*   Pl.85

Other names: Emblema, Mountain or Painted Finch.

Field marks: 105–115 mm. Distinctive with its strong colouration, unfinchlike pointed partly-red bill and white eye. Brown above, *black below, heavily spotted white, set off by brilliant, almost glossy, scarlet face, throat and irregular scarlet line or patch on centre of breast, and scarlet rump.* Bill deep-crimson, base of lower-mandible blue. Female: duller, much less red on throat and breast, larger white spots on sides. Imm: duller, little or no red on face and breast, none on rump; bill blackish. Pairs, or flocks to 30 + ; usually feeds on ground among rocks and spinifex, perches on boulders, bare branches. Flushes with quick chattering notes; flight fast, direct, slightly undulating, glowing red rump noticeable against dark plumage. Occasionally enters homestead gardens, especially for water.

Similar species: Crimson Finch (671), male: duller-red, dark eye and crimson, not black, flanks; longer reddish tail; female; grey below. Crimson Chat (646), male: white throat, no white spots below. Note range.

Voice: Perhaps harshest and loudest of family; when flushed, scratchy staccato 'chek chek', rapid 'chek-did-did-dit' or reedy 'ched up, cheddy up'. Male animated wheezy chattering song, described as 'che che che-che-che-che-che, werreeeeee-oweeeeee'.

Habitat: Usually associated with spinifex; favours rugged rocky spinifex-clad gorges near permanent water, but at times in open sandy spinifex plains or dense scrubs. In places e.g. Gascoyne R., WA, in citrus orchards.

Breeding: Nest: small, globular, poorly constructed, wide opening, no entrance tunnel but occasionally with verandah of spinifex straws; of small twigs, bark rootlets, spinifex stalks and softer grasses; lined with plant-down, vegetable material and feathers; on platform of bark, roots with earth attached and twigs in spinifex, less than 1 m high, occasionally in other vegetation or on ground. Eggs: 3–5; white, rounded.

Range and Status: Arid inland regions of Q, NT, and SA, possibly to far-nw. NSW, and through the more arid parts of WA to w. coast. In Q, ranges n. to Mt Isa–Cloncurry and e. to near Winton–Opalton. In NT, n. to Nicholson R.–Alexandria–Wave Hill, and s. through Macdonnell Ras. and other rocky ranges to n. SA, s. to L. Frome–n. Flinders Ras. (Arkaroola)–Oodnadatta–Musgrave Ras., and (recently) to Corunna Station, near Iron Knob on ne. Eyre Pen. In WA it ranges s. (? occasional) to Leonora–Menzies–upper Murchison R. to coast at Gascoyne R. (Carnarvon), n. to Pilbara region and Kimberleys. Near Carnarvon said to be extending s. Common but patchy, occurring only in suitable habitat, and absent from substantial areas in its indicated range.

669 DIAMOND FIRETAIL *Emblema guttata*   Pl.85

Other names: Diamond Java Sparrow or Sparrow; Spotted-sided Finch.

Field marks: A robust firetail with a *pale-grey head and bold black band across white breast, joining white-spotted black flanks.* Female: breastband narrower. Imm: browner, breastband absent or shadowy; flanks olive-brown, barred grey-white with indistinct spots; bill black at first. Pairs to small flocks; feeds mostly on ground with bouncing hops. When disturbed, usually flies up to high dead branch of nearby tree; often calls from such a point. Flight strong, undulating, scarlet rump prominent.

Voice: Main contact-call, penetrating long-drawn mournful rising note, 'p-a-i-r-r'; also described as 'twooo-hee' rising slightly, then falling.

Habitat: Open eucalypt forests and woodlands; grasslands with large trees, typically river red gums; larger more open mallee, sheoak, native pine and acacia scrubs; orchards, golf-courses, parks, gardens.

Breeding: Nest: bulky, bottle-shaped, with entrance spout to 150 mm long; well-constructed of grasses picked when green; lined with finer grasses, feathers and down; 2–3 m high in dense shrubs or low trees, citrus, garden shrubs and creepers, or 15–30 m high, in foliage of eucalypt, mistletoe clump, underside of hawk's nest; occasionally in deserted nest of babbler, or under roof of shed. Eggs: 4–6, occasionally up to 9; white.

Range and Status: E. and se. Aust.: in Q, from drier tablelands inland of Tully (Kirrama), s. on drier parts of Divide to inland environs of Brisbane, and w. to about Pentland–Muttaburra–Longreach–Charleville–Cunnamulla; in NSW mostly w. of Divide, to near coast in suitable drier habitats in parts e.g. Port Stephens, Hunter R. Valley, Illawarra district; w. to Moree–Nyngan, (occasional) w. to Ivanhoe Euston; sparse in river red gum forests of Murray R. downstream into SA; in Vic. patchy in drier open forests and woodlands; mostly *absent* from wetter parts of ne. high country (but recorded near Lake Mountain at 1500 m), and from coastal s. Gippsland, Mornington Pen., Otways and far-nw.; in se. SA, n. to s. Flinders Ras. and w. to s. Eyre Pen., also Kangaroo I. Generally uncommon and patchy; apparently much affected by clearing and settlement. Sedentary.

670 STAR FINCH *Neochmia ruficauda* Pl.85

Other names: Red-faced, Red-tailed or Rufous-tailed Finch (Firetail).

Field marks: 100–120 mm. Distinctive: *a small white-spotted pale olive-green finch with scarlet bill, crimson forehead, face and throat, dull-purplish red tail*; legs yellowish. Female: duller, less red on face. Imm: crown, cheeks and breast greyish, dull olive-brown above. Nominate race: olive-brown above, no yellow on underparts. Race *clarescens*: more greenish olive above, brighter-red face and centre of breast, golden-yellow abdomen and under tail-coverts. There is much individual variation; older birds are brighter and more clearly-marked. Pairs to large flocks; feeds mostly among grasses and low vegetation; takes flying insects. When disturbed, flies to cover in undulating flight, but large flocks fly swiftly with rapid changes of direction. Often at water in parties and flocks.

Similar species: Red-faced Gouldian Finch (677): purple breast, yellow underparts.

Voice: Flock-call, loud penetrating 'ssit' or 'sseet'; single contact-call, 'tlit'.

Habitat: Mostly restricted to vegetation beside watercourses and swamps; grassy flats or rank grass with few bushes and low trees, rushes etc; irrigated crops, sugar cane.

Breeding: Nest: domed, rounded, without entrance tunnel; of dry or green-plucked grass; thickly lined with feathers; 1–6 m high in tall grass or shrubby trees. Eggs: 3–6 or 7; white.

Range and Status: Disjunct distribution in coastal nw., n. and ne. Aust.: the race *clarescens* ranges from Barlee Ra., and the Henry and Ashburton Rs, WA, through Pilbara region and Kimberleys to top end NT s. to Katherine; in Q, Gulf coast to w. coast C. York Pen. n. to Watson R., inland to the upper Mitchell R. and (? formerly) on e. coast n. of Coen. The nominate race occurs in ce. Q near Rockhampton on the upper Dawson and upper Mackenzie Rs. It was recorded by Gould on the Namoi R., ce. NSW, in 1839, but thereafter disappeared and was not seen in NSW this century until a recent sight-record near Inverell. Locally common, in suitable habitat, but extremely patchy. The range in e. Aust. has apparently contracted since settlement; in NT and n. WA it is reported to have become abundant in irrigation areas.

671 CRIMSON FINCH *Neochmia phaeton* Pl.85

Other names: Blood Finch, Pale or White-bellied Crimson Finch.

Field marks: 125–140 mm. Richly coloured and long-tailed. Male: *deep-crimson with dark-grey crown and nape*; *back, wings and tail earth-brown, washed crimson*; few small white spots on flanks; *centre of abdomen and under tail-coverts* black. Bill crimson, eye pale-brown. Female: browner above, breast grey-brown with few small white spots on flanks; face, throat, rump and tail dull-crimson; bill crimson. Imm: brownish, secondaries, rump and tail washed dull-crimson; bill blackish. Race *evangelinae*, 'Pale' or 'White-bellied Crimson Finch': much *paler and greyer*; *male has centre of abdomen and under tail-coverts white*. Both sexes: base of bill pale-blue. Pairs, small parties or flocks in which uncoloured imms usually outnumber adults; associates with other finches. Active, aggressive; longish tail constantly flicked up and down or sideways. Feeds on ground and long grass; when disturbed, *flies to trees, scarlet rump and tail conspicuous*. Has adapted well to settlement, often lives near habitation, nests in houses, sheds.

Similar species: Painted Firetail (668): longer bill, shorter tail, black flanks prominently spotted white.

Voice: Usual call described as a brisk clear 'che-che-che-che'; alarm-call, sharp 'chip'; flocks make brittle tinkling when flushed; song described as low-pitched, very rapid series of squeezing rasping note 'ra-ra-ra-ra. reee', or ending with three melodious descending calls.

Habitat: Vegetation by water, typically canegrass and pandanus; tall rank growth on margins cultivations and roadsides, and in tall crops; gardens.

Breeding: Nest: domed, bulky, flatter than wide, without entrance spout, typically with landing platform; of broad strips or blades of grass; occasionally including strips of paperbark, and leaves; lined with plant-down, grass or feathers; usually 3–16 m high at base of leaves in pandanus or paperbark or in other trees, shrubs, tall grass, hollow limbs; in settled districts, in pineapples or bananas; sheds, or under eaves, rafters of verandahs, even inside rooms of houses, hotels. Eggs: 5–8; white, smallish.

Range and Status: Coastal n. and ne. Aust.: from Broome, WA, through Kimberleys; top end NT s. to Mataranka and e. along Gulf coast to Leichhardt R. in nw Q, inland along streams up to 300 km from coast; rare irregular visitor to Mt Isa. On e. coast, s. from Cairns to Proserpine, inland to Herberton and Herbert and Burdekin Rs., formerly s. to Rockhampton and Fitzroy R. On C. York Pen., race *evangelinae* s. from Watson to Mitchell R. on w. coast, and to Claudie R. on e. coast. Common, mostly sedentary. Also s. NG.

672 ZEBRA FINCH *Poephila guttata* Pl.85

Other name: Chestnut-eared Finch.

Field marks: 100 mm. A stocky little finch, familiar to many as a cage-bird. Male: greyish, with wax-red bill; *vertical white-and-dark streak on face, orange-tan cheek-patch and flanks*, latter finely spotted white; rump white, sides black, *tail blackish, barred white*; throat and breast grey, finely barred black and with black band separating whitish underparts. Female: no red in plumage, plain fawn-grey below; black-and-white face and tail markings similar. Imm: like female, bill black. Pairs to sometimes very large flocks, specially at water. Often perches in rows on fences; hops briskly on ground; takes flying insects. Flight fast and direct with slight undulations; *rump and tail-pattern prominent*.

Similar species: Southern Whiteface (568): bill black, upperparts and rump chestnut-brown; squeaky calls.

Voice: Usual call, described as loud 'tya', like toy trumpet; large flocks make blizzard of such calls, heard at some distance; song, series of such notes connected with chattering trills, uttered by displaying males.

Habitat: Seldom far from water; from arid mulga, spinifex and gibber of far inland to grasslands, open woodlands, scrubs and shrublands; saltbush, saltmarsh vegetation; pastoral country; crops; orchards, parks, gardens; tame round settlement.

Breeding: Nest: untidy, domed, of grasses, small twigs, rootlets; lined with feathers, plant-down, wool or fur; 2–4 m high singly or semi-colonial in low shrub or tree, often prickly; occasionally in hollow branch or fence-post, hole in termite-mound, tussock, or in nest of hawk, crow, babbler or Fairy Martin or in a building. Eggs: 3–7; blue-white to very pale dull blue.

Range and Status: Open habitats throughout interior of mainland Aust., drier coastal regions and coastal islands of same. Except during dry periods inland, usually *absent* from wetter and/or cooler coastal districts, although the picture is confused in parts by local colonies probably established from aviary escapes. In general, its range appears to be expanding as a result of clearing and the installation of stock-tanks. Uncommon to extremely abundant. Mostly sedentary. Introduced Kangaroo I., SA *c.* 1937; no recent records. Also Lesser Sunda Is.

673 DOUBLE-BARRED FINCH *Poephila bichenovii* Pl.86

Other names: Bicheno, Banded, Black-ringed, Owl, Owl-faced or Ringed Finch.
Field marks: 100–110 mm. Distinctive and somewhat owl-like. Face and underparts white, *with two black rings, one enclosing face and crossing lower throat, the other across breast.* Upperparts pale-brown with fine black-and-white checkering on wings; rump white, under tail-coverts black, tail blackish. Bill silver-grey, legs grey. Imm: duller, plain-fawnish below or with indistinct bar. Race *annulosa*, 'Black-ringed Finch': similar but rump black. Pairs to flocks, in which imms often predominate; feeds much on ground or among seeding grasses. Retreats in bouncing flight to leafy cover, nominate race showing *conspicuous white rump against black tail.*
Similar species: Banded Whiteface (570): forehead white, only one breastband, back and rump chestnut-brown. Note range. White-fronted Chat (649): more white on head, grey above and single broad black breastband; in flight, grey rump, broad white tip to black tail. Note range.
Voice: Usual call, toot like toy-trumpet, described as long-drawn-out 'tiaat, tiaat', longer than somewhat similar call of Zebra Finch (672).
Habitat: Vegetation along watercourses; drier grassy woodlands and scrublands; open forests and adjacent cleared lands: in settled areas canefields, roadsides, wastelands, golf-courses, plantations, parks, gardens.
Breeding: Nest: small bottle-shaped and rather scruffy; of dry grass; lined with soft grasses, plant-down and feathers; usually 1–5 m high; situations vary in nw. Aust. may be in pandanus, tall grass or open shrubby tree; in e. Aust. often under verandahs, in gardens. Throughout range, in low, fairly small, shrubs, occasionally in hole in stump or fence-post; sometimes in old nest of another finch or babbler and often near wasp's nest. Eggs: 4–5; occasionally to 8; white.
Range and Status: N. and e. Aust. and some coastal islands, from Broome, WA, through Kimberleys, WA, top end NT s. to Banka Banka–Alexandria; n. and e. Q from C. York through e. Aust. to Sydney area and Blue Mts Plateau, s. coastally to Jervis Bay, and an area s. of Moruya. Inland in Q to Mt Isa–Longreach–Charleville; in NSW inland to Walgett–Macquarie Marshes–Warren–Cowra, s. to s. tablelands and ACT; vagrant s. to Warby Ras., Vic. Race *annulosa* intergrades with nominate race in coastal e. NT, some vagrants in nw. Q e. to Leichhardt R. and Mt. Isa. From Kimberleys e. to Pine Creek, NT, and on Groote Eylandt, are only black-rumped birds; s. and e. from Katherine, NT, white-rumped birds increase to e. Q and NSW where they alone are found. Common; mostly sedentary, but nomadic in response to dry conditions.

674 MASKED FINCH *Poephila personata* Pl.86

Other names: Masked Grass-finch; White-eared Finch.
Field marks: 125–135 mm. Modestly coloured but handsome; cinnamon-brown above, paler below, note *rich yellow-orange bill, black forepart of face and throat;* white rump and abdomen contrast with black flank-mark and long pointed tail. Female: smaller. Imm: duller-brown, washed grey, no black mask; bill blackish at first. Race *leucotis*, 'White-eared Finch': *distinct white ear-coverts, white upperbreast and flanks,* upperparts redder-brown. Sociable, in parties to flocks of 20–30, usually of mated pairs and imms. Forms loose breeding colonies, birds coming together during day to drink, bathe and indulge in mutual preening. Under dry conditions may gather in large numbers near waterholes. Feeds much on ground. In flight, note prominent white rump and longish black tail.
Similar species: Long-tailed Finch (675): grey head, large black patch on throat; note range. Black-throated Finch (676): black bill, grey head, large black patch on throat.
Voice: Contact-call, described as low 'twat, twat' the 'a' as in 'have'; also loud call like Zebra Finch (672); chattering calls when pairs join groups.
Habitat: Dry, lightly timbered grassland with small shrubs or scattered higher trees; always fairly near water.

Breeding: Nest: bulky, globular, with side entrance, no well-developed entrance spout, but sometimes a platform at entrance; of soft broad grasses, shorter stiff stems and seed-heads; lined with plant-down, fur, feathers, or string, rags, newspaper; often contains charcoal that may blacken eggs during incubation; in bushes, low trees and on ground under or near stump or log; usually on thick layer of dry grass and well camouflaged; occasionally uses old nest-hole of parrot or kingfisher in termite mound. Eggs: 4–6; white.

Range and Status: N. Aust.: nominate race from Derby, WA, occasional to Broome, through Kimberleys; NT s. to Victoria R. Downs–Newcastle Waters–Brunette Downs; and through lowlands of nw. Q s. nearly to Camooweal and upper Leichhardt R. Race *leucotis* confined to C. York Pen. n. from about lower Leichhardt R. to Watson R. on w. coast and Princess Charlotte Bay in e., and s. to about Georgetown–Chillagoe. Fairly common; probably sedentary.

675 LONG-TAILED FINCH *Poephila acuticauda* Pl.86

Other name: Blackheart.

Field Marks: 150–165 mm. An elegant pinkish fawn finch with a rich-orange to yellow bill, grey head, small white ear-patch, and large *black patch on throat and upperbreast*; *white rump and long finely-pointed black tail*. Imm: bill blackish at first, tail shorter. Bill yellowish in nw. Aust. grading to orange in NT. Pairs to small or occasionally very large flocks, in which pairs persist. Active and graceful; feeds on ground and in grass, takes flying insects.

Similar species: Masked Finch (674): black 'mask'. Black-throated Finch (676): bill black, tail short, giving a more dumpy appearance. Only likely to be confused with imm. Long-tailed, and only in nw. Q, in range of white-rumped nominate race.

Voice: Somewhat mournful far-carrying descending 'peew', with distinctive quality; alarm-call, staccato chattering 'cheek-chee-chee-cheek'.

Habitat: Dry grassy woodlands near watercourses or permanent water; near coast, open grassy plains with pandanus.

Breeding: Nest: domed, with fairly long (50–100 mm) entrance-spout; of dry grass, occasionally with stems of creepers; lined with finer grass, plant-down and feathers; sometimes contains charcoal that may blacken eggs during incubation; usually 5–20 m high in foliage, mistletoe or pandanus or in grasses, including spinifex, near ground. Eggs 5–6 or 8; white.

Range and Status: N. Aust: from Broome, WA, through Kimberleys and NT s. to Dun-marra–Macarthur R.; nw..Q. e. nearly to Burketown–Leichhardt R., s. to Mt Isa district. district. Common; sedentary.

676 BLACK-THROATED FINCH *Poephila cincta* Pl.86

Other names: Blackthroat, Black-rumped, Black-tailed or Parson Finch.

Field marks: 100 mm. Very like the Long-tailed Finch (675), which it replaces in ne. Aust., but *black bill and short black tail give it a more stumpy look*. Nominate race, widespread in e. Q and into NSW, has a distinctive white rump; race *atropygialis*, 'Black-tailed Finch', (and others) on C. York Pen. has a *black* rump. Imm: like adult, but paler. Habits like Long-tailed Finch.

Similar species: Long-tailed Finch (675).

Voice: Like Long-tailed Finch, but slightly deeper, hoarser; one call, possibly alarm, escort or contact-call, soft 'beck-beck-beckadeck'.

Habitat: Open grassy woodlands, grasslands with few large eucalyptus, also grassy scrublands, usually near watercourses; nearer coast, open grassy plains with pandanus.

Breeding: Nest: like Long-tailed Finch; in similar situations but also sometimes in hollow dead limbs and occasionally in holes in termite mounds, or underside of large nest of bird of prey. Eggs: 5–9; white.

Range and Status: Ne. Aust.: from C. York Pen. w. to Gulf coast and s. to se. Q and far ne. NSW; absent from or patchy on humid e. coast lowlands. Nominate race occupies the larger (s.) part of the range, from Inverell–McIntyre R., ne. NSW, where it is rare but perhaps spreading, n. to about Ingham–upper Burdekin R.–Richmond, Q, and inland to Cunnamulla–Barcaldine. Race *atropygialis* (and others) occupy remainder of range w. to Leichhardt R. in nw. Q and n. to Watson and Rocky Rs. on C. York Pen.; reported to intergrade with nominate race in a zone through the upper Einasleigh R.–Forsayth–Croydon. Common locally, but patchy. Sedentary.

677 GOULDIAN FINCH *Erythrura gouldiae*   Pl.85

Other names: Painted, Purple-breasted or Rainbow Finch.

Field Marks: 125–135 mm. One of Australia's most gorgeous birds, better known in captivity than wild. There are three distinct phases of head colours. *Black-headed*, male: *head black, finely margined pale-blue, grass-green above with pale-blue rump, tail black, ending in two long fine points; breast deep-lilac, rich-yellow below, shading to white*. Bill whitish. Female: duller, colours of underparts washed out. Imm: head greyish, shading into greenish olive back, wings and tail; pale-greyish brown below; bill blackish above, pale below. *Red-headed*, male: similar, but *forehead, crown and cheeks dull-crimson*, throat and chin black. Female: similar but duller, shade of crimson varies. Imm: as above. *Golden-headed*, male: *forehead, crown and cheeks rich ochre-yellow*. Female: duller. The colour-phases occur in all parts of range, frequently in mixed parties. Black-headed outnumbers Red-headed by about 3:1, Golden-headed very rare. Small parties or flocks in breeding season; larger flocks in non-breeding season, in which dull-coloured birds predominate. Feeds in grass and other low growth, rather than ground. Birds of a group often gather in late afternoon to feed, bathe or sit together. Fond of hot sunshine; sunbathes, and active in heat of tropical day, when most birds quiet. Shy; when disturbed flies directly to cover usually in tops of nearby trees. During wet season feeds much on flying insects.

Similar species: Star Finch (670). Blue-faced Finch (678): much deeper green; face blue; rump and tail reddish.

Voice: Quiet; contact-call, sibilant 'sitt', of one to four syllables; alarm-call, sharp repeated version.

Habitat: Grassy flats and trees near water, tall vegetation along watercourses; in wet season, drier woodlands, scrublands with spinifex.

Breeding: Nest: globular, poorly made, without entrance-spout and occasionally without roof; of dry grass with softer grasses for lining; 6–14 m high in tree hollow or hollow in termite mound, occasionally in low scrub or tall grass; eggs sometimes laid on debris in hollow, with little or no nest-material. Colonial; several pairs may breed in same tree or even same hollow. Eggs: 4–8; white.

Range and Status: N. and ne. Aust.: from Derby, WA, through Kimberleys and NT s. to Negri R. and Daly Waters, to Gulf coastal areas and n. Q s. to Cloncurry, Hughenden and Upper Burdekin, e. to middle Herbert R., Atherton Tableland (where rare) and Coen, n. to lower Arther R. Partly migratory; formerly fairly common, now scarce.

678 BLUE-FACED FINCH *Erythrura trichroa*   Pl.86

Other names: Blue-faced or Tri-coloured Parrot-finch, Green-backed Finch.

Field marks: 120–125 mm. *A rich grass-green finch with black bill, cobalt-blue forehead and face; tail olive-brown, washed dark-red*. Female: duller, less blue on face. Imm: dull-green, without blue face. In NG and elsewhere, pairs to flocks of up to 20–30; in Aust., note range and rarity.

Similar species: Gouldian Finch (677): no colour-phase has a blue head, plumage not uniformly green.

Habitat: Coastal mangrove fringes through jungled foothills to clearings and fringes of

rainforest on tablelands. In NG, low sub-stage trees of forest, or dense secondary growth.
Breeding: Most recently in Aust. (March 1944) in rainforest at altitude of *c*. 1000 m on
foothills of s. slopes of Mt. Fisher, Atherton Tableland, ne. Q. Nest: rather pear-shaped,
more pointed toward bottom, with side-entrance; of curly green moss, dark fibrous
horsehair-like material and dead lawyer-vine strands; lined with dead grass; 7 m high in
slender saplings. Eggs: 3; (incomplete clutch?) swollen oval, white.
Range and Status: In Aust., a disappearing species or recent immigrant to Lloyd and
Double Is., highlands and foothills between Cairns and Innisfail. In addition to above
record, a pair, possibly with young, Ravenshoe, Dec. 1942. Few other Australian records,
none recent. Also Micronesia, Solomons, NG to Moluccas and Celebes.

679 PLUM-HEADED FINCH *Aidemosyne modesta* **Pl.86**

Other names: Cherry, Diadem, Plain coloured or Plum-capped Finch, Modest Grass-
finch.
Field marks: 100–112 mm. The most sombre Australian grass-finch. Male: *bill black,
forehead and chin dark-reddish purple or plum-coloured, cheeks white*; upperparts brown
with white spots on wings, indistinct whitish barring on rump; tail blackish, tipped white;
underparts almost wholly barred brown and white. Female: smaller purplish patch on forehead *separated from eye by fine white line* from bill; throat whitish; underparts less distinctly barred. Imm: brownish above, without or with less plum-coloured markings on
head; grey-white below, almost without barrings. Pairs, parties to flocks of several hundred. Feeds sedately on ground; climbs grasses. Flight fairly strong, slightly undulating.
Small parties quiet, big flocks reported to be noisy. Associates with other finches, especially Double-barred (673).
Similar species: Nutmeg Mannikin (683).
Voice: Reported to be a single 'tlip' or 'tleep', uttered perched or in flight: at times drawn-
out and high-pitched, like a Chestnut-breasted Mannikin (681). Song high-pitched,
scarcely audible.
Habitat: Taller grasslands, reeds, cumbungi and similar growth fringing riversides and
swampy areas; grassy flats with shurbs and some eucalypts at edge; lowlands, pastoral
country, to tablelands.
Breeding: Nest: small, rounded, taller than wide; no entrance-spout; of grass plucked
when green; sometimes lined with feathers; usually under 1 m high in tall grass or low
shrub or tree. Grasses growing round nest are frequently interwoven. Not known to make
roosting nests. Eggs: 4–7; white.
Range and Status: Mostly sub-inland e. Aust.: s. from about upper Burdekin R., Q, (rare
n. to Atherton), coastally s. from about Bowen to Rockhampton, mostly avoids coastal
districts of se. Q and ne. NSW; inland in Q to Winton–Opalton–Windorah–Quilpie and
the Paroo R.; inland in NSW (probably exceptionally) to Warrego Crossing (55 km w. of
Bourke), 60 km nw. and 12 km w. of Cobar, s. to Gooloogong (Forbes–Cowra)–Caper-
tree (ne. of Bathurst), occasional to ACT, and to near e. coast in lower Hunter R. Valley
and middle Hawkesbury R. (Richmond–Pitt Town) nw. of Sydney; vagrant (with Diamond Firetails–669) near Edenhope, w. Vic. Within these extremes very patchy, confined
to pockets of suitable habitat. Generally scarce, but locally abundant; apparently
nomadic according to conditions.

680 YELLOW-RUMPED MANNIKIN *Lonchura flaviprymna* **Pl.86**

Other names: Yellow-rumped, Yellow-tailed or White-headed Finch; Yellow-rumped
Munia.
Field marks: 100 mm. Distinctive; note large silvery grey bill, *fawnish white head and
plain whitish underparts washed yellow-buff on sides*. In the field, rump does *not* appear to
be distinctly yellower than that of Chestnut-breasted Mannikin (681). Imm: like imm.
Chestnut-breasted. Pairs or flocks; associates and in places interbreeds with Chestnut-
breasted, producing intermediates. The habits of the two 'species' are similar.

Similar species: Chestnut-breasted Mannikin (681): adult immediately distinguished by black face; imms difficult to separate in field.

Voice: Calls reported to resemble those of Chestnut-breasted, only more penetrating.

Habitat: Tall grasses near watercourses, grassy flats with widely spaced shrubs and trees; in places in rice and other crops.

Breeding: Nest and nest-sites like Chestnut-breasted. Eggs: 4–5; white.

Range and Status: Coastal nw. Aust.: from Derby, WA, through Kimberleys and coastal NT to King R. in Arnhem Land and beyond. Generally scarce, but abundant in parts e.g. irrigated areas on Ord R. Nomadic.

681 CHESTNUT-BREASTED MANNIKIN *Lonchura castaneothorax* Pl.86

Other names: Barleybird, Barley Sparrow, Bullfinch, Chestnut or Chestnut-breasted Finch.

Field marks: 100 mm. *Robust silvery bill contrasts with black face*; *broad chestnut band across breast above a narrow black band.* Crown and nape grey with fine black marks, back chestnut, *rump and tail yellowish rufous*; under tail-coverts black. Female: paler, duller. Imm: dull olive-brown above, tail ashy-brown; brownish buff below. Pairs to large flocks in nonbreeding season, imms often predominating. Feeds mostly in grass, and on ground, roosts in grass or reeds; takes flying insects. Normal flight undulating, but large flocks fly fast with swift simultaneous turns, somewhat like Common Starling (687).

Similar species: Yellow-rumped Mannikin (680): whitish head. Pictorella Mannikin (682): much greyer with whitish-scalloped breastband.

Voice: Bell-like notes, becoming a merry tinkling when a flock is put to flight; song of male very high-pitched wheezing, not easily heard.

Habitat: Grasslands near water, swamp-vegetation, coastal heaths, mangroves; overgrown wastelands and roadsides, pastures and cultivation, canefields, ricefields and other cereal crops; lantana thickets.

Breeding: Nest: small, globular, no entrance-spout, but entrance may be protected by hood; of green and dead grass; lined with finer grasses and plant-down; usually within 1 m of ground in long grass, reeds, crops, bushy shrub or bamboo. Eggs: 5–6, occasionally to 8; white.

Range and Status: Disjunct distribution in coastal n. and e. Aust. and some coastal islands: from Derby, WA, through Kimberleys and top end NT, and from Mitchell R. on w. coast C. York Pen. n. to Weipa (? and C. York proper) and s. on most of e. coast to Sydney area and Illawarra district, NSW; inland to Rolleston, Q, and Gloucester-middle Hawkesbury R. area, NSW. Common in Q and n. NSW and parts of Kimberleys, scarce in NT. Resident, nomadic, or part migratory. Feral from aviary escapes in several disricts e.g. some outer-Melbourne suburbs; Yellingbo, Vic.; and near Finniss, SA. Also NG. Introduced (? from Aust.) to Tahiti, New Caledonia and Society Is.

682 PICTORELLA MANNIKIN *Lonchura pectoralis* Pl.86

Other names: Pectoral or White-breasted Finch.

Field marks: 110–115 mm. Distinctive; male: bill robust, silvery-grey; *face and throat black, separated by a broad band of white scallops, from pinkish fawn underparts.* Upperparts grey, black on tail. Female: face brownish black, scallops on breast black and white. Imm: dark grey-brown above, whitish to fawn-buff below; face grey, no markings on breast, legs dull-pink. Pairs, small parties to large flocks in non-breeding season. Rather wary; feeds in tall standing grasses and on ground; takes flying insects. Associates with Yellow-rumped (680) and Chestnut-breasted (681) Mannikins.

Similar species: Yellow-rumped Mannikin (680): whitish head, yellow-brown rump and tail.

Voice: Usual call, single 'chip' or 'pik'; flock in flight lets fall continual rain of little 'chip' calls.

Habitat: Grassy woodlands, open grassy flats with sparse tall trees and bushes, occasionally in spinifex; favours taller grasses and similar growth near water; in places in crops.
Breeding: Nest: bulky, untidy, bottle-shaped without spout; of dry grass, rootlets, small twigs; lined with few feathers; usually under 1 m high in low bushes or tall grass, occasionally in spinifex. Eggs: 4–6; white.
Range and Status: N. Aust.: from Derby, WA, through Kimberleys and NT s. to Banka Banka–Alexandria; Gulf coast of Q, irregular summer visitor s. to Mt. Isa; se. to Richmond–Charters Towers, n. to Croydon–Georgetown. Nomadic, uncommon to locally common.

683 NUTMEG MANNIKIN *Lonchura punctulata* Pl.86

Other names: Nutmeg or Spice Finch; Spicebird, Ricebird; Common, Scaly-breasted or Spotted Munia.
Field marks: 105–115 mm. An introduced species, now well-established in coastal e. Aust. Rich-brown above, back and wings with a few whitish streaks, rump grey-brown, tail greyish yellow; *underparts whitish, heavily freckled dark-brown*; bill blue-grey. Imm. pale-brown above, plain-brownish yellow below. Pairs or flocks, sometimes very large. Feeds among grass, climbs tall grass or weeds; flicks wings, swings tail from side to side; perches fences, overhead wires. Associates with Chestnut-breasted Mannikin, (681), Plum-headed (679) and Zebra Finches (672), said to hybridize with Chestnut-breasted. Flight of single birds somewhat fluttering and undulating, but flocks fly fast and directly with simultaneous turns.
Similar species: Plum-headed Finch (679): purplish red forehead; wings more spotted with white; underparts barred brown on white. Chestnut-breasted Mannikin (681), imm: plain buff-brown below.
Voice: Contact-call, described as penetrating high-pitched 'kit-tee'; alarm-call, sharp creaking 'tret-tret'; jingling song.
Habitat: Wetter grasslands, cultivated areas, green crops; tall untidy growth along roadsides; enters urban areas.
Breeding: Nest: substantial, bottle-shaped, of coarse green grass, leaves and bark; lined with softer grasses and seed-heads; usually 1–10 m high in shrub or tree, often in colonies; also in sheds or other buildings. Eggs: 4–7; white.
Range and Status: Native to se. Asia from India to s. China, Philippines and Malay Archipelago e. to Tanimbar Is. Feral populations became established, apparently from aviary escapes, in parts of coastal e. Aust. after about 1940. Now locally common and abundant coastally from about Cooktown, ne. Q. to Moruya, s. coast NSW; inland to Miles–Meandarra, se. Q. In Q and coastal ne. NSW it may be displacing related grass-finches like the Chestnut-breasted.

684 RED BISHOPBIRD *Euplectes orix* Pl.85

Other name: Grenadier Weaver.
Field marks: 125 mm. Male, breeding plumage: spectacular; *head and lower breast black, contrasting with short orange-red cape extending from nape round upper breast*; lower back to upper tail-coverts scarlet; wings and tail pale-brown; under tail-coverts orange-red. Female: very different; sparrow-like, *including yellow-buff eyebrow*; *plumage buffish, with heavy dark streaks above*; *upperbreast and flanks streaked brown*; abdomen whitish, bill horn-coloured. Imm: similar, but feathers of upperparts with broader pale edges. Male eclipse 'winter' plumage: like female. Small to large flocks throughout year; polygamous, breeds in small colonies of one male and several females. Male has distinctive slow display flight; puffs feathers; wings make buzzing sound; darts after intruding males or chases females; on wing said to resemble enormous bumble-bee.
Similar species: House Sparrow (663), female.
Voice: Wheezing, mewing or twittering calls; in mating display, sizzling 'zik-zik-zik'.

Habitat: In Aust. reported in riverside reedbeds. In Africa, open grass-country and tall coarse vegetation usually near water; tall crops, open plains and short grass; bush-country, after nesting.

Breeding: Nest: domed with side entrance; woven of grass or reed-blades; slung between upright reeds over water; usually in groups of 2–7 or more nests, some of which may be old and in disrepair. Eggs: 4; uniform pale green-blue. More than one female may attend a nest.

Range and Status: Native to Africa from Senegal and Sudan s. to Cape. In Aust. a colony or colonies became established from aviary stock along the Murray R. near Murray Bridge, SA, in the late 1920s. Birds were occasionally reported elsewhere in se. SA. The colony is said to have succumbed during floods in 1956.

685   WHITE-WINGED WIDOWBIRD   *Coliuspasser albonotatus*

Other name: White-winged Wydah.

Field marks: ♂ 170 mm. ♀ 150 mm. Male, breeding plumage: *black with golden yellow shoulders and white on wing, tail broad and rather long* (*c.* 100 mm.). Female: very different; smaller, shorter-tailed and somewhat like a *large-billed yellowish female House Sparrow* (663). Note the yellow-buff eyebrow, upperparts broadly streaked yellow-buff and black, feathers of shoulders edged yellow; throat and upperbreast plain yellow-buff, underparts whitish. Male eclipse: like female but larger, and retaining the shoulder and wing-markings of breeding plumage. Imm: feathers of upperparts edged fawn; under-parts buff, chest and flanks darker. In e. Africa, desribed as 'Conspicuous birds locally common on open ground with long grass, usually seen sitting on grass-heads and spread-ing their long split tails'. In Aust. the polygamous males are reported to fly into the air above their large territories, fluttering down to an elevated perch, flipping wings and spreading tails; females also flip wings. Reported to form flocks in autumn–winter; when disturbed these swiftly wheel and turn.

Similar species: In Aust., except for possibility of related species of windowbirds feral near cities, it is only likely to be confused with House Sparrow (663), female.

Voice: Described as cheerful trilling.

Habitat: In Aust., open areas with rank vegetation bordering paddocks and swamps.

Breeding: Nest: spherical with large side-entrance; of woven grass-blades, lined with fine thin grass-heads with a few projecting as a sort of porch. Eggs: 2–3; pale-greenish blue, spotted and streaked brown and grey. (African data).

Range and Status: Native to Africa, nominate race ranging from s. Zaire and Tanzania s. to Natal. In Aust., a feral population, said to be from liberated aviary stock, first noted 1931 in Hawkesbury R. district, NSW (Wilberforce, Cattai, Pitt Town). Spasmodic reports from this area up to 1953 included breeding records and observations of a flock of males and *c.* 50 'brown birds' near Windsor; males in breeding plumage and partial eclipse subsequently caught and banded. In Jan. 1968, courtship activity observed. No further published reports up to July 1975.

Starlings and Mynas   Family *Sturnidae*

A varied family of medium-sized, often glossy blackish birds. Some African species in particular have brilliant eyes and gorgeous plumage, fleshy wattles or bare coloured skin on heads. Voices are mainly squeaky, creaking, wheezy or rattling, but some utter pleas-ant whistling notes; many mimic. Mostly gregarious, they feed in flocks and often breed in colonies. Nesting habits vary; most select hollows in trees, but some tunnel in banks; Common Starling (687) and Common Myna (688) often nest in buildings. The one native species, Shining Starling (686), builds hanging nests somewhat like those of weavers, in colonies. Since their introduction to e. Aust., Common Starling and Common Myna have extended well beyond settlement. Starling in particular displaces many native species from nest-hollows, and is doubtless partly responsible for their decline. It is a serious economic pest in orchards and vineyeards. Both it and Common Myna eat quantities of insects and larvae. For this reason the last was introduced to cane-growing and other agricultural areas of Q.

Food: Omnivorous.

Range: Most species in Eurasia and Africa; fewer in tropical Australasian region; one genus extends to Polynesia. One or two species introduced to other parts of the world including n. America and e. Aust.

Number of species: World 106; Aust. 3, including 2 introduced.

686 SHINING STARLING *Aplonis metallica* Pl.87

Other names: Glossy or Metallic Starling, Whirlwindbird.

Field marks: 215–240 mm. Distinctive: *brilliant glossy black with bright-red eye and longish sharply pointed tail*; feathers on neck long, pointed and slightly shaggy. Bill and legs blackish. Imm: differs; *duller and brownish above, whitish below, streaked darker and mottled grey on flanks*. Highly social, usually in chattering flocks that become very large after breeding. Feeds noisily on fruit of rainforest trees, also on nectar, insects. Conspicuous when nesting, with noisy chatterings and incessant coming and going. Breeds while still in imm. plumage. Flight swift and direct; flocks hurtle through and over rainforests. In sustained flight e.g. when passing between mainland and offshore islands, flocks travel very swiftly, rising and falling, from distance like Common Starling (687). Suns itself in high exposed positions, takes flying insects. Tame about settlement; roosts in street trees and on overhead wires in coastal towns in ne. Q; raids cultivated fruit, e.g. mulberries, paw paws.

Similar species: Spangled Drongo (692) distinct 'fishtail'; different demeanour and calls. See also Satin Bowerbird (694), male; Koel (373) and Trumpet Manucode (703).

Voice: Reedy wheezings, jeerings and chatterings; song somewhat canary-like, briefer but more fluty.

Habitat: Rainforest, coastal woodlands and scrubs, mangroves; gardens.

Breeding: Colonially, usually in tall isolated and often sparsely foliaged trees. Nest: hanging, bulky, oval; suspended from branch; of straws or vine-tendrils, pieces of palm-leaves, hair-like fibres and occasionally paper, lined with finer grass. Sometimes three or more nests joined together. Eggs: 2–4; pale blue-white, spotted and speckled brown and grey.

Range and Status: Coastal ne. Q and many coastal islands: from C. York s. to Mackay and occasionally to Gladstone, vagrant NSW; inland to Big Tableland near Cooktown and Atherton Tableland. Migratory, moving s. July–Sept. to breed and n. Feb.–April, to NG. Fairly common in coastal lowlands to 750 m; less common s. of Ingham. Also NG, Solomon Is. and Moluccas.

687 COMMON STARLING *Sturnus vulgaris* Pl.87

Other name: English Starling.

Field marks: 210 mm. A familiar pest in e. Aust. Note the longish *fine, pointed bill and short tail*; *plumage blackish, glossed bronze-green and purple*. In new autumn plumage, feathers of upperparts tipped buffish, those of underparts tipped white, *giving a general finely spotted appearance*; as tips become worn, spotted appearance decreases until in spring the birds are *mostly glossy black* with browner flight feathers. Throat-hackles longer and more pointed in male than female. *Bill pale-yellow in summer*, (base of mandible blue or blue-black in male, pinkish in female) *blackish in winter, legs red-brown*. Imm: plain dull mouse-brown, paler below, whitish on throat, bill and legs blackish. Usually in flocks, often very large in autumn, with imms. predominating. Jaunty, garrulous, quarrelsome; walks or runs about jerkily with quick jabs of bill into soil in sewing machine action. Flight swift; *travelling flocks typically rise and fall*. Noisy flocks conspicuous at roosts in reedbeds, large dense trees, city buildings, where nocturnal noisy chatter and mess often create a nuisance. Highly adaptable; feeds in many situations. Typical singing perch is top of dead tree, ridge of roof, chimney or TV aerial. Attracted to soft fruits, berries, grapes; serious pest in some areas, but probably beneficial in pastures.

Similar species: Blackbird (436): wholly black without spots; bill and eyering yellow to bright-orange throughout year; tail longer. Shining Starling (686), adult: wholly glossy black without spots; longer pointed tail; eye bright-red. Note range.

Voice: Song by male with slowly flapping wings; of wheezes, clicks, small thin rattles, some barely audible, and with characteristic descending whistle; accomplished mimic. Common scolding note, harsh descending 'tcheer', uttered in alarm by adults and insistently by imms; other alarm-call, sharp 'dick!', singly or staccato. Other notes.

Habitat: Urban areas: settled, cleared lands; pastoral country; many other open habitats including more open mallee; reedbeds; tidal mudflats, beaches; islands; alpine areas; gardens, orchards.

Breeding: Nest: rough, untidy open cup; often like a heap of grass, straw, wool, feathers and leaves, in tree hollow, stump of fence post, from which it often excludes or ejects native hollow-nesting birds; also old nests of babblers; holes in cliffs, walls, ceilings, roofs of buildings, abandoned farm machinery. Eggs: 4–5; plain blue-white.

Range and Status: Native to Europe and n. and w. Asia, introduced S. Africa, NZ, Oceania and N. America, and to Aust. in 1860s. Now well-established in e. Aust. and many coastal islands from about the Tropic in Q to Eyre Pen., Kangaroo I. and w. SA. In Q, inland to about Roma; in NSW, Vic., Bass Strait islands and Tas., nearly throughout; in SA n. to Oodnadatta–Birdsville Track, and w. to Ooldea; records from Bight coast at Nullarbor Station, far-w. SA and small numbers recently w. to near Eucla, WA; also extending coastally n.: occasional records from Innisfail, Cairns, Port Douglas, Iron Ra., and Port Moresby, NG. Common, very abundant. Dispersive, nomadic, or migratory. Several long-distance banding recoveries, e.g. bird banded Oatlands, Tas., on 12 Sept. 1959, recovered Brisbane, Q, 11 Oct. 1959, a distance of 1960 km in 29 days.

688 COMMON MYNA *Acridotheres tristis*   Pl.87

Other names: Indian Myna or Mynah.

Field marks: 230–255 mm. A sturdy *cocoa-brown bird with yellow bill, bare yellow skin behind eye, glossy black head and throat; legs yellow.* Imm: duller. Pairs or flocks; gregarious and garrulous; feeds much on ground; scavenges, walking bandily or exaggeratedly hopping. In flight, note *large white patch on rounded black wings, broad white tips to black tail.* Raids soft fruits and berries; can cause economic loss. Forms communal roosts, in street-trees, under bridges, in factory buildings; in some situations, several thousand birds may be involved, creating serious nuisance.

Similar species: None, but do not confuse by name with Noisy Miner (590) and congeners; these are honeyeaters.

Voice: Various raucous creaky notes, growls and rattles, often strung together as song; on taking flight, a mellow liquid note. Alarm-call, harsh 'scairr!', somewhat like tearing cloth.

Habitat: Urban areas; pastoral and agricultural districts near towns; in e. Q commonly in canefields.

Breeding: Nest: of grass, twigs, straw and feathers, sometimes including paper; in cavity of building, tree-hollow or as bulky open nest in dense foliage. Eggs: 4–5; glossy, pale-blue.

Range and Status: Native to Afghanistan, Russian Turkestan, India, Sri Lanka, Indo-China and Malaysia. Introduced S. Africa, NZ and Pacific islands; to Aust. in early 1860s and later. Now present in many urban and agricultural areas of e. Aust.: well-established in ne. Q, coastally from about Mossman–Atherton tableland s. to Mackay; in se. Q, from Darling Downs to Brisbane area (? recently) and coastal ne. NSW; well established in Newcastle–Sydney–Illawarra region, inland at least to Blue Mts. plateau; ACT (recently); well-established in Vic., becoming widespread, from Melbourne e. to Orbost, w. to Geelong–Ballarat, through c. Vic., and extending in Murray Valley between Cobden–Swan Hill (where rare); in Tas., an early introduction near Hobart apparently failed, but reported near Launceston 1967, and elsewhere in n. Tas. In SA, first reported n. suburbs of Adelaide in 1957, where a small (? expanding) colony persists. Locally common, often very abundant. Sedentary.

Orioles and Figbirds Family *Oriolidae*

A closely knit, mostly tropical family of rather robust birds the size of large thrushes. Wholly aroboreal, they feed mostly on fruit, berries and insects. In orioles the bill is longish, slightly curved and often pink; many have bright-yellow and black in their plumage, a conspicuous and widespread member being the Golden Oriole *O. oriolus* of the Old World. American orioles *Icteridae* are a different family. The two Australian orioles are more softly coloured than typical members and have dark streaks. The other genus in the family, the figbirds *Sphecotheres*, confined to the Australasian region, has one species only. Figbird (691), distinguished by shorter bill, bare coloured skin round the eye, and by different plumage-pattern. Males are unstreaked, females brownish or greenish and heavily streaked. Figbirds are gregarious, travelling and feeding in parties or flocks; calls and nest also differ. In Aust., as elsewhere, members of the family are either nomadic or migratory in response to seasonal availability of fruits and insects.

Food: Chiefly fruits, insects and their larvae.

Range: Eurasia, Africa, Indonesia and the Australasian region, excluding NZ.

Number of species: World 27; Aust. 3.

689 OLIVE-BACKED ORIOLE *Oriolus sagittatus* Pl.87

Other names: Cedarbird, Cedar Pigeon, Greenback, Green Thrush.

Field marks: 260–280 mm' A graceful largish thrush-shaped bird; *crown, cheeks and back olive-green, finely streaked black*; *underparts creamy white with dark tear-shaped streaks* (male washed olive-green on throat and breast). Tail grey-green, tipped white. Bill longish and slightly arched; deep-pink in male, duller pink in female; eye red, legs black, Imm: bill and eye blackish; greyish above, feathers edged rufous. Singly, pairs or small autumn –winter flocks. Usually heard before seen, often rather wary. Feeds in foliage on insects, larvae and fruits; takes flying insects; raids soft fruit in gardens, orchards; in n. parts of range associates in these activities with figbirds. Flight strong and undulating.

Similar species: Yellow Oriole (690): mustard yellow-green above *and below*; call even more distinctive. Figbird, (691), female: browner above, bill black, eye brown, surrounded by bare skin; throat looks brown at a distance; calls differ. Striped Honeyeater (582): call can be confused.

Voice: Usual call: highly characteristic rolling mellow quick and oft-repeated 'olly, ollyole', 'orry, orry-ole' or simply 'olio', that also forms basis of sustained song. Subsong includes mimicry, interspersed with scratchy warbles; harsh peevish scolding note.

Habitat: Wooded areas generally: rainforests, eucalypt woodlands, swamp woodlands, timber along watercourses; taller scrubs, including mallee; orchards, golf-courses, parks, gardens.

Breeding: Nest: deep somewhat untidy slung cup; of strips of bark, leaves, grass, moss and spiders' web, egg-sacs, occasionally wool or string; lined with grass or hair; suspended in or woven to a fork, 7–20 m high usually among hanging outer foliage. Eggs: 2–4; pale-cream, spotted and blotched brown, red-brown and grey.

Range and Status: N. and e. Aust. and some coastal islands: from Kimberleys WA, (s. to C. Baskerville, *c.* 80 km n. of Broome) to about Adelaide, SA; inland to upper Ord R., WA; Larrimah–Mallapunyah, NT; Mt. Isa–Barcaldine–Charleville–lower Moonie R.,

Q; e. NSW, inland to about Moree–Condobolin–Moulamein; vagrant Ivanhoe, Menindee; extends w. along Murray R. and associated red gum forests to Renmark–Waikerie, SA. In Vic., most forested districts n. to Murray R., but rare in nw.; through sw. Vic. into se. SA, w. to L. Alexandrina, Mt. Lofty Ras. and Adelaide Plains, occasionally breeding, Fairly common; mostly summer migrant in s., arriving Aug.–Sept., departing Apr.–May, with some overwintering; evidence of winter passage across Torres Strait. Also resident in NG.

690 YELLOW ORIOLE *Oriolus flavocinctus* Pl.87

Other names: Green or Yellow-bellied Oriole.

Field marks: 260–295 mm. Colour alone should simplify recognition: *rather dense mustard yellow-green above and below, head and breast finely streaked black*; flight-feathers black, these and wing-coverts margined and tipped pale-yellow. Bill longish, slightly arched, reddish pink; eye red; legs grey. Imm: more boldly streaked with yellow tips to wing-feathers. Bill browner. Singly, pairs or small flocks; feeds mainly in foliage of native trees on fruits, often with Figbird (691). Call is a characteristic sound near water in many parts of coastal n. Aust.

Similar species: Olive-backed Oriole (689). Figbird (691), female: browner, with dull-grey skin round eye; bill blackish.

Voice: Distinctive: often irritatingly repreated, a loud bubbling call of 3–4 notes on one level: 'yok-yok-yoddle'; also a clear 'pee-kweek'; aggressive call, a harsh 'scarab', also a sustained subsong of soft warbling notes.

Habitat: Rainforests, mainly in lowlands, luxuriant vegetation on watercourses, open woodlands, swamp woodlands, mangroves; plantations, orchards, gardens.

Breeding: Nest: deep, cup-shaped; of strips of bark and vine-tendrils; lined with twigs and rootlets; suspended in leafy outer branches, to 5–16 m high. Eggs: 2; creamish, spotted and blotched brown and grey.

Range and Status: Coastal n. Aust. and coastal islands: from about Derby, WA, to near Ingham, Q; through Kimberleys and top end NT s. to about Pine Ck. In ne. Q, C. York Pen., s. to Staaten R. on w. coast and s. to Ingham on e. coast, inland to upper Archer R.–Laura–Atherton Tableland. Common to fairly common. Also s. NG and Aru Is.

691 FIGBIRD *Sphecotheres viridis* Pl.87

Other names: Green, Northern, Southern or Yellow Figbird; Banana-bird, Mulberry-bird; Shrike.

Note that two forms, long regarded as good species, are now combined in a single species because they regularly interbreed in a broad zone in coastal e. Q between about Proserpine and Cardwell. S. of that zone, the race is *vieilloti*, 'Green Figbird', n. of the zone the race is *flaviventris*, 'Yellow Figbird'. In the hybrid-zone, and to the n. and s. of it, males with more-or-less green or yellow underparts may occur. Females of both races are fairly similar. Although females of both Australian races are illustrated, they are treated together in the following account.

Field marks: 275–295 mm. Male: *crown and cheeks black, with a patch of reddish skin round eye; olive-green above*. Race *vieilloti*, 'Green Figbird': throat, upperbreast and collar round hind-neck *dark-grey*, lower breast and flanks *olive-green*; abdomen and under tail-coverts creamy white. Race *flaviventris* 'Yellow Figbird': *throat and breast are bright-yellow*. Bill black, legs dull-pink, eye reddish. Female (both races): *dull grey skin round eye*; brown above, often washed olive-green; dirty white below, *with broad brown streaks, more finely and densely on throat, giving that area a brownish look*. Imm: like female, young males attain adult plumage at end first year; facial skin red, back becomes greener, Usually in flocks of ten to *c.* 50; feeds in foliage mostly on fruits; acrobatic, flutters, hangs head down; presence indicated by oft-repeated contact-note; perches overhead wires. Very mobile, flocks fly over rainforest or cross cleared country to reach isolated trees or other feeding area. Flight direct, undulating, *note prominent white corners* *to black tail.* Associates with other fruit-eating birds; raids soft fruit in gardens.

Similar species: Olive-backed Oriole (689). Yellow Oriole (690): from female Figbird by dull-pink bill, more uniform mustard yellow-green plumage; peculiar song.

Voice: Squeaky emphatic 'chyer!' or 'jokyer!' with downward inflection; also loud, clear, slightly-descending 'see-kew, see-kew' irregularly but often at times every 6–7 secs. Song, described as a strong mellow 'tu-tu-heer, tu-heer, tu-heer, tu-heer'; other small squeaky notes. Most calls have gay pleasant if squeaky quality; common sounds of parks and gardens in Sydney, Brisbane and many coastal towns in e. and n. Aust.; mimics.

Habitat: Rainforests, eucalypt forests and woodlands, swamp woodlands, vegetation on watercourses, mangroves; leafy trees on farms; in parks, streets and gardens; often in orchards.

Breeding: Nest: shallow, cup-shaped; fabric often loose enough to see eggs against light; of vines, stems, twigs, and roots; 6–20 m high in horizontal fork among outer foliage, several nests may be built in adjoining trees. Eggs: 2–3; dull apple-green to olive-brown, spotted or irregularly blotched in shades of red-brown, usually heavier at large end.

Range and Status: A species of several races, two occurring in Aust. Race *flaviventris*: coastal n. Aust. and islands in several (?isolate) populations, from Kimberleys, WA, in region of Prince Regent R., Mitchell Plateau and Manning Ck.; top end NT, s. to about Katherine; C. York Pen., s. to Normanton on Gulf coast, and s. to about Cardwell on e. coast. Race *vieilloti*: from about Proserpine, Q, coastally s. to about Kiama, s. coast NSW; vagrant Wellington, NSW, Berwick, Vic. The *species* is generally common, locally nomadic. Also Torres Strait islands, NG, Kai Is. and e. Lesser Sunda Is. Nominate race occurs Timor and Roti I.

Drongos   Family *Dicruridae*

A distinctive family of largish usually black, glossy, active birds that make spectacular swoops, curves and twists after flying insects. They are aggressive and our species has been reported to kill small birds. Wings are longish and the tail varies greatly: typically longish, forked and flared outwards at the corners, giving a fishtail appearance. Bill stout, somewhat arched and hooked, with luxuriant bristles. Voice usually harsh and metallic; nest is a fragile cup of stems, slung from small branches in outer foliage. The one Australian representative, Spangled Drongo (692), migrates n. in winter to NG and elsewhere.

Food: Mainly insects, often taken on wing.

Range: Mainly tropical, in Africa, Asia and the Australasian region excluding NZ.

Number of species: World 20; Aust. 1.

692 SPANGLED DRONGO *Dicrurus hottentottus*   Pl.87

Other names: Drongo-shrike, Fishtail, King Crow.

Field marks: ♂ 320 mm; ♀ 295 mm. An often frantically active *black bird with large head and longish 'fishtail'*; head and back dull-black, wings and tail more glossy; subtle glossy-green spots on crown, neck and upperbreast. Bill black, robust, with prominent hairlike feathers, eye bright-red. Imm: dull smoky black, with brown eye, scattered white spots and blobs on underwing, central abdomen and under tail-coverts; these disappear slowly with age; some adults retain white spots on underwing. Singly, pairs, migratory parties or open companies. Noisy and pugnacious; sits motionless, shrugs shoulders, flicks tail, dashes in pursuit of insects (or small birds) in air, on trunks, limbs and in foliage of trees. The red eye and raised feathers of crown give it a slightly mad look. *Flight swift, swooping, erratic.* Courting male performs unusual display-flight, climbing to about 30 m before diving with wings arched back and tail cocked, calling. Pairs display facing, with spread wings. Takes nectar from blossoms.

Similar species: Koel (373), male: pale bill. Shining Starling (686): smaller, glossier, with pointed rail. Black Butcherbird (716): larger blue-grey bill; short, straight tail.

Voice: Harsh chattering notes; a tearing 'shshashash', while perched and in flight; strange metallic notes, some like a well strained wire-fence being twanged.

Habitat: Rainforest, mainly at edges; isolated leafy trees in farmland, eucalypt forests and woodlands, swamp woodlands, coastal scrubs, mangroves; also leafy trees along watercourses, roadsides; parks, garden.

Breeding: Nest: delicate, basket-shaped; of twigs and vine tendrils, bound with spider's web; slung in horizontal fork in outer foliage 10–20 m high. Eggs: 3–5; pinkish or purplish white with blotches and wavy streaks of pinkish red, brown and purple. Shows tendency to return annually to same nest-site.

Range and Status: Coastal n. and e. Aust. and coastal islands: from Kimberleys e. through top end NT, s. to Pine Creek and occasionally to Katherine; e. to Oenpelli and probably along Gulf coast into Q; w. coast C. York Pen., and all Q e. coast; inland to Coen–Laura–Atherton middle Burdekin R.–Chinchilla–Toowoomba; in NSW mostly e. of Divide, occasional s. in summer to far-e. Vic. (Mallacoota); summer vagrant elsewhere, once to an unnamed location 560 km nw of Sydney. Common s. to ne. NSW, regularly breeding s. to about Macksville; uncommon s. to Sydney, rare s. of Syndey. Strongly migratory, with a general movement in Sept.–Oct. and n. movement in Apr.–May, many north-bound birds apparently crossing Timor Sea and Torres Strait. But there are other puzzling movements. Regular wintering has been noted at Moreton Bay, Q, and on c. coast NSW, (from Forster–Hunter R. Valley–Newcastle–Sydney, s. at least to Moruya); winter vagrants recorded near Melbourne and in n. Tas, also mid-n. SA (Koolunga, 13 May '74), the only SA record. Also Solomon Is. and from NG through Indonesia to Malaysia and s. Asia.

Birds-of-paradise and Bowerbirds   Family *Paradisaeidae*

A remarkable family confined to Aust. and NG. Above all else, bowerbirds are distinguished by construction of bowers in which displays and mating take place. These are not 'playgrounds' as so often stated, but form the psychological centre of male territory. In Aust. they are mostly of two types. Avenue-bowers: a double avenue of twigs or grass built on a platform of sticks on ground. Maypole-bowers: a single or double column of sticks built round saplings. The owners of bowers deposit in them natural or artificial objects usually of a particular colour, or reflective. There is correlation between these shades and textures and the plumage of the species concerned. Thus male Satin Bowerbird (694) with glossy dark-blue plumage, blue eyes and blue-white, yellowish-tipped bill, chooses mostly blue or yellowish display-objects, whereas the differently coloured Spotted Bowerbird (696) chooses pale-coloured, reddish or shiny objects. During display, males react to these objects as they would to intruding rival males. The instincts that in male bowerbirds lead to bower-construction and painting are thought to be derived from those formerly directed to nest-building and feeding of young, now the province of females alone. Bowerbirds are highly active and vocal and claim territory by voice and display. In avenue builders, this is typically a strange, stiff-legged dance, accompanied by flaring wing-movements, whirrs, wheezes and hisses. In maypole-builders, represented in Aust. solely by Golden Bowerbird (693), it is a spectacular hovering over and near the bower. In contrast, Tooth-billed Catbird (699), a species without strong markings, displays mainly while singing, perched over the simple display arena. Nests of bowerbirds are shallow cup-shaped structures of twigs in foliage or branches, usually near bower. Eggs are usually cryptically marked and coloured. As a rule bowers fall into disrepair after the breeding season, and adults and imms form loose mobile parties or flocks. An appetite for cultivated fruit and grapes has often turned the hand of man against bowerbirds and great numbers have been shot. Probably as a result, Satin Bowerbird has been virtually exterminated in Melbourne's Dandenong Ras., and Spotted Bowerbird has declined to near-extinction in nw. Vic. and the fruit-growing districts of the Murray Valley. Both are still common elsewhere. Birds-of-paradise are confined to NG, adjacent islands, and coastal e. Aust. The true birds-of-paradise of NG are spectacular and varied, typically with brilliant glossy shot-colours and exaggerated plumes. The family is represented in Aust. by Trumpet Manucode (703) and by two species of riflebirds (701–2). Male riflebirds have spectacularly rich-plumage, moss-like on the head, and gorgeously shot with colours; one species has long flank-plumes; females are brownish. Riflebirds are active, feeding on trunks, rotting stumps and logs somewhat like treecreepers but also taking fruit and berries. As in bowerbirds, the outstanding behavioural feature is the (arboreal) display of males. Nesting is the province of the female alone. The nest is scanty and often hard to locate; eggs are distinctive, marked with longitudinal streaks. The remaining bird-of-paradise in Aust., Trumpet Manucode (703), is much less spectacular and noted mostly for its strong voice.

Food: Mostly fruits, berries, leaves and insects and their larvae.

Range: NG and adjacent islands to the Moluccas; coastal e. and ne. Aust.

Number of species: World 61; Aust. 11.

693 GOLDEN BOWERBIRD *Prionodura newtoniana* Pl.88

Other names: Golden or Queensland Gardener, Newton's Bowerbird.

Field marks: 230 mm. Male: striking; *pale golden-olive above, with a small erectile patch of bright yellow on rear of crown and a much larger patch on the nape. Throat and under-parts golden yellow*, pale lower; intensity of yellow varies: rich golden in some, paler in others. Central tail-feathers brown or part-brown, *outer feathers wholly yellow*. The plumage is glossy and opalescent, flashing in sunlight. Bill brown, eye pale-yellowish white, legs slate-blue. Female: olive-brown above, ashy grey below; tail shorter than male; bill brown, legs black. Imm: like female, but imm. males have slightly golden tinge above. Singly or pairs, usually seen at or near bower. Active when feeding, takes fruit and insects among foliage and on ground. When bower is in use, mostly Sept.–Feb., male spends much time rearranging decorations; he displays in spectacular vertical hovering over bower or nearby; postures on vines and trunks, crest raised, tail fanned, wings raised or fluttered; head jerking, or thrust forward until head and tail form a bow-shape round perch. When not at bower or feeding, male typically sits for long periods on nearby perch, preening and calling. Smaller sub-bowers are built in vicinity.

Bower: the only Australian example of a maypole-bower; despite the size of the bird it is by far the largest structure made by an Australian bowerbird. Construction differs according to site. Roughly U-shaped, of two tall columns of sticks up to 3 m high and usually of uneven height, built round vertical saplings a metre or more apart and usually joining in mass at base. Between walls at heights from 150 mm to about 1.2 m from ground is a horizontal display-perch, usually branch or vine, the centre of which is kept bare by bird's constant attendance. On either side of perching position, bird places pale-green, sometimes brownish, lichen and freshly plucked pale flowers, usually orchids, on walls of bower.

Voice: Near bower, male utters a frog-like croak, preceded by rattling noise like rubbing together of branches or the ratcheting noise of a fishing reel; a single call like Grey Shrike-thrush (472) is reported; like other bowerbirds, it uses accomplished mimicry in its vocal displays.

Habitat: Tropical highland rainforests.

Breeding: Nest: shallow cup; of dead leaves, ferns and dry moss, lined with thin twigs; usually in cavity in protected position near ground against tree-trunks. Eggs: 2; oval, glossy; white without markings.

Range and Status: Confined to a small broken range in highlands of ne. Q, from Mt. Cook, near the Endeavour R., s. to about Mt. Spec, near Townsville; the range includes rainforests in parts of Atherton Tableland and the Bellenden Ker Ra. Usually above 900 m, occasionally lower in winter. Locally fairly common; sedentary.

694   SATIN BOWERBIRD   *Ptilonorhynchus violaceus*   **Pl.88**
Other names: Satinbird.
Field marks: 280–320 mm. Male: *wholly glossy blue-back*; *exposed part of bill bluish white, yellowish at tip*; *eye blue, legs pale-greenish yellow*. Tail rather short, and this is noticeable in flight. Female differs: blue-grey to olive green above, wings and tail tawny brown; fawn-white below with feathers margined dark-brown, *giving a fine scaly appearance*. Bill dark-brown, eye purplish blue, legs dull-greenish yellow. First-to-third year imm are like female, but fourth year males have chin and throat green with fine white spots and streaks and a green zone across the lower throat and breast. After fourth year, bill becomes paler and blue or partly-blue feathers appear in plumage. Adult male plumage is assumed in about the seventh year. Usually noticed in autumn–winter flocks of 20–50+, mainly of green birds, occasionally with a few blue males; often raids fruit, roadside blackberries. A robustly active bird; on ground hops vigorously; leaps between branches; flies strongly with marked undulations and swoops, wings thrown out and closed repeatedly, wingtips markedly unswept on each downstroke; note shortish tail. During breeding season (variable, but mostly within July–Feb.) imms associate in construction of 'practice' bowers, but adult males and females more solitary, former building, maintaining and displaying at bower, latter nest-building and feeding young. Males are promiscuous, attempting to mate with any submissive female attracted to bower.
Bower: of avenue type; a convex layer of twigs on ground roughly 1 m in diameter, but usually longer than wide, and 50–75 mm deep. Toward one end, two parallel arched walls of twigs form an avenue about 350 mm high and 450 long. Twigs of inner walls often partly crusted with dried macerated green leaves, wood-pulp or charcoal, applied by the bird. Inside avenue and on platform, bird deposits blue, greenish blue or yellow display-objects: flowers, feathers, parts of insects, berries, broken glass, crockery, plastic stolen from habitation. Bower rebuilt from mid-winter on and usually maintained until early summer, sometimes re-oriented. Owner spends hours perched overhead, uttering territorial call or mimicry, interspersed with bower-maintenance and display, mostly in mornings. During display, a female typically stands inside avenue at rear: male seizes a display object in bill and adopts trance-like poses with feathers partly raised and head low, eyes flushing lilac-pink; leaps sideways, flashing open wings and tail, performs repetitive mechanical dancing motions, uttering wheezing whirring notes. Mating takes place in or close to bower.
Similar species: Koel (373), male: longer tail, red eye; habits and calls differ. Spangled Drongo (692): black with greenish gloss, black bill, red eye, fish-like tail; habits and call differ. Green Catbird (700).
Voice: Territorial call of male, loud ringing 'wee-ooo'; at bower, many strange calls, including peculiar mechanical wheezes, whizzings and whirrings, also hissing notes; and mimicry.
Habitat: Rainforests, wetter eucalypt forests and woodlands of Divide; in autumn–winter, lower, more open woodlands and scrubs and nearby cleared paddocks, also orchards, parks, gardens.
Breeding: Nest: shallow, saucer-like; of sticks, lined with leaves; usually in fork in head of tree in forest; occasionally in mistletoe, to 16 m; usually within a few hundred metres of active bower. Eggs: 2, occasionally 1, rarely 3; cream to buff, spotted, blotched or streaked brown and slate-grey.
Range and Status: Broken range on Gt. Dividing Ra. and coastal e. and se. Aust. (1) Highlands of ne. Q, mostly above 600 m, from Atherton Tableland s. to the Seaview Ra., near Townsville, inland to Herberton Ra. (2) Coastal e. Aust., larger coastal islands, and wetter forests and valleys of the Divide, from about Cooroy, Q, s. coastally to about the Gippsland Lakes, Vic. and w. in the high country of e. and ne. Vic. to about Eildon–Marysville–Garfield; occasionally vagrant w. to Dandenong Ras., Melbourne suburbs and Creswick, Vic. (3) Otway Ras., Vic., sw. from about Airey's Inlet. Common, but extinct since settlement in parts of former range, e.g. Dandenong Ras., Vic. Still fairly

common in suitable habitat in the vicinity of Brisbane, Sydney, Canberra; (?) local autumn–winter dispersal mostly by 'green birds' to more open lowland habitats, with subsequent near-total disappearance from these areas in spring. But at Leura, Blue Mts., NSW, large winter concentrations occur from May until late Sept., before dispersal.

695 REGENT BOWERBIRD *Sericulus chrysocephalus* **Pl.88**

Other name: Australian Regentbird.

Field marks: 250–300 mm. Male: one of our most striking birds; velvety jet-black, with *crown, nape and inner part of wings bright golden-orange*; bill and eye yellow, legs black. Female: slightly larger and longer-tailed; olive-brown above with *large black patch on rear of crown, pale-grey mottling on mantle*; fawn-white below, black mark down centre of throat; feathers of underparts margined blackish brown, looks patterned. Bill blackish, skin at gape golden-yellow in breeding season, *eye yellow with brown flecks*; legs blackish. Imm: like female, eye dark-brown, but imm males may have bill and eye yellowish; imms of both sexes may have yellow feathers on crown and nape. Dark-eyed females known to breed. Males probably attain full adult plumage at about five years: often seen only as a flash of gold-and-black in quick, starling-like, flight betwen cover; in mornings and evenings, they perch conspicuously at or near the top of tall living or dead forest trees. Otherwise singly, pairs to flocks of 40+ in the nonbreeding season, predominantly of 'brown birds'; typically feed in low thickets on margins of rainforests, cleared lands, or dense growth in gullies. Attracted to fruit in orchards and gardens; tame in gardens where fed.

Bower: smallest Australian avenue-type; a platform of twigs on ground, 50 mm thick, into which are securely anchored two parallel walls of twigs 150–200 mm long, 50–75 mm wide (100 mm wide at base) and 240–300 mm high, forming avenue 90 mm wide at platform level and 65 mm wide at top of walls, some twigs forming an arch overhead; area round bower often has carefully swept appearance, but bower frequently untidy; rather few display-objects: shells, seeds, fresh leaves and coloured berries. Display consists of dance, often with display-object in bill, wings spread. Bower secluded, seldom found.

Voice: Seldom heard: in display, low chattering like Common Starling (687); a tearing rattle when chasing. Captive male reports to warble softly and sweetly. Also scratchy wheezy ventriloquial calls; mimics.

Habitat: Rainforests and vegetation round their margins; coastal scrubs; thickets of wild raspberries, wild tobacco, inkweed; secondary growth in clearings; orchards, gardens.

Breeding: Nest: somewhat loosely made saucer; of twigs, lined with finer twigs; usually 4–10 m or more high in mass of creepers in rainforest. Eggs: 2; pale-brownish buff, marked and marbled with irregular lines of dark-brown and purple.

Range and Status: Wetter parts of Gt. Dividing Ra. and coastal areas of e. Aust. from Eungella Ra. near Mackay, Q, s. to Gosford area, and to near Cattai, c. 35 km nw. of Sydney, NSW. Fairly common, sedentary or locally nomadic.

696 SPOTTED BOWERBIRD *Chlamydera maculata* **Pl.88**

Other names: Mimicbird; Western Bowerbird.

Field marks: 250–300 mm. A robust brown bird with a *strong, slightly arched dark bill and with bold rufous-buff spots on wings, upperparts and rump*; on nape, iridescent rose-pink crest, usually visible only in display, when shaped like inverted fan. Female: similar, crest smaller, said to become larger with age. Imm: more heavily marked on throat and breast; without crest. Race *guttata* 'Western Bowerbird': more richly coloured; *blackish above, on throat and upperbreast, with prominent pattern of large golden-cream to rich-buff spots*, smaller on throat and upperbreast; underparts yellowish buff. Singly or loose parties; active and rather shy.but bold round habitation and camps. Feeds in foliage and branches; may display in these as well as at bower. Flight strongly undulating and swooping, wingtips upswept.

Bower: avenue type; usually beneath overhanging branch of tree or in such low cover as lignum; thick layer of sticks and twigs, at one end a double, arched wall of twigs and grass-stems (sometimes wholly of grass) 375–750 mm long; 150–225 mm apart and 250–500 mm high. On platform, and in bower itself, many display-objects, typically reddish, whitish or shiny: faded bones, snail or mussel shells, small green native figs or berries. Bowers near habitation contain broken glass, cartridges, nails, spoons, coins etc. etc.

Similar species: Great Bowerbird (697).

Voice: An extraordinary variety of calls. During displays, loud churring grating hissing or 'throat-clearing' noises; mimicry in vocal display.

Habitat: Inland scrubs, drier open woodlands, timber on watercourses; in interior, rocky hills where water is present and native figs occur.

Breeding: Nest: shallow flimsy saucer; of twigs, scantily lined with leaves; in fork to 16 m high, usually within few hundred m. of active bower. Eggs: 2, occasionally 3; grey to greenish, usually with dark-brown wavy or thread-like markings.

Range and Status: Inland e., and interior and w., parts of continent. Nominate race: widespread inland e. Aust.; in Q, n. to Mt. Isa–upper Flinders R., e. to Barker's Knob–Charters Towers–Nebo–lower Dawson R.–Inglewood; in NSW, e. to about Warialda–Gilgandra–Barellan–Moulamein, becoming very rare in sw. NSW, occasional Moula-mein, Barham, Euston areas and adjacent nw. Vic. (Murrabit, Benjeroop and Kulkyne State Forest); rare stragglers w. along the Murray R. into SA, where once numerous downstream to Swan Reach; extends far-w. in Q and NSW, but precise limits little-known. Race *guttata*: in interior, mostly confined to rocky hills where native figs occur; from Everard and Musgrave Ras., nw. SA, through ranges of s. NT, e. to Jervois Ra. and n. to MacDonald Downs–Mt. Allan, thence w. to Rawlinson and Warburton Ras., WA, and (? separate population) n. to Pilbara region, w. to about Exmouth Gulf, and s. and w. to North-West Cape Ra., the middle Gascoyne R. and Cue–Kathleen Valley–Leonora. Locally common, generally rather uncommon. Sedentary, or nomadic in nonbreeding season.

697   GREAT BOWERBIRD   *Chlamydera nuchalis*   Pl.88

Other names: Great Grey or Queensland Bowerbird.

Field marks: 340–375 mm. A large, active plain-coloured bowerbird with dark, strongly arched bill, plain unmarked throat; upperparts greyish fawn, with darkish marks on crown; wings, back and rump brown, *greyish-white margins and tips to feathers giving heavily mottled appearance*, tail tipped whitish. Lilac crest on nape usually visible only as small patch; in aggression or display, spread into inverted fan. Female: slightly smaller, paler, less mottled, often without crest. Imm: like female. Singly, pairs, small flocks in non-breeding season. Active, inquisitive, almost reptilian; cranes neck, bounds on ground, springs between branches. Often waters at cattle troughs or in gardens. Flight strongly undulating, wings abruptly out-thrust with eagle-like upswept tips; note arched bill. Displays on ground or branches away from bower; half-spreads wings, up-and-down 'knees-bends'. Display at bower includes upright and forwardly stretched postures, plumage flat, neck out-stretched; holds object in bill, or flicks tongue; ticks and hisses loudly, head lowered, turned, jerked abruptly to accompaniment of ticking sound; crest expanded. Circles bower in peculiar strutting walk, runs or bounds with raised wings; ruffles feathers, droops wings, cocks tail. Female may watch from overhead branch, or in bower.

Bower: Largest Australian avenue-type; more substantial than Spotted (696); under shrub or low leafy branch; a large platform of twigs, on one end two arched walls *c.* 100 mm thick, 600–1200 mm long and about 450 mm high, forming avenue 150 mm wide. At each end of platform, extensive display-ground with bones, shells, stones, pale leaves, occasionally flowers; also glass, nails, cartridge-cases etc. Collections sometimes enor-mous, often small green fruits, occasionally red objects, kangaroo droppings and other round things. When not displaying, male often quietly rearranges twigs or shifts objects; paints inner twigs with saliva mixed with coloured substances.

Similar species: Spotted Bowerbird (696): smaller, more richly-coloured and spotted, with fine streaks or spots on chin and throat. Ranges seldom met, but both occur in vicinity of Flinders R. near Hughenden and Barker's Knob, ne. Q.

Voice: Extraordinary song of high-pitched whistling notes; cacklings, chatterings, explosive hisses, noises like paper being crumpled or silk being shaken; liquid churring noises; mimicry of many other birds and other animals included in vocal displays. A harsh alarm-like White-winged Chough (712), uttered by several birds during threat-display.

Habitat: Drier eucalypt woodlands, scrubs and thickets, seldom far from water; timber along watercourses, drier coastal scrubs and in apparently waterless habitat on Cockatoo I., nw. Aust.

Breeding: Nest: a wide frail saucer; of twigs, lined with few leaves or finer twigs; eggs can often be seen from below; up to about 6 m in rather open tree, usually lower. Eggs: 1–2; oval; grey-green with brown, blackish brown and purplish slate squiggles and twists.

Range and Status: Coastal n. Aust. and islands: from area of Broome, WA, (? s. to Hamersley Ra.) through Kimberleys, top end NT s. to Larrimah; Gulf coast of Q, s. to Nicholson, O' Shannassy and upper Flinders Rs.; occasional s. to Mt. Isa, Q; n. to Cape York and coastally s. to near Mackay. Common; sedentary.

698 FAWN-BREASTED BOWERBIRD *Chlamydera cerviniventris* **Pl.88**

Field marks: 290–305 mm. A typical bowerbird: pale grey-brown above, feathers of mantle and wings finely margined and tipped buffy white, giving patterned appearance; throat streaked grey-brown and buff, *breast fawn, underparts yellow-buff*. Bill black, eye brown, legs pale-apricot. Singly, pairs or small parties; shy and wary, more often heard than seen; said to be noisy while feeding in vine-scrub but quiet at bower.

Bower: of avenue-type; compactly built, but varying greatly in size: an extensive platform of sticks, 50–100 mm (or more) deep, with walls 220–300 mm high, 375 mm long and about 75 mm apart; avenue narrow. Sticks of inner walls painted with coloured saliva. The bower itself, and platform are typically decorated with small green fruit or berries, sometimes many; also greyish leaves, leaf-shoots, pieces of shells; bleached bones or other pale objects. Usually in scrub, occasionally mangroves. In display, the male runs through and round bower with wings trailing, occasionally with display-objects.

Similar species: Great Bowerbird (697): larger, head and underparts more uniform fawnish grey.

Voice: Song described as slightly ventriloquial, weak but penetrating; includes harsh grasshopper-like notes overlaid by a kind of hoarseness; mimicry included in vocal displays. Alarm-call, harsh scolding churr.

Habitat: Mangroves, tea-tree scrubs, with areas of tall grass and scattered bushes; adjacent vine scrub; thickets along watercourses.

Breeding: Nest: bulky open saucer; of fine sticks, twigs and bark, usually to 10 m in tree or pandanus. Egg: 1; creamy white, prominently scribbled with bold and fine lines of various browns and greyish purple.

Range and Status: In Aust. only on n. C. York Pen. coastally s. to Jardine and Chester Rs. Locally fairly common; sedentary. Also NG.

699 TOOTH-BILLED CATBIRD *Ailuroedus dentirostris* **Pl.88**

Other names; Queensland Gardener; Stagemaker; Tooth-billed Bowerbird.

Field marks: 260 mm. Unspectacular: olive-brown above; *fawn below, streaked and mottled brown. Bill dark brown, robust,* with three serrations on cutting edge near tips of both mandibles; eye red-brown. Singly, to parties in non-breeding season. Seldom seen or heard from Jan.–July but from Aug.–Dec., when males maintain display-grounds, usually easily located by calls. Male occupies song-perch 1–6 m above display-ground: a roughly oval cleared space 1–3 m in diameter, decorated with many large leaves, pale underside uppermost, picked green by bird chewing with its serrated bill. In display, bird sits erect on song-perch with open bill pointed skywards, pouring out medly of sound; in the gloom, *pale palate and yellowish bases of throat-feathers* prominent. Where birds are abundant, several display-grounds may be placed within a few hundred metres of one another. Habits away from display-ground little known.

Voice: Powerful, varied and strange; song begins with low chuckling notes, develops into medly of sound described as beautiful whistling notes against background of noise like cloth being ripped; loud cheerful chirp, also soft low rasping notes. Vocal display includes accomplished mimicry of birds, other animals.

Habitat: Tropical highland rainforests and vine-scrubs; occasionally to nearby thickets and plantations.

Breeding: Nest: flimsy saucer of twigs; in vines or canopy of rainforest, 5–30 m high, often difficult to locate. Eggs: 2; oval; cream to creamy brown.

Range and Status: Highlands of ne. Q, from 600–1400 m, occasionally lower; from Cooktown s. to Mt. Spec near Townsville, Q. Common; sedentary.

700 GREEN CATBIRD *Ailuroedus crassirostris*   Pl.88

Other name: Spotted Catbird.

Field marks: 310 mm. *A robust deep-green bird with a sturdy pale bill, white spots on tips of secondaries and on outer tail-feathers*; *eye red-brown*, legs brown; pale streak on either side of throat. Imm: duller, bill greyer; eye browner. Race *maculosus* 'Spotted Catbird': smaller (290 mm); *head blackish with small buff spots*; *black patch on ear-coverts*; breast olive-green *spotted buff-white*. Pairs to small foraging flocks in autumn–winter. Often first noted by extraordinary calls; not shy, but often difficult to observe in foliage. Forages on fruit in rainforest canopy, vine-tangles and occasionally on ground; raids nearby orchards or fruit trees in gardens. Not known to construct a display-ground.

Similar species: Satin Bowerbird (694), female and imm: paler grey-green above with unspotted yellow-brown flight-feathers; fawnish below with scaly pattern; eye blue or brown; bill less robust.

Voice: Loud, harsh, extraordinary, varies locally. Typical call like yowling cat, frequently commencing before dawn: a nasal, drawling 'here-I-are'; uttered by single birds, pairs or several. During territorial display, male from display perch near ground utters one or more sharp clicking notes, followed by three very loud guttural cries, first longdrawn, last clipped. Also plaintive hissing notes. Calls of *maculosus* said to be less cat-like.

Habitat: Rainforests and margins, densely-foliaged gullies; nearby cultivated areas.

Breeding: Nest: substantial open cup; of vines and twigs with broad leaves or moss, lined with thin vines, rootlets or bark fibre; usually in tangle of vines or saplings but occasionally in fork of tree or top of treefern; usually 3–6 m high, but occasionally to 30 m. Eggs: 2; plain creamy white.

Range and Status: Broken range in coastal e. Aust., on Gt. Dividing Ra. and some coastal islands. Nominate race: from Mt. Dromedary s. of Narooma, NSW, n. to Kingaroy, Q. Race *maculosus*: from Mt. Spec. near Townsville, n. to Claudie R., far ne. Q. Common; sedentary. Also NG and Aru Is.

701 PARADISE RIFLEBIRD *Ptiloris paradiseus*   Pl.87

Other names: Lesser, Queen Victoria's or Victoria's Riflebird.

Field marks: 240–280 mm. Male: spectacular; longish curved bill and velvet-black plumage with *shimmering iridescent-green crown, throat, upperbreast and middle tail-feathers*; *feathers of underparts brightly margined rich olive-green*. Female: differs; brown above, wings and tail rufous; crown finely streaked white; long buff-white eyebrow, *dark-brown* *line down side of whitish throat*; *rest of underparts deep-buff*, with fine black arrow-like barrings. Imm: like female. Singly or in pairs; 'brown birds' tend to be seen most frequently. Usually first noted by unmistakable call or sound *like rustling silk* made by wings of male in flight. Behaves somewhat like a treecreeper; flicks tail, climbs trunks or branches; probes cavities, rotting logs and stumps; feeds on fruits, hangs acrobatically. Courting males fly between tree-tops, calling; display spectactularly on bare horizontal limbs lower in canopy, on dead limbs or tops of large stumps, expanding plumage, spreading wings, often hanging upside-down.

Similar species: Magnificent Riflebird (702): note range.

Voice: Typical call, a distinctive rasping 'y-a-a-a-ss' or 'yass yass'; a deep, mellow whistle.

Habitat: Rainforests, mostly in mountains and foothills; nearby wetter eucalypt forests, swamp woodlands.

Breeding: Nest: shallow cup; of green stems, vine-tendrils and few dead leaves, lined with fine stems and twigs; rim may be decorated with dry snake skin; usually in vines or canopy, 25–30 m high. Eggs: 2; pinkish buff, beautifully spotted and streaked chestnut, purplish red and purplish grey.

Range and Status: Broken range in coastal e. Aust., mostly in highland rainforests of Gt. Dividing Ra. to *c*. 1200 m. Nominate race: from upper Williams R., Barrington Tops, NSW n. to Cooroy, Q. The small race *victoriae*: from Mt. Spec NP near Townsville n. to near Cooktown; also some coastal islands. Fairly common in Q; uncommon to rare NSW. Sedentary.

702 MAGNIFICENT RIFLEBIRD *Ptiloris magnificus* Pl.87

Other names: Albert or Prince Albert Riflebird.

Field marks: 280–330 mm. Spectacular: plumage of male of a soft velvet-texture, parts very highly glossed; mostly black with *highly irridescent blue-green* crown, nape and central tail-feathers; centre of throat and upperbeast have small scale-like iridescent blue-green feathers, plumage of lower neck forming a broad erectile fan; *a narrow band of bronze-green to deep-red separates green upperbreast from blackish underparts*; *note long black hairlike tufts on flanks*. Bill longish and curved; tail short. Female: like female Paradise Riflebird (701) but more red-brown above, whiter below. Shy; habits like Paradise, but calls differ. Plumage of male also makes heavy rustling sound in flight. Males display spectacularly on high branches, shaking plumage like heavy silk, spreading wings, crouching and posturing. Display has also been noted between 'brown birds', possibly imm. males.

Similar species: Paradise Riflebird (701): note range.

Voice: Described as two loud sharp whistles for most of the year, but during breeding season, three loud clear whistles and long-drawn diminishing note; each of first three notes sounding like 'wheeoo', ending abruptly in note like 'who-o-o'. Both sexes utter this call, but voice of male louder.

Habitat: Tropical rainforest, monsoon forest and scrubs.

Breeding: Nest: deep but loose cup; of plant-fibres and large dry leaves, twigs and vines, lined with fine midribs of leaves and fibres; in fork of tree; butt of leaf of pandanus, or on stump among secondary growth, 1–10 m high. Eggs: 2; cream, streaked brown and greyish.

Range and Status: Coastal ne. Q, from C. York s. to Weipa on w. coast and to Chester R., n. of Princess Charlotte Bay, on e. coast. Fairly common; sedentary. Also NG.

703 TRUMPET MANUCODE *Manucodia keraudrenii* Pl.87

Other name: Trumpetbird.

Field marks: 315 m. A glossy blue-black bird with *slender elongated feathers falling from sides of head down nape and a pronounced violet-blue tone to the head, mantle and foreneck*;

tail rather long, 'gabled', Bill and legs black; eye of male red; of female orange; of imm brown. Singly or pairs; shy, usually feeds high in canopy, mostly on fruits; often hard to observe. Flight has been described as rather loose and disorganized. Call of male distinctive, usually uttered from a high branch. Display, spectacular; facing female, male raises and spreads wings, erects body-feathers, calls loudly.

Similar species: Koel (373) male: bill horn-coloured, no crest; calls and habits differ. Shining Starling (686): smaller, tail pointed.

Voice: A single, frequently-heard loud harsh call. Described as a resonant trumpet-like squawk, or a croaking 'yark'; its resonant quality is imparted by lengthening of the windpipe under the skin of the breast.

Habitat: Rainforest, vine-scrubs, eucalypt woodlands and forest.

Breeding: Nest: shallow basket; of vine-tendrils, rather open in construction, eggs often visible from below; usually in top of tree in tropical scrub or eucalypt forest, 6–22 m high. Eggs: 2; pale-pink, spotted red-brown and grey.

Range and Status: C. York Pen., in area of Cape York proper and e. coast and coastal islands from Claudie R. s. to Chester R., n. of Princess Charlotte Bay. Fairly common; sedentary, or partial summer migrant from NG. Also D'Entrecasteaux Archipelago, NG, Aru Is. and Indonesia.

Woodswallows Family *Artamidae*

A distinctive family of graceful, smallish songbirds that may have originated in Aust. They are not swallows, but may be distantly related to starlings. Alone among passerines they possess powder-down, which gives their plumage a distinctive bloom. Except for the chestnut-breasted White-browed Woodswallow (706), colours are generally soft browns and greys, with simple white or black markings. Their pointed bills are bluish with black tips. Their mannerisms are attractive; display consists of slow flapping with spread wings and opening and wagging tails. Highly social, they often perch close together in a group on a bare branch, preening, from time to time darting to take flying insects. On the wing their silhouette is rather like the Common Starling (687); the flight is graceful and absolutely diagnostic: quick shallow wingbeats, circling glides and soaring on shapely pointed wings and spread tails; but pursuing flight can be dashing. Most woodswallows are migratory or nomadic; during long-distance movements they often fly very high and a feature of spring and early summer in s. Aust. and winter in inland and n. Aust. is the sight and sound of open companies drifting far-overhead. In particular mass movements by Masked (705) and White-browed (706) Woodswallows often attract attention. In flowering woodlands of inland and sub-coastal n. Aust. in winter, they often associate with the Rainbow Bee-eater (406) and trillers (432–3), and frequently feed en masse on nectar of blossoms, gathered with the help of a brush-like, divided tip to the tongue. Insects are taken in flight and on the ground. Perhaps the most curious habit of woodswallows is that of forming swarms or clusters, a few to 50 or more gathering on the trunk or in a cavity of a tree, later arrivals clinging to those below, like bees. Such clusters are usually formed at night but they also occur on dull cloudy days, in both cold and warm weather. There is some evidence that clustering is practised to gain shelter from the wind, but the full significance of this curious behaviour is not understood.

Food: Mainly insects, also nectar.

Range: India, Sri Lanka and w. China through Malaysia and Indonesia to Aust. and islands of sw. Pacific, excluding NZ.

Number of species: World 10; Aust. 6

704 WHITE-BREASTED WOODSWALLOW *Artamus leucorhynchus* Pl.82

Other names: Swallow-shrike, White-rumped Woodswallow.

Field marks: 175 mm. Dapper; blue-grey above, browner on mantle, *white breast and* *underparts cut off sharply from grey throat*; *large white rump*; bill rather robust, pale blue-grey tipped blackish; tail has no white tip. Pairs or small flocks; often over water. In flight, *note sharply cut-off white underparts and white rump*; *wholly dark tail*.

Similar species: Masked Woodswallow (705): white border to black facial area; no pale rump; tail tipped white.

Voice: Brisk 'pirt, pirt' somewhat like toy-trumpet; soft plesant song includes mimicry.

Habitat: Usually near water; perches and nests in live and dead trees over rivers, lakes, swamps or floodwaters; islands in n. part of range, where often seen on jetties, channel markers; also mangroves, swamp-woodlands, river red gum forests.

Breeding: Often in companies or loose colonies. Nest: a rather substantial cup; of twigs and grass; situated at heights up to 25 m; in bunch of mistletoe, fork of a branch, at the end of a broken hollow or against trunk on protruberance or piece of bark; also in mangroves and occasionally in trees far out from shore in lakes or swamps; street trees in coastal towns, including palms. Often uses old nest of Magpie Lark (710) or less often of Welcome Swallow (420) as base; occasionally on a man-made support. Eggs: 3–4; creamish or pinkish white, freckled and spotted red-brown and dark-grey in zone at large end or evenly distributed.

Range and Status: Nw., n. and e. Aust. and coastal islands; from Shark Bay, WA, coastally n. and through Kimberleys; coastal NT s. to Elliott–Brunette Downs–Alexandria; most of Q s. from C. York. *except* waterless parts of w. and sw.; similarly through most of NSW *except* coastally s. of about Gosford, and s. Tablelands; n. Vic., mostly on lakes and tributaries of Murray R. w. of about Tallangatta; occasional s., e.g. to Werribee, Wyperfeld NP., vagrant King I., Bass Strait; in SA from far ne. and L. Eyre Basin s. to Murray R. and Lake Alexandrina. Regular migrant in s., arriving Aug.–Sept., departing Mar.–May; resident or irregular in n. Aust. Fairly common in suitable habitat, but distribution patchy in drier regions and dependent on the presence of water. Also Fiji to NG and Philippines.

705 MASKED WOODSWALLOW *Artamus personatus* **Pl.82**

Other names: Bluebird; Blue or Bush Martin; Skimmer.

Field marks: 175–190 mm. Male: beautiful mid-grey above, silvery grey or whitish below; *a large white-bordered black mask covers the forehead, face and throat*; all but inner two tail feathers broadly tipped white. Bill bluish, tipped black. Female: duller, lightly washed brown; shadowy grey mask, blacker round eyes, *without white border*. Imm: similar, mottled. Some adults paler than others, seeming almost aluminium-grey in sunlight. Pairs, parties to flocks of thousands; associates with White-browed Woodswallow (706) when migrating, feeding and breeding (occasionally interbreeds). White-browed usually predominates in such flocks in e. Aust., but the contrary in WA. Also associates with Black-faced (707) and Dusky (708) Woodswallows. In flight, *note black mask, pale-grey underparts and white tail tip*.

Similar species: White-browed Woodswallow (706), male: darker, with white eyebrow, chestnut underparts; female: small white eyebrow, rufous underparts. Black-faced Woodswallow (707): duller; much smaller mask without white border. Black-faced Cuckoo-shrike (427): much larger; no white border to black face; bill black, heavier.

Voice: Musical 'chap, chap'; also sweet, miner-like notes.

Habitat: Open forests, woodlands, scrubs, coastal heaths; pastoral country, orchards, vineyards, golf-courses. Travelling flocks temporarily inhabit many habitats from sparse inland mulga and spinifex to timbered ranges, farms, towns.

Breeding: Nest: scanty saucer; of twigs, grass and rootlets; in fork of low living or dead tree, against tree-trunk on bark, at end of hollow spout, on top of stump, in cavity in fence-post; usually 1–6 m high. Eggs: 2–3; variable; grey-white, green-grey or pale-brown, speckled or blotched brown and grey.

Range and Status: Widespread in mainland Aust.: migratory and nomadic, with very extensive but often irregular spring–summer movements into s. parts of continent to breed. Returns n. in autumn–winter, when large companies disperse through scrublands and woodlands of inland and n. Aust. In some years these movements involve many thousands of birds; in other years locally scarce or absent from many s. districts. Generally it is much less common in coastal e. and se. Aust. than Dusky (708) or White-browed but outnumbers the last in s. WA. In 1964, with the last, it reached King I. in Bass Strait for the first recorded time and occurred there again in 1970 and 1972–73, when several pairs bred. In WA it avoids the humid sw. corner, s. of Perth and e. of Albany, usually absent n. C. York Pen. and top end, NT.

706 WHITE-BROWED WOODSWALLOW *Artamus superciliosus* Pl.82
Other names: Blue Martin, Skimmer, Sky Summerbird.
Field marks: 190–210 mm. Male beautiful and distinctive: deep blue-grey above and on upperbreast, darker on head, paler on rump and tail, *with conspicuous white eyebrow*; *underparts rich chestnut to pale-rufous*, tail tipped white. Female: paler above, *smaller white eyebrow*; *underparts dull-rufous or mushroom-pink*. Imm: like female, mottled. Pairs, parties to flocks of thousands, often with Masked Woodswallow (705). White-browed usually predominates in e. Aust., the contrary in WA. Migrating, or nesting, companies may be encountered almost anywhere in s. Aust. in spring, summer and autumn, and nomadic flocks in inland and subcoastal n. Aust. in winter. The sound of their calls frequently attracts attention when overhead or when drawn together by abundant blossoming of eucalypts and other trees; when nectar-feeding, associates with honeyeaters, trillers (432–3); in flight, with Rainbow Bee-eaters (406). Overhead, *rusty underparts contrast with pale underwings*. Males high overhead can look almost blackish.
Similar species: Masked Woodswallow. (705).
Voice: Flight-call, musical 'chap, chap'; sweet miner-like notes and harsh scoldings; quiet song includes mimicry.
Habitat: Open forests, woodlands and inland scrubs; pastoral country, farms, vineyards, orchards, golf-courses; suburban parks and streets; occasionally coastal scrubs and margins of rainforests; travelling flocks occur in most habitats, from inland mulga-spinifex to coastal heaths, rainforests, towns.
Breeding: Nest: scanty shallow cup; of small twigs or grass; lined with rootlets; in horizontal fork, against tree-trunk on bark, at end of hollow spout, on top of stump, in cavity in fence-post; usually 1–6 m high. Eggs: 2–3; buff-white to grey green, spotted and blotched brown with underlying markings of grey, evenly or in zone at large end.
Range and Status: E. and inland Aust., irregular in WA, usually with Masked Woodswallows; uncommon and spasmodic coastal nw. Aust., C. York Pen. n. of Mitchell R. —Atherton Tableland, and coastal e. Q and ne. NSW, *except* as an irregular transient. There is a fairly regular movement into se. Aust. in spring and summer to breed, flocks reaching alpine and coastal areas. Total numbers in woodlands of red ironbark *E. sideroxylon* and other eucalypts in c. Vic. are frequently considerable, and this region is undoubtedly an important breeding-zone. In some years when ironbark blossom persists, many overwinter. In spring, 1972, unprecedented invasion by hundreds into coastal se. Q (Cooloola–Brisbane area), to King I., Bass Strait (where fairly regular spring visitor) and to n. Tas., (where previously unknown.) Bred King I. and (at least one pair) near Penguin, n. Tas. (Oct. 1972). Subsequent reports from Penguin, C. Portland, near Smithton, and from Memana, on Flinders I., (first record). Occasional spring visitor, Kangaroo I., SA. Regular n. movement in autumn, large nomadic companies winter in woodlands inland and sub-coastal n. Aust. May breed almost anywhere after suitable rains and blossoming. Fairly common; often very abundant locally.

707 BLACK-FACED WOODSWALLOW *Artamus cinereus* **Pl.82**

Other names: Grey or Grey-breasted Woodswallow.

Field marks: 175–200mm. The sombrest woodswallow: *smoky grey-brown, with small area of black round base of bill and eye*; wings grey, under tail-coverts black, often tipped white, *but wholly white* in race *hypoleucos* of e. Q. Some birds are more silvery-grey than others. Imm: mottled. Singly, pairs, small flocks and open companies. A bird of open country, usually flies lower in such habitat than other woodswallows; perches on tops of shrubs, telephone wires, fences, works into wind, darts after insects. Unlike other wood-swallows, often hovers up to 10 m high. In flight, pure-white underwings, but no white streak along leading edge; *black or white under tail-coverts*; black tail broadly tipped white.

Similar species: Dusky Woodswallow (708): browner, conspicuous white streak on wing; habits differ. Little Woodswallow: (709): smaller, chocolate-brown; different calls, habits and habitat. Masked Woodswallow (705): paler grey, with much larger black mask, margined white.

Voice: Not loud; sweet notes, scratchy 'chiff, chiff' or 'chap, chap'; animated small song includes mimicry.

Habitat: Open country generally: inland gibber, spinifex and sandhills to saltbush country and open grasslands, nearly treeless plains, often far from water; open wood-lands and scrubs, margins of lakes, swamps; irrigation areas.

Breeding: Nest: compact cup; of dry grass, stems and rootlets; lined with grass or occasionally horsehair; in shrub or small tree, on stump, in grass-tree or on a man-made structure. Eggs: 3–4; variable; glossy white to blue-grey, spotted and blotched red-brown with less distinct spots and dashes of purplish grey.

Range and Status: Widespread in drier open habitats in all mainland States and drier coastal islands: in Q, s. from Gulf coast and from Archer R. on w. coast C. York Pen. e. to Atherton Tableland, s. to about Rockhampton; seldom to coastal se.; inland NSW, e. to about Moree–Wellington–Cowra–Gundagai–Albury; occasional ACT and Kosciusko NP; in Vic., mostly on n. plains, e. to about Echuca, s. to about Charlton; in SA, s. to the Murray R. and (occasional) to L. Alexandrina in e. and to n. Eyre Pen.–Bight coast in w.; in WA, nearly throughout *except* forested areas of far sw.; in NT, throughout. Common; sedentary or part-nomadic. Also Timor; (?) vagrant to w. NG.

708 DUSKY WOODSWALLOW *Artamus cyanopterus* **Pl.82**

Other names: Beebird, Blue or Jacky Martin, Bluey, Cherry-bird, Skimmer, Summer-bird, Woodmartin.

Field marks: 170–180 mm. Smoky brown, shaded blackish round bill: wings blue-black with unusual gun-metal bloom; *white streak on leading edge of wing* (formed by white outer webs of second, third and fourth primaries) *immediately separates it* from other wood-swallows. Tail black, tipped white. Imm: paler mouse-brown, streaked pale-grey, specially on crown and above, mottled paler below. Pairs in loose colonies; small to large travelling flocks; in flight, *white leading edge and whitish wing-lining contrast strongly with dark body*. Associates with Black-faced (707) and other woodswallows.

Similar species: Little Woodswallow (709): noticeably smaller and darker, no white streak on leading edge of wing; calls differ; note habitat. Black-faced Woodswallow (707): greyer, no white streak on leading edge of wing; under tail-coverts either black or white.

Voice: Charming but hard to characterize. One call is described as soft, low 'vut, vut'; also brisk 'peet peet' or chirps and chirrups with slightly brassy tone; song quiet but animated; includes mimicry.

Habitat: Open grassy forests and woodlands; paddocks with dead timber, open coastal and sub-inland scrubs; golf-courses, orchards, roadside timber; street trees in country towns, suburbs.

Breeding: Nest: scanty untidy saucer; of twigs or rootlets; lined with finer rootlets; on horizontal branch of tree, against tree-trunk on piece of bark, on stump, in hollow end of broken branch, on fallen limb near ground, in cavity in fence-post; from 1–20 m high. Eggs: 3–4; rounded-oval, glossy; white or buff-white, spotted or blotched purplish brown or brown and grey, usually in zone round large end or centre.

Range and Status: E. Aust., Tas. and sw. Aust.; some coastal islands: in Q, s. from Atherton Tableland–Herbert R.–upper Lynd R., inland to upper Flinders R.–Clermont–Carnarvon Ra.–Southwood–Inglewood; in NSW, w. (occasional, mostly winter) to about Bourke–Warrego Crossing–Ivanhoe; nearly throughout Vic.; Flinders and King Is., Bass Strait; n. and e. Tas., s. to Strahan on w. coast; in SA, n. to Flinders Ras., w. to Eyre Pen., also Kangaroo I. In sw. WA, said to be contracting before expansion by Black-faced Woodswallow; ranges s. from about Moora, inland on Darling Ras. and to Wagin in the wheatbelt; e. coastally to about Caiguna; winter record from Payne's Find. Common; regular summer breeding migrant in coastal se. Aust. and Tas., arriving Sept., departing Apr., occasionally May. Details of movements unknown; there may be an inland movement in winter in se. Aust. but coastwards movement in winter reported in Q. and wintering recorded in Tas. and Vic., specially in woodlands of c. and n. Vic.; many apparently cross Bass Strait and in Apr., 1963, birds collided with lighthouse, Montagu I., NSW, in night gale. Movements in WA less marked; there may be an inland dispersal in winter.

709 LITTLE WOODSWALLOW *Artamus minor*   Pl.82

Field marks: 120–140 mm. Smallest and darkest woodswallow: *smoky chocolate-brown*; *wings, rump and tail a contrasting deep blue-grey, with unusual gun-metal bloom*, but no white streak on wing. Blackish shading round bill and eye, tail tipped white. Imm: paler, streaked. Small flocks or colonies; in woodland often on dead timber, lower limbs, stumps, or sailing round rock-faces of gorges, looking small against grandeur of surroundings; roosts and nests in rock cavities. Flight floating, graceful, with easy curves, dips and dives; *looks almost black, with contrasting silvery wing-linings*. Occasionally feeds on nectar, congregates to hawk insects over swamps, lagoons; can be confused at distance with swallows or martins.

Similar species: Dusky Woodswallow (708): larger: white streak on leading edge of wing.

Voice: A brisk 'peet,peet', usually in flight, somewhat like Azure Kingfisher (396); may be uttered as series of three or four evenly spaced notes or as single note followed by two quick notes; more rarely as four high-pitched notes; soft pleasing twittering song.

Habitat: Rocky gorges of inland and n. Aust., usually with permanent water; taller open scrubs and grassy woodlands, that usually include both living and dead timber; also tall ring-barked timber; belar, river red gums.

Breeding: Nest: flimsy saucer of twigs and rootlets; lined with rootlets or leaves, in rock-cavity, hole in tree or end of hollow limb. Eggs: 3; white, creamy white or buff-white, spotted and blotched brown and indistinctly with dark-grey, mainly in zone at large end.

Range and Status: Widespread in n. and inland Aust. and islands off w. and n. coasts. Approximate s. limits: in NSW, s. in cleared or ringbarked parts of coastal ranges to near Grafton, breeding recorded inland to Warrumbungle NP–Bourke; in sw. NSW, occasional wandering flocks s. to Wentworth, probably down Darling R. Perhaps from same source to w. Vic., near Dunkeld, (Mar. 1969), and near Edenhope (several records over 30 years, including breeding). In SA, mostly in rocky inland ranges (Everard Ras., Flinders Ras.); occasional s. to area of Renmark and n. Eyre Pen., (where, in a deep gorge, it prabably bred). In WA, s. to gorges of lower Murchison R.; Mileura Station, *c.* 150 km nw. of Cue; Gnow's Nest Ra., se. of Yalgoo and Mt. Kenneth, w. of Youanmi. In Q, reported to tend n. in winter, s. in spring. Uncommon, patchy and irregular; nomadic, part-migratory, sedentary in deep gorges with water.

Magpie Larks   Family *Grallinidae*

The true position of the two members of this family remains a mystery. Neither magpies nor larks, they take their name rather from their bold black-and-white plumage. The Magpie Lark (710) is conspicuous in most Australian environments. With the Australian Magpie (720), White-winged Triller (432) Willie Wagtail (489) and a few others, it is one of those characteristically Australian, strongly marked black-and-white birds that prosper despite, or perhaps because of, conspicuousness. These unrelated species all have bold calls, feed in open exposed situations and are aggressive toward many predators; smaller members often nest near one another. When feeding, Magpie Larks often associate with Australian Magpies, and the two frequently skirmish, when the slow but flexible flight of the former is so effective against the dashing attacks of the Magpie as to suggest a long history of association and protective adaptation by the smaller bird. Magpie Larks are typically birds of river valleys and fringes of freshwaters, but in a dry continent the Australian species is nevertheless very widely distributed. In more arid parts of range, it may nest in any month in response to adequate rainfall. The other member of the family is the Torrentlark *Pomareopsis* of NG.

Food: Small animal food, including small reptiles, insects and larvae, aquatic inverrates.

Range: Aust. and NG.

Number of species: World 2; Aust. 1.

710   MAGPIE LARK   *Grallina cyanoleuca*   Pl.83

Other names: Little or Murray Magpie, Mudlark; Peewee, Peewit, Pugwall; Soldiers, Tilyabit.

Field marks: 260–300 mm. Familiar and conspicuous. Male: contrastingly black-and-white, with black head and neck, *prominent white eyebrow and broad white panel down side of neck below eye*. Female: like male, *but all forehead and throat white, broad black band from crown down through eye to black breastband*. Both have whitish bill, pale-yellow eye, black legs. Imm to approximately 3 months: dark bill and eye; the plumage-pattern combines features of both adults; black plumage browner. Pairs, family parties to large, loose flocks (? of unmated adults and imms.) in autumn–winter. Noisy and demonstrative, particularly before roosting. Males typically, and pairs frequently, hold territories throughout year, and, particularly when breeding, are frequently in aerial skirmishes with neighbouring pairs, Australian Magpie (720) or hawks. Feeds mostly on ground; walking with back-and-forward head-movement. Flight distinctive, *round wings making pulsing strokes*; when skirmishing, flutters, lifts and dodges lightly. Territorial males call on wing while flying with exaggerated catchy wingbeats. In flight note tail-pattern: *white with broad subterminal black band pointing up centre*. Birds in n. Aust. are noticeably small.

Similar species: White-winged Triller (432): smaller; bill black, head wholly black, underparts wholly white. Pied Butcherbird (719): powerful straight hooked bill; head and throat wholly black; in flight, tail black with large white corners.

Voice: Calls distinctive and varied; the duet by mated pairs is a well-known bush-sound: one bird utters loud, somewhat metallic 'tee-hee', immediately followed antiphonally by the other, 'pee-o-wee', 'pee-o-wit'; each rhythmically opens and raises wings and spreads tail. Also liquid mellow 'cloop, cloop, cloop' or 'clue-weet, clue-weet'; alarm-call, strident emphatic 'pee! pee! pee!'.

Habitat: Wide: absent in general only from dense forests, waterless deserts; typically in and near trees by rivers and swamps; widespread in urban areas.

Breeding: Nest: bowl-shaped; of mud, bound with grass; lined with hair, grass and feathers; plastered to horizontal branch 6–15 m high, often over water or on artifical structure. Eggs: 3–5; white or pinkish, spotted and blotched reddish, purplish brown or violet. Often nests near two other conspicuous black-and-white birds, Willie Wagtail (489) and White-winged Triller (432).

Range and Status: Throughout Aust. and many coastal islands; rare or occasional on Bass Strait islands; vagrant to n. and e. Tas.; rare Kangaroo I., SA. Resident or seasonal nomad; common; often abundant. Also s. NG and Timor.

Australian Mud-nesters   Family *Corcoracidae*

Dissimilar in many ways from magpie larks: markings are not bold, plumage rather soft, sexes similar. Highly gregarious; they feed, nest and even breed in groups, the basis of which appears in White-winged Chough (712) to be a dominant male with one or more females and offspring of previous seasons. Such groups co-operate to build the large bowl-shaped mud-nest; one or more females may lay in it, the clutch being larger when more than one bird lays. They also co-operate in feeding the young. Members of the family have harsh contact-calls, frequently heard when the birds are disturbed from ground when feeding.

Food: Small vertebrates and invertebrates generally; also seeds.

Range: E. and se. Aust. mainland.

Number of species: World 2; Aust. 2.

711 APOSTLEBIRD *Struthidea cinerea*   Pl.83

Other names: CWA-bird, Grey Jumper, Happy Family, Lousy Jack, Twelve Apostles.

Field marks: 285–330 mm. *A dark ashy grey bird with short, robust black bill, brown flight feathers, and rather full black tail.* Usually in groups of 6–10, occasionally to 20; feeding associations of hundreds have been noted in non-breeding season. Garrulous, restless, aggressive; groups feed mostly on ground, walking slowly, running or occasionally hopping; til flicked upwards and slowly subsiding. When disturbed, flies low and direct to cover, *wingbeats broken by glides*, wingtips upswept; leaps from branch to branch with wings and tail spread and partly cocked, typically with harsh calls. Dust-bathes on roadsides, rests and preens in groups; associates with White-winged Chough (712). Tame round habitation, often feeds with poultry.

Voice: Harsh and scratchy, in quality like begging call of young Magpie Lark (710), or sound of tearing sandpaper. Many specific calls are described, including a loud discordant 'ch-kew, ch-kew'; on being disturbed, a rough nasal 'git-out!', repeated.

Habitat: Usually near water in drier open forests, woodlands and scrubs; timber along watercourses, including black box and redgum forests; in parts of sw. NSW, reported to be locally confined to native pine *Callitris* woodlands; also roadside timber, timbered paddocks; golf-courses; orchards.

Breeding: Nest: large bowl; of grass, heavily plastered with mud; lined with fine grass; plastered to horizontal branch 3–20 m high. Members of a small social group co-operate in nest-construction, incubation and feeding young. Eggs: 2–5, more when more than one female lays; white or blue-white, spotted, blotched and occasionally streaked blackish brown and dark-grey; some eggs are without markings.

Range and Status: Sub-inland and inland e. Aust. and (? isolate) population in NT, in area of Elliott–Katherine w. toward Top Springs, and e. to upper Roper R. In Q, widespread s. from lower C. York Pen. (Staaten R.–Laura), e. to Atherton Tableland–Conjuboy (near Townsville)–Rosewood (near Rockhampton)–Toowoomba, occasional to near Brisbane. In NSW, e. to Glen Innes–Tamworth–Sydney area (records from Lucas Heights, Annangrove, Northmead, Carringbah, Cronulla and Botany)–Cowra–Harden–Albury; vagrant ACT. Extends far-w. in Q and NSW; precise limits uncertain. In Vic., seldom s. of Murray Valley; records s. to Mystic Park–Kulkyne State Forest–Hattah; vagrant s. to Beaufort and (? formerly) Edenhope. In SA, s. to about Naracoorte, w. to part of Mt. Lofty Ras. and some outer suburbs of Adelaide, n. to about Barrier Highway. Fairly common but local and patchy; sedentary or locally nomadic.

712 WHITE-WINGED CHOUGH *Corcorax melanorhamphos* Pl.83

Other names: Apostlebird, Black Jay or Magpie, Muttonbird.

Field marks: 425–470 mm. Distinctive: largish black bird with *longish tail and white patch on flight-feathers, conspicuous in flight*. Bill black, slender and arched; eye orange-red, legs longish, black. Imm: smaller, tail shorter, eye brown to reddish. Usually in parties of 5–10, in autumn–winter where food is plentiful may form associations of up to 100+. Feeds mostly on ground, *moving ahead in spread-out formation, sometimes running. Swaggers with back and forward head-motion, tail carried horizontally, or raised and lowered.* Rakes over debris or digs with bill, leaving small depressions. Dust-bathes; indulges in anting. When disturbed, flies low for cover in irregular stream *with quick flaps and glides*; *large white wing-patches prominent*; on settling, tail raised and lowered.

Similar species: Pied Currawong (713): larger, heavier; bill more robust, eye bright-yellow; prominent white base of tail, under tail-coverts and tail tips. Ravens and crows (721–725): bills more robust, eyes white in adults; no white on wings.

Voice: Mellow mournful descending whistle, frequently accompanied when alarmed by a grating 'hass'. If close, small throaty clicks.

Habitat: Drier forests, woodlands, sub-inland scrubs, including mulga and mallee; timber along watercourses; plantations of introduced pines; may forage away from cover in new crops, pastures; round homesteads and poultry-runs; timbered outer suburbs of towns and cities.

Breeding: Nest: large bowl; of mud and occasionally other plastered material, including manure; bound and lined with shredded bark, grass and fur; plastered to horizontal branch, usually under cover of foliage and usually over 6 m high, sometimes on top of old nest of babbler or crow. Built by members of social group. Eggs: 3–5, or up to 9 when more than one female lays; creamy white with few large blotches of brown and lilac.

Range and Status: E. and se. Aust.: s. from middle Burdekin R., Q, inland to Richmond–Barcaldine–Hungerford; most of NSW and Vic. *except* denser forests and cleared, closely settled better-watered coastal areas; widespread in s. SA s. of Flinders Ras., w. to near Tarcoola and along coast of Gt. Australian Bight, w. to Penong and possibly to Eucla; in WA reported near Eyre Highway between Madura and Cocklebiddy. Common but patchy; affected by clearing of habitat. Sedentary or locally nomadic.

Australian Magpies, Butcherbirds and Currawongs
Family *Cracticidae*

A distinctive family of the Australian region: medium-sized to large songbirds with robust straight bills and black, white or grey plumage, boldly patterned in some. They have very distinctive voices. All are active predators; some are scavengers round habitation; several are aggressive to man when nesting. One or more species is common in most land environments, most having adapted well to altered habitats following settlement. In particular, Australian Magpie (720) has been favoured by the conversion of woodlands to grassland, pasture and agriculture. For clarity, each of the three distinctive genera in the family are introduced separately below.

Food: Small mammals, small birds, eggs and young, small reptiles, insects and their larvae, other invertebrates; fruits and berries.

Range: Aust. and NG.

Number of species: World 10; Aust. 8.

CURRAWONGS   Genus *Strepera*

Currawongs take their name from a common call of the Pied Currawong (713); in some districts they are known as 'jays', or less incorrectly as bell-magpies, from their ringing, wailing or whistling calls that beckon the distance in lonely woodland or in snow-mantled high-country. They are fairly readily distinguished by their robust pick-like bills, more powerful than those of magpies, and by their yellow eyes. They have plain dark-brown, grey or black plumage; in two species the presence and amount of white on wingtips and under tail-coverts or on the tail itself is diagnostic. They fly with characteristic deep pulsing wingbeats and swoops. They nest in solitary pairs but after breeding often form large flocks. In se. Aust. and Tas. there is a partial, if marked, winter dispersal from hills to lowlands, often far into open country. More omnivorous than magpies, they visit towns, gather in forests to feed on outbreaks of phasmid insects in the heads of eucalypts and dig for larvae in pastures. They take invertebrates from under the bark of trees, using their heavy bills as levers and chisels; they rob birds' eggs and nestlings, are attracted to rubbish dumps and picnic grounds and at times become a pest in orchards.

713   PIED CURRAWONG   *Strepera graculina*   Pl.84

Other names: (Pied) Bell-magpie, Black or Mountain Magpie, Tullawong, Chillawong, Currawang, Mutton bird, Otway Forester.
Field marks: 425–490 mm. A large black bird with a robust black bill and yellow eyes. Its immediate distinguishing mark is the *white base to the tail*, coupled with a large white window in the wing, white under tail-coverts and tail-tips. Mostly these markings are prominent in flight, but toward sw. end of range, *white in base of tail is progressively reduced; w. of Melbourne it is sometimes not visible in the field.* Imm: grey-brown, breast mottled, with less white; eye dark. Singly, pairs, autumn–winter flocks. Noisy and alert, feeds on ground and actively on tree trunks, larger limbs and in foliage of trees; flies with deep lapping wingbeats and swoops. Bold and tame round settlement, picnic areas etc. In winter, forms communal roosts, flights and calls before retiring, seemingly most stridently in stormy weather.
Similar species: White-winged Chough (712): white in wing only; general appearance, habits and calls should easily separate it. Grey Currawong (715): generally much greyer, with no white at base of tail. However, note that in w. Vic. a curious situation exists where Pied Currawongs with little or no white visible in the *tail* occur in same region as darkest mainland forms of the Grey, with little or no white in the *wing*. If in doubt, carefully note calls; they are quite diagnostic; see Grey Currawong, Voice.
Voice: A common call is the basis for the name 'currawong', but needs some imagination to perceive. Calls vary in type and geographically. A common call in Vic. is a loud falsetto 'crik, crik, bewaiir', the last note wailed and descending; in ne. NSW–se. Q, a guttural, wailing 'currar-awok-awok-currar', or 'jabawok, jabawok'. A widespread call is a long-drawn rising then falling wolf-whistle, 'weeeooo'. Various mellow whistles, guttural and conversational notes.
Habitat: Alpine woodlands to above 1500 m; forests, woodlands, inland and coastal scrubs; farmlands, croplands, rubbish dumps, picnic grounds, street, parks, gardens; recorded breeding in Sydney city parks.
Breeding: Nest, flattish, of sticks, lined with root-fibres, grass and bark; in fork of leafy tree; 5–15 m high. Eggs: usually 3; light-brown, freckled and blotched darker-brown. Nest frequently parasitized by Channel-billed Cuckoo (374).
Range and Status: E. mainland Aust. and coastal islands: from C. York, Q, to far-sw. Vic. (? and extreme se. SA); in Q, inland to about upper Mitchell R.–Richmond–Tambo–Morven; in NSW, inland to Narrabri–Warrumbungle NP–Cocoparra NP–Barham; in Vic., most of e. half of State, w. on Murray R. to about Murrabit, near Kerang, sw. to Grampians and coastally to SA border area. Common; altudinal migrant, breeding

mostly in ranges and in forests of coasts and foothills, many dispersing to more open country in coastal lowlands and sub-inland in Apr.–May, returning Aug.–Sept. (However, scavenging flocks occur round ski-resorts in winter). Many country towns have their wintering flocks; dispersal in Murray Valley and tributaries take place through river red gum forests. In Q, flocks move in., inland or to coastal lowlands in autumn; wintering reported at Moreton Bay.

714 BLACK CURRAWONG *Strepera fuliginosa* Pl.84

Other names: Black Bell-magpie, Magpie or Jay; Mountain Magpie; Sooty Crow-shrike or Currawong.

Field marks: 470 mm. A robust blackish currawong with *only a small amount of white on flight feathers and tips of tail.* Bill black, robust; eye bright-yellow. Female and imm.: similar; latter has yellow gape. Pairs, family parties; winter flocks of up to 50, sometimes to 100+. Noisy and alert; feeds much on ground, in paddocks and swampy areas, observed to wade in shallow water, like a heron; forages actively among branches and foliage of trees. It has the characteristic loose, easy currawong-flight.

Similar species: Grey Currawong (715), race *arguta*: greyer, with large white patch on wing and white under tail-coverts; call differs. Forest Raven (722): no white in plumage, eye white in adult; call distinctive.

Voice: Noisy; the notes are distinctive; usual call is described as musical 'kar-week, week-kar'; loud metallic conversational calls.

Habitat: Mountain and lowland forests and woodlands; high moors; coastal heaths; open grazing country, orchards, suburban areas. On Bass Strait islands, more open habitats; in places reported to feed among rotting kelp on beaches.

Breeding: Nest: large, deep; of sticks and twigs, lined with rootlets and grass; in upright fork from 3 to 20 m. Eggs: 2–4; pale grey-brown or purplish buff, spotted and blotched red-brown and dull purplish brown.

Range and Status: Confined to Tas. region: well distributed throughout State; the only currawong on King, Flinders and other Bass Strait islands; also Maatsuyker I. Common, altitudinal migrant or sedentary.

715 GREY CURRAWONG *Strepera versicolor* Pl.84

Other names: Black-winged, Brown or Clinking Currawong; Grey or Hill Bell-magpie or Magpie; Jay, Mountain Magpie, Rainbird or Squeaker.

Field marks: 450–500 mm. A large grey bird with a robust bill and *with darker shading round the yellow eye*; *white window in wing, flight and tail-feathers tipped white, white under tail-covers.* Female: smaller. Imm: duller and more brownish, eye dark, gape yellow. General plumage-tone varies geographically from pale-grey to brownish to sooty black. But *except* in w. Vic. and (possibly) nearby far-se. SA, this does not affect field-identification because the white markings remain constant. The problem-zone in Vic. about w. of Melbourne occurs because plumage *becomes progressively darker and white in the wings reduced.* These dark birds could, without care, be confused with the w. Vic. population of Pied Currawongs (713) which have little or no white *at base of tail.* But their calls easily separate them. The darkest mainland race of the Grey is *melanoptera*, of mallee and scrubby woodlands in far-w. Vic., and adjacent sw. NSW (e. to Griffith, n. to Mossgiel), se. SA and Kangaroo I. Pied Currawongs moving w. to winter in Riverina or inland in w. Vic. may overlap its e. limits, so take care. The largest and darkest Grey Currawong of all is the Tas. race *arguta*. It is easily separated from the other Tas. Currawong, the Black (714), but its characteristic white markings. Singly, pairs or family parties; forms winter flocks in parts, e.g. nw. Vic., on Kangaroo I., SA, and in Tas. See family introduction for flight and other details, *note that in flight, the white under tail-coverts can show as a white mark on side of rump*, causing possible confusion with Pied Currawong.

Similar species: Pied Currawong (713): see comments under *Similar species* about situation in s. Vic. w. of Melbourne. Black Currawong (714), Australian Magpie (720), imms, all races: dark eyes, back *paler* than breast.

Voice: Distinctive and immediately separable from the calls of the Pied Currawong: typical is a ringing 'chling, chling' or 'chding, chding', also a ringing 'cree'; when close many strange small reflective notes like the mewing of a cat, or a toy-trumpet. In Tas., the calls of the race *arguta* have been described as 'keer-keer-kink', or 'clink, clank', like an anvil being struck.

Habitat: Forests and woodlands generally; mallee, coastal scrubs and heaths; roadside timber, paddocks, with large trees; orchards, some suburban areas.

Breeding: Nest: large, shallow; of sticks, lined with coarse rootlets and grass; typically 3–15 m high on horizontal fork at top of slender sapling or in tree. Eggs: 2–3; occasionally 4; variable; light-brown to pinkish or reddish buff with spots and blotches of brown to reddish brown and lilac-grey, many markings as though beneath surface. Eggs of the race *arguta* dull-white to buff-brown or grey, markings as above.

Range and Status: The species ranges sparsely over much of s. Aust. and in Tas. proper (mostly n. and e. of a line from C. Grim to Dover). On mainland the approximate n. limits are—NSW: Blue Mts. Plateau–Mossgiel; SA: s. Flinders Ras.–Everard and Musgrave Ras.; NT: n. from adjacent nw. SA to Victory Downs–Mt. Olga; WA: Warburton Ras.–Wiluna–Shark Bay. Fairly common to sparse and local; sedentary or nomadic, with (? local) winter dispersal.

BUTCHERBIRDS Genus *Cracticus*

Butcherbirds are much smaller than magpies or currawongs; they have rather large flat heads and strong straight, finely-hooked bills. Their patters are mostly bold, their flight usually arrow-like, wingbeats shallow and quick. For their size, they are perhaps the most rapacious Australian passerines, killing small birds, mammals and reptiles as well as insects. They have frequently been observed hunting in unison with Little Falcons (153), in what seems deliberate intent to secure prey driven under cover by the presence and/or tactics of the raptor. Butcherbirds are so-called from their usual method of dealing with prey: items too large to swallow are dismembered after being wedged in a fork or wires of a fence or clothes-hoist, etc. They have also been observed to cache food like beetles and lizard-remains in cavities in limbs and bark. Butcherbirds are not gregarious, they form only family parties; they are often aggressive at their nests, which may be attended by more than two birds. All the species have splendid territorial calls and songs that differ markedly between species, and geographically.

716 BLACK BUTCHERBIRD *Cracticus quoyi*   Pl.83

Field marks: 325–450 mm. Distinctive: adult *wholly blue-black*, with robust, finely hooked bill, blue-grey, tipped black; eye black. Note that the race *rufescens* of coastal ne. Q has a phase that is wholly *deep-rufous firmly barred blackish below*, perhaps an example of prolonged imm. plumage, (imms otherwise dull-black). But rufous birds, presumed to be adults, have been observed feeding young at nest. Singly, pairs or family parties; hunts along edges of vegetation and in mangroves. Shy, comes to houses for food.

Voice: Described as rich, flute-like and somewhat like Pied Currawong (713); one call, 'caw-caw-cooka-cook'; song described as three distinct notes interposed with softer ones.

Habitat: Rainforests and margins, monsoon forests, vegetation along watercourses, coastal scrubs, mangroves; more open woodlands adjacent to the above; agricultural area.

Breeding: Nest: substantial; of sticks and twigs; in upright fork about 6 m high. Eggs: 4; creamish to grey-green, with largish spots of brown and dark-grey, heaviest at large end.

Range and Status: Coastal n. and ne. Aust. and islands: from Port Keats, NT, through top end Arnhem Land, inland up to 50 km on rivers and probably e. along Gulf Coast in mangroves. C. York Pen., Q, s. at least to Watson and Rocky Rs.; the race *rufescens* occurs on e. coast from Cooktown s. to Ingham and Hitchinbrook I., inland to Atherton Tableland; another race from near Proserpine coastally s. to near Rockhampton. Common to fairly common; sedentary. Also NG.

717 GREY BUTCHERBIRD   *Cracticus torquatus*   Pl.83

Other names: Silver-backed Butcherbird; Derwent, Tasmanian or Whistling Jack or Jackass; Durbaner, Grey Shrike.

Field marks: 240–300 mm. A smart grey, black-and-white bird with a *robust blue-grey bill; tipped black and finely hooked; crown and cheeks black*, (extending to side of neck in the form in s. WA), *separated from grey back by a whitish collar*; underparts white, washed pale-grey. Female: crown somewhat browner. Imm: brownish, with buff to dirty-white rear collar, rump and underparts; bill dark-grey. The small race *argenteus*, 'Silver-backed Butcherbird': silver-grey back, pure-white underparts. Singly, pairs or family parties; spry, bold but wary. Sits watchfully in branches, darts to ground or through trees after prey. Flight direct and swift, with rapid shallow wingbeats; *note whitish rump*. Tame round habitation when fed; aggressive near nest.

Similar species: Black-backed Butcherbird (718): patterned in black-and-white; no grey. Pied Butcherbird (719), imm. shading on throat and upperbreast traces pattern of adult. Red Wattlebird (578) should never be confused with it, but is, at least in flight.

Voice: Territorial song: beautiful deep mellow piping, the phrasing varying geographically; a quiet subsong includes mimicry. In aggression, a staccato rollicking descending shriek, difficult to describe, and a harsh grating 'karr, karr'.

Habitat: Margins of rainforest and eucalypt forests; open woodlands, coastal and inland scrubs, including mallee, vegetation along watercourses; shelter-belts on farms, roadside timber, golf-courses, parks, gardens.

Breeding: Nest: untidy saucer of twigs and rootlets, with shallow well-formed cup of dry grasses and rootlets; in saplings or scrubby tree e.g. native pine, banksia, tea-tree or clump of mistletoe, 2–10 m high. Eggs: 3–5; variable; dull-green to light-brown, speckled and blotched dull-red or chestnut brown or purplish red.

Range and Status: Suitable habitat in most parts mainland Aust. and Tas., *except* drier desert areas and denser rainforests; many coastal islands, but not Kangaroo I. SA, or Flinders or King I. Bass Strait; absent C. York Pen. The race *argenteus*: from Port Hedland in coastal nw. WA inland to Barlee Ra., n. through Kimberleys to top end NT. s. to about Katherine. Sight-records of a small, very pale silver grey form in Macdonnell R. s. NT. Fairly common, widespread but patchy; nowhere does it seem particularly abundant. Mostly sedentary.

718 BLACK-BACKED BUTCHERBIRD   *Cracticus mentalis*   Pl.83

Field marks: 275 mm. *Marked* like Grey Butcherbird (717), but *boldly black-and-white*, rump grey. Note: *small black mark on chin, white throat and underparts*. Habits like Grey: hunts for insects and small lizards in branches of trees and lower shrubbery; tame round camps and habitation. In s. NG reported to gather in flocks up to 6, flying up to about 70 m, wheeling and calling.

Similar species: Pied Butcherbird (719): black throat and upperbreast. Grey Butcherbird (717).

Voice: Calls described as soft mellow carolling notes, some resembling Grey Butcherbird, but weaker; accomplished mimic.

Habitat: Open forests and woodlands, vegetation along watercourses, agricultural areas and near settlements.

Breeding: Nest: shallow; of sticks, stems of creeper and rootlets, lined with finer rootlets; in fork of tree, once 25 m high. Eggs: 2–3; green-grey to pale greyish brown, spotted and blotched dark-brown over surface of shell and in zone at large end.

Range and Status: C. York Pen. s. to Mitchell R. in w. and to near Cooktown on e. coast. Common, sedentary. Also NG.

719 PIED BUTCHERBIRD *Cracticus nigrogularis* Pl.83

Other names: Black-throated Butcherbird; Break-o'-day-boy, Organ Bird.

Field marks: 325–375 mm. A conspicuous black-and-white bird with a glorious voice. White body set off by *wholly black head, throat and upperbreast*; *wings and back black, conspicuous white panel on wings*; *rump white, tail black with white corner.* Bill straight, finely hooked at tip; blue-grey, tipped black. Imm: duller, brownish grey replaces black, white areas greyish cream. Singly, pairs, family parties, loose companies where food abundant e.g. when paddocks are ploughed; often rather tame, but aggressive round nest. Perches in exposed positions, flies to ground to seize food. Often hunts in pairs and with Little Falcon (153) in pursuit of small birds. Flight strongly undulating; note *black triangle on back and large white corners to black tail*, making it look wedge-shaped.

Similar species: Black-backed Butcherbird (718); wholly white below except for black chin. Grey Butcherbird (717), imm Magpie Lark (710).

Voice: Superb: slow flute-like piping, of clear high-pitched and low mellow notes, throughout day and moonlit nights, best in early morning; often given by two or three birds alternatively, higher-pitched notes of one contrasting with more mellow notes of others. When calling, bill raised high, then sunk on breast, or ducked then raised high. Also accomplished mimicry, as part of quieter subsong.

Habitat: Drier woodlands, sub-inland and drier coastal scrubs; timber along watercourses, pastoral lands, plains with sparse trees; farms, croplands, roadsides, picnic areas.

Breeding: Nest: untidy, fairly deep; of sticks and twigs, lined with rootlets and dry grasses; in fork up to 15 m high. Eggs: 3–5; variable; olive-green to brownish, spotted and marked darker, occasionally blotched brown and spotted blackish at large end.

Range and Status: Widespread in mainland Aust. and many coastal islands: in Q, nearly throughout *except* ne. coastal areas from about Ingham to Helenvale, near Cooktown; in NSW, widespread *except* coastal se. and high country, s. of a line through Morisset–Windsor–Richmond–ACT (occasional),–L. Hume; in Vic., mostly confined to region of the Murray R., from above L. Hume downstream to SA; but s. to Wyperfeld NP in nw. Vic.; in SA, widespread, *except* s. coastal areas and Kangaroo I.; in WA widespread *except* sw. corner s. and w. of Gingin–L. Grace; occasional coastally s. to Rockingham–Busselton; in the NT, widespread, including parts of Simpson Desert. Common; sedentary, or partly nomadic.

AUSTRALIAN MAGPIES Genus *Gymnorhina*

Australian magpies are not related to European and n. American magpies (which are corvids), but the name was no doubt borrowed because of the supposed similarity of their bold black-and-white plumage. The three geographical forms, 'Black-backed', 'White-backed' and 'Western' Magpies, were long treated as good species, but they freely interbreed where their ranges overlap and are now treated as races of a single species. A notable feature of magpie-behaviour is the holding of territories by groups; these can vary from a single pair to six adults or more, and imms. The sex-ratio is variable, but in breeding territories females tend to predominate and typically a dominant male mates with several females, despite membership of the group by other males. Five types of groups have been recognized, territorial activity commencing with mobile associations of birds with only a nesting-roosting territory to defend. As opportunities permit, there is a kind of upward mobility leading to membership of a group holding a permanent territory. Such a social organization seems to ensure a continuing reliable supply of food, and safe roosting and nesting places. Females appear to need the security of the territory to breed successfully. In contrast to the members of these territorial groups are non-territorial birds in the lowest category of association: loose locally mobile flocks of imms. evicted from territories in their first or second year, and non-breeding adults, mostly males. Such companies may number hundreds, specially in autumn–winter, where food is locally abundant.

720 AUSTRALIAN MAGPIE *Gymnorhina tibicen* Pl.83

Other names: Black-backed, Western or White-backed Magpie; Flutebird, Organbird, Piper.

Field marks: 370–440 mm. A conspicuous large black-and-white bird with a pointed, whitish black-tipped bill. Nominate race 'Black-backed Magpie': male; *mostly glossy black*, with prominent white nape, white shoulder and wingband, white rump, under tail-coverts and tail, latter broadly tipped black; eye red-brown. (Some males reported to assume a white back with age). Female: like male, but nape greyer. Imm: duller and mottled; bill shorter, blackish. Race *hypoleuca* 'White-backed Magpie': male; *back wholly glistening white* from nape to tail. Female: like male, but white areas, particularly of nape, back and rump *greyer and indistinctly mottled*. Imm: like a dull, mottled female; bill shorter, blackish; eye black. Race *dorsalis* 'Western Magpie': male; *back wholly glistening white*, from nape to tail. Female: *back black, feathers edges white, giving a distinctive contrasting pattern*. Note: some females have greyer backs, with less contrast, probably indicative of interbreeding. Imm: like a dull female, but mottling on mantle absent or less distinct; bill shorter, blackish; eye black. Feeds mostly on ground; family parties often indulge in play. Becomes tame in parks, gardens. Flight direct and swift, with characteristic swish of wings; note *angled white bar on black underwing*.

Voice: Familiar and justly famous: rich mellow flute-like or organ-like carolling by one or several birds, usually best in late winter and early spring; sometimes by night. Quieter subsong by single birds, including imms, includes mimicry. During aggression, brisk high-pitched yodel. Alarm-call, a short harsh shout, repeatedly; also a loud drawn-out descending 'peww'.

Habitat: Almost wherever there are trees and open areas of bare ground or grass; orchards, golf-courses, playing fields, surburban areas, gardens.

Breeding: Nest: bowl-shaped; of sticks and twigs, lined with grass, rootlets, wool or hair; occasionally of wire; usually in fork or on branch in outer part of tree 5–16 m or more high; sometimes in shrubs near ground, rarely on ground. Eggs: 2–3; occasionally fewer and sometimes as many as 5 or 6; variable; grey to brown or pale-blue, but typically blue-green, spotted brown. Race *dorsalis*: bluish or greenish, blotched, smeared and streaked, with red-brown and brown.

Range and Status: Nominate race: widespread on mainland *except* for the following, where sparse or absent: coastal se. Aust. and sw. WA (see below); n. Kimberleys, WA; top end NT; coastal C. York Pen. and coastal ne. Q, n. of Staaten R. on w. coast and n. of about Cardwell on e. coast, but present on highlands of ne. Q and interior C. York Pen. Race *hypoleuca*: a coastal strip 100 km or more wide, from about Narooma–Cooma, s. NSW, through s. Vic. to Eyre Pen. and Kangaroo I., SA; also Bass Strait islands and Tas. A broad overlap-zone, in which the two races intergrade, extends from about the ACT s. and w. through Vic., on and inland of the Gt. Dividing Ra. The zone is apparently expanding or moving s. but not precisely understood. The picture is confused by a possible winter n. movement of *hypoleuca* to n. Vic. and s. NSW. Magpies with partly or wholly white backs have been recorded in recent years as far n. in NSW as Dungog–Orange–Forbes–Ivanhoe–Broken Hill, as well as nearer Sydney (Kanangra–Boyd NP; Hornsby, Fearnley's Lagoon). Magpies with partly or wholly black backs occur and breed s. in Vic. at least to Jamieson–Wallan–Maryborough. Probably because of the absence of a physical barrier like a Dividing Range, the zone(s) of intergradation in SA, s. NT and sw. WA are much more gradual and indeterminate than in se. Aust. In SA, *hypoleuca* is predominant from the coastal se., to the Mt. Lofty Ras., Kangaroo I., Eyre Pen. n. to Gawler Ras., w. along the Bight coast into WA and possibly n. of the Nullarbor Plain. However n. and w. of these limits the position is complex. White-backed birds are reported to predominate in ce. SA, n. to L. Callabonna. Black-backed or white-backed birds, or intergrades, are sparsely distributed n. to the Birdsville Track and margins of Simpson Desert in ne. SA, to the Everard and Musgrave Ras. in nw. SA, and into the sw. NT, n. and e. to Alice Springs–Harts Ra.; n. of that limit the population is predominantly black-backed, with occasional white-backed birds n. to about Barrow Creek. Race *dorsalis*: sw. WA, n. to about Murchison R., inland to Kathleen Valley and coastally e. to Esperance, extending range into the sw. forest-zone as a result of land-clearing. Appears to intergrade with *hypoleuca* in se. WA, probably n. and s. of Nullarbor Plain, and with nominate race in sub-inland and coastal areas n. of Perth. The species as a whole varies from rare and sparse in n. and more arid zones, to very common and abundant in better-watered areas. It has benefitted greatly from land-clearing and the development of pastures. Sedentary or (? locally) nomadic. Also NG; introduced NZ.

Ravens and Crows   Family *Corvidae*

A well-known family of large, predatory, scavenging passerines. Some overseas forms, including an occasional self-introduced species, House Crow (726), have grey or white in the plumage, but all native Australian corvids are glossy black, with white eyes when adult. Although the names 'raven' and 'crow' are used specifically for one or other Australian species, their differences are slight. In Australia, ravens differ from crows mostly in size and in the colour of the down at the base of the body-feathers. All are commonly called crows and all are so similar as to be safely identified in field only with care, practice, and often some difficulty. Until the 1960s, only three native Australian corvids were recognized: the 'Australian Raven', the Little Crow (724) and the Australian (now Torresian) Crow (725). But it has been found that the accepted Australian Raven population in fact consisted of three distinctive forms, whose breeding ranges partly or wholly overlapped, indicating that they had differentiated to the status of full species. The two 'new' species are the Forest (722) and Little (723) Ravens. The Little Raven is a gregarious species living largely in sympatry (sharing the same country) with the Australian Raven (721) and maintaining its separate status by different habits, appearance, displays and calls. The Forest Raven, in many ways similar to Little Raven and of same stock, is confined to Tas. and parts of coastal Vic., with an isolate race in the ne. tablelands of NSW.
Food: Omnivorous.
Range: Cosmopolitan except for NZ and Pacific and many other islands.
Number of species: World 103; Aust. 6, including 1 introduced.
Identification of native Australian ravens is based on:
   1. Colour of down at the base of feathers on neck and body: *ashy-brown in ravens, snow-white in crows*, usually visible in field only when wind ruffles feathers of head and neck.
   2. Presence or absence of long pointed feathers on neck and throat (throat hackles) and whether throat expands in a shaggy bag when calling.
   3. Posture and actions when calling and position from which call is made.
   4. The nature of the main aggressive or territorial call.
   5. Relative length and massiveness of bill.
   6. Other aspects of behaviour, including wing-settling, flock and nesting behaviour, nest-site and construction.
   7. Distribution.

721 AUSTRALIAN RAVEN   *Corvus coronoides*   Pl.84
Other names: Crow, Kelly.
Field marks: 460–560 mm. Largest Australian crow, familiar to many. Distinguished by call, *by long pointed feathers on throat that become conspicuous when throat bags out during calling* and by position and posture bird adopts when uttering the main aggressive or territorial call: usually in a high position; *lowers head so that head, body and tail are*

nearly horizontal; wings seldom flipped. Bill black, robust, longish, slightly-curved; eye white. In hand, or when seen in wind, note ashy grey down at base of feathers and loose bare black skin under chin, between bases of lower mandible. Female: slightly smaller. Imm: duller black, eye brown until about 15 months; hazel (mottled brown and white) until nearly 3 years; then white. Unlike Little Raven (723), mated pairs are sedentary in breeding territories throughout year, but imms and unmated adults form small nomadic flocks of usually no more than 30; these tend to be much less-cohesive than flocks of Little Ravens. Established and bold round urban areas, otherwise notoriously wary. When approached at nest, slips quietly off and flies away low. Flight strong, direct and heavy; in a common display flight, flies on shallow-beating, almost quivering wings, uttering wailing calls.

Voice: Aggressive or territorial call: deep powerful 'aah-aah-aah-aaaaahh', last note drawn out descending and ending in a gargle; tempo much slower than Little Raven. Many other notes, including a high-pitched descending wail, and when heard nearby, throaty rattles.

Habitat: Most habitats, except dense wet forests, alpine areas up to 1500 m to coasts, dunes and beaches; islands; urban areas.

Breeding: Breeding territory large, 70–150 ha, nests thus usually well separated. Nest: substantial, flattish; of sticks, lined with bark, hair and wool felted in thick mat. Usually over 13 m high in secondary fork of tall tree, or on pylons, cross-arms of telephone poles, occasionally in dead tree in water of lake or in treeless districts lower, in top of shrub, often dense introduced boxthorn; rarely, on ground, in or beside coil of wire, fence-post. Eggs: 3–5; pale blue-green, blotched and freckled dark-brown and olive-brown, indistinguishable from other ravens and crows except by size from Little Crow (724).

Range and Status: Widespread on Australian mainland *except* e. Aust., present on some e. coastal islands: throughout Vic. and NSW, *except* coastal ne. NSW. In Q, mostly *absent* from coastal areas e. of Divide, but to coast in some places e.g. Townsville; widespread inland, *absent* n. C. York Pen., rare Gulf coast. In e. NT, n. to Nicholson R., Brunette Downs and Andado Station in w. Simpson Desert. In SA, w. to Oodnadatta–Tarcoola–Gawler Ras.–Eucla, apparently rare Eyre Pen.; occasional Kangaroo I., resident on islands off sw. SA coast. In WA, w. along Bight coast to sw. WA, n. to mouth of Murchison R. and inland to about 250 mm mean rainfall line, also some islands off w. coast. Common; mated pairs sedentary; unmated adults and imms. nomadic.

722 FOREST RAVEN *Corvus tasmanicus*

Other names: Tasmanian, New England Raven.

Field marks: 520 mm. Like Little Raven (723), but bigger and much heavier; calls differ. There are two widely-separated races: *the s. (nominate) race has most massive bill of any Australian corvid and by far the shortest tail*; these, coupled with call, small range and specialized habitat, should help identification. The n. race, *boreus*, has somewhat less massive bill and longer tail: proportions more like Australian Raven (721). Except for more specialized choice of habitat on mainland, habits generally like Little Raven. In non-breeding season flocks (up to 250+ in Tas.) forage in open paddocks.

Voice: Deeper than any other Australian corvid; a slow deep 'korr-korr-korr-korr' with tendency for last note to be drawn-out, like Australian Raven.

Habitat: In Tas. where it is not in competition with any other corvid, from alpine forests and high moors to wet eucalypt forests, drier woodlands, coastal scrubs and beaches; pasturelands and orchards. Habitat on mainland more specialized: breeds in wet eucalypt forests, possibly extending to more open country in nonbreeding season.

Breeding: Solitary like Australian Raven; nest and eggs similar.

Range and Status: Nominate race confined to (1) Tas. and some coastal islands – the only corvid in Tas. proper, where it is described as probably the most widely-distributed species. It does not occur on King Is. (2) Flinders and other islands of Furneaux Group,

(3) Otway Ras. and Wilson's Promontory in Vic. The n. race *boreus* is apparently confined to fringes of e. forested area of New England tablelands, NSW, from about Nowendoc in s. to 18 km n. of Guyra, and from Armidale in w. to Dorrigo State Forest in e., abutting range of the Australian Raven in w. and Torresian Crow (725) in e., on foothills of Divide. Common; sedentary or locally nomadic.

723 LITTLE RAVEN *Corvus mellori* Pl.84

Other name: Crow.

Field marks: 500 mm. Slightly smaller than Australian Raven (721), with a somewhat less-massive bill. Unlike the larger bird, *throat-feathers are not noticeably long, and do not fan out in a shaggy bag when calling.* But note that when feeding, *a small food-pouch is just* visible under the base of the bill, and this gives the head a subtly 'different' silhouette. The calls (see Voice) and manner of calling are diagnostic: the bird typically gives *a quick upward flip with the wings with each note*; *it does not adopt a special posture and may call from any position.* When parted by wind, note the ashy-brown down at the bases of the body-feathers. In hand, note the extensive loose bare skin on chin between bases of lower mandible. Imm: duller black, skin on mouth pinkish; eye brown for most of first year, then hazel, then white. Usually sociable, even when breeding; several pairs typically nest in proximity, sometimes in the same tree. After breeding, mixed flocks of adults and imms leave the breeding area and wander, adults later returning to breeding area. Such movements include dispersal from sub-inland to some coastal parts of Vic., where mobile flocks, sometimes numbering over 100, are common in summer, autumn and winter. Such flocks are typically larger and more cohesive than those of the Australian Raven. When moving far, Little Ravens typically fly fairly high, 70–100 m, in a consistent direction; they tend to forage more in trees than Australian Raven; other feeding habits are similar, but carrion is reported to be less important to them.

Voice: Aggressive or territorial call, a harsh rapid level 'car, car, car, car, car', *tempo much quicker than Australian Raven, notes harder, more clipped and do not tail off in throaty gargle.* Other harsh calls.

Habitat: Alpine woodlands over 1600 m to forests and woodlands of foothills, almost treeless plains, sub-inland scrubs and woodlands, pastoral country, farmlands and coastal lands.

Breeding: Nest: shallow cup; of sticks and twigs, lined with bark, grass and wool, felted into thick mat. Unlike Australian Raven, rarely over 10 m high and often in lighter fork in outer canopy. Typically semi-colonial or social, some nests only a few metres apart, breeding territory confined to near nest. Eggs: 4; pale blue-green blotched and freckled brown and olive; indistinguishable from other ravens and crows, except by size from Little Crow.

Range and Status: Shares range with Australian Raven *except* in se. high-country, where that species does not occur. Se. mainland Aust., King I., Bass Strait (possibly winter migrant): in NSW, n. to about Barrier Highway–Narrabri and e. to w. foothills of Divide (Mudgee–e. of Bathurst–Blue Mts. Plateau), s. tablelands and s. coast; in Vic., nearly throughout, to alpine areas over 1600 m, but *excluding* forested areas of Otway Ras. and Wilsons Promontory NP, where replaced by Forest Raven (722); in SA, w. to Eyre Pen. and Ceduna, Kangaroo I. and islands in Spencer Gulf, n. to about Port Augusta–Cockburn. Common, nomadic and part-migratory – see above.

724 LITTLE CROW *Corvus bennetti* Pl.84

Other name: Bennett's Crow.

Field marks: 410–480 mm. Smallest Australian corvid, identified when with other crows or Australian Magpie (720) by its *smaller size* and somehow much neater appearance. The bill is shorter and more slender than other corvids; J. N. Hobbs has pointed out that it makes the forehead look higher than Australian Raven (721), which has a sloped forehead. Down, at base of feathers, *white.* Imm: duller; eye brown for most of first year, hazel (mottled brown and white) until end of second year, then white. Behaviour and calls are helpful: often remarkably tame, particularly in country towns, but also in the bush; will frequently allow an observer to walk under tree where it sits. Reported to be aggressive round nest, hovering over intruder, occasionally swooping, calling continually overhead and from tops of nearby trees. Sociable when breeding; in nonbreeding season forms mixed flocks of adults and imms., numbering hundreds or even thousands when food is locally abundant e.g. during grasshopper swarms. Like Little Raven (723), flocks of 100+ often travel fairly high, 70–100 m, in a steady direction, calling; at other times, flocks soar high, swoop and dive in undulating flight, behaviour not shared by Torresian (725) Crow. In flight, the wingbeats are quick and shallow; when overhead, underwing reported to show a *two-toned look*.

Voice: Described as a very nasal 'nark-nark-nark-nark'.

Habitat: Inland scrubs, coastal woodlands, timber along watercourses; open grasslands, farmlands; gathers near settlement and in many inland and w. coastal towns, wherever pickings are to be had.

Breeding: Nest: small, of sticks with *mud or clay between these and lining*; latter of feathers, fur, strips of bark, or clean white wool. Often in fairly low scrubby tree like a mulga or mallee; several nests often situated in nearby trees, as a loose colony; occasionally uses a windmill-platform or cross-trees of a telephone-pole; rarely, on ground. Eggs: 4–6; noticeably smaller than those of other Australian corvids; rounded; greenish blue, heavily freckled, spotted and blotched olive-brown, evenly or heavily at large end.

Range and Status: Throughout interior and w. Aust.; coastal islands in WA: n. in WA to Pilbara region and s. Kimberleys (Halls Ck); in NT, n. to Tennant Ck–Brunette Downs; in Q, n. (? occasional) to Burketown and e. to Cunnamulla; in NSW, e. to Moree-Gilgandra–The Rock NP–Berrigan; in Vic., occasional to far nw.; in SA, s. to about the Murray R., w. to Morgan and to Sutherlands–Port Germein–n. Eyre Pen.; in WA, coastally s. to Murchison R., and through subcoastal sw. WA and the Nullarbor Plain. A migratory movement s. in spring–summer is reported in the Darling Ras. s. to Boyup Brook, and in wheatbelt; many remain until June–July. Common; nomadic, breeding in response to suitable conditions.

725 TORRESIAN CROW *Corvus orru* Pl.84

Other name: Australian Crow.

Field marks: 500–550 mm. Like Australian Raven (721), but throat does not expand in a shaggy bag when calling. In hand, and when wind ruffles plumage of the head and neck, it can be separated from the ravens by the *snowy white down at the base of the feathers*. From the Little Crow (724), it is best separated by size, calls and behaviour. More than other it *repeatedly and exaggeratedly lifts and shuffles the wings on settling; but does not flip wings when calling*. Imm: duller black; eye brown for most of first year, hazel (mottled brown and white) to end of second year, then white. In arid c. and w. Aust. where the Little Crow also occurs, the Torresian is usually in resident pairs, although the two species are also seen together in flocks. In coastal n. Aust., e. Q and ne. NSW, where Little Crow does not occur, Torresian forms flocks of up to 60 or more in nonbreeding season, gathering where food is plentiful or round towns, habitation, slaughteryards, rubbish dumps.

Habitat: Open forest, woodlands and coastal scrubs, beaches and mudflats; in arid inland and w., often confined to isolated ranges and taller timber along larger watercourses, taller mulga scrubs. Exploits food round habitation; in coastal w., n. and e. Aust. flocks attracted to crops of grain, peanuts and fruit.

Voice: Described as nasal high-pitched clipped 'uk-uk-uk-uk-uk', 'ok-ok-ok-ok-ok', or 'oh-oh-oh-oh-oh', never an 'a' sound as in Australian Raven.

Breeding: Nest: of sticks, usually smaller than Australian Raven; usually high in tall eucalypt; no mud used. Eggs: 3–5; pale-blue, lightly spotted and blotched dark-brown and olive-brown; in WA pale-blue, unmarked eggs are reported.

Range and Status: The species has an unusual range: (1) Humid zone of summer rainfall from ne. NSW, e. Q including C. York Pen. and islands of e. coast, top end NT, to Kimberleys, WA, and coastal islands. The s. and inland limits are from about Forster–Laurieton on the n. NSW coast, inland to Dorrigo State Forest–Inverell and, in Q, Chinchilla–Charleville–Winton–Hughenden–Normanton. This range does not overlap that of the Little Crow. The bird frequently occurs in large flocks, particularly in cultivated areas. (2) In NT, nw. SA and WA, away from the humid n. coastal zone, it occurs in sympatry with the Little Crow and is usually in pairs in taller timber along watercourses. Distribution patchy: occurs from n. to s. in the NT, but reported not to occur in an arc bounded by Victoria R. Downs–Attack Creek–Barrow Creek–the w. tip of the Macdonnell Ras., the George Gill Ra. and the Petermann Ras., nor in the Simpson Desert. In nw. SA, occurs in Musgrave and Everard Ras. and probably further s. In WA, from Kimberleys to Pilbara region, s. coastally to North West Cape, and s. inland to L. King, near s. coast. Adults probably sedentary, imms nomadic. Also Bismarck Archipelago, NG and Moluccas.

726 HOUSE CROW *Corvus splendens*

Other names: Colombo or Indian Crow.

Field marks: 430 mm. A smallish crow with *a dark eye*; *the mouse-brown nape, back and breast emphasise the blackness of crown, face and throat*. Bill fairly short, forehead looks high; legs fairly long compared to Australian Raven (721); eye blackish. In India and Ceylon it lives in close association with man; a familiar bird of towns and villages; a scavenger, destructive of eggs and nestlings of other birds. Forms communal roosts.

Voice: A short 'caw', repeated.

Habitat: Urban areas, dockyards; farmlands, shores.

Breeding: Nest: (Indian data) a platform of twigs often including wire, with cup-like depression lined with tow, coir fibre; 3 m or higher in tree, occasionally several nests in same tree. Eggs: 4–5; pale blue-green speckled and streaked brown.

Range and Status: Native of India and S. Asia. Occasionally self-introduced to Australian ports on ships, principally Fremantle, WA, but also at Geelong, Vic. Although apparently none has become established, it should immediately be reported or destroyed wherever positively identified.

DISTRIBUTION MAPS

These distribution maps show the area or region in Australia where the bird in question usually occurs. Of necessity they are oversimplified and arbitary, and except in a few cases, do not differentiate between summer and winter ranges, or between breeding and non-breeding ranges. It is obvious that in many cases the bird in question may occur only in widely separated areas of suitable habitat within the coloured area.

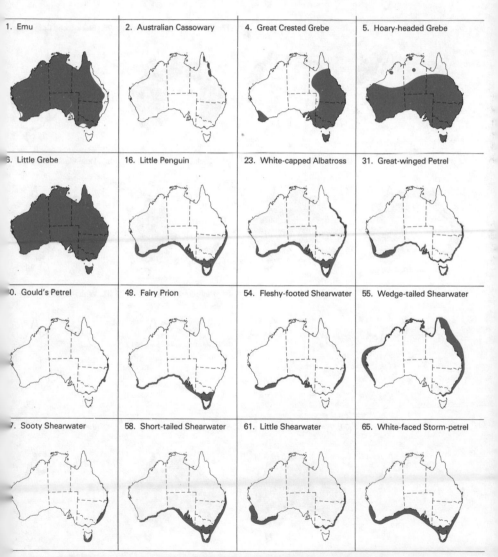

1. Emu   2. Australian Cassowary   4. Great Crested Grebe   5. Hoary-headed Grebe

6. Little Grebe   16. Little Penguin   23. White-capped Albatross   31. Great-winged Petrel

0. Gould's Petrel   49. Fairy Prion   54. Fleshy-footed Shearwater   55. Wedge-tailed Shearwater

7. Sooty Shearwater   58. Short-tailed Shearwater   61. Little Shearwater   65. White-faced Storm-petrel

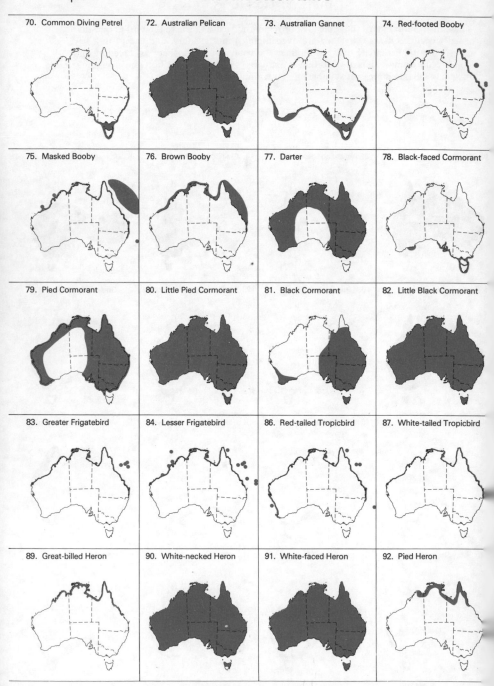

70. Common Diving Petrel

72. Australian Pelican

73. Australian Gannet

74. Red-footed Booby

75. Masked Booby

76. Brown Booby

77. Darter

78. Black-faced Cormorant

79. Pied Cormorant

80. Little Pied Cormorant

81. Black Cormorant

82. Little Black Cormorant

83. Greater Frigatebird

84. Lesser Frigatebird

86. Red-tailed Tropicbird

87. White-tailed Tropicbird

89. Great-billed Heron

90. White-necked Heron

91. White-faced Heron

92. Pied Heron

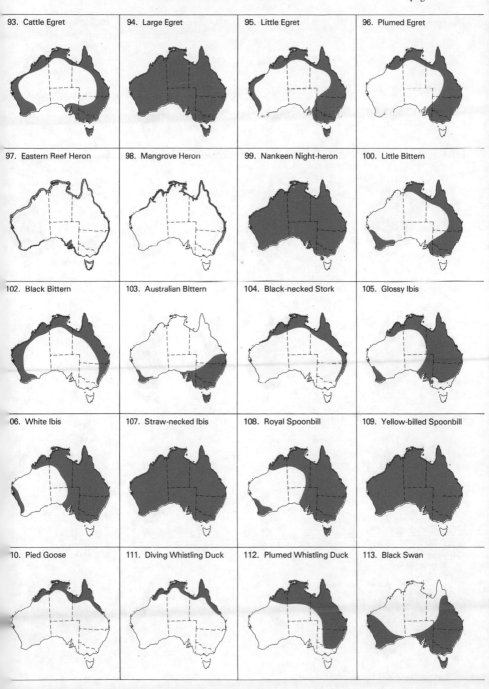

93. Cattle Egret
94. Large Egret
95. Little Egret
96. Plumed Egret
97. Eastern Reef Heron
98. Mangrove Heron
99. Nankeen Night-heron
100. Little Bittern
102. Black Bittern
103. Australian Bittern
104. Black-necked Stork
105. Glossy Ibis
06. White Ibis
107. Straw-necked Ibis
108. Royal Spoonbill
109. Yellow-billed Spoonbill
10. Pied Goose
111. Diving Whistling Duck
112. Plumed Whistling Duck
113. Black Swan

115. Freckled Duck

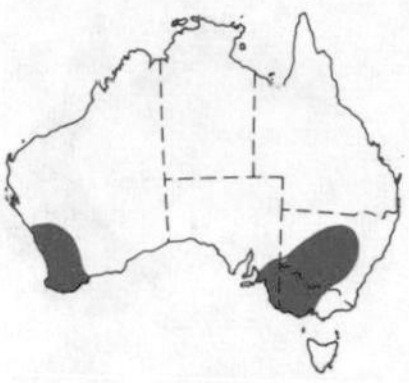

116. Cape Barren Goose

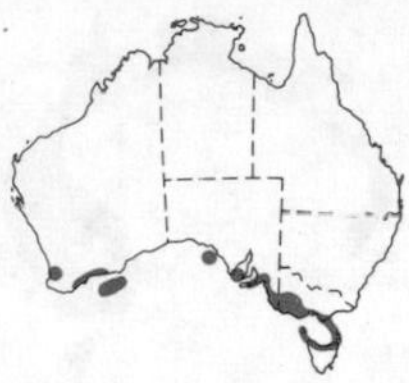

117. Chestnut-breasted Shelduck

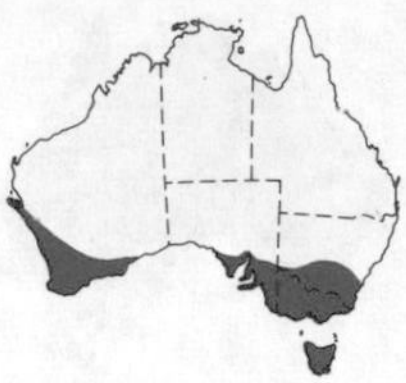

118. White-headed Shelduck

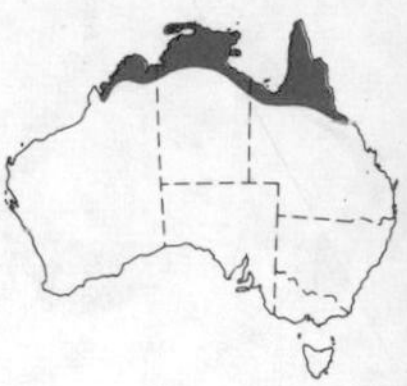

119. Black Duck

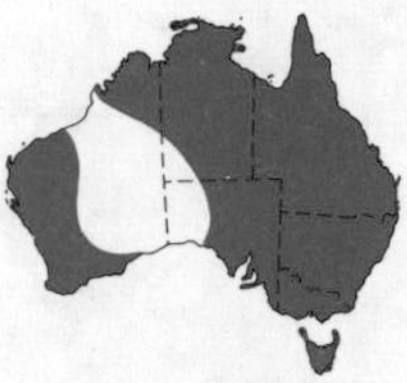

121. Grey Teal

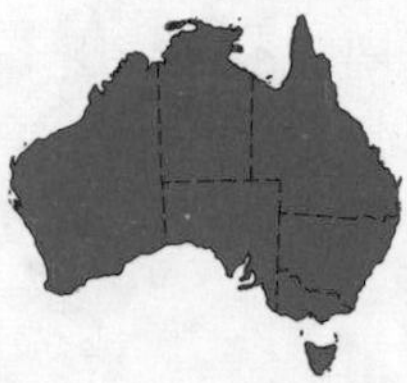

122. Chestnut Teal

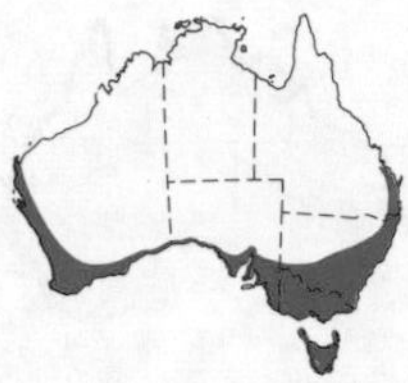

123. Southern Shoveller

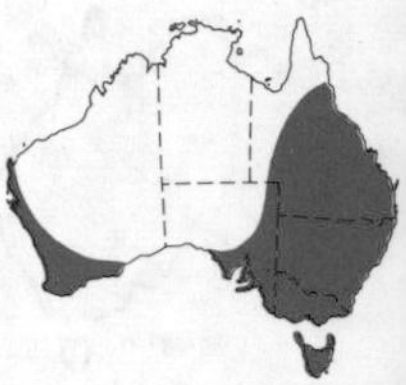

126. Pink-eared Duck

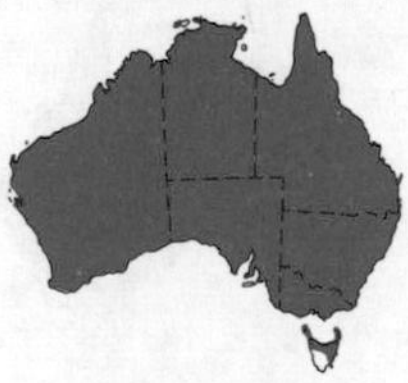

127. White-eyed Duck

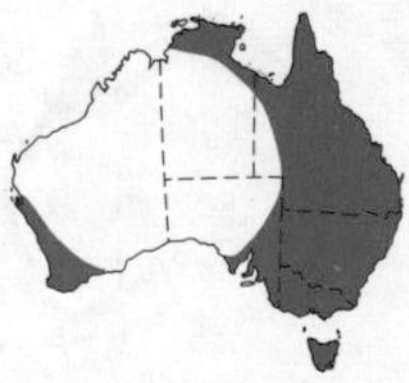

128. Australian Wood Duck

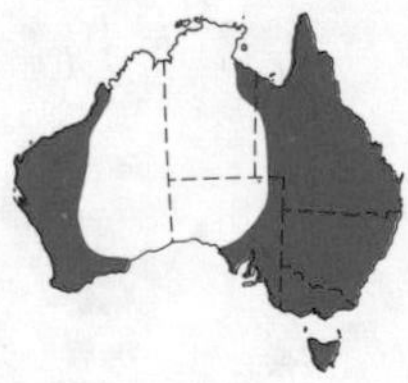

129. White Pygmy Goose

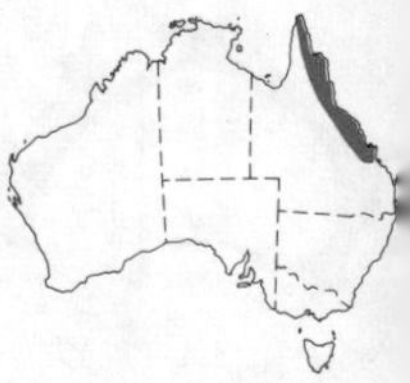

130. Green Pygmy Goose

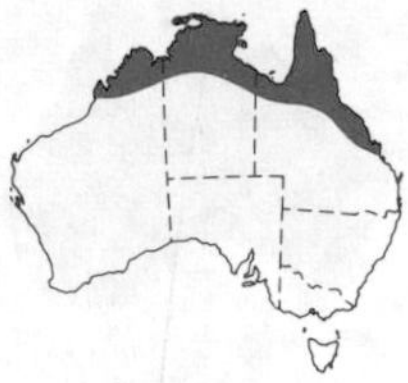

131. Blue-billed Duck

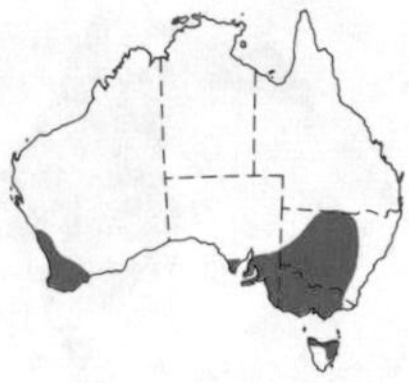

132. Musk Duck

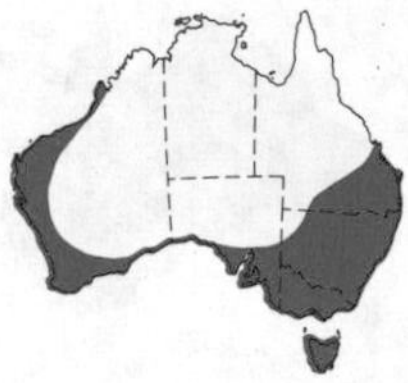

133. Osprey

134. Australian Black-shouldered Kite

135. Letter-winged Kite

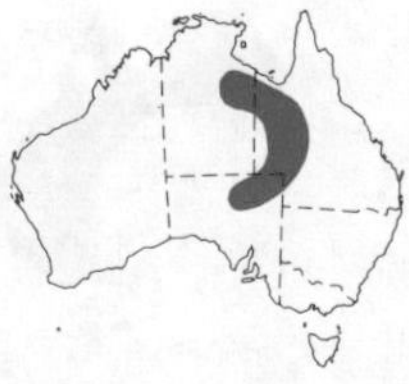

136. Crested Hawk

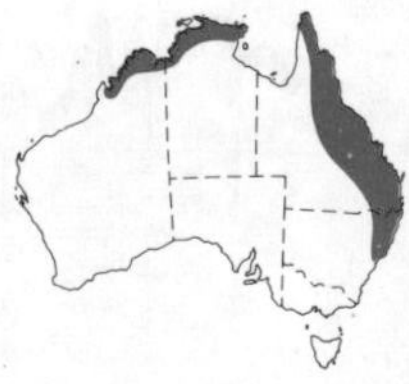

137. Fork-tailed Kite

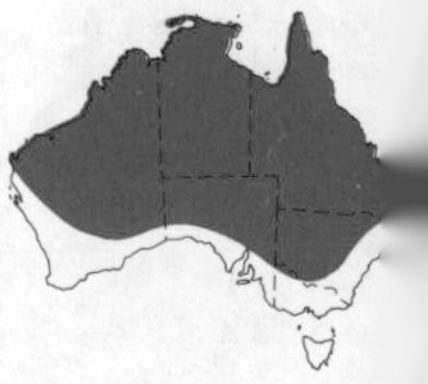

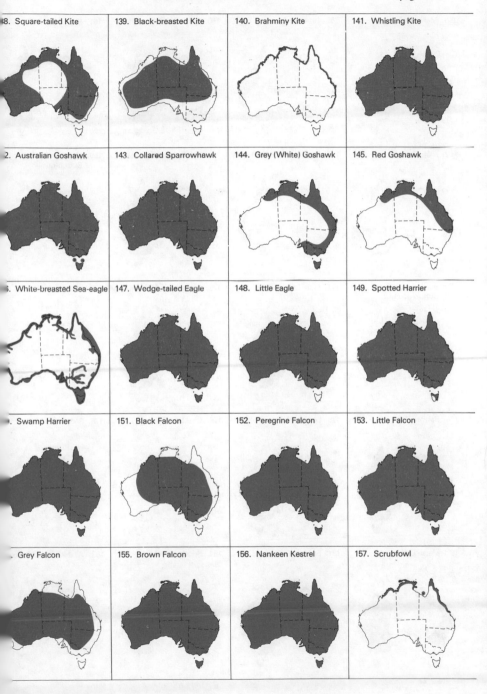

138. Square-tailed Kite
139. Black-breasted Kite
140. Brahminy Kite
141. Whistling Kite

142. Australian Goshawk
143. Collared Sparrowhawk
144. Grey (White) Goshawk
145. Red Goshawk

146. White-breasted Sea-eagle
147. Wedge-tailed Eagle
148. Little Eagle
149. Spotted Harrier

150. Swamp Harrier
151. Black Falcon
152. Peregrine Falcon
153. Little Falcon

154. Grey Falcon
155. Brown Falcon
156. Nankeen Kestrel
157. Scrubfowl

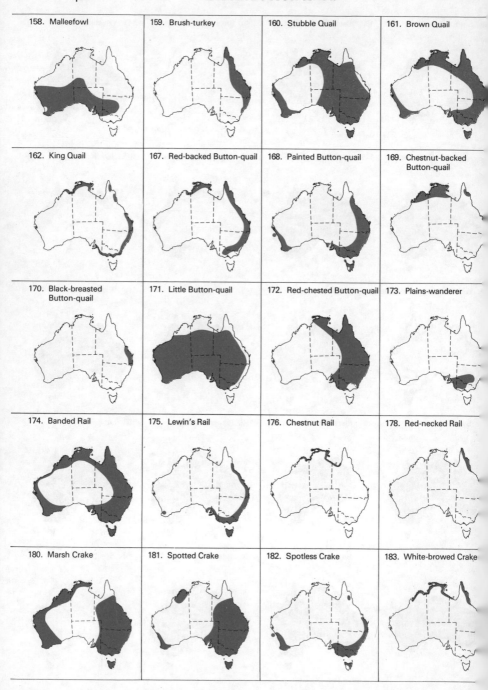

158. Malleefowl

159. Brush-turkey

160. Stubble Quail

161. Brown Quail

162. King Quail

167. Red-backed Button-quail

168. Painted Button-quail

169. Chestnut-backed Button-quail

170. Black-breasted Button-quail

171. Little Button-quail

172. Red-chested Button-quail

173. Plains-wanderer

174. Banded Rail

175. Lewin's Rail

176. Chestnut Rail

178. Red-necked Rail

180. Marsh Crake

181. Spotted Crake

182. Spotless Crake

183. White-browed Crake

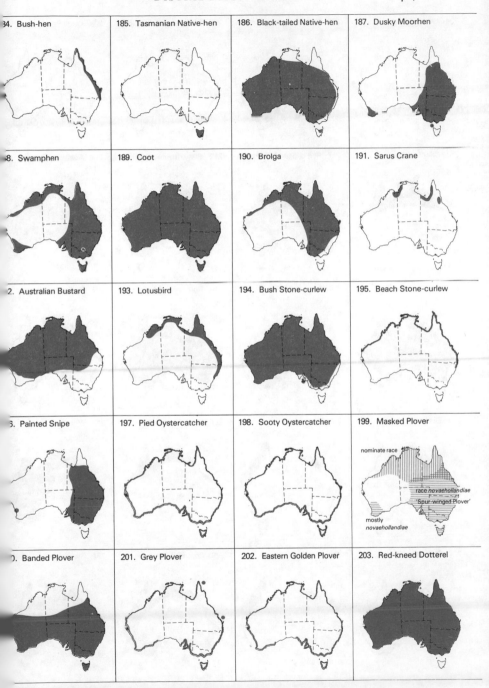

184. Bush-hen
185. Tasmanian Native-hen
186. Black-tailed Native-hen
187. Dusky Moorhen

188. Swamphen
189. Coot
190. Brolga
191. Sarus Crane

192. Australian Bustard
193. Lotusbird
194. Bush Stone-curlew
195. Beach Stone-curlew

196. Painted Snipe
197. Pied Oystercatcher
198. Sooty Oystercatcher
199. Masked Plover

nominate race
race novaehollandiae 'Spur-winged Plover'
mostly novaehollandiae

200. Banded Plover
201. Grey Plover
202. Eastern Golden Plover
203. Red-kneed Dotterel

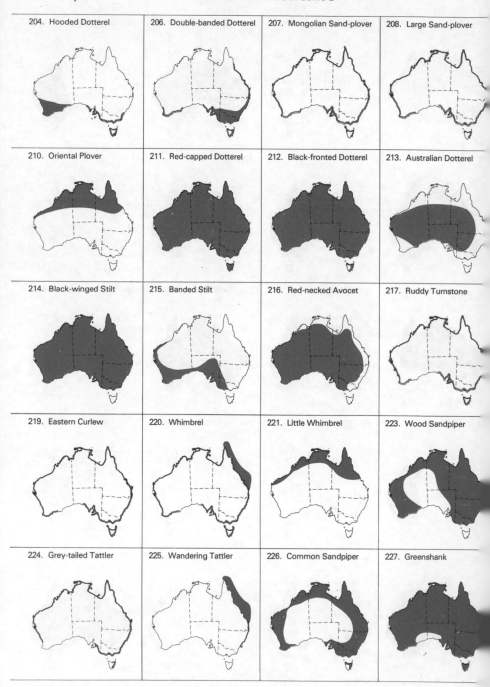

204. Hooded Dotterel

206. Double-banded Dotterel

207. Mongolian Sand-plover

208. Large Sand-plover

210. Oriental Plover

211. Red-capped Dotterel

212. Black-fronted Dotterel

213. Australian Dotterel

214. Black-winged Stilt

215. Banded Stilt

216. Red-necked Avocet

217. Ruddy Turnstone

219. Eastern Curlew

220. Whimbrel

221. Little Whimbrel

223. Wood Sandpiper

224. Grey-tailed Tattler

225. Wandering Tattler

226. Common Sandpiper

227. Greenshank

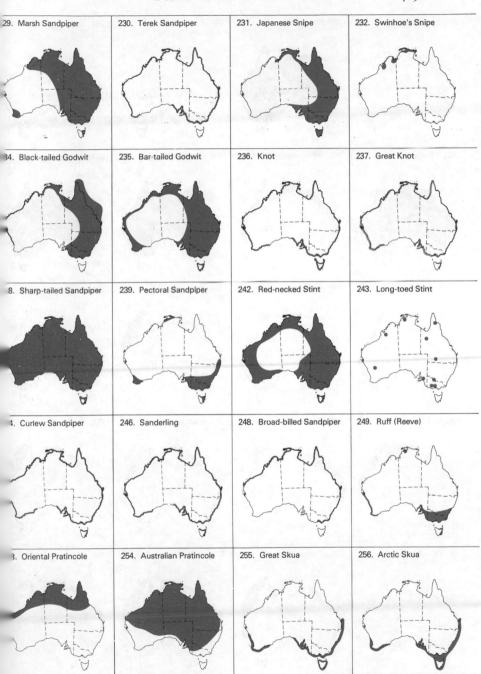

229. Marsh Sandpiper

230. Terek Sandpiper

231. Japanese Snipe

232. Swinhoe's Snipe

234. Black-tailed Godwit

235. Bar-tailed Godwit

236. Knot

237. Great Knot

238. Sharp-tailed Sandpiper

239. Pectoral Sandpiper

242. Red-necked Stint

243. Long-toed Stint

244. Curlew Sandpiper

246. Sanderling

248. Broad-billed Sandpiper

249. Ruff (Reeve)

253. Oriental Pratincole

254. Australian Pratincole

255. Great Skua

256. Arctic Skua

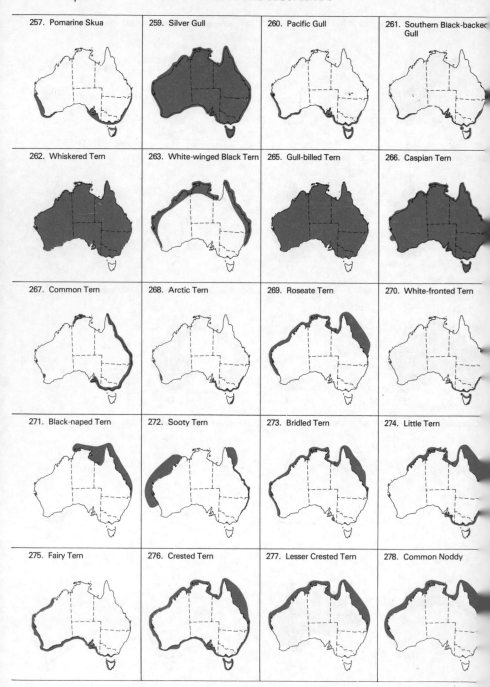

257. Pomarine Skua

259. Silver Gull

260. Pacific Gull

261. Southern Black-backed Gull

262. Whiskered Tern

263. White-winged Black Tern

265. Gull-billed Tern

266. Caspian Tern

267. Common Tern

268. Arctic Tern

269. Roseate Tern

270. White-fronted Tern

271. Black-naped Tern

272. Sooty Tern

273. Bridled Tern

274. Little Tern

275. Fairy Tern

276. Crested Tern

277. Lesser Crested Tern

278. Common Noddy

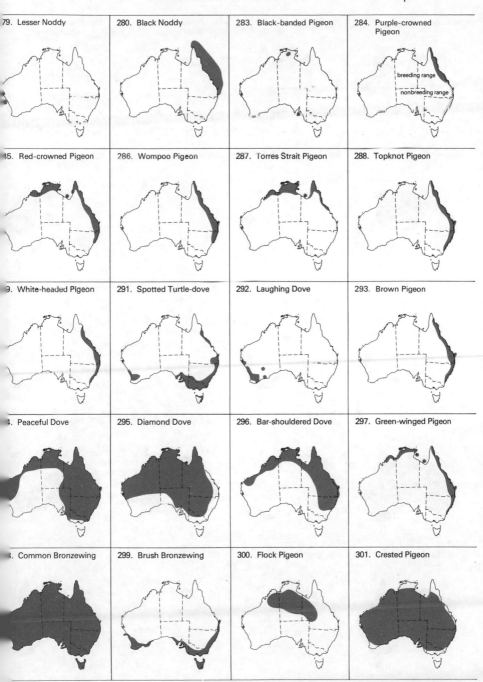

279. Lesser Noddy

280. Black Noddy

283. Black-banded Pigeon

284. Purple-crowned Pigeon

breeding range

nonbreeding range

285. Red-crowned Pigeon

286. Wompoo Pigeon

287. Torres Strait Pigeon

288. Topknot Pigeon

289. White-headed Pigeon

291. Spotted Turtle-dove

292. Laughing Dove

293. Brown Pigeon

294. Peaceful Dove

295. Diamond Dove

296. Bar-shouldered Dove

297. Green-winged Pigeon

298. Common Bronzewing

299. Brush Bronzewing

300. Flock Pigeon

301. Crested Pigeon

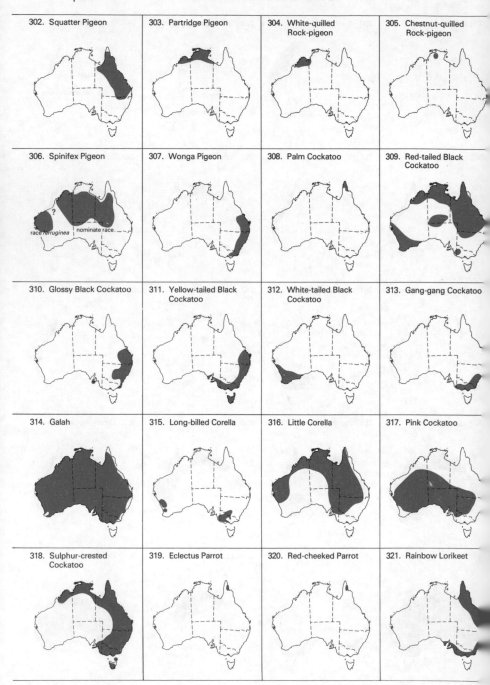

302. Squatter Pigeon

303. Partridge Pigeon

304. White-quilled Rock-pigeon

305. Chestnut-quilled Rock-pigeon

306. Spinifex Pigeon

race *ferruginea* nominate race

307. Wonga Pigeon

308. Palm Cockatoo

309. Red-tailed Black Cockatoo

310. Glossy Black Cockatoo

311. Yellow-tailed Black Cockatoo

312. White-tailed Black Cockatoo

313. Gang-gang Cockatoo

314. Galah

315. Long-billed Corella

316. Little Corella

317. Pink Cockatoo

318. Sulphur-crested Cockatoo

319. Eclectus Parrot

320. Red-cheeked Parrot

321. Rainbow Lorikeet

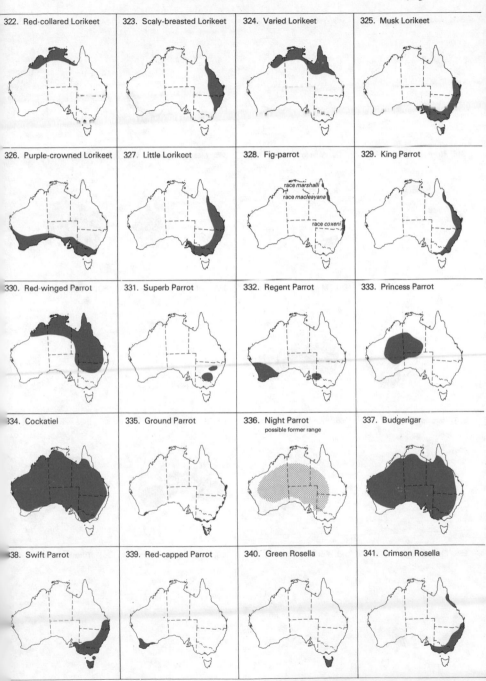

322. Red-collared Lorikeet

323. Scaly-breasted Lorikeet

324. Varied Lorikeet

325. Musk Lorikeet

326. Purple-crowned Lorikeet

327. Little Lorikeet

328. Fig-parrot
race *marshalli*
race *macleayana*
race *coxeni*

329. King Parrot

330. Red-winged Parrot

331. Superb Parrot

332. Regent Parrot

333. Princess Parrot

334. Cockatiel

335. Ground Parrot

336. Night Parrot
possible former range

337. Budgerigar

338. Swift Parrot

339. Red-capped Parrot

340. Green Rosella

341. Crimson Rosella

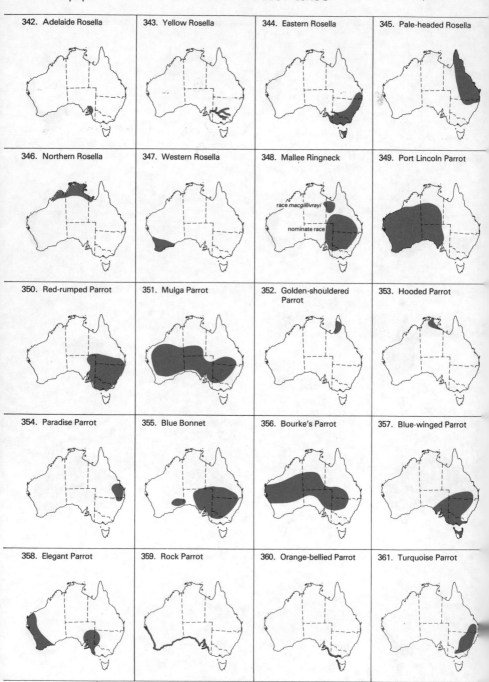

342. Adelaide Rosella

343. Yellow Rosella

344. Eastern Rosella

345. Pale-headed Rosella

346. Northern Rosella

347. Western Rosella

348. Mallee Ringneck

race *macgillivrayi*

nominate race

349. Port Lincoln Parrot

350. Red-rumped Parrot

351. Mulga Parrot

352. Golden-shouldered Parrot

353. Hooded Parrot

354. Paradise Parrot

355. Blue Bonnet

356. Bourke's Parrot

357. Blue-winged Parrot

358. Elegant Parrot

359. Rock Parrot

360. Orange-bellied Parrot

361. Turquoise Parrot

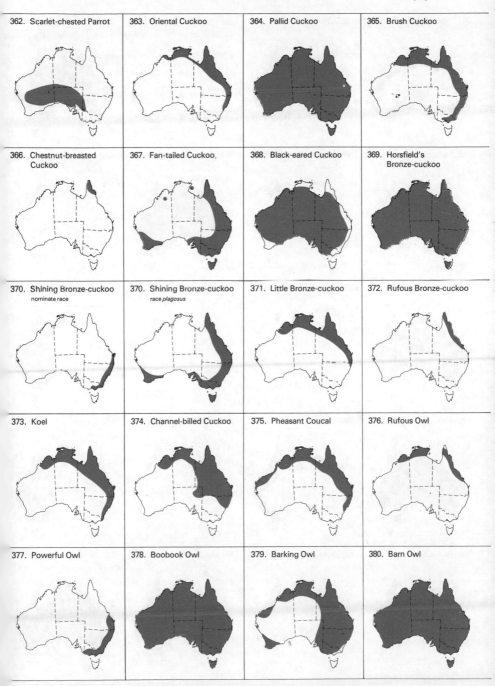

362. Scarlet-chested Parrot

363. Oriental Cuckoo

364. Pallid Cuckoo

365. Brush Cuckoo

366. Chestnut-breasted Cuckoo

367. Fan-tailed Cuckoo.

368. Black-eared Cuckoo

369. Horsfield's Bronze-cuckoo

370. Shining Bronze-cuckoo
nominate race

370. Shining Bronze-cuckoo
race plagosus

371. Little Bronze-cuckoo

372. Rufous Bronze-cuckoo

373. Koel

374. Channel-billed Cuckoo

375. Pheasant Coucal

376. Rufous Owl

377. Powerful Owl

378. Boobook Owl

379. Barking Owl

380. Barn Owl

381. Masked Owl

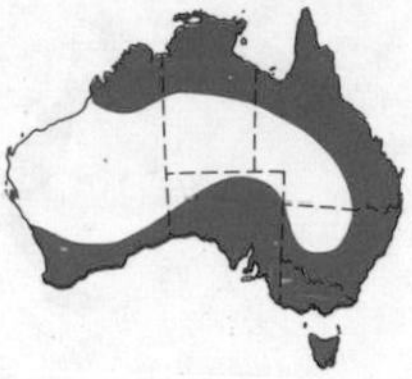

382. Grass Owl

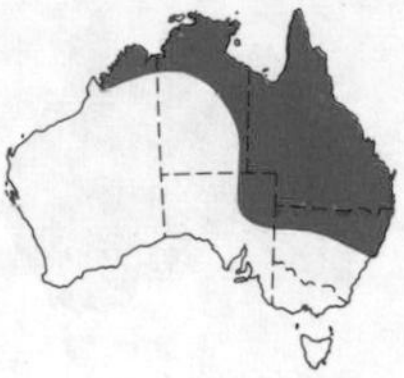

383. Sooty Owl

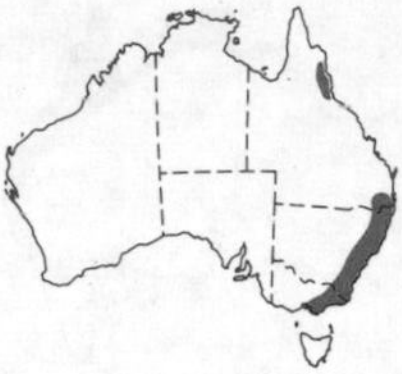

384. Tawny Frogmouth

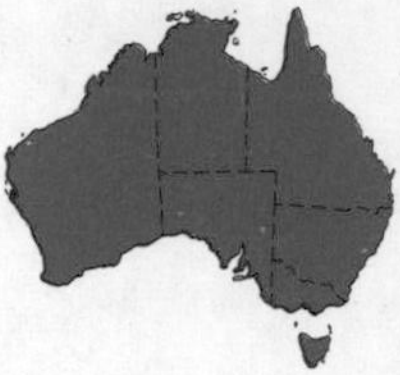

385. Papuan Frogmouth

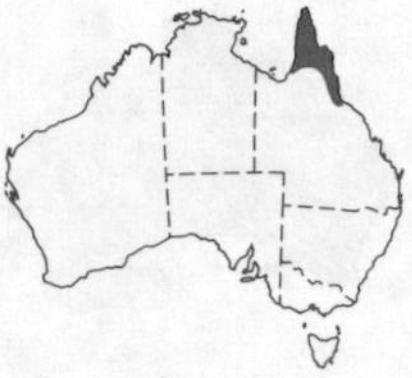

386. Marbled Frogmouth

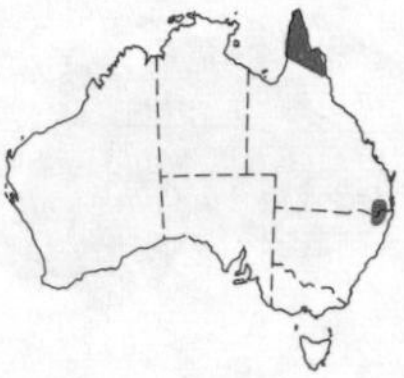

387. Owlet-nightjar

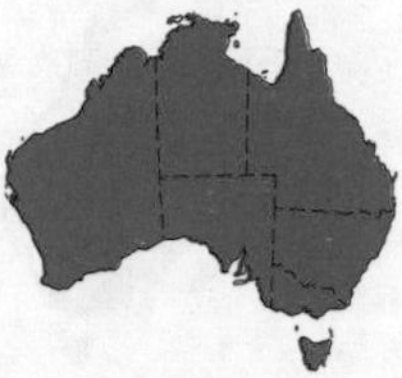

388. White-throated Nightjar

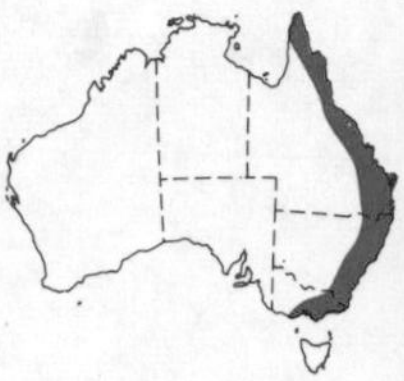

389. Spotted Nightjar

390. White-tailed Nightjar

392. Grey Swiftlet

394. Spine-tailed Swift

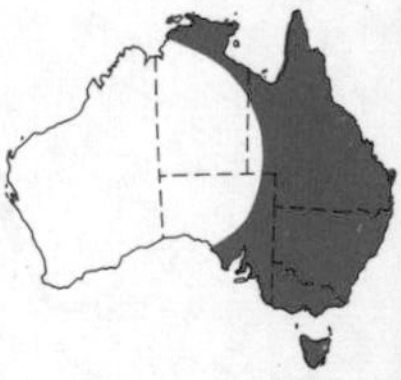

395. Fork-tailed Swift

396. Azure Kingfisher

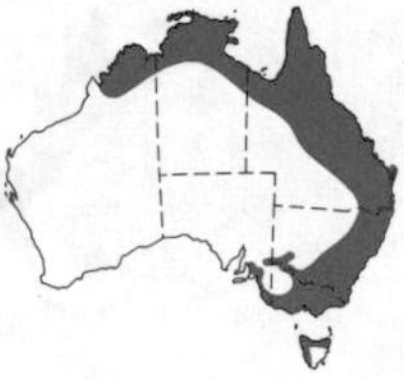

397. Little Kingfisher

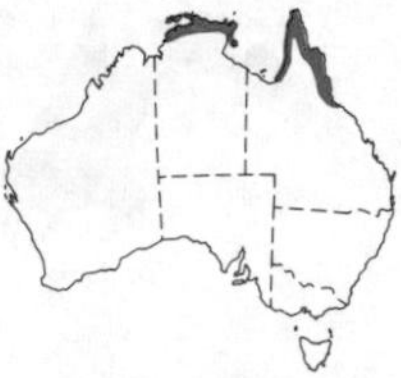

398. Laughing Kookaburra

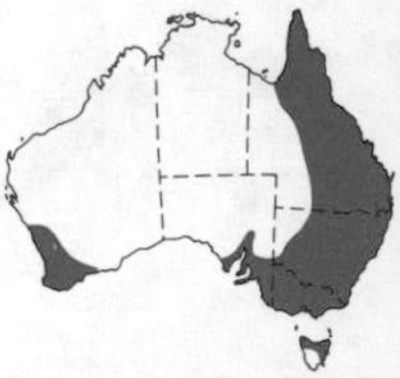

399. Blue-winged Kookaburra

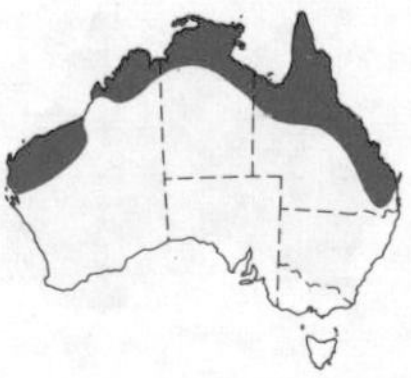

400. Forest Kingfisher

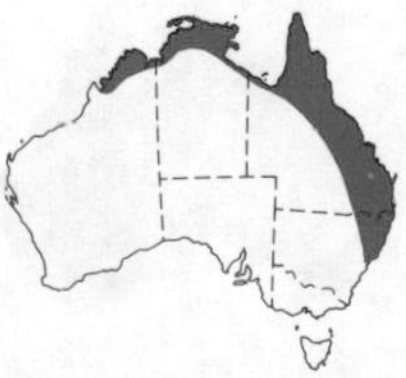

401. Red-backed Kingfisher

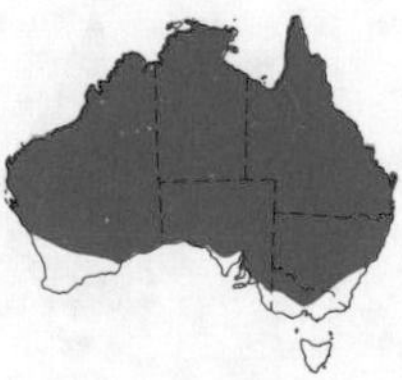

402. Sacred Kingfisher

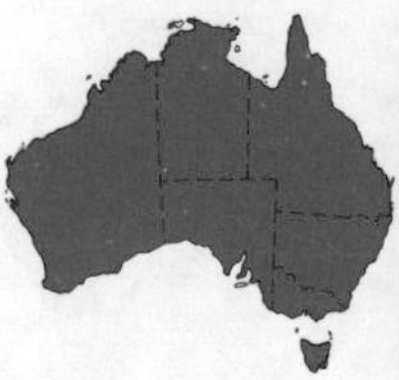

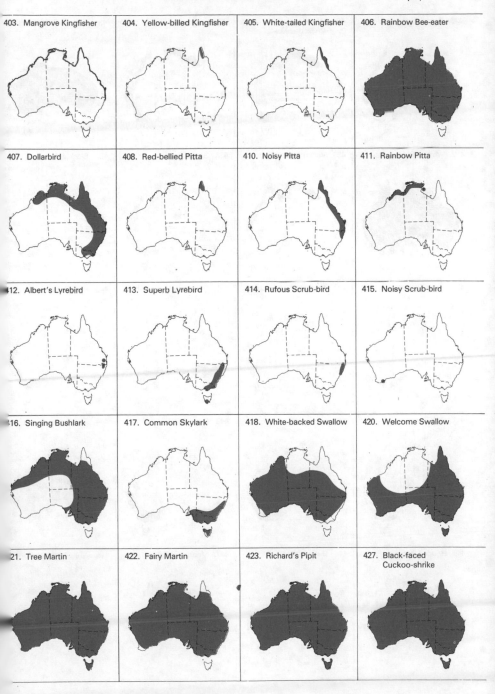

403. Mangrove Kingfisher
404. Yellow-billed Kingfisher
405. White-tailed Kingfisher
406. Rainbow Bee-eater

407. Dollarbird
408. Red-bellied Pitta
410. Noisy Pitta
411. Rainbow Pitta

412. Albert's Lyrebird
413. Superb Lyrebird
414. Rufous Scrub-bird
415. Noisy Scrub-bird

416. Singing Bushlark
417. Common Skylark
418. White-backed Swallow
420. Welcome Swallow

421. Tree Martin
422. Fairy Martin
423. Richard's Pipit
427. Black-faced Cuckoo-shrike

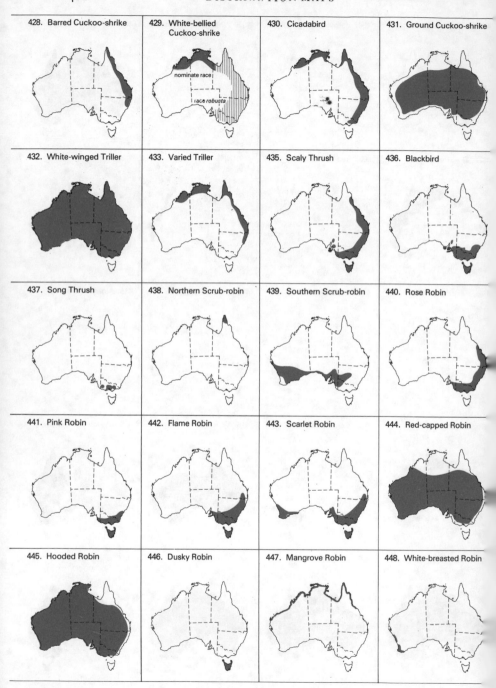

428. Barred Cuckoo-shrike

429. White-bellied Cuckoo-shrike

nominate race

race robusta

430. Cicadabird

431. Ground Cuckoo-shrike

432. White-winged Triller

433. Varied Triller

435. Scaly Thrush

436. Blackbird

437. Song Thrush

438. Northern Scrub-robin

439. Southern Scrub-robin

440. Rose Robin

441. Pink Robin

442. Flame Robin

443. Scarlet Robin

444. Red-capped Robin

445. Hooded Robin

446. Dusky Robin

447. Mangrove Robin

448. White-breasted Robin

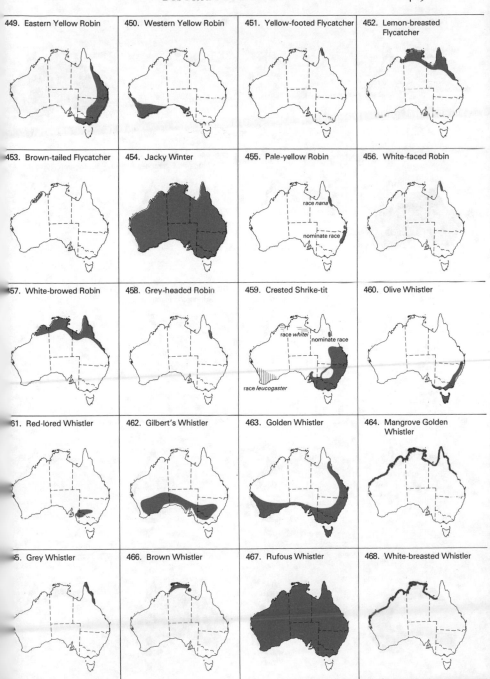

449. Eastern Yellow Robin

450. Western Yellow Robin

451. Yellow-footed Flycatcher

452. Lemon-breasted Flycatcher

453. Brown-tailed Flycatcher

454. Jacky Winter

455. Pale-yellow Robin

race nana

nominate race

456. White-faced Robin

457. White-browed Robin

458. Grey-headed Robin

459. Crested Shrike-tit

race whitei

nominate race

race leucogaster

460. Olive Whistler

461. Red-lored Whistler

462. Gilbert's Whistler

463. Golden Whistler

464. Mangrove Golden Whistler

465. Grey Whistler

466. Brown Whistler

467. Rufous Whistler

468. White-breasted Whistler

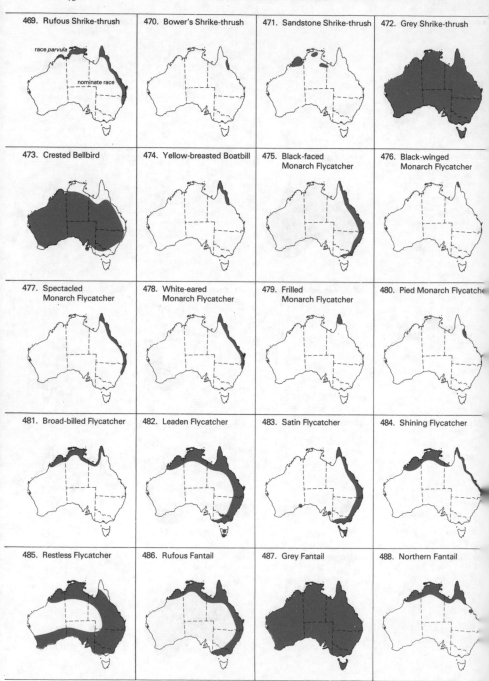

469. Rufous Shrike-thrush

race *parvula*

nominate race

470. Bower's Shrike-thrush

471. Sandstone Shrike-thrush

472. Grey Shrike-thrush

473. Crested Bellbird

474. Yellow-breasted Boatbill

475. Black-faced Monarch Flycatcher

476. Black-winged Monarch Flycatcher

477. Spectacled Monarch Flycatcher

478. White-eared Monarch Flycatcher

479. Frilled Monarch Flycatcher

480. Pied Monarch Flycatcher

481. Broad-billed Flycatcher

482. Leaden Flycatcher

483. Satin Flycatcher

484. Shining Flycatcher

485. Restless Flycatcher

486. Rufous Fantail

487. Grey Fantail

488. Northern Fantail

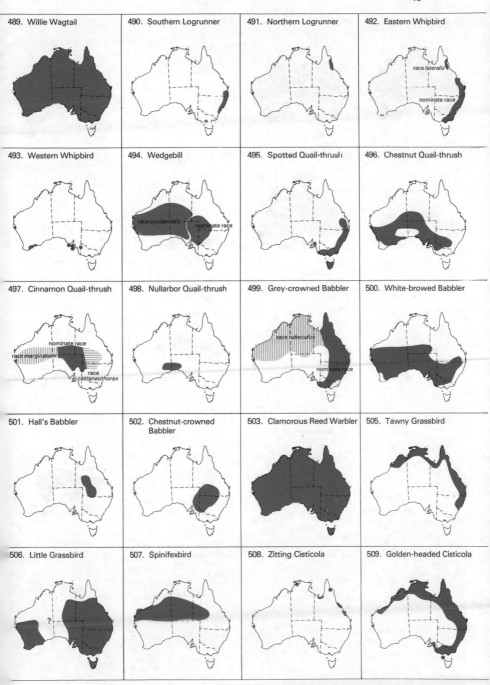

489. Willie Wagtail
490. Southern Logrunner
491. Northern Logrunner
492. Eastern Whipbird

race *lateralis*
nominate race

493. Western Whipbird
494. Wedgebill
495. Spotted Quail-thrush
496. Chestnut Quail-thrush

race *occidentalis*
nominate race

497. Cinnamon Quail-thrush
498. Nullarbor Quail-thrush
499. Grey-crowned Babbler
500. White-browed Babbler

nominate race
race *marginatum*
race *castaneothorax*

race *rubeculus*
nominate race

501. Hall's Babbler
502. Chestnut-crowned Babbler
503. Clamorous Reed Warbler
505. Tawny Grassbird

506. Little Grassbird
507. Spinifexbird
508. Zitting Cisticola
509. Golden-headed Cisticola

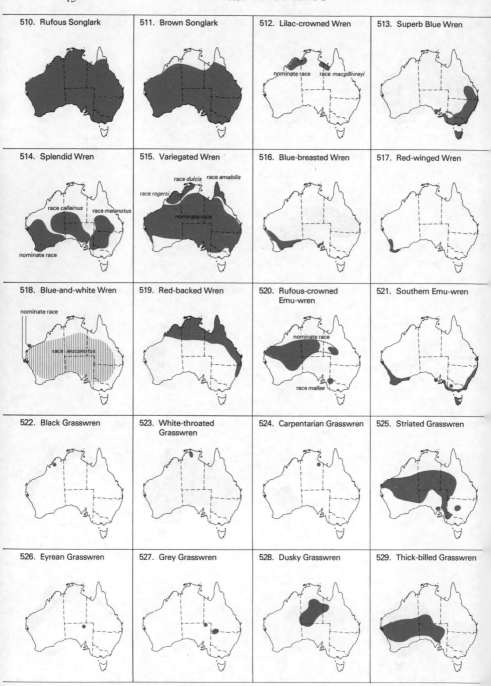

510. Rufous Songlark

511. Brown Songlark

512. Lilac-crowned Wren

nominate race   race *macgillivrayi*

513. Superb Blue Wren

514. Splendid Wren

race *callainus*   race *melanotus*

nominate race

515. Variegated Wren

race *dulcis*   race *amabilis*

race *rogersi*

nominate race

516. Blue-breasted Wren

517. Red-winged Wren

518. Blue-and-white Wren

nominate race

race *leuconotus*

519. Red-backed Wren

520. Rufous-crowned Emu-wren

nominate race

race *mallee*

521. Southern Emu-wren

522. Black Grasswren

523. White-throated Grasswren

524. Carpentarian Grasswren

525. Striated Grasswren

526. Eyrean Grasswren

527. Grey Grasswren

528. Dusky Grasswren

529. Thick-billed Grasswren

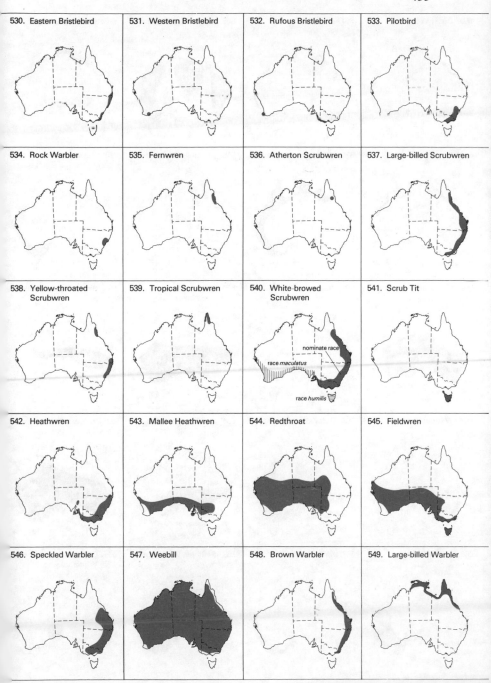

530. Eastern Bristlebird

531. Western Bristlebird

532. Rufous Bristlebird

533. Pilotbird

534. Rock Warbler

535. Fernwren

536. Atherton Scrubwren

537. Large-billed Scrubwren

538. Yellow-throated Scrubwren

539. Tropical Scrubwren

540. White-browed Scrubwren

nominate race

race *maculatus*

race *humilis*

541. Scrub Tit

542. Heathwren

543. Mallee Heathwren

544. Redthroat

545. Fieldwren

546. Speckled Warbler

547. Weebill

548. Brown Warbler

549. Large-billed Warbler

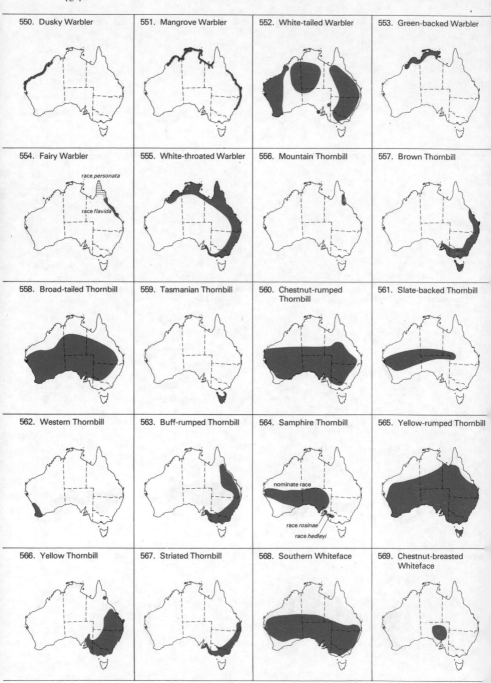

550. Dusky Warbler

551. Mangrove Warbler

552. White-tailed Warbler

553. Green-backed Warbler

554. Fairy Warbler

race *personata*

race *flavida*

555. White-throated Warbler

556. Mountain Thornbill

557. Brown Thornbill

558. Broad-tailed Thornbill

559. Tasmanian Thornbill

560. Chestnut-rumped Thornbill

561. Slate-backed Thornbill

562. Western Thornbill

563. Buff-rumped Thornbill

564. Samphire Thornbill

nominate race

race *rosinae*

race *hedleyi*

565. Yellow-rumped Thornbill

566. Yellow Thornbill

567. Striated Thornbill

568. Southern Whiteface

569. Chestnut-breasted Whiteface

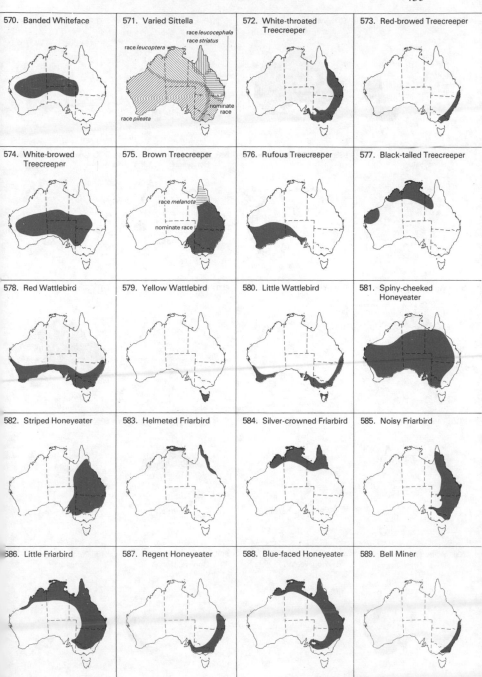

570. Banded Whiteface

571. Varied Sittella
race *leucocephala*
race *striatus*
race *leucoptera*
nominate race
race *pileata*

572. White-throated Treecreeper

573. Red-browed Treecreeper

574. White-browed Treecreeper

575. Brown Treecreeper
race *melanota*
nominate race

576. Rufous Treecreeper

577. Black-tailed Treecreeper

578. Red Wattlebird

579. Yellow Wattlebird

580. Little Wattlebird

581. Spiny-cheeked Honeyeater

582. Striped Honeyeater

583. Helmeted Friarbird

584. Silver-crowned Friarbird

585. Noisy Friarbird

586. Little Friarbird

587. Regent Honeyeater

588. Blue-faced Honeyeater

589. Bell Miner

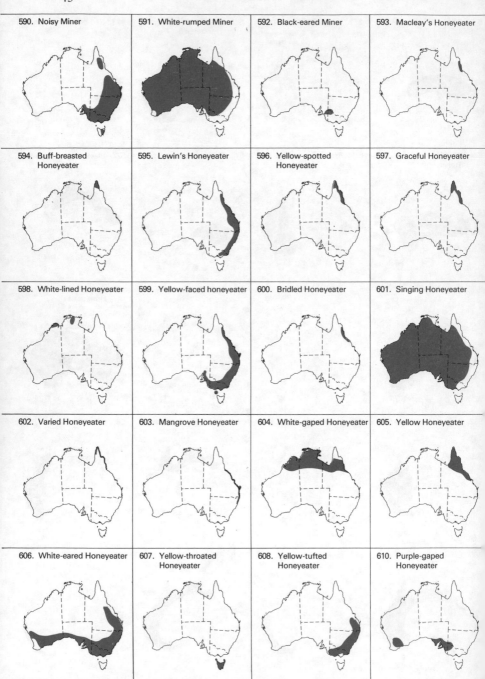

590. Noisy Miner

591. White-rumped Miner

592. Black-eared Miner

593. Macleay's Honeyeater

594. Buff-breasted Honeyeater

595. Lewin's Honeyeater

596. Yellow-spotted Honeyeater

597. Graceful Honeyeater

598. White-lined Honeyeater

599. Yellow-faced honeyeater

600. Bridled Honeyeater

601. Singing Honeyeater

602. Varied Honeyeater

603. Mangrove Honeyeater

604. White-gaped Honeyeater

605. Yellow Honeyeater

606. White-eared Honeyeater

607. Yellow-throated Honeyeater

608. Yellow-tufted Honeyeater

610. Purple-gaped Honeyeater

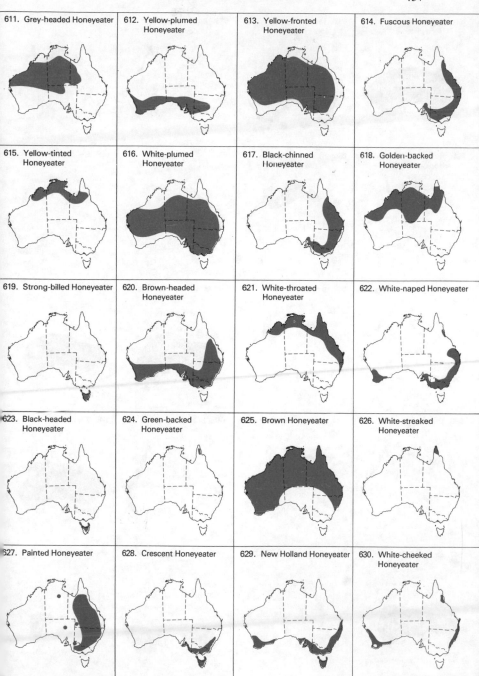

611. Grey-headed Honeyeater

612. Yellow-plumed Honeyeater

613. Yellow-fronted Honeyeater

614. Fuscous Honeyeater

615. Yellow-tinted Honeyeater

616. White-plumed Honeyeater

617. Black-chinned Honeyeater

618. Golden-backed Honeyeater

619. Strong-billed Honeyeater

620. Brown-headed Honeyeater

621. White-throated Honeyeater

622. White-naped Honeyeater

623. Black-headed Honeyeater

624. Green-backed Honeyeater

625. Brown Honeyeater

626. White-streaked Honeyeater

627. Painted Honeyeater

628. Crescent Honeyeater

629. New Holland Honeyeater

630. White-cheeked Honeyeater

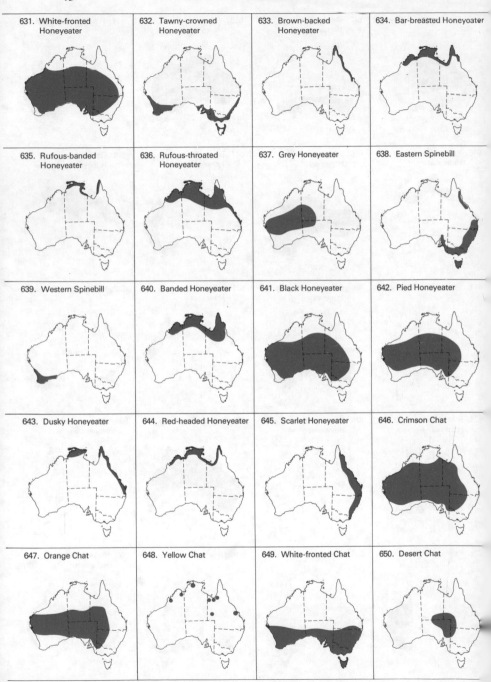

631. White-fronted Honeyeater

632. Tawny-crowned Honeyeater

633. Brown-backed Honeyeater

634. Bar-breasted Honeyoater

635. Rufous-banded Honeyeater

636. Rufous-throated Honeyeater

637. Grey Honeyeater

638. Eastern Spinebill

639. Western Spinebill

640. Banded Honeyeater

641. Black Honeyeater

642. Pied Honeyeater

643. Dusky Honeyeater

644. Red-headed Honeyeater

645. Scarlet Honeyeater

646. Crimson Chat

647. Orange Chat

648. Yellow Chat

649. White-fronted Chat

650. Desert Chat

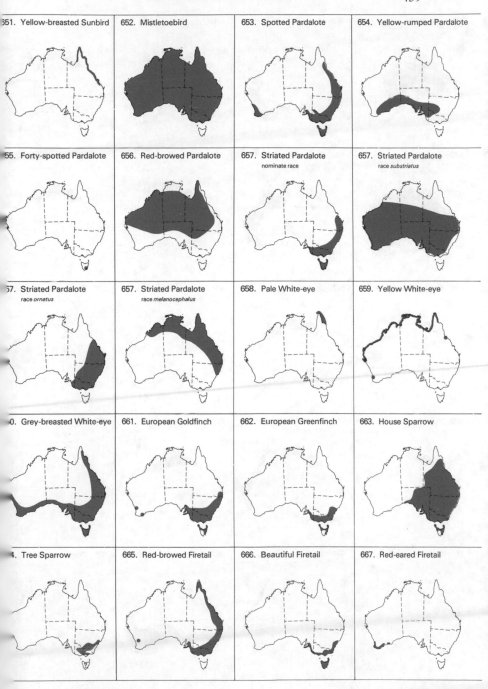

651. Yellow-breasted Sunbird

652. Mistletoebird

653. Spotted Pardalote

654. Yellow-rumped Pardalote

655. Forty-spotted Pardalote

656. Red-browed Pardalote

657. Striated Pardalote
nominate race

657. Striated Pardalote
race *substriatus*

657. Striated Pardalote
race *ornatus*

657. Striated Pardalote
race *melanocephalus*

658. Pale White-eye

659. Yellow White-eye

660. Grey-breasted White-eye

661. European Goldfinch

662. European Greenfinch

663. House Sparrow

664. Tree Sparrow

665. Red-browed Firetail

666. Beautiful Firetail

667. Red-eared Firetail

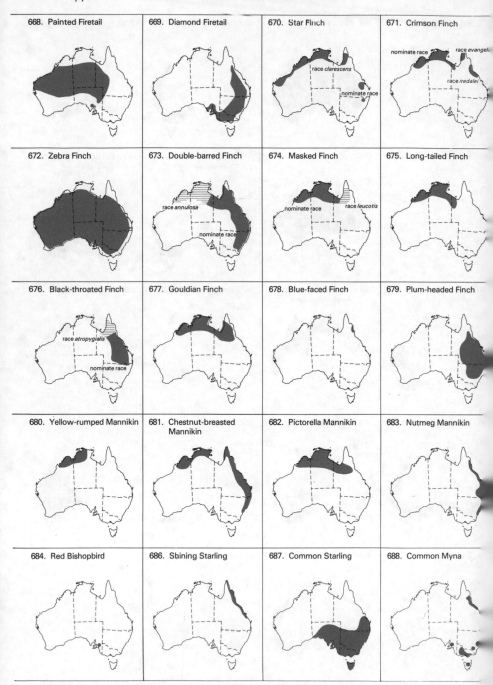

668. Painted Firetail

669. Diamond Firetail

670. Star Finch
race *clarescens*
nominate race

671. Crimson Finch
nominate race race *evangel.*
race *iredalei*

672. Zebra Finch

673. Double-barred Finch
race *annulosa*
nominate race

674. Masked Finch
nominate race race *leucotis*

675. Long-tailed Finch

676. Black-throated Finch
race *atropygialis*
nominate race

677. Gouldian Finch

678. Blue-faced Finch

679. Plum-headed Finch

680. Yellow-rumped Mannikin

681. Chestnut-breasted Mannikin

682. Pictorella Mannikin

683. Nutmeg Mannikin

684. Red Bishopbird

686. Shining Starling

687. Common Starling

688. Common Myna

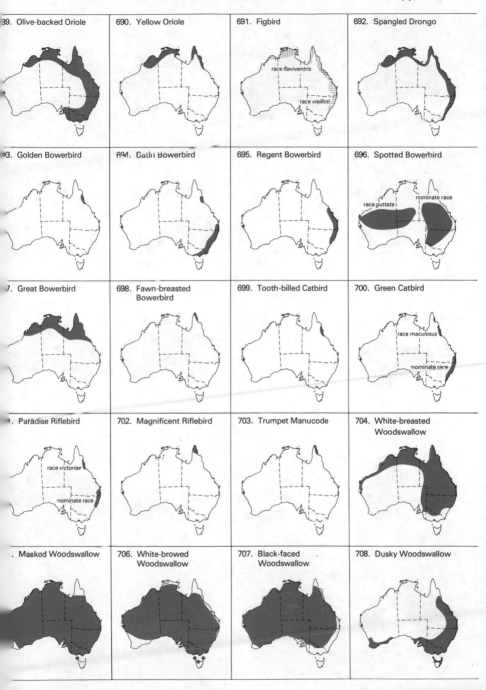

689. Olive-backed Oriole

690. Yellow Oriole

691. Figbird

race *flaviventris*

race *vieilloti*

692. Spangled Drongo

693. Golden Bowerbird

694. Satin Bowerbird

695. Regent Bowerbird

696. Spotted Bowerbird

race *guttata*

nominate race

697. Great Bowerbird

698. Fawn-breasted Bowerbird

699. Tooth-billed Catbird

700. Green Catbird

race *maculosus*

nominate race

701. Paradise Riflebird

race *victoriae*

nominate race

702. Magnificent Riflebird

703. Trumpet Manucode

704. White-breasted Woodswallow

705. Masked Woodswallow

706. White-browed Woodswallow

707. Black-faced Woodswallow

708. Dusky Woodswallow

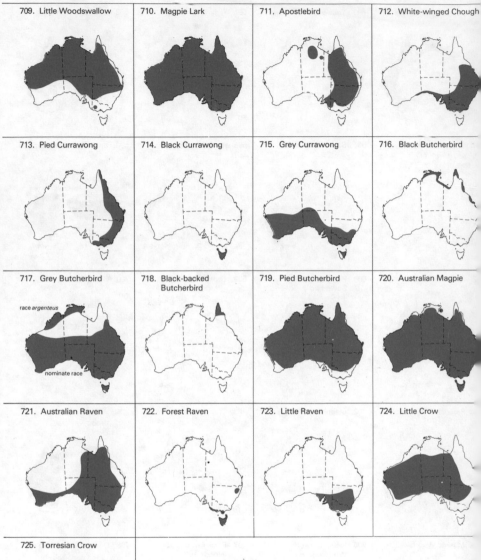

709. Little Woodswallow
710. Magpie Lark
711. Apostlebird
712. White-winged Chough

713. Pied Currawong
714. Black Currawong
715. Grey Currawong
716. Black Butcherbird

717. Grey Butcherbird
race *argenteus*
nominate race
718. Black-backed Butcherbird
719. Pied Butcherbird
720. Australian Magpie

721. Australian Raven
722. Forest Raven
723. Little Raven
724. Little Crow

725. Torresian Crow

Indexes

There are no page numbers in these indexes. The numbers in ordinary type are those given to species in the text and refer also to the maps of distribution for the species. Numbers in bold type are the numbers of the plates on which the birds are depicted. In the Index of English Names, those names recommended by the RAOU (1978, Emu Suppl. Vol. 77:245–307), where they differ from those used in this Guide and even if they do not appear in the text, are indexed separately or indicated (bracketed) with the names used in this Guide.

Index of Scientific Names

Index of English Names

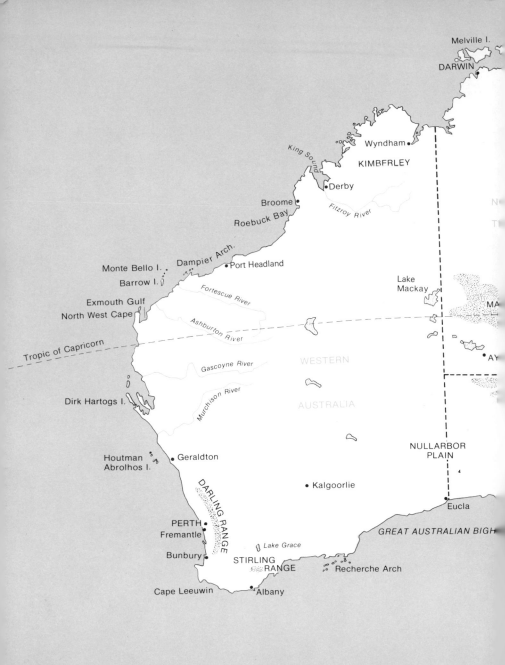